"One of the most learned, yet most readable history of psychology textbooks on the market today. Woody and Viney cover psychological thought from the ancient world to the present day with uncommon flair."

—**Christopher D. Green**, *Professor of Psychology, York University, Canada*

"In this latest edition of their successful textbook, the authors include their important chapter on historiography along with a clear chronological history of psychology. In addition, they provide a description of emerging fields and new research methods allowing us to re-examine historical findings."

—**Richard L. Miller**, *Professor and Chair of Psychology and Sociology, Texas A&M University–Kingsville, USA*

"This sixth edition continues the tradition of superb scholarship set by the first five editions. Responsibly placing psychological thought into the complex trajectory of the history of humanity, it deserves a place of honor among the longer and more thorough texts in the field. Excellent and up to date!"

—**Michael Wertheimer**, *Professor Emeritus of Psychology and Neuroscience, University of Colorado at Boulder, USA*

A History of Psychology

A History of Psychology: The Emergence of Science and Applications, Sixth Edition, traces the history of psychology from antiquity through the early twenty-first century, giving students a thorough look into psychology's origins and key developments in basic and applied psychology.

This new edition includes extensive coverage of the proliferation of applied fields since the mid-twentieth century and stronger emphases on the biological basis of psychology, new statistical techniques and qualitative methodologies, and emerging therapies. Other areas of emphasis include the globalization of psychology, the growth of interest in health psychology, the resurgence of interest in motivation, and the importance of ecopsychology and environmental psychology. Substantially revised and updated throughout, this book retains and improves its strengths from prior editions, including its strong scholarly foundation and scholarship from groups too often omitted from psychological history, including women, people of color, and scholars from outside the United States. This book also aims to engage and inspire students to recognize the power of history in their own lives and studies, to connect history to the present and the future, and to think critically and historically.

For additional resources, consult the Companion Website at www.routledge.com/cw/Woody where instructors will find lecture slides and outlines; testbanks; and how-to sources for teaching History and Systems of Psychology courses; and students will find a timeline; review questions; a complete glossary; and annotated links to relevant resources.

William Douglas Woody is Professor of Psychological Sciences at the University of Northern Colorado, USA. He has received Early Career Achievement Awards from the Society for the History of Psychology and the Society for the Teaching of Psychology.

Wayne Viney is Professor Emeritus of Psychology and Emeritus University Distinguished Teaching Scholar at Colorado State University, USA. He has served as President of the Society for the History of Psychology.

A History of Psychology

The Emergence of Science and Applications

Sixth Edition

William Douglas Woody and Wayne Viney

Routledge
Taylor & Francis Group

NEW YORK AND LONDON

Sixth edition published 2017
by Routledge
711 Third Avenue, New York, NY 10017

and by Routledge
2 Park Square, Milton Park, Abingdon, Oxon, OX14 4RN

Routledge is an imprint of the Taylor & Francis Group, an informa business

First edition published by Allyn & Bacon 1993
Fifth edition published by Routledge 2016

Library of Congress Cataloging in Publication Data
A catalog record for this book has been requested

ISBN: 978-1-138-68371-6 (hbk)
ISBN: 978-1-315-54440-3 (ebk)

Typeset in StoneSerif
Typeset in StoneSerif
Printed and bound by CPI Group (UK) Ltd, Croydon, CR0 4YY

Visit the companion website: www.routledge.com/cw/Woody

To Michael Wertheimer
—a mentor for both of us who serves as a continuing inspiration

And to
Lisa Woody for her enthusiasm, support, and encouragement

Finally
In loving memory of Wynona Rose Viney

Brief Contents

Preface		xvii
Acknowledgments		xxiii
Part I Historiographic and Philosophical Issues		**1**
1	Critical Issues in Historical Studies	3
2	Philosophical Issues	14
Part II Early Psychological Thought		**39**
3	Ancient Psychological Thought	41
4	The Roman Period and the Middle Ages	70
5	The Renaissance	98
Part III Modern Intellectual Developments That Contributed to the Birth of Psychology		**123**
6	Empiricism, Associationism, and Utilitarianism	125
7	Rationalism	151
8	Mechanization and Quantification	172
9	Naturalism and Humanitarian Reform	197
Part IV Psychology from the Formal Founding in 1879		**237**
10	Psychophysics and the Formal Founding of Psychology	239
11	Developments after the Founding	262
12	Functionalism	288
13	Behaviorism	322
14	Gestalt Psychology	359

15 Psychoanalysis   385
16 Humanistic Psychologies   423
17 Beyond the Systems of Psychology   447
18 Prospects for the Twenty-First Century   479

References   497
Illustration Credits   568
Index   570

Contents

Preface xvii

Acknowledgments xxiii

Part I Historiographic and Philosophical Issues 1

1 Critical Issues in Historical Studies 3

Why Study History? 3

History Enriches Our Sense of Time 3

History as a Contribution to Liberal Education 4

History Teaches Humility 4

History Teaches a Healthy Skepticism 4

History Influences Human Thought Processes 4

Some Problems in Historiography 5

The Development of Historical Consciousness 5

What Is History? 6

Can History Be Objective? 7

The Tyranny of the Present 8

Is There a Pattern or Direction in History? 8

What Makes History? 10

The History of the History of Psychology 11

Review Questions • Glossary 13

2 Philosophical Issues 14

Epistemology 14

A Priori and A Posteriori Knowledge 14

Nativism versus Empiricism 15

Instinct versus Learning 15

What Are the Criteria by Which We Claim to Know Truth? 16

The Role of Emotions in Knowledge 18

Science and Epistemology 19

Relevance of Epistemology to Psychology 23

The Problem of Causality 23

Free Will and Determinism 25

The Mind–Body Problem 27

Monism 27

Dualism 28

Pluralism 30

Psychogeny 31

The Problem of Explanation 32

Explanation by Analogies and Comparisons 33

Review Questions • Glossary 35

Part II Early Psychological Thought 39

Timeline: c. 600 BCE to AD 1600 40

3 Ancient Psychological Thought 41

Early Chinese Psychologies 41

Babylonia 42

Egypt 43

Other Ancient Eastern Psychologies 44
The Hebrews 44
Persia 45
Greece 46
The Cosmologists 46
Early Greek Concepts of Illness 51
Relativism 54
The Golden Age of Greece 55
*Psychological Thought Following
    Aristotle 66*
Review Questions • Glossary 66

**4 The Roman Period and the
    Middle Ages 70**
Roman Medicine 71
Galen 71
Roman Philosophy 73
Stoicism 73
Epicureanism 74
Neo-Platonism 75
Skepticism 77
The Fall of Rome 78
The Early Christian Faith 78
The Medieval Period 79
Aurelius Augustine 81
Islam 84
Judaism in the Middle Ages 88
The Rise of the European Universities 89
Conclusion 95
Review Questions • Glossary 95

5 The Renaissance 98
The Black Death 98
A New Worldview: Expanding
    Geographic Knowledge 100
Influence of the Greek Classics 100
Diffusion of Authority 101
Growth of Empirical Studies 102
Quantification 102
Changing Visions of the World 103
The Heliocentric Theory 104
Galileo Galilei 104
*The Larger Meaning of the Copernican
    Revolution 106*
Psychological Thought in the
    Renaissance 106

Petrarch 106
Niccolò Machiavelli 107
Juan Luis Vives 109
Leonardo da Vinci 111
Paracelsus 113
Michel de Montaigne 113
Oliva Sabuco 117
Juan Huarte 118
Conclusion 119
Review Questions • Glossary 120

**Part III Modern Intellectual
Developments That Contributed to
the Birth of Psychology 123**
Timeline: 1600 to 1879 **124**

**6 Empiricism, Associationism,
    and Utilitarianism 125**
Empiricism 125
Francis Bacon 125
John Locke 129
George Berkeley 132
David Hume 135
Empiricism on the Continent 138
Étienne Bonnot de Condillac 139
Claude-Adrien Helvétius 139
Associationism and Utilitarianism 140
David Hartley 140
Jeremy Bentham 141
Mary Wollstonecraft 142
James Mill 145
John Stuart Mill 145
Contributions of Empiricism 148
Review Questions • Glossary 148

7 Rationalism 151
Emphasis on A Priori Knowledge 151
Theory of the Active Mind 152
Deduction versus Induction 152
René Descartes 152
Descartes's Method 154
Baruch Spinoza 156
Gottfried Wilhelm Leibniz 159
Monadology 160
Immanuel Kant 162
Sense Experience and Reason 163

Social Psychology   164
Johann Friedrich Herbart   165
Thomas Reid and Commonsense
   Philosophy   166
Enfranchising Curiosity   167
Contributions of Rationalism   168
Review Questions • Glossary   169

**8   Mechanization and
     Quantification   172**
Thomas Hobbes   172
René Descartes Revisited   175
Jan Swammerdam   177
Niels Stensen   178
Stephen Hales   178
Robert Whytt   178
Johann August Unzer   179
Julien Offray de La Mettrie   180
Mapping the Central and Peripheral
   Nervous Systems   181
Localization of Function   181
Extending the Powers of Observation   186
Speed of a Nervous Impulse   188
Measuring Behavior   188
*Applications of the New Measurement
   Techniques   192*
Review Questions • Glossary   193

**9   Naturalism and Humanitarian
     Reform   197**
Evolutionary Theory   198
Evolution of the Solar System   198
Geological Evolution   198
*Evolution in Other Arenas of Intellectual
   Discourse   199*
Organic Evolution   200
Charles Darwin   202
Significance of Evolutionary Theory for
   Psychology   207
Comparative Psychology   207
Developmental Psychology   208
Emphasis on Adaptation   209
Individual Differences   210
Herbert Spencer   211
Naturalistic Approaches to Emotional
   Disorders   212

Demonology   212
The Witches' Hammer   212
The Demise of Witchcraft   216
Humanitarian Reform   216
*Reform in the Treatment of People with
   Emotional Disorders   217*
Reform in Other Places   224
*Reform Becomes a Social Movement:
   Dorothea Dix   225*
*Reform in the Care and Treatment
   of People with Cognitive
   Disabilities   228*
Women's Reform Movements   229
Review Questions • Glossary   232

**Part IV Psychology from the
Formal Founding in 1879   237**
   Timeline: 1875 to 2016   **238**

**10 Psychophysics and the Formal
     Founding of Psychology   239**
Psychophysics   239
Ernst Heinrich Weber   240
Weber's Work on the Sense of Touch   241
Gustav Theodor Fechner   242
Hermann von Helmholtz   245
Wilhelm Wundt   249
*General Characteristics of Wundt's
   Thought   252*
The Laboratory and the Broader Vision   254
Some Key Concepts in Wundt's System   255
Wundt's Legacy   256
*The Legacy of Wundt's Students in
   Applied Psychology   257*
Review Questions • Glossary   259

**11 Developments after the
     Founding   262**
Systems   262
Edward Bradford Titchener   264
Titchener's Psychology   266
Margaret Floy Washburn: A Broader
   Psychology   272
Franz Brentano and Act Psychology   274
Brentano's Psychology   275
Carl Stumpf   278

Georg Elias Müller 279
Oswald Külpe and the Würzburg
   School 280
Hermann Ebbinghaus 282
Wundt's Contemporaries and Applied
   Psychology 285
Review Questions • Glossary 285

12 Functionalism 288
William James and Harvard
   University 288
*General Characteristics of James's
   Thought 291*
Jamesian Psychology 294
James's Legacy 298
Hugo Münsterberg 299
Münsterberg's Psychology 299
G. Stanley Hall and Clark University 301
Hall's Psychology 303
Functionalism and the University of
   Chicago 305
John Dewey 306
James Rowland Angell 307
Harvey A. Carr 308
Psychology at Columbia University 309
James McKeen Cattell 309
Robert Sessions Woodworth 311
Mary Whiton Calkins 313
The Growth of Applied Psychology 314
Leta Stetter Hollingworth 315
Helen Wooley 316
Binet and Intelligence Testing 316
Influence of Functionalism:
   An Evaluation 318
Review Questions • Glossary 318

13 Behaviorism 322
Intellectual Antecedents of
   Behaviorism 323
Ivan Petrovich Pavlov 323
Edward Lee Thorndike 329
Formal Founding of American
   Behaviorism 331
John B. Watson 332
Neobehaviorism 340
Clark Leonard Hull 341

Edwin Ray Guthrie 344
Edward Chace Tolman 345
Burrhus Frederic Skinner 347
Behaviorism and Applied
   Psychology 354
Review Questions • Glossary 355

14 Gestalt Psychology 359
Max Wertheimer 359
Wolfgang Köhler 360
Kurt Koffka 362
Intellectual Background of Gestalt
   Psychology 363
Philosophy 363
Science 363
Psychology 364
The Fundamentals of Gestalt
   Psychology 365
Principles of Perceptual Organization 366
Thinking 368
Learning 369
*Insight: A Further Challenge to the S–R
   Formula 370*
Developmental Concepts 370
Gestalt Perspectives on Scientific
   Method 372
Mind and Brain: Isomorphism 373
The Influence of Gestalt Psychology 373
Kurt Lewin and Field Theory 374
Lewin's Field Theory 375
Tension Systems and Recall 376
Group Dynamics 377
Extension of Gestalt Principles 378
Common Misunderstandings of
   Gestalt Psychology 379
*Gestalt Psychology and Gestalt
   Therapy 379*
*Gestalt Psychology and Scientific
   Analysis 379*
Gestalt Psychology and Nativism 379
The Role of Past Experience 380
Gestalt Psychology and Applied
   Psychology 380
The Continuing Relevance of Gestalt
   Psychology 381
Review Questions • Glossary 382

xiv

15 Psychoanalysis   **385**
Sigmund Freud   385
General Characteristics of Freud's Thought 389
Freud's System of Psychology   390
Life's Major Goal and Its Inevitable Frustration 390
The Structure of Personality 392
Motivation and Unconscious Processes 393
Anxiety 395
Defense Mechanisms of the Ego 396
Stages of Psychosexual Development 398
Psychoanalysis as a Therapeutic Technique 400
Freud's Social Psychology 401
Appreciative Overview 403
Critical Overview 403
Future Perspectives 404
After Freud   405
Alfred Adler   405
Adler's System of Psychology 405
Carl Gustav Jung   407
Jung's Analytic Psychology 409
Evaluation 413
Karen Danielsen Horney   413
Horney's System of Thought 414
Other Developments   417
Review Questions • Glossary   418

16 Humanistic Psychologies   **423**
Intellectual Traditions   424
William James 424
Existentialism 424
Phenomenology 429
The Formal Emergence of Humanistic Psychologies   430
Abraham Maslow 430
Gordon Allport 435
Carl R. Rogers 436
Viktor Frankl 438
Joseph F. Rychlak 440
Overview of Third-Force Psychologies: Major Positions and Criticisms   441
Review Questions • Glossary   444

17 Beyond the Systems of Psychology   **447**
The Systems of Psychology in Retrospect   448
Psychoanalysis 448
Humanistic Psychology 449
Neobehaviorism and the Psychology of Learning 450
Cognitive Psychology   452
Intellectual Traditions 452
Themes and Content Areas of Cognitive Psychology 454
Critical Appraisal of Cognitive Psychology 455
Clinical Psychology and Related Fields   457
Critical Developments 458
Biopsychology   463
Enriched Environment Studies 463
Split-Brain Research 464
Studies of Synaptic Transmission 464
Direct Electrical Stimulation of the Brain 464
Measuring Brain Activity 465
Psychopharmacology 466
Behavioral Genetics 467
Psychoneuroimmunology 468
Social Psychology   468
Intellectual Traditions 468
Muzafer Sherif and the Autokinetic Effect 469
Solomon Asch and Conformity 470
Stanley Milgram and Destructive Obedience 471
Current Developments 472
Industrial-Organizational Psychology   473
Intellectual Traditions 473
Current Developments 476
Review Questions • Glossary   476

18 Prospects for the Twenty-First Century   **479**
Globalization and Multiculturalism: Psychology in an Expanding World   480
Changing Perspectives on Gender 481
Intersectionality in the Psychology of Prejudice and Privilege 482

Health Psychology 482
Positive Psychology 484
Ecopsychology 484
Psychology and the Law 486
Intellectual Traditions 486
*Hugo Münsterberg and Eyewitness
  Testimony 487*
Elizabeth F. Loftus 488
Current Developments 489
Resurgence of Motivation 489
Evolving Scientific Methodologies 490
Science and Faith 491

Recent Events: EITs and the Hoffman
  Report 492
Diversity and Pluralism in Modern
  Psychology 493
Conclusion 495
Review Questions • Glossary 495

References 497
Illustration Credits 568
Index 570

Preface

This book grew out of five earlier editions published under the title *A History of Psychology: Ideas and Context*. The first five editions included numerous distinctive features that we have preserved and amplified, but we believe the new title, *A History of Psychology: The Emergence of Science and Applications*, more accurately captures major developments in the history of the field. Substantial revisions have been necessary as a means of updating the book to include recent historical scholarship and enhanced pedagogical techniques.

Specifically, the current edition includes a more extensive review of the proliferation of applied fields since the mid-twentieth century. There are also stronger emphases on the biological basis of psychology, new statistical techniques and qualitative methodologies, and emerging therapies. The globalization of psychology, the growth of interest in health psychology, the resurgence of interest in motivation, and the importance of ecopsychology and environmental psychology are also emphasized. As with previous editions, this text strives for comprehensive examples of psychological thought from ancient Eastern and Western cultures, the Roman Empire, the Middle Ages, and the Renaissance. In the modern world, from about 1600, the focus is on intellectual traditions that contributed to the formal founding of psychology as an independent discipline. These traditions include rational and empirical philosophies, advances in physiology, development of quantitative techniques, evolutionary theory, naturalistic approaches to emotional problems, and significant humanitarian reform movements in the nineteenth century.

The text provides in-depth coverage of intellectual trends that followed psychology's formal founding in the late 1870s, with an emphasis on the major systems of thought and key developments in basic and applied psychology. We explore declining interest in systems of psychology beginning in the mid-twentieth century while recognizing the persistence of neobehavioristic, humanistic, and psychoanalytic approaches. The origin and development of the cognitive approach to psychology is pursued in detail along with what we regard as an age of specialization.

This book opens with a brief chapter on historiography that explores philosophical issues pertinent to disciplinary histories: What is history? Why study history? Is there a pattern in history? Can history be objective? We believe discussions of such questions result in more critical, engaged and informed readers who think not only about historical content, but also about the complex methodological tasks confronting the historian.

Chapter 2 introduces enduring philosophical problems encountered throughout the history of psychology: Do humans have free will? What are the methods by which we make truth claims? What is an explanation? What is the subject matter of psychology? The history of psychology is more meaningful to students who have a working knowledge of classic positions on fundamental philosophical problems. A careful reading of the materials in Chapter 2 will clarify and lend richness to topics encountered in subsequent chapters.

Psychological thought existed long before the founding of the formal discipline in the late nineteenth century. Like many comprehensive texts, this book presents examples of psychological thought encountered in ancient cultures. Greek and Roman periods are covered, but this book adds two critical features to the scholarship on ancient thought: First, psychological contributions of important early women such as Theana, Myia, and Hypatia are included. Second, in addition to reviewing the usual materials from the Greek and Roman periods, this text provides overviews of psychological thought from ancient Chinese, Indian, Babylonian, Persian, Egyptian, and Hebraic cultures. This emphasis on the broad scope of psychological thought is continued in later chapters that include contributions of Arab scholars such as Avicenna and Rhazes, Spanish scholars such as Juan Luis Vives and Juan Huarte, and neglected scholars such as Oliva Sabuco and Héloise.

The chapter on the Renaissance includes a consideration of the context that contributed to intellectual developments in this remarkable period. The plague, geographic discoveries, new inventions such as the telescope, the breakdown of authority, and the rediscovery of Greek classics had enormous influence. The works of important thinkers such as Galileo Galilei, Niccoló Machiavelli, and Michel de Montaigne are highlighted. Montaigne, a neglected figure in the history of psychology, is presented as a pivotal figure because of his powerful influence on subsequent thinkers such as Francis Bacon and René Descartes. The Renaissance period was progressive in some arenas, but the Inquisition and the witch hunts amounted to a holocaust for women.

In Chapters 8 and 9, this text devotes extensive space to the intellectual contexts that contributed to the development of psychology. We examine the influence of empiricism, rationalism, physiology, and evolutionary theory. We trace these developments in traditional detail and highlight the changing fortunes of doubt and curiosity in the works of the empiricists and rationalists. Curiosity, once regarded as a mark of vanity, was increasingly regarded as a virtue. We also include an emphasis on the key roles played by the growth of quantitative techniques and early applications of statistics by Florence Nightingale and Dorothea Dix. We call attention to the fact that psychology, as a formal discipline, was founded in an age of humanitarian reform movements (e.g., suffrage, abolition of slavery, new prison standards, universal education, and agitation by reformers for better treatment conditions for people with mental impairments and emotional disorders). We believe that extensive humanitarian reforms created a climate that helped legitimize the new discipline.

The second half of the text outlines the major classic schools or systems of psychology, emphasizing the basic and applied contributions of each school, and then examines psychological thought and applied psychology from the mid-twentieth century to the present. A description of the formal founding of psychology begins with nineteenth-century advances in psychophysics and voluntarism, an early school of psychology founded by Wilhelm Wundt. Additional consideration is given to scholars who shaped the new discipline of psychology, including Edward Bradford Titchener, Franz Brentano, Margaret Floy Washburn, Oswald Külpe, and Hermann Ebbinghaus.

The seminal works of William James and his American contemporaries figure strongly in the chapter on functionalism. The chapter on behaviorism reviews Russian reflexology, Edward Lee Thorndike's learning theory, John B. Watson's

xviii

behaviorism, and then neobehaviorists such as Clark Hull and Edward Tolman. The chapter culminates with an overview of B. F. Skinner's experimental analysis of behavior. The next chapter focuses on Gestalt psychology, an innovative school that challenged mechanistic and elementaristic approaches to psychology.

The advent of the psychodynamic school is detailed in the evolution of Sigmund Freud's psychoanalytic theory as well as resourceful challenges to his work from Alfred Adler, Carl Jung, and Karen Horney. The philosophical underpinnings of humanistic psychologies are traced in the works of scholars such as Unamuno, Kierkegaard, and Heidegger. These materials are followed by overviews of the works of Abraham Maslow, Gordon Allport, Carl Rogers, Viktor Frankl, and Joseph Rychlak.

Following the overview of humanistic psychologies we turn to a discussion of developments in the second half of the twentieth century. It is in this period that we witness a proliferation of specialized studies across basic and applied areas of psychology. The specialization is manifested partly in fifty-six divisions of the American Psychological Association that are extant as of this writing. We focus on developments in cognitive psychology, clinical psychology, biopsychology, behavioral genetics, psychopharmacology, psychoneuroimmunology, social psychology, and industrial-organizational psychology.

A final chapter, "Prospects for the Twenty-First Century," explores emerging new developments and prospects for the future. Current trends toward globalization and multiculturalism are included along with a discussion of continuing and growing work on sex and gender issues and the growing recognition of intersectionality in the psychology of prejudice and privilege. Health psychology is emerging as one of the most important developments in the opening years of the twenty-first century. We then examine positive psychology as a new and rapidly expanding field. This chapter also includes a section on ecopsychology, a central topical area for psychologists in a century where large populations must come

to grips with climate change and associated geographic changes along with crowding, extinction of species, and degradation of natural resources. Next, psychologists have long been interested in the law, and we see a continuing and growing emphasis on psychology and law. We then examine recent events in psychology, including the resurgence of motivation research and innovative new quantitative and qualitative research methods. Psychologists cannot ignore religious dimensions of human life, and the psychology of religion will continue to grow in importance. We examine a recent dark moment in the history of psychology: the findings of the Hoffman Report and the revelations of psychologists' involvement in enhanced interrogation techniques. The chapter closes with a discussion of the problem of unity and disunity in the sciences including psychology.

More than five hundred new references have been added. Study questions and a glossary of terms appear at the end of each chapter. Major sections of the text are introduced with a timeline. Moreover, numerous luminaries are covered in this text that were not included in previous editions. This edition includes more images and supporting materials as well.

Some final words are in order regarding some of the historiographic and philosophical biases of the authors. Disciplinary histories, such as those about art, music, philosophy, or psychology, are commonly *internal* histories that focus on historical developments within a discipline. Although emphasis on internal developments may be the primary goal in disciplinary histories, these works are nevertheless richer if attention is also directed to *external* history—that is, to contextual political, economic, religious, philosophical, scientific, and social forces that help shape the flow of events within a discipline. In this spirit, we identify some external forces that helped shape psychology. The complex, multidimensional characteristics of the task, however, guarantee that it cannot be carried out totally successfully. The historian who may be versed in economic context for a given period of time may not be so well versed, for example, in religious history and context. The complicated rich texture of the past is beyond the grasp of most of us. Nevertheless, an awareness that our discipline did not develop in a vacuum is itself valuable.

Another historiographic bias is illustrated in the organization of this text. We believe that nature and history are filled with real discontinuities, disjunctions, and surprises. Events, especially in the intellectual arena, seldom flow with measured, uniform, unvarying regularity. But even if the flow of events had been linear and logical, it would be impossible to present the story in such a fashion because the historian has little choice but to be selective with respect to the materials to be presented. The past is marked by a burly, robust accumulation of materials, some apparently more relevant and some less relevant to our interests. To present the story in all its thick detail would require more time than most of us could devote to the subject; hence, we must resort to the thinness of concepts. If the historian could function more as a photographer than as an artist, the product would still be based on many arbitrary decisions. In the main, we attempt to allow chronology to dictate the flow of ideas and we hope, from time to time, to capture some of the rich detail of the past. At other times, we will break with strict chronology to follow a single idea forward in time and then backtrack to follow another idea forward in time. Thus, the interests of coherence sometimes trump the dictates of chronology.

Study aids are provided in each chapter to help students focus on important materials and concepts. Key words in the text are presented in boldface to help the reader focus on major ideas. A phonic pronunciation guide for difficult names (e.g., Xenophanes [*zeh NAH fuh neez*]) is included to assist students in feeling more "at home" with the materials.

New to This Edition

This edition of the text retains all the unique features that appealed to students in previous editions but also includes numerous distinctive additions as follows:

- We have reviewed and incorporated over five hundred new references. This text remains one of the most heavily referenced texts in the field.
- New materials have been included on the nature of historical consciousness to highlight research into an area with important pedagogical and substantive consequences for historical studies in general and the history of science and psychology in particular. Additionally, we have incorporated new scholarship on the historical, present, and future unity and diversity of psychology.
- There is now an outpouring of new work in biological psychology, and our text reflects this explosion. We evaluate possible neurophysiological determinants of intention and implications for free will and determinism, an issue that occupies increasing attention of historians and philosophers of science and psychology. We also address the recent history of these and related research areas such as psychoneuroimmunology, psychopharmacology, and recent technological advances in neuroscience.
- We have added a section on the significance of evolution in the development of psychology. There are now growing numbers of new books and courses on behavioral genetics, evolutionary psychology, and evolutionary interpretations of such topics as the determinants of mate selection and mate guarding.
- Beginning with the first edition, we have focused on the significance of humanitarian reform movements in shaping the development of psychology. That emphasis has been expanded in this edition by reference to the work of Alice Paul and others in the women's suffrage movement. We also call attention to likely changes in the historiography of the Inquisition based on the opening of the Vatican archives.
- There are numerous updates in this edition on the philosophy and psychology of William

James. The addition of recent scholarship on James complements a section of the text that has been recognized as a strength.

- We have incorporated new scholarship about the origins of Gestalt theory, potential outcomes of Watson's Little Albert study, particularly the claims about Albert's identity, and innovative therapies that have generated positive and rigorously studied outcomes.

Acknowledgments

We deeply appreciate the literally thousands of students at the University of Northern Colorado, Colorado State University, and the University of Colorado Boulder who have studied previous editions of this text and have provided helpful, critical, and appreciative commentary. Their enthusiasm, generosity, and insights have played a major role in shaping this sixth edition.

We express our sincere gratitude to Dr. D. Brett King who has been involved in multiple ways with this project since its inception in the early 1990s and who served as co-author of the second and third editions of this text and as senior author of the fourth and fifth editions. Sincere appreciation is also extended to Dr. Cheri King who has made extensive contributions to this project through the first to the fifth editions. Priorities for other intellectual projects have prevented the Kings from participation in the writing of this sixth edition, but their influence remains in numerous parts of this work.

We also express appreciation to the many scholars who have offered suggestions for each of the editions of this book. A considerable number of reviewers who have helped us over the years include Thomas M. Atkinson, Lisa Best, Phillip Causey, James Choca, Steve Coleman, Edward Crossman, Robert Dippner, Marsha B. Driscoll, David Edwards, LeAnne Epling, Matthew Fanetti,

Laurel Furumoto, Allan M. Hartman, Mary Henle, Margaret Ingate, Tim Koeltzow, Howard Markowitz, Michelle Merwin, John Mueller, Robert Presbie, Darrell Rudmann, Charles Jeffrey Sandoz, Elizabeth Scarborough, David Schneider, John Terrizzi, Margaret Thomas, Sara Ann Tompkins, Michael Wertheimer, and William Woodward. The intellectual resources of our reviewers have made an immeasurable contribution to this book.

It has been a pleasure to work with the publication and production teams at Taylor & Francis as we developed this edition. We are especially grateful to Editor Christina Chronister for her encouragement and strong support. Editorial Assistant Julie Toich has been extremely patient and supportive. The entire team has been admirably personable and professional throughout the entire process. We would also like to thank Jill W. Payne, who has built the supplementary materials for the companion website.

We express our gratitude to several archivists and historians for their help in providing archival materials including David Baker, Robert Harper, Mott Linn, Carlos and Mai Parada, Lizette Royer, Fordyce Williams, and Nanci Young.

A few additional individuals merit a special word of thanks. We would like to share our appreciation to Lisa Woody for her enduring good humor, patience, support, and wisdom.

We have each benefited immeasurably from our association with Donald A. Crosby, philosopher and Professor Emeritus from Colorado State University. Crosby's extensive expertise in the history of philosophy and his authoritative work on William James have contributed to the scope and to many of the details of this work. We express deep gratitude to Professor Emeritus Michael Wertheimer of the University of Colorado at Boulder. Both of us have been influenced by his love of history, energy, generosity, wisdom, and wit. This edition, along with the previous five editions, reflects his continuing influence.

We also express our appreciation to our children: philosophers Donald Wayne and Marcus Viney for their many contributions, especially to the first half of this work; biologist Michael David Viney for helpful and thoughtful discussions on philosophy of science and evolution; and to Nate and Ian Woody for generously sharing their father with the very demanding requirements of this project.

Finally, in loving memory of Wynona Rose Viney (1934–2009).

W.D.W and W.V.

Part 1

Historiographic and Philosophical Issues

1 Critical Issues in Historical Studies

If we cling to our ignorance of history, error crushed to earth, will rise again, and we will have to go on solving the same old problems again and again.

—Mary Henle (1976)

The story of psychology begins in ancient times. As a self-conscious formal discipline, psychology is little more than a century old, but the subject matter captured the human imagination long before psychology became a science. In our journey, we will travel back thousands of years to visit the epic work of philosophers and scientists who wrestled with issues that continue to fascinate modern psychologists. Examining the work of early scholars on topics such as memory, emotions, dreams, perception, brain activity, learning, and mental disorders adds scope and richness to our understanding of psychology.

Our story will be more compelling if we examine problems associated with the study of history itself. A number of questions come to mind. What is history? Can the historian offer anything more than opinion? Why study history at all? Developing sensitivity to such philo-sophical questions makes for a more stimulating intellectual journey.

Why Study History?

The study of history is an important pursuit and numerous arguments have been proposed about why we should investigate it (see Wertheimer, 1980a). Let's take a look at a handful of the more compelling arguments.

History Enriches Our Sense of Time

In his book *The Future of an Illusion*, Sigmund Freud (1927/1961c) observed that "the less [we know] about the past and the present the more insecure must prove [our] judgment of the future" (p. 5). We live in a world of spatial, cultural, and temporal dimensions. We enrich our spatial sensitivities by traveling to other countries or studying geography. We enrich our cultural sensitivities in studies of subjects such as anthropology,

3

comparative religion, and sociology. If we hope to live in a broader time frame, we engage in historical studies.

In a way, history is memory. Just as there is a freedom that comes with a healthy and functional memory, so there is an intellectual freedom that comes with a broad historical perspective. In a later chapter on humanistic psychology, we'll explore the value of living in the present moment, but an exclusive emphasis on the past, the present, or the future could result in a naïve, uninformed, and isolated temporal prison. We live most fully in the here and now if we have a rich knowledge and memory for past events that contributed to the present. To neglect the past or to fail to think about the future is to impoverish the present.

History as a Contribution to Liberal Education

Robert I. Watson (1966), a historian of psychology, once remarked that psychologists, of all people, should seek to avoid "subjugation to influences of which [we are] unaware" (p. 64). Historical studies promote perspective, integration, context, and sensitivity to the fact that everything is in a complex environment of other things. Knowledge of the history of a discipline such as psychology helps us overcome the narrowness of specialization (Benjamin & Baker, 2009).

History Teaches Humility

When we study history, we are humbled by the genius, the effort, and the creative insight of previous thinkers. Helson (1972) reminds us that in history "student[s] may meet better minds in the literature than any [they] may have contact with in person" (p. 116). We may also encounter minds that have worked through problems we assumed were fresh or original. History all too often reveals that our innovative idea is a redis-

covery of something known long ago. History can teach humility.

History Teaches a Healthy Skepticism

When we have an understanding of history, we are less likely to fall prey to grandiose notions, utopian dreams, and schemes that promise more than they deliver. Psychology has suffered its share of unworkable schemes, including mesmerism, phrenology, craniometry, and even some modern therapies. History teaches us to be wary of the big claim, the single method to end all methods, and the one and only definition. Helson (1972) cautioned against easy acceptance that our future lies with a solitary panacea, such as "computer models of brain function, or that there is only one psychophysical law, or that trend analysis is the last answer to statistical treatments" (p. 116). Historical knowledge counsels against the glib acceptance of the latest fad or inflated idea. Jaynes (1973a) pointed out that history may help us "liberate ourselves from the persuasions of fashions" (p. xi). At the very least, we can hope that historical knowledge will make us less gullible (Goodwin, 2005) and that historical thinking will extend into other questions in our lives.

History Influences Human Thought Processes

Henle (1976) pointed out that most of us find it difficult to see our errors or question our assumptions. She argued that human cognition is often resistant to criticism and prone to a degree of inertia or self-preservation. According to Henle, knowledge of history "gives us distance not only from our immediate objective, but from our own thinking" (p. 16). History heightens awareness of the errors of others, but also keeps us thinking straight. As Henle warned in the quotation that opened this chapter, if we are blind to the lessons of history, then we will be doomed to solve the same old problems again and again.

Some Problems in Historiography

The term **historiography** has multiple meanings. In a narrow and literal sense, it refers to the writing of history, including techniques and strategies for investigating specific content areas. The term also encompasses philosophical questions about history and historical method (later, we will review some philosophical questions encountered in historical studies). A third meaning of *historiography* refers to the characteristics of a body of historical writings. For example, historical accounts of psychology have sometimes neglected the contributions of women, scholars from outside the United States (Burman, 2015), and other cultural minorities, and these systematic omissions and distortions carry consequences at every level of history education (Loewen, 2007). Fortunately, critical awareness of our biases has led to research that addresses how psychology has profited from the contributions of women (see Bohan, 1992a, 1992b; Gavin, 1987; O'Connell & Russo, 1983, 1988, 1990; Scarborough & Furumoto, 1987), African-American psychologists (see Guthrie, 2003; Phillips, 2000; Sawyer, 2000), and Hispanic psychologists (see Martinez & Mendoza, 1984), among others.

We will now examine questions and issues about history and historical method. What is history? What is historical consciousness? Can historians be objective? What is objectivity?

The Development of Historical Consciousness

Gilderhus (1992) suggests that peoples in traditional societies often lacked historical consciousness because immediate survival was their primary concern. Even so, survival depends on memory along with an awareness of time-based events. Temporal awareness clearly has survival value. Historical consciousness grows partly from beliefs in the significance of pivotal events in religion, politics, or science. In Hebraic literature, for example, people are encouraged to remember events associated with their delivery from Egyptian bondage. In more recent history, phrases such as *never again, lest we forget, 9/11,* and *united we stand* serve as reminders of the horrors of the Holocaust or the sacrifices of war and terrorism.

Gilderhus (1992) observed that historical consciousness in Greek times grew out of attempts to separate history from mythology. The legendary Greek historian **Herodotus** (*hi RAH duh tuhs*) (c. 484–c. 425 BCE) became the first to attempt a comprehensive history of the world. Documenting contemporary episodes as well as past events, he traveled widely, made extensive notes, and gained access to eyewitness testimony whenever possible. Herodotus described physical and psychological ailments (Pridmore, 2014), and he wrote history with an emphasis on natural rather than supernatural causes.

The naturalistic approach to history was extended in the work of **Thucydides** (*thoo SIHD ih deez*) (c. 460–c. 401 BCE). Remembered for his classic *History of the Peloponnesian War*, a classic still emphasized in military science education (Wither, 2010), Thucydides documented the war between Athens and Sparta from 431 to 404 BCE. Thucydides had a passion for accuracy and for naturalistic explanations stripped of theological overtones. Aware of previous attempts to write history in terms of miracles, mysteries, and divine purposes, Thucydides insisted on discovering positive facts and presenting them in a naturalistic context. Faith in the accuracy of historical writings creates respect for written histories and may foster historical consciousness. We turn now to one of the most fundamental and challenging issues in historiography—the problem of defining history.

Historical consciousness is more than knowledge of specific histories such as the history of the American Civil War, the history of a country, or the history of an academic discipline such as psychology. At a minimum, historical consciousness includes a sensitivity to the great range of philosophical problems associated with the writing of history, an endeavor to approach history with both critical and appreciative orientations, awareness of the dynamic ever-changing nature of historical inquiry, and an attempt to approach every subject historically (Viney, 2010). American philosopher and psychologist William James (1911) argued that "we give humanistic value to almost anything when we teach it historically. Geology, economics, [and] mechanics are humanities when taught with reference to the successive achievements of the geniuses to which these sciences owe their being. When not taught in this way, literature remains grammar, art a catalogue, history a list of dates, and natural science a sheet of formulas and weights and measures" (pp. 312–313).

What Is History?

In popular usage, the term **history** sometimes denotes the chronology of events that provides a raw material for the historian. The term also refers to stories we tell about our past. Dictionary definitions typically emphasize both meanings (i.e., history as a chronology of previous events and history as a narrative or interpretive study of the past). History has both empirical and explanatory components. The *empirical* component includes data such as unpublished letters; newspaper and Internet accounts; audio, video, or digital recordings; and official documents. The *explanatory* component refers to the efforts of historians to make sense of data. Additional perspectives about history are provided in Table 1.1.

So, how are we to define *history*? Let's begin with the idea that history has an empirical component. That is, real events that took place in the past can enter our present experiences through records. The empirical component can also include eyewitness accounts or personal experiences for more recent events. For instance, where were you on September 11, 2001? If you remember, chances are

the episode is vivid in your memory. Events such as the terrorist attack on the World Trade Center resonate, in part, because they provide a way of aligning ourselves with the yardstick of history.

The task of the historian is to become acquainted with as much data as possible. Data collection may include interviews, traveling to archives to examine unpublished letters and documents, and reading old newspapers. After collecting data, the historian must engage in an interpretive study. Such study includes examining contradictions, discriminating between what is relevant and what is not, and assigning weights to different bits of evidence. In a way, the process is like working on a complicated jigsaw puzzle when we know in advance that there will always be missing pieces.

The working definition of *history* suggested here is as follows: History is the interpretive study of the events of the human past. The definition assumes empirical and explanatory components in the work of a historian.

Table 1.1 Some Perspectives on the Nature of History

History as Subjective Study

We read history through our prejudices.
—Wendell Phillips

What is history but a fable agreed upon.
—Napoleon I (Bonaparte)

History as a Record of the Past

History is not history unless it is the truth.
—Abraham Lincoln

History as Cyclical

History repeats itself; that's just one of the things that's wrong with history.
—Clarence Darrow

The Importance of History

Who cannot give an account of three thousand years remains in the darkness of inexperience.
—Wolfgang Goethe

The less we know of the past, the more unreliable our judgment of the present and future.
—Sigmund Freud

The Value of History

If I have seen farther than others, it is because I have stood on the shoulders of giants.
—Isaac Newton

History is the witness that testifies to the passing of time; it illumines reality, vitalizes memory, provides guidance in daily life, and brings us tidings of antiquity.
—Cicero

[W]ithout history there can be no psychology.
—Carl Jung

A Presentist View of History

Let the past serve the present.
—Mao Tse-tung

A Historicist View of History

We cannot escape history. We . . . will be remembered in spite of ourselves . . . The fiery trial through which we pass will light us down, in honor or dishonor, to the last generation.
—Abraham Lincoln

Can History Be Objective?

If we agree that history is the interpretive study of the human past, we nevertheless encounter the problem of the faithfulness or truthfulness of our interpretations. Abraham Lincoln (1856/1950) said, "History is not history unless it is the truth" (p. 149). But how can we be assured that a historical narrative is an accurate reflection of the landscape of the past? The question of objectivity is a critical issue in the philosophy of history. Historians do not usually make direct observations. Even if they did, there is no guarantee of objectivity. Historians must be selective about what they report and we are all creatures of the present and, as such, may write history in the light of present personal and cultural perspectives.

Still, we can't easily close the case against objectivity. Objectivity is a desirable yet elusive ideal in most intellectual endeavors. If we reject attempts at objectivity, we run into the assumption that one person's opinion is as good as another's. Objectivity offers the hope that

historical narratives can rise above the prevailing climate of opinion. If such an ideal can be achieved, history can uncover mistakes of the past and can repudiate, disagree with, or tell unpopular stories. Chinese leader Mao Tse-tung (1893–1976) believed that history should serve the Communist revolution (Lifton, 1968, p. 144). But history serves best when it is free to treat political, religious, and philosophical ideologies in critical as well as appreciative ways.

Before proceeding, we should explore possible meanings of **objectivity in history**. The term *objective* could refer to a correspondence between a historical narrative and the events of the past it describes. If objectivity refers to such a correspondence, then the work of the historian is sure to be deficient. A historical narrative can never recapture the fullness of lived experience. Objectivity then, as correspondence, is suspect. Perhaps historians are more like painters than photographers. Even if they were like photographers, historical events would always offer another angle for a shot, a different way to frame the subject, a new magnification, or different films with varying sensitivity to color.

Another meaning of *objectivity* involves the attempt to portray all sides of an issue in a fair manner, even if something disagrees with the author's perspective. Objectivity, viewed in this way, is an attitude, one we may expect of a historian. In this context, the historian is reminded to be aware of ulterior motives and to hold them in check.

Before leaving the question of objectivity, let's return to Abraham Lincoln's contention that "History is not history unless it is the truth." Most historians might agree if we could add that, for any event, there is more than one possible true history. For example, the American Civil War can be regarded not as one war but as many wars. It was a different war for the South than for the North. The two sides could not even agree on the causes of the war. It was also a different war for each of the various states. From this line of reasoning, there can be multiple "true" histories of the American Civil War, each disagreeing on countless details.

The Tyranny of the Present

As noted earlier, historians are creatures of the present, but can they free themselves from natural biases imposed by current worldviews? Historians, like psychotherapists, must have a well-developed empathy for their subject. If such empathy is possible, then historians may be capable of suspending or neutralizing present biases; that is, they may literally "feel" their way back into the past so that deep and authentic understandings become a possibility. In short, we follow a commitment of "understanding the past for its own sake" (Stocking, 1965, p. 212). Stocking adds that a past-minded approach places emphasis on *understanding* the past rather than *judging* it; this perspective also avoids the temptation to use the past to glorify the present. As noted earlier, an adequate history can tell an unpopular story that is damaging to present interests. But is this ideal of past-mindedness possible? Can a historian suspend the present frame of reference with its possible distortions and prejudices? Put another way, can the historian capture an earlier era or frame of mind in all its intricacy, richness, and context? As noted, the problem resembles a common issue debated among clinical psychologists. Can we empathically "crawl into the mind" of another person or do individual differences prohibit genuine congruence of thought and feeling?

Related to this idea, **presentism** emphasizes the difficulty in divorcing historical facts from current perspectives. The presentist questions whether the historian can recapture the past with true objectivity. Buss (1977) wrote, "There is no such thing as hard-core, indubitable facts that are invariant across different theoretical explanations" (p. 254). The presentist is tuned to the effects of inevitable selective, judgmental, and contextual forces in historical scholarship. Scholars with a more past-minded orientation might counter that *because* we are aware of such forces, we can neutralize their effects.

Issues surrounding presentism and past-mindedness have stimulated discussion in the historiography of the behavioral sciences (see Ash & Woodward, 1987; Dewsbury, 1990; Furumoto, 1989; Harrison, 1987; Henle, 1989; Young, 1966). As with most issues, extremes of past-mindedness and presentism create difficulties. William James (1890/1981) once referred to absolutism as "the great disease of philosophic thought" (p. 334). Sounding a similar theme, Dewsbury (1990) raised doubts about the superiority of either approach and argued for a moderate and tolerant approach to historiography with room for past-minded and presentist orientations. Such an approach is sensitive to the role of present beliefs in our understanding and writing of history but also insists that authentic history will challenge and shape our present beliefs.

Is There a Pattern or Direction in History?

To ask whether history has a pattern or direction is to ask something about the meaning of history. Patterns offer information and the discovery of a pattern can be useful. We'll take a look at a few hypotheses about the direction of history that are applicable to the history of psychology.

CYCLICAL HYPOTHESIS   As the name suggests, the **cyclical hypothesis** claims that history repeats itself. We find an ebb and flow in events marked by endless repetition. Kingdoms rise and fall, only to rise again; freedom is gained and lost, only to be regained once more. Cycles of poverty and plenty play out along with war and peace, discovery and intellectual stagnation, innocence and corruption, and revolution and stability. Even our ways of understanding, according to this view, are cyclical. A rational and scientific era may arise in one era before falling to arbitrary political or religious authority, only to see the rational-scientific method return to prominence at a later time.

Cycles exist in every science, and psychology has seen its share. For example, neuroscientists in the twentieth century wondered if the right and left hemispheres of the brain mediate different emotional and intellectual processes, or do the hemispheres function in a more integrated fashion? Interest in lateralization of function in the cerebral hemispheres is not new. Long before modern neuroscience took an interest, Brown-Sequard (1890) wrote an article titled "Have We Two Brains or One?" The article is only one of many from that period to struggle with the problem of the lateralization of function. Another example from the history of psychology came in the early emphasis on conscious and experiential processes, only to face later rejection with the advent of behaviorism before an interest in consciousness and experience reemerged in the closing decades of the twentieth century.

LINEAR-PROGRESSIVE HYPOTHESIS A linear hypothesis can be either progressive or regressive, but let us assume optimism and consider only a linear-progressive view. According to the **linear-progressive hypothesis**, each generation builds upon discoveries from previous generations. Each new generation works up from a stronger base, giving rise to growth and progress in human knowledge and among human institutions. Brief regressions and setbacks may ensue, but the overall victory belongs to progress and growth. In a book entitled *The Good Old Days—They Were Terrible*, Bettmann (1974) recounts the hardships of American life from the end of the Civil War to the early 1900s. It was an era made almost unbearable with filth and pollution in major cities from factories, coal-fired steam engines, city streets teeming with horse manure, insects, and poor sewerage. In a time before air-conditioning, poorly ventilated houses and apartments claimed many lives during summer and winter months. Crime flourished, often beyond control, in major cities and on the frontier. "Dominating the record was, of course, the West, where the gun-happy barbarity was damned by observers both foreign and native for producing a 'great dismal swamp of civilization'" (Bettmann, 1974, p. 87). Education for women was little more than a faint hope, and school conditions remained deplorable for all

but wealthy men. In the absence of refrigeration, food spoiled, and diets were lean and inadequate. Epidemics of yellow fever, tuberculosis, smallpox, whooping cough, and measles raged throughout the country. Child labor laws had not yet been enacted, and unsafe factories took an enormous toll in injuries and death, with little recourse for victims or their families. The problems, of course, intensified for people enslaved in Southern states or, earlier in United States history, across the nation. Given the adversities of earlier times, most people today would probably rather not return to the "good old days."

CHAOS HYPOTHESIS The coming of the nuclear age dampened earlier optimism about the inevitability of human progress. It became clear that the entire structure of human achievement could be brought to ruin by a chance technological accident or by the design of political systems deficient in world perspective. The Nazi genocide of European Jews during the Holocaust tested the hypothesis that progress is inevitable.

According to the **chaos hypothesis**, history itself has no overall identifiable and universal meaning. History is, as noted by Fisher (1936), simply "the play of the contingent and the unforeseen" (p. v). The meanings found in history are the meanings we impose, not meanings that inhere in history itself. This idea was captured in a letter from Jean-Paul Sartre to Albert Camus. Sartre (1965) observed, "History, apart from the man who makes it, is only an abstract and static concept, of which it can neither be said that it has an objective, nor that it has not . . . The problem is not to *know* its objective, but to *give* it one" (p. 103).

Critics maintain that chaos theory discourages any attempt to take responsibility for our future. If what happens in the future is independent of individual human belief and action, what incentive exists to shape our future?

In addition to the theories outlined earlier, providential theories claim that a deity plays a role in shaping the direction of history. Providential theories vary of course, depending on the particular religious beliefs from which they are derived. One criticism of such theories is that they may undermine human efforts to improve the world. If the world is fordone by a decree of deity, why bother?

What Makes History?

We turn now to an issue of controversy among historians, one that holds special relevance for students of psychology. The central question here asks whether history is fashioned through the bold actions of exceptional people or the "spirit of the times" in which they live. The **great-person theory** suggests that uncommon individuals transcend the conditions of their day and shape history through their courage or wisdom or some other virtue. In contrast, the German terms **Zeitgeist** (spirit of a time) and **Ortgeist** (spirit of a place) argue that prevailing conditions, not individuals, forge historical events.

American philosopher Ralph Waldo Emerson's optimistic work titled *Self-Reliance* makes a compelling case for the great-person theory. For Emerson (1841/1981), history "resolves itself very easily into the biography of a few stout and earnest persons" (p. 138). He tells us that with Caesar, we have a Roman Empire; with Luther, the Reformation; with Fox, Quakerism; and with Wesley, Methodism. Following his lead, it is with Wundt that we have the formal discipline of psychology; with Freud, psychoanalysis; with Rorschach, the inkblot test; and so on. The great-person theory emphasizes the causal role of particular persons in particular circumstances and the ability of the individual to control or to change the direction of events.

Critics argue that the great-person theory results from an unsophisticated view of forces at work in the world; late in his life, E. G. Boring (1966) noted that the sudden insights of great people may serve as memory aids for students rather than accurate depictions of history (Rosenzweig, 1987). Causation in history is complex, so we must be tuned to multiple forces that

create an idea, event, or institution. Seldom can a critical occurrence or invention be credited to the labor of a single individual. As an example, powered flight could never have developed from individual effort prior to invention of the internal combustion engine. A relevant background of invention, material, culture, education, and social support must be present to nurture a significant historical happening. In addition to promoting hero worship, the idea that one person alone is responsible for any substantial contribution ignores the complexities of life and history. The place (*Ortgeist*) and time (*Zeitgeist*) must be conducive before advances can be made.

English philosopher Herbert Spencer (1873) believed in the possibility of a "science of history" where context played a central role in historical causation. Likewise, the Canadian naturalist Grant Allen (1878a, 1878b) argued that the great intellectual achievements in ancient Greece were due to geography and other external forces rather than specific individuals. Herman Melville's *Moby-Dick* captures this philosophy of history when a crew member advises Captain Ahab to call off the chase for the albino whale. Ahab replies, "This whole act's immutably decreed. 'Twas rehearsed by thee and me a billion years before this ocean rolled. Fool! I am the Fates' lieutenant; I act under orders" (Melville, 1851/1976, pp. 548–549). Such fatalism may, of course, have its origin in a theological or naturalistic context. We should note that an extreme emphasis on environmental context may overlook the importance of individual actions in the stream of historical causation.

William James (1880) provides a different approach to the problem of historical causality. He argued that historical development is a causal interplay between people and their environment. He agreed that our environment sets boundaries, but added that human effort changes our world. According to James, any account of history that neglects the individual dissolves into vagary and incoherence (see Viney, 2001). James proposes a balanced approach where an individual's idea cannot achieve fruition without social and material support. On the other hand, some ideas might never make a historical impact if not born in the mind of a unique and creative individual.

Disagreements over the forces that make history continue as a topic in historical scholarship. In an article titled "Genius without the 'Great Man,'" Ball (2012) suggests ways to engage with eminent figures without resorting to *hagiography* (a term originally meaning the worshipful and celebratory descriptions of the lives of saints). In this context, hagiography refers to a tendency to pedestalize individuals by giving them excessive credit for new historical developments. Continuing efforts to explore more comprehensive understandings of historical causation can be found in the ways psychology has been understood in a variety of countries (see Pickren, 2012).

The History of the History of Psychology

Interest in the history of psychology is as old as the discipline itself. Early textbook writers such as Wilhelm Wundt and William James acknowledged earlier contributions from disciplines such as physics, physiology, and philosophy. As noted, people discussed psychological topics centuries before psychology became a formal discipline. So it's no surprise that early psychologists were interested in the history of psychological ideas even while the formal discipline was in its infancy.

In addition to earlier and modern texts, numerous books of readings in the history of psychology have been published (Benjamin, 1997; Dennis, 1948; Diamond, 1974b; Fancher, 1996; Henle, Jaynes, & Sullivan, 1973; Herrnstein & Boring, 1966; Pickren & Dewsbury, 2002; Sahakian, 1968; Sexton & Misiak, 1971). Some helpful books trace the development of psychology in various countries (Hiroshi, 2002; Misiak & Sexton, 1966; Sexton & Misiak, 1976). With the growth of interest in the history of psychology, other resources have appeared that are useful to students writing term papers and to scholars conducting research. Select bibliographies show how

to find biographical information on various psychologists (Benjamin, 1974; Benjamin & Heider, 1976; Zusne, 1984), and numerous guides and sourcebooks outline how to discover other kinds of information on the history of psychology. For example, Viney, Wertheimer, and Wertheimer (1979) produced a large bibliography of sources in English on the history of psychology; Watson (1974/1976, 1978) compiled three volumes that provide lists of major works from the world's great psychologists (Volume 1, 1974), a bibliography of sources about these same psychologists (Volume 2, 1976), and resources for the study of the history of psychology (1978). Benjamin and colleagues (1989) prepared a bibliography of sources in the history of psychology compiled from notes and news sections from major journals. Sokal and Rafail (1982) published a guide to manuscript collections in the history of psychology for scholars interested in archival materials. From 1927 to December 2006, the *Psychological Abstracts* was the primary guide to world literature in psychology, but the electronic search tool PsycINFO has replaced it (see Benjamin & VandenBos, 2006). In addition to PsycINFO, a wealth of source materials is available to students interested in the history of psychology. Selected examples are presented in Table 1.2.

Prior to the 1960s, scholarly work on the history of psychology was disjointed and restricted to a few isolated researchers. Only a handful of journals accepted historical articles and only a few textbooks and books of readings hit the market. Informal meetings of interested individuals occurred at the annual conventions of the American Psychological Association, but opportunities were scarce.

The mid-1960s ushered in a dramatic change. During this period, the *Journal of the History of the Behavioral Sciences* was first published in January 1965 and, ten months later, the Archives of the History of American Psychology were established in Ohio at the University of Akron. That same year, the American Psychological Association approved the formation of Division 26, the Division of the History of Psychology, later renamed the Society

Table 1.2 Selected Source Materials for Students Interested in the History of Psychology

Source	Brief Description
PsycINFO	Primary electronic search tool and guide to world literature in psychology. Includes extensive references on historical materials.
History of Psychology	Flagship journal for the Society for the History of Psychology.
Journal of the History of the Behavioral Sciences	Includes articles on the history of psychology as well as histories of other behavioral sciences.
History of the Human Sciences	Interdisciplinary journal with historical articles in fields such as anthropology, political science, psychology, and sociology.
Theory and Psychology	Bimonthly journal with articles on the conceptual foundations of psychology including historical underpinnings.
Journal of the History of the Neurosciences	Organ of the International Society for the History of the Neurosciences. Includes historical articles on basic, clinical, and behavioral neurosciences.
American Psychologist	Flagship journal of the American Psychological Association. Includes archival documents, obituaries of well-known psychologists, and occasional historical articles.
American Journal of Psychology	Founded by G. Stanley Hall in 1887, explores the basic science of psychology. Often includes articles on the history of psychology.
Classics in the History of Psychology	A website containing hundreds of full-text classic articles in the history of psychology (http://psychclassics.yorku.ca/).
This Week in the History of Psychology	Podcasts consisting of twenty-five-minute interviews with experts on landmark events in the history of psychology (www.yorku.ca/christo/podcasts/).

for the History of Psychology. Psychologists interested in history quickly established physical, organizational, and social support for scholarly activities. In 1967, the first graduate program offering a Ph.D. in the history of psychology was established at the University of New Hampshire. A year later, another important society was launched—Cheiron, the International Society for the History of Behavioral and Social Sciences (the inspiration for the society's name came from Cheiron, a centaur in Greek mythology known for wisdom, knowledge, and immortality). As the history of psychology has grown into a self-aware discipline that integrates psychological scholarship with historical research techniques, these changes have brought important benefits, particularly in the rigor of our scholarship (Berrios, 2014) as well as potential costs (Pettit & Davidson, 2014).

In the twenty-first century, the history of psychology remains an invaluable topic of study. A survey of more than seven hundred psychology departments in American colleges and universities revealed that over 80 percent offer undergraduate courses in the history of psychology (Fuchs & Viney, 2002). Such courses are typically taught during the junior or senior year and sometimes serve as capstone courses for psychology majors. Further, accredited graduate programs in counseling and clinical psychology include instruction on the history of psychology as a core part of graduate education. Most departments of psychology offer a history course as a component of undergraduate and graduate education. Though professional organizations such as Cheiron and Division 26 (History of Psychology) of the American Psychological Association have weathered ups and downs in membership, researchers remain interested in the area. Because of the growth of scholarly work, the American Psychological Association approved a journal, *History of Psychology*, launched in 1998 under the initial editorship of Michael M. Sokal, a prominent historian of science who also served as president of the History of Science Society. Today, the history of psychology can be considered as an important facet of the history of science.

Despite these ongoing gains, the history of psychology as a field faces important challenges. Unlike many subtopics, external funding is extremely limited. A study published at the outset of the twenty-first century found that many departments plan to eliminate the course in the history of psychology when the current instructor retires (Fuchs & Viney, 2002). In some ways, the administrative aspects of universities challenge the place of the history of psychology in the larger discipline.

The history of psychology is an intrinsically interesting subject, covering groundbreaking thinkers and a wealth of ideas about human and animal nature. From the ideas of the earliest Greeks about mental illness, to concepts of childhood in the Middle Ages, to the nineteenth-century vision of a new discipline called psychology—the story is a fascinating and worthwhile adventure. Finally, and perhaps more urgently, the historical study of psychology provides an invigorating perspective on the present scene that would be difficult if not impossible to achieve in any other way.

Review Questions

1. List and briefly describe five reasons for the study of history.
2. What is historiography? What issues are typically studied in historiography?
3. What is history? Do you agree that history has an empirical component?
4. In what sense can the historian be objective?
5. List and describe three hypotheses regarding the pattern or direction of history.
6. Describe specific developments in the latter part of the twentieth century that contributed to the advance of scholarly work in the history of psychology.

Glossary

chaos hypothesis The belief that there is no pattern or direction in history; history has no meaning except that attributed to it by humans.

cyclical hypothesis The belief that history can be understood in terms of repetitive patterns or cycles. For example, it might be argued that freedom is lost, only to be regained and lost again; thus, there is endless repetition.

great-person theory The view that unique individuals play a causal role in history. Contrast with *Zeitgeist* and *Ortgeist*.

Herodotus (c. 484–c. 425 BCE) First great Greek historian to write history with an emphasis on natural rather than supernatural causes.

historiography The writing of history along with the study of the methodological and philosophical issues that are pertinent to the work of the historian.

history The interpretive study of the events of the human past.

linear-progressive hypothesis A view of history marked by belief in the inevitable growth and progress of human knowledge and institutions.

objectivity in history An attitude of the historical researcher marked by an attempt to present fairly all sides of an issue.

Ortgeist The spirit of the place. Contrasts with the great-person theory of history and emphasizes the importance of place and time (*Zeitgeist*) as conditions for the production and acceptance of new ideas.

presentism An orientation toward history emphasizing the pervasive influence of current prejudices on the interpretation of past events.

Thucydides (c. 460–c. 401 BCE) Greek historian and author of the *History of the Peloponnesian War*. He worked to achieve accurate naturalistic accounts of historical events.

Zeitgeist The spirit of the time. Contrasts with the great-person theory of history and emphasizes the importance of time and place (*Ortgeist*) as conditions for the production and acceptance of new ideas.

2 Philosophical Issues

But man, proud man, Drest in a little briefe authoritie, Most ignorant of what he's most assur'd (His glassie Essence) like an angry Ape Plaies such phantastique tricks before high heauen, As makes the Angels weepe.
—William Shakespeare (1604–1605/1964)

A study of the history of psychology is much more meaningful if you are aware of perennial psychological themes and issues that have emerged and re-emerged since antiquity (Robinson, 2013). In this chapter, we'll examine critical historical and philosophical problems and issues that shaped psychology's development.

Epistemology

The term **epistemology** is derived from the Greek *episteme*, which means to understand or to know. Epistemology is a branch of philosophy concerned with theories of knowledge. As you might guess, psychologists have had a long-standing curiosity about epistemological issues. For example, Jean Piaget (1896–1980) was trained in zoology and gained fame for his studies of human cognitive development, but he didn't consider himself a biologist or a psychologist. Instead, Piaget viewed himself as a student of **genetic epistemology**, the study of the ways we solve problems as a function of our age and level of development. As a genetic epistemologist, Piaget demonstrated that our understanding of the world and our ways of solving problems evolve as we mature. Let's take a look at epistemological issues that hold special relevance for psychologists.

A Priori and A Posteriori Knowledge

As you read the history of psychology, you'll encounter the idea that certain truths are presumed to be known a priori. What does that mean? The philosophical term **a priori** comes from the Latin meaning "from what is prior" or "from what comes before." By contrast, the term **a posteriori** means "from what comes later." *A posteriori* refers to that which is derived from or comes after experience and *a priori* refers to self-evident truths given in experience without learning. For example, if A is larger than B and B is larger than C, then A is larger than C. The truth of the proposition seems intuitively obvious. No one would deny that the proposition itself is known through experience. That is, without experience, we would not even know about the proposition. But we can still claim to know the truth of the relationships among A, B, and C through intellectual insight alone. In other words, we can grasp certain relationships without learning or benefit of prior experience. According to the theory of a priori knowledge, it can be argued, for example, that one could immediately grasp the truth of a statement such as "We cannot both exist and not exist at the same time."

Philosophers and psychologists have struggled with the role of the a priori in human knowledge. Extreme claims contribute to the problem. For instance, some thinkers argue that knowledge of good and evil is known a priori. On the other extreme, we encounter the argument that all knowledge is dependent on experience. Psychologists emphasize the centrality of experience as the basis of knowledge. But like philosophers, we wrestle with evidence that some relationships are discerned without learning or previous experience.

Nativism versus Empiricism

This issue is a close relative to the issue of a priori and a posteriori knowledge. **Nativism** holds that some perceptions are operational from birth, built in as a natural outcome of the structural and functional properties of the nervous system. By contrast, **empiricism** holds that all perceptions are learned or developed from experience. The problem of depth perception illustrates the dispute between nativists and empiricists. We have the ability to see our world in three dimensions, but do we learn to see in depth or is depth perception a natural or unlearned ability? Classic research suggests that newborns have perceptual abilities that may not be learned. Gibson and Walk (1960) constructed a visual cliff, a platform that ended in a steep drop but was covered by a bridge of transparent glass. Although it was

safe to cross the transparent bridge, baby goats and chicks only a few hours old avoided the visual cliff. Wertheimer (1961) demonstrated that newborn human infants, only minutes old, will turn their heads in the direction of a sound. Is the turning of the head learned or is it a native ability? Later in the text, we explore the work of philosophers and psychologists who examine these issues.

Instinct versus Learning

The problem of **instinct** versus **learning** has had a turbulent history during psychology's modern era (see Diamond, 1971, 1974a). Many early psychologists stressed the role of instincts in human and animal psychology. William McDougall (1871–1938) was perhaps the best example of an early theorist who believed that instincts play a central role in human life. McDougall (1908/1960) claimed that instincts operate in diverse behaviors such as curiosity, fighting, and maternal behavior. After a time, a group of psychologists called behaviorists replaced instinct theories with an emphasis on learning. Behaviorists assumed that we learn to be aggressive, to be inquisitive, and to be good parents. Behaviorist research showed that some behaviors assumed to be instinctual were subject to learning. In early studies, Zing-Yang Kuo (1898–1970) demonstrated that rat killing by cats is more subject to learning than anybody of the time had believed (1921, 1924). Depending on rearing conditions, baby kittens may grow to become rat killers but may also grow up fearful of rats or may grow tolerant or even cooperative, living peacefully in the same cages with rats and eating and drinking from the same dishes. Kuo showed that the conditioning history of the individual kitten is a key to understanding that kitten's later interaction with rats. Across these and other studies, Kuo (1924) sought to break down the nature–nurture distinction in psychology (Honeycutt, 2011).

Although behaviorism demonstrated the importance of learning, it did not banish instinct theory from psychology. Interest in the topic accelerated after World War II. Ethologists such as Konrad Lorenz (1903–1989) and Nikolaas "Niko" Tinbergen (1907–1988) and sociobiologists such as Edward O. Wilson (b. 1929) contributed new insights to the area. Desmond Morris's 1967 best-selling book *The Naked Ape* also stimulated public awareness of instinct theory.

Terms such as *a priori*, *nativism*, and *instinct* refer to abilities or capacities built into living systems. Important differences appear in the capacities denoted by these terms. For example, a priori knowledge is more cognitive than an instinct, which appears with a high degree of automaticity. A native ability such as the innate capacity to see in depth also seems less cognitive than a priori knowledge, which refers to real intellectual insight or the capacity to discern certain fundamental relationships. Terms such as *a posteriori*, *empiricism*, and *learning* are somewhat comparable because they stress the importance of experience.

What Are the Criteria by Which We Claim to Know Truth?

As human beings, we live our lives and make decisions based on epistemological categories that serve as guides to knowledge. On what grounds can we claim to have knowledge? On the grounds of authority? What about reason? Faith? Personal observation? Science? A clash of epistemologies provides the essential ingredient in disputes between science and law, between science and religion, and even between scientists and other scientists. Let's take a look at common epistemological criteria used as a basis for knowledge.

AUTHORITY Reference to **authority** is the most common method of assessing truth. During childhood, we incorporate the values, beliefs, and judgments of our parents. They serve as original authorities during our formative years. As we mature, we find authority everywhere in modern culture—teachers, sacred texts, the media, cultural institutions, political and religious leaders, and legal codes. We often neglect independent verification or substantiation—the word of the authority is sufficient.

In his 1947 book *Man for Himself*, psychologist Erich Fromm (1900–1980) provided a thoughtful analysis of the problem of authority. For Fromm, the great sin in authoritarian epistemology is to become too much like the authority. If we become as knowledgeable as the authority, we no longer need its information and direction. As a means of survival, some authorities discourage questions and restrict information so followers will not discover contradictory opinions. Authorities may encourage study, but only if it is sanctioned and determined to be "safe." Abuse often begins when an authority claims to be the exclusive and complete basis of knowledge.

History uncovers countless examples of the abuse of authority. The Spanish theologian Michael Servetus (1511–1553) was branded a heretic for not conforming to accepted scripture. He was burned at the stake. Almost a half-century later, Giordano Bruno (1548–1600) was condemned to the same fate for unorthodox religious, scientific, and political opinions. The executions of Bruno and Servetus exemplify how commitment to authority can crush threatening ideas. Shakespeare's quotation at the beginning of this chapter may have been rooted in outrage at the abuse of authority.

Unfortunately, authoritarian abuse is not a historical relic. Abusive authoritarian forces steal into art, literature, science, religion, politics, and people themselves. The 1978 mass suicide of over nine hundred Americans in Jonestown, Guyana (see *Time*, 1978; Layton, 1998) remains a tragic example of abusive authoritarian control. The balance between necessary and abusive authority is a critical problem confronting every human group, particularly because people easily rationalize or even idealize authority, even abusive authority (Woody, 2009).

Within the history of psychology, we will encounter the problem of authority over and over again. Despite potential for abuse, authority has utilitarian value. The scientist, for example, may rely on other scientists and experiments for fresh insights. Authority can be useful, but there is a potential for problems when it cannot be tested, questioned, or doubted.

EMPIRICISM   The term *empiricism* is derived from Greek and Latin terms that were close in meaning to our word *experience.* In contemporary usage, empiricism refers to a theory of knowledge where experience plays a central role. Experience of the world depends on sensory information. According to empiricism, knowledge is based on observable facts represented in experience. As the story of the history of psychology unfolds, we will see that empiricism is often contrasted with rationalism, our next topic. Empiricists can be discovered in most historical periods and places, but Great Britain boasted a line of thinkers who gave priority to experience. John Locke (1632–1704) argued that there is nothing in the intellect that was not previously in the senses. An earlier British empiricist, Francis Bacon (1561–1626), has been called the Great Herald of the Empirical Spirit because of his campaign to encourage observation and data collection. For Bacon, we should rely less on authority and more on the empirical method.

From an uncritical standpoint, empiricism seems an obvious alternative to authority as a way of obtaining knowledge. But empiricism as a way of knowing is not free of problems. First, as discussed with a priori and a posteriori knowledge, certain forms of knowledge may not depend on sensory information. We also know that sensory information can be unreliable. The senses are easily conditioned by emotion, social context, learning, and motivation. It is little wonder that philosophers and psychologists raised questions about the adequacy of empiricism as a way of knowing.

RATIONALISM   The term **rationalism** comes from the same Latin root as the term *reason.* Rationalists argue that the mind has innate organizing principles so information from the senses is filtered and patterned in ways that shape thinking. Rationalists believe sensory information alone is not an adequate basis for knowledge. They emphasize the activity of mind, the capacity to reason, and the ability to discern some meanings on an intuitive basis. Early philosophers and scientists such as Descartes, Galileo, Leibniz, and Kant advocated rationalism.

Early psychologists and philosophers debated whether the new psychology should be based on empiricism or rationalism. As early as 1732, Christian von Wolff wrote a book titled *Empirical Psychology*; two years later, he wrote a complementary book titled *Rational Psychology.* In the United States, Laurens Hickok also wrote separate books under the titles of *Rational Psychology* (1849) and *Empirical Psychology* (1854). Early writers believed rationalism and empiricism offered useful but different methods. As we will see in Chapters 6 and 7, the tensions between rational and empirical psychology remain with us.

AESTHETICISM   **Aestheticism** is a doctrine that the principles of beauty apply to other arenas of thought. In this sense, aestheticism is an epistemology or way of knowing; for aestheticists, inquiry itself is a search for truth and beauty. This perspective is well illustrated in the book *The Double Helix* by Watson (1968). After Watson and Crick constructed the DNA model, the comment was made that the model was "too pretty not to be true" (Watson, 1968, p. 134). The aesthetic test has been of historical importance in the humanities— especially in art and music— but scientists also seem to delight in a beautiful model or theory. Physicist Paul Dirac, as quoted by Brush (1974b), "stated that a theorist should prefer beautiful equations to uglier ones that yield closer agreement with experimental data" (p. 1167).

PRAGMATISM   Pragmatic philosophy offers still another perspective on epistemology. The term **pragmatism** is derived from a Greek root, translated as *pragma*, which refers to "things accomplished" or "things done." In this tradition,

Francis Bacon believed we should emphasize theories and propositions that can be tested. Immanuel Kant used the term *pragmatic* to refer to that which is prudent. Under the late nineteenth-century leadership of Charles Sanders Peirce (pronounced *purse*) and William James, pragmatism became a major philosophical movement. Peirce and James emphasized the practical consequences of theories, definitions, ideas, and concepts. In typical American fashion, James talked about the "cash value" of an idea. Does the idea produce real productive work that makes a difference in the world of experience? Or does it lead to dead ends and muddled thinking? James believed that viable ideas produce sustained intellectual and physical work. He argued that a definition does not close our intellectual quest; on the contrary, a good definition raises questions and invigorates additional work (see James, 1907/1975b).

For the pragmatist, the world is in flux, and concepts must be altered and updated to be responsive to new discoveries. Concepts can outlive their usefulness and may need to be discarded. As methods improve and cultural biases shift, truth itself changes. Pragmatism judges truth in terms of utility or workability, but this is not the whole story. Rather, pragmatism calls for a deep awareness of change, particularly changes in methods and worldviews, and a suspicion of big claims that cover too much territory. James (1876b) revealed his pragmatic side when he defined philosophy as the "habit of always seeing an alternative" (p. 178).

One problem with pragmatism is that an idea or concept may appear sterile or unworkable in the present intellectual context but may yield important truths at a later time. The Copernican model of the solar system appeared unworkable at first, but later revolutionized our knowledge of astrophysics. A naïve, extreme, or corrupted dose of pragmatism may discourage inquiry. William James and other pragmatists, however, would never permit such a consequence. James was more interested in opening than in closing doors (see James, 1909/1977).

SKEPTICISM According to **skepticism**, all truth claims are suspect and must be questioned. So it might appear counterintuitive to include skepticism as a way of knowing, but in the words of Rauch (1993), "all of your conclusions, every single one of them, may need to be corrected" (p. 45). Rauch argues for an epistemic humility that encourages skeptical analysis as an essential part of science and all honest inquiry. We need not surrender provisional knowledge, but we must be suspicious of certitude because there is always a new perspective or a fresh discovery that challenges old conclusions. Skepticism, as a method of discovering problems, can serve as a potent source of progress and knowledge. A society that discourages critical analysis and skepticism risks freezing the knowledge industry. In contrast, a society that encourages a skeptical ethic along with an evolutionary epistemology will be dynamic and open to the discovery mission (see Harrison, 2006). A productive and progressive science thrives on adversarial positions, conflicting theories, healthy curiosity, and a sincere skeptical attitude. Later in the text, we'll see how curiosity was considered a sin for centuries and how such a view resulted in intellectual stagnation. We will also show how skepticism in the late Renaissance period stimulated the development of modern science.

The Role of Emotions in Knowledge

Emotions play in our belief structures, complicating the problem of human knowledge. It can be challenging to sort out our competing beliefs when we are dispassionate. When emotions such as hate, fear, love, and anger enter the picture, our knowledge problems are compounded. Throughout this text, we will visit tensions between authority and reason. Though emotions may attach to either authority *or* reason, strong emotions are more likely to be associated with authority than with reason. Nevertheless, the dissonance associated with the violation of reason may be a source of emotion.

Let us return, however, to a consideration of emotion and its relation to authority. Authority is visible in our most vulnerable moments such as birth, marriage or other long-term commitments, illness, tragedy, and death. We sing to authority songs of praise, gratitude, thanksgiving, worship, and allegiance. Though protest music attacks authority, it is rare to encounter music inspired by claims of reason or logic, but it is common to encounter music inspired by claims of authority. We create symbols inspired by authority and then idolize those symbols and pledge our allegiance to them. We set aside special holidays to celebrate authority, and we participate in self-denial and in rituals that underscore our loyalty and commitment. Failure to observe a ritual is often a source of the most intense anxiety and self-criticism. Our personal identity is seldom tied to reason like the character of Mr. Spock in the classic *Star Trek* movies and television series. Personal identities of the overwhelming majority, even in matters such as dress and food, reflect authorities. Deviance may trigger legitimate fears of social ostracism. For example, people who undergo a dramatic conversion from one belief to another may be disowned by parents or other authorities (Jacoby, 2016). Though science values openness, a scientific community may ostracize a scientist who deviates from standard practice.

Emotional problems are compounded when we believe that authority is absolute and immune from questioning. When reason and authority clash, as they often do, the problem is both intellectual and emotional (Viney & Woody, 2017). The emotional power of authority is reflected in memory. Memorization is a valued activity in authority systems, and those who can recite the words of authority from memory are held up as role models. Children, especially, are encouraged to commit the words of authority to memory. A mechanical recitation is often more valued than a reflective and creative analysis.

We will see that the history of science generally and of psychology specifically, is partly a history of shifting epistemologies. Few topics are as important to human welfare and survival as

epistemology, yet the subject is avoided or neglected because of its vexing questions. Unfortunately, emotion coupled with ignorance and the inevitable blind spots encountered in all belief systems undermine the critical reflection necessary to understand belief structures. The problem of knowledge is not a trivial or irrelevant metaphysical issue. It is a practical problem relevant to daily life and should thus be confronted in a vigorous and honest fashion. The Shakespeare quotation is a poetic reminder of the certitude that often accompanies ignorance and its consequences.

We come full circle to our original question. On what grounds can we lay claim to knowledge? We turn now to the interplay between science and epistemology.

Science and Epistemology

Conceived as a way of knowing, science can be understood in terms of epistemological assumptions and commitments that include empirical, rational, pragmatic, and aesthetic components. From the beginning of the modern period, philosophers of science have studied scientific methodology, but they could not agree on what science is or how it operates. Later, we will observe disagreements about the nature of science, particularly between Francis Bacon and René Descartes, two of the original modern philosophers of science. Because of long-standing disagreements about scientific methodology, we must caution against assuming that there is only *one* traditional view of science. In what follows, we will examine three critical thinkers to gain insight into their philosophies about science and epistemology.

KARL RAIMOND POPPER Sir **Karl Raimond Popper (1902–1994)** was born in Vienna, where he studied mathematics, physics, and philosophy at the University of Vienna. His 1935 book *The Logic of Scientific Discovery* is a classic in the philosophy of science. He had a long and distinguished career and enjoyed extensive

19

acclaim for his unique work in the philosophy of science.

Popper argued that consistent positive observational evidence does not justify universal conclusions. For example, every observed swan (thus far) may have been white, but we are not therefore justified in making a claim that *all* swans *must be* white. The observation of a single black swan falsifies the claim. According to Popper, the integrity of science hinges on an honest quest for negative instances or disconfirmation. Survivability is not the first task of a good theory; rather, a good theory possesses the virtues of simplicity, clarity, testability, and falsifiability. A theory that is not falsifiable is a theory that is vague and that cannot be subjected to rigorous tests. For example, during the witch hunts in the late Renaissance a numb or insensitive part of the body was sometimes explained as the point of entry of demons into the body. Such an explanation is vague; it does not lend itself to empirical testing. How would one set up an experiment to test such an explanation?

Popper (1959) was basically offering a "theory of theories" (p. 59). His larger vision of the scientific enterprise is that it is by no means a basis for certitude. What Popper offers is an evolutionary epistemology that emphasizes the crucial role of explicit and rigorous theories in scientific thought. He likened scientific theories to "nets cast to catch what we call 'the world': to rationalize, to explain, and to master it. We endeavor to make the mesh ever finer and finer" (p. 59). There is the hope of progress, but no grounds for certainty. According to Popper, genuine scientific theory is not invulnerable, and a major characteristic of science is that it does evolve.

Popper's philosophy of science has been criticized (Toulmin, 1972; Kitcher, 1982) but it has served as an important attempt to set up a demarcation between science and those pseudosciences that focus exclusively on confirmation but that ignore negative instances.

THOMAS S. KUHN As the author of *The Structure of Scientific Revolutions*, **Thomas S.**

Kuhn (1922–1996) wrote one of the most influential books in the history and philosophy of science. Kuhn was initially interested in theoretical physics, but after assisting with an elementary science course for nonscientists, his interests shifted to the history and philosophy of science. Specifically, he confessed that historical scientific studies "radically undermined some of [his] basic conceptions about the nature of science and the reasons for its special success" (Kuhn, 1970, p. v).

Kuhn's work emphasized the importance of understanding science in terms of community structures and historical development. The scientific community shares an intellectual background, standard reference sources, textbooks, ways of solving problems, and values. The community exerts pressures on the individual, especially during student years and in early scientific-professional years when the young scientist is establishing a reputation. Kuhn did not mean that the scientific community is a closed club. Such an interpretation is an unfortunate "popular caricature of Kuhn's position" (Kitcher, 1982, p. 168). Kuhn recognized the diversities that exist in the scientific community. Nevertheless, there is much that community members share in common.

Kuhn was interested in the evolution of science over time. Competing schools of thought mark early prescientific development and are prone to quarrel over basic definitions, methods, and assumptions. He noted that the early stages of electrical research gave rise to competing views about the nature of electricity. The same is true in psychology as early psychologists engaged in vigorous debates over subject matter and appropriate methods.

Kuhn (1970) notes that the early search for research consensus is difficult because "all of the facts that could possibly pertain to the development of a given science are likely to seem equally relevant. As a result, early fact-gathering is a far more nearly random activity than the one that subsequent scientific development makes familiar" (p. 15). In time, one competing school will prevail over the others. The dominant school attracts a loyal following while promising a set of problems worthy of sustained study. The leading school now dictates the intellectual agenda, ushering in a transition to what Kuhn called **normal science**.

Normal science has a record of past achievement; it defines problem areas and provides methods of practice. Most scientists work in this tradition. When the time is right, Kuhn tells us, a **paradigm** emerges as an elaboration on the meaning of normal science. In a sociological sense, paradigm refers to "the entire constellation of beliefs, values, techniques, and so on, shared by members of a given community" (Kuhn, 1970, p. 175). The term also refers to conventional ways of approaching and solving problems. Paradigms define boundaries within which scientists do their work and clarify the legitimate methods of analysis and ways of looking at problems.

In the course of normal science, serendipitous findings and anomalies cannot be ignored. Sometimes discoveries occur through accidents and at other times are theory driven. Kuhn (1970) noted that X-rays are "a classic case of discovery through accident, a type that occurs more frequently than the impersonal standards of scientific reporting allow us easily to realize" (p. 57). He described events that led German physicist Wilhelm Conrad Röntgen (1845–1923) to discover X-rays and how even a notable scientist such as Lord Kelvin (1824–1907) believed they were a hoax. The prevailing paradigm had not predicted or anticipated Röntgen's X-ray discovery, but it was a finding that could not be ignored.

In most cases, efforts are made to assimilate new discoveries or anomalies into the prevailing paradigm. Such efforts are understandable because the scientific community has a vested interest in the traditional paradigm. It has commanded loyalties and lifetimes of hard work. However, tests of competing theories that lead to a succession of anomalous findings can become so compelling they cannot be ignored (Joireman & Van Lange, 2015). Such a turn of events creates a crisis that causes some members of the community to lose faith. The community response is

predictable: Some try to find ad hoc hypotheses to rescue the paradigm, whereas others search for new ways to organize the larger picture.

According to Kuhn, scientific revolutions are marked by new and more successful organizations of the world. With a paradigm shift, a new vision replaces the old way of seeing things. Kuhn (1970) noted that his "book portrays scientific development as a succession of tradition-bound periods punctuated by noncumulative breaks" (p. 208). Following a revolution, the old paradigm is rejected and scientists return to a normal science that operates within the new paradigm.

Both Kuhn and Popper advanced evolutionary epistemologies, and both challenged absolutistic approaches to science. Kuhn has a broader interpretation of what counts as legitimate science than does Popper. Mopping-up activities, accidental discoveries, and descriptive studies all comprise the business of science. Kuhn has been criticized for covering too much ground with the term *paradigm*. He acknowledged the criticism and attempted to correct it. Kuhn's model of science was subjected to the same criticism leveled against Popper—namely, that it does not do justice to the extreme diversity in the history of science. We turn now to a third orientation that offers a radical difference from Popper and Kuhn.

PAUL K. FEYERABEND In his book *Science in the Making*, Joel Hildebrand, a chemist and former president of the American Chemical Association, challenged the idea that there is *one* scientific method. Hildebrand (1957) argued that "to be successful in unlocking doors concealing nature's secrets, a person must have ingenuity. If [we do] not have the key for the lock, [we] must not hesitate to pick it, to climb in a window, or even kick in a panel" (p. 26). Hildebrand argues that scientific success values ingenuity and determination more than method.

Hildebrand's statement is by no means esoteric. In *Reflections of a Physicist*, Percy W. Bridgman (1955) said, "there is no scientific method as such" (p. 416). In that same source, he pointed out that scientists do not follow

21

"any prescribed course of action . . .[;] science is what scientists do, and there are as many scientific methods as there are individual scientists" (p. 83). Zoologist P. B. Medawar (1984) shared the same sentiment in his book *The Limits of Science*: "There is indeed no such thing as 'the' scientific method. A scientist uses a very great variety of stratagems . . . [and] no procedure of discovery can be logically scripted" (p. 51).

Medawar challenged the idea that breakthroughs follow a calculus of discovery. Perhaps some discoveries arrive in such a neat fashion, but he argued for the role of serendipity in science. Consider again the discovery of X-rays. Medawar (1984, p. 46) asks us to imagine a scientist prior to 1900 approaching a funding agency with a proposal "to discover a means of making human flesh transparent." The idea would be greeted with scorn. Still, the discovery of X-rays didn't follow any preplanned logical pathway connected to scientific goal setting.

Hildebrand, Bridgman, and Medawar do not wish to undermine respect for science. Quite the contrary, they have a keen interest in scientific advancement. What they are saying is that science is not as tidy, objective, and coherent as we have been led to believe. Similar themes are advanced by Brush (1974b), Cartwright (1999), and Swan (2015).

In a 1975 book titled *Against Method*, **Paul K. Feyerabend (1924–1994)** outlined an anarchistic theory of knowledge. Although acknowledging the negative implications of anarchism, especially for political science, he finds appropriate and healthy implications for anarchism in epistemology and science. His analysis of the history of science offers a vigorous disagreement with Popper and Kuhn. Feyerabend (1975) contended,

> The idea of a method that contains firm, unchanging, and absolutely binding principles for conducting the business of science meets considerable difficulty when confronted with the results of historical research—there is not a single rule, however

plausible, and however firmly grounded in epistemology, that is not violated at some time or other. It becomes evident that such violations are not accidental events; they are not results of insufficient knowledge or of inattention which might have been avoided. On the contrary, we see that they are necessary for progress.

(p. 23)

Feyerabend went on to say that conscious decisions to break from conventional wisdom and method are not only facts in the history of science but necessary to the progress of science. In his thinking, successful and creative scientists break or reverse rules, defend ad hoc hypotheses, work inductively and then deductively, and work sometimes for unity and sometimes for plurality. The rule, he tells us, is *anything goes*.

Feyerabend (1975) argued that "even a law-and-order science will succeed only if anarchistic moves are occasionally allowed to take place" (p. 26). Drawing on examples from the history of science as evidence, he suggested that "the idea of a fixed method, or of a fixed theory of rationality, rests on too naive a view of [human beings and their] social surroundings" (Feyerabend, 1975, p. 27, 1988).

Feyerabend's position should not be viewed as a debunking or skepticism regarding science. However, his position calls for closer scrutiny of the history of scientific discovery. He also encourages more detailed empirical analysis of what scientists actually do. For example, is the hands-on lab work of the chemist the same method as the astronomer calculating the trajectory of a comet? Does the theoretical mathematician use the same methods as the marine biologist who studies the feeding habits of sharks? Is there one scientific method adapted for various fields of science or is there a diversity of methods within specific disciplines? Does this assumption of a single method inhibit our inquiry (Hood, 2013)? If there is no *one* scientific method, are there at least features (e.g., the importance of quantification) that all methods share?

Relevance of Epistemology to Psychology

Early psychologists disagreed about the appropriate methodology for the new psychology. Should there be one method or many? If there is but one, which should it be? The philosophy of science dictates such questions. From some points of view, the scientific status of psychology hinges on methodological purity. Other philosophy-of-science considerations dictate psychology's status among the sciences. Within Kuhn's scheme, psychology could be regarded as a pre-paradigmatic science. It enjoys higher status in Feyerabend's scheme if for no other reason than that the methodological purity of all the sciences is called into question. Further, there is wider latitude of acceptance in Feyerabend's scheme about what constitutes "normal science."

The issues raised here are of historical interest, but they also command the attention of contemporary scientists and philosophers. As we proceed through the history of psychology, we will encounter questions about the nature of science and the scientific status of psychology.

The Problem of Causality

From the time of Aristotle to the present, philosophers and scientists have debated the nature and meaning of causation. Contributing to the richness of the problem are questions concerning the possible influence of unconscious processes in human life, the role of intention or purpose in determining behavior, and the question of whether the individual can be an agent of change (i.e., a cause). In what follows, we will review classic and modern approaches to the problem of causation.

Aristotle struggled with the meaning of causation, paving the way for centuries of debate and speculation on the issue. He believed that causation is not a simple one-dimensional affair. To know the cause of anything, we must understand several things. First, we must understand what conditions led up to the event. Aristotle referred to antecedent conditions as the **efficient cause**, essentially that which sets a thing in motion. When domino B falls after being hit by A, we can say that the movement of A is the efficient cause of the fall of B. Aristotle also believed we need to understand the material structure of a thing to understand causation. When a physician takes a hammer and strikes the patellar tendon, the knee reflex will cause the patient's leg to kick. If the physician's hammer is the efficient cause of the reflex, there must also be a material cause. In this case, we would not observe the reflex if there had been nerve or muscle damage. So part of the cause of the reflex is the material structure of the knee including the nerves, tendons, and muscles. In other words, the reflex depends on a physical substrate, which Aristotle called the **material cause**. Domino A (an efficient cause) impacting domino B could knock B over if both were made of the same material. But if B were made of lead and A of light wood, then B would not fall when impacted by A. The so-called causal sequence depends on a material structure as well as antecedent conditions.

Aristotle described a third kind of cause known as the **formal cause**. This refers to the form, shape, or identifying properties of a thing. A sculptor may chisel away at two pieces of granite, using one to create a bust of Beethoven and the other to shape a likeness of Mozart. For both busts, the material is the same but the form is different. The formal cause carries information value. The functional or causal properties of a thing depend on form. Domino B would not fall when impacted by A if it were too short or different in form than A. So form may also be essential to an understanding of a causal sequence. An airplane could be constructed of appropriate material (material cause) and have an excellent propulsion system (efficient cause), but if the wing were damaged or poorly designed (formal cause), the plane would not fly.

According to Aristotle, if you want to understand a sequence of events, you need to know its goal or purpose. Let's return to the knee reflex example. The physician was conducting a neurological exam, so she used a small hammer to tap the patient's knee. That was her purpose. Aristotle called this the **final cause**, the end or purpose for which a change was produced. Aristotle might say you cannot understand the knee reflex, or rather the cause of the knee reflex, until you understand the physician's intention or purpose.

For Aristotle, knowledge of causation rests on understanding antecedent conditions, material, form, and the purpose for which a thing was intended. Aristotle believed in a balance of all four dimensions of causation. His student, Theophrastus, believed science should concern itself primarily with material and efficient causation and not with final causation.

The Aristotelian notion of final causation should not be confused with teleological interpretations of the world encountered in numerous theological beliefs. The term **teleology** refers to purpose or design. Technically, *teleology* can be defined as the investigation of evidence that there is design or purpose in nature. The assumption of design leads to the next question: What was the origin of the design or purpose? There are two types of teleological answers to that question. **Intrinsic teleology** is the position that design, order, and purpose are immanent in nature—simple manifestations or characteristics of nature. But **extrinsic teleology** makes the claim that any design in nature reflects the work of a designer and that the designer has imbued the design with the designer's own purpose. Though Aristotle believed in an unmoved mover (God), it is questionable as to whether he would subscribe to the kind of teleology encountered in some theologies.

Intrinsic teleology has become archaic in physics and chemistry. Psychologists can't dismiss intrinsic teleology as easily. Despite attempts by behaviorists to build a psychological science like physics based on material and efficient causation, teleology or purpose has constituted a persistent problem for psychologists. Even if the *will* is rarely discussed in contemporary psychology, many psychologists have found it difficult,

if not impossible, to resist expressions such as *goal-directed, intention, plans, purposive behavior, anticipation,* and *expectancy.* Such terms, unless defined in unusual ways, suggest intrinsic teleology or final causation. But can human behavior be explained with the same material and efficient causation used to explain the movement of a billiard ball, the trajectory of a comet, or the changes in the metabolism of a cell? Or must we invoke some form of final causation to account for the complexity of human behavior? We will encounter opposition to teleological explanations in the works of theorists such as Jacques Loeb, John B. Watson, Clark Hull, and B. F. Skinner, while theorists such as William McDougall, Edward Chace Tolman, and Gordon Allport favor teleological explanations. Rychlak and Rychlak (1990a, 1990b) and Rychlak (1994) insist that teleological assumptions play a critical role in psychology.

You may have heard the familiar warning that correlation does not imply causation. But neither does correlation imply that there is not a causal relationship between two events. Correlation is neutral with respect to the question of causation. Perhaps causation is not a scientific construct. Maybe it is simply a historical and philosophical curiosity. To be sure, there are those who are content to study correlations or functional relationships. But the idea of causality is so entrenched in common sense that it refuses to vanish. Some still argue that science entails a search for fundamental processes that underlie and explain correlational data.

In psychology, questions associated with the problem of causality will show themselves time after time. Some of the questions are as follows: To what extent do events influence us that are not a part of our consciousness? If unconscious processes influence us, then can we claim to be rational or free? Is it possible to build an adequate science of human experience and behavior on the basis of material and efficient causes? Can we rise above cause-and-effect relations and exercise freedom of choice? This question will recur throughout the book.

Free Will and Determinism

Do we have some degree of control over the direction of our lives or are all things, including human experience and behavior, subject to the laws of causation? Is there anything that is uncaused? Such questions lie at the heart of one of philosophy's oldest problems. Several of psychology's greatest figures have dedicated serious consideration to this issue. Sigmund Freud, John Watson, Ivan Pavlov, and B. F. Skinner stand in the determinist camp, whereas William James, Carl Jung, Gordon Allport, and Carl Rogers are committed to a belief in freedom of choice. The issue of free will and determinism is an issue with far-reaching implications for psychology, science, the law, and theories of punishment. If humans have some degree of freedom, then a psychology based on strict determinism cannot do justice to its subject matter. On the other hand, if causality exists in nature—including human nature—then belief in freedom of choice is unwarranted or may even work against scientific investigations. This issue is more alive now than a half-century ago. It has been the subject of numerous books and articles in psychology (see Bloom, 2014; Boyer, 2014; Burns, 2014; Eagleman, 2011; Harris, 2012; Lawton & Churchland, 2013; Viney & Parker, 2016).

The doctrine of **free will** assumes that people make choices that are to some degree independent of antecedent conditions. It assumes we can, at least somewhat, rise above genetic, chemical, physical, and social influences. We can anticipate alternatives in the decision-making process and weigh their possible outcomes. Behavior may be predictable, but there's an element of unpredictability in our actions. If we feel we can rise above causal forces, we're more likely to view ourselves as rational or responsible creatures. By the way, most advocates of free will do not attribute this quality to animals.

Most people who believe in free will agree that environmental and genetic forces impose limitations on us, but they still believe in at least some freedom of choice. Although free will proponents may disagree about the power of the causes that affect our lives, they are likely to believe that the person or the self is not simply passive or reactive. Instead, the self acts on the environment with awareness and purpose. Let's take a look at arguments in support of free will.

1. *Argument for an adequate explanation of human experience.* Psychologists have never been able to make perfect predictions of simple, let alone complex, behavior. For example, there's no way we can write biographies in advance. Such predictive failure challenges the adequacy of strict determinism. The determinist position struggles with the spontaneity and unpredictability in human behavior. Those who endorse free will claim that their position offers a better fit with our observations and theories about experience and behavior. The free will perspective is embarrassed by neither our regularities nor our irregularities, uncertainties, and novelties.

2. *Logical contradictions in determinism.* Proponents of free will argue that if determinism is true, a determinist cannot logically declare that he or she *believes* in determinism. Why? Because the determinist is not the real believer. Belief is a mere consequence of antecedents. According to determinism, the very words *I believe in determinism* are conditioned by more fundamental forces. It is not that one believes in determinism, but that consequences have transpired to result in the statement *I believe in determinism.* Strict determinism implies a passive nature about the self that is well illustrated in B. F. Skinner's (1983a) statement, "If I am right about human behavior, I have written the autobiography of a nonperson" (p. 32).

3. *Argument from morality.* Free will believers argue that determinism makes a mess of morality. According to determinism, any immoral behavior can be explained in terms of causes that had no prevision of the ends they were achieving. In other words, individuals are not responsible for their actions.

Indeed, the term *responsibility* is a hollow term—it means little more than ability to respond.

4. *Argument from indeterminism.* Promoters of free will argue that strict determinism is a pre-twentieth-century concept that is no longer applicable in the physical sciences. Following quantum theory and Heisenberg's uncertainty principle, the physical world must now be viewed from a probabilistic rather than a strictly causal framework. The doctrine of **indeterminism** holds that it is not possible to apply strict cause-and-effect explanations in the world of subatomic particles. This well-known doctrine has led some individuals to argue that indeterminism applies to psychology. Although indeterminism is not identical with purposive free will, an indeterminist would tell us that human behavior is characterized by an inherent uncertainty.

As you can guess, the free will perspective has not gone unchallenged. **Determinism** states that there are causes, both known and unknown, for every behavior or experience. Taylor (1967b) defined *determinism* as the philosophical doctrine that "states that for everything that ever happens there are conditions such that, given them, nothing else could happen" (p. 359).

The great physicist Albert Einstein (1879–1955) proclaimed, "God doesn't play dice with the universe" (Michelmore, 1962, p. 128). As a determinist, Einstein believed that the law of cause and effect operates at every level of reality. He once remarked that "God is clever, but . . . not malicious" (Michelmore, 1962, p. 111). Einstein is suggesting that the world, because of its lawfulness, is knowable. It may be difficult to discover causes and laws, but with persistence we *can* make discoveries. This is the optimistic side of determinism: Nature is knowable, and problems can be solved when cause-and-effect relations are discovered.

Belief in freedom of the will may discourage inquiry (such a belief may have delayed the development of a scientific psychology). In this respect, the determinist offers the following rebuttal to indeterminism: Even if indeterminism applies to the world of fundamental particles, it is not applicable in larger physical systems. A system as complicated, say, as a basketball remains as a reliable and determinate system, even if the behavior of the smallest physical units sustaining it is indeterminate. Historically, science has always proceeded on the assumption of the lawfulness or statistical regularity of its subject matter. But now let us turn to a few major arguments in defense of determinism.

1. *Historical argument.* The history of the free will–determinism controversy is a history of victories for determinism and retreats for the theory of free will. With increasing knowledge of brain structure and function, lawful explanations are extended to an ever-widening spectrum of behaviors. The term *will* once occupied a great amount of space in psychology textbooks, but as knowledge progressed, we had less need for the term. In the history of neuroscience, for example, mechanistic explanations have replaced explanations based on the will on countless occasions.

2. *Argument from morality.* The determinist can counter free will arguments by stating that belief in free will can also make a mess of morality. Many of history's most barbaric practices were justified on the grounds that the victim had made a free choice and now deserved punishment. From medieval times, aggressive witch-hunts led to the persecution of people who allegedly used free will to make a pact with the devil.

3. *Argument from reasonable expectancy.* As we think about our world, we develop reasonable expectations that things are lawful. The world is not capricious; given a specific set of weather conditions, we can have a reasonable expectation that a Chinook wind will hit Boulder, Colorado, within a specified period of time. In a similar manner, we may

reasonably expect stress and other circumstances to contribute to an emotional breakdown. We don't need to attribute the breakdown to an act of free choice. Most of us live our lives on the basis of reasonable expectations. If an expectation is not confirmed, we assume we neglected to take some variable into consideration. Without determinism, we have no grounds for reasonable expectations about the world.

The free will–determinism debate is a defining issue for psychology. Throughout the book, we will outline where various psychologists stand on this issue. As noted, the issue is alive and well in contemporary psychology. With the advance of the neurosciences, the debates over free will and determinism have, if anything, intensified and grown more technical (see Baer et al., 2008; Libet, 1985; Schlosser, 2012; Wegner, 2002). Many of the recent debates have centered around research on neurophysiological precursors of intentions. If intentions lack automaticity and some degree of causal efficacy, do we have free will? If the conclusion is negative, we are still haunted by vexing existential questions raised by William James (1979a). Am I the author of nothing? What does it mean to face a world foredone?

The Mind–Body Problem

The mind–body problem belongs to a subdisciplinary area of philosophy known as *ontology*. Philosophers have used the term **ontology** in diverse ways. For our purposes, we can define it as the study of the nature and relations of being. When we ask, "what is real?" we are asking an ontological question. Is the mind real? Is there a mind that is somehow independent from the brain? What is the relationship between the mind and the brain? Is there one fundamental reality (monism), two (dualism), or perhaps many (pluralism)? If there is more than one reality, how do the various types of reality coexist—and do they influence each other? Do psychologists study the mind or do they study only behavior? All of these are ontological questions because they ask the essential question: What is real? Let's explore some traditional solutions to ontological problems.

Monism

According to monistic philosophy, everything belongs in some intimate way to everything else. As an elegant solution to the problem of ontology, **monism** suggests that reality, whatever it is, is all of one piece. If everything belongs in an intimate way to every other thing, then nothing is alien or foreign because all things are part of one thing. What appears as foreign or alien is only a product of the present gaps in our knowledge. Monism offers hope for a unity of knowledge because we all study the same thing, but at different levels and from diverse perspectives. One form of monism nurtures the belief that psychology is reducible to the field of physics. Although monism appeals to simplicity, a major problem arises because monists can't agree about what the one and only reality is. Monism, in fact, comes in oppositional forms. Let's consider them and their implications for the mind–brain problem.

MATERIALISM **Materialism** is a monistic ontology characterized by the belief that matter is the fundamental constituent of all things. A material monist might argue that the body exists, but not the mind. Terms such as *mind*, *spirit*, and *consciousness* are understood in terms of the material, efficient, and formal operations of brain activity (Lawton & Churchland, 2013). It follows that there is no mind–brain problem as such because all so-called mental activity is reducible to physical, chemical, or physiological processes. Many key figures such as Democritus, Thomas Hobbes, Julien Offray de la Mettrie, Herman von Helmholtz, Ivan Pavlov, and John B. Watson were materialists.

IDEALISM As an alternative to materialism, **idealism** emphasizes mind or spirit as the preeminent feature of life. It represents a radical departure from materialism and a different emphasis with respect to the mind–body problem. According to idealism, as the term is employed in philosophy, the mental world of experience is foundational to all science and, for that matter, all knowledge. It would be impossible to know anything apart from consciousness or experience. Thus, the mental world (experience, awareness, consciousness) has priority—it is the only world to which we have immediate access. The material world is regarded as derivative—an intellectual or philosophical product that has its origin in the world of experience. For the idealist, psychology is the science that studies mental processes and experience. Further, an idealist would argue that all science begins with experience and is about experience. Thus, it is the mind or the mental world that has ontological status. The material world is a construction—a mere by-product of a more important reality. Several key figures, including Plato, George Berkeley, and Gustav Fechner, identified with idealism.

DOUBLE-ASPECT MONISM This variety of monism displays sensitivity to the claims of materialism and idealism. **Double-aspect monism** emphasizes the idea that there is a language for mental processes and a language for underlying physical processes, but both languages refer to the same reality. We use words such as *mind, experience, consciousness, awareness*, and *thinking*. We also have a rich and growing language that refers to fundamental physical structures and processes such as neurons, neurotransmitters, cell assemblies, and synaptic transmission. According to double-aspect monism, both languages are legitimate but both refer to the same underlying reality approached from two perspectives. Benedict Spinoza, an early advocate of double-aspect theory, argued that human beings may be described in mentalistic terms or in the language of the physical sciences. The two languages provide different perspectives just as one may describe a coin from the perspective of either side. According to double-aspect theory, the mind–body problem is a problem of language. The ontological problem, however, remains. What is real? Is reality reduced to words? Despite its problems, double-aspect theory can embrace a tolerant and robust approach to psychology that includes legitimate roles for descriptions that refer to mental and to physical processes.

EPIPHENOMENALISM A final version of monism, **epiphenomenalism**, is often classified as a dualistic position, but for reasons that shall soon be apparent, it is more accurately classified as a monistic position. An *epiphenomenon* is an appearance or a kind of "overflow" resulting from the operation of something that is more basic or fundamental. According to epiphenomenalism, mental processes (e.g., thought, consciousness, cognitions) are a kind of "overflow" or by-product of brain activity. The mental world has no independent status; it is a mere epiphenomenon or appearance. According to epiphenomenalism, causality always runs one way, from the physical to the mental. There is no mental causation because the mind has no independent status apart from its physical substrate. Epiphenomenalism is clearly a variation of materialism.

Dualism

In contrast with monism, **dualism** asserts that there are two fundamental orders of reality—mind and body. Each has ontic (i.e., real) status. Naïvely, most of us experience the reality of mental processes; we also experience the reality of the physical world. According to the dualistic position, we are assured that neither the mental nor the physical world is a mere appearance. For all its popular appeal, at least to the Westerner, dualism presents a major problem. If there are two orders of reality, how do they get along with each other? Can one influence the other? Or can each influence the other, and if so, how? Most dualistic mind–body positions address the issue of how mind and body collaborate. Let's examine the better-known positions.

INTERACTIONISM According to **interactionism**, sometimes called the *commonsense* position, mental events are real—they influence each other and they influence bodily events. Bodily events also influence each other and mental events. Although interactionism sometimes appeals to common sense, it is not without problems. First, interactionists have difficulty specifying how an immaterial mental system can be causal with respect to a physical system (or, for that matter, how a material system can be causal with respect to an immaterial one). Second, a major problem centers around the locus of interaction. Where do mind and body influence each other? René Descartes, history's most famous interactionist, addressed this problem with considerable courage and suggested that the pineal gland, located in the center of the head, is the seat of interaction. Centuries later, we have found that people can function fairly well following a pinealectomy. In this sense, Descartes's theory of the locus of interaction was testable but was demonstrated to be wrong. Descartes also failed to show how a mental event can influence physical events and vice versa. His followers' subsequent attempts also proved unsuccessful. For all its commonsense appeal, interactionism leaves us with more questions than answers.

PSYCHOPHYSICAL PARALLELISM According to **psychophysical parallelism**, mental events are real, and they influence other mental events. Bodily events are also real, and they influence other bodily events. Mental events cannot, however, influence bodily events, and bodily events cannot influence mental events. The two orders of reality are nevertheless, by definition, parallel with each other. That is, whatever is happening in one order is happening simultaneously in the other order. The philosopher Gottfried Wilhelm Leibniz, the best-known advocate of this position, provides an intriguing allegory. Imagine that mind and body are like two clocks on a wall, each displaying the same time. They are synchronized but independent. One clock has no causal influence over the other, yet they function in agreement with each other. According to Leibniz, mind and body are by definition parallel, but there is no causal influence between these two independent orders of reality.

Parallelism avoids the problems encountered in the interactionist position, but at a considerable expense—it flies in the face of common sense. Most of us, for example, assume that the experience of pain is connected to the chance encounter with the hot stove top and the resulting burn. The burn is both mental and physical, and there appears to be a causal connection between them, even though the supporter of parallelism must argue that they are independent yet harmonious. The larger problem is that parallelism implies a kind of preestablished harmony between mind and body. Explaining how preestablished harmony works might prove more difficult than explaining an interaction.

EMERGENTISM The philosophical position known as **emergentism**, in at least one of its variations, argues that mental processes are produced by brain processes, but are qualitatively different. For example, the experience of a toothache emerges out of complex neurological activity that may have been activated by decay or some kind of damage. The experience itself, though emerging out of bodily activity, is not captured by descriptions of bodily activity. The experience seems to have a career of its own and a reality that is qualitatively set apart. To clarify, let's take an analogy from chemistry. Salt is a product of sodium and chloride, yet the compound salt has unique properties that differ from sodium and chloride. Sodium alone or chloride alone can be lethal to the living organism, yet when combined in the form of salt, they can prove vital to life. The compound seems to have "emergent" properties of its own that are not a simple summation of separate elements. In a similar manner, mental processes, though produced by brain processes, are radically and qualitatively different. The experience of a sunrise, a poem, or a symphonic passage emerges from brain activity, but the global mental experience with its inspirational, affective, and associative meanings appears to be a reality unto itself quite different qualitatively from the underlying firing of neurons or the neurochemical activities in the synapse.

Emergentism is by no means a unified or consistent philosophical orientation. There are varieties of emergentism such as epiphenomenalism that are more consistent with monism (Crick, 1994), but other varieties that are more consistent with dualism. Thus, an emergentist might argue that causal forces work from the parts to the whole and from the whole to the parts. Such an argument is consistent with a functional or pragmatic dualism, if not a metaphysical dualism. Let us turn now to another approach to the problem of ontology.

Pluralism

A final commonsense belief is that we live in a "multiverse" of separate orders of things. Ontological **pluralism** embraces the reality of mind and body but also insists that these two orders do not exhaust the possibilities. In a discussion of ontological pluralism, MacCormac (1990) pointed out that concepts arise "from physical brain processes . . . but they do not always find their origin solely in brain activity" (p. 417). A concept may have its origin in any of a great number of cultural sources, but because it depends on the physical system for its expression, its causal sources can be diverse. An ontological pluralist may believe that there are many separate real things, including different types of conscious experience and other orders of reality that do not obey rules that we know. Pluralism raises even more problems than interactionism. For each separate reality we posit, we must now struggle with the problem of the interaction of that reality with others. For example, as the mind–body theorist must struggle with how mind and body influence each other, a pluralist may struggle with mind–body interactions as well as the problem of theodicy (the relation of God to the world) and other actual or potential interactions.

It is little wonder that those with unity-loving natures are repulsed by pluralism—it is a messy philosophy. But the pluralist would insist that the world is not simple and that our complex and messy world can only be described by similar theories. Pluralism has been a continuing subject of interest in philosophy and science throughout the twentieth century and into the twenty-first century (see Ford, 1990; James, 1909/1977; Reck, 1990).

A major variation on pluralism could be labeled **attributive pluralism**. This position emphasizes the relationship between an object and the words used to describe the object. People, as users of words, may attribute various qualities to an object. For example, let's take the question, *what is a sunset?* A plurality of possible descriptions exists as an answer. Now imagine that we pose this question to a sample of different professionals. If we called on a physicist, a musician, a neuroscientist, an artist, a psychologist, and a poet, we would find a delightful array of explanations. The musician might invite us to listen to a new composition, "The Sunset Symphony," capturing the sunset as an auditory experience. Not to be outdone, the artist shows us a canvas depicting a sun fading above a seascape, revealed in vivid oil paint. Both are aesthetic representations, but we may ask, what is the real sunset? Does the physicist have the answer with all her elegant mathematical formulae? What about the neuroscientist who shares impressive monitoring of retinal images and occipital activity? Does the psychologist's analysis of the perceptual process offer the answer? Or even his normative testing on what sunsets mean to different people. Or shall we give the poet the final word? To adjudicate the claims of our scholars, we might convene a panel of philosophers consisting of two monists and two pluralists. The monists agree that the true sunset is one thing but disagree on what that one thing is—for one it is physical, for the other, experiential. One of the pluralists argues that there are many objective sunsets. The other contends that there are many legitimate descriptive modes: Sunsets are, after all, what we describe them to be. The most fundamental reality is, therefore, our words. But the other pluralist insists that realities exist beyond our words.

Let us now leave the mind–body problem, with the comment that the various schools and systems of psychology we encounter will disagree with each other on this issue. We will encounter materialists, double-aspect theorists, pluralists, interactionists, and others. A major key to understanding a given school or system will be to assess that school's or system's position on the mind–body problem.

Psychogeny

A close relative of the study of mind–body relations is encountered in the problem of psychogeny (*sy KAW gin ee*). The term **psychogeny** is derived from the Greek term **psyche** (*sy kee*), which has been translated as *spirit*, *soul*, *mind*, or *consciousness*. Each of these terms has different connotations, but they also share something in common in that they each refer to a principle of existence that embodies mentalistic concepts such as awareness, consciousness, sentience, or experience. Psychogeny may be defined as the study of the origin of psyche or the study of theories of the origin of psyche. Two very broad theories are briefly reviewed in the materials that follow, but more detailed discussion is available (see Viney & Woody, 1995).

PSYCHOGENIC IDENTITY THEORY Two key features of **psychogenic identity theory** are that (1) psyche is instilled in the primitive biological substratum of the organism at a given point in time, and (2) there is continuity or identity between the psychically endowed biological substratum and the later mature, self-reflective, fully conscious adult. Psychogenic identity theorists have never been able to agree with each other about the time of infusion of psyche into the body. For centuries, theologians argued that an embryo becomes human at forty days if it is male and eighty days if it is female (see De Rosa,

1988). More recently, a popular belief claimed that psyche is instilled at fertilization. Kuhse and Singer (1993), in their work on embryo experimentation, note, "what this claim amounts to is that the newly fertilized egg, the early embryo, and I are in some sense of the term, the same individual" (p. 66). Because of its emphasis on the independence of psyche, psychogenic identity theory is consistent with idealism and some forms of dualism. Although identity theory has popular appeal, it is not without a host of problems, many of which surfaced from recent work in embryo experimentation.

An example of a major problem with psychogenic identity theory is encountered in research on microsurgical sectioning of fertilized eggs. According to some forms of psychogenic identity theory, conception (the fertilization of an egg) marks the entry point of psyche into its material substrate. A colony of cells (a morula or blastocyst) develops following conception and results, according to psychogenic identity theory, in one body and one psyche. But we now know that following conception the morula can be surgically divided resulting in two, three, four, or more individuals. Each piece can be transplanted into a host, and we can artificially create twins, triplets, or quadruplets. Such procedures have long been used in the production of dairy cattle (see Seidel & Elsden, 1989) and are in theory, if not practice, available to humans (see Elmer-DeWitt, 1993). At conception, according to psychogenic identity theory, there was one psyche and one body. But assume now that the developing blastocyst is cut in half and there are now two bodies. If both bodies possess a psyche, the second psyche must have been instilled *after* conception. Thus, the theory of the entry of psyche exclusively at the time of conception raises important questions.

There are other problems for psychogenic identity theory. For example, in the early days of pregnancy, two separate colonies of cells (twins) developing in the uterus may float together and now form one individual—a chimera (see Austin, 1989). If both bodies possessed a psyche prior to floating together, what happened to the second psyche after the two came together? Clearly, for all of its popular appeal, psychogenic identity theory is not without serious problems. We now consider a second theory of psychogeny.

PSYCHOGENIC EMERGENTISM **Psychogenic emergentism** is an alternative theory of the origin of psyche. Psyche, according to this position, has no independent origin of its own, but rather develops with the developing body. Further, the complexity and the functional properties of the mental arena are dependent on the health and well-being of the organism. Psychogenic emergentism avoids the problems of identity theory, but comes with a set of problems of its own.

One of the major problems associated with psychogenic emergentism has to do with the arbitrary time of emergence. According to the theory, psyche is associated with some arbitrary level of neural complexity, but how much complexity is required? Is there some remote sense in which a single cell is conscious? Is a colony of cells, without a nervous system and without a circulatory system, conscious? At the other end of the scale, one might insist that consciousness is not consciousness until it is aware of itself. But how do we know when an organism has the capacity for reflective self-awareness? Psychogenic emergentism suffers the same problem as identity theory. Neither theory provides a satisfactory scientific answer regarding the time of infusion or emergence of psyche into a material substrate.

Another problem for psychogenic emergentism has to do with the experienced continuity of consciousness. I am the same *I* or *me* today as many years ago. Although my world may have been unstable resulting in experiences I could never have imagined and although I may not believe the same things I once did, it is nevertheless the same me who has changed. The persistent and obstinate nature of experienced continuity challenges psychogenic emergentism. We live in a constantly changing world that should result in major shifts in psyche, yet most of us experience ourselves to be remarkably consistent over time.

The psychogenic emergentist might argue that pathological discontinuities and disassociations exist in personality, often resulting from environmental changes or neurological damage. Such a rebuttal appears appropriate. Discontinuities in personality may well present a challenge to identity theory with its emphasis on a somewhat autonomous psyche. But it is also true that continuity of personality, especially in the face of change or even crisis, presents a challenge to emergentism with its emphasis on a more fragile and dependent psyche. There are many other problems and issues, including some interesting moral issues, associated with both theories (see Viney & Woody, 1995).

The relationship of mind and brain, like the problem of free will and determinism, is neither a relic of the past nor exclusively a philosophical problem. Indeed, there may be a greater outpouring of scholarly work on this problem at the dawn of the twenty-first century than at any other time in history. Contemporary philosophers, biologists, neuroscientists, computer scientists, and psychologists have produced a wealth of thoughtful approaches to the problem (see Buncombe, 1995; Crick, 1994; Dennett, 1991; Edelman, 1992; Searle, 1992, 1995a, 1995b; Tye, 1995). The mystery of the mental arena remains as elusive as ever, but contemporary advances in the neurosciences, the computing sciences, biology, psychology, and philosophy may provide additional pieces for a puzzle that is of unparalleled complexity.

The Problem of Explanation

The word *explain* comes from the Latin *explanare*, which means to make plain, flatten, or spread out. As we use it, the word *explain* refers to attempts to interpret or understand events or relationships. If you've worked with small children, you know a single word can satisfy as a nominal explanation. A child may be content to learn that "this dog is a collie, but that one is a golden retriever." Before long, we learn that words are arbitrary, so deeper understandings and more nuanced interpretations are needed. Simple words or phrases seldom explain anything. For example, throughout history and in the present, the word *free will* is offered as an explanation for desirable and undesirable behaviors—many legal and religious systems draw on this explanation. However, scientists often hold nagging and legitimate concerns about whether free will can explain anything (see Viney, 1990). Explanations based on the words of an authority are also problematic but very common in most cultural settings. Aristotle's causes, covered earlier in this chapter, can be regarded as the "four be-causes" in that they explain why things happen. For example, the billiard ball rolls into the pocket because external forces propelled it. This explanation is based on material and efficient causation. Now consider a different example: Wynona decided to go for lunch because she was hungry. This is a teleological explanation based on intention or purpose. Four additional explanatory modes encountered in science and in psychology are covered in the following section. Whether there is any explanatory mode free of problems is arguable.

Explanation by Analogies and Comparisons

The term *analogy* comes from the Greek *analogia*, referring to proportion or equality of ratios. In everyday use, *analogy* refers to the idea that one thing is somewhat like another thing even though the two are also different. Scientists have drawn analogies between the structure of atoms and the structure of our solar system. René Descartes compared nerves to water pipes. In medical circles, cholesterol is compared to sticky deposits that clog pipes.

Explanations by comparisons are central to the development of human cognitive processes. Small children use comparisons to form concepts. A kitten is to a cat as a puppy is to a dog, or a car is to a driver as an airplane is to a pilot. In politics, comparisons are used in pejorative ways when Democrats are compared to Communists and Republicans to Fascists. Such comparisons underscore the danger of thinking in terms of comparisons and analogies. An emphasis on the similarities between one thing and another can lead to overgeneralization, faulty thinking, or outright error.

Let's consider a greater problem that happens when we overemphasize the explanatory legitimacy of presumed similarities. A judge, while sentencing a teenager, acknowledged that the juvenile came from a disadvantaged home. The judge added that scores of other teenagers come from disadvantaged backgrounds but don't commit crimes. What are the problems with the comparison made by the judge? Further careful analysis will reveal all kinds of differences between the subject and the comparison targets. One purpose of science (and all critical and responsible thinking) is to engage in the relentless pursuit of the hidden and visible differences that make real differences in the world. Superficial and shallow comparisons based on presumed likenesses are unworthy of serious thinkers. Analogies may be helpful, but they should evoke deep suspicions (see Simanek, 2014). At best, analogies and comparisons offer programs for more intellectual work. At worst, they promote intellectual laziness.

MODELS AS EXPLANATIONS Models in science are comparable to analogies (see Eacker, 1975; Hesse, 1967), but more sophisticated. The term *model* in scientific literature refers to a conceptual framework marked by attempts to find logical, structural, or functional similarities between one thing and another. Psychologists have used steam boiler models to explain emotional expression. The greater the pressure generated in a steam boiler, the greater the need for a release of energy, or an explosion will occur. The model suggests that the pressures of living generate energy. If such energy is "bottled up" or not released through healthy exercise and verbal expression, then a nervous breakdown may

33

result. The same cautions that apply to simple analogies apply to models. A model may be helpful, but it may fail to do justice to the target it seeks to explain. Later, we will encounter a school of humanistic psychology that rejects all models in favor of a direct study of human beings.

NUMERICAL EXPLANATIONS Science has made remarkable progress in quantifying an increasing range of natural phenomena. This development is so critical that later sections are devoted to often surprising quantitative breakthroughs that influenced the emerging science of psychology. An early pioneer in the area named Francis Galton believed that every bodily and mental attribute could be quantified and summarized in a mathematical formula. In this tradition, formulae have been written to describe sensory thresholds, intellectual ability, mortality expectations, the relative contributions of heredity and environment to specific behaviors, and a host of other areas. Such formulae provide descriptive and predictive tools for the scientist, but can a mathematical formula unpack the deeper nature of the target it seeks to explain? Is intelligence the same as an intelligence quotient? In a way, we return to the same problem we encountered with analogies. When can we be sure we have a real identity between one thing and another? Quantitative explanations are integral to science, but may leave us grasping for more nuanced truths.

NEUROLOGICAL AND PHYSIOLOGICAL EXPLANATIONS The advent of brain sciences brought a growing faith that human experience and behavior can be explained in terms of underlying neurophysiological processes. As explored in later chapters, recent history has witnessed unprecedented advances in our understanding of the relationship between the nervous system and psychological processes. But can we believe that underlying neural processes offer adequate explanations for psychological events? There's no question we benefit from knowing that deposits of amyloidal plaques in nerve structures are asso-

ciated with Alzheimer's disease. The discovery of such plaques may uncover a piece of the puzzle and even suggest intervention techniques, but we may still lack an adequate explanation for the disease's role in experience and behavior. We must still struggle with the possible roles of heredity, diet, exercise, a more penetrating analysis of the chemistry of amyloidal proteins, immune reactions to such proteins, and so forth. Biochemical explanations, though useful, may leave us without a satisfactory explanation of the ultimate causes and characteristics of the disease and, particularly, the experience of the disease. The virtue of neuroscience centers on its practical and heuristic values. A concept or a theory with heuristic value is one that leads to productive new ideas and hypotheses. Neurological and physiological explanations lead to questions of a biochemical, chemical, or physical nature. Each level of analysis presents new mysteries but may fail to provide an adequate explanatory framework relevant to all the dimensions of a problem. As noted earlier, no explanation is free of problems. As we explore how scholars throughout history have explained psychological phenomena, it is helpful to think critically about the problem of explanation. In what sense are analogies and models helpful and in what sense are they misleading? Does the identification of a physiological or neurological correlate of a psychological event do justice to the complexity of that event? There are schools of thought (e.g., the Gestalt school and the psychology of William James), as well as cognitive psychologists (Lombrozo, 2015), and neuroscientists (Uttal, 2001, 2013), who question whether one level of explanation (e.g., the neurological level) can ever do justice to another level (e.g., the psychological level). We will revisit the problem of explanation in new and interesting ways.

In addition to the philosophical problems mentioned in this chapter, additional problems are of special interest for psychologists. Do human beings have an essential built-in moral nature (i.e., are we morally good, evil, or simply neutral at birth)? What is the appropriate unit of study in psychology? Should we focus on part processes such as reflex activity or should we focus on the whole organism in its natural environment? Such issues and others like them will surface as we consider the various systems of psychology. If you are interested, several resources focus on philosophical issues in psychology (Eacker, 1972, 1975; Rubenstein & Slife, 1988; Wertheimer, 1972).

Review Questions

1. Define the term *epistemology.*
2. Distinguish between a priori and a posteriori knowledge.
3. Differentiate between nativist and empiricist accounts of depth perception.
4. Briefly explain at least five different ways of assessing truth.
5. What risks come with the reliance on authority for knowledge?
6. According to Karl Popper, what is the key distinguishing feature between a legitimate science and pseudoscience?
7. Trace Kuhn's view on the development of science. What does Kuhn mean by terms such as *normal science* and *paradigm*?
8. If you were arguing for Feyerabend's philosophy of science, what evidence would you employ?
9. List and briefly describe Aristotle's four kinds of causation.
10. Distinguish between intrinsic and extrinsic teleology.
11. Advance three arguments in support of determinism and three arguments in defense of free will.
12. Outline two monistic and two dualistic approaches to mind and brain.
13. Which of the various mind–brain positions seems most adequate to you? What are some of the problems with this position?
14. Outline two major problems for psychogenic identity theory encountered in recent research on embryo experimentation.
15. What are the strengths and weaknesses of arguments by analogy?

Glossary

aestheticism The belief that the principles of beauty are applicable to other arenas of thought. In epistemology, aestheticism attempts to integrate truth and beauty.

a posteriori Literally, *from what is later.* Generally refers to the belief that knowledge is dependent on experience and past learning. Contrast with *a priori.*

a priori Literally, *from what is prior.* Generally refers to the presumed capacity to discern truths through intellectual insights with minimal dependence on past experience and past learning. Contrast with *a posteriori.*

attributive pluralism Emphasizes the varieties of descriptive modes applicable for most phenomena. For example, a sunset may be described in the language of physics, anthropology, psychology, or any of a variety of other disciplinary languages. Events can also be described poetically or musically.

authority One of the most common tests of truth. Reference to books, institutions, legal codes, or other people as appropriate and adequate repositories of knowledge.

determinism The belief in universal causation. Implies that whatever happens is based on antecedents such that, given them, nothing else could happen. Contrast with *free will.*

double-aspect monism A mind–brain position emphasizing the availability of two languages to describe the same phenomena. In this case, there is the language of physiology versus language that employs mentalistic concepts. The position assumes that both refer to the same underlying reality.

dualism The belief that there are two fundamentally different realities. For example, mental processes are considered by the dualist to be largely independent and qualitatively different from brain processes.

efficient cause According to Aristotle, the force that sets a thing in motion. Thus, domino *A*, impacting domino *B*, is the efficient cause of the fall of *B*.

emergentism A mind–brain position embracing the idea that mental processes are produced by brain processes. Some emergentists believe that mental processes, though produced by brain processes, are qualitatively different from the physical system from which they emerge.

empiricism A philosophical position that emphasizes the importance of experience, observation, and learning in the acquisition of knowledge.

epiphenomenalism A mind–body position marked by the belief that physical events are causal with respect to mental events. Mental events are viewed as completely dependent on physical functions and, as such, have no independent existence or causal efficacy.

epistemology A branch of philosophy concerned with problems of knowledge such as what can we know or how can we know?

extrinsic teleology The view that design or order in nature reflects the work of a designer.

Feyerabend, Paul K. (1924–1994) Philosopher of science who has argued for an anarchistic epistemology marked by belief that there is no such thing as a single unified and unchanging scientific method.

final cause According to Aristotle, the goals or purposes for which an action was intended.

formal cause The form or shape that contributes to a causal sequence. Thus, an airplane could not fly if critical components were not shaped properly.

free will The assumption that human beings make choices that are to some degree independent of antecedent conditions. Contrast with *determinism*.

genetic epistemology The study of ways of knowing and ways of solving problems as a function of developmental level.

idealism A philosophical orientation emphasizing mind or spirit as the preeminent feature of life. Contrast with *materialism*.

indeterminism The doctrine that it is impossible to apply strict cause-and-effect explanations to events at the subatomic level.

instinct An organized sequence of behaviors characteristic of a given species. It is assumed that instinctive behaviors are not learned.

interactionism A commonsense belief in the interdependence of the mental and the physical realms. According to this position, mental events may be causal with respect to physical events and vice versa.

intrinsic teleology The position that design, order, and purpose are immanent in nature.

Kuhn, Thomas S. (1922–1996) A philosopher of science who emphasized the importance of understanding science in terms of its community structures and evolutionary processes. His book *The Structure of Scientific Revolutions* is one of the most influential works in its field in the twentieth century.

learning Any change in performance or behavior that is attributable to the effects of practice or experience.

material cause Aristotle's contention that things behave as they do partly because of their material structure. For example, a billiard ball could not function properly if it were made of cork or rubber.

materialism A monistic ontology characterized by the belief that all real things are composed exclusively of matter. Implies that all being can be understood in terms of the principles of material structure.

monism The position that reality is one thing. Thus, everything relates to everything else in a completely interconnected world. Contrast with *pluralism*.

nativism The position that there are perceptions that are built in or operational from birth and that are informative about the world. For example, the nativist argues that we have an innate capacity to see in depth. Contrast with *empiricism*.

normal science A notion introduced by Thomas Kuhn that refers to conventional ways of solving problems in science at a given time or during the reign of a particular paradigm.

ontology A branch of philosophy that studies the nature and relations of being. Considers the question, "what is real?"

paradigm According to Thomas Kuhn, the beliefs, attitudes, values, methods, and assumptions that guide the intellectual community at a given time.

pluralism The belief that there are many real things and many different orders of reality. Contrast with *monism*.

Popper, Karl Raimond (1902–1994) Mathematician and philosopher noted for a hypothetico-deductive approach to science. His book *The Logic of Scientific Discovery* is one of the classics in the philosophy of science.

pragmatism A U.S. philosophical movement associated with the work of Charles S. Pierce and William James. James emphasized the close connections between empiricism, pluralism, and pragmatism. According to pragmatism, concepts must be judged in terms of their cash value or the practical work they do in the world. Thus, truth is judged by utility and the practical consequences achieved by an idea.

psyche The Greek term for soul or mind. Includes mental processes such as thought, memory, sensation, and perception.

psychogenic emergentism The idea that mental processes develop or emerge with the development of the body.

psychogenic identity theory A theory of the origin of psyche that stresses the continuity or identity of the psychically endowed biological substratum of the organism and the later mature, self-reflective, fully conscious adult.

psychogeny Literally, the origin of psyche. Theories of the origin of psyche.

psychophysical parallelism A mind–brain doctrine that assumes the independent existence of mental and physical events. According to parallelism, the mental and the physical are, by definition, congruent. They do not interact with each other; rather, they are like two clocks that always agree on the time, but are nevertheless independent systems.

rationalism A philosophical orientation deriving from the Latin *ratio*, meaning to reason or think. Rationalist philosophers emphasize a priori knowledge, deduction, and an active mind that selectively organizes sensory data.

skepticism The philosophical position that all truth claims are suspect and must be questioned.

teleology Refers to purpose or design. According to Aristotle, design or purpose is an intrinsic part of the natural order. Thus, it is the purpose of a seed to sprout under the proper conditions and grow into a plant. Such a teleology can be thought of as intrinsic and is in contrast with the extrinsic teleology encountered in certain religions. Extrinsic teleology implies that things do what they do because they fulfill purposes imposed by a deity.

Part II
Early Psychological Thought

Chapters 3 through 5 provide an overview of psychological thought from ancient times through the late Renaissance period, ending about 1600. Psychology developed as a formal academic and professional discipline in the late nineteenth century, but a deep interest in psychological topics developed long before then. Though our methods and tools of inquiry have expanded, we'll find surprising continuities across time with respect to questions about psychology. What is an emotion and how can we control our emotions? How do we learn and how can we improve learning? Is there one motive (maybe the will to power or sexuality) that dominates all other motives? What is the mind and how can two minds know the same thing? What is the relation of the brain to mental processes? Who can best investigate the problems of psychology and what methods should be employed? The thoughts and discoveries of past thinkers enrich the history of science, including psychology, revealing that we do not live in complete temporal isolation. A comprehensive appreciation for the history of psychology is greatly enhanced by knowledge of the content of the following three chapters. The timeline highlights important developments in early psychological thought.

TIMELINE 3.1

c. 600 BCE to AD 1600

600–470 BCE	Era of the Greek cosmologists and early Greek medics
470–322 BCE	Golden Age of Greece—philosophy features the work of Socrates, Plato, and Aristotle
c. 175	*On the Diagnosis and Cure of the Soul's Passions* by Galen
354	Birth of Augustine
c. 380	Christianity becomes official religion of Rome
415	Martyrdom of Hypatia of Alexandria
570	Birth of Mohammed
711	Muslims invade Spain
732	Charles Martel defeats Muslims near Tours (stops northern expansion)
965	Birth of Alhazen (his *Book of Optics* later becomes a classic)
980	Birth of Avicenna
c. 1095	*The Incoherence of the Philosophers* by Al-Ghazali
1095	Beginning of Crusades
1215	Magna Carta is issued
1225	Birth of Thomas Aquinas
1232	Inquisition is established by Pope Gregory IX
1252	Innocent IV allows torture as part of Inquisition interrogations
1304	Birth of Petrarch (one of the founders of Renaissance humanism)
1347	Beginning of great plague (contributes to growth of skepticism)
1354	Mechanical clock installed at Strasbourg Cathedral
c. 1400	Aristotle's works translated into Latin, bringing philosophy to a wider audience
1409	Founding of University of Leipzig, later to become birthplace of psychology
1431	Joan of Arc burned as a witch
1456	Gutenberg prints the first Bible, feeding the development of a larger reading public
1486	*The Malleus Maleficarum* by Kramer and Sprenger (Bible of the witch hunts)
1492	Columbus sails to America
1500	Leonardo da Vinci draws a model of a musket, a precursor of guns
1513	*The Prince* by Machiavelli (a classic in political theory and social psychology)
1517	*Ninety-Five Theses against Indulgences* by Martin Luther challenges church authority
1519	Ferdinand Magellan starts voyage that results in first circumnavigation
1543	*On the Revolutions of the Celestial Spheres* by Nicolaus Copernicus
	On the Structure of the Human Body by Andreas Vesalius
1561	Birth of Francis Bacon
c. 1576	*Apology for Raimond Sebond* by Michel de Montaigne helps initiate a skeptical crisis
1583	University of Edinburgh (an early secular university)
1587	*New Philosophy on the Nature of Man* by Oliva Sabuco
1588	Birth of Thomas Hobbes
	Francis Drake defeats Spanish Armada
1596	Birth of René Descartes
1600	Beginning of modern period
	Giordano Bruno argues for a sun-centered cosmos and is burned at the stake

3 Ancient Psychological Thought

We must not be too sure of the ignorance of our ancestors.

—Will Durant (1954)

The story of psychology is told in ancient manuscripts and documents such as the Vedas of the Hindus, the Talmud of the Hebrews, the Avesta of the Zoroastrians, and early Greek epic narratives and poems such as the *Iliad*. Ancient writings are rich in speculative as well as practical psychology. Psychological thought is global and is one of the ways humans deal with the mysteries of life.

Early Chinese Psychologies

In a survey of the social history of Chinese psychology, Petzold (1987) called attention to "the special sensitivity of psychology to political and ideological influences" (p. 213). Early psychological thought in China was tied to a larger worldview organized around the number 5. The Chinese believed in five basic elements consisting of wood, fire, metal, earth, and water. Five basic organs were identified, including the ear,

eye, nose, mouth, and body. These organs corresponded with sensations of hearing, vision, smell, taste, and touch. Ancient Asian scholars also organized colors, smells, sounds, tastes, and tissues around the number 5. For example, they identified the five tastes as sweet, sour, salt, bitter, and acid. Basic colors were thought to consist of green, red, yellow, black, and white. Smells were identified as burning, fragrant, goatish, rank, and rotten. Later developments included attempts to identify the basic emotions, parts of the body, and virtues. Emotions were designated as anger, joy, desire, sorrow, and fear (Fernberger, 1935, p. 547).

The number 5 also guided an analysis of human relationships. **Confucius (551–479 BCE)** proposed five kinds of human relations including "ruler and minister, father and son, elder brother and younger brother, husband and wife, and one friend and another" (Chan, 1967, p. 189). These five prototypes illustrate the paternal emphasis in Chinese culture. Confucius was interested in the moral life and harmony among people. Although a great humanist, his teachings were counterproductive for the development of some sciences.

41

For example, his belief that the body is sacred discouraged the practice of dissection.

One of the greatest Chinese philosophers, **Hsün Tzu (c. 298–c. 212 BCE)**, is sometimes compared with the Greek philosopher Aristotle. Like Aristotle, Hsün Tzu was a naturalist who emphasized the regularity and orderliness of nature. He argued for rational and empirical methods and opposed superstition. For Hsün Tzu, we cannot count on divine intervention because nature goes its own way. Given his thinking, it makes no sense to pray for rain because natural phenomena cannot be controlled. Hsün Tzu was a strong advocate of learning and self-advancement. He believed basic human nature is evil, but we can attain goodness through education.

The concepts of **yin** and **yang** dominated ancient Chinese philosophy and psychology. At first, yin and yang were viewed as antagonistic cosmic forces, but later thinkers recognized them as both opposite and complementary (Yun, 2012). Yang is associated with qualities such as force, hardness, masculinity, heat, and dryness. Yin is related to qualities such as weakness, softness, femininity, hearing, coldness, and moistness. Physical and psychological well-being and social balance depended on equilibrium between yin and yang. Early Chinese medicine worked toward restoring and maintaining this essential balance. For example, acupuncture, dating from the third millennium BCE, was designed to stimulate or drain energy flow or *chi* necessary to maintain balance and health. Other therapies, including diet, herbs, sleep (Yanjiao et al., 2015), and disciplined activity such as *Tai Chi* (Tong, 2003), focused on restoring a balance of yin and yang forces. Castiglioni (1941), for example, noted the importance of organ therapy by pointing out that warriors "drank blood or ate the liver of tiger" (p. 103). Consuming the tiger's blood or liver was thought to intensify yang in the warrior, leading to greater courage.

Early Chinese scholars stressed the importance of cognitive processes. In Chinese thought, the mind plays a dominant role, whereas the body acts as its servant. This doesn't imply a radical separation of mind and body because mental processes are nurtured inside the body. Mind and body are integrated and inseparable. Chinese thought opened the door to a physiological psychology where the mind is as significant as the body. These ideas continue to permeate psychological science and practice in contemporary China (Hsueh & Guo, 2012).

Babylonia

Babylonia, regarded as one of antiquity's greatest civilizations, wielded a far-reaching influence on other nations in the Mediterranean basin. The authority of Babylonian ideas colored the intellectual traditions of the Greeks, Egyptians, Jews, and Arabs. Close to the old riverbeds of the Tigris and Euphrates, the ruins of Babylon are situated about sixty miles south of the present city of Baghdad.

The Babylonians studied mathematics, geography, astronomy, law, medicine, and language. Writing was an important art among their elite and skilled citizens. During the last century, scholars deciphered many of their cuneiform writings on clay tablets including two famous Babylonian works—the *Epic of Gilgamesh* and the *Code of Hammurabi*.

Thousands of major and minor gods populated their belief system. Deities were thought to rule over everything from astronomical events to taxation. Only human imagination, it seemed, could limit the gods of Babylon. Sometimes friendly and other times hostile, Babylonian deities were anthropomorphic and engaged in human affairs. Help from the gods was invoked through magic rites, prayers, incantations, and the special powers and methods of priests and physicians.

A universe of demons challenged the power of Babylonian gods and threatened humanity. Alexander and Selesnick (1966) mention that "each disease had its specific demon. Insanity was caused by the demon Idta" (p. 20). Demons were exorcised through special medicines (e.g., certain plants were thought to have the power to kill demons), confessions, magic rites, and other procedures designed to restore harmony with divine forces. The Babylonians encouraged prevention as well as treatment. Charms, religious symbols, and virtuous behavior could ward off demons. In keeping with prevailing opinions of the day, it was wise to avoid women because they were said to have the power to inspire demonic possession.

The Babylonians studied personality differences (Millon, 2012), offered accurate descriptions of diseases, including epilepsy (Magiorkinis et al., 2010), and their astronomy was sufficiently advanced to permit predictions of eclipses. They were interested in human and animal anatomy and sophisticated mathematics. As with other early cultures, the Babylonians offered a curious blend of empirical and superstitious explanations of their world.

Egypt

In many ancient civilizations, science cannot be easily separated from religion. In ancient Egypt, prevailing religious perspectives influenced many ideas about psychology. When it came to religion, the polytheistic Egyptians had no trouble finding things to worship. A variety of plants and animals, the sun, the moon, the stars, rivers, mountains, and people served as objects of worship. A belief in immortality was a centerpiece of Egyptian religions, guiding the art of mummification and elaborate burial customs. The quality of bodily preservation was thought to enhance the soul's ability to survive after death and to facilitate the transition to immortality.

Though ancient Egyptians often resorted to mystical and religious views of illness, they were among the first to conduct detailed naturalistic studies of the body including the heart and the brain (see Trueman, 2015). It was apparent that blood vessels connected the heart to the entire body including the brain. As a result, evidence suggests that Egyptians understood the importance of the heart in cognitive activity (see

Laver, 1972). Perhaps the brain was subservient to the heart, but the ancients did observe correlations between head injuries and disorders of speech, memory, and movement (Rose, 2009). Confusions over the roles of the brain and the heart in cognitive activity would later spill over into Greek medicine.

It is clear that Egyptian medicine was a blend of superstition and observation. They believed that insects, filth, and devils spread disease. They treated disease with rituals, incantations, rest, surgery, enemas, and medications designed for ingestion or external applications. Medications were created from plants, honey, animal dung, oil, blood, and animal organs, and Egyptians pursued alchemy for mummification and other goals (Cavalli, 2016). They placed considerable emphasis on hygiene and regularly practiced circumcision and fumigation of the vagina. Alexander and Selesnick (1966) noted that the Egyptians "recognized the emotional disorder that the Greeks later called 'hysteria'" (p. 21). A woman's emotional disorder was believed to result from a uterus that had wandered to another part of her body. Egyptian doctors fumigated the vagina in an attempt to return the uterus to its normal resting location. This explanation for hysteria (named after the Greek word for uterus, *hysteron*) persevered for centuries, even into the late Middle Ages.

The import of names is not lost on modern cultures. First and last names are pivotal to our sense of self and our religious and cultural identities. Egyptians were among the first to emphasize the close identity of an object and its name. The cursing of a name, the succession of names from one generation to the next, or the destruction of a name, had great psychological significance. The early emphasis on names and their deep cultural and existential meanings continues in modern cultures.

Egyptian women achieved higher social status than their counterparts in most ancient and modern cultures (see Thompson, 2010). Women held political offices, took the initiative in courtship if they wished, owned property, made formal proposals for marriage, and, in general, wielded considerable power in their homes. Although pharaohs and some wealthy citizens had harems, women enjoyed unparalleled status and power in the majority of monogamous Egyptian families.

A hallmark of Egyptian civilization was its superior engineering. Even in the twenty-first century, we are in awe of their canals and pyramids. Egyptian science—with the possible exception of geometry—was less impressive than their engineering.

Other Ancient Eastern Psychologies

Some of the oldest civilizations, dating from the fourth millennium BCE, existed in what is now India and Pakistan. Some early cultures enjoyed well-constructed houses connected to sewers, streets, shops, and baths. Anthropologists have discovered a variety of bronze and copper utensils and pottery along with jewelry and copper weapons.

During this time, psychological thought flourished in the area that is now India and Pakistan. We can find pronounced psychological themes in the ancient **Vedas**, the oldest sacred books of India. The term *Veda* means "knowledge." Although orthodox Hindus date the books from the beginning of time, historians are more likely to date them from earlier than 1000 BCE. The Vedic treatises contain a philosophic knowledge known as the **Upanishads**.

Selected verses from the Vedas and Upanishads offer a glimpse of early Indian beliefs about psychology. A major theme centers on the problems of knowledge and desire. As we will see, the Greeks debated the relative merits of the senses versus the intellect. In ancient Indian philosophy, neither is to be trusted. The ancient Indians emphasized respect for the mystery of life and encouraged intuition and the development of spiritual sensitivities. People who became too involved with the sensory world developed false consciousness, inordinate desire, and an undisci-

plined nature. The Indians advocated austerity, self-denial, and cleansing of excessive desires of the senses through fasting and meditation.

Early Indian thinkers showed little interest in studying sensory phenomena, owing perhaps to their distrust of the senses. Anatomical studies were also rare. The Indians were, however, careful observers of pregnancy, and the Vedas include pre-natal recommendations (Rakhshani et al., 2015). Ancients in India believed an infant's personality could be traced to maternal characteristics during pregnancy. For example, an ill-tempered mother might give birth to an epileptic child, while an alcoholic mother might deliver an infant with a weak memory. An immoral mother could give birth to an effeminate son. Women were subjected to stringent controls, perhaps because of their potential for influence. The *Code of Manu* illustrates the point: "No act is to be done according to her own will by a young girl, a young woman, or even by an old woman . . . The good wife of a husband . . . must never do anything disagreeable to him" (see Welles, 1957, p. 33). In contrast to Egyptian culture, Indian women were subjected to the will of their father, husband, or sons.

Indians believed that diseases resulted from devils, filth, or imbalance of humors. Excessive emotional expression could produce mental disorders. The Indians used charms, incantations, meditation, and exorcism to combat disease. They emphasized personal hygiene and, following the teachings of Siddhartha Gautama (the Buddha or Enlightened One), they engaged in psychotherapeutic yoga and meditation exercises designed to induce a quiet spirit and resignation (Chaturvedi, 2015). Knowledge of yoga was slow to come to Western psychology, although one finds early discussions by Leuba (1925) of yoga not as a practice but as a religion.

The Hebrews

Jewish philosophy and psychology developed in the context of radical monotheism. Their belief in a single god contrasted with the polytheisms of the Babylonians, Egyptians, and Greeks. Jewish life and thought were conditioned by one of the most famous religious expressions in history, "Hear, O Israel, the Lord our God, the Lord is One." The task of every Jew was to know the one God by understanding the word of Jehovah as set forth in the Torah. Scholarly activity was held in high regard and has remained so for several millennia.

The Hebrews viewed Jehovah as an all-powerful source of reward and punishment. At the same time, they stressed human responsibility and freedom of choice. People were viewed as victims of a natural duplicity. On the one hand, we are creatures of the flesh, but we are also spiritual creatures with a spark of the divine and are capable of self-renunciation for community benefit. On occasion, the Hebrews embraced a kind of fatalism, but the stronger tradition might be characterized in terms of an if–then belief system. *If* the people obey God's commandments, *then* beneficial consequences follow. Failure to obey, however, results in punishment. The future is open and rewards or punishments depend on human behavior. This basic perspective has shaped much of Western thought.

Ben-Noun (2004) claimed that the roots of psychiatry are traced to ancient Israel. Likewise, Rotenberg and Diamond (1971) found evidence that the Hebrews advanced a concept of moral insanity. Hebraic thinkers also considered disorganized behavior, as illustrated in Daniel 4:33 where Nebuchadnezzar was isolated from people and fostered a delusion that he was an animal. According to the Hebrews, the anger of Jehovah might cause mental illness (Deut. 28:28), but human disobedience was thought to produce such vengeance. Demonological explanations of mental and physical ailments can be found in Hebrew thought and in later Christianity, but such perspectives conflict with Hebraic concepts of the absolute oneness of God. We come across this tension in the later philosophy of Spinoza (discussed in Chapter 7) and other Jewish mystical traditions (Bakan, 1958).

The Hebrews gave the leading role to the man in marriage but the Talmud admonished men to honor their wives above themselves. The Hebrew people were unique in their regard for children. The "fruit of the womb" was viewed as a gift from God (Psalms 127:3) and children's children as "the crown of old men" (Proverbs 17:6). At the same time, extensive duties were imposed on children. "Honor thy father and thy mother: that thy days may be long upon the land" was literally true, because the actions of wayward or rebellious children were tantamount to a capital crime.

Most ancient cultures practiced infanticide. Influenced by Egyptian and Babylonian beliefs, the Hebrews may have performed child sacrifice in a limited fashion. In most countries of the Mediterranean basin, unwanted children were abandoned on hillsides, sacrificed to the gods, thrown into rivers, or sold to strangers (see DeMause, 1974). Children were sacrificed because of real or imagined defects, sometimes at the direction of religious beliefs. Consistent with prevailing views about women, girls were victims of infanticide far more than boys.

Persia

At one time, the great Persian Empire was as large as the continental United States. It encompassed the countries surrounding the eastern Mediterranean and extended east to the Indus River in India, including much of what is now Iran and Afghanistan. The Persian Empire had its beginnings about 900 BCE and thrived from about 600 BCE until Alexander the Great's conquest in 331 BCE. For nearly two centuries, the Persians existed as contemporaries and rivals with the Greeks.

Persia was the birthplace of the Zoroastrian religion, which originated in the teachings of a prophet named **Zarathustra**. According to legend, the god Ahura-Mazda revealed his teachings to Zarathustra, resulting in the Zoroastrian holy book called the **Avesta** (sometimes called the **Zend-Avesta**). This work includes rules and ethics for medical practice (Hatami et al., 2013a) and divides physicians into three groups, including those who used holy words to treat people; the Avesta also describes the use of a stimulant to induce euphoria as a treatment for depression, which Zargaran et al. (2012) describe as early psychiatry. Although Zarathustra taught that there is one God, his followers saw the world in terms of a struggle between Ahura-Mazda and Angro-Mainyus, the prince of devils. Persian culture drew considerable influence from this theological dualism. Diseases and emotional disorders were viewed as the work of the devil, giving rise to predictable treatments involving exorcism, incantations, and magical and religious rites. Humans were viewed as the testing ground for the forces of good and evil. According to Zarathustra, people have free will, giving them the liberty to follow Ahura-Mazda or Angro-Mainyus.

Crimes were viewed as offenses against Ahura-Mazda and punishments could be severe. Public whippings, crucifixion, mutilations, and stonings were commonplace. The intellectual climate in Persia was not friendly to the growth of philosophy or science.

Greece

MacLeod (1975) is one of many historians who suggested that the period from 600 to 300 BCE in Greece represents one of the great creative periods in human history. We can trace many intellectual Western traditions to the Greeks. The earliest Greeks evidently occupied the island of Crete and other smaller islands off the coast of the mainland as early as 3000 BCE. As with other cultures, the distinction between legend and history is blurred. For centuries, the legendary figure of Agamemnon and the city of Troy were thought to exist only in Homer's epic tales. That view was shattered when treasure hunter and amateur archeologist Heinrich Schliemann (1822–1890) made the greatest archeological discovery of the nineteenth century. At the age of eight, Schliemann had claimed that one day he

would excavate Troy. In 1871, his prediction came true when he uncovered the ruins of the ancient city (see Schliemann, 1875/1968; Schuchhardt, 1891/1971). His discovery underscores the difficulties of assessing legendary stories from the past. Our incredulity can be unwarranted as often as our credulity.

Ancient Greece produced an explosion of intellectual curiosity, but we're not really sure how it happened. From a geographical standpoint, it was neither the best nor the worst of locations to support civilization. Only about a quarter of the rocky peninsula was fit for growing crops; fishing and hunting provided food, and forests supplied fuel. As in other parts of the ancient world, the institution of slavery provided leisure time for the elite classes. For a variety of reasons, the Greeks produced remarkable accomplishments in science, literature, philosophy, political theory, and the arts. In addition, the earliest hints of naturalistic psychology are found in the Greek mind.

The Cosmologists

The earliest Greek philosophers were interested in the nature of the universe (cosmology) and the origin of the universe (cosmogony). In addition to introducing concepts such as evolution and an early theory of atoms, Greek cosmologists speculated about many topics of a psychological nature.

THALES   **Thales** (*THAY leez*) of Miletus was probably born a few years before 625 BCE. He was a pivotal figure who insisted on scientific interpretations of the world over mystical ones. Possibly influenced by Egyptian cosmology, he believed the earth resembled a flat-rimmed saucer floating on the sea. But another question haunted him: Is there a single element from which everything is derived? Many ancient Greek thinkers obsessed over finding the fundamental stuff of the universe. In this tradition, Thales believed that water was the primal substance (Green & Groff, 2003). It made sense. Plants and animals depend on water for survival. It appears in a diversity of forms from rain to snow to steam; water seemed to characterize the world.

Thales also developed an interest in the problem of movement. How could creatures move? His fascination with movement evolved from his curiosity about magnets. Writing later, Aristotle suggested that Thales believed a magnetic stone possessed a soul (Kirk & Raven, 1957, pp. 93–95). Apparently, he believed a soul has kinetic and motive force that makes movement possible. So far as we know, Thales did not speculate about how water—the primal physical substrate of the world—interacts with soul. While staring at the stars, the story is told, Thales met his death after plummeting into a well. A cautionary tale, it seems, to keep in mind for philosophers.

ANAXIMENES Like Thales, the early Greek philosopher **Anaximenes (c. 588–c. 524 BCE)** was a member of the Milesian school and shared their interest in cosmological problems. Anaximenes (*uh NAHK suh meh neez*) taught that air is the primal substance of the universe and can be transformed to other things through rarefaction and condensation. Following condensation, air becomes clouds. Through further condensation, clouds become rain. Rain becomes hail. With subsequent condensation, air condensed into rain then becomes land and condensed land becomes rocks. Through rarefaction, heavy, windy air becomes lighter air, and very light air becomes fire. Condensation is associated with coldness and rarefaction with heat. He concluded that earthquakes could result from disturbances of air, the result of too much moisture or extensive drought.

Anaximenes taught that the soul is rarefied air and that the soul holds the body together (Kirk & Raven, 1957). Maybe he believed this because of how the body decomposes when the breath of life or soul leaves the body. He also claimed that cosmic air holds the world together and even suggested that air is a god.

ANAXIMANDER Thales's immediate successor was **Anaximander of Miletus (610–c. 547 BCE)**.

Like his mentor, Anaximander (*an Ack suh man der*) wondered about a basic element in nature, but he rejected water and air as primary substances. He questioned, for example, how water could be the basic substrate of fire. If water was not the basic substance, neither could it be any other thing that we observe. Anaximander believed that when we look at nature, we're actually seeing a manifestation of something basic, but not something the senses can understand. As a result, Anaximander claimed the basic stuff of the universe was infinite and formless, so he named it *apeiron* (meaning "without boundary").

Anaximander believed in a succession of worlds, each evolving through a cyclical process of beginning, maturation, and decay. In the beginning, oceans dry up and form land, giving home to creatures to inhabit its surface. In this process, life develops out of the interaction of opposites—moisture and fire, coolness and heat. Anaximander claimed that the first creatures were encased in a protective hard surface. As they aged, the creatures crawled out of the waters onto dry land, producing a gradual change in their protective body surfaces. Often viewed as the first evolutionary theorist, Anaximander believed that the first humans came from fishlike creatures (see Kirk & Raven, 1957, p. 141). He observed that, unlike many other creatures, humans have a long period of dependency after birth. Because human infants are so dependent, he believed the first humans could not have survived by themselves. So how did they endure? Anaximander concluded that another creature must have nurtured the first human infants.

He is often credited with constructing the first world map. He may also have been the first Greek to construct a sundial. Although only fragments of his writings exist, Anaximander's interests ranged over all the sciences in his culture, from astronomy to biology.

PYTHAGORAS Born on the island of Samos, **Pythagoras (c. 580–c. 500 BCE)** is remembered as a legendary figure in mathematics and philosophy. In fact, Pythagoras likely coined the term

47

philosophy, constructed from *philo* (meaning love) and *sophia* (meaning wisdom). As a philosopher—one who loves knowledge—Pythagoras was known for pure and applied interests. He had a deep love for the search for abstract and universal principles. As the founder of a religious society, he also applied philosophy and science to ethical conduct and the good life.

Pythagoras and his followers shifted the perspective from cosmology to an interest in human problems. Formal mathematical explanations replaced an emphasis on primordial substances. The Pythagoreans believed that all things in the universe have numerical qualities. Pythagoras claimed that numbers are absolute and unchanging and can affect the existence of objects on earth. For example, Pythagoras argued that although humans cannot draw a perfect triangle, the lengths of the sides of a drawn triangle relate to each other in ways that depend on the perfect relations of sides in an abstract triangle. The

Pythagoras

unchanging, perfect world of numbers affects the changing temporal world here on earth. For Pythagoras, even psyche was a "mathematical entity" (Green & Groff, 2003, p. 22). Unlike some other scholars of their day, the Pythagoreans viewed the brain as the seat of mental life. They also count among the first Westerners to use music as therapy.

In terms of religious assumptions, the Pythagoreans believed in immortality and the transmigration of souls. For this reason, they advised against eating animals; killing an animal might mean that you are invading the habitat of an ancestor's soul. They encouraged discipline and balance and avoided excessive laughter. Presumably, the expression of strong emotions undermined dignity and character. The Pythagoreans valued study, especially before speaking on matters pertaining to their beliefs. They imposed prohibitions on their followers that may have resulted in compulsive behavior. The Pythagoreans warned against putting the left shoe on first, wearing rings, looking in mirrors beside lamps, eating beans, or allowing swallows to nest under your roof.

The Pythagoreans assumed important stands on cultural issues. Despite its critical role in the Greek economy, Pythagoras condemned slave labor. And at a time when women were often prohibited from studying science and mathematics, he invited them to his school. According to Waithe (1987b), numerous women were associated with Pythagorean societies from the sixth to the second century BCE, and many assumed leadership roles. Fortunately, these traditions continued after his death, with several women joining neo-Pythagorean schools as late as the third century CE.

Unlike their sisters in Egypt, most Grecian women did not enjoy social status in antiquity. Perhaps Pythagoras encouraged the education of women because his wife and daughter were both accomplished thinkers. Pythagoras's wife **Theana** was a philosopher who played a key role in the society's educational activities. Their daughter **Myia** focused on moderation and

48

balance (see Waithe, 1987b, pp. 15–16), and provided some of the earliest advice on the care of infants. Myia emphasized the importance of milk and bland foods, moderation in temperature, good ventilation, and soft clothing. A later Pythagorean scholar named **Aesara** also discussed balance. In a fragment of her writing, she argued that physical and mental health result from harmony, making her one of the first to emphasize a balance theory of health.

XENOPHANES   Based in Elea, a town in southern Italy, another group of philosophers called the Eleatics contemplated different questions related to epistemology. The first of the Eleatics was **Xenophanes** (*zeh NAH fuh neez*), born about 560 BCE in Colophon. Known for his epistemological skepticism, he distinguished between knowledge and opinion, insisting that humans do not have certain knowledge, only opinion. A strict monotheist, Xenophanes attacked Homer's portrayal of anthropomorphic gods in epic poems such as the *Iliad* and the *Odyssey*. It troubled him how the gods of Homeric polytheism indulged in corrupt human actions and emotions including jealousy, deceit, and adultery. In an early work on psychology and religion, Xenophanes noted that Ethiopians' gods appear Ethiopian while Thracians' gods appear Thracian. He thought it strange that people conceptualize their gods as wearing clothes. He argued that if animals could draw, they would draw their gods to look like themselves. The one god above all gods, according to Xenophanes, was in no way similar to mortals.

Although known for epistemology, Xenophanes also studied meteorological and astronomical problems. He taught that a new sun, made of ignited clouds, arises each morning and proceeds in a straight line forever.

PARMENIDES   Born around 515 BCE, **Parmenides** (*pahr MEHN ih deez*) of Elea influenced several later philosophers, especially Plato. In a poem likely titled "On Nature," Parmenides shares a message from a goddess on "the way of truth" and "the way of seeming." The way of seeming is the way mortals view their world. The way of truth is the way an immortal might see the world. Although controversy surrounds the interpretations of Parmenides's poem, he teaches that reason and the senses provide contrasting information about the world. Through the senses, we are aware only of plurality, division, and change but through reason we can discover the real world of permanent truths. Reason provides the means through which we move beyond the realm of mere appearance, an idea that marks him as an early rationalist.

Parmenides was one of the first to emphasize a philosophy of *being* as opposed to a philosophy of *becoming*. A philosophy of becoming emphasizes process, change, variety, and transition. Few things are more *apparent* than the inevitability of change. The word *apparent*, however, is well chosen, especially to those who embrace a philosophy of being. For such a philosophy, the change we observe with the senses may be an illusion. A philosophy of being emphasizes unity, permanence, and a perfect reality that forms the backdrop of transient things. Philosophies of being and becoming offer different implications for psychology. In a statement that could almost have been written by an early Greek cosmologist, the American psychologist Abraham Maslow (1962) contrasted being-psychology with becoming-psychology as "the perfect with the imperfect, the ideal with the actual . . . the timeless with the temporal, end-psychology with means-psychology" (p. iv).

Parmenides also studied the mechanisms of perception. He apparently believed that "like" perceives "like," whereas some early philosophers taught that we perceive by virtue of opposites. For example, the theory of opposites holds that we experience the heat of hot water by virtue of the contrast between the temperature of the water and the temperature of the skin. Parmenides argued that we perceive light because we have fire or light within us. The light in the pupil of the eye responds to "its own kind." A corpse could not perceive light because the light or fire is deficient in the corpse. But the corpse could know coldness and silence (see Kirk & Raven, 1957, p. 283).

ZENO **Zeno of Elea**, a student of Parmenides, is best known for his paradoxes of motion. None of the remaining fragments of Zeno's teachings contains all of his arguments about motion, but the essential idea is illustrated as follows. Suppose an archer releases an arrow at point A and the arrow is aimed at a target at point B. To get to point B, the arrow must first traverse half the distance. Once it has gone halfway, to reach the target it must now travel half of the remaining distance, at which point it must travel halfway again, and so forth. Because we can continue dividing the remaining distance indefinitely, there is a logical problem about whether the arrow can ever reach its goal. By infinitely dividing the distance into progressively smaller pieces, Zeno approached the foundations of differential calculus over two thousand years before Leibniz and Newton. How does such a paradox relate to Parmenides?

Although motion is apparent to the senses, it violates logic and reason. Zeno's paradoxes also cast doubt on all of experience, particularly experience of change. When the senses conflict with reason, which should we choose? Reason, according to Parmenides, is superior to the senses; therefore, motion must be an illusion like other forms of change and becoming. Vlastos (1967) argues that "commonplaces may conceal absurdities and hence [we have] the need of reexamining even the best entrenched and most plausible assumptions" (p. 378).

HERACLITUS Whereas Parmenides was the best-known early philosopher of being, **Heraclitus** (*hehr uh KLY tuhs*) was the best-known philosopher of becoming. Most biographical information about Heraclitus is suspect. His dates are unknown, but he was probably active around 480 BCE. Known as the "Dark Philosopher," he is often portrayed in sculptures and paintings as weeping in anguish over the folly of human nature (Lurie, 1979). Possibly blind, he apparently lived in Ephesus and was an elitist who had little respect or liking for other philosophers. The feeling was mutual. Other philosophers often disparaged his work. Heraclitus proved unpopular because of his arrogance, his attacks on fellow philosophers and their works, and a philosophy that countered prevailing opinion. Although later philosophers such as Plato and Aristotle belittled his work and characterized him as morose, Heraclitus was treated with greater respect in recent centuries.

Heraclitus is most famous for his statement, "Upon those that step into the same rivers different and different waters flow" (Kirk & Raven, 1957, p. 146). In his thinking, constancy is illusory; experienced change is real, and his empiricism focuses on a world that is becoming. Fire is the metaphor by which Heraclitus understood the world. Fire is a natural choice because fire is ever changing and can transform one thing into another, causing something to burn or melt or rise in steam. Like Xenophanes, Heraclitus believed a new sun appears in the sky at the beginning of every day.

Heraclitus believed that souls could be wet or dry and that wetness is harmful; in fact, complete wetness means death. Partial wetness interferes with normal functioning. For example, drunkenness wets the soul and interferes with judgment. A dry soul is wise. Heraclitus seems to be arguing against excessive emotions in one of his fragments that asserted, "It is hard to fight with anger; for what it wants it buys at the price of soul" (Kirk & Raven, 1957, p. 211). Heraclitus trusted the senses more than his contemporaries or successors, but he found some senses to be more trustworthy than others. For example, he believed vision to be more accurate than audition. Heraclitus believed that the senses become clogged in sleep leading to memory loss. Memory, however, returns with the reactivation of the senses when we awaken.

Heraclitus had little respect for the knowledge and opinions of others. He saw humans as apes when compared with a god. The moralistic Heraclitus had contempt for the masses that lack

50

discipline as evidenced by overeating. He mocked conventional religion. Blood sacrifices and prayers to idols offended him; he likened the practice to talking with inanimate objects such as houses. It is little wonder Heraclitus lived in semi-isolation and, according to one account, committed suicide at age sixty (Kirk & Raven, 1957). Although disliked in his times, Heraclitus's influence in later science, philosophy, and even theology has been extensive, with continued influence on the study of such topics as the nature of theory (Ajit, 2008), people who dissociate (Mendelowitz, 2008), self-identity (Skolnick, 2008), and existentialism (Heidigger & Fink, 1970/1979).

LEUCIPPUS AND DEMOCRITUS The story of early Greek philosophy, science, and psychology takes a modern flavor with the early atomists Leucippus (*loo KIHP uhs*) and Democritus (*duh MAHK rih tuhs*). **Leucippus**, who lived around 500 BCE, was the founder of atomic theory, later refined by **Democritus (c. 460–c. 370 BCE)**. Although we know little about the life of Leucippus, it is known that Democritus was a citizen of Abdera in Thrace. He traveled around the Mediterranean world and had diverse interests including science, religion, and ethics. Whereas Heraclitus was characterized as weeping over the misery and foolishness of the human condition, Democritus is often portrayed as laughing at it. Lurie (1979) claimed, "To ancient writers, the two philosophers personified two contrasting approaches to *vita humana*, the contemplation of which evoked weeping in the one and laughter in the other" (p. 279).

According to Leucippus and Democritus, reality is composed of both the void and atoms. The void is empty space, and Leucippus noted that movement would be impossible without the void. Atoms were thought to be so small as to elude human perception. If any tangible object could be divided again and again, one would finally arrive at the atom, a unit that could not be divided (*atom* comes from the Greek word *atemmein, a* meaning "not" and *temmein* "divide"). Leucippus and Democritus taught that atoms vary in arrange-

ment, position, and shape. There were hooked atoms, rough atoms, smooth atoms, and so on. The sensible qualities one experiences result from the arrangement and shapes of atoms. For example, a dense and heavy object is more compact, possibly consisting of many atoms hooked together. Fire consists of smooth atoms, and the soul, according to Democritus, is material and consists of smooth atoms that disperse at death (Katona, 2002).

The atomists taught that all things come into existence out of a great whirl of atoms. Atoms in the whirl begin to separate, like being attracted to like, and in time worlds are generated. They believed in many worlds, some moist, some dry, some supporting plants and animals, and others devoid of life.

Democritus argued for a strict determinism. He believed that randomness was an appearance. When he spoke on psychological topics, he employed the language of causation. For example, small spherical atoms cause a bitter taste while large jagged atoms create a salty taste. In an early statement on the psychology of religion, Democritus argued that fear motivated a belief in popular Greek gods.

Democritus believed all objects give off images of themselves, consisting of thin layers of atoms shaped like the object (Wade, 2005). As these thin layers move through the void and impact our senses, we develop a perception of the object, provided we have like atoms that can respond to the layer of projected atoms—like responds to like. Democritus's ethical system consisted of a sophisticated pleasure theory. Pleasure is desirable but may be attained through discipline rather than indulgence and through austerity rather than possessions.

Early Greek Concepts of Illness

Early Greek concepts of illness often emphasized the roles of fate and divine ordination. Sometimes humans were viewed as little more than puppets of the gods, but in time, naturalistic approaches to illness competed with more mystical views.

AESCULAPIUS The earliest mythic figure in Greek medicine was **Aesculapius** (*EHS kuh lop ee uhs*) (or Asclepius), the son of Apollo, the god of Greek medicine. Homer described Aesculapius as the father of Machaon and Podaleirius, two surgeons who served with the Achaean forces in their war with the Trojans. Aesculapius is also reputed to be the father of Hygieia, regarded by Greeks and Romans as the goddess of health.

Over three hundred temples were built in Greece and Rome to carry on the healing traditions associated with Aesculapian mythology. The temples, always located in places of beauty, were designed to fill people with expectations of imminent recovery. Therapy consisted of sleep, suggestion, diet control, medications, massage, and baths. Suggestion likely played a role and remission of symptoms was common. The Aesculapian physicians encouraged their patients to dream about Aesculapius, making their dreams prophetic of actual cures.

Like many ancients, the Aesculapians used the snake (a symbol of mystery, power, and knowledge) in their healing rites. A statue in the Vatican museum depicts Aesculapius with a serpent coiled around a rod—a symbol of medicine persisting into modern times and incorporated in 2015 by the American Psychiatric Association as a celebration of the medical roots of psychiatry (Keshavan, 2015). The Aesculapians practiced both rational and supernatural techniques, but focused more on mystical procedures that bring to mind the methods of contemporary faith healers.

ALCMAEON The work of **Alcmaeon** (*ALK mee on*) of Crotona offers a major milestone in Greek medicine. His exact dates are uncertain, but his work is believed to originate around 500 BCE. He practiced dissection, making him one of the first to use an empirical approach to anatomy and physiology. Although only fragments remain of his work, it appears he attempted to trace sensory channels to the brain. Unlike many scholars of the time, he understood that the brain was involved in thinking and intelligence (Celesia,

2012; Rose, 2009). He believed sleep occurs when blood travels from the brain to large blood vessels. Juhasz (1971) noted that this is the first known theory of sleep. Alcmaeon also believed that many sensory defects result when the channels to the brain become clogged.

In addition to anatomical work, Alcmaeon advanced a homeostatic-equilibrium theory of health. He believed health prevails so long as there is balance between coldness and warmth, wetness and dryness, and sweetness and bitterness. His ideas make empirical sense. A common illness can bring dehydration or excessive moisture. Sickness can also produce a fever and shivering as well as bitterness or a bad taste in the mouth. According to Alcmaeon, death results when any of the paired opposites is too strong. He also emphasized the lack of moderation (e.g., eating too much or too little) as a cause of disease.

EMPEDOCLES **Empedocles** (ehm PEHD uh kleez) **(c. 490–c. 430 BCE)** was another early homeostatic theorist influenced by Parmenides and Pythagoras. Empedocles taught that four basic elements (fire, earth, air, and water) are born out of two first principles (love and strife). The idea of four basic elements may have been borrowed from earlier Mediterranean cultures, but the principles of love and strife are original with Empedocles. According to Empedocles, the principles of love and strife act as forces of attraction and repulsion that interact with the four basic elements. If all things are composed of fire, earth, air, and water, we still need principles to account for the organizations and combinations. Love, or the force of attraction, accounts for organic unity, whereas strife or repulsion accounts for disintegration and the breakdown of objects or events. These tensions led Freud to celebrate Empedocles and his depiction of the tensions between love and strife (King, 2013). Empedocles believed that thought and reason have their substrate in the blood because, according to this theory, the four elements are perfectly blended in blood. Blood represents a near equal mix of fire, earth, air, and water. This opens the possibility that an imbalance of elements in the blood can cause a thought disorder.

Because he believed in the transmigration of the soul, Empedocles was a vegetarian. He taught that there is a "greatest god" that is not anthropomorphic. He believed that the principles of love and strife operate in the cosmos as well as within the individual life. Thus, principles of attraction and harmony are responsible for the birth and organization of the world.

Empedocles, like Anaximander, also believed in a form of evolutionary theory. He argued that creatures survive who are "accidentally compounded in a suitable way; but where this did not happen, the creatures perished and are perishing still" (Kirk & Raven, 1957, p. 337). Empedocles believed nature had experimented with grotesque creatures without necks, partly male and partly female, with eyes "strayed alone" and with animal-like features. As the result of strife and improper mixtures of the elements, these creatures perished. But when like chanced to meet like, appropriately, and when there was harmony in the process of organization, then creatures survived. Despite later rejection of these ideas by Aristotle (Smith, 2010a), Empedocles proposed an early variation of natural selection, even if he did not apply survival of the fittest in the manner Darwin would over two thousand years later.

Empedocles spoke against animal and human sacrifice as the primal sin. The following condemnation is but one of several expressing Empedocles's outrage: "Father lifts up his own dear son, his form changed, and, praying, slays him—witless fool; and the people are distracted as they sacrifice the imploring victim" (Kirk & Raven, 1957, p. 350). Some accounts suggest that he hanged himself or drowned after falling overboard from a ship. In the best-known legend, he jumped into an active volcano in a failed attempt to prove his immortality, a deed memorialized in Matthew Arnold's 1852 poem, *Empedocles on Etna*.

HIPPOCRATES **Hippocrates** (hih PAHK ruh teez) **(c. 460–c. 377 BCE)** was the most famous

physician of antiquity. Born on the island of Cos, he practiced medicine there and in Athens. He helped establish an empirical approach in the medical school of Cos, where he was the leader of a large group of priest-healers (Ventegodt & Merrick, 2013). The body of writings attributed to Hippocrates (*Corpus Hippocraticum*) covers a breadth of medical subjects. Scholars are torn about the degree to which his work was written by Hippocrates or by his colleagues (Green & Groff, 2003). We'll discuss his work at the school of Cos with the understanding that other physicians contributed some of the ideas.

Sometimes called the founder of medicine, Hippocrates devised a naturalistic account of all disease, both physical and mental. Like Empedocles, he taught that disease results from a disturbance of balance in the elements that make

Hippocrates

53

up our bodies. To treat a patient, you must restore balance (Maher & Maher, 2003). He believed that intelligence results from a proper blend of fire and water. However, an excess of water causes stupidity, as revealed in symptoms such as slowness, weeping without reason, and suggestibility. An excess of fire could result in an impulsive person who rushes from one thing to another without focus or concentration. Hippocrates believed this condition could turn into madness without proper treatment. Treatment for an excess of fire included eating fish in place of other meats, moderate (natural) exercise, induction of vomiting after surfeits, eating barley bread rather than wheat, and reduction of sexual intercourse.

For Hippocrates, dreams represent the activity of the soul. "When the body is awake the soul is its servant . . . but when the body is at rest, the soul, being set in motion and awake, administers her own household" (Goshen, 1967, p. 12). He saw dreams as indicators of illness. The greater the contrast between dream and reality, the greater the illness. The sleeping soul can, through dreams, reveal a host of important messages about the body. For example, dreams of abnormal rivers may signify blood disorders, trees barren of fruit may foretell reproductive problems, and troubled seas may indicate disorders of the stomach.

The Cos school accepted Empedocles's four-element theory of fire, earth, air, and water. They believed these elements were manifest in four bodily humors: black bile, yellow bile, blood, and phlegm. In turn, the four elements and humors were associated with four qualities of cold, hot, dry, and wet. Differences of opinion emerged about how the humors were associated with various qualities. According to one classification (Castiglioni, 1941), blood is associated with heat, phlegm with coldness, yellow bile with dryness, and black bile with wetness (p. 162). Health was thought to result from an organic balance of the four humors, and disease from an imbalance. The empirical basis for Hippocratic thought is evident. High body temperatures, sweating, jaundiced conditions, pallor, discoloration of urine, and excess of phlegm—conditions associated

with illness—can be related to the four-humor theory. Some theorists continue to argue for a four-factor personality theory rooted in the psychological qualities that Hippocrates associated with the four humors (Merenda, 1987).

After careful and systematic observation (Nutton, 2006; Millon, 2012), Hippocrates employed many treatments to restore balance. He was a strong believer in diet control, honey being a favorite prescription. He advocated therapies such as exercises, fresh air, rest, laughter, baths, and bleeding. Hippocrates also employed a variety of surgical techniques, including trephining to relieve pressure from brain tumors. He taught that the brain is the seat of intellectual activities and he was the first to classify emotional disorders, earning him recognition as an early neurologist (Breitenfeld et al., 2014). His classification included mania, melancholia, paranoia, and epilepsy, and he described people with the symptoms of cerebral palsy (Panteliadis et al., 2013). Hippocrates challenged popular supernatural assumptions of the time that epilepsy was a "sacred disease" (Todman, 2008) and instead concluded it was a natural disorder of the brain. Hippocrates and the school at Cos arrived at a medicine without gods and demons, one that replaced mysticism and superstition with naturalistic and holistic treatment. He also introduced a terminology for spinal structures (Panourias et al., 2011), and treated psychological and emotional problems within the framework of a thorough naturalism (Green & Groff, 2003). Hippocrates argued that if physicians could do no good, they should do no harm. Accordingly, his treatments undoubtedly offered beneficial and pleasant consequences, making the Hippocratic period a brief era of enlightenment.

Relativism

Ancient Greek thinkers explored another issue in epistemology that centered on the status of truth. The question here asks: Is truth relative or are there independent and enduring truths that reason can discern? In this section, we will discuss the relativistic doctrine of Protagoras, and in the materials that follow, we will consider the arguments against **relativism** offered by Socrates.

PROTAGORAS Born in Abdera, **Protagoras (c. 485–c. 410 BCE)** lived most of his adult life in Athens. He was a famous **sophist** or teacher remembered for a relativistic doctrine summarized in the anthropocentric belief that the human being is the measure of all things. Protagoras argued that the world we know is a world conditioned by the senses. Truth itself is a product of sensory information. If pizza tastes good to one person but not to another, then it is true that pizza is good and it is also true that it is bad. Truth is relative. If a painting appears ugly to one person but beautiful to another, then it is true that the painting is both ugly and beautiful. Protagorean relativism, extended to groups, contributed to democratic notions of majority rule. If a group votes for a given legislation, then that legislation has truth value for that group.

The philosophical basis of Protagorean relativism inspired Hume, Mill, and other later thinkers (Hocutt, 2013) and had major implications for psychology. Psychologists have always had an interest in how people see their world. Techniques such as projective tests, free association, introspection, and phenomenological descriptions are a few ways we have attempted to understand the world of the individual—a world that has a face value and legitimacy all its own.

The Golden Age of Greece

As the work of early cosmologists and physicians diminished, a more comprehensive philosophy emerged in the work of Plato and Aristotle. The range of their interests covered topics in the physical and biological sciences, psychology, political science, and sociology along with traditional philosophical issues such as logic, metaphysics, and ethics.

SOCRATES The pivotal work of **Socrates (c. 470– c. 399 BCE)** is like a saber slashing through the history of philosophy, dividing all Greek thinkers before him as pre-Socratic philosophers and all those who followed as post-Socratics. Despite his remarkable fame, little is known about the man himself. At various times, this brilliant but polarizing figure has been described as a saint and a martyr, as well as grotesque, degenerate, independent, ugly, courageous, dignified, and deranged. What is known about the historical Socrates comes from differing sources that often contradict each other. His best-known student, Plato, provides the most reliable source of information, although his philosophy might influence the portrait of his mentor.

Socrates was born about 470 BCE in Athens and died in 399 BCE in the same city. His mother was a midwife and his father was possibly a sculptor. A young female philosopher named Aspasia had a profound influence on Socrates. He regards her as his teacher and she appears throughout his dialogues. In an early work on women in science, Mozans (1913) suggested that Aspasia's emphasis on equality and the rights of women influenced both Socrates and Plato.

Socrates served time in the Athenian army during the Peloponnesian War and won distinction for his courage (which he later demonstrated

Socrates

55

during his imprisonment and execution). His passion for philosophy was so great, Socrates loved philosophy more than his wife and children and craved it more than material comfort or social success. He was so wholly dedicated to the pursuit of truth and ideas that he devoted little thought to ordinary needs such as food and clothing. He was disciplined, independent, simple in his tastes, and an engaging conversationalist. The picture emerges of a person with a powerful social presence complemented by a discriminating ability to entertain and evaluate other viewpoints.

Socrates enticed people into conversation on topics such as the nature of justice, virtue, or prudence. He asked simple questions about how a person defined terms, and then listened with care to the answers. After the person offered a definition, Socrates asked questions about how the definition covered a variety of situations. Often his probing questions proved embarrassing, revealing the individual's untenable grasp of the concept. But the nature of the dialogue was so captivating that curious listeners surrounded Socrates. Like many young people of any era, the youth of Athens were attracted to ideals, integrity, intellectual excitement, and inspiration. Socrates provided that and more for his disciples.

Although an inspiration to Athens's younger minds, Socrates was a nuisance and a threat to the political and religious establishment. Wielding his merciless and biting intellect, Socrates criticized powerful Athenian political and military leaders, exposing their incompetence. Because most conservative Athenians preferred answers to questions, his constant probing into established wisdom proved an unbearable irritation. As a consequence, he was brought to trial on three trumped-up charges: (1) corrupting the youth of Athens, (2) denying Greek gods, and (3) attempting to establish new gods. Historians have argued that the indefensible charges concealed the true reason for Socrates's trial; namely, he had incurred too many personal enemies.

In characteristic style, Socrates turned his trial into a condemnation of his judges and accus-

ers. He refused to compromise on any point as he steadfastly maintained his innocence. Had Socrates made a gesture of appeasement, he might have been rewarded with a light sentence and the whole affair would have been forgotten. His uncompromising integrity would never permit that kind of concession. He found no grounds for yielding on any point, even at the expense of his life. Upon receiving the death sentence, Socrates faced his enemies and stated, "For my part I bear no grudge at all against those who condemned me and accused me" (*Apology*, 41d). He argued "that the difficulty is not so much to escape death; the real difficulty is to escape from doing wrong" (*Apology*, 39a). The long thirty days that followed his sentence offered countless opportunities for escape, but, as emphasized in *The Crito*, he refused to break the law in any manner (Silverman, 2010). In *The Phaedo*, Plato provided a moving account of the execution. When several of Socrates's disciples wept bitterly, he reprimanded them for their weakness. When it was his time to die, the seventy-year-old philosopher drank the hemlock without drama. He walked around the room, making observations about the poison's effects before it claimed his life.

During his life, Socrates had rebelled against the teachings of the sophists. As professional teachers, the sophists received money for their instruction. Although disagreements persist about the sophists' range of topics, their teachings undoubtedly included rhetoric and argument. In an article on the beginnings of psychotherapy, Pivnicki (1969) pointed out that Antiphon, a sophist, had a doorplate advertising his qualifications to heal grief and melancholia by means of words. Guthrie (1960) noted, "the Sophists were not a particular philosophical school, but rather a profession. They were itinerant teachers, who made a living out of the new hunger for guidance in practical affairs" (p. 66). Socrates believed the sophists' practical concerns with winning arguments and making money from teaching overshadowed their love of wisdom. He also took issue with their emphasis on sensation and relativism. This point deserves elaboration.

As we saw in the previous section, the sophist Protagoras argued that individual perception is the source of knowledge. Socrates claimed we obtain knowledge through analysis of concepts. For example, we may ask someone to define a triangle. Individual triangles may be small or large, and they may come in a variety of colors or materials. In defining an appropriate concept of triangles, we must abstract only those qualities that all triangles have in common. For Socrates, there are objective and universal qualities that participate in a correctly framed concept, and following the appropriate conceptual work, we can assess whether a specific shape is or is not a triangle. As noted by Stace (1962), "It is no longer open to anyone to declare that whatever he chooses to call a triangle is a triangle . . . The Sophist can no longer say 'whatever seems to me right, is right for me'" (p. 145). Socrates emphasized the power of reason; he believed that through the rational process, we can discern objective truths. This orientation exerted an enormous influence on Plato and Aristotle and later thinkers.

Socrates found little interest in physics, astronomy, or the biological sciences. For this reason, some scholars charge that he had a detrimental effect on these disciplines. His central inquiries were psychological and philosophical rather than physical or biological. Whereas most of Socrates's thought was directed inward, his quest for truth was in keeping with the scientific spirit.

Socrates believed that self-knowledge is vital to virtue. He believed that human beings do not knowingly engage in evil but rather that evil results from ignorance. It follows that the role of the good teacher is crucial. The teacher assists the student in the quest for knowledge. As knowledge increases, virtue increases. Because virtue includes a host of socially desirable behaviors, knowledge is the means by which the individual and society may advance. But true knowledge is elusive. Socrates believed himself to be ignorant but still wiser than those who were blind to their ignorance. The tensions between Socrates's personal admission of ignorance and any claims he might have made to be a virtuous man are still topical in philosophy (Brickhouse & Smith, 1990). He believed that most people are informed by half-truths, misinformation, and false concepts. Smith (1974) argues that Socrates was among the first to formulate a scientific approach to psychology that emphasized multiple (moral, social, anatomical, and physiological) causes of behavior. In explaining his reasons for choosing death by poison, Socrates insisted that his decision was not based on any one simple set of factors but rather a combination of mental, physical, and social concerns. Smith insists that Socrates would have opposed twentieth-century reductionism.

One of the students present at Socrates's death was **Aristippus**, head of a school of philosophy at Cyrene. Following the death of Aristippus, his daughter **Arete** headed the school. Waithe (1987a, p. 198) noted that we know nothing about Arete's personal views, but we do know something about the teachings of her school at Cyrene. It was one of the first to advance a systematic treatment of the roles of pleasure and pain in human life. The Cyrenaics advanced a sophisticated approach to pleasure, arguing that discipline, knowledge, and virtuous actions are more likely to result in pleasure, whereas negative emotions such as anger, fear, and remorse should be avoided because they multiply pain. In her thirty-five years as a teacher, Arete was thought to have "written forty books, and to have counted among her pupils one hundred and ten philosophers" (Waithe, 1987a, p. 198). The school at Cyrene provided one of the first approaches to psychological hedonism—a doctrine that would surface again as a systematic philosophical position in the eighteenth and nineteenth centuries under the leadership of Jeremy Bentham. Richardson (1990) notes, "Towards the end of the *Protagoras*, Socrates suggests that the 'salvation of our life' depends upon applying to pleasures and pains a science of measurement" (p. 7). The meaning of hedonism (or the pursuit of pleasure) in the works of Socrates and Plato continues to provide lively discussion (see Richardson, 1990; Weiss, 1989).

PLATO Unlike most philosophers of his time, many of Plato's writings have survived to the present day. **Plato (c. 428–c. 347 BCE)** typically presented his ideas in the literary form of the *dialogue* often set on the streets of Athens or at a gathering of friends. Participants in the dialogue argued the various facets of concepts such as justice or virtue. Some dialogues turned into monologues as one participant held forth on a topic for a lengthy period. The collected works of Plato include a few letters as well as the numerous dialogues, including well-known works such as *The Apology, The Crito, The Laws, The Meno, The Phaedo, The Republic, The Sophist, The Symposium, The Theaetetus*, and *The Timaeus*. In addition to his recognition as a Western philosopher and teacher, Plato is regarded as a significant literary figure.

Plato was born to a wealthy family in Athens between 429 and 427 BCE. Few details are known about Plato's youth, but he doubtless received an excellent early education befitting a member of an aristocratic family. As a young man, he served in the war effort against Sparta, but little is known about his military activities. Everything changed for Plato when Socrates entered his life. As a young man, Plato was present at Socrates's trial (*Apology*, 34a) and witnessed his teacher's death. Afterward, Plato, embittered and disillusioned, traveled to numerous Mediterranean countries. Upon his return to Athens, he founded what can be regarded as the first European university, a remarkable school known as the **Academy**. The exact date of his university's founding remains in dispute, but it was here that Plato spent the remaining forty years of his life. At the Academy, he produced important philosophical works and taught students without charging tuition (a tradition inherited from Socrates). Plato died at age eighty-one, probably in 347 BCE. His nephew, Speusippus, succeeded him as head of the Academy.

Plato's early dialogues reveal the stamp of Socrates's influence. Plato's originality did not assert itself until his later works. His transformation from student and recorder to an established philosopher remains difficult to discern. In his mature philosophy, we encounter discussions of ethics, politics, law, art, religion, epistemology, and psychology. He is critical to the history of psychology, partly because he introduced an early conflict model of psychological disorders.

Method It's often said that Plato rejected empirical knowledge or knowledge based on sensory information. Such a point doesn't misrepresent Plato, yet the claim is too strong without qualification. Plato's *The Timaeus* included materials on astronomy based on observation and materials on anatomy based on dissection. Additionally, descriptive sciences were taught in the Academy. It seems Plato accorded a more important role to the senses in practice than in theory. Nevertheless, he believed rational processes provide true knowledge, whereas sensory information alone offers only appearance and opinion. But opinion and appearance are not without value. For example, a person may have a correct opinion about tomorrow's weather or the stock market. The correct opinion, though not certain knowledge (i.e., justified, true belief), may still offer practical value.

Theory of Forms According to Plato, sense objects always have a particular or individual quality. Furthermore, objects of sense are always changing. They are in the process of becoming— either growing or decaying. In contrast with the world of sense is the world of forms, known through intuition or rational processes. The **theory of forms**, according to Plato, points to the true world, a world of absolute being, perfect, unchanging, and independent of individuals and particulars and known only through reason. If there were no individual triangles available to us, this would not undermine the principles of triangularity or the form of the triangle, which, for Plato, has absolute being. Sense objects (e.g., particular triangles) may participate in or partially represent the real world of forms, but individual objects of sense are always incomplete, temporal, spatial, and changeable. The form is timeless, immutable, and unextended. In this way, Plato bridges the seemingly irreconcilable gap between the empirical justification for a world of becoming, as argued by Heraclitus, and rational justification for a world of being, as argued by Parmenides and Zeno. Even if the world as we know it ceased to exist, there would be formal ontological truths such as the abstract principles of triangularity. If the world of forms is not known through the senses, how is it known?

Whereas it is the body, via the senses, that reveals the changing, illusory, temporal world, it is the activity of the soul that reveals the world of forms through reason (Leahey, 2005). Plato believed the souls of human beings are immortal and that souls may be reincarnated into other bodies. In its new incarnation, the soul may have dim recollections of the real world of forms that it once knew. Now, chained to the body and the senses, it is a difficult task for the soul to comprehend true forms. Juhasz (1971) noted, "the metaphor 'eye of the soul' was originated by Plato in the *Republic*" (p. 51). The **eye of the soul** perceives the real world of forms through memories, images, and higher cognitive functions. The soul's vision of true reality is diminished when it concentrates on the welter of sensory information. The qualitative division between the permanent and perfect world of forms and being known only through reason and the temporal and changing world of becoming known through experience remains a strong theme in Western philosophy.

Nature of the Soul Plato's thoughts on the nature of the soul are complex and often appear contradictory. Reasons for the apparent contradictions are readily identified. First, Plato's writings cover several decades, and, like the changing degree of influence that Socrates had on his views, his thought on the nature of the soul evolved. Because scholars cannot always agree on the chronological order of Plato's writings, we can't be certain how his thought developed. To complicate matters, Plato enjoyed speaking in metaphors. He used different metaphors during different periods in his career. At one point, he compared the soul to a scribe. At another time, it was compared to a charioteer (reason) trying to rein in two powerful horses (appetite and spirit)

in competition against each other. We'll consider the problem of the definition of *soul* in Plato before looking at the functional and structural properties of the soul.

Plato's term **psyche** is typically translated as soul. But scholars disagree about the exact meaning of *psyche*. Soul is a reasonable translation in the sense that Plato believed that psyche was immortal. But Plato also ascribed mental properties to psyche so that the terms *mind* or *consciousness* could serve as reasonable translations. Unfortunately, Plato did not provide an unambiguous definition, so analysts attempt to understand the functional and structural properties of psyche. To complicate matters further, translations have been influenced by the temporal and cultural contexts of the translators. In the Middle Ages, for example, church scholars consistently translated *psyche* as soul.

We encounter many functional qualities of the soul in Platonic literature. The soul is active; it compares, discriminates, organizes, exercises control, and masters. In a helpful article on the Platonic model of the mind and mental illness, Simon (1972) enumerated the soul's mental processes, characterized in terms of higher and lower activities. Sleeping is a lower activity, whereas waking is higher. Childishness, conflict, and appetite are lower. Adulthood, harmony, and rational processes are higher activities. Plato conceptualized the soul as engaged in psychological activities, including memory, ideation, knowing, feeling, and willing.

Plato divided the psyche into three major functions (Smith, 2010a). The rational soul is highest among the three and the appetitive soul is lowest. Intermediate between the other two is the affective soul. In this structural arrangement, the rational soul is located in the head. Appetite resides in the gut. The affective soul can be found in the chest. The tripartite division was illustrated with the famous example of the charioteer and the two horses mentioned earlier. Plato favored metaphors that emphasize the entrapment of the soul in the body, such as in his famous allegory of the cave in *The Republic*. For Plato, we

59

are all chained like prisoners in a darkened cave, unable to see the real world. Relying only on sensory experience, we glimpse little about our world beyond flickering shadows cast on a cave wall. Reason, however, can liberate us. Although chained as a prisoner of the senses, our soul can overcome its limitations and escape captivity through reason. Only with reason, can we know the real world of unchanging forms outside the cave.

Memory Plato believed that prior to birth, the soul dwells in perfection in the world of forms. His views about memory are built around the idea that the rational soul can recall material from this perfect world. He draws upon the technology of his day to conceptualize memory. In his time, people would write on a wooden surface coated in a layer of wax. Likewise, Plato proposed the metaphor of the soul as a wax slate. Juhasz (1971) pointed out that "in different persons the quality of the wax as well as the quality of the pattern varies" in our memories (p. 52). The metaphor of the scribe in Plato's *Philebus* implies processes of storage and retrieval as well as comparison. Plato offers an early model of memory that bridges the world of sensation with the world of forms.

Learning and Education Plato believed education was central to effective political leadership. In the ideal Platonic state, only accomplished philosophers could serve as leaders. Learning was also critical for the attainment of individual virtue and for development of good habits by the people, which are in turn essential for good government (Cusher, 2014). He accepted the Socratic notion that ignorance is the major culprit in wrongdoing. For Plato, learning and education are important in their own right but they also serve utilitarian ends. Virtue, harmony in society, harmony within the individual, and knowledge of universal forms are all products of learning.

Perception For Plato, perception provides, at best, an approximation to reality and, at worst, outright illusion. He was not greatly concerned with sensation and perception, but *The Timaeus* contains passages devoted to how the senses

operate. Vision takes place, for example, when fire in the eye communicates with fire in the world. In other words, we see by virtue of the correspondence of like elements (Wade, 2005). In vision, fire from the eye proceeds outward, but in audition, shock propagated by the air impacts the ear. He believed we see through the eyes, but not with them. The eyes, as the other senses, provide a chaos of sights, sounds, tastes, and so on. Plato's emphasis on the separation of body and psyche permeates his views of perception, and seeing is not simply visual but involves comparisons, organization, memory, and other activities of the rational soul (Caston, 2015).

Motivation Plato recognized the roles of pleasure and pain in human life (see Weiss, 1989). Although these belonged to the lower appetitive realm, he nevertheless believed that pleasure in moderation represents harmony and balance, whereas pain signifies discord. A particular motive might involve a complex interaction of appetite, spirit, and reason. For example, fear might be present in the appetitive dimension, but depending on spirit and reason might or might not manifest itself in behavior. Spirit and reason might complement fear with courage and with a rationale to stand one's ground. But if courage is deficient in the affective division of the soul, then cowardly behavior might be associated with fear. Plato believed that human beings seek pleasure, but the source of pleasure may change with growth. With maturity, the greatest pleasure results from the highest activities of philosophy—the comprehension of the ideal world of forms.

Mental Disorders From the time of Homer to the time of Plato, thinking about people with mental disorders evolved from supernatural to more natural models of psychopathology—a development that would repeat itself as the Middle Ages gave way to the modern era. Moving beyond earlier ideas about supernatural forces and imbalances of humors, Socrates and Plato focused on psychological forces involved in mental disorders. Simon (1972) outlined several important contributions of Plato's work: (1) the recognition that powerful irrational and asocial forces may dominate the mind; (2) the view that mental disorder results from discord among the rational, appetitive, and affective components of the psyche; and (3) the belief that mental problems result from ignorance.

Plato believed that irrational and primal forces exist within all people. As evidence, he suggested that dreams reveal bizarre instincts such as incest with a parent or unnatural unions with gods or beasts. In *The Timaeus*, Plato spoke of mental disease as a lack of intellectual function. Madness results when the appetitive psyche dominates a weak rational psyche. The impulsive and unbridled appetitive psyche was viewed as asocial. It is of a lower order, being tied to the selfish aims of the body. It is the rational soul, capable of participating in the real world of forms, that brings coherence into the system. Plato spoke of justice in the soul, apparently referring to the importance of an appropriate relationship between the divisions of the soul (Seeskin, 2008). Lack of justice results in madness for the individual just as lack of justice produces a troubled social order (Irwin, 2013).

Simon (1972) outlined two kinds of ignorance that, for Plato, play a role in mental disorder. The first is the ignorance associated with deficiencies in self-knowledge. Socrates also condemned this brand of ignorance, reportedly telling the jury at his trial that "the unexamined life is not worth living" (*Apology*, 38a). A second type involves ignorance of the ideal and of the world of forms. Reliance on the sensual, the temporary, the illusory world of the senses is a form of ignorance, one that may ultimately promote the ascendance of the appetitive soul—an unfortunate consequence for emotional health.

Plato saw philosophy, including critical dialectical explorations of alternative views, as an ideal basis for changing cognitions about the world. In this sense, philosophy becomes a kind of therapy, or talking cure, for dysfunctional thinking. Plato also recognized the role of learning in mental disturbance, warning that many children's stories and fairy tales offer contaminating influences; he understood there can be toxic aspects of family life that have negative effects on children. In *The Republic*, Plato saw a role for the professional in the care and rearing of children. He was not impressed with the qualifications of the typical parent.

Love The Platonic vision of love and its significance remains a dominant theme in Western thought. Plato advocated higher and lower forms of love, an approach that follows a hierarchical arrangement consistent with his entire philosophical system (Perper, 2010). Eros, or erotic love, is bound to the body or the senses and can enslave people to their passions (Soble, 2009), but the soul can progress in its capacity to love (*The Symposium*). Stace (1962) noted that in all love, Plato believed we are searching for beauty. We may find beauty first in eros, but then in people, then in knowledge, and finally in philosophical study of love as an abstract ideal.

Plato's impact on Western thought has been extensive. Although Alfred North Whitehead (1979) may have overstated his claim that Western philosophy "consists of a series of footnotes to Plato" (p. 39), Plato's emphasis on the conflict between rational and irrational forces foreshadowed the work of Sigmund Freud. Plato's lasting influence on Western thought is illustrated by the terms *Platonism* and *neo-Platonism*, referring to the philosophies of individuals or groups who emulate Plato. Though some contemporary scholars find much to criticize in Plato (Rauch, 1993), others argue that the ancient sage has much to teach us about contemporary topics such as ecology, ethics, and virtuous behavior (see Ali, 2012; Lane, 2012; Ophuls, 2011).

ARISTOTLE This brilliant philosopher was born in Stagirus in 384 BCE. After his physician father died when **Aristotle** was a small boy, he lived under the care of a guardian. At age seventeen, he joined Plato's Academy in Athens where he remained until age thirty-seven. Following Plato's death in 347 BCE, Aristotle left the Academy and resided for brief periods in Atarneus in Asia Minor and in Mytilene (located on the island of Lesbos in the eastern Aegean Sea). At the invitation

Aristotle

of Philip of Macedonia, Aristotle tutored a young prince named Alexander III (356–323 BCE), later to gain infamy as the conqueror Alexander the Great.

Following a five-year period as Alexander's mentor, Aristotle returned to Athens and founded a school known as the **Lyceum** (the name honors a wolf deity known as Apollo Lyceus, the god of shepherds). As the former teacher of a prince, Aristotle enjoyed many benefits and opportunities, including political protection and an abundance of supplies. During his most productive years, he established a library and scientific laboratories at the Lyceum. This prolific period inspired many of his four hundred books, most rather modest in length.

Aristotle taught at the Lyceum for thirteen years, but was forced to leave Athens when the political climate turned volatile. Following Alexander the Great's death in 323 BCE, the pro-Macedonian party was overthrown. Because Aristotle had once tutored Alexander, the new leadership viewed him as pro-Macedonian. In order to escape persecution and the fate of his intellectual grandfather Socrates, Aristotle fled Athens and took up residence in Chalcis. He died shortly thereafter, in 322 BCE, at sixty-three years of age.

Unlike his teacher Plato, Aristotle was much more a creature of this world. As such, he focused attention on the immediate world more than the abstract world of forms. Although sympathetic to select features of Platonic rationalism, he was an unapologetic empiricist. The comprehensive nature of Aristotle's thought is revealed in his work. He was educated in the mathematics, astronomy, and physics of his day and made many original contributions in the physical sciences. As a founder of zoology, he was the first known collector and classifier of zoological specimens. Single-handedly, he founded formal logic. He was also creative in political philosophy, metaphysics, and axiology, and was acquainted with the medical wisdom of his day. Aristotle's intellectual activities and achievements—impossible in an age of specialization such as our own— remain impressive. He stands among the leading scholars of all time, perhaps the last person to know all or at least most of the available scholarship in his or her culture at a given time.

Earlier, in Chapter 2, we discussed Aristotle's notions of material, efficient, formal, and final causation. The concept of final causation, for which Aristotle has been severely criticized, attempted to establish reasons, purposes, or ends for which things in the world exist. Aristotle rejected the idea that the universe is irrational or chaotic. Development is also a key feature in Aristotle's thinking; for example, he proposed three separate seven-year periods of development prior to adulthood (Lerner, 2009). Additionally, he emphasized the idea that there is direction in nature and that this direction is toward reason. Let us now turn to a consideration of some of Aristotle's psychological concepts.

Soul and Body Robinson (1989a) noted, "It is a mark of Aristotle's intellectual independence that, after no less than twenty years of instruction in the Academy, he would arrive at a conception of soul so radically different from the Socratic one passed down in Plato's dialogues" (p. 44). Guthrie (1960) pointed out that for Aristotle "we cannot understand the soul if we neglect the body . . . so, with a particular sense; we cannot understand sight unless we examine the structure and workings of the eye" (p. 147). In an early model of physiological psychology, Aristotle claimed that soul and body are as interdependent as matter and form (Leahey, 2005). Jager and VanHoorn (1972) noted that in the natural philosophy of Aristotle, there is material and form and "in the phenomenal world there can be no real separation between the two; no shape without some solid material; no solid material without some shape" (p. 321); Aristotle's views are sometimes called **hylomorphism**, a term derived from *hule* meaning matter and *morphe* meaning form. Aristotle applied the matter–form interdependence to the soul–body question. In *De Anima*, Aristotle affirmed that "we can wholly dismiss as unnecessary the question whether the soul and the body are one: it is as meaningless as to ask whether the wax and the shape given to it by the stamp are one" (412b, 5). So that which is mental is not separable from that which is physical. Aristotle's hylomorphism, applied to the mind–body problem, establishes the legitimacy of both domains, but at the same time, sounds a cautionary note to those who flirt with extreme materialism or idealism. Either extreme can result only in a strained and fragmentary psychology. Whereas mind, according to Aristotle, is closely tied to the body, it is more than a set of organizational properties operating in a physical substrate (see Green, 1998). Indeed, mental processes are more than a mere addition of their physical elements. Formal processes depend on a physical structure, but also enjoy some degree of independence and causal efficacy.

Aristotle proposed a hierarchy of the psyche. At the most elementary level, all life forms have a nutritive function. Even in plants, the basic processes of growth and reproduction are necessary for survival. Beyond the nutritive function, animals have sensitive (sensing or perception) and movement (locomotion) functions (Smith, 2010a). Over and above these there is the function of reason, which is further divided into passive and active components. Passive reason is closely associated with the senses and with the function of common sense, which ties one sense to another through the ability to compare

or make judgments. Aristotle argued that the passive mind is "related to what is thinkable, as sense is to what is sensible" (*De Anima*, 429a, 15). Scholars strongly disagree with each other about the meaning of Aristotle's concept of active reason. Some believe Aristotle tied some dimensions of the soul to that which is transcendent or even immortal. Others deny that this was Aristotle's intent.

Memory In his work *On Memory and Reminiscence*, Aristotle reminds his audience that the object of memory remains in the past, whereas the object of perception stands in the present and the object of expectation waits in the future (in this context, Aristotle noted the possibility, one day, of a science of expectation). He argued that memory must be based on something within us like an impression or a picture. If the receiving surface is too soft, too hard, frayed, or decaying, memory will be defective. Aristotle believed that elderly people have poor memories because of decay and the very young have poor memories because of rapid growth. He noted that defects of memory point to symptoms of mental derangement. A common symptom is the inability to discriminate a mere phantasm or picture in the head from a real memory. Aristotle argued that memory is a faculty of sense perception— a faculty that perceives time. Aristotle makes a distinction between memory and recollection. For him, recollection is a "searching for an 'image' in a corporeal substrate" (*On Memory and Reminiscence*, 453a, 15–16). Recollection involves effort and an active process of searching. Aristotle pointed out that memory can occur without recollection (i.e., there can be a spontaneous quality about memory). Recollection, however, cannot take place without memory; Aristotle probably meant that recollection is successful only when the so-called imprint, or picture, is found. He pointed out that failures of recollection imply a need for relearning.

In his discussion of the pragmatics of recollection, Aristotle outlined important laws of association that are still with us today. How are we to proceed most efficiently with the task of recollection? He noted that an ordered event is easy to remember, but "badly arranged subjects are remembered with difficulty" (*On Memory and Reminiscence*, 452a, 3). Recollection is facilitated by similarity, contrast, contiguity, and frequency (*On Memory and Reminiscence*, 451b, 15, 452a, 30). Aristotle also pointed out that recollection is more efficient if we begin with the first item in a series, but failing that, we may be successful if we recover a middle item. Mistakes in memory result from the numbers of associations that can be made for any event.

Sensing Aristotle noted that sensation depends partly on passive reception of sense objects and on the nature of the sense objects themselves (Tuominen, 2014). Some sense objects, such as color or timbre, are of such a nature that they can be detected by only one sense. Aristotle said that, "such objects are what we propose to call the special objects of this or that sense" (*De Anima*, 418a, 15). In addition to special objects, Aristotle argued that there are "common sensibles" or activities that are common to all the senses. Robinson (1989a) pointed out that common sense "is not a separate and distinct sense in itself but a mode of perceptual integration" (p. 75). The "common sensibles" were thought to be figure, number, magnitude, movement, and rest. If the term *figure* refers to a sensory pattern, then one could well imagine that patterns of various sorts could be detected within any sensory domain. Aristotle was not specific about how each "common sensible" operates in each sensory domain. Jager and VanHoorn (1972) pointed out that Aristotle's general theory of sensing must be understood in terms of his theory of actuality and potentiality. Potential sensing is present, for example, when one listens for the chime of the clock, while actual sensing happens when hearing and chiming occur together. Smith (1971) stated that Aristotle's theory "requires an object–organism interaction through a medium of contact" (p. 375). Aristotle was not always clear about the nature of that medium. For sound, the medium was air; for smell, he said, the medium had no name (*De Anima*, 419a, 30). He found evidence

for a medium in the fact that the object of sense "sets in movement only what lies between, and this in turn sets the organ in movement: If what sounds or smells is brought into immediate contact with the organ, no sensation will be produced" (*De Anima*, 419a, 28–30). But if there is a medium for sight, smell, and sound, what are the media for taste and touch? Aristotle argued that these latter two do have media, "for we do perceive everything through a medium" (*De Anima*, 423b, 5).

He argued that the skin and tongue are merely related to the real organs of touch and taste. Thus, the skin is the medium of touch, but not the organ of touch. Presumably, the same is true for the tongue—it is simply a medium. Aristotle found evidence for this conclusion in the fact that direct contact with the skin produces a sensation of touch. The skin must therefore be the medium rather than the organ of touch (Green & Groff, 2003). Recall that Aristotle believed that direct contact with the sense organ itself results in no sensation. It is noteworthy that Aristotle was troubled over whether touch is a single sense or a group of senses (*De Anima*, 422b, 15). As for gustation, he believed that there are two contrary simple tastes, sweet and bitter. Secondary tastes include saline on the side of bitter and succulent on the side of sweet. Between the extremes are other secondary tastes such as harsh, pungent, astringent, and acid. He believed that smells follow the same patterns as tastes: sweet, bitter, pungent, and so on.

Aristotle was one of the first to study perceptual illusions and his writings include several examples (see Johannsen, 1971). The first, possibly discovered by Aristotle, is obtained by crossing the second finger over the first. With the eyes closed, the adjacent sides of the fingers are then stimulated by a common object, creating a tactile illusion of two objects. Aristotle believed that the illusion possibly results from the fact that, in natural finger position, the same object seldom stimulates the two outer sides of the fingers simultaneously. Another illusion reported by Aristotle was one of movement, described in his work on dreams. It is illustrated when we turn away from a moving object and fix our eyes on something steady, we may continue to perceive motion.

Imagination and Thought In Aristotle's writings, the term *phantasia* can be translated as "imagination" (Juhasz, 1971), so we may use *phantasia* as a synonym for "mental image." Aristotle drew a sharp distinction between imagination and perception or sensation. Unlike the way the latter two terms are used today, they are equivalent for Aristotle. He argued that "perception of the special objects of sense is always free from error" (*De Anima*, 427b, 10). But imagination, which we can employ anytime, can lead to falsehoods. Juhasz (1971) pointed out that imagination in Aristotle's theory "is pure appearance without the subject of the perception. As such it is at once highly susceptible to error" (p. 54). Perception, according to Aristotle, cannot be called up anytime because it is dependent on the correspondence between the sense object and the sense organ. Because thinking often happens in the absence of the objects of perception and because it is impossible to think without mental images, thinking is also susceptible to error. Thus, perceiving, as a correspondence between external and internal movements, is accurate, but imagination does not have the corrective influence of the external world; so additions, deletions, and distortions are possible in thought. Thinking that is dependent on images or imagination can easily go astray.

Dreams In many traditional cultures, dreams were explained as prophecies or signs from a deity, but Aristotle argued that dreams are not divine messages. He suggested that lower animals also dream and that persons of the most inferior type claim to foresee the future in dreams sent by God. Such persons, he said, are "garrulous and excitable" and given to so many prophetic experiences that they, like gamblers, find occasional luck. But it is only chance when a vision predicts some event in the world.

Aristotle called attention to the persistence of movement observed in nature. Waves from a pebble thrown into a pond persist across the pond; something heated by a fire loses its heat only gradually. Aristotle believed that the same principle holds for the senses. Thus, if we look at a bright light, and "we close the eyes, then, if we watch carefully, it appears in a right line with the direction of vision (whatever this may be), at first in its own colour; then it changes to crimson, next to purple, until it becomes black and disappears" (*On Dreams*, 459b, 10). Aristotle also called attention to the persistence of the perception of movement and strong odors. He concluded that "the dream proper is a presentation based on the movement of sense impressions, when such presentation occurs during sleep" (*On Dreams*, 462a, 25).

But do dreams have significance beyond the fact that they represent complicated afterimages? The answer is yes. If they fail to convey divine messages in a theological sense, they nevertheless have biological significance. The dream may be a message of the development of pathology. When large movements of the body (e.g., walking) have subsided, we have in the dream a special sensitivity to small movements. Aristotle noted that the smallest residual light image may register in the dream as lightning or the smallest sound as thunder. By extension, small changes in the body may be represented in the dream—so he agrees with the popular medical thought of his day that physicians as well as speculative philosophers "should pay diligent attention to dreams" (*On Prophesying by Dreams*, 463a, 5).

Motivation and Values The subject of motivation concerns why people do what they do. Aristotle believed that we are motivated to seek pleasure and happiness, but in so doing we should also seek the good. Stace (1962) observed, "For Aristotle an action is not good because it yields enjoyment. On the contrary, it yields enjoyment because it is good" (p. 315). But what is the good? Unlike other animals, we have a unique capacity for reason. One manifestation of the good is the development of our rational capacity. Goodness and virtue also consist partly of subordinating the appetites and passions to rational control (Sobel, 2009). Sometimes, he believed, our failure to achieve goodness is rooted in excess or lack of moderation. We should seek a golden mean between extremes. As Guthrie (1960) adds, "Courage is a mean between cowardice and foolhardiness, temperance a mean between abstinence and self-indulgence, generosity between meanness and extravagance, proper pride between abjectness and arrogance" (p. 155). Aristotle recognized the importance of at least four sets of contributing factors in achieving the good: individual differences, habit, social supports, and freedom of choice. Individual differences are manifested in his idea that the mean between extremes may vary from person to person. Thus, what is courage for one person would be foolhardiness for another. For Aristotle, learning and habit are keys to good or ethical behavior. In his discussion of ethics, he refers to the importance of habit (*Nicomachean Ethics*, 1095b, 1–9) and to the close correspondence between happiness and virtuous actions (*Nicomachean Ethics*, 1100b, 10). Aristotle believed that social supports and good fortune (e.g., friends, riches, power, good children, beauty, good family) help us to find happiness; those who are childless, solitary, or physically unattractive will have greater difficulty attaining happiness. But even in the face of misfortune, we can find redemption in effortful and habitual virtuous activity. We can attain happiness in spite of circumstance and "bear the chances of life most nobly and altogether decorously if [we are] 'truly good' and 'foursquare beyond reproach'" (*Nicomachean Ethics*, 1100b, 20). Aristotle's emphasis on habit would be echoed over two thousand years later in the work of American psychologist William James. Critical and appreciative work on Aristotle's views on character formation continues to find its way into contemporary literature in psychology (see Lewis, 2012).

Psychological Thought Following Aristotle

After Aristotle's death, Stace (1962) noted, "the rest of the story of Greek philosophy is soon told, for it is the story of decay" (p. 339). The decay was illustrated by a loss of interest in the pursuit of wisdom for its own sake and a growing demand for the achievement of immediate gratification. Investigation of great questions in science and metaphysics was replaced by narrow self-centered concerns such as how to be happy and how to maximize personal gains. New ideas diminished. Long after the Golden Age of Greece, philosophy was largely derivative.

The schools of stoicism, Epicureanism, and neo-Platonism took center stage after the passing of the Golden Age. As Stace (1962, p. 340) noted, each school shared a focus on individuals and their concerns. On occasion, a figure emerged who addressed great issues, but such pursuits counted as secondary concerns for them.

Review Questions

1. Discuss psychological thought as it is encountered in documents and manuscripts from ancient cultures such as China, Egypt, and India.

2. Many of the early Greeks were interested in the primal substance of the world. Contrast Thales, Democritus, Anaximander, and Anaximenes with respect to their views on the primal substance.

3. Myia of the Pythagorean school provided some of the earliest advice on the care of infants. Briefly summarize her advice.

4. Contrast the philosophy of becoming as advanced by Heraclitus with the philosophy of being as advanced by Parmenides.

5. Trace the development of Greek medical thought from Aesculapius to Hippocrates.

6. How did Socrates argue against the relativism of Protagoras?

7. Briefly outline the contributions of Socrates to psychology.
8. Outline Plato's conflict model of mental disorders.
9. Discuss Plato's methodology. Include in your discussion a statement about Plato's theory of forms and explain the meaning of his metaphor "eye of the soul."
10. Briefly state Plato's position on memory, perception, and motivation.
11. Contrast Plato with Aristotle with respect to their approaches to knowledge.
12. What was Aristotle's approach to the soul–body question?
13. Outline Aristotle's positions on memory, sensing, and motivation.
14. Briefly discuss Aristotle's approach to dreaming.
15. What are the essential features of psychological and philosophical thought following Aristotle?

Glossary

Academy A facility purchased by Plato by a park named Academeca in Athens. Plato taught students at this facility, which became known as the Academy. The Academy flourished during Plato's life and for hundreds of years after his death.

Aesara One of the first Greek philosophers to emphasize the importance of balance to health.

Aesculapius Possibly a historical figure, but the name comes from the Greek mythical god Aesculapius, son of Apollo. Aesculapius was a great physician who, in Greek mythology, was killed by Zeus because he sinned by raising a man from the dead. Many temples were built in honor of Aesculapius.

Alcmaeon Early Greek physician who worked around 500 BCE. He advocated an empirical, rational, and naturalistic approach to medicine. One of the first to practice dissection.

Anaximander of Miletus (610–c. 547 BCE) Greek scientist and philosopher and one of the first to advance a theory of organic evolution.

Anaximenes (c. 588–c. 524 BCE) A cosmologist who taught that air is the primal substance and that this substance is transformed into other things through condensation and rarefaction.

Arete Daughter of Aristippus and head of the school of philosophy at Cyrene following the death of Aristippus.

Aristippus Student of Socrates who headed the school of Cyrene following the death of Socrates.

Aristotle (384–322 BCE) The pupil of Plato and one of the great philosophers who is especially noteworthy for his work in physics, biology, and psychology. Aristotle also founded logic and set forth an original and comprehensive view of causality.

Avesta Holy book of the Zoroastrian religion.

Confucius (551–479 BCE) Well-known early Chinese philosopher interested primarily in the moral life with a focus on methods that promote personal and interpersonal harmony.

Democritus (c. 460–c. 370 BCE) Refined the atomic theory set forth earlier by the philosopher Leucippus. Taught that reality was based on atoms and the void. Atoms were thought to be indivisible and invisible. Their basic structures accounted for the nature of the observable material world.

Empedocles (c. 490–c. 430 BCE) Early homeostatic theorist who taught that four basic elements (air, earth, fire, and water) combine with two first principles (love and strife). Love unites and organizes, whereas strife results in disintegration and disorganization.

eye of the soul A metaphor employed by Plato to convey the idea that the soul can sometimes apprehend true reality.

Heraclitus Probably active around 480 BCE, Heraclitus was the first process philosopher. Emphasized the idea that only change is real.

Hippocrates (c. 460–c. 377 BCE) Sometimes regarded as the Father of Greek Medicine, Hippocrates advanced a thoroughgoing naturalistic account of all illness, both physical and mental. Advanced the first classification system of mental disorders.

Hsün Tzu (c. 298–c. 212 BCE) An early Chinese philosopher who advanced a thoroughgoing naturalistic philosophy. He is sometimes viewed as the Chinese Aristotle.

hylomorphism A mind–body position advanced by Aristotle—it comes from *hule* meaning matter and *morphe* meaning form. Aristotle stressed the interdependence of matter and form. Thus, seeing as a mental process cannot be separated from the physical structure of the eye.

Leucippus Greek philosopher who lived around 500 BCE. He was the founder of atomic theory later refined by Democritus.

Lyceum A school near Athens founded by Aristotle.

Myia Daughter of Pythagoras and Theana. One of the first to give advice on child rearing.

Parmenides Early philosopher who did his work shortly after 500 BCE. He was one of the first to attempt to distinguish between appearance and reality. According to Parmenides, the senses reveal only appearances, whereas reason leads to real truths. In contrast with Heraclitus, Parmenides emphasized a philosophy of being as opposed to a philosophy of becoming.

philosophy A term likely coined by Pythagoras from *philo* (meaning love) and *sophia* (meaning knowledge or wisdom). Hence, the love of wisdom.

Plato (c. 428–c. 347 BCE) The student of Socrates and the teacher of Aristotle. One of the great philosophers of all time, remembered, among other things, for his emphasis on the importance of reason as a means of discerning the formal abstract nature of truth. Advanced an early conflict model of mental illness and speculated on numerous psychological topics such as memory and sensation.

Protagoras (c. 485–c. 410 BCE) A sophist (teacher) who emphasized the doctrine of relativism. Protagoras argued that the world is conditioned by our senses and hence truth is relative.

psyche The Greek term for soul or mind. Includes mental processes such as thought, memory, sensation, and perception.

Pythagoras (c. 580–c. 500 BCE) An enduring figure in Western intellectual history who did his work around 550 BCE. He is remembered for his emphasis on the importance of quantification and for specific contributions such as the famous Pythagorean theorem. His beliefs in the primacy of reason and the nature of the soul were influential later in the work of Socrates and Plato.

relativism The doctrine that knowledge is not absolute; rather, it is a product of human mental processes with all their inherent limitations. Thus, according to relativism, truths change as a function of time, place, and circumstance.

Socrates (c. 470–c. 399 BCE) Teacher of Plato and so important in Greek thought that all philosophy before him is called pre-Socratic. He reacted against the relativism of Protagoras and taught that reason is the basis of true knowledge. He emphasized the importance of self-knowledge and is thus an important figure in the history of psychological thought.

sophist A type of teacher in ancient Greece. The sophists often emphasized relativism and how to live successfully. They often offered plausible but fallacious arguments. Hence, terms such as *sophistry* and *sophistic* refer to arguments that appear to be sound but are later found to be superficial or fallacious.

Thales An early Greek cosmologist active around 600 BCE. Thales was known for his contention that water is the primordial substance. He was also interested in the problem of movement and the nature of motive forces that make movement possible.

Theana An accomplished philosopher and wife of Pythagoras who played a key role in the educational activities of the Pythagorean school.

theory of forms According to Plato, there are universal and true principles comprehended through reason. For example, the senses reveal only particular triangles, but reason reveals the principles of triangularity. A goal of education is to uncover the true formal properties of things.

Upanishads Vedic treatises dealing with philosophical and psychological matters. See *Vedas*.

Vedas Oldest sacred books of India setting forth many early ideas on psychological matters.

Xenophanes (c. 560–c. 478 BCE) An early Greek philosopher remembered for his epistemological skepticism. He argued that human beings do not have certain knowledge and he scoffed at anthropomorphic concepts of deity.

yang Ancient Chinese concept representing qualities such as force, hardness, masculinity, and heat. Contrasts with but also complements the concept of yin.

yin Ancient Chinese concept representing qualities such as softness, coldness, passivity, and moistness. Contrasts with but also complements the concept of yang.

Zarathustra Major prophet of the Zoroastrian religion.

Zend-Avesta See *Avesta*.

Zeno of Elea Active around 450 BCE, Zeno was a follower of Parmenides. He is remembered for paradoxes that supposedly revealed contradictions between reason and the senses. His paradoxes of motion are particularly noteworthy. For example, an arrow on its way toward a target presents a certain paradox. It must first travel half the distance, but then it must travel half the remaining distance. Because Zeno thought it is possible to divide forever, the arrow should never reach its target.

4 The Roman Period and the Middle Ages

But soul is not in the universe, on the contrary the universe is in the soul.
—Plotinus, *Enneads*, V, p. 411

In ancient times, the Roman Empire held a great deal of the world in its iron grip. Its period of dominance spanned more than ten centuries, beginning in obscurity in the seventh century BCE and ending with the unseating of Rome's last emperor in 476 CE. At the height of its power in 100 CE, the Roman Empire occupied the countries surrounding the Mediterranean Sea and ran to the western shores of Spain. Its border stretched as far east as the Persian Gulf and, to the north, it encompassed the British Isles. Its southern command stretched to Africa, reaching well past the pyramids of Egypt.

As early as the second century BCE, one million people lived in Rome, but the population of the greater empire boasted fifty to one hundred million people. Early in its history, Roman society was grounded in superstition and polytheism. Citizens were expected to uphold the qualities of conformity, duty, order, loyalty, and perseverance. In this paternalistic society, the father of a family enjoyed complete legal power. An unfaithful wife could be sentenced to death. A disobedient child could be brutally punished or sold into slavery.

By the first century CE, the Roman way of life embraced material comfort and amusement. The Romans indulged in baths, swimming, and exercise facilities as well as soaps, cosmetics, exotic clothing, jewelry, and music imported from Greece. A proliferation of holidays offered citizens the chance to attend games and circuses. For the delight of bloodthirsty crowds, exhibitions pitted wild animals imported from Africa and the North against professional gladiators and people who were enslaved. A handful of citizens protested the slaughter of humans and animals, but their voices were drowned in the cry for greater spectacle.

The scientific spirit didn't flourish in a population addicted to games and bloodlust. The Romans adored technology, but had little use for science. There was some interest in geology, possibly because Italy was prone to earthquakes and volcanic eruptions. The Romans used geometry in their architecture, but did little to extend the discipline beyond the pioneering discoveries of Euclid (325–265 BCE) and Pythagoras (c. 580– c. 500 BCE). Astrology motivated some attention to the stars. The Romans had an interest in medicine, mostly because of its practical applications. The study of medicine also fueled some curiosity about psychological questions. Across these domains, the Romans embraced practical uses of ideas rather than inquiry for its own sake.

Roman Medicine

Medicine flourished during this period, owing to the practical need for sustaining Rome's formidable armies. Despite it all, medicine in the early Roman Period was primitive. Barbers conducted surgery along with captives from other countries. Superstition and miracle cures triumphed over scientific inquiry. As with other sciences, Roman medicine borrowed from earlier Greek advances.

An influential Greek physician named **Asclepiades (c. 124 BCE)** was an early figure in the study of mental disorders whose practice in Rome attracted numerous patients and students. Asclepiades distinguished between delusions and hallucinations and argued that therapy for mental disorders should be pleasant and expedient. Like Hippocrates, he relied heavily on diet, music, massage, baths, and exercise. An Aesculapian temple erected in the third century BCE proved popular with the Romans, who basked in its gentle and relaxed atmosphere.

The Greeks contributed to Roman medicine, but the relationship was turbulent. Although Greek physicians were better trained, Romans became suspicious when their surgeries or medicines failed. Greek doctors were viewed with a mixture of admiration and paranoia. In that context, the work of Rome's best-known physician flourished.

Galen

In the history of Western medicine, Claudius **Galenus (c. 129–c. 199 CE)** stands as second

in importance only to Hippocrates. Galen studied philosophy in Pergamum and anatomy in Alexandria, Egypt. He studied and commented on earlier philosophical and medical works while developing his own ideas (Green & Groff, 2003). Roman law prohibited dissection of human cadavers, so Galen conducted anatomical studies on pigs, apes, and other animals, even dissecting the eyes of oxen (Wade, 2005). When he became physician and surgeon for the gladiators, Galen was allowed to conduct limited studies on human anatomy. He wrote nearly four hundred treatises covering numerous medical issues and conditions. Today, unfortunately, only eighty-three of his works exist. From his remaining work, we can conclude that he was a dedicated student of psychology.

Galen subscribed to the Greek four-humor theory of black bile, blood, phlegm, and yellow bile. In addition to humors, he argued that four

Galen

71

qualities (cold, warm, dry, and moist) play a role in sickness and wellness. When one is in good health, he believed, humors and qualities remain in balance. An imbalance produces illness.

But what affects the balance? Galen claimed that various foods could increase or decrease the humors and qualities. Geography, occupation, and age could also play a role. Even seasonal changes might make a difference. For example, Galen associated the springtime with blood, warmth, and moistness. The winter months brought phlegm, coldness, and moistness.

Drawing on his studies of the humors and qualities, Galen proposed an early personality theory. The four humors were associated with four personality traits or temperaments (a word derived from the Latin verb *temperare*, meaning "to mix"). An individual with a *choleric* temperament would be quick tempered and fiery. The *phlegmatic* type would be described as sluggish and unemotional. A sunny person who is cheerful and optimistic would possess a *sanguine* temperament. The *melancholic* person would be sad with a tendency toward depression.

As with physical illness, Galen believed most mental disorders result from an imbalance in humors and qualities. For example, an imbalance of black bile may produce melancholia. Mania (frenzied excitement) was thought to be a "hot disease" related to an excess of yellow bile and heat. How do you treat an excessive humor? He proposed treatments that relied on the opposite of the excess. A physician might counteract a "hot dry disease" by wrapping the patient in cold wet towels. A "cold wet disease" might be treated with warm and dry remedies.

Galen believed in a physiological basis for mental disorders, but also thought that our minds can influence our bodies. As an example, Jackson (1969) cites the case in which Galen treated a woman for insomnia. During his examination, Galen was ready to conclude that the woman had an excess of black bile resulting from melancholia. At that moment, another person in the examining room mentioned seeing the famed dancer Pylades at the theater. Galen noted that

the woman's expression changed and her heart rate became irregular. In subsequent examinations, he mentioned other dancers, but found no jump in her heart rate. Whenever Pylades was mentioned, however, Galen documented a reliable physiological reaction. He concluded the woman was in love with the dancer. In his mind, it served as proof that mental states have important physiological consequences.

Galen's book *On the Diagnosis and Cure of the Soul's Passions* contains advice on seeking another person's counsel for emotional problems. The other person, as noted by Jackson (1969), should be "an older man—mature, respected, free from passions—who would point out the person's faults in regard to his passions" (p. 380). Galen seems to advocate an early psychotherapy. Although authoritarian and direct, his therapy stressed a confrontation of passions. Galen believed that passions (powerful experiences such as greed, anger, and jealousy) burned with greater intensity than typical emotions (Maher & Maher, 2003) and were the root of psychological problems.

As a vitalist, Galen believed the universe was dynamic and alive. His vitalism is apparent in his ideas about the **pneuma**. In his time, *pneuma* referred to air drawn in as breath that is distributed to bodily tissue. Galen used pneuma to describe three vital principles of life (Smith, 2010a). The first, known as **natural spirit**, is found in all plant and animal life. Largely unconscious, natural spirit is involved in simple, day-to-day processes of vegetative maintenance and survival. Pneuma also functioned in the **vital spirit**, a process that regulated body heat. Galen also spoke of the *psychic pneuma*, usually translated as **animal spirit**. Whereas the vital spirit was in the heart, the animal spirit had its seat in the brain. Not surprisingly, this type of pneuma controlled higher cognitive functions. Although Galen believed that the substance of the brain was involved in mental activity, his emphasis on the actions of the pneuma in the ventricles (brain cavities) may have influenced the later medieval notion that the mental faculties were located in the ventricles of the brain (Green, 2003; Rose, 2009).

For the time, Galen was a rigorous scientist. He conducted empirical studies on animals and traveled to search for medications and new ideas. His emphasis on empirical work inspired later Renaissance anatomists, including Vesalius (Lanska, 2014). He thoroughly studied his patients' physical symptoms, and he was a "tireless interrogator of his patients" to better understand their histories and symptoms (Mattern, 2011, p. 479). Galen was a flexible thinker, but subsequent generations pressed his work into the confines of narrow dogma.

Early Christian leaders interpreted Galen's concept of the pneuma (especially animal spirit) as consistent with church doctrine that the body is subservient to the soul. As a result, Galen's ideas were assimilated into Christian doctrine. For centuries, his teachings were praised and became the basis of dogmatism in a climate that forbade medical research and dissection. In the absence of experimentation, errors in Galen's work went unnoticed. For 1,500 years, major psychological topics such as thought, movement, and perception were explained in terms of vital principles or animal spirits. Galen's pneuma theory remained unchallenged until the discoveries of the seventeenth- and eighteenth-century physiologists.

Roman Philosophy

The Roman Period featured several schools of philosophy including stoicism, Epicureanism, skepticism, and neo-Platonism. All were derivative and practical (Henley & Thorne, 2005). Unlike their Greek predecessors, Roman philosophers were not known for original contributions or for great world questions. The individual became the primary focus, especially how one could escape the ills of the world and live a good life.

Stoicism

The school of **stoicism**, founded by **Zeno of Cyprus (c. 335–c. 263 BCE)**, thrived for over five hundred years. The early leaders of the stoic school focused on discipline, self-control, and the absolute lawfulness of nature. The stoics advocated suppression of self-will and appetite. Virtue was found in duty, reason, principle, and the suppression of all passions. Rather than seeking outright pleasure, happiness was supposed to be found in a life of austerity and discipline, resigning ourselves to our unchangeable fate, an attitude that would later shape cognitive behavioral therapy (Murgui & Díaz, 2015), as discussed in Chapter 17. According to Laertius (1972), Zeno injured a toe while walking, interpreted this as a sign that his life was to end, and willingly took his own life as a meaningful gesture of acquiescence to duty (see Kaplan et al., 2007).

The stoics disliked the idea of arbitrary boundaries that divide geographical regions into states. People should identify with each other rather than identifying with nations. True wisdom can never come from subordinating oneself to a state. With resignation, however, they noted that the number of the wise in the world is a mere trifle. Most human beings, the stoics believed, are fools.

EPICTETUS A slave by birth, **Epictetus** (*EHP ihk TEE tuhs*) **(c. 50–c. 135 CE)** taught stoic principles that appealed to poor Romans and possibly to early Christians who identified with the plight of slaves. His birth is estimated to have been between the years 50 and 55 and he died about 130 CE. He had movement limitations, possibly due to mistreatment as a slave. After finding freedom around his late teen years, he was permitted to attend lectures. He devoted himself to philosophy, which he viewed as a cure for the soul. According to Meredith (1986), Epictetus conceived the lecture room of the philosopher as a kind of hospital, a place offering restoration and healing.

As a slave, Epictetus developed deep sensitivities to things beyond human influence and control. There is wisdom, he believed, in resigning ourselves to events we cannot change. All we can do is place faith in larger forces, even if we don't understand their purpose. Rather than rage against unalterable forces, we must trust that events unfold according to some critical design. His stoicism echoes today whenever someone says, "things happen for a reason."

The early Christian writer Paul also hints at a stoic message in his prison epistles, such as Philippians 4:11, where he writes, "I have learned in whatever state I am, *in this* to be content." Despite parallels between stoicism and Paul's teachings, there are major differences (see Wilson, 1997). After orthodox (i.e., literally "right thinking") Christianity was established at the Council of Nicea under the direction of Emperor Constantine (Pagels, 2003), most Christians expressed hostility toward beliefs that deviated from rigidly defined views of Christianity. In practice, however, many were stoic. Yet below the surface, the differences may be far greater than any similarities (see James, 1902/1985, p. 45).

Epictetus loved simplicity, order, moral courage, self-control, and discipline. Hallie (1967) noted that he demanded daily self-examination as a means of promoting self-knowledge. He insisted that people take responsibility for the things they can control. Though we often find ourselves in circumstances we cannot change, we can control our attitude toward such events and avoid complaining. James (1902/1985), for example, cited stoic resignation and acceptance of life's events as an optimistic approach to spiritual experience.

Epictetus had a strong influence on the Roman emperor **Marcus Aurelius (121–180 CE)**, who argued that we should accept disagreeable events beyond our control. We must recognize that such things are a significant part of a larger whole. If we could but see the whole picture with clarity of mind and careful evaluation (Suibhne, 2009), we would discover the selfishness of a grumbling and critical attitude. Such ideas also run through the work of Albert Ellis and his Rational Emotive Therapy (Still & Dryden, 2012), as we discuss in Chapter 17.

Stoic philosophy—if conscientiously followed—may foster an admirable tranquility in the face of difficulties. On the other hand, could stoicism lead to passivity? Or perhaps even a tendency to underestimate our ability to make changes that would benefit ourselves and others? Could stoicism have provided an adequate philosophical base for later scientists, scholars, and humanitarian reformers, outraged at suffering and injustice and eager to understand and control natural forces?

Epicureanism

Named after **Epicurus of Samos (341–270 BCE)**, **Epicureanism** arose around the same time as stoicism, approximately three hundred years prior to Christianity. The Epicureans believed pleasure is good and pain is an evil to be avoided (Bergsma et al., 2008). They warned against excesses such as gluttony that may produce temporary pleasure but long-term discomfort. Other things that interfere with pleasure include false opinions, fear of death, and excessive fear of the gods. The Epicureans advised against heavy social responsibility. Instead, one should strive for an uncomplicated existence. The school of Epicureanism survived until at least 200 CE.

LUCRETIUS The philosophy of **Lucretius (c. 96–c. 55 BCE)** is expressed poetically in his work *De Rerum Natura* ("On the Nature of Things" or "On the Nature of the Universe"). The work is composed of six books that cover matter and space, movements and shapes of atoms, life and mind, sensation and sex, cosmology and sociology, and meteorology and geology. Across these wide-ranging topics, Lucretius argues that nature can be understood by using reason and the senses (Wood, 2010).

Lucretius argued that if body and mind were independent, why do they parallel each other? He insisted that mind cannot exist apart from body: "Mind and body as a living force derive their vigour and vitality from their conjunction"

(Lucretius, *On the Nature of the Universe*, p. 113). He insists that the mind comes into existence with the birth of the body and grows with the body. For those who believe that spirits are slipped into the body from outside, he points out that, "it is surely ludicrous to suppose that spirits are standing by at the mating and birth of animals—a numberless number of immortals on the lookout for mortal frames, jostling and squabbling to get in first . . . or is there perhaps an established compact that first come shall be first served?" (*On the Nature of the Universe*, p. 119).

Like Leucippus and Democritus of old, Lucretius believed all things are composed of different sizes and shapes of atoms. However, he wasn't a conventional determinist. He argued that as atoms fall through space, they swerve from their path; these swerves interfere with a determinist order of things and serve as a theoretical basis for free will. Latham (1967) claims Lucretius wanted to demonstrate that "voluntary action arises from within and ultimately from the unpredictable movement of a single atom" (p. 101).

Lucretius believed that sensation was the basis of knowledge. Senses provide information about the material world, so the senses and their functions are keys to understanding the mind. He concluded that vision is activated when we see thin atomic films emanating from objects. Latham (1959) believed Lucretius would likely say, "psychologists are wrong in thinking that the mind is anything other than an assemblage of very mobile particles that easily group themselves into patterns or images in conformity with other images that impinge upon them from outside objects" (p. 11). Lucretius also described epilepsy, sleep, and vision in epic poetry (York, 2011), and he described the neurology of movement in ways surprisingly consistent with contemporary views (Hyam et al., 2011).

Taste results "when we squeeze it out by chewing food, just as if someone were to grasp a sponge full of water in his hand and begin to squeeze it dry. Next, all that we squeeze out is diffused through the pores of the palate and the winding channels of the spongy tongue" (Lucretius, *On the Nature of the Universe*, p. 149). Different tastes result from blending food atoms with the interatomic atoms found in sensory channels. As a result, a food that excites the taste of one person may disgust another.

As an Epicurean, Lucretius was interested in ethics and a way of life that maximizes pleasure and minimizes pain. He argued against immediate gratification and for the value of discipline. He valued true piety, which for him was the capacity to philosophize with an undisturbed mind. Lucretius lamented the superstition that parades as piety, the "oft repeated show of bowing a veiled head before a graven image; this bustling to every altar; this kowtowing and prostration on the ground with palms outspread before the shrines of the gods; this deluging of altars with the blood of beasts; this heaping of vow on vow" (Lucretius, *On the Nature of the Universe*, p. 208). He taught that fear of death and fear of hell are great evils to overcome.

In his book on cosmology and sociology, Lucretius proposed a theory of the evolution of social groups, religion, and language. Early human groups evolved because of a necessary contract to protect defenseless offspring and others who were weak. Any group breaking the contract failed to survive. As for religious beliefs, Lucretius argued that many are born in fear of the forces of nature. He proposed that language evolved gradually; we first imitated the sounds of animals and gradually recognized the convenience of communication through verbal symbols.

As an empiricist, a materialist, and an Epicurean, Lucretius was a creature of this world. His philosophy conveys his love of nature and his preference for simple explanation. His ideas are clearly derived from earlier Greek thought, but some scholars suggest we underestimate his originality (Latham, 1967, p. 99).

Neo-Platonism

In terms of lasting influence, **neo-Platonism** was the most important school of philosophy following Aristotle. It married early Greek traditions with Jewish and Christian mysticism. For good or ill, it was a participant in the wedding of philosophy and religion that characterized thinking in the Middle Ages. Neo-Platonism fueled theological discussions on the activities of the soul, the corruption and transience of the material world, the problem of evil, and the illusory nature of sense perception.

PLOTINUS Considered the founder of neo-Platonism, **Plotinus (205–270 CE)** was probably born an Egyptian but received a Greek education in Alexandria. His extensive travels cultivated knowledge of Indian and Persian philosophies. About 245, he settled in Rome and befriended the emperor Gallienus. During two productive decades there, Plotinus attracted numerous students. With his student Porphyry, he produced six volumes titled *Enneads* (Green & Groff, 2003). Plotinus probably left Rome following the assassination of Gallienus in 268 CE.

Inspired by Plato, Plotinus argued that the "Soul is not in the universe, on the contrary the universe is in the Soul" (*Enneads*, V, p. 411). In other words, mental processes, or activities of the soul, have a certain primacy; they are not to be regarded as derivative from the material world. Quite the opposite, we know about the material world only through the activities of the soul.

Plotinus merged Platonic thought and religion (Leahey, 2005). For him, a world of matter is a world of multiplicity and divisibility. Nonmaterial things, according to Plotinus, rank above matter. For example, the abstract principle of triangularity rises above particular triangles. If there were no observable triangles, the principles of triangularity would still exist. Plotinus believed the body could be a burden to the soul and weigh it down or alienate it. In time, the soul transcended the body and would be reincarnated in a later body. Plotinus also believed in direct communication between souls through extrasensory means.

Moore (1946) pointed out that Plotinus recognized an active quality in perception. For example, eyes are important for visual perception,

but what we see with the eyes is also actively organized around memories, emotions, and cultural settings. Seeing is not just passive registration; it is active organization. Plotinus argued for a similar approach to memory: In his words, "Sensation and memory, then, are not passivity, but power" (*Enneads*, IV, p. 341).

Plotinus also addressed the interplay of happiness and self-understanding. Happiness is attained in knowing the "true-self" through self-knowledge. Merlan (1967) notes, "the concept of the unconscious plays a decisive role in the system of Plotinus" (p. 358). Self-knowledge is elusive; it is attained through contemplation and in the consistency of action and thought. We do not have self-knowledge when we are torn by multiplicity or when we fail to be guided by intelligence.

In a brief essay, Plotinus speculated about "how distant objects appear small" (*Enneads*, II, p. 8). He also noted that as an object recedes, its color or brightness fades, and details grow fuzzy. With distance, we lose perspective on individual parts and respond to the thing as a whole. Plotinus believed that when details are seen, perception becomes more accurate.

Finally, Plotinus argued for freedom of choice and against astrology. He admitted small influences from the stars, but believed that much of astrology was not rational. Plotinus influenced the emerging religion of Christianity and, in turn, shaped psychology and philosophy during the Middle Ages (Kemp, 1996).

HYPATIA OF ALEXANDRIA The celebrated philosopher–mathematician **Hypatia (c. 370–415 CE)** was the most important leader of the neo-Platonic school in the fourth century. She was the daughter of Theon, a mathematician–astronomer who worked at the legendary Royal Library of Alexandria. Though little is known about Hypatia's education, she likely benefited from her father's instruction and the cultural opportunities afforded by the library. By her late twenties, Hypatia was the leader of the neo-Platonic school at Alexandria. She lectured to

Hypatia of Alexandria

students from all parts of the world and mentored several prominent philosophers of her era.

Hypatia is remembered for her expertise in geometry and astronomy, but she probably accepted most of the teachings of the neo-Platonic tradition. Indeed, Hypatia's use of music therapy in the treatment of mental disorders may have been one of several heresies that led to her murder (see Richeson, 1940). Hypatia lived in a time of tension between the Christian church and other religions, and music therapy was associated with various forms of non-Christian thought. Following complications both ideological and political, Hypatia came under the suspicion of Cyril, the Bishop of Alexandria. During Lent in 415, a group of monks attacked Hypatia, dragged her into a church, killed her, dismembered her body at the altar, and then burned her corpse. Hypatia's tragic story offers a reminder of the all-too-human reluctance to allow philosophical freedom (Viney, 1989; Waithe, 1987a). Her

story, told in the motion picture *Agora*, continues to inspire and captivate the imagination (see Bovaira & Augustin, 2010).

Skepticism

Skepticism is rooted in the works of Socrates as well as pre-Socratic philosophers such as Anaximander, Xenophanes, and Heraclitus, all of whom emphasized the changing nature of things. It was **Pyrrho (c. 360–c. 270 BCE)**, however, who introduced a systematic philosophy of skepticism that attacked philosophical certitude. Pyrrho believed we must live our lives on the basis of opinion, appearance, and probability. The skeptics noted that every argument has a counter-argument. Authorities disagree with each other and, furthermore, our sensory impressions are not consistent. Skeptics also called attention to the fact that different animals have different sensory systems. How do we know that our sensory system is superior to all others? If we cannot trust our senses, neither can we trust reason, because reason is based on initial propositions that are plain assumptions. The skeptics also called attention to the fact that circumstances condition our reactions to the world.

SEXTUS EMPIRICUS The birth and death dates for the Greek physician **Sextus Empiricus** are uncertain, but he became the leader of the skeptical school in the late second and early third centuries. Sextus argued that human beings should suspend judgment on most matters and live on the basis of probable truths. Skepticism does not have to deny an immutable truth, but even if there is one, how do we know with certainty that we possess it? Roman skepticism presented followers with a way to live such that conflicts and disappointments would be minimized. Dogmatic certainty could lead to anxiety, frustration, unhappiness, and disillusionment if confronted with overwhelming contrary evidence. The role of human certainty in war, terror, and genocide provides powerful evidence for these concerns. On the other hand, the openness that goes with suspended judgment can lead to contentment, happiness, and tranquility, and these views may have helped people cope with danger, uncertainty, and sometimes rapid changes that were common in their cultures. According to Sextus, the skeptic is free to consider all sides of an argument and to weigh everything as probable in an open and honest fashion. One can even live life on the basis of a probability, always aware, however, that one may be wrong.

The skeptics tried to avoid the pretension, presumption, and rash personal qualities found in popular philosophies of their day. They admired the humility associated with the admission of human frailties in matters of knowledge. In later historical periods, skeptics argued that pretension is the original human malady, one that leads to personal and social strife including war. The rise of Christianity and Islam diminished the influence of skepticism. We will see that in the sixteenth century, an outraged French humanist named Montaigne resurrected Pyrrhonian skepticism to challenge religious certitude during the Protestant–Catholic wars.

The Fall of Rome

At the height of its power, the Roman Empire seemed invulnerable. It is a curiosity that such an awesome political, economic, and military experiment could falter. Ironically, Rome's success contributed to its downfall. For centuries, its crushing military success had won vast territories, but at a price. The empire reached far distances, making the defense of its borders an unbearable economic and military burden.

In the midst of the need for economic growth, Rome experienced a staggering decline in population and, consequently, in the tax base. As early as the second century, masses of people enjoyed the luxury of smaller families. In the third century, the plague decimated the Roman population. It is also likely that infanticide checked population growth; female infants especially

were killed in large numbers. Extensive military campaigns and emasculation of men who were enslaved also reduced the population. Rome's downfall was the result of a complex pattern of crumbling economic, moral, social, and political institutions. In addition, Roman authority faced new challenges. Judeo-Christian monotheism defied the worship of multiple gods and polytheism began to fade. In addition to Christianity and Judaism, other competing influences came from the Greeks, Ethiopians, and northern tribes. In fact, the growing tension between Rome and Christianity would produce a later unification, one that would transform the Catholic Church into a dominant force during the Middle Ages.

The Early Christian Faith

The early Christian faith was never a single system of thought (Ehrman, 2003; Pagels, 2003), but rather a movement beset with internal strife during its first three centuries of life. Rival Christian faiths and other philosophies such as Gnosticism, Marcionism, and Montanism competed for disciples. Prominent leaders such as Iranaeus, Tertullian, and Origen differed on matters of doctrine.

During the fourth and fifth centuries, church councils made progress toward a unified theology. However, the early church was embroiled not only with internal conflict, but in conflict with secular powers in Rome. Widespread persecutions began with the burning of Rome in 64 CE. These persecutions had far-reaching implications for the development of doctrine. It is unknown whether the doctrines that became ascendant in the face of persecution would have prevailed in a more hospitable environment. In any case, church leaders emphasized otherworldliness such that existence in the material world was viewed as without value. Life was but a temporary testing ground for human souls on their journey to an afterlife that would compensate for the injustice of this world; peace and happiness await the righteous in heaven, whereas torment awaits the wicked in hell. With the value of this life and world called into question, science and practical inquiry were viewed as trivial. One was advised to attend to the affairs of the soul rather than engage in such frivolities.

On occasion, church doctrine in the Roman era departed from teachings attributed to Jesus of Nazareth. For example, scholars point to discrepancies between attitudes toward women in the patristic church and attitudes displayed by Jesus (Christen, 1984; Daly, 1968; Southard, 1927). Customs of the day forbade speaking to women or even looking at them. Ignoring the prohibition, Jesus spoke to women—even foreign women—in public (see Jeremias, 1975, p. 363). He also accepted women as travel companions and included them in instructional activities. Both practices were violations of existing gender barriers. Jesus also struck at existing divorce standards that favored men. His parables sometimes accorded greater moral status to women and other socially devalued groups than to the conventionally religious and powerful. The patristic church was obsessed with blaming woman for the "fall," but in no instance does Jesus indulge in this practice. The original teachings of Jesus regarding women are not readily apparent in the later church dominated by men.

In the fourth century, the Roman emperor Constantine converted to Christianity, issuing a declaration of religious freedom and restoration of church property. At the same time, "barbarians" pushed against the borders as the Roman Empire lapsed into ruins. Authority shifted from state to church. Gradually, the church defined the legitimate boundaries of the intellectual arena. Now, church leaders such as Augustine and Aquinas in the Christian faith, Maimonides in the Jewish faith, and later Avicenna in the Islamic faith established the intellectual agenda. Before turning to their teachings, we will discuss general characteristics of the **medieval period**.

The Medieval Period

The term *medieval* is derived from the Latin terms *medius* (middle) and *aevium* (age). The Middle Ages refer to a period of European history between the fall of Rome and the rise of the Renaissance. The dates are arbitrary because no one historical event marks the Middle Ages. For our purposes, we may regard the Middle Ages as a period from about 400 CE to about 1300 CE.

The Middle Age period in the West covers a vast expanse of time and space—over a thousand years of history, a geographic region extending from the western shores of Spain to kingdoms in the Northern and Baltic Seas, to Islamic territories (after the seventh century) in the south and east, to what some people regard as "holy land." Three major religious traditions (Christian, Islamic, and Jewish) as well as variations in the economic, social, physical, and political dimensions of cultures contributed to a diversity among peoples. Scholars and historians in psychology often dismiss or overlook this period (see Henley & Thorne, 2005). We must be cautious about making easy generalizations or sweeping epitaphs such as "the Dark Ages."

Curious and contradicting trends shaped the period. It was a time of mischievous and corrupt influences within the church, but also a period of religious compassion and charity. Historians searching the Middle Ages for intellectual stagnation or regression will find ample evidence. As with all historical periods, we can discover isolated islands of enlightenment surviving in a sea of ignorance (see Henley & Thorne, 2005). Magical and superstitious thinking was widespread, resulting in beliefs that seem primitive compared with the earlier naturalistic approaches of Hippocrates and Galen. As an example, White (1896/1910) described a medieval treatment rooted in superstition: "If an elf or a goblin come, smear his forehead with salve, put it in his eyes, cense him with incense, and sign him frequently with the sign of the cross" (p. 102). Medications were chosen for their presumed ability to drive out an indwelling demon. Patients were encouraged to drink or use bitter or offensive materials, including the saliva of a priest or wolf dung, to combat the forces of evil.

Throughout the Middle Ages, people believed in prophecies, soothsaying, astrology, and palmistry. The smallest event could be interpreted as a sign or omen—a fly landing on a person's forehead, a sneeze, the prolonged stare of a dog, a change in weather, the spilling of food, or an accidental encounter with unlucky numbers such as 666 or 13. Swift action could ward off the harmful effects of signs and symbols. The sign of the cross, a quick prayer, the wearing of a cross, the rubbing of a stone, the repetition of a verse or formula, compulsive adherence to rules, and countless other superstitious actions were used as defenses against mischievous spirits or as placations to benevolent forces.

At the time, trial by ordeal and trial by combat were used as tests of truth. Trial by combat— different in intent than a duel—was based on the assumption that God would not permit an injustice; therefore, truth and God would favor the winner of combat. In a dispute, the winner would be seen as chosen by God rather than determined by fighting skill; therefore, a given party could hire a champion or professional to fight on his or her behalf. Insults, challenges, disputes, and even political decisions were decided with "God's will" based on the outcome of trial by combat. The church opposed this practice, but to little avail. Trial by ordeal, a practice common during witch hunts, often involved the infliction of an injury or burn on an accused individual. If the individual showed evidence of the injury after a specified time, say three days, he or she was guilty. If evidence of the injury could not be found, it was taken as a sign of God's intervention and the individual might be judged as not guilty.

The legendary poet and author Dante Alighieri (1265–1321) captured the spirit of divine justice and retribution in his *Divine Comedy*, perhaps the greatest literary work of the Middle Ages. Dante describes an earth-centered universe with God dwelling in the highest realm of a paradise for the righteous. Beneath the earth, a terrifying inferno

is designed to punish its inhabitants for their earthly sins. Dante's famous work shaped the medieval mind-set about issues of divine justice and intervention. For most of the time, revealed truth came from bizarre tests and rampant superstition as well as Dante's masterpiece. Far fewer found answers in science.

Despite the superstitious age, real discovery and progress happened during the Middle Ages (Bjornsson, 2004). Precursors of the modern university emerged as did precursors of the modern hospital. Eyeglasses and clocks were created. Gunpowder and magnetized needles for the compass were rediscovered in Europe, long after their introduction by Chinese scholars. Advances in practical chemistry led to improved glues, dyes, inks, cosmetics, and enamels. The medieval period also witnessed impressive architectural achievements. We can find pockets of imaginative and speculative thought. In the thirteenth century, Roger Bacon discussed the possibility of submarines and airplanes. Two centuries earlier, Oliver of Malmesbury crashed when he launched a "flying machine" from a high place (Mumford, 1934). In many cases, scientific discoveries played out in the context of reason and revelation.

Bizarre tests of truth exist on the fringes of societies in all periods of history including the present. People have always believed in weird truths and embraced esoteric and superstitious patterns of knowing (see Shermer, 2002). The Middle Ages were no exception. For example, a long medieval tradition supported the idea that some dreams can tell the truth or prophesize the future (Kemp, 1996). Still, medieval thinkers accomplished important epistemological work. The Middle Ages witnessed almost every conceivable solution to the reconciliation between revelation and reason including some of the following:

1. Revelation provided by scriptures (whether the scriptures be Jewish, Christian, or Islamic) leads to more acceptable conclusions than those provided by reason.

2. Proper reason and the authentic authority

of scripture complement one another, providing a synthesis. This was probably the dominant position in the Middle Ages.

3. The two-domain theory was proposed. Here, reason provides little support for the revelation contained in scripture and vice versa. There are two different kinds of discourse, and though both may be gifts of God, they are often difficult to reconcile. This raises the difficult question as to whether there can be a double truth. In other words, could a truth affirmed by reason contradict another truth confirmed by revelation? Those who were thought to believe in double truths could face accusations of heresy.

4. The final position stresses the primacy of reason. This was a dangerous position to defend at this time.

The extensive and relentless quest during the Middle Ages for a satisfactory solution to the tensions between the claims of reason and revelation will be illustrated in the works of most of the scholars discussed in this chapter. It is a tension that is not foreign in the twenty-first century, with continuing debates, at least in some parts of the United States and the world, about the age of the earth, human origins, the origins of sexual orientation, genetic editing, and stem cell research. Many widespread debates are motivated by divided loyalties between scientific and religious worldviews.

TERTULLIAN **Tertullian (c. 155–230)** was an early Christian scholar, called by some the first Christian psychologist (Roback & Kiernan, 1969), who addressed the problem of reason in relation to the authority of revelation. His position served as a foil for subsequent scholars and offered a key to understanding knowledge in the Middle Ages. Tertullian was a well-educated literate resident of Carthage who experienced a dramatic conversion to Christianity around the year 197. He is remembered for enlightened criticism on topics such as child sacrifice, the brutality of the Roman games, and the persecution of Christians. He is also

remembered, however, for attacking Greek philosophers such as Socrates, Plato, and Aristotle. He viewed the Greeks as heretics who advanced grievous false doctrines that produced skepticism and despair. By contrast, he believed the revelation of scripture offered hope and optimism. Tertullian was one of the first scholars to set the stage for the Middle Ages by emphasizing the futility of reason and placing "the truth of revelation" at the center of his worldview. His position would frustrate later efforts to elevate the role of reason in philosophy and science. Tertullian stands at the headwaters of a virulent and often deadly misogynist movement that persisted through the Middle Ages and the Renaissance, reaching its pinnacle in European witch hunts from 1500 to 1700 (see DeRosa, 1988; Ranke-Heinemann, 1990).

Aurelius Augustine

Although there was no all-prevailing medieval viewpoint on psychological topics such as learning and mental illness, a handful of prominent thinkers made contributions to the study of human nature. Commonly known as Saint Augustine (*AW guh steen* or *aw GUHS tihn*), **Aurelius Augustine (354–430)** was a pivotal figure in the transition from the Roman Period to the Middle Ages. Augustine was born in the town of Tagaste in northern Africa to parents who proved a study in contrasts. His mother, Monica, was a devout Christian and his father was a man of the world with only a limited dedication to wife and family. In his early years, Augustine followed the path of his father, but Monica held the lasting influence on her son's life.

At great financial expense to his parents, Augustine attended schools in northern Africa, first in Madura and later in Carthage. In his famous *Confessions*, one of the first autobiographical works in Western culture, he spoke with candor about his wayward youth. He relished sexual exploits and basked in praise from rowdy friends. Following his Carthage schooling,

Augustine taught grammar and rhetoric and lived with a concubine, a legal arrangement under Roman law. He fathered a son he named Adeodatus (meaning "given of God"). Augustine's respect for his son represents a rare case of loyalty in his early life. His experiences, both with women and philosophies, were transient. He separated from his concubine and then found another mistress while engaged to still another woman. He described himself as "a slave of lust" and as "in bondage to a lasting habit" (*Confessions*, p. 132); throughout his life, he viewed sexual thoughts as a threat to reason (Soble, 2009). Augustine read Aristotle, studied astrology, and, for a time, embraced Manichaeism, a religion rivaling Christianity. Augustine flirted with skepticism before finding himself drawn to the teaching of neo-Platonism and Plotinus. Throughout his youthful journey, he remained dissatisfied. Augustine described himself as sick and tormented, particularly between his faith and his sexual drives.

And then everything changed.

Pushed to the brink, Augustine considered dedicating his life to God. Total commitment to the faith meant giving up what the sensuous Augustine loved most: "My old mistresses, trifles of trifles and vanities of vanities . . . still enthralled me. They tugged at my fleshly garments and softly whispered: 'Are you going to part with us?'" (*Confessions*, p. 174). In a moment of tearful crisis, Augustine heard the voice of a child say, "Pick it up, read it" (*Sume, lege*). He took this as a divine command to open the Bible and read the first passage that came to his eyes. The random selection of a biblical passage (*sortes sanctorum*) was, for centuries, justified as the basis for an authentic communication from God. Augustine grabbed a Bible and opened it. He read a scripture that condemned the carnal activities he most adored. He was immediately converted. In 387, a prominent theologian named Ambrose baptized Augustine. Since that time, scholars have dissected the conversion of Augustine as a classic case study in the psychology of religion (see Coe, 1900).

Aurelius Augustine

Augustine returned to Africa. He lived his life in poverty and celibacy as a writer and defender of Christian faith. Perhaps more than any other, Augustine set the tone of Western thought for centuries to come. Coe (1900) observed, "Augustine, always intemperate where feeling was concerned, was now intemperately temperate" (p. 212). As an example, Coe cites Book 10, Chapter 33 of *Confessions*, noting that Augustine now felt guilt anytime he was moved by the aesthetics of church music rather than its message. Augustine's views of women and sex became increasingly negative, fueling an already misogynistic church. Augustine founded the first monastic order and worked faithfully for the church until his death in 430.

Augustine understood the obvious differences between Christian and Platonic thought, but he recognized parallels that create workable combinations of the two perspectives. In this context, he discussed psychological topics including the active role of the mind in perception (Silva, 2014), infant motivation, grief, habit-breaking, memory, and unconscious motivation in dreams.

INFANT MOTIVATION Augustine viewed infants as self-seeking, asocial, and even brutish. Recalling his infancy, he reported feelings of selfishness, jealousy of other children, temper tantrums, and a consuming desire to win at any cost. He analyzed the self-serving nature of his childhood prayers, noting that he "prayed with no slight earnestness that [he] might not be beaten at school" (*Confessions*, p. 39). By most accounts, it seems this prayer was seldom answered.

Augustine protested the use of punishment in schools, despite its commonplace practice in his day. He argued that fear of punishment interfered with curiosity and was not conducive to learning. He speculated that threats and classroom punishment had interfered with his learning of Greek. By contrast, he had learned Latin in a supportive environment free from punishment and felt it had facilitated his mastery of the language.

GRIEF Augustine plumbed the extremes of many emotions, but his account of grief shows unusual sensitivity and understanding. With characteristic honesty, he describes his bitter grief and religious turmoil following the death of a beloved friend (see *Confessions*, pp. 81–83). During his grief, he experienced severe death anxiety because he reasoned that his friend now lived only in Augustine's consciousness. If Augustine died, his friend would be all the more dead. Augustine observed that the consolation of friends and new associations and ideas made his grief vanish over time.

HABIT BREAKING Consistent with his belief in the will as a force unto itself (Cary, 2007), Augustine (*Confessions*) tells the story of a young man who was addicted to watching gladiatorial games. By chance, the addict heard a speech where Augustine reprimanded spectators who were obsessed with attending gladiator arenas. The young man accepted the rebuke and stopped attending the games. Augustine concluded that a rebuke may play a role in habit breaking, but recognized it can also have the opposite effect, leading to rebellion (social psychologists would later name this phenomenon "reactance"; Brehm, 1966).

MEMORY Augustine devoted considerable space to the topic of memory in Book 10 of *Confessions*. He referred to memory as a storehouse and drew a clear distinction between recognition and recall. He argued that in our memories of sensory experiences we do not remember things themselves, but only the images of things. However, he believed emotion obscures the memory of images. What, for example, is the image involved in a memory of joy or sadness?

Augustine was also troubled by topics such as the tip-of-the-tongue phenomenon in memory (Kemp, 1990) and the mechanism that makes it possible to remember a previous joyful state when we are in a state of sadness. Although most memories are mediated by images, he believed there are things we "intuit within ourselves without images and as they actually are" (*Confessions*, p. 212). Mathematical relations and certain moral truths are included in such intuitions, but memory even for these things must be exercised. Otherwise, they become dispersed or submerged and are recalled only with great effort. Augustine believed in a priori knowledge, but rejected Plato's idea that the soul recalls knowledge of the forms encountered in a previous existence. This latter idea was inconsistent with Augustine's Christian theology.

DREAMS With typical candor, Augustine shared that dreams of forbidden pleasures didn't stop after his conversion (Bulkeley, 2008). His thoughts about fornication were subdued while awake, but such fantasies had greater power in sleep. Indeed, some of his dreams about sexual intercourse were as real as the act itself. Such dreams depend on memory, and in his discussion, he alluded to deeply buried or repressed memories. He doubted that such hidden memories could be controlled by reason during sleep. Augustine was also aware of self-deception. For example, he pointed out that the soul prepares an excuse as a defense; we may say we need a certain portion of food for our health when it is really for our pleasure (see *Confessions*, p. 227).

Augustine's works are rich in psychological insights and he has been celebrated as one of the great psychologists (see Brett, 1912–1921/1965, p. 225). He nevertheless promoted ideas that took root in medieval thought while working against the development of science. Harrison (2001) reminds us that Augustine viewed worldly curiosity as a spiritually dangerous vice dating back to the sin of Adam and Eve. Consequently, Harrison notes that medieval curiosity was associated with sins of pride, vanity, conceit, and lust. Humility, submission, meekness, and self-abasement were promoted as more noble virtues than curiosity. A few thinkers embraced doubt and curiosity, but wider acceptance of the scientific spirit waited in the distant future.

Islam

The seventh century witnessed the rise of a powerful new religion on the Arabian Peninsula. In middle age, the prophet Mohammed was said to have received a revelation from God. He founded a religion named Islam, meaning "surrender to God." Islam united the Arab peoples (at least until Mohammed's death in 632) and posed a serious challenge to the Jewish and Christian traditions. Within a century of the birth of Mohammed in 570, the Islamic faith had a holy book (the Koran), three holy sites (Mecca, Jerusalem, and Madinat an-Nabi), and hundreds of military victories that claimed vast territories including the entire Arabian Peninsula, Syria, the northern coast of Africa, most of Spain, part of southern France, and the Persian Empire (including what is now Iran, Afghanistan, and Pakistan). Islam's military momentum was finally checked by the Franks under the leadership of Charles Martel (686–741) in the north near Tours, France, in 732, in one of history's most pivotal battles. Had the Islamic armies won the battle of Tours and conquered France, the distribution of Muslims, Jews, and Christians in Europe would have changed dramatically. Aside from military victories, Islam produced notable contributions in medicine and philosophy, many of which incorporated Islamic notions of the divine (Hatami et al., 2014).

RHAZES   Abu Bakr al-Razi **(c. 854–c. 925)**, better known as **Rhazes** (*RAH zees*), was a physician and author of medical textbooks who had wide-ranging interests in psychology, philosophy, and religion. In Baghdad's religious culture, he spoke out against demonological concepts of disease and the arbitrary use of authority in science. Ronan (1982) noted that Rhazes was "quite prepared to criticize ancient authorities, whoever they were, and even wrote a book with the title *Doubts Concerning Galen*" (p. 236). Rhazes attacked superstitious religious beliefs and the concept of miracles. He argued for scientific rationalism and against fanaticism and arbitrary authority.

Rhazes followed in the traditions of Democritus, Empedocles, and Hippocrates. He subscribed to the atomic theory, the four-element (fire, earth, air, and water) theory, and the humor theory. He stressed the importance of distractions, music, diet, bathing, and chemical remedies in treating illnesses. Gordon (1959, p. 158) noted that Rhazes advocated games such as chess playing and music as diversions for melancholia.

Rhazes wrote about social influences on therapy and offered explanations for why some place faith in impostors rather than legitimate healers. He claimed that quacks sometimes produce visible results in treating a medical complaint. People then overgeneralize and credit the dubious healers with greater medical knowledge than they deserve. He noted that legitimate healing is often slow and without immediate visible results.

Rhazes was an empiricist, but religious constraints on freedom of inquiry limited his medical investigations. Religious conservatives believed all questions worth asking were already answered by the Koran. As in previous times, dissection was forbidden. Despite the restrictive conditions, Rhazes described the reflex action of the pupil in response to light (Riese, 1959) and was renowned for his accurate descriptions of many diseases, including facial palsy (Sajadi et al., 2011; Pearce, 2015) and epilepsy (Zohalinezhad & Zarshenas,

2015), and for his studies on the relationship between hygiene and pathology. According to Gordon (1959, p. 163), he was the first person to apply chemistry to medical research.

As Gordon points out, Rhazes's chemical writings had an unfortunate consequence. He presented one of his chemistry books to Prince Al-Mansur. The prince was delighted and even asked Rhazes to demonstrate one of the chemical experiments described in the book. The experiment failed and the prince was furious. In a rage, he bashed Rhazes over the head. The beating produced blindness from which Rhazes never recovered. He died in poverty around 925.

AVICENNA The most influential Arabian philosopher and physician of the Middle Ages was **Avicenna** (*AH vuh SEEN uh*) **(980–1037)**, a mercifully shortened Western version of Abū 'Ali al-Husayn ibn 'Abd Allāh ibn Sīnā. Avicenna's interests ranged over medicine, metaphysics, cosmology, logic, political and religious philosophy, and psychology. Ronan (1982) pointed out that Avicenna has been called "the 'Galen of Islam' partly because of his encyclopedic book entitled *Canon of Medicine*" (p. 236). *The Canon* reflected the ideas of Galen and others (Dols, 2006) and included treatments for a wide range of conditions including migraines (Zargaran et al., 2016) and heavy menstrual bleeding (Tansaz et al., 2016). According to Gordon (1959), it became the medical textbook of choice in European universities (Hatami et al., 2013b). Avicenna is remembered less for originality than for his ability to integrate and systematize past knowledge.

Avicenna was a child prodigy with an unusual memory and a great appetite for learning. By age ten, he memorized the Koran and displayed considerable skill in literature and science. In his late teens, he was well studied in the medical arts and was already practicing medicine. He was also an avid reader of Greek and Roman literature and philosophy. The political strife of tenth- and eleventh-century Persia complicated Avicenna's life. For a brief time, he lived close to the Caspian Sea near Teheran. He moved to Hamadan, but political

Avicenna

unrest interfered with his work and Avicenna was forced to move to Isfahan. A later shift in the political climate made it possible for him to return to Hamadan. In spite of the turmoil of his times, Avicenna practiced medicine and wrote nearly one hundred books on science, medicine, and philosophy.

Avicenna's greatest intellectual contribution may be his attempt to reconcile faith and reason. Afnan (1958) stated that "nowhere in Islamic philosophy are the problems of reason and revelation better contrasted, and an agreement in essentials more consistently attempted, than in the system of Avicenna . . . He was deeply animated by the desire to see [philosophy and theology] brought into harmony" (p. 168). Temperamentally, Avicenna was both a rationalist and a mystic. As a rationalist, he was interested in a subject for its own sake and believed reason should guide human nature. As a mystic, he had a love of mystery and used symbolism and allegory in his work. For Avicenna, people find truth through reason and intuitive or mystical processes. He believed the two are not necessarily contradictory.

As a physician, Avicenna encountered many psychological problems in his patients. Like Galen, he observed a relationship between emotions and physiological states such as heart rate. He also accepted humoral explanations of the mind. According to Gordon (1959), Avicenna believed that "unconsumed bile and black bile will cause melancholia . . . abundance of yellow bile leads to irritability, confusion, and violence. An increase of putrefied phlegm causes a morose and serious mood" (p. 175). He also identified a "disorder of love" that appeared to include facets of depression, anxiety, and obsession (Shoja & Tubbs, 2007). For Avicenna, good health must include good mental health (Sanati & Abou-Saleh, 2012).

Despite his limited knowledge of anatomy, Avicenna speculated on the brain's role in psychological disorders. He concluded that disturbances in the middle ventricles produce a diminished intellect such as in feebleminded patients. Frontal regions of the brain governed perception and common sense, whereas the brain's posterior regions process memory. Avicenna believed that mental representation of external objects occurred in the ventricles (Kemp, 1998).

Avicenna understood the role of psychology in treating patients. According to Gordon (1959, p. 176), he tried to cheer melancholic patients by reading to them or using music as therapy. Alexander and Selesnick (1966) share a story that reveals he wasn't afraid to use unconventional treatments. One of Avicenna's patients believed he was a cow. As part of his psychotic delusion, the man even bellowed like one. Playing along, Avicenna told the patient a butcher was coming over to slaughter him. The man's hands and feet were bound in preparation for the butcher's visit. At the last minute, Avicenna declared the patient too thin and unfit for slaughter. After Avicenna untied him, the man abandoned his delusion and recovered (see also Aggarwal, 2011).

Avicenna's view of the soul echoes Aristotelian faculty psychology. Afnan (1958, p. 136) pointed out that Avicenna believed in soul as a single genus divided into three species. Different faculties of functions exist within each species. The *vegetative soul* manages the functions of nourishment, growth, and reproduction. The *animal soul* guides active perception (Kaukua, 2014) and motor functions of movement. The *human soul* governs powers unique to human beings such as intellectual and rational powers and the ability to comprehend universals. Avicenna believed that faculties serve and sustain each other. For example, nutrition serves growth and reproduction, whereas perception serves imagination. His hierarchical arrangement of faculties hints at the influence of Plato, although Avicenna rejected the Platonic notion of the transmigration of the soul.

In all, Avicenna preserved elements of Aristotelian and Platonic thought on the soul and attempted to integrate these older ideas into Islamic thought. He believed in the oneness of the soul, although multiple faculties exist within that oneness. Consistent with Islamic teaching, he argued for the separation of soul and body at death and the immortality of the soul.

ALHAZEN The Islamic scientist and physician Ibn Al Haitam **(965–1039)** is one of the most critical figures in the study of optics and vision. Known in the West as **Alhazen** (*AL haze uhn*), few details are available concerning his life. He was apparently born in Basra (located in what is now eastern Iraq), but lived most of his life in Egypt. Alhazen's *Book of Optics* describes many important advances in visual science (Aaen-Stockdale, 2008) and marks him as one of Islam's great scientists. He is important because of his emphasis on theory and hypothesis testing (Cucina et al., 2014), his originality, and his influence on later science.

Crombie (1961) noted that Alhazen rejected the idea that the transmission of light is instantaneous and also refuted the Platonic theory of extramission (the notion that the eye emits light rays) (p. 102). Gordon (1959) credited Alhazen with being the first to show that light comes to the eye from external objects. Alhazen conducted original experiments on angles of refraction and the perception of objects. For example, he determined that objects appear larger on the horizon than at the zenith because of differences in the density of the atmosphere.

Alhazen's *Book of Optics* was a major source of inspiration to later European scientists. Roger Bacon's work on optics (e.g., see his *Opus Majus*) clearly built on the foundations established by Alhazen (Wade, 2005). Time and time again, Bacon quoted Alhazen on topics such as binocular vision, apparent size, double vision, and color perception. Alhazen is, unfortunately, a neglected figure in the history of visual perception.

AL-GHAZALI One of the most influential philosophers in Islamic intellectual history confronted the problem of knowledge while departing from predecessors such as Alhazen and Avicenna. **Al-Ghazali** (*AL gah zel i*) **(1058–1111)**, a respected mystic and legal scholar, was a prominent teacher in Baghdad, lecturing to hundreds of students on legal, philosophical, and religious issues; additionally, themes of education and moral education run through his writings (Alavi, 2007). Disillusioned by personal religious uncertainties and concerns over legal corruption, Al-Ghazali abandoned teaching to seek solitude and meditation. We know little about this period of his life, but he did devote himself to solitude and spiritual exercises, writing, and teaching to select audiences. Al-Ghazali's prodigious scholarship covered many subjects, but arguably his most important work was known as *The Incoherence of the Philosophers*. Completed about 1095, this work reinforced conservative suspicions about Greek works and Islamic scholars such as Avicenna who attempted to reconcile Greek thought with religious doctrine.

Rubenstein (2003) notes that Al-Ghazali argued that "the very idea of cause and effect is a manmade illusion, since God, not nature, produces every effect" (p. 85). Al-Ghazali was specific on this matter: "Take for instance any two things, such as the quenching of thirst and drinking;

satisfaction of hunger and eating; burning and contact with fire . . . They are connected as the result of the Decree of God (holy be his name), which preceded their existence" (c. 1095/1963, p. 185). He challenged the idea of any kind of natural connection *in itself*. It follows that one can conclude little about the natural order by studying the regularities of the world. Further, because God's nature is inscrutable, empirical and rational structures are also limited and suspect. Watt (1965) notes that following Al-Ghazali's criticism of the philosophers, "there are no further great names in the philosophical movement in the Islamic east" (p. 1041). Al-Ghazali's book was one of several forces that fueled intense fundamentalist movements to silence the voices of rationalist philosophers in the Arab east. Fifteen years after the death of Al-Ghazali, however, another great Islamic scholar made a profound impact on intellectual development in Western Europe.

AVERROËS The last Arabian philosopher–physician of the Middle Ages whom we will consider is ibn Rushd **(1126–1198)**, known in the West as **Averroës** (*uh VEHR oh eez*). Tsanoff (1964) called Averroës "the greatest Arabian philosopher" (p. 186). In terms of his influence on Western thought, he may be the greatest among many important Arab philosophers.

Averroës was born in Cordoba, Spain. Little is known of his life, but apparently he spent most of his years in Spain and in Marrakesh, Morocco. He served as chief justice in Seville and also as court physician for the caliph of Marrakesh. He wrote extensive commentaries on the works of Aristotle that became a major intellectual force in Europe. Averroës worked in the Aristotelian tradition, especially in his attempts to reconcile faith and reason. Arguably, Averroës's most important philosophical work was *Tahafut Al-Tahafat* (*The Incoherence of the Incoherence*), written to refute many of the claims of Al-Ghazali's *The Incoherence of the Philosophers*. Averroës elevated the role of reason and the importance of the discovery of compatibilities between the claims of reason and the claims of faith (see c. 1180/2008). Perhaps, more than any other, he was responsible for introducing Aristotle to the West, but his work was met with continuing criticism and rejection in much of the Islamic world.

Aside from his celebrated commentaries, Averroës made substantive scientific contributions. Crombie (1961) credited him with being the first to discover that "the retina rather than the lens is the sensitive organ of the eye" (p. 102). He wrote a major treatise on medicine that was translated into Latin and used in European universities. He was one of the first to observe that patients become immune to smallpox if they survive an attack of the disease.

Toward the end of Averroës's life, hardheaded fundamentalist religious authority was prevailing over reason. Averroës and other philosophers were persecuted and their books were burned. The intellectual traditions of the Greeks were rediscovered in Europe even as the Muslim world discarded them. The age-old cycle between authority and reason was repeated with predictable consequences for both Arab and European cultures.

Judaism in the Middle Ages

Jerusalem in the Middle Ages, as today, hosted a battleground for conflicting religious claims between Christians, Jews, and Muslims. Deprived of a peaceful home of their own, Jewish emigrants settled in other countries of the Mediterranean basin. By the seventh century, Jewish settlements were established in major cities of northern and southern Europe.

For brief periods, Jewish citizens lived in peaceful and friendly surroundings in isolated regions in Christian and Muslim countries. Unfortunately, such times proved rare. More often than not, Jews found themselves in the crossfire of social, political, and religious hostilities. They typically paid more than their fair share of taxes and were often blamed for natural disasters and social ills. During periods of tension, they were

sometimes forced to either convert to the socially dominant religion (Islam or Christianity) or find a new home. Converted Jews faced constant suspicion and were seldom treated well (Friedrich, 1982). Outright pogroms against Jews were commonplace in the Middle Ages. In spite of the hardship, Jewish culture was rich in depth and variety with a powerful emphasis on education, the family, cleanliness, and faith.

Like Christians and Muslims, the Jewish community was often torn between rival claims of faith and reason:

> The medieval Jews, like the Moslems and the Christians, covered reality with a thousand superstitions, dramatized history with miracles and portents, crowded the air with angels and demons, practiced magical incantations and charms, frightened their children and themselves with talk of witches and ghouls, lightened the mystery of sleep with interpretations of dreams, and read esoteric secrets into ancient tomes.
>
> (Durant, 1950, p. 416)

In this context, our next figure struggled to reconcile faith and reason and became a critical philosopher of the Middle Ages.

MAIMONIDES Rabbi Moses ben Maimuni **(1135–1204)** stands as the greatest Jewish philosopher–physician of his time. Known in Europe as Moses **Maimonides** (*my MAHN ih deez*), he was born in Cordoba, Spain. Maimonides was well versed in Hebrew literature and tradition, but also excelled in secular education provided by his Arab teachers.

When Maimonides was thirteen, Cordoba's moderate political leadership was overthrown. New fanatic leaders gave heretics a choice of conversion to Islam or exile. This was the first of many occasions when Maimonides felt the sting of religious bigotry. He chose exile in Morocco and even pretended to be a convert to Islam for a time. During this period in the early 1160s, he began studying medicine, including psychological disorders, and these interests continued through the end of his life (Gesundheit et al., 2008). He became well known as a scholar during his exile in Morocco, but understood the danger of pretending to be Islamic. Maimonides moved to Palestine, then to Alexandria, and later to Cairo. While in Egypt, he distinguished himself as an author of medical texts, a commentary on Jewish laws and traditions, a systematic treatise on Jewish religious beliefs, and as a contributor in the fields of law, government, and public administration (Newbold & Schortgen, 2011). However, his best-known work was *Guide for the Perplexed*, a book destined to create storms of protest in Christian, Jewish, and Muslim cultures.

The *Guide* was written for knowledgeable Jews caught in the intellectual bind between Greek rationalism and religious traditions based on authority and revelation. Although written for Jews, the book was relevant for Muslims and Christians torn between rival epistemologies. The *Guide* was widely read and used in European universities where it was praised or burned depending on the local temper.

In the *Guide*, Maimonides argued that ancient scriptural texts were written to enlighten simple and unlearned people. Great truths were presented as symbolic or fictional stories and parables to ensure their meaning as spiritual messages. Jehovah was even presented in anthropomorphic terms. Maimonides believed conflict between reason and faith results when people interpret scripture in a literal manner. But a marriage of faith and reason is possible for intelligent people who discern the essential spiritual truths behind concrete picture-like representations in scripture. The "perplexed" had experienced the dissonance between faith and reason and needed a workable resolution.

Maimonides was an intellectual elitist who believed that many people had little need for his book and little need for reason. He thought it best for such people to live their lives under the authority of a primitive childlike faith. Although elitist, Maimonides's work legitimized reason and helped pave the way for the coming scientific revolution.

The Rise of the European Universities

European universities began to emerge in the tenth and eleventh centuries. The term *university* was derived from the Latin *universitas*, referring to a whole or a group organized around a common goal. Students who attended early universities sometimes met in European cathedrals or in small gatherings with self-appointed masters who taught in marketplaces or rented rooms. Initially, there were no diplomas, no entrance requirements, and no set curriculum. In most cases, the reputation and eloquence of the teacher attracted students.

By the twelfth century, universities gained momentum throughout Europe. Formal curricula were established, degrees were conferred, guilds were formed to protect both teachers and students, and campus buildings were founded. Students often traveled great distances to witness a debate or hear an inspired teacher. William of Champeaux, Peter Abelard, and Robert Grosseteste were known as legendary teachers.

The rise of the European university was one of the most critical intellectual developments of the Middle Ages. Theology, law, and medicine were soon complemented by liberal arts. Learning became important in its own right. In isolated quarters, students again heard the fragile but persistent voice of reason.

PETER ABELARD Born at Pallet in France, **Peter Abelard** (*AB uh lahrd*) **(1079–1142)** was the most renowned teacher and scholar of the early twelfth century. He is remembered for his original work in the fields of ethics, logic, and theology. He lectured at well-known centers such as St. Geneviève and Notre Dame and founded an important convent for women.

Abelard wrote about his life in a brief autobiography titled *Historia Calamitatum* (*Story of My Calamities*), translated under the title *The Story of Abelard's Adversities* (see Muckle, 1992). Abelard was known for his eloquence and polemic style in the lecture hall, and he was charged with heresy on several occasions. In his inflammatory style, he attacked "the shortcomings of the clergy, the immorality of priests and monks, the sale of indulgences, [and] the invention of bogus miracles" (Durant, 1950, p. 946). In the midst of an ultraconservative age, it seemed inevitable that calamity would fall upon such a fierce and uncompromising scholar.

The calamity intensified when Peter Abelard was introduced to Héloise, a striking woman with unusual intellectual gifts and an insatiable love of learning. Héloise was the delight and pride of her uncle, a man named Fulbert. As a canon of the church, Fulbert valued religious education and wanted Europe's most renowned teacher to educate his niece, so he hired Abelard to tutor her. What Fulbert didn't realize was that Abelard had fallen desperately in love with Héloise.

Any attraction between the two seemed unlikely to Fulbert. Abelard was almost two decades older than his beautiful student. And as a teacher of sacred theology, he had taken a vow of celibacy. When Abelard suggested he move into Fulbert's home, it must have seemed like an appropriate arrangement. Before long, Abelard's tutoring sessions with Héloise became intense romantic interludes. Up to this point in his life, Abelard had dedicated himself to the life of the mind. But now? He compared himself to a ravenous wolf consumed with love.

Héloise's uncle was furious when he learned about their affair. He separated them, but that did nothing to quiet their romance. After a time, it was impossible to conceal their relationship. Héloise was pregnant. Abelard proposed to her, but Héloise refused his offer of marriage. She placed Abelard's career above her own desires, knowing that a public marriage would end his career.

Héloise gave birth to a son they named Astralabe (after an instrument used for charting the heavens). In time, Héloise consented to marry Abelard, but Fulbert's anger against Abelard was unrequited. Not only had he been deceived but, as legal guardian of Héloise, he could have enjoyed a substantial profit if she had married a wealthy suitor.

Fulbert couldn't allow this indignity. In his lust for a reckoning, he hired a gang of thugs to hunt down Abelard and castrate him. Humiliated, Abelard blamed himself for his calamity and withdrew into the monastic life. He prevailed on Héloise, against her wishes, to become a nun. In time, she agreed. Their son was raised by Abelard's sister.

Abelard's work as a monk was no less controversial than his work as a teacher. He alienated church authorities and they, in turn, accused him of treating God as an object that could be sliced apart with the scalpel of cold reason. Though such an accusation was not entirely true, Abelard's methods must have seemed harsh to those who preferred an uncritical, faith-based theology. Finally, the hierarchy had had enough. Pope Innocent II ordered a burning of Abelard's books and demanded that Abelard be placed under house arrest and forced to accept the imposition of perpetual silence. Although he had been castrated, his enemies accused him of continuing to lust after Héloise. Abelard was condemned as a heretic but his reputation as a theologian and his works survived despite the book burnings.

Although tragic, the story of Abelard and Héloise is considered one of the great love stories of all time. The novel *Stealing Heaven* (Meade, 1979) captures the details of their celebrated relationship and inspired a motion picture with the same title (see George & Donner, 1988). Abelard and Héloise are buried side by side in the celebrated Père Lachaise cemetery in Paris, where lovers still leave letters at their grave.

Abelard's Work The battle between faith and reason reached a new intensity in the work of Abelard and his followers. Abelard believed reason was no less a gift from God than the scriptures. We know truth through reason, and we know truth through scriptures. Both truths come from God, and God cannot be self-contradictory. Nor can truth contradict itself. What are we to do when scripture and reason contradict each other? Abelard took the position that revelation and scripture must be interpreted by reason and that reason will always undergird an adequate faith.

His work established a declaration of independence for logic and philosophy. For much of the Middle Ages, religious interpretations of Greek philosophy served as handmaidens of theology, but Abelard insisted that scripture and revelation must be exposed to the light of reason.

If reason is a gift of God and if reason is conveyed through Greek thinkers such as Socrates, Plato, and Aristotle, then it follows that truth and God's wisdom are not the exclusive property of the Hebrews, Christians or Muslims. Abelard argued that the God of conventional theology was too small. Such liberal thoughts guaranteed retaliation from those who placed scripture and revelation in higher priority than reason.

Abelard approached theological problems through an early variation of the dialectical method. One of his best-known works, titled *Sic et Non* (*Yes and No*), employed the method of opposition to explore theological and philosophical questions. A given question or scripture was stated in a simple way. Contrasting and supporting arguments, scriptures, and authorities were then set forth with scripture pitted against scripture and authority against authority. Rather than obscuring potential disagreements, Abelard openly contrasted famous church leaders and their positions on various issues, and he left synthesis to the reader. The effect of the work was to create doubt and uncertainty. The church had taken the position that doubt, especially in theological matters, was a sin. Abelard, however, saw doubt in positive terms as a motive for inquiry. He believed that doubt followed by inquiry and reason leads to a more informed faith. Abelard argued that we should not believe a thing because we think God said it. Rather our beliefs should be based on the solid rock of reason, which was also a gift of God.

According to Clanchy (1997), "Abelard was the first modern 'theologian' in the sense that he was the first teacher to promote the word 'theology' and to use it to mean the reconciliation of human reason with Christian revelation" (p. 5). Abelard had an intellectual thirst for religious and philosophical issues. He criticized the chants,

prayers, and rituals of his day as little more than mindless repetition. Abelard raised embarrassing questions that were troublesome to those who placed authority and revelation in higher priority than reason. Why would those who had never had a chance to hear the Christian message be condemned to hell? How could subsequent generations inherit the sin of Adam and Eve? If God knows everything in advance, what is the meaning of confession? His detractors believed that Abelard raised too many questions, including ones that should best remain buried. Church officials believed that vain curiosity had been the original sin of Adam and Eve. Ignorance and humility were preferred to the pompous faith in human reason manifested in the works of Abelard.

Abelard was one of the first to imbue his listeners with a spirit of independence and the courage to use reason in the quest for knowledge. He paid dearly for his epistemological bravery and his earlier affair with Héloise, but he is remembered as a bold spirit who integrated Greek and Christian thought.

HÉLOISE **Héloise** (*EL uh weese*) **(c. 1098–1164)** is typically known only for her relationship to Abelard. In truth, she was a gifted scholar with knowledge of Latin, Greek, and Hebrew. She had extensive knowledge of Greek and Roman philosophy and Christian theology. In his brief autobiography, Abelard notes that in terms of literary excellence, Héloise was "the most renowned woman in the whole kingdom" (Muckle, 1992, p. 26). Although the authenticity of Héloise's writings has been disputed, scholarship suggests she did write the works attributed to her (Waithe, 1989, pp. 68–72). She may have even made substantive contributions to Abelard's writings.

Some of Héloise's intellectual concerns grew out of her love affair with Abelard. In letters exchanged with Abelard, she explored social, psychological, and ethical issues (Radice, 1974) and is a precursor of modern psychologists who study love and attraction. In letters to Abelard, Héloise discusses tensions between love as a means to

91

an end (e.g., satisfaction of sexual appetites) and what she called *indifferent love*. This latter term refers to love in its own right or love for the sake of love and not mere physical gratification. Indifferent love transcends society's limitations and regulations. For example, a marriage certificate in the Middle Ages granted conjugal rights to the man. The woman was expected to "perform her wifely duties." Héloise understood the necessity of contracts and social conventions but believed they distort our understanding of love.

Héloise's psychology and philosophy of love played out in an interesting way. Under pressure from Abelard, she acquiesced to marriage but did not approve of it. Héloise understood that marriage would interfere with Abelard's desire to conform to the religious constraints of the time. As noted by Waithe (1989), "she prefers prostitution, as she calls it, to marriage because marriage would not be for Abelard's good" (p. 79). Abelard preferred a secret marriage that would permit him to work as a teacher, but also sustain access to Héloise.

Like Abelard, Héloise embraced a teleological psychology where human action must be understood in terms of intention. Abelard had argued that actions, even one that might result in the tragic death of another, are not necessarily immoral. Héloise believed immoral actions result from a purposeful violation of conscience. According to such a view, a psychology based on material, efficient, and formal causes is inadequate to adjudicate moral issues. The issue remains as critical today as it was in the Middle Ages (see Rychlak & Rychlak, 1990).

Although Abelard believed the "hand of God" guided his calamities, Héloise did not subscribe to such intervention. If the castration of Abelard was divine chastisement, then she did not wish to know or serve this God. Nevertheless, she became a nun to please Abelard. Héloise played the part to perfection. In the shadow of this façade, she thought herself a hypocrite because she loved Abelard, but not God.

ROGER BACON Like Abelard and Héloise, controversy and brilliance marked the life and work of **Roger Bacon (c. 1220–c. 1292)**. Only fragments of information survive about his early life. Evidence is inconclusive about his family background or the exact location of his birth in England. It is known that he studied at Oxford and the University of Paris. He was an independent scholar until age forty when, for unknown reasons, Bacon joined the Franciscan order. It was a troubled union.

Bacon took a radical stand in supporting mathematics and science as keys to understanding theology and God. He was indiscreet in condemning the educational backgrounds of fellow members in the order. Aside from wild speculations, Bacon's alchemy experiments and his belief in astrology offended his superiors. In 1278, the General of the Franciscan order imprisoned Bacon for "certain suspected novelties" (Bridges, 1976, p. 32). The "suspected novelties" may have been Bacon's beliefs that Providence had guided the Greeks and Jews, that the stoics showed a personal morality superior to many Christians, that ethical values can be found in Islamic literature, and that changes in religious faith follow conjunctions of the planets Jupiter and Mercury (Bridges, 1976).

Completed around 1267, Bacon's *Opus Majus* covers topics such as optics, philology, mathematics, experimental science, and moral philosophy and emphasizes observation over theory (Cucina et al., 2014). Wade (2005) pointed out that Bacon understood the magnifying powers of convex lenses. Bridges (1976) argued that Bacon "imagined, and was within measurable distance of effecting, the combination of lenses which was to bring far things near, but which was not to be realized till the time of Galileo" (p. 39). Christopher Columbus (c. 1451–1506) discovered a passage from Bacon's *Opus Majus* quoted in Pierre d'Ailly's *Imago Mundi*. Bridges (1976) claims that Bacon's words may have inspired Columbus to make his famous voyage.

In Part One of the *Opus Majus*, Bacon offers important contributions to epistemology (see Burke, 1962) with a discussion of four general causes of human ignorance and error (pp. 3–35).

The first involved an unjustified reliance on authority. Another cause can be found in the human tendency to remain a slave to habit, tradition, and custom. In addition, popular prejudices blind people and contribute to ignorance. A final cause springs from conceit about our knowledge or wisdom. On this latter topic, Bacon championed breadth of experience and advocated the importance of learning from common people and the humbling advances of technology. To combat smug preconceptions about our knowledge, he also encouraged a broad curriculum including languages, mathematics, science, and philosophy.

The ideas of Bacon form an intellectual bridge between the Middle Ages and modern thought. Like other influential thinkers of his time, he hoped to reconcile faith and reason. For centuries, the Christian church had vacillated between tolerating and condemning Aristotle's psychology and philosophy. Bacon dreamed of reforming the church on this matter. In his mind, the Greeks did not pose a threat. In fact, their ideas could only strengthen Christian theology. Although a few church authorities tolerated Bacon's radical thought, many in his time considered him a misfit. Like other historical rebels, his voice would find acceptance only after the passing of many years.

THOMAS AQUINAS   Another stellar figure from the University of Paris became the greatest church doctor since St. Augustine. Born into an influential family, **Thomas Aquinas** (*uh Kwy nuhs*) **(1225–1274)** received an impressive education at a Benedictine abbey before studying liberal arts at the University of Naples. At age twenty, Aquinas joined the Dominican order with the expectation of becoming a scholar who would teach and serve God in absolute poverty.

His decision came as a bitter disappointment for his family. In fact, they kidnapped Aquinas. For one year, his family imprisoned him in an effort to steer him toward a more acceptable profession. He was unmoved. After their failed attempt, the family released their captive son.

Undeterred, Thomas Aquinas earned a doctorate in theology at the University of Paris in 1256.

He enjoyed the bulk of his teaching and writing career at Paris and in several Italian monasteries. Though he lived a mere fifty years, his writings are extensive. Without question, his most famous work is the *Summa Theologica*. In 1323, Pope John XXII canonized Aquinas as a saint of the Catholic Church a century after his birth.

Like Bacon, Maimonides, and Avicenna, Aquinas was committed to a reconciliation of faith and reason. He believed that revealed truths are not discernible from reason. On the other hand, he urged that the voice of reason be given an open and sympathetic audience. Aquinas was the foremost Aristotelian of his time, but he was also a moderate who constructed a system of thought that accommodates reason and faith. He encouraged an open consideration of rival positions on intellectual issues. Like Aristotle, Aquinas was fascinated with psychology.

Thomas Aquinas studied topics that today would fall under headings such as philosophical psychology and philosophy of science. His psychological interests ranged from intelligence, emotion, the senses and hallucinations (McCarthy-Jones, 2011), sex and gender (Soble, 2009), and motivation to the study of social influences on human beings, consciousness, and habit. His frequent comparisons between humans and animals reveal his interest in comparative psychology. He reestablished the scientific approach to nature found in Aristotle's empiricism. Although his psychology follows Aristotle, Aquinas's reflective philosophical work is a continuing source of inspiration (see McCool, 1990).

Body and Soul Copleston (1962) claimed that Thomas Aquinas accepted Aristotle's soul–body hylomorphism (García-Valdecasas, 2005). *Hylomorphism* refers to the complete interdependence of form and matter. In Aquinas's view, the "name 'man' applies neither to the soul alone nor to the body alone, but to soul and body together, to the composite substance" (Copleston, 1962, p. 94). He rejected the Platonic and later Cartesian idea that the soul is imprisoned inside the body

(Butera, 2010). Instead, he saw the union of body and soul as natural and desirable. His Aristotelian emphasis on the unity of soul and body informed his psychology. Emotion must be understood in terms of physiological and psychological qualities—the two are inseparable. Likewise, Copleston (1962) notes that sensation "is an act not of the soul using a body, but of the *compositum*; we have no innate ideas, but the mind is dependent on sense-experience for its knowledge" (p. 102). Although Aquinas did not advance a system in the modern sense, his psychology assumed a relationship between the material substrate and experience or mental activity. For example, he argued that emotions disturbed thought (Mandler, 2003). Aquinas stressed that personality meant wholeness or completeness.

All of this raised an important question: How could Thomas Aquinas believe in the unity of body and soul while, at the same time, believing in the survival of the soul following death? It is debatable whether he provided a satisfactory answer to the question. He did argue that the soul is immortal and that its mode of knowing is conditioned by the state in which it finds itself. While the soul is united with the body, the soul knows via the senses, and cognition results from the interdependence of physiological and psychological processes (Kemp, 1990). But in another state it has other modes of cognition. Therefore when separated from the body, the soul could still have cognitive capacity.

Theory of Knowledge Gerard (1966, p. 318) noted that Thomistic psychology is based more on empiricism than authority. For Thomas Aquinas, the sensory image was a key building block in knowledge, but he also emphasized intellectual activity in organizing sensory information. McInerny (1990) argued that "Thomism is solidly based on the assumption that we know the world first through our senses and then via concepts formed on the basis of our sense experience" (p. ix). Aquinas sought a middle road between the extremes of empiricism and rationalism.

For Aquinas, scientific activity begins with simple sensory components and practical conceptual processes that organize sensory information. He accepted a moderate form of realism, contending that it is reasonable to believe in a conformity between the mental and physical worlds. He understood, however, that human accounts of the world are variable and may contradict each other. But in his view, diversity and disagreements stimulate further study (das Neves & Melé, 2013). In matters of science, Aquinas believed each serious viewpoint should receive a fair hearing along with a search for new data pertinent to disagreements. At the time, his positions were controversial and dangerous but made a significant contribution to the reconciliation of faith and reason.

Scholars disagree about the work and influence of Thomas Aquinas. Russell (1959) offered both an appreciative and a critical analysis. He agreed that the Thomistic version of Aristotle dominated the Renaissance, but unlike his predecessors, Aquinas was at least a "thorough and intelligent student" of Aristotle. Russell contended that the conclusions in Aquinas's philosophy "are inexorably imposed beforehand by Christian dogma. We do not find the disinterested detachment of Socrates and Plato, where the argument is allowed to take us whither it will. On the other hand . . . opposing points of view are always stated clearly and fairly" (p. 156).

We should note that Aristotle's work was often forbidden prior to Thomas Aquinas. Papal edicts banned the teaching of Aristotle even in cosmopolitan centers such as the University of Paris. In this historical context, Aquinas's work is notable. According to Ronan (1982), "Almost alone he was able to make the theological faculty [at the University of Paris] change course and come to terms with Aristotelian teaching" (p. 260). Aquinas elevated the role of reason and broadened the concept of revelation. God could be revealed in nature and through reason.

Gerard (1966) noted that Thomas Aquinas "reveals an approach to behavior which would seem to be described more accurately as an observational empiricism than as a blind Aristotelianism or a religious dogmatism" (p. 327). As a leading theologian, Aquinas emphasized moral courage in intellectual endeavors (Irizar, 2014), and he took the position that an adequate theology has little to fear from science and reason. He made contributions to the reconciliation of faith and reason, yet was surprisingly empirical for his times. Thomas Aquinas represents a challenge to those who treat the medieval period as a void without psychological contributions.

WILLIAM OF OCKHAM Before concluding the medieval period, we should mention another Franciscan, **William of Ockham (c. 1285–1349)**. Born near London around 1285, he studied at Oxford University. Like Roger Bacon, William was suspected of embracing heretical ideas. After a time, he was excommunicated because of repeated conflicts with the church over questions of papal authority and succession.

William carried on the empirical tradition set forth in the work of Thomas Aquinas, and his interests included cognition, memory, and mental representation (Kemp, 1998). However, he is best remembered for proposing the law of parsimony or **Ockham's Razor**. William argued that an explanation containing fewer assumptions is preferable to one containing more assumptions. Other things being equal, simplicity is superior to complexity, which should never be posed without necessity. As if wielding a razor, William of Ockham was notorious for shaving away unnecessary assumptions to find the simplest explanation.

Ockham's Razor holds a potent lesson for science and is especially relevant for psychology. For example, psychologists have sometimes attributed human traits to animals, thus violating the law of parsimony. We shall return to this issue throughout the course of this book.

Conclusion

Gerard (1966) noted that even historians once wrote off the medieval period as a time dominated by theological preoccupation, blind allegiance to authority, superstition, and ignorance. It is true that if the historian is looking for such qualities in medieval thought, they are easily found. In recent years, however, scholars have come to view the Middle Ages in a different light (e.g., Henley & Thorne, 2005). In an insightful book, Bjornsson (2004) traced critical achievements in antiquity and the Middle Ages that set the stage for the coming scientific revolution. We can no longer dismiss this period of history. Its proper rediscovery is an important task for historians of science.

Review Questions

1. List and briefly define (in a word or two) Galen's constitutional types.
2. Explain Galen's pneuma concept of the soul.
3. Describe the basic teachings of Epicurus, Zeno, and Pyrrho. In what sense are their teachings comparable?
4. What did Plotinus mean when he argued that the "soul is not in the world, rather the world is in the soul"?
5. Describe four possible solutions to the tensions between revelation and reason.
6. What is the significance of Augustine's *Confessions* for psychology? Explain Augustine's thought on infant motivation, grief, dreams, and habit breaking.
7. Why, according to Rhazes, do people trust charlatans rather than legitimate healers?
8. List and describe major substantive contributions coming out of the works of Avicenna, Averroës, and Alhazen.
9. What is the essential message contained in Maimonides's book *Guide for the Perplexed*?
10. Outline Abelard's position with respect to the roles of faith and reason.
11. What did Héloise mean by indifferent love?
12. According to Roger Bacon, there are four causes for human ignorance and error. What are they?
13. Briefly outline the views of Thomas Aquinas on methodology.
14. Outline some of the general intellectual characteristics of the Middle Ages and the Roman Period.

Glossary

Abelard, Peter (1079–1142) One of the best-known university teachers in the twelfth century. His book *Yes and No* illustrated contradictions in the positions of past authorities. He argued for a stronger role for reason in Christian epistemology.

Al-Ghazali (1058–1111) Author of *The Incoherence of the Philosophers*. Attacked the rationality of the Greeks and the concept of causality. Worked against scientific progress in Islam.

Alhazen (965–1039) One of the greatest Islamic scientists whose *Book of Optics* is one of the most influential classic works on vision. He made many original contributions on topics such as depth perception, apparent size, and binocular vision.

animal spirits A concept that has enjoyed wide usage, especially in premodern times. In Galen's pneuma concept of the soul, the expression *animal spirits* was used to account for a vital psychological function, namely, the operation of higher cognitive functions. Animal spirits contrasted with *natural spirits*, which account for vegetative functions. See *vital spirit*.

Aquinas, Thomas (1225–1274) One of the greatest doctors of the church, remembered for his heroic efforts to reconcile faith and reason. He is also remembered for advancing an empirically based system of psychological thought.

Asclepiades A popular Greek physician who practiced in Rome around 124 BCE. He distinguished between delusions and hallucinations and argued that therapy for emotional problems should be pleasant.

Augustine, Aurelius (354–430) One of the great doctors of the church who wrote extensively about a number of psychological topics including memory, grief, speech, and dreams.

Aurelius, Marcus (121–180 CE) Roman emperor and stoic philosopher who emphasized the importance of enduring hardships that undoubtedly serve a larger purpose. The expression *stoic resignation* characterizes an important dimension of his thought.

Averroës (1126–1198) An Islamic scholar very influential in Europe because of his commentaries on the works of Aristotle. Known also for many substantive scientific discoveries. He discovered that patients once infected with smallpox become immune if they survive the initial infection. He also discovered that the retina is the part of the eye sensitive to light.

Avicenna (980–1037) An influential philosopher of the Islamic world who attempted to reconcile the tensions between revelation and reason. Also remembered for his Aristotelian approach to psychological problems.

Bacon, Roger (c. 1220–c. 1292) One of the first to write on the sources of error in human thought. His catalog of errors included things such as being a slave to habit, relying too much on authority, giving in to popular prejudices, and conceit about one's own knowledge.

Empiricus, Sextus Roman physician and skeptic who criticized dogmatic certainty and argued for the virtues associated with an attitude of suspended judgment.

Epictetus (c. 50–c. 135 CE) A Roman stoic philosopher, popular in his day, who emphasized the stoic virtues of order, discipline, and resignation in those matters beyond our control.

Epicureanism A philosophy based on the goodness of pleasure and the evil of pain. Epicureanism emphasized moderation and the capacity to forgo immediate pleasures for long-term gains.

Epicurus of Samos (341–270 BCE) An important post-Aristotelian philosopher who founded a school of thought that focused largely on how to live the good life by maximizing pleasure and minimizing pain.

Galenus (c. 129–c. 199 CE) Rome's greatest physician, remembered for his early anatomical theories and his speculation on a host of medical problems including the problems of emotional illness.

96

Héloise (c. 1098–1164) A gifted scholar known primarily for her tragic love affair with Peter Abelard. Her letters illustrated a deep philosophy and psychology of the nature of loving relationships.

Hypatia (c. 370–c. 415 CE) Neo-Platonic philosopher noted for her expertise in astronomy and geometry. Possibly one of the first to recommend music therapy for emotional disorders.

Lucretius (c. 96–c. 55 BCE) Roman Epicurean philosopher who wrote on a variety of psychological topics, often from the vantage point of the atomic theory of Democritus.

Maimonides (1135–1204) Influential Jewish philosopher who attempted to reconcile the conflicting claims of reason and revelation. His book *Guide for the Perplexed* was widely read and highly controversial.

medieval period The historical period from approximately 400 to 1300. Though it was a period marked by reliance on tradition, revelation, and authority, scholars attempted to find an acceptable role for reason and for observational studies.

natural spirit In Galen's pneuma concept of the soul, natural spirit refers to those vital principles responsible for vegetative functions of the body.

neo-Platonism A school of philosophy founded in the third century that combined selected features of Platonic philosophy with Jewish and Christian mysticism.

Ockham's Razor The contention of William of Ockham that explanations containing fewer assumptions are to be preferred to those containing more assumptions.

Plotinus (205–270 CE) Founder of neo-Platonic philosophy and author of a six-volume series entitled *Enneads*. The works of Plotinus are a rich source of psychological thought on topics such as perception, sensation, memory, and thinking.

pneuma Refers to the air we draw in as we breathe, but also refers to those vital principles that make life possible.

Pyrrho (c. 360–c. 270 BCE) Founder of a systematic philosophy of skepticism. Also emphasized the importance of finding means to live a calm and untroubled existence.

Rhazes (c. 854–c. 925) Physician and author of medical texts. Argued against demonology, superstitious religious beliefs, and the arbitrary use of authority in science. He advocated a rational and empirical approach to the problems of medicine and psychology.

skepticism One of the major systematic approaches to philosophy following the death of Aristotle. The concerns of the skeptics were largely focused on the problems of epistemology and the good life.

stoicism A major post-Aristotelian philosophy emphasizing discipline and suppression of desire as means to the greatest happiness and virtue.

Tertullian (c. 155–230 CE) An early Christian scholar remembered for his attacks on child sacrifice, the persecution of Christians, and the brutality of the Roman games. Also remembered for his attacks on Greek philosophy and his emphasis on faith as opposed to reason.

vital spirit In Galen's pneuma concept of the soul, vital spirit refers to activities located in the heart that regulate or control body heat.

William of Ockham (c. 1285–1349) An early philosopher friendly to empirical methods and strongly influenced by Thomas Aquinas. See *Ockham's Razor*.

Zeno of Cyprus (c. 335–c. 263 BCE) Founder of the post-Aristotelian school of stoicism, which emphasized self-control, austerity, and suppression as guides to virtue and happiness.

5 The Renaissance

No truth [is] so sublime but it may be trivial tomorrow in the light of new thoughts.
—Ralph Waldo Emerson (1841/1969)

In the twilight of the Middle Ages, European culture witnessed the emergence of a dramatic scientific and philosophical revolution. Beginning in the fourteenth century and stretching to the sixteenth, the **Renaissance** (meaning "the rebirth") inspired an unprecedented growth and shift in perspective. MacLeod (1975) noted, "The metaphor of the Rebirth suggests that freedom had been born and had flourished during the time of the Greeks, that it had subsequently died, and that it was now being reborn" (p. 87).

The Renaissance period witnessed revolutionary trends in art and architecture with a new emphasis on human life and on the natural world. Renaissance music was broadened to include folk music, art songs, love songs, madrigals, court music, and street music. New developments in music theory accompanied a growth in the number of music schools and an increasing demand for musical instruments.

When German goldsmith Johannes Gutenberg (1398–1468) invented the printing press around 1440, it proved to be an innovation that forever changed communication. The new technology lowered the expense of publishing and encouraged new intellectual vistas. No longer the exclusive possession of the elite, books found their way into the hands of a broader population. Renaissance literature evolved from tales about God and the afterlife to the interplay of human beings and their lives.

New geographic discoveries expanded intellectual boundaries along with the rediscovery of Greek classics. Another major development during the Renaissance was the powerful revolt against authority as a way of discerning truth. Despite the intellectual rebirth, the Renaissance was stagnant and even regressive in certain ways. And new challenges emerged as Europe faced a devastating pandemic.

The Black Death

One of the most destructive calamities in human history ushered in the Renaissance. Throughout history, the plague (sometimes called the "Black Death") has struck with ruinous consequences, but the brief period from 1347 to 1350 witnessed a biological and medical holocaust that decimated the European population. Hundreds of communities were destroyed or deserted. The toll in human numbers is difficult to calculate because population statistics were not well established. Even reliable counts of the dead in some localities did not provide a basis for estimating mortality statistics in other regions. We do know that the fatalities across Europe during this tragic period numbered in the millions. Evidence suggests that one-third of the European population was lost between 1347 and 1350. For some communities, the death rate ran far higher.

The plague brought economic and social consequences that scarred Europe's intellectual landscape (see Herlihy, 1997). Following the loss of one-third of the population, the number of workers diminished, disrupting the equilibrium between supply and demand. Wealth was redistributed with the loss of entire families (Cantor, 2001). As with natural disasters such as earthquakes and floods, law and order crumbled in the wake of theft and violent crime. The soaring death rate pushed community services beyond capacity. Although severe under the best of circumstances, the problems of sanitation in many communities were exacerbated by inadequate burial services and the resulting accumulation of corpses. European streets were cluttered with decomposing victims of the Black Death.

What was the human reaction to the Black Death? Many viewed it as the end of the world (Hall, 2009). One encounters examples of stoic resignation, self-sacrificing heroism, opportunism, and reckless abandon to short-term pleasure in the face of inevitable death. The wealthy could flee from cities and communities to take isolated shelter in remote estates. Angry and desperate, some searched for a scapegoat (Mora, 2008). As in other times, Jewish citizens became the target of choice. According to Ziegler (1969/1991), "The massacre [of Jews] was exceptional in its extent and its ferocity; in both, indeed, it probably had no equal until the twentieth century set new standards for man's inhumanity to man" (p. 80).

European Jews provided a familiar scapegoat. Christian teachings had denigrated Jews and they were also resented for their financial success. For centuries, the church followed a strict literal approach to scripture that opposed loans of interest. Based on passages such as Deuteronomy 23:1 and Luke 6:35, church leaders viewed it as a sin to make money on money. St. Ambrose even suggested that money lending for interest was in the same league as murder (see White, 1910). However, Jewish businessmen who were not scriptural literalists were free to lend money for interest. This advantage contributed to their financial success, which in turn fostered resentment and jealousy. In 1349, the men, women, and children in the Jewish community of Strasbourg were executed in a mass burning. In addition, the city canceled all debts owed to Jews and confiscated all property belonging to Jewish citizens (Friedrich, 1982). For a host of theological, social, and economic reasons, Jews were blamed for the plague. They were tortured, imprisoned, and massacred sometimes at "the mere news that the plague was approaching" (Ziegler, 1969/1991, p. 77). According to Kelly (2005), Jews sometimes avoided brutality by killing themselves and their children before the angry mobs arrived.

When hostility was not directed at others, it was sometimes turned inward. As in other tragedies, people searched for an explanation for their misfortune. Many believed God had sent the plague as a punishment for the sins of people. If you accept that line of thinking, what would be the next step? For some, self-punishment seemed a solution. Perhaps an act of a sincere, self-inflicted flogging could appease God's wrath. Earlier catastrophes had inspired a similar reaction, but during the plague years it achieved new levels of zealotry among the brotherhoods of the flagellants. Vast numbers of flagellants marched through towns beating themselves with sharpened pieces of metal attached to leather thongs. In the words of Ziegler (1969/1991), "Each man tried to outdo his neighbor in pious suffering, literally whipping himself into a frenzy in which pain had no reality. Around them the townsfolk quaked, sobbed and groaned in sympathy, encouraging the brethren to still greater excesses" (p. 66).

At best, flagellation may have salved a guilty conscience, but open wounds and crowds of people would only favor the spread of the Black Death. Tragically, an understanding of the cause of the epidemic disease had to wait until a later generation of scientists discovered *Yersinia pestis*, a vector-borne enterobacteria transmitted from fleas (*Xenopsylla cheopis*) carried on the backs of infected black rats (see Biddle, 1995).

An interesting outcome of the plague is that it contributed to doubts about authorities and institutions. People were told that the Black Death was God's punishment for sin. But no one could ignore that even the most godly in their midst—including priests and other church officials—were stricken with the same ferocity as the general population. Trusted institutions, especially the church, seemed helpless to protect people against a nightmare of terrifying proportions. The resulting doubts and resentment directed at authorities formed the intellectual backdrop of the Renaissance. We will now consider other characteristics that contributed to Renaissance science in general and psychology in particular.

A New Worldview: Expanding Geographic Knowledge

Imagine that the year is 1522 and you are living in Europe. You believe the earth is the center of the universe. You believe the sun is red in the evening because it reflects the fires of hell (see White, 1896/1978). Now imagine hearing that Ferdinand Magellan's ship has returned after a grueling sea voyage that claimed his life. Magellan's voyage, completed under the leadership of Juan Sebastian del Cano, has become the first to circumnavigate the globe. Although sailing with a crew of more than two hundred and fifty in 1519, a remnant of only thirty-five sailors has returned.

Hearing the news about the first-known voyage around the earth reinforced skepticism about the old cosmology. The world was now a different place, better known and far bigger than before.

These journeys exposed Europeans to groups of humans for whom the existing Western theological and political worldviews could not account. If it became necessary to expand geographic boundaries, perhaps it was also necessary to expand intellectual boundaries. Perhaps some people could enlarge one without expanding the other, but in many cases new geographic knowledge contributed to a new curiosity and openness to revolutionary ideas. In that context, the Renaissance flourished.

Influence of the Greek Classics

By the fifteenth century, Greek texts were commonplace in European centers of learning and in private libraries. A handful of wealthy bibliophiles went to great trouble and expense to acquire private collections of old manuscripts. When Constantinople fell in 1453, Byzantine scientists were forced to leave, and many brought Greek manuscripts to Italy (Delaunay, 1958). Other texts found their way to Europe in the hands of traders who profited from the Crusades.

However they arrived, the writings of the ancient Greeks influenced the Renaissance imagination. The classics stimulated an interest in the Greek language and in editing and translation. They also invigorated new ways of thinking. It was refreshing to witness the Greek courage to allow speculation to run its course without having to affirm dogmatic conclusions that had been imposed beforehand. The classics quickened the reemergence of a naturalistic approach to psychology. Delaunay (1958) offered the opinion that the birth of Renaissance humanism echoed the return of Hellenic values. Whatever their precise roles, the rediscovery of the classics kindled interest in human problems and reduced the appeal of theological matters.

Diffusion of Authority

During the medieval period, the Roman Catholic Church dominated the political, intellectual, and religious life of Europe. During the Renaissance, the church saw its power and authority diminish. Forces at work within the church and external cultural developments contributed to its declining influence.

Emerging nation-states likely posed the single most important challenge to church authority. The leaders of the new nation-states sometimes viewed the church as a foreign competitor and jealously protected their territory and assets. Some people felt resentment about sending money to support a church with a base of power in a distant land (Manchester, 1992).

As noted previously, Gutenberg invented the printing press around 1440. This invention stimulated a growing number of readers and made available new translations of the Bible, and provided an important underpinning for the development of the sciences. Translations of the Bible prepared by Martin Luther and others were sometimes condemned and placed on the **Index of Forbidden Books** (see Haight, 1978), but nevertheless found their way to the public. The increased availability of the Bible may have contributed to the idea that human beings have direct access to God without need for a church-based intermediary. The concept of the "individual priesthood of the believer" carried the assumption that all persons could read and interpret scripture for themselves. Even so, Protestants who were allowed to read scripture were often not free to read Catholic literature. Censorship remained rampant in both Protestant and Catholic countries (see Grendler, 1988).

As mentioned, forces within the church contributed to the demise of its influence and power base. As a large institution, the church struggled with enormous financial demands. To satisfy those needs, religious leaders raised money through the sale of political or religious offices and indulgences. An **indulgence** involved an exchange of money for a spiritual favor. After

committing a personal sin, an individual might beg forgiveness by paying a sum. Or, in some cases, a wealthy individual could decide to sin but pay in advance for forgiveness of this "indulgence." Another person, worried about the soul of a deceased relative, might pay for intercession to improve the relative's status in the afterlife. It's no surprise that the practice of granting indulgences offended some faithful Europeans.

During the fourteenth and fifteenth centuries, church leaders wrestled with debilitating power struggles. Important questions were raised as to whether authority should be vested in a single leader or in church councils. Such conflict contributed to the rupture that inspired the Reformation.

A succession of earlier dissidents had called attention to problems within the church, but none had the impact of **Martin Luther (1483–1546)**, an Augustinian monk and theologian. In 1517, Luther nailed ninety-five theses on a church door in Wittenberg, Germany. His bold gesture ushered in a protest movement known as the **Reformation**. Luther hoped to reform Catholic doctrine and practice rather than start a new church. However, authorities within the church interpreted his actions as anti-Catholic. Despite such condemnation, Luther's reform movement found support from emerging nations struggling for political and economic freedom from Rome (Manchester, 1992) as well as from an emerging group of women who wrote in favor of the Reformation (Zitzlsperger, 2006). After ongoing conflicts with the church, Luther was excommunicated and then exiled to Saxony. Following his excommunication, he spearheaded the Protestant movement until his death in 1546.

How great was the Reformation's influence on the development of science? Scholars hold legitimate differences of opinion. Watson and Evans (1991) concluded that Renaissance science and philosophy gained nothing from the Reformation. They point to the Protestant John Calvin and his well-known justification for ordering the torture and burning at the stake

101

of Michael Servetus (Buchanan, 1885). Servetus had "described the Holy Land as a barren wilderness (which it was), thus contradicting the scriptural description of it as a land of 'milk and honey'" (Watson & Evans, 1991 p. 151). Many Reformation leaders were as intoxicated with authority as those against whom they rebelled. MacLeod (1975) argued, however, that "just as Luther . . . could exhort his followers to read the Bible and draw their own conclusions, so could other Protestants exhort their followers to look at nature (as Aristotle had done) and draw their own conclusions" (p. 91). In this way, the Reformation may have contributed to the growing importance of the individual in Renaissance humanism (Jansz, 2004). The role of the Reformation in Renaissance science remains subject to interpretation and debate.

Growth of Empirical Studies

A host of empirical discoveries were introduced during the Renaissance period (Bjornsson, 2004). During this time, mapmaking was reestablished as a scientific activity. Based on the careful observations of explorers, descriptions and drawings of coastlines, harbors, and peninsulas were created with a fair amount of accuracy.

Freed from the prohibitions of earlier times, the study of human anatomy flourished during the Renaissance. In 1543, the Belgian scientist **Andreas Vesalius (1514–1564)** prompted cultural turmoil (Bazan, 2016) and dramatically improved knowledge of human anatomy when he published his classic *The Fabric of the Human Body*, a text based on his painstaking dissections (Schillace, 2014). By including the anatomy of the central nervous system, Vesalius is credited as an early neuroscientist (Catani & Sandrone, 2015). Other researchers such as Gabriello Fallopio (1523–1562), Bartolommeo Eustachio (1520–1574), and Michael Servetus (1511–1553) also made significant contributions to anatomical knowledge. And, as we'll see later, Leonardo da Vinci (1452–1519) and others used art to com-

plement traditional studies on anatomy (Ginn & Loruso, 2008).

During the late Renaissance, empirical work in botany and zoology made numerous advances. Descriptions of plants and many animal species were more detailed and accurate than in previous generations. The Greeks of antiquity and medieval scholars such as Roger Bacon and Moses Maimonides had articulated a robust empirical spirit. It was now being realized on a scale they could never have imagined.

Quantification

Commenting on a debate about whether there really was a Renaissance, Bochner (1973) declared that "there was indeed a mathematics of the Renaissance that was original and distinctive in its drives and characteristics" (p. 178).

Interest in Renaissance mathematics was fueled by practical demands of navigation along with business, banking, and commercial activities. Ronan (1982) noted that "between the years 1472 and 1500 no less than 214 mathematical books had been published to feed the increasing demand for mathematics by banking houses, merchants, workshops, public administrators, astrologers and scholars" (p. 322). Public contests were even staged where participants competed against each other to solve mathematical problems (Ronan, 1982).

Major schools in Germany, Italy, and France valued mathematics in its own right, independent of practical application. Mathematicians had a strong interest in the discipline for its own sake, leading to original contributions, especially in algebra and geometry. The Renaissance witnessed the development of new mathematical symbols and the solution of numerous equations. The rediscovery of Pythagoras and Euclid, along with new mathematical discoveries, offered new optimism about quantitative methods. Such optimism later served as a decisive force in psychology's development.

Changing Visions of the World

As with mathematics, the late Renaissance witnessed revolutionary changes in cosmology. The term **cosmology** refers to theories about the nature of the universe, including earth's relation to the rest of the solar system. Changing beliefs about the universe provide an important intellectual backdrop for the history of the social sciences because our world visions have far-reaching consequences for how we view ourselves (see Berenda, 1965).

For centuries, the prevailing view was that earth was positioned in the center of the universe. According to this model, the earth was encircled by the sun, the moon, and the other planets. The **geocentric** (earth-centered) cosmology was a dominant intellectual feature of the Middle Ages and early Renaissance. The model was a curious combination of theology wedded to the work of Aristotle and an Egyptian astronomer, geographer, and mathematician named **Ptolemy (c. 100–c. 165)**.

Working in Alexandria during the second century, Ptolemy (*TAHL eh mee*) argued that earth sits motionless in the center of the cosmos. The stars beyond the immediate planetary system were regarded as fixed points of light. If one assumes that such bodies follow strict circular pathways around earth, then we should be able to predict the motion of heavenly bodies. But such predictions fail to match observations. Following the thinking of earlier Greeks, Ptolemy constructed an elaborate though awkward theory to account for locations and movements of celestial bodies (see Thurston, 1994). Although Ptolemy was aware of the possibility of visual illusions, having devoted much of his *Optics* to the topic (Coren, 2003), he argued that human impressions of astronomy were accurate.

One of Ptolemy's proofs for the immovability of earth centers on the following argument: If our planet moves, then an object tossed up should fall in a different location from where it was tossed. Ptolemy's proof fails to account for one fact. If earth is moving, then the thrown object is moving at the same speed as earth at the time of the toss. Hence, even with a moving earth, the object should fall in the same relative location from which it was tossed. Despite this now-evident fallacy, Ptolemy's argument retained its intuitive power for centuries.

Ptolemy's arguments for a stationary earth located in the center of the universe squared beautifully with many theological beliefs of the Middle Ages. Such beliefs were grounded in scripture and church tradition. Some raised questions about the shape of earth (e.g., was it disc-like, or spherical?), but most agreed it was stationary and central in the scheme of things. By the later Middle Ages, the prevailing belief was in a central, stationary, and spherical earth.

Although popular and accepted, geocentric cosmology was not without nagging biblical perplexities. Does the earth hang on nothing as mentioned in Job 26:7, does it rest on foundations as implied in Job 38:4, Psalms 102:25, and Psalms 104:5, or is it founded on the seas as implied in Psalms 24:2? Would the earth abide forever as proclaimed in Ecclesiastes 1:4, or would it someday be burned as prophesized in II Peter 3:10? If some biblical texts were taken literally, others must be taken metaphorically.

The geocentric worldview was integral to larger philosophical and theological notions. The model was an abiding source of emotional and intellectual comfort. A stationary earth was fixed at the center of the universe, and Jerusalem was the central point on earth. People were confident in the belief they were the key players in a lawful universe designed for their benefit. The heavens, literally *up there* (not *out there*), radiated the perfection of God. In the medieval conception of hell, Dante took over from Ptolemy. Despite a lack of physical description in the Bible, the complicated architecture of hell was described in graphic detail in the pages of Dante's *Divine Comedy*.

Questions about the structure of the universe were not just questions about astronomy or physics, but questions about human destiny, theology, philosophy, and the purpose of life on earth. The task of disentangling science from theology in this period was not only vexing from an intellectual standpoint, it was fraught with danger to the well-being of scientists who dared raise questions.

The Heliocentric Theory

The Greek astronomer Aristarchus of Samos (310–230 BCE) was one of the first to advance the idea of a sun-centered cosmos. The idea, however, was not taken seriously until the sixteenth century. **Nicolaus Copernicus (1473–1543)**, a Polish astronomer and canon of the church, is sometimes regarded as the founder of modern astronomy. His book *On the Revolution of the Celestial Spheres*, published days before his death in 1543, proposed that earth turned once daily on its axis and traveled in an annual path around the sun. As a challenge to the old geocentric universe, Copernicus had advanced a new **heliocentric** (sun-centered) cosmology.

In terms of calendar predictions, Copernican theory represented little improvement over Ptolemy's geocentric model. Like Ptolemy, Copernicus believed that the circle is the most perfect geometric figure. It seemed inconceivable to both men that a lawful universe would be based on anything other than perfect circular motion. **Johannes Kepler (1571–1630)**, a German astronomer and mathematician, later demonstrated they were wrong. He discovered that planets travel in elliptical or oval-shaped motions around the sun. Kepler's calculations were instrumental in delivering a deathblow to the aging geocentric theory. Clinging to the old theory, religious supporters did not give up without a fight. The stage was set for a battle between theology and science, and one man was caught in the crossfire.

Galileo Galilei

The Italian astronomer and physicist **Galileo Galilei (1564–1642)** is one of the most celebrated

Galileo Galilei

figures in the history of science. Born in Pisa, Galileo (*Gal uh LAY oh*) received his early education near Florence. In 1581, he returned to the University of Pisa to study medicine. Because of shifting interests and shortage of funds, Galileo withdrew from medical training before receiving a degree. After 1585, he studied mathematics and physics. In 1586, he achieved widespread recognition for his work on a hydrostatic balance, an instrument designed to measure the specific gravity of objects. Galileo held a professorial position in mathematics at Pisa from 1589 to 1592. In 1592, he was awarded a chair in mathematics at the University of Padua.

Early in his career, Galileo believed in Copernican theory, but he was afraid of going public with his convictions. By 1609, he had built an excellent thirty-two-power telescope and was the first to use this instrument in a systematic study of astronomy. After collecting data with his telescope, Galileo developed greater confidence in Copernican theory. The old geocentric theory had predicted that the moon's surface would appear perfect and unblemished. Instead, Galileo, a skilled artist, discovered and painted the irregular lunar surface pocked with craters and littered with rocks and mountains (Harris, 2010). The old theory had taught that all objects in the heavens were visible to the naked eye. But gazing through his telescope, Galileo discovered sunspots along with the moons of Jupiter and the rings of Saturn. One of his students had predicted that, if the heliocentric model is correct, the planet Venus should exhibit phases that resemble lunar phases. Galileo confirmed his student's predictions (Gribben, 2006, p. 97). Galileo's observations proved a daunting challenge to geocentric theory as well as to the prevailing worldview. He pioneered the idea that raw experience can be productively amplified through the use of tools such as the telescope and quantitative descriptions. Galileo's views helped set the stage for the development of other sciences including scientific psychology.

In 1610, Galileo returned to Florence as philosopher and mathematician in the employment of the Grand Duke of Tuscany. Already, his observations were generating acclaim. A year later, he visited the pontifical court in Rome where he demonstrated his telescope. The friendly atmosphere in Rome emboldened Galileo to take a stand in supporting Copernican theory.

Subsequently, academic enemies greeted Galileo's support of Copernicus with fierce criticism and personal attacks. Five years after demonstrating his telescope in the pontifical court, he was summoned back to Rome. In 1616, he faced official charges of possible heresy. Although he was not found guilty, he was ordered to refrain from *holding* or *defending* Copernican doctrine. Select members of the church hierarchy defended Galileo, but a larger and more influential conservative group dominated the proceedings.

In 1624, Pope Urban VIII denied Galileo's request to reverse the prohibition of 1616. However, the Pope granted Galileo the right to publish a work comparing geocentric and heliocentric theories. Galileo was instructed to treat the heliocentric view as a mere hypothesis while keeping his conclusions consistent with prevailing theological truths. With the Pope's permission, Galileo devoted years of research and writing to creating a masterpiece in cosmology. His book *Dialogue Concerning the Two Chief World Systems—Ptolemaic and Copernican* was published in 1632. The story of how the book survived church censors and obstacles on its way to publication is a lengthy and contradictory tale of intrigue (see Shea, 1986).

Although hailed as a literary and scientific achievement, *Dialogue* generated a storm of controversy. Within a year of *Dialogue's* publication, Galileo was forced to travel to Rome to stand trial before the Inquisition. In open defiance of the Pope, Galileo had used his book to support Copernican cosmology. He was found guilty of believing and teaching the hated doctrine. The Roman Inquisition ordered him to recant.

At the age of seventy, Galileo was forced to his knees as he faced the holy cardinals. Before his accusers, he placed his hands on the Bible and abjured and cursed his errors. Galileo was made to swear he would never again do anything to arouse suspicion regarding his orthodoxy.

Because of his advanced age, Galileo avoided imprisonment. Removed from family and friends, he was placed under house arrest in his remote country estate. There, he spent the final eight years of his life before dying in 1642. Though he avoided a physical prison, Galileo was placed in a cruel intellectual prison as he was forbidden to continue his work on the problems that had captured his imagination for so many years.

To no one's surprise, Galileo's *Dialogue* and Copernicus's *On the Revolution* were placed on the Roman church's *Index of Forbidden Books*. The controversy over rival cosmologies went beyond a dispute about the nature of the universe. The scope of a larger controversy centered on matters of authority. Under the guise of competing epistemologies, the authority of literal scripture was pitted against the authority of the new observational sciences.

The complexity of the debate becomes clear in the arguments against Galileo and the Copernican system. Conventional wisdom assumed that the moon generated its own light. However, the heliocentric view claimed that the moon reflects light from the sun. Religious authorities countered with the Genesis 1:16 passage that refers to a lesser light that rules by night. Galileo's discovery of the moons of Jupiter was denounced as an illusion caused by the telescope or perhaps Satan himself. Some authorities raised doubts about telescopic observations on the grounds that the telescope itself possibly added to or distorted the objects in its field of view. In response, Galileo observed hundreds of items close up with the naked eye and at a distance with the telescope (see Gribben, 2006, p. 97). Galileo could find no evidence that the telescope added anything to objects as revealed to the naked eye.

Galileo's observations coupled with his powerful arguments for the Copernican system brought him into conflict not only with the Roman Catholic Church but with Protestant reformers as well. The Protestant response to heliocentrism was mixed and less organized than the Catholic reaction (see Westman, 1986). Martin Luther (1539/1967) complained that "whoever wants to be clever must agree with nothing that others esteem . . . This is what the fellow does who wishes to turn the whole of astronomy upside down . . . I believe the holy scripture, for Joshua commanded the sun to stand still and not the earth" (pp. 358–359). But just as some devout Catholics opposed biblical literalism and favored Galileo's beliefs, some liberal Protestant reformers found no incompatibility between the new cosmology and the essential Christian message.

The Larger Meaning of the Copernican Revolution

Prior to the Copernican revolution, people had little appreciation for natural causes. As Deason (1986) tells us, Reformation theologians Luther and Calvin, who echoed the earlier claims of Al-Ghazali, believed that nothing in nature happens through natural inherent forces. For example,

Luther "chided physicians and philosophers for ascribing procreation to 'a matching mixture of qualities, which are active in predisposed matter'" (Deason, 1986, p. 176). According to Catholic and Protestant theologies, active causal power resides in God alone, not in natural forces.

Copernican cosmology, however, described inherent, lawful, predictable, and quantifiable natural forces that exist independently. Such forces can be studied without reference to any extrinsic causal force. Geographic discoveries, rather than the new astronomy, fed a growing belief that the dominant theology had been wrong about cosmology. Was it not also possible that it had been wrong about the philosophy that was so closely connected to that cosmology?

Such questions and doubts promoted a new openness, first to the physical sciences and later to the life sciences. Galileo's telescopic studies also influenced the study of vision (Wade, 2009a). Copernicus and Galileo brought us one step closer to understanding the grand mysteries of the universe, including the mysteries of human experience and behavior.

Psychological Thought in the Renaissance

Along with discoveries in other sciences and a new emphasis on humanistic studies, several figures prepared the intellectual groundwork for Renaissance psychology. The period also witnessed the first treatise on individual differences. In addition, a trend deemphasized what was called the "will" in favor of broader influences such as intelligence, aptitude, social influence, temperament, and learning. A flood of original ideas contributed to an optimism about a science of human nature.

Petrarch

Francesco Petrarch (1304–1374), an Italian poet, scholar, and moralist, was an early leader in **Renaissance humanism**. From his earliest years as a student, Petrarch (*PEH trark*) was obsessed with the recovery and study of ancient Roman and Greek manuscripts. In his mind, intellectual Christianity had epistemological limitations. Medieval scholasticism used hairsplitting logic to study remote theological problems that shed little insight into human nature. Hellenistic philosophy, science, literature, and poetry offered a refreshing contrast. Petrarch embraced Roman and Greek concerns with this world and with the immediate and practical problems of life. Although a loyal Christian, he hoped to widen the horizons of the faithful, focusing attention on the importance of the present and the compatibilities between Christian and classic thought.

Petrarch set the stage for the expansion of humanistic studies in the Renaissance. Human beings should be understood not just in the context of theology, but also in the context of their natural setting. Petrarch found joy in nature, society, secular studies, and travel. He believed we have the right to be creatures of this world. Such a claim is foundational to the development of a science of human nature.

Niccolò Machiavelli

The Italian civil servant **Niccolò Machiavelli** *(MAK ee uh VEHL ee)* **(1469–1527)** is often regarded as the founder of modern political science. He also was a founder of modern military science. So why is he important for the social and behavioral sciences? Machiavelli established descriptive and objective methodologies that

Cesare Borgia and Niccolò Machiavelli

107

rejected moralistic approaches to human behavior. His views on the malleability of human behavior suggested new possibilities for understanding and control—key elements in any science. He was one of the first to recognize the role of social influence in human life. In many respects, he was an intellectual ancestor to modern social psychology.

In 1502, Machiavelli served as the Florentine secretary for Cesare Borgia (c. 1475–1507). Imposing and ruthless, Borgia was the duke of Valentinois and the captain general of the papal army. He was also the son of Pope Alexander VI (despite a vow of celibacy, the Pope made no secret that he had fathered several children). Machiavelli had a firsthand look at Borgia's leadership style. Cunning and self-reliant, Borgia could also be cruel and manipulative in running political and military affairs. During this time, Machiavelli developed a fascination with the social psychology of power, leadership, and authority. His fascination would result in major treatises on these topics.

During Machiavelli's lifetime, the political climate was unstable. In Italy, a host of city-states competed for power. At the same time, France, Germany, and Spain tried to influence political developments in Italy. Some Italian city-states formed an alliance with foreign powers, whereas others allied with the Vatican. In the early sixteenth century, Florence was allied with France, but forces loyal to the papacy tried to drive the French from Italy. Machiavelli trained and led a small Florentine army to defend Florence. Despite a hard-fought battle, superior papal forces crushed his army and the French were driven from Italy. A new political order was established in Florence. Machiavelli was imprisoned and then tortured. He managed to avoid being burned at the stake.

After his release, he moved to a rural estate near Florence where he lived in poverty. During a fourteen-year exile, Machiavelli wrote books that earned him a place in history. He wrote his best-known works, *The Prince* and *The Discourses*, in 1513. *The Prince* (1532/1977) offered a monarchical ruler advice on how to stay in power based on

methods Machiavelli doubtless saw while working with Cesare Borgia. His other books included *History of Florence* and *The Art of War*. He also wrote comedies, plays, biographies, and short stories, and these works as well as his letters reveal his interests in love and sex (Ruggiero, 2007).

During his exile, Machiavelli tried to regain a civil service position in Florence. He enjoyed a brief return to public service in 1525, but an unstable political situation prevented him from regaining his former position. He died in 1527.

Machiavelli's works aroused indignation and controversy. Thorne (1969) noted that Pope Clement VIII condemned *The Prince*. Gilbert (1967) pointed out that Machiavelli's works were placed on the *Index of Forbidden Books* in 1559 and that "Cardinal Reginald Pole said that Machiavelli 'wrote with the finger of the devil'" (p. 121). The indignation against Machiavelli's works may lie partly in their objectivity. For example, Machiavelli observed that religion may be employed to invoke obedience and control. A successful leader can use religion to call people back to their roots and founding principles. Such action serves to unite and to weed out corruption. For Machiavelli, religious values are subordinate to political values. The clever leader can manipulate religious people to achieve desired ends. Some leaders who condemned Machiavelli nevertheless used his principles without hesitation.

We noted that Machiavelli emphasized the malleability of human nature. If he held a somewhat cynical view about human nature, he was nevertheless optimistic about attaining a good social order. The suggestibility of the masses could work for the good of humankind. So could the proper use of political and social influence, even in the hands of a leader who may violate moral norms (Cunha et al., 2013). Machiavelli was interested in the larger social good. He believed that an ideal society was within reach.

Machiavelli contributed to the belief that human behavior can be understood in a naturalistic–scientific context. His views on human nature contained an interesting blend of pessimism and hope. On the pessimistic side, basic human nature was regarded as brutish, selfish, shortsighted, vain, and imitative. Machiavelli believed that self-preservation is the strongest motive. Self-preservation can induce violence and destruction or, under proper leadership, great industry and accomplishment. He taught that the human tendency to imitate others is inconsistent with creative thought, but it can make the masses malleable for shaping.

Wood (1968) addressed the common misconception that Machiavelli advocated immoral acts. Such acts are sometimes excused if a larger good is attained. For example, deception in Machiavelli's treatment is never an end in itself, but its use is acceptable if a larger good can be achieved. In some degree, most of us are Machiavellian when we use mild deception to avoid a "hard truth" (e.g., "that hat looks good on you") because we believe the former will do no harm, whereas the latter may result in unnecessary pain.

In psychological literature, the term **Machiavellianism** refers to "an amoral, manipulative attitude toward other individuals" (Gutterman, 1970, p. 3; Jones, 2016). When used in such a manner, the term is a corruption. Machiavelli was not, strictly speaking, amoral. At one level, he simply advanced a descriptive science of human social and political behavior without regard to the morality or immorality of such behavior. He attempted to describe what people actually do. Thus, he worked much as today's social scientists. Machiavelli went a step further to show what we *can* do. In this regard, he served as an intellectual forerunner to later psychologists, including behaviorists such as John B. Watson and B. F. Skinner, who strived to predict and control human behavior. For Machiavelli, efficiency, practicality, and the common good take precedence over all moral principles as ends in themselves.

Machiavelli placed strong emphasis on development, socialization, and suggestibility. These processes could be exploited to mold a desirable character and to ward off evils that result from unbridled human nature. His emphasis on socialization would be reflected in the later works of philosophers, sociologists, educators, and psychologists. Let us now turn from Machiavelli's social psychology to a Renaissance thinker with a broader range of psychological interests.

Juan Luis Vives

Watson (1915) has argued that the Spanish humanist **Juan Luis Vives (1492–1540)** should be viewed as the true originator of modern psychology. Vives was born in Valencia, Spain, in 1492, the same year that Columbus launched his fateful voyage, and Jews were expelled from several Spanish cities. Although of Jewish ancestry, Vives was given a Christian education, likely due to his mother's conversion to Christianity a year before his birth. Vives attended school in Valencia where he studied Latin grammar, rhetoric, poetry, and the Greek classics. At age seventeen, he left Valencia to continue his studies at the University of Paris.

Tragically, his parents were later victims of the Spanish Inquisition, a tribunal dealing with religious heresy. A Dominican monk named Tomás de Torquemada (1420–1498) served as First Grand Inquisitor. Unapologetically anti-Semitic, his oppressive and cruel tactics guided the Inquisition long after he stepped down. Though records are incomplete, Vives's father was likely burned at the stake. His mother faced a different fate. Having converted to Christianity, she was buried in a Christian cemetery. Years after her death, however, witnesses testified that they had seen her enter a Jewish synagogue after her conversion, casting doubt on her status as a Christian (Norena, 1970). As a result of her posthumous Inquisition trial, his mother's body was removed from a Christian cemetery and burned. So far as we know, Juan Luis Vives never returned to Valencia.

His education at the University of Paris was a disappointment. At the time, secular and religious forces wrestled for control of the university, undermining the institution and the quality of its programs. He completed only the three-year arts course before leaving with few pleasant memories. In 1512, Vives worked in the Netherlands, first as a student and later as a teacher. In 1520, he was granted a license to give public lectures at the University of Louvain. Vives earned a reputation as a sought-after teacher and scholar. The intellectual climate in the Netherlands was a haven of freedom compared with much of Europe. During this period, Vives established a friendship with Desiderius Erasmus (1466–1536), the most respected scholar of his day.

In 1523, Vives moved to England where he received an appointment at Oxford University. He hoped to settle into teaching and scholarly activities, but a thorny political situation with the king of England interfered with his plans. Vives had established a close friendship with Henry VIII and his first wife, a Spanish princess named Catherine of Aragon. After twenty years of marriage, Catherine had given birth to only one child, a daughter named Mary (later known as "Bloody Mary"). Henry needed a son to succeed him as heir to the throne and demanded a divorce.

Vives befriended Sir Thomas More (1478–1535), a respected English scholar who opposed the king's plans for a divorce. More insisted that Henry could not legally become head of the Church of England if he divorced Catherine. The king disagreed and More was executed as a traitor. No such misfortune befell Vives, but he lost the friendship and protection of both Henry and Catherine during their divorce proceedings. Catherine had asked Vives to be one of her advocates. Vives advised that she forgo any defense, leaving the queen disappointed and enraged. In 1528, Vives left England to return to the Netherlands.

His final years were spent in relative seclusion, but were highly productive, resulting in the publication of *De Anima et Vita (On the Soul and Life)* among other works. According to Norena (1970), this book "inaugurated in European thought the study of man based on reflection and observation without any metaphysical scheme" (p. 117). Vives died in 1540, just two years after the publication of *De Anima*.

Brett (1912–1921/1965) argued that Vives went beyond the theologians of his day to examine the capabilities of the mind or soul rather than to logically deduce its powers. Clements (1967) added that sometimes Vives's "writings seem to show brief but almost brilliant flashes of physiological and psychological insights, e.g., his insistence that medication first be tried on rats and guinea pigs, and his casual observations of the conditioned responses of animals" (p. 234). Clements noted, however, that at other times Vives's writings seem unfocused because of his tendency to pursue moral, religious, or poetic tangents. Let us now explore Vives's psychological work.

EMOTIONS Vives's interest in human emotion was based on empirical studies (Mandler, 2003). He believed there are inherent temperamental differences that influence emotions, but he also emphasized environmental or social influences. For example, he suggested emotions are influenced by climate, material culture (including our houses and belongings), and our relationships with other people. Vives believed emotional processes and the body influence each other. For example, he thought that "sadness causes black bile and black bile increases sadness" (Norena, 1970, p. 273). Vives believed we must learn to control emotion because unbridled emotions interfere with perception, judgment, and reason. Clements (1967) stated that Vives was also sensitive to the beneficial consequences of emotion. Even emotions such as pride, so often judged in a negative light, have their origin in the quest for good. Clements claimed that Vives's physiological emphasis and his work on emotions had a substantial impact on Descartes.

MEMORY Vives's work on association and memory is a neglected chapter in the history of psychology (Murray & Ross, 1982). Zilboorg (1941) pointed out that Vives "cites example after example of associations through similarity, contiguity, and opposites. The first in the history of psychology, he recognizes the emotional origin of certain associations" (p. 192). Vives recalled that as a youth, he had eaten cherries while ill with a fever. Years later, the taste of cherries resulted in such vivid recall of the fever, it was as if he experienced it again (see Zilboorg, 1941). Vives is among those philosophers dating to Aristotle who stress the roles of association and emotion in cognitive processes.

Vives's work on memory was characterized less by an interest in what memory is than in how it works. Anything that disturbs the spirits of the brain may have an impact on memory. Illness, alcohol, age, and intelligence are but a few of the factors associated with our ability to remember. Vives believed a memory image can be erased, in which case relearning is necessary to reinstate the image. In most cases, memory images are not completely lost but simply weakened. In these cases, recollection is facilitated when we recover any image strongly associated with the to-be-recalled image.

LEARNING Vives was a pioneer in pedagogy, education, and educational psychology (Weinstein & Way, 2003). Unique in his time, Vives supported education for women and the poor, despite his culturally typical views about women's inferiority (Ljungqvist, 2012). He believed in secular education and emphasized the importance of individual instruction. Vives's thoughts on education came from his conviction that knowledge and education were necessary to create social reforms.

Vives's significance in the history of psychology should not be underestimated. He influenced a large number of later scholars, including René Descartes, and the British associationists. His book remained popular even a century after his death.

Leonardo da Vinci

The contemporary expression *Renaissance person* describes a versatile individual with proficiency in multiple disciplines. Such polymaths are rare in our age of specialization. The intellectual breadth of **Leonardo da Vinci (1452–1519)** embodied the true ideal of a Renaissance per-

son. Remembered for world-famous paintings such as *The Mona Lisa* and *The Last Supper*, he was also a mechanic, architect, engineer, inventor, and scientist. His extensive notes (see Richter, 1970) testify to Leonardo's originality and to the breadth of his scientific and engineering interests. His notebooks are filled with sketches of flying machines (including an early conception of a helicopter), numerous drawings of physical geography (da Vinci had advised Columbus to navigate the globe), detailed anatomical drawings based on over thirty dissections he had conducted, sketches of irrigation systems and various military weapons, and architectural drawings that included plans for towns, canals, streets, churches, and palaces. In the history of psychology, Leonardo's contributions center on his studies of the senses, especially vision.

Leonardo da Vinci

111

Leonardo was born in the vicinity of Vinci, between Florence and Pisa. He was the illegitimate son of Pietro da Vinci, a notary. His father and members of his father's family raised Leonardo. Little is known about his mother. He showed early signs of artistic talent and was apprenticed to a well-known Florentine artist, Andrea de Verrocchio. Da Vinci received most of his education from Verrocchio.

In 1483, Leonardo moved to Milan where he enjoyed a sixteen-year period of creative activity. Following his years in Milan, he moved back to Florence for six years. During this period, Cesare Borgia hired da Vinci as an architect and military engineer. Machiavelli was also working for Borgia at this time, and he befriended the artist. Leonardo made military maps and offered suggestions for the military defense of Florence. Although a pacifist, da Vinci designed a host of deadly weapons and machines. He drew up plans for armored tanks, catapults, submarines, rapid-firing crossbows, cannons, and bottles of poison gas. One of his most notorious weapons was a horse-drawn chariot with revolving scythes that could shred enemy soldiers like a field of grain.

Continuing his anatomical studies, Leonardo conducted autopsies at the Hospital of Santa Maria Nuova. Leonardo's six-year stay in Florence was followed by a second Milan period from 1506 to 1513. He then moved to Rome for three years where he painted *The Mona Lisa*. Da Vinci's last years were spent in France where he enjoyed status as a recognized artist in the court of Francis I. Leonardo worked with enthusiasm and energy until his death on May 2, 1519, presumably from the recurrent strokes he suffered (Coralli & Perciaccante, 2016).

For Leonardo, vision was sovereign among all the senses. The eye was the premier instrument of human knowledge. He struggled with the ancient notion that "vision is power" or that the eye emits rays, but rejected this in favor of the idea that the eye is simply responsive to light energy. Although apparently unsatisfied with his own accounts of the processing of images (Wade, 2005), Leonardo believed that images are inverted prior to reaching the lens and reinverted by the lens so they are right side up on the retina (we now know he was wrong and that images on the retina are inverted). He made many anatomical drawings of the visual system (see Calder, 1970), including cross-sections of the human eye and illustrations of the optic chiasma. Da Vinci was interested in comparative vision and dissected the eyes of animals including a lion, dogs, and an owl in an attempt to understand their visual capacities.

Boring (1942) pointed out that Leonardo da Vinci made many contributions to our understanding of visual perception. As an example, Leonardo illustrated contrast effects by showing that white can appear whiter when contrasted with a darker color. Interestingly, Leonardo also argued that "beauty and ugliness seem more effective through one another" (Zubov, 1968, p. 137). Boring (1942) stated that Leonardo also contributed to our understanding of *aerial perspective*, the effects of atmosphere on distance perception (p. 266). Leonardo understood that colors fade with distance. He also noted that objects lose clarity with distance. There are disputes (see Boring, 1942; Wade et al., 2001) about whether da Vinci understood the possible role of retinal disparity in space perception. He wrote many rules for painters pertaining to contrast effects and aerial perspective, but although he was interested in the practical applications of his rules, his interests were more scientific. He was interested in perception in its own right as a guide to understanding nature.

Leonardo also wrote about the other senses and had a strong interest in human emotional expression. In his work *Leonardo da Vinci and a Memory of His Childhood*, Sigmund Freud (1910/1957b) pointed out that Leonardo sometimes accompanied "condemned criminals on their way to execution in order to study their features distorted by fear and to sketch them in his notebook" (p. 69). Leonardo often infused emotional and moral characteristics into his medical illustrations (Lorusso, 2008).

Some of da Vinci's other psychological interests are represented in scattered maxims. For example, he pointed out that "the part always has a tendency to reunite with its whole in order to escape from its imperfection" (Richter, 1970, vol. 2, p. 238). He emphasized the unity of body and spirit by pointing out that "the spirit desires to remain with its body, because, without the organic instruments of that body, it can neither act nor feel anything" (p. 238).

In many respects, Leonardo was an important forerunner of Francis Bacon and René Descartes. Long after da Vinci, both philosophers struggled with the problem of human knowledge and the nature of the scientific method. In a set of maxims, Leonardo outlined a method closer to Bacon's later ideas than to those advocated by Descartes. Leonardo argued that we should first consult experience and then reason. He believed that reason and judgment are more likely to err than experience. More in line with Cartesian thought, he argued that there can be no certainty without mathematics. He also maintained that practice without science is like a sailor without a compass (see Richter, 1970, vol. 2, pp. 239–241).

Leonardo da Vinci was an artist and a man of science. In both capacities, his interests turned to matters that would fascinate later psychologists. His influence in psychology may not have been extensive, because many of his contributions were discovered long after his death in unpublished notes. He does, however, illustrate important psychological discoveries during the Renaissance.

Paracelsus

One of the most enigmatic figures of the Renaissance was the physician–alchemist–astrologer–scientist Philippus Aureolus Theophrastus Bombastus von Hohenheim, who mercifully went by the nickname **Paracelsus (1493–1541)**. Paracelsus was born in Switzerland and it appears he studied at several European universities before completing a doctorate in medicine. He argued against demonology but accepted the possibility that stars influence personality. On

psychological matters, he believed that mental processes impact the health of the body and vice versa. He taught that harmony with nature is the key to human happiness. Thus, "if nature takes its proper course, we are happy [but] if nature follows the wrong course we are unhappy" (Jacobi, 1958, p. 203). Paracelsus believed in the role of external physical forces in human health. This part of his theory, and his astrology, had an impact later on Franz Anton Mesmer. He also shared with Mesmer a strong interest in his own fame and legacy (Hooley et al., 2013).

Paracelsus is also known for his radical or even fanatic comments on epistemology. He presented the strongest polemics against the ancients and appealed for a new science based on experience rather than the rational schemes of antiquity. The term *bombastic* is possibly derived from Paracelsus's name Bombastus. If so, the term characterizes his style as he denounced older authorities in a near rage. On one occasion, he publicly burned the books of Avicenna. As Ronan (1982) pointed out, Paracelsus insisted "that knowledge comes not from books in the old scholastic sense but from a study of nature" (p. 310).

His major contribution may have resided in his agitation for mastery over nature. Such mastery was achieved through wisdom based on observation. Rogers (1912) stated, "Paracelsus is the type of a host of men who sprang up all over Europe—men of enthusiasm for nature, and to some extent of original and high ideal, but men whose undisciplined imaginations led them beyond the bounds of sober thinking" (p. 231). People such as Paracelsus represent an important bridge from medieval scholasticism to modern science.

Michel de Montaigne

We mentioned earlier that many Renaissance scholars placed an emphasis on human beings in this world rather than on God and the afterlife. This new emphasis defined the writings

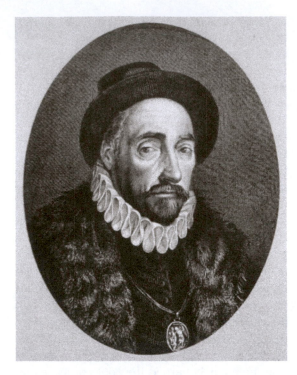

Michel de Montaigne

of the French skeptic **Michel Eyquem de Montaigne** *(mahn TAYN)* **(1533–1592)**. According to Bloom (1987), "Montaigne, until the advent of Shakespeare, is the great figure of the European Renaissance, comparable in cognitive power and in influence to Freud in our century" (p. 1). Groethuysen (1963) pointed out that he attempted to "comprehend life in its own immediate terms without recourse to religious or metaphysical postulates" (p. 634). Many of the world's scholars, including Shakespeare, Burton, Byron, Emerson, and Aldous Huxley, have expressed their debt to Montaigne.

He was born near Bordeaux in the southwest region of France. Montaigne received his formal education at the Collège du Guyenne and then at the University of Toulouse. He practiced law in Bordeaux, but decided to retire from public life in 1571. After his retirement, he began work that would secure for him a place in intellectual history. Montaigne expressed his views in the form of *Essais (Essays)*, a new literary form of his

invention that reflected the intellectual and spiritual upheaval of the times (Starr, 2012). His essays are masterful introspective studies, each projecting a spontaneous and informed opinion on a variety of topics. As we'll see, many probe the depths of psychology and philosophy.

MONTAIGNE'S SKEPTICISM Montaigne's most important philosophical essay was "Apology for Raimond Sebond." This essay resurrected earlier Greek and Roman skepticism about the possibility of attaining genuine knowledge. The "Apology" was motivated in part by Montaigne's attempts to work through his own bitterness over the religious wars between Protestants and Catholics. In the summer of 1572, tens of thousands of French Protestants or Huguenots were slaughtered, and Huguenot homes and shops were pillaged during the St. Bartholomew's Day Massacre. Like other religious atrocities of the time, the massacre fed increasing bitterness and hatred between Catholics and Protestants. The intense rivalry troubled Montaigne. Although Catholic, he was friendly to some Protestant ideas and maintained a keen intellectual interest in all religions. His moderate theology aroused suspicion on both sides.

The "Apology" was also motivated by attacks on Raimond Sebond's *Theologia Naturalis (Natural Theology)*, a work that Montaigne had earlier translated from Latin. Sebond, like many theologians of the time, argued that reason could support the Christian faith. His work, however, was subject to criticism and arguments that his reasoning was unsound. Montaigne, who grounded his religion in faith alone, disagreed with Sebond's contention about reason in support of faith. Nevertheless, he believed Sebond's arguments were as good as those of his critics. Frame (1960, vol. 2, p. 113) noted that the "Apology" is misnamed. Montaigne used "Apology" from the Greek to mean "defense." He did not apologize for Sebond's mistakes. Instead, he wrote a limited defense of Sebond, arguing his errors are no greater than the errors of his critics. The "Apology" itself turns into a trenchant attack on the arrogance of human beings who claim knowledge even when such knowledge is supposedly based on experience or reason.

Montaigne was fearful of those who believed their faith was buttressed by reason. He found too many people who, out of religious zeal, are willing to march in armies. He lamented that "there is no hostility that excels Christian hostility" and contended that "our religion was made to extirpate vices; [but] it covers them, fosters them, incites them" (Apology, p. 120). Montaigne believed virtue is the real product of truth. Given his beliefs, we may view the "Apology" as an attack both on the arrogance of reason and on the impotence of reason.

Montaigne opened his attack by pointing to presumption as the original human malady. Humans are arrogant and filled with unjustified vanity. He devoted over thirty pages to anecdotes and demonstrations showing that animal virtue and intelligence are superior to such qualities in humans. He concluded we have no grounds to believe we are superior to animals. According to Montaigne, humans are, in many respects, not as good or as knowledgeable as animals. Following his comparison of humans with animals, Montaigne moved to arguments relevant to his skeptical thesis.

After examining the ideas of countless thinkers, Montaigne listed the most blatant contradictions in the work of over two dozen famous scholars and philosophers. Next, he reviewed contradictions in philosophies of government, the variability of customs, and the defects of language that render it difficult to convey clearly a single thought to another person. Indeed, Montaigne argued that most of the troubles of the world are grammatical; lawsuits, wars, and interpersonal difficulties stem from doubts about meanings. Montaigne pointed out that it is with the "mad arrogance of speech [that humans seek] to bring God down to their measure" (Apology, p. 217), and asked the reader to consider the sheer nonsense of early religious beliefs and practices. Montaigne quoted, with approval, St. Paul's contention that those who profess to be wise become fools (Romans 1:22).

Montaigne outlined the effects of emotions and motives on beliefs. Pay a lawyer a bit more, he contended, and that lawyer will find new interest in your case, declaring it more believable. Ministers who preach with emotion become more convinced of their doctrines. A proposition defended in anger may thereby be made more memorable and convincing. Montaigne found that the cognitive-rational apparatus is weakened by wishful thinking.

He declared that change overtakes even science. How can we be sure what is now taken for scientific truth will not be replaced tomorrow? Montaigne attacked claims about the accuracy of sensory information: There may be realities for which we have no sense; we are subject to illusions and do not always recognize them as such; bodily conditions and emotions bias sensory information; and our upbringing affects our opinions. We are always changing and that metamorphosis governs the way we see our world.

Montaigne embraced a kind of epistemological humility—the ability to admit that in matters of knowledge we are all beggars. In her biography of Montaigne, Bakewell (2010) notes that the qualities he embraced included curiosity, the capacity to entertain a variety of perspectives, and adaptability. The arrogance of certitude was, for Montaigne, the underpinning of violence, terrorism, war, unjustified feelings of religious and political superiority, and ignorance.

Montaigne's attack on human knowledge was influential. Popkin (1967) characterized the "Apology" as a pivotal essay that structured seventeenth-century thought by serving as a foil for the work of René Descartes and Francis Bacon. Indeed, according to Durant and Durant (1961), Montaigne's "influence pervaded three centuries and four continents" (p. 413). Winter (1976) observed that the essays were especially well received "in Holland and in England, where at the time a less restrictive political and religious climate prevailed" (p. 106). Popkin (1967) pointed out that Montaigne "succeeded in intensifying the doubts already produced by the religious crisis of the Reformation, the humanistic crisis of the Renaissance, and the philosophical–scientific crisis of revived Pyrrhonism . . . Bacon, Herbert of Cherbury, and Descartes were to seek new philosophical systems to provide for human knowledge a basis impervious to Montaigne's doubts" (p. 368).

MONTAIGNE'S PSYCHOLOGY Aside from skepticism, Montaigne explored psychological topics such as thought, emotion, motivation, and conflict. His essays use a fresh introspective analysis that is remarkable in contrast with St. Augustine's introspective technique. Augustine's introspections took the reader to the innermost parts of the troubled soul. By contrast, Montaigne's lighter approach, though introspective, was not morbidly introverted. The reader does not just observe, but actively participates with him in the psychological analysis of topics such as anger, fear, happiness, and folly. Montaigne consistently emphasizes experience as part of inquiry; for example, he used his own experiences with kidney stones to argue for the importance of experience in medical diagnosis (Robert, 2015). Though Montaigne did not pretend to develop a coherent psychology, he did consider topics of psychological interest. We will briefly examine Montaigne's views on child rearing and education, the impossibility of pure experience, and the inconsistency of human action.

CHILD REARING AND EDUCATION In Montaigne's time, children were often disciplined in a violent manner (DeMause, 1974). He lamented cruel child-rearing practices and questioned why the courts ignored the physical abuse of children. He believed many parents use brutal punishment not for correction, but for revenge. He also condemned the schools of his day for their strict discipline. Such schools, he argued, were like prisons where wrathful teachers tortured the inmates. Montaigne believed children should find pleasure in learning. Punishment, by contrast, turned children into dullards. He believed the cruelty begins with parents who laugh when their child torments a pet or bullies a peer. After

surveying seventy children living prior to the eighteenth century, DeMause (1974) concluded that "all were beaten except one: Montaigne's daughter" (p. 40).

EXPERIENCE IS NEVER PURE Several of Montaigne's essays raise an issue of concern for many early psychologists. The issue is whether there are pure experiences of simple or elementary things, or whether experience is always composed of a mixture of elementary things. For example, is there a pure feeling of joy or is there a pure sense of sweetness? Are there elements in our experience that are not mixed with other elements or that present themselves in an undiluted form? Montaigne's answer, based on his self-observations, is an unqualified "no."

In his essay "We Taste Nothing Pure," he compared human experience to metals such as gold that serve best when they are debased or combined with other materials. Similarly, Montaigne declared that on close examination, experiences always reveal an admixture of a combination. Thus, "our utmost sensual pleasure has an air of groaning and lament about it" (see Frame, 1960, vol. 2, p. 381). Indeed, we are so constituted, according to Montaigne, that we cannot endure intense or sustained pleasure; we escape to more neutral, safe ground. He quoted, with approval, Socrates's contention that some god must have become confused during the creation of pain and pleasure, and, after botching the job, tied the two together by the tail. As we cannot sustain intense pleasure, pain also has its accompanying satisfactions. Over three hundred years later, Sigmund Freud pointed to the tensions and confusions between pleasure and pain. Both men would have been keenly interested in late twentieth-century research demonstrating the release of endorphins (opiatelike neurotransmitters) that apparently stimulate feelings of well-being or even pleasure following hard work or painful experiences.

The thoroughness with which Montaigne rejected pure experience is illustrated by his confession that his "best goodness . . . has some tincture of vice" (Frame, 1960, vol. 2, p. 383).

Throughout his essays, we find evidence of Montaigne's suspicion that a manifest behavior or experience serves as a cover for its opposite counterpart. He was close to an awareness of what would later be called a *reaction formation*. Though such awareness was evident in his writings, Montaigne did not bring himself to the analysis of the human psyche that Freud would later undertake.

INCONSISTENCIES OF HUMAN ACTIONS

As a close observer of human behavior, Montaigne found that consistency of actions within individuals is rare, whereas inconsistency is almost a rule of action. Few of us demonstrate stability of conduct or opinion and that irresolution is "the most common and apparent defect of our nature" (Frame, 1960, vol. 2, p. 1). Montaigne finds several reasons for human inconsistency; the first is the result of the variations and vicissitudes of appetite. We follow our appetites, but our appetites constantly change.

Changes in situation or circumstance bring about inconsistency. Montaigne observed that an individual may be bold and adventurous in one context, but fearful or cowardly in another. Context and circumstance play powerful roles in courage, fear, valor, and other human virtues and vices. His emphasis on circumstance and context would be verified by later social psychological experiments.

Though Montaigne saw conduct as a product of circumstance, he also argued our inconsistencies result from different roles we play and different masks we wear. Montaigne's work on inconsistency went beyond earlier work in that he identified some of the sources (e.g., variability of appetite, context, role-playing, influence of authority) that contribute to the problem. Growth toward consistency and integrity was, in his view, one of the greatest challenges confronting human beings. He believed that most of us are unable to bridle appetite, resist flattery, or avoid prostituting ourselves in the marketplace to whatever advantages might be offered. Montaigne valued the integrity associated with self-directedness.

Montaigne introduced important psychological insights in the late Renaissance period. However, his major contributions consisted of his attitudes about people and life and his recognition of the individual as part of the growing Renaissance humanism (Jansz, 2004). As we noted, his skepticism stimulated other scholars to give serious consideration to the problem of human knowledge. His ability to describe behavior and experience opened the door to more naturalistic studies of human beings. For that reason, he is a key figure in the history of the cognitive and behavioral sciences.

Bakewell (2010) captures a central feature in Montaigne's pragmatic psychology—he teaches us how to live! It's okay to be imperfect, reflect on a wider range of phenomena and question everything, be temperate and humble, live in the moment, read voraciously, avoid being a control freak, and work to overcome the blindness and the sleep of habit and traditionalism. Montaigne would also counsel us to question authority and to live appreciatively and critically in the stream of experience.

Oliva Sabuco

Work attributed to **Oliva Sabuco** (*SUH bu ko*) de Nantes Barrera **(1562–1590)** has been the subject of a long-standing and difficult historiographical problem. An influential book dedicated to Phillip II titled *New Philosophy on the Nature of Man* was first published in 1587 in Madrid under her authorship. Shortly after the original publication, Oliva's father Miguel Sabuco issued a legal statement claiming that he was the sole author of the work, and that he had allowed the book to be published under his daughter's name as a way of honoring her. Miguel's subsequent attempts to gain recognition as author, including an attempt to publish an edition of the book in Portugal, met with no success. In fact, the book went through four editions, including one that was edited extensively (with deletions and interpretive commentary) by the Spanish Inquisition. All editions were published under the authorship of Oliva Sabuco. The question of authorship is still subject to debate, and there are scholars who believe Miguel Sabuco is the author (see Norena, 1975). There are, however, compelling reasons to believe the book was indeed authored by Oliva Sabuco (see Waithe, 1989). Given the gender inequalities of the times, it seems unlikely the legitimate claims of a man would have been ignored.

Little is known about the personal lives or the educational backgrounds of Miguel or Oliva Sabuco. Most of Oliva's education may have been of an informal nature. She was apparently one of the eight children of Miguel Sabuco and Francisca de Cozar. Oliva was married when she was eighteen, and *New Philosophy on the Nature of Man* was published when she was twenty-five.

Oliva Sabuco was one of the first to write on the subject of the passions and their effects. She had a deep sensitivity to the physical and psychological consequences of emotions such as anger, fear, jealousy, hatred, and depression. She pointed out that such emotions, unchecked, lead to physical and emotional imbalance and even death. She also addressed the salutary consequences of love, hope, happiness, and moderation. Sabuco understood the wisdom of avoiding emotional extremes and the importance of environmental context as a means of maintaining balance and harmony. She believed extremes in sounds, colors, tastes, and odors contribute to illness, whereas moderate and harmonious surroundings promote health.

Oliva Sabuco understood the close connection between physiology and psychology. According to Waithe (1989), Sabuco also viewed "human nature as a microcosm of nature itself" (p. 268). It follows that psychology must be based on a broad epistemological foundation. Sabuco stressed introspection as a way of knowing, but also emphasized close observation of the physical causes of psychological states. She underscored the importance of intellectual processes and the imagination, but she placed equal, if not greater, emphasis on the central role of emotions in human life. Above all, she emphasized the wisdom of moderation in all things and a broad-based approach to knowledge.

Juan Huarte

A significant breakthrough in late Renaissance psychology came from the pen of **Juan Huarte (c. 1530–c. 1592)**, a contemporary of Montaigne. Huarte (*WAHR tae*) can properly be regarded as a pioneer in the study of aptitude, temperament, and individual differences. His book *Examen de Ingenios para las Sciencias* (*The Examination of Men's Wits*) (1594/1959) stands as a classic in differential psychology as well as educational psychology, neuropsychology, and psychiatry (Virués-Ortega et al., 2011).

Like others in this chapter, little is known of Huarte's personal life. He was apparently born in San Juan de Pie del Puerto in Navarre, but spent most of his life in Baeza, Spain. He earned a medical degree at the University of Alcala and enjoyed a successful practice. Throughout his medical career, he was interested in psychological topics set forth in the *Examen*. The book was translated into many languages, went through dozens of printings, and shaped popular discourse; Cervantes used Huarte as a source for the medical difficulties faced by Don Quixote (Palma & Palma, 2012). Some printings were placed on local indexes of forbidden books during the Inquisition because they offended religious authorities. An example, as noted by Rogers (1959), was Huarte's contention that poetic skill has a natural rather than a divine origin.

In the *Examen*, Huarte states that some children are capable of one kind of knowledge or aptitude but not another. Given such differences, he argues that we should study children at an early age to discover the nature of their abilities and to determine what studies fit their natural capacities. Huarte was sensitive to the importance of introducing subjects at appropriate developmental levels. For example, language (which Huarte viewed largely as a memory task) may be introduced early because small children have excellent memories. Logic requires the development of understanding and should be introduced later in the curriculum.

Huarte believed that humoral temperaments influence individual differences. Heat, cold, moistness, and dryness were thought to produce all individual differences. Humoral temperaments were used to account for differences in age, ethnicity, and intellect. For example, Huarte used his theory to tackle age differences in memory and understanding. Memory was dependent on moistness and understanding was dependent on dryness. He believed the brain of an old person is dry and filled with understanding, but such a brain is poor when it comes to memory. By contrast, children whose brains are endowed with moisture have excellent memory, but poor understanding. Huarte insisted that for all of us, memory is superior in the morning because moisture accrues during sleep. Through the day, the brain dries and hardens. As a result, memory becomes less facile.

Diamond (1974b) pointed out that Huarte emphasized "somatic determinants of behavior" that have their origin in the brain (p. 368). Although Huarte quoted Galen, Aristotle, and Hippocrates, he had the courage to refute them. His final product represented a curious blend of Greek philosophy with emphasis on the natural determinants of behavior and Christian theology that emphasized miraculous enlightenment. Huarte's orientation toward natural determinants of behavior marks him as an important pioneer of differential psychology.

Huarte, as a product of the sixteenth century, perpetuated prevailing views on gender differences. He counseled that women are not to be blamed for their dullness, for they can do nothing about the coldness and moistness that characterize their gender. Huarte's efforts to understand individual differences, coupled with his paternalistic biases, underscore the importance of raising gender-differentiated questions as one reads history.

Conclusion

Huarte's views on women and men were consistent with the contention of Kelly-Gadol (1977) that there was no Renaissance for women. If anything, their social status declined during the three hundred years that are so often viewed as a period of intellectual rebirth. We thus come back to the question about whether the period deserves the extravagant title of *Renaissance*. The reasoned response must surely be "yes and no." There was a Renaissance in some areas, but in others, human beings remained in darkness.

On the positive side, the Renaissance ushered in new geographic and technical advancements that contributed to an expansion of intellectual boundaries. The era witnessed a rediscovery of Greek classics and strong rebellions against existing authorities. Such rebellion may have reinforced the growth of empirical studies and a new confidence in individual judgment. The resurrection of Greek skepticism, particularly as set forth in Montaigne's widely distributed essay "Apology for Raimond Sebond," stimulated interest in the problem of human knowledge. Pioneers in both empirical (e.g., Francis Bacon) and rational (e.g., René Descartes) traditions created a basis for knowledge that challenged the criticisms of the skeptic. In an indirect way, Renaissance skepticism contributed to the epistemological foundations of contemporary science.

The Renaissance produced noteworthy contributions to psychological thought, though generally as a few isolated islands in a sea of ignorance. As we move to the modern period (from 1600), we will discover more clearly discernible threads of psychological thought marked by ideas building on each other. Such threads of thought will be evident in the chapters that follow on empiricism, rationalism, and the growth of the mechanistic perspective. Returning to the discussion on patterns in history in Chapter 1, history may indeed be sometimes chaotic and sometimes linear.

Review Questions

1. Describe five general characteristics of the Renaissance period.
2. How did the plague contribute to the changing climate of opinion in the Renaissance?
3. Contrast geocentric and heliocentric worldviews and their implications for a science of human nature.
4. Discuss Machiavelli's importance to the history of the social and behavioral sciences.
5. Outline at least three of Vives's contributions to psychological thought.
6. Discuss Leonardo da Vinci's contributions to perception. What are some specific ways in which Leonardo contributed to the growth of empirical studies?
7. In what way does the thought of Paracelsus serve as a bridge from scholasticism to modern science?
8. Outline some of Montaigne's skeptical arguments. Why was Montaigne's skepticism important to the development of modern science?
9. Briefly describe Montaigne's position on child rearing.
10. In what way does Juan Huarte serve as an important pioneer in the study of individual differences?

Glossary

Copernicus, Nicolaus (1473–1543) Polish astronomer, physician, and minister remembered as the founder of a scientific revolution marked by the belief that the sun, rather than the earth, is the center of the solar system.

cosmology The study of theories of the nature of the universe including the relation of earth to the rest of the solar system.

da Vinci, Leonardo (1452–1519) Broad-ranging Renaissance scholar who was an artistic genius, engineer, sculptor, and architect. He is also remembered for his careful studies of human anatomy and his artistic skill in capturing human emotions.

Galilei, Galileo (1564–1642) Italian astronomer and physicist remembered for improving the telescope and using it systematically in the observation of the solar system.

geocentric Literally, *earth centered*. Generally refers to the ancient view of Ptolemy that the earth is the center of the solar system.

heliocentric Literally, *sun centered*. Typically refers to the work of Nicolaus Copernicus who taught that the sun is the center of the solar system.

Huarte, Juan (c. 1530–c. 1592) One of the first to write on the subjects of individual differences, aptitude, and temperament.

Index of Forbidden Books Generally refers to books forbidden by the Catholic Church because they were regarded as dangerous to faith and morality. Though censorship was practiced from the early days of the church, the *Index* started in the sixteenth century and continued until 1966.

indulgence Refers to various means of raising money practiced by the Catholic Church prior to the Reformation. Generally involved payment of money in exchange for a spiritual favor.

Kepler, Johannes (1571–1630) German astronomer and mathematician who discovered the elliptical or oval-shaped motions of the planets.

Luther, Martin (1483–1546) The founder of the Reformation and leader of the Protestant movement. Arguably, Luther contributed to the growth of the empirical spirit by advancing the doctrine of the individual priesthood of the believer, in which people have the right to read and interpret scriptures for themselves.

Machiavelli, Niccolò (1469–1527) Founder of modern political science and modern military science. One of the first to emphasize the importance of socialization and the techniques for molding public opinion. He advocated the utility of a descriptive social science.

Machiavellianism Refers to the application of the principles set forth by Niccolò Machiavelli. Sometimes implies amoral, manipulative attitudes, but, strictly speaking, such an implication is a corruption of the teachings of Machiavelli.

Montaigne, Michel de (1533–1592) Late Renaissance scholar who launched a powerful and influential attack on human knowledge. His skepticism was to have a strong influence on Francis Bacon and René Descartes. Montaigne also speculated on a number of psychological topics such as how to rear children, education, motivation, and emotion.

Paracelsus (1493–1541) Radical Renaissance epistemologist who argued that observational studies should replace old scholastic techniques and blind allegiance to authority.

Petrarch, Francesco (1304–1374) Italian poet, scholar, and moralist who was a founder of Renaissance humanism.

Ptolemy (c. 100–c. 165) Egyptian astronomer, geographer, and mathematician known for an early geocentric cosmology that was widely accepted for over 1,400 years.

Reformation A sixteenth-century religious movement founded by Martin Luther and motivated by an attempt to reform the Catholic Church. Luther's failure to bring about the changes he desired ultimately led to a major split in the church and the beginnings of Protestantism.

Renaissance Literally, *rebirth*. That period in history from approximately 1300 to 1600 marked by the rediscovery of Greek classics, a new interest in mathematics, expanding geographic knowledge, and a wider epistemology.

Renaissance humanism Refers to a new interest in human affairs. It was manifested in art as the subject shifted from theological figures to human figures, and in music as the subject shifted from the sacred to the secular. In science, there was a new interest in physiological and anatomical studies and a general new focus on topics of human concern.

Sabuco, Oliva (1562–1590) Late Renaissance writer who emphasized the wisdom of moderation. Sabuco was among the first to understand the role of emotions in physical and psychological health.

Vesalius, Andreas (1514–1564) Physician and anatomist known for his empirical approach to anatomy based on actual dissections. He revolutionized the study of the human body much as Renaissance explorers such as Columbus and Magellan revolutionized knowledge of geography.

Vives, Juan Luis (1492–1540) Spanish humanist who advocated an empirical approach to psychology. His book *De Anima et Vita* is a rich source of Renaissance thought on psychological topics.

121

Part III

Modern Intellectual Developments That Contributed to the Birth of Psychology

Chapters 6 through 9 will explore specific developments in the modern period (from 1600) that contributed to the birth of psychology as a science and a profession. Each development created a social and intellectual context that nurtured and promoted the need for a scientific psychology. As you proceed through the following chapters, try to identify ideas and issues that captured the imaginations of scientists and philosophers, resulting in the later subject matter of psychology. We will cover developments in empiricism, rationalism, advances in neurology and physiology, evolution, the discovery of new measurement techniques, and humanitarian reforms.

TIMELINE 6.1

1600 to 1879

1609	Invention of telescope in Holland
c. 1610	Emergence of work of Galileo, Bacon, Descartes—the scientific revolution
1620	*Mayflower* lands in New England
	Novum Organum by Francis Bacon
1632	*Dialogue on the Two Chief Systems* by Galileo
1633	Galileo condemned in Inquisition
1636	Founding of Harvard College
1642	Death of Galileo
1651	*Leviathan* by Thomas Hobbes
1662	Royal Society founded in London
1664	*Treatise on Man* by René Descartes
1690	*An Essay Concerning Human Understanding* by John Locke
1701	Founding of Yale University
1705	*Observations on Man* by David Hartley
1709	*Essays on the Mind* by Claude-Adrien Helvétius (emphasizes sensation in mental life)
1710	*An Essay Towards a New Theory of Vision* by George Berkeley
1739	*A Treatise of Human Nature* by David Hume (links experimental method to psychology)
1752	Benjamin Franklin conducts his "kite experiment"
1775	Beginning of American Revolution
1776	Declaration of Independence signed in the United States
1781	*Critique of Pure Reason* by Immanuel Kant
1784	Mesmerism condemned
1789	Beginning of French Revolution
1792	*A Vindication of the Rights of Woman* by Mary Wollstonecraft
1796	Edward Jenner develops smallpox vaccine
1798	*Essay on the Principle of Population* by Thomas Malthus
1806	*A Treatise on Insanity* by Philippe Pinel
1809	Charles Darwin and Abraham Lincoln are born on February 12
	Diseases of the Mind by Benjamin Rush
1821	Catholic Church lifts its ban on teaching Copernican physics
1830	Lyell begins his work on geological evolution
1841	Beginning of Dorothea Dix's humanitarian reform movement
1842	Birth of William James
1843	After testimony from psychological experts, Daniel M'Naughton is found not guilty by reason of insanity
1845	Founding of the journal *Scientific American*
1856	Birth of Sigmund Freud
1859	*Origin of Species* by Charles Darwin
1860	*Elements of Psychophysics* by Gustav Fechner
1861	Beginning of American Civil War
1863	Founding of the National Academy of the Sciences in the United States
1874	Franz Brentano's *Psychology from an Empirical Standpoint*
1875	William James offers first American psychology course at Harvard University
1879	Wundt founds psychology laboratory at Leipzig, Germany

6 Empiricism, Associationism, and Utilitarianism

I admit nothing but on the faith of eyes.
—Francis Bacon (in Anderson, 1960, p. 26)

In this chapter, we will begin with the empirical-inductive philosophy of Francis Bacon and conclude with the radical empiricism of David Hume. We will then examine associationism and utilitarianism, two intellectual traditions inspired by empiricism. In Chapter 7, we will explore rationalism, beginning with Descartes and ending with Immanuel Kant. We will then examine commonsense philosophies that are close intellectual relatives of rationalism. We will find that both empirical and rational traditions made unique and clearly identifiable contributions to psychology's development.

Empiricism

The English term *experience* is roughly equivalent to the term **empiricism**, which was derived from the Greek *empeirikos* and its Latin equivalent *empiricus*. Empirical philosophy elevates the roles of observation and experience in human knowledge. Empiricists also reject the idea that the mind at birth is already furnished with knowledge. Modern empiricism, beginning with Francis Bacon, was conceived partly as a promising method for the new inductive sciences and partly as an alternative to the traditions and authorities of the past.

Francis Bacon

Few figures in intellectual history have evoked as much controversy among scholars as **Francis Bacon (1561–1626)**. Mathews (1996) has provided a historical overview of the disagreements over Bacon's contributions. On the appreciative side, Bacon has been regarded as the "Great Herald of the Empirical Spirit," the first to emphasize the methodological unity of the sciences, the first to advocate social support for scientific education, and the first to appreciate the human benefits derived from scientific discovery. Philosophers and scientists such as Charles Darwin, René Descartes, John Locke, and Sir Isaac Newton have acknowledged their intellectual debts to Bacon. And despite vast philosophical differences, Immanuel Kant dedicated his book *Critique of Pure Reason* to Francis Bacon.

Bacon has also been the subject of criticism. For example, he was not a scientist and had little appreciation for the mathematical foundations of science. He failed to appreciate or acknowledge major scientific breakthroughs of his day, such as John Napier's logarithms or William Harvey's work on blood circulation. Bacon failed to accept Copernican theory and Galileo's contributions. At the same time, Bacon's emphasis on induction charted an intellectual path for the development of science. He clearly stands at the crossroads between Renaissance ideas and emerging modern notions of inductive science (MacDonald, 2007).

Francis Bacon was born on January 22, 1561, in London. Following two years of study at Cambridge University, Bacon worked in Paris on the staff of Sir Amias Paulet, ambassador to France. By 1582, Bacon was back in England practicing law with a firm in London. In 1584, he was elected to Parliament. Bacon's best-known work, *Novum Organum*, meaning "new instrument of the mind," was published in 1620. The triumph of *Novum Organum* was followed, however, by a major reversal. Bacon was convicted of participating in bribery and was forced to resign his office, pay a heavy fine, and serve a brief prison sentence. At age sixty, Bacon turned his attention from legal and legislative matters to science and philosophy. In his remaining years, he published three major works, including *History of the Winds* (1622), *History of Life and Death* (1623), and a Latin translation of his earlier book *The Advancement of Learning*, first published in 1605. At age sixty-five, Bacon was conducting research on the preservation of flesh while stuffing a chicken with snow. He caught a chill that brought on pneumonia. Bacon never recovered. He died on April 9, 1626.

Francis Bacon

Bacon dedicated himself to the problem of human knowledge. He was dismayed that centuries of intellectual activity had produced such a paucity of useful knowledge. The problem, according to Bacon, was that prevailing methods of inquiry were flawed. Authority held the human intellect in bondage and the scholastic and philosophical traditions were insufficiently wedded to experience. Bacon even joined ranks with the skeptics in calling attention to sources of error that fostered ignorance. At the same time, Bacon believed that with proper methods, there is room for optimism regarding human knowledge.

Bacon is often remembered for his list of **Idols**, phantoms of the human mind or common sources of error that lead us astray in the quest for knowledge. Some Idols reflect weaknesses in the human intellect, whereas others illustrate the unfortunate consequences of social forces. On this latter topic, Bacon recognized that a supportive social and economic structure is required for science to flourish. But let us now turn to an examination of the Idols.

Bacon used the term **Idols of the Tribe** to refer to limitations to knowledge based on weaknesses in human nature. For example, sensory processes may distort external objects when their images are transported to the brain. Another example is illustrated by intellectual inertia, which manifests itself when human beings are satisfied with limited information and surface rhetoric.

A second type of error, called the **Idols of the Cave**, includes prejudices along with preferred theories and explanations that blind us to alternative interpretations. Bacon believed that data should be the investigator's first concern. Individuals should be more interested in truth and less interested in confirming a favored hypothesis. Bacon argued that generalizations should be developed only after extensive data collection. We should also be open to alternative interpretations of data.

The **Idols of the Marketplace** include the so-called nominal fallacy: the temptation to take words too seriously or to believe that the mere naming of a thing explains it. Too often, the common usage of terms and definitions misleads us. Bacon would approve the constant reexamination of definitions and classification systems. He recommended vigilance to how we use words and how we allow ourselves to be used by words.

Bacon called the final set of errors the **Idols of the Theatre**. He was referring to "the mischievous authorities of systems, which are founded either on common notions, or on a few experiments, or on superstition" (1620/1960, p. 63). Bacon cautioned against the easy acceptance of faddish systems or paradigms. He cared little whether such paradigms had rational or empirical basis (pp. 60–61) or whether "superstition and an admixture of theology" had corrupted them (p. 62). Bacon's Idols of the Theatre challenged the individual to avoid the uncritical acceptance of authority.

Bacon (1620/1960) found it understandable that in the quest for knowledge the human mind

at "first distrusts and then despises itself" (p. 103). There are, however, many grounds for hope and for challenging the skepticism that can hinder our quest for knowledge. He was an optimist despite the forces that work against human knowledge, the lack of progress, and the inadequacy of past methods. He envisioned a positive science that would benefit human life. Bacon realized that his work was outside the mainstream of such a science; he was a prophet who had a vision of the possibilities of science.

Bacon believed that skepticism was flawed, leading the skeptic to commit the same intellectual errors as others. For example, skeptics often demonstrated how sensory illusions deceive our perceptions. Some illusions are natural, but many are based on careful manipulation of materials. The existence of illusions, according to Bacon, does not justify an attack on all sensory information. Bacon was correct in pointing out that skeptics were guilty of overgeneralization. In fact, his defense of the senses represented little more than a commonsense faith in the validity of sensory data. Bacon pointed out that instruments can aid the senses and can correct information revealed to the unaided senses. This was a bold claim in a time when there were suspicions of the telescope and the microscope. Bacon argued that one type of sensory information can be used to cross-check another type. He might have added that even the skeptic must place faith in some form of sensory information in order to call attention to the truth of an illusion.

Bacon did not formulate an explicit and coherent statement of scientific methodology. Nonetheless, he provides sufficient commentary to construct an outline of his beliefs. He realized he was making a provisional statement regarding scientific method. He anticipated that methodology would further evolve, as illustrated in his insightful statement that "the art of discovery may advance as discoveries advance" (1620/1960, p. 120).

Bacon's positive approach to science is illustrated in a metaphor characterizing researchers. Some, he said, are like ants who collect and use materials. Others are like spiders, busy spinning webs from their own substance. Between the extremes is the bee who gathers a variety of materials and transforms and digests them in community (Bacon, 1620/1960). Bacon advocated the way of the bee. He understood the limitations of mere collection and cautioned that empirical philosophy can give rise to misinformation as much as rational philosophy, especially when empirical philosophers leap to hasty generalizations based on inadequate experiments. Bacon reserved his most vigorous attacks for the rationalists, whose methods divorced them from the data of experience. Bacon's middle road is best described as a new inductivism that rejects the big leap, the temptation to entertain, or the temptation to place excessive trust in the intellect. The new inductivism demands the "reform of human understanding by grounding it solidly in experience" (Stephens, 1975, p. 60). He was accused of advancing a naïve empirical inductivism that entails the mere collection of facts. Such an accusation, however, is inaccurate. Bacon emphasized assimilation and generalization, but cautioned that such activities should not be premature; they should follow massive data collection from many sources.

Bacon cautioned against hastiness when claiming to have attained knowledge. Thus, Bacon's conservatism regarding scientific claims tempered his optimism regarding the possibilities of knowledge. He recommended that investigators commit to two rules before conducting an inquiry: "first, to lay aside received opinions and notions; and second, to refrain the mind for a time from the highest generalizations" (1620/1960, p. 119). Bacon's emphasis was first and foremost on extensive data collection. A massive number of observations should be collected and, if possible, organized for presentation in tabular form. Due attention should be given to negative instances. The second step in Bacon's method was the search for generalizations or higher principles, but, again, the researcher should exercise caution.

Bacon was also interested in the communication of scientific results. With a long-standing interest in rhetoric, he cautioned against the "grand style" and argued for a subdued approach emphasizing objective data based on observation. He recognized that style may seduce human beings. Accordingly, the researcher should forgo style for substance.

The Baconian inductive method, with its emphasis on observation, occupies a niche in the evolution of modern science. For example, his emphasis on data and his hesitancy to suggest grand theories inspired the atheoretical psychology of B. F. Skinner (Moore, 2005). The deficiencies of the method—the failure to appreciate hypotheses and mathematics—are now well understood, but the new emphasis on observation was crucial in a time marked by the tendency to rush toward first principles, those things we think we know beforehand. Bacon also helped restore confidence in human knowledge. His optimism influenced several succeeding generations of philosophers and scientists.

Francis Bacon found his way into the history of psychology via another route. In his classification of the sciences, he included topics that still interest contemporary psychologists. He believed society should support empirical studies of medicine (Thorpy, 2015); sleep and dreaming; development from infancy to old age; the senses; affections such as anger, love, and fear; and cognitive abilities such as imagination, thinking, and memory. Bacon called for the construction of complete natural histories of each of these areas. He believed that understanding the natural history of an area provides scientists with the foundation to erect new knowledge structures and to improve people's lives (Weston, 2009). Bacon believed that well-researched and well-written natural histories would provide the background necessary to initiate his great plan for the restoration or renewal of the sciences. At the same time, natural history without the new empirical instruments would grow sterile.

Brett (1912–1921/1965) points out that "the ideas which [Bacon] expressed ruled the progress of inductive or experimental psychology all through its development" (p. 351). We turn now to Bacon's successor, John Locke, one of the most influential scholars in Western intellectual history.

John Locke

A number of seventeenth- and eighteenth-century philosophers tackled the possibilities and limitations of empiricism as a way of knowing. Bacon's followers, empiricists, deemphasized his methodological focus. Instead, they explored the larger metaphysical dimensions of empiricism. Bacon's most important immediate successor, **John Locke (1632–1704)**, has been described as "the most widely influential philosopher of English speech" (Tsanoff, 1964, p. 329). If Bacon can be viewed as the Great Herald of the Empirical Spirit, it is Locke who launched a serious inquiry into an empirical theory of knowledge.

John Locke was born in Wrington, Somerset, on August 29, 1632. At age fourteen, Locke pursued

John Locke

classical studies at Westminster School. In 1652, he entered Oxford University, where his interests shifted from classical studies to the natural sciences. His bachelor's degree was conferred in 1656 and his master's degree two years later. Following the death of his father and younger brother, Locke inherited most of the family estate. The small inheritance provided independence.

After completing his master's degree, Locke studied natural sciences and medicine. Though he did not extensively practice medicine, he did accept a few patients, including his close friend Lord Ashley, the Earl of Shaftesbury. In addition to serving as Shaftesbury's personal physician, Locke accepted administrative and political responsibilities and tutored Shaftesbury's grandson. These positions left time for the study of philosophy. In the period from 1689 to 1704, he produced an outpouring of scholarship including psychological works such as *An Essay Concerning Human Understanding* (1690/1959) and *Some Thoughts Concerning Education* (1693/1989).

Locke's philosophical interests focused on the problem of epistemology. He saw himself as an early "philosopher of science with the self-appointed task of providing epistemological foundations for the emerging empirical sciences" (Soles, 1985, p. 339). His work on education may also be viewed as an extension of his epistemological interests. Though he never married, he had a deep interest in children, especially in how they acquire knowledge, and he engaged in extensive discussions about education with friends who were parents (Benzaquén, 2015). He argued for the improvement of the teaching–learning process. Politically and religiously, Locke was a liberal who argued for natural rights to life, liberty, and property for all individuals (Tigiripalli & Kadarla, 2009). He advocated public education for all people as well as majority rule and the right of all individuals to study religion and hold opinions that are not imposed by religious or political authority.

One of the most celebrated and controversial ideas in Locke's work centers on his belief that, at birth, the mind is as "white paper, void of all characters, without any ideas" (1690/1959, p. 121). Fraser (1959, p. 121) suggested that Locke did not mean the mind is without latent capacities; he simply meant that the newborn's mind is not furnished with knowledge or ideas. Locke's position, though not new, was set forth in a persuasive way. The *Zeitgeist* of the seventeenth century was ripe to entertain the "white paper" hypothesis. If the hypothesis is true, experience and education become preeminent social and individual ideas. The poet Dante had claimed we have innate knowledge of good and evil; such claims inspired Locke to launch a vigorous attack on belief in innate ideas.

In his *Essay on Human Understanding*, Locke argued that there are no innate moral ideas, no innate ideas of God (though he believed that the wise of all nations have come to believe in God), no innate speculative principles, and no innate practical principles. Locke insisted that we cannot find universal agreement on any topic, but even if we could, such agreement would not prove innate ideas. Universal agreement, if it did exist, might indicate little more than common experience. Locke worried that belief in innate ideas discourages inquiry into possible exterior sources of ideas and, consequently, produces intellectual laziness.

If ideas are not innate, what is their origin? Locke contended that some ideas come to the mind via only one sense. Two events in the same sensory domain in close temporal or spatial conjunction may be associated. Locke called this result an idea. Other ideas result from the operation of two or more senses. He believed that some ideas result from reflection, which is based on extrapolations from previous sensory information. A given idea may also originate from a complicated combination of sensation and reflection.

Locke's strong empirical position on the origin of knowledge emphasized learning and education as well as their social and environmental context. Ward (2010, p. 17) argues that with John Locke we encounter a democratization of mind. Under Locke's treatment, the individual does not shoulder full responsibility for deficits in knowledge—the requisite information may never have been provided. If individual responsibility is somewhat diminished in Locke's system, social responsibility for others— especially children—is enhanced.

Locke's search for the origin of ideas led him to consider the relationship between ideas and stimulus objects that produce ideas. The validity of human knowledge and the relationship between the physical world and the psychological world (the world of ideas) concerned him deeply. *Validity* here refers to the correspondence between ideas and objects. Locke hoped to demonstrate that ideas can correspond to the physical world; otherwise, in his words, "The visions of an enthusiast and the reasonings of a sober man will be equally certain" (1690/1959, p. 227). Locke believed that our brains are crammed with imaginations, dreams, chimeras, and illusions, but we may also possess real knowledge. What then are the grounds for believing in a correspondence between ideas and stimulus objects?

Locke believed that the senses furnish certain simple ideas that accurately reflect the nature of things. For example, we have a simple idea of solidity, and Locke said, "If anyone asks me *what this solidity is*, I send him to his senses to inform him" (1690/1959, p. 156). Solid objects are known by the sense of touch. The idea of solidity is not a fiction but the inevitable result of conformity between psychological and physical realities. Two solid objects struck together produce a real effect, and we can know that effect. Locke also argued that our knowledge of mathematical truths represents real knowledge.

Though Locke may be the first to present a formal empirical philosophy, he found it impossible to be a consistent empiricist. Just as he took a commonsense approach to the existence of certain qualities of physical objects, he took an intuitive approach to his own existence. Like Descartes, he believed that to think, we must exist. Locke was also open to rationalist ideas about God's existence. Although we have no innate idea of God, we can nevertheless demonstrate

God's existence through reason (Locke, 1690/1959, Book 4, Ch. 10).

Locke's interest in the problem of knowledge led him to agree with earlier scientists such as Galileo and Boyle that two kinds of qualities characterize stimulus objects in the physical world. **Primary qualities** reside or inhere in an object and are independent of perception. Although there were disagreements about primary qualities, some examples include extension, figure, mobility, and solidity. **Secondary qualities** are hidden powers of an object that result in specific sensations; these are dependent upon the perceptions of the observer. Thus, color, sound, warmth, and taste are examples of secondary qualities. If we examine a red cube, its shape and solidity may be taken as primary qualities, but the redness is a secondary quality. To illustrate, if we lower the lights in a room, the color of the object seems to change, but the solidity and shape of the object do not change. Color, as a secondary quality, seems to emerge as a result of the interaction among light conditions, the object, and the perceiving subject. The characteristics of the perceiver contribute in a substantial way to the perception of secondary qualities, but such is not the case for primary qualities. For example, consider our red cube: Certain color-blind animals would not see the color red; they would see only shades of gray. Thus, the redness resides in the perceiver and not as an inherent quality of an object, though the object has the power to evoke the perception of redness in some perceptual systems.

The following example from comparative psychology might clarify the nature of secondary qualities. People may delight in the taste of vine-ripened tomatoes or fresh cucumbers or radishes, but most dogs would not find them appealing. Similarly, humans avoid odors that appeal to dogs. To summarize, secondary qualities emerge in interactions of sensory systems and external objects. Primary qualities, by contrast, reside or inhere in an object and are independent of the perceiver.

In other words, it would be difficult to separate a primary quality from an object without destroying the object. Indeed, Galileo suggested a subtraction test as a means of distinguishing between primary and secondary qualities. If a quality can be subtracted from an object without destroying its identity, then that quality is secondary. We could subtract the color orange from a triangle and the triangle would retain its identity as a triangle. The subtraction of figure, however, a primary quality, cannot be accomplished without destroying the object's identity. The distinction between primary and secondary qualities raises all kinds of problems, and as we will see, this distinction captured the attention of Locke's successors.

Sahakian and Sahakian (1975) claimed that Locke's book *Some Thoughts Concerning Education* (1693/1989) "was destined to have a profound influence during the course of two centuries upon the education of children in all classes of society throughout the [W]estern world" (p. 86). The ideas for the book had originally been set forth in Locke's letters to his friend, Edward Clarke, who had asked the philosopher for advice on raising Clarke's eight-year-old son. Garforth (1964) pointed out that we know little about the sources of inspiration for Locke's thoughts on education, but we can be certain he drew from his experiences at Oxford. The writers François Rabelais, John Milton, and John Drury influenced Locke. The Spanish humanist Juan Luis Vives may also have influenced his educational writings. Locke discussed subjects including the relations between parents and children, methods of training, the role of reward and punishment in discipline, curriculum, and the personality characteristics of the tutor.

Locke's ideas on education were generally consistent with his empirical philosophy. He argued that children are natural learners (Gregoriou & Papastephanou, 2013) and that, for the majority of human beings, education contributes more to character than does nature. Locke recognized that there are individual differences in natural abilities and that these are sometimes difficult to overcome (Thompson et al., 2012). Nevertheless, it is the environment that largely determines what we will become. For this reason, it is important to attend to a range of environmental influences, from the food we eat, to parental influences, to pedagogical technique.

According to Locke, children should have plenty of sleep, fresh air, and exercise. The educator should scrutinize the child's diet: He discouraged eating between meals and consuming too much sugar. Locke clearly understood the relationship between learning and good health. He adopted older notions of **hardening**, a rigorous conditioning where the child endures pain, hardship, and fatigue. Thus, a bed should be hard because feathers may contribute to physical weakness. Forcing the child to endure reasonable amounts of coldness or wetness also accomplished hardening. Consistent with his views on hardening, Locke believed crying is a fault that should not be tolerated. If crying cannot be abated with harsh or disapproving looks, then blows are acceptable if applied in a rational, dispassionate manner (van Drunen & Jansz, 2004). Persuasion, however, is preferable to physical punishment.

Although Locke believed in the judicious use of physical punishment, he emphasized reward and a positive, affectionate relationship between children and adults. He believed that unwarranted punishment works against learning and good character development. Locke argued that excessive punishment may undermine confidence and interfere with vigor and industry. Punishment in educational situations may result in an aversion to learning. Locke also counseled against reward that is not genuine, but he viewed credit for real accomplishment as a cardinal rule of education. Locke recognized that excessive and rigorous assignments result in avoidance of the lesson. A good teacher will be sensitive to the pace of the assignments and make learning enjoyable.

Many of Locke's educational views, especially his ideas on hardening and physical punishment, have been discounted by later scholars. He nevertheless represents an important turning point in the history of educational psychology. In *Letters Concerning the English Nation* (1733/1980),

Voltaire extolled Locke's systematic approach to education. Voltaire credited Locke for advocating step-by-step progress in the development of a child's understanding. He praised Locke for examining what humans have in common with animals and how we differ. In Locke's work, we have an emphasis on topical areas that will later form an important part of the new discipline of psychology. We also encounter an early emphasis on the idea that the environment shapes personality and behavior.

George Berkeley

Like Bacon and Locke, **George Berkeley (1685–1753)** emphasized the primacy of experience in human knowledge. With Berkeley, empiricism is not only a method, it is a radical statement about what it is that's real. Experience has an ontological primacy; everything, including the material world, is known in experience, and it is experience that is real.

Born in Kilkenny, Ireland, in 1685, Berkeley enrolled in Trinity College, Dublin, at age fifteen, where he earned his B.A. in 1704 and M.A. in 1707. Berkeley then held several university posts, but he was drawn to the New World. Inspired by missionary-religious views, he wanted to convert people who were enslaved, spread the Protestant faith, and educate colonists.

Finally, in 1728, he was ready to sail for America. One month prior to departing, Berkeley married Anne Forster, the daughter of an Irish magistrate. He and his wife resided in America for only three years. During that time, he lived on his farm in Rhode Island, preached sermons in the Episcopal Church, and organized a philosophical society. He hoped to found a college in the New World, but funding promised by Parliament never materialized. As a result, his stay in America was brief. In 1731, Berkeley and his wife and their infant son Henry set sail for London. Another child—a daughter born in America—died shortly after birth. Berkeley donated his farm to Yale University and contributed books to the Yale and Harvard libraries. A major California city and university would later adopt Berkeley's name. Berkeley died in January of 1753. Biographers describe him as a vigorous and handsome man with the rare combination of humility and genius.

Berkeley employed empiricism as a tool to battle materialism and skepticism. He wanted to restore faith in spiritual interpretations of the world. Interestingly, Locke's empiricism revealed to Berkeley an opening for an attack on materialist perspectives. For Locke, primary qualities reside in objects and are independent of the observer. To be sure, primary qualities are observed by the senses, but Locke's assertion was that such qualities reside in an object whether we discover them or not. With Berkeley, this distinction between primary and secondary qualities became untenable. He argued that it is absurd to ask what the world is like, independent of experience. The shape of the triangle must be experienced just as the color must be experienced. Furthermore, a figure or shape changes depending on the angle of perspective, just as color changes, depending on illumination. In a book titled *Three Dialogues between Hylas and Philonous* (1713/1935), Berkeley argued his case through Philonous (love of the mind) against materialist philosophy as voiced by Hylas (matter). Berkeley placed in the mouth of Hylas, his adversary, the idea that real things "have a fixed and real nature, which remains the same notwithstanding any change in our senses, or in the posture and motion of our bodies" (1713/1935, pp. 55–56). Such, of course, was the materialistic assumption about primary qualities; they were assumed to reside in a material substance independent of the perceiver. But in *Three Dialogues*, we find Philonous responding to Hylas by declaring that *all* sensible qualities, including size, shape, and color, are continually changing and are conditioned by the context or the medium through which we make our observations. So-called primary qualities vary as much as secondary qualities; the distinction between the two could not be established through experience.

Berkeley challenged more than the distinction between primary and secondary qualities. He also called into question the existence of primary qualities independent of experience. Extension, figure, and motion, the so-called primary qualities, exist in experience, as do color, taste, sound, or temperature. In an earlier, more innocent time, people could take refuge in a host of absolutes, including primary qualities. But the absolutes, one by one, were challenged. At one time, Europeans could believe that Jerusalem was the absolute center of the universe, but following the Copernican revolution, there was no absolute location; location was relative and changing as the earth spins on its axis and follows its orbit around the sun. How many miles do you suppose you have traveled since you started reading this chapter, or, for that matter, how far have you traveled just in the past five minutes? If there were no absolute location, we could still hold on to the idea of absolutes that exist in objects around us. But with Berkeley, these absolutes were challenged. An object viewed one way is a square but from another perspective appears to be a trapezoid. From one perspective an object is large, but from another it is quite small. Berkeley thus contributed to the demise of absolutes, but it is the absolutes of materialism that he attacked. He left his readers with spiritual absolutes, which remained for Hume to attack.

Berkeley argued that there are no legitimate grounds for assuming that some ideas represent real properties of an object. How can an idea (that which is mental) in any way represent the property of an object (that which is physical)? Thus, for Berkeley, there was no empirical evidence for the world-in-itself that is separate and distinct from the lived world of experience. In fact, the *only* real world is the world of experience or the world of the mind. Berkeley is remembered for his famous dictum *esse est percipi*: "to be is to be perceived." Such was the case even for Locke regarding secondary qualities such as color, taste, and odor, which had no absolute being in themselves. Rather, they depend for their existence on a perceiver. But for Berkeley, the expression "to be is to be perceived" applied to everything.

Following the conclusions of Berkelean empiricism, we encounter a new skepticism regarding claims for the materialist interpretation of the world. In his dialogues between Hylas and Philonous, Berkeley, speaking through Philonous, declared that he was convinced "that there is no such thing as what philosophers call *material substance*" (1713/1935, p. 11) and later added that "all that we know or conceive are our own ideas" (p. 61). Subjective experience becomes the centerpiece of empiricism pushed to the extreme. The real world is not a nonperceptible world of material substance; rather, the real world is the world as we know it in our own experience. There is an elegant simplicity in this philosophy, just as there is in materialism or any other monistic orientation. But simplicity comes with a price. A philosophy that meets our needs for simplicity sometimes falls short of meeting our equally valid demands for adequacy.

A major problem in Berkelean empiricism centers on the consistency and coherence of experience. There is no principle in experience per se that explains the orderliness of our subjective world. Yet, the world of experience holds together in an orderly way. When I finish this cup of coffee, I will leave this restaurant, get in my car, drive one mile south, turn right into the faculty parking lot, find a parking space (if I'm lucky), get out of the car, walk to the office, and meet my 9 a.m. appointment. I do not now perceive the car or any of its parts, the street, the stoplights, the parking lot, my office, or desk, but I am convinced all these things exist and the world of my immediate future experience will be reasonably coherent and orderly. How can I account for such order and coherence if my experiences are not driven by the orderly world as such, out there, that makes its step-by-step contributions to the content of my subjective experience? Surely, the orderly content of the mind must be tied to the world of objects and such objects contribute to the coherent succession of experiences that accompany my getting from the restaurant to my first appointment.

Berkeley anticipated this criticism. Before we consider his reply, let's caution against the popular misconception that Berkeley denied the existence of the real world. What Berkeley denied was the objective and independent status of primary qualities. If secondary qualities are known only in experience, so also are primary qualities known only in experience. In taking such a step, Berkeley also denied that primary qualities represent a material substance that has objective and independent status.

John Locke believed that material substance forms the world of objects. The qualities of objects to which we respond are either primary or secondary. A secondary quality resides in subjective experience, but a primary quality is supported by a material substance that is not directly perceived. What is perceived is an attribute (e.g., a figure or solidity of an underlying material substance). Asked what this material substance is, Locke declared that it is "something, he knew not what."

Berkeley denied the existence of any mysterious metaphysical material substance that has objective or independent status. Berkeley did not deny the existence of the real world; rather, he gave us a new vision of the real world. It is the materialist account of the world that is rejected, an account that paradoxically uses experience to declare that experience is derivative, and that accords primacy to a mysterious metaphysical material substance that is not directly perceived. The real world for Berkeley was the intimate world of ideas and experience, whereas the material world is derivative.

How did Berkeley respond to the criticism mentioned earlier concerning orderliness of experience? First, Berkeley did not discount the existence of other perceiving minds. Second, as a religious individual in the early 1700s, Berkeley believed in an omnipotent and omniscient God whose apprehension of the world extends throughout space and time. The world operates in an intelligible and orderly way through God's perceptions of the world. Therefore, all of the things that exist are perceived at all times. The glue for Berkeley's empiricism is found in his theism, which is itself supported on rational rather than empirical grounds. It will remain for David Hume to provide us with an empirical philosophy that is stripped of theistic and rational support.

The accusation is made that Berkelean empiricism leads to solipsism. **Solipsism** refers to the philosophical position of extreme subjectivism, which holds that only knowledge of one's own mind is possible. But Berkeley recognized other minds or other perceivers and was explicit in his recognition of God as the permanent perceiver. Thus, we participate in a wider reality and are not necessarily consigned to solipsism. The problem, however, is how we participate. The reader who takes a leap of faith with Berkeley that we live in a wider reality tied to God's perception is rescued from solipsism. Others may find it difficult to reject the contention that Berkelean empiricism leads to solipsism.

In 1709, Berkeley published a classic psychological treatise *An Essay Towards a New Theory of Vision* (1709/1948). In his essay, he argued against Descartes's contention that there are geometric principles known innately that contribute to depth perception. Berkeley argued that we learn to see in depth. Berkeley's approach to depth perception is now recognized as a classic. Although Berkeley was not experimental in his visual research and did not cite the experimental studies of his day (Wade, 2009b), he argued that there is a close relationship between sight and touch (see Pastore, 1965) and that a vivid visual sensation will be associated with a tactile sensation of closeness, whereas a less vivid visual sensation may be associated with a sensation of reaching. We thus learn to interpret sensations of nearness or distance through the medium of touch. The implications of Berkeley's theory are that distance in and of itself cannot be seen and that cues for distance must be learned (Wade, 2005). Berkeley believed that one who was born blind and who later gained sight would not be able to immediately perceive depth. Berkeley also believed that associations between visual and auditory sensations provide clues to depth perception.

Berkeley's work on depth perception anticipated later psychological investigations of the senses. Though most psychologists and philosophers rejected Berkeley's metaphysical scheme, his questions stimulated their work. Like other empiricists, he also encouraged the importance of human learning and association. As noted before, his extreme emphasis on empiricism also stimulated further work on the problem of knowledge.

David Hume

David Hume (1711–1776) offers one of the most complete and radical statements of empirical philosophy. More than any other, Hume provided an untempered empiricism. We also find in Hume a real concern with psychological topics.

Born near Edinburgh, Scotland, in 1711, David Hume was the second of the three children of Joseph Hume and Catherine Falconer. When David was three years old, his father died, leaving the resolute and devoted Catherine to raise and educate her children. David matriculated in the University of Edinburgh when he was twelve. Despite family pressure to pursue law, Hume displayed an unusual interest in literary and philosophical studies. After leaving the university at about age fifteen, Hume suffered a nervous breakdown. The treatment suggested to him included fresh air and exercise with attention to a balanced diet. Within two years, Hume had regained his health and was engrossed in reading literature and philosophy. In 1734, he went to France, where he wrote his first philosophical work, *A Treatise of Human Nature*. *A Treatise* was divided into three parts, with Part 1 devoted to the problem of human knowledge, Part 2 to the passions, and Part 3 to morals. The first two parts were published in 1739, but their reception was a disaster. Reviews were hostile, the book did not sell, and Hume later claimed the book fell deadborn from the press. If the book was an initial failure, history rescued it so that we now view it as a classic. In 1740, Hume published Part 3 of

A Treatise, dealing with moral subjects such as justice, virtue, and objects of allegiance.

Although Hume's first publication was a disappointment, his later works enjoyed success. In 1748, he published a revision of Part 1 of *A Treatise* under the title *Philosophical Essays Concerning Human Understanding*, and in the same year he published *Three Essays, Moral and Political*. Hume died in 1776, the year of the American Declaration of Independence, a cause he supported.

David Hume supported many unpopular causes and was reviled for his unorthodox religious views. All of his books were placed on the *Index of Forbidden Books*. He was the victim of harsh and unfair criticism that prevented him from obtaining university positions because of his religious beliefs. However, friends viewed him as energetic, enthusiastic, cheerful, good-natured, generous, and amiable. His sense of humor is illustrated in his reply to a colleague who was complaining about the spitefulness of the world. Hume jokingly insisted that things were not so bad, for he had written on all sorts of subjects—moral, political, religious—that could excite hostility, and yet he "had not made a single enemy; unless, indeed, all the Whigs, and all the Tories, and all the Christians" (Burton, 1846/1967, p. 443). Hume's self-appraisal is illustrated in the following letter. Hume was apparently asking a friend to find him lodging for a forthcoming visit to London, suggesting "a room in a sober discreet family, who would not be averse to admit a sober, discreet, virtuous, regular, quiet, goodnatured man of a bad character—such a room, I say, would suit me extremely" (Huxley, 1898, p. 40).

Following Berkeley's lead, Hume agreed that experience constitutes the primary subject matter of philosophy. But the events of experience, according to Hume, are not held together by any "necessary connection" that can be established through reason. Neither can it be established that a meaningful sequence of events in experience is driven by an external succession of events that reflect cause–effect relations. Thus, causality, in Hume's treatment, reduces to a psychological

problem. Causality cannot be viewed as a primary quality. If domino *A* impacts domino *B*, and domino *B* falls, Hume finds nothing in *A* that could be labeled as a cause. Causality does not inhere in an object; rather, causality is more like one of Berkeley's secondary qualities. Causality is what *we* see and what *we* attribute to things, but it does not reside in objects as a substantial quality. Thus, there are no necessary connections "out there," but only our ways of making sense of succession or sequence. All we know is that when *A* hits *B*, *B* falls over. What we take to be objective causality reduces to our habitual ways of seeing things. Hume noted that our notions of causal connections are based on temporal priority (*A* precedes *B*), spatial contiguity (*A* and *B* are close together), and constant conjunction (*B* regularly falls when impacted by *A*). We form the idea of objective necessary connection only from the regularity of our impressions. We'll return to causality as we explore other dimensions of Hume's views on psychology.

Mental life for Hume could not be verified through reason. Following his radical empirical approach to knowledge, Hume found only impressions and ideas. *Impressions* present themselves directly with considerable force. They include sensations, passions (motives), and emotions. A taste, a color, a hunger pang, a sound, a startling stimulus that results in fear, or an odor could each produce an impression. *Ideas* are fainter images of impressions. The recollection of a taste thirty minutes after eating would constitute an idea, which in this case is a weaker recollection of the original impression. Impressions or ideas may be simple, such as a single clear tone, or compound, such as we might encounter as we respond simultaneously to the color, taste, odor, and feel of a food object such as an apple.

His views on causality, coupled with his position on the sources of knowledge, led to an interesting psychological question. What, according to Hume, is the nature of the self? Most of us experience a sense of personal identity and a causal connection between one idea and another and between our ideas and our actions. According to Hume, this sense of personal identity cannot be based on any mysterious mental substance; neither can it be based on objective causality. How, then, do we explain personal identity?

First, Hume believed the sense of personal identity may be exaggerated. Tsanoff (1964) summarized Hume's position: "All that we find in inspecting our so-called 'selves' is a bundle of sensations, a collection of different perceptions. As in a kind of theatre, they pass, re-pass, glide away, and mingle in boundless variety" (p. 361). Hume is not describing a stream of consciousness but a parade of impressions and ideas that present themselves in no logical order. The parade is ongoing with a mixture of entertaining, sad, vivid, and dull entries of which we are hardly conscious. Thrown into the mix, the parade may include an intense emotional and ecstatic entry followed by a sobering entry that we watch with resentment. In some entries, we may perceive ourselves as active observers, as if we were in the parade being observed by others, whereas in other entries, we may perceive ourselves as passive observers. There is no necessary or logical connection between one entry and another. We do not know from where the parade begins or where it will end. Happily, some seem to enjoy the whole nonsensical succession, but others are not so blessed.

Most of us can muster the intellectual empathy to feel our way into this radical empirical Humean world. If you reflect on your day, you might remember punctuated bits and pieces that succeed each other without meaningful connections, flickering on and off like tiny flashbulbs. Maybe you're jostled from sleep by a new ringtone on your cell phone alarm. You drag yourself out of bed before grabbing a protein shake and a bagel as you rush out the door to class at eight. Abruptly, you're riding the bus to campus, streaming a new song on your smartphone while discreetly sizing up the other students. After class, you head to a coffee shop, ordering while telling the barista about your sleep deprivation. Quite illogically, the next major awareness seems to

be sitting in a classroom where twenty people are critiquing your thesis statement. Between classes, you run the usual online routine, switching between email, social media, class notes, and your bank account while texting a friend. Time disappears until you leave your last class, heading for the bus stop as you contemplate whether or not graduate school is the right choice. You collapse on the sofa, and before long, you're sucked into some awful reality show while ignoring the massive amounts of homework.

Who knows what the next focal point will be in this disjointed parade? It would seem like an accident if the next entry had even the appearance of being causally related to the current entry. But if you perceive a causal connection, it reflects your attempts to make connections in your day-to-day experiences.

Let's go back to Hume's account of self-identity. As we said, he rejected any notion of a substantial self. He failed to find a single impression or idea that can account for our sense of continuity or identity. In Hume's system, we encounter a succession of selves. But in normal experience, these selves are one and the same. It is the same *you* who enjoys dinner tonight and later enjoys watching a movie this weekend, even if there are gaps between your two experiences. In the final analysis, continuity or personal identity is, according to Hume, a product of the imagination, and one cannot make an objective claim on behalf of such an imagination. The sense of personal identity is a product of the peculiar way we attend to the succession of impressions and ideas. In the end, personal identity is a construction that grows out of the ways we organize the entries and gaps in our experiences.

Hume devotes the second volume of *A Treatise* to a study of what were commonly called the passions. He discusses emotions such as pride, humility, love, hate, respect, and contempt. He emphasized comparative studies in his work on emotion. Hume notes that studies of animals have been useful to anatomists and physiologists and that comparisons of the "anatomy of the mind" may also be useful (see 1739–1740/1978,

Book 11, Sec. 12). He argued that some emotions in animals have the same origins as comparable emotions in humans (see pp. 326, 363, 398, 448). Generalizations from one species to another may not always be permissible, but he was ahead of his time in recommending comparative psychological studies.

Another important feature of Hume's approach was his assumption that all emotions "are founded on pain and pleasure" (1739–1740/1978, p. 438). Hume believed emotions such as joy, desire, and hope are derived from pleasure, whereas sorrow, aversion, and fear are derived from pain. He believed that values had their basis in desires (Curry, 2006) and that emotions could drive humans to moral actions even at personal cost (Frank, 2011). Hume provided what he called experimental demonstrations. In a subtitle to his *A Treatise of Human Nature*, he declared that the book is "an attempt to introduce the experimental method of reasoning into moral subjects." Hume's so-called experiments consisted of anecdotes or demonstrations, but even so, here and elsewhere he attempted to tie his propositions to observable events (Demeter, 2012). In discussing the transfer of an emotion from one object to another, he gives the example that a quarrel with one family member may produce hatred for other family members even though they have done nothing to deserve it.

Hume's originality, intellectual courage, and integrity contributed to his greatness as a philosopher. His work on the problem of causation was the most original work on that topic since Aristotle. Hume exuded courage and integrity in his uncompromising efforts to construct a philosophy of experience.

He is a central figure in the history of psychology for several reasons. More than any empiricist since Bacon, Hume focused on emotion. He hoped to understand the origins of emotions and their role in intellectual life as well as establish a nomenclature for them. The problems of self and self-identity may have been elevated in importance because subsequent scholars considered Hume's treatment of these topics a disaster.

Hume's emphases on habit and association as well as his scientific approach to human minds (Froese, 2009) marked him as a contributor to topics of lasting psychological interest. Finally, Hume's work on the problem of causation left a mark on scientific metatheory. Following Hume, the debate over what scientists study would never be the same.

Hume's legacy created an intellectual crisis in the eighteenth and early nineteenth centuries, comparable to the crisis Montaigne's skepticism had created a century before. Bozeman (1977) pointed out that Hume demonstrated "with an awful cogency, that 'the common Lockean philosophy,' when driven to an ultimate conclusion, supplied a sandy foundation for such crucial premises of inductive science as the actual 'existence' of an external world of objects or the operation of causes in that world" (p. 9). Philosophy's compelling task was to reconstruct the conceptual foundations of science. Chapter 7 will examine reactions to Hume's thought.

Empiricism on the Continent

The British are credited with founding modern empirical philosophy, but thinkers on the continent also made contributions. The French philosopher **François-Marie Arouet de Voltaire (1694–1778)** praised British empiricism and was instrumental in importing it to the continent. In the works of Bacon and Newton, Voltaire found a means to challenge the oppression and dogmatic philosophies that had dominated European thought. Voltaire's literary and philosophical works conveyed suspicion of untestable theories and theological dogma. Instead, he supported a philosophy established on observation and experimentation. His vocal support of British thought, especially his praise for John Locke, resulted in a warrant for his arrest and a lengthy exile from Paris. Voltaire's enthusiasm for the new empirical philosophy influenced two French empiricists, **Étienne Bonnot de Condillac (1715–1780)** and **Claude-Adrien Helvétius (1715–1771)**.

Étienne Bonnot de Condillac

Étienne Bonnot de Condillac (*Kohn de YAHK*) was born in Grenoble, France, on September 30, 1715. He studied theology, philosophy, and science at a Catholic seminary at Saint-Sulpice and at the Sorbonne. Later, he was appointed to the French Academy and the Royal Academy of Berlin. Condillac's writings on education were in demand, adding to his esteem as tutor for the children of royalty. He devoted his later years almost exclusively to writing. He died in 1780 after completing a major treatise on logic.

The task of philosophy, according to Condillac, is not to discover the nature of the mind but to find out how the mind works. In this emphasis, he can be viewed as a forerunner of functional psychologies (see Chapter 12). Condillac, like John Locke and René Descartes (see Leary, 1980), attempted to establish a moral basis for the new psychology. He wanted a mental science that could make a difference in people's lives.

Condillac avoided lengthy consideration of metaphysical problems of causality and the nature of the real world that had so captivated Berkeley and Hume. Instead, he studied the genetic basis of knowledge. With a thoroughness unequaled even by Locke, Condillac sought to analyze the origins of knowledge.

Condillac asked us to imagine a marble statue that represents a human. Imagine further that the statue's intellect includes no innate ideas and can only passively sense the world (Riccio, 2012). He proposed we chart intellectual growth by opening one sensory channel at a time. He began with the sense of smell and presented one stimulus event (the smell of a rose) to the statue. Condillac argued that with one stimulus, his statue displays intellectual functions such as attention and a sense of existence. When the smell of a rose is followed by the smell of a sweet pea, the statue is now capable of discrimination and a sense of contrast. Condillac proceeded by opening other sensory channels one at a time to demonstrate the emergence of all cognitive functions. If a given stimulus is too intense or painful, the statue

is motivated to minimize the pain. Likewise, if a given stimulus yields pleasure, the statue is motivated to maximize the pleasure. He believed we understand the external world through the sense of touch, which produces compelling sensitivities to resistance, solidity, motion, hardness, softness, and so on. As noted, Condillac did not trouble over whether this awareness is subjective or objective. As a practical philosopher, his sensationist theory was focused on learning and education, and his ideas about language and mind influenced eighteenth-century philosophers as well as later scholars (Hardcastle, 2009).

Condillac is also remembered for his studies on the origin and meaning of human language. He argued that language provides symbols that represent sensations, needs, or desired actions. Condillac argued that the excellence of science was based partly on the excellence of scientific language. Scientists must work to avoid common language with its many errors. Instead, scientific concepts should be grounded in the precise language of mathematics. Condillac also emphasized the importance of accurate classification systems and taxonomies in science.

Condillac's focus on the language of science influenced thinkers in the late eighteenth and early nineteenth centuries. It pointed in the direction of positivism, which developed later in the nineteenth century. Under his guidance, empiricism became more practical and psychological, and that may be his greatest legacy within the history of psychology. Condillac demonstrated practical uses of empiricism in the investigation of problems such as the development of language and the learning process.

Claude-Adrien Helvétius

In the work of Claude-Adrien Helvétius (*ehl VA shus*) (1715–1771), we encounter an early version of a radical behaviorism (see Chapter 13) that emphasized the Lockean white paper hypothesis carried to the extreme of denying all inborn capacities. In his essays on the history of

139

materialism, Plekhanov (1967) suggested that Helvétius was so consistent in his materialist philosophy that he "horrified other materialists" (p. 92). Perhaps other materialists were horrified by Helvétius's candid approach to the moral implications of his psychology. Under his treatment, our most treasured virtues are the simple product of education. Human vice and corruption result from poor legislation and a failure to educate the masses. Helvétius gives us an environmental psychology that challenges freedom of choice and autonomy. Such extreme perspectives are seldom popular, even today.

In his book *De l'espirit* (*On the Mind*), Helvétius argued that humans are controlled by society's system of rewards and punishments. At the root of all behaviors are self-interest, the pursuit of pleasure, and the avoidance or the threat of pain. As noted, Helvétius denied hereditary influences, much like the behaviorist John Watson in the early twentieth century (Jahoda, 1992; Roback, 1937). He even suggested that genius resulted from environmental influence. Either we learn to learn or we develop a negative attitude toward learning and remain ignorant. How, then, is it possible that two people given excellent educations should turn out differently, with one being brilliant and productive and the other mediocre? Helvétius argued that chance (an encounter with the right teacher or just the right experience) plays a role in producing such differences. Under his treatment, we all have the potential to be geniuses.

Although not original, Helvétius was influential. His environmentalism and hedonism had a profound effect on the development of utilitarianism (to be discussed next) and his emphasis on the malleability of human beings elevated the importance of learning and education.

Associationism and Utilitarianism

The practical implications emerging from the thought of empiricists such as Locke, Berkeley,

and Hume inspired the associationists and utilitarians of the eighteenth and nineteenth centuries. If knowledge is acquired through experience, then the means of its acquisition is elevated as a topic of study. Knowledge can no longer be taken for granted as a mere given, a gratuity bestowed by God or the benevolent forces of nature. The specifics of how we acquire knowledge now becomes a central focus in any science of human nature.

David Hartley

David Hartley (1705–1757) is regarded as the founder of modern **associationism**. He also studied motivation and the structural and functional characteristics of the nervous system.

Hartley was born in Armley, Yorkshire, England, and was educated at Cambridge. Originally, he planned to pursue theology, but doctrinal questions drove him away from the ministry and into medicine. His most noteworthy treatise was titled *Observations on Man, His Frame, His Duty and His Expectations* (1749/1966). This work drew inspiration from Locke's work on sensation. Hartley elaborated on the doctrine of association and speculated about how it worked. He also set forth an early classification system of pleasures and pains. He practiced medicine, but had interests in history, music, philosophy, poetry, and religion. Hartley's son, also named David (1732–1813), described his father as a gentle, caring physician who treated both mind and body. Hartley was a liberal who argued in favor of inoculation at a time when it was regarded with suspicion. His son carried on Hartley's liberal perspectives with his opposition to the slave trade and England's war with America. Hartley died in Bath, England, in 1757.

Hartley was one of the first to classify the varieties of pleasure and pain. He identified seven sources of pain and pleasure from (1) the external senses, (2) imagination, (3) opinions of us held by other people, (4) our possession of the means of happiness, (5) sympathy or empathy with the status (joy or suffering) of other people, (6) the sense of our relationship with God, and (7) our moral sensitivities toward goodness and beauty or evil and deformity. Hartley thought the greatest pleasures derive from the latter three categories. As a religious man, he downplayed the pleasures associated with the first four categories and encouraged the cultivation of the so-called higher pleasures.

Newtonian physics inspired Hartley's views on neurophysiology and these views complemented his associationism (Buckingham & Finger, 1997). Newton had argued that vibrations in nerve fibers transmit sensory information to the brain. Hartley extended Newton's idea. Hartley contended that vibrations from the senses trigger miniature vibrations, or *vibratiuncles*, that persist for brief periods following the initial stimulus. Smith (1987) noted that Hartley thought "the vibrations set up by external energies gradually die away leaving only miniature vibrations or vibratiuncles" (p. 127). According to Hartley, memory is based on vibrations that fade unless appropriate conditions reactivate the vibration. Vibrations in one region may be associated with vibrations in another region resulting in extensive sources of reactivation. And these numerous sources support learned connections and memories. Hartley also connected these vibrations to categories of psychological disorders (Berrios, 2015). Smith (1987) pointed out that Hartley's associationism mirrors concepts included in Ivan Pavlov's *Conditioned Reflexes* (though there is no evidence Hartley influenced Pavlov). Hartley did, however, have a major influence on later utilitarians and empiricists such as Jeremy Bentham, James Mill, and John Stuart Mill.

Jeremy Bentham

British empiricists doubted the validity of innate knowledge. Later associationists and utilitarians joined in this suspicion. In this tradition, **Jeremy Bentham (1748–1832)** called for massive reform in jurisprudence and legal philosophy.

Jeremy Bentham

Lawmakers and court officials in Bentham's day prided themselves on their intuitive grasp of absolute moral principles. Bentham challenged this belief with the same zeal John Locke displayed when attacking the concept of innate ideas.

In Bentham's day, punishments bore little relationship to the social consequences associated with specific crimes. Instead, as Bentham points out, punishments were based on revulsion at the particular crime under litigation. Thus, same-sex interaction between consenting adults might be punished with great severity, whereas a crime with major social consequences might receive a mild reprimand. Bentham advocated a more empirical and objective basis for legal decisions. Therefore, punishment would be based on the measured social consequences of the crime.

Jeremy Bentham was born in Houndsditch, London, on February 15, 1748. He was a precocious child who learned Greek and Latin by age four. He entered Queens College at Oxford in 1760 and graduated with a B.A. when he was sixteen. In 1766, he was awarded an M.A. from

141

Oxford and in 1767 he went into legal practice. Bentham disliked practical law because, with minimum effort, most cases could be settled out of court. Despite Bentham's distaste for practical law, he pursued abstract problems of jurisprudence, including questions of interrogation and confession as well as other evidence (Weiss, 2012). In 1789, he published a major theoretical work titled *Introduction to the Principles of Morals and Legislation*. Friends published most of Bentham's work after his death. Some of his most thoughtful work focused on utilitarian approaches to reward and punishment. Bentham exemplified his own philosophy. Even in old age, he exuded a buoyant and optimistic spirit. He died on June 6, 1832, and, in characteristic altruism, donated his body to science.

Bentham argued that the intuitive approach to jurisprudence results in subjectivity and inequality. He contended that there are objective grounds for political, social, and legal theory. He summed up these objective grounds in a single principle of **utilitarianism**, sometimes called the *hedonic calculus*. The basic idea is that actions should be judged in terms of their social consequences for pleasure and pain. We should maximize pleasure and minimize pain. At the same time, we must seek the greatest pleasure for the greatest number of people. Punishment should be administered in terms of utilitarian principles. For example, a leader who conspires illegally with a political enemy deserves more punishment than another leader who, for instance, engages in a consensual same-sex relationship with another adult (Soble, 2009), even though same-sex relationships were generally not accepted during Bentham's lifetime. A wealthy person caught embezzling a large sum of money from a financial institution should receive more severe punishment than a person who steals to provide food for his or her children.

Bentham's utilitarian approach to punishment conflicted with intuitionism and retribution theory. Though there are varieties of retribution (see Cottingham, 1979), the purpose of retribution is generally to inflict a penalty on an individual as punishment or vengeance. For Bentham, the goal

of punishment is to protect society and reform the offender. The merits of the two theories are open to debate (see Benn, 1967), but Bentham provided a new perspective on punishment and his theory served to correct extreme retribution. His work contributed to the curbing of cruel and unusual punishments (Foucault, 1979) and shaped the legal systems of emerging nations (Oviedo, 2012). It also produced varying standards regarding the idea that punishment for children should differ from punishment for adults.

Bentham also believed in **psychological hedonism**, the idea that people seek pleasure and avoid pain. Although later psychologists embraced this principle, none stated it more eloquently than Sigmund Freud (1930/1961a), who noted that "the purpose of life is simply the programme of the pleasure principle. This principle dominates the operation of the mental apparatus from the start" (p. 76).

Can we quantify pleasure and pain? Can a theoretical and practical balance of pleasure and pain guide our justice system? Bentham and his followers debated such issues. His critics were not optimistic; not until the twentieth century would social psychologists engage in systematic assessment of happiness (Veehoven, 2011). Such debates are of less historical significance than Bentham's attack on intuitionism. Following Bentham, one could conceive that closer scrutiny could benefit social systems and lead to more objective standards of punishment. With his work, a psychological analysis of human motivation is also elevated in importance.

Mary Wollstonecraft

The empirical vision of a world that can be improved through proper education served as a challenge and inspiration to **Mary Wollstonecraft (1759–1797)**, the most visible early pioneer in the battle for the emancipation of women. Though Wollstonecraft did not identify with any single philosophical system, she grasped the value of empiricism. Indeed, she stands at the headwaters of a complex late twentieth- and early twenty-first-century movement known as Feminist Empiricism (Duran, 2006). If the mind at birth is as "white paper," as Locke contended, then the role of education in shaping character is paramount. Further, the white paper hypothesis suggested that perceived differences between men and women may be attributed to differences in educational opportunities.

Gender differences had long been explained in terms of **essentialism**. The term *essence* refers to "the intrinsic nature or character of something; that which makes it what it is" (Brown, 1993, p. 852). As noted by Braaten and Viney (2000), "An essentialist philosophy applied to gender emphasizes natural differences neatly boxed and separated by clear boundaries" (p. 576). Women were regarded as essentially more emotional than men, deficient in judgment and in scientific and mathematical skills, and unconcerned about politics. The essentialist philosophy was used to argue against educational opportunities for women and against the right of women to vote or own property. Empirical philosophy could provide a plausible alternative for the understanding of gender differences. Perhaps the differences could be explained in terms of the scarce opportunities for women. Wollstonecraft, in her classic book, *A Vindication of the Rights of Woman*, seized on this alternative explanation and challenged the assumed hierarchy of men and women (Taylor, 2003). Botting (2006) argues that despite the difficulties Wollstonecraft faced in her lifetime, she contributed to twenty-first-century views of a more egalitarian family.

Mary Wollstonecraft was the second of the seven children of Edward John Wollstonecraft and Elizabeth Dixon. Edward, a weaver, inherited a large sum of money from his father, but squandered it on gambling, alcohol, and inept business ventures. Some of Mary Wollstonecraft's earliest memories, in the words of Jacobs (2001), were of "her parents as unequal warriors, her mother weak and pretty, her father a sentimental tyrant who fawned over his family one moment, then beat them the next because he was drunk

or out of sorts" (p. 18). She resented her father's tyranny and her mother's martyrdom. They displayed favoritism toward her oldest brother and made him sole heir to their estate (he had already inherited money from his grandfather). Under English law, women had no property rights and only limited educational opportunities. Mary Wollstonecraft sensed her intellectual superiority to her older brother and was offended that her brothers enjoyed a classic education while she and her sisters toiled on cooking and sewing.

Despite social barriers, Wollstonecraft acquired an informal education through extensive reading and friendship with progressive thinkers. Fighting career limitations, she served as a teacher before beginning her writing career. Regrettably, her new

Mary Wollstonecraft

143

career provided insufficient funds to cover debts and to provide for her younger sisters. Writing, however, allowed her to unleash her rage over the presumptions, ignorance, and injustices of her day.

A Vindication of the Rights of Woman was written in only six weeks. According to one biographer, "It is ill arranged and full of repetitions, yet its directness, its sincerity and the terse militant strength of some passages make it one of the creative books of its age" (Brailsford, 1963). In her introduction, Wollstonecraft (1792/1929) points to her "wish to persuade women to endeavor to acquire strength, both of mind and body, and to convince them that the soft phrases [of the day such as], susceptibility of heart, delicacy of sentiment, and refinement of taste, are almost synonymous with epithets of weakness, and that those beings who are only the objects of pity . . . will soon become objects of contempt" (p. 5). Her book condemned those who keep women in a state of ignorance, stupid acquiescence, and "childhood" as a means of preserving their innocence. According to Wollstonecraft, "Ignorance is a frail base for virtue!" (p. 69). She digs into the depths of feminine experience as she warns that passive women who serve as toys to please their husbands will find little fulfillment after their charms evaporate and the honeymoon ends. Wollstonecraft detested that women had been trained to be deceitful, coquettish, delicate, and docile pets.

Her book pleads for fierce honesty on the part of men and women to confront ruinous social conventions. Such practices rob women of genuine personhood and rob men of rich and meaningful companionship. She insisted that social conventions must change to reach a just and equitable system. Despite technical faults, insights roll off every page of this hastily written but original book. In the words of Jacobs (2001), it is the first "feminist manifesto in the history of human rights" (p. 99). Wollstonecraft demanded educational equality in coeducational systems (Laird, 2008) and economic independence for women through wider employment opportuni-

ties. She observed that beyond domestic duties, women of her day did little in society except loiter in a graceful fashion. The antidote was to train women in fields such as medicine, business, government, and politics, and she also promoted exercise and sports for women (Park, 2010). She believed that social change would benefit everyone. She believed that good men would find a more satisfying relationship with a competent woman than with an obedient one.

Wollstonecraft spoke with power and passion about parent–child relations. She observed that "meek wives are, in general, foolish mothers; wanting their children to love them best, and take their part, in secret, against the father, who is held up as a scarecrow" (1792/1929, p. 166). She notes that, in such cases, the wife seldom disciplined the child, leaving it to the husband. She lamented the fact that, in many cases, parental affection "is but a pretext to tyrannize." Children are rational creatures in their own right and must not be subjected to selfish and demanding authority, but too often this is the case, especially for girls. She argued that the subjection of a person to "the mere will of another . . . is a most cruel and undue stretch of power, and perhaps as injurious to morality as those religious systems which do not allow right and wrong to have any existence, but in the Divine will" (p. 168). Wollstonecraft believed that love should be merited, not coerced.

Both *A Vindication of the Rights of Woman* and its author faced severe criticism. Wollstonecraft was disparaged for being overly sentimental, impulsive, and indelicate in her love affairs (Stephen, 1993). Most criticisms were *ad hominem* attacks on the drama of her personal life rather than on the substance of her work. She was, for a time, the common-law wife of Gilbert Imlay, an American traveler and merchant. Her first child, Fanny, resulted from this relationship. When Imlay deserted her, Wollstonecraft attempted suicide. After recovering from her despondency over Imlay, she married the philosopher William Godwin. Their short-lived but happy relationship resulted in the birth of a daughter,

144

also named Mary. Tragically, medical attempts to recover the undescended placenta caused an infection that ended Mary Wollstonecraft's life at the age of thirty-eight. Her first daughter, Fanny, committed suicide. Her second daughter, Mary Wollstonecraft Godwin (1797–1851), married the Romantic poet Percy Bysshe Shelley in 1814 (Seymore, 2001). As Mary Shelley, she referenced her mother's work in a celebrated Gothic novel, *Frankenstein; or, The Modern Prometheus*, first published anonymously in 1818.

James Mill

James Mill (1773–1836), a close disciple, trusted colleague, and friend of Jeremy Bentham, played a key role in popularizing and expanding Hartley's associationism and Bentham's utilitarianism. Mill was born the eldest son of James Mill, a cobbler, and Isabel Fenton on April 6, 1773. Though Mill studied for the ministry and was licensed to preach, he had no enthusiasm or success in this work. In 1802, Mill moved to London, where he embarked on a career as an editor and a writer. In 1805, he married Harriet Burrow. The first of their nine children, John Stuart Mill, was born in 1806.

James Mill's meager income came from his writing. His best-known literary work was *History of India* (1818). Because of his extensive knowledge of India, Mill received an appointment as an official in India House. He educated his own children in a stern, businesslike atmosphere with an emphasis on cognitive learning and a repression of emotion. Though he was a disciple who amplified the ideas of others, his work heightened visibility of the new philosophy's emphasis on education. Mill died on June 23, 1836.

James Mill's best-known psychological work, *Analysis of the Phenomena of the Human Mind* (1829), presents an uncompromising mechanistic approach to mental processes. Beliefs, memories, and expectancies—even purposes and aesthetic preferences—are grounded in association or conditioning. Character and cognitive ability are

the products of proper educational procedures, and Mill rigorously educated his son in accordance with these beliefs. In his autobiography, John Stuart Mill (1873/1969) credited his father for adding "greater length and depth" to David Hartley's associationism (p. 43). Inspired by the implications of associationism, Mill became a staunch advocate for education for the masses.

John Stuart Mill

According to Robinson (1982), **John Stuart Mill (1806–1873)** "contributed directly and indirectly to any number of turns psychology would take toward the end of the nineteenth century. His philosophy of science put the older empiricism of Bacon and Locke on modern footing and lent plausibility to the claim that an *experimental* science of mind was within reach" (p. 75). Mill was one of the great liberal thinkers of the nineteenth century. He argued for freedom of expression, representative government, and the importance of the individual in politics (Busse et al., 2015) and economics (Schabas, 2015). Mill defied popular opinion in his support of the emancipation of women. His interests ranged from epistemology and logic to history, political theory, literature, and psychology. He ranks as one of the great British philosophers.

John Stuart Mill was born on May 20, 1806. The story of young Mill's early life is well known. He was a precocious child, who, in the words of Bertrand Russell (1959), "had his father's educational doctrines ruthlessly inflicted on him. 'I never was a boy,' he complained later in life" (p. 266). Mill, educated by his father, started Greek at age three. At age eight, he was learning Latin and reading the Greek classics. The pace of learning was strained, even for a child with such gifts. "I was continually incurring his displeasure by my inability to solve difficult problems for which he did not see that I had not the necessary previous knowledge" (Mill, 1873/1969, p. 9). Harsh by twentieth-century standards, young Mill benefited from individual instruction and an erudite teacher. He viewed his education as a mixture of praise and criticism. Mill lamented the absence of holidays, the neglect of manual arts and skills, and the failure to recognize emotions. At the same time, he appreciated his father's interest, diligence, and knowledge.

The Examiner's Office of India House hired Mill, where he labored, once again, under his father's supervision. He wrote for the press, commenting that "the writings by which one can live, are not the writings which themselves live" (1873/1969, p. 51). He was nevertheless able to earn a living and to find ample time for philosophy. Together with his father, Mill was a member of a small fraternity of influential thinkers known as "Benthamites," who supported utilitarian ideas promoted by Jeremy Bentham. Later, John Stuart Mill coined the term *utilitarian* to describe nineteenth-century liberal thought representing Hartleian metaphysics, complete freedom of discussion, representative government, universal education, full employment, and voluntary birth control. In supporting his ideals, John Stuart Mill was once jailed overnight for distributing birth control information.

In the autumn of 1826, Mill suffered a severe depression, declaring later that "the whole foundation on which my life was constructed fell down . . . for some months the cloud seemed to grow thicker and thicker" (1873/1969, p. 81). He lamented having no one to talk with, no one who would understand, least of all his father. In the midst of depression, he realized that the cultivation of feeling had been lacking in his education. He then explored his feelings by turning to art, poetry, and music, and he experienced an epiphany. He was reading a passage from Marmontel's *Memoirs* describing his father's death and the subsequent inspiration of a son to replace the father. Mill said, "A vivid conception of the scene and its feelings came over me, and I was moved to tears. From this moment my burden grew lighter" (1873/1969, p. 85).

In 1830, Mill met **Harriet Taylor (1807–1858)**, a woman unhappily married but unable to divorce due to the strict laws of the day. Their friendship deepened over a twenty-year period. Taylor's first husband died in 1849 and she married Mill two years later. In his autobiography, Mill claimed his companionship with Taylor enhanced his intellectual and emotional development. She served as a sounding board and often as a foil for Mill's intellectual work. Speaking in glowing terms, he regarded her as a genius, "a woman of deep and strong feeling, of penetrating and intuitive intelligence, and of an eminently meditative and poetic nature" (Mill, 1873/1969, pp. 111–112). Tragically, Harriet Taylor lived a mere seven years after her marriage to Mill. Devastated but still productive, Mill lived another fifteen years in a house he built to overlook Harriet Taylor's grave. One of Taylor's children by her first husband attended to Mill in his final years. Mill died on May 8, 1873.

Robinson (1982) argued that "Mill anticipated and encouraged the sort of research ordinarily identified as 'behavioristic' . . . he avoided the temptation to rush psychology into scientific status by biologizing it" (p. 75). Instead, the central organizing themes in Mill's conception of psychology are association and pleasure. Mill accepted his father's and Hartley's principles of association, joining the belief that scientific methods can demonstrate elementary laws of the mind. But Mill raised doubts about whether the mechanical approach to association could do justice to the more complex mental phenomena. He observed that "the phenomena of mind are sometimes analogous to mechanical, but sometimes also to chemical laws" (1843/1974, p. 853). By this, he conveyed the idea that elements are not necessarily identifiable in complex ideas. He noted, for example, that when prismatic colors are properly mixed we may see white rather than each of the individual colors. According to Mill, this is an example of "mental chemistry: in which it is proper to say that the simple ideas generate, rather than that they compose, the complex ones" (p. 854). Mill warned, however, that psychological chemistry does not relieve us of the responsibility of identifying the basic properties of complex ideas any more than the chemist is

146

relieved of the responsibility of identifying the elements of a chemical compound.

Mill's optimism about the possibility of a scientific psychology was illustrated in his belief that natural laws affect us, even those about which we have little or no knowledge. He compared human nature with meteorology. The laws of heat, pressure, and electricity govern the weather. When we understand these laws, we can better understand the weather. By the same rule, biological and sociological laws govern human nature. According to Mill, it is no disparagement against certain sciences such as meteorology or a science of human nature that predictions must be couched in terms of probabilities or approximations.

Mill raised a question about the reality of a scientific psychology. He answered, "All states of mind are immediately caused either by other states of mind, or by states of body" (1843/1974, p. 849). There is not only a science of psychology that studies successive states of mind or bodily influences on mind, but there is also a science of character formation, which Mill called *ethology*. Ethology, like psychology, can be studied by observational and experimental methods. Mill embraced the concept of an applied psychology (ethology) and a basic psychology.

As noted, Victorian attitudes toward women deeply concerned Mill. His book *The Subjection of Women* (1869/1988) called for radical change and generated predictable hostility from men who wished to conserve the status quo. He argued that "the principle which regulates the existing social relations between the two sexes—the legal subordination of one sex to the other—is wrong in itself, and now one of the chief hindrances to human improvement; and that it ought to be replaced by a principle of perfect equality, admitting no power or privilege on the one side, nor disability on the other" (p. 1). Mill believed that male chauvinism parades in the sciences as natural law or in religion as true theology based on divine ordinance. He had faith, however, that sexism would yield "before a sound psychology, laying bare the real root of much that is bowed down to as the intention of Nature and the ordinance of God" (p. 2).

The origin of Mill's feminist perspective is grounded in his empiricism and utilitarianism (Soble, 2009). In Mill's day, inequality was justified by citing presumed deficiencies in the nature of women. As a staunch empiricist, Mill argued that we cannot claim adequate knowledge about the nature of women so long as they live in political and social circumstances that undermine their abilities. Speculating on the origin of Mill's feminism, Okin (1988) pointed out that "it is certain that, from the time they met, Harriet Taylor was a major influence on the development of Mill's feminism" (p. ix). Mill also credited Taylor for sharpening his sensitivities to the practical, day-to-day consequences of sexism.

Mill's philosophical work and his interest in sexism are vital for a science of human nature. His views on the subjection of women suggest the possibility of a social psychology that could enlighten us on the benefits of gender equality. His philosophical work, economic writings (see Schabas, 2015), and social interests are intellectual forerunners of basic and applied psychology. Like many philosophers included in this chapter, Mill was interested in a new science of human nature that would enable us to "understand in order to improve human behavior" (Leary, 1980, p. 292).

Mill influenced a Scottish colleague named **Alexander Bain (1818–1903)** who founded the journal *Mind* in 1876. This journal, initially edited by George Croom Robertson (1842–1892), is recognized as the first psychological journal (King, 2000). *Mind* served as an important outlet for early scholars in psychology and furthered the professionalization of psychology in Great Britain (Neary, 2001) but shifted focus toward a more philosophical journal. Bain not only founded the first psychological journal, but also wrote early critical psychology texts and promoted a psychology of physiology and behavior (Malone, 2014; Wade, 2012a). His books *The Senses and the Intellect* (1855) and *The Emotions and the Will* (1859) influenced the early generation of psychologists.

147

Contributions of Empiricism

Under Bacon, empiricism started in part as a reaction to Montaigne's skepticism. Empirical philosophy's emphasis on personal experience and observation influenced all sciences including psychology. A summary of the influences of empiricism includes, at a minimum, the following:

1. Empiricism provided a new methodology (in Bacon's words, *Novum Organum*) that corrected years of intellectual stagnation and challenged scholasticism, authority, revelation, and tradition.
2. With empiricism came a new emphasis on learning and universal education. If the mind at birth is as "white paper" as Locke contended, then mental content depends on environment and social structures friendly to education.
3. John Locke's philosophy helped open the door to the study of children and their learning processes.
4. The work of empiricists such as Berkeley and Condillac emphasized the scientific study of the senses. If knowledge is acquired through the senses, we must investigate these "windows to the mind."
5. Early empiricists were important pioneers in the study of motivation and emotion. David Hartley provided a classification of pleasures, and Jeremy Bentham was a critical figure in the study of punishment. David Hume furthered the study of the emotions.
6. John Stuart Mill and Harriet Taylor, following the tradition of Mary Wollstonecraft, challenged stereotypes about the abilities of women. Empiricism established an intellectual context that encouraged the liberation of women.
7. Hume's work on causality might properly be regarded as the most creative work on that subject since Aristotle.

Many intellectual components necessary for psychology to develop as a formal science were in place following the work of early empiricists and utilitarians.

Review Questions

1. Briefly describe Bacon's four Idols. What are some of the Idols in our day?
2. What is the Baconian approach to scientific methodology?
3. Distinguish between Locke's primary qualities and secondary qualities. Give examples of each.
4. Discuss some of the implications of Locke's contention that there is nothing in the intellect that was not previously in the senses.
5. What was Berkeley's objection to primary qualities? Briefly argue in defense of Berkeley's position.
6. Outline Hume's general approach to the problem of causality.
7. Show how empiricism evolved from a method (epistemology) under Bacon's treatment to a position on the nature of being (ontology) in the work of Berkeley and Hume.
8. Outline contributions to empiricism made by continental philosophers Condillac and Helvétius.
9. Briefly discuss the nature of the legal problems that contributed to the development of utilitarianism. What were the implications of utilitarianism for a science of human nature?
10. Review Hartley's seven varieties of pleasure.
11. Briefly outline Hartley's contributions to associationism.
12. Distinguish between the concepts of mental mechanics (James Mill) and mental chemistry (John Stuart Mill).
13. In what ways did John Stuart Mill contribute to the development of applied psychology?
14. Describe the early feminist thought of John Stuart Mill.
15. Outline some of the ways empiricism contributed to an intellectual climate friendly to the development of psychology as a discipline.

Glossary

associationism Systematic emphasis on the idea that human knowledge is not innate but grows inevitably out of the gradual buildup of associations from sensory data.

Bacon, Francis (1561–1626) Early modern philosopher of science who called for a close examination of the problem of knowledge and increased sensitivity to sources of error. A powerful advocate of a critical empirical-inductive method.

Bain, Alexander (1818–1903) Founded *Mind*, the first journal devoted extensively to psychological topics. Also the author of some of the first psychological texts.

Bentham, Jeremy (1748–1832) Founder of utilitarianism. Argued against intuitive approaches to jurisprudence that resulted in punishments that do not fit the crime and argued for a rational system of punishments and rewards and the need to maximize pleasure for the greatest possible number of people.

Berkeley, George (1685–1753) British philosopher who argued that the real world is not the world of matter but the world of experience. His dictum *esse est percipi* (to be is to be perceived) marks him as one of the most radical of the early empiricists. Advanced an early empirical approach to depth perception, attempting to demonstrate that we learn to see in depth.

Condillac, Étienne Bonnot de (1715–1780) French radical empiricist who attempted to show specifically how all knowledge could derive from associations that start with simple sensations.

empiricism A philosophical position that emphasizes the importance of experience, observation, and learning in the acquisition of knowledge.

essentialism Belief in the possibility of discerning the fundamental character or intrinsic nature of something.

hardening An early concept that emphasized the beneficial role of self-imposed hardships (e.g., sleeping on an uncomfortable bed, exposure to cold weather) as means of preparing for subsequent tasks. Hardening is not quite the same as conditioning in that it involved practices that were more likely to be damaging.

Hartley, David (1705–1757) Founder of modern associationism and one of the first to establish a classification system of pleasures and pains.

Helvétius, Claude-Adrien (1715–1771) French materialist who argued that human actions can be explained on the basis of rewards and punishments. His views were considered radical in his day and he was forced to recant his position.

Hume, David (1711–1776) British empiricist who advanced the view that causality is not a property of objects, and therefore, there are no necessary connections. Causality is thus reduced to a psychological problem and is based on consistent conjunction and our ways of making sense of the successive events in the world.

Idols A term employed by Francis Bacon referring to "phantoms of the mind." Idols are sources of error, such as excessive reliance on authority, that blind us in our quest for truth.

Idols of the Cave Local prejudices or strongly preferred hypotheses or theories that interfere with objective responses to data.

Idols of the Marketplace The temptation to take words too seriously so that naming is confused with explaining. To guard against the Idols of the Marketplace, one must constantly reexamine definitions and understand the deceptive dimensions of language.

Idols of the Theatre Errors of thought based on the easy acceptance of authority or the naïve acceptance of a popular paradigm.

Idols of the Tribe Errors of thought resulting from inherent human limitations such as sensory distortions and the tendency to overgeneralize.

Locke, John (1632–1704) One of the greatest philosophers of English speech who insisted that the mind at birth is like a blank slate devoid of characters or ideas. His emphasis on the centrality of experience and learning elevated the importance of universal education.

Mill, James (1773–1836) British philosopher who advanced an uncompromising mechanistic approach to association. Argued strongly for the education of the masses.

Mill, John Stuart (1806–1873) One of the great philosophers of English speech who envisioned a science of human nature based on probabilistic notions. Also one of the first to deplore the subjugation of women.

primary qualities Qualities such as figure, extension, and solidity that are presumed to inhere in objects.

psychological hedonism Belief that human beings seek in all things to gain pleasure and avoid pain.

secondary qualities Powers of objects that contribute to specific sensations such as colors, tastes, and sounds.

solipsism A subjective philosophical position that makes the claim that the only possible knowledge is self-knowledge.

Taylor, Harriet (1807–1858) Wife of John Stuart Mill. Collaborated with Mill and likely influenced his thought on feminism.

utilitarianism A philosophy advanced by Jeremy Bentham emphasizing the idea that the moral basis of action should be the greatest good for the greatest number.

Voltaire, François-Marie Arouet de (1694–1778) French philosopher who advanced the cause of new philosophies based on observation and experiment. His sharp attacks on untestable theories and theological dogma continually placed him at risk.

Wollstonecraft, Mary (1759–1797) The most visible early pioneer in the battle for the rights of women. Author of *A Vindication of the Rights of Woman*.

7 Rationalism

A desire which springs from reason can never be in excess.

—Benedict Spinoza
(in Gutmann, 1949, p. 233)

As discussed in Chapter 6, seventeenth-century philosophy confronted the task of combating skepticism and restoring faith in human knowledge. Empirical philosophers such as Bacon and Locke argued that we can attain knowledge through experience and the association of sensory data. Rational philosophy, the subject of this chapter, turns to axiomatic first principles and reason as guides to knowledge. The term **rationalism** is derived from the Latin *ratio*, which means to reason or to think. Major differences separate rationalism and empiricism. First, rational philosophy emphasizes a priori knowledge, whereas empiricism claims that all knowledge is derived from experience. We'll discuss this in a moment. Second, rationalists regard the mind as active in the sense of its capacity to select, organize, and discriminate, whereas empiricists argue for a more passive mind dependent on the laws of association and conditioning. Finally, deductive reasoning is emphasized in rationalism, whereas inductive reasoning is emphasized in empiricism. Let's take a look at these contrasting perspectives.

Emphasis on A Priori Knowledge

According to rationalism, certain essential truths are apprehended in an a priori manner, independent of experience. For example, statements such as *All bachelors are unmarried* or *A line cannot be perpendicular to itself* are grasped as necessarily true once we understand the terms. Granted, we have had experience with language and with specific terms such as *bachelor* and *unmarried* or *line* and *perpendicular*, but according to rationalism, the self-evident nature of the proposition is grasped a priori and such a priori knowledge forms the foundation of knowledge (Hatfield, 2009). In the first example about bachelors, we do not need to question all of the bachelors about their marital status; we understand that the predicate completely unpacks the subject. In a similar manner, we may grasp more complex relationships. Thus, if A is larger than B and B is larger than C, we know also that A is larger than C. Rationalists also emphasize certain innate capacities and preferences such as the capacity to see in depth or the preference for sweet rather than bitter tastes.

Theory of the Active Mind

According to empiricism, our senses bring information to the mind. Knowledge about the world is built through associations based on external influences such as contiguity, similarity, contrast, and reinforcement. Rationalists would not disagree, but they also argue that the mind is more than a passive repository of sensory information. Instead, the mind organizes, selects, rejects, discriminates, and acts on sensory data. An **active mind** is tied to rationalism's emphasis on a priori truths. Such truths would hold little significance if they did not translate into action.

Deduction versus Induction

Reason and experience play roles in both rationalism and empiricism. Nevertheless, rationalism stresses deductive reason, whereas empiricism is more concerned with the rules of induction. In a **deductive argument**, the premises are claimed to provide definitive grounds for the conclusion. If a deductive argument is valid, then it is impossible for the premises to be true while the conclusion is false. Consider the following simple syllogism. All humans are mortal, Socrates was a human, and therefore Socrates was mortal. If the two premises are true, then the conclusion follows with certainty. An **inductive argument**, by contrast, relies on probability rather than certainty. If an inductive argument is strong, then the conclusion is shown to be probable, given the premises. It is characteristic of induction to reason from samples to populations. In induction, conclusions use the language of probability. Did the differences between two groups occur by chance, or is it more probable that the predictor variable caused the differences? In contrast, conclusions can be offered as "proved,"

in a strict sense, in deductive reasoning as in mathematics.

Rationalism and empiricism result in contrasting views of human beings and in different philosophies of science. This chapter will examine the leading rationalists of the seventeenth, eighteenth, and nineteenth centuries. We'll also take a look at the implications of rational philosophy for psychology.

René Descartes

Born on March 31, 1596, **René Descartes (1596–1650)** was the fourth child of Joachim Descartes and Jeanne Brochard. Tragically, his mother died fourteen months later while giving birth to her fifth child. We know little about Descartes's early years, but his childhood was marked by continued illness. Because of his frail condition, he was pampered and his formal education delayed. Joachim Descartes, a practicing lawyer and judge, recognized an unusual curiosity and intellect in his son. In 1604, when Descartes was eight years old, his father enrolled him in a Jesuit School at La Flèche, north of Touraine. Still in frail health, he was excused from morning activities and allowed to sleep in, giving rise to a lifelong habit of sleeping ten hours a day (Rodis-Lewis, 1999), possibly due to a chronic sleep disorder (Damjanociv et al., 2015). Descartes was a brilliant student with unusual skills in mathematics. He discovered his deepest satisfaction in this area because it offered greater certainty than other subjects.

The period from 1612 to 1628 held no hint that Descartes would one day secure fame in philosophy. In 1616, he earned a law degree from the University of Poiters, but the legal profession did not captivate him. Filled with self-doubt, he turned from academic life to the "book of the world" and to careful introspection. During this period, he experimented with military life, volunteering for duty in Holland under the Prince of Orange. Next, he served in the Bavarian Army and, still later, in the Imperial Army of Hungary.

152

René Descartes

Descartes traveled throughout Western Europe, all the while engrossed with the problems of human knowledge. As noted by Damjanovic et al. (2015), Descartes learned "that he preferred wielding thoughts over swords" (p. 296). By the late 1620s, Descartes's proficiency in mathematics gained attention. A renowned cardinal named Pierre de Berulle encouraged Descartes to immerse himself in scholarly activity.

After moving from France to Holland, Descartes began work on his book *The World* (Gaukroger, 1997). Written from 1629 to 1633, this treatise was in essential agreement with Galileo's conclusions. Like Galileo and Copernicus, Descartes did not believe that the earth is immovable or that it rests at the center of the universe. In 1633, he learned the fate of Galileo at the hands of the Inquisition. The disturbing news ensnared Descartes between his loyalty to Catholic authority and his passion for truth. Vrooman (1970) believed it unlikely that Descartes would have suffered his "Italian

contemporary's fate, which was first strict confinement and later, while still under surveillance, weekly recitation of the seven penitential psalms for a period of three years" (p. 84). Descartes's letters reveal his intense anxieties in the aftermath of the Galileo affair as well as his identification with the ideas presented in Galileo's *Dialogue* (see Grayling, 2005, pp. 143–147). His worries might have been compounded through inappropriate comparisons with the work of Giulio Cesare Vanini (1585–1619) who had proposed a naturalistic philosophy in his book, *The Secrets of Nature*. Vanini had not hesitated to trample on sacred ground by denying the immortality of the soul and raising doubts about miracles. Vanini was burned at the stake in 1619.

The fates of Galileo, Vanini, and other scholars underscore the danger in challenging religious authority during the early seventeenth century. For Descartes, authority conquered reason and he decided against publishing *The World*. His decision was, in all likelihood, based on intense loyalty to the church rather than on a lack of courage. In a letter to his friend Marin Mersenne, Descartes declared that his argument for the movement of the earth was based on clear proofs. Nevertheless, he said, "I would not wish, for anything in the world, to maintain them against the authority of the church" (see Kenny, 1970, p. 26). Despite four years of work, Descartes made the fateful decision to suppress his treatise. Fortunately, it would not remain so. *The World* was finally published in 1664, fourteen years after his death. Shorto (2008) notes that "Reason vs. faith may be the chronic fever of modernity" (p. 79). It is a fever that has remained virulent into the twenty-first century.

In 1635, Descartes had a brief relationship with a Dutch servant that resulted in the birth of a daughter named Francine. Although he decided against marriage, Descartes became a dedicated father. Unfortunately, Francine suffered an illness at age five and, according to one account, died in Descartes's arms (Rodis-Lewis, 1999).

Crushed with grief, Descartes withdrew from intimate relationships to immerse himself in work. Between 1628 and 1649, he produced the major works that secured his place in history. During this prolific period, he wrote *Rules for the Direction of the Mind*, probably completed around 1628, but published posthumously in 1684; *Discourse on the Method of Rightly Conducting One's Reason and Seeking the Truth in the Sciences, and in Addition the Optics, the Meteorology and the Geometry, Which Are Essays in This Method*, first published anonymously in 1637; *Principles of Philosophy*, 1644; *Description of the Human Body*, published posthumously in 1664; *The Passions of the Soul*, 1649; and Descartes's most celebrated work, *Meditations on First Philosophy*, 1641 (see Cottingham et al., 1984–1985).

By the late 1640s, Queen Christina of Sweden (1626–1689) had developed an interest in Descartes's work. In 1649, she invited him to Stockholm to become her personal tutor. Descartes was filled with reservations about the northern climate, the voyage itself, and the demands of courtly life. As a Catholic, he was also apprehensive about living in a Protestant country. His greatest concern centered on whether his need for privacy and solitude would be compromised in the queen's court. Despite reservations, he accepted the invitation and landed in Stockholm in October 1649.

It proved a greater challenge than he had imagined. The queen insisted Descartes conduct her tutorials at 5 a.m. Although never a morning person, he agreed to her demand and awakened early to tutor her for almost five months, despite the difficulties brought by these changes in his sleep schedule (Damjanovic et al., 2015). The inconvenient schedule and a harsh Stockholm winter took their toll. In January, Descartes admitted in a letter, "I am not in my element here" (Rodis-Lewis, 1999, p. 188). Less than a month later, he contracted pneumonia. René Descartes died in the early hours of February 11, 1650.

In his work, Descartes managed to shape modern science and philosophy with an integrated system of thought. From his earliest years, he was interested in the problem of knowledge. He was troubled about the threat to science and philosophy posed by skeptics such as Charron and Montaigne. As noted by Popkin (1979), Descartes hoped to establish an "intellectual fortress capable of withstanding the assaults of the skeptics" (p. 173). In part, his "intellectual fortress" was built from the labors of his unusual mathematical gifts (unlike Bacon, he appreciated the unique role that mathematics plays in science). Descartes was also well versed in the discoveries of the empirical sciences of his day. In terms of both interest and intellect, he was well qualified to construct a philosophy that would influence the new sciences.

Descartes's Method

Descartes is regarded as a rationalist because he promoted reason as the means of attaining foundational scientific knowledge. His major works emphasize innate ideas, a priori truths, and a preference for deduction. In this philosophical context, his method is grounded in a rebellion against skepticism.

Descartes's search for an intellectual edifice that could withstand the assaults of skepticism began with the methods of skepticism itself. He agreed with Montaigne that it is possible, as an intellectual exercise, to doubt many things—the past, the world, one's own body, the existence of other people, and even the existence of God. Descartes's real goal was to push skepticism to its limit, to engage in a kind of hyperbolic doubt to see if he could discover something that was immune to doubt. In the course of his work, he found something he could not doubt—namely, the fact that he was doubting. But in order to doubt, one must think. In order to think, one must exist. On the basis of this reason, Descartes (1641/2010) arrived at his celebrated axiom, *cogito ergo sum* (I think, therefore I am).

Like Bacon, Descartes believed we should lay aside old prejudices and opinions. He was, however, quick to separate science and faith. As noted by Mahaffy (1969), "In the first he is a sweeping reformer; in the second a strict conservative"

(p. 24). Here we emphasize Descartes the reformer who, in his *Discourse on Method*, established procedural rules for the intellect and a "strong and unswerving resolution never to fail to observe them" (Cottingham et al., 1984–1985, p. 120). The four rules, also emphasized in his *Meditations*, are as follows:

1. Never accept anything as true unless it is so clear and distinct as to be immune from doubt.
2. Divide all difficulties into as many parts as possible.
3. Start with the easiest and best-known elements and proceed step by step to knowledge of the more complex.
4. Make complete enumerations and comprehensive reviews to ensure that nothing is left out.

Descartes declared that his method was modeled on mathematicians who alone provided "certain and evident reasonings" (Cottingham et al., 1984–1985, p. 120). He believed his method could be extended to a great range of problems and usher in a new era of discovery of certain knowledge. His inquiry led him to argue that categorical differences exist between mind and body (which he argued interact through the pineal gland), humans and animals, and God and the world. Questions about the nature of the interactions between qualitatively different substances plagued and inspired his contemporaries and continue to challenge scholars today.

Although Descartes's system betrays a preference for deduction starting from self-evident truths, this foundation reserves a role for experience in scientific procedure. To be sure, he was conservative in his views of experiments because he realized that an experiment is only a special form of observation that can be poorly conceived and thus result in misinformation. Clarke (1982, p. 18) pointed out that Descartes is quick to reject the results of experiments that defy reason. At the same time, Clarke insists that Descartes "commends the appropriateness of ordinary

experience as a foundation for physical science" (p. 23). Mahaffy (1969) calls attention to one of Descartes's letters to the philosopher Marin Mersenne where Descartes expresses his wish "that some patient person would write down an exact description of the actual state of the heavens, without hypotheses or conjecture, after the manner of Bacon. This would be the greatest help to the theorist" (p. 55; see also Kenny, 1970, p. 24). Shorto (2008) notes that Descartes was "foundational to *both* the rationalist and the empiricist traditions" (p. 78).

The Cartesian method includes a place for ordinary experience and simple day-to-day observation. Indeed, Descartes trusted ordinary experience more than experiments and believed that the foundation for science is grounded in simple observation of natural events followed by critical reflection. Descartes noted that at the beginning of an investigation "it is better to resort only to those [observations] which, presenting themselves spontaneously to our senses, cannot be unknown to us if we reflect even a little. The reason for this is that the more unusual observations are apt to mislead us" (Cottingham et al., 1984–1985, p. 143). Clarke called attention to Descartes's simple anatomical observations on beasts killed in butcher houses and to his claim that in unambiguous situations "reasoning is useless without experience" (Clarke, 1982, p. 205). The role of experience in Descartes's method provides material for reflection based on sensory information that is the source of scientific procedure. Sensory information alone cannot be trusted; it leads only to surface appearances (see Green, 1985). Descartes applied his methods to many topics; some argue that he was the first to systematically investigate consciousness (Frith & Rees, 2007).

Descartes did not deny that discoveries may result from chance observations or blind trial and error. However, such discoveries are not, in a formal sense, part of his scientific worldview. For Descartes, scientific knowledge presupposes a conceptual or theoretical framework. Clarke (1982) called attention to Descartes's dismay that "the telescope was discovered by experimental manipulation of lenses without a theory to explain the result: 'To the shame of our sciences, this discovery, which is so useful and admirable, was initially made only by experimenting and by chance'" (p. 37).

To summarize, Descartes's emphasis on deduction, mathematical proofs, and self-evident truths betrays a rationalist approach to the philosophy of science. Nevertheless, for Descartes, simple experiences play a key role in the initial stages of inquiry. If one wants to initiate geographic inquiry, Descartes would undoubtedly counsel that one should begin by making observations of coastlines, mountain ranges, and the courses of rivers. Just as a map of the heavens would be helpful to the science of astronomy, so would a well-constructed map benefit a science of geography. Descartes reserves a role for simple experience; what he opposes is premature, poorly conceived, or meaningless experiments that lack adequate conceptual bases. With his emphasis on the role of common experience, Descartes does not fit the role of Bacon's "rationalist spider," that spins webs out of its own substance.

Descartes provided conclusions that emphasized the role of the individual (Jansz, 2004), and it's no surprise that he influenced later philosophers who studied the problem of knowledge and the new sciences. His immediate successor, Benedict Spinoza, drew inspiration from Descartes's philosophy of science and views of mind and body, forging an important conceptual basis for a science of human nature.

Baruch Spinoza

Intense religious persecution prompted a mass exodus of Jews from Spain and Portugal during the late sixteenth century. One of the greatest philosophers of the seventeenth century came from a Jewish family who had fled the cruelty of the Inquisition to find a new home in Holland, known at the time as a haven of religious freedom. **Baruch Spinoza (1632–1677)** was born

in Amsterdam on November 24, 1632. He later changed his Jewish name, Baruch, to its Latin equivalent, Benedict.

The young Spinoza was an outstanding student, making him the subject of admiration for the orthodox Jewish community. In time, he became a source of consternation. An unabashed radical, Spinoza raised penetrating questions about fundamental beliefs and criticized ideas based on authority and tradition (Meymandi, 2010). In desperation, the rabbis offered Spinoza a sizable scholarship for his education, but added the condition that he abandon his unorthodox views and conceal his doubts. But Spinoza, as much as any figure we have encountered, was caught in the grip of an irresistible urge to take ideas seriously. The life of the mind could not be compromised. In a bold move, he refused the scholarship.

Brutal consequences followed Spinoza's decision, leading to aggressive public ridicule. On one

Baruch Spinoza

occasion, a knife-wielding fanatic attacked him. In 1656, he was excommunicated from the synagogue. In the wake of this censure, the Jewish community was prohibited from speaking with Spinoza or reading his works. Goldstein (2006) argues that the persecution of the anti-Semitic Inquisition and of Spinoza himself shaped his philosophical views.

Spinoza's uncompromising dedication to truth was tested repeatedly. He refused most offers of financial support because they held stipulations that compromised his intellectual integrity. As a consequence, he was forced to earn a meager living as a lens grinder. In his remaining free time, he worked on philosophy. By 1663, he had published his *Principles of the Philosophy of René Descartes* (see Curley, 1985, pp. 221–346). He also wrote two controversial works published after his death, *Treatise on the Emendation of the Intellect* (see pp. 3–45), and his best-known work, *Ethics* (see pp. 401–617). A central theme is the denial that an epistemology based on revelation has special status as a means of attaining truth. In contrast, rigorous rational inquiry held promise as a way of ascertaining truth and knowing God. *Ethics* employed methods of inquiry perceived as the most advanced in his day, and therefore it proceeded in step-by-step geometric proofs of the nature of God and existence. By the 1660s, Spinoza's fame had spread, and he corresponded with numerous intellectual figures including the philosopher Gottfried Wilhelm Leibniz. However, few of Spinoza's contemporaries appreciated his arguments, so it is little wonder his works were banned.

In 1672, he became enraged when a mob assassinated Jan De Witt (1625–1672), a politician Spinoza admired. Damasio (2003) described the execution: "Assailants clubbed and knifed [De Witt and his brother] as they dragged them on the way to the gallows, and by the time they arrived there was no need to hang them. They proceeded to undress the corpses, suspend them upside down, butcher-shop style, and quarter them. The fragments were sold as souvenirs, eaten raw, or eaten cooked, amid the most sick-

ening merriment" (pp. 20–21). Although the riot troubled Leibniz, Damasio (2003) called it "probably Spinoza's darkest hour" (p. 21). His landlord worried when the philosopher planned to march to the site of the execution to protest the mob's savagery. Realizing that his friend would be no match for the bloodthirsty mob, the landlord locked Spinoza in a room in their canal townhouse and prevented him from staging a protest. His friend no doubt saved Spinoza from certain death.

In 1673, Spinoza was offered a chair in philosophy at Heidelberg University. The offer was accompanied, as usual, with an expression of trust that Spinoza would refrain from controversial religious statements. In characteristic fashion, Spinoza refused. In 1673, a representative from the court of Louis XIV promised a pension if Spinoza would dedicate a new work to the king. As yet another testimony to his unflinching integrity, Spinoza declined.

In 1675, Spinoza completed his greatest work, *Ethics*. However, his efforts to publish resulted in such a storm of protest from the clergy that he abandoned the project. *Ethics* was published posthumously and was promptly banned. During his lifetime, he became accomplished at cutting, grinding, and polishing glass for the construction of microscopes and telescopes. Legend has it that Spinoza had to work with glass in order to earn a living, but Gullan-Whur (1998, p. 90) suggests that scientific interests motivated his work in optics. Tragically, his profession shortened his life as exposure to fine glass particles from grinding and polishing contributed to a lung disease and his death at the age of forty-four on February 21, 1677. During his life and for long thereafter, his name was anathema to orthodox Catholics, Protestants, and Jews. As we note in a later chapter, even more than two centuries afterward, young Max Wertheimer's parents refused to let him read Spinoza due to Spinoza's excommunication. Though he was not a resident of Spain, Spinoza's name was placed on the "wanted list" in the Spanish Inquisition. He was accused of atheism and of denying revelation. Strictly speaking, neither charge was true; Spinoza simply gave the world a new vision of God and revelation.

In Descartes's philosophy, we encounter a dualism of soul and body, at least where humans are concerned. Such a radical separation of soul and body leaves room for free will in humans, but animals may be viewed as automata. Such a split between humans and animals contributes to a polarization of the free will–determinism issue. There was still another split between the sacred realm that includes a transcendent God and the secular world. What is most evident in Spinoza is an unrelenting quest for unity, a quest that results in a denial of the legitimacy of distinctions between sacred and secular, mind and body, humans and animals, and free will and determinism. Let us begin with Spinoza's vision of the union of the sacred and the secular.

During his life, people with mental disorders were thought to be possessed by demons. Spinoza, however, denied the metaphysical basis of demonology. He argued that there is only one ultimate reality and that reality is God. There are not separate spiritual powers that control natural events such as the weather, earthquakes, or mental illness. Rather, God, the only spiritual power, is immanent in nature and inseparable from truth. What is true is of God, indeed *is* God. When we discover a natural truth, we are thereby discovering something about the infinite substance that is God. With Spinoza, it is not God *or* nature or God *in* nature; rather, God *is* nature. Spinoza believed that the common view that God is separate from nature was a product not of reason but of imagination. It was also imagination that projected the popular anthropomorphic God with human needs and a human form. Spinoza's view is essentially pantheistic; it argues that God is all things. Thus, any distinction between sacred and secular is false. The scientist or the rationalist can discover as much or more about God as the theologian.

Such radical ideas made Spinoza the subject of ridicule and contributed to his excommunication. Due to his denial of a God separate from the world, Delahunty (1985) noted, "To his

immediate successors, his 'hideous hypothesis' seemed a ruseful version of atheistic materialism, honeyed words coating poisoned messages" (p. 125). But Spinoza was neither an atheist nor a materialist, and within a century of his death, he was viewed as a "God-intoxicated man" (p. 125).

Spinoza also challenged Cartesian notions about separate substances for mind and body and their interaction in the pineal gland. How, he asked, can a nonphysical mind be causal with respect to a physical substance and how does causal interaction take place in the pineal gland? According to Spinoza, mind and body are not radically separate; rather, they are two aspects of the same fundamental reality. Thus, psychological and neurophysiological processes coexist in double-aspect monism, and the world of experience (the psychological world) and the world of behavior (the physiological world) are but two expressions of the same thing. Such a position provides a foundation for psychology as a scientific discipline. Mental processes are a part of the natural order—the human mind is a part of nature and is subject to nature's laws.

If the human mind is subject to nature's laws, there is no absolute or unconditioned free will. There is, however, a kind of freedom associated with knowledge of the laws of nature. For example, knowledge of the cause of a disease greatly enhances our freedom to deal with the disease. Spinoza also believed we are freer when not dominated by our passions. Spinoza's book, *Ethics*, deals with ways in which freedom has meaning within a deterministic context. We will encounter this approach later in the thought of Sigmund Freud who, like Spinoza, believed in the lawfulness of the mind, but also embraced the possibility of a hard-won but weak form of freedom that emerges when the ego is not dominated by irrational forces (see Viney & Parker, 2016).

Spinoza's psychological thought as set forth in his *Ethics* is rich in insight. For example, he claimed, "anything may be accidentally the cause of either hope or fear" (Gutmann, 1949, p. 163). He connected this proposition with the development of superstition. Spinoza contended that

158

the strength of an emotion is a function of the number of simultaneous causes (p. 259). In a discussion of the origin and nature of emotions, he noted that if we develop hatred for a thing once loved, we hate with greater intensity than had we never loved it in the first place. Why? It is because the greater hatred is fueled by sorrow over the loss of love (p. 156).

Spinoza's rationalism is evident in his use of the geometric method. His ideas were often set forth in terms of axioms, numbered propositions, and demonstrations. Like Descartes, he emphasized the capacity to grasp certain essential truths intuitively. Spinoza also insisted on careful examination of definitions and a procedure that begins with what is self-evident or grasped a priori. He was as suspicious of unexamined sense data as he was of authority or tradition. He argued for the role of an active mind in many ways, even including sensation (Viljanen, 2014). Relevant examples come from contemporary demonstrations that those who are highly competent in a given skill see things differently than those who are less competent. For example, expert baseball players may see the ball as larger or slower than those who are less skilled (see Witt et al., 2014; Witt & Sugovic, 2013). Spinoza romanticized rationalism, claiming that reason produces "just, faithful and honorable" people (Gutmann, 1949, p. 203). Also he declared, "a desire which springs from reason can never be in excess" (p. 233).

It can be argued that Spinoza contributed more to the philosophical and intellectual spadework necessary for modern psychology than any thinker we have encountered. His philosophy challenges the separate status of mental processes implied in earlier dualistic theories. Though reviled in his day, Spinoza inspired later scholars including many of the founders of experimental psychology (Bernard, 1972). Alexander and Selesnick (1966) suggest that Spinoza understood ideas such as repression, overcompensation, reaction formation, and the role of pleasure that materialized in later Freudian psychology. Spinoza's influence extended beyond psychology and philosophy, inspiring Albert Einstein to

assert, "I believe in Spinoza's God who reveals himself in the harmony of all being" (Brian, 1997, p. 127).

Gottfried Wilhelm Leibniz

A contemporary of John Locke and Sir Isaac Newton, **Gottfried Wilhelm Leibniz (1646– 1716)** was a genius who shaped European thought in diverse areas such as mathematics, law, history, politics, religion, philosophy, and psychology. Leibniz and Newton are remembered as independent inventors of the differential calculus. Leibniz is also remembered as one of the first to develop a calculating machine. His work can be characterized as a quest for the world's unity. Unlike Spinoza, his philosophy allows a stronger role for diversity within unity.

Leibniz's concern for unity extended to practical problems. For example, he sought to reconcile Protestants and Catholics and to unite medicine and science. He also envisioned a universal language. Leibniz saw the possibility of a united world ruled by reason, science, and an essentially Christian ethic. His practical quests for unity were, of course, frustrated. His metaphysical quest for unity, anchored as it was in theology, fared no better.

Leibniz was born in Leipzig, Germany, in 1646. His father, a professor of moral philosophy at the University of Leipzig, died when his son was six years old. When Leibniz was eight, he was allowed to explore his father's library. It opened a new world, bringing him into contact with his father's work and values. Leibniz was a precocious student with a broad appetite for studies in language, mathematics, history, religion, and philosophy. At age fifteen, he enrolled in the University of Leipzig, where he earned a doctorate of law in five years. However, university authorities were reluctant to award the doctoral degree to a man of only twenty years. Consequently, Leibniz immediately withdrew and enrolled at the University of Altdorf. Within months of his enrollment, he presented a dissertation and successfully defended it. His doctorate was awarded on February 22, 1667, when he was only twenty-one years of age (Fancher & Schmidt, 2003).

Leibniz refused university positions, believing he could accomplish more goals and live in comfort if he worked for ruling political authorities. Though courtly routine often compromised his intellectual interests, he enjoyed a productive career. He worked four years for the archbishop of Mainz, but most of his time was spent in Hanover where he served under a succession of three rulers. The lives of Leibniz and Spinoza were as dissimilar as the public perceptions of their work; these differences are captured in the title of Stewart's (2006) account of their lives, *The Courtier and the Heretic*.

Leibniz enjoyed countless honors in his lifetime. To name a few, he was elected to the Royal Society, the Paris Academy of Sciences, and the Accademia Fisico-Matematica in Rome. He was nominated president of the Paris Academy of Sciences, the Society of Sciences in Vienna, and the Berlin Society, and he was offered the position of custodian of the Vatican library (Aiton, 1985, p. 159). Leibniz died in 1716 at the age of seventy. Later, the town of Hanover erected a marble bust to Leibniz's memory to commemorate his forty years of work in their community.

Monadology

As we noted in the previous section, Spinoza's solution to the mind–brain problem avoided the difficulties of Cartesian interactionism but introduced new problems. In Spinoza's system, mind and brain come down to the same thing. Leibniz was critical of Cartesian interactionism, but neither could he accept the singular vision of Spinoza. Though both shared a belief in reason, Leibniz disagreed with Spinoza's contention that all things are part of one fundamental substance. Leibniz sought to give equal status to the claims of the mental and physical realms and at the same time preserve the world's unity—no small

task. He also rejected Spinoza's determinism and the idea that plurality is nothing but appearance.

Leibniz's approach to mind and brain must be understood in the context of his concept of the monad. Leibniz probably adopted the term **monad** (*monas*) from the philosophers Anne Conway and F. M. Von Helmont (see Merchant, 1979). Lady Anne Conway (1631–1679), an influential philosopher in her day, found middle ground between the extreme dualism of Descartes and the extreme monism of Spinoza and likely had a strong influence on Leibniz. The term *monad* refers to a principle of existence or an ultimate unit of being, each unit of which is distinct (Marshall, 2015). Now, how does the concept of monads relate to the mind–brain problem? According to Leibniz, mind is a unit of being, a principle of existence. The same is true of the body. Both are real, but they do not interact. How do these two principles exist together? This question leads to the concept of preestablished harmony.

Leibniz believed that the universe was created with a **preestablished harmony** of its individual parts. Leibniz chose the analogy of independent synchronized clocks to illustrate his idea of preestablished harmony. Imagine that mind and body are like two clocks set for the same time. Although synchronized, neither clock depends on the other to function. Both are independent while existing in parallel harmony. Following the analogy, both mind and body exist and are perfectly synchronized. The mental is truly separate, yet it corresponds perfectly with the physical. Our cry of pain parallels our searing physical burn, and the burn parallels the cry of pain. In his psychophysical parallelism, every individual monad brings the universe along with it.

Leibniz avoids Descartes's problems of interactionism by proposing a separate solution (Weik, 2010): monads in preestablished harmony never interact. His brand of psychophysical parallelism leaves us with real diversity or individuality within unity. But, we now encounter violence to causality. In Leibniz's system, no monad is causal with respect to any other monad. Monads do not interact in any way, and all monads are in harmonious accord by virtue of preestablished harmony. But how are we to account for preestablished harmony? Leibniz's answer is found in theology. The synchronicity of monads reflects a divine order. Somewhat like Newton's notion of a "clockwork universe," God is the great clockmaker, now responsible for establishing preestablished harmony.

Poma (2013, p. 3) notes that Leibniz coined the term *theodicy*. Broadly conceived, theodicy refers to the relationship of God to the world and often focuses on the problem of evil. If God is omnibenevolent (i.e., all-loving), omniscient, and omnipotent, then God wants the best of all possible worlds, knows what the best possible world is, and can create the best of all worlds. Therefore, the currently existing world, arranged in a preestablished harmony by a perfect God, *must be* the best of all worlds despite widespread suffering and evil. In his novel *Candide*, Voltaire (1759/1991) mocked Leibniz's optimism in the guise of Candide's tutor, the character Professor Pangloss. Throughout *Candide*, after each fresh disaster in an ongoing series of tragedies, with people suffering and dying around him, Pangloss remains convinced that all things are for the best and that this must be the best of all possible worlds. Additional difficulties with Liebniz's position are explored by Poma (2013).

It is testimony to Leibniz's influence that some early psychologists rejected preestablished harmony, but still embraced psychophysical parallelism. It offers a practical solution to the mind–brain problem that avoids the tangled difficulties of interactionism, yet enfranchises both mental and physical realms.

Aiton (1985) pointed out that Leibniz "distinguishes between perception, which consists in being conscious of something, and apperception, which consists in being aware of a distinct perception" (p. 283). On the other end of the scale, Leibniz believed there are **petites perceptions**, French for "small perceptions," of which we are not aware. But many small perceptions in concert form the basis of perception. We may not hear a

single drop of water at a waterfall, but thousands of drops in chorus form a mighty roar. The idea of *petites perceptions* suggests the importance of unconscious processes, absolute thresholds, and difference thresholds—all concepts that would serve important roles in the early development of psychology (Rand, 2004).

Leibniz quarreled with the Aristotelian and Lockean emphasis on the role of the senses in knowledge. To Locke's famous dictum "Nothing is in the intellect that was not previously in the senses," Leibniz quipped, "Nothing save the intellect itself." Leibniz's emphasis on the activity of the intellect was driven by his views of energy. All monads were viewed as being invested with energy. Accordingly, the mind could not be a passive receptacle; rather, it is active, and its nature is to be involved in cognitive activities. One cannot pour knowledge into the mind through the senses as one pours water into a bowl. This is not to argue that sensory activity is unimportant, but it is not *all*-important as suggested by Locke or the French materialists. The active thinking process itself is not the result of something poured in from outside; rather, it is an inherent part of the mental monad. In Leibniz's view, sensory input is not causal (he denied interactionism); instead, it is parallel with thinking processes. Leibniz would find no accident in the fact that sensory enrichment is correlated with certain mental advantages and that sensory deprivation is correlated with certain mental deficits. For him, sensory enrichment and sensory deprivation illustrate the harmony or the parallelism of the monads.

In an idea that has important implications for psychology, Leibniz argued that "nature never takes leaps" (see Aiton, 1985, p. 283); rather, natural processes are characterized by a law of continuity. This same principle later guided Sir Charles Lyell (1797–1875) in his classic *Principles of Geology* as he struggled with tensions between **uniformitarianism** (i.e., the concept that change is gradual and occurs over long periods of time) and special creation with its emphasis on abrupt change or radical discontinuity. In psychology, Leibniz's view emphasized lawful and gradual gradations from unconscious processes to conscious processes. It also underscored the importance of growth and development but emphasized the maintenance of identity in change. You are the same individual today as yesterday as last week and last year. There is continuity of identity within an evolution that emphasizes the importance of the past to the present and the present to the future. Needless to say, there was a de-emphasis on miracles in a system that emphasized preestablished harmony and continuity. At the same time, such a system provides a rich intellectual framework that preserves the uniqueness of psychological processes, yet brings them within the province of science. Such a view nourished the development of a science of psychology.

Indeed, **Christian von Wolff (1679–1754)**, who elaborated on the Leibnizian model, was one of the first to use the term *psychology* in a major publication where he discussed the measurement of mental and emotional experiences (Konstantin, 1960). In 1732, Wolff published a book titled *Empirical Psychology*, and in 1734 he complemented it with a publication titled *Rational Psychology*. According to Wolff, empirical psychology studies the facts associated with the powers of the soul. It includes events in the senses, feelings of pain and pleasure, and so forth (Klempe, 2011). Rational psychology, clearly superior to empirical psychology, according to Wolff, involves the use of reason in the metaphysical study of the soul. Through rational psychology, one might hope to discover principles and laws. Wolff accepted the Leibnizian concept of preestablished harmony. He also advanced an early faculty psychology that influenced subsequent thinkers such as Immanuel Kant and Franz Joseph Gall, as we discuss in Chapter 8.

Immanuel Kant

Based on criteria such as originality and lasting influence, **Immanuel Kant (1724–1804)**

takes his place among the great philosophers of all time. Though we include him here as a rationalist, he was a consolidating figure between the extremes of empiricism and rationalism. He rejected the radical empiricism of David Hume, recognizing that it leaves us with nothing but an incoherent parade of sensations. At the same time, in his *Critique of Pure Reason*, he accepts the idea that "all our knowledge begins with experience" (1781/1965, p. 41). Even so, he believed that sensory information is shaped or filtered by a priori considerations. Kant's major work is of an epistemological nature, but like Descartes, his contributions reach far beyond psychology.

The story of Kant's life is an uncomplicated one. He never married. On the rare occasions when he traveled, he seldom journeyed far from Königsberg, the East Prussian city where he was born on April 22, 1724. He attended the University of Königsberg where he lived in poverty as a student, often interrupting his studies

Immanuel Kant

to gain a meager income as a tutor. After his doctorate in 1755, Kant taught a variety of subjects as a private instructor. Only in later years did he secure a professorial position with a decent income.

Kant's early years were defined by rigorous routine, privation, and an absence of individual freedom. Religious instruction was extensive and aversive, dwelling on heaven and hell rather than the value of life. In a biographical sketch, Cassirer (1981), quoting from Kant, pointed out that "the sum of pleasure is 'less than nothing' and the goal of life is not 'happiness' but self sufficiency and independence of will" (pp. 15–16). If we may believe his student Johann Gottfried Herder, Kant as a teacher had overcome his somber youth. Herder described Kant as having "at his service, jest, witticism, and humorous fancy, and his lectures were at once instructive and most entertaining" (cited in Durant & Durant, 1967, p. 532). Perhaps reacting to the religious dogmatism of his past, Kant appeared to Herder as a tolerant objective thinker. "No cabal or sect, no prejudice or reverence for a name, had the slightest influence with him in opposition to the extension and promotion of truth. He encouraged and gently compelled his hearers to think for themselves; despotism was foreign to his nature" (p. 532).

After years as a private instructor, he was offered a professorship in 1770. The following decades witnessed an outpouring of work including *Critique of Pure Reason* (1781/1965); *Critique of Practical Reason* (1788/1956); *The Critique of Judgment* (1790/1952); and *Religion Within the Limits of Reason Alone* (1793/1960). This last work aroused the ire of Frederick the Great, who accused Kant of undercutting the authority of scripture. Not possessing the fiery spirit of Spinoza, Kant assured the king he would refrain from talking or writing about religion.

After living the whole of his life in Königsberg, Immanuel Kant struggled with dementia (Miranda et al., 2010) and then died on February 12, 1804. Cassirer (1981) illustrated the philosopher's fame: "His funeral turned into a great public ceremony, in which the whole city and the inhabitants of all quarters of it took part . . . Amid the tolling of every bell in Königsberg, young students came to Kant's house to take up his body, from whence the innumerable procession, accompanied by thousands, wound to the university cathedral" (pp. 414–415). An inscription on Kant's grave reads "The starry heavens above me, the moral law within me."

Sense Experience and Reason

The goal of Kant's epistemological work can be understood partly on the basis of a distinction between analytic a priori knowledge and synthetic a priori knowledge. **Analytic a priori** knowledge refers to formal truths in which a predicate completely unpacks a subject, for example, *All bachelors are unmarried.* Such formal statements play important roles in deductive logic, but taken alone can be trivial or tautological. A *tautology* is an expression that contains a redundancy or pleonasm—that is, a word and its synonym are placed in close conjunction. Examples include statements such as *She was a sophomore in her second year* or *It is a true fact.*

Kant hoped to establish **synthetic a priori** truths that are not trivial but informative. Descartes's statement *I think therefore I am* may be regarded as an example of a synthetic a priori truth in that it is informative. It is not tautological in the same sense as a statement such as *If A is larger than B, then B is smaller than A.* Kant believed that many basic propositions in mathematics are of a synthetic a priori nature and are genuinely informative about the world (Otte, 2009). An example is provided by a statement such as *A straight line is the shortest distance between two points.*

Kant believed knowledge begins with sensory experience. However, sensory experience by itself would not be intelligible apart from certain a priori considerations. For example, we grasp in an a priori way that one object succeeds another in time or that there are spatial differences between objects. Kant also believed there is an intuitive or a priori sense of causality so that the mind itself imposes an if–then judgment. In other words, there are ordering principles of the mind that are yoked with sense experience, and the two together—sense experience and ordering principles—contribute to knowledge and provide a foundation for science (Robinson, 2014) and for both the self and consciousness (Northoff, 2012). Kant referred to a priori ordering principles such as the intuition of time, space, and causality as **categories of understanding**. The ordering principles envisioned by Kant can be viewed as filters that compromise any kind of one-to-one direct access to the world (Worburton, 2011, pp. 110–114). Kant differentiated between the **noumenal** world and the **phenomenal** world. The noumenal refers to "a thing in itself" or the world as it is, independent of perception. The phenomenal world is the world as it appears to us in experience. According to Kant, the world we know as outside of ourselves is the phenomenal world (Masrour, 2013). He rejected the idea that we have direct access to the noumenal world.

In contrast with John Locke, Kant regarded the mind as an active agency rather than a passive receptacle. In Kant's view, the mind as an active agency transforms sensory materials into meaningful configurations, connections, and structures. For Kant, reason and experience alone are suspect as sources of knowledge; rather, knowledge results from the interaction of reason and experience.

Social Psychology

Kant kept a watchful eye on both the American and French Revolutions. In particular, the formation of an American federation of states fascinated him. It is well known, of course, that the American experiment succeeded over the protests of people who demanded sovereignty for individual states. The fear was that such diversity would be impossible within a unified nation and that a remote and insensitive federal government would undermine basic freedoms. America represented

a microcosm of what Kant envisioned for Europe and the world. If the American experiment could work, then perhaps the same could emerge on a larger scale (see his 1795 essay titled *To Perpetual Peace: A Philosophical Sketch* [in Humphrey, 1983, p. 341]). Kant's vision called for a world order that could intervene during a war between states but would nevertheless be constituted to permit sovereignty for states to pursue nonhostile activities. He envisioned plans for international conflict resolution that would not be attempted until the twentieth century.

Kant extended his categorical thought to people. His views of non-Europeans were typical of the negative views of his time and culture; more broadly, he contributed to the development of typical eighteenth-century social views of race (Larrimore, 2008). Kant looked with disdain on any nationalism that undermines humane values. Human beings should work for educational, historical, and humane perspectives that transcend local biases. He was optimistic that, through good education, people could enjoy the moral progress that comes from identifying themselves with humanity rather than with local tribes, states, or nations.

Kant was one of the first to advance a theory of moral development. He believed that human beings are caught in tensions between heteronomy and autonomy. **Heteronomy**, or government from the outside, is manifested by goodness based on authority, rules or threats, or rewards and punishments. The task of the individual is to grow into moral autonomy manifested in sensitivity to moral maxims or imperatives. **Autonomy** refers to self-government, will, and the ability to act in a moral manner, not just to please an authority or not just because such action is rewarding but because of an intrinsic moral requirement in a given situation (Häyry, 2005). Kant's theory of moral action is related to his belief in the possibility of individual freedom in spite of external causal forces (Slife, 2005). Kant also believed that moral actions are based on our regard of other human beings as ends rather than as means. To regard someone as a means carries the risk that we will use them for our own purposes, whether these be economic, sexual, or political. By contrast, when we view another human being as an end, we emphasize the person's intrinsic worth.

Kant is remembered as one of the great philosophers, and he is also important in the history of science. Along with Descartes and Laplace, he believed in the evolution of the solar system. Kant believed in geological and biological evolution, though he failed to pursue these topics. He made contributions to meteorology, geology, and geography. His most important legacy, however, is that he found a center between the poles of empiricism and pure reason. Kant's middle ground provided the opening for generations of psychologists and philosophers to build the intellectual foundation for contemporary philosophies of science.

Johann Friedrich Herbart

Imagine the challenge of succeeding Immanuel Kant. That daunting task fell to **Johann Friedrich Herbart (1776–1841)**, a mathematician, philosopher, and psychologist. Herbart's interests in psychology ranged from its applications to clinical and educational problems to the quantification of mental functions. He was also interested in the unconscious. Herbart was born in Oldenburg on May 4, 1776. He studied at the University of Jena and later earned his Ph.D. in philosophy at the University of Göttingen. The bulk of Herbart's academic career (1809–1832) was at the University of Königsberg where he became Kant's successor. His final appointment was at Göttingen where he died in 1841.

Herbart was a critical pioneer in educational psychology and mathematical psychology (Huemer & Landerer, 2010; English, 2013) as well as the psychology of music (Kim, 2014), and in Germany he is viewed as an originator of social psychology (Jahoda, 2006). His educational psychology is set forth in a book titled *The Science of Education* (1902/1977), first published in English

in 1902. Herbart outlined pedagogical techniques designed to facilitate learning and retention. He believed that good teachers must help students review familiar material and then relate new materials to older, more familiar material. He also advocated the importance of demonstrating practical applications whenever possible.

One goal of education, according to Herbart, involved building what he called the **apperceptive mass** (Jahoda, 2009). The term **apperception** typically referred to mental operations more complex than those involved in perception. According to Herbart, apperception sets humans apart from other animals. He regarded apperception as more than passive awareness or a mere set of complex associations. It implies an active capacity to assimilate ideas from one arena and apply them to another. It also involves the ability to apply lessons learned from old problem situations to new problems. Mental illness or a head injury might interfere with apperception because the individual may then be capable of facing only concrete problems. For Herbart, apperception implies a capacity to operate at higher levels of abstraction.

Herbart also saw moral development as the central goal of education. By this he meant that education should instill a capacity for effort, the ability to forgo present pleasure for future gain, the development of sensitivities to moral issues, the capability to see things from a variety of vantage points, and the evolution of goodwill. The latter involves the capacity for empathy and a willingness to abide by laws for the larger good.

Herbart's mathematical psychology attempted to account for the fusion of concepts. For Herbart, mathematical formulae played the same role in psychology as in Newton's view of the solar system (Boudewijnse et al., 1999). Although his mathematical approach was initially positive, criticism of his approach emerged after experimental methods entered psychology in the mid-1800s with the work of Fechner, Wundt, and others (Boudewijnse et al., 2001). Herbart's mathematical formulae hold little interest today, but the problems that occupied his thought influenced psychology's early development. For example, he believed that concepts or components of concepts lie beneath the surface of awareness or in the unconscious. He believed concepts strive to break into consciousness and that more or less permeable barriers separate the conscious and unconscious. In his work, we encounter concepts of suppression, repression, threshold, and unconscious processes. All of these were, of course, part of the stock-in-trade for later psychologists like Freud. Herbart did not have a clear grasp of the possibility of a truly experimental psychology that manipulates variables. However, his work invigorated the founding of psychology.

Thomas Reid and Commonsense Philosophy

Thomas Reid (1710–1796) bridged the extremes of empiricism and rationalism with a **commonsense philosophy**. The expression *common sense* has multiple meanings, and it is likely that most philosophers and scientists believe their systems appeal, in one way or another, to common sense. The expression sometimes refers to the unreflective or naïve opinions of ordinary people or to collective opinion. These meanings do not, however, resonate with how philosophers use the term. In philosophy, common sense often refers to an opposition to beliefs that are counterintuitive or that do violence to our experience of the world. Robinson (1982) used the term *necessity* to refer to Thomas Reid's concept of common sense. According to Robinson, "When Reid spoke of the principles of common sense he was referring neither to opinion nor [even] to judgment. Rather, he was proposing those very activities of mind and laws of conduct by which life becomes possible" (p. 48). For example, Reid argued for a number of propositions that he referred to as "first principles" that make life possible, including beliefs in an external world, in causation, and in the self as an active manipulator (see Lehrer, 1989, pp. 160–161). According to Reid and his followers, the radical

Thomas Reid

empiricism of Berkeley and Hume had left us with a world that was unnatural and that violates common sense at every turn.

Thomas Reid grew up in rural Scotland and graduated at age sixteen from Marischal College in Aberdeen. He then turned his attention to theological studies. For a number of years, Reid had a pastorate in New Machar, but in 1751 he accepted a position at King's College in Aberdeen. In 1758, he helped form the Aberdeen Philosophical Society, a group of scholars that met regularly over a period of fifteen years. In 1764, Reid succeeded Adam Smith (1723–1790), a prominent philosopher in his own right (Gonin, 2015), in the chair of moral philosophy at Glasgow. He remained at Glasgow until his death in 1796. Reid's best-known works include *An Inquiry into the Human Mind* (1764/1970), *Essays on the Intellectual Powers of Man* (1786), and *Essays on the Active Powers of Man* (1790).

According to Reid, an adequate empiricism would not arrive at the skeptical crisis that we find in Hume's work. Indeed, an adequate empiricism will discover important truths in experience that Hume failed to envision. What Reid discovered in experience, according to Lehrer (1989), "are innate principles of our constitution yielding conceptions and convictions of the operations of our own minds, of the minds of others, of the qualities of external objects, and of the laws of nature" (p. 8). Thus, according to Reid, there are innate principles of the mind leading to convictions that we find as a natural part of experience and common sense. In other words, there are natural necessities. Robinson (1982) concluded, "even skeptical Hume took for granted that he had sensations and this not out of choice or opinion but because of a natural *necessity*. He could not think otherwise" (p. 48).

Reid believed that a truly empirical philosophy, one that resonates to what is found in human experience, reveals natural necessities that are more complicated than mere sensations. For example, it is experience itself that contributes to belief in the external world. Reid (1764/1970, p. 24) asked why the smell of a rose is more vivid in the presence of the rose than it is in memory. He pointed out that the same question can be asked of any sensation. Why is the taste of an apple more vivid during the act of eating than in memory a few hours later? Reid (1764/1970) argued, "I could as easily doubt of my own existence, as of the existence of my sensations" (p. 24). He went on to say that sensation compels "our belief of the present existence of the thing, [and] memory a belief of its past existence" (p. 25). Thus, through experience itself and common sense, Reid attempted to restore faith in the external world (Wade, 2010b), a self with real continuity, and a belief in causality.

Reid's views elicited some interesting biases. For example, psychologist and historian E. G. Boring appeared surprised that such influential philosophy could emerge from a minister (Robinson, 1989b). Reid's influence was extensive in Europe and America. His admirer, Dugald Stewart (1753–1828), believed that Reid had restored the Baconian vision, clearing the way for an intelligible science of human nature. Stewart's influential book *Elements of the Philosophy of the Human Mind* (1792/1802) extended Reid's thought and applied it to psychological topics such as attention, memory, association, and imagination. Reid and Stewart believed that the mind can be divided into faculties or powers. We'll see in Chapter 8 that Franz Joseph Gall (1758–1828) developed this concept in an attempt to associate each faculty with a specific brain region.

Enfranchising Curiosity

In earlier chapters, we explored the issues of curiosity and forbidden knowledge. For centuries, curiosity about the natural world had been regarded as an intellectual vice, a mark of foolish pride, and an affront to God. Numerous scriptures were taken as warnings against those who probed the secrets and mysteries of the world. The Koran in Surah 5:101 says "do not put questions about things which if declared to you may trouble you." Paul warned in I Corinthians 1:20, "The wisdom of this world is foolishness with God." Such scriptures, taken in a literal and concrete fashion, could undermine the quest for new truths and new perspectives.

The empiricists and rationalists disagreed on many things, but they shared in a new interpretation of the role of human curiosity. To be sure, the climate of opinion had shifted. The public hungered for a fresh perspective on old questions. Empiricists and rationalists were eager to outline such an approach. Harrison (2001) pointed out that Francis Bacon linked curiosity to charity, softening attitudes regarding worldly wisdom. Bacon opened his defense of curiosity by agreeing with those who had spoken against it. Curiosity could indeed motivate investigations and produce knowledge that results in pride, conceit, and arrogance, but that is only half the story. God, after all, had made the world. Further, the benefits from studying the world could be used for charitable purposes to aid the poor, the sick, and the disadvantaged. Surely charity was among the most valued of religious virtues. Of course, some doubted the sincerity of Bacon's theological justification of curiosity. It seems probable that in his private thoughts, Bacon would have valued curiosity in its own right. But he did resort to theological justifications and these no doubt appealed to many quarters. In his book *Curiosity: How Science Became Interested in Everything*, Ball (2012) carefully traced the history of changing attitudes toward curiosity from early condemnations of such attitudes to widespread modern beliefs that curiosity is a virtue that contributes to progress and that is intrinsic to human nature.

Philosophers, following Bacon, such as John Locke, David Hume, René Descartes, and Benedict Spinoza, defended curiosity as a natural human quality, one that demands nurturing and discipline. In time, the virtues of curiosity and wonder were celebrated as a hallmark of modern thought (see Keen, 1973). Relentless curiosity seems now firmly and legitimately attached to all categories of human thought. Indeed, the reversal in attitudes toward curiosity is so complete that it now seems possible that older attitudes could slip from the grasp of our comprehension.

Contributions of Rationalism

Born in the late Renaissance, the skeptical crisis of Montaigne stimulated a response from rationalists and empiricists. They hoped to restore faith in human knowledge and construct a philosophical base for the new sciences. In the process, they constructed intellectual foundations that would ultimately support the new discipline of psychology. Though the rationalists concentrated on the problem of knowledge, they also wrote thoughtful works dealing with theoretical and practical questions of psychology. Their pervasive influence is illustrated in extensive references to their work by early pioneers in psychology such as William James and Wilhelm Wundt. At a minimum, the specific contributions of the rationalists to an intellectual atmosphere friendly to the development of the human sciences should include the following:

1. René Descartes, like Francis Bacon, sought to overcome the extreme skepticism of Montaigne by advancing a new method designed to restore faith in human knowledge. Thus, modern rationalism, like empiricism, begins as a new methodology supportive of a scientific approach to the world.

2. Philosophers such as Leibniz and Herbart were among the first to investigate concepts of thresholds, a topic later to become a preoccupation of some of the early psychologists.

3. The concept of thresholds also supported the idea that there is real mental activity not currently in consciousness. The investigation of subconscious and unconscious processes took root in later systems of psychology.

4. By emphasizing the lawfulness of psychological processes, Spinoza laid the conceptual groundwork for a science of psychology. His attacks on demonology contributed to naturalistic approaches to the study of emotional disorders.

5. Some of the earliest treatises with specific psychological content came from rationalists. For example, Christian von Wolff's *Empirical Psychology* (1732) and *Rational Psychology* (1734) were among the early modern attempts to elevate the study of mental powers as a foundational part of philosophy.

6. Some of the rationalists were pioneers in educational and mathematical psychology. Herbart's book *The Science of Education* was an early attempt to explore pedagogical techniques designed to foster learning and improve memory.

7. Rationalists provided a broad vision of the world of experience. They did not deny that observation and association are important in the acquisition of knowledge, but argued that some connections are grasped intuitively or in an a priori fashion.

Like the empiricists, the rationalists contributed to the intellectual and cultural context from which psychology as a formal discipline was born. We'll revisit their influence in later chapters.

Review Questions

1. Identify three ways in which rationalism differs from empiricism.
2. Briefly list four procedural rules for the intellect set forth by Descartes in his *Discourse on Method*.
3. Outline Spinoza's contributions to the intellectual spadework necessary to the development of psychology.
4. What are the advantages and disadvantages of Leibniz's approach to the mind–body problem?
5. Outline Kant's distinction between analytic a priori and synthetic a priori knowledge. What is the significance of the distinction?
6. Briefly describe Kant's theory of moral development.
7. Distinguish between the terms *apperception* and *perception*.
8. Explain what Thomas Reid meant by common sense and explain how Reid argued against Hume's skepticism.

Glossary

active mind Refers to intelligent, self-organizing properties of mental processes. Contrasts with the "blank slate" hypothesis encountered in empirical philosophies.

analytic a priori Refers to formal truths in which a predicate completely unpacks a subject. A statement such as *All bachelors are unmarried* is an example.

apperception Historically a term with many meanings, but it commonly refers to mental processes that are more complex than those involved in perception. It implies a high level of awareness and activity of the mind so that relationships are clearly understood. Contrasts with mere passive awareness.

apperceptive mass A term employed by Johann Friedrich Herbart (1776–1841) to refer to the goal of education to produce not only knowledge of facts but also a higher level of awareness of relationships.

autonomy A term employed by Immanuel Kant (1724–1804) that refers to self-government or the ability to act in a moral and responsible manner, not to please an authority but because the individual recognizes the inherent or intrinsic worth of certain actions.

categories of understanding An expression employed by Kant to refer to inherent ordering principles of the mind that contribute to knowledge. For example, Kant believed that human beings have intuitive understandings of causality and temporal and spatial relationships.

commonsense philosophy A term referring to the philosophical orientation of philosophers such as Thomas Reid (1710–1796) and his followers. The expression refers to a deeply held opposition to beliefs that are counterintuitive or that do violence to our experience of the world.

deductive argument Any argument in which the conclusion is claimed to follow necessarily from the premises. A deductive argument is valid if, and only if, it is not possible for the premises to be true and the conclusion false. Otherwise, the argument is invalid.

Descartes, René (1596–1650) French philosopher who is often regarded as the founder of modern philosophy. Descartes made extensive original contributions in a great variety of areas. He helped elaborate early scientific methodology, provided rich and often testable hypotheses about the relationships between behavior and physiology, and is regarded as one of the key figures in modern rationalism.

Herbart, Johann Friedrich (1776–1841) German mathematician, philosopher, and psychologist. Herbart was among the first to attempt to quantify mental functions. He was also interested in the role of unconscious processes in human life and in the application of psychological studies to clinical and educational problems.

heteronomy A term employed by Kant to refer to the varieties of forces outside the organism

169

(e.g., rewards, punishments, authority) that often regulate behavior.

inductive argument Any argument in which the conclusion is claimed to be more probable than not given the truth of the premises. Inductive arguments are said to be strong or weak, depending on whether the conclusion is or is not made probable according to the truth of the premises.

Kant, Immanuel (1724–1804) One of the great German philosophers, remembered for his attempts to reconcile empirical and rational approaches to knowledge. Kant believed that knowledge begins with experience, but in his view, there are meaningful connections in experience itself. Kant also advanced an early theory of moral development and was interested in problems associated with nationalism.

Leibniz, Gottfried Wilhelm (1646–1716) German rational philosopher and mathematician who sought ways to reconcile the legitimate claims of monism and pluralism. Leibniz advocated a universal language and a world united by reason and international government. Leibniz and Isaac Newton independently discovered the differential calculus.

monad A term employed by Leibniz to refer to a principle of existence. Leibniz believed that the world consisted of many independent monads, but all monads are harmonious with all other monads. Thus, for him, there is a real mental world and that world is completely harmonious with a real physical or physiological world. Hence, mind and body are both real but completely harmonious and independent.

noumenal In Kant's philosophy, the term *noumenal* refers to a "thing in itself," an object or event independent of experience or perception.

petites perceptions French term meaning *small perceptions* used by Leibniz to refer to small perceptions below the level of awareness. Leibniz believed that small perceptions in concert form the basis of perception. His concept of *petites perceptions* represents an early concept of unconscious processes.

phenomenal The term *phenomenon* is similar to the term *appearance*. In Kant's philosophy, the term *phenomenal* refers to the world as it appears in experience.

preestablished harmony A concept employed by Leibniz to account for the congruence or harmony of different orders of reality. He believed, for example, that mind and body do not influence each other but they are always congruent. Leibniz believed that God had ordered the world in such a fashion as to permit the simultaneous and harmonious operation of many independent principles of existence.

rationalism A philosophical orientation deriving from the Latin *ratio*, meaning to reason or think. Rationalist philosophers typically emphasize a priori knowledge, deduction, and the concept of an active mind that selectively organizes sensory data.

Reid, Thomas (1710–1796) Leader of Scottish commonsense philosophy that sought to reconcile the conflicting claims of empiricism and rationalism.

Spinoza, Baruch (Benedict) (1632–1677) A key figure in the rationalist tradition, Spinoza sought to demonstrate the artificiality of many of the dualisms introduced by Descartes. For Spinoza, there is no gulf between God and the world or mind and body. He believed that most dualities result from problems of language, but different language systems may simply represent different ways of looking at the same reality.

synthetic a priori According to Kant, a synthetic a priori truth is known intuitively and is informative about the world. Descartes's statement "I think, therefore I am" may be regarded as a synthetic a priori truth. The truth of the statement is grasped intuitively, but the statement is not a mere tautology; rather, it is informative about the world.

uniformitarianism The belief that evolutionary changes on earth occur gradually over vast stretches of time.

Wolff, Christian von (1679–1754) German philosopher and author of early books titled *Empirical Psychology* (1732) and *Rational Psychology* (1734). Wolff believed in both empirical and rational approaches to psychology, but argued that rational approaches would be more fruitful and lead to the discovery of principles by which the mind operates.

8 Mechanization and Quantification

There is no bodily or mental attribute . . . which cannot be gripped and consolidated into an ogive with a smooth outline.

—Francis Galton (1883/1907)

Going back to earliest times, human beings have been interested in the measurement of things. Innovations in measurement provided answers for countless questions, both simple and complex. For example, practical questions motivated an interest in knowing how many days would be spent on a trip. And how far and how fast will I need to travel? How much of this product in exchange for that product? How many pieces of wood of what sizes and shapes will I need to build a house? How many of our soldiers will be needed to battle their soldiers? Measurement plays a critical role because errors are devastating to economic, social, and physical well-being.

Breakthroughs in measurement influenced science, technology, and even the ways we view ourselves. One of the most important breakthroughs came in the nineteenth century when **Hermann Ludwig Ferdinand von Helmholtz (1821–1894)** measured the speed

of conduction of a nervous impulse. Boring (1950) wrote that this accomplishment laid the groundwork "for all later work of experimental psychology on the chronometry of mental acts and reaction times . . . It brought the soul to time, as it were, measured what had been ineffable, actually captured the essential agent of mind in the toils of natural science" (p. 42). The claim that Helmholtz "captured the essential agent of mind" may be excessive, but his work stimulated optimism about the possibility of a science of human nature.

This chapter examines the measurement of physiological and behavioral events that were regarded for centuries as ineffable and, hence, resistant to quantitative studies. The mechanistic perspective inspired new quantitative studies in physiology and behavior, a philosophy that begins in the modern period with Thomas Hobbes.

Thomas Hobbes

Thomas Hobbes (1588–1679) argued that the goal of philosophy should involve numerical

Thomas Hobbes

comparisons to assess magnitudes, distances, motions, and proportions. Hobbes adored the mechanical model. For him, "The heart is a spring, the nerves are strings, the joints are wheels giving motion to the whole body" (Peach, 1982, p. 840). A mechanical model holds promise for psychologists to discover material and efficient causes. Hobbes has been characterized as a fearless intellectual adventurer who was given the extravagant title of the "Great Columbus of the Golden Lands of New Philosophies" (see Reik, 1977).

Hobbes was educated at Oxford, but had little interest in the scholastic curriculum. He earned his bachelor's degree when he was twenty and accepted a position as tutor to Baron Hardwick, son of William Cavendish. As a tutor in a well-to-do family, Hobbes enjoyed good pay, access to libraries, travel, and considerable leisure. Aside from brief positions as Francis Bacon's secretary and tutor in the family of Sir Gervase Clinton, Hobbes was associated with the Cavendish family throughout his life.

Hobbes was a contemporary of many great minds of the seventeenth century. Around 1635, he visited with Galileo, who may have inspired Hobbes to extend the concept of motion to all

natural philosophy. Hobbes invited controversy. He was regarded as a corrupter of morals because he spoke against biblical literalism, the authority of the Pope, and excessive reliance on authority. Despite charges against him, people who knew Hobbes held him in high regard and defended him even when disagreeing with his philosophy. Published in 1651, his masterpiece, *Leviathan*, remains an important psychological and political work. He died in 1679 at the age of ninety-one, still a controversial figure.

Like his contemporaries, Hobbes was fascinated with the puzzle of human knowledge. He argued that knowledge has its origin in sensory impressions. Such impressions result from external physical movements that activate the sense organs. The sense organs in turn activate the brain via the nerves. Thus, bodies in motion in the external world set off motions in the sensory channels, and these set off motions in the brain. Ideas, or what Hobbes called "phantasms," result from motions in the brain. Superficially, the emphasis on the sensorial origins of knowledge places him in the empirical tradition. However, Hobbes defies this easy classification because he argued that experience alone is incapable of establishing anything of a universal nature (1650/1962a). Through experience, we can have knowledge only of specific events, and such knowledge can hardly serve as an adequate basis for science. Thus, it is a mistake to classify Hobbes as an unqualified empiricist.

Tsanoff (1964) noted that "Hobbes, like Bacon, demanded the fullest survey of the facts in order to apprehend their basic characteristics, but he sought demonstrative conclusions by strict deductions from evident principles" (p. 264). Matson (1982) commented that the Hobbesian view of science is that it "is a body of organized knowledge, for which geometry provides both the model and the starting point" (p. 852). Hobbes's deep admiration for the method of geometry with its emphasis on axioms and deduction places him in the rationalist tradition. In fact, Hobbes loved geometry as a way of reasoning and believed its method was crucial to understanding all sciences including a science of human nature (see Jesseph, 2004). In tearing apart his complicated epistemology, Mintz (1962) contended that Hobbes also represents a nominalist approach to knowledge. According to Hobbes, we begin with knowledge from the senses from which we get information about singular things such as houses, animals, and vehicles. Through reason, we establish all-inclusive names and classification systems that provide order for specific experiences. According to Mintz (1962), "The truth which reason yields for Hobbes is the truth about words, not things; it is a hard truth to find because words are such notorious snares" (p. 25). Epistemologically, Hobbes's work represents a complicated mix of rationalism, nominalism, and empiricism. Fortunately, his ontology is more straightforward than his views on knowledge.

As noted, Hobbes was a dedicated materialist. Whatever exists must have a material nature, including God. A material God could, of course, serve as a first or efficient cause, setting in motion the rest of material reality. But after serving as first cause, a deity has few remaining duties in Hobbes's mechanistic and materialistic philosophy. Hobbes may have reserved room for humans to honor God, but there is little real work left for the deity. For understandable reasons, Hobbes's theism troubles people who believe in an active God who continuously interacts with the world.

Although some would question Hobbes's theism, there could be no question about the seriousness of his views on human nature. Set forth with characteristic vigor and clarity, his views sent shock waves through the intellectual world. Cambridge Platonists joined Catholics and Protestants in a constant assault on Hobbes's works. Zagorin (1968) noted, "In 1683 the University of Oxford condemned a number of his works to the flames" (p. 485).

Hobbes's views of human nature were derived from his materialist metaphysics and buttressed by his friend William Harvey's work on the circulation of the blood. Hobbes took the centrality of motion in Galilean and Keplerian physics and Harvey's physiology and extended

them to psychology. As noted, sensations and thoughts are understood in terms of motions in the sense organs and brain. But Hobbes assumed other psychological processes are also based on movements that, in theory, are quantifiable. For example, "Feelings of pleasure and pain result from alterations in the vital motion of the body" (Watkins, 1965, p. 115). For Hobbes, psychological processes depend on a physical substrate; thus, the same quantitative science that Galileo used to study the physical world can be used to study the behavior of human beings.

Hobbes also assumed that powerful drives toward self-interest and self-preservation governed human nature. Our fear and awe of collective power restrains us from inflicting our selfish interests on others. In *Leviathan*, Hobbes (1651/1962b) warns that without a civil state there is the danger of war of everyone against everyone. But with a powerful state that holds us in awe, egoism is held in check. Because of the civil state, we can have invention, industry, culture, navigation, the arts, and knowledge, and we can become better people (Reagan, 2012). Without the civil state, we have "continual fear, and danger of violent death; and the life of man [is] solitary, poor, nasty, brutish, and short" (p. 113). Hobbes chides readers who are shocked by his pessimism and asks them to consider whether they lock their doors when they sleep. He also reminds them that they probably secure their valuables and protect their children. He then argues that such actions betray the same accusations against humankind as do the words in his manuscript.

Hobbes's reduction of philosophy to the study of bodies in motion marks him as an important figure in the history of psychology. Matson (1982) pointed out that "Philosophy to Hobbes, is simply science" (p. 851). Hobbes's work offers a psychology uncompromised by dualistic or theological considerations. He is a key figure in the intellectual genealogy of behavioral psychologies and classic psychoanalysis. In a broader sense, Hobbes suggests the importance of studying physiological and social influences with the same quantitative methods that proved so successful in the physical sciences.

René Descartes Revisited

Like his contemporary Thomas Hobbes, **René Descartes (1596–1650)** was obsessed with the problem of movement. But unlike Hobbes, Descartes did not restrict himself to philosophic inquiry. In Chapter 7, we covered his epistemological work, but he also devoted time to groundbreaking research on anatomy and physiology. In a telling story, Huxley (1874) described how a friend of Descartes, "once calling upon him in Holland begged to be shown his library. Descartes led him into a sort of shed, and, drawing aside a curtain, displayed a dissecting-room full of the bodies of animals in the course of dissection, and said, 'There is my library'" (p. 725). Based on his investigations, Descartes advanced provocative and testable theories about the mechanisms responsible for movement in living organisms. As we will see, most of his theories were wrong, but they stimulated other researchers and contributed to physiological knowledge that was relevant to psychological questions.

Although familiar with Galen's concept of pneuma, Descartes was not satisfied with explanations of movement. Perhaps his dissatisfaction can be traced to the technology of his day. Popular mechanical inventions included toys, clocks, and windmills that dazzled the public with their intricate movements. Strandh (1979) describes a fourteenth-century clock that was once on the Cathedral at Lund in Sweden: "Two medieval knights on the dome of the clock hourly exchange blows to the number of the hour. At twelve o'clock, after the twelfth blow, a hymn resounds from a mechanical trombone, a little door beside an image of the madonna opens, and the three kings from the East come out, followed by servants, and file, bowing, past the virgin Mary" (p. 51). If such elaborate movement could be accomplished on a mechanical basis—and understandable in terms of material and efficient

causation—could animal and human movements be better explained from a natural or mechanistic perspective rather than a vitalistic one? If so, the pneuma concept of movement was wrong. Descartes looked for a simpler explanation.

He found inspiration while visiting the royal gardens at Saint-Germain-en-Laye, a western suburb of Paris. For the queen's amusement, the Francini brothers had designed elaborate mechanical statues throughout the gardens, making it a kind of seventeenth-century Disneyland. When Descartes stepped on a hidden plate, it triggered the release of water into a complex network of hydraulic pipes that caused the statues to move. In his *Treatise on Man*, Descartes describes a statue of Diana bathing at the water's edge. Move too close and the shy Roman goddess would hide in the surrounding reeds. Move closer still, and an intimidating statue of Neptune charged at you, poised to strike with his trident.

Powered by hydraulic forces, the statues served as a model for Descartes's theory of bodily movement (Jaynes, 1973b). Although the details of the model are difficult to decipher (see Popplestone, 1995), Descartes drew specific comparisons between nerves and the water pipes that caused movement in the statues.

The discovery of the nerve cell would not come until the nineteenth century, but large nerve fibers (consisting of bundles of axons in a kind of conduit) were visible to the naked eye and had been identified since early times. Descartes believed that nerve fibers, like the water pipes in the statues, were filled with fluids that activate muscles and tendons, the basic machinery of movement. In the case of the nerves, however, the fluids were refined and distilled from the finest elements of the blood. In turn, the blood had been distilled from the finest elements of the digestive juices. He referred to the fluids in the nerves as "spirits" or "animal spirits." Descartes (1637/1985a) argued that the spirits were composed of minute fast-moving particles, which he likened to fine wind or a pure and lively flame.

As noted by Jaynes (1973b), Descartes believed "the nerve pipe fed into the muscle, and when the fluid came down, it billowed the muscle out like a balloon, and so made the limb move" (p. 171). In addition to fluids inside the nerves, Descartes believed small threads ran through the length of the nerves. The threads, when activated by a stimulus, triggered valves in the endings of the nerves in the ventricles of the brain. When the valves opened, the spirits stored in the ventricles were released to move through the nerves to the muscles. The statues at Saint-Germain, which moved by both mechanical and hydraulic action, may have encouraged Descartes's belief in the threads and animal spirits.

Descartes believed that many human movements and all animal movements are mechanical or nonreflective (Leiber, 2011; Steiner, 2006). Thus, many movements have their origin in the senses that activate the so-called spirits in the ventricles of the brain and these, in turn, result in automatic actions. The automatic actions may include sighing, yawning, startle patterns, or more complex activities such as walking or eating. All such activities are shared in common with animals and follow from the actions of nerves, muscles, and senses "in the same way as the movement of a watch is produced merely by the strength of its spring and the configuration of its wheels" (Descartes, 1649/1985b).

Descartes envisioned the body as a machine, comparing body parts such as nerves, ventricles, muscles, and tendons to pipes, storage tanks, springs, and wheels. He applied the mechanical-hydraulic explanation to all animal movement and to involuntary human movement. In his view, there was only a difference of degree between animals and the moving statues. To be sure, animals, as God's creations, were better machines than those machines made by humans, and the superiority of animals to moving statues was manifested in smooth and complex movements. But there were not categorical differences between machines and animals. As noted by Jaynes (1973b), "Animals were mere water statues, not conscious, not really living—machines without will or purpose or any feeling whatever. He dissected them alive (anesthetics were far off in

the nineteenth century), amused at their cries and yelps since these were nothing but the hydraulic hisses and vibrations of machines" (p. 170). But if a mechanical-hydraulic model could explain animal motion, why couldn't the same model account for human motion? Descartes was unable to take that step.

Descartes (1664/1985c) argued that, in the case of humans, God had united a rational soul with the bodily machine, a dualistic assumption that raised important questions in philosophy as well as physiology, and an assumption that some argue limited the science and practice of psychology (Ventriglio & Bhugra, 2015). How could the material interact with the immaterial? Caught in the irresistible grip of curiosity about the mechanics of soul–body interaction, Descartes (1649/1985b) declared that "there is a little gland (the pineal gland) in the brain where the soul exercises its functions more particularly than in other parts of the body" (p. 340). He believed the soul is joined to the whole body, but specific soul–body interactions take place in the pineal gland, which is not divided into halves like other regions of the brain. Descartes also believed, erroneously, that animals do not have pineal glands.

For Descartes, the pineal gland is supplied with nerves that permit it to influence the body even as the body influences the pineal gland. He claimed, for example, "When the soul wants to remember something, this volition makes the gland lean first to one side and then to another, thus driving the spirits toward different regions of the brain until they come upon the one containing traces left by the object we want to remember" (1649/1985b, p. 344). When the spirits find the traces, the informed gland recognizes the stored information. The soul can also exercise will via the gland, but cannot in all cases fully control the passions. The reason is that strong passions affect the heart, blood, and animal spirits in such a violent way that the soul cannot prevent some movements. The soul is tied to the body and cannot exercise complete autonomy. No amount of willpower can easily divert attention from a fractured ankle.

Empirical studies, as much as his original work on epistemology, secured Descartes's fame as founder of modern philosophy. His legacy was set forth in provocative and testable theories about the mechanics of movement. He influenced the course of neurology and physiology long after his death. What were some of his testable theories? First, he argued that animal spirits inflate muscles; second, he tied the muscular system to the ventricles of the brain via the tiny threads or strings that he thought he observed in nerves; third, he ascribed both sensory and motor functions to the same nerve; fourth, he spoke of some nervous transmission as being instantaneous or extremely fast; fifth, he claimed that the pineal gland is infused with nerves, can move from side to side, and exists only in humans; and sixth, an early concept of the reflex is clearly evident in his work. Finally, his speculations about the beast-machine, in the words of Rosenfield (1968), "became a fountainhead of inspiration for many years" (p. 64). Rosenfield's book *From Beast-Machine to Man-Machine* documents the war of ideas about animals and animal rights in the years following Descartes's death (see also Leiber, 2011). Descartes envisioned a gulf between humans and animals that produced an unwitting but intense range of intellectual activity from poetic celebration of animals to investigations in comparative anatomy, physiology, and psychology (see King & Viney, 1992). His provocative theories inspired many studies to which we now turn.

Jan Swammerdam

A Dutch physician named **Jan Swammerdam (1637–1680)** conducted one of the first tests of Descartes's theory of movement. Remembered for his expertise in entomology and respiration (Cobb, 2006), Swammerdam devised brilliant demonstrations that proved embarrassing to Descartes's notion that a flow of animal spirits from the brain inflates muscles. In his classic work *The Book of Nature* (1758), Swammerdam showed that a muscle with an attached nerve

from a frog's leg continues to contract even when separated from the body. This demonstration rules out the ventricles of the brain as a source of animal spirits. He also proved that the muscle contracts even after small cuts sever some of the fibers. Swammerdam (1758) comments that "Tho' the muscle be cut, and its moving fibers separated from each other, all these parts move again, as it were naturally, as soon as the nerve which belongs to them is irritated" (p. 124). If Descartes's theory were correct, animal spirits would escape through the cuts and fail to inflate the muscle. These works established Swammerdam's place as one of the most influential seventeenth-century scholars of the nervous system (Pubols, 1959).

The most conclusive evidence against Descartes' idea that animal spirits literally inflate a muscle comes from a more complicated demonstration. Swammerdam prepared a cylinder that opened at the top into a narrow pipette. A frog's muscle with attached nerve was placed in the cylinder with connecting wires that allowed Swammerdam to make the muscle contract. A drop of water is placed in the pipette. If the muscle grows in size when contracted, as predicted by Descartes's theory, the drop of water should be forced upward. The water did not move upward; if anything, it dropped a bit. These results were clearly inconsistent with Descartes's prediction that a muscle is inflated by animal spirits.

Swammerdam (1758) concluded that at least no "sensible or comprehensive bulk flows through the nerves to the muscles . . . From these experiments therefore, it may, I think be fairly concluded, that a simple and natural motion or irritation of the nerve alone is necessary to produce muscular motion whether it has origin in the brain, or in the marrow, or elsewhere" (p. 125).

Pubols (1959, p. 134) pointed out that Swammerdam anticipated the distinction between sensory and motor nerves and challenged the distinction between voluntary and involuntary activity that had been central to Descartes's theory. In fairness, Descartes may also have recognized the distinction between sensory and motor nerves, but he also believed individual nerves have both sensory and motor functions. Swammerdam was far ahead of his time, both conceptually and methodologically. His work demonstrated the importance of well-conceived experiments and paved the way for naturalistic studies on the measurement and mechanics of physiological and behavioral events.

Niels Stensen

Further work on Descartes's speculations about the pineal gland came from Jan Swammerdam's friend **Niels Stensen (1638–1682)**, sometimes called Nicolaus Steno. Though Stensen respected Descartes's philosophical method, he exposed the great philosopher's anatomical errors. Descartes had said that the pineal gland leans from one side to another and by such action drives the spirits toward various parts of the brain. Stensen argued that the pineal gland could not possibly lean from side to side. He also understood that the pineal gland is not richly supplied with nerves and, therefore, could not be implicated in complex cognitive functions. Finally, Stensen was aware that animals have pineal glands. His anatomical critique destroyed another building block in the Cartesian system.

Stensen took no delight in attacking Descartes. Even in his criticisms, he was careful to protect the philosopher's memory. Yes, Descartes had made mistakes, but he was the first to attempt a completely natural account of human and animal actions (see Fearing, 1970, p. 40). If Descartes and others had made mistakes about the basis of movement, should they be believed if they "talk about God and the Soul" (see Scherez, 1976, p. 33)? That question was undoubtedly on the lips of many people following geographic and scientific findings that contradicted earlier explanations.

Because of past errors in anatomy, Stensen called for a new program of anatomical studies that included less extravagant terminology (terms such as *animal spirits* were vague and unacceptable), a more careful and detailed cataloging of anatomical parts, and greater conservatism with respect to assigning functions to anatomical structures. Though open to the rationalism and geometric method of Descartes and Spinoza, Stensen called for a more empirical science of anatomy that looked for structures and efficient causes. Stensen also struggled with tensions between science and religion, and he sought a different resolution than others; he eventually abandoned science and became a bishop, despite remaining in contact with scholars, including Leibniz, who encouraged him to return to scientific pursuits (Cobb, 2006).

Stephen Hales

McHenry (1969) pointed out that English physiologist **Stephen Hales (1677–1761)** first demonstrated a spinal reflex. Unfortunately, he did not publish his experiment, but, according to McHenry, "Hales decapitated a frog and found that reflex movements of the hind leg could still be obtained by pricking the skin, and that the headless frog would hop about" (p. 112). Such a finding would hardly surprise anybody who has observed decapitation of animals. Reflex activity remains for periods of time, depending on the ambient temperature and the species of animal (spinal reflexes remain for hours or even days in some creatures such as snakes or turtles). But Hales took another step and found that such activity vanishes if the spinal nerves are destroyed. Hales's research demonstrated that reflexes could be carried on without the brain but not without the spinal cord.

Robert Whytt

Probably the most accomplished neurophysiologist of his day, **Robert Whytt (1714–1766)** replicated Hales's experiment and subjected it to closer scrutiny. Whytt (*white*) studied medicine at Edinburgh, London, Paris, and Leiden and earned medical degrees from Rheims and St. Andrews.

Revered as one of the foremost experimental physiologists of the time (Rocca, 2007), he practiced and taught medicine in Edinburgh and was named fellow of the college in 1737. In addition to his physiological work, Whytt appears to have conducted early observational studies of people with anorexia nervosa and bulimia nervosa (Silverman, 1976) and to have been the first to systematically describe a person with multiple sclerosis (Lincoln & Ebers, 2012).

When Whytt repeated Hales's experiment, he ran a red-hot wire lengthwise through the spine of a decapitated frog. He noted that following this procedure "there is no sympathy between the different muscles or other parts of the body as was observed when the spinal marrow was entire" (McHenry, 1969, p. 114). Whytt also observed some reflex actions remain if small segments of the spinal cord are left intact. Many motions persist after removal of the brain and some persist if small segments of the spinal cord are left intact following decapitation, but all motion stops when all spinal nerves are destroyed. Based on his research, Whytt emphasized the idea that movement has its origin in the action of a stimulus that excites nervous activity. Herrnstein and Boring (1966), commenting on Whytt's work, remarked, "One can now perceive the essentials of the chain of events that ultimately established the reflex as a fundamental concept: a stimulus acts on nervous tissue, leading to a muscle movement whose magnitude is in some way proportional to the strength of the stimulus" (p. 283). In a lasting contribution, Watson and Evans (1991) credited Whytt with introducing "the terms 'stimulus' and 'response'" (p. 248).

Whytt drew distinctions between voluntary and involuntary actions and actions based on habits, which he viewed as being somewhere between voluntary and involuntary actions. Among involuntary actions, he included digestive processes, coughing and sneezing, blushing, salivation, heart action, respiration, and pupillary reactions. Because he did the first complete analysis of pupillary dilation and contraction, the pupillary reflex is called *Whytt's reflex* (Eling,

2016a; McHenry, 1969). He emphasized the protective or adaptive nature of reflexes and anticipated the empirical findings that formed the foundation of nineteenth-century work on classical conditioning. Whytt, as quoted by Fearing (1970), noted that "The sight or even the recalled idea of grateful food, causes an uncommon flow of spittle into the mouth of a hungry person; and the seeing of a lemon cut produces the same effect in many people" (p. 80).

Johann August Unzer

Though Whytt researched the concept of the reflex, it was **Johann August Unzer (1727–1799)** who popularized the concept. Though Unzer's work was not original, it was systematic. According to Fearing (1970), "The concept of reflection seems firmly established in Unzer, and implies an element of necessity. The conversion of an afferent impulse into an efferent impulse by a mechanism of reflexion gives us a concept of reflex action which is adequate even in the modern sense" (p. 92). McHenry (1969) credited Unzer as "the first to employ the word *reflex* in connection with sensory-motor reactions" (p. 119). Clarke and O'Malley (1968) also noted that Unzer introduced the terms **afferent**, meaning to move inward toward the central nervous system, and **efferent**, meaning to move outward toward the muscles or glands.

Unzer earned his M.D. degree from the University of Halle in 1748. He is best remembered for his 1771 book *Principles of Physiology*. Aside from his medical research, Unzer indulged in philosophical interests, particularly the nature of mind and consciousness. His work on reflex action led him to study the relationship between consciousness and nervous activity. He wondered if consciousness was involved in all nervous activity or a product only of high-level, integrated activities mediated by the brain.

The relevance of such questions emerged from a social interest in capital punishment. In 1792, a thief named Nicholas-Jacques Pelletier became the first victim of the guillotine. Before long, the public took a morbid interest in France's notorious beheading machine, named after its advocate, Dr. **Joseph Ignace Guillotin (1738–1814)**, who developed the tool to provide a more humane method of execution. During the French Revolution, record crowds flocked to see a criminal's appointment with "Madame Guillotine." People even brought their children to witness the grisly spectacle. Despite its widespread use, the deadly machine inspired controversy. One question stood out from the others: Was death by guillotine really painless? This question was based on the idea that movement, regardless of its location, may represent some degree of consciousness. After the blade dropped from inside its tall wooden frame, a curious thing happened. Newly severed from its head, the condemned's body would sometimes go into a violent convulsion. Finding both curiosity and fear in the moment, spectators wondered if such thrashing revealed a consciousness of pain. Walker (1973) noted that "there were suggestions that the victims' heads responded after severance—Charlotte Corday's face was slapped [following decapitation] and [reportedly] showed annoyance" (p. 103). Popular curiosity about the sensitivity to pain and consciousness undoubtedly stimulated scientific inquiry. Unzer was one of the first to address the issue.

Unzer concluded that reflexes may be identical in decapitated and intact people and animals. He reasoned that if an impression moving toward the brain cannot reach its destination because of decapitation, it may get turned around and follow an efferent path to produce the same motion had the animal been intact. But he argued that such reflexes in decapitated animals are unconscious and, therefore, produce no pain. Unzer believed the conscious experience of pain depends on brain activity. Thus, the movements following decapitation are purely mechanical.

The pioneering work of Hales, Whytt, and Unzer opened discussion that led to the modern understanding of the reflex. The concept of reflexive activity played a role in early psychological research, including the psychology of Pavlov and American behaviorism. The concept of the reflex was a central building block in the mechanistic viewpoint because it sharpened the distinction between voluntary and involuntary action. More and more, early physiologists denied that the soul has an influence in involuntary actions. We now turn to an eighteenth-century mechanistic view that extends the picture initiated by Descartes.

Julien Offray de La Mettrie

The French physician and philosopher **Julien Offray de La Mettrie** (*lah MEH tree*) **(1709–1751)** was one of the most important materialists of the eighteenth century. He studied anatomy and medicine at the University of Paris and earned his medical degree at Rheims. He also studied under the great Dutch anatomist and physiologist Hermann Boerhaave (1668–1738). La Mettrie's most important book, *Man a Machine* (1747/1912), included human beings in a mechanistic program that can be traced back to Descartes. His work set forth a deterministic, evolutionary, mechanistic, and atheistic viewpoint that created an outrage even in liberal Holland (Walusinski, 2012). As a result, La Mettrie moved to Berlin, where he obtained security through Frederick the Great and where he was named to the Royal Academy of Sciences. After a bout of severe indigestion brought on a virulent fever, La Mettrie died at the age of forty-two. Though vilified by his enemies, his radical mechanistic theory lived on to inspire and outrage (Gray, 1967) and to provide a mechanistic foundation for the neurosciences.

La Mettrie argued that mental events depend on bodily ones. While in the French army, he observed during an illness that the clarity of his thought seemed related to his body temperature. He concluded that we are more likely to enjoy good mental health when we are in good physical health. After observing people with brain injuries, he realized that mental abilities sometimes suffer with physical injuries. According to Vartanian

(1967), La Mettrie saw the brain in terms of "the model of a 'thinking machine' into which sense perceptions feed ideas in the form of coded symbols that are, in turn, stored, classed, compared, and combined by the cerebral apparatus in order to engender all the known varieties of thought" (p. 381). The work of La Mettrie completes the journey from beast-machine to human-machine.

Unlike Descartes, La Mettrie failed to find a qualitative gap between humans and animals (Greenwood, 2016). The possession of language marks us as human, but even here he was not convinced of our uniqueness. As noted by Rosenfield (1968), "Could they [the apes] but be taught language, he [La Mettrie] suggested and the task would not be too difficult—they would be identical with primitive man" (p. 146).

La Mettrie was a determinist. He had little use for judges who pass sentences on others and suggested replacing them with intelligent doctors who look for causal connections and ways to heal. Society must be protected from those who are ill or poorly socialized, but state-enforced punishment as retribution makes little sense. La Mettrie believed that happiness and health are the supreme goals of medicine and philosophy. Old notions of sin and evil, vice and virtue, must be replaced with more scientific concepts. La Mettrie was a major figure in the intellectual genealogy of neuroscience, behaviorism, reflexology, cybernetics, information processing, and health psychology. La Mettrie's work represents the logical extension of Descartes's animal-machine model, giving bold expression in a move toward a quantitative-mechanical approach to life.

Mapping the Central and Peripheral Nervous Systems

The early nineteenth century marked a growing optimism about discovering a neurophysiology of mental and physical functions. The methodological tools of science were now to be employed in the search for the soul or the mind. As with most scientific discoveries, false starts tempered the optimism, although some proved to be productive.

Localization of Function

A major breakthrough in the mapping of the nervous system came with the discovery of the sensory and motor tracts in the spinal column. In a series of independent experiments, Sir **Charles Bell (1774–1842)** of Britain and **François Magendie (1783–1855)** of France demonstrated that the ventral or anterior roots of the spinal column influence muscular contraction. Though Bell was first to make the discovery (a fact acknowledged by Magendie), Bell's initial experiment established only the motor function of the ventral root. Magendie's experiments established the sensory functions of the dorsal or posterior root and the motor functions of the ventral or anterior roots. Despite bitter controversies over priority, their discovery—one of the most important in physiology—is now called the **Bell–Magendie Law**.

SIR CHARLES BELL Born in Scotland, Charles Bell attended school in Edinburgh and studied anatomy with an older brother who was a surgeon. In 1804, Bell established residence in London where he served as principal lecturer at the Great Windmill Street School of Anatomy. Bell worked in London until 1836, when he returned to Edinburgh University as professor of surgery. His best-known book is *Idea of a New Anatomy of the Brain*, published in 1811. In addition to his work on sensory and motor tracts, Bell is remembered for shaping views of emotions (Dixon, 2012), his unusual gifts as an anatomical artist, and his drawings of faces that reflected his moral and emotional perceptions of the subject, including the subject's psychological health (Huddleson & Russell, 2015; Lorusso, 2008). He is also known for his discovery of the thoracic nerve, which goes by his name, and for his analysis of facial paralysis (Bell's palsy) resulting from injury to the seventh cranial nerve (Sajadi et al.,

2011). Extensive controversy has emerged regarding whether Bell himself suffered from Bell's palsy (Korteweg et al., 2010; Resende & Weber, 2010).

In 1811, Bell published his views on neural transmission in a pamphlet that he shared with friends. One hundred copies were printed, but all remained inside the network of Bell's friends and associates. A little more than a decade later, François Magendie began work on nerve physiology, unaware of Bell's research.

FRANÇOIS MAGENDIE Born in Bordeaux, France, François Magendie (*muh zhon DEE*) was the son of a surgeon. He was raised according to the liberal precepts outlined by Rousseau in his famous book *Émile*. Though he did not start school until age ten, he progressed so rapidly that by age sixteen he was hired to conduct anatomical dissections in a Paris hospital. At age twenty, he was accepted as a medical student and he received his medical degree at age twenty-five. Magendie worked briefly on the medical faculty of Paris. After interpersonal difficulties, he founded a private practice while also providing private instruction in anatomy and physiology. In 1821, he was honored with elections to the Royal Academy of Medicine and the Academy of Sciences.

Magendie was a pioneer in modern experimental physiology. He founded a publication outlet called *Journal of Experimental Physiology* and argued for well-controlled experiments. In addition to his neurological work, Magendie contributed to the physiology of digestion, to the measurement of blood pressure in animals, and to early attempts to measure mechanically the cerebrospinal fluid pressure (Stahnisch, 2008). Grmek (1974) noted that "Magendie introduced into medical practice a series of recently discovered alkaloids: strychnine, morphine, brucine, codeine, quinine, and veratrine. He also generalized the therapeutic use of iodine and bromine salts" (p. 9).

Animal rights activists may have hampered Bell's research in Britain. Magendie did not face as much scrutiny in his native France (although later scientists such as Charles Darwin and T. H. Huxley criticized his practices and the vivisection reformer Albert Leffingwell blamed Magendie for animal abuse). In his vivisection experiments on several species of animals, Magendie developed techniques that permitted him to sever the anterior and posterior roots of the spinal column one at a time and in combination. The results revealed that severing the anterior roots interferes with movement and severing the posterior roots interferes with sensation. Severing both results in loss of sensation and movement.

The discovery of separate sensory and motor functions of the spinal roots suggested the possibility that other nerve channels are specialized. Indeed, Sir Charles Bell set forth a statement on specific energies of nerves in 1811, but the doctrine of specific energies, implying radical separation of various senses, became a centerpiece in the work of our next figure.

JOHANNES MÜLLER The legendary physiologist **Johannes Müller (1801–1858)** was born on July 14, 1801, in Coblenz, Germany. In 1818, he enrolled at the University of Bonn, and he earned his medical degree in 1822. Following further studies in anatomy in Berlin, Müller returned to Bonn where he taught comparative anatomy, physiology, and pathology. By 1830, Müller was full professor with a comfortable salary. In 1833, he moved to Berlin University as professor of anatomy and physiology. Müller is best remembered for his massive *Handbuch der Physiologie des Menschen* (1833–1840), which, according to MacLeod (1968a), became "the standard reference work for physiologists throughout Europe" (p. 525). As testimony to Müller's influence, Steudel (1974), claimed that "almost all German scientists who achieved fame after the middle of the nineteenth century considered themselves his students" (p. 568).

Müller had broad interests in anatomy and physiology as well as the psychology of visual hallucinations (Berrios, 2005), but we'll focus on his work on the neurophysiology of the senses. Influenced by Sir Charles Bell, Müller elaborated

182

Johannes Müller

on the doctrine of **specific energies of nerves** in his *Handbuch*, where he argued that, for each of the five senses, there is a "specific nerve energy" such that the nerve itself imposes the quality of sensation on mental processes (Finger & Wade, 2002). According to Müller, a nerve is capable of transmitting one and only one kind of sensation. No matter how the nerve is stimulated, it will transmit *only* its quality of sensation (Cassedy, 2008). For example, pressure on the eye will result in a visual sensation, whereas a blow to the ear will produce an auditory sensation such as ringing. It follows that one nerve could not substitute for another. Indeed, Boring (1950) noted that Emil du Bois-Reymond, one of Müller's students, "went so far as to say that, were it possible to cross-connect the auditory and optic nerves, we ought to see sounds with our ears and hear light with our eyes" (p. 93).

The influence of the doctrine of specific energies was not limited to physiology. The philosophical implication was that the sense organs conditioned knowledge. Elaborating on the point, Boring (1950) wrote: "The central and fundamental principle of the doctrine is that we are directly aware, not of objects, but of our nerves themselves; that is to say, the nerves are intermediates between perceived objects and the mind and thus impose their own characteristics upon the mind" (p. 82). Such a doctrine represents another important step in the transition from vitalism to mechanism because it ties the mind to the machinery of the body.

Müller's doctrine was one of the most widely accepted physiological notions of the early nineteenth century. As such, it shaped the direction of many later physiological and psychological theories. The doctrine was extended to the idea that specific nerve fiber energies correspond to various psychological qualities (Cassedy, 2008). Thus, Thomas Young and Hermann von Helmholtz suggested that the primary colors possess three different optical fibers (see Herrnstein & Boring, 1966, pp. 40–44). Helmholtz also suggested that thousands of specific auditory energies correspond to each discriminable tone. Other investigators extended the idea of specific energies to other sensory modalities, resulting in the belief that each elementary sense quality was associated with specific nerve fibers. By 1896, a youthful psychologist named Edward Bradford Titchener calculated a kind of psychological table of elements that included thousands of visual and auditory qualities. Titchener found far fewer qualities associated with the other senses (e.g., four taste qualities and four skin qualities), but his total number of elementary qualities for all senses was formidable.

The doctrine of specific energies shaped early psychological thought in other ways. For example, it suggested a radical isolation of the senses from each other. According to Helmholtz, the sense qualities were so heterogeneous that there were no meaningful transitions from one to another. Thus, questions such as whether "sweet is more like blue or red, can simply not be asked" (Helmholtz, 1896, p. 584). Despite later challenges to the idea that sense qualities have nothing in common with each other (see Hartshorne, 1934; Köhler, 1947; Viney, 1991), such a view prevailed in mainstream psychology for a long time. The doctrine of specific energies was also consistent with nineteenth-century faculty psychologies, including phrenology.

GALL AND SPURZHEIM: A PRODUCTIVE FALSE START A German anatomist, physiologist, and physician, **Franz Joseph Gall (1758–1828)**, gave psychology its most extreme theory of *localization of function*, the idea that different regions of the brain carry out different functions. Imagine that only one region of your brain controls your sense of self-esteem. Similarly, a region toward the back of your head controls your talent at forming and maintaining friendships. Gall was convinced that *faculties* (personality traits and abilities) are localized in specific regions of the brain (Sizer & Drayton, 1892). A person's faculties could be evaluated by examining the corresponding parts of the skull immediately above specific locations. Are you a spiritual person? If so, that region of your brain would swell, leaving a bump in the skull topography. Awful at math? The cortical area around your left eye would shrink, producing a concave dent. Gall's "doctrine of the skull" insisted that skull indentations and protrusions reveal our greatest strengths and weaknesses, and this information could be used for academic, career, or couples counseling (Hershenson, 2008; Sizer & Drayton, 1892). Although faculties were typically viewed as separate, complex cognitive activities, such as the creation of fine art, could involve a combination of faculties (Eling & Finger, 2015).

Gall and his student **Johann Kaspar Spurzheim (1776–1832)** mapped out elaborate charts to guide the assessment of intellectual abilities and personality characteristics based on the shape of the head. Originally, Gall referred to his techniques for measuring the skull as cranioscopy and later as *faculty psychology*. Under Spurzheim's leadership, however, the name changed to **phrenology**, from the literal Greek roots *phrenos* ("the mind") and *logos* ("the study of a thing"). Between 1810 and 1819, Gall and Spurzheim published a four-volume work titled *The Anatomy and Physiology of the Nervous System in General and the Brain in Particular, with Observations on the Possibility of Discovering the Number of Intellectual and Moral Dispositions of Men and Animals through the Configurations of Their Heads*. Brevity was not among their collective faculties.

From the outset, phrenology was controversial among scientists and some physicians while proving offensive to many religious and political leaders. Indeed, Gall was forced out of Vienna and his works were banned shortly after the turn of the nineteenth century. Scientists were suspicious of Gall's methodology, whereas religious and political officials were concerned with the moral implications of a theory that emphasized the role of natural causes in human experience. Despite all the scientific doubts, phrenology enjoyed great popularity in much of Western Europe and the United States (Eling et al., 2011), and many enthusiastic promoters, including George Combe (Wright, 2005) and Nelson Sizer (Sizer & Drayton, 1892), added their own scholarship. The public attended phrenology lectures and read journals devoted to the topic. Voters interested in the campaign leading to the 1852 American presidential election could consult the phrenological *Journal of Man* for an analysis of each candidate. Countless people, rich and poor, consulted practitioners who provided diagnostic services and advice on personal growth and development (giving rise to the taunt, "you ought to have your head examined"). In short, phrenology became a cultural phenomenon.

Many notable Victorians, including Jane Addams, Louisa May Alcott, Susan B. Anthony, Clara Barton, Henry Ward Beecher, Thomas A. Edison, Nathaniel Hawthorne, Andrew Jackson, Helen Keller, Abraham Lincoln, Henry Wadsworth Longfellow, Horace Mann, Karl Marx, Samuel F. B. Morse, Edgar Allan Poe, Theodore Roosevelt, and Booker T. Washington, visited phrenological parlors for readings (Bryan et al., 2003). Conan Doyle's character Sherlock Holmes interacted with phrenologists (Wagner, 2006). The poet Walt Whitman solicited American phrenologists Lorenzo Fowler (1811–1896) and Orson Fowler (1809–1887) to examine his head. Whitman was so delighted with the glowing results that he published them five times as a means of announcing himself as the "Poet of America" (later, the Fowlers and their brother-in-law, Samuel Wells, published Whitman's seminal *Leaves of Grass* in 1855). American writer and humorist Mark Twain was more skeptical. No stranger to hoaxes, he paid multiple visits to phrenologists including Lorenzo Fowler. Following his informal single-blind test of phrenology, Twain found it wanting. In a delicious bit of irony, Fowler discovered a cavity on Twain's head that "represented a total absence of the sense of humor" (Neider, 1959, p. 116).

Phrenologists joined other scholars in endorsing the gender and racial biases of the late 1800s, providing "scientific" evidence of the superiority of some groups and the inferiority of others (Sizer & Drayton, 1892; see also Cornel, 2014; Gibbon, 1878), even as women practitioners contributed to the movement (Lilleleht, 2015). Before long, phrenology became the stuff of quacks, hucksters, and crass moneymaking. The craze faded as the world moved into the twentieth century. Phrenology was branded a pseudoscience and was thus condemned to join other questionable folk sciences such as palmistry, astrology, physiognomy, alchemy, mesmerism, and craniometry.

Phrenology is an example of a productive false start in the quest for an understanding of the relationship between the mental and physical worlds. There can be little question that the work of Gall and Spurzheim mobilized other scientists to investigate localization of function, including such pioneers as Paul Broca (Eling, 2016b). Further, and equally important, phrenology helped shape public opinion regarding the central role of the brain in intellect and personality. Leading educators and reformers of the day embraced phrenology as a foundation for progressive reform (Tomlinson, 2005). Although flawed methodologically and substantively, phrenology inspired later neuroscientists (Quick, 2014) and contributed to the growing climate of opinion that there could be a science of human nature (Sokal, 2001).

PIERRE FLOURENS French physiologist **Pierre Jean Marie Flourens** (*flew RAHNS*) **(1794–1867)** delivered some of the most credible scientific evidence against phrenology. Although trained in medicine, Flourens devoted himself to neurophysiology research. His distinguished career resulted in numerous honors, including election to the French Academy of Sciences.

In his neurological research, Flourens used the surgical method of *ablation*, which involved removing a specific brain structure to determine its function. Through this method, he discovered that respiratory functions are located in the medulla oblongata. He learned that the cerebellum mediates muscular coordination and that the cerebrum governs perceptual and cognitive functions. At first glance, Flourens seems to be advocating localization of function. Although recognizing some localization, he found no reason to agree with phrenologists (Price, 2012). Instead, Flourens argued that the brain functions as a whole (Pearce, 2009a). As a sort of action commune, the brain is an interconnected network of activity. He even determined that the brain shows plasticity so that—within limits—select regions of the brain could take over for other injured parts.

Flourens is also remembered for many other scientific achievements. He discovered the anesthetic properties of chloroform after such properties had been demonstrated for ether and nitrous oxide. His research led to an understanding of the role of the semicircular canals in equilibrium. He was also well known as a biographer of renowned scientists. His studies with the method of ablation had a lasting influence on neurophysiology.

PAUL BROCA Flourens challenged the phrenological claim that intellectual and personality abilities are localized in specific regions of the brain. Now it remained for another French physician to demonstrate that there are some localized functions. **Paul Broca (1824–1880)**, like Flourens, was an eminent physician–scientist with versatile interests. Indeed, he is often considered one of the founders of modern physical anthropology. He was also elected to the French Senate as a representative for science. Broca published in many fields of medicine, including anatomy, pathology, and surgery.

In 1861, Broca met a mental patient who had been locked in the Bicêtre psychiatric hospital for some thirty years. Although not struggling with severe symptoms, the man was unable to speak except for sputtering the word *tan*. He didn't seem to have a problem comprehending what was said to him; he simply could not speak. Broca could not find any problems with the patient's speech apparatus and larynx. Less than a week after coming into Broca's surgical unit, the man died. Broca performed an autopsy on the patient, later named "Tan" in neuroscience literature. Broca's autopsy revealed a fluid-filled cavity in the left frontal lobe of Tan's brain. After researching cases with similar lesions, Broca concluded that this region of the brain played a vital role in the production of speech (LaPointe, 2013, 2014). He discussed his work at the early 1861 meetings of the Paris Society of Anthropology, even though much of these meetings were devoted to the study of craniometry and race (Lorch, 2011). Although there is evidence that Marc Dax preceded Broca in identifying the left hemisphere as the area of speech localization (Buckingham, 2006; Manning & Thomas-Antérion, 2011), this region of the brain was later named *Broca's area* in his honor. Damage to Broca's area produces *expressive aphasia* or a loss of articulate speech.

By 1874, the German neurologist and psychiatrist **Carl Wernicke (1848–1905)** showed that damage to the superior portion of the left temporal lobe interferes with speech comprehension (the region was later named *Wernicke's area*). Unlike Broca's patients, Wernicke's patients had no trouble speaking. They did, however, have difficulty comprehending language. Broca's work, although not rigorous by scientific standards, is viewed as the birth of neuropsychology (Cubelli & De Bastiani, 2011), and his clinical method was clearly more credible than the methods of the phrenologists. Broca's discovery embarrassed phrenology on two counts—the methodology was superior and the speech area was not located in the front of the head as phrenologists had claimed. However, Broca's discovery challenged the claims of Flourens by demonstrating that when it comes to some functions, specific regions of the brain are localized, and this finding was embraced by later phrenologists (Sizer & Drayton, 1892).

Extending the Powers of Observation

Progress in understanding nature inevitably follows new ways of seeing the world. For example, new instruments such as the telescope, X-rays, and microscope broadened human powers of observation. Much of our progress in mapping the nervous system has depended on developing new observational techniques.

FRITSCH AND HITZIG In 1870, German researchers **Gustav Theodor Fritsch (1838–1927)** and **Julius Eduard Hitzig (1838–1907)** collaborated on the electrical stimulation of the cortex. Their classic paper established the field of electrophysiology and, inspired by the work of Broca and others (Gross, 2007), provided a breakthrough in our understanding of the localization of function. Fritsch and Hitzig applied small electrical currents to specific regions of a dog's cortex, producing reliable movements on the side of the body opposite the source of stimulation (Hagner, 2012). It is now well understood that damage to the right side of the brain results in loss of motor functions on the left side of the body, and vice versa. Fritsch and Hitzig provided additional evidence in favor of localization of function (Gross, 2007), though their findings did not support the phrenologists. More importantly, electrical stimulation of the brain, pioneered by Fritsch and Hitzig, has been refined and remains a powerful methodological tool in the neurosciences. According to Clark (1972), Hitzig influenced psychology in another way. He demanded more humane treatment and a more scientific approach to the study of people with emotional disorders.

CAMILLO GOLGI AND SANTIAGO RAMÓN Y CAJAL The Italian pathologist and histologist **Camillo Golgi** (*GOHL gee*) **(1843–1926)** offered another example of how new observational techniques influence our study of nature. Because of their fine structure and embeddedness in other tissue, nerve elements are extremely difficult to observe, even with a microscope. Golgi provided an original approach to the problem. He developed a staining procedure that enhances the features of nerve elements. Bearing his name, the Golgi stain revealed for the first time central features of the fine anatomy of nerve cells (Kruger et al., 2011).

Santiago Ramón y Cajal (1852–1934), a Spanish physician, histologist, and anatomist, was one of the first to use and refine Golgi's staining methods in the study of the fine structure of the nervous system. Ramón y Cajal (*ro MOHN ee ka HALL*) discovered the anatomical gap between nerve cells, and he understood that transmission proceeds from the synapse to the axon. His extensive productive research and his prolific publication record establish him as the central figure in the discovery of the modern theory of the neuron (Rapport, 2005). In 1906, the Nobel Prize was shared by Golgi and Ramón y Cajal for their extensive contributions to our understanding of the anatomy of the nervous system (López-Muñoz et al., 2006); oddly, their intertwined legacy continued as a souvenir stamp of Ramón y Cajal was mislabeled as an image of Golgi (Triarhou & del Cerro, 2012).

SIR CHARLES SHERRINGTON The work of pioneers such as Flourens, Fritsch, Hitzig, Golgi, and Ramón y Cajal had provided important new study methods and substantive knowledge about the nervous system, but the knowledge was highly fragmented and disjointed. The most comprehensive and integrative research on nervous system properties came from the English

neurophysiologist Sir **Charles Sherrington (1857–1952)**. In 1906, Sherrington published a monumental work titled *The Integrative Action of the Nervous System*. His work did for neuroscience what Newton's *Principia* did for classical physics. Indeed, Sherrington's book has been called the "Principia of Physiology" because it defined the field and set the stage for future work. He is remembered, among other things, for coining terms that are still used in the language of neuroscience (e.g., *synapse, proprioceptive, neuron pool, neuron threshold, nociceptive*), for mapping a variety of neural pathways, and for his investigations on the integrative work of the reflexes (Molnár & Brown, 2010).

Even a simple task such as standing upright involves a complicated network of reflex activities carried on without conscious awareness. Reflexes are not necessarily isolated or discrete events, but are integrated in an adaptive fashion with ongoing routine activities. Sherrington identified

Sir Charles Sherrington

187

a new type of receptor that detects information in the interior of the muscles and the joints. He referred to information from such receptors as *proprioception*. He showed that the role of proprioception in complex motor activities involves a kind of reciprocity. For example, when one set of muscles is stimulated, another antagonistic set may be automatically inhibited. Following Sherrington, there was a greater appreciation for the complexity and the integrative activity of reflexes. His work also deepened appreciation for the role of reflexes in "higher nervous functions" though, as noted by Swazey (1975), Sherrington resisted reductionism. Thus, "the physical is never anything but physical, or the psychical anything but psychical" (p. 401). Nevertheless, Sherrington believed that the two domains are integrative, and he received many honors throughout his long and productive career, including the 1932 Nobel Prize in recognition of his pioneering work on the nervous system.

Speed of a Nervous Impulse

As mentioned, Descartes believed the pulling of a thread running the length of a nerve resulted in the release of animal spirits. Following Descartes, it was assumed that the rate of nervous transmission was comparable to the speed of light. Johannes Müller believed that nervous transmission was so fast as to be unmeasurable, but Müller's student, Hermann von Helmholtz, initiated a laboratory investigation that laid to rest still another Cartesian doctrine. Helmholtz's method was fairly simple. He had invented a device called a myograph that consisted of a rolling chart recorder. Moving at a known rate, the recorder registered the action of a stimulus and a response. Using the myograph, Helmholtz recorded the time lag between stimulation of a nerve and muscle contraction. Next, he stimulated the nerve at a point far from the muscle and then at a point near the muscle. The difference in contraction time between the far and near points divided by the distance between

points yielded a measure of velocity. The rate of transmission calculated by this method was surprisingly slow. Rates ranged from fifty to one hundred meters per second, so the velocity that was supposed to have approximated the speed of light was not even as fast as the speed of sound. What is important about Helmholtz's work is not only the speed of the nervous impulse per se, but that scientific technology had quantified another important physiological process.

By the mid-nineteenth century, there was a heady optimism in scientific circles about the ascendance of materialistic philosophy and the appropriateness of that philosophy to a science of human nature. Several of Johannes Müller's students captured the new optimism, even going so far as to take an oath that there were no forces in the living organism except those of a physical–chemical nature (Wertheimer, 2011). These radical young scientists soon convinced much of the older generation that faith in vitalism limited scientific progress (Kesselring, 2013).

Faith in the quantitative methods of science was complete, at least in the minds of nineteenth-century luminaries such as Hermann von Helmholtz, Emil DuBois-Reymond, Karl Ludwig, and Ernst Brücke. Specific quantitative methods, so successful in physiology, were now needed in the science of psychology. Such methods had already surfaced in the work of scientists who studied probability theory.

Measuring Behavior

What has sometimes been labeled the *origin myth* is nowhere better illustrated than in probability theory and statistics. What was the origin of the science of **statistics**? The term itself comes from a Latin root meaning "state." Political facts and figures, including population and census data, have always been associated with the term *statistics*, but its origins probably lie in dicing and gaming more than census activities.

Games of chance date to early times. People who studied the laws of chance made an impor-

188

tant step in developing modern statistics. Among the best-known pioneers in modern probability theory were Blaise Pascal (1623–1662), a French scientist–philosopher, and Galileo Galilei (1564–1642), the Italian astronomer–physicist. Galileo worked on the probabilities of obtaining given numbers associated with throws of dice. For example, in the throw of two dice, the number 12 is less likely than, say, the number 8. The reason is that there is only one way to obtain 12; both dice must fall to display the number 6. But the number 8 can come about in a number of ways: 4 and 4, 3 and 5, and 2 and 6. Galileo was one of the first to calculate probabilities involving dice.

Pascal also made many contributions to the formalization of probability theory. His work, along with the work of other early probability theorists, provided a means for making educated predictions under conditions of uncertainty. Such thinking makes it possible to discover law-like principles behind apparent irregularities and uncertainties.

The bell-shaped curve proved to be a critical development in statistics. The French mathematician Abraham DeMoivre (1667–1754) set forth the original derivations in 1733. Pierre Simon de Laplace (1749–1827) and Carl Friedrich Gauss (1777–1855) also contributed to the development of the curve that is typically called the *Gaussian curve* or sometimes the *normal curve*.

JACQUES QUÉTELET Gauss and Laplace worked on human errors of observation, but it remained for a Belgian mathematician and astronomer to see the wider applications of the Gaussian curve. Lambert Adolphe **Jacques Quételet** (*kat LUH*) **(1796–1874)** is one of the most underestimated figures in the history of psychology. Tylor (1872) claimed that two broad contributions to "physiological and mental science" can be attributed to Quételet. First, according to Tylor (1872), Quételet

has been for many years the prime mover in introducing the doctrine that human actions, even those usually considered most

arbitrary, are in fact subordinate to general laws of human nature . . .; second, he has succeeded in bringing the idea of a biological type or specific form, whether in bodily structure or mental faculty, to a distinct calculable conception, which is likely to impress on future arguments a definiteness not previously approached.

(p. 45)

If individual behavior appears arbitrary or even capricious, such behavior could nevertheless be shown to display amazing regularity. Quételet found interest in the orderliness between variables such as age and criminal activity. He determined that people in the twenty-one to twenty-five age group commit far more thefts than those between the ages thirty-five and forty. Such a relationship between biological and ethical dimensions of behavior suggested important hidden causal links. Quételet also found lawful relationships between literacy level and crime, age of offender and type of crime, time of day and frequency of suicide attempts, and type of crime and sex of offender. On the issue of literacy level and crime, Quételet showed in one study that 61 percent of people accused of various crimes in France in 1828–1829 could not read or write, 27 percent could read or write imperfectly, and 12 percent could read or write well or had superior education (1842/1968). He believed that such a finding implicates society and suggested a causal link between illiteracy and criminal activity.

Quételet conducted studies on the physical characteristics of human beings. He collected data on chest measurements, height, weight, grip strength, heart rate (relative to age peers), respiration, and length of leap. He also investigated mortality statistics and medical epidemiology, and he developed the Body Mass Index, which is still used today and which furthered the emerging science supporting physical education (Delheye, 2014). He found not only that many physical qualities are distributed in the familiar bell-shaped curve but also that moral or psychological qualities are distributed in exactly the same way. He found regularities in nature that were heretofore unsuspected, suggesting the possibility of a new science. Tylor (1872) pointed out that with Quételet's work, we have "the introduction of scientific evidence into problems over which theologians and moralists have long claimed jurisdiction" (p. 49).

One of Quételet's more celebrated concepts is that of the *homme moyen*, typically translated as the "average man." He tells us that there is a central type in every population and that variation around that central type is lawful. Most people tend to cluster close to the average and departures on either side of the average occur with decreasing frequency. Quételet's quantitative work offered practical benefits. For example, accurate mortality statistics prove useful to the insurance industry. And the knowledge that more people wear a size medium shirt than other sizes holds value for the mass production of clothes.

The practical consequences of Quételet's work were important, particularly the uses of statistics to evaluate and further the goals of government (Bartholomew, 2012; Louckx & Vanderstraeten, 2014), but the theoretical consequences were more so. Quételet (1842/1968) spoke of determining "the period at which memory, imagination, and judgments commence, and the stages through which they successively pass in their progress to maturity; then, having established the maximum point, we may extend our inquiries to the law of their decline" (p. 74). Quételet proposed that scientists research memory, and asserted his belief in its lawfulness and its relationship to age. He also proposed a scientific study of reason and imagination, cautioning that "we can only appreciate faculties by their effects; in other words, by the actions or works which they produce" (pp. 74–75). His importance in statistics is undisputed, but he occupies an equally relevant position in psychology's intellectual ancestry. As much as any other, he advanced the idea that behavior can be measured.

SIR FRANCIS GALTON Gould (1981) remarked, "No man expressed his era's fascina-

tion with numbers so well as Darwin's celebrated cousin, Francis Galton" (p. 75). His fascination bordered on obsession, fueled by the belief that "there is no bodily or mental attribute . . . which cannot be gripped and consolidated into an ogive with a smooth outline" (Galton, 1883/1907, p. 36). At times, Galton's enthusiasm for measurement ran ahead of his better judgment. For example, his views on racial and gender attributes were based on inadequate data and reflected prejudices of the day. He nevertheless made significant contributions to the psychological study of individual differences and to the theory and practice of measurement; he is considered the founder of educational and behavioral statistics (Clauser, 2007).

Sir **Francis Galton (1822–1911)** was born in England, in the vicinity of Birmingham. His legendary intellect showed itself at an early age. He learned to read at age two-and-a-half and could read any book in the English language at age five. Growing up in a family of considerable wealth, he was given a sizable inheritance that allowed him to pursue any interest of his choice. He studied medicine, but interrupted his training in favor of a liberal arts degree. Although American psychologist Lewis Terman (1917) estimated that Galton possessed an amazingly high IQ, he struggled in his studies at Cambridge University and found it a challenge passing his mathematics examinations. He suffered an emotional breakdown while in his third year at Cambridge. Health problems prevented him from taking an honors degree in mathematics, but Galton eventually completed a degree at Cambridge. Afterward, he returned to medical school in London, but experienced a renewed ambivalence about medicine. Once again, he failed to complete his medical training. It didn't matter. A different education was to follow.

After his formal schooling, Galton traveled throughout Africa and the Middle East. He led an exploration into the interior of Africa and produced some of the first accurate maps of central southwest Africa. In recognition of his contributions, the Royal Geographical Society awarded him a gold medal and later made him a Fellow.

Sir Francis Galton

In 1853, Galton married Louisa Butler, who came from a family distinguished for academic and intellectual achievements. Galton enjoyed relations with his scholarly in-laws and maintained contacts in London with leading scientists of his day. He corresponded with his cousin Charles Darwin and often visited with Admiral Fitzroy, who had been Darwin's captain on HMS (Her Majesty's Ship) *Beagle*. Galton settled into an enthusiastic work routine that resulted in a bibliography of over three hundred popular and scholarly publications on a wide range of topics. His restless curiosity always pushed him toward intellectual exploration.

Galton developed a keen interest in the weather, inspired in part by his travels. As a pioneer meteorologist, he drew some of the first weather maps and discovered the importance of low- and high-pressure gradients in weather prediction. His skill as an inventor complemented his interest in scientific instrumentation. He developed an improved heliostat for flashing signals on sunny days, proposed a printing telegraph, and improved several meteorological instruments (see Forrest, 1974, p. 294). Galton (1909) also was a pioneer in the use of fingerprinting as a means of identification. He estimated that the odds of two individual fingerprints being identical were one in sixty-four billion. He consulted with his friend Edward Henry, leading to the development of the Galton–Henry system of fingerprint identification. Their work influenced Scotland Yard's criminal investigations and Sir Arthur Conan Doyle's Sherlock Holmes stories. All of this is part of Galton's larger interest in developing new statistical techniques. Before turning to his measurement theory, let's discuss Galton's obsession with counting.

No matter where he found himself, Galton could be counted on to count. In 1885, he attended a crowded public meeting with a tiresome speaker. He wrote that the "communication proved tedious, and I could not hear much of it, so from my position at the back of the platform I studied the expressions and gestures of the bored audience" (1885, p. 174). In an early work of nonverbal social behavior, he observed the crowd, cataloging fidgeting (such as swaying from side to side) as a measure of boredom. Galton (1885) concluded with a word of advice: "Let me suggest to observant philosophers when the meetings they attend may prove dull, to occupy themselves in estimating the frequency, amplitude, and duration of the fidgets of their fellow-sufferers" (p. 174).

Like his cousin Darwin, Galton (1872) had a flair for controversy as seen in his work "Statistical Inquiries into the Efficacy of Prayer." Galton observed that length of life is not related to the amount of prayer offered on a person's behalf. He noted that missionaries often die early, even though they are the subject of considerable prayer. He also found no differences in the life spans of clergy, lawyers, and physicians and argued that public prayers for state leaders are ineffective because such leaders had shorter than average life spans.

Galton's paper was part of a larger debate in the early 1870s that raged over experiments (see Brush, 1974a) proposed by well-known scientists such as the physicist John Tyndall. The proposed experiments, designed to test the efficacy of prayer, triggered an emotional debate among some scientists and the clergy. The clergy were quick to point out that all outcomes of the proposed experiments would be subject to a hopeless array of interpretations. The debate illustrated an unbounded Victorian optimism about the application of measurement techniques to human problems. Such optimism would, of course, accommodate or even mandate a science of psychology. Galton was a chief representative of that optimism.

His contributions to measurement theory and practice had implications for experimental design and the kinds of problems psychologists could investigate. Diamond (1977) stated that without Galton's contributions, "it would have been a far more difficult task to give psychology its new directions, that is, to change it from a normative science, which had been conceived as the propaedeutic basis for philosophy, into a functional science of behavior, independent of philosophy" (p. 47). His most important discoveries were in the areas of regression and correlation, both concepts growing out of his interests in heredity. He used scattergrams to characterize the relationship between the heights of parents and the heights of their adult children. In a scattergram, values of one variable (height of a parent) could be laid out along an x axis and values of another variable (height of an adult child) could be displayed on the y axis. Galton was the first to use the term *co-relation* (later changed to *correlation*) and he contributed to the mathematical development of correlations. In his early work, he was interested in correlations of physical traits (e.g., height, weight, circumference of head), but he later realized that correlation had wider significance, with implications for a host of sociological and psychological problems. In addition to his contributions to the development of correlation techniques, Galton was the first to use the term

median, an important contemporary measure of central tendency. Galton also made extensive use of percentiles, and indeed introduced the term *percentile*, although the concept itself was not new with him.

Applications of the New Measurement Techniques

The emerging nineteenth-century faith in new measurement techniques and new methods of analysis shaped psychology. Furthermore, early discoveries of the lawful distribution of physical and behavioral measures of human beings contributed to optimism about the extension of science into the human arena, including education of students who are gifted (VanTassel-Baska, 2014). Of course, abuses tempered the benefits associated with advances in measurement. Galton and others who studied individual differences at this time viewed differences in ability as genetic rather than environmental; therefore, they perceived their social success as the result of superior genes instead of wealth and privilege (Massey, 2015). In his book *The Mismeasure of Man*, Gould (1981) traced abuses of psychological measures of intelligence. He documented the unfortunate results of early craniometry, which attempted to relate intelligence to cranial capacity. Gould showed that carelessness and poor sampling techniques resulted in beliefs that whites possessed larger brains than other racial groups. Therefore, craniometry was used in the service of racial and sexual prejudices.

Racism also found its way into intelligence testing. As discussed in Chapter 12, Binet viewed intelligence scores as assessments of learning and therefore as changeable. H. H. Goddard and others, however, reified IQ. Intelligence as measured by an IQ test was now viewed as something real, genetic, and unchangeable (Gould, 1981). Many prominent psychologists, including Lewis Terman, Robert M. Yerkes, David Wechsler, and E. G. Boring, promoted this view of intelligence and intelligence tests. Their interpretations and findings both promoted and reflected the virulent racism spreading through the United States during the early 1900s (Loewen, 2005; Sussman, 2014).

Despite widespread and systematic abuse, measurement techniques did serve as new scientific research tools. Simple descriptive social statistics paved the way for a public awareness that many events, when seen in numerical context, are best conceived in terms of the operation of natural causes. We'll illustrate this point with examples of the early use of social statistics.

One of Quételet's admirers was the famous nurse Florence Nightingale (1820–1910), who is remembered for her efforts to improve sanitary conditions in hospitals and in battlefield emergency hospitals designed to care for sick and wounded soldiers, for her influential model of nursing education (Ervin, 2015), and for her successes as a woman employed outside the home in the nineteenth century (Mak & Waaldijk, 2009). Nightingale was fascinated with Quételet's efforts to quantify human behavior and saw an application of statistical techniques in the field of nursing. Nightingale deplored the failure of hospitals to keep uniform statistical records on births, deaths, and number of days for convalescence. As a consequence of her concerns, she agitated for reforms in medical recordkeeping. She demonstrated that during war, disease and poor sanitary conditions produced more deaths among British soldiers than did the enemy. She was among the first to illustrate her arguments with graphs. Because of Florence Nightingale's contributions to descriptive social statistics, she was elected to fellowship in the Royal Statistical Society and as an honorary member of the American Statistical Association. Nightingale saw a role for statistics in moral and political reform efforts and other questions of social and psychological significance.

Drawing on her admiration of Florence Nightingale, the American reformer Dorothea Lynde Dix (see Chapter 9) used descriptive social statistics in her campaign to improve the treatment environment for mental patients. In her memorials to state legislatures, Dix presented tabular information on admissions, mortality, cure rates, age of onset of illness, and hospital costs. In her reports to legislative bodies, Dix sometimes included frequency data from hospitals on presumed causes of mental illness, including factors such as loss of property, domestic difficulties, grief, unemployment, head injuries, and extravagant religious excitement.

The increasing use of social statistics in the nineteenth century was an important development. Events that had been viewed as capricious, or as acts of the will, or as acts of God, could now be seen in a naturalistic context. Discovery of such regularities in human behavior contributed to the acceptance of the possibility of a science of psychology.

Review Questions

1. Briefly discuss Hobbes's position on epistemology.
2. In what way did Hobbes's work encourage naturalistic and quantitative studies?
3. Briefly describe Hobbes's beliefs about basic human nature.
4. Outline Descartes's views on reflex activity.
5. List and describe four testable hypotheses found in Descartes's views on the physical basis of movement.
6. Briefly describe why Swammerdam's experiment on the nerve-muscle preparation was embarrassing to Descartes's theory.
7. List three arguments advanced by Niels Stensen against Descartes's views on the role of the pineal gland.
8. Briefly characterize Hales's and Whytt's contributions to reflex theory.
9. According to Unzer, the guillotine provided a painless death. What was Unzer's rationale?
10. Why is the work of La Mettrie important to the development of scientific psychology?
11. Briefly describe the Bell–Magendie Law and how it was discovered.
12. What is the doctrine of specific energies and who was its chief advocate?

13. Briefly outline Helmholtz's technique for measuring the speed of conduction of a nervous impulse. Approximately what was the speed?
14. Why is the work of Jacques Quételet so important in the history of psychology?
15. Briefly outline Francis Galton's contributions to the development of quantitative techniques.

Glossary

afferent In neurology, the term *afferent* refers to movement inward toward the central nervous system.

Bell, Charles (1774–1842) Co-discoverer with François Magendie that spinal nerves are specialized. The ventral root handles motor functions and the dorsal root handles sensory functions.

Bell–Magendie Law The discovery by Sir Charles Bell in Britain and by François Magendie in France that motor functions are localized in the ventral root of the spinal cord, whereas sensory functions are localized in the dorsal root.

Broca, Paul (1824–1880) A French physician who is remembered, among other things, for his discovery that the anatomical locus for articulate or spoken speech is in a small region of the left frontal lobe—the inferior frontal gyrus, subsequently named *Broca's area*.

Descartes, René (1596–1650) French philosopher who is often regarded as the founder of modern philosophy. Descartes made extensive original contributions in a great variety of areas. He helped elaborate early scientific methodology, provided rich and often testable hypotheses about the relationships between behavior and physiology, and is regarded as one of the key figures in modern rationalism.

efferent Refers to neurological activity that moves outward from the central nervous system toward the muscles and glands.

Flourens, Pierre Jean Marie (1794–1867) French physician and neurophysiologist who employed the method of ablation (surgical removal or isolation of specific structures) as a means of establishing the functions performed by various parts of the brain.

Fritsch, Gustav Theodor (1838–1927) German physician and physiologist who, together with Eduard Hitzig, established the field of electrophysiology. Fritsch and Hitzig were pioneers in the use of direct electrical stimulation as a means of establishing brain functions.

Gall, Franz Joseph (1758–1828) German anatomist, physician, and pioneer in faculty psychology. Gall believed that faculties of the mind were localized in specific regions of the brain and that well-developed or deficient regions were manifested in protrusions or indentations on the skull. Gall was the founder of phrenology, the attempt to assess character by examining the shape of the head.

Galton, Francis (1822–1911) A key figure in the discovery of new quantitative techniques for the study of behavior. He pioneered many early concepts in statistics including the concept of correlation.

Golgi, Camillo (1843–1926) Italian physician and histologist famous, among other things, for developing a staining technique that made it possible to distinguish fine nervous structures from surrounding tissue. His methods made a singular contribution to the advance of knowledge in neurophysiology.

Guillotin, Joseph Ignace (1738–1814) Famous French physician who invented the instrument named after him and used for decapitation.

Hales, Stephen (1677–1761) One of the first to demonstrate clearly a spinal reflex and the dependence of that reflex on the integrity of the spinal cord.

Helmholtz, Hermann Ludwig Ferdinand von (1821–1894) One of the great German scientists of the nineteenth century. Among other contributions, he was the first to measure the speed of conduction of the nervous impulse.

Hitzig, Julius Eduard (1838–1907) German psychiatrist and neurophysiologist who collaborated with Gustav Theodor Fritsch to establish the field of electrophysiology. Fritsch and Hitzig were pioneers in the use of direct electrical stimulation to study brain functions.

Hobbes, Thomas (1588–1679) One of the first of the modern philosophers to advance a thoroughgoing mechanistic account of human behavior. He also argued that self-interest serves as the primary basis for motivation.

La Mettrie, Julien Offray de (1709–1751) French physician whose famous book *Man a Machine* advanced a deterministic, evolutionary, and mechanistic approach to human mental processes.

Magendie, François (1783–1855) Demonstrated that motor functions are handled by the ventral root of the spinal cord and that sensory functions are handled by the dorsal root. Sir Charles Bell made the same discovery, now referred to as the Bell–Magendie Law.

Müller, Johannes (1801–1858) Great pioneer in experimental physiology. Remembered, among other things, for his doctrine of specific energies, which argues that each nerve is highly specialized to carry out one kind of function.

phrenology Literally, *science of the mind*. A theory developed by Franz Joseph Gall and Johann Kaspar Spurzheim that character and personality traits are related to specific regions of the brain. It was also believed that the surface features of the skull (e.g., protrusions and indentations) can be used as a means of assessing character.

Quételet, Jacques (1796–1874) Early pioneer in statistics who was one of the first to realize that there were quantitative procedures applicable to human behavior. He understood that there are lawful regularities operating in moral and psychological arenas earlier regarded as capricious.

Ramón y Cajal, Santiago (1852–1934) Spanish physician, histologist, and anatomist who discovered the synapse and developed the modern theory of the neuron.

Sherrington, Charles (1857–1952) Sherrington was awarded the Nobel Prize in 1932 for his monumental work on the integrative action of the nervous system. He laid the foundations for modern work in neurophysiology and coined many of the terms that are common in the field today.

specific energies of nerves Early belief that nerves are highly specialized so that they can carry out only one kind of function.

Spurzheim, Johann Kaspar (1776–1832) A student and disciple of Franz Joseph Gall, Spurzheim helped develop and popularize the theory of personality and character known as *phrenology*. Spurzheim developed elaborate charts designed to assess personality via analysis of the shape of the skull.

statistics Literally, *characteristics of the state*. A branch of mathematics devoted to the study of appropriate means of collecting and interpreting data. A common focus is on establishing the probability of occurrence of a given event.

Stensen, Niels (1638–1682) Sometimes known as Nicolaus Steno. He exposed the anatomical errors of Descartes by demonstrating that animals have pineal glands and that the pineal body is not richly supplied with nerves. He further argued that, contrary to the predictions of Descartes, the pineal gland could not possibly move from side to side. Such findings dealt a severe blow to Descartes's theory of nervous action.

Swammerdam, Jan (1637–1680) With a nerve-muscle preparation, Swammerdam performed a series of classic experiments demonstrating that a flexed muscle could not possibly grow larger because of the inflow of animal spirits. Swammerdam's demonstrations were contrary to predictions derived from the theory of nervous action advanced by Descartes.

Unzer, Johann August (1727–1799) First to apply the word *reflex* to simple sensorimotor functions. Also introduced the terms *afferent* and *efferent*.

Wernicke, Carl (1848–1905) German neurologist and psychiatrist who discovered the speech comprehension area in the left temporal lobe of the brain.

Whytt, Robert (1714–1766) First to identify clearly the components of a reflex in terms of the action of a stimulus on nervous tissue, resulting in a response.

9 Naturalism and Humanitarian Reform

In no case may we interpret an action as the outcome of the exercise of a higher psychical faculty, if it can be interpreted as the outcome of the exercise of one which stands lower in the psychological scale.

—Conwy Lloyd Morgan (1894/1977)

Naturalism, as a philosophical perspective, states that scientific procedures and laws apply to all phenomena. Naturalism assumes that all events have a history that is understandable in terms of identifiable forces. The early modern period and late Renaissance witnessed new naturalistic accounts of the histories of the earth and solar system. Later in the modern period, the naturalistic perspective accounted for the origin of life, the origin of physical diseases, and the causes of emotional disorders. As we will see, evolutionary theory and naturalistic accounts of mental disorders play a crucial role in the background of psychology.

The appeal of naturalism in the sciences is based partly on its heuristic value. A **heuristic theory** is one that fosters discovery, learning, and predictive efficiency. Rogers (1960) illustrates

the value of naturalism along with the deceptive appeal of non-natural approaches to the world. Imagine you are talking to a medieval scholar named Faustus who believes that invisible demons cause friction. "Really? Demons?" you ask. "Well, how is there more friction if I push a brick over a rough surface?" Faustus answers that the number of demons pushing against you as you move the brick over the surface determines the amount of friction and that more demons live on rough surfaces. "But wait a minute," you say, trying to trap him. "What if I pour oil over the surface? That would decrease friction." "Of course," Faustus answers, "oil drowns demons so now there are fewer demons to push against the brick."

In all likelihood, the "oil drowns demons" notion was not in the original theory; Faustus came up with it as an ad hoc explanation to rescue his theory. Faustus can explain everything with invisible demons that you can explain using standard naturalistic concepts with identifiable components.

Now ask yourself the following questions: Which theory will have the greatest heuristic value? Which theory will generate more believable, workable, and quantifiable hypotheses regarding the operation of friction? Consider another example. For centuries, demons were used to explain weather phenomena such as destructive hail, lightning, and windstorms (see Kramer & Sprenger, 1486/1971). Gradually, with the advent of the scientific revolution, demonological explanations were replaced by naturalistic explanations based on measurable low-pressure centers, high-pressure centers, jet streams, pressure gradients, humidity, sea temperatures, and ambient temperatures. Although observers may perceive supernatural forces as causes of major weather events, heuristic values have led to productive hypotheses about how the weather works and to accuracy in predicting hurricanes, tornados, and droughts. We turn now to a consideration of naturalistic accounts of human origins and emotional disorders and how they have influenced the development of psychology.

Evolutionary Theory

As we have seen, evolutionary thinking can be traced back to ancient Greece. As early as the fifth century BCE, Anaximander proposed a protoevolutionary theory that anticipated later models of evolution, and Empedocles promoted similar ideas soon afterward. Goudge (1973) noted that the roots of protoevolution can be found in early Buddhism, Taoism, and the teachings of Confucius. Our focus will be on the development of evolutionary theory in modern times.

Despite a precedent from earlier cultures, modern theories of organic evolution were a relatively late development. In fact, the idea of evolution is a part of the broader discipline of **cosmogony**—the study of the origin of the cosmos or the universe. We'll examine modern theories of the evolution of the solar system, geological evolution, and organic evolution.

Evolution of the Solar System

By the mid-seventeenth century, scholars attacked the Aristotelian view of the immutability and permanence of the sun and stars. Bold and imaginative new cosmogonies accompanied the new Copernican cosmology, including theories proposed by **René Descartes (1596–1650)**, **Immanuel Kant (1724–1804)**, and **Pierre Simon de Laplace (1749–1827)**. Each theorist believed that our solar system had a natural history. Descartes, perhaps fearful of the Inquisition and the fate of Galileo, denied any intention of contradicting the Genesis account of creation.

Kant and Laplace supported the **nebular hypothesis**. According to this cosmogony, matter in the form of gaseous clouds was once distributed throughout the solar system. In conformity with known laws of motion, attraction, and repulsion, it was assumed that denser regions attract lighter ones and that at some point a series of concentric rings became well elaborated. Forces of attraction within each ring formed spheres corresponding to our planets. The material in the center of the field formed the sun. The same laws responsible for our solar system were assumed to operate in other systems as well. The idea that the solar system evolved according to natural laws was an important first step in modern evolutionary thought. The next step was a natural evolutionary account of the history of the earth itself.

Geological Evolution

George-Louis Leclerc **(1707–1788)** enjoyed a life of unusual wealth and is better known by his title, **Comte de Buffon**. Along with Diderot, Voltaire, and Rousseau, Buffon is regarded as a premier thinker in eighteenth-century French history. He published on vision and its development (Wade, 2008), and, drawing on his encyclopedic knowledge, he produced the massive *Histoire Naturelle*, a forty-four-volume effort that covered topics in zoology, botany, geology, meteorology, theology, philosophy, and psychology (see Buffon, 1780–1785/1977). Buffon was one of the first modern figures to propose an evolutionary model.

Buffon claimed that during the course of natural history, the earth evolved through a series of epochs. At one time, it existed in a molten stage. A universal sea came later and then a volcanic stage. In time, continents formed and were later populated with animals and finally human beings. Buffon realized it would take a great deal of time for such a large mass to cool from a molten stage. To estimate the cooling time, he heated spheres of different sizes and then calculated the time for them to cool. Based on an extrapolation from the differential cooling times of the spheres to his estimate of the size of the earth, Buffon concluded it would take the earth just under 43,000 years to cool from a molten stage.

More than fifty years before Buffon's birth, Archbishop James Ussher (1581–1656) studied biblical chronology to calculate the date of creation. Ussher (1650/2003) estimated that the world had been created on October 23, 4004 BCE. Many scholars and religious authorities accepted his estimate as an irrefutable fact. Buffon did not. He determined that the total age of the earth was almost 75,000 years, far older than Ussher's estimate.

Troubled by Buffon's geological heresies, theologians at the University of Paris condemned his estimate of the earth's history. In response, Buffon published a retraction: "I abandon whatever in my book concerns the formation of the earth, and in general all that might be contrary to the narration of Moses" (Fellows & Milliken, 1972, p. 82). The king of France may have saved Buffon from further harassment. When the theology faculty denounced Buffon's *Époques*, the king urged a special investigative "committee to proceed with circumspection, an admonition that so impressed the assembled doctors that their committee never reported, some few taking covert revenge in dropping hints that the work had been judged the harmless product of senility" (p. 83).

Buffon demonstrated anatomical similarities among animals and speculated about common ancestries. Yet, Goudge (1973) pointed out that Buffon "publicly denied that species are mutable" (p. 177). So organic evolution remained, for him, a weak hypothesis. Had he made a stronger statement, it would have led to undesirable repercussions with ecclesiastic authorities. Clodd (1897/1972) insisted that we must read between the lines to understand that Buffon offered modern ideas before the world was prepared to hear them, making him "the most stimulating and suggestive naturalist of the eighteenth century" (p. 111).

The period following Buffon's death nurtured bold new theories about geological evolution. French biologist **Georges Cuvier (1769–1832)** proposed in his **catastrophe theory** that earth-wrenching catastrophes had annihilated entire species and transformed the earth's topography. A challenge to this idea came with the landmark publication of the *Principles of Geology* (1830–1833) by Sir **Charles Lyell (1797–1875)**. He argued for **uniformitarianism**—the belief that evolutionary changes on earth occur gradually over vast stretches of time. Uniformitarianism replaced catastrophe theory and became the orthodox position for well over a century, establishing Lyell as the founder of modern geology. In time, his theory played a central role in Charles Darwin's work.

Evolution in Other Arenas of Intellectual Discourse

The idea of evolution as a process of natural change is applicable to many intellectual arenas. On many occasions, the history of ideas has embraced evolutionary thought, sometimes leading to fierce intellectual battles. For example, a naturalistic perspective was evident in debates about the origin of language. For many cultures, it was considered a divine gift, where "each people naturally held that language was given directly or indirectly by some special or national deity of its own; thus, to the Chaldeans by Oannes, to the Egyptians by Thoth, to the Hebrews by Jahveh" (White, 1896/1910, pp. 168–169).

For centuries, Western scholars had insisted that Hebrew was a divine language used by God and Adam in the Garden of Eden. All other languages were thought to be derivatives of Hebrew. However, a more naturalistic conception emerged as philologists viewed language from an evolutionary perspective. Acceptance of the evolution of language came easier than a belief in organic evolution. In part, this was because we can more easily see how words are derived from earlier languages as well as how new words are coined and how new meanings get attached to older words.

The idea of natural change arose in a time of rapid cultural evolution and fiery debates over topics such as slavery, powered flight, the origin of disease, the roles of women in society, the nature of mental illness, and capital punishment. On this last topic, we do not have to look far into history to encounter the practice of executing ten- and eleven-year-old children for minor crimes. Drawing and quartering and burning at the stake were common practices. By contrast, in recent times, many countries have outlawed capital punishment altogether. Where it is practiced, its efficacy and morality are subjects of intense debate. Recognition of these and other cultural changes helped set the stage for biological evolution.

Organic Evolution

As early as the Renaissance, the stage was set for theories of organic evolution. The period ushered in fruitful questions about the beginnings of life. Even within the Christian community, there was not universal agreement about the details of a sacred theory of origins. For centuries, theologians debated creation theory among themselves. In heated quarrels, the questions they raised were numerous and significant: What was the mode of creation? Did God speak things into existence as implied in the first chapter of Genesis or work

like a sculptor as hinted in the second chapter of Genesis? Were the fowl brought forth out of the waters (Genesis 1:20) or out of the ground (Genesis 2:19)? What was the order of creation of life? The first chapter of Genesis lists the order as plants, fish, birds, cattle, wild beasts, and people. The second chapter announces the order as plants, the human male Adam, beasts, birds, and finally the human female Eve. Early theologians attempted to reconcile these differences.

Scientific findings posed challenges to popular doctrinal assumptions. For example, theologians had claimed that dangerous objects such as thorns, stingers, and poisonous fangs did not appear until after God had expelled Adam and Eve from the Garden of Eden. The fossil record, however, proved otherwise. Abundant evidence revealed that animals had devoured other animals long before humans existed on the planet. Many theologians had argued no species could ever become extinct because God is not in the habit of making mistakes. Further, they argued that no new species had appeared since creation. For a time, they also resisted findings about the sexual nature of plants, but overwhelming evidence gradually crushed any opposition. The distribution of animals in remote regions such as South America and Australia posed another problem. Presumably, the fossil remains of the ancestors of all animals should be found in the vicinity of the mountains of Ararat, the supposed resting place of Noah's Ark. All animals should have fanned out from that point, but there is no evidence for such a presumption. The sacred theory of origins, like the sacred theory of the structure of the universe, was beset with problems that divided biblical scholars. The need arose for alternative explanations.

As before, the Comte de Buffon proposed a naturalistic approach to the question of origins. It's true he denied the mutability of species and did not endorse a doctrine of organic evolution (at least not publicly). Yet, he pondered whether humans and apes shared a common ancestry.

Buffon was one of the first modern figures to study the developmental history of individuals, a

200

common interest among evolutionary theorists. He wrote on intrauterine development, infancy, and puberty. He investigated mortality statistics of infants, noting that Simpson's mortality tables, published in London in 1742, showed that "a fourth of [infants] died in the first year, more than a third in two years, and at least one half in the first three years" (Buffon, 1780–1785/1977, p. 393). In his mind, those who survive should consider themselves favored by the Creator. He added, however, that infant survival in France was better than in England. Thus, he hints at a geographic or naturalistic determinant of survival even after suggesting that God influences our survival rate. Such duplicity suited Buffon, who repeatedly pulled readers into tensions between natural and supernatural worldviews. In an early work on gerontology, Buffon wrote in detail on the changes in physiology associated with aging.

The English physician and biologist **Erasmus Darwin (1731–1802)** also contributed to the theory of organic evolution. He married twice and had fourteen children, producing a complex family tree that included his grandsons, Charles Darwin and Francis Galton. Erasmus Darwin was a dabbler, allowing his broad interests to drift from botany to poetry to natural philosophy. He experimented with galvanism, the use of electricity to stimulate nerves and muscle contraction (his studies allegedly inspired Mary Shelley to write *Frankenstein*), and he wrote extensively about visual phenomena and vertigo (Gardner-Thorpe, 2006; Wade, 2010a, 2015). He designed carriages and copy machines, speaking machines, and rocket engines, but didn't patent his inventions, fearing it might damage his reputation as a physician.

Erasmus Darwin was a member of England's Lunar Society, a group of intellectuals and industrialists who met around the time of a full moon to better see their way home after a meeting (Ronan, 1982). Some members were known for scientific achievements as well as for their political and theological work. The society included about a dozen eminent scientists such as James Watt, developer of the steam engine; astronomer

Sir William Herschel; and Joseph Priestley, known for the isolation of oxygen, ammonia, and carbon dioxide.

Discussions in the Lunar Society were carried on in an atmosphere of honesty and intellectual freedom. However, many of the group's ideas were anathema to the larger society. The fate of Joseph Priestley provides a dramatic example.

Despite his fame as a scientist, Priestley was attacked from pulpits and the House of Commons for his sympathetic words about the American and French Revolutions. Many in England branded him a traitor and the anti-Christ. In 1791, a mob torched his Birmingham home and laboratory. The inferno consumed his library, taking with it some of his unpublished works. After growing weary of harassment, Priestley emigrated to the United States a few weeks after his sixty-first birthday.

The persecution of his friend made an impression on Erasmus Darwin. He was a deist after all, believing that natural processes evolved from the time of creation without divine intervention. Perhaps fearful of repercussions, Darwin did not present his views on organic evolution until the latter part of the eighteenth century, a few years before his death.

Darwin believed that plant life preceded animal life and that all animals evolved from the same basic organic material. He rejected the idea of separate creations for various species. He believed human beings were not far removed from a former existence as quadrupeds. The mechanism for such evolution, according to Erasmus Darwin, was **inheritance of acquired characteristics**. In this model, a given trait is acquired from a specific need. To survive in an arctic climate, for example, an animal must grow a thick coat to stay warm. The acquired trait is then passed on to subsequent generations. Darwin observed evidence for evolutionary changes in domestic breeding, in climatic effects on animals, and in breeding anomalies. His notion of the inheritance of acquired characteristics was destined to become a source of controversy. Still, it prevailed long after his death and reached its apogee in the work of our next figure, Jean-Baptiste Pierre Antoine de Monet Lamarck.

French biologist **Jean-Baptiste Lamarck (1744–1829)** is remembered for an early theory of organic evolution and as a pioneer in invertebrate paleontology. Lamarck's name is associated with *progressionism*, the idea that there is a steady linear advance in nature from simple to more complex forms of life. Taylor (1983) wrote that, in later developments of his thought, Lamarck believed in a "branching evolution and the vanishing of many forms" (this was a bolder claim than it looks; the orthodox claimed God could not make mistakes, and therefore, there could be no vanishing forms) (p. 39). No thinker before Lamarck so well appreciated the importance of extinction of species and adaptation.

Lamarck argued that species are human constructions based on our need for convenient classificatory schemes; individual plants or animals in nature are simply steps in an ongoing process. Each individual may differ from its ancestors, and its offspring may acquire still different characteristics.

The most controversial aspect of Lamarck's theory was the proposed mechanism of evolution. Like Erasmus Darwin, Lamarck believed that environmental changes (e.g., changes in climate or food supply or in predator populations) had an obvious and profound impact on the needs of living organisms. Once a need is created, such as a behavior pattern to avoid a new predator, adaptive mechanisms are set in motion. The adaptations that are acquired are then transmitted genetically to the offspring. Traits such as a rough skin or armor, a longer coat for warmth, or avoidance behaviors are passed on to subsequent generations. The sequence, according to Lamarck, is that changes in the environment influence the animal's needs. Changing needs alter the animal's behavior and new behaviors impact biological organization and structure. The new organizations and structures are then passed along.

Taylor (1983, pp. 39–40) pointed out that Lamarck did *not* say that environmental con-

ditions per se affect heredity. Nevertheless, Lamarck's proposed mechanism was not accepted by mainstream biologists, though the idea of the inheritance of acquired characteristics has remained quite compelling. It appeared later in the work of William McDougall, and for many years, it had strong appeal in Soviet science because of its perceived consistency with Marxist–Leninist thought. More recently this notion has reemerged as scientists have mapped the human genome and learned more about how the environment affects the functions of genes and how genes shape our interactions with the environment (Chang & Ota Wang, 2014).

Charles Darwin

As we have seen, theories of cosmological, geological, and organic evolution were well entrenched in scientific literature prior to Darwin. The missing pieces in the puzzle involved a theoretical mechanism of evolution along with adequate supporting biological evidence. Darwin provided it and, simultaneously with **Alfred Russel Wallace (1823–1913)**, proposed a mechanism for evolution that appealed to the scientific community. Their independent work gave foundation to one of the great epochs in the history of science.

Charles Darwin (1809–1882) was born on February 12, 1809, the fifth of the six children of Robert Waring Darwin and Susannah Wedgwood. Charles's mother came from a family with an international reputation for excellence in pottery, fine china, and ceramics. Charles was eight years old when his mother died in 1817. Robert Waring Darwin was the third son of Erasmus Darwin and his first wife, Mary Howard. Robert was a successful physician known for treating patients with sympathy and understanding. Indeed, Wichler (1961) claimed that "his greatest success was a new method of treatment that is today called psychotherapy" (p. 153). Robert Darwin had a forceful personality, and he played a strong role in his son's life.

There is little evidence in Charles Darwin's educational life to suggest he would later achieve eminence in the scientific world. He had no love for primary school, and most of his work was perfunctory at best. At age sixteen, he entered Edinburgh University to pursue a medical degree. It didn't last. Darwin grew bored with classroom experiences and developed a profound aversion to observing surgical procedures. After two years he abandoned his studies at Edinburgh. Subsequently, he enrolled as a theological student at Cambridge University, but discovered he disliked theology as much as medicine. Nevertheless, he managed to complete a theology degree in 1831, but never found use for it.

From his early years, Darwin had a keen interest in natural science, driven by a special fondness for organization and collection. He cultivated an extensive knowledge of birds, insects, plant life, and sea fauna. During his time at Cambridge, Darwin suffered through lectures before escaping

Charles Darwin

to study nature. He labored long hours collecting and identifying beetles, a curious hobby for a theology student. He soon commanded respect in the natural sciences. In 1831, Captain Robert FitzRoy (1805–1865) of the Royal Navy wrote to a botany professor named Henslow, asking for a naturalist to accompany him on a South American voyage. Henslow recommended Darwin. Although his father considered it a waste of time, Darwin signed on as an unpaid crewmember on the second survey voyage of HMS *Beagle*.

He was a few months shy of age twenty-three when the survey voyage began. In the opening lines of his account of the voyage of HMS *Beagle*, Darwin (1897) described the demanding beginning and purpose of the expedition:

> After having been twice driven back by heavy south-western gales, her Majesty's ship *Beagle*, a ten-gun brig, under the command of Captain Fitz-Roy, R.N., sailed from Devonport on the 27th of December, 1831. The object of the expedition was to complete the survey of Patagonia and Tierra del Fuego . . . to, survey the shores of Chile, Peru, and of some islands in the Pacific—and to carry a chain of chronometrical measurements around the world.
>
> (p. 1)

The *Beagle* sailed southwest past the Canary Islands to the coasts of Brazil and Argentina and further south to the Falkland Islands and Tierra del Fuego, the southern tip of South America. The voyage proceeded up the west coast of South America to the Galapagos Islands, the most important natural laboratory for Darwin. As the *Beagle* sailed westward, Darwin visited many islands of the Pacific before reaching New Zealand and Australia. By early May 1836, the Cape of Good Hope was in sight, but unfavorable winds carried the brig-sloop off course. On October 2, the shores of England were in sight. Darwin suffered seasickness throughout much of the journey, but the rewards of his excursions on land more than compensated for his misery at sea.

Darwin's account of the voyage of the *Beagle* reveals his keen ability to observe along with his geological, botanical, and zoological knowledge. Anthropological interests punctuate many passages and reflect his scientific and humane interests. For example, he noted that the people of Tierra del Fuego faced scarce food supplies during the winter. To Darwin's dismay, the Fuegians cannibalized their elderly women before resorting to eating their dogs. Darwin dwelled on the lives of the Fuegians, whom he regarded through the racial biases of his day as the most wretched of people. He was interested in how they arrived at Tierra del Fuego and what they could know of pleasure. Commenting on the Fuegians, Darwin (1897) observed,

> The different tribes have no government or chief, yet each is surrounded by other hostile tribes, speaking different dialects, and separated from each other only by a deserted border or neutral territory: the cause of their warfare appears to be the means of subsistence. Their country is a broken mass of wild rocks, lofty hills, and useless forests: and these are viewed through mists and endless storms. The habitable land is reduced to the stones on the beach; in search of food they are compelled unceasingly to wander from spot to spot, and so steep is the coast, that they can only move about in their wretched canoes. They cannot know the feeling of having a home, and still less that of domestic affection; for the husband is to the wife a brutal master to a laborious slave. Was a more horrid deed ever perpetrated, than that witnessed on the west coast by Byron, who saw a wretched mother pick up her bleeding dying infant-boy, whom her husband had mercilessly dashed on the stones for dropping a basket of sea-eggs!
>
> (pp. 215–216)

Darwin's evolutionary approach to life was based on extensive field experience and masses of geological, botanical, zoological, and anthro-

pological data. One can see his new perspective taking shape in his recorded thoughts. At every turn, the importance of the environment in shaping life forced itself on his thinking. But how does evolution work? What is the mechanism? In Tierra del Fuego, Darwin (1897) speculated, "Nature by making habit omnipotent, and its effects hereditary, has fitted the Fuegian to the climate and the productions of his miserable country" (p. 216). The conclusion that the effects of habit are hereditary would have to be modified at a later date.

In the Galapagos Islands, Darwin encountered one of the world's finest natural laboratories for the study of species variation. The Galapagos are located about five hundred miles west of Ecuador, and the equator cuts through the northern part of the largest island. There are ten major islands, with neighboring islands often less than ten miles away. Climate, altitude, and soil conditions are comparable throughout the archipelago, yet Darwin found surprising and unexplained differences in plant and animal life from island to island. For example, finches on one island had developed a heavy parrot-like beak, whereas their relatives on a nearby island possessed a long and graceful beak. Darwin found plant and animal species that were unique to given islands or groups of islands and other species that were common to all the islands, but that varied from one island to the next. Strong currents probably prevented most animals from traveling from island to island. Darwin (1897) stated, "Most of the organic productions are aboriginal creations, found nowhere else" (p. 377). He speculated that with these islands, "We seem to be brought somewhat near to that great fact—that mystery of mysteries—the first appearance of new beings on this earth" (p. 378). Nevertheless, for the time, the mechanisms of change and adaptation eluded him.

Darwin's account of his voyage sensitizes us to his emphasis on environmental setting, adaptation, and the sheer indifference and brutality of nature and people. At times, Darwin as the detached observer–naturalist surrendered to

Darwin, the empathic human being. After witnessing beatings of people who were enslaved and the separation of families at auctions, Darwin (1897) bitterly remarked, "I thank God, I shall never again visit a slave country . . . These deeds [atrocities against people who were enslaved] are done and palliated by men who profess to love their neighbours as themselves, who believe in God, and pray that his will be done on earth!" (p. 499).

On his return to England, Darwin prepared and classified numerous plant and animal collections from his voyage. During this time, he began writing the results of his voyage in scientific papers and books. Published years before his *The Origin of Species*, Darwin's early works were admired in scientific circles and established him as a promising new voice.

His personal life was evolving as well. Darwin considered proposing to his older cousin, Emma Wedgwood. He debated it on scraps of paper under the columns of "Marry" or "Not Marry." Darwin (1958) concluded that one advantage of marriage would be a "constant companion and a friend in old age . . . better than a dog anyhow" (pp. 232–233). Disadvantages included "less money for books" and a "terrible loss of time." He finally decided in favor of marriage and proposed to Emma.

After marriage in 1839, the couple moved south of London and settled into the rural Down House on a small acreage with greenhouses for botanical work and facilities for his biological studies. The Darwins had ten children, although two died in infancy and his daughter, Annie, died at age ten. Throughout Darwin's time at Down, the condition of his health dictated the pace of his life and work. Plagued by nausea, headaches, insomnia, and dizziness, Darwin retreated from conventional social activities into the routine of scientific work. His strict work-oriented schedule was no doubt a source of therapy, but it also formed the basis of a productive career.

After returning to England, he couldn't fit together several pieces of the evolutionary puzzle. A breakthrough of sorts came in 1838, when Darwin read *An Essay on the Principle of Population* by English economist **Thomas Robert Malthus (1766–1834)**. Malthus provided one of the first mathematical models of population growth (Pollard, 2012) and argued that population increases geometrically while food supply tends to increase in a slower arithmetic progression (at best). In other words, without proper checks, populations outgrow their food resources. The result is an inevitable struggle for survival that may lead to catastrophe. Although Malthus anticipated the catastrophic effects of unlimited population growth, he nevertheless rejected birth control, regarding it as a mortal sin. Darwin, long an observer of the struggle for existence in plant and animal populations, felt an immediate debt to Malthus. As deBeer (1964) pointed out, "Darwin had already grasped the importance both of variation and of selection; the effect [of Malthus's work] was to suggest to him the inexorable pressure exerted by selection in favour of the better adapted and against the less well adapted" (p. 99).

Even with the impetus from Malthus's essay, Darwin's work moved at a slow pace. In 1844, he shared his ideas with botanist Joseph Hooker. Concerned about his friend's reaction, Darwin admitted it felt like he was "confessing a murder" (cited in Colp, 1986, p. 9). More than twenty years after returning from the Galapagos, he still had not published his ideas.

In 1858, English biologist Alfred Russel Wallace sent a manuscript, asking for critical comments. Darwin was shocked when he read it. Based on his work in the Amazon basin and other regions, Wallace's manuscript spelled out a model of evolution that paralleled Darwin's ideas in remarkable detail. Like Darwin, Wallace had found inspiration in Malthus's essay on population. Eiseley (1957, p. 206) claimed that Darwin, though shaken, was tempted to let credit for the theory go to Wallace. But Charles Lyell and Joseph Hooker were determined to announce the work of Darwin and Wallace and their new approach to evolution. In July 1858, Hooker and Lyell presented essays by Darwin and Wallace at a conference of the Linnean Society of London. Distraught over the death of his infant son, Darwin did not attend. Their work was published in the *Journal of Proceedings* of the Linnean Society on August 20. Like the conference presentation, the joint publication attracted little attention.

Now under great pressure and in delicate health, Darwin dedicated the next thirteen months to summarizing his extensive work. When his now famous *On the Origin of Species by Means of Natural Selection* was published in 1859, the entire stock of 1,250 copies sold out. Scholars continue to ask questions about priority in the discovery of the Darwin–Wallace evolutionary theory, differences in ideas between Darwin and Wallace (see, for example, Cézilly, 2015; Hoquet & Levandowsky, 2015), and the historical treatment of Alfred Russel Wallace (see Brackman, 1980), particularly given Wallace's acceptance of supernatural intervention in the evolution of humans (Bickerton, 2014).

A dozen years after the publication of *The Origin of Species*, Darwin came out with a second book on evolutionary theory titled *The Descent of Man*. Additional publications followed, several outlining the promise of an evolutionary psychology. More and more, nagging health concerns cut into his productivity. After struggling through months of illness, Charles Darwin died on April 19, 1882. One day later, his remains were interred in Westminster Abbey, close to the final resting place of Isaac Newton.

Darwin's *The Origin of Species* ignited a firestorm of controversy that burns to the present day (Hoquet, 2015), but it also advanced a revolutionary new way of thinking about evolution. In the first edition, he described the mechanism as *descent with modification* and did not use the phrase *evolution* until the concluding paragraph. As a rich heuristic theory, Darwin's model is built on a foundation of four essential technical features. One might regard the following as a family of theories, each subject to empirical testing.

First, populations of all species tend to produce more members than can possibly survive.

Second, variation appears in all populations.

Third, a struggle for survival ensues, but in specific environmental niches some variations are, by chance, better adapted to survive than others.

Fourth, those variants that are better adapted will tend to endow their offspring with genetic advantages. The outcome is a **natural selection** both for survival and for extinction.

Taylor (1983) pointed out that Darwin said "(1) that *all* changes which become fixed did so in this way, (2) that all changes occurred by *imperceptible gradations*, and (3) that all changes arose in the first instance by *chance*" (p. 17). Darwin assumed that species are always in more or less tension with their environments, making evolution an ongoing affair. He found much evidence in support of the theory—the extinction of entire species, the fact that offspring are similar to their parents but also depart from their parents, and the production of variations through selective breeding. Given sufficient time, Darwin assumed that such variations may result in new species. We should note that some of the original technical features have been called into question, most notably the assumption that all change is gradual. Nevertheless, the broader outlines of the Darwin–Wallace theory have formed an integral part of biology since the publication of *The Origin*. The heritage of Darwin had a profound impact on many other intellectual contexts including philosophy, religion, history, morals, and science (see Kohn, 1985; Richards, 1987).

After more than a century and a half, Darwinian evolution is canonical (in the sense of being an accepted theoretical and unifying standard) for the overwhelming majority of scientists. Despite scientific acceptance, large segments of the population—especially in the United States—regard the theory with disdain. Ideologists clash in landmark legal cases, bitter school board meetings, the creation of special schools, and attempts to control textbook content. The National Science Teachers Association (2013) addresses how the evolution controversy intimidates K–12 science teachers and how public opposition to teaching evolution threatens the scientific literacy of students. Despite the difficulty in teasing out facts among the claims and counterclaims, evolution has shaped and continues to shape psychology and other scientific disciplines.

Significance of Evolutionary Theory for Psychology

In an early paper titled "The Influence of Darwin on Psychology," Angell (1909) related that in Darwin's time there was already "a disposition to view mental life as intimately connected with physiological processes, as capable of investigation along experimental and physiological lines, and finally as susceptible of explanation in an evolutionary manner" (p. 152). Angell went on to state that Darwinian thought brought new emphasis to functional, developmental, and comparative processes as opposed to the simple analysis of the normal adult mind that had interested some early psychologists. The influence of Darwin and evolutionary ideas on psychology may be even greater than Angell could have imagined, particularly given the growing emphasis on application and pragmatism in the United States (Green, 2009).

During the present day, evolutionary theory remains vital in organizations such as the Center for Evolutionary Psychology (CEP) located at the University of California at Santa Barbara. An open-access, peer-reviewed journal titled *Evolutionary Psychology* has enjoyed success, along with a wealth of books (see Buss, 2016; Crawford & Krebs, 2008; Ray, 2013; Workman & Reader, 2008; Zeigler-Hill et al., 2015) and encyclopedia entries on the topic. Buss (2016) observes that evolutionary psychology has emerged as a prominent theory guiding productive research. Evolution has grown to become a central organizing feature in all the biological sciences. Such growth is due in part to a balanced treatment of genetic and environmental influences and a strong emphasis on the centrality of adaptation in a world that is anything but static.

Buss (2016) notes that evolutionary psychology challenges the blank slate hypothesis originating in the modern period with John Locke and embraced by many of the behavioral psychologies. He also acknowledges that evolutionary psychology often focuses attention on the dark sides of human behavior. Evolution also emphasizes the continuities between humans and other animal groups in many areas, including sexual selection (Harris & Vitzthum, 2013). For example, mate guarding is evident throughout much of the animal kingdom where steps are taken to isolate females from male competitors (see Thornhill & Alcock, 1983). Buss (2002) and Buss and Shackelford (1997) note that mate-guarding strategies are evident in humans when potential competitors are denigrated, threatened, or even killed. Mate guarding is also a factor in the isolation of females as when they are forced to remain indoors unless accompanied by a male or when they are forced to thoroughly cover themselves so as to be nearly invisible to potential male poachers. The influence of evolution on psychology is further manifested in the importance of topical areas summarized in the following materials.

Comparative Psychology

Darwin's *The Origin* triggered an explosion of interest in comparisons between animals and humans (Wasserman, 2013). A decade before his death, Darwin (1872/1998) published a captivating book on *The Expression of Emotions in Man and Animals*. In this comparative work, he used satire to challenge views of human exceptionalism, arguing that our moral expressions have amoral evolutionary sources (e.g., our smile reflects our evolutionary ancestors' hunger; see Dupouy, 2011), and he concluded that human and animal emotions are universal and innate and offer real survival value. In collaboration with a psychiatrist named James C. Browne (1840–1938), Darwin even analyzed the facial expressions of people experiencing psychosis to better understand emotion.

Inspired by this and other works in Darwin's legacy, comparative psychology had widespread popular appeal and was the subject of many articles in popular or cultural magazines, often written by well-known psychologists. The articles investigated an impressive range of subjects: the mental capacity of the elephant (Hornday, 1883), the intelligence of ants (Romanes, 1881), queen ants and queen bees (Wheeler, 1906), the formation of habits in the turtle (Yerkes, 1900), babies and monkeys (Buckman, 1895), and morality in animals (Leuba, 1928). Important theoretical issues surfaced in the early literature of comparative psychology. However, much of the early work was anecdotal in nature, consisting of interesting stories about an individual animal told by an owner or a hunter or naturalist. The stories typically revolved around the animal finding its way home or "solving" some other kind of problem. Based on the anecdote, enthusiastic observers made hasty inferences about the animal's psychological traits. Too often, the same writers indulged in *anthropomorphism*, attributing human characteristics to animals.

Many scientists were interested in comparative psychology (see Dewsbury, 1989), but arguably the most visible was English biologist **George John Romanes (1848–1894)**. For his *Mental Evolution in Animals* (1883), he used some of Darwin's notes and published a chapter from *The Origin* as part of an appendix (Smith, 2010b). Romanes's books *Animal Intelligence* (1882) and *Mental Evolution in Man* (1888) were enthusiastic attempts to found a science of animal behavior and reason built on a continuum between humans and animals. Romanes inferred that animals had minds (Forsdyke, 2015), and he opened the door to comparative psychology, but he was criticized for focusing on anecdotal evidence of remarkable animal feats. The American psychologist Joseph Jastrow (see Cadwallader, 1987) and German physiologist Wilhelm Wundt (1894/1977) were among his most aggressive critics. Romanes was aware of a need to establish definite principles and to avoid anecdotes. Still, he couldn't avoid the charge that anecdotalism

and anthropomorphism—if not sensationalism—contaminated his work.

The English scientist **Conwy Lloyd Morgan (1852–1936)** advanced a more disciplined comparative perspective. Morgan (1894/1977) contended that "in no case may we interpret an action as the outcome of the exercise of a higher psychical faculty, if it can be interpreted as the outcome of the exercise of one that stands lower in the psychological scale" (p. 53). Thomas (2001) points out that Morgan initially described this idea as a "basal principle," but later referred to it as a "canon of interpretation." Subsequently, it has come to be known as *Morgan's canon*, and it continues to guide discussions of animal intelligence (Zentall, 2011), despite being the subject of widespread misinterpretation. Morgan was not advocating simplicity *for its own sake*, and he understood that interpretive efforts must, of necessity, have a human face. He was arguing for cautious interpretations of data and for the development of deep sensitivities to the adequacy of explanations offered for natural events. The tensions between what Wertheimer (1972) discussed as richness versus precision have been salient from the earliest days of comparative psychology. In the *precision orientation*, we run the risk of oversimplification and of thus doing violence to our subject matter. In the *richness orientation*, we run the risk of reverting to constructs that have no scientific basis. In the final analysis, we agree with Alfred North Whitehead (1920/1971) who reminds us that the "aim of science is to seek the simplest explanations of the facts. We are apt to fall into the error of thinking that the facts are simple because simplicity is the goal of our quest. The guiding motto in the life of every natural philosopher should be Seek simplicity and distrust it" (p. 163).

Developmental Psychology

As we have seen, philosophers such as Rousseau and Locke were interested in the development and care of children. As with comparative psychology, an interest in developmental issues grew out of the Darwinian model of evolution. In addition to his work on naturalism, Darwin also gained a reputation as a pioneer in the study of individual development. His 1877 article "A Biographical Sketch of an Infant," first published in the British journal *Mind*, was based on careful observations of his infant son's sensory acuity, reflexes, moral sense, emotions, and associations. This classic in developmental psychology set the stage for later studies that provided normative data on the physical and psychological development of children. Following Darwin, a child study movement emerged with leaders often acknowledging their debt to evolutionary theory.

German zoologist **Ernst Heinrich Haeckel (1834–1919)** proposed an early attempt to tie evolutionism and psychology that had implications for the study of development and comparative psychology. As one of the first to embrace and promote Darwin's theory, Haeckel proposed that **ontogeny** (the origin and history of the individual) **recapitulates phylogeny** (the origin and history of the species). In other words, the development of the individual of every species repeats the evolutionary development of that species. In *The Evolution of Man*, Haeckel (1905) demonstrated the difficulty of differentiating between human embryos at various stages of development and the embryos of other animals. Although Haeckel's recapitulation theory is not completely accurate, it nevertheless inspired the emergence of developmental psychology (Koops, 2015) and provided the foundation of G. Stanley Hall's claims about childhood development (Green, 2015a). Haeckel argued strongly for a scientific psychology based on physiology and the assumed lawfulness of mental processes and evolution.

German physiologist **William Thierry Preyer (1841–1897)** was a colleague of Haeckel at the University of Jena. He extended Haeckel's ideas to child psychology in his classic textbook *Die Seele des Kindes* (1882), later translated into English as *The Mind of the Child*. Similar to Darwin, Preyer observed the mental growth and language development of his son over a four-year period (Dennis, 1985). Zusne (1975) contended that "Preyer's book provided the greatest single impetus to the development of modern ontogenetic psychology" (p. 161).

The study of infant and child development, like comparative psychology, had understandable popular appeal. Psychological works on infancy and childhood found their way into popular and cultural magazines, with titles such as "The Imitative Faculty of Infants" (Preyer, 1888), "Lingual Development in Babyhood" (Taine, 1876), "Children's Vocabularies" (Gale & Gale, 1902), "The Origin of Right-Handedness" (Baldwin, 1894), "Helen Keller: A Psychological Autobiography" (Jastrow, 1903), and "Development of the Moral Faculty" (Sully, 1886). In addition to popular articles, other psychologists informed the public about the child-development movement. In *Harper's Magazine*, American psychologist G. Stanley Hall (1910) outlined the history of the systematic study of development and discussed specific content areas such as growth norms, language development, and moral development. Sully (1894, 1895, 1896) wrote a series of articles for *Popular Science Monthly* that conveyed the need for a science of childhood and also discussed research areas on imagination, play, childhood art, and childhood fears. The world of the child became a major interest for pioneers such as G. Stanley Hall and William Preyer, who acknowledged their debt to Darwin.

Emphasis on Adaptation

Darwin's emphasis on survival, adaptation, and the shaping forces of the environment played a major role in defining the directions of the new psychology. Following Darwin, the frontiers of psychology were expanded. The detailed study of sensory processes that occupied much of the attention of the earliest psychologists was complemented by a more worldly psychology interested in education, the workplace, the

209

home, and all those institutions and circumstances that influence adaptation, including the role of sympathy and social approval in human adaptation (Brooke, 2013; Marsh, 2013). Scholars also extended evolutionary perspectives into questions about evolution of consciousness (Smith, 2010b), adaptive cognitive traits (Croston et al., 2015), and altruism as well as other moral behavior (Flescher & Worthen, 2007; Harman, 2014). Darwin had a profound influence on the early leaders of American psychology, including William James, John Dewey, James McKeen Cattell, and G. Stanley Hall. As we will see later, each acknowledges a debt to Darwin.

Individual Differences

Sir **Francis Galton (1822–1911)** was not immediately affected by his cousin's book, *The Origin of Species*. In time, however, Darwin's continued scholarship on biological variation inspired Galton to emphasize individual differences in inherited intellectual abilities (Fancher, 2009). Prior to the publication of Darwin's *The Origin*, differences among individuals were often attributed to differences in the will. Older psychologies had stressed the importance of training the will, and expressions such as *diseases of the will* and *defects of the will* were common. Even Darwin, prior to reading Galton's work, had emphasized passion and a rigorous work ethic as the major determinants of individual differences. But after considering Galton's ideas, Darwin wrote to his cousin, "You have made a convert of an opponent in one sense, for I have always maintained that excepting fools, men did not differ much in intellect, only in zeal and hard work" (quoted in Pearson, 1914, p. 6).

Galton believed that differences among individuals are enormous and many are innate. In his classic *Hereditary Genius*, a work he later wished he had called *Hereditary Talent* (see Forrest, 1974, p. 88), he showed that exceptional accomplishment runs in families, suggesting the operation of a powerful hereditary influence. In this prominent

work in early gifted education (VanTassel-Baska, 2013), Galton demonstrated that musicians tend to come from families of musicians, judges from families of judges, poets from poets, commanders from commanders, and so on, but he did not consider environmental influences. Based on these observations, he promoted *eugenics*, the selective breeding of humans to improve the species (Gould, 1981), an idea that became prominent throughout the United States, where many states passed legislation to forcibly sterilize people viewed as unfit, largely women who were impoverished and not white (Kohlman, 2012; Singleton, 2014). Darwin did not support eugenic ideas (Shields & Bhatia, 2009), and many observers view Galton's uses of evolution as one of many "perversions of science" perpetuated to justify racism (Wade, 2014, p. 16). Still, Galton launched the study of individual differences as a field of psychological inquiry. Differences in memory, mathematical ability, musical ability, literary ability, and the like were then regarded less as matters of willpower and individual responsibility and more as questions amenable to science. His radical emphasis on the hereditary basis of individual differences would later be challenged with a radical emphasis on environment in shaping individuals.

Galton's work, a product of the late nineteenth century, had strong sexist and racist biases. Galton's biases fit into a Victorian public attitude that attributed white men's accomplishments to innate superiority rather than to their educational and other privileges. Though Galton left unfortunate legacies about race that have continued to reemerge in psychology (Gould, 1981; Winston, 2003; Wade, 2014), he also opened the door to methods that were used to challenge his biases. He also pioneered in the study of identical twins as a method for the investigation of the differential effects of heredity and environment, and as noted in Chapter 8 he introduced correlation methods and, following Quételet, sensitized us to the importance of statistical measures of variability as scientific tools.

Herbert Spencer

Prior to the publication of Darwin's *The Origin*, English philosopher **Herbert Spencer (1820–1903)** advanced his own evolutionary theory based on Lamarckian thought. The publication of Darwin's *The Origin* in 1859 further sharpened Spencer's enthusiasm for evolution as a unifying principle and he embarked on applying the theory to all branches of human knowledge (Smith, 2014). He wrote on psychology, sociology, biology, ethics, and other topics, always stressing growth from simplicity to complexity. In his 1864 *Principles of Biology*, Spencer coined the expression *survival of the fittest*, giving rise to arguably the most popular catchphrase in the evolutionary literature. As with Darwin, the themes of species adaptation, survival, and continuity ran through his writings, including his work on brain size and race, which he used to argue for racial superiority of Europeans (Gondermann, 2007).

Herbert Spencer

Spencer, often regarded as a forerunner of functionalism (see Chapter 12), came from the British utilitarian tradition. He believed that goodness gives long-term pleasure. He also believed we tend to repeat activities that result in pleasurable circumstances, an idea rediscovered in later research on learning, and he anticipated many principles of behavior analysis (Leslie, 2006). Like Darwin, Spencer believed that chance mutations produce many evolutionary changes. Spencer's two-volume *Principles of Psychology*, first published in 1855, was standard reading for many early psychologists.

Goudge (1973) pointed out that "evolutionism is a family of conceptions having great vitality and viability" (p. 188). One part of that family is Darwin's technical biological theory. But evolution is more than a technical theory; it is an attitude, an intellectual paradigm. As we have seen, it opened doors to the study of developmental psychology, comparative psychology, individual differences, and adaptation. Its contribution to the biological sciences and to psychology has been enormous. Darwin's work placed human experience and behavior in an uncompromising naturalistic context. It is probably no accident that the first laboratory in psychology opened within twenty years of the publication of *The Origin of Species*.

Though Darwinism places mind and behavior in a naturalistic context, the resulting image of human beings need not be pessimistic. Indeed, numerous scholars (Richards, 1987; Teilhard de Chardin, 1961) have argued that evolutionary theory need not result in moral and ethical nihilism (see Richards, 1987). In fact, moral concerns shaped much of Darwin's thinking. He was distressed by human suffering, animal suffering, the seeming indifference and brutality of nature, and the selling and owning of slaves even by those who were members of recognized religious organizations.

Naturalistic Approaches to Emotional Disorders

The naturalistic perspective gave depth and scope to many intellectual arenas including astronomy, geology, meteorology, and biology. Before it could exert influence, however, naturalism had to dislodge prevailing explanations based on the presumed operation of mysterious, paranormal, or supernatural forces. It wasn't a quiet cultural war. People held deeply entrenched beliefs that spiritual forces caused both physical and emotional problems. Literal interpretation of sacred books and institutional authority encouraged such beliefs. Consequently, naturalism faced unusual resistance. To appreciate naturalistic accounts of psychopathology, let's explore how older beliefs about demons and various spirit forces accounted for emotional disorders.

Demonology

When we think of explanations of mental illness based on demonic possession, we tend to think of people in early times and the Middle Ages. However, Kirsch (1978) contended that demonological beliefs became more widespread during the Renaissance than in earlier times. He argued that **demonology** reached its apogee in the mid-seventeenth century. For example, in 1609, the year Kepler published his accounts of the elliptical motion of planets, *pricking* was announced as a method of diagnosing demonic possession (Kirsch, 1978). Pricking consisted of sticking a suspected witch with a pin until finding a spot that proved insensitive to pain or did not bleed. Such a spot was regarded as the point through which a devil had gained access to a witch's body. This method was added to an arsenal of earlier diagnostic techniques set forth in an influential "bible" on demonology known as *The Witches' Hammer*.

The Witches' Hammer

In 1484, Pope Innocent VIII became troubled that many people in northern Germany had "abandoned themselves to devils" (see Summers, 1971, p. xiii). In response to this threat, the Pope commissioned two Dominican friars and professors of theology to serve as inquisitors. Based on their inquisitorial work, Heinrich Kramer and James Sprenger wrote the **Malleus Maleficarum**, translated as *The Witches' Hammer* or *The Hammer against Witches*. First published in 1486, the *Malleus* was one of the most influential books of the fifteenth and sixteenth centuries. It went through fourteen editions by 1520 and was translated into several European languages. Motivated by paranoia and a fear of anarchy, the *Malleus* was a response to individuals and groups who were perceived as revolutionary and corrupt. In this context, witches were viewed as conspirators against civilization. In his introduction to the *Malleus*, Summers (1971) cited examples of witchcraft techniques that inspired fear. One involved the age-old method of creating an image of someone the witch wished to destroy and then thrusting pins into the image or melting it. That the techniques of witchcraft "worked" should come as no surprise in view of widespread beliefs about magical and supernatural techniques.

Nearly all European countries passed laws against witchcraft, lending it credibility as a perceived threat. Laws were deemed necessary because common people could be moved to panic at the mere suggestion that a witch could manipulate their lives. The credulity and fear of the people made it possible to use witchcraft as a form of blackmail. It is little wonder that forceful action was taken to combat these terrifying forces.

The *Malleus* itself was divided into three parts, devoted to (1) a classification of devils and witches and how their influence in the world can be reconciled with God's omnipotence; (2) methods by which devils and witches accomplish their work, along with defenses and remedies against these methods; and (3) interrogation,

212

judicial, and ecclesiastical procedures for bringing witches to justice. In Part II of the *Malleus*, Kramer and Sprenger suggested that devils can enter the heads of people to manipulate their mental images. Such entry may come about at the request of a witch. It was suggested that demonic possession may be the price one pays for a life of sin. Entry may also result from the light or heavy sin of another person. For example, a devil may possess a child if the parent has engaged in a sin. Some possessions, according to the *Malleus*, are for an individual's greater advantage. For example, Kramer and Sprenger told the story of one priest who had a gift for expelling devils. Because of his ability, he became famous and fell victim to the vice of vanity. Overcome with guilt, he prayed that, as punishment for his sin, he might be possessed by a devil for a period of five months. According to the *Malleus*, "He was at once possessed and had to be put in chains, and everything had to be applied to him which is customary in the case of demoniacs. But at the end of the fifth month he was immediately delivered both from all vainglory and from the devil" (Kramer & Sprenger, 1486/1971, p. 130).

The *Malleus* warned that demonic possession could result in symptoms such as sterility, impotence, loss of sensory functions, loss of motor functions, mental disorganization, pain, somnambulism, epilepsy, mania, and death. In practicing her mischief, it was said that a witch could cast a spell with a mere look or glance. Charms, incantations, poison, or a hex all served as imagined weapons in her arsenal. In addition to causing bodily harm, a witch could conspire with a devil to create emotional disorders or perceptual distortions. For individuals with sufficient credulity, the verbal threat of a witch could induce intense anxiety and stress. Based on the will to believe, numerous early records reported the gradual or speedy death of a threatened victim.

To battle this sinister influence, prescribed treatments were designed to cast out demons. Such treatments included exorcisms with sacred words, confessions, prayers, visits to holy shrines, repetitions of approved scriptures, and reverent participation in church ceremonies. The pages of the *Malleus* are filled with admonitions against the use of superstitious practices in combating devils and witchcraft. In general, one could be assured that a practice was not superstitious if it was in good accord with church doctrine. Not surprisingly, the same methods used to fight demonic possession were also employed to counter other events perceived as works of witches or devils, including hailstorms and illness in animals. The sprinkling of holy water, the ringing of church bells at an approaching storm, the making of the sign of the cross, or the utterance of prescribed prayers were encouraged as interventions.

Not all physical and psychological disturbances were viewed as the work of demons or witches. The *Malleus* recommends treatments for disorders caused by something other than witchcraft. For example, a man made sick by inordinate love for a woman may be treated in several ways. "He may be married to her, and so be cured by yielding to nature . . . his love [may be directed] to a more worthy object . . . He may be directed to someone who . . . will vilify the body and disposition of his love, and so blacken her character that she may appear to him altogether base and deformed. Or, finally, he is to be set to arduous duties which may distract his thoughts" (Kramer & Sprenger, 1486/1971, p. 171).

In many cases, witches were viewed as enemies of civilization and were accused of visiting natural calamities and great suffering upon the world. Authorities felt an urgent need to identify witches, expose their work, and bring them to justice. As a result, witch trials spread across Europe during the sixteenth and seventeenth centuries. Virtually all European countries were caught in a frenzied campaign to stamp out witchcraft. In its various incarnations, the Inquisition targeted members of vilified outgroups, including heretics, witches, intellectuals, and people who were not heterosexual (Murphy, 2012). Consistent with these traditions, the witch trials besieged many of the same individuals, particularly Jews and women, who suffered disproportionately (Burns, 2003; Friedrich, 1982).

Fueled with paranoia and hostile retribution, witch hunts stand among the great crimes in the history of civilization. The true scale of the barbarism remains a mystery. Historians have tried to estimate the number of women who were executed in the name of witchcraft. The numbers prove elusive. Kieckhefer (1976) listed over five hundred European witch trials during the relatively inactive period between 1300 and 1500. Many trials included multiple defendants, and the court records are often piecemeal and incomplete, failing to specify the exact charge or verdict of a case.

Summers (1965) pointed to another reason why the numbers are elusive: "The people, frantic with superstitious fears, may often have taken the law into their own hands" (p. 359). Despite the obstacles, we have compelling evidence that European witch hunts, especially at their height through the sixteenth and seventeenth centuries, amounted to a holocaust that resulted in tens of thousands or even hundreds of thousands of executions. Many towns throughout Europe were decimated. Summers (1965), quoting the commissary Claude de Musici of Treves, pointed out that "from 18 January, 1587, to the 18 November, 1593, there were executed for witchcraft in the diocese of Treves three hundred and sixty-eight persons of both sexes; this does not include the number of sorcerers who were burned at Treves itself" (pp. 486–487). Bromberg (1954) tells of a French judge who "boasted that he had burned eight hundred women in 16 years on the bench" (p. 52). Documentary evidence of large numbers of executions can be found in the legal records but again, exact numbers remain elusive. Fortunately, scholars may gradually be able to provide more accurate data on many facets of the Inquisition including executions. The Vatican archives, closed for more than four centuries, were opened to researchers in 1998. The archives house a vast collection of records that, according to Murphy (2012), fills about twenty rooms located in a large underground bunker.

Unfortunately, legal codes were written with little thought of protecting innocent people. It was hardly necessary given the prevailing theological view that God protects the innocent. Although comforting in its time, this belief contributed to a judicial inquisition that would bring condemnation from later generations. Let's take a look at some procedures used to prosecute witchcraft.

Part III of the *Malleus* outlined the typical procedure for initiating a trial where one party accused another and then offered evidence in court that supported the accusation. If the accusing party was irresponsible or if that party initiated a frivolous charge, it was liable to a countersuit. In the search for witches, however, this procedure could prove dangerous. Why? The *Malleus* tells us that an individual who accused a witch and served as witness might be vulnerable to the witch's retaliatory powers. From this perspective, Pope Boniface VIII decreed that in heresy trials, including witch trials, the inquisitor may withhold names if there was reason to believe that such witnesses or accusers faced danger.

A second procedure used in witch trials was for an individual simply to serve as an informer. Such an individual provided evidence to the court but did not serve as a witness, thereby enjoying protection from the suspected witch. The third procedure, most common in witch trials, was to initiate a process without an accuser or an informer. This procedure began when there was a suspicion that witches were active in a given region. Based on a suspicion, a judge could bring charges and proceed with a trial. The citizens were given warnings that an inquisition was beginning when a general citation was posted on parish churches or town halls. Any person, under any kind of suspicion, could be placed on trial. For example, if a person touched or cradled a baby—and that baby later became ill—the individual could be tried on grounds of witchcraft.

Deceptive techniques were advocated in the questioning of suspected witches. In advising interrogators, Kramer and Sprenger (1486/1971) suggested, "Let her [a suspected witch] be asked why she persists in a state of adultery or concubinage; for although this is beside the point [in a particular trial], yet such questions engender more suspicion than would be the case with a chaste and honest woman who stood accused" (p. 213). Inquisitors employed many forms of deception and placed great weight on an individual's reactions to questions. Denials were interpreted as cover-ups. On the other hand, if the witch gave an impassioned defense, that could also be taken as a sign of guilt.

In addition to deceptive interrogation procedures, certain signs or tests were taken as evidence of demonic possession and witchcraft. For instance, suspected witches were sometimes thrown into water. Floating was taken as evidence of guilt or demonic possession, whereas sinking revealed the witch's innocence. Another test was to determine whether a suspect could weep. It was believed that witches had an inability to shed real tears. The judge nevertheless had to use the weeping test with caution and with close supervision of attendants, because it was said that witches were capable of false tears or of assuming a weeping posture and then smearing spittle on their faces. Still other signs of possession or witchcraft included birthmarks, unusual growths, scars, or moles.

Even sober courtrooms at times deteriorated into theater, the drama coming when witnesses fell into hysterics, denouncing others as witches. Inquisitors often demanded that witches confess their crimes. To this end, and despite their grave concerns about the possibility of false confessions, torture was employed and with such efficiency that many accused confessed to what the inquisitors wanted to hear. Russell (1980) suggested that, in Lorraine, "only 10% persisted in denying their guilt to the moment of death" (pp. 79–80). Inquisitors tortured witches using thumbscrews, toe screws, leg vices, racks, whippings, and sustained imprisonment. The confessions often went into lurid detail about how the victim had sworn allegiance to the devil, attended witches' sabbats and other diabolical assemblies, engaged in intercourse with Satan, or eaten the flesh of infants. Such confessions were often made with the expectation that they would

sway the court to impose a more humane death sentence. In most cases, confessions served only to reinforce popular stereotypes about the power of witches and provided further justification to support belief in witches. Many confessions included lists of accomplices, often enemies of the defendant. Such accomplices were then, of course, also subject to trial. Russell (1980) told of one defendant who named all the court officials as being secretly involved in witchcraft.

Fear of the power of witches was so extensive that unusual precautions surrounded most legal proceedings. Jailers were cautioned against letting a witch touch or stare at them. If they touched the witch's bare hand, they were advised to immediately apply a remedy such as salt that had been consecrated on Palm Sunday or a "blessed disc of wax" stamped with a lamb and blessed by the Holy Father. Witches were led into the courtroom backward so that their eyes might not fall on the judge before his eyes fell on them. Otherwise, the judge might succumb to the witch's power and offer a lighter sentence. Witches were sometimes carried in a basket, under the assumption that their power was diminished so long as their feet did not touch the ground. Many suspects were stripped of all their clothes and all hair was shaved from their bodies. This humiliating exercise was enforced under the assumption that devils or evil spirits might hide or lurk in hair, especially pubic hair.

Most of those convicted of witchcraft were executed, although the sentence might be lighter for those accused of using magic or witchcraft to accomplish a good purpose, such as healing. Executions were often by burning, although other techniques were also employed. Most of the witch hunts and executions had ceased by the close of the eighteenth century.

The vast literature on witchcraft includes much discussion on the causes of such a belief system. Harris (1974) suggested that "the best way to understand the witch mania is to examine its earthly results rather than its heavenly intentions" (p. 237). It is true there was a theological backdrop that supported demonological views, but in addition, any problem—a death, a natural calamity, a financial failure, a physical or emotional illness—could be blamed on demons. Harris also noted that there was an economic basis for the witch hunts. Property was confiscated and sold and profits were made from the legal proceedings. Szasz (1970) claims that in many cases the idea of witchcraft was used to justify the execution of a person perceived to be atypical. Whatever the causes, the ideological basis of witchcraft was stubborn and died a slow death.

The Demise of Witchcraft

Russell (1980, p. 84) wrote that as early as 1563, the physician Johann Weyer (1515–1588) wrote a treatise *On Magic* arguing that witches were harmless old women suffering from mental disorders and that natural causes could explain most alleged cases of witchcraft. Because of such a bold claim, Weyer was himself accused of being a witch.

Two rationalist philosophers presented a stronger challenge to witchcraft. Baruch Spinoza denied any intermediate forces between human beings and God (Lea, 1957, p. 1361). If God is infinite, then God occupies all points in space and in time, and there can be no forces at work in the world other than God. Therefore, Spinoza denied the existence of the devil and demons and viewed belief in demons as nonsense (Almond, 2014). In an attempt to undermine biblical authority on demonology, he suggested that Jesus acquiesced to popular superstitions when he referred to demons.

Spinoza transformed the radical monotheism of his Jewish heritage into a monistic naturalism. There was a unity between God and nature and an emphasis on natural causality. Spinoza wished to understand all things, including human actions, in terms of natural forces. There were no other forces with which to contend. In his emphasis on causality and on the unity of nature, Spinoza constituted a challenge to the kind of dualism, animism, and vitalism inherent in demonology. His perspective was similar to later scientific thought.

René Descartes provided another major challenge to demonological viewpoints. His emphasis was on the relationship between the activities of the soul, presumably seated in the pineal gland, and the soul's interactions with other parts of the body. Lea (1957) concluded that Descartes's beliefs about the relationship between brain activity and psychological processes (e.g., dreams, images, memory) left no room for other agencies such as demons.

Humanitarian Reform

Numerous intellectual traditions provided a friendly context for the birth of psychology in the late nineteenth century. Empiricism, rationalism, advances in physiology, the development of new quantitative tools (especially statistics), evolutionary theory, and the naturalistic approach to mental and emotional disturbances all contributed to an intellectual climate supportive of a new science and profession. In addition to these intellectual developments, psychology arose and was nourished in an age of social agitation. Known as the Progressive Era in the United States, it was a time of vigorous social activism with a variety of agendas (Gendzel, 2011). Teeming with optimism, progressive causes inspired dramatic reform on issues such as universal education, improved sanitation, equality for women, birth control, animal rights, prison reform, work conditions in factories, the treatment of the mentally ill, and child protection.

Each reform movement raised questions that called for the development of new knowledge and for scientific investigation into new kinds of problems. For example, labor movements were a response to deplorable eighteenth- and nineteenth-century factory conditions, but there were legitimate concerns on the part of both management and labor about how to balance their respective interests. A growing need emerged for studies on workplace environments, work behavior, work motivation, efficient organizational structures, and equitable distribution of profits. The naturalistic approach to mental and emotional problems opened the door to studies on etiology and the effects of various treatment environments. The reformers themselves realized the need for controlled studies and sometimes collected informal data pertinent to their reform agendas. For example, Dorothea Dix observed that loss of employment and unusual religious excitement often preceded emotional breakdowns.

It is no accident that psychology was born in an age of humanitarian and progressive reform. Once established, though, concerns arose about whether the new discipline was prepared to assist with practical problems. We'll see in subsequent chapters that some psychologists believed the first step should be to build a fund of basic knowledge. Others were impatient to apply psychology to problems in education, mental disorders, industry, and the law. The United States provided fertile soil for attempts by the new discipline to answer the problems of daily life. In particular, a reform agenda built around the humane treatment of mental disorders played a critical role in the social and cultural background of the new psychology.

Reform in the Treatment of People with Emotional Disorders

The metaphysical challenge to witchcraft and demonology paralleled a challenge of a different sort in a reform movement designed to provide humane care for people with mental illness. Revolutionary in its scope, the idea was to treat patients not as witches or demons or animals, but as human beings. Although beliefs and practices varied, the humanitarian reformers brought sweeping changes both in psychiatric treatment and in the public perception of people with mental disorders. As we will see, Europe and the United States played host to some of the more dramatic advances in humanitarian care. Such treatment grew partly out of a naturalistic approach to people with emotional disorders, as illustrated in the work of Franz Anton Mesmer.

FRANZ ANTON MESMER   The son of a forester, **Franz Anton Mesmer (1734–1815)** (*MEZ mur*) was born on May 23, 1734, in Iznang in the German province of Swabia. He began preparing for the ministry at age nine, but music and other interests distracted him. In 1759, Mesmer journeyed to Vienna where he earned a medical degree seven years later. At age thirty-two, Mesmer had earned an M.D. as well as a Ph.D. with his doctoral dissertation titled "The Influence of the Planets on the Human Body" (Buranelli, 1975). In the tradition of the Renaissance alchemist Paracelsus, Mesmer believed that celestial bodies affect the health of our minds and bodies.

Like many scholars of his day, Mesmer had a long-standing interest in electricity and magnetism. In the 1770s, he consulted a professor of astronomy named Maximillian Hell (an ironic last name given that Hell was also a Jesuit priest). Mesmer was entranced as Hell described his use of magnets in healing the sick. Curious, the young physician conducted his own investigations on restoring the magnetic balance inside the body to eliminate sickness. Mesmer's magnetic therapy would soon bring fame beyond his wildest dreams. To no avail, Hell protested that Mesmer unfairly borrowed the idea from him.

Mesmer believed that the magnetism of iron, like the planetary bodies, affected a magnetic fluid in the body that controlled health and disease. He ran magnets across the bodies of his patients and found that some drifted into a trance. Bolstered by his findings on "animal magnetism," he treated patients with a variety of physiological symptoms including deafness, paralysis, blindness, rheumatism, headaches, and chronic pain. He even claimed to cure epilepsy and hysteria.

Although popular with Viennese society, the scientific community greeted Mesmer's animal magnetism with skepticism and scorn. In a celebrated case, he treated a blind concert pianist named Maria Theresia von Paradis, who happened to be a friend of Mozart. After Mesmer claimed he had restored her sight, several eminent physicians challenged his results and branded him a charlatan. In 1777, he was expelled from the medical faculty of the University of Vienna and barred from the practice of medicine. With his gift for controversy, it would not be the last time Mesmer clashed with medical authority (Oon, 2008).

By 1778 Mesmer was in exile in Paris where he caused an immediate sensation. Brimming with confidence and charisma, his flair for grandiosity was perfectly suited to the extravagance of pre-Revolutionary Parisian society (Hoffeld, 1980). Nestled in a suite at the Place Vendôme and later at the fashionable Hôtel Bullion, his clinic introduced the idea of psychotherapy as theater. In a dimly lit salon, patients gathered around a *baquet*, a large wooden tub filled with chemicals that Mesmer described—with a Cartesian flourish—as "animal spirits" (the tub contained nothing more than water and bits of metal, stone, and ground glass).

In one of the earliest attempts at group therapy, patients were instructed to take an afflicted part of their body, a paralyzed arm, say, and press it against iron rods rising from the sides of the *baquet*. As music from a glass armonica soothed in the background, supposedly enhancing the therapeutic effects (Zeitler, 2013), Mesmer made his grand entrance dressed in a lilac robe and brandishing a long iron wand, looking more like a sorcerer than a physician. He wandered from person to person, touching them with the wand and staring deep into their eyes. When he gave the command *Dormez* ("sleep"), his patients would slip into a trance. In the spell of this "crisis," some would tremble or twitch as if in the throes of a seizure. Others would groan or laugh or scream. A few would spin in a frenzied dance or collapse in a cold faint. But after the crisis had passed, most appeared to be free of their affliction.

Before long, Mesmer and his therapy were celebrated in both rich and poor circles. Among the wealthy and titled, Marie Antoinette and the Marquis de Lafayette joined the thousands who flocked to the clinic for the privilege of being mesmerized. As Mesmer's popularity soared, Mozart made mesmerism the stuff of friendly satire in his comic opera, *Così fan tutte* (Landon, 1990).

As in Vienna, however, the French medical community came to detest the practice of animal magnetism. Armed with a keen wit and the sort of bombast that might have impressed Paracelsus, Mesmer did not concede defeat. With characteristic audacity, Mesmer challenged the French Academy of Medicine to select twenty patients at random; he would treat ten and academy members would assume care for the remaining patients. Mesmer believed the clinical results would demonstrate the validity of his therapy (Hooley et al., 2013). The academy declined to participate in his contest. For Mesmer, their reluctance must have seemed a small victory in itself.

By 1784, the rift between Mesmer and his medical colleagues swelled into a heated confrontation that traveled all the way to the court of King Louis XVI. Sympathetic to Mesmer's cause, a group calling itself the "Society of Harmony" called on the monarchy to investigate. The king convened a panel of experts to determine if mesmerism was a legitimate medical practice or little more than a dangerous magic trick. The panel boasted intellectuals such as the American diplomat and scientist Benjamin Franklin (an ambassador to France at the time), the chemist Antoine-Laurent Lavoisier, the astronomer Jean-Sylvain Bailly, and Joseph Guillotin, a physician and proponent of the beheading machine (both Lavoisier and Bailly would be guillotined during the French Revolution). After examining the evidence, a verdict was issued on August 11, 1784:

The commissioners have ascertained that the animal magnetic fluid is not perceptible by any of the senses; that it has no action, either on themselves or on the patients subjected to it . . . Finally, [the commissioners] have demonstrated by decisive experiments that imagination apart from magnetism produces convulsions, and that magnetism without imagination produces nothing.

(Binet & Féré, 1887/1891, pp. 16–17)

Unable to find support for mesmerism, the commission insisted that any positive effects of the treatment were the product of deception or the power of suggestion (Bromberg, 1959). Interestingly, the committee also drafted a secret report for the king only, in which they observed that early practitioners were often, like Mesmer, highly charismatic men (Musikantow, 2011) and that mesmerism generally led to more intense reactions from women than men. In this secret report the committee raised questions about the threat to morals due to the physical closeness of "the magnetizer" to the woman, the practice of touching the woman's knees, back, and abdomen (including "the ovarium"), the excitation both parties felt with intense physical contact, and the potential for sexual coercion by magnetizers (Bailly et al., 1784/2002, p. 365).

The commission's decision shattered Mesmer's reputation and career. Denounced as an impostor, Mesmer closed his notorious practice and left Paris in disgrace. After a move to London and later Germany, he practiced animal magnetism but never regained the fame and fortune he had enjoyed in Paris. Mesmer died in obscurity in 1815, but his legacy is well preserved in the modern use of hypnotherapy (Gezundhajt, 2007).

Did Mesmer practice hypnosis? In the formal sense, no. But the practice of mesmerism relied on methods of suggestion that would be refined and investigated by a number of later hypnotherapists including Mesmer's follower Marquis de Puységur (1751–1825), who promoted more psychological explanations of these phenomena (Gielen & Raymond, 2015), as well as James Braid (1795–1860) and Jean-Martin Charcot (1825–1893). Charles Poyen brought mesmerism to the United States, where he faced similar threats to his credibility, compounded by the biases against working-class women, his most common participants (Quinn, 2012). Outside of psychology, Mesmer's ideas remained a source of fascination for the public and notable intellectuals of the nineteenth century. The novelist Charles Dickens (1812–1870) dabbled with mesmerical experiments, as did Ada Lovelace (1815–1852), a British mathematician and daughter of Lord Byron (Woolley, 1999). Interestingly, magnetic brain stimulation has recently been applied, with extensive limitations, as treatment for people with depression who have not had success with other approaches (Martens et al., 2013); Mesmer would likely approve.

PHILIPPE PINEL   After Mesmer, the face of humanitarian reform shifted to the work of a bold physician named **Philippe Pinel (1745–1826)** (*pe NEL*), who spearheaded widespread reform in French asylums. A scientist more than a performer, Pinel enjoyed a medical respectability that forever eluded Mesmer, joining the ranks of Freud and Kraepelin in historical prominence in psychiatry (Messias, 2014).

Born near Castres, France, in 1745, Pinel was the first of seven children and the product of a rich medical heritage—Pinel's father was a surgeon and his mother's family included several physicians. Following an early literary education, Pinel studied theology at Toulouse in 1767 and then switched to medical studies and earned his medical degree in 1773. Condillac's analytic method had a profound impact on Pinel's thinking (Riese, 1951), as did the ideas of Locke, Hippocrates, Rousseau, and Voltaire. A new way of thinking was taking shape with an emphasis on equality, freedom, education, and the improvement of all societal institutions. People with disadvantages were no longer regarded as possessed or evil, but rather as sick or as victims of cruel and uncaring social institutions.

In this climate of optimism about human perfectibility, Pinel introduced legendary reforms at the Bicêtre hospital and later at the Salpêtrière. Prior to his arrival in 1792, inmates at the Bicêtre hospital were confined in cramped, poorly ventilated, foul-smelling quarters where they lived in accumulations of filth. Disturbed by the horrible conditions, Pinel petitioned the French government about a plan to experiment with new methods of treatment. At last, an official visited the Bicêtre hospital and witnessed firsthand the spectacle of patients chained in cells and shouting obscenities. The government official granted the freedom to experiment, but warned that Pinel would likely become the victim of his own show of mercy.

The time had come for dramatic reform. Slowly and cautiously, Pinel liberated fifty patients. The poignant release of one man is illustrated in a memoir from Pinel's son as translated and abridged by Dix (1845/1971):

> The experiments commenced with an English captain, whose history was unknown; he had been in chains forty years! As he was thought to be one of the most dangerous, having killed, at one time, an attendant with a blow from his manacles, the keepers approached him with caution; but first Pinel entered his cell unattended. "Ah, well captain, I will cause your chains to be taken off; you shall have liberty to walk in the court, if you will promise to behave like a gentleman, and offer no assault to those you will meet." "I would promise," said the maniac; "but you deride me, you are amusing yourself at my expense; you all fear me, once free." "I have six men," replied Pinel, "ready to obey my orders; believe me, therefore, I will set you free from this duress, if you will put on this jacket." The captain assented; the chains were removed, and the jacket laced;—the keepers withdrew, without closing the door. He raised himself, but fell: this effort was repeated again and again; the use of his limbs, so long constrained, nearly failed: at length, trembling, and with tottering steps, he emerged from his dark dungeon. His first look was the sky! "Ah," cried he, "how beautiful!" The remainder of the day he was constantly moving to and fro, uttering continually exclamations of pleasure;—he heeded no one: the flowers, the trees, above all the sky, engrossed him. At night he voluntarily returned to his cell, which had been cleansed, and furnished with a better bed: his sleep was tranquil and profound. For the two remaining years which he spent in the hospital, he had no recurrence of violent paroxysms, and often rendered good service to the keepers, in conducting the affairs of the establishment.
>
> (pp. 30–31)

In dealing with patients, Pinel emphasized logical consequences. For example, when released from confinement or chains, patients were informed that continued freedom would depend on their behavior. Patient after patient responded to his humane treatment. In time, the fame of the reformer was ensured and his techniques were sometimes revered as an original discovery. In truth, Pinel's methods signaled a return to the psychological medicine of the ancient Greeks.

Based on clinical observation, Pinel's classic book *A Treatise on Insanity* (1806/1977) outlined a simplified and improved classification of mental disorders (Shorter, 2013). Influential in its time, his classification system distinguished five major clinical categories that he called "species." The first was *melancholia*, a disorder that includes depression and/or delusions, especially delusions of persecution or involving suspicion (Telles-Correia & Marques, 2015). The second species was *mania without delirium*, a disorder characterized by poor impulse control or acts of fury. Pinel's third species involved *mania with delirium*, characterized by continuous or intermittent nervous excitement and intellectual deterioration. He called the fourth species *dementia* and described it as "marked by ideas unconnected amongst themselves and without relation to external objects" (p. 161). The final category, *idiotisme*, involved a general reduction of intellectual capacity.

With regard to etiology, Pinel rejected the popular belief of his day that all mental disorders have an anatomical or physiological basis. Although he believed that some disorders are associated with malformed skulls, his own research revealed that many mental patients have no identifiable physiological or anatomical

Philippe Pinel in the courtyard of the Salpêtrière

atypicality. An individual's environment and lifestyle, Pinel argued, play powerful roles in the creation of mental illness.

Because the home environment might contribute to mental disorders, he encouraged the admission of patients to mental hospitals. In a 1794 address before the Society for Natural History, Pinel appealed to the Revolutionary French government to construct institutions designed for humane care (Weiner, 1992), a cause later taken up by the American reformer Dorothea Dix. Pinel concluded that hospitals should group patients according to the nature and severity of their disorders. Hospital management and treatment should be interrelated so that patients live in clean and uncrowded quarters with a chance to enjoy fresh air and sunlight as well as opportunities to engage in work. Physical restraint should be used only when necessary.

As one of the founders of *moral therapy* (a precursor to psychotherapy), Pinel dedicated a major section of his *Treatise* to "The Moral Treatment of Insanity." Moral therapy consisted of *talk treatment* in a supportive atmosphere with a therapist who respected the patient's dignity and responsibility. In several respects, Pinel's therapeutic philosophy foreshadowed the modern school of humanistic psychology discussed in Chapter 17.

BENJAMIN RUSH **Benjamin Rush (1745–1813)** was born on the outskirts of Philadelphia, the fourth of seven children. His father, John Rush, died when Benjamin was only five. During the next three years, he lived with his mother, Susanna Hall Harvey Rush, before joining a boarding school run by his uncle, Samuel Finley.

After boarding school, Rush entered the College of New Jersey (now Princeton University),

221

where he earned his bachelor's degree in 1760. He served in a medical apprenticeship from 1761 to 1766 and took courses at the College of Philadelphia. In the fall of 1766, he enrolled at the University of Edinburgh, where he received his medical degree two years later. In 1776, Rush returned to Philadelphia and practiced medicine, primarily among the poor. He was appointed chair of chemistry at the College of Pennsylvania, where he established a national reputation as a medical educator. As a member of the Continental Congress, Rush was an original signer of the Declaration of Independence. He briefly served as surgeon general of the army under George Washington. Disagreements with Washington over the quality of medical service, however, led to Rush's resignation.

During his lifetime, Rush pursued many social causes and wrote articles for the popular press in support of his reform interests. Rush was active in the abolition movement (Plummer, 1970),

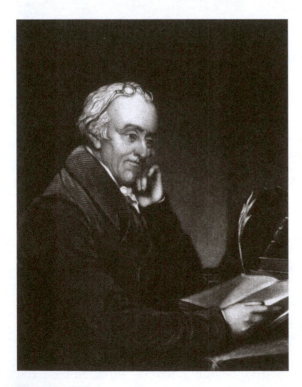

Benjamin Rush

joining the Pennsylvania Abolition Society in 1787 even though he owned a slave at the time (Horton & Horton, 2005). He also advocated for improved education for women, a national university system, flexibility in school curricula, and a stronger emphasis on practical subjects. He questioned the utility of Greek and Latin and encouraged the teaching of modern languages.

Rush (1806) protested the use of punishment as a means of controlling behavior. He called for reform of inhumane prison conditions and opposed public and capital punishment. He also disliked corporal punishment in schools because it interfered with learning and seemed contrary to the best ideals of a free people. Rush thought disruptive classroom behavior could be better handled through a private conversation with the student or a period of detention after school.

Although dedicated to political and social issues, Rush was also a visible leader in the care and treatment of people with psychological disorders. In 1812, he wrote *Medical Inquiries and Observations upon the Diseases of the Mind*, the first psychopathology textbook in America. He is recognized as the first American psychiatrist, and his image is immortalized in the official logo of the American Psychiatric Association.

In contrast with Pinel, Rush's approach to mental disorders is a curious blend of conservative Christianity and scientific materialism. On one hand, he believed in a theocentric universe and in a doctrine of original sin (see Carlson, 1977, pp. 74–104; Carlson & Simpson, 1964, pp. 290–214). On the other hand, Rush (1812/1818) claimed that all psychopathology was the product of physiological processes. As suggested in the title of his classic 1812 book, Rush viewed psychopathology as the study of "diseases of the mind." Mental disorders were thought to have their origin in the blood vessels of the brain. In his opinion, disturbances of circulation were the cause of all disease including mental disorders. As evidence for his theory, he compared the symptomatology of mental disorders with disorders such as strokes that have a known blood vessel pathology. When Rush observed abnormalities of pulse in mental patients, he took it as further proof for his circulation theory.

Rush sometimes departed from his circulation model when studying certain types of mental disease, although he seldom strayed from organic explanations. He also conducted early studies on multiple personality disorder, today called "dissociative identity disorder." The diagnosis of an American woman named Mary Reynolds (1793–1854), in 1811, is often regarded as the first case study of someone with multiple personalities. In fact, Rush had described three earlier cases of dissociation in which he accounted for this "doubling" as the product of an abnormal brain (Carlson, 1981).

He also conducted the first medical studies on alcohol and described them in a treatise called "An Inquiry into the Effects of Ardent Spirits upon the Human Body and Mind" (Keller, 1943). At a time when physicians believed drunkenness was neither a disease nor a compulsive condition, Rush became the first to claim that alcoholism was both an addiction and a progressive disease (Levine, 1978).

Rush was open to a variety of treatments and even considered ones his colleagues had discredited. Years after his friend Benjamin Franklin had failed to find value in Mesmer's work, Rush researched animal magnetism in 1789 and 1812 (Schneck, 1978). Although he rejected Mesmer's theory, he believed in the validity of suggestion and imagination and incorporated them into his clinical practice.

Like many physicians of his day, Rush practiced bloodletting, a method dating to Hippocrates. An excess of blood was thought to be responsible for both mental and physical disease, and Rush used bloodletting extensively to treat patients during the Yellow Fever outbreak in 1793. After George Washington developed a throat infection, his physicians drained almost two-thirds of his blood. Washington died hours later at Mount Vernon (Morens, 1999). Ironically, Rush was on trial in Philadelphia at the time for malpractice charges relating to his use of bleeding.

Some of Rush's more notorious and unorthodox treatments were inspired by his circulation theory. He invented a device known as the *gyrator*, a machine that whirled the patient in a circle to stimulate blood flow in the brain. Not surprisingly, many patients passed out after taking a spin in the gyrator. Rush also designed a *tranquilizing chair*, a large wooden chair used to temporarily restrain people experiencing mania. A person's arms and legs were strapped to the chair. A headpiece attached to the chair's back held the person's head in a rigid upright position. In case the individual was restrained for long periods, an opening in the seat contained a pail that caught urine and fecal matter. This treatment likely appears cruel and unusual to today's readers, but Rush had few effective treatments for comparison and believed his tranquilizing chair was more humane than binding people in straitjackets or handcuffs.

Although Rush's methods appear inhumane, he was motivated by sincere humanitarian concern. Rush had a genuine regard for his patients' dignity and demanded they receive adequate heating, baths, and employment. His treatments were not always physical; Rush recognized the importance of a supportive social and psychological environment (Mackler & Hamilton, 1967).

Despite attention to his views on mental disease, Rush's work on psychology has been unduly neglected. His lectures on the mind reveal far-reaching psychological interests (Carlson, Wollock, & Noel, 1981). His syllabus for a course on "physiology, pathology, hygiene, and the practice of medicine" covered topics such as the history of the nature of mind, instinct, memory, imagination, perception, association, hunger, thirst, dreams, sleep, somnambulism, reason, and volition.

Although not generally recognized, Rush coined the word *phrenology* (Noel & Carlson, 1970). He believed that phrenology need not refer to spirits or to an abstract philosophy of being; instead, he saw it as an intelligible and useful science of the mind (Carlson et al., 1981). Rush argued that phrenology was useful to the physician because disorders of the mind influence diseases of the body (Noel & Carlson, 1973).

223

As with his circulation theory, Rush's ideas about phrenology and psychology were grounded in physiology. He observed that physiological states influence moods. For example, a person may be irritable prior to breakfast, but affable afterward. Diet was important to mental outlook. Rush claimed that vegetables rather than meat had beneficial consequences for our moods. Climate also played a role in human emotional life, with foggy and rainy seasons triggering negative emotions and sunshine producing happiness. Rush believed that light and darkness, music, cleanliness, and pain influenced human emotions. So did idleness, which he considered the parent of all vice.

Like Philippe Pinel, Benjamin Rush's work shaped the development of psychiatry and humanitarian reform. Despite their influence, the reforms of both men did not translate into a social movement. For a time, reform was restricted to select medical circles. Before long, the call for humanitarian reform began to challenge abusive treatment of psychiatric patients.

Reform in Other Places

From the seventeenth through the nineteenth century, a number of mental hospitals became notorious for their treatment of patients. Although founded in 1247, the General Hospital of St. Mary of Bethlehem didn't become England's first royal hospital to specialize in treating the mentally ill until 1403. In 1547, King Henry VIII granted Bethlehem Hospital to London for the exclusive care of the insane provided the city fund an expansion of the facilities. Better known by its nickname "Bedlam" (now meaning a place of uproar and confusion), the hospital degenerated into a place where patients were treated like animals. In a climate of squalid and inhumane standards, patients were whipped and chained to walls. The hospital's indignities made their way into cultural awareness as evidenced in William Shakespeare's references to Bedlam in *King Lear* and other plays. Still, the public seemed unmoved

by the inhumane and squalid conditions. In 1675, Bedlam moved to Moorfields, London, where it became a popular tourist attraction with visitors paying to observe and even taunt the patients. Bedlam was not alone in its mistreatment of mental patients. Later in the United States, violent or hysterical patients at the New York State Lunatic Asylum were locked inside the "Utica Crib," a wooden cagelike box that resembled a coffin but with a little more breathing room.

In 1790, a Quaker widow named Hannah Mills struggled with melancholy and was confined to the York Asylum in Leeds, England (Digby, 1983). Her Quaker friends were not allowed to visit her and the young woman died a short time after her admission. Distraught over Hannah's improper care, the Quaker merchant and philanthropist **William Tuke (1732–1822)** resolved to create an alternative to "madhouses" like Bedlam and the York Asylum.

Tuke appealed to the Society of Friends to help establish the York Retreat in 1796. Without benefit of a medical background, he designed it as a place of moral and humane treatment that resembled the methods of Pinel (at the time, Tuke was unfamiliar with the French reformer's work) but was more personal and individual (Charland, 2002, 2007). In contrast with other European asylums, the York Retreat resided on a sprawling, picturesque country estate where patients enjoyed fresh air, rest, and the tranquility of nature. Tuke opposed the use of manacles and chains, and he did away with the widespread practice of bloodletting. Gentle supportive treatment and meaningful occupations were encouraged, along with education programs for attendants.

Later, Tuke's grandson, **Samuel Tuke (1784–1857)**, wrote *Description of the Retreat: An Institution Near York for Insane Persons of the Society of Friends* (1813), the first book-length description of a residential psychiatric institution (Raad & Makari, 2010). Subsequently, Tuke's great-grandson, **Daniel Hack Tuke (1827–1895)**, ran the York Retreat. Daniel Hack Tuke earned a medical degree from Heidelberg University in 1853. He distinguished himself as a leading authority on mental disorders and served as an editor of the *Journal of Mental Science*. He wrote numerous papers and wrote or edited several classic books including *A Dictionary of Psychological Medicine* (1892), *Illustrations of the Influence of the Mind upon the Body in Health and Disease* (1872), and *Insanity in Ancient and Modern Life, with Chapters on Prevention* (1878).

New models of humane care began to spread throughout Europe. In Italy, **Vincenzo Chiarugi (1759–c. 1820)** instituted humanitarian reform while working at Bonifazio Hospital and was one of the first to employ psychodrama as a clinical tool. Chiarugi's classification system and studies on etiology and treatment were similar to (and in many cases more advanced than) Pinel's work. At about the same time, Germany played host to several reform movements as well as a few important theoretical works. Some of the most influential ideas flowed from the pen of **Johann Christian Reil (1759–1813)**, a neuroanatomist (Fusa-Poli et al., 2009), one of the founders of modern psychotherapy, and the individual who coined the term *psychiatry* (Kaplan, 2012). Harms (1967) described Reil as a "psychological phenomenologist for whom the modern concepts of *Ganzheit*, totality, unity, centricity are basic elements of scientific interpretation" (p. 86). Reil viewed mental illness in terms of a failure of the basic unity of psychological processes. The failure of unity or centricity may result from either physical or social–psychological disturbances. Reil's approach to therapeutic intervention included psychodrama, occupational therapy, music therapy, and the encouragement of socially acceptable means of expressing emotion, and he strongly endorsed publicly supported residential treatment (Schochow & Steger, 2014). Although it would not arrive until a half-century later, Reil anticipated a time when worthwhile experiments would be conducted on the senses. He felt that such research would aid in understanding mental processes and psychopathology (see Harms, 1967). He saw a practical role for scientific psychology in the study of people with mental disorders.

Reform Becomes a Social Movement: Dorothea Dix

Reform in the care and treatment of mental disorders was, for a time, restricted to local settings. But by the mid-nineteenth century, humanitarian reform became a social movement throughout the United States and Europe. More than any other figure, an American named **Dorothea Lynde Dix (1802–1887)** was the catalyst for making the enlightened techniques of Pinel and Tuke available on a large scale. Prior to Dix, only the upper classes could afford the best treatment. If the "insane poor" were given treatment at all, it was usually of the brutal variety offered at inhumane asylums.

Dorothea Dix, the first of three children of Joseph Dix and Mary Bigelow Dix, was born on April 4, 1802. Her father, unsuccessful in several business ventures, underwent a climacteric religious conversion to become an itinerant Methodist preacher. He was moody, high strung,

Dorothea Dix

225

filled with evangelistic zeal, and often absent from the home. Dorothea's mother was an invalid who had little energy for normal household chores or for the care of Dorothea or her two younger brothers. Dorothea felt no love from her parents and once remarked that she never knew childhood. Gollaher (1995) suggests that Dix, like so many children in the early nineteenth century, was very likely subjected to considerable "physical and emotional mistreatment" (p. 20).

For reasons that are not entirely clear, Dorothea Dix left home at age twelve to live with her widowed paternal grandmother in Boston. In 1816, Dix traveled to Worcester to live with an aunt. Dix proved to be a brilliant student with a voracious appetite for knowledge. Indeed, at the young age of fourteen, she was allowed to start a private school for small children. She attempted to hide her youth with adult dress and mannerisms. As a teacher, she adopted the stern techniques of her time, demanding strict obedience, punctuality, respect, extensive drills, and memory work. Discipline was enforced with a birch rod. After three successful years as a teacher in Worcester, Dorothea Dix returned to her grandmother's home. In Boston, Dix continued her studies, seizing every possible educational opportunity. She took private instruction and enrolled in public lecture courses offered by Harvard professors. She made extensive use of public libraries and enjoyed the intellectual and spiritual stimulation provided by the preaching of the well-known Unitarian preacher William Ellery Channing. Dix developed a special fondness for history, science, and literature and established considerable expertise in botany and astronomy.

By 1821, Dix had opened a "dame" school at her grandmother's home in Orange Court. This school was one of many that prepared students for public grammar schools. Students were expected to read prior to entering the public schools; hence there was great demand for private preparatory schools. In addition to her dame school responsibilities, Dix opened a free evening school for poor children who could not afford the usual private schools. She was a devoted teacher who sought to expand her knowledge so that she might be more effective in the classroom. In spare hours, she worked on a book designed to provide parents and teachers with useful, well-researched information on how to answer children's questions on common natural topics. Her book featured over three hundred questions that children ask: What causes a rainbow? What are clouds? Where do diamonds come from? Her little book was perfect for parents and teachers of the day who struggled to find answers for such questions. First published under the title *Conversations on Common Things*, Dix's book went through sixty editions.

By 1841, it appeared that Dix's career was over. A chronic pulmonary disorder had forced her to take leave of teaching activities for enforced periods of bed rest. In March, she was recovering from an extended illness but had nevertheless agreed to substitute for a Unitarian ministry student who was unable to teach his Sunday School class at the East Cambridge jailhouse.

What Dorothea Dix observed at the jail on that cold New England morning in 1841 changed her life.

In that day, hardened criminals were crammed into the same cell with alcoholics and people with mental illnesses, as well as people who had been diagnosed as "feebleminded" (a then-popular classification used to describe individuals with cognitive disabilities). The stench of human waste arose from overcrowded cells filled with filth. Shivering from the cold, prisoners huddled together to stay warm in the unheated cells. The stench and misery shocked Dix. She pleaded with the jailer to heat the cells. He refused, declaring that these inmates were incapable of feeling heat or cold and the criminals deserved to freeze. The inhumane conditions compelled Dix to seek court action. Her appeal was victorious, and conditions at the East Cambridge jailhouse improved. The facility was cleaned and the cells were heated for the prisoners.

Invigorated by her accomplishment, Dix investigated the conditions of mental patients and prisoners throughout Massachusetts. The former schoolteacher consulted with authorities and studied the available literature to learn the most advanced views on mental illness. The work of the Tukes in England and Pinel in France impressed Dix. Their enlightened techniques contrasted with the prevailing custodialism in most almshouses and jails.

During extensive travels throughout Massachusetts, Dix discovered that many facilities matched the appalling conditions she had encountered in the East Cambridge jailhouse. Quarters in almshouses and jails were unfurnished, sanitation was neglected, heat was seldom provided, and diets were inadequate. Many mentally ill and "feebleminded" people roamed the countryside. In some respects, they may have been more fortunate than mental patients confined in asylums.

Conducting some of the earliest social research in America, Dix armed herself with data from her extensive investigations and prepared a "memorial" for the lawmakers of Massachusetts. With the help of powerful political figures such as Horace Mann, Senator Charles Sumner, and Dr. Samuel Gridley Howe, she convinced legislators that additional facilities and personnel were needed to provide for the care and treatment of the mentally ill. As a result of Dix's research and her memorial, funds were set aside for an expansion of the state hospital at Worcester. Instead of the one hospital at Worcester, Dix would have preferred an additional smaller hospital in a different location. Nevertheless, her memorial was successful and her career as a reformer was launched.

After the victory in Massachusetts, Dix continued her investigations in other states. Her reform activities followed a familiar pattern: extensive research into existing conditions, contact with key political figures, preparation of a memorial describing existing conditions, and requests for new or additional facilities. Dix didn't make public speeches; instead, she asked respected political figures to read her memorials to legislative bodies. Her forty years of reform work produced extensive accomplishments. She played a key role

in the founding of thirty-two mental hospitals, several schools for those with cognitive deficits, training facilities for nurses, and improvements in prisons and mental institutions.

In part, her achievements were due to a prevailing mood that proved receptive to humanitarian reform. Dix was also well organized, energetic, and persuasive. Her extensive knowledge of psychopathology contributed to her success. Indeed, Dain (1964) contended that her knowledge compared favorably with leading authorities of her day. Her memorials (see Viney, 1996b; Viney & Bartsch, 1984) reveal an understanding of mental illness and acquaintance with the legal aspects of the subject. Her views on etiology recognized physiological, psychological, and social contributions. She believed the brain was the organ of the mind but mental illness was also *the offspring of civilization*. She was particularly impressed with the role of unemployment, loss of family or possessions, and abnormal religious excitement in the etiology of mental disorders. She believed that treatment should include good diet, exercise, amusement (including music, games, and reading), and meaningful occupation. Dix opposed custodialism, except for hopelessly incurable cases. Her memorials focused on treatment and curability. Accordingly, she raised money, not only for buildings but also for libraries, musical instruments, museums, and in one case, a bowling alley. She had a keen interest in anything that would facilitate therapeutic intervention.

Stevens and Gardner (1982) claimed that Dorothea Dix represented the conscience of early psychology. They argued that without Dix and other humanitarian reformers, psychology might have been restricted to laboratory investigations or might have stagnated altogether. Popular and practical concern created a friendly atmosphere for the development of a new discipline. Her ability to mobilize public opinion about psychological issues makes Dix's contributions greater than has been recognized.

During the American Civil War, Dix's reform activities were interrupted while she served as Superintendent of Union Army Nurses. Following

227

the war, she returned to work as a reformer, but didn't enjoy the influence of her earlier years. This was partly due to the devastating economic effects of the Civil War. Funds for social projects such as the building of hospitals were no longer available. Interest in the needs of the mentally ill faded after her death in 1887. During the next decades, conditions in mental hospitals deteriorated. Unfortunately, many hospitals became almost as custodial as the jails and almshouses they had replaced.

Others joined Dix in the movement toward humane residential treatment of people with psychological disorders, most prominently **Thomas S. Kirkbride (1809–1883)**. Kirkbride also brought the approaches of Pinel to the United States, and he emphasized the built environment of the hospital itself. To maximize healing he believed that well-designed buildings and grounds could provide beauty as well as meaningful work, and his plans (Kirkbride, 1994/1845) set the standards for institutions across the United States, which are now largely shuttered (Payne & Sacks, 2009). Additionally, in 1844 at his home in Pennsylvania, Kirkbride and others founded the Association of Medical

Superintendents of American Institutions for the Insane, which later evolved into the American Psychiatric Association (Silver, 2009), the organization that publishes the *Diagnostic and Statistical Manual of Mental Disorders* (2013). Large residential institutions remained the primary method of treating people with psychological disorders until deinstitutionalization in the mid- and late twentieth century.

Reform in the Care and Treatment of People with Cognitive Disabilities

Prior to the modern era, physical and mental disabilities were regarded as the work of demons or as evidence of the sins of the parents. For example, engaging in intercourse during menstruation was viewed as a sin that produced defective children. Ranke-Heinemann (1990) documented the teachings of numerous thirteenth-century theologians who attributed birth defects to the poisonous effects of menstrual blood on the male seed. Children born with disabilities were sometimes regarded as *changelings*, a term referring to

Fergus Falls Asylum, a Kirkbride institution in Fergus Falls, MN

a substituted infant. Some believed that an evil force replaced a legitimate and normal child with a defective one. Tragically, children branded as changelings were often neglected, abused, abandoned, or sacrificed.

More naturalistic approaches to people with cognitive disabilities occurred alongside reforms in the care and treatment of people with mental illnesses. A pioneer in the study and training of mental deficiency was **Jean-Marc Gaspard Itard (1775–1838)**, a French physician and teacher of the deaf, who anchored his medical views on the primacy of the senses (Newman, 2006). An accidental discovery stimulated Itard's work on people with mental deficiencies. In 1799, three hunters found a naked boy covered in scars. He tried to escape but was captured. The boy, about ten years of age, had apparently been abandoned by his parents, but had somehow managed to survive in the wild near Aveyron in southern France. When he was first captured, he displayed characteristics of a wild animal and appeared unmanageable.

The "wild boy of Aveyron" aroused interest among scientists and the public. After considering his case, Philippe Pinel diagnosed the boy as an "incurable idiot" (Gaynor, 1973, p. 439). Itard disagreed.

He worked with the boy, Victor, for years (Constant, 2014). Itard was not able to teach the boy to speak, but progress and desirable changes were made. The boy became affectionate and responsive. He learned to understand many words and could engage in useful tasks but was unable to acquire language skills. Later scholars have suggested that Victor likely had a form of autism (Thompson, 2014). Additionally, in 1825 Itard evaluated people who exhibited involuntary movements in what later observers called the first clinical study of Tourette Syndrome (Newman, 2010). Across these domains, despite limited success, Itard's work was suggestive of what might be accomplished on a larger scale with other individuals with cognitive disabilities.

Another Frenchman, **Édouard Séguin (1812–1880)**, developed a systematic approach for sensory training and self-care skills for individuals with cognitive disabilities (Toth & King, 2010). Séguin sought ways to assist individuals in developing their innate sensory and motor capacities so they could engage in useful skills. He worked first in France and later in the United States where his work attracted public attention. Soon, fund-raising efforts made by reformers such as Dorothea Dix resulted in training facilities for people with mental deficiency. Scholars realized the need for the systematic study of learning processes and the development of training techniques. Thus, another reform movement created a need for the systematic study of topics such as learning, sensory and motor processes, and motivation that were later to become standard content areas of psychology.

Women's Reform Movements

In Chapter 6, we discussed Mary Wollstonecraft's classic work *A Vindication of the Rights of Woman* and John Stuart Mill's work *The Subjection of Women*. These visionary writers were reacting to the long history of the subordination of women. Women, compared with men, were commonly regarded as less intelligent, less creative, more emotional, and relatively uninterested in commercial, political, economic, and philosophical questions. Gender stereotypes were used to justify restrictions on property rights, educational opportunities, voting privileges, and work opportunities for women. It was further argued that women were incapacitated once each month because of the menstrual cycle.

By the mid- to late nineteenth century, there was growing agitation for women's rights and a corresponding public interest in the abilities of women. Public interest was stimulated by an outpouring of popular magazine articles on topics such as the education of women, the intelligence of women, gender differences in emotional expression, and voting rights for women. Many articles were written in defense of old stereotypes, but several challenged older ways of thinking. Such challenges, along with the demands of reformers in the women's movement, stimulated a climate conducive to impartial studies of gender differences. In fact, many of the sex stereotypes lent themselves to experimental investigation and some of the early psychological research delivered a deathblow to many of the old attitudes about women. For example, Leta Stetter Hollingworth (see Chapter 12) conducted research demonstrating that the menstrual cycle did not mentally or physically incapacitate women.

The women's reform movements grew out of a long and painful history with entrenched traditions regarded by many as sacred. Following the American Civil War, religious magazines presented an ongoing debate about whether women should be allowed to speak in church services (see Knowlton, 1867; Torrey, 1867). Disputes grew out of the interpretive difficulties of scriptures such as I Corinthians 14:34–35, which was used as a source of authority for those who forbade women to speak in church. If women could not speak in church, there was little possibility for them to assume positions of spiritual leadership. The undercutting of leadership roles for women in the religious arena was common in Western as well as Middle Eastern and Islamic traditions (Lippman, 1995, p. 96). It may be argued that the subordination of women in some religious traditions did not reflect true interpretations of those traditions, but as a practical fact, such subordination took place and continues to take place in some traditions. In many religious and cultural traditions, women were and are required to lower their eyes, cover their heads, veil their faces, avoid adorning themselves with jewelry, and cultivate habits of humility, obedience, submission, domesticity, and chastity. Only men could fill leadership roles in religious venues.

The late nineteenth century witnessed an unprecedented battle for a new orientation toward women and a new and informed appraisal of their intellectual abilities and personal and spiritual gifts. Such an appraisal, of course, would become grist for the work of psychologists. The battle itself was waged on many fronts (e.g.,

access to university education, new employment opportunities, property rights), but the most visible facet of the battle was in the arena of suffrage or the right of women to vote. American reformers such as Susan B. Anthony (1820–1906) and Elizabeth Cady Stanton (1815–1902) spearheaded the battle. The intensity of the battle is graphically illustrated in the film *Iron Jawed Angels* featuring the story of Alice Paul and other young activists who were jailed and force-fed when they went on a hunger strike (see Pilcher, 2004). Their story shocked the conscience of lawmakers and the nation and played a significant role in the change of attitudes ultimately resulting in the passage of the Nineteenth Amendment. Even so, progress was slow as legislation was introduced in Congress each year for more than forty years before the Nineteenth Amendment to the U.S. Constitution was finally passed in 1920. Opponents of the legislation made radical claims that illustrate the depth of feelings and the fervor of the battle. In *The Ladies Home Journal*, former president Grover Cleveland (1837–1908) argued that "sensible women" (p. 7) had no desire to vote, always avoided any situation in which women could talk unsupervised by men, and understood their divinely appointed subordinate roles (Cleveland, 1905).

MARGARET SANGER AND FAMILY LIMITATION Another facet of the women's movement was as intense and controversial as suffrage and, in some quarters, remains controversial to the present day. The dynamics of family life and the effects of family structures on individual personality development would later become important areas for social and developmental psychologists, but early sensitivities to these topical areas are found in the work of reformers in the women's movement.

Margaret Sanger (1883–1966), as the sixth of eleven children, was convinced that the birthing (she and her ten siblings *all* weighed more than ten pounds at birth) and rearing demands of a large family contributed to her mother's premature death at age forty-nine. Sanger observed critical differences between large and small families in her New York neighborhood, especially related to economic concerns. Large families were generally poor; smaller families were not. In her early years, she developed a concern with issues pertaining to the quality of life for children and women. Her mother remained a devout Catholic to her death while her father was best described as an intellectual, an impractical artist, a fiercely independent thinker, and an atheist. Sanger identified with the plight of her mother and with her father's intellectual independence. Her home life prepared her for a career as a reformer with its demands to fight for a cause while standing firm against critical attacks.

Educated as a nurse, Sanger was moved by the plight of poor women. Her work brought a renewed awareness of the poverty associated with large families. She also faced continuing inquiries from poor women about how to control conception. Women sometimes begged for the secrets of birth control, but Sanger had no satisfactory answers. Doctors often advised women simply to avoid sex, but the effectiveness of such advice assumed the cooperation of husbands. A turning point came when Sanger was called to the apartment of Sadie Sachs who fell ill after a self-induced abortion. Following her recovery, Sachs pleaded with her physician about information for avoiding another pregnancy. The doctor gave the usual unsatisfactory answer. Later, Sanger was called back to the apartment. This time, Sachs slipped into a coma and died from yet another self-induced abortion. As in earlier periods, such tragic events were common in the late nineteenth and into the mid-twentieth century. Sachs's death was pivotal and Sanger devoted herself to women's health issues. She focused on disseminating information on women's health and on safe and effective reproductive control.

Sanger believed that women's health and their social equality depended, in part, on birth control. In her campaign to improve public knowledge, she published pamphlets that described safe birth control methods (Eig, 2014). Later, she formed organizations such as the National Birth Control League, the Voluntary Parenthood League, and the American Birth Control League, subsequently to become the Planned Parenthood Federation of America. Just as resistance greeted the suffrage movement, Sanger's work endured strong and vocal opposition.

During Sanger's time, a conservative reformer named Anthony Comstock (1844–1915) led a crusade against literature that he deemed as obscene. Known as the Comstock Law, a ruling forbade the U.S. Postal Service from delivering obscene materials. Because Sanger's pamphlets contained explicit descriptions of birth control devices, the Postal Service deemed them obscene and confiscated them. In 1916, Sanger opened the first birth control clinic in the United States for the purpose of distributing contraceptive materials. Crowds of desperate women lined up to take advantage of clinic services. Little more than a week after the clinic opened, Sanger was arrested and jailed on charges of creating a "public nuisance."

Grounded in compelling moral issues, her trial aroused public interest. The final outcome was a small but significant victory. Though the Comstock Law itself was not thrown out, the court ruled that physicians could provide contraceptive advice as a means of preventing disease. In 1937, the American Medical Association endorsed the teaching of contraception in medical schools. Shortly after Sanger's trial, birth control information could be sent through the mail, but it was not until 1967 that the Supreme Court extended the right of birth control to married couples (Garraty & Carnes, 1999).

Sanger and her work remain highly controversial. Like Mary Wollstonecraft, Sanger's detractors call attention to what they regard as disagreeable features in her character and personal life, such as her support for testing medication on psychiatric inmates (May, 2010). Because she promoted birth control for minorities, critics accused her of eugenics. Such an accusation is questionable; poverty and its effects were the true focus of Sanger's efforts, and she was not a leader in the broader eugenics movement (O'Brien, 2013). Sanger was known to be a socialist, she had affairs, her first marriage ended in divorce, and she was as vocal in her criticism of her detractors as they were of her. Hostility to Sanger was based partly on the fact that her work challenged doctrines regarded by many as sacred though leaders in numerous religious traditions supported her work. Sanger deepened public sensitivities to issues pertinent to human health and particularly to the health of women. Her reform program opened the door to increased reproductive freedom by challenging the restrictive legal structures of her day. Her work also had a direct effect on scientific work. Indeed, she provided the funding that led directly to the development of the first birth control pills. Sanger also helped shape the intellectual context for later research on health psychology and human sexuality.

The naturalistic perspective provided a foundation for the study of the nature and origin of life and emotional disorders in addition to fostering an intellectual climate responsive to the development of psychology. As a formal discipline, psychology was born in an age of unprecedented humanitarian reform and on the heels of Darwin's revolutionary work. Understanding of the formal birth of psychology is enhanced by an awareness of these intellectual and social developments.

Review Questions

1. Outline the development of evolutionary thought regarding the solar system and geology.
2. Trace key developments in the theory of organic evolution prior to Darwin.
3. List and describe four technical features of Darwin's theory of evolution.
4. Discuss the significance of evolutionary theory to psychology and show specific influences of evolutionary theory on the development of psychology.
5. List at least six major social reform movements that took place in the nineteenth century.

6. Briefly describe the three major subdivisions of the *Malleus Maleficarum*.
7. How did Spinoza and Descartes challenge beliefs in witchcraft?
8. Outline the contributions of Benjamin Rush and Philippe Pinel to reforms in the understanding of mental illness.
9. Dorothea Dix was a great social reformer but also had substantive views on mental illness. What were her views on the origin and treatment of people with psychological disorders?
10. Briefly, how did Jean Itard and Édouard Séguin advance our understanding of people with cognitive disabilities?

Glossary

Buffon, Comte de (1707–1788) One of the great French scientists of the eighteenth century remembered, among other things, for an early theory of geological evolution that challenged the strict biblical chronology advanced by Archbishop Ussher. Buffon was also one of the first of the modern scientists to offer a theory of organic evolution.

catastrophe theory View of evolutionary change advanced by the French scientist Cuvier that earth-wrenching catastrophes may have annihilated entire species and that such catastrophes have produced abrupt changes in populations and their characteristics. Contrast with *uniformitarianism.*

Chiarugi, Vincenzo (1759–c. 1820) Italian humanitarian who instituted reforms in the treatment and care of the mentally disturbed prior to Pinel in France. Chiarugi was one of the first to employ psychodrama as a therapeutic tool.

cosmogony The study of the origin of the cosmos or the universe.

Cuvier, Georges (1769–1832) French biologist who argued that evolutionary change is often abrupt because it is brought about by great natural catastrophes.

Darwin, Charles (1809–1882) Modern evolutionary theorist who supported his theory of evolution with a wealth of empirical evidence. Darwin and Alfred Russel Wallace also proposed a mechanism for evolution based on natural selection that was acceptable to a large number of scientists. Darwin was also a pioneer in the study of developmental processes in small children.

Darwin, Erasmus (1731–1802) Grandfather of Charles Darwin and a member of England's Lunar Society who argued that natural processes evolve without divine intervention. Erasmus Darwin's theory of evolution was based on the concept of inheritance of acquired characteristics.

demonology Literally, *the study of demons*, but the term also refers to belief in demons as causal agents.

Descartes, René (1596–1650) French philosopher who is often regarded as the founder of modern philosophy. Descartes made extensive original contributions in a great variety of areas. He helped elaborate early scientific methodology, provided rich and often testable hypotheses about the relationships between behavior and physiology, and is regarded as one of the key figures in modern rationalism.

Dix, Dorothea Lynde (1802–1887) American humanitarian reformer who worked for over forty years on behalf of the insane poor. Dix advocated a therapeutic climate for curable patients and humane living conditions for all patients.

Galton, Francis (1822–1911) Cousin of Charles Darwin and pioneer in the study of individual differences. Galton emphasized the hereditary basis of individual differences.

Haeckel, Ernst Heinrich (1834–1919) German zoologist, one of the first to emphasize the importance of evolutionary theory to psychology.

heuristic theory A heuristic theory fosters discovery, learning, and predictive efficiency.

inheritance of acquired characteristics Belief held by many early theorists such as Erasmus Darwin and Lamarck that acquisitions of parents are passed on to offspring. This explanation of evolutionary change was rejected in mainstream biology at the beginning of the twenty-first century.

Itard, Jean-Marc Gaspard (1775–1838) A French teacher of hearing-impaired individuals and early pioneer in the training and treatment of mental deficiency.

Kant, Immanuel (1724–1804) German rationalist who is remembered for his naturalistic account of the origin of the solar system.

Kirkbride, Thomas S. (1809–1883) Builder of large residential treatment complexes and founder of the Association of Medical Superintendents of American Institutions for the Insane, which later became the American Psychiatric Association.

Lamarck, Jean-Baptiste (1744–1829) French biologist remembered for his early original work on the nature of species and for an early theory of organic evolution based on the inheritance of acquired characteristics.

Laplace, Pierre Simon de (1749–1827) French scientist who advanced an early naturalistic account of the solar system known as the *nebular hypothesis.*

Lyell, Charles (1797–1875) Often regarded as the founder of modern geology. His classic three-volume *Principles of Geology* presented a view of the evolution of the earth marked by the belief that change occurs over vast stretches of time. This view is sometimes called *gradualism* or *uniformitarianism.*

Malleus Maleficarum Literally, *The Hammer against Witches*. A book published in 1486 by Dominican friars Heinrich Kramer and Jacob Sprenger that served as a guide for detecting and prosecuting suspected witches during the Inquisition.

Malthus, Thomas Robert (1766–1834) Author of *An Essay on the Principle of Population* that set forth the hypothesis that populations may outgrow their food supply because food supply tends to increase arithmetically while populations increase geometrically.

233

Mesmer, Franz Anton (1734–1815) French physician who proposed a magnetic therapy that allegedly eliminated sickness by restoring magnetic balance inside the body. Although his career was marked by controversy, he pioneered an early form of hypnosis that became known as *mesmerism*.

Morgan, Conwy Lloyd (1852–1936) English biologist, philosopher, and psychologist who made extensive contributions to comparative psychology. He is remembered for a regulative principle that came to be known as *Morgan's canon* which states: "In no case may we interpret an action as the outcome of the exercise of a higher psychical faculty, if it can be interpreted as the outcome of the exercise of one which stands lower in the psychological scale."

naturalism The doctrine that scientific procedures and laws are applicable to all phenomena.

natural selection A concept employed by Darwin to account for survival and extinction. Darwin believed that in the population of any species, some variants are, by chance, better adapted to certain niches; other variants may, by chance, be less well adapted. Advantages or disadvantages of parents will be passed on genetically to offspring. Thus, there is a natural selection for survival and extinction.

nebular hypothesis In astronomy, the hypothesis that the solar system evolved from bodies of rarefied gases and dust in interstellar space.

ontogeny recapitulates phylogeny Belief advanced first by Ernst Haeckel that the history of the individual (ontogeny) recapitulates the history of the species (phylogeny).

Pinel, Philippe (1745–1826) French physician and humanitarian reformer who advanced an early modern classification system of mental disorders. Pinel is typically remembered for cleaning up living conditions for those who were mentally ill and advocating therapy instead of custodialism.

Preyer, William Thierry (1841–1897) Pioneer in child psychology whose classic book *The Mind of the Child* served as a powerful impetus for the study of developmental processes.

Reil, Johann Christian (1759–1813) One of the founders of modern psychotherapy and an early advocate of experimental studies of basic psychological processes.

Romanes, George John (1848–1894) English biologist and Darwinian who helped found a science of comparative psychology. He is often criticized for his anecdotal methods, but he was aware of the problems of anecdotalism and argued for a broad methodology.

Rush, Benjamin (1745–1813) Early American physician who argued for liberal reforms such as the abolition of slavery and of public whippings. His book *Medical Inquiries and Observations upon the Diseases of the Mind* advocated humane treatment for mentally ill patients. He understood the value of warm baths, meaningful employment, and a supportive psychological environment as part of the treatment program for patients.

Sanger, Margaret (1883–1966) American reformer deeply concerned about women's health issues. She was instrumental in making accurate information about contraception available to the public and was a founder of the Planned Parenthood Federation of America.

Séguin, Édouard (1812–1880) French pioneer in the study and treatment of mentally deficient individuals. Séguin's efforts helped inspire fund-raising for training facilities for mentally deficient people. His work also encouraged the development of scientific studies of basic psychological processes.

Spencer, Herbert (1820–1903) English philosopher who attempted to apply evolutionary thought to all branches of human knowledge. Evolution was thus a unifying principle for his philosophy. He is sometimes regarded as a forerunner of American functionalism.

Tuke, Daniel Hack (1827–1895) For many years, the head of the York Retreat in England and a key figure in promoting scientific studies of mental illness and humanitarian treatment of people who are mentally ill.

Tuke, Samuel (1784–1857) William Tuke's grandson, who wrote the first book-length description of an institution that provided residential care to people with psychological disorders.

Tuke, William (1732–1822) Philanthropist who helped found the York Retreat in England. The York Retreat incorporated the most advanced humanitarian treatment techniques available in its day.

uniformitarianism The belief that evolutionary change is gradual and that most change occurs over vast stretches of time. Contrast with *catastrophe theory*.

Wallace, Alfred Russel (1823–1913) Simultaneously with Darwin, advanced a theory of organic evolution based on the concept of natural selection.

Part IV

Psychology from the Formal Founding in 1879

Chapters 10 through 18 cover the history of psychology from the time of its formal founding by Wilhelm Wundt in Leipzig, Germany, in 1879 to early developments in the twenty-first century. The timeline includes the dates of major publications and events within psychology as well as critical historical events that help provide a larger sense of cultural context. Notice that this section of the text covers major systems of psychology such as functionalism, behaviorism, Gestalt psychology, and psychoanalysis. Events listed on the timeline are associated with developments within some of the major systems, but others are of general interest to all psychologists regardless of theoretical orientation.

TIMELINE 10.1

1875 to 2016

1875	William James teaches psychology at the graduate level
1879	Wilhelm Wundt founds the first psychology laboratory in Leipzig, Germany
1881	Wundt founds the journal *Philosophical Studies*
1885	*Memory: A Contribution to Experimental Psychology* by Hermann Ebbinghaus
1890	*Principles of Psychology* by William James
	Mental Tests and Measurements by James McKeen Cattell
1892	G. Stanley Hall helps found the American Psychological Association (APA)
	Edward Bradford Titchener accepts a position at Cornell University
1895	Mary Whiton Calkins passes her unauthorized dissertation defense
1896	"The Reflex Arc Concept in Psychology" by John Dewey
1900	*The Interpretation of Dreams* by Sigmund Freud
1902	*Varieties of Religious Experience* by William James
1905	Mary Calkins becomes first female president of the APA
	Alfred Binet and Théodore Simon publish first usable intelligence test
1908	*On the Witness Stand* by Hugo Münsterburg
1909	Clark University Conference organized by G. Stanley Hall
1912	Max Wertheimer launches the Gestalt psychology movement
1913	"Psychology as the Behaviorist Views It" by John B. Watson
1914	Beginning of World War I
1917	Robert Yerkes introduces Army Alpha and Army Beta tests
1920	Nineteenth Amendment providing voting rights for women
1924	*The Mentality of Apes* by Wolfgang Köhler
1928	*Lectures on Conditioned Reflexes* by Ivan P. Pavlov
1929	U.S. stock market crashes and Great Depression begins worldwide
1933	Adolf Hitler becomes chancellor of Germany
1936	Otto Loewi and Sir Henry Hallett Dale share the Nobel Prize for the discovery of the neurotransmitter acetylcholine
1938	*The Behavior of Organisms* by B. F. Skinner
1941	United States enters World War II
1942	*Counseling and Psychotherapy* by Carl Rogers
1945	*Productive Thinking* by Max Wertheimer
1949	Boulder Conference on Graduate Education in Clinical Psychology
1950	*The Authoritarian Personality* by Theodor Adorno
	The Individual and His Religion by Gordon Allport
1952	First edition of the *Diagnostic and Statistical Manual of Mental Disorders (DSM)*
1954	Social scientists contribute to the case of *Brown v. Board of Education*
1958	*Psychotherapy by Reciprocal Inhibition* by Joseph Wolpe
1967	*Cognitive Psychology* by Ulric Neisser
1973	The last combat soldiers from the United States officially leave Vietnam
1979	*Eyewitness Testimony* by Elizabeth Loftus
1988	Founding of the American Psychological Society (APS)
1994	American Psychiatric Association publishes *DSM-IV*
2000	Scientists map human genome
2006	Final publications of *Psychological Abstracts*; the abstracts are replaced by an electronic guide to the world's literature in psychology known as PsycINFO
2013	American Psychiatric Association publishes *DSM-5*
2015	Hoffman Report

10 Psychophysics and the Formal Founding of Psychology

I have proceeded on the conviction that law and order even if they are not fundamentally sound are better than contradictions and lawlessness.
—Hermann Von Helmholtz (1896)

As we have seen in previous chapters, many important intellectual forces contributed to a climate friendly to the birth and nourishment of psychology. The most direct influences, however, came from developments in physiology, pointing to the possibility that mental processes could be measured (Evans, 2000). This chapter reviews selected scientific projects in physiology that led to the founding of the new discipline of psychology. The chapter then examines the formal founding of psychology and the first systematic approach to the discipline.

Psychophysics

The term **psychophysics** refers to the study of the relationships between physical properties of stimuli and the psychological or subjective impressions of those stimuli. Psychophysics began as informal speculation and wonder about the nature of the relationship between objects in the world and our perceptions of those objects. In Chapter 2, we reviewed theoretical positions regarding what we can claim to know about objects in the world. One extreme position is encountered in the solipsistic claim that we can know only our own private experience. Another extreme position, naïve realism, contends that we see external things as they are. In a limited and modest way, early studies in psychophysics challenged both extreme positions.

Psychophysics involves the study of the properties of stimuli as measured by a physical scale and psychological impressions of those stimuli. For example, we can measure a series of tones in terms of vibrations or frequencies. With proper equipment, a graded series can be presented with known physical characteristics. One of the most obvious discoveries about any graded series is that there are values on the lower and upper extremes that do not register in experience. For tones, the term *hertz (Hz)* is used as the international unit equal to one cycle per second, and the typical young person hears values from approximately 20 Hz to 20,000 Hz. In other words, there are lower and upper thresholds. The measurement of thresholds provides a small quantitative opening into the world of private experience. Such **thresholds** were defined operationally as that minimal or maximal stimulus intensity that is detected 50 percent of the time. Although psychophysics emerged in the context of the study of thresholds and other phenomena in music (Hui, 2013; Kim, 2014), part of the early work in psychophysics was directed at investigating *lower* and *upper thresholds* for varieties of stimuli in all sensory modalities.

Another type of threshold that was investigated was called the **difference threshold**—the minimal stimulus difference that is detectable 50 percent of the time. For example, an experimenter may stimulate the surface of the skin of a research participant with two points of an adjustable compass known as an **aesthesiometer**. The participant, under certain conditions, may report the presence of a single sensation, even though both points of the aesthesiometer contact the skin. The task of the experimenter is to assess the two-point threshold (that distance where two points are experienced as two points instead of one point). It has been found that there are relatively insensitive areas (e.g., the back) where the two-point threshold may be well over 40 millimeters (mm) (over 1.5 inches). At the other extreme, the two-point threshold may be as small as 1 mm in a sensitive area (e.g., the tip of the tongue or the tips of the fingers).

Psychophysical methods permitted quantitative assessments of selected mental processes. By assessing absolute thresholds, the limits of possible experiences within a single dimension could be established for each of the senses. Early psychophysics challenged naïve realism because it demonstrated measurable stimulus values below or above the threshold of awareness, and psychophysics, as a field, figured prominently in early psychology, even in the earliest plans for the first international congress (Nicolas & Söderlund, 2005). As illustrated with the aesthesiometer, there are differences that cannot be experienced by the unaided senses. In fact, some stimulus differences must be surprisingly large to be experienced. Studies in psychophysics also uncovered lawful relationships between stimulus differences according to a physical scale and experienced differences. Such lawful relationships showed promise for a science of the mind. The discovery of lawful relationships between physical values of stimuli and experience also challenged extreme solipsistic views. Such discoveries suggested that our experiences are tied to the physical world in lawful ways and that comparisons between individuals are meaningful.

The work of German physiologist **Ernst Heinrich Weber (1795–1878)** and physicist–philosopher Gustav T. Fechner (1801–1887) ushered in the formal beginnings of psychophysics.

Ernst Heinrich Weber

Ernst Heinrich Weber was born on June 24, 1795, the third of thirteen children. At age sixteen, Ernst enrolled at the University of Wittenberg. He later transferred to the University of Leipzig where he completed a thesis on the anatomy of the sympathetic nerves. Impressed with Weber's work, university officials offered him a faculty position. He accepted and stayed at Leipzig for the remainder of his career.

Weber worked in the fields of anatomy, physiology, physics, and biology. He collaborated with his brother, Eduard, on one of his most important contributions. They discovered the inhibition of heart action following stimulation of the peripheral end of the vagus nerve. Kruta (1976) noted that this discovery, together with

Ernst Weber

that we are less sensitive if the two points of the compass are applied longitudinally along the length of a limb than if they are laid transversely or in a crosswise direction to the axis of the limb. He noted that our sensitivity is greater when the two points of the compass contact contiguous body parts, such as the inside of the lip and the skin adjacent to the lip. Weber showed that the two compass points appear to spread apart when moved over the surface of insensitive areas. By contrast, a convergence of the two points is experienced if the two points are moved over sensitive areas. These phenomena are known as **Weber's illusion**, which continues to be the focus of research (Longo & Haggard, 2011).

Weber also found less sensitivity when two points are presented simultaneously and greater when they are presented one after the other. Similarly, perceived differences in the weights of objects are greater when such weights are presented successively. The same holds for perceived temperature differences.

Weber's work on two-point thresholds demonstrated that the world as experienced does not directly correspond to the physical characteristics of the stimuli presented by the experimenter. In further explorations of the relationship between the physical and psychological worlds, Weber investigated just noticeable differences of weights of small containers filled with lead.

Imagine that a researcher asks you to lift a small jar weighing 50 grams. You pick it up and get a sense of about how much it weighs. Now how much weight could the researcher add to the jar before you could tell the difference between the original (standard) weight and the new (comparison) weight? The smallest detectable difference between the standard and the comparison is called the **just noticeable difference (jnd)**.

After conducting many experiments with many stimulus values, Weber observed a law-like relationship between standard and comparison stimuli. The amount that must be added in order to produce a jnd was a function of the amount of existing stimulation. For example, you might reliably detect a difference between a standard

subsequent research, "showed that inhibition is a common phenomenon in the central nervous system and that an adequate balance between excitation and inhibition is indispensable for its normal function" (p. 200). In 1826, Weber turned his attention to the skin and muscle senses. His pioneering work led to a book called *The Sense of Touch*, a classic in experimental psychology. Weber retained his chair in anatomy at Leipzig until 1871, just eight years before the university recognized Wilhelm Wundt's laboratory in psychology. Weber died on January 26, 1878.

Weber's Work on the Sense of Touch

Weber (1834/1978) employed the two-point threshold technique to systematically map the cutaneous sensitivity of the human body. As noted earlier, sensitivity varies depending on where we stimulate the body. Weber observed

241

jar weighing 50 grams and a comparison jar weighing 1 gram more. But what would happen if you lifted a jar weighing 100 grams? How much would the comparison jar have to weigh before you could detect a difference? The comparison jar would need to weigh about 102 grams. Again, the jnd is a function of the amount of existing stimulation. Based on this research, Weber created the first formula to bridge the physical and psychological worlds:

$$\frac{\Delta R}{R} = K$$

where R = the amount of existing stimulation

ΔR = the amount of stimulation that must be added to produce a jnd

K = a constant

Presumably, one could establish a fraction and then predict the jnd for any new stimulus value. As an example, for lifted weights, the fraction is about 1/50 (.02). Thus, for a 300-gram standard weight, the comparison should be about 306 grams.

Weber opened a door into an unexplored world. We cannot directly measure a psychological event, but we can quantify perceived differences in relation to scaled physical stimulus values. Psychological events, or jnds, can be studied in conjunction with measurable physical stimulus values. Although Immanuel Kant believed psychological processes could not be quantified, Weber demonstrated otherwise.

Weber's work inspired hundreds of early research projects investigating jnds for each of the sensory modalities. His work also triggered new and more rigorous methodologies for the study of thresholds. More than any other researcher, Gustav Fechner fulfilled Weber's vision of psychophysics.

Gustav Theodor Fechner

The relationship between mind and body captivated **Gustav Theodor Fechner (1801–1887)**.

He devoted much of his career to studying relationships between the mental and the physical realms. Mind and body suggest a duality in nature, but Fechner was "a thoroughgoing monist, regarding body and soul as but a double manifestation of one and the same real thing" (Ward, 1876, p. 452). His psychophysics research represents a vital building block for the new discipline of experimental psychology.

After completing his gymnasium studies, Fechner enrolled at the University of Leipzig. He completed an M.D. degree in 1822, but physics claimed his early scientific interests. He had established a reputation in physics by 1831. Three years later, he was appointed professor of physics at Leipzig.

The year 1839 posed an unfortunate turning point in Fechner's life. Haunted by a profound emotional disturbance, Fechner resigned from his university position. It seems that partial blindness may have initiated his mental collapse. Fechner had sustained visual problems

Gustav Fechner

242

while using improper lenses to gaze at the sun during his study of afterimages. Beginning in 1839, Fechner was plagued by a persistent illness that forced him to resign his chair of physics the following year. Adler (1996) notes:

> It started with photophobia. Light hurt Fechner's eyes so much that he spent most of his days in a darkened room, venturing out only when he was wearing self-constructed metal cups over his eyes. He communicated with the family through a funnel-shaped opening in the door. His digestive system presented another problem. Fechner could not eat or drink and he was in danger of dying of starvation. Doctors tried animal magnetism, homeopathy, and moxibustion (the burning of herbs on the skin) without avail. About the only food he was able to keep down was a mixture of chopped raw ham with spices, soaked in Rhine wine and lemon juice. The recipe for this concoction had appeared to a lady acquaintance in a dream. Fechner's worst problem was his mind. He suffered from a flight of ideas; he was unable to concentrate, to speak coherently, or to tame his wild thoughts.
>
> (p. 5)

Throughout the process, Fechner kept detailed notes on his struggles. In October 1843, he began speaking again. Fechner gradually overcame his mystery illness, but did not resume his academic responsibilities, save for occasional public lectures.

Five years later, Fechner resumed work at the University of Leipzig, but now as a philosophy professor. In his new position, he explored both philosophical and scientific interests. On the philosophical side, Fechner profiled two opposite views of the universe. He viewed the basic stuff of the universe as inert matter. He referred to this extreme materialistic position as the *night view*. A contrasting view would suggest that all things have a psychic component. Fechner argued that plants have a psychic life and that any organic whole has psychic qualities. He referred to his panpsychism as the *day view*. He created a pseudonym, *Dr. Mises*, to express his mystical beliefs in the day view. In "Proof That the Moon Is Made of Iodine," his first paper as Mises, he satirized a popular medical notion that iodine was a panacea. For more than thirty years, the writings of Dr. Mises provided a whimsical outlet for Fechner's humanistic and aesthetic interests in art, music, dance, and poetry as well as more satirical topics (e.g., the comparative anatomy of humans and angels). Indeed, in 1851, Fechner first outlined his psychophysics program in a book on human immortality, the *Zend-Avesta, or Concerning Matters of Heaven and the Hereafter* (see Boring, 1963). He hoped his work in psychophysics would provide evidence for the day view.

In 1860, Fechner published his *Elements of Psychophysics*, a book widely recognized as the first major publication to demonstrate that experimental methods could fruitfully be applied to psychological phenomena (Robinson, 2010) and destined to become a classic in psychology. In 1876, he published *Vorschule der Aesthetic*, a seminal work in the experimental approach to aesthetic judgments, and he remains recognized as a pioneer in this field (Shimamura, 2012). He continued work in psychophysics and experimental aesthetics until his death in November 1887. Angell (1913) called attention to Wundt's memorable words in his funeral oration for Fechner: "We shall not look upon his like again" (p. 49).

October 22, 1850, was a critical day in the life of Gustav Fechner. He commemorated it as the date when he realized there must be a discernible quantitative relationship between sensations and stimuli (Meischner-Metge, 2010). Unaware of Weber's research, Fechner believed there was not a one-to-one relationship between perceived increases in stimulus intensity and physical increases in stimulus values. Indeed, he concluded that perceived increases were related to the amount of existing physical stimulation. His conclusion is consistent with Weber's discovery.

Following this insight, Fechner discovered Weber's work and launched a vigorous experimental program. Fechner reported that "for several years I considered it a daily task to experiment about an hour for the purpose of testing Weber's Law and for elaborating new methods of research" (cited in Angell, 1913, p. 47).

Weber's formula provided the intellectual spadework for Fechner to develop a more ambitious formula for the measurement of sensation. By integrating Weber's formula, Fechner generated the new formula:

$$S = k \log R$$

where S is the mental sensation and R is the *Reiz* or stimulus magnitude. The formula specified that the strength of a mental sensation is a constant logarithmic function of the stimulus. It further specified that as a mental series increases arithmetically, the stimulus series must increase geometrically. Fechner's formula predicted the observation that is familiar to anyone who has turned on a three-way light bulb, advancing it from 100 to 300 watts. Equal increments in a physical scale are experienced in terms of a diminishing series called **response compression**. The difference between 100 and 200 watts appears greater than the difference between 200 and 300 watts. Fechner, deferring to Weber's pioneering work, called his formula **Weber's law**. Today, we think of it as **Fechner's law** and the earlier simpler formula that inspired it as *Weber's law.*

In subsequent years, research on Weber's and Fechner's laws occupied a central place in early psychology laboratories. Investigations on these laws contributed to the construction of sensory scales, such as the decibel scale for dealing with the intensity of auditory stimuli. This research program also produced a greater understanding of the capacities of the sensory systems. Research confirmed that Weber's and Fechner's laws were accurate primarily for the middle ranges of sensory information. Predictions are less accurate for the lower and upper extremes of physical intensity, and in the mid-twentieth century these and other difficulties led to the emergence of new approaches (Stevens, 1961).

Additionally, much of Fechner's classic 1860 work was devoted to inner psychophysics, and definitions of this term remain difficult (Billock & Tsou, 2011). Although Fechner argued that "Inner psychophysics would go beyond the physics and physiology of stimuli, to the mind's interpretation of sensation" (Robinson, 2010, p. 425), and that it was a more important field of study than external psychophysics, scholars did not pursue these ideas. For Fechner, inner psychophysics also included unconscious (or literally subliminal, i.e., below threshold) phenomena, but his robust body of scholarship on these topics remains largely unknown (Romand, 2012).

FECHNER'S METHODS Fechner's investigation of thresholds produced important methodological contributions, becoming an integral part of experimental psychology. In part, his methods were important because they were applicable to a variety of problems.

The Method of Limits Fechner referred to this method as the method of *just noticeable differences (jnd)*. A researcher named Delezenne had used it in tests of tonal intervals and Weber had used it as well in research on weights, touch, and vision (see Fechner, 1860/1966, p. 62). The **method of limits** consists of presenting a standard stimulus along with variable or comparison stimuli of greater and lesser value than the standard. The comparison stimuli are presented in ascending and descending series. For example, a standard weight of, say, 100 grams may be presented along with a comparison weight of 105 grams. As you can guess, it's easy to detect a difference between these two weights. In a descending series, subsequent comparison weights of 104, 103, 102, and 101 grams may be presented with the standard weight. Then, an ascending series may include comparisons of 100, 101, 102, 103, and 104 grams. In each series, the experimenter can assess the point at which a difference is no longer detected or the point at which the difference is first noticed. The average for several ascending and descending series defines the jnd.

This method also applies to absolute thresholds. In this case, single stimulus values are presented in ascending and descending series. For example, tones of 17, 18, 19, 20, and 21 Hz may be presented in an ascending series and the task is to report when the tone is first detected. In a descending series, starting above threshold (e.g., 25, 24, 23, and 22 Hz), the participant must specify the frequency at which the tone is no longer heard.

Fechner believed that the method of limits is the method of choice for preliminary studies but that other methods are superior for more rigorous studies (see Fechner, 1860/1966).

The Method of Constant Stimuli Fechner referred to this method as the *method of right and wrong cases*. In this method, comparison stimuli are coupled with the standard stimulus in a random fashion. The participant's task is to report whether the comparison stimulus is equal to, greater than, or weaker than the standard, or alternatively, detected or not detected. For absolute thresholds, single stimulus values above and below threshold are presented randomly. The participant simply reports whether the stimulus is detected. The **method of constant stimuli** avoids certain errors commonly associated with the method of limits. For example, errors of habituation (i.e., falling into the habit of saying that one stimulus is of greater or lesser value than the other) are easily established in a graded series. Such errors are eliminated when comparison values are randomized.

The Method of Average Error Sometimes called the *method of adjustment*, the **method of average error** permits the participant to manipulate a comparison stimulus until it appears to match a standard. Following the adjustment, the remaining difference between the standard and the comparison stimuli can be measured. For example, a standard might consist of a light of a given brightness. The comparison could be a light source activated by a variable switch that permits the participant to adjust brightness. The brightness of the comparison stimulus can be adjusted until it appears to match the brightness of the standard. Normally, several ascending and descending series are employed and a mean is determined. Thus, in one series, the comparison starts at a higher or brighter value and is adjusted downward, and in a subsequent series, the comparison starts at a lower or dimmer value and is adjusted upward.

Although Fechner's methods generated criticism (Adler, 1998; Michell, 1999; Zudini, 2011), his work had wide application and became standard in training experimental psychologists. Fechner raised issues more than a century ago that still resonate in modern psychophysics research and signal detection theory (Adler, 1998; Link, 1994; Murray, 1993). Contemporary psychologists use variations of Fechner's methods when investigating problems as divergent as perception of air quality and the discrimination capacity of a particular species. Some argue that Fechner instead of Wundt should be viewed as the first experimental psychologist (Asthana, 2015a). Although Fechner's dream of solving the mind–brain problem proved too ambitious, he did create the foundation for an experimental psychology. On occasion, in the history of science, a major research goal goes unrealized even as other fortunate benefits emerge through productive accident.

Hermann von Helmholtz

Psychology owes an immense intellectual debt to **Hermann Ludwig Ferdinand von Helmholtz (1821–1894)**, one of the most celebrated scientists and inventors of the nineteenth century. His original contributions in physics, physiology, and psychology mark him as one of the last scholars who could produce cutting-edge research in multiple scientific fields.

Helmholtz studied under Johannes Müller and established close friendships with Müller's other students including Ernst Brücke, Emil DuBois-Reymond, and Karl Ludwig. Helmholtz

245

completed his M.D. in 1842 and served until 1848 as an army surgeon, when he was released early from military duty to accept a faculty position in physiology at Königsberg. In 1855, he accepted a position in anatomy and physiology at the University of Bonn. One year after arriving at Bonn, he published Volume I of his classic *Handbook of Physiological Optics*. Kahl (1967) pointed out that this seminal work is "frequently called the *principia* in its field" (p. 469). The handbook established Helmholtz as one of Europe's most promising young scientists. By 1858, he accepted an appointment to the chair of physiology at the University of Heidelberg. He remained in that position for thirteen productive years before accepting a position in 1871 as professor of physics at the University of Berlin. Turner (1972) stated, "By 1885 Helmholtz had become the patriarch of German science and the state's foremost advisor on scientific affairs" (p. 243). Helmholtz died on July 12, 1894.

Hermann von Helmholtz

HELMHOLTZ'S CONTRIBUTIONS Helmholtz rejected the idea that vital forces or mysterious energies influence physiological or psychological processes. He believed all movements within the organism are, in principle, understandable in terms of physical laws (Turner, 1977). He demonstrated that a simple muscle contraction generates a slight increase in temperature. The total energy expended in a given unit of time is related to the way the organism metabolizes food. Helmholtz believed the conservation of energy applies to living organisms just as it applies to physical phenomena. Furthermore, there are no mysterious forces or unknowable energies that activate the organism. The psychology that Helmholtz envisioned was grounded in physiology. Physiology, in turn, was grounded in physics and chemistry. Helmholtz's vision of the unity of the sciences was such that, according to Wertheimer (1991), "he hardly knew when he was doing psychology, physiology, or physics."

Visual Perception Although accomplished in many provinces of science, Helmholtz's most enduring contribution may have been in the study of perception (Wade, 1994). His masterpiece, *Handbook of Physiological Optics*, showcases the breadth of his interests in psychological, physiological, and physical problems. The physics and physiology of vision are covered in chapters on topics such as the physical characteristics of light, the crystalline lens, the cornea, refraction in the eye, mechanisms of accommodation, and the retina. His discussion on the retina includes detailed descriptions of rods and cones along with an analysis of their distributions. On psychological matters, the handbook contains chapters covering topics such as illusions (Gregory, 2007; Wade, 2005), the perception of depth, and color vision.

The handbook also covers methodological topics. Helmholtz provided a methodological breakthrough when he invented the **ophthalmoscope**, an instrument for viewing the retina (Pearce, 2009b). His genius is illustrated in the handbook as he discussed the theory of the ophthalmoscope (see Southall, 1962). Helmholtz noticed that light reaching the retina is partly

246

absorbed and partly reflected, and he investigated the optical properties of the eye as though the eye were an optical instrument (Wade & Finger, 2001). Thus, an observer could, for the first time, see images and anatomical details of the retina of another person's eye. If the senses are the windows of the mind, then Helmholtz's contributions made it possible to peer into those windows and to entertain the hope that science could forge ahead into another frontier.

Helmholtz's empirical approach to perception was set forth in an 1894 article titled "The Origin and Correct Interpretation of Our Sense Impressions" (see Kahl, 1971; Stromberg, 1989). He notes that a child hears sounds in the form of common names associated with objects in the world. Countless repetitions forge a connection between sounds (words) and objects in the world. Subtleties are slowly developed through connection of descriptive adjectives with nouns, allowing finer and finer discriminations. Helmholtz (1894/1971) pointed out that, in time, "we are able to follow the subtlest, most varied shadings of thought and feeling. If, however, we tried to say how we acquired this knowledge, we could explain it only in the form of a general proposition: we always found certain words used in certain ways" (p. 502).

Helmholtz argued that something similar takes place with respect to sense impressions. For example, a baby gains different information when grasping a ball rather than a cube. At the same time, reaching and grasping are associated with visual cues. When connections are consistent, the baby gains a sense impression of a sphere and a cube. Helmholtz (1894/1971) concluded "from these facts that the meaning of some of the simplest, most important visual images for a human infant must be learned" (p. 506). Even if the baby were articulate, it could not specify how it gained sense impressions. As a result, Helmholtz emphasized "unconscious inferences" in perception that are built through countless repetitions of stimulus and response events.

Helmholtz employed this reasoning to explain depth perception. For example, we learn that object A is more distant than object B because of invariant connections between A and the feeling of the outstretched arm and B and the feeling of the arm when it is closer to the body. There are other connections (visual, proprioceptive, and perhaps verbal) that occur together and that gradually contribute to sense perceptions. It would be nearly impossible to specify all the cues that contribute to a given perception, but we draw unconscious inferences that are exquisitely conditioned by our interaction with objects in the environment.

Helmholtz was particularly interested in depth perception including the study of monocular cues such as size, contours, shadows, and aerial perspective. He also discussed binocular cues, some of which could be demonstrated with the **stereoscope**, an instrument that produces a compelling three-dimensional effect by simultaneously presenting slightly different views of a visual scene to the left and right eyes. Much of Helmholtz's discussion of depth perception is still relevant today.

Color Vision One of the first naturalistic theories of color was attributed to Aristotle, who apparently believed that all colors result from admixtures of lightness and darkness (see Barnes, 1984). Modern theories of color date from the work of Isaac Newton (1642–1727), whose classic work in optics described the properties of light. Newton demonstrated that a beam of sunlight passing through a prism is dispersed into a spectrum of colors. He also demonstrated that white light is attained again when the dispersed colors are recombined with a converging lens. Newton's demonstration was damaging to the then popular belief that white light was pure and devoid of color.

In time, it was understood that colors are associated with specific wavelengths. But how do we see in color? Do we have a specific structure for each discriminable wavelength? If so, the physiology of color vision would be complex because it is possible to split the visible spectrum into hundreds of different hues. A much simpler solution was proposed in 1802 by the physiologist

Thomas Young (1773–1829), who argued that all colors can be produced with various combinations of red, green, and blue (violet). Young suggested three types of specialized retinal structures, each sensitive to a specific primary color. Boring (1942) pointed out that by positing specialized nerves for color primaries, Young's theory "anticipated Johannes Müller's theory of specific nerve energies" (p. 112).

Interestingly, little experimental work was conducted on color vision in the two-hundred-year period from Newton to Helmholtz. Indeed, Young's studies on color vision, although provocative, were speculative in nature. By the middle of the nineteenth century, Helmholtz conducted experiments on color mixtures (Finger & Wade, 2002). As in other research on visual perception, Helmholtz held to the empiricist position, bringing him into conflict with the German physiologist Ewald Hering (1834–1918), who defended nativism in the study of color vision. In one of the most impassioned debates in modern science, Helmholtz clashed with Hering over issues such as space perception, color blindness, optical illusions, and the therapeutic practices of clinical ophthalmology (Turner, 1994). Helmholtz was interested in discovering the minimum number of primaries from which one could obtain all colors of the spectrum. Initially, he argued against Young's belief in three primaries, opting instead for five: red, yellow, green, blue, and violet.

Scottish physicist **James Clerk Maxwell (1831–1879)** provided experimental work favoring Young's trichromatic theory (Finger & Wade, 2002). With sophisticated experimental techniques, Maxwell matched any spectral value with mixtures of red, green, and blue. Subsequently, Helmholtz embraced Young's trichromatic theory. Since that time, it has been known as the **Young–Helmholtz trichromatic theory**, although a more appropriate name might have been the Young–Maxwell–Helmholtz theory or even the Young–Maxwell theory. Helmholtz's contributions to color theory, however, should not be minimized. He tied Young's theory to

possible physiological mechanisms and, in the words of Beck (1968), "extended the theory to account for color blindness, negative afterimages, and successive contrasts" (p. 347). The Young–Helmholtz theory remains an important theory in color science.

Acoustics and Hearing Helmholtz's great breadth of interest in physics, physiology, and psychology is evident in his original work *On the Sensations of Tone*. His resonance theory of hearing, for example, identified possible physiological structures for pitch perception. Helmholtz observed that a string on a musical instrument such as a harp or piano is activated by an external sound source of the same frequency as the one to which it is tuned. Helmholtz speculated that fibers in the basilar membrane of the inner ear, like the strings of a piano or harp, may also resonate to specific frequencies. Thus, pitch discrimination is based on vibration of fibers in sympathy with external sources. In yet another extension of Müller's doctrine of specific energies, Helmholtz argued that each discriminable pitch activates separate specialized nerves, and his work was foundational for later psychologists, physiologists, and physicists who studied sound and audition (Palmieri, 2012).

He also accounted for the timbre or quality of sound. He reasoned that a specific pitch, say middle C, sounds different on different instruments because of the harmonics or overtones produced by the structural properties of the instrument.

Beck (1968) pointed out, "From the perspective of posterity . . . Helmholtz made his most significant contributions to the fields of sensory physiology and psychology. In particular, he laid the foundations for the experimental investigation of the sensory processes in audition and vision" (p. 345). These contributions, coupled with his measurement of the speed of the nervous impulse and his commitment to the doctrine of the conservation of energy, mark him as one of the most pivotal figures in the history of experimental psychology (Stumpf, 1895).

Wilhelm Wundt

The formal beginnings of experimental psychology can be traced to 1879 when the University of Leipzig recognized Wilhelm Wundt's laboratory (Boring, 1950; Wade et al., 2007). Weber, Fechner, and Helmholtz had already established many conceptual and methodological tools for the new discipline. Additionally, in the late 1790s there had been a productive start on an empirical and teaching psychology by Ferdinand Ueberwasser (1752–1812), which had been cut short by political upheaval (Schwarz & Pfister, 2016). What remained was for someone with vision and knowledge to tackle the risky business of agitating for institutional space and recognition. **Wilhelm Maximilian Wundt (1832–1920)** had the requisite vision, knowledge, and energy for such an undertaking. He faced an uphill battle because conservative university officials expressed only lukewarm interest in the new

Wilhelm Wundt

science. Some even voiced administrative concerns that Wundt's introspective methods might cause students to suffer mental breakdowns. To say the least, the outlook for the new laboratory was not optimistic.

Wundt's persistence produced monumental consequences. From a single room on the Leipzig campus, Wundt was the key player in launching a new discipline that would become international in scope. Who would have predicted that, within a century, a course in psychology would be required for many university majors or that psychology as a major would be among the most popular on university campuses? Of course, we can't credit Wundt with sole responsibility for psychology's popularity. But more than any other, he had the vision, talent, organizational skill, and enthusiasm for establishing psychology as a formal discipline. Accordingly, he occupies a singular place in psychology's history.

Wilhelm Wundt was born on August 16, 1832, in Neckarau, a small village located in a German principality close to the present city of Heidelberg. Wundt was the youngest of four children of Maximilian Wundt (1787–1868) and Marie Friederike née Arnold (1797–1868). Typical for the times, only two of the four children survived, Wilhelm and his older brother Ludwig (1824–1902).

Maximilian was a Protestant minister known for his moderate or even liberal theology. Diamond (1980) noted that "Wundt grew up in effect as an 'only child'" (p. 10). His brother Ludwig, who was eight years his senior, started work in the gymnasium at Heidelberg when Wilhelm was only two years old. Wundt's earliest years were marked by loneliness and poor health (he had a severe case of malaria in his first year). As a consequence of isolation from other children and loneliness, he reveled in his own fantasy world. Indeed, his habit of daydreaming interfered with his high school and early college studies.

In 1836, Maximilian received an appointment to a large parish in Heidelsheim, a rough town that did nothing to allay Wilhelm's shyness or his fear of other children. He had a single friend his own age, a gentle boy with apparent cognitive deficits and speech deficiencies. Wundt entered grammar school at age six, but the poorly socialized youngster struggled with his lessons. The school's oppressive atmosphere forced him to retreat deeper into his own thoughts. Wundt's personal difficulties were compounded at age eight when his father suffered a massive stroke. The resulting family hardship had a dramatic effect on Wundt's early education.

As a consequence of the stroke, Maximilian's young assistant, Friedrich Müller, assumed a large share of the parish responsibilities, and also took an interest in young Wilhelm. According to Bringmann et al. (1980), Müller "made his appearance when the boy must have been under considerable stress. His grandfather had just died, his brother remained away from home, and his mother's time was taken up with the care of her crippled husband" (p. 18).

Müller, who shared a room with Wilhelm in the parsonage, assumed the responsibilities of tutor. He assigned and graded lessons and often discussed the youngster's performance. Their bond was so intense that Wundt was overcome with grief when Müller was assigned to a church in Münzesheim. Wundt, then twelve years old, was allowed to go to Münzesheim to live with his tutor. Later, he enrolled in the gymnasium in Bruchsal. Again, the result was disastrous. Wundt enrolled in the equivalent of the first year of high school and promptly failed. His teachers regarded him as lazy, inattentive, and poorly fitted for any career. Wundt became all the more deeply withdrawn.

Wundt's academic prospects were dim, to say the least, following the disastrous year at Bruchsal. Within one year, however, a radical transformation had taken place. Diamond (1980) stated, "Wundt's family—which is to say, his Mother's family—saw to it that he was given another chance. At thirteen, he joined Ludwig in their aunt's home, to attend the Heidelberg gymnasium and do his studying in the same room with his industrious brother, with no daydreaming

nonsense allowed" (p. 13). For whatever reasons (e.g., greater maturity, the presence of a good role model, new determination), Wundt's prospects improved. His attention was gradually directed outward, as evidenced by a newfound ability to make friends. His academic performance improved, but was still below expected standards.

Following graduation from the Heidelberg Lyceum in 1851, Wundt was still undecided about a career. However, he was accepted as a premedical student at the University of Tübingen where his uncle, Friedrich Arnold, taught anatomy. Following a year at Tübingen, Wundt was accepted for premedical studies at the University of Heidelberg. For the first time in his troubled academic career, Wundt surrendered himself to his studies. As a result, he completed the medical program in three years, obtaining his M.D. in 1855 with highest honors.

Wundt found he had little interest in the practice of medicine. As a consequence, in 1856, he sharpened his research skills in physiology in postdoctoral work at the University of Berlin under Johannes Müller and Emil DuBoisReymond. Back at Heidelberg later in the year, he was hired as a docent with teaching and research opportunities. The monetary reward was meager, but Wundt at last found work suited to his interests. In 1858, Wundt published his first book, *The Doctrine of Muscular Movement*. In that same year, he applied for a position in Helmholtz's physiology laboratory. He was given the appointment and remained as Helmholtz's assistant until 1865 (Araujo, 2014a). During this period, Wundt conducted research, instructed medical students, and offered his own courses. In 1862, he taught a course titled "Psychology as a Natural Science."

During this period, Wundt's research interests shifted from physiology to psychology. Two of his most important psychological contributions from the period are *Contributions to a Theory of Sensory Perception* (1862) and *Lectures on Human and Animal Psychology* (1863). The introduction to the book on sense perception announced the need for a new discipline of experimental psychology.

Wundt remained at Heidelberg for almost a decade after leaving Helmholtz's laboratory. The period from 1865 to 1874 was productive with the most noteworthy academic achievement coming from Wundt's 1873 publication of Volume I of *Principles of Physiological Psychology*. The second volume appeared the following year. Around the same time, Wundt married Sophie Mau in 1872 after several years of engagement.

In 1874, Wundt accepted an appointment as chair of inductive philosophy at Zurich, but in less than a year he received a call to the larger, more prestigious University of Leipzig. Wundt's growing reputation in psychology prompted the call to Leipzig. According to Bringmann et al. (1980), the dean at Leipzig hoped Wundt would bring prestige and recognition to the university. In one letter, the dean wrote, "I hope that your call to the university will one day be viewed as [the beginning of] an epoch in the history of German philosophy, especially of psychology and epistemology" (p. 128). The dean's hopes were realized when the forty-two-year-old Wundt embarked on work that fulfilled the promise of a new science.

In his first four years at Leipzig, Wundt taught an average of two courses per semester, over a wide range of topical areas including psychology, anthropology, logic and methodology, history of modern philosophy, brain and nerve physiology, and cosmology. Wundt supervised dissertations and conducted his own research. He produced almost two publications a month, amounting to eighty-eight publications during the four-year period at Leipzig, including four books. Few scholars in any field or period of history can match Wundt's productivity.

In 1879, Wundt established the psychological laboratory at Leipzig. Much of the early equipment was provided by Wundt himself. By December, the first experiments were under way.

Wundt recognized the need for a scholarly journal to publish the numerous research papers emerging from his new laboratory. The new research didn't fit with established journals in physiology or philosophy. In 1881, Wundt published the first issue of *Psychological Studies*. Immediately, the title was changed to *Philosophical Studies* to avoid confusion with a parapsychology journal. Wundt's journal was primarily an outlet for research from the Leipzig laboratory.

Wundt's work stretched over the next four decades, and the high productivity in the first four years offered promise about coming research. In his years at Leipzig from 1875 to 1920, Wundt directed one hundred and eighty-six doctoral theses (see Tinker, 1980). Wundt revised his magnum opus, *Principles of Physiological Psychology*, through six editions, the last being issued in 1911. If all this were not enough, Wundt taught large classes. Indeed, Angell (1921) reported "there was no lecture room in the university large enough to hold the audience that 'subscribed' to the lectures on psychology" (p. 164).

Wundt devoted much of his later years to his long-term interest in sociocultural psychology (*Völkerpsychologie*). The result was a ten-volume work covering areas in anthropology, psycholinguistics, forensic psychology, the psychology of religion, personality, and social psychology. In this massive work, he tackled issues that included the origin of belief in gods, the growth of complexity of rewards and punishments, the development of legal systems, marriage and family systems, the beginnings of language, and primitive societies. Part of *Völkerpsychologie* is available in English (see Wundt, 1916), and it remains understudied, likely from a combination of issues related to translation, cultural and scientific barriers across history, and the lack of a strong synthesis of ideas (Diriwächter, 2012). Criticisms of Wundt's *Völkerpsychologie* by Houston Stewart Chamberlain (who was a political but not a psychological figure) affected the trajectory of this research program. After Wundt, *Völkerpsychologie* became an applied area of research in ethnic differences (Klautke, 2010), and Chamberlain and others expounded upon differences perceived as racial, particularly between Jews and others (Guski-Leinwand, 2009), all of which were substantial changes from Wundt's *Völkerpsychologie*.

In view of his enormous productivity, one might conclude that Wundt was a social recluse, but such is not the case. He was active in politics twenty years before founding his psychology laboratory. In Heidelberg, he was elected to a parliamentary seat, which he held from 1866 to 1869. He was interested in social concerns of his day, such as improving education and working conditions. Wundt's adult personality is a matter of considerable interest, especially in view of his troubled and solitary childhood. Despite his dramatic turnaround and successful years in the M.D. program, the young scientist remained socially awkward. Indeed, Titchener (1921) referred to Wundt's Heidelberg period as "seventeen years of depression" (p. 171).

Did Wundt's turbulent childhood and early adult years leave noticeable scars? The answer is not simple. Wundt did have difficulties with colleagues and was overly reactive to criticism (see Diamond, 1980). However, many positive personal qualities balanced negative traits. Wundt was patient and helpful with students and showed genuine concern about their progress and success. Although friendly and warm, he never allowed students to lose sight of the formal master–student relationship. He was generous in devoting time to student laboratory projects and theses. One student, Edward A. Pace (1921), celebrated Wundt's lack of ostentation even while students from around the world were flocking to his laboratory. Howard Warren (1921) and Walter Dill Scott (1921) commented on his encyclopedic knowledge and breadth of vision (see also Sokal, 1980a).

Walter Dill Scott (1921) summed up Wundt's legacy as follows: "When he began his work psychology was thought of as a branch of philosophy. His work changed it into an experimental science" (p. 183). Wundt's life and work mark a turning point in intellectual history. At the time of his death in 1920, the formal discipline he established was rooted in major universities around the world. By that time, psychology was both an experimental science and a fledgling professional discipline with branches extending into education, industry, the military, and the clinic.

General Characteristics of Wundt's Thought

Several general characteristics distinguish Wundt's philosophical and psychological vision. Although he changed positions on specific topics in psychology, many broader philosophical underpinnings remained stable.

MIND AND BODY In *Principles of Physiological Psychology*, Wundt speculated about the evolution of mental function. He rejected the extreme positions of **hylozoism** (the view that mind is manifested in all material movement—e.g., even the falling of a rock) and the dualistic Cartesian view that only humans have mental functions. Wundt believed the lower limits of mental function are illustrated in movements that have a voluntary basis. He pointed out that voluntary movements, unlike simple reflexes or vegetative functions (like respiration), "are varied to suit varying conditions, and brought into connection with sense-impressions previously secured" (1910/1969b, p. 28). For example: "The amoeba, which is regarded morphologically as a naked cell, will sometimes return after a short interval to the starch grains that it has come upon in the course of its wanderings" (p. 29). Wundt noted that such a phenomenon argues for continuity in mental processes. He believed that the origin of mental processes dated to the origin of life itself.

Wundt also speculated about the metaphysical or ontological status of mental processes. He recognized the popular assumption that mind is a separate substance or being but argued that such an assumption is unnecessary. He noted that we do not treat virtue or honor as substances, yet that does not prevent our doing intelligent and logical work with these topics. In a similar manner, we may simply treat mind "as the logical subject of internal experience" (1910/1969b, p. 18).

In Wundt's psychology, experience is central. Mind is one meaningful subject of discourse and the physical system is another meaningful subject of discourse. Mental *and* physical processes are both known in experience, but psychology cannot, in its immaturity, specify the metaphysical basis of either process, and Wundt believed that the tools used to study the brain in his day could not provide a foundation for psychology (Wong, 2010). Wundt believed in the unity and interdependence of mental and physical processes. His perspective came closer to Spinoza's double-aspect monism than to a mind–body dualism.

BREADTH OF VISION Wundt's philosophical and psychological vision offered enormous scope. In addition to teaching a wide range of courses, he published in diverse fields such as ethics, logic, sociocultural psychology, and physiology. Frank Angell (1921), one of Wundt's students, said, "For depth and range of learning, for capacity for generalization, for power of scientific imagination, he was the ablest man I ever met" (p. 166). Wundt's breadth of vision for the new psychology was illustrated in several ways. First, he employed a variety of methods. It is true that much of the work of the laboratory for which he is remembered was based on a rigorous form of what we often call introspection; however, he was quick to recognize other methods, including naturalistic observation such as in astronomy or field biology. He also recognized the historical methods employed in archeology and geology. In his laboratory work, Wundt emphasized precise measurements and the importance of being able to replicate findings. Although his laboratory work focused on sensory processes, perception, and reaction time, he nevertheless had the vision of a wider psychology that included social and cultural variables.

VOLUNTARISM The name Wundt preferred for his system of thought was **voluntarism**. It is important to point out that voluntarism is *not* the same thing as free will. Wundt wrote in his *Ethics* (1892/1901) that "To be free, an action must be voluntary" (p. 38). It does not follow, however, that all voluntary acts are free. Wundt declared that volition was not a sufficient condition for freedom.

Thus, a person with a substantial psychological disorder "may balance motives one against another, and proceed with thoughtful circumspection, yet we do not call his decisions free" (p. 38). Wundt did, in fact, believe some people possess a free will, but free will is possible only when we attain a truly reflective self-consciousness. According to Wundt, true reflective self-consciousness is based on deep cognitions that are hard won through experience. Such a free will could hardly be expected to exist in children, people with mental illness, individuals with cognitive disabilities, or those under unusual duress.

If voluntarism is not the same as free will, then what is it? A *voluntaristic psychology* is one that emphasizes psychological causality. For example, one may stand at the ice cream counter and choose chocolate over vanilla. Asked why, the individual may say, "Well, I love both, but it's been a long time since I've had chocolate. Plus, I caught a whiff of this wonderful fresh chocolate aroma." Wundt did not deny that there are underlying material and efficient physiological and biochemical causes for a choice. But, as psychologists, we study psychical motives, or in Wundt's (1892/1901) words, "ideas accompanying the voluntary act" (p. 52). Such ideas are the stuff of psychical causality. In one sense, Wundt's voluntarism affirms the legitimacy—even the primacy—of the world of experience and its causal forces.

WUNDT AND DARWIN Wundt's emphasis on volition, with its obvious implications for adaptation, hints at the influence of Darwin. Such a conclusion, however, is unwarranted. Despite parallels between Darwinian theory and Wundt's system (see Richards, 1980), it's not clear that Wundt assimilated Darwinian ideas. References to Darwin in Wundt's major works are sparse and sometimes critical.

In his *Lectures on Human and Animal Psychology* (1894/1977), Wundt agreed with Darwin on the importance of the principle of adaptation. However, Wundt claimed his notion of voluntary action adds to Darwin's concept of adaptation.

He pointed out that Darwinian adaptation is a passive concept. Plants, for example, are altered by the interplay of environmental forces and adapt or die out. The same forces apply to animals, but in addition to passive adaptation, animals display a more active adaptation. In animals, volition has an object toward which it is directed and there is an "interaction of external stimulus with affective and voluntary response" (Wundt, 1863/1907, p. 409). Thus, the animal is not merely passive but acts on its world on the basis of affect and past associations. Acting on the world does not, of course, necessarily imply that animals have free will.

The Laboratory and the Broader Vision

Wundt's laboratory work was directed toward manageable, well-defined problems that lent themselves to available techniques and equipment. The goals of laboratory investigation were somewhat modest, but the basic canons of scientific research were not compromised. Wundt's broader vision included topics such as linguistics and social influences on behavior that did not lend themselves to his conception of laboratory research. Unfortunately, Wundt's psychology is often portrayed largely in terms of his laboratory work. The result is that his system has often been represented as narrow in terms of methodology and subject matter. There are numerous helpful criticisms of the stripped-down versions of Wundt presented in early history texts (see Blumenthal, 1975, 1998; Danziger, 1979; Farr, 1983; O'Neil, 1984). Wundt's experimental psychology is perhaps best illustrated with concrete examples of his research. Studies on the speed of reflexes, associations, and vision are typical of experimental work that Wundt conducted or supervised during his years at Leipzig.

Before the formal founding of his laboratory, Wundt (1876) published an article in the journal *Mind* that presented research on the speed of different types of reflex action. During this time, the creation of scientific technology became a "hallmark for the new psychology of the laboratory" (Evans, 2000, p. 322). Wundt contributed to this trend by conducting research on reflex action with the assistance of the *pendulum myograph*, an instrument that permitted precise measures of stimulus and response. In this case, the stimulus was an electric current and the response was reflex activity of a frog. Among the topics investigated, Wundt compared unilateral spinal conduction, transverse conduction, and longitudinal conduction. In unilateral conduction, excitation is from the sensory root to its corresponding motor root on the same side. Transverse conduction is from the sensory root on one side to the motor root on the opposite side. Longitudinal conduction follows the spinal axis from a lower sensory root to a higher motor root, or vice versa. Longitudinal conduction can follow unilateral or transverse paths. Wundt also studied the effects of temperature on the speed of reflexes. In addition, he examined the reflex process when adjacent nerves were receiving simultaneous stimulation.

Among the findings, Wundt reported that simultaneous stimulation of neighboring nerves had mixed effects on reflex activity. Simultaneous stimulation or compounding of stimulation may have excitatory or inhibitory effects. This finding was important because it demonstrated the critical role of inhibitory processes in the nervous system. Wundt saw inhibition as an equal partner with excitation in lower and higher mental processes. For example, ordered voluntary behavior is based on a mix of inhibitory and excitatory processes. Wundt realized that the growth of inhibition is central to adaptive and voluntary behaviors. One of his abiding curiosities concerned the physiological and psychological nature of inhibition (see Diamond et al., 1963).

Wundt's laboratory research was focused on sensation, perception, and reaction time, and this narrow focus eventually led to perceptions of stagnation and a search in the United States for another foundation for psychological science; American functionalists emphasized Darwin rather than Wundt for these reasons (Green,

2009). Nevertheless, studies were conducted on topics such as attention, emotion, association, and dreams. Wundt also directed many dissertations in philosophy.

Some Key Concepts in Wundt's System

Certain terms occur again and again throughout Wundt's experimental work. Such terms represent themes in his thinking and provide keys to understanding his laboratory work. However, his laboratory work is but one phase of Wundt's larger psychological perspective. To use a metaphor once employed by Freud, it is as if Wundt recognized that the house has more than one floor. Insofar as the work of the laboratory was concerned, Wundt was content to remain on the lower floor. The constructs to which we now turn pertain to this lower floor.

DEFINITION OF PSYCHOLOGY As far as the laboratory is concerned, Wundt defined *psychology* as a science that investigates "the facts of consciousness" (Wundt, 1912/1973, p. 1). He pointed out that psychology has two tasks: the first is to discover the elements of consciousness and the second is to discover the combinations that elements undergo and the laws that regulate combinations. He referred to a combination of elements as a *psychic compound* (see Wundt, 1912/1973, p. 44). Although Wundt agreed with his contemporaries, such as James, Freud, and Titchener, that psychology involves the study of consciousness, there was little agreement about definitions of consciousness. The emphasis on consciousness in psychology would diminish in the early twentieth century and not return for over half a century (Ferrari & Pinard, 2006).

ELEMENTS The term **element** in Wundt's thinking is a difficult abstraction that requires further comment. We normally think of an element as something simple, pure, and irreducible. Wundt believed that there are mental elements,

or pure sensations such as the sensation of the beat of a metronome. However, he recognized that a single simple sensation on the psychological side—that is, a psychological element—is by no means simple on the physiological side. Nevertheless, we may treat simple sensations (e.g., blueness, redness, or sweetness) as elements.

SENSATIONS AND PERCEPTIONS Wundt (1912/1973, p. 45) defined **sensation** as an element of consciousness. In addition to sensations, there are perceptions and ideas. He noted that the term *perception* generally refers to combinations of outward sense impressions (e.g., an object of a particular shape and color may be called an apple). An *idea*, by contrast, generally refers to combinations that may come from memory, previous associations, and so on. Wundt questioned the validity of the distinction between *idea* and *perception*. In both cases, we observe compounds or combinations and both can be equally lively as experienced phenomena.

ASSOCIATION AND APPERCEPTION Wundt believed that compounds or combinations of elements may be passive or active. He described *passive combinations* as associations and *active combinations* as apperceptions. The distinction between *association* and *apperception* is important in Wundt's thought and carries implications for his larger psychological system.

Association and apperception are illustrated in the distinction between mere rote memory and memory with real awareness. Wundt (1912/1973) pointed out that in rote memory, separate words "are joined to each other by mere association. In the consciousness of the child they do not form a unified whole" (pp. 127–128). Association is manifested in the flight of ideas of a person struggling with delusions or in the immediate response to a simple stimulus. Wundt pointed out that a simple series of words such as *school, house, garden, build, stones, ground, hard, soft, long, see, harvest, rain, move,* and *pain* illustrate association. He then asked the reader, "Compare with this a context like the following out of the seventh book of Goethe's *Wilhelm Meister*: 'Spring had come in all its glory. A spring thunderstorm, that had been threatening the whole day long, passed angrily over the hills'" (pp. 124–125). What is the essential difference between these series? The first illustrates associations, but they are haphazard, aimless, not well connected, and only moderately intelligent. The second illustrates **apperception** marked by intelligent direction within a larger context. Apperception is characterized by activity with intelligent direction and inner unity—these are lacking in association. Wundt criticized British empiricism and associationism for failing to grasp the important distinction between association and apperception.

THE TRIDIMENSIONAL THEORY OF FEELING In addition to studying cognitive concepts such as sensation, perception, ideas, associations, and apperceptions, Wundt was deeply interested in feelings and emotions (Araujo, 2016). Wundt (1912/1973) warned that feelings must not be overlooked because they are tied to more complex psychological processes such as apperception, memory, imagination, perception, and cognition.

Through introspective studies, Wundt developed a **tridimensional theory of feeling** based on three dimensions: pleasure and pain, strain and relaxation, and excitation and quiescence. Certain sensations result in specific feelings. Thus, a bitter taste or a smell like ammonia is unpleasant almost to the point of pain, whereas sweetness is usually pleasurable. Wundt noted that red is exciting and blue is quieting. Colors, like music, may produce relaxation or strain.

Rarely are feelings isolated or partial with respect to the dimensions specified by Wundt. Instead, they combine to form a meaningful compound. Thus, a given sensation may be pleasurable and exciting or pleasurable and relaxing. Varieties of combinations are possible. So-called emotions such as joy or hope represent pleasurable feelings tied to a particular cognitive content. Anger or fear may represent feelings of strain and unpleasantness tied also to a particular cognitive content.

THE PRINCIPLE OF CREATIVE SYNTHESIS
Whereas Wundt hoped to identify the elements of consciousness and to discover the laws that govern connections of elements, he nevertheless believed that there are inherent indeterminations in psychic compounds. In other words, there is real novelty and creativity in higher mental operations (Asthana, 2015b). Wundt's term for such novelty is the principle of **creative synthesis**. He wrote that this principle refers to "the fact that in all psychical combinations, the product is not a mere sum of the separate elements that compose such combinations, but it represents a new creation" (1912/1973, p. 164).

Wundt noted that one of the major manifestations of creative synthesis is illustrated in the principle of the **heterogony of ends**. This principle is exemplified in the emergence of new motives during the course of a chain of activities. Let's say you're invited to a friend's surprise birthday party. Your motives are to go, surprise your friend, and have a great time. But after surprising your friend, you meet someone you're attracted to at the party. Now a whole new set of motives emerge that exist alongside and in addition to the original motive (Should you ask the person out? Where would you go after the party?). The interplay of motives in our immediate experience defines our social behavior as well as our cognitive reaction to the world. Wundt also called attention to the changing motivational structure attached to the practice of ancient habits or customs. Original motives for a practice such as a religious rite or ceremony may be obscured or even be replaced by new motives that bear little relation to the original motives. For example, baptism in some Christian religions was once viewed as a way of casting out evil spirits; such motives for the practice are now only rarely encountered.

Wundt's Legacy

If there is one central dominating figure in the history of experimental psychology, it is Wilhelm Wundt. Under his leadership, psychology gained status as a separate discipline in a major institution of learning. Undergraduates packed into classrooms and graduate students from around the world flocked to the Leipzig laboratory and then disseminated his ideas and methods around the world. For example, his student Vladimir Bekhterev took Wundt's perspectives back to Russia before breaking away from voluntarism and launching *reflexology*, which would in turn influence behavioral work by Pavlov and others (Araujo, 2014b). Other students (e.g., Edward Bradford Titchener, James McKeen Cattell) took Wundt's methods to the United States. Under Wundt's guidance, the new discipline was soon on a firm footing and the Leipzig experiment proved a viable model for other schools. Psychology gained recognition in other major universities.

There have been questions about the lasting effects of Wundt's substantive contributions (e.g., theories and laboratory findings). The fact is, however, that many laboratory findings were cited in early textbooks and some results held up remarkably well. For example, the finding, cited earlier, regarding the locus of retinal stimulation and perceived brightness is widely accepted. Blumenthal (1975) also called attention to additional lasting influences. For instance, factor analytic studies of feelings have yielded results that correspond closely to the predictions of Wundt's tridimensional theory. His work was also a central influence in the development of applied cognitive psychology (Hoffman & Deffenbacher, 1992). Unfortunately, his rigid view of memory as an imprecise and overly popular concept with little value for scientific psychology served to alienate some contemporaries (Danziger, 2001). Still, Wundt's substantive contributions to the new discipline cannot be dismissed. Indeed, additional historical work should be focused on the lasting effects and generalizability of Wundt's many substantive contributions.

Wundt's laboratory emphasis on sensory processes and reaction time was criticized for its narrowness. But, as noted by Wertheimer (1987), "This criticism may be somewhat inappropriate.

After all, this was just the beginning of genuine experimental psychology. Wundt can hardly be blamed that there were no studies of learning in the early years at his laboratory; that kind of work was not yet in the Zeitgeist" (p. 69). Besides, as noted earlier, Wundt's larger vision did include a broader and encompassing psychology. It is perhaps no accident that many of Wundt's students helped implement his wider vision.

From the early 1970s, there has been an outpouring of scholarly work on Wundt's system of psychology (see Rieber & Robinson, 2003). Most of the scholarly projects have been designed to "correct misconceptions and distortions" (see Araujo, 2012, p. 33). As a pioneer in a new discipline marked by all kinds of uncertain boundaries, it is understandable that Wundt struggled with a host of substantive and methodological issues and that his ideas would evolve over the course of more than sixty years of his active work in psychology. There are clear discrepancies and different points of emphasis between many of his early and later works. Further, as noted by Araujo, Wundt, though not formally trained in philosophy, sought to establish a psychology consistently informed by a coherent philosophical framework, and he warned psychologists about the risks of separating from philosophy to form an independent discipline (Wundt, 2013), as psychologists in the United States have done since his warning (Lamiell, 2013a, 2013b).

The Legacy of Wundt's Students in Applied Psychology

In his major works, Wundt (1897/1969a, 1863/1907) made numerous references to pathological psychology, so it is little wonder that some of his students pursued this area. Wundt (1863/1907) even argued that "pathological psychology has as good a claim to rank as an independent discipline beside normal psychology, as has the pathology of the body to be separated from its physiology" (p. 316).

The renowned psychiatrist **Emil Kraepelin (1856–1926)** learned experimental methodology from Wundt and, according to Blumenthal (1975), advanced a theory of schizophrenia derived specifically from Wundtian psychology. Kraepelin was awarded his M.D. at twenty-two, one year before Wundt established his laboratory at Leipzig. At twenty-seven, despite facing challenges as a promoter of Wundt's work in new academic settings (Steinberg & Himmerich, 2013), Kraepelin wrote a treatise on psychiatry that produced multiple editions (Boring, 1950). His early studies on the psychological effects of alcohol and morphine established Kraepelin as a pioneer in the field of psychopharmacology (Healy, 1993; Müller et al., 2006). He pioneered clinical observation and categorization of people with mental illnesses (deVries et al., 2008), and in 1883, he published an early taxonomy of psychiatric disorders that anticipated current classification systems. This work introduced enduring diagnostic terms such as *paranoia* and *manic-depressive psychosis*, a mood disorder later called bipolar disorder (Marneros, 2009). However, Kraepelin's clinical term *dementia praecox* (premature deterioration) was later, at an April 1908 meeting of the German Psychiatric Association (Kaplan, 2008), renamed *schizophrenia* (splitting of the mind) by Swiss psychiatrist Eugen Bleuler (1857–1939) (Palha & Esteves, 1997). Bleuler also broadened the nature of the definition and defined the disorder in a less pessimistic manner (Hoff, 2012). Kraepelin made a substantial impact on psychiatry and his ideas soon spread through Europe (Healy et al., 2008) and across the United States (Kendler, 2016).

Kraepelin's interest in dementia led to pioneering studies on a disorder that would later be called *Alzheimer's disea*se (Cipriani et al., 2011). Prior to the definitive research of the German neurologist Alois Alzheimer (1864–1915), Kraepelin conducted early clinical work on presenile dementia (Weber, 1997). After Alzheimer published his classic description of the disorder in 1907, Kraepelin named it "Alzheimer's disease" in honor of his colleague.

As forensic research made an impact in Europe at the end of the nineteenth century (see Bartol & Bartol, 1999), Kraepelin played a crucial role in the development of criminal psychiatry. He was one of the first researchers to claim that criminal behavior should be considered a mental illness, and he became a vigorous opponent of the death penalty (Hoff, 1998). In a sentiment shared with modern clinicians, he urged the use of psychiatric treatment in rehabilitating prisoners. He envisioned a larger role for the psychiatrist in the courtroom and even suggested that clinicians have a voice in judicial decisions regarding the variety and length of imprisonment. Unfortunately, while supporting these views, he also supported racism and eugenics, and three of his students went on to become prominent scientific supporters of the Nazi regime before and during World War II (Strous et al., 2016).

Born the same year as Sigmund Freud, Kraepelin was a staunch opponent of psychoanalysis, which he saw as art but not science. Instead, he believed the root of psychopathology to be organic and drew on his findings to educate the German public about the health dangers of alcoholism and syphilis (Engstrom, 1991). Kraepelin was a pioneer in cross-cultural psychology in Germany (Machleidt & Sieberer, 2013; Steinberg, 2015), he wrote extensively about sleep (Becker et al., 2016), and his medical work remains a source of ongoing interest to psychiatrists (Jablensky et al., 1993; Engstrom & Kendler, 2015). Wundt's interests in pathological psychology were extended in the work of not only Kraepelin but also Lightner Witmer, the founder of clinical psychology.

Lightner Witmer (1867–1956) was born in Philadelphia. He earned a bachelor's degree from the University of Pennsylvania in 1888. Following a brief teaching career, he studied at the University of Pennsylvania, but later transferred to Leipzig where he earned a Ph.D. with Wundt in 1893. He returned to the University of Pennsylvania, where he worked until his retirement in 1937. He died at the age of eighty-nine in 1956.

Following his work at Leipzig, Witmer engaged in experimental work on topics such as the perception of pain and the special learning problems of children with cognitive disabilities (Wilkins & Matson, 2009). His work in this area held practical value for early school psychologists (Fagan, 1996), and D'Amato et al. (2011) credit Witmer for providing the interdisciplinary foundations of school psychology. In March 1896, Witmer opened the world's first clinic headed by a psychologist. In its first year of operation, the clinic handled about two dozen cases, primarily clients with learning disorders (McReynolds, 1996). Later, the caseload increased and a greater diversity of clients were tested and treated (see Levine & Wishner, 1977). In 1907, Witmer founded a new journal, which he called *The Psychological Clinic*. McReynolds (1987) pointed out that "Witmer's opening article in the first issue of his new journal . . . called for a new profession and proposed that it be termed *clinical psychology*" (p. 852). Summarizing Witmer's contributions, McReynolds (1997) noted that he was the first to see that scientific psychology could serve as the basis for a helping professional discipline. In addition to founding the first clinic and clinical journal, Witmer showed by his own involvement in clinical activities how clinical professionals might function independent of the medical profession. He also believed that there should be close ties between scientific psychology and clinical psychology. Some have suggested that his work anticipated later developments in industrial/organizational and counseling psychology (McWhirter & McWhirter, 1997).

In subsequent chapters, we will encounter additional examples of how students from Wundt's laboratory extended the boundaries of psychology. If such students departed from the strict focus of the Leipzig laboratory, many nevertheless carved out areas of application consistent with their mentor's larger intellectual agenda.

Review Questions

1. Psychophysics explores the relationships between the properties of stimuli as measured by a physical scale and the psychological or subjective impressions of those stimuli. List and describe two extreme positions about the nature of the relationship of experience to objects in the world.
2. How did early psychophysics challenge the two extremes referred to in the previous question?
3. Define the term *threshold*.
4. List some of the findings that came out of Weber's work on difference thresholds.
5. Write both the Weber formula and the Fechner formula and explain their meanings.
6. Briefly describe three of Fechner's psychophysical methods.
7. Briefly explain Helmholtz's approach to the understanding of color vision and his approach to audition.
8. Outline four general characteristics of Wundt's thought.
9. Give two examples of representative research coming out of Wundt's laboratory.
10. How did Wundt define *psychology*?
11. How did Wundt distinguish between perception and apperception?
12. Briefly explain Wundt's tridimensional theory of feeling.
13. What did Wundt mean by *creative synthesis*?
14. What role did Emil Kraepelin play in the study of psychiatric disorders?
15. Briefly outline Lightner Witmer's contributions to the formal development of clinical psychology.

Glossary

aesthesiometer A compasslike instrument used to measure tactile sensitivity. Two points can be stimulated simultaneously. The task of participants is to report whether they feel both points or only one.

apperception In Wundt's psychology, an apperception is an active set of associations marked by intelligent direction within a larger context. A simple associative combination such as *sky* and *blue* would be counted simply as a perception. Apperception, by contrast, carries far more meaning. Thus, a statement such as "If the weather is clear in the morning, we will go sailing" denotes an intelligent direction within a context, an apperception.

creative synthesis The principle advanced by Wundt that psychical combinations are not a mere sum of elements. Rather, a combination of associations includes new attributes not predictable from the sum of the elements.

difference threshold The minimal stimulus difference that is detectable 50 percent of the time.

element An abstraction referring to a simple irreducible sensation.

Fechner, Gustav Theodor (1801–1887) His *Elements of Psychophysics*, one of the great original classics in psychology, set forth a systematic approach to psychophysics. He proposed several early psychophysical methods and helped lay the conceptual and methodological foundations for the new discipline of psychology.

Fechner's law An integration of Weber's formula expressed as $S = k \log R$, where S is a mental sensation and R is a stimulus magnitude. Thus, according to the law, a mental sensation is a logarithmic function of the stimulus multiplied by a constant.

Helmholtz, Hermann Ludwig Ferdinand von (1821–1894) One of the great scientists of the nineteenth century who, along with Thomas Young, advanced a trichromatic theory of color vision. He also advanced a theory of pitch perception and was the first to measure the speed of conduction of the nervous impulse.

heterogony of ends Wundt's position that an ongoing behavioral sequence must often be understood in terms of an ever-shifting pattern of primary and secondary goals. For example, a cat chasing a mouse may suddenly find it necessary to compete with a partner, overcome an unexpected barrier, or avoid a danger. Ends, goals, and purposes keep changing.

hylozoism The view that mind is manifested in all material movement.

just noticeable difference (jnd) The smallest detectable difference between a standard stimulus and a comparison stimulus.

Kraepelin, Emil (1856–1926) A student of Wundt. He created an influential classification system of psychiatric disorders and made numerous contributions to psychiatry and psychopharmacology.

Maxwell, James Clerk (1831–1879) Scottish physicist who demonstrated that he could match any spectral value with various mixtures of red, green, or blue. He thus contributed directly to the Young–Helmholtz theory of color vision.

method of average error A psychophysical method that permits a participant to manipulate a variable stimulus until it appears to match a standard stimulus.

method of constant stimuli A psychophysical method in which comparison stimuli are judged against a standard stimulus. Various values of the comparison stimuli above and below the standard stimulus are presented on a random basis. The task of the participant is to specify whether each comparison stimulus is equal to, greater than, or less than the standard.

method of limits A psychophysical method whereby a standard stimulus is compared with various values of comparison stimuli presented in both ascending and descending series. The task of the participant is to specify when the standard and the variable appear to be the same. Also called the *method of limits* because it measured the quantitative limits of the variable stimulus values that appear to be greater than, less than, or equal to the standard stimulus.

ophthalmoscope An instrument designed by Hermann von Helmholtz for viewing the interior of the eye, especially the retina.

260

psychophysics The formal study of the relationship between the properties of stimuli as measured by a physical scale and the psychological impressions of those stimuli.

response compression In psychophysics, equal intervals on a physical scale may be experienced as a diminishing series. Illustrated in the experience of a diminishing series associated with a three-way light.

sensation According to Wundt, an element of consciousness referring to simple awareness of stimulation.

stereoscope An instrument that produces a three-dimensional effect by simultaneously presenting slightly different two-dimensional views to the left and right eyes.

threshold That stimulus intensity (or change in intensity) that is detected 50 percent of the time.

tridimensional theory of feeling According to Wundt, a theory of feeling marked by three fundamental directions: pleasure and pain, strain and relaxation, and excitation and quiescence.

voluntarism Technical term for the system of psychology advanced by Wilhelm Wundt. Voluntary behaviors are those that are varied to meet the demands of varying circumstances.

Weber, Ernst Heinrich (1795–1878) Well-known nineteenth-century physiologist who was the first to establish a quantitative relationship between the physical properties of stimuli and the experience of those stimuli. Weber's book, *The Sense of Touch*, launched the field of psychophysics.

Weber's illusion The perception that two points of a compass appear to move apart when the compass is moved over an insensitive area of the skin. By contrast, the two points appear to move together when the compass is moved over sensitive areas of the skin.

Weber's law First quantitative law in psychology expressed as

$$\frac{\Delta R}{R} = K$$

where R = the amount of existing stimulation

ΔR = the amount of stimulation that must be added to produce a jnd

K = a constant.

Witmer, Lightner (1867–1956) One of Wundt's students. Founded the first psychological clinic and coined the expression *clinical psychology.*

Wundt, Wilhelm Maximilian (1832–1920) The founder of the first psychology laboratory that functioned for a sustained period of time. Wundt also advanced the first systematic vision of psychology known as voluntarism. He is also the first person who, without qualification, can be thought of as a psychologist. His *Principles of Physiological Psychology* is one of the great classics in the discipline. More than any other, he can be viewed as the founder of modern psychology.

Young, Thomas (1773–1829) English physiologist who formulated the trichromatic (red, green, and blue) model of color vision. He speculated that retinal structures must therefore be specialized for color primaries.

Young–Helmholtz trichromatic theory Young's theory that color vision is produced by separate receptor systems on the retina that are responsive to primary colors (red, green, and blue-violet). Maxwell and Helmholtz supported Young's theory in the nineteenth century.

11 Developments after the Founding

How many evils could be remedied . . . by knowledge of the laws according to which a mental state can be modified!

—Franz Brentano (1874/1973)

A rapid growth of interest followed the formal founding of psychology at Leipzig. Within a few years, a host of new lecture courses, laboratories, and degree programs emerged in Europe and the United States. In 1898, Edward Bradford Titchener, writing for the journal *Mind*, reminded readers, "It is now twenty years since Prof. Wundt instituted the first psychological laboratory in the University of Leipzig. A revolution, radical and far-reaching, was thus quietly inaugurated . . . Laboratories have been established in most of the principal universities of Germany and in all the principal universities of the United States" (p. 311). Excitement about laboratories ran high as journals carried descriptions of research plans, announcements regarding the establishment of new laboratories, and descriptions of laboratory equipment. Titchener celebrated the fact that "to carry on the psychological work of a modern university the psychology profes-

sor must have acquired a body of what one may call 'technical' knowledge, knowledge of applied mechanics and applied electricity" (p. 311).

Wundt played a pivotal role in founding psychology, but not everyone agreed with his approach to the new discipline. There were heated debates on topics such as methodology, the appropriate subject matter of psychology, theoretical positions, definitions, and basic assumptions.

Before we consider alternatives to Wundt's psychology, let us explore the meaning of expressions such as *systematic thought* and *systems of psychology*. Courses in the history of psychology are sometimes called "History and Systems of Psychology." What do we mean by a system of psychology or, for that matter, a system of anything? The answer moves us into a rich intellectual arena.

Systems

A **system** may be defined as an *organized way of envisioning the world or some aspect of the world.*

There are integrated, all-encompassing systems that are nothing less than a "philosophy of life," or what German scholars call a *Weltanschauung* ("worldview"). More commonly, however, we encounter less-ambitious, single-domain systems that provide an organized way of envisioning a limited dimension of human experience. For example, we have political systems, religious systems, economic systems, philosophical systems, and psychological systems. Subsequent chapters will be more meaningful after we explore the characteristics of systems. We'll draw upon the discussion of Wilhelm Wundt in Chapter 10 to illustrate our mission here.

First, systems provide definitions. Wundt defined *psychology* as the "science that investigates the facts of consciousness." Of course, different systems offer different definitions of psychology. We can uncover countless terms in psychology that are defined in multiple ways depending on a given systematic position. For example, as we will see in a later chapter, two notable learning theorists, Clark Hull and B. F. Skinner, defined the term *reinforcement* in different ways. Psychology is not alone with regard to such discrepancies; for years, physicists quarreled over the definition of a positron.

Second, systems include assumptions. Wundt thought that humans possess only a limited free will. By contrast, Sigmund Freud built his system of psychoanalysis on the deterministic assumption that all mental phenomena are caused. Systems of psychology vary with respect to assumptions about issues of nature and nurture, mind and brain, and free will and determinism. Assumptions are sometimes explicit and other times implicit. The behaviorist John B. Watson preferred to not waste time talking philosophy, but implicit philosophical assumptions are nevertheless evident in his system.

A third characteristic of systems is that they prescribe methodologies or ways to conduct research. Most of us know about the different methods and assumed sources of truth in religious and political systems. The same is true in the sciences where a variety of methodologies

are associated with different disciplinary areas. For example, historical sciences such as paleontology and geology employ different methods than meteorologists testing a weather model or chemists manipulating materials and instruments in a laboratory. Wundt's psychology emphasized controlled introspection, but his research team used additional methodologies in the laboratory. Introspection, naturalistic observation, and controlled laboratory experiments are among psychology's many methodological tools. Presumably, the methodologies employed by scientists result in observations that can be checked and replicated. Thus, the methods of science are associated with certain constraints and expectations that may not always be evident in nonscientific methods.

Fourth, systems also specify the subject matter of a disciplinary area. Among other things, Wundt was concerned with the discovery of the elements of consciousness and the way these elements combine. By contrast, Freud emphasized the unconscious mind and its influences, whereas the behavioral psychology of John B. Watson focused on observable behavior of humans and other animals. Humanistic psychology criticized these systems as narrow and insisted that joyfulness, peak experiences, and self-actualization are legitimate topics for study in psychology.

Fifth, a system may be construed as open or closed. An open system is responsive to new and multiple sources of information, whereas a closed system restricts or even censors the flow of ideas. Systems of thought also exist in a hierarchical arrangement. For example, one may embrace several single-domain systems, but one system is often dominant and serves as a filter for what is acceptable in other systems. Thus, a political or a religious system may serve as a filter for a scientific system or vice versa. A deep and critical awareness of the effects of such a hierarchy can be expected in a more open system of thought.

Sixth, systems of thought sometimes differ with respect to their treatment of time. Some psychologists explore the past to understand the present. Psychoanalytic theory emphasizes the power of childhood trauma in coloring adult experiences and behavior. By contrast, behaviorism stresses the importance of present facts—new conditioning begins *now*, so there is not always a need to dwell on the past. Some humanistic psychologists will emphasize their clients' hopes for the future.

Seventh, systems of thought also vary along a liberal–conservative continuum. Conservative thought seeks to preserve stability by emphasizing traditions that have proved workable in the past. In this context, the term *liberal* means "worthy of a free person." Liberals do not reject tradition "out of hand," but they may argue that contemporary problems are not always solved by traditional methods. Systems tell us how to dress, what to eat, what to regard as primary or secondary, what to regard as relevant or irrelevant, and how to interact with others. Systems may also attach special significance to specific times, locations, and symbols. In many cases, our systems of thought even define, for better or worse, who we are.

Edward Bradford Titchener

Edward Bradford Titchener

Edwin G. Boring (1927) noted that "the best key to Titchener's life . . . lies in the fact that he emulated Wundt" (p. 504). One might conclude that **Edward Bradford Titchener (1867–1927)** had devoted years of study with the master. In fact, his studies in Leipzig were limited to the two-year period from 1890 to 1892. The relationship between the two men in that period could be described as businesslike and professional. Nevertheless, Titchener identified with Wundt's personal and professional style and with the elementary dimensions of his psychology. He did not admire Wundt's larger philosophical vision, especially his emphasis on social, cultural, and linguistic studies. Rather, he identified with the hard-core scientific work in Wundt's laboratory.

More than any other disciple, Titchener brought Wundt's experimental thought and work to the United States. Unfortunately, Titchener's psychology has often been mistaken as a close version of Wundt's psychology. Although similarities exist in their respective work, historical scholarship has clarified important differences between them (see Blumenthal, 1975, 1979; Leahey, 1981).

Edward Bradford Titchener was born in Chichester, England, on January 11, 1867, the son of John Titchener and Alice Field Habin. He studied at Malvern College in Worcestershire. Later, at Oxford University, he studied physiology, the classics, and philosophy. After graduating from Oxford in 1890, he studied at Leipzig where he embarked on doctoral studies with Wundt. Following the completion of his Ph.D. program in 1892, Titchener returned to England. At that time, job opportunities in psychology were sparse. Despite its robust empirical heritage, England was one of the last European countries to recognize the new discipline of psychology. Unable to secure a British appointment, Titchener accepted a position at Cornell University in Ithaca, New York. He remained at Cornell until his death in 1927. For a time, Titchener was a powerful force in American psychology. His books were widely read and, like Wundt, he produced a large number of doctoral students. Even so, his system faded after his death.

Titchener thrived despite frustrations in setting up a new laboratory and establishing a new program. By 1895, he had advanced to the position of full professor, an impressive accomplishment for a twenty-eight-year-old. He translated several of Wundt's works into English and produced a steady stream of publications that included eight books and over two hundred articles, in addition to his many translations.

Titchener also headed one of the most vigorous doctoral programs in the United States. Boring (1927) listed fifty-six doctoral students who graduated from Cornell in the period from 1894 to 1927 (records before 1910 were incomplete, so the actual number of doctoral students may have been higher). Titchener's first graduate student was Margaret Floy Washburn (1871–1939), later to establish a reputation for her work in comparative psychology. In all, nineteen of Titchener's fifty-six graduates were women. In the context of the times, this was a remarkable record. Evans (1991) reminds us that "Titchener took women into his graduate program at Cornell at a time when Harvard and Columbia would not. More women completed their Ph.D. degrees with him than with any other male psychologist of his generation" (p. 90).

Students who earned their degrees under Titchener came away with colorful anecdotes. Evans (1991) added, "Titchener's was an overpowering personality. He seemed bigger than life and often overwhelmed his students and colleagues by sheer strength of character" (p. 89). Boring (1961) remembered that "psychology at Cornell—at least the orthodox psychology that centered in the laboratory—revolved around and was almost bounded by the personality of E. B. Titchener" (pp. 22–23). He took a keen interest

in the progress of his students and gave generous time to their research projects. Young (1972) told of "weekly conferences with Titchener in his home" (p. 334). Titchener conducted a small orchestra on Sunday evenings and students who could play an instrument were encouraged to participate. After the music, Sunday evenings were devoted to casual conversation, generally on topics other than psychology.

Titchener's erudition and brilliance are typical themes in the biographies of his students. Boring (1961) stated,

> He always seemed to me the nearest approach to genius of anyone with whom I have been closely associated . . . He was competent with languages, and could ad lib in Latin when the occasion required it. If you had mushrooms, he would tell you at once how they should be cooked. If you were buying oak for a new floor, he would at once come forward with all the advantages of ash. If you were engaged to be married, he would have his certain and insistent advice about the most unexpected aspects of your problems, and if you were honeymooning, he would write to remind you, as he did me, on what day you ought to be back at work.
>
> (pp. 22–23)

Boring noted that Titchener, like Freud, demanded loyalty from his students. At Cornell, there was a strict European code on matters of decorum and conduct and those who violated the code could pay a severe penalty. Most students decided that the benefits of working with a man such as Titchener far outweighed the inconveniences brought about by his paternalistic nature. Titchener's closest relationships were with students rather than with colleagues. By temperament, he was not one who thrived in a rugged, democratic climate. Titchener also strongly promoted the new science. In 1904, in part due to his frustrations with the American Psychological Association, he and others created the Society of the Experimentalists, later named the Society of Experimental Psychologists, to reflect his narrower definition of laboratory psychology as discussed subsequently (Goodwin, 1985, 2005). Despite Titchener's advocacy for women in psychology and his acceptance of many women as doctoral students (Proctor & Evans, 2014), women were excluded from the Society of Experimental Psychologists until after his death; in 1929, his former student, Washburn, and another woman became charter members of the newly reorganized society.

After the first decade of the new century, the tide was turning against Titchener's systematic psychology. John B. Watson called for a radical new approach to psychology. The new Gestalt psychology from Germany issued devastating critiques that challenged Titchener's systematic vision. American functionalism provided an approach to psychology with broader appeal than his narrow approach to the discipline. Titchener died in 1927 and, though he produced many doctoral students, no one carried on his legacy. Accordingly, his systematic vision died with him. Some have speculated about how Titchener's system might have evolved had he lived a longer life (see Evans, 1972).

Titchener's Psychology

The technical term employed by Titchener for his system of psychology was **structuralism**. Like other systems, structuralism embraced a specific methodology, advanced definitions of the subject matter of psychology, and made assumptions regarding age-old philosophical problems. Titchener drew parallels between the physical sciences (especially physics and chemistry) and psychology. He hoped to establish the new discipline on the same conceptual footing that had proved so successful in the established sciences.

THE SUBJECT MATTER OF PSYCHOLOGY Titchener (1910) argued that "all the sciences have the same sort of subject-matter; there can be no essential difference between the raw materials

of physics and the raw materials of psychology" (p. 6). All science, according to Titchener, begins with experience. Without experience, there can be no cognition, no knowledge. Though all the sciences begin with experience, experience itself can be considered from different points of view. For example, we can consider a unit of time, say an hour, from the point of view of physics. The hour, from such a point of view, is a measured unit of time. The actual unit of measurement has fixed qualities (e.g., 60 minutes or 3,600 seconds) that are independent of human judgment. But an hour, from the point of view of psychology, may be long or short, pleasant or unpleasant. The subject matter of psychology, thus, is experience, dependent on the experiencing person. Titchener (1910) stated that formal study from the first point of view (stated previously) "gives us facts and laws of physics; [the] second gives us facts and laws of psychology" (p. 8).

THE PROBLEM OF PSYCHOLOGY Science, according to Titchener, always seeks to answer three sorts of questions: what, how, and why? *What* questions deal with the basic, most uncomplicated elements of the subject (e.g., what is water made of?). *How* questions deal with the appearances of things. For example, how do the basic elements that compose water combine with each other? Finally, Titchener (1910) stated that "science enquires, further, why a given set of phenomena occurs in just this given way, and not otherwise; and it answers the question 'why' by laying bare the cause of which the observed phenomena are the effect" (p. 37). The first problem for psychology is to identify the basic **elements** of experience, such as irreducible sensations or simple images. The second task is to assess the ways in which elements combine. The third is to determine causal relations in these phenomena. We shall return later to a more detailed consideration of these problems.

THE METHOD OF PSYCHOLOGY The method of psychology, in Titchener's view, is really no different from the method employed by any other science. All scientific work begins with observation of the phenomena that have been designated as the subject matter of a particular science. The type of observation employed by the physicist is called *inspection*, whereas the type of observation employed by the psychologist is called **introspection**. Needless to say, special training is required for the unique observational tasks of any discipline. For an observation to be scientific, it is important that it be possible to isolate it, vary it experimentally, and repeat it. For example, the stimulation of a particular receptor site on the tongue with a particular substance may produce a specific response. Maybe a research participant declares that she or he experienced a taste of sweetness. Presumably, the site can be isolated, the substance can be varied many ways (e.g., with respect to quality or concentration), and the response for a particular isolated stimulus can be repeated. The observation, in this case, is a variety of introspection, but in Titchener's view, this need not be viewed as radically different from inspection.

THE SCOPE OF PSYCHOLOGY Because Titchener's method was limited to introspection, it might be argued that psychology, in his view, is limited in scope. For example, how can we ask a baby or nonhuman subject such as a cat or a dog to introspect? For that matter, how can we ask someone struggling with distorted thinking to introspect? It appears that Titchener's psychology is limited to the study of normal human beings. Further, it appears superficially, at least, that introspection reveals only the contents of the individual mind and that we are trapped in a kind of solipsism. Titchener was aware of the problem and took steps to ensure that his system did, in fact, have considerable scope. To argue that Titchener was interested only in the adult human mind is to caricaturize his system of thought.

Titchener believed that psychologists must make ample use of analogy. Although we have direct access only to our own experience, we have every reason to believe that a specific behavior

(e.g., the expression of fear) in another is comparable to our own experience of fear. Such an argument provides the conceptual basis for social psychology and a similar line of argument provides the basis for comparative psychology. On this topic, Titchener (1910) wrote:

> If however, we attribute minds to other human beings, we have no right to deny them to the higher animals. These animals are provided with a nervous system of the same pattern as ours, and their conduct or behaviour, under circumstances that would arouse certain feelings in us, often seems to express, quite definitely, similar feelings in them. Surely we must grant that the highest vertebrates, mammals and birds, have minds.
>
> (p. 27)

In the same passage, Titchener argued that the range of mind seems to be as broad as the range of animal life. His view on the scope of psychology, then, was broader than what might be derived from an uncritical acceptance of his definition of psychology as human experience dependent on the experiencing individual. The architecture of the nervous system and analogies drawn from behavior provide the glue for the breadth of his vision. Titchener (1910) told his readers that there is

> a psychology of language, a psychology of myth, a psychology of custom, etc; [there is also] a differential psychology of the Latin mind, of the Anglo-Saxon mind, of the Oriental mind, etc.
>
> And this is not all: the scope of psychology extends, still further, from the normal to the abnormal mind. Life, as we know, need not be either complete or completely healthy life. The living organism may show defect, the lack of limb or of a sense-organ; and it may show disorder and disease, a . . . lapse from health. So it is with mind.
>
> (pp. 28–29)

267

As Titchener's thought evolved, he realized the importance of the study of different types of consciousness. For example, he argued that studies of people with sensory impairments or with morbid fears are important in their own right. Furthermore, such studies may shed light on our understanding of more typical conscious processes. In fact, the study of normal conscious processes commanded the most attention in Titchener's laboratory. In the words of Evans (1991), Titchener's "lasting contribution to American psychological thought was his championing of psychology as science and of the laboratory as the primary source of data for psychological research" (p. 102). Titchener drew a distinction between science and technology, and although he did not oppose technology as such, he preferred that psychology identify—especially in its infancy—with laboratory science. We turn now to some of the major content areas explored by Titchener and his students.

ELEMENTARY MENTAL PROCESSES The first task of any science, according to Titchener, is to investigate the basic elements of its subject matter. His first concern was the nature and number of the elementary mental processes. Following the Leipzig tradition, Titchener focused on the senses as windows to the mind. His most immediate concern was to identify the basic elements associated with each of the senses. According to Titchener (1910), a true element "must remain unchanged, however persistent our attempt at analysis and however refined our method of investigation" (p. 46). The next task of the psychologist is to arrange "the mental elements precisely as the chemist classifies his elementary substances" (p. 49).

Though the senses occupied a central place in Titchener's system, he identified two additional elementary processes: images and affections. Sensations were regarded as elements of perceptions, whereas images were regarded as elements of ideas, memories, and thoughts. Affections were treated as the elementary processes of emotions. The relative emphasis of Titchener on these elementary processes is illustrated in the amount of page space devoted to each. For example, in *A Textbook of Psychology* (1910), Titchener devoted 293 pages to sensation and perception, seventy pages to affection and emotion, and seventy-two pages to memory and thought. In that same book, twenty-one pages were devoted to association, thirty-seven pages to attention, and forty-one pages to a discussion of reactions and actions.

In addition to the identification and classification of elements, the psychologist, according to Titchener, must discover the **attributes of elementary mental processes**. For example, he found that all sensations, at a minimum, have four attributes: quality, intensity, clearness, and duration. *Quality* is the major identifying property of a sensation—its saltiness, sweetness, redness, coldness, and so on. *Intensity* simply refers to the fact that the sensation exists in some amount or strength. *Clearness* refers to the transparency or the distinctiveness of a sensation; a clear sensation is easily identified. *Duration*, of course, is a temporal attribute. As noted, all sensations share these four basic attributes, but some sensations have additional attributes. For example, certain solutions such as alcohol applied to the skin may have an attribute that could best be described as penetratingness. Such a solution stimulates the surface of the skin as well as areas below the surface.

Titchener also believed that the attributes of quality, intensity, clearness, and duration are associated with images. He found quality, intensity, and duration in association with affections, but clearness was not easily identified as an attribute of affection. Titchener and his students identified other attributes with specific elements. For example, he noted that "certain sensations have been credited with an attribute of insistence. They are self-assertive and aggressive; they monopolise consciousness . . . We speak of the penetratingness of odours like camphor and naphthalene; of the urgency . . . of certain pains" (1910, p. 55).

One way to gain an appreciation for Titchener's system is to examine his position on some key issues of the day.

MIND AND BRAIN Titchener admitted that common sense tells us that we lose consciousness as a result of inhaling ether or that we run because of fear. In other words, the physical system influences the mental and vice versa. Titchener's position, however, was "that mind and body, the subject-matter of psychology and the subject-matter of physiology, are simply two aspects of the same world of experience. They cannot influence each other, because they are not separate and independent things" (1910, p. 13). Titchener referred to his position as *psychophysical parallelism*, but it is not completely clear that the label is accurate. Titchener could also be viewed as a double-aspect theorist because he declared that mind and body are but "two aspects of the same world of experience." A true psychophysical parallelist would posit both the physical and the mental but deny that the two interact.

Ambiguities are evident in Titchener's position. Heidbreder (1933) was correct when she declared that his "emotions were not involved in the problem for its own sake . . . He is almost perfunctory in his discussion of the topic" (p. 127). At every turn, Titchener emphasized the primacy of experience. He studied experience in relation to the physical system and because he rejected commonsense interactionism. For all of these reasons, he is viewed as a psychophysical parallelist, just as he described himself. His psychophysical parallelism, however, may be of a pragmatic rather than a metaphysical variety.

ATTENTION Like many early psychologists, Titchener was very interested in attention (Posner et al., 2007). He distinguished between passive or involuntary attention and active or voluntary attention. He referred to involuntary attention as *primary* and to voluntary attention as *secondary*. Both represent types of consciousness that are identifiable at different stages of development. **Primary attention**, according to Titchener (1910), is brought about by strong stimuli and is "an attention that we are compelled to give and are powerless to prevent" (p. 268). Titchener believed that certain qualities are irresistible and

observed that, in his own case, attention was commanded by stimuli such as the smell of musk, a bitter taste, or the sight of yellow. Examples of other factors that control involuntary attention include novelty and suddenness.

Secondary attention involves a focus on a subject that would not normally call attention to itself. For example, Titchener (1910) pointed out that "a problem in geometry does not appeal to us as a thunderclap does" (p. 271). Thus, "Secondary attention is attention under difficulties, attention in the face of competitors, attention with distraction" (p. 272). Clearly, secondary attention is associated with a more advanced stage of development. The infant is capable of primary attention but may not yet be capable of secondary attention.

Titchener (1910) found still a third stage in attention, and that stage, he tells us, consists in nothing else than a relapse into primary attention. As we work our problem in geometry, we gradually become interested and absorbed; and presently the problem gains the same forcible hold over us as the thunderclap has from the moment of its appearance in consciousness. The difficulties have been overcome; the competitors have been vanquished; the distraction has disappeared. For Titchener, there could hardly be stronger evidence of the growth of secondary out of primary attention than this fact of everyday experience that secondary attention is continually reverting to the primary form.

His laboratory investigated numerous topics such as the duration and effort of attention, the inertia of attention, and bodily conditions conducive to Titchener's attention. This area of scholarship remained robust until the 1920s, when the study of attention faded from the United States with the rise of behaviorism (Moray, 2007).

ASSOCIATION If Titchener's primary experimental focus was on sensory processes, he didn't neglect the importance of association. He acknowledged the debt of psychology to Aristotle and to British thinkers from Hobbes

269

to Bain who emphasized the centrality of association. Furthermore, he quoted, with approval, the contention of David Hume that association is to the mental world as gravitation is to physics (see Titchener, 1910). Titchener's emphasis on associationism shaped his views and uses of introspection as a research method (Beenfelt, 2013).

Titchener recognized traditional attempts to establish laws of association but argued that all association can be reduced to the law of contiguity. He pointed out that even the so-called law of similarity really involves contiguity. In Titchener's (1910) treatment, association is characterized by the following statement: "Whenever a sensory or imaginal process occurs in consciousness, there are likely to appear with it (of course, in imaginal terms) all those sensory and imaginal processes which occurred together with it in any earlier conscious present. This we may term the law of association" (p. 378).

Titchener immediately recognized a possible objection to his law. What about affective processes? Feelings most assuredly play a role in associative processes. Titchener (1910) agreed but noted that feelings play a role in association only "by virtue of their sensory and imaginal components, and not in their affective character" (p. 378). However, he admitted that little is known about feeling and that his position was tentative.

THE EXPERIMENTAL STUDY OF ASSOCIATION
Titchener noted that, prior to the work of Hermann Ebbinghaus on memory, the experimental study of association was confounded because of the presence of previously acquired meanings. In a celebration of Ebbinghaus's contribution, Titchener (1910) offered the opinion that "it is not too much to say that the recourse to nonsense syllables, as means to the study of association, marks the most considerable advance, in this chapter of psychology, since the time of Aristotle" (p. 381). Nevertheless, according to Titchener, the nonsense syllable is not a complete panacea because we human beings find

intrinsic meanings everywhere. Thus, even in a set of nonsense syllables, we may find that one has more meaning than another and the one with the greater meaning forms an impression. The impression then helps mediate associations. He argued that associations must be understood in the context of impressions that result from the fact that some stimuli, even some nonsense syllables, have a unique capacity to impress themselves on the brain. Accordingly, impression and associative processes supplement each other. In Titchener's view, the mere study of association without careful introspective analysis of what is taking place is inadequate. He also warned that our knowledge in this area will remain inadequate until such future time as we are able to devise means to study the physiology of association.

MEANING According to Titchener (1910), "Meaning, psychologically, is always context" (p. 367). In Titchener's **context theory of meaning**, meaning is understood as a function of the laws of attention in combination with the laws of the association of sensations. An aggregate of sensations will also be supplemented by images that result from memories of previous encounters with the particular aggregate of sensations. The group of sensations and images, according to Titchener (1910), "has a fringe, a background, a context; and this context is the psychological equivalent of its logical meaning" (p. 371).

Titchener (1910) acknowledged that many psychologists would not accept such a narrow associationistic approach to meaning:

A square, they say, is more than four linear extensions, sensibly of the same length, and occupying certain relative positions in the visual field; a square is square; and squareness is a new character, common to all squares, but not to be explained by attention, or by the laws of sensory connection, or by those of imaginal supplementing. A melody, again, is more than rhythm and consonance and scale; a melody is melodic; we recognize its melodic character as such; the melodic character is something new and unique, common to all melodies, but not found elsewhere.

(p. 372)

Titchener (1910) noted that he could not find this extra character in his own introspections. That is, he found no need for a new distinct mental content based on a combination or synthesis of the parts. He was nevertheless open to future research on the matter and added that it is "only right to say that the belief in a new mental content, or new mental character, peculiar to perception, is shared by many psychologists of standing" (p. 373).

EMOTION The most widely discussed theory of emotion in Titchener's day was a rather paradoxical theory (see Chapter 12) advanced by William James (1884b) and propounded independently by Carl Lange (1885/1922). Widely known as the **James–Lange theory of emotion**, the view stressed the dependence of emotions on bodily responses. According to the theory, we experience emotions such as fear, anger, or love because of bodily events (e.g., muscular arousal, discharge of adrenaline, and increase in heart rate) that interpose between one mental event and another. Thus, to use one of James's examples, we see a bear, we run, and we are afraid. The experience of emotion is a product of the running and the multitude of physical events that accompany it. We refer to the theory as paradoxical because it contradicts the commonsense idea that we see the bear, are afraid, and then run. The theory will be examined in more detail in Chapter 12, but it is sketched briefly here because it serves as a foil for Titchener's position.

Titchener noted that the so-called James–Lange theory was not really new. It had been anticipated, at least in part, by figures such as Malebranche, Descartes, Spinoza, Lotze, and Maudsley. Despite its venerable history, Titchener found flaws in the theory.

The first problem, according to Titchener (1910), was that "the bodily changes to which

James refers may appear identically in very different emotions. There are tears of joy and tears of rage, as well as tears of sorrow; we may strike in fear or in cruelty, as well as in anger; we may run as hard to overtake a friend as we run from a pursuing bear" (p. 477). In response to such criticisms, James modified his theory and admitted that stimuli themselves may produce responses with avoidance or approach characteristics (James, 1894).

Titchener also argued that mere sensations of organic conditions can hardly be identified with the richer, more complex experience of an emotion. Titchener did not deny the importance of biological correlates of emotion but argued for a much broader conception. He believed some experiences are automatically toned with **affect**—a position James also accepted. Such affect occurs in an environmental context, is associated with biological conditions, and may be associated with images or earlier memories. Thus, according to Titchener, the experience of emotion may have multiple causes.

Titchener discussed the difficulties of classifying emotions as well as emotional types. The major difficulty is that any classification scheme may serve only the convenience of the person doing the classifying and have nothing to do with the science of emotions. For example, he referred to the ancient typology advanced by Galen. Recall from Chapter 4 that Galen's temperamental types included the choleric, the sanguine, the melancholic, and the phlegmatic. Titchener (1910) referred to other possible classification schemes but noted that they are "of interest rather for an applied than for a general psychology" (p. 498), which, for Titchener, indicated lesser value.

Titchener (1910) pointed out that the sentiment "represents the last stage of mental development on the affective side, as thought represents the highest level of development on the side of sensation and image" (p. 499). A sentiment, according to Titchener, is more complex than emotion; it includes discrimination, a critical dimension, possible conflicting claims, and

271

so on. For example, if patriotism counts as a sentiment, it includes emotions, but there are also tensions. What are the relationships between loyalty to state, to nation, or to humankind? What is substantive and what is mere symbolism? Clearly, the sentiment involves emotion but is a much more complicated manifestation of the affective dimension.

AFFECT AND EMOTION Earlier, we noted that Titchener identified three elementary mental processes: sensations, images, and affections. **Affections** were initially regarded as the elements of emotions. As Titchener's theory developed, the relationship between affect and emotion became troublesome. Titchener was suspicious that affections are really nothing more than sensations of pleasantness or unpleasantness (see Henle, 1986). The same suspicions had also been directed at the so-called images; perhaps they were but a species of sensation.

In the final years of his life, Titchener moved away from the concept of elements and thinking in terms of the dimensions or attributes of experience. As noted by Evans (1972), "As early as 1918 the system started out from 'the ultimate dimensions' of psychological subject matter" (p. 172). These ultimate dimensions consisted of what were earlier called attributes: quality, intensity, duration, and so on. Titchener's final approach to psychology was much closer to what we find naturally in experience. It could be argued that what is most immediate is a quality such as redness or sweetness or a sense of pleasantness or unpleasantness. Images, sensations, and feelings are not the ultimate elements or dimensions of experience but abstractions discovered through dissection or discrimination.

Though Titchener was moving toward a new organizational approach to psychology, there is no evidence that he would have changed his rigorously scientific approach. Indeed, though his original system did not survive, his rigorous scientific attitude enjoyed prominence among experimental psychologists. In his final years, Titchener celebrated the growing independence of psychology from physiology. The confidence betrayed in such celebration may have had salutary effects on psychologists who found security in the new discipline.

Margaret Floy Washburn: A Broader Psychology

Titchener's first graduate student, **Margaret Floy Washburn (1871–1939)**, became a significant figure among a new generation of psychologists. Washburn had earned a bachelor's degree from Vassar in 1891. Science and philosophy dominated her academic interests, and she found that the new field of experimental psychology joined her two interests in a near perfect union. Following graduation, she studied psychology at Columbia University where a few women were accepted as "hearers," but not as degree candidates. Accordingly, Washburn transferred to Cornell University, where she would be permitted to work toward an advanced degree. She arrived in the fall of 1892 just as the twenty-five-year-old Titchener became a new faculty member. Washburn completed her degree with Titchener in 1894 and became the first woman in the United States to be awarded a Ph.D. in psychology. After brief positions at Wells College, Cornell, and the University of Akron, Washburn accepted an appointment at Vassar, where she remained for the rest of her illustrious career.

Washburn accepted Titchener's emphasis on the central role of consciousness in psychology though she doubted that consciousness consisted of irreducible static elements. She was too much of an empiricist, in the classic sense of that word, to reject the mental world or consciousness as a legitimate topic in psychology. In spite of this, she could not accept Cartesian interactionism with its emphasis on a mental substance that can "go it alone." She accepted epiphenomenalism because it is friendly to both the mental and the physical worlds but assumes that real causal force always works from the physical to the mental. Nevertheless, in her opinion, we learn about

Margaret Floy Washburn

consciousness and its physical underpinnings by relying on introspection and other psychological techniques. Her willingness to seek harmony between conflicting systems of psychology was rare in her day (Viney & Burlingame-Lee, 2003).

Washburn became a leader in comparative psychology with the publication of *The Animal Mind* (first published in 1908 with substantial revisions in 1917, 1926, and 1936) and joined the growing trend toward animal research (Baker & Serdikoff, 2013). Her book provided a wealth of information on animal sensory systems, animal memory, intelligence, attention, behavior, and adaptation. The book's strong evolutionary thrust is evident in her speculations about the role of distance receptors such as the eye and the ear in the development of higher cognitive processes. Early species who had only contact receptors could never afford the luxury of the delay involved in cognitive processes. Physical contact for such

organisms demanded an immediate and appropriate response or else the organism would die or lose the chance to acquire food. By contrast, the development of distance receptors provided the luxury of delay because one may see or hear an enemy or prey at a great distance. With delay, adaptation is facilitated by the development of cognitive strategies, memory, discrimination, and plans. If she were alive today, Washburn would relish metaphors for intelligence that rely on visual and auditory imagery—expressions of cognition where we "gain insight," "see through," "truly hear," or develop a "visionary strategy."

As suggested in the title of her book, Washburn (1908) believed animals possess consciousness that can be accessed via inference, the same way we study human consciousness. In her view, animal consciousness is an appropriate research topic for psychologists. Washburn always argued, however, for a rigorous methodology that challenges simplistic and anthropomorphic inferences. She recognized that facts may be distorted by people who attribute human qualities to animal consciousness. Washburn's *The Animal Mind* is a masterful work in comparative psychology as well as a primer in the evolutionary study of higher cognitive processes. In a review titled "The Animal Mind at 100," David Washburn (2010) (no relation) reminds us that the work remains remarkably relevant 100 years later "both as an introduction to animal psychology and as a marker of changes in the discipline that spanned the book's four editions" (p. 369).

Margaret Floy Washburn (1916) is also known for a book titled *Movement and Mental Imagery* that set forth a "motor theory of consciousness." According to the motor theory, mental activity has its origin in, and is supported by, subtle neurophysiological movement systems. An example is found in the work of Walter Samuel Hunter (1889–1954), who allowed a hungry but restrained dog to watch as meat was placed inside a goal box. As it stared hungrily at the goal box, the dog displayed what Washburn called "persistent tentative movements" in the direction of the box. We can assume that the dog "anticipates" food as it salivates and strains at the leash. The dog's behavior is "goal directed" and "purposive." If we release the dog, it will scramble toward the food and eat it. But if we introduce a delay, the dog may become distracted by other things and stop straining in the direction of the goal box. If released after losing its postural set, the dog no longer heads directly to the goal box. In other words, incipient muscular movements appear to support ongoing mental activity and purposive behavior has a motor or muscular component. Consider a different example. Even without an instrument, a musician might practice moving her fingers as if playing a piece, engaging in incipient muscular movements that serve as a kind of rehearsal for an actual performance. Washburn's motor theory of consciousness is sometimes regarded as counterintuitive, but it becomes more plausible the more it is studied (see Viney & Burlingame-Lee, 2003, for a more detailed explanation of the theory).

Margaret Floy Washburn was one of the leading American psychologists in the first three decades of the twentieth century. She served as president of the American Psychological Association (APA) in 1921, the second woman to hold that position. (Mary Whiton Calkins, the first female APA president, will be discussed in Chapter 12.) In 1931, Washburn was named to the National Academy of the Sciences, one of the highest honors for any scientist. Washburn acted as president of the Psychology Section of the American Association for the Advancement of Science and served on the editorial boards of numerous journals. Scarborough (2000) claims that Washburn was regarded as the best lecturer at Vassar. She was a powerful force not only in the science of psychology but also for the full participation of women in the intellectual community.

Franz Brentano and Act Psychology

Franz Brentano (1838–1917) provided a striking alternative to Wundt's and Titchener's

psychology. As early as 1874, his system, known as **act psychology**, rejected the exclusive alignment of scientific psychology with physiology. It also rejected older interpretations of empiricism that emphasized the content of experience and the building of experience through exclusive mechanical associations. According to Brentano, an authentic empirical psychology will find more in experience itself than mere contents or passive associations. A truly empirical psychology will discover that experience is forward looking, active, manipulative, and intentional. A psychology that does not recognize these dimensions of experience is not a true empirical psychology. According to Sussman (1962), Brentano insisted on the Aristotelian approach to empiricism, "reviving the concept of activity as the fundamental essence of empiricism. In this sense is the oft used quote from him: 'Experience alone influences me as a mistress'" (p. 504). Brentano's

Franz Brentano

best-known psychological work is his book *Psychology from an Empirical Standpoint*, first published in 1874.

Franz Brentano, born on January 16, 1838, was one of the five children of Christian and Emilie Brentano. Young Franz was educated in the Gymnasium at Aschaffenburg following private tutoring by a Catholic priest. Brentano excelled in language and mathematics but was also drawn to theological and philosophical studies. Rancurello (1968) noted that Brentano studied at four universities in six years to complete his Ph.D. in 1862, before seeking the priesthood and being ordained in 1864.

Brentano's career as a university professor included a seven-year period at Würzburg and a twenty-year period at the University of Vienna. Although Brentano's research earns him a place in the history of psychology, he enjoyed unusual success as an inspiring teacher (Huemer & Landerer, 2010). His better-known students included Edmund Husserl, a philosopher whose work in phenomenology had a profound influence in psychology (Broome et al., 2012); Alexius Meinong, the founder of the psychology laboratory at Graz (Radler, 2015); and Sigmund Freud, who took courses with Brentano at Vienna (Dewalque, 2013). Though scholars disagree about the extent of Brentano's influence on Freud, a case can be made (see Domenjo, 2000; Fancher, 1977) concerning similarities in their thought. Additionally, Brentano clearly influenced Carl Stumpf and Christian von Ehrenfels, who in turn influenced some of the later founders of Gestalt psychology.

Though Brentano was a brilliant teacher, his was by no means an untroubled career. Prior to the December 1867 meeting of Vatican Council I, debates raged in the church about the relative authority of the papacy versus church councils. Some scholars argued that, in selected spiritual matters, the word of the Pope should be regarded as infallible. Catholics were deeply split on the issue, and Brentano sided with those who challenged the dogma of papal infallibility. Those opposed to the dogma of infallibility argued that

popes had contradicted each other on spiritual matters and that the doctrine of infallibility was not necessary to the Catholic faith.

On July 18, 1870, the council voted 433 to 2 in favor of a doctrine of infallibility. Brentano's former teacher, Ignaz von Dollinger, also opposed the doctrine of infallibility and was excommunicated for his refusal to accept the council's decision. Brentano, like Dollinger, could not subordinate reason to faith, but neither could he suppress earlier theological doubts now exacerbated by Vatican I. As a consequence, Brentano resigned from the priesthood and separated from the church in 1873.

All of this was not irrelevant to Brentano's academic life. He had been appointed to his position on the Würzburg faculty as a priest. As noted by Puglisi (1924), he felt "morally bound to resign his chair" (p. 416). Brentano's former affiliation with the church haunted him in his subsequent position at the University of Vienna. In 1880, at age forty-two, he was engaged to marry Ida Lieben but, as pointed out by Puglisi (1924), she "as a Catholic could not contract in Austria a religious marriage with one who had formerly been an ecclesiastic. Brentano was therefore obliged to assume Saxon citizenship, and consequently to resign the title of *professor ordinarius* in the Austrian university. On September 16 of the same year, 1880, he was married in Leipzig to Miss Lieben" (p. 417). Brentano was allowed to work at the University of Vienna, but his status was reduced to that of lecturer. Brentano remained at Vienna until the death of his wife in 1894. In retirement years, he lived first in Florence and later in Zürich, where he died on March 17, 1917.

Brentano's Psychology

In *Psychology from an Empirical Standpoint*, Brentano (1874/1973) clearly separated the physical and the mental (Broome et al., 2012) and defined *psychology* as "the science of mental phenomena" (1874/1973, p. 100). In an elaboration of the meaning of *mental phenomena*, he referred to John Locke's famous experiment on the perception of coldness and warmth. Locke warmed one hand while simultaneously cooling the other. Then he placed both hands into a pan of lukewarm water, experiencing warmth in the hand that was previously cool and cool in the hand that was previously warm. Brentano argued that the experiment "proved that neither warmth nor cold really existed in the water" (p. 9).

Brentano provided other examples of the effects of context on experience and noted that the term *phenomenon* is close in meaning to the word *appearance*. In the example of the water basin, we experience the water as warm or cold, depending on the previous conditions to which the hands have been subjected. Brentano (1874/1973) believed that the succession of mental phenomena follows yet-to-be-discovered lawful patterns and that there is "a vast range of important problems for the psychologist" (p. 12). According to Brentano, mental phenomena are real and inherently intentional. He rejected the idea that the only real things are those that exist in the outside world. We know all things through experience.

Brentano was optimistic about what a science of psychology could accomplish. He envisioned the development of a discipline broad in scope. For example, he asked, "How many evils could be remedied . . . by knowledge of the laws according to which a mental state can be modified!" (1874/1973, p. 22). He considered the enormous value of early diagnosis of aptitudes. Brentano argued that "for the individual and even more for the masses, where the imponderable circumstances which impede and promote progress balance each other out, psychological laws will afford a sure basis for action" (p. 24). Brentano saw psychology as the science of the future, a science both theoretical and practical. He repeatedly conveyed optimism about the potential applications of psychology and noted that "the practical tasks I assign to psychology are far from insignificant" (p. 22). Brentano's optimism is seldom appreciated, but in attitude and orientation, he must be considered as a forerunner of applied psychology.

On questions of method, Brentano advocated a pluralistic and developmental epistemology. He recognized that the history of science involves the adaptation of scientific method to ever more complex phenomena. Scientific method is not static and Brentano mentioned several psychological methods that could be valuable. Included are observations on the newborn, studies of primitive societies, studies of those with congenital disorders such as congenital blindness to assess the effects of sensory deprivation, animal research, and studies of diseased mental states.

In the study of normal phenomena, Brentano advocated a variety of methods such as the use of biographies and what he called *inner perception*. Brentano distinguished between *inner perception* and *inner observation*. The latter term he equated with introspection and declared it an impossibility. We can observe external objects, but it is pretentious to say we observe psychological phenomena in the same manner. We perceive inner events by focusing attention on the immediate past and on the flow of events. Thus, retrospection is involved in inner perception. Brentano noted that all sciences must consult memory in the course of their work, so psychology is not uniquely disadvantaged if it must trust memory to describe mental phenomena.

Brentano provided an example of inner perception by calling attention to the way we study our own anger. We do not observe it directly, but we can report our perception of the flow of events and their effects. We retrospect about those things that just took place, the things that preceded them, and the perceived consequences. We can know about the inner state of others through verbal reports and behavior. Indeed, he argued that behavior or practical conduct is often the most reliable guide to inner states (1874/1973, p. 39). He also recognized involuntary physical indices such as blushing as guides to the nature of inner states.

If the content of Brentano's psychology was broad in theory, it was nevertheless fairly focused in practice. His unique approach is still informative and provocative. Chances are that if Brentano were devising a curriculum in psychology, he would prefer that course titles, where possible, employ verb forms rather than noun forms. Rather than teaching a course titled "Sensation and Perception," we might better give the course a title such as "Sensing and Perceiving." The reason for Brentano's preference for the active verb form rather than the passive noun form is based on what he encountered in experience itself. Experience is an active, participatory, creative, and constructive process. It does not consist simply of inert, static, or passive contents.

Fancher (1977) noted that, for Brentano, "physical phenomena are always objects such as sounds or colors, while mental phenomena are always *acts* that 'contain' *objects*, such as hearing a sound or admiring a color" (p. 208). Physical phenomena, such as the sounds of music over a stereo system, are mere facts in consciousness, but mental phenomena are much more. They may include admiration, reflections over the phrasing or rhythms of a passage, memories, comparisons, wishes, and so forth. The unique features of a mental act are its complexity, involvement, and particularly its intentionality (Gantt & Thayne, 2013). It does not consist of mere awareness.

Brentano was interested in the classification of mental phenomena and provided an excellent overview and critique, beginning with Plato, of the history of classification schemes (1874/1973, pp. 173–193). His classification system divided mental phenomena into presentations, desires, and judgments. **Presentations** are basic because there could be no desires or judgments without them. A presentation is simply an event or a presence in experience. He pointed out that a presentation and a judgment "are two entirely different ways of being conscious of an object" (p. 201). **Judgment** clearly involves belief or disbelief and it helps define our relationship with a presentation. Similarly, **desire** further delineates our relationship to an object and is still another mode or dimension of consciousness. Presumably, one could desire an object in consciousness, such as an item of food, yet judge the food negatively in terms of its nutritional value.

One might also encounter positive judgments or beliefs coupled with negative desires.

Brentano argued that the three types of mental phenomena are intertwined. Indeed, in *Psychology from an Empirical Standpoint*, he contended that "there is no mental act in which all three are not present . . . but it is conceivable without contradiction that there might be a form of mental life which is missing one or even two of these kinds of mental activities and lacks all capacity for them as well" (1874/1973, p. 265). Later, Brentano changed his mind and expressed the belief that there are visual and even auditory sensations lacking in affect (see Rancurello, 1968).

Brentano, as much as any theorist in the history of psychology, struggled with the question of the unity of experience. Is experience, as we encounter it, a mosaic of bits and pieces that add together somehow to form the whole, or are all the parts intimate with each other? Brentano was a strong believer in the unity of consciousness and in the existence of a self in possession of experience. To deny such a self would reduce us to a kaleidoscope of sensations, much as we encounter in the philosophy of David Hume. The self, according to Brentano, is a reality that appropriates and integrates other realities. It ties past and present together, along with intentions about the future.

Brentano is a key figure in the history of psychology because he described an alternative approach that placed appropriate conceptual work in higher priority than experimental work. Brentano would have agreed with Descartes, who counseled that in any conflict between the results of an experiment and reason, we should embrace reason. Brentano did not oppose experimentation but believed that it should be preceded by appropriate conceptual homework.

Brentano's influence on the discipline of psychology is remarkable in view of the sparseness of his written work. He is remembered for his *Psychology from an Empirical Standpoint* and his lectures. Nevertheless, he had a direct and profound influence on phenomenology as a philosophical movement (Siewert, 2015) as well as phenomenological psychology and existential psychology (Gilbert, 1968). There are clear-cut intellectual affinities between his work and the psychology of William James, American functionalism, existentialism, Gestalt psychology, and, arguably, Freud's psychoanalytic thought. Although his ideas about mental phenomena did not always mesh with the positivistic temper of nineteenth-century psychology, Brentano has been rediscovered as a viable alternative to contemporary models of cognition (Macnamara, 1993).

Carl Stumpf

Born on Good Friday, 1848, to a distinguished family of scholars, **Carl Stumpf (1848–1936)** remarked that "the love of medicine and natural science was in my blood" (1930, p. 389). Despite a natural interest in science, his childhood passion was music. By seven, he had learned to play the violin and, without formal instruction, had taught himself another five instruments. At ten, he composed the words and music for an oratorio. Stumpf's fascination with music proved to be an instrumental part of his professional career.

Stumpf studied law at the University of Würzburg because it was a career that would provide leisure time for his music. His interest shifted after Franz Brentano joined the faculty. Under Brentano's influence, Stumpf became a critical thinker devoted to the study of philosophy and psychology. Following his mentor's advice, Stumpf made scientific studies a priority and engaged in work on chemistry. Unfortunately, he made "some careless reaction" that nearly burned down the chemistry laboratory. Stumpf (1930) remembered that the blaze "might have spread over the whole building if the attendant had not come to the rescue" (p. 392).

Brentano encouraged Stumpf to study with Lotze at the University of Göttingen. In addition to research on physics and physiology, he pursued a long-standing interest in Plato as the basis for his 1868 dissertation. His fascination with Plato might have been fed partly by their common interest in music. A year following the completion of his dissertation, he entered an ecclesiastical seminary at Würzburg. Like Brentano, Stumpf lost faith in orthodox religion and left the ministry before his ordination. A chance encounter with Ernst Weber stirred his interest in psychophysics, as did an opportunity to serve as a participant in Gustav Fechner's studies on aesthetics.

After accepting a teaching position at Würzburg, Stumpf began pioneering work on acoustic psychology. He later accepted a position at Prague and published his classic book *Tonpsychologie* in 1883, followed by a second volume in 1890. This classic book in the psychology of music focused on topics such as the evolution of music, primitive instruments, and sound perception. In 1894, Stumpf moved to the University of Berlin and converted three modest rooms into an impressive Psychological Institute; in 1920, the Institute moved into twenty-five rooms in the former Imperial Castle. Although more than a decade younger than Wundt, Stumpf's tenacity helped establish Berlin as a dominant competitor to Leipzig for leadership in European psychology. By the time of Stumpf's retirement in 1921, the Berlin Institute was recognized as a preeminent center for psychological research. Stumpf died on Christmas Day in 1936.

As a disciple of Brentano, Stumpf made an impassioned protest against the artificial nature of reductionism and developed an approach to philosophy and psychology that placed emphasis on the value of holism. Stumpf shared Brentano's zeal for the study of mental events from an empirical or experiential standpoint, especially one that considered the rich, dynamic quality of human cognition. His work was founded on the holistic assumption that all aspects of consciousness are connected and perceivable as a unity. He was convinced that the attributes of any sensation—such as quality, brightness, or intensity—form a whole rather than a simple aggregate of the parts.

Stumpf made significant contributions to areas such as space and auditory perception, emotion, psychophysics, aesthetics, and phenomenology. However, music remained the central focus of his psychology. He wrote extensively on music, including its forms and origins (Stumpf, 1911/2012), and he became a leading figure in the emerging discipline of musicology.

In addition to the two-volume work on tone psychology, in 1898 he founded a journal devoted to musicology, *Beiträge zur Akustik und Musikwissenschaft*, and amassed one of the world's leading ethnomusicological collections, housed at Berlin's Psychological Institute. Founded in 1900, the Phonograph Archives consisted of a large assembly of Edison cylinders containing the musical recordings of a vast number of cultures. Stumpf provided the initial funding himself and named the young Berlin psychologist and musicologist Erich Moritz von Hornbostel (1877–1936) as director of the archives. Under the supervision of Stumpf and von Hornbostel, the archives grew from a few wax cylinders to a collection of more than ten thousand gramophone recordings from all over the world (Lewin, 1937). The revolutionary phonograph became a popular resource for the psychological and anthropological study of native dialects and the musical culture of indigenous tribes. Stumpf also considered music to be an important tool in the holistic study of mental phenomena (see Ringer, 1969).

The American psychologist William James admired Stumpf's work on tone psychology. Although Stumpf proposed a cognitive-evaluative theory that opposed James's famous theory of emotion, the two scholars enjoyed an extensive correspondence (Reisenzein & Schonpflug, 1992). Like James, Stumpf was a strident critic of Wundt's research, especially his work on acoustics. Stumpf challenged the Leipzig school's assumption that a trained but nonmusical introspectionist could make more valid judgments about tone than a trained musician. For Stumpf, the sophisticated perceptual judgments of musical experts were far superior to those generated in laboratory studies of introspection. Wundt was upset by

the critique and engaged Stumpf in a bitter and scathing debate. Decades later, Stumpf (1930) wrote that "Wundt's methods of procedure had been repellent to me even since his Heidelberg days, and continue to be so, although I admire his extraordinary breadth of vision and his literary productivity" (p. 401).

Beginning with studies of his own children, Stumpf devoted considerable time to research on the mental life of children. In 1897, he studied a four-year-old boy with exceptional memory and in 1900 helped found the Berlin Association for Child Psychology. In 1903, Stumpf combined his interest in music with developmental psychology when he began investigation of several musical child prodigies.

Like Brentano, Stumpf's psychology offered a holistic alternative to structuralism that inspired many European scholars, especially the Gestalt psychologists (Sprung & Sprung, 1996); Max Wertheimer, Wolfgang Köhler, Kurt Koffka, and Kurt Lewin were graduate students of Stumpf (Bonacchi, 2009). Stumpf was a critical inspiration to Edmund Husserl (Fissette, 2009). Langfeld (1937) noted that Stumpf's death signaled that the "last important link with the early decades of experimental psychology, which produced Wundt, Müller and Ebbinghaus, was broken. It was a great period in which virgin soil was tilled and Stumpf had an important part in guiding the plow and sowing the seed from which our present day psychology has developed" (pp. 316–317).

Georg Elias Müller

There have always been diverse roads to greatness in any intellectual enterprise, but **Georg Elias Müller (1850–1934)**, by placing emphasis on extensive laboratory work, took the road less traveled. Many early psychologists were not strangers to the laboratory, but most were interested in providing encompassing systematic visions of the discipline. By contrast, Müller was content to focus on the rigorous experimental investigation of several important problem areas.

As a result, some of the most productive work in the new experimental psychology came out of the University of Göttingen. Müller was head of the laboratory there for a fifty-year period from 1881 to 1931 and, according to Boring (1950), "As a power and an institution he was second only to Wundt" (p. 379); Haupt (2001) makes the stronger claim that by the 1890s Müller's laboratory had more advanced apparatus and greater research output than Wundt's laboratory at Leipzig. Boring also pointed out that Müller, unlike many of the other pioneers, "was little else than an experimental psychologist" (p. 379). His interests were directed almost entirely to problems of a psychological nature.

Müller, born on July 20, 1850, studied first at the University of Leipzig, and then at the University of Göttingen. He earned his Ph.D. under Hermann Lotze at Göttingen in 1873. In 1881, Lotze gave up his position at Göttingen to accept a position at the University of Berlin. He was succeeded by Müller, who remained at Göttingen for the remainder of his life. Müller retired in 1931 and died on December 23, 1934.

Müller, together with Friedrich Schumann and Alfons Pilzecker, was prolific in the areas of memory and association (McGaugh, 2000). Indeed, as noted by Diamond (1974b), the reports of the work on memory and association "run to over 2000 pages" (p. 271). Müller's early work on memory anticipated later work in the area of retroactive inhibition. For example, in an article published in 1900, Müller and Pilzecker reported studies of memory for an initial learning task along with memory for a second task. With the particular problems employed, memory was always better for the second task. Müller and Pilzecker noted that later unrelated material may weaken or inhibit the associations necessary for the recall of the initial material. They went on to say, "For lack of any shorter expression we shall designate this type of inhibition as *retroactive inhibition*" (1900, p. 273).

Müller was also one of the first to conduct extensive studies on the problem of perseveration. He noted that some individuals shift easily from one task to another, whereas others tend to perseverate on an initial task. According to Diamond (1974b), Müller's work on perseveration provided "the first experimental breach in the theory that the 'train of thoughts' is determined solely by association, and it also points to the existence of a separate short-term memory process" (p. 271). Müller noticed that there was perseveration on materials presented to a subject, but there was also rapid decay in attention to the materials. His work is clearly an early precursor of later work on short-term memory.

As noted, Müller conducted extensive work in psychophysics and color vision as well as on memory and association (Haupt, 1998). According to Boring (1950), he helped shape these areas and enjoyed leadership in all these fields. Sprung and Sprung (2000) call attention to Müller's liberal approach to science marked by his unusual "openness to women as scientists and colleagues" (p. 86). They note that, unlike many early pioneers in psychology, Müller promoted applied psychology along with a variety of methods so long as such methods were consistent with the canons of natural science. Unfortunately, most of Müller's work has not been translated, and as a result has not received the widespread recognition it deserves.

Oswald Külpe and the Würzburg School

Oswald Külpe (1862–1915) provided another important European alternative to the psychology of Wundt. Külpe's approach to psychology combined some of Brentano's act psychology with Wundt's experimental approach. Külpe's focus on the experimental investigation of thinking presented a direct challenge to elementaristic psychologies.

Oswald Külpe was torn between history, philosophy, and psychology. In 1881, he enrolled at the University of Leipzig, intending to pursue a career in history, but he was also interested in the work of Wilhelm Wundt and his new psychology laboratory. The period from 1881 to 1887 found Külpe studying first at Leipzig, then at the University of Berlin, followed by a year and a half at the University of Göttingen under G. E. Müller. Finally, Külpe returned to Leipzig, where he earned his Ph.D. with Wundt in 1887. He remained at Leipzig to help run the laboratory until 1894, when he received an appointment at the University of Würzburg.

Külpe established a laboratory at Würzburg and remained there for fifteen years, including time with Karl Popper as a student (Kumar, 2010). He later established laboratories at Bonn and Munich. Külpe's dedication to psychology was complete. He never married but once declared that science was his bride. Like William James in the United States, Külpe was regarded as one of psychology's most affable figures. He died in Munich on December 30, 1915.

Lindenfeld (1978) pointed out that in his early years, Külpe "was a tough-minded experimentalist whose definition of psychology aroused the objection even of Wilhelm Wundt as being too narrow" (p. 132). In later years, Külpe adopted a different approach to the discipline, and it is this later work for which he is known and to which we will direct our attention.

Külpe's philosophical interests extended to the fields of ontology, epistemology, and aesthetics. All of these interests complemented his work in psychology. Philosophically, he represented a middle road between the extremes of naïve realism and idealism. Külpe assumed the independent existence of objects and processes in the world and argued that such an assumption is basic in all sciences. At the same time, we know about objects in the world only through conscious experience, which contributes to our understanding of the world. Külpe's position might be described as a kind of representational or critical realism in contrast with naïve realism.

Some of the best-known work coming out of the Würzburg laboratory was clearly related to Külpe's philosophical realism. The work, on **imageless thought**, was a source of controversy because it challenged the elemental or building-block approach. *Imageless thought* refers to the belief that there are objective meanings in experience that are not associated with specific words, symbols, or signs. There are, for example, meaningful abstractions in science that have no direct unambiguous images. The worlds of theoretical physics, theology, and psychology are full of such abstractions. The Würzburg researchers might agree that there are images associated with many thoughts. For example, most of us probably experience images in connection with simple noun forms such as *dog*, *cat*, *car*, *pencil*, and *book*. It may be more difficult, however, to find an image in connection with terms such as *ontology* or *epistemology*. Furthermore, in simple word-association tasks, the word given as a response to a stimulus word (e.g., *table–chair* or *sky–blue*) may be given rapidly and without any introspective awareness of its image. Lindenfeld (1978) pointed out that Külpe believed that "our ability to recognize something we have seen before . . . is quite independent of our ability to remember an image of it" (p. 133).

Students at Würzburg also conducted experiments on the effects of mental set on problem solution. **Mental set** refers to a predisposition to respond in a given manner. For example, Külpe briefly presented stimulus materials that varied along several dimensions. If subjects are given a mental set to look for a specific dimension, such as a color, a pattern, or a number, they inevitably find it and may be only minimally aware of the other dimensions that they were not instructed to see. In time, it was recognized that mental set is a powerful factor that accounts for a great deal of the variation in the way people solve problems. The pioneering studies on mental set at Würzburg inspired many subsequent studies on these questions.

Like Gustav Fechner, Külpe was interested in experimental aesthetics. It was a natural interest because Külpe loved sculpture and painting and, according to Ogden (1951), "was himself a musician and played the piano expertly" (p. 7). Külpe believed that mental economy played an important role in the perception of beauty. Thus, harmony, orderliness, and symmetry require less perceptual effort than their opposites and are more likely to be associated with objects judged to be beautiful.

Though Külpe's students worked on higher mental operations, he was open to a psychology with a much wider scope. He spoke of a need for animal psychology and social psychology, and argued for openness to a variety of methods and topics, including cultural studies (Valsiner, 2007). He also argued that *psychogenesis*, or the study of the development of mental phenomena, "forms an indispensable supplement to our knowledge of the developed consciousness" (1893/1973, p. 17).

Külpe's influence on the discipline of psychology was extensive. His name is associated with two productive laboratories and a well-equipped institute. Experimental psychology, once confined to the study of simple sensations and reaction times, now included more complex cognitive processes. Külpe also influenced the discipline through his students. His most famous student was Max Wertheimer, the founder of Gestalt psychology. Other students included Kaspar Ach and Henry Watt, both of whom worked on the effects of mental set on problem solving; Robert Morris Ogden, who was instrumental in introducing Gestalt psychology in the United States; and Kurt Koffka, one of the founders of the Gestalt school, who did postdoctoral studies at Würzburg.

Hermann Ebbinghaus

In terms of lasting influence, **Hermann Ebbinghaus (1850–1909)** ranks as one of the most important pioneers in psychology. Such a strong claim is all the more remarkable in view of the fact that Ebbinghaus was not a prolific writer, nor is his fame evident through the works of his students. He is remembered for the development of the nonsense syllable and the first quantitative studies of memory. Postman (1973) pointed out, however, that Ebbinghaus's influence on the

discipline was far broader. We will examine this influence and his pioneering studies of memory.

Biographical information on Ebbinghaus is sparse, but we know he was born near Bonn in 1850 and that his early interests were in language, literature, and philosophy. He served in the military in the Franco-German War (1870–1871) and earned his Ph.D. in philosophy from the University of Bonn in 1873. He then traveled for several years before taking his first academic position at the University of Berlin. Ebbinghaus worked at Berlin from 1880 to 1893 and then took a position at the University of Breslau, where he worked until 1905. His final position was at the University of Halle. He died of pneumonia in 1909, only four years after assuming his position at Halle.

Roback and Kiernan (1969) described Ebbinghaus as "a radiant personality, prepossessing in appearance and cooperative, he was

Hermann Ebbinghaus

practically the antithesis of Wundt" (p. 73). They also noted that at the time of his death he was "revising his first volume of a textbook which in point of lucidity and literary flavor was of a piece with William James's *Principles of Psychology*" (p. 73).

Ebbinghaus is remembered almost exclusively for his pioneering studies on memory, but the importance of that work should not block awareness of other important contributions. Postman (1973) outlined several guiding principles in the writings of Ebbinghaus that foreshadowed later developments in psychology. The first is that the discipline of psychology should be divorced from philosophy and take its place alongside the natural sciences. Ebbinghaus valued controlled quantitative studies much more than philosophical speculation. The second guiding principle outlined by Postman is that Ebbinghaus broadened the scope of experimental inquiry. No longer was psychology limited to the study of simple sensations and their relations to physiological structures. Now, higher mental operations could be subjected to experimental scrutiny.

Other principles that Postman identified in the work of Ebbinghaus include methodological and theoretical eclecticism. Ebbinghaus eschewed efforts to find the grand theory and the grand method applicable to the entire discipline. Instead, he focused his efforts on identifying more modest methodological and conceptual tools appropriate to a limited domain such as memory. A final principle in the writings of Ebbinghaus, according to Postman (1973), "is the reconciliation of pure and applied psychology" (p. 223). Ebbinghaus believed that problems were important in and of themselves. It is context that dictates whether a problem will be regarded as pure or as applied, but Ebbinghaus regarded the distinction as somewhat artificial.

Ebbinghaus contributed to applied psychology with work in mental testing. He was a pioneer in the use of the *completion test* as a way to assess the cognitive capacities of schoolchildren. Completion tests provide a context from which a student is asked to draw a logical conclusion.

One form of the completion test is the analogy. For example, a child might be asked to respond to a simple problem such as "If an elephant is big, then a mouse is _____." This type of question has found its way into all kinds of assessment instruments, from those used with small children to ones designed for adults.

Ebbinghaus's research on memory is set forth in his classic work *Über das Gedächtnis*, which was translated as *Memory: A Contribution to Experimental Psychology*. The original work was published in 1885 and an English translation was made available in 1913. The lengthy preexperimental scholarship on memory produced many impressive insights (see Herrmann & Chaffin, 1988), but until Ebbinghaus's work, the problems of memory were still intractable from a scientific viewpoint.

Gustav Fechner's *Elements of Psychophysics* inspired Ebbinghaus to conduct an experimental study of memory. In the preface to *Memory*, Ebbinghaus (1885/1913) pointed out that "in the realm of mental phenomena, experiment and measurement have hitherto been chiefly limited in application to sense perception and to the time relations of mental process" (p. v). His goal was to apply Fechner's methods to a new dimension of mental life. In order to achieve his mission, he warned at the outset that "the term, memory, is to be taken here in its broadest sense, including learning, retention, association and reproduction" (p. v).

Ebbinghaus acknowledged that memory's capricious and private nature offered challenges for the scientific method. Weber and Fechner had faced the same problem in the study of sense perception. We cannot gain direct access to the private sensation of another person, but we can discover the relationship between values as they exist on a physical scale and values as they are reported in experience. In a similar manner, we may not be able to gain direct access to the specific memory of another person but, according to Ebbinghaus, external conditions of memory are accessible to measurement.

Prior to Ebbinghaus, memory was studied only after it had developed. Then, introspective or retrospective study assessed what had taken place. Ebbinghaus's new approach involved the memorial process from start to finish. Thus, we may easily count the number of repetitions or amount of time it takes to memorize a list of words. Following a lapse of time, we may count the number of repetitions or the amount of time it takes to relearn the list.

Initial learning of material was important to Ebbinghaus's entire project and he exercised unusual caution in controlling its conditions. He recognized that previous associations contaminate speed of initial learning, so he developed the nonsense syllable in an attempt to neutralize the effects of prior associations. Chapter 3 of his book describes other ways in which he controlled the conditions of initial learning. For example, he controlled learning speed by memorizing and reciting to the beat of a metronome. He minimized the effects of intonation or accent by rehearsing with due sensitivity to the stress of the voice. He controlled motivation and effort and reduced efforts to use mnemonic devices to memorize nonsense syllables. He conducted his work at the same time each day and kept all conditions of his life as constant or stable as possible. Despite likely boredom from the rigid and repetitive nature of this work, Ebbinghaus persevered and provided a strong foundation for later scholars of memory (Newman & Loftus, 2012).

Ebbinghaus's diverse memory investigations opened the door to research on a host of additional problems. For example, he found that distributed practice leads to better recall than massed practice (Simon, 2013); as you may have observed in your own life, consistent daily study for an exam leads to better recall than a night of cramming. One of the more interesting findings involved the time it takes to memorize items as a function of the length of a list. In one study, he learned lists of seven, twelve, sixteen, twenty-four, and thirty-six syllables to a criterion of mastery (one perfect repetition). Ebbinghaus found that, for him, seven syllables was the number he could typically recite after only one recita-

Table 11.1 Number of Repetitions as a Function of Numbers of Syllables

Number of Syllables in Series	Number of Repetitions Necessary for First Errorless Reproduction
7	1
12	17
16	30
24	44
36	55

tion. The numbers of repetitions, respectively, to memorize the syllables in each of the lists are presented in Table 11.1. It is clear from an examination of the table that the greatest difference occurs between the list of seven and the list of twelve. It took only one repetition to learn the list of seven, but it took 16.6 repetitions to learn the list of twelve syllables.

Ebbinghaus also found rapid forgetting of nonsense syllables over the first two days after initial learning before slowing over subsequent days. The famous **Ebbinghaus forgetting curve** shown in Figure 11.1 documents rapid initial forgetting followed by a slowing so that there is little difference in the amount of forgetting after one week versus the amount of forgetting after one month.

Ebbinghaus was a significant figure, not only because of his seminal memory research (Einstein et al., 2012) but also because of the new methodology and orientation he brought to the discipline (Danziger, 2001). Following Ebbinghaus, there was an exciting breadth of vision as to what could be included in the new discipline of psychology. Many psychologists might be tempted to agree with Titchener's (1910) opinion when he argued that Ebbinghaus's "recourse to nonsense syllables, as means to the study of association, marks the most considerable advance, in this chapter of psychology, since the time of Aristotle" (p. 381). There can be little question that he is a pivotal figure who changed the discipline.

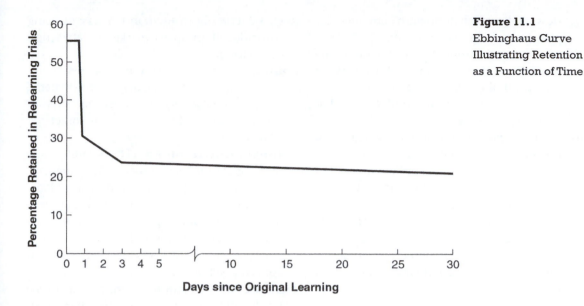

Figure 11.1
Ebbinghaus Curve
Illustrating Retention
as a Function of Time

Wundt's Contemporaries and Applied Psychology

Titchener has seldom been regarded as a friend of applied psychology and it is true that his primary scientific interest was the adult normal mind. At the same time, as noted at the beginning of the chapter, Titchener recognized the importance of abnormal psychology, social psychology, animal psychology, and other subdisciplinary areas. He argued that all of these fields must be "cultivated, if psychology is to progress" (1910, p. 29). He did not find time to include applied areas in his own research programs and placed the greatest value on purely scientific studies. At the same time, he was not closed to the future development of a psychology much broader in scope than he cultivated at Cornell University.

Wundt's other contemporaries also focused on basic scientific problems, but were open to a psychology larger in scope. Brentano was optimistic about the prospects of applied psychology. As noted, Ebbinghaus thought that the distinction between pure and applied studies is a function of context and not a basic or logical distinction. In one context, a problem could be regarded as basic or pure, but in another context, the same problem might be regarded as applied. With the study of a growing number of topical areas, it was inevitable that psychology, like the other sciences, would find it impossible to remain in the important but restricted environment of the laboratory. In Chapter 12, we will encounter a system that, from the beginning, advocated a psychology equally at home in the laboratory and in the world of daily life.

Review Questions

1. Contrast Titchener and Brentano with respect to methodology.
2. Give a typical example of a type of laboratory problem that might have been explored in Titchener's laboratory.
3. Outline Titchener's distinction between primary and secondary attention. Do you regard the distinction as useful?
4. Briefly review Titchener's theory of meaning.
5. What were some of Titchener's criticisms of the James–Lange theory of emotion?
6. What was Washburn's "motor theory of consciousness" and how did her ideas about consciousness differ from Titchener's theory?

7. How did Brentano distinguish between inner perception and inner observation?
8. Briefly describe Stumpf's contributions to the psychology of music. How did his work on tone psychology differ from Wundt's ideas?
9. Outline two of Georg Elias Müller's contributions to psychology.
10. Define *mental set* and show how it plays a role in problem solving.
11. Why was the work at the Würzburg school on imageless thought so crucial to the psychologies of Wundt and Titchener?
12. List five ways that Ebbinghaus influenced the field of psychology.
13. Briefly describe two important experimental findings coming out of Ebbinghaus's work on memory.

Glossary

act psychology A system of psychological thought advanced by Franz Brentano emphasizing the forward-looking, intentional, planful character of experience. Brentano strongly rejected the simplistic characteristics of many of the early systems of psychological thought.

affect (affection) According to Titchener's early theory, affections are the elementary mental processes associated with emotions. Later, he viewed affections primarily as sensations of pleasantness or unpleasantness.

attributes of elementary mental processes According to Titchener, elementary processes such as sensations include four attributes: quality, intensity, clearness, and duration.

Brentano, Franz (1838–1917) Founder of a system of psychological thought known as *act psychology*. Brentano emphasized a developmental and pluralistic methodology and the active, participatory, creative, and intentional characteristics of mental life.

context theory of meaning According to Titchener, meaning depends on context or the association of a stimulus with other relevant surrounding stimuli.

desire According to Brentano, a way of being conscious of an object marked by attraction or repulsion.

Ebbinghaus forgetting curve A curve demonstrating that forgetting of nonsense material is rapid immediately after learning. After an initial rapid decline, the rate of forgetting slows down.

Ebbinghaus, Hermann (1850–1909) One of the great pioneers in psychology, remembered for developing the nonsense syllable as a means of studying memory experimentally while minimizing past associations. Also developed an early form of a completion test and argued for the legitimacy of pure and applied psychology.

element An abstraction referring to a simple irreducible sensation. See also Chapter 10 Glossary.

imageless thought Belief that there are objective meanings in experience that are not associated with specific words, symbols, or signs.

introspection A species of observation, but the subject to be observed is in experience itself. Thus, introspection is a kind of "looking in" to identify elements of experience and the way these elements combine, or the processes and adaptations of experience.

James–Lange theory of emotion A theory of emotion advanced independently by William James and Carl Lange. The theory emphasizes the somatic substrate of emotional experiences and argues that the experience of emotion is the experience of the activity of the body—thus, the famous statement: We see a bear, we run, and we are afraid. James's later vision of emotion emphasizes constitutional determinants and the impossibility of separating cognition and emotion.

judgment According to Brentano, consciousness of an object marked by belief or disbelief.

Külpe, Oswald (1862–1915) Student of Wilhelm Wundt and well-known founder of an early psychological laboratory and school of thought at Würzburg. Külpe's experiments on imageless thought challenged the simplistic characteristics of other early systems.

mental set Predisposition to respond in a given manner or tendency to organize an event in terms of an existing bias.

Müller, Georg Elias (1850–1934) Prominent German psychologist remembered for his work in psychophysics, memory, learning, and vision. Numerous early psychologists studied with Müller at the University of Göttingen.

presentation According to Brentano, consciousness of an object marked by simple awareness of the presence of the object.

primary attention According to Titchener, primary attention is involuntary and typically activated by a sudden or strong stimulus.

secondary attention According to Titchener, secondary attention is learned and persists under difficult conditions (e.g., staying alert while studying even under noisy circumstances).

structuralism A system of psychological thought associated primarily with Edward Bradford Titchener, who attempted to model psychology after the more mature sciences, especially chemistry. Structuralism employed the method of introspection to search for the elements of consciousness and the rules by which elements combine.

Stumpf, Carl (1848–1936) Student of Brentano and pioneer in the psychology of music. His holistic orientation focused on meaningful mental phenomena rather than arbitrary elements of consciousness.

system An organized way of envisioning the world or some aspect of the world.

Titchener, Edward Bradford (1867–1927) One of Wilhelm Wundt's best-known students and founder of a system of psychological thought known as structuralism. Titchener was a dominant force in U.S. psychology from the early 1890s until his death in 1927.

Washburn, Margaret Floy (1871–1939) First woman to earn a doctorate in psychology and the second female president of the American Psychological Association. Washburn made significant contributions to the study of comparative psychology and was well known for her "motor theory of consciousness."

12 Functionalism

Nothing includes everything or dominates over everything. The word "and" trails along after every sentence.

—William James (1909/1977)

In times of antiquity, process-oriented philosophers emphasized the fluid, changing, mutable, and dynamic nature of the world. The world of human experience is also a world of change, somewhat like a flowing stream. Psychologists in the functionalist tradition emphasized the developmental, adaptive, and dynamic features of experience. The result was a psychology radically different from structuralism. This chapter explores the loosely knit school of thought known as *functionalism*.

The term **functionalism** is difficult to define, but its meanings will unfold throughout the chapter. Whereas structuralism focused on *what* questions, functionalism explored *how* questions. The functionalists encouraged both basic and applied science and adopted a variety of methods. If there was one central focus, it was adaptation. Functionalism's most important original scholar was the American psychologist and philosopher William James.

William James and Harvard University

Many Americans paid close attention to the birth and development of psychology in Germany. No one watched the emergence of the new science with a more careful eye than a brilliant young American named **William James (1842–1910)**. As early as 1875, James wrote articles for popular American magazines that informed the public about German psychology. In unsigned notices, he called attention to the publication of Wundt's *Principles of Physiological Psychology* (James, 1875) and to developments in applied psychology such as Franz Von Holtzendorff's work on the psychology of murder (James, 1876a).

James is difficult to characterize as a professional. His degree was in medicine, but he did not practice it. He trained in physiology, but spent little time teaching or researching it. He was not trained in psychology—indeed, the first lecture he heard on the subject was his own—nor was he trained in philosophy. Yet he held professorships in psychology and philosophy and enjoyed international acclaim in both disciplines. If American psychology had a favorite academic son, James would be the overwhelming choice. The philosopher Alfred North Whitehead (1938/1968) identified four great thinkers for "their achievements in philosophical assemblage . . . These men were Plato, Aristotle, Leibniz and William James" (p. 2). The term *assemblage* refers to the sheer breadth of the contributions of these thinkers. As we will see, James delivers a psychology with enormous breadth in terms of both subject matter and methodologies. His influence connects in one way or another with general psychology, educational psychology, the psychology of religion, developmental psychology, psychopathology, and social psychology. Many of his mature perspectives are highly relevant to later developments in existential psychology (May, 1969) and ecopsychology (Viney & Mullen, 2017). With the work of William James, psychology would no longer focus primarily on the typical adult mind.

William James, the first of five children of Mary Robertson Walsh and Henry James Sr., was born in New York City on January 11, 1842. William was named after his grandfather William James of Albany, who migrated to the United States from Ireland around 1789 and quickly made one of the original American fortunes by investing in tobacco, salt works, and the Erie Canal. A robust inheritance permitted Henry and Mary to live a luxurious existence including extensive travel and high quality private education for their children. According to Perry (1954), Henry and Mary produced a tolerant, stimulating, and even indulgent environment including the stimulation of famous friends such as Ralph Waldo Emerson. Other biographers (e.g., Simon, 1998) describe Henry as an overly protective father involved in a consuming struggle to keep "his children isolated from a world that offered them choices, temptations, and satisfactions" (p. 63). Richardson (2006) called attention to "intellectual chasms" between William and his father (pp. 83–84). Henry was a monist with God as the all-pervasive feature in the center of his universe, whereas William was a pluralist who took seriously the many things encountered in experience—a real God, a real moral life, a real material world, real evil, and so forth. For Henry, individualism was an evil to be overcome, but William celebrated the individual and denigrated the social forces that undermine authentic selfhood (see Coon, 1996; James, 1899/1920b). As noted in Perry's early biography, the James home was stimulating and offered enormous intellectual opportunities, but William's path was not uncomplicated as he worked through personal and philosophical differences with his father.

In the fall of 1861, William enrolled in the Lawrence Scientific School at Harvard University and studied the usual subjects: chemistry, biology, anatomy, and physiology. But, as noted by Perry (1954), "He was perpetually grazing and ruminating, wandering wherever the pasturage was good . . . [James's interests ranged] over the whole field of literature, history, science, and philosophy. They indicate a mind as energetic and acquisitive as it is voracious and incorrigibly vagrant" (p. 71). James's breadth of interest and

William James

extensive travel, including trips to South America and Europe, interfered with his medical training but helped refine his own vocational inclinations. He joined Louis Agassiz on a biological expedition to Brazil and discovered a profound distaste for mere collecting and classifying. In Europe, he became acquainted with leading figures such as Emil DuBois-Reymond, Wilhelm Wundt, and Hermann von Helmholtz. He also discovered a distaste for the rigors of routine laboratory work in physiology. James finally completed his M.D. in 1869, submitting a dissertation on the effects of coldness on the human body.

In 1870, James found himself in a state of intellectual and emotional turmoil, still uncertain about his vocational or personal prospects. During this period, he suffered intense anxiety and depression (see McDermott, 1968). In 1872, James accepted an appointment as instructor of physiology at Harvard, but by 1873 he was expressing ambivalence about his career. Though a successful teacher, he knew that physiology was not his first love. In 1875, he offered a graduate course called the "Relations between Psychology and Physiology" and founded the psychology laboratory at Harvard. In 1876, James taught his first undergraduate course in psychology. Two years later, he signed a contract with Henry Holt and Company to write a psychology text. In 1878, James married Alice Howe Gibbens, a twenty-seven-year-old Boston schoolteacher who had been introduced to James by his father.

Initial plans called for the text to be completed in two years, but James's classic *The Principles of Psychology* did not appear until 1890. The delay in publication was caused by the usual distractions of settling into a new career and James's wish to produce a significant work, not a mere collection of existing ideas and findings (King, 1992). His family obligations between 1878 and 1890 also colored the writing process. In that period, three sons and two daughters were born to William and Alice, and in 1885, their third child, Hermann, died of complications from whooping cough. Given such conditions, the gestation of *The Principles* was lengthy, but its success

was nearly instantaneous. Called "The James," it became the leading text in the United States and was translated into many foreign languages. A briefer version of *The Principles* (called "The Jimmy"), published in 1892, was also a major success. *The Principles of Psychology* (1890) influenced generations of psychologists. Over seventy years after its publication, MacLeod (1969) said that it "is without question the most literate, the most provocative, and at the same time the most intelligible book on psychology that has ever appeared in English or in any other language" (p. iii). It was also notable for advancing a psychology much broader in scope than most of the existing psychologies of the day.

Highly significant books followed in the wake of *The Principles*, including *The Will to Believe* (1897), *Talks to Teachers* (1899), and *The Varieties of Religious Experience* (1902). After 1900, James's publications were philosophical, though each one returned to specific psychological themes first discussed in *The Principles*. His key philosophical works include *Pragmatism* (1907), *A Pluralistic Universe* (1909), *The Meaning of Truth* (1909), and *Essays in Radical Empiricism*, published posthumously in 1912. The pattern of James's publications reveals the shift of his interest from psychology to philosophy. Even so, James the psychologist remained alive in James the philosopher. His acute mind returned to psychological topics time after time in his major philosophical works (Crosby & Viney, 1990). As a philosopher, he remained interested in the welfare of the new discipline he helped found at Harvard University. James retired from Harvard in 1907 and died from a heart condition in 1910.

James embodied the Victorian ideal of a gentleman scholar. For his work and personality, appreciation has always outweighed criticism. He is eulogized for tolerance, industry, warmth, generosity, and intellectual conscience. The most common criticisms are directed at inconsistencies in James's system. Such criticisms are valid, but less so when James's psychology is understood in the context of his larger philosophical vision. We will now consider general characteristics of James's thought before focusing on his psychology.

General Characteristics of James's Thought

James's general philosophical orientation grew out of his sensitivity to people, their experiences, and their problems. Earle (1967) pointed out that "James addressed himself to the people . . . and he listened to the people to find out what life meant to them. He respected not so much their common sense as their common feelings and hopes" (p. 240). What emerged was a philosophy with face validity—a philosophy unique for its openness to differences and its willingness to experiment with methods. It is a philosophy that is integrated with the character of American thought. It is not pessimistic or overly optimistic—it is, above all, practical—but it leaves ample room for theoretical and nonutilitarian intellectual endeavor. Perhaps its major hallmark is its believability. Seldom is there anything in James that seems strained, narrow, superficial, or one-sided, and his ideas are rich and complex and include apparent contradictions that have long inspired psychologists (Allport, 1943). James's psychology and philosophy are cut from the same cloth (McDermott, 1968), so it is important to grasp the themes that run throughout all his writings.

INDIVIDUALISM   A strong individualistic quality runs throughout James's writings. His emphasis on the importance of the individual was illustrated earlier in Chapter 1 in our discussion of the philosophy of history. James believed that a purely *Zeitgeist* theory of history causes us to go beyond scientific determinism into fatalism. He believed that circumstances shape individuals but, in turn, individuals shape the world in ways that would not happen without the unique contribution of the individual. Thus, individuals *and* circumstances make history.

James made extensive use of biographies and case studies to illustrate the importance of the individual. He believed experience and reality are not easily separable. Indeed, we come down to reality, as such, in the experience of the individual. When we get away from individual experience, we study abstractions and are thus removed from what is most fundamental. James did not rule out normative analysis, but such analysis should itself be tested against experience. James took experience seriously, and often started his inquiry with an examination of his own experiences; in these ways he broke ground as an early qualitative researcher (Carol & Owens, 2007; Leary, 2014).

Another strand of James's individualism arrives in his fierce denunciation of the impersonal and hollow forces found in large bureaucratic organizations. He has sometimes been portrayed as an insulated academic removed from the concerns of daily life. Coon (1996), however, documents James's active political involvement in the 1890s and his vigorous resistance to the growth of imperializing and dehumanizing forces in government, the military, and large corporations. One of his greatest concerns was with the failure of large institutions to recognize and honor traditional values of freedom, individuality, and pluralism.

MULTIPLE LEVELS OF ANALYSIS   Trained in physiology and medicine, James was a strong believer in emphasizing the biological and physiological correlates of behavior. Nevertheless, he was not a reductionist. He understood, with great vigor, the importance of both the broad psychological world of experience and the biological underpinnings (Hawkins, 2014). For James, there is a real sense in which experience cannot be reduced and cannot be explained by resorting to an alien biological substrate. His classic book *The Varieties of Religious Experience* illustrates this point. In James's day, it was popular to "explain" religious experiences in terms of neurological processes. James (1902/1985) insisted that neurological processes are also applicable to atheistic beliefs. Even if one were to discover the biological basis of belief, that would not undermine its validity. He argued that the claims of theism and atheism must be adjudicated based on the differences these ideas make in the lives of individual believers. James affirmed multiple levels of analysis: molecular, biological, psychological, sociological, philosophical—all are legitimate and have their special value and application. For James, error begins when we believe that all things can be subsumed under any one rubric. This latter point leads to the next major characteristic of James's thought—his pluralism.

JAMESIAN PLURALISM In *Pragmatism*, James (1907/1975b) argued that the monism–pluralism issue is "the deepest and most pregnant question that our minds can frame" (p. 141). Although James was open to the possibility that there may be only one real thing and that all else is derived from that one reality (monism), he was nevertheless a pluralist and repeatedly referred to himself in that way (see 1909/1975a, pp. 124–125; 1909/1977, p. 26; 1912/1976, p. 133).

James's **pluralism** had implications for his psychology (Woody & Viney, 2009). The first implication is methodological. If we survey James's psychological and philosophical works, we discover a pragmatic pluralism in which methodology becomes subservient to vision. James embraced a variety of methods and was a methodological pluralist (see Viney, 1989). James's pluralism also had profound implications for the subject matter of psychology (see Viney et al., 1992). Though experience is primary in his philosophy, there is no one content area (e.g., learning, sensing, and emotion) or worldview (Wiggins, 2009) that is foundational for all other areas; questions of pluralism or unification remain important in psychology (Gaj, 2016; Sternberg, 2005). James's psychology had enormous scope, including basic and applied problems, the psychology of religion, and even paranormal phenomena (Sommer, 2012)—much to the dismay of his colleagues who believed psychic research was a pseudoscience that embarrassed the scientific integrity of psychology (Coon, 1992).

FREE WILL Few psychologists have struggled with free will and determinism with the intensity that James devoted to the issue. On one hand, he agreed that science, including psychology, may conduct business on the assumption of determinism. At the same time, James (1890/1981) insisted that science "must be constantly reminded that her purposes are not the only purposes, and that the order of uniform causation which she has use for, and is therefore right in postulating, may be enveloped in a wider order, on which she has no claims at all" (p. 1179). So James leaves room for a methodological determinism for psychology and science. But at the same time he argued that we will probably never write a biography on an individual life in advance.

Although James reserved a place for methodological determinism in science, he rejected metaphysical determinism. In his early years, he was a determinist. During an emotional crisis in the early 1870s, he abandoned metaphysical determinism with the declaration, "My first act of free will shall be to believe in free will" (1920a, p. 147). The idea for the affirmation of free will by an act of free will came to James through the philosopher Jules Lequier via Charles Renouvier (Viney, 1984, 1997).

James's best-known statement on the free will–determinism issue is in his article "The Dilemma of Determinism" (1884a, 1979a, pp. 114–140). For James, determinism is more consistent with monism, whereas belief in free will, even a limited free will, is more consistent with pluralism. James argued that the concept of causality, from a philosophical perspective, is as ambiguous as the concept of freedom. He believed there are ambiguities associated with the future and real possibilities. He believed in regularities, so his was not an untrammeled free will. Indeed, he found that freedom is hard won and exercised only through effortful striving.

MORALISTIC PSYCHOLOGY AND PHILOSOPHY Rambo (1980) has pointed out that James's concern with what people *should* or *ought* to do influenced his writings. For example,

James distinguishes between *easygoing* and *strenuous moods*. In the easygoing mood, we become perfunctory and lazy, but in the strenuous mood, we seize the opportunities for action and work with energy and enthusiasm. James believed we all have the capacity for the strenuous mood, but that capacity must be cultivated. In his famous chapter on habit in *The Principles*, he counseled, "Keep the faculty of effort alive in you by a little gratuitous exercise every day . . . do every day or two something for no other reason than that you would rather not do it, so that when the hour of dire need draws nigh, it may find you not unnerved and untrained to stand the test" (1890/1981, p. 130). One of James's concerns was with those who believed that they had the absolute truth. He argued that such beliefs could lead to "moral holidays" manifested in absolutistic one-size-fits-all philosophies that overlook shades of grey and the complexities and ambiguities encountered in real life situations. James seldom lost an opportunity to apply psychology to human nature. He wanted a basic experimental psychology but one that made a useful difference in daily life and culture including such topics as war and peace (Deutsch & Coleman, 2012).

RADICAL EMPIRICISM James lamented the misleading nature of brief names, but preferred that his philosophy be called *radical empiricism*. A fundamental postulate of **radical empiricism**, according to James (1909/1975a), is "that the only things that shall be debatable among philosophers shall be things definable in terms drawn from experience" (p. 6). The term *radical* means that things that are experienced must not be ignored. From this perspective, it is not surprising that he investigated mystical and psychic experiences (Junior et al., 2013). It also implies our right to exclude things that are not definable in terms drawn from experience. James was quick to admit, however, that there may be many real things that are not experienced. He was open to new possibilities and to borderline phenomena or to things that some people claim to experience and that others claim not to experience. Radical

empiricism, for James, meant that we must find a place for everything that is a genuine part of experience. The term *radical* also implies that monism will be regarded as a hypothesis (James, 1897/1979b, p. 5). For James, any monism is a hypothesis open to the test of experience.

James did not believe, however, that monistic conceptions square with experience. He argued that monism, born in rationalism and logic, tells us what to count and what not to count. Thus, if one is a materialistic monist, the whole mental realm is either not counted at all or is rationalized away. If one is an idealistic monist, the physical realm is intellectualized. James failed to find any monistic vantage point so encompassing that it could include everything—hence, his statement at the opening of this chapter: "Nothing includes everything" (1909/1977, p. 145). Monistic orientations, whether they be inspired in political, religious, psychological, economic, philosophical, or scientific arenas, are never sufficiently comprehensive or responsive to the ever-growing breadth and fullness of human experience in a changing and sometimes promiscuous world. According to James (1897/1979b), something "is still wrong and other and outside and unincluded, from *your* point of view, even though you be the greatest of philosophers" (p. 145).

Given James's view of process, it is questionable that he could ever believe in the adequacy of any monism. He truly believed that the world is in process, that creation was not an event but is an ongoing process, happening now as always; for better or worse, we are all participants. James once asked, "What has concluded, that we might conclude in regard to it?" (1910/1978, p. 190). Since the world is in process, there is no vantage point from which one can make the big claim for truth with a capital *T*, because our vantage points are themselves in constant flux. As a consequence, we must be content with provisional and practical truths that are subject to change. James's radical empiricism was nascent in *The Principles* (see Crosby & Viney, 1990) and is a key to understanding his system of psychology.

PRAGMATISM The final general characteristic of James's worldview is his pragmatic philosophy. For James, **pragmatism** is a method, a theory of truth, and a way of thinking about the world. It opposes absolutistic schemes and contents itself with provisional (but workable) concepts and methodologies. James (1907/1975b) instructed his readers as follows: "If you follow the pragmatic method, you cannot look on any such word [e.g., *energy*, *reason*, and *God*] as closing your quest. You must bring out of each word its practical cash-value, [and view it] as a program for more work" (pp. 31–32). For James, words, theories, concepts, and the like are "instruments, not answers to enigmas."

The Varieties of Religious Experience (1902/1985) illustrates the pragmatic method in which beliefs and practices are judged by the work they accomplish in the world. If good work is accomplished, then a belief or practice is vindicated. James (1907/1975b) rejected the idea that any belief or theory could make the claim to be "absolutely a transcript of reality" (p. 33).

James's pragmatism and pluralistic empiricism found a receptive intellectual climate in the United States. The commonsense nature of his philosophy, his unusual ability to communicate with both academics and the public, and the sheer charm of his personality combined to make him a powerful force within psychology as well as philosophy.

Jamesian Psychology

James (1890/1981) defined *psychology* as "the science of mental life, both of its phenomena and of their conditions" (p. 15). By *phenomena*, James meant feelings, cognitions, desires, and so on, and he centered psychology on personal consciousness (Taylor, 2010). By *conditions of mental life*, he meant bodily and social processes that influence mental processes. James defined *psychology* as the study of mental processes, but such processes take the psychologist into behavioral, physiological, and cultural dimensions.

HABIT James believed that much of human life is understandable in terms of habits acquired through learning and education. He stressed the physical basis of habit by pointing out that stimulation follows the path of least resistance in living tissue. For example, a joint once sprained becomes more vulnerable to future stress. Similarly, a pathway once established in the nervous system is likely to be used again.

James discussed habit in functional terms, as essential to civilization and to the economy of individual action. Our lives follow habitual patterns in manner of dress, ways of greeting and departing, ways of getting to and performing work, and ways of eating and even sleeping. In a famous analogy, James suggested that habit does for the individual and for society what the flywheel does for an internal combustion engine. The flywheel smooths the operation and keeps the engine running just as habit keeps us in our niche even when circumstances are difficult.

For James, the goal of education was instilling good habits. He believed individual success or failure depends on the development of good habits. The commonsense quality of Jamesian psychology is best illustrated in his famous chapter on habit. We have, at every turn, an abundance of examples: the accomplished pianist who practices eight hours a day, the Olympic gold medal winner who tells of years of training, and the winner of a Nobel Prize who, for years, labors through eighty-four-hour workweeks.

James's chapter ends with practical suggestions for launching productive habits and breaking bad ones. He counseled his readers to move toward a new habit with great initiative, enlist social support by making a public pledge, and never suffer an exception to occur. We should schedule activities, if possible, to decrease the expression of the old habit. Likewise, we should invite opportunities that promote the new habit.

THE STREAM OF THOUGHT James contended that psychologists abandon the empirical method when they dissect mental life into simple sensations. The reason for this contention is that, in our normal experience, we do not have simple sensations. Rather, according to James, continuities, relations, and complexities define consciousness. Psychology's starting point is not simple sensations but thinking itself. From such a starting point, James discussed five general characteristics of the **stream of thought**.

First, James found that thoughts are personal and *owned*; they are *our* thoughts. Such a contention runs headlong into difficulty. We are reluctant to own some dreams or intrusive thoughts, and there are obvious cases of people whose perceptions of their thoughts as outside of themselves challenge James's belief in the personal nature of consciousness. James recognized the difficulty. His explanation illustrated an early recognition of unconscious processes. He argued that hysterical anesthesias, automatic writing, and multiple personalities are manifestations of what he called *secondary personal selves* that are sometimes out of touch with the self as it typically appears. But James believed that the various forms of dissociation do not constitute an exception to his position that thought tends to be part of a personal consciousness. He noted that within a so-called secondary personality there is some degree of organization and a sense of identity. He also argued that there is some limited communication between primary and secondary personalities.

A second characteristic of the stream of thought is that thoughts are constantly changing. James believed that the experience of constancy is an illusion that results from inattention. He was convinced that our state of mind is always in process; thus, a present state is not like a previous state. It may appear that we have the same view out a window each day, but *we* are a bit different each day, and the view itself is slightly different. James's emphasis on process joins him in a tradition that extends from Heraclitus to contemporary process philosophy.

A third characteristic is that thought is characterized by continuity rather than division or separation. Again, difficulties arise with such a contention, but James anticipated the difficulties.

A loud clap of thunder might appear as a separate and discrete event that breaks in on the continuity of thought. But James argued that what we hear "is not thunder *pure*, but thunder-breaking-upon-silence-and-contrasting-with-it" (1890/1981, p. 234). Time gaps such as we encounter in sleep would appear to contradict James's third characteristic, but he argued that consciousness following a time gap "belongs to" or is continuous with consciousness before it. It is the same thought that takes up the problem this morning that was put to rest last evening. James shared with Brentano an emphasis on the active, intentional, and flowing nature of experience.

A fourth characteristic is that human thought conveys a sense of something other than itself. In other words, it is cognitive. The term *cognitive* is derived from a Latin verb *cognoscere*, which means "to know" or "to become acquainted with." James contended that the bridges we build between our past thoughts of an object and our present thought of the same object condition our belief in an outer reality.

The final characteristic of thought, according to James, is that selectivity, discrimination, choice, and shifting interests are in its very nature. James believed that selectivity is based on the nature and characteristics of the stimulus, aesthetics, and personal values. He argued that we find it quite impossible to be impartial in terms of how we direct our interest and attention.

THE SELF For James, the *self* includes the totality of all things that belong to us: friends, children, a home, clothing, a pet, reputation, memory, perception, and a physical structure. He identified three constituents of the self: the material self, the social self, and the spiritual self. In addition to these, and in a class apart, was the pure ego.

The most intimate part of the material "me" is the body—and some parts are more "intimately me" than others. Clothing is also part of the **material self** (Watson, 2004), as well as family, furniture, collections, and other possessions. So, we lose or gain aspects of our selves with the ebb and flow of our possessions.

The **social self**, according to James, is not one but a variety of selves. He contended that we have a different social self for each person who recognizes us. He emphasized context and role-playing as determinants of social selves. Although a child may be shy or polite in the presence of parents or teachers, he or she may be "appropriately rude" or assertive in the presence of friends. For this reason, many descriptive adjectives assigned to us are names for a particular social self. We are honest, loyal, obedient, courageous, competent, but not all at once and not in every social situation. An athlete who is brash and courageous in competition may stand weak and inept in front of a speech class. All of us have experienced such duplicity or multiplicity, but James's theory of the spiritual self points to a way out of such experiences.

The material and social selves are outward manifestations, but the **spiritual self** is personal, subjective, and intimate. It is an inner citadel that sits in judgment on the other selves. Indeed, the other components of the self belong to the spiritual self, and it is more permanent than the rest. In James's view, the spiritual self is a source of effort or will; it is a source of change and desire for change.

James believed that the selves engaged in tensions and rivalries. Tensions also flourish among potential selves. We might wish to be wealthy, athletic, scholarly, witty, philanthropic, adventurous, and beautiful. We cannot, however, appropriate the energy to be everything. We must be judicious and direct energy in ways that strike a balance between our ideals and reality.

James argued that our **self-esteem** is a function of the ratio of our success and our pretensions as follows:

$$\text{Self-esteem} = \frac{\text{Success}}{\text{Pretensions}}$$

James pointed out that the greatest burdens are lifted by adjusting our expectations downward. We may experience great release when we accept imperfection on some activity or when

we realize we can drop the endeavor. James called attention to the different pretensions associated with the different selves. The material self may find esteem in wealth, the social self may find esteem in recognition, and the spiritual self may find esteem in purity or moral superiority.

Under the topic of pure ego, James contended that psychology encounters its most puzzling question: What is the nature of personal identity and the sense of continuity that runs through the present self and reaches backward and forward? Is there an arch-ego and, if so, what is its nature? James reviewed spiritualist theories of a substantive soul, transcendentalism, and associationism, finding difficulties in each. He concluded that psychology must content itself for the time with a mere functional approach to the self. Such an approach can do real work in the world and can be scientifically productive and satisfying. For his part, James was open to many ways of knowing and never demanded that any perspective, including science, provide totality.

THE EMOTIONS James's original paper, titled "What Is an Emotion," published in 1884, inspired controversy. The reaction to the 1884 paper prompted James to publish another paper in 1894, titled "The Physical Basis of Emotion." The focus of the early papers was on the physiological correlates of emotion, but he explored some of the rich experiential dimensions of emotion in later works such as: *The Varieties of Religious Experience*, *The Will to Believe*, *Talks to Teachers*, and *Essays in Radical Empiricism*. In these later works, he examined topics such as the value of emotions, the control of emotions, paradoxical emotions, and what he called *the stream of feeling*. His larger view of emotion goes far beyond his physiological theory (see Viney, 1992).

A hallmark of Jamesian psychology is its commonsense appeal, but his physiological approach to emotion seems counterintuitive. The theory, advanced independently by Danish physiologist **Carl Georg Lange (1834–1900)**, has come to be called the **James–Lange theory of emotion**. James admitted that his theory departs from common sense. Let's say you are hiking in the woods when you encounter a bear. Common sense would say that you see the bear, become afraid, and then run. But the James–Lange theory insists that bodily changes precede the experience of emotion. In other words, you see the bear, run, and then experience fear. Or, as James tells us, "We feel sorry because we cry, angry because we strike, afraid because we tremble."

James could not imagine a disembodied emotion. If there were no activation, no arousal, how could there be an experience of emotion? This problem puzzled him. In his 1894/1983 article, James pointed out that his theory "assumes (what probably everyone assumes) that there must be a process of some sort in the nerve-centres for emotion" (p. 306). For James, the experience of emotion *is* the experience of the activity of the body. He never denied that stimuli evoke emotional behavior. We see a bear and run! The stimulus provokes emotional behavior. James did not deny the importance of context, either. If we see a bear in a zoo, or if we see a bear in the wilderness and we are well-trained on how to respond, we may not run. In James's view, a stimulus situation (a chance encounter with a bear in the woods or a view of a bear in a cage at the zoo) provokes an adaptive response. We may run or stand in admiration, depending on context.

We could see a bear and freeze in fright or we could see a bear and run. James would not deny that either reaction is possible but contend that the emotions associated with freezing are different from the emotions associated with running. The bodily conditions in the two circumstances are different and hence should be associated with different feelings.

James's physiological theory of emotion is still debated in the twenty-first century (Wassmann, 2014), and Papanicolaou (1989) has argued that there is still no evidence "indicating that the body is not a necessary condition of emotion . . . Reports of affect, when detailed, are also reports of somatic sensations" (p. 127). James's vision of emotion, as set forth in *The Varieties* and

in his philosophical works, recognized that some individuals are disposed to an optimistic outlook, whereas others are prone toward the darker side of things. James also found difficulty in separating emotion from cognition. The two, in his view, are interwoven.

INSTINCTS James believed in instincts and was interested in events that play a role in their evolution within the individual. For example, habit and conditioning may gradually build on and replace instincts. The organism may become partial to the first stimulus to which it reacted. As an illustration, James cited Spalding (1873), who demonstrated that chicks born in the absence of a hen "will follow any moving object. And, when guided by sight alone, they seem to have no more disposition to follow a hen than to follow a duck or a human being.

James discussed the transiency of instincts. For example, the instinct to follow fades after a brief but critical period of time. Here again, he cited Spalding who placed hoods over chicks' heads and showed they would not follow after being hooded for a period of four days.

James believed that the principle of transiency is important in human and animal life. An instinct is ripe for only a brief period. The mode of expression first utilized is most likely to be followed or fixed and, according to James, there is an optimal moment for attaching an instinct to an appropriate stimulus and this optimal moment or moment of readiness has clear implications for educators. James believed instincts were important in early development and less important later. He believed that behaviors such as sucking, biting, clasping, crying, imitating, and certain fears are instinctive.

Dewsbury (1992) in a helpful overview traces the origins of James's interest in instincts, some of the details of James's theory, and his influence on subsequent theorists. Dewsbury notes that while instincts are not at the center of Jamesian psychology, they are nevertheless present in the developmental core of the individual though they play changing roles as life proceeds.

MEMORY James opened his chapter on memory with a distinction between primary and secondary memory. **Primary memory**, according to James, is memory for the immediate past or the events that have most recently been in consciousness. He believed in a close connection between primary memory and afterimages—a topic of considerable interest in early perception research. **Secondary memory**, for James, was memory proper. He defined it as knowledge of previous events that are not currently a part of thought or attention. James contended that the exercise of memory presupposes two things: first, the retention of a fact, and second, the demonstration of retention through reminiscence, recollection, reproduction, or recall.

James cited what he called the "heroic" work of Ebbinghaus on memory and concluded his chapter with a section on forgetting. He focused on the utility and the irregularities of forgetting. Under this latter subject, he included topics such as the difficulty of recall that sometimes occurs with strenuous effort and the subsequent ease with which the to-be-remembered material comes back when we relax. (Psychologists later described such forgetting as the "tip-of-the-tongue phenomenon.") James believed that memory is facilitated by quality of organization, interest, and active (as opposed to passive) repetition. He agreed with French psychologist Théodule Ribot that we have memories rather than memory. He believed that different individuals have different gifts for visual, auditory, tactile, verbal, and muscular memories.

In a lengthy footnote, James described his study on the transfer of learning. Briefly, he investigated whether learning lines from Victor Hugo's "Satyr" would shorten the time to learn lines from a different kind of material (Milton's *Paradise Lost*). He found that the learning of the first task did not facilitate the learning of the second task. This study foreshadowed later transfer of learning studies that proved embarrassing to the doctrine of formal discipline.

James's Legacy

James's leadership stimulated the expansion of the methodological, conceptual, and substantive boundaries of psychology. Some psychologists returned to a narrow, unified psychology after James. But in pluralistic America, such visions suffered at the hands of those infected with a Jamesian suspicion of grand, all-embracing schemes. James left us with a legacy that monism—any monism, be it spiritual, material, political, psychological, scientific, or religious—is but a hypothesis. The positive side of James's legacy is that he encouraged us to pursue alternatives. One of the greatest tributes to James is that his major works are in print a century after his death. He remains relevant!

James's continuing relevance is illustrated in scholarship on the ecological implications of radical empiricism, pluralism, and pragmatism (see Crosby, 1996; Heft, 2001; Viney & Mullen, 2017). Though ecology, as a formal discipline, surfaced long after James's work, some scholars now argue for identifiable affinities between ecological perspectives and Jamesian metaphysics. James did call for the development of a deep and solemn sensitivity to the complexities of our relation to the world. For example, in a speech to a men's club at Harvard, he reminded his audience of the "innocent beasts [who] have had to suffer in cattle-cars and slaughter pens and lay down their lives that we might grow up, all fatted and clad, to sit together here in comfort and carry on this discourse" (1897/1979b, p. 47). James embraced the idea that human experience is not the highest or only type of experience extant in the universe, and he argued that humans may share more than we realize with other animals, perhaps even including immortal souls (1898). Neither are humans the only creatures with valuative types of experiences. Humans, he argued, "are tangents to the wider life of things" (1907/1975b, p. 144). James was not an ecologist and one can find isolated statements in his work that illustrate insensitivities to things we take for granted a century later. Nevertheless, his mature philosophy, with its strong emphasis on the importance of feelings, relations, particularity, diversity, perspective, and balance, provides a relevant metaphysical frame of reference for ecology.

Hugo Münsterberg

Though William James founded the first experimental laboratory in the United States, he was not suited to direct its activities or conduct experiments. Nevertheless, he wanted Harvard to maintain visible leadership in psychology at a time when competing universities established laboratories. A key to Harvard's leadership was to find an outstanding young scholar to direct the laboratory. James was impressed with the early career and promise of a feisty young psychologist named **Hugo Münsterberg (1863–1916)**,

Hugo Münsterberg

a former student of Wilhelm Wundt. James was aware that Münsterberg was critical of Wundt's work and also that his action theory of behavior was compatible with the James–Lange theory of emotion (Landy, 1992). Largely through James's efforts, Münsterberg was invited to join the Harvard faculty in 1892. He accepted and remained at Harvard until his death in 1916.

Münsterberg was born in Danzig, East Prussia (now Gdansk, Poland). He received his Ph.D. under Wilhelm Wundt in 1885 at age twenty-two and then earned an M.D. at the University of Heidelberg two years later. He moved to Harvard following a brief but productive assignment at Freiburg. His major assignment at Harvard was to run the laboratory but, like James, Münsterberg's interests ranged wide. As discussed in Chapter 18, he is celebrated as a significant figure in the history of applied psychology (Landy, 1992).

Though Münsterberg established residence in the United States well before his thirtieth birthday, he never relinquished his strong German identity. As World War I approached, Münsterberg's German sympathies became widely apparent. He had initially won favor in the United States, but fell into disfavor because of his public support for Germany (Spillmann & Spillmann, 1993). Münsterberg died of a stroke in 1916 at the age of fifty-three. His early death may well have been hastened because of the tensions he experienced over his divided loyalties and public rejection.

Münsterberg's Psychology

Though Münsterberg rejected the larger philosophical implications of James's pragmatism, he delivered a psychology that was tuned to the daily lives of people (Morawski, 1983). For example, Münsterberg (1916) wrote a book, *The Photoplay*, that analyzed "moving pictures," marking it as an early work on the psychology of film. He went on to be a pioneer in several applied fields (Benjamin, 2006). His applications of psychology to daily life were often not grounded in solid experimental work, but they legitimized a broader vision of psychology. Münsterberg can be counted as a pioneer in educational psychology, industrial psychology, psychotherapy, and psychology and law. He argued that psychologists should acquaint themselves with the world of work, the school environment, and the courtroom before undertaking applied research.

Münsterberg's book *On the Witness Stand* (1908) is a classic in legal psychology. The book explores problems associated with topics such as eyewitness testimony and suggestibility of witnesses in court, and he was the first to raise important questions about methods of interrogation and false confessions (Kassin, 2016). Münsterberg also believed that the day would come when psychological experts would be invited to the courtroom to testify, just like chemists, physicians, and other expert witnesses, and he encouraged courts to consider psychological research (Bornstein & Meissner, 2008). Münsterberg's (1913) work in this area was a precursor of efforts in the 1970s to establish formal scientific and professional organizations and educational programs in psychology and the law (see Packer & Borum, 2013).

In addition to legal psychology, Münsterberg was fascinated with clinical psychology. His text *Psychotherapy* (1909) is broad in scope with a discussion of the causes of emotional disorders along with treatment strategies and case histories. It also examines the role of religion in treatment, the role of the physician, and the interest of the community. On treatment strategies, Münsterberg advised against a strict, systematic approach. He argued that the therapist should adjust the treatment to the special needs and abilities of the patient. Though hypnosis and suggestibility played strong roles in his therapy, he recognized other techniques. For example, the patient experiencing depression might be asked to go through the motions of joyful expression. Münsterberg (1909) believed that such a process, though artificial, might open "the channels of motor discharge" (p. 218). He also noted that the confidence of the therapist, the capacity of the therapist for empathy, and the expectations of the patient all played crucial roles in psychotherapy.

In his final chapter on psychotherapy and the community, Münsterberg discussed the problems of prevention of emotional disorders. He noted the destructive effects of social and legal injustice and the problem, for the individual and for society, of finding a middle road between the extremes of inhibition and expression. Those extremes, also recognized by Pavlov and Freud, play pivotal roles in emotional disorders. Münsterberg contended that society should give due attention to processes that block emotional expression. On the other hand, he recognized that society is impossible without inhibition. In his view, the "middle way is again the real hygienic ideal" (1909, p. 397).

Münsterberg's *Psychology and Industrial Efficiency* (1913) is another classic in applied psychology (Landy, 1997). His aim, as stated at the outset, was "to sketch the outlines of a new science which is intermediate between the modern laboratory psychology and the problems of economics: the psychological experiment is systematically to be placed at the service of commerce and industry" (p. 3). The book covers content areas that would later comprise the subject matter of industrial and organizational (I-O) psychology. He explored topics such as vocational fitness, economy of movement, the problems of monotony and fatigue, job satisfaction, and advertisement, and he remains a pioneer in vocational counseling (Porfeli, 2009). He believed work can be one of the greatest sources of joy, pride, and satisfaction, but can also produce great depression and discouragement. The pioneering work of Hugo Münsterberg on industrial efficiency lives on around the world, and though I-O psychology has expanded and evolved in terms of content and methods, it thrives as one of the most vigorous topical areas in applied psychology (see Bryan & Vinchur, 2013).

Some of Münsterberg's scholarly activities, particularly his efforts to popularize psychology, contributed to the backlash from other scholars, leading to allegations of "yellow psychology" (Spillman & Spillman, 1993, p. 329). Additionally, although Münsterberg "left no legitimate intellectual heir" (Spillman & Spillman, 1993, p. 334) to his experimental research program, Münsterberg's "illegitimate heir" (Bunn, 1997, p. 93), **William Moulton Marston (1893–1947)**, continued Münsterberg's popularization of psychology. Marston (1917) developed the polygraph as a lie detection tool, acted as the resident psychologist for *Family Circle* magazine, and used his popular writings to promote the psychological well-being of the public as well as to advocate for greater freedom and opportunity for women (Bunn, 1997, 2007). These goals guided the development of Marston's other popular creation: Wonder Woman, a mighty Amazon princess who breaks gender roles and uses her magic lasso to make people tell the truth, perhaps not a surprising superpower created by the inventor of the polygraph.

Münsterberg remains a giant in the history of applied psychology. His most original contributions were in forensic psychology and industrial psychology—two areas that gained momentum in the latter part of the twentieth century (Moskowitz, 1977). Though he did not identify with functionalism, his sympathies and contributions are more related to that tradition than to any other. Münsterberg had no wish to compromise experimental psychology; he simply had a larger vision of what counts as genuine experimental psychology.

G. Stanley Hall and Clark University

The functionalist spirit in psychology is nowhere better illustrated than in the work of **Granville Stanley Hall (1844–1924)** who, according to Averill (1990), explored "every human area and relationship: genetics, childhood, adolescence, family, education, aberration, and religious phenomena" (p. 125). No longer was psychology concerned solely with the dissection of consciousness. Expanding on the pluralistic and pragmatic tradition of his teacher William James, Hall challenged the conservative and stuffy psychology

of his day and delivered a process-oriented evolutionary perspective. In his autobiography, Hall (1923) said, "As soon as I first heard it in my youth I think I must have been almost hypnotized by the word 'evolution,' which was music to my ear and seemed to fit my mouth better than any other" (p. 357). Because of the freshness of his evolutionary perspective and his breadth, organizational skills, energy, and enthusiasm, he was an enormous force in the new discipline.

Granville Stanley Hall was born on February 1, 1844, in Ashfield, Massachusetts and educated in the rural setting of western Massachusetts. At age sixteen, he was examined by a school committee and awarded a certificate of competence to teach in the public schools. He taught briefly in Chapel Falls, Massachusetts, before enrolling in college preparation studies at Williston Academy in Easthampton, Massachusetts. Hall graduated from Williams College at age twenty-three and enrolled that fall in Union Theological Seminary in New York City.

The liberal climate of Union and the cosmopolitan setting combined to challenge his conservative and orthodox values. Ross (1972) called attention to Hall's "clandestine excursions" during the first two years of seminary (p. 32). He attended the theater, sampled a variety of religious services, and immersed himself in New York City's diverse cultural and intellectual opportunities. In 1869, Hall took a leave from the seminary to engage in philosophical studies in Germany. This period of personal and intellectual growth marked a shift from theology to natural philosophy. In 1870, Hall was back in New York to complete his final year at Union.

Following graduation, Hall's struggle to follow an academic career was beset with compromises between his real interests and his financial limitations. Tall and imposing, Hall engaged in private tutoring and a four-year teaching assignment in the humanities at Antioch College in Yellow Springs, Ohio. With savings from his teaching assignment, Hall, at age thirty-two, enrolled in graduate studies at Harvard University. He did most of his work with William James but also studied physiology and psychopathology. Ross (1972) noted that in 1878 Hall's handwritten dissertation on the muscular perception of space was "the first [doctorate] in the field of psychology to be given in this country" (p. 79). Always strained, the relationship between Hall and James grew increasingly volatile over the years.

Following completion of his doctoral studies at Harvard, Hall returned to Germany where he worked with luminaries such as Emil DuBois-Reymond, Karl Ludwig, Hermann von Helmholtz, and Wilhelm Wundt. In 1881, Hall delivered a series of lectures at Johns Hopkins University, and these were followed by a full-time professorial appointment. Johns Hopkins offered space and money for a psychology laboratory that Hall (1923) described as the "largest and most productive laboratory of its kind in the country up to the time of my leaving" (p. 227). Hall and James continued to quarrel over priority in establishing the first American psychology laboratory. At considerable personal expense, Hall founded *The American Journal of Psychology*, the first of its kind in English, with an emphasis on reporting research, and it included research on child development, attention, and mental chronometry (O'Shea & Bashore, 2012; Young & Green, 2013). The first volume was published in 1889 and he served as the journal's first editor, publishing works from psychologists as well as from other scholars in related fields (Green & Feinerer, 2015). Three years later, he founded *Pedagogical Seminary*, a journal dedicated to research and discussion about education (Young & Green, 2013).

Within a decade of completing the first Ph.D. in psychology, Hall was such a visible figure in the academic world that he received an invitation to become the first president of Clark University. As president of a new university, Hall was not hesitant to be chauvinistic for the new science, shaping the program at Clark into a dominant force in U.S. psychology.

Across Hall's writings, his sexist and racist biases clearly fit the existing prejudices of his times (Cravens, 2006), focusing on gender and largely on "only two 'racial' minorities, Jews and Blacks" (Hogan, 2003, p. 30). Despite racist themes that emerge in his writings (Youniss, 2006), his behavior revealed a complex individual who reached across the cultural divides he appeared to support, and Hall's actual views remain frustratingly obscure. Not only did he supervise women doctoral students while promoting sexism (Diehl, 1986), he engaged in other similar activities. For example, despite his public support for racism, he published an anonymous paper in his journal, *Pedagogical Seminary*, that challenged racist assumptions as well as the quality of the intelligence testing methods cited to support racist views (Anonymous, 1916; Ware, 2006). He also challenged prevailing stereotypes by providing opportunities to faculty and students who were underrepresented at universities. During a period of ripe anti-Semitism on college campuses, Hall invited three Jewish scholars to join the Clark faculty: anthropologist Franz Boas (1858–1942), physicist Albert A. Michelson (1852–1931), and chemist Morris Loeb (1863–1912). He also strongly supported his Jewish doctoral student, Samuel Moses, as a student and in Moses's struggles to find an academic position. Hall corresponded with Moses through Moses's decision to change his name to Morse in an effort to hide his Jewish heritage (Hall, 1907; Moses/Morse, 1907); this decision led to Morse's successful hiring in a faculty position in South Carolina. Hall was also the first psychologist in the United States to work with Japanese and Chinese doctoral students (Hall & Motora, 1887; Sato et al., 2012). Additionally, as noted by Guthrie (2003), prior to his doctoral work Hall had sought to teach at Howard University, a historically black university in Washington, D.C., for reasons he described as personal, and Hall was one of the few psychologists to encourage African-American students to enroll in graduate studies at other institutions as well. Under his direction, **Francis Sumner (1895–1954)** was awarded a Ph.D. from Clark University in 1920, making him the first African American to earn a doctorate in psychology in the United States.

Sumner's productive career resulted in more than forty-five publications on topics such as perception, advertising, and the psychology of religion. He proposed strategies for the higher education of African-American youth, an issue he struggled with against the smothering backdrop of segregation (Sawyer, 2000). Sumner headed the psychology department at Howard University from 1930 until his death in 1954 (Guthrie, 2003). During Sumner's tenure, Howard was dubbed the "Black Harvard" and played a role in training influential psychologists such as Mamie Phipps Clark (1917–1983) and Kenneth B. Clark (1914–2005), later to become the first African-American president of the American Psychological Association (Phillips, 2000). After earning their Ph.D.s from Columbia, the Clarks continued to study prejudice and the impact of segregation on children, research that was cited in the 1954 Supreme Court case *Brown v. Board of Education* (Jackson, 2006). Although Hall died thirty years prior to this landmark legal decision, he likely would have applauded the outcome.

Beginning with his status as the first to earn a doctorate in psychology, Hall was in the vanguard of several important developments in psychology. Wapner (1990) provided an overview of Hall's career in psychology during his thirty-one years as president of Clark University. Let's look at a few of his more noteworthy achievements:

1. Hall founded and often edited journals such as those discussed above as well as the *Journal of Religious Psychology and Education* and the *Journal of Applied Psychology.*
2. He founded and organized the American Psychological Association (APA) and served as its first president in 1892 and as its thirty-third president in 1924 (Sokal, 1992).
3. Hall brought Sigmund Freud and Carl Jung to the United States in 1909, introducing U.S. psychologists to psychoanalytic thinking.
4. His department at Clark University was a leader in producing many doctoral students in psychology.

5. His enormous scholarly output, consisting of a great many books, articles, and lectures, helped shape the direction of American psychological thought. We will examine this achievement in more detail as we turn to a consideration of Hall's viewpoint in psychology.

Hall retired from the presidency of Clark in 1920 but continued to work on personal and psychological projects. He completed *Senescence* in 1922 and his autobiography, *Life and Confessions of a Psychologist*, in 1923. He died of pneumonia on April 24, 1924. Ross (1972) noted, "At the small funeral in Worcester, the local minister caused a brief scandal by criticizing Hall for not having appreciated the importance of the institutional church, a scandal which Hall surely would have relished" (p. 436).

Though Hall's accomplishments were extensive, personal difficulties and tragedies tortured him. His first wife and an eight-year-old daughter were accidentally asphyxiated in 1890 (Hogan, 2003). Later, Hall's second wife was hospitalized with a severe mental disorder. Following the loss of his first wife, Hall immersed himself in work and failed to develop a close relationship with his oldest child, Robert Granville Hall. Throughout his life, Hall was torn between passivity and aggression and between depression and stormy manic-like periods. He had an apparent need to surround himself with people who were dependent and accommodating. In an informative article, Sokal (1990) discussed these traits and their influence on the development of psychology at Clark. For all of his personal difficulties, Hall ranks as a key figure in U.S. psychology. We turn now to a further consideration of some of his contributions.

Hall's Psychology

Hall did not deliver a tightly reasoned system of psychology with clear-cut definitions and rigid methodological prescriptions. However, his published works and the experimental program he advocated had a definite thematic quality. In discussing Hall's laboratory at Johns Hopkins, Pauley (1986) noted that the major research topics included "binocular vision, perception of time, coordination of action between the two halves of the body and the relationship between psychological attention and muscular movement" (p. 28). Pauley pointed out that Hall envisioned a much wider experimental program, but most students, in fact, worked on these topics. Hall published in all these areas, but the focus of his early research was on the psychology of childhood (White, 1992). His long-term interest was in the emerging field of life-span development (Thompson et al., 2012).

In the preface to his classic *Adolescence*, Hall (1904) celebrated the "extension of evolution into the psychic field" (p. v). He argued that knowledge of the soul is dependent on knowledge of the history of the soul in the world. Thus, the study of the history of the individual should be complemented by studies of the history of the species. Hall (1904) repeatedly expressed the belief that "the child and the race are each keys to the other" (p. vii). He adopted the idea that ontogeny (the history of the individual— postnatal development through childhood) recapitulates phylogeny (the evolutionary history of the species; Green, 2015a). Such a belief comes ready-made with methodological and substantive prescriptions, including beliefs that mirror the intense cultural prejudices of his time. On the methodological side, Hall argued that, "animal, savage, and child-soul can never be studied by introspection" (p. vii). To address these limitations, Hall became one of the pioneers of the use of self-reports, particularly open-ended self-reports from children, as psychological data (Young, 2013). The methodology of psychology would have to become broader and more biological. On the substantive side, Hall declared, "We must go to school to learn the folk-soul, learn of criminals and defectives, animals, and in some sense go back to Aristotle in rebasing psychology on biology" (pp. vii–viii). Clearly, Hall's approach

to psychology represents a radical departure from Titchener's psychology. Hall's developmental-evolutionary approach gives concrete expression to ideas in the philosophy of William James but not always translated into specific programs for action.

His vision for an experimental child psychology was set forth in a popular magazine article titled "A Children's Institute." In that article, Hall (1910) campaigned for institutes devoted to broad-based studies of children. Such institutes would have divisions or specializations on a host of topics such as growth norms, language development, special diseases of children, hygiene, juvenile crime, and educational techniques (Brooks-Gunn & Johnson, 2006). Much of Hall's personal research was designed to expand the public awareness of what children know and what they do. Thus, he published studies on topics such as children's vocabulary and number abilities when they enter school (Hall, 1891), children's lies (Hall, 1890), showing off and bashfulness (Hall & Smith, 1903), and several works on children's concepts (Hall & Browne, 1903; Hall & Wallin, 1902). Hall was one of the first to view adolescents, particularly boys, as vulnerable rather than threatening (Kett, 2015). As noted by Arnett (2006), although many of Hall's ideas no longer have scholarly support, his discussions of delinquent behavior, sensation seeking, and vulnerability to peer and media influences in adolescence are particularly similar to twenty-first-century scholarship.

Hall's research work on children covered a variety of additional topics (e.g., fears, pets, curiosity, and companions), and he involved himself in the education of parents, particularly mothers, who in the 1920s were expected to provide almost all childcare (Brooks-Gunn & Johnson, 2006). His bibliography reveals a massive and programmatic effort to understand the mind and behavior of the child (see 1923, pp. 597–616). Hall's experimental and conceptual work on children apparently owed much to Theodate Louise Smith, who headed the Children's Institute at Clark. According to Sokal (1990), her interests "meshed effectively with Hall's . . . and contributed to some excellent science" (p. 121). The work of Hall, Smith, and others in the child study movement met a great public need and elevated the visibility and status of psychology. Hall's work contributed to the impression that psychology had something important to say about the real problems of living.

The child study movement was not restricted to the United States. Indeed, Hall had many counterparts in other countries. In Germany, Wilhelm Preyer (1841–1897) was an important pioneer in childhood studies. His book *The Mind of the Child* (1882) is one of the great classics in the field. In England, James Sully (1842–1923) wrote numerous books and articles on childhood. In France, Hippolyte Adolphe Taine (1828–1893) wrote an important early paper on lingual development in infancy. These early pioneers and others paved the way for the continuing emphasis on childhood in the work of people such as Binet, Freud, and Piaget.

As noted earlier, Hall's larger interest was in life-span development from infancy to old age, and he described his own aging process in an article that he intended to be anonymous (Hall, 1921), at least until he was identified by former students (Morse, 1920; Hall, 1921). His final book, *Senescence*, first published in 1922, is a classic work in the study of aging (Cole, 1993). Hall examined the treatment of the elderly in various cultures, along with literature by and on elderly people. He then turned to actuarial and mortality tables and pointed to the inevitable problems associated with the changing age demography, already evident in his day. He reviewed national old-age pension plans in other countries and stated, "The United States is the only nation that has no retirement system or provision for old age, even for its employees, save for soldiers and for judges of the Supreme Court" (1922, p. 180). On this matter, Hall was ahead of his time. It had been argued that a national retirement plan would undermine individual responsibility and that it ran counter to the best interests of a capitalistic society. Then, with the Great Depression,

responsible families were devastated through no fault of their own. As a result of such widespread financial disaster, especially for the elderly, the Social Security Act of 1935 brought the United States into line with other nations. Hall would have approved because he was aware of countless elderly people in his day who were financially destitute.

Hall (1922) called for the creation of a kind of "senescent league of national dimensions" (p. 194) with educational, political, and social divisions that would serve an advocacy role for the elderly. The latter part of *Senescence* presents results of an attitude survey that Hall conducted on topics such as sources of pleasure, belief in an afterlife, death anxiety, beliefs about longevity, and recognition of the signs of aging.

Hall had many other interests, especially in education and pedagogy (Fagan, 1992), the history of psychology (Bringmann et al., 1992), and the psychology of religion (Vande Kemp, 1992). He was especially interested in the effects of religious education on youth. His book *Jesus the Christ, in the Light of Psychology* (1917) represents a kind of "working through" of tensions between his early Calvinistic background and his natural-science approach to psychology.

In terms of his influence on both the basic and the applied dimensions of psychology, his innovations, his selling of psychology to the public, and his specific developmental-evolutionary perspective and its subsequent influence, Hall must be counted as one of the great psychologists.

Functionalism and the University of Chicago

In her classic book *Seven Psychologies*, Edna Heidbreder (1933) referred to the University of Chicago as "the capital of a new school" (p. 201). The term *capital* is appropriate because, whereas the functionalist perspective dominated thought in many U.S. and European universities, it was nowhere more articulated than at the University of Chicago. The two elder leaders of the Chicago

305

school, John Dewey and James Rowland Angell, studied respectively with G. Stanley Hall and William James. The third leader of the Chicago school, Harvey Carr, completed his degree under Angell at Chicago.

John Dewey

Regarded by many as America's most important philosopher of education, **John Dewey (1859–1952)** played a key role in launching functionalism. Dewey was born in Burlington, Vermont, and he graduated from the University of Vermont in 1879. Following a brief teaching career, he enrolled in the graduate program in philosophy at Johns Hopkins University. During that period, he studied with G. Stanley Hall and wrote a doctoral dissertation on the psychology of Immanuel Kant. He earned a Ph.D. from Johns Hopkins in 1884 and accepted a teaching assignment in psychology and philosophy at the University of Michigan. In 1894, he accepted an appointment as chair of psychology and philosophy at the University of Chicago. During his decade at Chicago, Dewey made his most visible contributions to psychology's functionalist viewpoint. In 1904, he moved from Chicago to Columbia University where he focused on the philosophy of education as well as a wide range of social, philosophical, and political topics (Cochran, 2010). Dewey's long and productive career came to an end in his ninety-second year, on June 1, 1952.

Dewey's classic article "The Reflex Arc Concept in Psychology," published in 1896, is so pivotal in the history of the functionalist school that Edwin G. Boring (1953) referred to it as "a declaration of independence for American functional psychology" (p. 146). In obvious celebration of Dewey's general philosophical and psychological orientation, William James wrote in 1903, "It rejoices me greatly that your school (I mean your philosophic school) at the University of Chicago is, after this long gestation, bringing its fruits to birth in a way that will demonstrate its great unity and vitality"

(1903/1980, p. 204). What features of Dewey's thought warranted such praise?

Like James, Dewey believed that philosophy must begin with experience. Furthermore, experience must be understood in a naturalistic context (Brinkmann, 2013). Dewey was critical of earlier idealistic philosophers whose concepts were not wedded to observable events in the world. As with James, Dewey was friendly to a pluralistic view that placed emphasis on the irreducible and unique features of the experiences of individual human beings. Dewey's article "The Reflex Arc Concept in Psychology" criticized attempts to dissect experience into artificial piecemeal units. Such dissection is inappropriate even for simple reflexes, let alone more complicated behaviors. Furthermore, such dissection violates what is found in experience and departs from an empirical approach to psychology.

Dewey asked his readers to consider the term *reflex*: Do we ever really consider the stimulus as a thing in itself or the response as a thing in itself? Such a distinction is unlikely except in a highly artificial laboratory situation. Dewey (1896) argued that a reflex is not "a patchwork of disjointed parts, a mechanical conjunction of unallied processes" (p. 358). Instead, what we encounter is "a continuously ordered sequence of acts, all adapted in themselves and in the order of their sequence, to reach a certain objective end" (p. 366). The ends we seek, such as reproduction, safety, and locomotion, call attention to motivation and to observable behaviors associated with motivation. Shook (1995) has documented Wundt's influence on Dewey's earliest writings. However, Dewey found too much reduction and abstraction in the older psychologies and a failure to appreciate the special ends or functions of psychological processes.

Boring (1953) offered the opinion that "after Dewey went to Columbia in 1904 his mission to the new psychology was largely accomplished, like the mission of any parent when the child has grown up" (p. 147). Boring's statement is applicable to Dewey's mission to academic psychology; he continued, however, to have an influence on applied psychology, especially in educational circles (Jackson, 1998). Dewey's continued interest in the applied arena was fueled by a combination of interests in U.S. democracy, economics (Tilman & Knapp, 1999), schools, art (Jackson, 1998), the nature of learning, and his own six children.

According to Soltis (1971), Dewey believed "democracy was more than a form of government; it was a way of living that went beyond politics, votes, and laws to pervade all aspects of society" (p. 84). Accordingly, Dewey believed schools should afford firsthand opportunities for children to learn democracy and see it in action. Dewey's cardinal rule of education was that we learn by doing and by reflecting on what happened. So if we want to promote democracy, it should be learned in schools. Dewey believed that the educational system should respect individuality and promote individual rights but at the same time should challenge our ethnocentrism (Blackmore, 2013). He opposed mere imitation, regimentation, and rote learning. Such learning, he felt, prepares us not for democracy but for totalitarianism. Dewey was a premier figure in the founding of functionalism and progressive education (Hilgard, 1996).

James Rowland Angell

Like Dewey, **James Rowland Angell (1869–1949)** was born in Burlington, Vermont. Angell's college work was at the University of Michigan, where he completed a B.A. in 1890 and an M.A. in 1891. Miles (1949) noted that a highlight in Angell's experience at Michigan was "a seminar with Dewey on William James' recently published *Principles of Psychology*" (p. 1). In fact, Angell declared that James's "book, more than any other, profoundly influenced his thinking for the next twenty years of his life" (p. 1). Following the completion of his work at Michigan, Angell enrolled at Harvard University where he worked with William James and the philosopher Josiah Royce (1855–1916). In his autobiography, Angell (1930/1961)

reflected on studying Kant with Royce and abnormal psychology with James (p. 7).

Following his year at Harvard, Angell traveled to Germany where he enjoyed lectures from leading scholars in psychology, philosophy, and physiology. At the University of Halle, Angell submitted a dissertation on the meaning of freedom in Kant's philosophical work. His work was accepted, subject to revision. Rather than revising the dissertation, he accepted a position as instructor of philosophy and psychology at the University of Minnesota. Ironically, Angell received several honorary doctorates and was instrumental in granting many doctorates, but he never completed the formalities associated with his own Ph.D.

After one year at Minnesota, Angell joined the faculty at the University of Chicago where he and Dewey crossed paths again. Angell was discouraged because, in his words, "For seven years I received no promotion in rank and no advance in salary" (1930/1961, p. 13). He was finally promoted to associate professor in 1901 and to professor in 1904. Angell believed his promotion was granted because other universities such as Princeton had offered him faculty positions. In 1905, Angell became head of the psychology department at Chicago and then dean of the faculties in 1911. After that point in his career, Angell remained in administrative work. He served as dean at Chicago and then acting president. In World War I, he served with Walter Dill Scott on the Committee on Classification of Personnel. In 1921, Angell became president of Yale University where he served with distinction until his retirement in 1937. Following retirement, Angell worked as an educational counselor for the National Broadcasting Company. He died in New Haven, Connecticut, on March 4, 1949.

Angell's contributions to psychology are all the more remarkable in view of his enormous time commitments to administration (Dewsbury, 2003). His most visible contributions to psychology were produced during his tenure at the University of Chicago. In 1904, he published a text, *Psychology*, that went through four editions.

In 1907, Angell published an article titled "The Province of Functional Psychology" based on his presidential address to the American Psychological Association. This work is regarded as a classic exposition of the functionalist school.

Although Dewey is often viewed as the founder of the Chicago school of functional psychology, Angell is recognized for making these views more systematic (Backe, 2001). Angell argued that functionalism was really not new: It had been around since Aristotle and, in modern times, since Spencer and Darwin. The first mark of the functionalist orientation, according to Angell (1930/1961), is that it involves "the identification and description of mental *operations*, rather than the mere *stuff* of mental experience" (p. 28). The second mark of functionalism is that it is concerned with the conditions or circumstances that evoke a mental state. A mental state does not exist in isolation; it must be understood in social and biological context. Finally, Angell argued that mental states or events must be understood in terms of how they contribute "to the furtherance of the sum total of organic activities, considered as adaptive" (1930/1961, p. 28). In other words, he asked, what contributions do mental events make to our adjustment to the world? These three marks of a functionalist psychology go a long way from a merely descriptive psychology of the stuff of consciousness. Although Angell did not adhere to an explicit evolutionary psychology (Gangestad, 2012), his emphasis on adaptation in the functionalist approach is illustrated in studies of animal behavior, developmental psychology, and psychopathology. A functionalist psychology is inherently social and biological and emphasizes experience and behavior in the service of adaptation.

In his autobiography, Angell commented on other developments in his day. He found that psychoanalysis offered some sound contributions, but was troubled about parts that seemed romantic and unscientific. As for the testing movement, he was concerned about its premature application in industry and education, but saw potential if used properly.

Angell and Dewey were forces in U.S. psychology despite the fact that other activities outside psychology commanded their interests. They both served as president of the American Psychological Association (Dewey in 1899 and Angell in 1906). Also, both were named to the most prestigious scientific society in America—the National Academy of Sciences. According to Miles (1949), Angell, who was elected in 1920, was the sixth psychologist named to the academy. Others were James McKeen Cattell (1901), William James (1903), Josiah Royce (1906), John Dewey (1910), and G. Stanley Hall (1915).

Harvey A. Carr

The consolidation and extension of the functionalist position took place under the leadership of Angell's student, **Harvey A. Carr (1873–1954)**. Born in Indiana, Carr was educated at DePauw University and later at the University of Colorado at Boulder where he came under the influence of Arthur Allin, a disciple of G. Stanley Hall. After completing a master's degree at Colorado, Carr enrolled in the doctoral program at the University of Chicago. His dissertation, directed by Angell, was completed in 1905. Carr worked in a high school in Texas and then at the Pratt Institute before returning to the University of Chicago in 1908. He remained at Chicago until 1938, chairing the department through much of that period. Under his leadership, Chicago became one of the leading schools in psychology.

Carr contended that psychology is concerned with mental activity. By *mental activity*, he referred to "the acquisition, fixation, retention, organization, and evaluation of experiences, and their subsequent utilization in the guidance of conduct" (1925, p. 1). Both experience and behavior (conduct) are central features of functionalism as interpreted by Carr. He argued, "The type of conduct that reflects mental activity may be termed adaptive or adjustive behavior" (p. 1). Adaptation or adjustment, according to Carr, involves a response that alters a situation so as to satisfy a motivating stimulus. A motivating stimulus may be a hunger pang, an itch, excessive temperature, pain, and so forth. Clearly, the subject of motivation is elevated in the functionalist system.

Carr accepted a variety of methods, including introspection and objective observation, and he investigated animal as well as human cognition (Dewsbury, 2000). He questioned whether the methods of all the sciences are really comparable. For example, he noted that "geology, astronomy, and mathematics are usually regarded as sciences, but are they experimental in the usual laboratory sense of the term?" (1930/1961, p. 80). Carr expressed doubt "that the experimental method—in the usual sense of that term—is the only scientific method" (p. 81). In his view, psychologists should not be doctrinaire about method, but attend, first and foremost, to the nature of the problem.

Carr, like Angell, believed in a psychology broad in scope, encompassing problems in learning, motivation, psychopathology, education, sensation, perception, and development. Like Angell, he believed all problems should be examined in terms of biological and social context.

The Chicago functionalists devoted little space to the metaphysical problems that occupied other psychologists. Carr, in his book *Psychology: The Study of Mental Activity*, discussed free will and determinism, but seemed most interested in the ways freedom might have meaning and utility. Such a position is consistent with the functionalist agenda. The metaphysical status of the two positions was not of great interest, but the meanings of the two positions—their utility, the work they accomplish, or the various meanings they convey—were important problems. Believing that freedom is acquired through knowledge, he quoted with approval the injunction, "Seek the truth and the truth shall make you free" (1925, p. 332).

Psychology at Columbia University

We encounter another clear expression of functionalism in the early psychology at Columbia University. Nurtured and developed by James McKeen Cattell, the psychology department at Columbia became one of the most visible and productive in the United States.

James McKeen Cattell

One of psychology's more colorful and controversial figures, **James McKeen Cattell (1860–1944)** found his way to fame in his chosen discipline via an unusual route. His research program failed and, compared to others, he published few papers. Yet, for a time, he was one of the most visible and powerful figures in the discipline. He won his place in history through editorial and administrative skills. Through his editorial efforts, the experimental and conceptual work of psychologists was brought to the attention of other scientists and the public. The discipline of psychology enjoyed center-stage attention that might not have been possible without Cattell's unique contributions.

Cattell was a gifted student, graduating in 1880 with honors from Lafayette College in Easton, Pennsylvania. Following two years of travel and study in Europe, Cattell returned to the United States to enroll in philosophy at Johns Hopkins University. Despite excellent work in G. Stanley Hall's laboratory at Hopkins, his fellowship for the second year was not renewed. Reasons for the transfer of the fellowship from Cattell to John Dewey are not clear. Sokal (1980b) referred to Cattell's "continual bickering with Daniel Coit Gilman, the university president" (p. 43) as well as Cattell's arrogance and his antagonistic manner (2016), and Ross (1972, p. 145) implicated G. Stanley Hall in the decision. For whatever reason, Cattell moved from Baltimore to Leipzig and, as noted by Sokal (1980b), "became the first

American to earn a Ph.D. in experimental psychology from Wilhelm Wundt at Leipzig" (p. 43).

Following his work at Leipzig, Cattell went to England, where he worked with Francis Galton. Galton's obsession with the measurement of bodily and mental attributes had a profound influence on Cattell. On the philosophical side, he had earlier been influenced by a Baconian vision for an empirical approach to the study of mental processes. Galton's work helped Cattell translate his philosophical biases into an experimental program (Young, 2013).

Following work with Galton, Cattell returned to the United States in 1889 to accept an appointment at the University of Pennsylvania. In 1891, he accepted a position at Columbia University, which he held until 1917. Cattell's research programs at Pennsylvania and Columbia focused on the development of *mental tests*, a term he coined in 1890 (see Beins, 2010; Cattell, 1890). In Cattell's day, there were high expectations that mental abilities could be measured and that such measurements would have the most salutary consequences for schools and industry. The problem was to develop mental tests with demonstrated predictive efficiency. Cattell, following the lead of Galton, measured simple reaction times, complex reaction times, visual acuity, auditory acuity, strength of grip, and the like.

As noted by Sokal (1980b), Cattell's measurements "literally correlated with nothing. The result killed his career as a psychological tester and redirected his efforts away from experimental psychology" (p. 47). As we will see later, Binet and Henri reviewed Cattell's work and then developed different tests with predictive efficiency (Nicolas, Coubart, & Lubart, 2014). Though Cattell's research program failed, he established laboratories at the University of Pennsylvania and at Columbia University. Also, at Columbia, he helped promote one of the most active doctoral programs in psychology.

In 1894, Cattell embarked on work as an editor, a career that would span a half-century. One of his greatest accomplishments involved the journal *Science*. A New York journalist named John Michaels founded the interdisciplinary journal in 1880 with financial support from inventor Thomas Edison and later from Alexander Graham Bell. Despite such support, *Science* fell into serious financial difficulty. In 1894, Cattell purchased the journal for $500. *Science* provided an outlet for research in many fields, including physics, chemistry, biology, geology, and psychology. Cattell took over as editor of *Science* and established policies that rescued the journal and improved its visibility (see Sokal, 1980b). It was remarkable that a psychologist edited such an important outlet for all the sciences. As a result, psychology articles found their way into the prestigious journal alongside research from more established scientific disciplines.

In 1893, Cattell joined forces with James Mark Baldwin (1861–1934) to purchase G. Stanley Hall's *The American Journal of Psychology* (Sokal, 1997). When Hall refused to sell, Cattell and Baldwin founded the *Psychological Review* one year later, a journal that still occupies a central place in the discipline. In time, Cattell and Baldwin went on to found a family of successful journals including the *Psychological Index* and *Psychological Monographs*. According to Johnson (2000), Hall's journals had a broader focus, whereas "the Baldwin and Cattell journals represented a narrower view of psychology, publishing more specialized experimental articles than general or theoretical articles and considerably fewer applied articles" (p. 1146). After years of feuding, Cattell and Baldwin dissolved their partnership in 1903. *Psychological Review* was sold to the American Psychological Association in 1925.

Cattell edited a variety of other journals. From 1900 to 1915, he served as editor of the magazine *Popular Science Monthly*. Under Cattell's leadership, *Popular Science Monthly* included articles on psychology to satisfy an ever-growing public demand for information on topics such as child rearing, animal behavior, psychopathology, and mental testing. Cattell also served as editor of the *American Naturalist* from 1907 to 1944 and *School and Society* from 1915 to 1939. Although not exhaustive, this list of his editorial responsibilities conveys the central role he occupied with respect to communication of scientific information. How did Cattell edit so many journals? He enlisted his graduate students and his wife and children to run his science publication machine. Most notably Cattell's wife, Josephine Owen Cattell, played a key role in the publication of *Science*.

In 1921, Cattell founded the Psychological Corporation as a "commercial firm designed to implement his 1904 call for an applied psychology" (Sokal, 2006, p. 32). The corporation made psychological services such as consulting and testing available in business and industrial settings. Cattell (1937/1992) correctly predicted in the first volume of his *Journal of Consulting Psychology* that professional psychology would thrive in the twentieth century (Garfield, 1992). Another of Cattell's most noteworthy achievements was his work to recognize outstanding achievement in science. He founded the reference series *American Men of Science*, later to become *American Men and Women of Science*, and developed a rating system as a means of establishing eminence (Sokal, 1995). His system, however, was not always received with enthusiasm. For example, in 1903, Cattell asked William James to participate in an exercise to rank psychologists. James complied but expressed his suspicion about fine-tuned rankings. He also argued that the nature of the work of different individuals is not always homogeneous enough to warrant meaningful comparisons. With characteristic Jamesian honesty, he said, "Permit me to say that in my private breast *you* stand lower now than you did before I got this problem from you!" (1903/1986b, p. 313).

Many honors came to Cattell during his life. One of the original founders of the American Psychological Association, he served as its fourth president. As a powerful advocate for science and academic life, Cattell held strong opinions on many issues and did not hesitate to express them. Indeed, his stinging criticisms of key political and university officials ultimately led to his dismissal from Columbia University. There have been disagreements over the justifications for the firing of Cattell (see Gates, 1968; Sokal, 2009, 2011), but there can be little question that he made some important and unique contributions to the early development of psychology.

Robert Sessions Woodworth

One of the essential features of functionalism is that it broadened the scope of psychological inquiry. Both basic and applied problems were legitimate and there was an extension of research into areas such as learning and motivation. **Robert Sessions Woodworth (1869–1962)** became a key figure in the subject area of motivation.

Woodworth was born in Belchertown, Massachusetts. Even as a youngster, Woodworth had broad-ranging academic interests that included music, philosophy, mathematics, and science. Initially, he planned to follow his father into a career in the ministry. On graduating from Amherst in 1891, he still considered the ministry as he taught science and mathematics classes to raise money for additional education.

Woodworth's experiences as a teacher caused him to reassess his vocational plans. Poffenberger (1962) claimed, "He entered Harvard in the autumn of 1895, fairly well committed to a teaching career in philosophy and psychology" (p. 678). Poffenberger pointed out that, while at Harvard, Woodworth worked with William James and developed friendships with fellow graduate students E. L. Thorndike and W. B. Cannon. He earned an M.A. degree from Harvard but then transferred to Columbia, where he graduated with a Ph.D. in psychology in 1899. Woodworth studied in Scotland and in England where he worked with the famous physiologist Sir Charles Sherrington. Woodworth held temporary instructorships before accepting a regular faculty position at Columbia in 1903. With the exception of the brief temporary assignments, Woodworth spent his entire academic career at Columbia University. Woodworth's lengthy career spanned six decades until his death at age ninety-two on July 4, 1962.

Woodworth is often categorized as a functionalist. However, he did not think of himself as a member of a school, but as an experimental psychologist seeking to understand cause–effect relationships in experience and behavior. Woodworth's published contributions to psychology extend over two hundred papers and ten books. Though he made substantive contributions in many areas, three areas are noteworthy.

First, as noted by Murphy (1963), under Woodworth's leadership, "the term *experimental* was extended to more and more kinds and fields of research endeavor" (p. 131). In 1938, he published *Experimental Psychology*, a book so influential it was known as the "Columbia Bible" (Winston, 1990). In the introduction to the revised edition, Woodworth and Schlosberg (1954) noted that the field of psychology started with a few scattered experiments conducted by scientists from several other disciplines, but after years of hard work, experimental psychology encompassed the fields of learning, memory, thinking, attention, emotion, and motivation. Though Woodworth extended experimental psychology to a widening field of subjects, he narrowed the concept of what counts as an experiment. We return to this topic later.

Woodworth's second contribution relates to the first but deserves special treatment. Specifically, in his work, we encounter a new and broader emphasis on the concept of motivation. Like the study of emotion, research on motivation had carried over from the previous century as a popular topic for psychologists (Edwards, 1999). Woodworth took issue with an exclusively biogenic approach to motivation. He did not believe that all motives have their origin in instincts or in metabolic processes. He drew attention to learned drives and to the idea that there are "activities that have intrinsic incentive value" (Woodworth & Schlosberg, 1954, p. 685). Thus, play, manipulation, exploration, and even some forms of work may, in his words, "function autonomously" (p. 686).

The notion of **functional autonomy**, encountered later in the psychology of Gordon Allport (1937, 1955), refers to the idea that a means or mechanism for satisfying a motive may acquire drive properties. For example, a person may work at a bookstore as a means of earning a living. In time, however, he or she becomes acquainted with a good book and develops a strong drive to spend time each day reading. What started as a mere "means" has now become an acquired motive and is sustained because of its own intrinsic merits.

Woodworth's concept of motivation extended into the realm of the unconscious. Seward and Seward (1968), for example, pointed out that Woodworth "anticipated Freud in considering the dream to be the result of perseverating wishes; however, his theory rested on a broader base than Freud's, inasmuch as he believed that wishes underlying dreams might pertain to any area of interest" (p. 562). Thus, the wish behind a dream, according to Woodworth, need not be sexual; rather, it might be based on any strong human need such as a need for achievement, recognition, and security.

Woodworth called his approach *dynamic psychology*. The term *dynamic* refers to the importance of understanding the causes of behavior. Woodworth assumed that causes are not always reducible to a simple stimulus–response (S–R) formula. He argued that the S–R concept should be replaced by a stimulus–organism–response (S–O–R) concept. The S–O–R formulation emphasizes the crucial role of the organism in the sequence. Examples of organismic variables, according to Woodworth, include learned motives, expectations, readiness to respond, and personal characteristics such as cautiousness or fearfulness.

A third contribution came through Woodworth's influential textbooks. His introductory text titled *Psychology*, first published in 1921, was widely used, but the text that had the greatest influence on academic psychology was his *Experimental Psychology* (Winston, 2006). For over two decades, the book served as a standard reference for students preparing for graduate school. Noteworthy for its breadth, Woodworth's text reviewed classic studies and methodologies in a host of content areas including psychophysics, association, emotion, sensation, learning, motivation, memory, and problem solving.

Though Woodworth expanded sensitivity to the scope of experimental psychology, he also narrowed what counted as an experiment with a distinction between correlational and experimental research (Winston, 1990). Woodworth emphasized the importance of independent and dependent variables and experimental control. Winston (1990) noted that "nearly all textbooks, both introductory and experimental, adopted Woodworth's conceptualization of 'experiment'" (p. 397). Woodworth's definition of an *experiment* elevated the importance of "wet-lab" approaches to psychology and enhanced the scientific image of the discipline. In later years, however, the term *experiment* often has broader meanings. Thus, there are activities of astronomers that could possibly be viewed as experimental, even though variables are not manipulated in the usual sense. The discovery of a new planet, for example, may arise from hypothesis testing and controlled observation, but the procedure is not readily comparable to the typical experiment.

Woodworth made many additional contributions to the discipline of psychology. For example, he developed an early personality test to evaluate soldiers in World War I (Gibby & Zickar, 2008), but he may be best known for his famous studies with Edward Lee Thorndike on the transfer of training (discussed in Chapter 13). He did extensive editorial work for psychological journals and served as president of the American Psychological Association in 1914. In 1956, the American Psychological Foundation awarded Woodworth the Gold Medal for his outstanding contributions to the discipline.

Mary Whiton Calkins

Shortly after 1900, functionalism gained momentum as the dominant orientation in numerous universities. However, some scholars sought to preserve the best in structuralism and functionalism. One such person was **Mary Whiton Calkins (1863–1930),** the founder of an early psychology laboratory in the United States.

In the 1880s and 1890s, progressive colleges and universities encouraged the growth and development of psychology laboratories. Calkins, a young Greek and philosophy instructor at Wellesley College, was given the opportunity to establish a laboratory on the condition that she take time off and pursue advanced studies in psychology. She explored numerous options but encountered restrictions against women in most leading institutions in Europe and the United States. Initially rejected at Harvard, she was finally permitted to enroll on the condition that the courses would not count for a degree. She took a course with William James and later conducted research in Hugo Münsterberg's laboratory. Her work was of a distinguished quality and, in 1895, she presented a thesis and was given an unauthorized examination. The examining

Mary Whiton Calkins

313

committee included distinguished faculty: James, Münsterberg, Josiah Royce (1855–1916), and George Santayana (1863–1952). They affirmed that she met all doctoral requirements, but Harvard refused to grant the degree. Furumoto (1979) has outlined the details of her studies and the controversy over the degree.

Though she never received the Harvard doctorate she had earned, Calkins established the laboratory at Wellesley and became a productive scholar. In 1905, she was elected as the fourteenth president of the American Psychological Association. She taught at Wellesley College until her retirement in 1929.

Calkins believed that *psychology* should be defined as the science of the conscious self. Although not a popular cause at the time, she was, for three decades, the most visible advocate of self-psychology. Wentworth (1999) concluded that Calkins's vigorous defense of the science of selves was, in part, rooted in her beliefs about ethics, religion, and morality. She viewed mind or consciousness as the ultimate reality and, in that sense, belonged to the idealist tradition and to a philosophical tradition known as *personalism*. Calkins (1906) argued that if the self is the focus of psychology, then there is room for reconciliation between structuralism and functionalism. Calkins believed that human consciousness is understood in terms of its environmental contexts. The functionalist engages in such explorations and thus makes valuable contributions. Consciousness must also be understood in its own terms as a reality unlike any lower reality from which it emerged. The structuralist is more likely to provide insights into the unique and irreducible dimensions of consciousness, but even in the search for elements of sensation she emphasized the role of the self of the perceiver (Calkins, 1906). She found a place for both functionalism and structuralism, a theme echoed in Calkins's presidential address before the American Psychological Association in 1905.

Calkins made additional contributions to psychology, including early development of the *paired associate method* as a means of studying retention. This method required research subjects to learn an association between a pair of stimulus–response terms such as *desk–moon* or *orange–hat*. When given the stimulus term *desk*, the participant would be expected to respond with the term *moon*. Calkins's short-term memory studies anticipated later developments in memory research (Madigan & O'Hara, 1992).

Calkins (1893) also conducted one of the first formal studies of dreams. She kept track of her dreams for fifty-five nights, waking herself up at various intervals to record dreams in a journal. Her colleague, Edmund Clark Sanford (1859–1924), recorded his dreams for forty-six nights, and together they made several insightful findings. She accurately concluded that people dream every night, that four dreams are common in an average night, and that we can, to a degree, control our dreams. Several years later, Sigmund Freud acknowledged Calkins's seminal work in his book *The Interpretation of Dreams*. She is remembered appropriately as one of the pioneers who, in the words of Pratola (1974), demonstrated despite tremendous obstacles that "women have a rightful place in scientific and academic endeavors" (p. 780).

The Growth of Applied Psychology

Earlier we encountered Münsterberg's contention that psychological experiments should be placed in the service of practical day-to-day interests. Inspired by functionalism, many psychologists geared their research to problems and issues of daily living. Such research left its mark on public institutions and helped mold public and scientific attitudes about the practical value of psychology. An example of research that attacked and helped change public and scientific attitudes is visible in the work of Leta Stetter Hollingworth.

Leta Stetter Hollingworth

In the late nineteenth and early twentieth centuries, the so-called **variability hypothesis** formed part of the explanation for the differential achievements of men and women in science, music, law, and so on (Shields, 1975). Briefly stated, the variability hypothesis held that men are physically and psychologically more variable than women. According to the hypothesis, women tended toward averages in all things, whereas men showed greater variety; men were thought to be more courageous but more cowardly, more virtuous but more corrupt, more intelligent but more stupid, and more violent but more peaceful. Superficial support for the variability hypothesis was found in the achievements of men compared to women and in the finding that more boys compared to girls were diagnosed with cognitive disabilities. Evidence against the variability hypothesis had been set forth in a classic study by Karl Pearson (1897). Pearson calculated means and measures of variability on literally thousands of boys and girls ages six through ten. Among other things, he examined height, weight, strength of grip, visual acuity, and numerous cranial measures. He found no reliable evidence for differential variability between boys and girls; despite these findings the variability hypothesis persisted.

Leta Stetter Hollingworth (1886–1939) was aware of Pearson's work, but decided to test the contention that males are physically and psychologically more variable than females at birth (Shields, 1975). She conducted this study with the support of her advisor, Edward Lee Thorndike, despite Thorndike's support of the variability hypothesis (Shields, 1991). Hollingworth's study, unlike Pearson's studies, reduced possible effects of environmental influences on variability. It is altogether fitting it would be a woman who would deliver the deathblow to the variability hypothesis. Born Leta A. Stetter, she was reared in Nebraska and earned her bachelor's degree at the University of Nebraska and her Ph.D. at Columbia University in 1916. Benjamin (1975)

called attention to the fact that many early psychologists made claims for the inferiority of women. Such claims were sometimes derived from the predictions of the variability hypothesis.

As a means of investigating the variability hypothesis, Hollingworth compared male and female infants on a variety of physical characteristics such as height, birth weight, and cranial circumference. She found no differences in variability on any of the physical characteristics she explored. Male infants were slightly larger than females at birth, but were not more variable. Hollingworth acknowledged that more boys than girls were admitted to residential treatment for people with cognitive disabilities, but in early twentieth-century America, more was expected of boys and hence a boy with a cognitive disability was more likely to be detected. She argued that greater male achievements are the result of unequal educational opportunities. Girls had almost no vocational options; hence, achievement was next to impossible.

Hollingworth (1914) also conducted research that showed that the perceptual, motor, and mental abilities of women are not adversely affected during the menstrual cycle, a discovery that undercut another early twentieth-century myth that women could never compete with men because of a monthly incapacity brought about by menstruation. Hollingworth's studies together with Pearson's studies now count as classics in the psychology of women and made important contributions to the reduction of prejudices that had prevented equal educational opportunities for women.

Following World War I, Hollingworth became active in clinical research on individual differences in intelligence, an area like the psychology of women that was "fraught with myth and misunderstanding" (Shields, 1991, p. 248). During the course of her prestigious career, Hollingworth (1920, 1942) focused on two extreme populations of children—children with cognitive disabilities and gifted children with IQs above 180. She was one of the first to apply intelligence testing and longitudinal studies to questions of gifted

315

education (Berman & Schultz, 2013), and she applied psychological research to curriculum development and other aspects of educational practice (Hertberg-Davis, 2014). Her work resulted in the celebrated book *The Psychology of the Adolescent* (1928) as well as a variety of conceptual issues that remain relevant for contemporary professionals (Klein, 2000).

Helen Wooley

Like Leta Hollingworth and Margaret Floy Washburn, **Helen Wooley (1874–1947)** was one of the first generation of women to receive a Ph.D. in experimental psychology (see Furumoto & Scarborough, 1986; Milar, 1999). After receiving her doctorate from the University of Chicago in 1900, Wooley became a pioneer in educational psychology and the study of gender differences.

As a backdrop to her work, child labor laws played a critical role in humanitarian reform movements during the time psychology emerged as a new discipline. In that tradition, Wooley served as the director of the Vocation Bureau in the public schools in Cincinnati, Ohio, from 1911 to 1921. As director, she worked on numerous problems such as the consequences of dropping out of school (Wooley & Hart, 1921) and how to best match educational programs with the intellectual and vocational abilities of children. Milar (1999) reviewed Wooley's work on a massive longitudinal study of students who remain in school compared with adolescents who drop out of school to enter the workforce. Because of measurement issues, her study did not yield clear-cut results and conclusions. Such a disappointing outcome comes as no surprise to those who follow scientific attempts to investigate problems of a much simpler nature (e.g., trials on the effects of drugs often do not yield unequivocal results).

Milar (1999) points out, however, that despite the disappointing results of the longitudinal study, Wooley was singled out for praise as a pioneer in childhood education and welfare. Further, "The Vocational Bureau [headed by Wooley] was

one of the earliest psychological clinics in a public school and was used to support special education classes of various types and to consult with the juvenile courts" (Milar, 1999, p. 232). Wooley, as a part of the functionalist tradition, demonstrated strengths and limitations of psychology as a means of investigating practical social issues.

Binet and Intelligence Testing

Arguably, the measurement of intelligence became the most significant psychological research in terms of its lasting impact on public institutions. Earlier in the text, we referred to Galton's work on individual differences and to Cattell's unsuccessful attempts to measure intelligence. Shortly after 1901, the French experimental psychologist, **Alfred Binet (1857–1911)**, declared his intention to measure intelligence by means of special tests. Early in his career, Binet flirted with research on physiognomy, the theory that physical appearance can reveal aspects of character (Collins, 1999), and he explored reaction times and sensory acuity as assessments for children (Esping & Plucker, 2015). After numerous failures, Binet and his collaborator, Théodore Simon (1873–1961), constructed a scale generally regarded as the first successful intelligence test to assess individual differences.

Binet is not associated with any of the dominant systems of psychology but, in her biography on Binet, Wolf (1973) argued that "he was in fact completely absorbed by the ideas of the functional viewpoints and terminology, by concerns about the nature of consciousness, and by the need for comparative and developmental studies" (p. 4). As an experimental psychologist, Binet's interests were wide ranging. In addition to work on intelligence, he conducted studies on topics such as hypnosis, attention, creativity, graphology, handwriting analysis, and eyewitness testimony (Nicolas, Gounden, & Sanitioso, 2014; Nicolas et al., 2015). He assisted in the founding of the first French journal of psychology, *L'Année Psychologique*, and he helped found a laboratory

Alfred Binet

at the Sorbonne, which was not associated with a degree program and therefore struggled to attract students (Nicolas & Sanitioso, 2012).

After considerable trial and error, Binet attempted to measure intelligence in a way that departed from the earlier approaches of Galton and Cattell (Nicolas et al., 2014). According to Wolf (1973), Binet realized it might be possible to find differences "in complex superior processes rather than in elementary ones" (p. 146). Instead of studying simple reaction times, Binet looked at memory for numbers, ability to solve spatial or conceptual problems, and memory for designs. Test items were related to daily tasks. Binet also gathered normative data on types of problems that typical children in various age groups could solve. This approach yielded the first usable intelligence test, published in 1905 and revised in 1908 and again in 1911. The Binet–Simon scales, though ignored and even ridiculed in France,

were translated into other languages and hailed as a major achievement (Schneider, 1992).

Unlike later theorists, Binet viewed a child's score on the test as simply a score on a particular test on a particular day (Gould, 1981). From Binet's point of view, a child's intelligence test score could change with additional education. As discussed in Chapter 8, later thinkers, including Goddard, Terman, Yerkes, and others, reified IQ and viewed it as a genetic, unchangeable aspect of an individual, and this change had long-term consequences for both psychology and the larger culture.

Wolf (1973), quoting Simon, noted that educational psychologist and eugenicist Lewis Terman (1877–1956) purchased the rights to publish the first U.S. version of the Binet–Simon scale for $1. Terman translated the test, made adaptations, and standardized the test on a large group of American children. The first Terman adaptation was published in 1916 and was called the *Stanford–Binet Intelligence Scale*. (The name of the test was based partly on Terman's affiliation with Stanford University.) Later editions of the Stanford–Binet were published in 1937 and 1960. Alternatives to the Stanford–Binet test quickly surfaced and often featured special conveniences or applications. For example, in World War I, a paper-and-pencil test designed for group testing and known as the *Army Alpha* was developed by Robert M. Yerkes (1876–1956) and his associates as a means of screening large numbers of service personnel. An alternative, known as the *Army Beta*, was designed for personnel who were illiterate in English. Despite extensive racial and other biases, these tests were used as means of rejecting individuals for service and as an aid in making special assignments. Following the war, a steady growth in the use of intelligence tests led to a proliferation of different tests.

Though many theoretical and practical problems of measuring intelligence were solved early in the century, the social consequences of large-scale testing remain a concern. In his book *Even the Rat Was White*, Guthrie (2003) outlined the warnings of African-American psychologists about the dangers of mental testing and the pitfalls of cultural biases in tests. In his book *The Mismeasure of Man*, Gould (1981) outlined the history and social consequences of conceiving intelligence as a single thing and of characterizing human beings in terms of an abstract number that serves as a symbol of merit. Numerous additional sources on the history of testing (DuBois, 1970; Sokal, 1987; Sussman, 2014) are recommended reading.

Influence of Functionalism: An Evaluation

Functionalism grew out of a pluralistic, pragmatic, and radically empirical context and thus, as a philosophical psychology, was more inclined to open doors than to shut them. It entertained a host of interesting problems that affected the daily lives of people: the problems of child rearing, education, aging, the work environment, and emotional disorders. Furthermore, it refused to be restricted by narrow conceptions of the scientific method. Functionalism did not persist as an organized school or system of thought, but its values and vision were incorporated into subsequent schools. Indeed, as we will see in Chapter 13, John B. Watson, the founder of American behaviorism, specifically spoke of the functionalist nature of behaviorism (see 1913, p. 166).

There are numerous legitimate criticisms of functionalism. One of the more common criticisms is that it seems vague. Indeed, the typical student may read about functionalism and then experience difficulty expressing what the school is all about. A related criticism is that functionalism was eclectic and often inconsistent or even incoherent. The functionalists did not work within a tightly reasoned, rigidly prescriptive system of thought. The resulting looseness and inevitable ambiguities are sources of frustration. Examples abound, but we might illustrate the point by considering the functionalist treatment of freedom and determinism. Many psychologists took clear-cut and unequivocal stands on the issue so that there were no further questions to be asked.

James believed in free will, but thought it appropriate that scientists postulate the operation of lawfulness within their investigations. Harvey Carr left his readers with even greater ambiguities than James on the free will and determinism issue. He was willing to use both positions to see where they led.

Perhaps one of the appeals of the behaviorist system (which we will review in Chapter 13) was that it was more straightforward. The functionalists were not concerned about criticisms regarding their inconsistencies. In *The Principles*, James (1890/1981) argued that absolutism "is the great disease of philosophical thought" (p. 334). He believed that there are genuine ambiguities in the world and that systems that hide or cover up such ambiguities may achieve coherence and consistency, but these are won at the expense of adequacy.

Functionalism was also criticized for ignoring basic problems and focusing instead on applications. It is true that functionalists were interested in applications, but they also valued basic studies. What they rejected was a psychology that focused exclusively on basic science. Their emphasis was on the discovery of facts (basic science) and the understanding of what differences the facts make (applied science). This balance of emphasis became a hallmark of American psychology. In a real sense, much of the mainstream psychology of the early twenty-first century can be regarded as functionalist. Some psychologists worked within the tradition of basic science, whereas others were free to conduct research on practical day-to-day problems. Following the work of William James, G. Stanley Hall, and the Chicago and Columbia functionalists, there was a virtual explosion of interest in applied psychology.

Review Questions

1. List and briefly describe six general characteristics of William James's philosophy.
2. What advice might James give to someone who wishes to get rid of an undesirable habit?

3. List five characteristics that James found with respect to the so-called stream of thought.
4. What were the constituents of the self, according to William James?
5. Briefly explain James's concept of self-esteem and how self-esteem might be improved.
6. Explain and criticize the James–Lange theory of emotion.
7. What did James mean by the transiency of instincts? Give an example.
8. Distinguish between primary and secondary memory in James's psychology.
9. List five of G. Stanley Hall's major achievements.
10. How did Hall's book *Senescence* anticipate contemporary developments in the psychology and sociology of aging?
11. Outline the essential features of John Dewey's arguments in his classic article "The Reflex Arc Concept in Psychology."
12. List three characteristics of functionalism according to James R. Angell.
13. In what way did James McKeen Cattell contribute to the scientific stature and visibility of psychology?
14. Outline three major contributions to psychology made by Robert Sessions Woodworth.
15. What was the variability hypothesis and how did Leta Stetter Hollingworth study it?
16. According to Mary Calkins, how might structuralism and functionalism be reconciled?
17. Discuss three major criticisms of functionalism and explain how a functionalist might respond to each criticism.

Glossary

Angell, James Rowland (1869–1949) A powerful advocate of the functionalist viewpoint in U.S. psychology. He argued that psychology should emphasize mental operations rather than the "stuff of experience." His book *Psychology* and his classic article "The Province of Functional Psychology" are important expositions of functionalism.

Binet, Alfred (1857–1911) Early pioneer in intelligence testing. Binet and his collaborator, Théodore Simon, developed early assessments for children.

Calkins, Mary Whiton (1863–1930) First woman president of the American Psychological Association, who argued for a reconciliation of structuralism and functionalism. Advanced a personalistic psychology in which the self is the primary focus of study.

Carr, Harvey A. (1873–1954) The thirty-fifth president of the American Psychological Association, Carr helped consolidate and amplify the functionalist viewpoint in psychology. At the University of Chicago, he headed a powerful department of psychology that was one of the most prolific in Ph.D. production.

Cattell, James McKeen (1860–1944) A prominent leader in the U.S. functionalist tradition. Though he published little, he established a laboratory at Columbia University and headed a strong department in that institution. Cattell served as editor of numerous journals and magazines, including *Science*, *Popular Science Monthly*, *Psychological Review*, and *School and Society*. Through his efforts, psychology became more visible in the public consciousness and in the scientific community. He also advanced the cause of applied psychology, most notably by founding the Psychological Corporation.

Dewey, John (1859–1952) U.S. psychologist and philosopher and a key pioneer in the functionalist school of thought. Dewey argued for a process-oriented psychology emphasizing the study of adaptation. He argued against the concept of elements, whether they be units in consciousness or in the reflex.

functional autonomy Refers to the idea that the means for satisfying a motive may acquire drive properties. Thus, one might hunt to satisfy hunger, but later hunting acquires drive properties of its own and one now hunts for "sport."

functionalism A loosely knit system of psychology having its origin in the work of U.S.

319

scholars such as William James, John Dewey, and G. Stanley Hall. Functionalism emphasized a broad-based methodology applied to basic and applied problems associated with experience and behavior.

Hall, Granville Stanley (1844–1924) Pioneer U.S. psychologist and founder and first president of the American Psychological Association. Hall was awarded the first doctorate in psychology, founded several journals, and served as president of Clark University. One of the first developmental psychologists, Hall was the author of classic books such as *Adolescence* and *Senescence*.

Hollingworth, Leta Stetter (1886–1939) Psychologist and educator who was one of the first to subject gender differences to rigorous experimental scrutiny. Her work exposed several nineteenth-century myths regarding the intellectual status of women. She is also remembered for pioneering studies on gifted children.

James, William (1842–1910) U.S. psychologist and philosopher who was the author of several classics in both fields. James's two-volume *The Principles of Psychology* is one of the most influential books in the field. His *The Varieties of Religious Experience* and *Talks to Teachers* are pioneering efforts in the psychology of religion and educational psychology. His philosophical pluralism, pragmatism, and radical empiricism are still deeply imprinted in U.S. psychology and philosophy.

James–Lange theory of emotion A theory of emotion advanced independently by William James and Carl Lange. The theory emphasizes the somatic substrate of emotional experiences and argues that the experience of emotion is the experience of the activity of the body—thus, the famous statement: We see a bear, we run, and we are afraid. James's later vision of emotion emphasizes constitutional determinants and the impossibility of separating cognition and emotion.

Lange, Carl Georg (1834–1900) Danish physiologist remembered for a theory of emotion

comparable to one proposed by William James and subsequently known as the James–Lange theory. See also *James–Lange theory of emotion*.

Marston, William Moulton (1893–1947) Student of Hugo Münsterberg who popularized psychology, invented the polygraph, and created Wonder Woman.

material self In James's theory, the material self is the body, friends, and possessions such as clothing, house, and automobile.

Münsterberg, Hugo (1863–1916) German American psychologist and a pioneer in applied psychology with his research on forensic, clinical, and industrial psychology.

pluralism A philosophical position that emphasizes the importance of alternative perspectives (methodological pluralism) and the existence of many realities (metaphysical pluralism).

pragmatism A U.S. philosophical movement associated with the work of Charles S. Pierce and William James. According to pragmatism, concepts must be judged in terms of their cash value or the practical work they do in the world. Thus, truth is judged by utility and the practical consequences achieved by an idea.

primary memory According to William James, primary memory is memory associated with nerve vibrations that have not yet ceased. It is memory associated with the specious present, what is immediately held in consciousness, and somewhat akin to an afterimage.

radical empiricism The name William James employed to characterize his larger philosophic vision. Radical empiricism emphasizes the primacy of experience and argues that things genuinely encountered in experience must not be excluded from philosophical and scientific inquiry. Radical empiricism treats various monisms as hypotheses.

secondary memory In James's psychology, secondary memory is memory proper or memory of past events that are not in present consciousness.

self-esteem A topic explored by William James and discussed in his work as a function of the ratio of success to pretensions.

social self In James's view, a dimension of self-hood born in various social contexts. Thus, the self in the presence of a parent may be different in some respects than the self in the presence of a friend.

spiritual self In James's view, the self that is "the home of interest" or that sits in judgment of other selves. The spiritual self, for James, is also the source of effortful striving.

stream of thought A concept advanced by William James that illustrates his view that consciousness is not composed of static elements. According to James, even a strong stimulus, such as a clap of thunder, is not pure; rather, it is "thunder-breaking-upon-silence-and-contrasting-with-it." James regarded consciousness as ever changing; each successive thought, even of the same object, changes by some degree.

Sumner, Francis (1895–1954) A pioneer in the study of black psychology and the first African American to earn a doctorate in psychology in the United States.

variability hypothesis A commonly held nineteenth-century belief that, in all things physical and mental, men are more variable than women. The research of Leta Stetter Hollingworth effectively dismantled the variability hypothesis.

Woodworth, Robert Sessions (1869–1962) A pioneer psychologist in the functionalist tradition who greatly extended the domain of experimental psychology. Woodworth was one of the first U.S. psychologists to emphasize the centrality of motivation. His text *Experimental Psychology* may be the most important classic in the field.

Wooley, Helen (1874–1947) American psychologist who emphasized practical social problems in her research on educational psychology.

13 Behaviorism

Psychology as the behaviorist views it is a purely objective experimental branch of natural science. Its theoretical goal is the prediction and control of behavior.

—John B. Watson (1913)

The late twentieth and early twenty-first centuries have witnessed rapidly accelerating technical advances in robotics aided by space-age miniaturization and computer technology. Robots can now mimic the functions of the human hand and are increasingly endowed with sensory functions such as seeing, hearing, and touching. They execute extremely dangerous tasks such as undersea exploration or the disarming of bombs. They perform repetitive, mundane, and boring tasks and are adept and valuable in replacing body parts that are injured. They fly airplanes and play frightening, dangerous, deadly, and complicated roles in warfare. They drive cars, guide spaceships, monitor satellites, and help assemble complicated machinery such as automobiles.

The study of robotics once belonged largely to the fields of mechanical engineering, electronic and electrical engineering, and computer science, but increasingly other disciplines such as economics, sociology, philosophy, and psychology are key players in this highly successful field. An example of the role of psychologists is set forth in an article by Wang et al. (2015) who explore some of the dimensions of human–robot interaction. They refer to the pioneer roboticist Masahiro Mora who spoke of a possible "uncanny valley" in human–robotic relations. One might predict that our fondness for robots might grow as they become increasingly like us, but this may not be the case. The likeability of a robot might increase up to a point, but then fall into negative appraisal—the so-called uncanny valley. Why? There are many possible explanations, but robots often replace us, they do things we cannot do, and they have major economic implications for all of us. In becoming like us, they may become uncanny. Wang et al. refer to the uncanny in the circus clown, who is somewhat like us, but who often evokes fear or avoidance, especially in small children.

Computers and robotics raise all sorts of philosophical questions. What does it really mean to be human? To what extent can we make meaningful comparisons between human structures and functions and robotic functions and structures? Can a robot be almost human or develop consciousness and self-awareness? If so, does such a robot have moral claims? What was once wild imaginative material on robots and androids set forth by science fiction writers is now reality. The philosophical and psychological questions surrounding robotics lead us to a particular school of psychology. Behaviorism, in many of its classic manifestations, is a school of thought that is friendly to a thoroughgoing mechanistic view of life. It is no accident that the title of a biography of John B. Watson, often regarded as the founder of American behaviorism, was *Mechanical Man*: *John B. Watson and the Beginnings of Behaviorism* (see Buckley, 1989). As noted earlier in Chapter 8, Julien Offray de la Mettrie, one of the philosophical precursors of behaviorism, titled his classic book *Man a Machine*. Albert Paul Weiss (1924), an early American behaviorist, argued, "human conduct and achievement reduces to *nothing but* (a) different kinds of electron-proton groupings characterized according to geometric structure; [and] (b) the motions that occur when one structural or dynamic form changes into another" (p. 39).

Intellectual Antecedents of Behaviorism

Behaviorism's philosophical roots go back to ancient Greek atomic theory, the first complete mechanistic and materialistic psychology. Leucippus and Democritus argued that reality consists exclusively of atoms and the void. The world as it appears, including psychological processes, is based on mechanical atomic combinations and the complex interplay of atoms creates psychological processes. Stewart (2014) notes that mechanistic atomic theory was also embraced by Epicurus and Lucretius and that these philosophers had a profound and little understood influence on early Americans such as Thomas Young, Ethan Allen, and Thomas Jefferson. Over the centuries, various thinkers rediscovered, refined, and amplified these basic ideas, and in time advances in neurophysiology reinforced behaviorism's modern mechanistic foundation (see Chapter 8).

Behaviorism is often viewed as an American school of thought, but Wertheimer (1987) pointed out that "its predecessors were Europeans rather than Americans" (p. 121). In previous chapters of this text we have been reminded at every turn of materialists such as Condillac, Helvétius, and Hobbes; empiricists and associationists such as Locke and Hartley; and physician philosophers such as La Mettrie. Although Russian contributions remain systematically underrepresented, the roots of behaviorism extend into Russian physiology, particularly as encountered in the works of Vladimir Bekhterev, Ivan Sechenov, and Ivan Pavlov (see Aleksandrova-Howell et al., 2012).

Vladimir Mikhailovich Bekhterev (1857–1927) earned a doctorate in Leipzig and brought Wundt's methods back to Russia (Araujo, 2014b), where he advanced **reflexology**, a psychology based on the reflex as the fundamental category of inquiry in psychology (Zhuravel, 1995). Though Bekhterev worked to reconcile his system with Marxist–Leninist thought, his work was gradually discredited for failure to comply with Soviet ideology (Misiak & Sexton, 1966), and he died under mysterious circumstances (Shereshevskii, 1994).

The Russian physiologist Ivan Mikhailovich Sechenov (1829–1905) has been regarded as "the father of Russian physiology" (Tsagareli, 2012, p. 394) and was one of the first to envision a scientific psychology based on physiology. Esper (1964) argued that Sechenov "became the first 'behaviorist' of modern times" (p. 324). In his book *Reflexes of the Brain*, Sechenov makes the case that the reflex, consisting of affective activity, central connective processes, and efferent (motor) activity, is the fundamental unit of study. It would remain for Ivan Pavlov to demonstrate the complexity and reach of a psychology based on reflexive processes. We turn now to a consideration of Pavlov's extensive contributions.

Ivan Petrovich Pavlov

Born in Ryazan, Russia, **Ivan Petrovich Pavlov (1849–1936)** was the eldest child in a poor

Ivan Pavlov

family that endured more than its share of adversity and sorrow. Six of the eleven children did not survive childhood. Young Ivan sustained a severe head injury that delayed formal schooling until he was eleven. Fortunately, Pavlov's father, a lover of books, took a keen interest in the boy's education.

Pavlov's early education was in a theological seminary, backward in some respects, but also known for its liberal atmosphere (see Todes, 2014, p. 24). Students who did not excel in one subject were encouraged in other areas. Seminary officials who were not always well-qualified teachers nevertheless inspired vigorous exchanges of ideas, permitting students to discover their unique talents and interests. Drawing influence from Darwin and other scientists, Pavlov dedicated himself to science (Windholz, 1997). In 1870, he entered St. Petersburg University, where he pursued a degree in the natural sciences. Subsequently, he enrolled in the Medico-Chirurgical Academy "not for the

purpose of becoming a physician, but with the idea that after getting the degree of doctor of medicine, [he] would qualify for a chair in physiology" (1955, p. 42). His doctoral thesis focused on the role of cardiac nerves in circulation. His medical degree was granted on December 19, 1879. He also won a gold medal and a scholarship for postgraduate studies.

Pavlov's early studies centered "on the physiology of circulation, digestion, and higher nervous activity" (Samoilov & Zayas, 2007, p. 75) and led to his 1904 Nobel Prize (see Miyata, 2009). In his acceptance speech, he hinted at the conditioning research that would dominate his scientific life. In fact, as noted by his assistant and co-worker Boris Babkin (1949), the years from 1902 to 1936 were "devoted almost exclusively to the study of the functions of the cerebral cortex by the method of conditioned reflexes" (p. 273).

PAVLOV'S PSYCHOLOGICAL WORK
Pavlov's work on the gastric and salivary glands resulted in unexpected observations that led to work on "higher nervous activity." Pavlov and his colleagues measured the amount and quality of salivary and gastric secretion in relation to the nature of stimulus materials placed in a dog's mouth. There was evidence that secretions are "intelligent" in the sense that they depend on the nature of stimulus materials. The fundamental fact, in Pavlov's words, was that "the kind of substances getting into the digestive canal from the external world, that is, whether edible or inedible, dry or liquid, as well as the different food substances, determined the onset of the work of the digestive glands, the peculiarities of their functioning in each case, the amount of reagents produced by them and their composition" (Pavlov, 1955, p. 131).

Pavlov observed another way in which salivary activity is "intelligent." In his Nobel speech, Pavlov (1955) noted that "it has long been known that the sight of tasty food makes the mouth of a hungry man water" (p. 139). He added that though such an observation is commonplace, its implications and mechanisms had never been investigated. Pavlov and his colleagues observed after multiple trials that dogs salivated at the mere sight of food used in gastric experiments. Furthermore, other stimuli such as containers and noises associated with food also produced salivation. Salivation produced in early trials as a result of the direct action of the food is understandable in terms of classic reflex theory. That is, food has a direct action on the receptor system and the response is understandable in terms of material and efficient causes. But salivation at the mere sight of the food or at the sight or sound of a stimulus associated with the food is a different matter, and these events were interfering with Pavlov's interpretation of salivary responses. He became increasingly interested and then launched his well-known classical conditioning paradigm; the debate continues about whether he used an actual bell, as typically reported in textbooks (Jarius & Wildemann, 2016; Todes, 2014). Pavlov referred to salivation at the mere sound of a stimulus as **action at a distance** and in his early work also referred to it as a **psychical reflex**. Later, these terms were replaced with more precise terminology.

The concept of *action at a distance* was troublesome for Pavlov just as similar terms had been troublesome for other scientists such as Descartes and Newton in physics. The issue in physics centered on the action of magnets, gases, gravitational fields, and the transmission of light. How could such actions be explained in terms of direct action or efficient causes? (See Hess, 1967, for a brief but helpful discussion of the problem.) Action at a distance appeared to challenge material and efficient causality, so central to science as Pavlov conceived it. Specifically, what was it that stimulated the salivary glands when the animal salivated at the mere sight of the food? The expression *psychical reflex* provided only a nominal solution. The term didn't really explain anything; it provided only a name for an observed relationship. Pavlov wanted to understand the mechanisms.

Pavlov concluded that he was dealing with two kinds of reflexes. He regarded the physiological

reflex as unconditioned or unlearned. An external stimulus (food) stimulates an organism's nerves, acting on the effectors through connecting nerves. The second type of reflex also originates in external stimuli, but activates the eye, ear, or nose rather than taste and smell receptors. Pavlov (1955) observed that the new reflex "is permanently subject to fluctuation, and is, therefore, *conditioned*" (p. 144). He argued that conditioned or learned reflexes, like the unconditioned reflexes, "can be easily conceived from the physiological point of view as a function of the nervous system" (p. 145). The task was then to discover the functional relations between the two types of reflexes.

Pavlov (1928) observed that "nervous activity consists in general of the phenomena of excitation and inhibition" and argued that either phenomenon can spread, or irradiate, over the cortex (p. 156). Such irradiation provides a conceptual basis for connections between stimulus events from various sensory modalities. Thus, through the spread of nervous activity over the cortex, visual, auditory, or other signals may be associated with the unconditioned reflex.

In time, Pavlov's basic paradigm was elaborated in terms of an **unconditioned stimulus (UCS)** that reliably produces an **unconditioned reflex (UCR)**. The unconditioned stimulus is a biologically adequate stimulus that has the capacity to automatically induce the reflex activity that terminates with the unconditioned reflex. The **conditioned stimulus (CS)** was at one time a neutral stimulus, but after repeated pairings with the UCS, the CS produces a reflex similar to the UCR, the **conditioned reflex (CR)**. These findings remain a continuing topic of research on learning (Bitterman, 2006).

The temporal relations between the UCS and the CS resulted in findings that surprised Pavlov and his coworkers. They discovered that conditioning was optimal when the CS precedes the UCS by a fraction of a second (see Figure 13.1A). This arrangement of the CS and the UCS is called *delayed conditioning*. Another temporal arrangement, much less efficient than delayed conditioning, is called *simultaneous conditioning* (Figure 13.1C). The most interesting discovery regarding the relationship of the CS and the UCS is called *trace conditioning*. In this arrangement, the CS and the UCS are initially paired, as in Figure 13.1A, but then the temporal interval between the two is increased so that the CS occurs prior to the UCS and is terminated before the UCS occurs (Figure 13.1B). As the temporal interval between termination of the CS and the onset of the UCS increased, Pavlov's dogs sometimes became drowsy or even fell asleep. Pavlov argued that the CS may be associated with local cortical inhibition and that, in the absence of the excitatory UCS, the inhibition associated with the CS may irradiate over the surface of the cortex. Sleep resulted from the spread of inhibition.

Pavlov studied other topics that continue to inspire research on the nature of learning. Some of the key areas are extinction, spontaneous recovery, stimulus generalization, and discrimination.

Extinction occurs when the CS is presented repeatedly in the absence of the UCS. Pavlov found that the CS loses its ability to produce salivary activity. Pavlov also observed, however, that after extinction of a response, following a period of rest, the CS may again elicit the CR; Pavlov called this phenomenon **spontaneous recovery**. The CR, however, is extinguished if the CS is again presented several times without the UCS.

Pavlov observed other phenomena that inspired him and prompted study by later learning theorists. He observed **stimulus generalization**: Stimuli similar to the original CS may also elicit the CR. Thus, if the original stimulus is a bell that produces a given pitch, then a bell that produces a similar pitch may also elicit the CR. Despite generalization, Pavlov observed that **discrimination** between stimuli, sometimes even remarkably similar stimuli, can be conditioned. Thus, a circular shape (the CS) may be reliably associated with food (the UCS), whereas an ellipse may never be associated with the UCS. The dog soon learns to salivate to a circle, but not to an ellipse. If the ellipse is gradually changed so that it looks more and more like the circle,

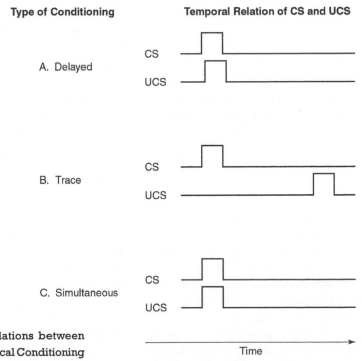

Figure 13.1 Temporal Relations between the CS and the UCS in Classical Conditioning

326

the discrimination becomes increasingly difficult. Such a procedure tests the discriminatory capacity of the animal. It also serves as a major frustration, especially if it is important to make the discrimination, as it may well be for a hungry dog. The behavior of the dog in difficult discrimination tasks became a major curiosity for Pavlov and contributed to his interest in the problems of psychiatry (Wolpe & Plaud, 1997). Prior to elaborating on this topic, it is important to examine another dimension of Pavlov's theory.

Temperament As noted earlier, Pavlov believed in two fundamental processes in the nervous system: inhibition and excitation. Both were manifested in different ways in dogs with different temperaments. For example, he observed that some dogs, such as terriers, are nervous, excitable, quick, short-tempered, and alert. Pavlov believed that such dogs have more excitation than inhibition. By contrast, other dogs are timid, hesitant, and shy. He believed that such dogs are dominated more by inhibition than excitation. Other dogs are warm, friendly, and affable. They represent a balanced temperament marked by an even mix of inhibition and excitation. Pavlov accepted a theory of temperaments derived from the work of Galen that was applicable to both humans and dogs. Pavlov's version of Galen's scheme is illustrated in Table 13.1.

In accepting the idea of temperamental differences, Pavlov departed from Sechenov's radical

Table 13.1 Galen's Classification of Temperaments

Temperamental General Type	Characteristics
Choleric	Excitable, touchy, quick-tempered; marked by excess of excitation
Sanguine	Marked by warmth, balance of excitation and inhibition
Phlegmatic	Not easily excited, also balanced between excitation and inhibition
Melancholic	Tendency toward depressed moods, excess of inhibition

environmentalism. Pavlov concluded that temperamental differences interact with learning processes. More importantly, temperamental differences dictate how a dog will respond to laboratory-induced stress caused from difficult discrimination problems.

Experimental Neurosis Although many writings about Pavlov focus exclusively on his medical and classical conditioning work, beginning in the 1920s until his death in 1936, Pavlov's interests shifted to clinical problems resulting from difficult discriminations or conditions of stress. Resistance to stress was clearly a function of general health and temperament. Some dogs were naturally more resistant to stress than others. Pavlov's work on experimental neurosis is an excellent illustration of how applied science sometimes grows directly from basic science.

Pavlov (1941) found that severe stress-producing situations resulted in what he called **ultramaximal inhibition**, a state of inhibition that occurs when we have exceeded our maximum capacity for physical and psychological stress. Just after a severe crash or life-threatening situation, an individual may show shock-like symptoms such as a vacant stare, unresponsiveness, or stereotyped responding. Pavlov believed that a powerful assault on the nervous system may take the brain into a state of protective inhibition. If the entire cortex is in an inhibitory mode, then one could expect that the organism would be unresponsive. In the face of overwhelming threat, inhibition can be protective, at least in the sense that it may block the input of a still more threatening stimulation.

Pavlov's laboratory studies revealed three different after-effects of ultramaximal inhibition. First, some animals display the **equivalent phase**, whereby the dog responds with the same amount of saliva regardless of the strength of a stimulus. Sargant (1957) pointed out that "the observation is comparable to the frequent reports by normal people in periods of intense fatigue, that there is little difference between their emotional reactions to important or trivial experiences" (p. 64). Following a more profound biological or psychological insult, the dog may display the **paradoxical phase**. In this phase, a strong stimulus produces a weak response (very little saliva) and a weak stimulus produces a strong response (much saliva). The paradoxical phase has counterparts in humans in stress situations. A whisper may produce an explosive outburst, whereas a shout may result in little more than an eyeblink (Sargant, 1957). The paradoxical phase makes sense in terms of Pavlov's notion of ultramaximal inhibition. Perhaps there are circumstances in which a weak stimulus gets through the inhibitory barrier and is fully processed, whereas a strong stimulus does not get fully processed. If such were the case, then one might predict a weak response to a strong stimulus and a strong response to a weak stimulus.

Pavlov had the most interest in the **ultraparadoxical phase**. Following severe trauma, Pavlov observed a radical shift in the personality of the dog and its response system. In this phase, stimuli that previously produced a positive response now produced a negative response and vice versa. Sargant (1957) observed that in this phase the dog may "attach itself to a laboratory attendant whom it had previously disliked, and try to attack the master whom it has previously loved" (p. 65). The ultraparadoxical phase is all the more interesting in that its effects may be long-lasting.

In his book *Battle for the Mind*, Sargant (1957) applied Pavlov's work to psychiatry and argued that the ultraparadoxical phase may explain political and religious conversions, false confessions, and similar phenomena, especially when such conversions follow an intense and prolonged assault on the nervous system. Such an assault, at the human level, may include rhythmic chanting or singing, fatigue, and threats of damnation or death in an atmosphere that undermines individual adequacy and judgment. Sargant (1957) sought to use similar methods therapeutically to improve the condition of people with severe psychological illnesses, and he generated extensive controversy with his enthusiastic support of insulin and electric shock therapies, among

others (Dally, 2004). Some of Sargant's most controversial treatments involved narcosis therapy, chemically induced sleep that he believed placed clients in a state of inhibition, so that they could be reconditioned into psychological health. Sadly, he never evaluated his techniques or outcomes, and he destroyed his records before his death in the 1980s (Read, 2010). Sargant's work has generated a recent storm of controversy, with some former narcosis patients reporting gratitude for his methods while others describe narcosis as torture (Davies, 2013).

Pavlov became increasingly concerned that inhibition and excitation interact with temperament to produce a variety of psychiatric illnesses. He believed that choleric and melancholic individuals were more vulnerable to breakdown, whereas those who were sanguine and phlegmatic were more resistant to stress. However, any individual, subjected to sufficient stress, would likely break down. Pavlov's work in this area had a major impact on the field of neuroscience (Gray, 1999; Grimsley & Windholz, 2000; Pickenhain, 1999) as well as the development of behavioral therapy in Russia and abroad (Sukhodolsky et al., 1995; Wolpe & Plaud, 1997).

Problem Solving In his final years, Pavlov became increasingly interested in the nature of problem solving. The Gestalt psychologist Wolfgang Köhler (see Chapter 14) had argued that higher primates do not solve problems in a mechanical stimulus–response fashion. Rather, in open situations, such as field settings, primates show evidence of true insight achieved not mechanically but through creative, novel, and flexible response modes. Such a holistic approach to problem solving represented a direct challenge to Pavlov's mechanistic and reductionistic system. As a consequence of Köhler's work, Pavlov initiated research in 1933 with two chimpanzees named Raphael and Rosa (see Windholz, 1984). During the last three years of his life, Pavlov replicated some of Köhler's experiments but offered his own explanations in terms of the mechanics of conditioning and trial and error (see Todes, 2014).

There were concerted efforts in the former Soviet Union to strongly favor scientific activities and theories guided by, and consistent with, Marxist–Leninist ideology (Academy of Sciences of the U.S.S.R., 1951). As a result, there were topical areas such as research in genetics that were deemphasized or even rejected altogether. Scientists such as Pavlov had to navigate continuing and complicated tensions between the nature of their scientific work and changing political ideologies (see Todes, 2014).

Edward Lee Thorndike

In the United States, **Edward Lee Thorndike (1874–1949)** advanced a system of thought consistent with some of the major behavioristic views. Educated in the functionalist tradition, Thorndike remained sympathetic to the tolerant spirit of functionalism but favored a more objective psychology focused on observable actions of living organisms. He didn't care for the method of introspection and the study of people's minds or inner states. He believed that anything that exists, exists in some amount, and is thus quantifiable. Inspired by other sciences, he applied scientific methods to such a host of problems that he has been called "America's most productive psychologist" (Jonçich, 1968). From a broad philosophical standpoint, Thorndike can be considered a functionalist, but his practical work is more consistent with behaviorism (Malone, 2014).

Thorndike grew up in a home marked by a serious emphasis on duty, industry, independence, discipline, honesty, and propriety. Such values were put to productive use in his adult years but his moral code was more liberal than that of his family, at least in matters of religion. He entered Wesleyan University in Middletown, Connecticut, in 1891 and graduated in 1895. Later, he received a master's degree in psychology from Harvard, where he kindled a friendship with William James. Following his work at Harvard, Thorndike enrolled in the graduate program at Columbia,

Edward Lee Thorndike

where he studied with James McKeen Cattell. He graduated with a Ph.D. from Columbia in 1898. After holding a brief faculty position at Western Reserve University, he accepted an appointment at Columbia, where he remained until his retirement in 1941. During his long and productive career, Thorndike was president of the American Psychological Association in 1912, was elected to the National Academy of Sciences, and won a gold medal award from Columbia for his distinguished research contributions to education. Thorndike died on August 9, 1949.

THORNDIKE'S WORK Thorndike's contributions ranged over a variety of problems in psychology and education (Hilgard, 1996). He was a pioneer in the experimental study of animal behavior and an early investigator of social intelligence (Kihlstrom & Cantor, 2011). He advanced an early learning theory but also emphasized genetic influences. He compared

329

identical twins on various tasks (see Thorndike, 1905) and was struck by similarities in their performance. He also observed that correlations between identical twins were greater than correlations between other siblings. Jonçich (1968) noted that he believed in individual differences, but "Thorndike's individual is already armed, well or poorly, by . . . genes" (p. 333). He understood that learning is critical to the individual and society, but learning alone will not achieve all things.

Thorndike, without knowing Pavlov's work, sought to study the effects of the environment on behavior (Donahoe & Vegas, 2011), and his learning theory arose from early laboratory studies with cats (Baker & Serdikoff, 2013; Chance, 1999). His doctoral dissertation at Columbia was published in 1898 under the title "Animal Intelligence." In his dissertation, Thorndike rejected earlier anecdotal and anthropomorphic work on animal behavior in favor of groundbreaking methods that remained the basis for comparative psychology more than a century later (Galef, 1998). His methods are classic in the psychology of learning, and set forth the basics of a theory of learning known as **connectionism**.

In his doctoral research, Thorndike placed a cat in a "puzzle box" constructed of wooden slats and hardware cloth. He positioned a fish outside the box as an incentive to escape. Once inside, the cat could open the door and escape by pressing a lever in one box or tugging on a wire loop in another. As the cats became "box wise," learning to escape from simpler boxes, Thorndike placed them in more challenging boxes. To escape a more complex box, a cat would need to depress a treadle, pull on a string, and push a bar up and down. While learning to escape from the fifteen different puzzle boxes, the cats exhibited behaviors that appeared random. (Thorndike preferred to describe the learning process as "trial and accidental success" rather than "trial and error," but the latter became the more popular expression.) In time, irrelevant movements dropped out and a specific series of actions became associated with the desired consequence.

Similar to Pavlov, Thorndike sought to understand complex events (e.g., learning complex tasks) through more simple processes (e.g., building learned connections) (Donahoe & Vegas, 2011); therefore, he emphasized the connections or bonds between sense impressions and response patterns. Learning, in his view, involved the strengthening of bonds or connections, which he believed were grounded in physiology. This was one of the earliest and most influential of the stimulus–response or S–R psychologies. Thorndike formulated the **law of exercise**, which states that connections are strengthened through repetition or use and weakened through disuse. Stated in more simple terms, you use it or you lose it.

Thorndike also proposed a **law of effect** to explain that connections are strengthened or weakened as a result of their consequences. In its early expression, the law of effect asserted that a connection is strengthened when followed by a "satisfying" state of affairs and weakened when followed by an "annoying" state of affairs. Thus, reward or reinforcement strengthens a connection and punishment weakens it. These two principal laws laid the foundation, in part, for his learning theory (Donahoe, 1999). Thorndike also recognized the importance of factors such as maturation or readiness to respond, the ability to generalize, and mental set or attitude.

Thorndike later modified both the law of exercise and the law of effect. He abandoned his law of exercise after determining that exercise alone (as mere blind repetition) does not strengthen a connection. Rather, exercise in conjunction with other conditions strengthens connections. For example, if information about the response's accuracy accompanies each repetition of a response then a connection might be strengthened. The modified law of effect, sometimes called the **truncated law of effect**, casts doubt on punishment as a means of weakening connections but acknowledges that a satisfying state of affairs will strengthen the behavior that it follows.

In other noteworthy research, Thorndike collaborated with Robert S. Woodworth on the transfer of training. Conventional wisdom held that knowledge of certain academic subjects improved intellectual ability in general. For example, studying Latin provided more than knowledge of the ancient language; it was thought to enhance logic and reasoning skills as well. The idea that certain subjects held beneficial general effects was called the **doctrine of formal discipline**.

The opposite view does not deny the importance of the exercise of intellectual functions, but holds that the transfer of abilities is more specific than assumed by the doctrine of formal discipline. This conflicting view, sometimes called the **identical elements transfer theory**, emphasizes the degree of identity between the first and second tasks. Thorndike and Woodworth (1901) demonstrated that the amount of transfer is a function of the similarities between two tasks. Transfer is sometimes small even when tasks are similar. For example, improvements in the accuracy of judgments of line lengths of 0.5 to 1.5 inches did not result in better subsequent judgments of line lengths of 6 to 12 inches.

Working with simple perceptual problems, Thorndike and Woodworth supported the identical elements transfer theory, but the concern remained that academic subjects such as Latin and geometry might have general transfer values in the real world. More than two decades after his work with Woodworth, Thorndike (1924) conducted a classic study on the transfer effects of specific high school courses. Using 8,564 high school students as participants, Thorndike investigated the relative effects of a great variety of courses (e.g., algebra, physics, psychology, Latin, French, biology) on subsequent problem-solving ability. He found surprisingly small transfer effects from various topical areas on later problem-solving ability. However, students in the upper levels of ability at the beginning of the study gained far more than students who entered the study with lower levels of ability. Thorndike's work had far-reaching implications for education.

Following Thorndike, educators emphasized the relationship between the content of a subject and the demands of daily life. The new educational rule was simple and practical: If you want to know English, study English; if you want to know algebra, study algebra; and so forth. Studies in the transfer of training remain an important area in the psychology of learning, and Thorndike is known as a pioneer of educational psychology (Beatty, 2005).

THORNDIKE'S OTHER INTERESTS As noted, Thorndike had interests in a host of topics in psychology and education. His publications on the psychology of labor (Thorndike, 1922) and the psychology of the profit motive (Thorndike, 1936) are important early contributions to industrial psychology. On the subject of labor, Thorndike argued that work is not necessarily aversive and encouraged research on worker satisfaction and dissatisfaction. He was interested in ways to humanize capitalism. He believed in the value of the profit motive but thought psychology could address social problems associated with it.

Perhaps stemming from his early background, he found interest in the meaning of education in a scientific and technological age. Thorndike (1920) expressed concern about twentieth-century adherence to dogmatism and beliefs in magic as well as beliefs guided by emotion rather than intellect. He believed that our great task is to improve the quality of life. This belief fueled his mature work on the effects of social context on lifestyle. His books, *Human Nature and the Social Order* (1940), *Man and His Works* (1943), and *Your City* (1939), demonstrate his social–psychological interests and optimism about psychology's role in addressing problems of daily life. Thorndike was a "sane positivist" who believed that a science of values can guide moral assessment, social policy, and the betterment of humanity (Beatty, 1998; Dewsbury, 1998).

Formal Founding of American Behaviorism

American behaviorism was rooted in familiar philosophical and scientific soil dating back to the early work of philosophical materialists (Leahey, 1992; O'Neil, 1995). Yet, when John B. Watson introduced his systematic vision in 1913, it seemed fresh and simple, even revolutionary. Behaviorism promised a radical break from the dominant psychologies of the day. Behaviorism was appealing because it offered a direct and unambiguous message. Watson promised a new and better way to do things—a way that offered hope for cutting through past complexities. Watson is often thought of as the founder of behaviorism, but he made no such claim, and as noted by Malone (2014), he is more appropriately regarded as an exemplar of the movement. Clearly, there had been several psychologists, including William McDougall (1871–1938), Edwin Bissell Holt (1873–1946), Walter Samuel Hunter (1889–1954), Albert Paul Weiss (1879–1931), and Max Frederick Meyer (1873–1967), who had favored a behavioral approach to psychology, but it was John B. Watson who captured the philosophic vision and set it forth in a rather stark, but commanding fashion.

John B. Watson

There is little in Watson's humble background to suggest he would become one of the most influential scientists of his age. **John Broadus Watson (1878–1958)** was born in Travelers Rest near Greenville, South Carolina, on January 9, 1878. He was the youngest of four children of Pickens Butler Watson and Emma Roe. In a candid autobiography, Watson (1961) described himself as a lazy and insubordinate youth. Nevertheless, he was allowed to enroll in Furman University in 1894. He worked his way through college and showed an improved but still undistinguished academic performance (Harris, 1999). In his autobiography, he explained why he took five years and graduated with an A.M. instead of taking four years and graduating with an A.B. One of his professors declared "if a man ever handed in a paper backwards, he would flunk him" (Watson, 1961, p. 272). Watson inadvertently handed his

John B. Watson

paper in backward, and the professor kept his word! Accordingly, Watson's graduation was delayed as he was forced to spend an extra year at Furman. But the delay afforded an opportunity to complete a master's degree.

Watson's earned his Ph. D. at the University of Chicago where he studied with an all-star cast: philosopher–psychologist John Dewey, the neurologist Henry Donaldson, and the well-known physiologist Jacques Loeb. However, James Rowland Angell had the most influence on Watson. Indeed, Angell became a father figure. Some years later, Watson discovered the pain of breaking intellectual ties with his mentor. Watson developed rigorous work habits at Chicago that persevered his entire life. His work was so intense, however, that it may have contributed to a nervous breakdown in his third year at Chicago. He called it "a typical Angst," marked by sleeplessness and fear of the dark. Watson noted that his breakdown caused him "to accept a large part of Freud, when I first began to get really acquainted with him" (Watson, 1961, p. 274). He recovered, completed his dissertation, and graduated magna cum laude in 1903.

After graduation, Watson was appointed as a laboratory assistant at Chicago, a position he held for five years before accepting an offer as chair of psychology at Johns Hopkins University. By 1908 he was achieving recognition for his research and was viewed as one of the country's most promising psychologists. Watson developed the essentials of behaviorism during his early years at Hopkins. In the classroom, he "taught a modified James type of general psychology" (Watson, 1961, pp. 276–277), but his research focused on animal behavior. Inspired by Pavlovian conditioning, Watson promoted behaviorism as a new method to compete with Titchener's method of introspection and Freud's method of psychoanalysis (Rilling, 2000a). In 1913, the *Psychological Review* published Watson's classic article, "Psychology as the Behaviorist Views It." The article, known as the "Behaviorist Manifesto," was initially received in a guarded way but in time has been celebrated as one of the most important classics in the history of the discipline (Lattal & Rutherford, 2013). The article included a trenchant attack on earlier mentalistic psychologies along with a call for a new "objective psychology" based purely on the material or physical assumptions that had proven to be so successful in other sciences such as chemistry and physics. We turn now to an overview of Watson's system.

WATSON'S PSYCHOLOGY Watson's criticisms of the older psychologies were aggressive and unapologetic. We'll consider some of his concerns.

1. *The divisions of consciousness are arbitrary.* Watson (1913) asked the reader to consider "the question of the number of isolable sensations. Is there an extremely large number of color sensations—or only four, red, green, yellow and blue?" (p. 164). He argued that if we count each just noticeable difference, then "we are forced to admit that the number is so large and the conditions for attaining them so complex that the concept of sensation is unusable, either for the purpose of analysis or that of synthesis" (p. 164).

2. *Psychology is too human-centered.* Another major criticism of the older psychology was that it had little use for observed facts outside of human consciousness. Animal behavior and comparative psychology were treated as embarrassments. In effect, the old psychology was too human-centered; he argued that early biology faced the same dilemma. Watson (1913) discussed the predicament that arose when "the whole Darwinian movement was judged by the bearing it had upon the origin and development of the human race" (p. 162). When emphasis shifted to the experimental study of adaptation and descent, biology was rescued from anthropocentrism. By the same token, behaviorism promised to rescue psychology from the same intellectual danger.

3. *Introspection is unreliable and esoteric.* Watson (1913) noted that if one person cannot replicate another's results, it is assumed that the introspectionist was poorly trained. Thus, "the attack is made upon the experimental setting. In physics and chemistry the attack is made upon the experimental conditions. The apparatus was not sensitive enough, impure chemicals were used, etc. In these sciences a better technique will give reproducible results. Psychology is otherwise. If you can't observe 3–9 states of clearness in attention, your introspection is poor. If, on the other hand, a feeling seems reasonably clear to you, your introspection is again faulty. You are seeing too much. Feelings are never clear" (p. 163).

4. *Older psychologies are dualistic.* Watson (1913) claimed that the older psychologies were fed on the relative merits of parallelism and interactionism. He then declared, "I should like to bring my students up in the same ignorance of such hypotheses as one finds among the students of other branches of science" (p. 166). He believed that if behavior is the subject matter of psychology, then mind–brain positions should be of no greater interest to the psychologist than to the chemist or physicist.

With characteristic brashness, Watson (1913) attacked structuralists as well as functionalists. "I have done my best to understand the difference between functional psychology and structural psychology. Instead of clarity, confusion grows upon me. The terms sensation, perception, affection, emotion, volition are used as much by the functionalist as by the structuralist. The addition of the word 'process' . . . after each serves in some way to remove the corpse of 'content' and to leave 'function' in its stead" (p. 165). Ambiguity characterized both structural and functional psychologies. What was required, according to Watson, was a radical break with both.

Definition of Psychology Watson (1924a) argued that "the definition of any one science, physics, for example, would necessarily include the definition of all other sciences" (p. 11). Then we "mark a ring around that part of the whole of natural science that we claim particularly as our own" (p. 11). Just like the physicist, the psychologist studies reactions, adjustments, movements, activities, and behaviors.

Relation to Other Sciences Watson (1913) declared in the opening of his manifesto that "psychology as the behaviorist views it is a purely objective experimental branch of natural science" (p. 158). Later, in his book *Behaviorism*, Watson (1924a) pointed out that "its closest scientific companion is physiology. It is different from physiology only in the grouping of its problems, not in fundamentals or in central viewpoint" (p. 11). He acknowledged the importance of studying behavior in social and cultural context and of seeking solutions to moral and social problems, thus recognizing that psychology is allied with social sciences (Rakos, 2013).

Goals of Psychology Watson (1913) declared that, as in other sciences, psychology's "theoretical goal is the prediction and control of behavior" (p. 158). On the practical level, Watson (1924a) looked to a time when "we will have a behavioristic ethics, experimental in type, which will tell us whether it is advisable from the standpoint of present and future adjustments of the individual to have one wife or many wives; to have capital

punishment or punishment of any kind; whether prohibition or no prohibition; easy divorce or no divorces" (p. 7).

Watson believed that prediction and control were best accomplished through environmental conditions. He was confident that environment shaped both human and animal behavior. During a Clark University address, Watson (1926) expounded on his radical environmentalism with the bold claim:

> I should like to go one step further tonight and say, "Give me a dozen healthy infants, well-formed, and my own specified world to bring them up in and I'll guarantee to take any one at random and train him to become any type of specialist I might select—a doctor, lawyer, artist, merchant-chief and, yes, even into beggarman and thief, regardless of his talents, penchants, tendencies, abilities, vocations and race of his ancestors." I am going beyond my facts and I admit it, but so have the advocates of the contrary and they have been doing it for thousands of years.
>
> (p. 10)

Methods of the Psychologist Unlike the structuralist method of introspection, Watson's behaviorism dovetailed with emerging techno-scientific ideals that stressed quantification and standardization (Coon, 1993). Watson found no place for introspection. Like all sciences, the object is to gather facts, verify them, and subject them to logical and quantitative analysis. Watson recognized the legitimacy of Pavlov's conditioning techniques, and he sought to bring these methods to the study of humans (García-Penagos & Malone, 2013). He also accepted psychological tests so long as they are not called "mental" tests. "To the behaviorist tests mean merely devices for grading and sampling human performance" (Watson, 1924a, p. 35). He approved of a variety of tests and considered them important assessment tools. Watson also approved of technical forms of social experimentation and naturalistic observation. His chapter "How to Study Human

Behavior" in *Behaviorism* includes a rather broad methodological agenda. The acid test for methods is that they be truly public and lead to measurable results.

Scope of Psychology Watson (1913) pointed out that the behaviorist "recognizes no dividing line between man and brute. The behavior of man, with all of its refinement and complexity, forms only a part of the behaviorist's total scheme of investigation" (p. 158). Psychology, then, according to Watson, has affinities with all the sciences and shares with biologists an interest in all life-forms; in this way, he provided part of the foundation for comparative psychology (Dewsbury, 2013).

Selected Content Areas As noted by Samelson (1994), the focus of Watson's research interests shifted across several content areas during the course of his career. Habit and learning were the foundation areas for behaviorism, but other topical areas were also important.

Habit The central concept of Watsonian behaviorism was habit. Watson (1924a) declared that at birth there is a stream of unlearned activities, but some of these activities begin to be "conditioned a few hours after birth" (p. 218). Ultimately, personality is a complex system of habits—and this applies to each arena of life. As an example, Watson asked what it means to say that a human being is religious. It may mean that the person attends church, reads religious literature, prays before meals, and perhaps tries to convert others. "Let us put all of these separate activities together and call them the *religious habit system* of the individual. Now each of these separate activities making up this system has a dating back in the individual's past and a history" (p. 219). Watson went on to show how the child may have been taught to pray and may have been rewarded for attending religious services and memorizing religious writings. Watson would not, of course, rule out sudden conditioning, perhaps through fear.

Watson argued that the so-called normal personality is based on a certain consistency of conditioning patterns. The person with the normal personality may have been fortunate enough to be reared in an environment free from excessive punishment and trauma. Weaknesses in personality or even illnesses result from habit conflicts. He quarreled with expressions such as *mental illness* or *mental disturbance*. Watson (1924a) pointed out that in many functional psychopathologies "there are no organic disturbances of sufficient gravity to account for personality disturbance. There may be no infections, no lesions anywhere, no absence of physiological reflexes (as there often is when there are organic diseases). And yet the individual has a sick personality" (p. 244). Watson argued that the expression *mental illness* raises the specter of interactionism. He preferred to emphasize conditioning in the acquisition and extinction of personality disturbances. His position is perhaps best illustrated in his infamous research on fear conditioning.

Fear Conditioning Watson devoted extensive time to child rearing (Root, 2008) and to the study of children (Watson & Rayner, 1928). His 1920 study with Rosalie Rayner titled "Conditioned Emotional Reactions" counts as one of the most extensively cited studies in the history of psychology and remains foundational in the study of children's fears and phobias (Ollendick & Muris, 2015). Harris (1979) noted, "This work was the final published project of Watson's academic career" (p. 152). Watson and Rayner conducted experimental work with an infant they identified as Albert B., whose mother was a wet nurse in a hospital environment. Watson and Rayner (1920) described Albert as "healthy from birth and one of the best developed youngsters ever brought to the hospital . . . He was on the whole stolid and unemotional. His stability was one of the principal reasons for using him as a subject in this test" (p. 1). As discussed below, the claim that Albert was healthy has since been challenged. Regardless of Albert's actual state of health, when he was about nine months of age, the researchers presented Albert with "a white rat, a rabbit, a dog, a monkey, with masks with and without hair, cotton, wool, burning newspapers, etc." (Watson & Rayner, 1920, p. 2). Albert showed no fear of any of these things. Also, at about nine months of age, Albert was tested to determine his reaction to a loud sound created by striking a four-foot-long suspended steel bar with a hammer. The sound characteristics (e.g., decibel level) were not specified, but sharp blows to the bar did result in a violent reaction, including crying and fear.

The stage was set to determine whether a conditioned emotional response could be established. Watson and Rayner hesitated for ethical reasons, but finally concluded that conditioned emotional responses occur in the world all the time. If such responses were to be understood, they must be subjected to experimentation. So, when Albert was eleven months and three days old, the white rat was presented to him. As Albert reached for the rat, the loud noise sounded. Albert jumped but did not cry. After seven repetitions, Albert displayed a conditioned emotional response to the rat. That is, when the rat was presented alone, Albert cried and crawled away. Watson and Rayner found that Albert then avoided other objects such as a rabbit, a fur coat, and a dog. Despite methodological problems (see Harris, 1979) in the Watson and Rayner experiment, it was generally accepted as a demonstration of fear conditioning. The study also demonstrated the generalization of a fear response from the original conditioned stimulus. Although these outcomes may feel predictable to today's readers, scholars of the day doubted that Pavlov's conditioning procedures could apply to humans, particularly to human emotions.

Watson and Rayner chided the Freudians, who they guessed would analyze a twenty-year-old Albert's fear of a sealskin coat in terms of repressed memories from a time when he was scolded for attempting to play with his mother's pubic hair. They argued, "Emotional disturbances in adults cannot be traced back to sex alone" (Watson & Rayner, 1920, p. 14). The researchers did not attempt to decondition Albert or desensitize him.

Beck et al. (2009, 2010) reported that they had discovered Little Albert's identity, although some have questioned their claims (Harris, 2011; Powell, 2010, 2011). Beck and colleagues contend he was Douglas Merritte, son of Arvilla Merritte, a wet nurse at the hospital where the research was conducted (2009, 2010; Fridlund et al., 2012a, 2012b). The child died at age six of hydrocephalus, a condition linked to neurological difficulties. A second child, Albert Barger, has also been identified as Little Albert (see Powell, 2011; Powell et al., 2014; Digdon et al., 2014). To complicate the historical analysis, both candidates share a birth date. Much of the debate rests on the appearance of Little Albert in film recordings. Does he show neurological impairment as suggested by Fridlund et al. (2012a, 2012b)? As noted by Griggs (2015), this assessment may rest on observers' expectations. Although the Little Albert study is rife with questionable ethical behavior, the deliberate selection and study of a child with neurological impairments, as well as the decision to obscure this from later scholars and the public, would raise additional important questions about Watson's legacy. Although these questions remain unresolved, Griggs and others believe that Albert Barger is more likely to have been Little Albert, particularly based on adult photos, evidence about his mother's identity, and, at least potentially, his adulthood aversion to dogs.

Later, Watson supervised research by **Mary Cover Jones (1896–1987)** involving the experimental elimination of fear (Jones, 1924a). In her most famous study, she worked with a boy she described as "Albert grown a bit older" (Jones, 1924b, p. 309). Unlike Watson and Rayner's study with Little Albert, Jones tried to remove fear rather than instill it. Three-year-old Peter had a profound fear of rabbits. After trying several methods, Jones used a "direct conditioning" approach with Peter. Through counterconditioning, she paired a pleasant stimulus (food) with a rabbit. In time, Peter's fear was extinguished. This study became the bedrock for later behavioral therapies (Beck et al., 2009). In the 1970s, Joseph Wolpe (see Chapter 18) described Mary Cover Jones as the "mother of behavior therapy" (Rutherford, 2006, p. 189). In later years, she made significant contributions to the study of child development.

Emotions As we have seen, Watson believed that most emotional attachments occur through conditioning. Anxieties and phobias may result from unfortunate early conditioning experiences. The same may be said for positive attachments. Love for another person, objects, animals, and so on occurs through associations of pleasant circumstances with the loved object or person.

Watson quarreled with earlier psychologists on the unlearned beginnings of emotional reactions. He argued that there are only three responses—fear, rage, and love—that can be brought forth in the infant. He cautioned, however, that these terms must be stripped of their old connotations. Fear is brought forth naturally by sudden or unexpected stimuli such as a loud sound or by a sudden loss of support. Rage is observed when bodily movement is hampered or a goal-directed activity is blocked. He pointed out that stimuli that provoke "love responses" include "stroking of the skin, tickling, gentle rocking, patting" (Watson, 1924a, p. 123). In each of these cases—fear, rage, and love—Watson referred to broad undifferentiated response patterns. Such patterns are later differentiated in specific ways through conditioning.

Instincts Watson's position on the existence of instincts changed over the course of his career. In an early article on instinctive activity in animals, Watson (1912) argued, "There are at least three great divisions or classes into which we may provisionally throw the acts of animals: Instincts essentially perfect upon their first appearance; instincts which must be supplemented by habit; and finally, random activity of instinctive origin" (p. 377). Watson found evidence for the first type of instinct in his early field studies on noddy and sooty terns. He argued that the very young birds eat food in the same species-specific way with or without the parents as models. The same was true for other characteristic behaviors such as preening feathers. Watson also believed that fear responses, fighting, and nest cleaning are examples of congenital instincts. He argued that pecking is

an example of the second class of instincts; it improves dramatically with practice. Examples of the third class are random responses to indefinite stimuli such as hunger, thirst, light, dark, warmth, and cold. More specifically, increased activity is normal when the organism is hungry. Random activity associated with hunger drops out when the right movements bring success.

Seven years after making these observations about instinct, Watson (1919) argued that "there is no sharp line of separation between emotion and instinct. Both are hereditary modes of action" (p. 231). In *Psychology from the Standpoint of a Behaviorist*, Watson (1919) defined *instinct* as "a hereditary pattern reaction, the separate elements of which are movements principally of the striped muscles" (p. 231). He contended that at the human level it is almost impossible to classify instincts because habit dominates human actions, but meaningful classifications can be made at the animal level.

Five years later, Watson devoted two chapters in *Behaviorism* to the topic of instincts. His chapter title "Are There Any Human Instincts?" betrays a new skepticism. Watson admitted that we inherit structures that interact with conditioning to determine what we can accomplish. He also admitted that there are unlearned responses such as hiccupping, crying, smiling, and grasping. He asked, however, whether there is any real utility in the concept of instinct. Smiling, for example, "begins at birth—aroused by intraorganic stimulation and by contact. Quickly it becomes conditioned, the sight of the mother calls it out, then vocal stimuli, finally pictures, then words and then life situations either viewed, told or read about" (Watson, 1924a, p. 104). He next raised the question of whether the whole concept of instinct is not meaningless. What is really important is conditioning and habit. Four years later, in *Psychological Care of Infant and Child*, Watson (1928) asserted, "There are no instincts" (p. 38). At least at the human level, he was embracing the Lockean blank slate viewpoint when he declared that "we build in at an early age everything that is later to appear" (p. 38).

The 1920s and 1930s afforded a friendly climate for Watson's skepticism about the utility and scientific legitimacy of instinct. Anti-instinctivism flourished in the early part of the century and may have served as a corrective to psychologies that placed too heavy an explanatory burden on instincts, such as the work of William McDougall (1923, 1926a). The anti-instinct movement may also have flourished because of newfound optimism about the power of conditioning and the importance of the environment. For whatever reasons, the 1920s and 1930s witnessed an outpouring of argument against the concept of instinct. Representative works included Kuo's (1924) "A Psychology without Heredity" and Bernard's (1924) *Instinct: A Study in Social Psychology*. Even at mid-century, questions remained about the usefulness of the concept of instinct (Beach, 1955). However, at the same time, behavioral researchers trained in zoology, often called *ethologists*, were marshaling powerful evidence for the role of instincts in animal behavior (Hess, 1962). For helpful overviews of the history of the concept of instinct, see Diamond (1971, 1974a).

Thinking and Speech In his book *Behaviorism*, Watson (1924a) warned readers that they have been taught to believe "that thinking is something peculiarly uncorporeal, something very intangible, very evanescent, something peculiarly mental" (p. 191). He further warned that "there is always a strong inclination to attach a mystery to something you can't see" (p. 191). It appears, at least superficially, that thinking would present a problem to a psychology that denies the existence of mental events. Yet Watson argued that a natural science approach to thinking is both possible and productive. Watson (1924b) admitted that "thinking, with the behaviorist, is and must remain until the advent of experimentation partly a logical formulation" (p. 339). He was confident, however, that with the advancement of science, more and more scientific experimentation on thinking would be possible. What, then, was the behaviorist view of thinking?

In an article titled "The Unverbalized in Human Behavior," Watson (1924b) noted that a person "learning to play golf learns (usually) simultaneously to talk golf" (p. 273). Words can substitute for actions and objects. The utility of the substitutability or equivalence of words for actions or objects is obvious. Watson pointed out that as we develop, we soon have verbal organizations for every object or situation we have encountered. He compared verbal habits or organizations with the kinesthetic organization of playing a tune on the piano. Initially, one must look at each note on the score and find the corresponding key on the piano. Soon, however, the initial stimulus note may trigger a response chain. One may even take away the music or play in the dark. Watson (1924a) argued that "the same thing happens in word behavior" (p. 188). After a few repetitions, the first line of a poem or a fairy tale may trigger a repetition of the entire passage.

Watson believed that we learn muscular habits when we learn to speak. Speaking is not just a central process, it is also a peripheral process. We speak as a consequence of the interaction of the brain and the musculature. The primary muscle groups involved in speech are those associated with the larynx, but Watson (1924a) was aware that "removal of the larynx . . . does not destroy whispered speech" (p. 191). He believed that we really speak with our whole body—our hands, shoulders, tongue, facial muscles, throat, chest, and so on. The brain does not function in isolation from the rest of the physical system.

Another component in Watson's theory of speech grew out of his observations of children at play. When young children play alone, they typically talk to themselves. Watson (1924a) noted that even "deaf and dumb individuals who when talking use manual movements instead of words use the same manual responses they employ in talking, in their own thinking" (p. 193). In time, young children cease to talk aloud, but "talking" goes on nonetheless. "Behind these walls you can call the biggest bully the worst name you can think of without even smiling" (Watson, 1924a, p. 193). In an article titled "The Place of

Kinesthetic, Visceral and Laryngeal Organization in Thinking," Watson (1924b) declared, "The behaviorist has preferred to call all verbalization that goes on behind the closed door of the lips 'thinking,' regardless of whether new verbal adjustments are effected or only old habits rehearsed" (p. 340). Thinking, then, as the behaviorist views it, is tied to speech. Indeed, thinking could be defined as subvocal speech.

Watson anticipated an important question about his theory: Do we think only in words? His answer was, "Yes, or in word substitutes, such as the shrug of the shoulders or other bodily response . . . When the individual is thinking *the whole of his bodily organization is at work*—even though the final solution shall be a spoken, written or subvocally expressed verbal formulation" (Watson, 1924b, p. 341).

Under Watson's treatment, thinking and all other psychological processes are subject to investigation by the established methods of the natural sciences. By deemphasizing the role of central (brain) processes in thinking, he opened the door to the use of new response measures (e.g., throat movements, verbalization) in the study of thinking. Following Watson, there were many studies on the role of peripheral processes in thinking. He may have had a small impact on the literature on thinking, but his narrow approach to the topic had a truncating effect on the types of questions that were raised. In the end, a broader, more cognitive approach proved more productive. The broader approach made room for the investigation of topics such as the role of cognitive strategies in problem solving, the effects of the structure of a situation on problem solving, and problem solving as a function of the capacity to transform and rearrange parts or to see alternatives. The Watsonian approach to thinking was driven by the dictates of the larger behavioristic vision rather than by the special nature and requirements of the phenomenon in question.

OTHER CONTRIBUTIONS We must return now to developments and vicissitudes in Watson's personal life in order to grasp a more comprehensive picture of his contributions. World War I interrupted Watson's work at Hopkins. He was inducted into military service and put in charge of aviation examining boards. A major task for such boards involved the selection of fighter pilots. He also worked on the use of homing pigeons in delivering military messages. Still later in his tour of duty, he worked on a medical project on the effects of oxygen deprivation. Watson was deeply troubled by, and critical of, military life, but he was at least allowed to do pioneering work on psychological problems that would later become a permanent part of military psychology.

Following the war, Watson was back at work at Johns Hopkins but his academic career came to an abrupt and dramatic halt following an affair with his graduate student Rosalie Rayner. Extensive negative publicity resulted in a request that Watson resign his position at the university. After divorcing his first wife, the forty-two-year-old psychologist married Rosalie Rayner in 1921. The loss of his academic position embittered Watson. Rumors also endured that Watson was fired not only for this affair, but for conducting inappropriate research on physiological responses during sexual intercourse. Despite the persistence of these rumors, the allegations may not be true (see Benjamin et al., 2007).

In his autobiography, Watson told of the hardships of the first few months after resigning from Hopkins: "I went to New York, stranded economically and to some extent emotionally" (Watson, 1961, p. 279). Watson lived briefly with his friend William I. Thomas (1863–1947), who had been dismissed from the University of Chicago following a career-threatening scandal. Thomas introduced Watson to Stanley Resor, president of the J. Walter Thompson Company, a prominent advertising firm. Watson was given a temporary assignment to study the boot market. Soon he was ringing doorbells and canvassing in the Mississippi River region to determine boot preferences. Following this work, he was given a permanent position in charge of the sales of Yuban coffee and Pond's facial creams. Within a year, Watson reported he had "found himself" and discovered that it was "just as thrilling to watch the growth of a sales curve of a new product as to watch the learning curve of animals or men" (Watson, 1961, p. 280). His behaviorism did not signal a revolution in advertising, though he rejected popular catchy slogans in favor of appeals to consumer attitudes about prestige and image (Coon, 1994). By 1924, Watson was vice president of the J. Walter Thompson Company. He was soon a wealthy man whose pioneering contributions to advertising and sales were as noteworthy in the business world as his contributions in psychology were to academia.

In an overview of the behaviorist's career, Bergmann (1956) declared that John B. Watson was second only to Freud as "the most important figure in the history of psychological thought during the first half of the century" (p. 265). Watson's contributions were substantial. First, of course, was the systematic objective approach to the discipline. His conceptual approach was also tied to important experimental work in comparative psychology, learning, and emotional conditioning in children (Morris & Todd, 1999). This latter work had a direct influence on the development of behavior therapy. All of this was accomplished in the relatively short span of Watson's academic career, from 1903 to 1920—a time interrupted by his service in World War I. Watson also influenced the world of advertising and, with his many popular articles, contributed to public awareness of psychology. His remarkable career came to an end when he died on September 25, 1958. His vision for a scientific psychology, however, continued to thrive in many ways in the work of neobehaviorists.

Neobehaviorism

Shortly after publication of Watson's behaviorist manifesto, it seemed that psychology, after more than three decades, might become a unified coherent discipline (or in the words of Kuhn, a "paradigmatic science"). Optimism flourished, especially among the younger generation, as psychology seemed poised to achieve scientific status. The behaviorist perspective offered a methodology that better resembled other sciences. The subject matter was observable and quantifiable. Yet, after the founding, the behaviorist school appeared far from coherent. Even as it dominated American psychology, behaviorism was far from a unified system of thought (see Mills, 1998). It was a house divided over numerous substantive and methodological issues. In spite of dissension, some harmony surfaced among behaviorists.

The neobehaviorists, for example, emphasized the centrality of learning as an important key to understanding behavior. We learn languages and skills such as writing, swimming, riding a bicycle, and playing tennis. It is also true that attitudes, fears, self-concepts, political orientations, and philosophical and religious positions are subject to learning. The behaviorists also insisted on precision and clarity as marks of scientific language. Though behaviorists often disagreed with each other over exact meanings of basic terms such as *learning*, *reinforcement*, and *extinction*, there was agreement on the importance of linking such concepts to experimental procedures. When an expression such as *hunger drive* was employed, there was agreement that such an expression should be treated as if it had no meaning across experiments. Instead, the expression was tied to a specifiable metric employed in an experiment. *Hunger drive*, for example, might be defined in terms of hours of food deprivation. A group that had gone without food for twelve hours would, by definition, have more hunger drive than a group without food for six hours.

The importance of establishing clear empirical meanings for scientific terms is found in the work of Nobel laureate **Percy W. Bridgman (1882–1961)**. In his classic book *The Logic of Modern Physics*, Bridgman (1927) set forth the principles of operationism. As envisioned by Bridgman, **operationism** is a programmatic attempt to tie scientific terms to the measurements or operations of an experiment. In physics, one might measure air pressure in terms of a meter reading, while in psychology, one might measure a concept such as hunger drive in terms of hours of food deprivation, number of stomach contractions in a specified time period, blood chemistry changes, or number of approaches to a food container in a specified block of time.

The neobehaviorists were largely in agreement with operationism and with a related movement in philosophy called **logical positivism**. Logical positivism, sometimes called *critical empiricism* or *scientific empiricism*, grew out of a school of philosophy known as the Vienna Circle. It was a discussion group comprised of scientists and philosophers such as Moritz Schlick, Otto Neurath, Rudolf Carnap, Herbert Feigl, and Philipp Frank. Members of the Vienna Circle hoped to achieve a unified science, devoid of ambiguous and meaningless metaphysical concepts. Such a science would insist, first and foremost, on clarity of expression in scientific work.

The logical positivists argued that many concepts are devoid of scientific meaning because they cannot be verified or confirmed. Such concepts are little more than collections of words without clear-cut references. The positivists were not referring to random collections of words as meaningless but to coherent statements that evoke feelings or trigger past associations. A statement such as *The rat is happy* illustrates the point. The statement may be coherent and may evoke past associations, yet it is scientifically meaningless. Why? Because, according to the logical positivists, we cannot scientifically study an inner world devoid of clear and explicit references. We could, of course, operationalize *happiness* and study such behaviors as vigor of response, amount of food consumed, or number of intromissions in a sexual episode. Each is measurable and confirmable by independent observers. By contrast, an expression such as *The rat is happy* calls for an assessment of the inner world of the rat. Such an expression cannot yield the same kind of quantitative, publicly verifiable data as, for instance, amount of food consumed. Though logical positivism would later succumb to its critics, the emphasis on publicly confirmable

propositions and a suspicion of inner experience was consistent with behaviorism.

A third characteristic of the neobehaviorists was their strong emphasis on the importance of experimentation. It was agreed that theories and hypotheses must be subjected to vigorous experimental scrutiny. Neobehaviorism's reign in the 1930s, 1940s, and 1950s produced an unprecedented outpouring of research. At the same time, the rapid growth of new statistical procedures contributed to innovative design techniques.

We now turn to four neobehaviorists who followed Watson and became dominant figures in American experimental psychology until the midpoint of the twentieth century.

Clark Leonard Hull

Clark Leonard Hull (1884–1952) was probably the leading figure in academic experimental psychology from about 1930 to 1950. According to Logan (1968), Hull earned this status because he "presented his theoretical ideas with a degree of rigor and analytic detail then unfamiliar in psychology" (p. 535). Logan claimed that Hull's theory drew from dominant influences of the day—Watson, Pavlov, Darwin, Thorndike, and even Freud. According to Logan (1968), Freud's emphasis on "the central role of motivation in behavior [was] a position Hull increasingly adopted" (p. 535). Hull's theoretical approach to learning and behavior was mathematical and deductive, illustrated in quasi-mathematical postulates and corollaries that lend themselves to experimental procedure.

Hull graduated from the University of Michigan in 1913 and received his Ph.D. in 1918 from the University of Wisconsin. In 1929, James Rowland Angell hired Hull to work at the Institute of Human Relations at Yale University. During this time, he produced his monumental work in behavior theory. Hull was recognized with many honors during the course of his academic career, including election as president of the American Psychological Association in 1935.

Hull had a singular impact on experimental psychology and expanded the scope of stimulus–response (S–R) psychology (Rashotte & Amsel, 1999) by emphasizing the intervening variables in the organism (S–O–R; see Moore, 2011). Later we discuss how this emphasis on the intervening variables opened the door to cognitive psychology (Moore, 2013). One of Hull's best-known students, Kenneth W. Spence (1952), claimed that 70 percent of all experimental studies on learning and motivation "reported in the *Journal of Experimental Psychology* and the *Journal of Comparative and Physiological Psychology* during the decade 1941–1950 made reference to one or more of Hull's publications" (p. 641). Hull clearly conceived of psychology as a natural science. Hull died of a heart condition on May 10, 1952.

HULL'S SYSTEM The intellectual background for Hull's general behavior theory was based partly on his love for quantitative predictions and his quest for scientific unity (see Mills, 1988). The theory is set forth in four books and a large number of scientific papers. His major books include *Mathematico-Deductive Theory of Rote Learning*, published in 1940, followed by the classic *Principles of Behavior* (1943), which became a powerful force in psychology into the mid-1960s (Kranz, 2005). Eight years later, *Essentials of Behavior* (1951) showed the maturity of Hull's system. Hull's final book, *A Behavior System* (1952), was published posthumously. According to Logan (1968), another book on "application to social and cultural problems remained to be written at the time of Hull's death in 1952" (p. 536).

Many of the anchoring concepts in Hull's system are set forth in quasi-mathematical formulae as follows:

$$_sE_R = {_sH_R} \times D \times V \times K$$

$_sE_R$ refers to action potential in a given situation; $_sH_R$ refers to **habit strength** or number of previous trials in the situation; D is drive strength (e.g., the number of hours of food deprivation); and

V refers to **stimulus intensity dynamism**. This last term recognizes that some stimuli have a stronger influence on behavior than others. For example, the rat, a nocturnal animal, might run more vigorously in a darkened runway than in a well-lighted runway. Thus, V would have a greater value in the darkened runway. Finally, K refers to incentive motivation. For example, a child might work harder for a marble than for a button. Presumably the marble would have more K, or incentive value.

Hull's formula indicates that reaction potential is a multiplicative function of habit strength, **drive** (an internal state that leads to action), the nature of the stimulus, and incentive motivation. Thus, a rat might be expected to be highly active in a familiar, slightly darkened runway working for a preferred food object under relatively high drive. The foregoing formula is somewhat simplified but provides a general sense of Hull's approach. Hullian formulae often generated precise predictions about what subjects would do in specific situations.

Hull's work in psychology began with simple observations (e.g., performance improves with practice, we learn better under some circumstances than others, and under certain circumstances we quit engaging in what was once a well-established response). The terms Hull used as intervening variables (e.g., *drive*, *incentive*, and *habit strength*) all have intuitive appeal and are tied to observable behaviors and stimulus events. Let us now consider Hull's position on specific problems in behavior theory.

Reinforcement Reinforcement played a key role in Hull's behavior system. He spoke of the law of reinforcement, which meant that stimuli that reduce drive stimuli are reinforcing. Thus, food reduces hunger stimuli produced by the depletion of solid material in the stomach, just as escape from shock reduces shock stimuli. Further, Hull recognized the crucial role of "secondary" reinforcement in the control of behavior: Any stimulus consistently associated with primary reinforcers takes on reinforcing properties. As noted earlier, Hull also recognized the role of incentive as an important dimension of reinforcement.

Experimental Extinction Because of its theoretical and possible practical applications, the study of experimental extinction has long been a topic of interest. The usual laboratory procedure is to establish a response through conditioning and then study the persistence of the response once reinforcement is terminated. The speed of extinction, the conditions that accelerate or retard it, and the explanations for why it occurs have occupied a prominent place in the literature of behavior theory.

Hull argued that each response generates some degree of inhibition, which he called **fatigue**. Such inhibition is an after-effect of the response and is akin to a negative drive, like pain. Hull referred to the inhibitory potential associated with each response as I_R, or *reactive inhibition*. Hull assumed that I_R dissipates with the passage of time, so it is a temporary state that follows each response. When responses are massed close together or when responses require high effort, I_R should be increased.

A second component of Hull's theory of extinction is called *conditioned inhibition*, or $_sI_R$. Hull assumed that $_sI_R$ builds up during the dissipation of I_R. To illustrate, assume that a rat during extinction has pressed an eighty-gram counterweighted bar several times. Such a bar would be fairly heavy for the typical laboratory rat. After such a response burst, the rat has presumably generated much I_R, or fatigue. Now the rat rests, and the act of resting is reinforcing. In other words, the dissipation of I_R is reinforcing. So $_sI_R$, or conditioned inhibition, gets built up. Hull accounted for permanent extinction in terms of conditioned inhibition. Hull's predictions on the roles of effort and inhibition in extinction received support in the literature (see Capehart et al., 1958; Fischer et al., 1968), but it is unlikely inhibition in its various forms is sufficiently robust to provide a complete account of extinction of responses.

The Role of Insight in Learning Hull believed that learning proceeds in a continuous

fashion and "the organism's own responses furnish the surrogates for ideas" (Hilgard & Bower, 1966, p. 183). Hull attempted to understand behavior mechanistically in terms of material, efficient, and formal causation. Although he did not deny that terms such as *purpose, insight,* and *intention* can be attributed to the behavior of organisms, his hope was to show that such terms are "secondary principles" that can be deduced "from more elementary objective primary principles" (Hull, 1943, p. 26).

How Does Learning Occur? As noted earlier, Hull believed that reinforcement plays a crucial role in learning. Hilgard and Bower (1966), in summarizing Hull's position, pointed out that "mere contiguous repetition does nothing but generate inhibition; all improvement depends upon reinforcement . . . [and] the number of reinforcements is the basic variable in acquiring habit strength" (p. 182). Nevertheless, Hull's theory is by no means a single-factor theory. Reinforcement may be necessary for learning in Hull's system, but it is not sufficient, nor is any other element, such as contiguity, sufficient. Hull's theory accounts for learning in terms of a complex interaction of a variety of organismic and environmental variables.

APPRAISAL OF HULL'S THEORY Although a leading figure in neobehaviorism during his lifetime, Hull's visibility in the psychological literature diminished after his death (Webster & Coleman, 1992). A number of critics outlined potential concerns in Hull's system. However, Spence (1952) stated that "no account of Hull's point of view would be complete which failed to emphasize his appreciation of what it was necessary to do in order to develop a science of psychology" (p. 646). Hull has even been criticized for the very scientific qualities some psychologists count as virtues. The rigor of his approach, specifically his emphasis on substantive and operational definitions, was both a strength and a weakness. Specifically, critics have argued that the approach is sterile, artificial, and irrelevant to real-life concerns. Spence (1952)

343

replied to such criticism: "Hull fully realized that, just as the physicist found it necessary to introduce such unworldlike conditions as the vacuum and the biologist such unnatural situations as an isolated piece of tissue 'growing' in a test tube, so likewise the psychologist must not hesitate to observe behavior, whether animal or human, under controlled conditions, artificial or otherwise" (p. 646). The comparison with early physics and biology is provocative, but it is perhaps still too early to gauge its legitimacy.

Edwin Ray Guthrie

Edwin Ray Guthrie (1886–1959) had an extensive background in mathematics, formal logic, and philosophy but ultimately settled for a career in experimental psychology (Clark, 2005). He was well known in his day and is remembered for a theory of learning that highlights many of the basic tenets of positivism and classic behaviorism. Guthrie taught at the University of Washington where he also served as Dean of the Graduate School. He was elected president of the American Psychological Association in 1945 and received the gold medal award from the American Psychological Association in 1958 for his distinguished contributions to the science of learning.

Guthrie's approach to learning is remembered for its commonsense emphasis on observable behaviors and his avoidance of the kinds of hypothetical constructs and intervening variables encountered in the work of Clark Hull. Guthrie avoided formalized theory and was skeptical of truths based exclusively on deduction. His position on many of the learning issues of his day was unique for its emphasis on the single law of contiguity. According to this law, we learn connections or associations based simply on close temporal or spatial conjunction between stimuli and desired responses. For example, a young student enters a classroom and immediately occupies a specific seat previously assigned by the teacher. The specific seat might well be in an entirely different location relative to the room than the seat the student occupies in a different classroom. In each case, entry into the classroom triggers cues associated with responses that lead to the appropriate seat. Guthrie believed that learned associations are established purely on the basis of the single law of contiguity without the need for drive reduction or reinforcement.

Guthrie doubted that reinforcement per se has any direct logical or causal relationship with actual learned associations. Reinforcement, of course, has activating effects and may help keep the individual in a position such that learning can take place, but Guthrie believed that learned connections, in themselves, are independent of reinforcements such as food or praise. Thus reinforcement is used because it is part of a complex stimulus arrangement that makes it possible to learn.

Guthrie was well known for his belief in "one-trial" learning. He argued that what is learned is learned in a single trial. Why then is there improvement with practice? According to Guthrie, improvement occurs because each trial affords opportunities to attach increasing numbers of stimuli to the relevant response. Thus, something is learned on each trial, but each trial is a bit different from the previous trial. Improvement occurs as larger numbers of cues are attached to the relevant response or set of responses.

As we have seen, learning theorists in Guthrie's day were deeply interested in extinction. Such interest is based on practical problems associated with the breaking of habits. How can we rid ourselves of undesirable or unhealthy behaviors? Guthrie's position on the problem was unique in his day. He did not believe that responses are weakened by the mere passage of time, the withdrawal of reinforcement, fatigue, or the effort required to make a response. According to Guthrie, what we call extinction really amounts to new learning that results from establishing new responses to old stimuli. For example, one may have developed a fear of dogs based on a single unfortunate incident. Guthrie's approach to such a fear would be to establish new stimulus situations, possibly with non-threatening puppies, that would afford opportunities for new learning.

One appeal of Guthrie's theory is his use of illustrations from everyday life. He was interested in the application of learning to psychotherapy, habit breaking, and a host of educational problems. His practical interests were illustrated in books such as *The Psychology of Human Conflict* (1938), *Educational Psychology* (1950), co-authored with Francis Powers, and his paper "Personality in Terms of Associative Learning" (Guthrie, 1944). Guthrie's approach to learning was carried on in the works of admirers such as Estes (1950) and Voeks (1950). In Guthrie's hands, learning is not just a sterile laboratory discipline. It is a vital and all-encompassing way of thinking about behavior in educational, clinical, industrial, and daily-life situations.

Edward Chace Tolman

Edward Chace Tolman (1886–1959) developed a "new formula for behaviorism" that accepted behavior as the proper subject matter of psychology but rejected Watson's stark stimulus–response system (see Tolman, 1922) as well as Hull's reductionistic and mathematical system.

Tolman was born to an upper-middle-class family in Newton, Massachusetts, on April 14, 1886. He graduated from Massachusetts Institute of Technology and immediately enrolled in philosophy and psychology courses at Harvard. Following completion of a Ph.D. at Harvard, Tolman worked for three years at Northwestern University before taking a faculty position at Berkeley that he would hold for the rest of his life. He was a committed pacifist, and in the early 1950s he publicly and successfully led the resistance to a requirement that University of California faculty take an anti-communist oath to retain their jobs (Carroll, 2012). Like other prominent neobehaviorists, Tolman enjoyed many honors in his lifetime. He served as president of the American Psychological Association

in 1937. Twenty years later, Tolman received the Distinguished Scientific Contribution Award from the American Psychological Association.

TOLMAN'S COGNITIVE BEHAVIORISM

A major complaint against Watsonian behaviorism was that it achieved scientific status at the expense of believability. Watson's system lacked appeal because consciousness, cognition, and goal-directedness were either banished altogether or redefined in ways that defied common sense. In contrast, Tolman retained the objectives of classical behaviorism, but with a greater sensitivity to events in our daily lives. Tolman characterized his system as a *molar behaviorism* in contrast with Watson's molecular behaviorism. The term *molar* referred to large units or the kind of global behavior that we observe in the everyday world. Tolman believed that behavior is a legitimate scientific topic of inquiry in its own right. He referred to his system as a **purposive behaviorism** because organisms are directed toward goals (Innis, 1999). Such goals have clearcut observable qualities that can serve as objects of scientific analysis. We need not get lost in the philosophical subtleties of teleology to explain the goal-directed features of behavior.

According to Tolman, **molar behavior** has a purposive quality but it is also *cognitive* and *docile*. These two terms distinguish molar behavior from rigid, reflexive, mechanical behaviors. Molar behavior is not like a reflex. Molar behavior has a multitude of causes; it has an intelligent "teachable" quality, and it is not blind. The term *teachable* is close in meaning to Tolman's term *docile*. The term *cognitive* refers to abilities such as the capacity to discriminate, the sense of locations, a sense of what leads to what, and the capacity to form expectations.

Intervening Variables Tolman believed we can identify meaningful psychological concepts that account for the behavior of living organisms. In other words, Tolman was not content to describe simple stimulus–response relationships and, like other neobehaviorists, emphasized the O in S–O–R (Moore, 2011). He believed psychological processes intervene between stimuli and responses. Such psychological processes are inferred from and tied to behavior. **Intervening variable** refers to psychological processes that direct behavior and mediate between stimuli and observable responses. For Tolman, examples of intervening variables include cognitions, expectancies, purposes, hypotheses, and appetite. To illustrate, consider the term *expectancy*. According to Tolman, an expectancy develops when a reward follows each successful response. Humans and animals develop expectancies anytime regular relationships occur between stimulus events or between responses and environmental stimuli. Once developed, an expectancy is involved in directing and controlling behavior. Many of Tolman's intervening variables had a mentalistic ring yet were always tied to observable events. We now turn to a consideration of Tolman's position on additional key issues in learning.

Reinforcement What we normally think of as a reinforcement (e.g., food) has nothing to do with learning as such, but reinforcements do regulate the performance of learned responses. Tolman, more than any theorist, drew a sharp distinction between learning and performance. Classic experiments on **latent learning** illustrate Tolman's position on the relationships among reinforcement, learning, and performance.

In a typical experiment (Tolman & Honzik, 1930), one group of rats was given a food reward following each successful run through a maze. Over the course of the experiment, the speed of running quickly increased and the number of errors decreased. Another group of rats received no food in the maze. After spending time in the maze each day, subjects in this group are removed and returned to their home cage. Speed of running and number of errors for this group did not improve significantly. At this point, one might conclude that the group that had been rewarded had learned while the group that had not been rewarded did not learn. Such an interpretation, however, confounds learning with performance. Perhaps the group that had not been fed had also learned the maze but had no reason to show

that they knew it. So, on day eleven, Tolman and Honzik introduced food in the reward box for rats that had not previously been rewarded. Their running speeds and error scores improved dramatically—so dramatically that Tolman concluded there was latent learning during the non-rewarded trials.

Tolman argued that rats learn spatial relationships or even develop a cognitive map of a maze by virtue of sheer exposure. Reinforcement influences motivation, and hence performance, but learning itself is an independent process. For practical purposes, he argued that we should still use reinforcement because of the important role it plays in motivation.

Experimental Extinction According to Tolman, extinction occurs largely because of changes in expectancies. Response strength remains high so long as conditioned stimuli serve as signs that food will be forthcoming. When stimuli no longer have value as signs, expectancies change and so do responses. One implication of Tolman's position is that extinction, in theory, can be a cognitive affair; that is, it could occur without responding. If one were in a position to see that a sign will no longer lead to a reinforcement, extinction could be accomplished without the necessity of responding. Experiments on latent extinction have provided evidence for cognitive interpretations of extinction.

In the typical experiment, rats were repeatedly placed in an unbaited goal box that was once a place where they had obtained reinforcement. Subjects who were exposed to an unbaited goal box extinguished faster in subsequent extinction trials than did subjects who had no such preextinction exposure to the unbaited goal box. Extinction, according to Tolman, results from changing cognitions that are influenced by sign stimuli in the environment. Such a position is in marked contrast with Hull's response-produced inhibition theory.

Cognitive Maps The emphasis in many early learning theories was on connections between stimuli and responses. Tolman accepted the idea that some learning involves stimulus–

response connections, but he also emphasized stimulus–stimulus connections. Complicated stimulus–stimulus connections are vital components in Tolman's concept of the **cognitive map**.

Consider the complicated maze that the typical college student must run in order to get from a dorm room to a classroom. The maze may involve many left and right turns, some diagonal pathways, stairs, or even elevators. In animal laboratories, comparable situations are sometimes created for rats. When the maze is successfully traversed, we may ask ourselves what has been learned. Have we learned a complicated chain of stimulus–response connections? According to Tolman, the answer is "no." In such a situation we learn a cognitive map.

For example, we do not learn that we must make three successive left turns, followed by two right turns, followed by a left turn, and so on. Instead, we develop a cognitive map that includes, at first, a vague sense of location and a sense of the layout of the situation, including many possible pathways connecting various locations. In other words, there is a rich and broad cognitive representation of the world in which we move (Nadel, 2013). We do not move about our world in a mechanical fashion; rather, we move in a flexible fashion, following first one pathway then another. Rats do the same thing. Again, Tolman did not deny that some learning involves stimulus–response connections, but he insisted we learn stimulus–stimulus connections that are vital to the development of cognitive maps.

The Role of Insight in Learning Tolman accepted the idea that learning is often marked by radical discontinuities. Most learning is not of the blind trial-and-success variety discussed in Thorndike's work. Tolman believed in the "*capacity* for grasping field-relationships" (Tolman, 1932, p. 200). He also spoke of the capacity for *inventive ideation*, which referred to "running back-and-forth, attempting alternatives, and making behavioral adjustments." Although Tolman avoided the term *insight*, he also rejected

the idea that learning is always a continuous, gradual, mechanical process.

APPRAISAL OF TOLMAN'S SYSTEM Tolman demonstrated that the desirable methodological rigor of classical behaviorism could be coupled with a richer, more believable psychology that recognizes the complexities and subtleties of human and animal life. His system provided the intellectual spadework that nurtured the cognitive movement in the 1950s. Hilgard and Bower (1966) noted that Tolman "gave a new cast to behaviorism by insisting that it be open to the problems created by cognitive processes, problem solving, and inventive ideation" (p. 228).

Finally, Tolman's work can be viewed as a springboard for developments in the 1950s and 1960s in such diverse areas as motivation (Festinger, 1962; Lawrence & Festinger, 1962), clinical psychology (Rotter, 1954), neuropsychology (Olds, 1954), and mathematical learning theory (Bower, 1962; MacCorquodale & Meehl, 1954). He was the first to publish research on selective breeding for maze-learning ability in rats, work that inspired his students such as Robert Choate Tryon (1901–1967) and influenced the field of behavioral genetics (Innis, 1992). Tolman's work is one of the most important bridges between classical behaviorism and contemporary psychology (Goldman, 1999; Fuller, 2013). Gleitman (1991) notes that Tolman was "clearly a forerunner of modern 'cognitive psychology'" and that he was well ahead of his time (p. 235).

Burrhus Frederic Skinner

Hull, Guthrie, and Tolman were not neobehaviorism's sole champions. In the latter half of the twentieth century, B. F. Skinner not only dominated neobehaviorism, but also became one of psychology's most celebrated figures.

Burrhus Frederic Skinner (1904–1990) was born on March 20, 1904, in Susquehanna, Pennsylvania. He lived a pleasant childhood

347

surrounded by a cordial family. Skinner hoped to become an author and, though a careless student, studied literature at Hamilton College in New York. He decided against a writing career despite the poet Robert Frost's favorable appraisal of his work. While at Hamilton, Skinner read Ivan Pavlov's *Conditioned Reflexes*, Bertrand Russell's *Philosophy*, and John B. Watson's *Behaviorism*. Despite the minimal emphasis on behaviorism, the graduate program at Harvard allowed Skinner autonomy in developing research interests. He completed all requirements for his master's degree in 1930 and received his Ph.D. the following year. From 1933 to 1936, Skinner continued his research in the prestigious position of junior fellow of the Harvard Society of Fellows. In 1936, Skinner joined the faculty of the University of Minnesota, where he continued development of operant conditioning. In 1945, he assumed the chair of the psychology department at Indiana University but after three years he returned to Harvard University.

In 1958, the American Psychological Association honored Skinner with its Distinguished Scientific Contribution Award. In the same year, he was appointed to the prestigious Edgar Pierce Professorship, named in honor of the affluent Harvard alumnus who established the William James lecture series. Skinner, however, found little gratification in such veneration. Indeed, his style of life was self-effacing and uncomplicated. He answered his own phone, refused to display medals or trophies, and stored honorary degrees in a box in the basement of his home; he published with many faculty and student co-authors (McKerchar et al., 2011). When he allowed interviews or appearances on talk shows (such as a 1971 debate with the physicist Donald MacKay on the TV program *Firing Line*), it was not for self-aggrandizement but for the promotion of behaviorism (Washburn, 1997).

Skinner retired in 1974 to become Professor Emeritus of Psychology and Social Relations. In August 1990, the American Psychological Association presented Skinner with the unprecedented Citation for Outstanding Lifetime Contribution to Psychology. B. F. Skinner died from leukemia on August 18, 1990, a mere eight days after accepting the APA award.

For six decades Skinner was a prolific and animated defender of behaviorism. His experimental behavior analysis was set forth in numerous scientific and nontechnical books, including *The Behavior of Organisms* (1938), *Walden Two* (1948), *Science and Human Behavior* (1953), *Verbal Behavior* (1957), *The Technology of Teaching* (1968), *Beyond Freedom and Dignity* (1971), and *About Behaviorism* (1974). In addition, he published a three-volume autobiography, *Particulars of My Life* (1976), *The Shaping of a Behaviorist* (1979), and *A Matter of Consequences* (1983a). Although his research was often marked with controversy and criticism (Rutherford, 2000), Skinner invested little time answering his critics. His preference was to collect data and work out the details of his position.

SKINNER'S PHILOSOPHY OF BEHAVIORISM

Skinner was a resolute positivist devoted to psychology as an objective natural science. According to Skinner (1963), behaviorism was more than the study of behavior; it was a philosophy of science.

B. F. Skinner

348

Like Watson, Skinner saw psychology as a natural science and, like Watson, he was a thoroughgoing determinist. Skinner (1971) insisted that behavior is lawful and argued that the romantic notion of free will is counterproductive both to behavioral science and to society at large.

Though Skinner's writings gave the impression of hard determinism, his research on reinforcers that increase the probability of a future response suggests an interest in probabilistic lawfulness rather than strict determinism. Nevertheless, emphasis on prediction and control was central to Skinner's entire system of thought. Furthermore, his goal was to demonstrate the detrimental features of aversive control and the advantages of positive control. Like most other neobehaviorists, Skinner was a student of behavior rather than of mental events.

Unlike Clark Hull, Skinner eschewed grandiose theory construction in favor of descriptive observations of behavior, and his bottom-up approach to the study of behavior has remained fruitful (Madden et al., 2012). More than any behaviorist, Skinner (1956) followed Bacon's critical inductivist tradition. He denied that he constructed hypotheses or that he tested formal theorems or models (Moore, 2013). He assumed that behavior was lawful and understood the difficulty of discovering its laws. We turn now to a consideration of Skinner's specific contributions.

OPERANT CONDITIONING Skinner (1938) established experimental behavior analysis in his classic work *The Behavior of Organisms*. Based on his published research since 1930, this book presented a comprehensive system of methods for the **operant conditioning** of animals. Although some critics attacked Skinner for making no effort to tie his ideas to existing data and concepts, *The Behavior of Organisms* was hailed as a significant contribution to the psychology of learning (Knapp, 1995). As far back as 1932, Skinner had distinguished between two major types of conditioning, and five years later introduced the term *operant* in contrast with Pavlovian **respondent conditioning** (Coleman, 1981).

Pavlovian conditioning probed the correlations between unconditioned and conditioned stimuli, whereas Skinner stressed the relation of the response and reinforcement. Thus, Skinner referred to Pavlovian conditioning as *Type II* or *Type S* (reinforcement correlated with a stimulus) and operant conditioning as *Type I* or *Type R* (reinforcement correlated with a response). Type S encompassed conditioning of autonomic behavior, whereas Type R was conditioning of voluntary behavior. From its genesis, operant conditioning involved modifying behavior as a consequence of reinforcement. Any consequence that increased the probability of a future response was deemed a reinforcer.

Because Skinner was not concerned with the antecedent association between stimulus and response, his work is not in the tradition of S–R psychology. Skinner denied this heritage: "I do not consider myself an S–R psychologist. The stimulus is only one among a lot of different variables. As it stands, I'm not sure that response is a very useful concept. Behavior is very fluid; it isn't made up of lots of little responses packed together . . . It is a mistake to suppose that there are internal stimuli and to try to formulate everything as S–R psychology" (quoted in Evans, 1968, pp. 20–21).

You might note the similarity between the research of Skinner and of Edward L. Thorndike (Chance, 1999). In a letter to Thorndike, Skinner (1967) acknowledged that his work was an elaboration of the former's puzzle box research. As in Thorndike's revised law of effect, Skinner favored reinforcement over punishment in the strengthening of behavior. Intermittent punishment may produce unfortunate by-products and only short-term gains. Nevertheless, Skinner (1953) asserted that society had made progress in diminishing the aversive influence of punishment. He celebrated the demise of angry avenging gods and threats of hellfire that terrorized previous generations. He was also pleased that the "dunce cap" and birch rod in schools were replaced by more enlightened positive incentives to learn. Skinner verified reinforcement principles with

349

data collected from various technological innovations. Indeed, his modification of ice chests into operant chambers revolutionized the study of animal behavior. The chamber allowed an animal to demonstrate a learned behavior (e.g., a bar press or key peck) that could be rewarded by a food dispenser. Interestingly, Clark Hull branded the operant chamber with the infamous title of "Modified Skinner Box," although in characteristic modesty, Skinner (1983a) protested usage of the eponym.

Skinner also constructed the cumulative recorder, a mechanical device that monitored patterns of operant behavior from a single animal. By the mid-1950s, operant instrumentation was manufactured by several companies. His experiences with operant technology led to new discoveries, such as the influence of different schedules of reinforcement on behavior (Crossman, 1991). Skinner (1956) reported that practical necessity motivated his early interest in schedules of reinforcement. One day it was clear that he was running out of food pellets, so he reinforced his subject once every minute. He saved his supply of pellets and observed a constant rate of responding. This serendipitous finding led to the study of fixed intervals and other schedules of reinforcement. Together with Charles Ferster, Skinner published a book on the specifications of these experimental reinforcement schedules (Ferster & Skinner, 1957).

Skinner's fundamental vision of operant conditioning did not radically change in the ensuing half-century (although ideas about drive and reflex were abandoned after the 1930s). However, Skinner's contribution extends beyond research on animal learning. In fact, the broad implications of his research on operant conditioning have served as the impetus for numerous applications.

SKINNER'S APPLIED RESEARCH One hallmark of B. F. Skinner's legacy is an effort to generalize his ideas from the domain of the laboratory to the complexity of the external world. Though initially he found little interest in the applications of operant conditioning (see Skinner, 1938), he later changed his position. Indeed, the 1968 debut of the *Journal of Applied Behavior Analysis* signaled one of many applications of the experimental principles of behavior analysis. Let's take a look at Skinner's more prominent applications.

Verbal Behavior One of Skinner's earliest applied efforts, started in 1935, was an analysis of verbal behavior. Although a disciple of Darwinian continuity, Skinner (1938) admitted, "The only differences I expect to see revealed between the behavior of rat and man (aside from enormous differences of complexity) lie in the field of verbal behavior" (p. 442). Skinner revealed his concept of language acquisition in his 1948 William James lectures, which were expanded into the controversial 1957 publication *Verbal Behavior*. He claimed that verbal behavior is learned and, like any operant behavior, is modified by ensuing consequences from a given community.

Critics, most notably psycholinguist Noam Chomsky, argued that Skinner's reinforcement explanation of linguistic development was simplistic and reductionistic. Chomsky (1959) believed that language was an abstract, rule-governed system. Chomsky's scathing review generated considerable attention while Skinner's work was largely neglected (Andresen, 1991). However, Skinner was convinced that Chomsky misunderstood the book and declined rebuttal to the psycholinguist's critique; these concerns persist (Palmer, 2006). Kenneth MacCorquodale (1970) later defended Skinner's verbal behavior perspective within the context of the nativism (Chomsky) versus environment (Skinner) debate. Despite criticism of the book, Skinner continued to support the reinforcement explanation of verbal behavior, and this explanation remains relevant in psychology (Schlinger, 2008).

Developmental and Educational Applications While at Indiana, Skinner gained notoriety for his invention of the aircrib, a large, well-lit chamber with proper temperature control for child rearing (Benjamin & Nielsen-Gammon, 1999). Originally called the "baby-tender,"

Skinner employed the chamber during the upbringing of Deborah, his second daughter. Contrary to rumors about trauma resulting from her upbringing, Skinner (1967) proudly noted that his daughter was a college graduate and an accomplished artist. Furthermore, Julie, his oldest daughter and an educational psychologist, raised Skinner's granddaughter in an aircrib.

Skinner took an active interest in the education of his children, and he hoped to promote a structured educational environment that employed the principles of operant conditioning. He also advocated a behavioral approach to classroom management (Peck, 2013; Skinner, 1958, 1968). In the 1920s, Sidney L. Pressey (1888–1979) had constructed programmed machines for testing intelligence. Skinner revised Pressey's idea by designing programs that dispensed immediate feedback for each student response. Skinner's programmed instruction promoted sustained activity with self-paced mastery of the material. The idea generated a great deal of media attention (Rutherford, 2000). Although IBM and other companies were interested in marketing teaching machines, negotiations collapsed along with Skinner's dream of reforming American education (Bjork, 1993); nonetheless, Skinner's attempts to improve education and culture through controlled, ethical application of his behaviorism to education anticipated computer-assisted instruction by several decades (de Melo et al., 2015). His programmed instruction inspired other researchers to develop innovative educational methods. Most notably, Fred S. Keller formulated a Personalized System of Instruction (PSI), which emphasized the individual student's responsibility for mastering the material (Keller & Sherman, 1974). Despite such pedagogical innovations, Skinner (1984) remained dissatisfied with the direction of U.S. education.

Finally, Skinner explored the process of aging. Together with Margaret Vaughan, he published a nontechnical book titled *Enjoy Old Age* in 1983. This book contained practical suggestions and insights on gerontological concerns such as diet, exercise, retirement, forgetfulness, sensory deficiencies, and the fear of death. Ironically, Skinner (1983a) recalled the rigorous composition of the book: "We met a self-imposed deadline and finished it in three months, thereby violating, for me, one of its basic principles: avoid fatigue. I was scarcely enjoying old age when we finished the book, but I soon recovered" (p. 394).

Military Applications Perhaps Skinner's most unconventional idea was his so-called Project Pigeon research during World War II. With the assistance of several outstanding students from the University of Minnesota (including Keller and Marian Breland and William K. Estes), Skinner trained pigeons to navigate an armed glider named the "Pelican" (so named because, like the bird, the glider had a large frontal store with a considerably smaller body). The enthusiastic researchers demonstrated the efficiency of their automated bombers to government officials but with disappointing results. Ironically, Skinner (1960) claimed that one military authority declared that the pigeons were more accurate than radar. Despite Skinner's certitude about the effectiveness of his "crackpot idea," the government rejected further support for the project. Despite initial funding by General Mills, the decision was made to discontinue funding in favor of other military projects.

However, the classified research did demonstrate the efficacy of operant conditioning. Skinner kept thirty pigeons and demonstrated immediate and accurate target strikes even after six years of inactivity. Franklin Taylor resurrected the research under the auspices of the Naval Research Laboratory in Washington, DC. A missile nose cone from Project Pigeon resides with a teaching machine in the Smithsonian Institution (Skinner, 1983b). Skinner's ideas were also implemented in an aerospace program that sent two bar-pressing chimpanzees into space (Rohles, 1992).

Walden Two: Another Behaviorist Utopia In an essay titled "A Behaviorist's Utopia," John B. Watson conceived of a society that controlled child care and social relationships from the time of birth to maturity (Buckley,

1989). Although far removed from Watson's utopia, Skinner proposed in detail a society based on the use of behavioral principles of reinforcement to support well-being and social justice (Altus & Morris, 2009). In his 1948 novel *Walden Two*, he described life in a hypothetical experimental colony designed by behavioral engineering. The novel centers on Professor Burris, who is reacquainted with T. E. Frazier, a maverick colleague from their graduate school days. Frazier is the founder of Walden Two, a community maintained and established on positive reinforcement. Workers labor for four hours daily, have a credit system of payment, and enjoy numerous opportunities for creative relaxation. Through the observations of Burris and Frazier, the reader is allowed insight into Skinner's vision of a behaviorist utopia.

Written in a mere seven weeks, *Walden Two* became one of Skinner's most popular books, especially during the quest for alternative lifestyles in the 1960s. The controversial nature of a behaviorally designed community aroused curiosity among the general public, college students, movie studios, and even the Central Intelligence Agency (Skinner, 1983a). An experimental community based on *Walden Two* was established in 1967 in Twin Oaks, Virginia. The community proved only marginally successful (Kuhlmann, 2005) but led Skinner (1967) to reformulate the role of incentive, education, and sexuality in a behaviorist community. Although fictional, Skinner's *Walden Two* provides an intriguing glimpse into behavioral engineering for the collective good, an early step toward positive psychology (Adams, 2012).

Additional Applications Skinner's experimental behavior analysis has also found application in psychotherapy. During the 1930s, he had an interest in employing operant techniques with individuals struggling with severe psychological disorders but was prevented from doing so by a rigorous schedule. In 1948, he delivered a series of lectures at Worcester State Hospital but was again unable to initiate a research program on behavior modification.

Finally in 1952, Skinner initiated a behavior therapy program at the Metropolitan State Hospital in Waltham, Massachusetts. Ogden Lindsley, one of Skinner's students, engaged in six hundred hours of successful behavior modification using candy, cigarettes, and pinup posters as reinforcers for people with psychoses (Skinner, 1983b). In November 1953, Skinner and his colleagues presented their research in the paper "Studies in Behavior Therapy," marking the first usage of the term *behavior therapy* (Reed & Luiselli, 2009). Today, Skinner is the "father of applied behavior analysis" (Morris et al., 2005, p. 99), and behavior therapy and modification remain an enterprising field of psychotherapy.

Skinner had two additional students who applied operant conditioning to animal training. While working with him on Project Pigeon, Keller Breland (1915–1965) and Marian Breland (1920–2001) recognized the commercial potential of operant conditioning. They decided against pursuing their doctoral degrees at Minnesota in favor of applying behavior analysis to train animals for commercial and entertainment purposes. Although Skinner tried to dissuade them, the Brelands formed Animal Behavior Enterprises (ABE) in 1943. Over the next few decades, ABE trainers trained more than one hundred and forty different species for advertising and public entertainment. After using operant conditioning to train dolphins, the Brelands wrote a 1955 manual that influenced later marine mammal training programs at Sea World (Bailey & Gillaspy, 2005). In the 1960s, they taught training skills to Navy dolphin trainers, allowing the Brelands to study dolphin communication, acoustics, and training methods. This venture brought them into partnership with Bob Bailey who became ABE's research director in 1965 and later its general manager.

The work of Breland and Breland stimulated interest in the media, exposing the public to operant conditioning. The popular press spotlighted their work in countless articles and the Brelands featured trained animals on *The Tonight Show with Johnny Carson* and the *Ed Sullivan*

Show, among other television appearances (Bailey & Gillaspy, 2005). In 1961, they wrote "The Misbehavior of Organisms," a controversial article that challenged operant researchers to investigate instinctive behavior. Breland and Breland (1961) insisted that the "behavior of any species cannot be adequately understood, predicted, or controlled without knowledge of its instinctive patterns, evolutionary history, and ecological niche" (p. 684).

APPRAISAL OF SKINNER'S BEHAVIORISM
The praise for Skinner's work has been joined with dissension from both public and scientific sectors. Following the 1971 publication of *Beyond Freedom and Dignity*, Skinner reached the height of his public exposure and found himself embroiled in controversy that spilled into the *New York Times* among other media (Rutherford, 2000). His ideas usually provoked skeptical or condemnatory reaction and, at times, detractors perceived him as a sort of "scientific despot." A legion of critics from psychotherapist Carl Rogers to former Vice President Spiro Agnew damned Skinner's ideology. He was branded a fascist and a Nazi, protestors picketed his talks, and his image was hanged in effigy. His open criticism of the Vietnam conflict during the 1960s nearly jeopardized government funding of his research and made him the target of an FBI investigation (Skinner, 1983a; Wyatt, 2000).

Skinner also provoked criticism from colleagues within the scientific community. Critics such as Chomsky contended that Skinner's "simplistic explanations" appear sound in an artificial laboratory context but have little validity in the real world. Furthermore, behavior analysis has been accused of indifference toward topical areas such as the self, personality, cognition, feelings, purpose, creativity, and nativism. Skinner has also been blamed for advancing a mechanistic science that dehumanizes the individual. In addition, Mahoney (1989) charged that the radical behaviorist's intolerant opinion of contemporary psychology had jeopardized its future and called for a tempering of ideology if the discipline

was to progress. Baron-Cohen (2015) has argued against all forms of radical behaviorism (presumably Pavlovian, Watsonian, and Skinnerian) by pointing out that behavior is a "surface level" phenomenon. Clearly, identical behaviors can have very different neurological underpinnings, different underlying motivations, different cultural origins, and altogether different meanings; Skinner viewed his behaviorism as autonomous from neuroscience (Zilio, 2016). It can be argued that exclusive emphasis on behavior is not truly empirical because there is so much in experience that such an emphasis ignores.

Rutherford (2003) provided a carefully researched study of the treatment of Skinnerian psychology in the popular press from the 1940s to the 1970s. It was clear that changing social contexts over the decades played a significant role in the reception of Skinner's work and often contributed to feelings of ambivalence among the public. Skinner's basic goals were often consistent with the goals of major social movements, but there were disagreements about how to achieve such goals. For example, Skinner opposed the Vietnam War, as did much of the United States in the late 1960s, but he was a vocal critic of counterculture protests and other tactics. Skinner, like humanistic psychologists (see Chapter 17), promoted a societal and political system that was supportive and responsive to human needs and interests. The humanistic school of thought simply disagreed with Skinner about how to achieve such a society. Rutherford (2009) has also argued that a substantial part of Skinner's contribution comes from the technology of behavior change. If we move beyond the stereotypes of Skinner as an unfeeling researcher, we find good reasons why he was named Humanist of the Year in 1972. Rutherford (2000) observed that in the 1980s there was a "shift in public opinion and a more philosophical evaluation of [Skinner's] impact on the popular culture of psychology" (p. 391). Following Skinner's death in 1990, scholarly studies are leading to a more nuanced view of his many innovations and connections between his ideas and other areas of psychology

353

(Toates, 2009). At present, no adequate generalization does justice to Skinner's lasting influence, but there can be no denying his contributions to both experimental and clinical psychology (Goddard, 2012; Brown & Gillard, 2015).

For his part, Skinner (1987a) was puzzled about the controversy surrounding his research. After all, anybody can go to the laboratory and check his results for themselves. That is the way science works! If there have been errors, they can be corrected through additional research.

Behaviorism and Applied Psychology

In his classic article "Psychology as the Behaviorist Views It," Watson (1913) declared, "One of the earliest conditions which made me dissatisfied with psychology was the feeling that there was no realm of application for the principles which were being worked out" (p. 169). In that same article, he pointed out that if psychology would follow his system, "the educator, the physician, the jurist and the business man could utilize our data in a practical way, as soon as we are able experimentally to obtain them" (p. 168). Watson lamented the sterility of the older psychology that explored such problems as the number of discriminable shades of gray. Watson (1913) argued that he would rather explore problems such as "the effect upon behavior of certain doses of caffeine . . . [and] the effects of recency upon the reliability of a witness's report" (p. 169).

In terms of the systems examined in this book, behaviorism ranks high in its contributions to applied psychology. As we have seen, Pavlov's later career involved studies of clinical problems, and Watson supervised the earliest research on the counterconditioning of fear (Jones, 1924a, 1924b). Following Watson, there was an explosion of interest in behavior therapy techniques, manifested in the founding of scholarly journals such as *Behavior Research and Therapy*, *Journal of Applied Behavior Analysis*, and *Behavior Therapy* (Rakos, 2013). Numerous scientific and professional organizations were also founded as vehicles for the exchange of ideas on behavioral therapy. Such organizations include the Association for the Advancement of the Behavioral Therapies, the Association for the Behavioral Treatment of Sexual Abusers, the Association for Behavior Analysis, and the Society of Behavioral Medicine. Watson's contributions to applied psychology extended into the field of advertising (see Larson, 1979). The extent of his contributions to the psychology of advertising and sales is still not sufficiently appreciated.

The neobehaviorists who followed in the tradition of Watson also worked on practical problems. Though he was keenly aware of the problems of assessing human ability and potential, Hull's book *Aptitude Testing* (1928) is a classic in that area. His book *Hypnosis and Suggestibility* (1933) is also one of the most informed and substantial books on the topic of hypnosis and continues to inspire researchers (Mohl, 2012). As we have seen, Skinner was dedicated to the application of operant conditioning to a broad range of areas, including education, linguistics, development, and military and clinical psychology. Along with Skinner, Guthrie had the broadest range of interests in applied problems. Guthrie's major works are filled with practical anecdotes on how to apply his learning theory to daily problems. His book *Educational Psychology* (1950), published with Francis Powers, is an application of learning theory to the classroom. He also wrote on the topics of personality, psychotherapy, leadership, the evaluation of faculty performance, and the function of the state university.

Though most of Tolman's published works dealt with theoretical issues in learning, his cognitive emphasis brought new breadth to behaviorism. His was a more psychological behaviorism and his followers explored a larger range of problems while retaining the methodological rigor that characterized behaviorism. Tolman's book *Drives Toward War*, published in 1942, just after the United States entered World War II, illustrates his interest in the psychological sources of conflict.

Behaviorism was the dominant force in U.S. psychology from the 1920s to the late 1950s. Though most behaviorists viewed learning as foundational to the field of psychology, their interests ranged broadly from the problems of psychopathology to the problems of social psychology. Even so, by the 1960s there was a growing consensus that their vision was too narrow and that they had closed too many doors, both methodologically and substantively. Their many positive contributions, however, carried on in new, broader approaches to the discipline.

Mental processes and experience as topical content areas in psychology were re-enfranchised with the advent of the so-called cognitive revolution in the late 1950s and 1960s, and we explore these changes in Chapter 17. Psychologists who once focused largely on the study of mental processes via introspection moved to the study of behavior via more objective methodologies. The cognitive revolution did not exclude behavior as an important topic, but also included studies of the relations between behavior, neurological processes, and experience. Accommodations and tensions between behavioral psychologies and the new cognitivism and the historical accounts of their relations remain a relevant historiographic problem (see Watrin & Darwich, 2012; Staddon, 2014; Moore, 2011, 2013).

Review Questions

1. Briefly outline some of the important intellectual antecedents of behaviorism.
2. Why was the concept of *action at a distance*, or *psychical reflex*, troublesome to Pavlov?
3. What are the four temperament types included in Pavlov's system?
4. Discuss Pavlov's approach to experimental neurosis and specify the meaning of terms such as *ultramaximal inhibition, equivalence phase, paradoxical phase,* and *ultraparadoxical phase.*
5. In what sense can Thorndike be considered a functionalist and in what sense can he be considered a behaviorist?

6. Distinguish between Thorndike's early law of effect and his later law of effect. Do you think he was correct in modifying the law of effect?
7. How did John B. Watson define *psychology* and what methods did he advocate?
8. Outline Watson and Rayner's classic work on fear conditioning.
9. Describe Watson's treatment of thinking. What criticisms can you offer of his approach?
10. Contrast Hull, Guthrie, Tolman, and Skinner with respect to their views on the subject of reinforcement.
11. Briefly explain the significance of the latent learning experiments.
12. What did Tolman mean by the expression *intervening variable*?
13. Contrast Skinner and Hull with respect to their views on the role of theory in science.
14. Discuss three applications of Skinner's research.
15. Outline some of the contributions of behaviorism to applied psychology.

Glossary

action at a distance Any apparent effect for which one cannot readily identify material and efficient causes.

behaviorism A system of psychology founded by John B. Watson and marked by a strong commitment to the methods and values of the natural sciences. Watson saw psychology as a branch of the natural sciences and defined the discipline simply as the scientific study of behavior.

Bekhterev, Vladimir Mikhailovich (1857–1927) A contemporary of Ivan Pavlov who advanced an objective psychology in which the reflex served as the fundamental category of inquiry. Bekhterev's system was known as reflexology.

Bridgman, Percy W. (1882–1961) U.S. physicist and mathematician, known for his classic book *The Logic of Modern Physics* and for his emphasis on operationism, or the attempt to tie scientific terms to precise measurements.

cognitive maps A term employed by Edward Chace Tolman referring to "mental representations" of the environment that make it possible for an animal to grasp relationships and locations.

conditioned reflex (CR) In classical conditioning, a learned reflex elicited by a conditioned stimulus. Also known as a conditioned response.

conditioned stimulus (CS) In classical conditioning, any stimulus that is psychologically or biologically neutral prior to conditioning trials. Such a stimulus may be paired repeatedly with an unconditioned stimulus. After repeated pairings, the previously neutral conditioned stimulus will elicit a reflex similar to the unconditioned reflex elicited by the unconditioned stimulus.

connectionism A formal term often applied to the theory of learning advanced by Edward Lee Thorndike. Thorndike believed that learning involved the development of connections or bonds between sense impressions and responses. Connectionism is one of the first S–R theories of learning.

discrimination In classical conditioning, subjects may be conditioned to respond to one stimulus and to ignore or withhold a response to another stimulus. Discrimination is generally established through differential reinforcement.

doctrine of formal discipline An early belief that the mind, like certain muscle groups, is developed most effectively by specific exercises such as the study of certain classics (e.g., Latin and geometry).

drive A term employed in different ways in different systems of psychology but generally referring to "inner stimulation" that results in action.

equivalent phase A Pavlovian term referring to the tendency of a subject to respond in a highly stereotyped fashion to any stimulus. The equivalent phase may follow a biological

insult that produces a shock-like reaction. In such circumstances, the subject may respond in the same way to all signals.

extinction The weakening or elimination of a conditioned response. The major means of achieving extinction is to present repeatedly the conditioned stimulus in the absence of the unconditioned stimulus.

fatigue In Hull's system, fatigue refers to the theoretical position that each response generates some inhibition to its own reoccurrence.

Guthrie, Edwin Ray (1886–1959) Well-known U.S. behaviorist and learning theorist remembered for a theory of learning based primarily on the law of contiguity. Guthrie served as the fifty-third president of the American Psychological Association in 1945.

habit strength A term employed by the learning theorist Clark Hull referring to the number of reinforced trials in a situation that have contributed to the strength of a connection between a stimulus and a response.

Hull, Clark Leonard (1884–1952) One of the most famous neobehaviorists, known for a mathematical-deductive approach to animal and human behavior. Hull, a member of the National Academy of Sciences, served as the forty-fourth president of the American Psychological Association in 1935.

identical elements transfer theory In contrast with the doctrine of formal discipline, the identical elements transfer theory holds that the learning of any new task will be facilitated most by experience with highly comparable previous tasks.

intervening variable An unobserved process that accounts for connections between stimulus events and responses. For example, response rate may slow down under conditions of high effort. According to Clark Hull, response rate is slowed down because of reactive inhibition (I_R), a fatigue-like state. Fatigue, in this case, might be regarded as an intervening variable.

Jones, Mary Cover (1896–1987) American psychologist famous for her work on counterconditioning fear responses in a boy named

Peter. Her research in this area established her as a founding figure in behavior therapy.

latent learning A term employed by Edward Chace Tolman referring to learning that has occurred but is not observed because environmental conditions have not been favorable to its display. When environmental conditions change appropriately, such learning, heretofore unobservable, may now show itself.

law of effect Refers to Thorndike's early view that connections are strengthened when followed by a satisfying state of affairs and weakened when followed by an annoying state of affairs. Later, Thorndike dropped the second half of the law and argued that satisfiers strengthen associations, but annoyers do not weaken associations.

law of exercise Refers to Thorndike's early belief that connections are strengthened through practice and weakened through disuse. Later, Thorndike denied that exercise alone controls the fate of connections.

logical positivism Sometimes called *critical empiricism* or *scientific empiricism*, this school of thought contends that scientific concepts must be explicitly and operationally tied to observable events. Publicly confirmable propositions were to replace "inner experience" in all phases of scientific activity.

molar behavior An expression employed by Tolman to designate the special domain of his psychology. Molar behavior is the behavior of the intact organism engaging in typical day-to-day activities. Molar behavior contrasts with molecular or isolated small units of behavior.

operant conditioning The term *operant* refers to behavior that is emitted. According to Skinner, operant conditioning occurs if reinforcement follows with a response that is emitted in a specific situation.

operationism A programmatic attempt to tie scientific terms to measurements or operations employed in experiments. Thus, abstract terms such as *anxiety* or *intelligence* are defined in terms of the measures or operations employed in research studies.

paradoxical phase According to Pavlov, a weak stimulus may sometimes produce a strong response and a strong stimulus may produce a weak response. The paradoxical phase sometimes follows shock induced by a biological insult.

Pavlov, Ivan Petrovich (1849–1936) The most significant figure in the history of Russian psychology and pioneer in research in classical conditioning. His *Lectures on Conditioned Reflexes* is a classic work setting forth a psychology and psychiatry based on the principles of conditioning.

psychical reflex An early term used briefly in Pavlov's laboratory to describe conditioned responses. See *action at a distance*.

purposive behaviorism An orientation advanced by Tolman in which behavior is regarded as the proper subject matter of psychology, but behavior is construed as goal-directed.

reflexology A psychology based on the reflex as the fundamental category of inquiry in psychology.

reinforcement A term highly subject to theoretical interpretation but generally referring to those objects or events that result, for whatever reason, in an increased probability of responding.

respondent conditioning Pavlovian conditioning that investigates correlations between unconditioned and conditioned stimuli.

Skinner, Burrhus Frederic (1904–1990) One of the foremost behaviorists of the twentieth century, who argued that scientific psychology must concern itself with the analysis of behavior rather than the study of the mind.

spontaneous recovery Following extinction trials, a conditioned stimulus may lose its ability to produce a conditioned response. However, following a period of rest, the conditioned stimulus may once again elicit the conditioned response.

stimulus generalization Stimuli similar to the original conditioned stimulus may also elicit a conditioned response.

stimulus intensity dynamism A term employed by Clark Hull referring to the capacity of a stimulus to energize or direct behavior.

Thorndike, Edward Lee (1874–1949) U.S. psychologist who studied with James at Harvard and Cattell at Columbia. Thorndike was a pioneer in the experimental investigation of animal behavior and advanced one of the earliest and most influential learning theories. His practical work focused on behavior, and he can be considered a forerunner of behaviorism. Nevertheless, he believed that psychology might be best served by a variety of methods and viewpoints.

Tolman, Edward Chace (1886–1959) One of the leading behaviorists of the twentieth century, remembered for his attempts to combine features of behaviorism, Gestalt psychology, and McDougall's psychology. Tolman emphasized the purposive nature of behavior. He is properly regarded as one of the precursors of late twentieth-century cognitive psychology.

truncated law of effect Thorndike's later theory that reward strengthens associations. In his later work, Thorndike raised doubts that punishment serves to weaken associations.

ultramaximal inhibition Sometimes called *protective transmarginal inhibition*, refers to the effects of a severe biological or psychological insult. Such insults may produce a shock-like state that Pavlov regarded as protective. Massive inhibition, in this case, may serve a protective function by blocking out further stimulation. In shock-like states, subjects may feel no pain and be incapable of intelligent response.

ultraparadoxical phase Following a severe shock, some subjects display an unusual reversal of values. Thus, a formerly positive or loved stimulus is regarded negatively or hated and a formerly negative or hated stimulus is regarded positively or loved. Such conversions may be relatively permanent.

unconditioned reflex (UCR) Any naturally occurring reflex to a strong stimulus. Examples include salivation when hungry in the presence of food, withdrawal from a painful stimulus, or constriction of the pupil with increasing light. Also known as an unconditioned response.

unconditioned stimulus (UCS) A stimulus that is biologically adequate to produce an unconditioned reflex.

Watson, John Broadus (1878–1958) Founder of American behaviorism and twenty-fourth president of the American Psychological Association. Watson's system is remembered for its identity with the natural sciences and extreme emphasis on the environment in shaping behavior. With a strong belief in determinism and materialism, Watson argued that complete prediction and control of behavior could be achieved by a truly scientific psychology.

14 Gestalt Psychology

Is the human mind to be regarded as a domain of mere indifferent facts? Or do intrinsic demands, fittingness, and its opposite, wrongness, occur among the genuine characteristics of its contents?
—Wolfgang Köhler (1938/1966)

The demand for a radically different orientation to psychology surfaced in Germany in 1910. The new orientation, called *Gestalt psychology*, was headed by **Max Wertheimer (1880–1943)** and supported by his close associates **Wolfgang Köhler (1887–1967)** and **Kurt Koffka (1886–1941)**. Wertheimer, Köhler, and Koffka envisioned a broader psychology that challenged many of the earlier assumptions about human and animal psychology. At first, the Gestalt psychologists rebelled against the elementary dimensions of Wundt's psychology. As voluntarism and structuralism faded into history, the Gestalt school targeted American behaviorism.

There is no exact English counterpart for the German word **Gestalt** although *configuration*, *form*, *holistic*, *structure*, and *pattern* are offered as potential translations. We should avoid the trap of seeking any one English word as an equivalent for the term *Gestalt*. For example, it can be misleading to translate the term *Gestalt* as "holistic."

Michael Wertheimer (1983) noted that there have been many holistic psychologies, but most lack the precision and rigor that characterize Gestalt psychology.

We'll begin with a biographical review of the school's leaders before examining historical antecedents and major themes in the Gestalt system. The chapter closes with an evaluation of the continuing relevance of Gestalt theory for contemporary psychology.

Max Wertheimer

Max Wertheimer was born in Prague, Austria-Hungary (later Czechoslovakia and still later the Czech Republic), on April 15, 1880, the second son of Wilhelm Wertheimer and Rosa (Zwicker) Wertheimer. Max's father was a prominent educator who pioneered a "kind of personalized system of instruction, a tutorial approach for the teaching of business practice, typing, accounting, shorthand, and the like" (Wertheimer, 1980b, p. 6). Following high school, the young Wertheimer attended Charles University in Prague to study law, but he explored other fields such as philosophy, music, physiology, and psychology. Max's

359

Max Wertheimer

son, Michael Wertheimer (1980b), noted that "among his most important teachers at this time was the philosopher–psychologist Christian von Ehrenfels, from whom Max took several courses" (p. 9); von Ehrenfels, like Stumpf and others, had been profoundly influenced by Franz Brentano and his emphasis on experience.

A career in law did not appeal to Wertheimer, although abstract ideas about justice, values, and ethics remained deep and lasting concerns. He shifted from law to philosophy, studying first at Prague, then later at Berlin, where he worked with notable figures such as Carl Stumpf; Friedrich Schumann, the co-developer with Georg Elias Müller of the memory drum; and Erich von Hornbostel, a musicologist. Following his time at Berlin, Wertheimer enrolled in the Ph.D. program at Würzburg, where he obtained his degree in 1904 with Oswald Külpe.

Wertheimer's academic career began at an institute in Frankfurt (later to become the University of Frankfurt). From 1916 to 1929, he worked at the Berlin Psychological Institute and, in 1929, returned to Frankfurt as a full professor. The Nazi movement and subsequent losses of academic freedom (see Gimbel, 2012; Henle, 1978b) inspired a mass exodus of Germany's brightest scholars. Such notable intellectuals as Albert Einstein, John von Neumann, Edward Teller, and Max Delbrück were among the émigrés from Germany to the United States.

In his book *Hitler's Mistakes*, Lewin (1984) illustrated the loss to German science by pointing out that "five of those who transferred to the United States had already won the Nobel Prize and six were subsequently to do so" (p. 56). Fifty-three-year-old Max Wertheimer was among the German émigrés along with his wife, Anne, and their three children. Wertheimer accepted a professorial position in New York City at the New School for Social Research. He held this position from 1933 until his death in 1943 (King & Wertheimer, 2005). His decade in the United States was productive, resulting in papers that extended the Gestalt vision into humanistic concerns such as the meaning of truth (1934), ethics (1935), democracy (1937), and freedom (1940). We will see that Wertheimer's Gestalt vision is more than a system of psychology—it is a worldview with implications for other intellectual arenas such as philosophy, science, and education.

Wolfgang Köhler

Wolfgang Köhler (*KUR lur*) was born on January 21, 1887, in Reval, Estonia (Allik, 2007), but his early formal education was in Germany at the Gymnasium at Wolfenbüttel. He earned his Ph.D. in 1909 at the University of Berlin under Carl Stumpf. Following his doctoral work at Berlin, Köhler took a position as assistant in the psychology laboratory at the Frankfurt Academy, soon to become the University of Frankfurt. From 1913 to 1920, he was director of the Anthropoid Research Station on the island of Tenerife located in the Canary Islands. His work on Tenerife resulted in one of the classic works in Gestalt psychology, *The Mentality of Apes*, first published in English in 1924, and his ongoing scholarship with animal models helped shape comparative psychology in Germany (Kressley, 2006).

Following work on Tenerife, Köhler returned to Germany to take a position as professor at the University of Göttingen. In 1922, he accepted a position as professor and director of the Psychological Institute at the University of Berlin, taking over the role of director from Carl Stumpf (Toccafondi, 2009). Henle (1978b) pointed out that the institute, under Köhler's direction, included an "all-star cast of characters" (p. 939). Faculty members present during all or part of Köhler's tenure included Max Wertheimer, Karl Duncker, Kurt Lewin, Otto von Lauenstein, and Hedwig von Restorff.

The 1920s and early 1930s at the Berlin Institute were productive years, but the delicate climate that encouraged scientific creativity was

Wolfgang Köhler

shattered in 1933 when the Nazi regime came to power. Hitler immediately invoked changes that wreaked havoc in the German university system. Jewish professors and any professors who were unfriendly to National Socialism were dismissed. Scientific theories, methods, and problems were favored on the basis of their agreement with political authority (Ash, 1995; Gimble, 2012). Professors found it difficult to obtain funds and the scientific enterprise was burdened with an unreliable bureaucratic structure marked by infighting and a continual breakdown of authority. Lewin (1984) remarked that as early as 1933, the great mathematician John von Neumann lamented that the Nazis would ruin German science for a generation. Psychology did not, however, disappear under National Socialism; in fact, professional psychology grew rapidly during the Third Reich (Geuter, 1984/1992).

In a thoughtful article titled "One Man Against the Nazis," Henle (1978b) called attention to Köhler's heroic struggles against the Nazi government. Among many activities of resistance, in 1933 Köhler wrote a powerful letter to protest the dismissal of Jewish professors, the last anti-Nazi article openly published in Germany. As Henle (1978b) noted, "everyone expected Köhler to be arrested for it" (p. 940). On the night of publication, he and his students and colleagues gathered to play chamber music and wait for the knock on the door, which, to their surprise, did not come. Later that year, when the regime demanded that professors begin classes with a Nazi salute, the Gestapo and their supporters filled Köhler's class to watch him give in. He did a caricature of the salute followed by a passionate lecture on the importance of academic freedom. Köhler's comments were greeted with thunderous applause from his students, but the Nazi brownshirts in the crowd were undoubtedly not in agreement. Köhler's work at the Berlin Psychological Institute continued until 1935, but by that time conditions were all but unbearable. Finally, Köhler resigned his position and emigrated to the United States, where he accepted a position as professor of psychology at Swarthmore College.

Köhler was a prolific writer and advocate for the Gestalt movement. In 1929 he published *Gestalt Psychology*, a classic statement that opened with a trenchant attack on behaviorism. The book brings to focus the extent to which behaviorism is based on the atomism and mechanism of nineteenth-century physics. Köhler then set forth the Gestalt position that took its lead from the newer concepts of field physics. He published *The Place of Value in a World of Facts* in 1938 and *Dynamics in Psychology* in 1940.

Many honors came to Köhler. Among the most significant were his delivery of the William James lectures at Harvard University and his delivery of the Gifford lectures at Edinburgh in 1958. He was named research professor of philosophy and psychology at Swarthmore College in 1946 and was elected president of the American Psychological Association in 1958. A year before his APA election, he received the Distinguished Scientific Contribution award from the same association. The estimate of his biographers is noteworthy. Asch (1968) said, "There are few in any generation of his stature" (p. 119), and Henle (1978b), referring to Köhler's struggles with the Nazis, said, "It shows us once more what a human being can be" (p. 944).

Wolfgang Köhler made his home in Enfield, New Hampshire, following his formal retirement from Swarthmore. In his later years, he continued to write, give lectures, conduct research, and consult with interested students and colleagues. He died in Enfield on June 11, 1967.

Kurt Koffka

Kurt Koffka was born on March 18, 1886, in Berlin, Germany. Koffka was expected to follow his father into the legal profession. Like Wertheimer, Koffka was drawn to more wide-ranging and theoretical interests. After beginning studies at the University of Berlin in 1903, he shifted from philosophy to psychology. Except for a year at Edinburgh, he stayed in Berlin, earning a Ph.D. in 1909 under Carl Stumpf. Afterward,

he worked a year in the Freiburg laboratory of Johannes Von Kries and another year as assistant to Oswald Külpe at Würzburg. In 1910, Koffka discovered Gestalt psychology while working for three semesters at Frankfurt with Wertheimer and Köhler. In 1912, Koffka accepted a position at the University of Giessen in central Germany. After several visits to the United States in the mid-1920s and after holding visiting professorships, including at Wisconsin, where he had a politely contentious relationship with Clark Hull (Gengerelli, 1976), Koffka accepted a position at Smith College in 1927. In 1932, he traveled with Soviet psychologist Alexander Luria to Uzbekistan to conduct cross-cultural studies of human perception; not only did Koffka and Luria disagree about the research (Lamdan & Yasnitsky, 2016), but Koffka acquired a recurrent illness (Harrower, 1984). He remained at Smith until his death in 1941.

In 1924, Koffka published *Growth of the Mind*, a creative and influential book that demonstrated

Kurt Koffka

362

the relevance of Gestalt principles to developmental psychology. In 1935, he published *Principles of Gestalt Psychology*, a major systematic treatise. Koffka was the first to write on Gestalt psychology in English. His article, "Perception: An Introduction to the Gestalt-Theorie," was published in the *Psychological Bulletin* in 1922. Unfortunately, the article gave the impression that Gestalt theory was concerned only with perception. To the contrary, the first problem addressed by Gestalt psychologists was thinking. But, as discussed earlier, it is a system of psychology with a broad vision and an interest in a host of topics that extend beyond the borders of psychology.

Intellectual Background of Gestalt Psychology

Several intellectual forces shaped the Gestalt school, but there are unique features in the system that cannot be identified with any one antecedent influence. We will now consider traditions in philosophy, science, and psychology that left their mark on the Gestalt psychologists.

Philosophy

Michael Wertheimer (2014a) starts his review of the history of holistic perspectives with early Greek culture. Holistic philosophies from Spinoza and others further shaped the intellectual foundations of Gestalt psychology (King & Wertheimer, 2005), and Wade (2012b) includes art as a precursor to Gestalt. A particularly relevant influence came from the philosopher Immanuel Kant (1724–1804), who argued that our mental processes are organized in an a priori fashion. Meaningful experiences are not always the result of the mechanical laws of association. Instead, ordering principles such as intuitions of causality, time, and space interact with sense experience. Sensory experiences are not necessarily disjointed affairs that await an external connecting principle; rather, organization is a natural, ongoing process, and meanings are often given in experience itself.

Kant also believed that experience is the foundation on which knowledge is built. As noted in Chapter 7, he is regarded as a rationalist, but his emphasis on experience found him seeking a moderate position between the extremes of rationalism and empiricism.

Gestalt psychology is also often regarded as a system that is more akin to rationalism than empiricism. This is a mistaken assumption. Gestalt psychologists challenge us to adopt a more adequate empiricism based on those things that are most real in our experience. Gestalt psychologists would argue that an adequate empiricism would deny the conclusion that meaningful experiences are built from separate mechanical elements held together with the glue of association. The Gestalt position emphasizes conjunctions, meanings, and patterns that are given in the natural flow of experience. We will later examine the detailed arguments for this position. For the time being, we will note that the Gestalt school should not be placed in either of the philosophical extremes of rationalism or empiricism. The starting point for this school is experience, and thus Gestalt psychology is empirical, but proper attention to experience itself will confirm select claims of the rationalists.

Science

In the latter part of the nineteenth century and the early twentieth century, powerful new currents of thought in the scientific world influenced the Gestalt founders. Wolfgang Köhler had a rigorous background in the physical sciences and had studied with the theoretical physicist Max Planck (1858–1947). Planck and Köhler shared personal and intellectual similarities. On the personal side, they openly resisted the Nazi movement. Planck also resisted Hitler by demanding the release of German scientists imprisoned because of their political or religious beliefs.

Because of his resistance, Planck was dismissed as president of the Berlin Physical Society. Later, the Nazi regime imposed a brutal penalty on the famous scientist by forcing him to attend the execution of his son, a member of the resistance movement against the Nazis.

Planck's approach to science, which included a critique of strict empiricism, also left its mark on Köhler. Planck argued that scientific progress is nurtured by creative theoretical work. An obsession with measurement for its own sake will interfere with scientific progress. Planck's emphasis was on the nature of the events and specific processes that underlie a measured effect. Like his teacher, Köhler was also critical of excessive emphasis on measurement. His position is illustrated in a scathing attack on operational definitions of intelligence defined as that which an intelligence test measures (see Köhler, 1929/1947, pp. 44–48).

Albert Einstein also influenced Gestalt psychology. As close friends, Einstein and Max Wertheimer spent long hours in conversation about the nature of science and creativity. Einstein once sought the company of Wertheimer and another friend, Max Born, to help him intervene in a dispute between the student council and the administration of the University of Berlin (see Clark, 1971). The larger intellectual implications of Einstein's work in physics undoubtedly left their stamp on Wertheimer. Indeed, more than any other psychological system, Gestalt psychology is sensitive to the importance of the context of the observer or the so-called frame of reference. These concepts evolved from Einstein's work on electrodynamics of moving bodies. Wertheimer and Köhler were also influenced by the concept of field forces in the new physics. The concept can be illustrated with a magnetic field, as when small iron filings sprinkled on a sheet of paper are distributed into a definite configuration when a magnet is placed under the paper. The focus of the scientist is on the field or the pattern rather than on single elements within the field.

The work of physicist **Ernst Mach (1838–1916)** also influenced Gestalt psychologists.

Although much in Mach's empiricism was disagreeable to Gestalt psychologists, his book *The Analysis of Sensations* (1886/1959) was a source of stimulation. Mach argued for space-form and time-form sensations that are essentially configural. An example of a time-form sensation is a melody, which is something different from its individual elements. The elements, or individual notes, can all be changed, as when one transposes to a different key signature, and yet the melody remains. The melody is not just a collection of separate elements, but a pattern with a clear identity of its own that transcends the individual notes. Similarly, a visual or space-form sensation maintains an identity independent of the elements. The form quality of a triangle persists regardless of one's spatial orientation to the triangle. Triangularity as a space form is thus something different from just lines that serve as the elements.

At the outset of the twentieth century there were developments in other scientific disciplines that challenged piecemeal, bit-by-bit, elementaristic approaches to the world. Field theory, along with a new emphasis on dynamic and evolving processes as opposed to an exclusive emphasis on static structures, was emerging in the philosophy of science.

Psychology

Christian von Ehrenfels (1859–1932), a philosopher–psychologist associated with the Austrian school of act psychology, elaborated on the concept of form qualities. Ehrenfels agreed with Mach that form qualities are different from the elements of which they are composed. In 1890, he published a pivotal paper "On Gestalt Qualities" (Kissinger, 2008) in which Ehrenfels coined the term *Gestalt* and took the position that form qualities are given immediately in experience and may persist even when the elements change (Boudewijnse, 2005). Ehrenfels held a position at the University of Prague where the young Wertheimer took several courses with him from 1898 to 1901 (Wertheimer, 2014a). Ehrenfels undoubtedly focused Wertheimer on the part–whole problem, though it would be over a decade before Wertheimer proposed a solution that was radically different from the one embraced by his teacher. To look back an academic generation, both Ehrenfels and Stumpf (with whom Wertheimer, Köhler, and Koffka all studied) studied with Brentano, whose experiential perspectives remain evident in Gestalt theory.

Ehrenfels, in accord with many holistic psychologists (Diriwächter & Valsiner, 2008), agreed that the whole is *more* than the sum of its parts, but the whole was still viewed as derivative or as another element. The unique feature of the Gestalt system, as noted by Michael Wertheimer (1983), is "the radical view that *the whole is psychologically, logically, epistemologically, and ontologically prior to its parts. A whole is not only more than the sum of its parts, it is entirely different from a sum of its parts: thinking in terms of a sum does violence to the very nature of the dynamics of genuine wholes*" (p. 43, italics in original).

The relationship between the psychology of William James and Gestalt psychology calls for more detailed scholarly review than it has received to date (Woody, 2001). The leaders of the Gestalt movement quoted from James's psychological and philosophical works and not only found some points of agreement, but also found much with which to disagree.

James's powerful attacks on atomism mark a point of agreement. In particular, James's mature philosophical vision, especially his radical empiricism, reveals rich parallels with the Gestalt school. In a compelling analysis of common sympathies between the two approaches, Woody (2001) observed that "both Gestalt psychologists and William James begin investigations with experience, argue that science and other epistemological endeavors should be grounded in experience, experientially evaluate the truth of a given claim, emphasize the personal nature of experience, and embrace experienced relationships across many levels" (p. 40). And just as experience plays a critical role in epistemology,

James and the Gestalt school agreed that methodological pluralism offers real promise for a robust science of psychology (Woody, 2001). The range of topical areas was clearly broader in these two systems than in many other systems. Among areas of disagreement, the Gestalt psychologists disagreed with James's pluralism as well as his position that instincts are little more than chained reflexes.

The Fundamentals of Gestalt Psychology

The formal founding of Gestalt psychology is generally dated to 1910, when Max Wertheimer was inspired by apparent movement he observed during a train ride to a vacation in the Rhineland. In typical accounts, he left the train, purchased a toy stroboscope, and subsequently initiated experiments on the **phi phenomenon**. The phi phenomenon, or apparent movement, is illustrated in the simplest form by two discrete lights. If the lights are flashed onto two different locations on the retina and if one light succeeds the other by a brief time interval, then the participant sees movement. Though the lights are stationary and though they represent two discrete points, the participant sees a sweeping movement in a direction from the first flash to the second. In this case, the observer does not see two separate lights. What is seen is radically different from the elements. Indeed, one could study the elements separately but fail by such a procedure to provide an adequate understanding of the experience of movement. This study is generally described as the start of the Gestalt movement (Wagemans et al., 2012a).

Michael Wertheimer (2014a) argues that this account is oversimplified and that Max Wertheimer's holistic approach emerged out of his upbringing, his studies with Stumpf and von Ehrenfels, and his observations about the structures of music and numbers from people in traditional societies. These influences occurred prior to the publication of the phi phenomenon

(Max Wertheimer, 1912/1950). Despite the common view, supported in part by claims that he made during seminars (Luchins & Luchins, 1982), new perspectives have emerged. Gundlach (2014) examines the evidence for the classical accounts but presents a more complex history. He argues that Wertheimer joined other students of Friedrich Schumann at Berlin who conducted studies of apparent motion with Schumann's tachistoscope, an early device used to present visual stimuli in very brief, precise intervals. This study then formed Wertheimer's *Habilitation* project, a unique feature of central European universities similar to an entrance examination for joining a university faculty. Given the evidence for this more complex series of events, why did Wertheimer not relay this history to his students? Gundlach (2014) suggests that the full story would include "the intricacies of *Habilitation* and acceptance of an unexpected offer to a research somewhat predesigned by his mentor but nevertheless executed with his personal ingenuity" and "would have been too complicated and perplexing for his American students" (p. 145). Regardless of these details, however, this study would gain recognition as the start of the Gestalt movement.

Max Wertheimer, working with Köhler and Koffka as research participants, collected data for his *Habilitation* experiments and published his classic paper, "Experimental Studies on the Perception of Movement" (1912). The phi phenomenon represents a particularly elegant demonstration that the whole is *different* from the sum of the parts. In this case, the parts are static elements, simply two stationary flashes of light. But given appropriate temporal and spatial relationships, we see movement, something fundamentally and qualitatively different. Gestalt psychologists believed that the whole could never be understood by piecemeal examination of the isolated elements. Thus, a piecemeal approach from part to whole would prove inadequate to the understanding of experience.

By contrast, analysis that begins with what is given in experience will lead to a more adequate and believable psychology. The Gestalt psychologists took the position that the whole is prior to its parts, and thus, that part processes are governed by the nature of the whole. If this position seems untenable, consider the phi phenomenon again. What we see is movement; we do not see the isolated elements. In our immediate experience, the whole is quite literally prior to its parts. Starting with what is given in our experience, we may then proceed "from above" and discover the natural parts and their relations.

Consider another illustration. If a theoretician of music asked for an analysis of a melody, we would begin by focusing on the melody itself. The melody, like the phi phenomenon, has a clear identity in our experience. With that identity as a starting point, we may proceed with a meaningful analysis of the relative arrangement of the parts. According to Köhler (1929/1947), "One of the main tasks of Gestalt psychology is that of indicating the genuine rather than any fictitious parts of wholes" (p. 168). We will now turn to an examination of Gestalt principles applied to various topics of psychology.

Principles of Perceptual Organization

In addition to the phi phenomenon, Wertheimer found Gestalt principles in many intellectual and sensory domains. Whether we are listening to a melody, perceiving movement, observing objects, or attempting to grasp an idea, we perceive our world in meaningful patterns or unified wholes. Organization is a given in our experience and not something to be added on by association to a collection of elements. The parts or elements are not what is most basic; what is most basic in our phenomenal world is the pattern or organization, and many scholars continue to view Gestalt phenomena as foundational in perceptual psychology (Pomerantz, 2006). In studying perceptual organization, the Gestalt psychologists discovered several principles that clarify the process, guided in part by Koffka's famous question

"Why do things look as they do?" (Koffka, 1935, p. 75; van Leeuwen, 2007). Some of the most important Gestalt perceptual principles are as follows:

1. *Figure–ground.* The Danish psychologist Edgar Rubin (1886–1951) examined figure and ground as part of a long complex career in philosophy and psychology (Pind, 2013). He argued that there are two components in perception. There is that which stands out or that dominates or that has a "thingness" about it. Rubin referred to this component of perception as *figure.* Other things recede into the background and Rubin referred to these as *ground.* He observed that there are sometimes reversible **figure–ground** relations, as observed in Figure 14.1A. The Gestalt psychologists and Rubin disagreed about some of the interpretations of figure–ground phenomena, but the finding has persisted as a recognized principle of organization and continues to inspire consideration of Gestalt principles (Wagemans et al., 2012a).

2. *Similarity.* One of the standard features of perceptual organization is that figures or *Gestalten* that are similar tend to be grouped together. **Similarity** is illustrated in Figure 14.1B.

3. *Proximity.* According to **proximity**, close temporal or spatial conjunction leads to a perception of togetherness. In Figure 14.1C, we tend to group *Gestalten* that are close together, so we tend to see three groups of three instead of nine squares.

4. *Closure.* According to the principle of **closure**, we tend to complete that which is

A. Figure–Ground

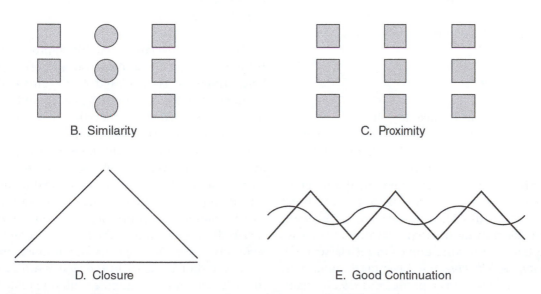

B. Similarity

C. Proximity

D. Closure

E. Good Continuation

Figure 14.1 Some Principles of Perception Emphasized in Gestalt Psychology

367

incomplete. In other words, we fill in the perceptual gaps. In Figure 14.1D, we tend to see a triangle rather than a series of disconnected lines.

5. *Good continuation.* In Figure 14.1E, it would be possible to see a series of broken lines if we transferred back and forth away from the wavy to the straight lines. However, we tend to see a **good continuation** of the wavy lines and a good continuation of angular lines.

Wertheimer's principles of organization contribute to what he called the **law of Prägnanz**. According to this law, perceptual organization tends to be as good as possible under prevailing conditions (Wagemans et al., 2012b). Thus, we see our world in as orderly, coherent, and economical a way as conditions permit.

It is important to emphasize that these principles of organization are givens in perceptual experience. Gestalt psychology does not deny that learning, association, and motivation influence perception, but it points to the importance of understanding what is given in experience. The Gestalt psychologists argued that the organization we find in psychological experience resembles physiological organizations. This topic will surface later in the discussion of the Gestalt treatment of the mind–brain problem.

Thinking

It is a common mistake to believe that Gestalt psychologists were interested first and foremost in perception. Michael Wertheimer (1980b) pointed out that the earliest Gestalt orientation of Max Wertheimer is found "in the psychology of thinking . . . rather than in perception" (p. 13; see also Max Wertheimer, 1912/1950). Wertheimer's most extensive work on the psychology of thinking arrived in his classic book *Productive Thinking*, published posthumously in 1945. The book was reprinted in 1959 and again in 1982 to include fragments and additions found

among Wertheimer's unpublished papers (King & Wertheimer, 2005).

Wertheimer was keenly interested in the distinction between **reproductive thinking** and **productive thinking**. The former is associated with mere repetition, conditioning, drills, habits, or the routine retracing of familiar intellectual territory. The latter, by contrast, results in new ideas, breakthroughs, or insights that make a difference (van Steenburgh et al., 2012). What really happens, asked Wertheimer, when productive thinking takes place? What are the conditions that foster it or that block it? How can we nurture it?

Wertheimer opened his book by reviewing traditional approaches to thinking. A widespread belief held that training in traditional logic nurtured thinking. Wertheimer encouraged such training because it stimulated rigor and a critical orientation, but he concluded that logic in and of itself does not give rise to productive thinking. One can be logical without being creative. He criticized associationist theories of thinking, pointing out that blind trials, drills, repetitions, and chance connections can hardly be construed as productive thinking. He recognized the historical importance of Hegelian, Marxist, and functionalist approaches but found that they do not offer satisfactory solutions to the problem of productive thinking.

Wertheimer declared that his approach to thinking would be understood in terms of field principles. He explored Albert Einstein's thinking that led to relativity theory and the thinking of Galileo that produced the law of inertia (Wertheimer, 1945/1982). In more common examples of productive thinking, Wertheimer explored such diverse problems as finding the areas of various geometric shapes to the thinking underlying the way we see ourselves in various social situations. *Productive Thinking* is filled with rich and experiential illustrations of alternative solutions to specific problems. For instance, the story is told of a teacher in the eighteenth century who presented this simple addition problem to a class of students:

$$1 + 2 + 3 + 4 + 5 + 6 + 7 + 8 + 9 + 10 = ?$$

Do you know the answer? Carl Friedrich Gauss (1777–1855), later to become a famous mathematician, but then only six years old, announced almost immediately that the answer is 55. Perplexed by his quick answer, the teacher asked young Gauss how he arrived at the solution. While other students added 1 + 2 + 3, and so on, Gauss looked at the whole string of numbers and observed a pattern of five 11s. In Gauss's novel solution, he combined 1 + 10, 2 + 9, 3 + 8, and so on. Gauss's solution illustrates Wertheimer's point that productive thinking results when we look for structural truths rather than piecemeal ones.

Wertheimer argued that productive thinking is based on the capacity to grasp structural features and to envision structural reorganization in meaningful ways. In the preceding problem, Gauss broke out of the usual lockstep approach to addition. He looked first at the whole problem then structurally transposed it by looking at the two extremes and found the number 11. He then found that the number 11 repeated itself four more times.

Productive Thinking is filled with examples of problems that arise in human life. The book's continuing relevance is illustrated in a later emphasis on schemas, plans, and knowledge structures—all reminiscent of Wertheimer's approach to thinking (German & Defeyter, 2000).

Learning

As mentioned, Gestalt psychologists launched many attacks against behaviorism. They opposed the connectionism of Thorndike, the reflexological emphasis of Pavlov, and the S–R psychology of Watson. Their opposition to these schools focused on learning theories that emphasized blind or mechanical connections as well as artificial methodologies.

Working independently, Karl Lashley (1942) and Wolfgang Köhler (1929/1947) made an important contribution to the Gestalt model of learning. The study begins by training a research subject, typically a pigeon or, for Köhler, working with the limited resources in Tenerife, a chicken, to select the darker of two shades of gray. Thus, as indicated in Figure 14.2, the subject is rewarded when it selects object 2, the darker of the two objects. The two objects are, of course, randomized with respect to position (left vs. right) so that the subject learns to respond to number 2 whether it appears on the left or the right. In phase 2, the formerly rewarded object is now paired with a new object 3 that is darker than number 2. The brightness interval between 2 and 3 is the same as the brightness interval between 1 and 2. Now confronted with 2 versus 3, subjects choose 3 in most cases.

Notice that number 3 has never been rewarded in the past, whereas number 2 has consistently been associated with reward. Yet the preference is for number 3. Such a finding is embarrassing to a strict S–R theory. In view of the reinforcement history with number 2, it should be the object that is firmly connected to the response. Yet the subject selects an object that has never been rewarded and ignores the one that has always been rewarded. Köhler's (1938) interpretation is that in the total configuration, what is learned is the relational discrimination "darker than" rather than a response to an absolute stimulus value. If that is the case, then the stimulus is not what the behaviorist defines it to be.

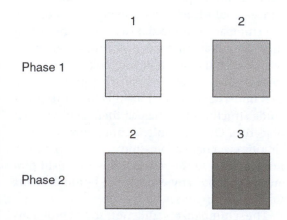

Figure 14.2 Discrimination Problem

369

Furthermore, the established connection is not a hardwired connection between object 2 and the response. Instead, what is seen is the pattern of the relationship rather than an isolated element. If the relationship is established in the first problem, then the subject simply transposes from the first problem to the second. In the transposition, it is "darker than" that wins. Although Spence (1937) provided an explanation of these findings with Hullian theory, the most parsimonious interpretation, according to Gestalt theory, is that relationships outweigh absolute stimulus values. The data suggest that what is learned is a cognitive structure rather than a response to an absolute stimulus value.

Insight: A Further Challenge to the S–R Formula

The best-known work on learning in the Gestalt literature is Köhler's classic book *The Mentality of Apes* (1925/1976). In his book, Köhler describes studies he conducted while on Tenerife. These studies demonstrated that animals envision a whole situation and then restructure parts of the situation to attain a goal. Without such restructuring, the goal would be unattainable.

For example, Köhler suspended a banana by a string several feet above the head of a chimpanzee. Jumping proved futile because the banana was suspended higher than the chimpanzee could leap. After a period of reflection, the chimpanzee noticed boxes on the ground. If the chimp dragged boxes beneath the banana, it restructured the situation and took a critical step toward solving the problem. Though chimpanzees understand little of architecture, they built crude structures that helped them achieve their objective. One of Köhler's chimpanzees named Grande even built a four-story structure of boxes. Köhler believed the restructuring of a field progresses without any evidence of reinforcements for discrete responses.

The chimpanzees did not solve problems by blind trial and success or in a mechanical fashion where a reward follows every response. Given an open situation (the ability to see the relevant parts of the field), Köhler's chimpanzees demonstrated the ability to solve problems in inventive and insightful ways. Köhler's stated criterion for **insight** is "the appearance of a complete solution with reference to the whole layout of the field" (1925/1976, p. 190).

Köhler argued that behavioral studies are often structured to preclude the possibility that animals could see the layout of the whole field. In a typical maze, the possibilities of visualization are limited and there is little way to learn except by trial and error. A human in a maze would also learn by trial and error, but imagine how different that learning curve would be if the entire maze were viewed, even for a brief moment, from above (an *optically given situation* in Köhler's language). Most natural learning occurs in field situations in which there are possibilities for pattern recognition and restructuring. Artificial laboratory situations may lead to false conclusions about crucial questions such as what gets learned, what conditions facilitate learning, and what are the learner's capacities.

These perspectives on insight led to conflicts with behaviorists, some of the most intense infighting in the history of psychology. Not only did they clash in scientific journals, they challenged each other's views in other contexts. For example, in his autobiography, Skinner (1979) parodied Köhler's research as unscientific, and Dunker engaged in similar attacks on behaviorists and behaviorism (King et al., 1998). At one point, Köhler and Hull even had an intense and negative personal interaction in a crowded bar outside of a conference (King & Wertheimer, 2005). Throughout the twentieth century, neither side came to readily accept the views of the other.

Developmental Concepts

Koffka's book *Growth of the Mind* provided a wider application of Gestalt principles by showing their operations and applications in developmental processes. The major emphasis of the book, in Koffka's words, is "upon the evolution of the child's mind" (1924/1980, Preface). He pointed out that without sound developmental and comparative psychologies, the psychology of normal adults will be defective. Koffka observed that the extreme positions of empiricism and nativism had undercut the study of development. Rather than attempting to understand the problems of mental growth as we find them, the empiricists and nativists searched for those things that fit their preconceptions.

METHODOLOGICAL CONSIDERATIONS IN DEVELOPMENTAL PSYCHOLOGY Koffka distinguished between the view *from without* and the view *from within*. The view from within is a descriptive concept (i.e., I know my toothache, my headache, or my feeling of elation; when someone else has a toothache, I cannot get out of my skin and know it directly). But Koffka contended that if people weep, we may be assured they are sorrowful; if they laugh, we may feel that they are happy; and if they are animated, we may have certain confidences about their experience of energy and well-being. When we say that someone is animated or active, we are using behavioral concepts, but such concepts are also functional in that they refer to underlying experiences. Functional concepts assume an intimate relationship between observable behavior and experience. When we study infants and young children, we employ functional concepts, but with the assurance that if an infant smiles and coos, his or her behavior corresponds to experiences of well-being. We will now turn to some examples of Koffka's work in developmental psychology.

THE GROWTH OF LEARNING Kurt Koffka believed that much of early learning is what he called *sensorimotor learning*. An illustration of sensorimotor learning is found in the maxim, "The burnt child shuns the flame." Koffka (1924/1980) argued, "The withdrawal of the burned hand is naturally reflexive, but what is learned is not to withdraw the hand, but to avoid the fire in the future" (p. 302). What is learned is a configuration relating fire and pain, not a reflex that occurs naturally. If there were no attention, the child would not learn and then the experience would have to be repeated. So even in so-called sensorimotor learning, we do not learn mere connections; rather, what is learned is a constructive achievement with future adaptive significance.

IMITATION In addition to sensorimotor learning, Koffka argued that a great deal of learning occurs by imitation. Such learning occurs in natural settings but is less likely in artificial settings such as many laboratory experiments on learning. Koffka contended that there is no need to explain imitation or its purposes; it simply occurs in the natural flow of events. What often is imitated is complex configurations, whether these be auditory or visual. We can observe children attempting to perfect their imitations. Koffka believed that the perceptual and motor systems are related so that configural recognition or transfer can go naturally from one to the other. Koffka was not talking about mere observational learning. Rather, for him, imitation implied a capacity to discern relevant relations.

IDEATIONAL LEARNING The highest type of learning in Koffka's developmental scheme is ideational learning, a type of learning that makes use of language. Koffka pointed out that it is a pivotal time in children's development when they grasp the idea that things have names. In early experience, the name is thought to inhere in the thing itself as an attribute. Koffka illustrated with a bit of humor that comes from an argument about the best language. One of the participants says, "The English language is the best, and I can prove it to you. Take the word *knife*; the French call it *couteau*; the Germans *Messer*, the Danes *kniv*, while the English say knife, and that's what it really is" (Koffka, 1924/1980, p. 324).

Following the naming stage, children enter a period marked by a new flexibility with respect to the application of language. A word, for example, that was originally associated with only one thing or event may now be applied to other things. Koffka related the case of Hilda Stern, who, after learning the word *nose*, applied it to the tips of her shoes. Such inventive manipulations are common in young children. Children also often generate words of their own in a playful manner. Michael Wertheimer's four-year-old daughter Karen preferred to describe a butterfly as a *flutterby*. Such a rearrangement illustrates verbal generation of ideational material that can play a role in learning. The new term *flutterby* is descriptive; it conveys an idea about the object that is not captured in the term *butterfly*. From a multitude of possible verbal rearrangements and new symbolic representations we have a powerful tool that extends our capacity to learn and to solve problems. We turn now from learning modes to one of Koffka's most speculative but interesting suggestions regarding developmental phenomena.

Gestalt Perspectives on Scientific Method

Gestalt psychology's approach to scientific methodology illustrates the thoroughness of its revolt against the established psychology of its day. In his book *Gestalt Psychology*, Köhler accused the established psychologies—particularly behaviorism and structuralism—of emulating physical sciences in their mature form. Such imitation, he argued, overemphasized quantitative methods while ignoring qualitative and experiential considerations that precede quantification. Köhler argued that psychologists should emulate physical sciences in early rather than later stages of development. Prior to sophisticated quantitative procedures, early physical scientists attended to the experiences of everyday life. As an example, Köhler discussed the work of Henry Cavendish (1731–1810) on electrical resistance. Prior to developing exact measures of resistance, Cavendish experienced shocks to his arm delivered through varying pieces of material inserted in an electrical circuit.

Köhler warned about the danger in copying the advanced quantitative form of established sciences without attending to the demands inherent in psychology's unique subject matter. A premature emphasis on measurement may compel us to overlook critical processes and phenomena. The net result is that we focus on things that lend themselves to measurement but neglect something of greater importance that cannot be quantified. Köhler (1929/1947) argued that "narrowness in observation protects narrowness in theory" (p. 54). Overvaluing quantitative techniques restricts the range of legitimate problems in the new discipline.

Köhler (1929/1947) was concerned that psychologists would conduct elegant but fruitless experiments. He found evidence in psychophysics where "thousands of quantitative psychophysical experiments were made almost in vain. No one knew precisely what he was measuring. Nobody had studied the mental processes upon which the whole procedure was built" (p. 44).

What, then, was the Gestalt solution to Köhler's methodological criticisms? First, according to Köhler (1929/1947), "a method is good if it is adapted to the given subject matter; and it is bad if it lacks regard for this material, or if it misdirects research" (p. 37). He warned that a successful methodological procedure in one science could prove useless in another discipline. Methodology should be adapted to the subject matter of a discipline rather than the other way around.

Köhler believed that Gestalt psychology occupied a central place among the natural sciences (Henle, 1993). Not surprisingly, we encounter a variety of scientific procedures within the Gestalt literature. For some problems, the Gestalt psychologists worked like astronomers or field biologists, employing naturalistic observation with minimum intrusion into their participants' ongoing activities. In other studies, Gestalt psychologists worked more like scientists in a wet-lab situation, manipulating and controlling variables.

Gestalt psychologists helped pioneer the phenomenological method, and they would likely be open to well-conceived questionnaire and interview techniques (so long as these methods are meaningfully tied to the problems under investigation). Their broad approach to methodology parallels William James's (Woody, 2001). As in Jamesian psychology, Gestalt science found inspiration in vision not method and in studies with meaningful applications to experience. In fact, the Gestalt psychologists argued for a greater metaconsciousness of science. They understood the dangers of losing critical perspective on methodology: We may restrict the range of legitimate problems or we could risk generating misinformation or even trivialize the scientific enterprise if we remove it from the flow of meaningful events.

The Gestalt concerns about methodology did not perpetuate differences between mission-oriented (applied) research and basic research. Indeed, the Gestalt school's philosophy of science might diminish the sharp dichotomy between applied and basic psychology. The dichotomy could disappear altogether because a truly basic science would yield sensible findings. Even if such findings are not immediately applicable, they would not strain credulity with respect to their eventual potential to make a difference somewhere in the world of our experience.

Mind and Brain: Isomorphism

The Gestalt perspective on the mind–brain problem has been called **isomorphism**. Köhler (1929/1947) defined the term as follows: "Experienced order in space is always structurally identical with a functional order in the distribution of underlying brain processes" (p. 61). Literally, the word *isomorphism* means having the same appearance or same form. In chemistry, two substances may be said to be isomorphic if they share similarities with respect to atomic structure. The term *isomorphism* in Gestalt psychology refers to the structural correspondence between experience and underlying brain processes. The

ordered nature of an experience does not exist in isolation but corresponds to an ordered distribution of cortical events. If we experience an auditory temporal sequence (a rhythm), we may also expect a pattern of events in brain processes that are isomorphic with the experience.

Gestalt founders discussed isomorphism in slightly different ways (Luchins & Luchins, 1999/2015), and it is often misrepresented (see Henle, 1984). A common erroneous belief is that isomorphism means we have pictures in our heads that correspond to physical structures. Some critics have asked whether color in the external world is isomorphic with some part of the brain that matches that color (Gregory, 1974). What is missed in many misrepresentations of isomorphism is the importance of the word *functional*. Köhler (1938/1966) took pains to add that the *functional* cortical counterpart of a color would not have to be a color. Likewise, the functional cortical counterpart of a sound of a violin would not need to replicate the physical features of such a sound. The Gestalt concept of isomorphism does not refer to a correspondence between physical events and brain processes, but to a correspondence between experience and brain processes, which Luccio (2010) connects to Spinoza's ideas. The position expresses faith in the fundamental structural similarity of two realms (experience and brain) that are vital to psychology.

The Influence of Gestalt Psychology

The 1920s proved to be a golden decade for Gestalt psychology. Wolfgang Köhler's Psychological Institute at the University of Berlin was the center for the Gestalt revolution. Henle (1977) said that "graduate students were coming to the Institute from a number of countries; the *Psychologische Forschung*, the journal of the Gestalt Psychologists, was founded, and work was progressing in many directions" (p. 3). During this time, the German school stretched to other cultures, including

Italy and Japan (Sakuma, 1999; Verstegen, 2000). Köhler and Koffka attended the 1929 International Congress of Psychology at Yale University, giving the Gestalt school greater visibility in the United States. Despite fragile economic conditions in Germany's crumbling Weimar Republic, the 1930s promised another productive decade for Gestalt psychology.

And then Adolf Hitler came to power in 1933.

Not content to dominate politics and the military, Hitler imposed his will on cultural, artistic, and scientific works as well. It was his ambition to replace "Jewish science" with "Aryan science." Although Wertheimer was not a practicing Jew, he was among the first generation of professors forced into "retirement" by the new Nazi government (King & Wertheimer, 2005). Historians can only speculate about the outcome had the Berlin Psychological Institute prospered in a friendlier environment. A continuing research program and the production of doctoral students would have formed the core of a significant research force, something Gestalt psychology never enjoyed. In the devastating wake of the Nazi regime, the world could no longer look to Germany as a rich source of scientific ideas.

The small nucleus of Gestalt theorists separated and went to isolated colleges that did not offer major doctoral programs (Koffka at Smith College, Köhler at Swarthmore, and Wertheimer at the New School for Social Research). The Gestalt movement faced an uphill battle in another way. The major leaders, isolated from each other and from graduate students, labored on foreign soil in a country in the grip of behaviorism. The vicissitudes of Gestalt psychology in the United States are discussed in thoughtful articles by Sokal (1984), Ash (1985), and Henle (1986).

Despite such obstacles, Gestalt research, argument, and theory had a telling influence. Its authority was felt in three important ways:

1. There were systematic approaches to subdisciplinary areas such as motivation, personality, social psychology, and cognitive psychology inspired by Gestalt psychology, though not a part of the classic core of Gestalt thought (King & Wertheimer, 2005).

2. Gestalt concepts and research discoveries found their way into textbooks that conveyed the mainstream of psychological knowledge.

3. Gestalt research findings served as a powerful stimulus for other systems, often forcing modifications in their positions.

We turn to an examination of an influential system that had roots and inspiration in Gestalt psychology.

Kurt Lewin and Field Theory

Wertheimer, Köhler, and Koffka made important contributions to the study of thinking, perception, learning, and development. As noted, however, the Gestalt vision is a worldview that reaches beyond the boundaries of psychology. In this tradition, **Kurt Lewin (1890–1947)** broadened the Gestalt perspective to include work on motivation, personality, social psychology, and conflict resolution.

Lewin was born in Mogilno, Prussia (later part of Poland), on September 9, 1890. When he was fifteen, his family moved to Berlin where Lewin completed his high school studies at the Kaiserin Augusta Gymnasium. After a semester at the University of Freiburg and another at the University of Munich, he enrolled at the University of Berlin where he completed the requirements for a Ph.D. in psychology under Carl Stumpf's direction. As with other Gestalt scholars, Stumpf's views affected Lewin substantially (Bonacchi, 2009).

Following graduate studies, Lewin enlisted in the German army and served through World War I. He was awarded the Iron Cross after being wounded in battle. Lewin's students (see Marrow, 1969) have pointed out that his experiences in World War I served as a basis for his later field theory. Concepts such as *boundary*, *force*, and *zone* are as real on the battlefield as in ordinary human experience.

Upon completing his military tour of duty, Lewin took a position at the Psychological Institute at the University of Berlin, even though he was denied a tenure track position due to his Jewish heritage (Marrow, 1969). At Berlin, he encountered Wertheimer and Köhler. Marrow (1969) pointed out that "Gestalt holism impressed Lewin. Though he was never a completely orthodox Gestalt psychologist, he did become a vital force in the new movement and contributed to it his own special insights" (p. 13). Lewin even was impressed with psychoanalysts because they worked with real-life problems, but he found flaws in their methods (Marrow, 1969). Lewin's work at the Berlin Institute continued with only minor interruptions until 1933. By that time, he had gained international visibility and an impressive publication record. Several articles brought widespread recognition, especially a paper contrasting Aristotelian and Galilean thought that continues to inspire debate (Lewin, 1931; Tateo, 2013).

At the outset of the Nazi movement, Lewin declared he could not continue to teach in a university where his children would not be welcome as students (see Marrow, 1969). Throughout his life, he continued to write about Jewish experiences in hostile environments (Krasner, 2016). In 1933, he joined the exodus of German intellectuals and took a temporary position at Cornell University. Two years later, he accepted a position at the Child Welfare Research Station at the University of Iowa, a position he held until 1944. That same year, he was named director of the Research Center for Group Dynamics at Massachusetts Institute of Technology (MIT). He died of a heart attack at his home in Newtonville, Massachusetts, on February 12, 1947.

Like William James, Lewin was an intellectual democrat. He took ideas too seriously to demand intellectual conformity or loyalty. Many students were attracted to him and, as noted by Marrow (1969), they could move in and out of his circle without guilt or accusations of disloyalty. Before World War II, he communicated with Vygotsky and Luria, among others, in the Soviet Union

(Yasnitsky, 2016), and Lewin drew many students from Russian laboratories, including many women, who faced extensive discrimination in academia regardless of nationality (Weiner, 2013). Lewin's openness could be characterized as a logical outgrowth of his philosophy of science, and his drive to understand the world remained inseparable from his desire to improve the world (Verstegen, 2015). He was strongly committed to the idea that science must continually change. He insisted that "the idea of an eventual unification of all sciences is wishful thinking" (Marrow, 1969, p. 19).

Lewin's Field Theory

Lewin's psychology was a corrective for earlier systems that emphasized traits, inherited predispositions, learning, agencies, or other intrapsychic events or processes. In contrast with extreme individualistic approaches, Lewin's **field theory** emphasized the interdependence of the person *and* the environment. His most characteristic formula, $B = f(p,e)$, states that behavior is a function of person *and* environment. According to the formula, an adequate psychology of behaviors and mental states can be developed only by appreciating the full scope of forces that play a role in human life, including the biological and physical environment (Smith, 2009). Lewin believed that earlier psychologists had placed too large a burden on the explanatory role of association and other limited concepts. He also believed that earlier psychologies had neglected affect, motivation, and social forces. Emphasis on Lewin's field theory faded after his death but returned in the 1990s (Burnes & Cooke, 2013). His larger views influenced both social psychology and rehabilitation psychology (Dunn, 2011).

One of the key concepts in Lewin's psychology is the **life space**, which refers to every psychological fact that is influential in the life of an individual at a given time. In any one slice of time, the life space consists of physical events (an impending storm, a new car, a cup of coffee, the aroma of cinnamon, a book), personal and biological facts (a toothache, a memory, fatigue, the exhilaration of a workout), and social facts (another person, membership in a group). It consists of the extensity of experience at a given moment. The life space of the child is limited both spatially and temporally, but with growth, the space expands. Lewin believed that the task of education is to extend the life space so that we can strive for goals that are further and further removed in time. Young children typically strive only for more concrete and visible things. With education and growth, the present can become more spacious, the future more pregnant with possibilities, and the past more enlarged. Lewin quoted with approval Goethe's famous statement, "Who cannot give an account of three thousand years remains in the darkness of inexperience, can live only from one day to another" (see Lewin, 1935, p. 173).

It is important to point out that the life space is not static. At a given time, its focal features may consist of a small group of people, a physical setting, food, and great conversation. In the midst of all that a phone call or email may bring salient information that changes the focus of attention, hence the life space.

Lewin referred to positive or negative features of objects in the life space as **valences**. A *positive valence* refers to the attractive or desirable qualities that reside in an object. In general, objects that satisfy a need possess positive valence and objects that frustrate or frighten have a negative valence. Valences fluctuate dynamically with needs. For example, a Pop Tart will have a higher positive valence for a hungry child. After consuming the snack, a favored toy may have a higher positive valence.

Lewin's emphasis on positive and negative valences led to some of the most productive work in the history of psychology on the nature of conflict. In the day-to-day world, we seldom encounter a simple pathway to a simple goal. Instead, we encounter complexities that require adjudication and choice. Lewin and his students called attention to common types of conflicts.

First, we may be caught between two objects with comparable positive valences. Though there may be considerable vacillation in such a circumstance, this type of conflict is usually regarded as fairly easy to resolve. Second, another type of conflict occurs when an object has positive *and* negative valences or when an object with a positive valence is surrounded by a physical or psychological barrier. The dynamics of conflict resolution in this type of situation are complex and depend on the relative weights of the positive and negative valences and the capacities of the individual. Lewin observed that individuals may attempt circuitous routes to the goal or, when the conflict is too intense, the individual may leave the field and search for an alternative goal. The third type of conflict surfaces when we are caught between two regions that both have negative valences. Lewin gave the example of the child who is required to perform an undesirable task and failure to do the task will result in punishment. This is a severe conflict, especially if escape from punishment is impossible and if the task is repugnant.

These types of conflict are easily recognized as part of the mainstream of psychological literature under the labels of **approach–approach conflict**, **approach–avoidance conflict**, and **avoidance–avoidance conflict**. Lewin's original work on conflict has inspired a great deal of research on simple conflict situations and on more complicated real-life situations in which there are multiple positive and negative valences associated with many regions.

Tension Systems and Recall

Lewin believed that needs are associated with tension systems and that the satisfaction of a need is associated with the dissipation of tension. Lewin's student Bluma Zeigarnik (1900–1988) tested one implication of his idea.

Under Lewin's direction, Zeigarnik gave her participants a series of simple tasks. At times, participants were interrupted before completing their task. In other instances, they were allowed to finish their work. Afterward, Zeigarnik tested her participants' memory about the various tasks. The researchers hypothesized that people would remember interrupted tasks better than completed work. The data supported their prediction. When we complete a task, tension dissipates. But tension persists for a longer period when we are not allowed to finish a job. The tension state produces a need for closure that begs for resolution. Someone who gets unexpectedly dumped might continue to mourn the broken relationship years after it ended. Or you might become addicted to a TV series or thriller novel because it leaves you hanging from one cliffhanger to the next. The tendency to recall uncompleted tasks better than completed tasks came to be known as the **Zeigarnik effect**.

One explanation for the Zeigarnik effect is that tension remaining from an uncompleted task may cause participants to persevere or rehearse the materials associated with that task. On the other hand, the completion of a task may free the individual to turn attention to other things. In other words, the uncompleted task serves as a barrier to interference. Regardless of why it works, the Zeigarnik effect suggests that a study unit might be ended most effectively with a question. A compelling question, by its very nature, means that something is not complete or that something is unanswered. A good question should result in a tension system that will keep the learner on task for a longer period of time than without the question.

In 1931, Bluma Zeigarnik moved to the Soviet Union, where she continued her psychological work for more than fifty years (Zeigarnik, 2007), particularly in pathopsychology, the study of mental processes exhibited by people with mental disorders (Nikolaeva, 2011).

Group Dynamics

As mentioned, Lewin was named director of the Research Center for Group Dynamics at MIT in 1944. During this period, he focused on group dynamics, a term he coined and popularized (Carron & Brawley, 2008) and a problem of long-standing interest. The expression **group dynamics** is not easily defined, but in general it includes the study of the effects of groups on individuals and individuals on groups. Groups modify individual behaviors and perceptions, and individuals modify groups, which change actively and fluidly (Forsyth & Diederich, 2014). Group dynamics also includes studies of the structures of groups with respect to leadership (e.g., democratic vs. authoritarian) and the effectiveness of leadership structures in various kinds of tasks and contexts.

Lewin's interests extended to wide varieties of groups, including industrial work groups, educational groups, and casual interest groups, and he was interested in destructive behaviors as well as prosocial actions (Wennberg & Hane, 2005). His 1939–1947 work with the Harwood Manufacturing Corporation helped bring group research from the laboratory to applied settings and was, among other things, an early study in organizational behavior (Burnes, 2007). Lewin was also invested in community action programs where psychological theory could be tested in the day-to-day world; in this way he contributed to the history of community psychology (Dalton et al., 2013). Lewin inspired a representative experiment on integrated housing conducted by his students. A few years after Lewin's death, Deutsch and Collins (1951) studied housing projects in which black and white residents were integrated in a random fashion. That is, houses were available on a first-come, first-served basis. In another condition, black and white participants were segregated in a block-type or checkerboard pattern. Results showed that integration resulted in more positive and accepting interracial attitudes. Segregated housing patterns resulted in increased resentment, prejudice, and a desire for greater segregation. Within integrated neighborhoods, people enjoyed more opportunities to build friendships and gain insight into the basic humanity of other ethnic members.

Extension of Gestalt Principles

Aside from the contributions of Wertheimer, Koffka, Köhler, and Lewin, a number of second-generation Gestalt psychologists extended the work of their mentors. Students of Gestalt psychology enjoyed a time of great productivity in Germany during the 1920s. Among the more influential students was **Karl Duncker (1903–1940)**, who under Wertheimer's influence and direction conducted an ingenious series of experiments on problem solving. Originally published in German in 1935, Duncker's research was translated a decade later into English (Duncker, 1935/1945). After conducting numerous experiments, Duncker found that many participants exhibited a **functional fixedness**, that is, an inability to find productive solutions to new problems (van Steenburgh et al., 2012). Duncker's research has continued to influence problem-solving research (German & Defeyter, 2000; Newell, 1985). Tragically, Duncker struggled after having immigrated to the United States from Germany following the rise of Nazism, and he ultimately took his own life (King et al., 1998). According to Mandler and Mandler (1969), "Apart from the personal tragedy, there is reason to believe that [Duncker] was the most brilliant of the Gestalt group . . . His main contribution has made a continuing impact on the psychology of thinking, both in the United States and elsewhere" (p. 393).

Another example of the extension of Gestalt principles is encountered in the work on memory of **Hedwig von Restorff (1906–1962)**, who served as a research assistant for Köhler at the Psychological Institute in Berlin. Like Duncker, she was dismissed by the Nazis in 1933. Köhler and von Restorff found that isolated items are recalled better than a series of homogeneous items. Participants in one of their experiments learned a list of nonsense syllables. However, when an individual three-digit item was presented with the nonsense syllables, participants recalled the three-digit number better than the nonsense syllables. According to Köhler and von Restorff (1935), the three digits acted as the figure to the ground of the homogeneous nonsense syllables. This phenomenon has been popularized with the eponym of the *Köhler–von Restorff effect* or the less accurate **von Restorff effect**. According to Baddeley (1990), the British Post Office even employed the research of Köhler and von Restorff in the design of its postcode. The von Restorff effect continues to inspire research (Bireta & Neath, 2008; Kelley & Nairne, 2001).

It is an unfortunate circumstance that many of the heirs of Gestalt psychology were severely affected by the Nazi regime. Henle (1986) lamented, "By the end of World War II, the first generation of young Gestalt psychologists was essentially wiped out" (p. 119). Some were lost in the war, but most had moved to other countries. The Gestalt journal, *Psychologische Forschung*, resumed production after World War II. In the United States, Solomon Asch found great success in the incorporation of Gestalt theory into his research on the effects of group pressure on problem solving. We'll discuss Solomon Asch's social psychology research in more detail in Chapter 17.

In a more indirect fashion, the work of other psychologists reflects the principal tenets of Gestalt psychology. Edward Chace Tolman, though a behaviorist, acknowledged that Gestalt psychology had been a major source of inspiration for his cognitive approach to learning. Muzafer Sherif's (*Sher-uhf*) conceptual approach to psychology, his experiments on the autokinetic effect, and his well-known boys' camp experiments (which incidentally inspired the novel *Lord of the Flies*) are best appreciated within a Gestalt orientation. Kurt Goldstein's organismic personality theory was directly influenced by Gestalt theory, as was Andras Angyal's theory of personality. Other theorists such as Fritz Heider (1896–1988), Hans Wallach (1904–1998), and Herman Witkin (1916–1979) drew inspiration from the Gestalt school. Henle (1985) has also demonstrated that contemporary cognitive psychology owes a large and often unacknowledged debt to Gestalt psychology, as does the study of social cognition that emerged in the 1970s

(Hamilton & Carlston, 2013). Rock and Palmer (1990) have outlined additional influences.

Common Misunderstandings of Gestalt Psychology

The Gestalt system perhaps offers greater complexity and subtlety than any other system we have covered. For this reason, a number of misunderstandings have arisen over the years. We'll summarize the most common misunderstandings.

Gestalt Psychology and Gestalt Therapy

Because of similarities in terminology, it would be reasonable to assume that Gestalt therapy, which had its origin in the work of Fritz Perls (1893–1970), is somehow related to Gestalt psychology. In an article titled "Gestalt Psychology and Gestalt Therapy" Mary Henle (1978a) examined **Gestalt therapy** and found it to be in marked contrast with the teachings of Gestalt psychology. Henle concluded that Perls borrowed terms from Gestalt psychology, stretching them beyond recognition. For her, the psychology advanced by Perls "is *not* Gestalt psychology" (Henle, 1978a, p. 31). In agreement with Henle, Michael Wertheimer (1987) found "*no* conceptual relationship between Perls' neoanalytic 'gestalt psychotherapy' and Gestalt psychology in the sense of the Wertheimer–Köhler–Koffka theory" (p. 139).

Gestalt Psychology and Scientific Analysis

Another common misunderstanding is that Gestalt psychology opposes analysis. This accusation is set forth in Pavlov's polemics against the Gestalt school (see Pavlov, 1955). Earlier, we pointed out that Gestalt psychology should not be confused with holistic psychologies that do oppose analysis. Gestalt psychology has never rejected analysis of the natural units of the phenomenal field. Thus, if a unit is a genuine part of a whole, it is a legitimate task of the scientist to understand that unit. Köhler (1929/1947) said, "Analysis in terms of genuine parts is a perfectly legitimate and necessary procedure in Gestalt psychology" (pp. 168–169). From a Gestalt perspective, analysis starts with a phenomenal event, then proceeds to its natural parts and their relations.

Gestalt Psychology and Nativism

Another common misunderstanding is encountered in the belief that Gestalt theory is a nativistic psychology, meaning that it places heavier emphasis on heredity than on environment. In fact, Gestalt psychologists reject the nature–nurture dichotomy and argue that it is misleading to treat events in the psychological world as if they were *simply* inherited or learned. In his last book, Köhler (1969) declared it an error to treat "the terms 'learned' and 'inherited' as though these words indicated an 'either–or' alternative" (p. 89).

The Gestalt position goes back to a neglected feature of evolutionary theory—namely, that the physical–chemical forces of nature are applicable to living organisms. Thus, physical conditions (e.g., gravitational forces, pH values, ambient temperature) and principles (e.g., conservation of energy) all contribute to the dynamic distributions or possibilities. For example, at a relatively low ambient temperature, gelatin is a semisolid, but at a higher temperature, it is a liquid. The dynamic distribution and movement of particles is a function, among other things, of temperature. Temperature is associated with limits or constraints within which we observe invariant dynamics.

Köhler (1969) argued that "it is three factors (not two) by which events in organisms, and therefore also in nervous systems, are generally determined. First, the invariant principles and forces of general dynamics, secondly, anatomical constraints which evolution has established, and thirdly, learning" (p. 89). If we focus only on what is learned or inherited, we neglect attention to what Köhler called *invariant dynamics*, something we share with the inorganic world. Köhler (1969) asked whether "processes in our nervous system follow the laws of nature because some genes compel such processes to do so" (p. 69). The answer is clearly "no." The upshot of the Gestalt position is that it calls for a psychology informed by life sciences *and* physical sciences.

The Role of Past Experience

A final misunderstanding of Gestalt psychology is that it neglects past experience. Gestalt theory has been accused of neglecting history because it stands in sharp contrast with other systems that overemphasize the importance of the past. If thinking, learning, and perception work as the Gestalt theorists believe they do, then present facts are important, though the past is by no means unimportant. If the Gestalt position is correct, we may not be tied in a blind and mechanical way to our individual and collective histories; insight and productive thinking can enable us to transcend our histories. Both insight and productive thinking would be impossible without the ability to integrate the past into ongoing activities.

Recall that Lewin quoted with approval Goethe's statement, "Who cannot give an account of three thousand years remains in the darkness of inexperience." Gestalt concepts such as insight and productive thinking give a new intimacy with the past. We are hardly intimate with the past if its events dictate (either through conditioning or unconscious motivations) the present flow of events. In the Gestalt perspective, the present is elevated in importance, but the past and the future are not neglected. Indeed, time perspective may have greater breadth within a Gestalt framework than in any other system of psychology.

Gestalt Psychology and Applied Psychology

Although focused on the study of perception, thinking, learning, development, and social psychology, Gestalt psychology was actively applied to topics such as the psychology of art, education, and psychotherapy. Behrens (1998) argued that the work of Cubist artists such as Pablo Picasso had an impact on Gestalt theory; Gestalt ideas also shaped architecture in the twentieth century (Steinert, 2014). Likewise, several illustrious artists including Paul Klee, Vassily Kandinsky, Josef Albers, and M. C. Escher found inspiration in the tenets of Gestalt theory (King et al., 1994). Like his mentor Max Wertheimer, Rudolf Arnheim (1943) saw the principles of Gestalt theory in the natural world and in the arts (Fitzek, 2013), not only in the rigorous constraints of the laboratory. Born in 1904, Arnheim earned his Ph.D. from Wertheimer at the University of Berlin at age fourteen; his dissertation project involved handwriting analysis, which marked the beginning of a lifetime of studying perception, cognition, and meaning (Gardner, 2008). In 1932, due to his Jewish descent, he emigrated from Nazi Germany to Italy and later to the United States, where he held a series of academic positions (Pariser, 2008).

Arnheim's greatest contribution involved his use of Gestalt theory to explore the psychology of art (Mandler & Mandler, 1969; Verstegen, 2005, 2007). His scholarly activities ranged from a molar study of architecture, music, film, radio, poetry, theater, and sculpture to a detailed Gestalt-inspired analysis of Picasso's creative thinking during the painting of his *Guernica* (Arnheim, 1962). Indeed, the majority of his books on the psychology of art bear the unmistakable stamp of Gestalt theory (Arnheim, 1966, 1974, 1986).

The Gestalt model also held important implications for education. The Gestalt perspective paralleled closely the functional ideology of progressive education as opposed to a more traditional approach based in repetition and rote memorization. Wertheimer's vision of a Gestalt theory of education had a profound influence on several students including George Katona.

Although he earned a Ph.D. under G. E. Müller at Göttingen, **George Katona (1901–1981)** came under the influence of Wertheimer and Köhler while studying in Berlin. In 1933, he emigrated to the United States and taught at the New School for Social Research from 1938 to 1942. Katona was a prolific researcher, particularly in the area of behavioral economics (Katona, 1959, 1979; Hosseini, 2011), in which he applied field theory to the study of economics in numerous books and articles. Katona's most dynamic contribution to Gestalt psychology was *Organizing and Memorizing* (1940). Like Duncker's research on problem solving, Katona's book complemented Wertheimer's work on productive thinking but with a greater application to educational psychology. Katona (1940) demonstrated that understanding of information based on insightful grouping (*meaningful* learning) would yield superior results to memorization of unorganized materials (*senseless* learning). Katona even challenged the utility of Ebbinghaus's retention curve by noting that the data were derived from nonsensical stimuli rather than meaningful material. Katona's work stands as an important precursor to research on organization in learning and memory (Baddeley, 1990).

The Gestalt contribution to psychotherapy is less evident than its applications to art and education. Although Wertheimer dismissed Freud's work as excessively associative and unscientific, several psychologists linked Gestalt theory with psychoanalysis and other psychotherapies. As with Fritz Perls's Gestalt therapy, most efforts bore no intellectual resemblance to the Gestalt theory of Wertheimer, Köhler, and Koffka (King et al., 1994). However, the Gestalt psychologists were not averse to the application of their ideas to a clinical setting. Select passages in Wertheimer's *Productive Thinking* reveal an interest in psychopathology. In the 1920s, Wertheimer supervised a student named Heinrich Schulte on a Gestalt theory about people with delusional beliefs (Schulte, 1938; Wertheimer, 1924/1986). According to Levy (1986), the Wertheimer–Schulte theory has relevance because it "claims to account for *all* forms of paranoid developments, regardless of whether they are exogenous or endogenous, psychogenic or somatogenic, and so offers a general theory which at present we do not seem to have" (p. 248). Furthermore, the work of Adhémar Gelb (1887–1936) and Kurt Goldstein (1878–1965) on brain injury and agnosia reflects the influence of Gestalt psychology, particularly in Goldstein's encouragement for psychologists to view humans as more than specific symptoms or test scores (Eling, 2012). Despite Gestalt therapy's mistaken identity, the Gestalt model can serve as a fruitful resource for the clinical psychologist (Crochetière et al., 2001).

The Continuing Relevance of Gestalt Psychology

In an address at a conference on the worldview of contemporary physics, the theoretical physicist Fritjof Capra (1988) contrasted the paradigm that has been dominant in the sciences and in society for the past several hundred years with an emerging new worldview. The old paradigm, according to Capra, included beliefs in a mechanical universe consisting of elementary building blocks, the human body as a machine, unlimited material progress through technological and economic growth, life as a competitive struggle, and the natural domination of the male over the female. Capra characterized the emerging new worldview under five points:

1. A shift from the part to the whole.
2. A shift from structure to process.
3. A shift from "objective science" to "epistemic science."
4. A shift in scientific metaphor from knowledge as a building block to knowledge as a network.
5. A shift from truth to approximate description.

Although there are many differences between Gestalt psychology and the new perspectives as outlined by Capra, there are also some important similarities. Long ago, Gestalt psychology rejected the view of the universe as a mechanical system consisting of elementary building blocks and the view of the human body as a machine. Gestalt psychologists could also offer a great deal of informed comment to all those who agree with Capra that there should be a shift of emphasis from the part to the whole, from structure to process, and from objective science to epistemic science.

The continuing relevance of Gestalt psychology is manifested in other later developments. Recall that one of the major positions of the Gestalt system is that there are internally determined organizations within physical forces. As stated by Henle (1985), "Physical interactions do not occur indiscriminately, but depend on the properties of the interacting events" (p. 105). In recent years there has been increasing awareness that there is latent order within apparent disorder. For example, there are repeated orderly patterns in chaotic physical events such as shattered glass, a rising heat current, and the distribution of matter in an explosion. The Gestalt concept of free dynamics is applicable to these and other physical events. In some cases, computer-generated models of chaos (see Gleick, 1987) reveal striking repetitions of consistent and orderly patterns and shapes occurring on large and small scales, and further evidence of hard-to-see patterns comes from new statistical methods of data mining to reveal complex patterns in massive data sets.

Though psychologists today do not typically claim allegiance to the Gestalt school, there is much in this school that is consistent with the scientific orientations that prevailed at the outset of the twenty-first century. According to Wertheimer (2014b), Gestalt principles have "been rediscovered in fields as diverse as the psychology of art, visual neuroscience, social psychology, cognition, personality theory, and attempts to model the processes of problem solving and other aspects of cognitive neuroscience" (p. 130). Indeed, Gestalt theory is more consistent with the scientific worldview of the twenty-first century than that of the 1940s. In an era marked by interest in ecological concerns and suspicion of reductionism, it would not be surprising if Gestalt theory continues to be rediscovered.

Review Questions

1. Trace some of the key influences on Gestalt theory coming out of science, philosophy, and psychology.
2. Why was the phi phenomenon so important to Wertheimer?
3. Distinguish between productive thinking and mere reproductive thinking.
4. What is the law of Prägnanz and how can it be illustrated?
5. Briefly review the evidence that learning is not based on strict point-for-point mechanical connections.
6. Outline three types of learning discussed in the work of Koffka.
7. Discuss the Gestalt approach to the scientific method. Contrast this approach to the behavioristic approach.
8. Explain the Gestalt approach to the mind–brain problem. Why is the concept of "pictures in the head" a misrepresentation of isomorphism?
9. Explain Lewin's concept of the life space and why it was important to his overall conceptual approach to psychology.
10. What is the Zeigarnik effect and what are some of its practical implications?
11. Discuss Lewin's concept of motivation and its relationship to his approach to conflict.
12. Outline four common misunderstandings of Gestalt psychology.

Glossary

approach–approach conflict A type of conflict marked by the presence of two attractive but mutually exclusive goals. Thus, the achievement of one goal precludes the possibility of attaining the other.

approach–avoidance conflict A type of conflict in which a positive goal is associated with some unattractive or undesirable feature.

avoidance–avoidance conflict A type of conflict marked by the presence of two unattractive or undesirable alternatives.

closure The tendency psychologically to complete that which is incomplete, to fill in the gaps, or to see wholeness even when it is not present.

Duncker, Karl (1903–1940) Gestalt psychologist remembered for his work on the nature of problem solving and for work on the relativity of perceived movement.

field theory Generally associated with the psychology of Kurt Lewin. Field theory emphasizes the interdependence of the person and the environment. It may be viewed as a corrective to extreme individualistic psychologies that neglect the role of context.

figure–ground A principle of perception characterized by the tendency of the subject to see some things as standing out and other things as forming background.

functional fixedness The inability to find productive solutions to new problems. May also refer to the inability to see alternative uses for a particular tool or method.

Gestalt There is no exact English equivalent for this German term, but English words such as *whole* and *configuration* are close in meaning.

Gestalt therapy A form of therapy coming out of the work of Fritz Perls and having little or nothing in common with Gestalt psychology.

good continuation The perceptual tendency toward linearity, continuity, or coherence. Good continuation is manifested when a perceptual pattern is tracked even in the presence of irrelevant or competing cues.

group dynamics In Lewin's psychology, this expression refers broadly to the study of the effects of groups on individuals and the effects of individuals on groups. It also includes the study of group structures and their effect on work, productivity, and achievement of group goals.

insight The capacity to see a problem in a large context and perceptually to restructure relationships necessary to the solution of the problem.

isomorphism The Gestalt position on the mind–brain problem. Literally, this term refers to similarity of form. Isomorphism, in the context of the mind–brain problem, refers to an assumed functional relationship between experience and underlying brain processes.

Katona, George (1901–1981) Gestalt psychologist who applied Gestalt principles to memory and education.

Koffka, Kurt (1886–1941) Pioneering Gestalt psychologist remembered especially for introducing Gestalt psychology to the English-speaking world and for the extension of Gestalt theory into the field of developmental psychology.

Köhler, Wolfgang (1887–1967) Principal advocate of the Gestalt school. Köhler is remembered for his pioneering work on the role of insight in learning, for his treatment of value theory from a Gestalt perspective, and for his broad systematic approach to science and psychology.

law of Prägnanz The law of Prägnanz, according to Wertheimer, refers to the idea that perceptual organization tends to be as good as possible under prevailing conditions. Thus, perceptual organization is as orderly, coherent, and economical as possible under prevailing conditions.

Lewin, Kurt (1890–1947) Inspired by Wertheimer, Köhler, and Koffka, Lewin attempted to extend the Gestalt vision to other subdisciplinary branches of psychology, including motivation, personality, social psychology, and conflict resolution.

life space Key concept in Lewin's psychology referring to all the psychological facts that are influential in the life of an individual at a given point in time.

Mach, Ernst (1838–1916) Nineteenth-century physicist who argued that there are space-form and time-form sensations that are configural in their nature. Mach's analysis served as an inspiration for the early Gestalt psychologists who also argued that there are wholes that are grasped intuitively and that are more than a mere collection of elements.

phi phenomenon Apparent movement illustrated by successive activation of two stationary lights placed in close spatial conjunction. Phenomenally, what is seen is movement from the first to the second light.

productive thinking Wertheimer's term for a bold and radical centering of a problem that results in creative new ideas, breakthroughs, insights, or solutions. Einstein's revolutionary theory of relativity serves as a classic illustration of productive thinking.

proximity The perceptual tendency to group figures or *Gestalten* that are close together in space or time.

reproductive thinking Wertheimer's term for the routine reproduction of familiar solutions that result in blind conclusions with no sense of direction.

similarity The perceptual tendency to group figures or *Gestalten* that are similar.

valence According to Lewin, the positive or negative characteristics of objects in the life space.

von Ehrenfels, Christian (1859–1932) One of the first to argue that form qualities are given immediately in experience. Although Ehrenfels believed that the whole is more than the sum of the parts, he still believed that it was derivative and thus acts simply like another part.

von Restorff, Hedwig (1906–1962) A second-generation Gestalt psychologist remembered for her study of memory with Wolfgang Köhler.

von Restorff effect Refers to superiority of recall for isolated items in a list compared to more homogeneous items.

Wertheimer, Max (1880–1943) Founder of the Gestalt school of thought and author of the influential book *Productive Thinking*.

Zeigarnik effect Tendency to remember incomplete tasks better than completed ones.

15 Psychoanalysis

The ego is not master in its own house.

— Sigmund Freud (1917/1955)

Like behaviorism, psychoanalysis moved beyond a system of psychology to become an intellectual movement. Psychoanalytic theory connected with many fields including literature, philosophy, art, religion, and history. And like behaviorism, psychoanalysis inspired both devotion and derision. Debate continues to rage about the influence and relevance of psychoanalysis, with some scholars insisting it is a vanishing system while others claim it is alive and robust (see Ciabattari, 2014; Crews, 1996; Dvorsky, 2013; Horgan, 1996). In terms of its influence in literature, general cultural studies, debates on clinical practices, and psychology texts, and the numbers of professional organizations, journals, and books, the evidence supports a continuing presence and influence of psychoanalysis. The original system has been subjected to a great many methodological and substantive modifications. Many of these have resulted from obvious deficiencies that surfaced in the classical theory and practice. We begin with a brief biographical sketch of Sigmund Freud.

Sigmund Freud

Sigmund Freud (1856–1939). Born on May 6, 1856, in Freiberg, Moravia, Sigmund was the first of the eight children of Jakob Freud and Amalie Nathansohn. In 1860, Jakob and Amalie settled in Vienna, a city that became Freud's home for the next seventy-eight years. Anti-Semitism colored day-to-day life and narrowed vocational opportunities for Jewish citizens. Jones (1953) relayed the story of a thug who knocked Jakob Freud's new hat into a puddle of mud and then demanded, "Jew get off the pavement" (p. 22). Jewish citizens were often victims of hostile acts and demeaning humor as well as housing, employment, and other types of discrimination. Such a climate had a profound effect on Sigmund Freud's thought and character (see Bakan, 1958; Miller, 1981; Phillips, 2014; Roith, 1987).

Always a precocious student, Freud graduated from high school summa cum laude at age seventeen. He excelled in literature, history, and science. His facility with languages was evident in his competence in Latin, Greek, French, English, Italian, Spanish, and Hebrew. In 1873, Freud matriculated in the University of Vienna, where he pursued a degree in medicine. Like William

Sigmund Freud

James, his interests ranged over the entire curriculum. He attended Franz Brentano's courses in philosophy and psychology as well as a course on evolution taught by zoologist Carl Claus and a course on the physiology of speech taught by **Ernst Brücke (1819–1892)**.

In the fall of 1876 Freud accepted a position as a research scholar in physiology in Brücke's laboratory, where he conducted original research on the histology of spinal nerves in fish. Freud's skills as a physiology researcher were rewarded with a grant that paid for two brief trips to Trieste, Italy where he engaged in research on gonadal structures in eels. It would have been Freud's preference to continue indefinitely as a researcher in neurology in Brücke's laboratory, but dismal prospects for advancement as well as personal financial exigencies forced him into a medical career. Accordingly, he served as a resident

in the Vienna General Hospital from 1882 to 1885 gaining experience in surgery, internal medicine, dermatology, and ophthalmology, but he had little interest in any of these fields. His interest picked up when he worked in Theodore Meynert's psychiatric clinic and in Franz Schol's department of nervous diseases.

During his residency, he fell in love with a young woman named Martha Bernays. Not long after meeting her, Freud had flowers delivered every day to his "princess." He dreamed of marrying Martha, but the poverty-stricken student couldn't support her. Around this time, Freud discovered a "magical substance" extracted from coca leaves. He noted that alkaloid cocaine gave him a sense of good cheer and energy, warding off depression and indigestion with "brilliant success." He initially denied its addictiveness (Cohen, 2012), and according to Jones (1953), Freud recommended the drug to "his friends and colleagues, both for themselves and their patients; he gave it to his sisters. In short, looked at from the vantage point of our present knowledge, he was rapidly becoming a public menace" (p. 81). Freud hoped his research on the drug's medicinal benefits might establish his reputation and provide the financial rewards that would allow him to marry (Markel, 2011; Lipsitt, 2016), but he soured on it after discovering cocaine's darker, more addictive side. After his disappointment, despite an available supply, no legal consequences for use, and no support to overcome his addiction, Freud impressively quit using cocaine.

While working in Brücke's laboratory Freud had met **Joseph Breuer (1842–1925)**, a respected physiologist who was treating a twenty-one-year-old woman who had developed some symptoms of hysteria while caring for her dying father. The woman, Bertha Pappenheim, experienced headaches, loss of sensation, partial paralysis, and hallucinations about skeletons and black snakes. Under hypnosis, Pappenheim relived traumatic events that had escaped her conscious memories. She made progress with what she referred to as her *talking cure or chimney sweeping* (Gay, 1988). But later, she announced she was pregnant with

Breuer's child, another symptom of her hysteria. The announcement of the false pregnancy caused Breuer to stop the therapy and to leave her to the care of a colleague. In time, she overcame the hysteria and became one of Germany's first feminists and a pioneer in the field of social work.

Breuer first described her case to Freud in 1882. Much later, Freud and Breuer, in a classic book, *Studies in Hysteria*, discussed the case under the pseudonym Anna O. As noted, Freud's training to this point had been in physiology and his predilections had been in the direction of purely physical and neurological approaches to mental problems. The analysis of the Anna O. case, however, did not lend itself easily to available neurological explanations. The case seemed to have clear-cut psychological underpinnings. As we will see, the transition from physiology and neurology to psychology would prove extremely difficult, even vexing, for Freud.

In September of 1885, Freud was appointed *Privatdozent* (a lecturer paid only by student fees) in neuropathology. In the winter months of 1885–1886 he worked in **Jean-Martin Charcot's (1825–1893)** neurology clinic at the Pitié-Salpêtrière Hospital in Paris. This opportunity reinforced Freud's interest in hysteria and hypnosis and shaped his later approaches to diagnosis (Lepoutre & Villa, 2015). The experience was pivotal because the Paris School focused on the psychological nature of emotional problems, whereas the Vienna faculty advocated physical interpretations. Following his time in Paris, Freud returned to Vienna, where he launched a private practice on April 25, 1886. That same year, following their lengthy engagement, he married Martha Bernays.

Freud's system of psychotherapy did not develop suddenly. In fact, the term **psychoanalysis** did not debut until a full decade after Freud had established his clinical practice (Jones, 1953). During the earliest phases of his practice, he used electrotherapy (not to be confused with electroconvulsive therapy). Conventional wisdom held that deficiencies in circulation produced mental disorders. As a remedy, *electrotherapy* consisted of passing small currents of electricity through the skin and muscles of the head to improve circulation. Freud came to the conclusion that electrotherapy was little more than a placebo. Later, Freud used hypnotic suggestion before trying Breuer's cathartic method. His technique of free association evolved from a growing disillusionment with other therapeutic methods.

Freud's best-known book, *The Interpretation of Dreams*, appeared in November 1899 as *Die Traumdeutung* (the publisher postdated the book as 1900 to reflect a new way of thinking for a new century). Freud advanced his familiar position that dreams represent wish fulfillments in disguise. Now regarded as a classic, the book did not bring instant fame to its author (Fancher, 2000). Initial reaction was sharp and hostile, especially in Viennese circles. In time, the book attracted attention, granting renown for Freud within a decade after its publication.

Freud's bibliography following *The Interpretation of Dreams* reveals an impressive output of books, shorter papers, and case histories designed to elaborate and extend his system of psychological thought. So prolific were his writings that the collected works are now contained in twenty-three volumes with an additional volume devoted to indexes and bibliographies (see Strachey, 1953–1974).

In 1909, Freud accepted G. Stanley Hall's invitation to speak at Clark University. Gay (1988) observed that prior to his American lectures, psychoanalysts "represented a small, embattled minority in the psychiatric profession; Freud's ideas still remained the property of the few, and a scandal to most" (p. 206). The Clark visit enfranchised psychoanalysis in America, especially in the psychiatric community, and helped turn psychoanalysis into an international movement (see Burnham, 2013). The success of the American visit prompted Freud to regard the Clark University ceremony as the "first official recognition of our endeavors" (Jones, 1955, p. 57). William James was one of many luminaries who attended Freud's five lectures. The two men later met for a walk but were interrupted when James experienced pain from the aggravated heart condition that would claim his life nearly a year later. Inspired by James's stoicism, Freud (1924/1959a) later wrote, "I have always wished that I might be as fearless as he was in the face of approaching death" (p. 52); Freud would have the chance to find out.

Freud's biographers paint the picture of a brilliant thinker with a complex personality (Gelfand & Kerr, 1992). He could appear shy almost to the point of lacking confidence, but could also be outgoing, joyful, enthusiastic, or even jubilant. His creativity was inconsistent as he suffered through periods when he was incapable of pro-

ductive work but such periods were eclipsed by bursts of creative industry. Though he worked unusually long hours, he found time for Martha and their five children, as well as his extended family. His close relationship with his wife's sister has prompted rumors of an extramarital romance since this allegation was first mentioned by Jung (Gale, 2016). Freud's tastes in music were narrow, but he had a deep appreciation for art, especially sculpture. Besides cigars, his major indulgence was a collection of antiquities, mostly sculptures of ancient figures that guarded his desk like battle-hardened sentries.

PSYCHOLOGY CONFERENCE GROUP, CLARK UNIVERSITY, SEPTEMBER, 1909

Beginning with first row, left to right: Franz Boas, E. B. Titchener, William James, William Stern, Leo Burgerstein, G. Stanley Hall, Sigmund Freud, Carl G. Jung, Adolf Meyer, H. S. Jennings. *Second row:* C. E. Seashore, Joseph Jastrow, J. McK. Cattell, E. F. Buchner, E. Katzenellenbogen, Ernest Jones, A. A. Brill, Wm. H. Burnham, A. F. Chamberlain. *Third row:* Albert Schinz, J. A. Magni, B. T. Baldwin, F. Lyman Wells, G. M. Forbes, E. A. Kirkpatrick, Sandor Ferenczi, E. C. Sanford, J. P. Porter, Sakyo Kanda, Hikoso Kakise. *Fourth row:* G. E. Dawson, S. P. Hayes, E. B. Holt, C. S. Berry, G. M. Whipple, Frank Drew, J. W. A. Young, L. N. Wilson, K. J. Karlson, H. H. Goddard, H. I. Klopp, S. C. Fuller.

The 1909 Conference at Clark University played host to some of psychology's most influential pioneers. In the front row, Clark's president G. Stanley Hall (center, hat in hand) stands next to Sigmund Freud (hat and cane); Carl Jung stands to the right of Freud. E. B. Titchener stands in the front row, second from the left. To his right is William James (holding hat and coat) and J. M. Cattell appears behind and to the right of James.

As with countless Jewish scholars, Freud's life and work faced upheaval with the rise of Adolf Hitler, and this upheaval had profound effects on the emergence of psychoanalysis (Gitre, 2011). On May 10, 1933, the Nazis burned Freud's books along with the works of other intellectuals (Gay, 1988). After hearing the news, Freud responded with characteristic gallows humor: "What progress we are making. In the Middle Ages they would have burnt me; nowadays they are content with burning my books" (Jones, 1957, p. 182). Tragically, the Holocaust would reveal that the Nazis conspired to destroy more than books. In 1938, a gang of Nazi authorities invaded Freud's home. His youngest daughter, Anna, escorted them to the family safe and opened it. The men emptied the safe, taking the equivalent of well over $10,000 in today's economy. "Freud ruefully commented on hearing of it later that *he* had never been paid so much for a single visit" (Jones, 1957, p. 219). At first defiant, Freud finally agreed to leave Vienna after the Gestapo interrogated Anna (Cohen, 2009). Before he was permitted to emigrate, the Nazis required that he sign a statement that he had not been mistreated. Taking a tremendous risk, he employed sarcasm, writing "I can most highly recommend the Gestapo to everyone" (Gay, 1988, p. 628). Despite his statement, he was permitted to leave.

Stricken with cancer of the jaw, his last months were spent in exile in London. His affiliation with B'nai B'rith, as well as his theories, made him a prime target for Nazi hostilities. Totalitarians such as Stalin and Hitler do not like to believe their intellectual constructions might have unconscious psychological origins. Freud's final days in London were undermined by the shrill cry of air raid sirens and his struggles with terminal cancer. He faced his own death as directly as had James. Finally, he convinced his friend and physician, Max Schur, to administer three centigrams of morphine on September 21, 1939 (Gay, 1988). After the final and fatal dose of morphine, Freud lapsed into a coma. He died on September 23 as a result of physician-assisted suicide.

General Characteristics of Freud's Thought

Though Sigmund Freud's psychology evolved over time, several philosophical assumptions guided his work. We'll review six defining characteristics of his theory and then consider details of his system.

DETERMINISM Freud was an unapologetic determinist. He argued for a methodology that assumes natural causes for all mental events (MacMillan, 1991). Gay (1988) wrote, "It is a crucial point in Freud's theory that there are no accidents in the universe of the mind" (p. 119). Sulloway (1979) noted that "Freud's entire life's work in science was characterized by an abiding faith in the notion that all vital phenomena, including psychical ones, are rigidly and lawfully determined by the principle of cause and effect" (p. 94). Other scholars (Brown, 1964, p. 3; Jones, 1953, p. 304; Wisdom, 1943) have emphasized Freud's strong commitment to determinism. As we will see later, however, meanings of freedom surfaced in Freud's clinical work.

BELIEF IN THE CONTINUITY OF THE ANIMAL KINGDOM In his autobiographical study, Freud (1924/1959a) basked in Darwinian theory because it suggested that knowledge of natural processes enhances our understanding of the world. In an open letter to Albert Einstein on the subject of war, Freud (1932/1964a) insisted that humans should not be excluded from the animal kingdom. According to Jones (1953), Freud subscribed to the evolutionary position that "no spirits, essences, or entelechies, no superior plans or ultimate purposes are at work. The physical energies alone cause effects—somehow" (p. 42). Freud believed a naturalistic study of human nature offered distinct advantages.

ROLE OF UNCONSCIOUS INFLUENCES Freud's belief in the unconscious is a defining feature of his psychology. He believed that irrational unconscious motives influence rational conscious processes. It's a troubling idea that challenges our cherished belief in human rationality (Grose, 2014). Even more disturbing, he insisted that unconscious forces can sometimes marshal the authority to dominate the conscious mind. When this happens, according to Freud (1917/1955), "the ego is not master in its own house" (p. 143). Nevertheless, he believed human beings can find ways to escape the bondage of unconscious influences. As we will see later, Freud's goal of psychoanalysis returns the ego to "its mastery over lost provinces of . . . mental life" (Freud, 1938/1964b, p. 173).

DEVELOPMENTAL EMPHASIS Classic psychoanalytic theory stressed the importance of development and growth. Freud understood that needs and abilities vary as a function of age. According to his theory, early childhood events color later adjustment, a statement that is widely accepted today but was inflammatory at the time (DeMause, 1974). At the same time, the child must negotiate critical developmental periods if she or he hopes to enjoy later psychological health and well-being.

EMPHASIS ON MOTIVATION We often identify major systems of psychology with a preferred area of study. For example, structuralists placed considerable emphasis on the senses and behaviorists on learning. In Freudian psychology, the study of human motivation is the privileged content area. What motivates us to do the things we do? Freud's discussions of patients and their clinical dilemmas are couched in the language of motivation. He never denied the crucial roles that learning, perception, and social influence play in our lives, but clearly his emphasis was on motivation.

APPLIED PSYCHOLOGY Freud's theoretical interests ran deep, but he hungered for a psychology that could speak to the daily problems of life. He dedicated a great deal of intellectual energy to problems of intervention and treatment. This applied emphasis is reflected in the term

psychoanalysis because it refers simultaneously to a psychotherapy and a system of psychology.

Freud's System of Psychology

Psychoanalytic theory and practice evolved over the forty-three years of Freud's professional career. At first, he hoped to advance a psychology anchored in neurology and physiology, a psychology that would prove worthy as a natural science (Connors, 2000). Freud (1895/1950) expressed his early ambitions in a manuscript titled "Project for a Scientific Psychology." He soon realized it was premature to establish rigorous connections between physiology and the world of experience. After vexing struggles he abandoned his cherished project in favor of a more psychological approach to the problems of living.

On numerous occasions, Freud pursued false leads that forced him to backtrack and start over. In terms of development, psychoanalysis did not travel a smooth linear progression of ideas. As we explore Freud's system, we'll begin with his mature thought because it opens the broadest vista. We'll then work back to earlier ideas to fill in details of his psychology.

Life's Major Goal and Its Inevitable Frustration

In his book *Civilization and Its Discontents*, Freud (1930/1961a) outlined his belief that the **pleasure principle** dominates human nature. From the beginning of life, we seek pleasure and try to avoid pain. We seek pleasure by satisfying basic needs such as hunger and sexuality, but the world doesn't always cooperate with our basic desires. Even our body betrays our best efforts to enjoy sustained pleasure. Freud observed that we know pleasure only through contrast, but we have a constitutional incapacity to experience contrast for sustained periods. If you're shivering from a winter's chill, you take a hot bath. You experience pleasure as you are submerged in the water's warmth, but the pleasure is short-lived. The constancy of the bath will itself grow aversive if we remain in it too long. Freud (1930/1961a) reminded his readers of Goethe's warning that "nothing is harder to bear than a succession of fair days" (p. 76). In addition to constitutional constraints on happiness, Freud outlined three sources of suffering that oppose the pleasure we so highly prize.

The first source of suffering is our own body. As we age, it fails more and more to satisfy our appetite for pleasure. Although resilient, the body is doomed to deterioration, sending relentless warnings of its frailty and inevitable demise. The outer world constitutes the second source of suffering. Consider the threats it poses: earthquakes, floods, tornados, drought, avalanches, landslides, hurricanes, wildfires, famine, and bacterial and viral invasions. Our world rages against us with unrelenting insults. Even the grandest surroundings are beset with natural disasters that compromise happiness, replacing it with misery.

Freud saves the greatest source of suffering for last. Think about where you find the most anguish in life. For Freud, the answer is simple: other people. To be sure, other people are sources of joy and happiness, but they can also inflict chaos, pain, and unhappiness. The sources of social suffering are extensive, arriving in the form of war, theft, assault, betrayals, injustice, prejudices, child and spousal abuse, daily insensitivities and hostilities, dishonesty, authoritarian structures and attitudes, and economic disparities. Given all the sources of unhappiness, Freud (1930/1961a) wondered if it was never intended that human beings should be happy.

So how do we cope with our difficult quest for pleasure? Freud suggested remedial actions that seek to preserve gratification (although most are flawed and temporary in their effects). One method is to withdraw from the world, savoring whatever satisfaction can be found in self-imposed isolation. Another approach—highly prized because it produces a small portion of happiness and independence from the world—is the

method of intoxication. Despite his experiments with cocaine, Freud was not impressed with artificial intoxicants because they blur our sense of reality and require energy that could have been put to better use. Unafraid of controversy, Freud compared religion to intoxication, arguing that both involve an escape from reality. In his view, religion places us in a state of mental infantilism that depreciates the value of this world while promising the illusion of a better world to come.

The word *illusion* in Freud's writings does not refer to something that is false by definition. Freud (1927/1961c) noted, "An illusion is not the same thing as an error; nor is it necessarily an error" (p. 30). Rather, an illusion is a belief motivated by a powerful wish that is divorced from normal realistic expectations. Freud believed that many religious beliefs are marked by blatantly obvious, but unrealistic wishes regarding the structure of reality and the fantastic acquisitions one might enjoy in an afterlife. It is no accident that cherished projected acquirements and fantasies concerning an afterlife (wealth, leisure, beauty, and unimaginable sustained pleasures) are the very things we long for, but do not possess in this life. Pervasive wishes for justice and compensation in most belief systems are almost impossible to ignore. Freud's major critiques of religion are outlined in his book *The Future of an Illusion* (1927/1961c).

We can create other methods for coping with the world. Freud included defenses such as loving and being loved, enjoyment of works of art, and the flight into mental illness. According to Freud, hard work and science offer the most admirable defense against the sources of suffering. Through both, we can make lasting contributions for the good of others (although Freud added that work is seldom valued by the masses).

Freud acknowledged that all strategies for attaining happiness and defending against suffering are incomplete. We are fighting a losing battle because the demands of the pleasure principle cannot be fulfilled. He believed different alternatives must be judged in an equation sensitive to short-term and long-term interests and to individual and social interests. Difficulties, complexities, and ambiguities in the pursuit of happiness confront every person. Freud's views on the pleasure principle and its vicissitudes provide a backdrop for understanding human personality.

The Structure of Personality

Freud conceptualized the structure of human personality in terms of three interrelated systems called the *id*, *ego*, and *superego* (meaning, respectively, the *it*, *I*, and *over-I*). The three systems are embroiled in frequent battle, delivering conflict that must be resolved if we hope to adapt to the world. Adjustment depends on harmony among the three systems. If any of the three gains excessive control, severe consequences will follow. The three systems offer differing strategies for coping with threats against the pleasure principle. Although Freud viewed the id, ego, and superego as hypothetical features of personality, he often spoke of them as if they were real entities.

THE ID In the beginning there is the **id**. It emerges as the first component of personality. Primitive and feral, it is driven by powerful biological needs necessary for physical survival. The needs of the id are common to all animal species and seek expression in the most biologically direct and efficient manner. Society can claim no permanent hold on the id, but customs, morality, values, conventions, and ethics restrain it. Impulsively and reflexively, it is directed toward immediate gratification. According to Freud, the id operates on the pleasure principle. The id is represented in impulsive and reflexive activity, but it also finds expression in **primary processes**, images, or memories of objects that satisfy needs. A dream of a sexual encounter illustrates primary processes at work. Such processes present themselves without the embellishment of polite social conventions and norms.

Freud employed the term *libido* to refer to the psychic energy that fuels our pursuit of need

gratification. In our hunt for pleasure, libidinal energy is often directed toward beloved or desired objects (*object libido*). However, the libido may attach itself to the ego. When this happens, an intense self-love called narcissism replaces object love.

THE EGO The **ego** is the *I* or *me* of the personality (taken from the Latin first-person singular pronoun of *I*, *ego* is used in English translations for Freud's German term *Das Ich*). The ego is the center of organization and integration. Whereas the id is tied to the pleasure principle, the ego operates on the **reality principle**. The ego must serve as a mediator, balancing the demands of the id with the demands of social convention. Caught between such powerful forces, it learns to appropriate, compromise, substitute, and delay. The ego makes use of the **secondary process**, devising strategies through which the id's primary process can be satisfied in a socially acceptable manner. Such techniques protect the individual and the social order by finding acceptable channels for the demands of the id. Often at odds, the demands of the id and society impose remarkable strain on the ego. To survive such aggressive and continuous conflict, the ego must be robust and stable. But this is not the complete story. In time, the ego must contend with still another force.

THE SUPEREGO Every bit as irrational as the id, the **superego** consists of internalized social norms, ideals, and standards that are not grounded in reality. Rather than seeking pleasure, the superego is a kind of conscience with an inhibitory function. Over and above this, it pushes the ego to achieve higher values embraced by society. No more realistic than the id, the superego is an intolerant taskmaster, driving the ego to reach impossible standards of perfection.

Like Plato, Freud used the example of a charioteer struggling to rein in powerful steeds (Simon, 1972). Freud was consumed with documenting the conflicts among the id, ego, and superego. All three serve important roles and each must find legitimate and acceptable expression. The id represents dimensions of biological life that cannot be ignored. On the other hand, we must inhibit primal desires if we are to live with other people. If the id dominates the ego, antisocial behavior results and society must take action to correct such behavior. Likewise, an aggressive superego may block the expression of basic biological needs. Freud believed the repression of biological drives results in emotional difficulties common to civilized societies. (We'll return to this topic later.) According to Freud, the ego must have sufficient strength to deal with the complex and sometimes capricious demands of the external world while permitting the compromised expression of both id and superego. He believed the volatile interplay among the id, ego, and superego had far-reaching consequences for the mental health of his patients.

Motivation and Unconscious Processes

Orgel (1990) tells us that "the core idea of psychoanalysis begins with the assumption that in every human being there is an unconscious mind" (p. 1). Freud's early experiences with hypnosis had telling effects on his theoretical development. Before the July 1889 Congress on Hypnotism in Paris, Freud visited the clinic of Hippolyte Bernheim (1840–1919), a rival of Charcot. In a typical demonstration, Bernheim hypnotized patients and gave suggestions to be carried out after awakening from the trance. For example, a patient was instructed that the next time Bernheim and his assistants entered the room, the patient would open the physician's umbrella (conveniently placed in the corner) and hold it over Bernheim's head. The patient was brought out of hypnosis. When Bernheim and the assistants returned to the room, the patient greeted them and then opened the umbrella and hoisted it above the physician's head.

After the posthypnotic suggestion was carried out, Bernheim asked the patient why he had opened the umbrella, an atypical behavior.

Embarrassed patients usually offered rationalizations. For example, a given patient might claim the weather forecast had called for rain and he or she needed to inspect the umbrella to make certain it didn't leak. In truth, patients couldn't account for their behavior because they could not consciously recall what had transpired during the hypnotic trance.

Commenting on such demonstrations, Freud said he "received the profoundest impression of the possibility that there could be powerful mental processes which nevertheless remained hidden from the consciousness" (cited in Jones, 1953, p. 238). The patients did not seem to understand the cause of their strange behavior. Bernheim's hypnosis demonstrations provided a graphic example of how unconscious forces can influence behavior. At the same time, conscious explanations of the behavior were superficial, even illusory, yet patients *believed* their fabricated explanations.

Freud described Bernheim's work with hypnosis as astonishing, and it had a clear influence on the development of psychoanalysis. No longer could consciousness be viewed as autonomous nor could we be certain we understood all that is in the mind. Freud viewed it as a mistake to equate mental processes with consciousness alone. To defend the powerful role of unconscious forces in human life, he drew from hypnotic phenomena, dreams, slips of the tongue, and everyday purposeful forgetting such as the forgetting of a dental appointment. No conscious event was sacrosanct, not even a religious experience. Freud provided an interesting case study to illustrate this latter point.

In the case study titled "A Religious Experience," Freud (1927/1961d) tells of a young physician who shared the story of his religious conversion in the hope of convincing Freud about the existence of God. In writing about his conversion, the doctor described seeing the corpse of an old woman carted to the dissecting room. The sight inspired indignation over the apparent injustice of the woman's death. The man decided then and there to abandon his belief in God. But after reflecting on the matter, he reported that a voice "spoke to my soul that 'I should consider the step I was about to take'" (Freud, 1927/1961d, p. 169). Following that event, he was overcome with fear and remorse. In a dizzying moment of conversion, he suddenly accepted a specific Christian belief.

In sharing his experience, the young doctor beseeched Freud to abandon his atheistic beliefs. Freud sent a polite reply to the doctor's letter and then proceeded to analyze the religious experience. Unable to accept the doctor's story at face value, Freud raised some important questions. Why had the young doctor been so outraged, and why had he renounced God at the sight of an old woman carried away for dissection? The questions are cogent because doctors see far more grisly sights than a corpse destined for autopsy. Why would this particular event initiate a renunciation of belief in God and a subsequent religious conversion? Wouldn't it prove a more stirring sight to witness the senseless death of a child or a young adult?

But Freud reasoned that this particular event was well suited to initiate the doctor's conversion because it aroused unconscious motives (Woody, 2003). Freud insisted that the sight of the old woman triggered associations of the doctor's mother. In this case, the cruel fate of the mother is the work of God the father. In a cry of outrage, the doctor rebelled against the source of the indignity and injustice. He vowed to deny the existence of God. But why, then, was the doctor so quickly converted? Conversion, in this case, represents obvious fear and surrender to God the father. The reason for the conversion, according to Freud, is found in an unconscious conflict that most human beings experience at an earlier stage in their lives (although this conflict can reemerge symbolically in later life).

Freud believed that Sophocles's ancient Greek tragedy *Oedipus Rex* is characteristic of conflicts that young children experience. He claimed that in the course of development, a child develops a strong emotional attachment to its opposite-sex parent but finds conflict with the same-sex parent.

For example, a boy with strong attachment to his mother may feel hostility toward his father because he is a usurper who robs the boy of exclusive rights to the mother. But hostility toward the father is fraught with danger. The boy is powerless while his father is formidable in comparison. How does the child resolve the Oedipus conflict? He might abandon his competitive stance and identify with the father. Identifying with power, even aggressive power, is a well-established psychological phenomenon. According to Freud, the Oedipus conflict may not be resolved in childhood and may rise again to haunt the person in adulthood.

Following Freud's analysis, it comes as little surprise that the young doctor could not sustain his anger at God. God was simply too powerful (the mere suggestion that the doctor should consider the step he was about to take led to fear followed by remorse for his childish rebellion). The doctor achieved resolution through an identification with God the father. Religious conversion was the end result. The case history illustrates Freud's beliefs about the possible weight of unconscious forces on mental processes. Critics, however, have raised understandable questions about Freud's approach to conversion (see Kovel, 1990; Meissner, 1984; Zilboorg, 1961).

The idea that reason serves unconscious motives comes as a blow to human pretensions. It is little wonder that Freud (1917/1955) claims that "the ego does not look favorably upon psychoanalysis and positively refuses to believe in it" (p. 143). Freud envisioned himself as a scientific champion like Copernicus and Darwin, challenging the frailties of human narcissism. With Copernican heliocentricity, our planet no longer occupied the center of the cosmos. With Darwin, we were no longer products of special creation. But Freud believed psychoanalysis posed the greatest challenge to collective human narcissism. Is there any more disturbing thought than the possibility that we are not always aware of the reasons for our beliefs and actions? Are we not in control of our own minds? Freud shattered our cherished belief that we are rational creatures with a free will that allows us to shape our destinies.

Though Freud stressed the influence of unconscious forces, his larger vision of human motivation was more complicated. We turn now to an important work titled "Instincts and Their Vicissitudes" (Freud, 1915/1957a). Unfortunately, the English term **instinct** is a poor equivalent for the German term *Trieb* used in Freud's original work. The term *drive*, as used in American psychology, comes closer in meaning to Freud's *Trieb*. Whatever the translation, Freud's concept of *Trieb* is an important key to his theory of motivation.

TRIEB Freud argued that *Trieb* originates in a stimulus that persists until it finds satisfaction. He suggested that the term *need* best describes such a stimulus. We have a basic need to reduce powerful drives. Think about times when you've been hungry or dehydrated. How great did it feel when you finally had the chance to eat and drink? You can see how drive reduction can be pleasurable. But how many drives do we have? In addition to biological needs like thirst and hunger, drives are behind social actions ranging from play to aggression. In short, Freud acknowledged many drives but noted that psychoanalysis, especially in its earliest development, focused largely on complications associated with drives toward pleasure.

He proposed four components associated with a drive or *Trieb*. The first component is the *source*. A drive has its source in a bodily stimulus. For example, mechanical and chemical changes in the body trigger hunger. The need for food will persist until the source is abolished. Satisfaction, however, is temporary because drives operate on a cyclical nature.

A second characteristic, known as the *impetus*, refers to the amount of energy associated with the drive. He also used the expression *motor element* to define the term *impetus*. Presumably, the impetus grows as a function of the amount of time that has lapsed since the drive was last experienced. In other words, the impetus will grow more intense the longer you go without food.

The third characteristic of a drive is its *aim*. Satisfaction is the aim of every drive. Freud (1915/1957a) noted that drives always seek satisfaction through altering the stimulation that produced them in the first place. Though satisfaction is the aim, it may be attained in multiple ways. The ego plays a crucial role in achieving the aim by making compromises, temporary delays, substitutions, and so forth.

The final, and most interesting, component of a drive is its *object*. This is where the drive achieves its aim. Freud (1915/1957a) argued that the objects of drives are highly variable. Indeed, the object is the most flexible component of a drive. A single stimulus may serve more than one drive. And a given drive may become attached to a great variety of stimulus objects. A particularly strong attachment to a stimulus is called a **fixation**.

Freud observed that drives undergo many vicissitudes or changes. For example, drives may be sublimated, repressed, or even reversed into their opposites. He claimed that the vicissitudes of drives have far-reaching consequences for human adjustment and health.

Anxiety

In Freud's psychology, interplaying tensions confront every human being. Various components of personality may bring tension. So can competing drives and different sources of pain and suffering. Freud believed such tensions could produce anxiety.

OBJECTIVE ANXIETY As noted, the outer world can rage against us. Our body is vulnerable to internal and external assaults. And most of all, other people can hurt us. Anxieties arise from such threats to our well-being, a process Freud called **objective anxiety**. It is part of the wear and tear of living in a world that can be hostile and forbidding. This brand of anxiety emerges when objective forces in the world threaten the ego. Its force is a function of the strength of the ego in relation to the perceived power of the threat. In a sense, this is healthy—even adaptive—anxiety. If you're hiking in the wilderness and you encounter a bear, it would seem abnormal if you didn't experience at least a little anxiety.

NEUROTIC ANXIETY Unlike objective anxiety, **neurotic anxiety** emerges from within our own personality and doesn't serve an adaptive or healthy purpose. Neurotic anxiety arises when the id dominates the ego. Because the source of threat arises from within, there is no obvious escape and no identifiable cause. Neurotic anxiety can have a mysterious quality because it can appear, for no apparent reason, at any time or place. Without noticeable cause, the individual may experience impending doom or a panicked feeling. Neurotic anxiety is more common when basic drives are thwarted or bottled up. During Freud's day, Victorian culture imposed rigid prohibitions on sexual expression. But if we stifle powerful drives at every turn, they will find expression in unwanted intrusions into the stream of experience.

MORAL ANXIETY As a counterpart to neurotic anxiety, **moral anxiety** results when the superego dominates the ego. Here again the source of moral anxiety arises within the personality, so escape seems impossible. The original source of moral anxiety comes from caregivers and the outside world. Over time, the superego incorporates society's norms, values, customs, and prohibitions and is the source of internalized moral authority capable of meting out punishment. Moral anxiety appears when we feel guilt over real—even imagined—violations of internalized values. The more robust the superego, the greater the likelihood a person will experience moral anxiety. Sometimes the most virtuous and exemplary people experience the greatest moral anxiety. On the opposite extreme, some people almost never experience moral anxiety. Such individuals risk placing their own instinctual needs ahead of the rights of others. They may end

up isolating themselves from others or, in some cases, being forcibly isolated from others by the criminal justice system. However, people ruled by excessive moral anxiety risk an existence that is colorless, overly controlled, hollow, or blindly submissive to the demands of authority.

The varieties of anxiety illustrate the importance of personality balance. Individual health and adjustment depend on a flow of channeled energy from the id and the superego. The ego must possess ample strength to deal with the harsh demands of the world and the nagging weight from its internal companions. But what happens when the id and the superego don't play nice? In those circumstances, the ego must resort to desperate measures to seize control over the irrational forces that challenge it.

Defense Mechanisms of the Ego

We mentioned that Freud believed work is the most admirable defense against pain and suffering. The capacity to work with vigor and joy is, in his view, a mark of good health. Freud believed the ego can employ admirable methods to cope with danger and anxiety. But everything may change if the id or superego overwhelms the ego, making it "no longer master in its own house." Moral and neurotic anxieties are hallmarks of neurosis (in psychosis, the id or superego may destroy the ego; Freud had no interest in treating individuals with such severe symptoms because he believed that psychoanalysis cannot resurrect a dead ego). To reclaim the human psyche, the ego may engage in disguises, distortions, falsifications, denials, and misrepresentations of reality. We'll now consider some of the ego's defensive strategies.

REPRESSION Freud (1914/1957c) proclaimed that "the theory of repression is the cornerstone on which the whole structure of psychoanalysis rests. It is the most essential part of it" (p. 16). As a defense against irrational unconscious forces, **repression** involves forcing out dangerous or anxiety-provoking thoughts, memories, or perceptions from consciousness into the unconscious realm. Gay (1988) compared the repressed unconscious mind to "a maximum-security prison holding antisocial inmates . . . [who are] heavily guarded, but barely kept under control and forever attempting to escape" (p. 128). For most of us, he believed, irrational thoughts and wishes escape from their unconscious lock-up before sneaking out to contaminate our dreams, slips of the tongue, and humor. Freud believed repression is involved to some degree in other defense mechanisms.

Whereas the ego makes use of repression, it may on occasion receive assistance from the superego. *Primal repression* refers to a class of ideas so painful and unthinkable they are barred from consciousness in the first place. Freud included ideas of incest and aggression against the same-sexed parent in this group.

PROJECTION   When personal motives or ideas are unacceptable or when they provoke anxiety, they may be repressed. In turn, the repressed materials may be ascribed to other people or events. **Projection** occurs when we attribute personal faults or weaknesses to other people, objects, or situations. For example, a husband tempted to have an affair with a coworker may instead accuse his wife of having unfaithful fantasies. Aggressive individuals or groups may claim that others are the real aggressors. The ego finds safety in projection because it distances itself from motives and ideas that provoke anxiety. It's not a perfect refuge. A dramatic distortion of reality is the high price the ego pays for such protection.

REGRESSION   If the present proves too harrowing, the ego may find sanctuary in the past. **Regression** involves the retreat to an earlier stage of development, resulting in attitudes and behaviors that defined that period. Regressions may be brief and episodic or, in the face of overwhelming threats, may persist over months and years. Brief or episodic regression may be

manifested in dreams or daydreams in which one returns to an earlier, more secure stage in life. Regression may be reflected in activities such as temper tantrums, easy submission to authority, masturbation, the need to be babied during an illness, or taking drugs as an escape from responsibility. The ego feels less accountable while operating in an earlier manner. In severe regression, the ego is removed from adult responsibility and is literally aided and assisted as in childhood.

REACTION FORMATION   In "Instincts and Their Vicissitudes," Freud (1915/1957a) talked about paradoxical situations in which a drive may undergo a reversal into its opposite. Because mental life is marked by polarities, reversals are always a possibility. Love may turn to hate, pleasure to pain, passivity to activity, and so forth. In the **reaction formation**, we encounter a defense in which the ego masks awareness of an anxiety-provoking motive by emphasizing its opposite. For example, a parent who harbors hostility toward a child may instead become overly indulgent and overprotective. A man troubled by homosexual fantasies may mask the threat by demeaning a gay man. In reaction formations, we find clear denials of certain motives. The idea that no one proclaims innocence louder than the guilty is a classic illustration of reaction formation. As with other defense mechanisms, this method can purchase the ego some degree of relief from anxiety, but the antagonistic extremes generate conflict of their own.

OTHER DEFENSES   The ego may practice a host of additional defensive strategies. Some involve less repression than those mentioned and may seem more realistic and adaptive. In **sublimation**, the ego takes a wish or thought that society deems improper and substitutes it with a more acceptable one. Many activities such as work, sporting events, art, and even philanthropic activities may involve a rechanneling of sexual energy into socially acceptable activities. Freud saw sublimation as important to the overall goals of civilization. Another defense, **rationalization**, involves the attempt to "explain away" personal shortcomings by providing logical but false reasons to excuse weaknesses or errors. Still another defense, **identification**, covers weaknesses by emulating significant or impressive role models. A teenager who admires a hip-hop artist may imitate his hero in everything from clothing, emcee style, and rap beats down to his loose-fingered wag while freestyle rapping. If the ego is not adequate in itself, it can at least borrow or steal from an idol. In cases of extreme psychopathology, the distinctions between self and model crumble until the person is lost in delusion, believing he or she is the object of identification.

In his work titled *The Ego and the Id*, Freud (1923/1961b) described the ego as "a poor creature owing service to three masters" (p. 56). Since those masters—the id, the superego, and the external world—are so powerful and uncompromising, the ego must amass a great psychological arsenal of its own. Yet it cannot make the necessary acquisitions without help. It must be nurtured and assisted in a supportive environment.

Stages of Psychosexual Development

Freud believed the quality of adult experience is connected to the quality of childhood experience. He is often accused of advancing a narrow view of psychology based on a narrow view of sexual motivation. Freud argued, however, that it is the common view of sexuality that is narrow. According to the common view, sex is limited to genital contact between adults. Freud believed that all surfaces of the body, not just the genitals, are erotogenic. Some regions such as the lips are especially erogenous. He tied sexuality to the pleasure principle, viewing the subject in broad terms. Sexuality, for Freud, broadly incorporated the notion of intense physical pleasure. As discussed, he believed that the object is the most flexible characteristic of a drive and there are many sexual objects. We turn now to Freud's stage theory of psychosexual development.

ORAL STAGE A child's mouth is the medium for initial interactions with the world. Hunger and thirst drives are satisfied through sucking and needs are expressed through crying. In this early stage, the child learns a good deal: The world is either responsive or unresponsive to cries for help, the nursing situation is friendly or cold, and pleasure is derived through food and liquids. A bit later, children experiment by shoving objects in their mouths. Freud assumed that neglect or overindulgence during this stage can produce negative consequences for later development. For example, overindulgence might result in unrealistic optimism whereas neglect might lead to a pessimistic or angry adult. Freud believed that later "oral characters" are based on fixations at early stages. Such fixations result from failures to meet basic needs during critical periods of development.

ANAL STAGE In the second and third years, children discover the gratification in the relief of bowel and bladder tension. But this simple pleasure is fraught with difficulty because the external world now imposes strict regulations concerning toilet training. Parent and child may clash during this stage. From the child's perspective, elimination is a source of pleasure; the feces are a curiosity and possibly even perceived as a part of one's self (the child might wonder, "If my parents love me so much, why are they so eager to dispose of this part of me?").

Freud's views on the anal stage are grounded in the historical context of toilet training. It is neither a pleasant nor an easy history to understand, especially in our time of disposable diapers, well-ventilated houses, indoor toilets, automatic washing machines, and hot and cold running water. In earlier centuries, proper toilet training was consequential to a well-ordered house. Children were forced to sit for long periods on training chairs, were subjected to enemas and purges, and were often the victims of beatings for failures to control bladder or bowel movements (see DeMause, 1974).

In this context, Freud was sensitive to the precarious balancing act confronting the small child.

398

The newly discovered pleasures of elimination and the curiosity about feces must be steadied against the controlling demands of the world. Freud believed this stage had consequences for later personality development. For example, if parents take a lenient and overly indulgent attitude and the child derives joy from releasing his feces, it might create an *anal-expulsive character*. Such a character is reckless, messy, disorganized, and careless. Another child might find gratification in retaining fecal matter. In an act of defiance, the child refuses to release excrement, leading to traits associated with the *anal-retentive character*. Such a character is likely to be stingy, neat, meticulous, precise, and compulsive about rules and regulations.

PHALLIC STAGE   From ages three to five, the **phallic stage**, children's interests turn to their sex organs and to the sex organs of the parents. In addition, the child begins to identify with the parent of the opposite sex. This identification involves positive sexual feeling of the boy for his mother and of the girl for her father. As children feel attraction for the opposite-sex parent, the parent of the same sex is viewed as a threat and evokes hostile and rebellious actions. The affection for the parent of the opposite sex and the hostility toward the parent of the same sex is called the **Oedipus complex**. Freud found inspiration in Sophocles's (c. 470–399 BCE) Greek tragedy about a young man named Oedipus who unwittingly kills his father, Laius, and marries his mother, Jocasta. (Oedipus had been separated from both parents since birth.) After realizing he has murdered Laius, Oedipus blinds himself with Jocasta's brooch as an act of repentance.

As noted, when we discussed religious conversion, desire for the mother leads to anxiety born in a fear of the father. The boy would like to replace his father, but he recognizes that his father holds the threat of awesome retaliation. In Freud's theory, such retaliation includes the threat of metaphorical castration. The father might castrate the boy, striking at the source of pleasure (in this case the genitals). Freud should not be taken literally with respect to the use of the word castration. Rather he seems to be referring to the sense of the overwhelming power and adequacy of the father to produce feelings of emasculation. Fearing the father's retaliatory power, the boy represses his feelings for his mother and then gradually identifies with the father. For the boy, repression and identification help resolve the Oedipal conflict.

According to Freud, this kind of crisis plays out in an entirely different way for girls. He believed that girls do not completely repress their striving for the father, nor do they thoroughly identify with the mother. Instead, the girl transfers her desire for the father to other men, making the father the prototype for her future husband. Freud insisted that the girl becomes envious of the protruding male sex organ and blames her mother for what she considers to be her castrated condition. Freud argued that so-called **penis envy** played an important role in the psychology of women. As with the male, the Oedipal situation may never be completely resolved. Although many sources present this as the *Electra complex*, the term originated in Jung and was rejected by Freud (Kilmartin & Dervin, 1997). Freud's views on feminine sexuality remain a controversial facet of his theory (see Roith, 1987). Additionally, psychologists have criticized Freud's assumptions that typical families and typical development must be heterosexual; he reflects the biased medical views of his times (Viney & Woody, 2017).

LATENCY PERIOD   In the aftermath of the phallic stage, the child enters a phase of development in which erotic interest becomes latent or dormant. Signs of sexual interest are not explicit during this **latency period**. From age four or five until the beginning of puberty, children busy themselves with intense physical activity and strong interest in peer groups. Sexual attachments are present but less noticeable than at other periods of development.

GENITAL STAGE   The **genital stage** of development begins as the person enters adolescence.

Residue from earlier periods may be present, but if development is normal, the individual will forge emotional ties with members of the opposite sex. At this age, the genitals become the focus of sexual energy. During the genital stage, the individual is preoccupied with object choices relating to friends, social institutions, and vocations. The major goal of the genital stage is reproduction and ancillary activities (work, socialization) critical to the propagation of the species.

Psychoanalysis as a Therapeutic Technique

Freud believed that the unconscious mind is a kind of storehouse containing powerful drives along with repressed sentiments going back to childhood. Drives and repressed materials are not revealed in naked meanings but find expression in symbolic, mediated, or disguised forms. The conscious mind has only indirect access to the dangerous materials that reside in the unconscious. Freud posited a **preconscious** containing materials that are readily available to consciousness. Material that is not now in consciousness, but can be recalled with relative ease, is stored in the preconscious area. Freud believed that certain dangerous materials (drives, wishes, repressions) in the unconscious are not readily available to consciousness but may, nonetheless, play a crucial role in psychopathology.

As noted earlier, Freud found evidence for unconscious processes in hypnotic phenomena, slips of the tongue, forgotten appointments, and dreams. In each area, however, unconscious content is disguised. One who harbors hostility toward another person may forget an appointment with that person. Freud believed that dreams are the most important means for expression of unconscious wishes and drives. He argued that dreams have **manifest content** and **latent content**. The former refers to the dream as described by the dreamer. It's the censored part of the dream that the ego wants you to remember. The latter refers to the specific way the dream

expresses an unconscious wish or drive. The art of dream interpretation is the art of translating manifest content into latent content.

Freud believed that human emotional problems result from a buildup of repressed material. Excessive pressure in the unconscious may show itself in terms of a host of symptoms such as phobias, skin rashes, obsessive or compulsive behaviors, depression, or anxiety. Because repressed materials in the unconscious were thought to be responsible for many emotional problems, it was important to explore the origins of those materials. Freud assumed that the cautious uncovering of repressions might rob them of their energy. Such energy would no longer be available to feed the troublesome psychological symptoms that brought the patient to analysis in the first place.

In his book *An Outline of Psycho-Analysis*, Freud (1938/1964b) contended that a major goal of therapy is to return back to the ego "its mastery over lost provinces of . . . mental life" (p. 173). Freud (1932/1964a) wrote that the goal of psychoanalysis is "to strengthen the ego, to make it more independent of the super-ego, to widen its field of perception and enlarge its organization, so that it can appropriate fresh portions of the id: 'Where id was, there ego shall be'" (p. 80). In other words, the goal of psychoanalysis is to free the ego, to widen consciousness, and to liberate the individual from destructive unconscious forces. Earlier, we spoke of Freud's strong commitment to determinism, but how can such a commitment be reconciled with the goal of the clinician to free the ego? Some scholars (e.g., Smith, 2003; Tauber, 2009; Mills, 2013) believe that Freud gradually accepted a concept of free will that allowed for an autonomous ego. Others (e.g., Jones, 1953; Brown, 1961; Jahoda, 1977; Sulloway, 1979; Viney & Parker, 2016) argue that Freud maintained his belief in strict causality, but embraced meanings of freedom consistent with determinism. For example there are freedoms associated with self-awareness, knowledge, emancipation from authority figures, and the capacity to sublimate. Freud believed that science has freed us from all sorts of threats that dominated the lives of our ancestors. How, then, was the goal of psychoanalysis to free the ego to be carried out in the context of a deterministic worldview?

As noted earlier, Freud believed that dreams provide the most important avenue for the expression of unconscious forces. He also believed there was therapeutic value in sharing one's story with another person. In addition, he developed **free association**, the uninhibited verbal expression of whatever is central in consciousness during therapy. For the typical patient, free association is no easy task. It requires trust and a weakening of inhibitions and resistances. One's intimate psychic world is laid bare, leaving a sense of vulnerability. Most normal conversation is guided by inhibition, convention, and a kind of meta-level awareness of what is appropriate to the situation. In free association, such defenses are suspended. Freud assumed that free association, such as the content of dreams, might provide a vehicle for the expression of unconscious processes. Patients in psychoanalytic therapy were encouraged to assume a comfortable position, often on a couch, and discuss their dreams and/or to free associate.

In time, patients build trust in the analyst and share the content of their dreams and free associate. For their part, analysts listen and provide interpretations of dream materials and free associations. Such interpretations are offered with caution and only when patients are ready to confront the dark side of their minds. Freud found that patients often develop emotional attachments to their therapists and that therapists may develop emotional attachments to their patients. He referred to the former as **transference** and the latter as **countertransference**. In successful therapy, the patient gradually works through the transference and develops an independence from the therapist. A major goal of psychoanalytic training is to teach therapists to learn how to cope with the issues of transference and countertransference.

Sometimes **resistance** slows or even halts the progress of psychoanalysis. There are presumably many symptoms of resistance: sustained inability to free associate; failure to talk about a dream because it is judged to be trivial, irrelevant, or simply humorous; out-of-hand rejection of the analyst's interpretations; or broken appointments. Freud found that resistance was weakened as patients gained trust.

In his brief essay titled "Family Romances," Freud (1908/1959b) remarked that one of the most painful and difficult tasks is to achieve liberation from parents or other significant authority figures. In successful psychoanalytic therapy, the individual is freed not only from the authority of the parents but also from the authority of the analyst. The influences of the id and the superego are also moderated as the ego grows in strength and authority. Ultimately, the goal is that the individual is able to enjoy loving and working and is an effective and contributing member within the human community. The balances necessary for the achievement of such a goal are hard-won because opposing forces from without and from within are powerful and ever-present. Freud's views on the difficulties facing the individual and humankind are set forth in his later works. As noted earlier, psychoanalysis is both a system of psychology and a therapy. We turn now to a consideration of his social psychological views.

Freud's Social Psychology

Although accused of neglecting social issues, Freud did tackle broad societal concerns in later works such as *Civilization and Its Discontents* (1930/1961a). The issue of war shaped his thinking, particularly after World War I and the detainment of one son in a prison camp at the end of the war (Fry, 2009). In particular, Freud argued for community support for veterans suffering the psychological effects of combat (Danto, in press). In 1932, Freud shared an open exchange of letters with Albert Einstein titled *Warum Krieg?* ("Why War?"). At the time, Einstein recognized developments in physics that foreshadowed nuclear weapon systems. He was distressed that such weapons would soon be available to a species that had been unable to abolish war as a means of solving its difficulties.

Einstein's letter explored the problem of war and speculated about one possible solution. He proposed an international legislative and judicial body with the power to settle disputes among nation states. Einstein insisted that he was personally immune to nationalistic bias, but that underscores a problem with his proposed solution. Only a minority can identify on such a broad basis with the world community of human beings; clearly the Einsteins and Gandhis of the world are few in number. The identities of great hosts of human beings are bounded by strict national, racial, religious, cultural, or even sexual lines of demarcation that set up rigid in-group and out-group distinctions.

Einstein noted other issues surrounding his solution to the problem of war. Namely, that in almost every nation there is a political minority "indifferent to social considerations and restraints [who] regard warfare, the manufacture and sale of arms, simply as an occasion to advance their personal interests and enlarge their personal authority" (Einstein, 1932/1964, p. 200). He questioned how a minority could work against the interests of the majority, excluding professional soldiers who believe they are working for the highest interest of their culture by choosing the military as their profession. He noted that the press, the churches, and the schools are also, in too many cases, under the control of the minority. Einstein also recognized a problem centering on the fact that some of history's greatest wars have been civil wars. Thus, he turned to Freud for a deeper analysis of the problem of war with its "collective psychosis" marked by a lust for violence, destruction, and hatred.

In a thoughtful reply, Freud agreed on the desirability of a world organization, but like Einstein, he was aware of the problems of instilling the broader base of identity humans need if they are to achieve such an ideal. In his mid-seventies at the time, Freud had witnessed the tribulation of the First World War along with countless examples of national and human interpersonal

conflict. He described two antagonistic forces that seize human nature in a struggle for survival. *Eros* is a life-preserving drive that seeks to preserve and unite. *Thanatos* is an internal aggressive force that seeks to destroy or kill (Mills, 2006). Freud viewed both drives as essential and found they seldom work in isolation from each other. For example, he argued that "the instinct of self preservation is certainly of an erotic kind, but it must nevertheless have aggressiveness at its disposal if it is to fulfill its purpose" (Freud, 1932/1964a, p. 209). He believed motivation is always complicated; it is not a simple unidirectional matter. Freud claimed that events that run counter to eros can automatically reinforce opposite destructive instincts.

Unfortunately, civilization imposes constraints on eros. The price of civilization is that erotic gratifications must be delayed, drives must be sublimated, and the range of object choices must be restricted. Civilization becomes a valued acquisition but also a source of frustration that feeds destructive instincts. Certain repressive systems or governments foster despair, hopelessness, and a general devaluing of life. Unfortunately, when repressive systems strangle erotic instincts (including love of others, valuing of nature, and opportunities for expressing of self-actualizing motives), they are likely to trigger destructive thoughts and behaviors. The ensuing destructiveness may be directed at the self or at other people or at the self *and* others. Destructiveness aimed at the self is manifested in individual suicides or in collective suicides as in the Heaven's Gate group led by Marshall Applewhite, who convinced thirty-eight followers to commit suicide while the Hale-Bopp comet blazed across the skies in 1997. Destruction aimed at others is manifested in wars and massacres, including blind attacks or drive-by shootings of total strangers. Some of the most bizarre examples of the destructiveness that Freud identifies are marked by a general anger and devaluation of life when the self *and* others are targets, as in the case of suicide bombers or in the all-too-common media accounts of murder–suicides.

Freud offers a complicated answer to Einstein's question. He agreed that an international government is a step in the right direction but pointed to conflicts of interest both within and between organizations. Freud argued that it is useless to attempt to rid ourselves of aggression because it is vital to our biological nature. However, social structures can be established to curb destructive instincts while permitting the expression of drives within reasonable constraints (Zilbersheid, 2013). Freud believed arbitrary religious and political authorities encroach on freedom of thought and work against world peace. In the end, he called for social structures sensitive to the intricacies of human nature that will not shut the door on reasonable interests.

Freud saw value in broadening identification by emphasizing common bonds and shared interests. He quoted with approval the golden rule, "Thou shalt love thy neighbor as thyself." Freud realized the difficulties in achieving such an ideal love and he doubted that this ideal could be realized through a simple command. He believed, however, that we might achieve the ideal through the hard work of reason, education, and emotional and intellectual insight.

Appreciative Overview

Freud leaves us with a complicated legacy. Psychoanalysis opened intellectual vistas with far-reaching consequences for psychology and other disciplines. The appreciative commentary that follows reflects the expanded scope that Freud offered psychology. What then were his major contributions?

1. *Emphasis on development.* Freud was one of the first to recognize the importance of childhood and the special needs associated with stages of human development. It makes little difference if his stage theory does not hold up. His larger developmental perspective and the continued developmental focus of later psychoanalysis have had an enduring influence on Western notions of emotions, the self, and families (Shapira, 2013).

2. *Unconscious processes.* Though many do not value Freud's model of the unconscious, it has been a continuing influence in psychology along with repression and the ego defense mechanisms.

3. *Focus on motivation.* Freud was not the only psychologist to emphasize motivation, but he contributed to this content area so that it soon took its place alongside sensation, perception, and learning as a principal topic of inquiry.

4. *Psychotherapy.* Though we can find much to criticize in Freud's therapy, he nevertheless contributed to the notion that human problems originate in everyday life. Proper therapy for such problems is not simply medical but psychological. This idea ran counter to medical thought in Freud's Vienna, so it is little wonder he was not popular with his contemporaries. Still, many of his insights endured and now occupy a respected and undisputed place in clinical texts and reference sources.

5. *Interdisciplinary contributions.* As noted, Freud's thought was influential in diverse fields such as history, philosophy, religion, literature, and medicine, and it powerfully impacted culture across the United States (Samuel, 2013). Although controversial, psychoanalysis forced psychology to be a less insular discipline. This in itself is a worthy achievement.

Critical Overview

A system as wide-ranging as psychoanalysis is bound to generate criticism, and reaction has ranged from thoughtful disapproval to sarcasm and mocking. We'll outline some of the better-known criticisms.

1. *Tendency to overgeneralize.* Freud often drew sweeping conclusions based on limited simple

observations. Our earlier discussion of a young doctor's religious conversion is a case in point. If you wanted to draw conclusions about the psychology of conversion, wouldn't it make more sense to study many cases? Even then, generalizations should be cautious and couched in language that encourages experimental work. This last point leads to the next criticism.

2. *Empirical verification.* Despite experimental studies designed to test Freud's predictions, psychoanalysis does not lend itself to experimental verification. Part of the problem is that many of the terms of the theory (e.g., *libido, eros, primary process*) are not easily operationalized. Freud relied largely on case studies to provide evidence in support of his views (Braakmann, 2014).

3. *Closedness.* Freud had an almost unmatched zeal in discovering new truths about the workings of the mental world. In time, however, he became dogmatic about his theory (Barratt, 2013; Rudnytsky, 2008). Freud's followers and associates were expected to be disciples dedicated to extending his theory. The range of acceptable ideas was truncated and any person who deviated too far from core concepts was viewed as disloyal. Scientists are rightfully suspicious of loyalty and orthodoxy but unfortunately these characteristics came to define classical psychoanalysis as an increasingly closed system. In its later developments, psychoanalysis would become more pluralistic (Bland & Strawn, 2014).

4. *Sexual emphasis.* Freud is accused of advancing a monistic theory where all behavior is derived from a single motivation—namely, sex. This criticism calls for greater scrutiny. Freud did explore sexual motives, but his view of such motivation was broader than many critics acknowledge, and he explicitly recognized the existence of many drives.

5. *Psychoanalytic treatment.* Psychoanalysis has been criticized on several grounds. One harsh criticism suggests that practitioners are a closed club isolated from the meaningful correctives of critical and scientific research (see Masson, 1991). Treatment has also been criticized because it is expensive and time-consuming. Beyond its prohibitive cost, critics have questioned whether it accomplishes more than other therapies.

6. *Theory of female sexuality.* Freud's concept of penis envy and his views on female sexual conflict have faced withering criticism (see Horney, 1967; Sprengnether, 1990). Scholarly work has attempted to clarify the context of Freud's views (see Roith, 1987). Nevertheless, his notion that women are "incomplete men" must now be regarded as an error driven more by theory than sensitivity to the complexity of human sexuality. Freud did welcome women into the psychoanalytic movement. Here as in other institutions, however, they did not enjoy equality (see Roith, 1987; Wolberg, 1989). Perhaps most telling is Freud's confession that a baffling mystery for him is what motivates a woman. Gay (1988) reports that Freud "had, he thought, sincerely tried to understand the 'sexual life of the adult woman,' but it continued to intrigue and puzzle him. It was something of 'a *dark continent*'" (p. 501).

Future Perspectives

At some level, perhaps, psychology will always retain some of the elements of Freud's vision. As noted, many psychoanalytic journals continue to explore almost every facet of classical psychoanalysis along with modern reinterpretations of Freud's continually relevant work (Reppen, 2006). The larger Freudian vision continues to evolve and is by no means dead. More recent work (Gabbard et al., 2012; Wallerstein, 1988/2006) celebrates the transition of psychoanalysis from its early narrow orthodoxy into an increasingly viable pluralistic discipline that welcomes conceptual and therapeutic innovations. Rudnytsky (2011) speaks of rescuing psychoanalysis from Freud as manifested by increasing diversity while retaining efforts to synthesize science and art. Appraisals of psychoanalysis will increasingly need to be informed by careful assessments of recent developments.

After Freud

As with behaviorism, psychoanalysis became a house divided. Many who were influenced by Freud disagreed with his emphasis on sexuality. Deep divisions emerged over a host of topics, such as the nature of unconscious processes, the autonomy of the ego, the stages of development, and the nature of therapy.

Alfred Adler

Alfred Adler

In 1902, **Alfred Adler (1870–1937)** was welcomed into Sigmund Freud's Wednesday Psychological Society. Adler believed the discussion group would offer a broad intellectual agenda with open debate on psychiatric issues. He was mistaken. In time, Adler discovered that Freud held strong views and seldom tolerated contrasting opinions. Although respectful of each other at first, tensions between Adler and Freud deepened over the years. An irritated Freud interpreted the young man's challenges as an affront and a "hostile competition" (Gay, 1988, p. 224). In 1911, Adler escaped Freud's shadow to develop an alternative system known as **individual psychology**. He was an original thinker who should not be remembered as a disloyal disciple (Ansbacher, 1994).

Adler was born near Vienna on February 7, 1870. His early years were marked by poor health aggravated by rickets. Adler graduated with an M.D. from the University of Vienna in 1895. After serving in the military during World War I, he opened Vienna's first child-guidance clinic. In 1926, he moved to the United States and joined the faculty at Columbia University and, later, the Long Island College of Medicine. Adler died after a heart attack on May 28, 1937, while on a lecture tour in Scotland. According to Gay (1988), "Freud was gratified to learn that he had outlived Alfred Adler ... He had hated Adler for more than a quarter century, and Adler had hated him for just as long, and as vocally" (p. 615).

Adler's better-known books are *The Practice and Theory of Individual Psychology* (1964b), *Understanding Human Nature* (1957), and *Social Interest: A Challenge to Mankind* (1938). Ansbacher and Ansbacher (1956) provided an important secondary source titled *The Individual Psychology of Alfred Adler*; scholarship continues in journals dedicated to individual psychology, and *Alfred Adler Revisited* (Carlson & Maniacci, 2012) provides helpful overviews of Adler's positions on a variety of issues.

Adler's System of Psychology

Adler's individual psychology is a study in contrast with Freud's classic psychoanalytic theory. In a paper devoted to these differences, Adler (1931/1964a) argued that "the Freudian view is that man, by nature [is] bad" (p. 210). By contrast, Adler insisted that we have a natural capacity to identify with the goals of society to achieve a common good. Adler was affected by the context of medical training and practice, including the social privilege afforded to physicians, as well as by cultural debates about democracy and equality (Angioli & Kruger, 2015). His **social interest** reflects a real concern for people and society. He also quarreled with Freud's use of pleasure as a regulative principle. According to Adler, happiness is a more important goal than pleasure, but more important yet is a striving for totality, unity, or wholeness. Another important difference is that Adler emphasized goal setting in human life. His theory is teleological, whereas Freud's theory emphasized material, efficient, and formal causes; even Adler's explanation of crime rests on his assumptions that perpetrators make purposeful and rational choices (Shon & Barton-Bellessa, 2015).

On the methodological side, Adler argued for a broader study of psychological phenomena than did Freud. Adler encouraged exploring old memories, but balanced this by studying plans or anticipations about the future. He also studied body language as manifested in postures and movements. He examined the role of birth order on personality. He studied dreams, interpreting them as forward-looking signs rather than backward-looking examinations of personal history.

His psychology contrasts with Freud's in additional ways. Adler's (1964a) article "The Differences between Individual Psychology and Psychoanalysis" provides a helpful overview on their differences concerning the Oedipus complex, the death wish, and dream interpretation among other issues. We turn now to key concepts in Adler's system.

GOALS AND THE STYLE OF LIFE In his book *The Practice and Theory of Individual Psychology*, Adler (1964b) advances the proposition that "every psychic phenomenon, if it is to give us any understanding of a person, can be grasped and understood only if regarded as a preparation for some goal" (p. 4). Adler believed psychological functions such as feeling and thinking are impossible unless they occur in the context of goals. In his radical stance on causality, he claimed that chaos would mark the psychological world if it

resulted only from antecedent causes. In his view, an integration of psychological processes meant that past, present, and future interests are brought together. Without future considerations, ongoing present activities—considered only as results of material and efficient causes—are meaningless.

Adler believed our experiences and behaviors must be understood in terms of our goals. He used the expression **fictional final goals** to describe how our future plans aren't always grounded in reality. For example, a student may believe she has potential to become a great mathematician, even after struggling through an elementary algebra course. She may start living and behaving with the goal of becoming a great mathematician. Stone (2011) elaborates on potential self-deceptive characteristics of some fictional goals. Adler used the term **style of life** to refer to all the unique behaviors that characterize personality and that move us in the direction of specific goals. Adler's psychology emphasizes processes, strategies, and functions rather than structures. A style of life includes strategies, plans, short-term and long-term projects, designs, and behaviors that are in the service of life's goals. For Adler, a person who does not have social interest is living a "mistaken style of life" or a "life lie."

INFERIORITY AS A SOURCE OF MOTIVATION
In his book *The Science of Living*, Adler (1929) suggested "all persons feel inadequate in certain situations" (p. 60). This is especially true in childhood when we may feel inadequate or inferior in many situations. We may perceive a weakness in specific organs or functions that sets the stage for special difficulties later on. Adler believed that the character and intensity of *organ inferiority* and other types of insecurities are keys to understanding personality. He described the **inferiority complex** as an intense or abnormal feeling of inferiority. Adler (1929, p. 79) pointed out that an inferiority complex may shroud a complicated set of motives such as feelings of superiority. People who act superior may be masking deep-seated feelings of inferiority.

Feelings of inferiority are normal and widespread, setting the stage for important life goals as we struggle to overcome our perceived inferiorities (Overholser, 2010). Adler argued that many of our thoughts and activities are guided by compensation and overcompensation. With **compensation**, we overcome specific inferiorities by developing strengths in alternative areas. For example, a debilitating disease confined Stephen W. Hawking (b. 1942) to a lifetime in a wheelchair, but it did not prevent him from becoming an innovative thinker in theoretical astrophysics and cosmology. Sometimes there are *compensation ideals* in the form of others, such as Stephen Hawking, who embody the traits we most desire. Such ideals become models, although extreme identity with such models is a form of pathology. **Overcompensation**, in Adler's view, involves attempts to develop strength in an area beset with difficulties. Despite a sickly childhood, the American president Theodore Roosevelt (1858–1919) became the embodiment of William James's concept of the strenuous life. (Roosevelt had taken a class with James at Harvard.) Likewise, James Earl Jones (b. 1931) conquered childhood stuttering before honing his talent as an actor in movies and theater. His rich and booming baritone gave life to Darth Vader, making Jones one of the most recognizable voices in the world.

BIRTH ORDER   Adler believed the family constellation played a critical role in forging personality. He believed that birth order influences the way we see our world and how we respond to it. A first child enjoys favored status in the family constellation until the fateful arrival of another sibling. The new sibling can produce devastating or salutary consequences. First children can develop a caring attitude or can have difficulty overcoming the shock of being displaced. No longer the center of attention, first-born children may view new arrivals as usurpers. In adulthood, the first child might exhibit a rigid and authoritarian personality. (Adler noted, with some satisfaction, that Sigmund Freud was a first-born child.) The second child may develop a competitive style while attempting to keep up with the older sister or brother. Not as pampered as his or her older sibling, the middle-born child cultivates a healthy sense of competition and has the best chance at positive development. (Incidentally, Adler was a middle child.) The youngest child grows up thinking older siblings have more freedom and superior status. The youngest is typically more spoiled and protected than the other children. From Adler's view, that's not a good thing. Despite apparent biases in his theory, Adler's birth-order model remains one of his most productive contributions (Ekstein & Kaufman, 2012) and has had a continuing influence on research (see Ernst & Angst, 1983; Grey, 1998).

LIFE'S MAJOR PROBLEMS   Adler argued that most human problems center around issues of work, interaction with others, and sexual intimacy. He viewed it as a mark of health when we pursue meaningful work-related goals. Adler also argued that life's problems must be understood in terms of social context and societal well-being (Ferguson, 2010). The prejudices, injustices, and preferences encountered in almost every society have devastating consequences for individual development. Adler thought all human beings strive for superiority in certain arenas both to overcome their own weaknesses and to overcome social barriers and injustices. He saw the capacity for sexual intimacy as a mark of one's larger relationship with humankind. Sexual intimacy may have a selfish and abusive component, or it may reflect social interest in true caring about the happiness and welfare of another person. A primary task of psychology, according to Adler, is to foster the development of social interest (Ansbacher, 1997). These facets of Adler's ideas continue to influence psychological practice (Carlson et al., 2006).

Carl Gustav Jung

Though **Carl Gustav Jung (1875–1961)** was associated with Freud's psychoanalytic movement from 1907 to 1913, it is a mistake to view

407

Jung as a disciple or as a defector. Many ideas in Jung's psychology were formulated before he met Freud. Despite some theoretical similarities between the two psychologies, Jung's system is far from derivative (Shamdasani, 2012).

Jung was born in Keswil, Switzerland, on July 26, 1875. Later, the Jung family moved near Basel, where Jung received his formal education. In 1895, he enrolled at the University of Basel, and he received his medical degree five years later (this was normal timing for the attainment of the M.D. in the late nineteenth century). After receiving the medical degree, Jung accepted an appointment at a psychiatric hospital in Zürich, where he studied with Eugen Bleuler (1857–1940), one of the premier authorities in psychiatry (Hayman, 2001). In 1902, while at Zürich, he completed his dissertation, "The Psychology and Pathology of So-Called Occult Phenomena," which shaped his thinking for the rest of his life (see Shamdasani, 2015a). After two years with Bleuler, Jung took a brief leave to study with Pierre Janet (1859–1947) in Paris.

On his return to Zürich, Jung initiated experiments using Galton's word-association tests. He put a spin on Francis Galton's concept, claiming that the speed and content of associations revealed pent-up unconscious dynamics. Let's say you administer the test, asking a client who is a man to offer an immediate response to your stimulus word. When you say "up," he says "down." When you say "far," he says "near." When you say "father," he says "murder." As embarrassment washes across his face, the man tries to convince you he meant to say "mother," not "murder." Jung believed that such responses, or failures to respond, may be diagnostic of conflict.

Jung proposed that word association could be used as a lie detection device, an idea that brought him into conflict with the Gestalt psychologist Max Wertheimer who had conducted similar forensic work (see Wertheimer et al., 1992). Jung's work with the word-association test was of interest to Freud, and Freud's classic *Interpretation of Dreams* had been of interest to Jung.

In 1907, Jung traveled to Vienna after a friendly exchange of letters with Freud. Their first meeting was legendary, lasting something like a marathon thirteen hours. Freud hoped to find a "crown prince of psychoanalysis" who would extend the range and application of his developing system of thought. Additionally, unlike Freud and other central figures of psychoanalysis, Jung identified with Protestant Christianity rather than Judaism. Like Adler, Jung was an original thinker and not well suited to discipleship. The friendly side of their relationship lasted only about five years. By 1912, strong theoretical differences had surfaced. Some scholars argue that the agreements and disagreements of Freud and Jung incorporated the later questions and debates about psychoanalysis that continue to guide research and embroil practitioners into the present (Henderson, 2015). In part, these tensions emerged when Jung shared his interest in mystical phenomena.

At first, Freud feigned interest in Jung's mysticism. In a 1909 letter, Freud wrote that he looked "forward to hearing more about your investigations of the spook-complex, my interest being the interest one has in a lovely delusion which one does not share oneself" (cited in Jung, 1961/1973, p. 363). Like Adler, Jung disagreed with Freud about the role of the sex motive in human nature. Ideology finally overshadowed personal bonds, dissolving their volatile relationship around 1914. Freud (1914/1957c) and Jung (1961/1973) published independent and sometimes conflicting reasons for their separation.

The conflict with Freud took its toll on Jung. In 1913, however, Jung had a series of revelations that transformed his life and career. Jung began practicing trancelike meditations he called "active imagination" (Shamdasani, 2015b). During one dreamlike state, he encountered a wise old man named *Philemon*, a spiritual guide with a flowing white beard and held aloft by kingfisher wings. In his autobiography, Jung (1961/1973) wrote:

Philemon represented a force which was not myself. In my fantasies I held conversations with him, and he said things which I had not consciously thought . . . Psychologically, Philemon represented superior insight. He was a mysterious figure to me. At times he seemed to me quite real, as if he were a living personality. I went walking up and down the garden with him, and to me he was what the Indians call a guru.

(p. 183)

In trancelike visions, Jung's eyes were opened to the power of the unconscious mind (see Shamdasani, 2009). After the break with Freud, he recorded inner visions and ideas that flooded from his unconscious during active imagination sessions. From around 1914 until 1930, Jung collected his illustrations and calligraphic text in a red leather-bound manuscript. Known as *The Red Book*, it raised questions about relationships with people who have died, the nature of creativity, and more; the manuscript remained private until his heirs allowed publication in 2009 (Hillman & Shamdasani, 2013; Kirsch & Hogenson, 2014). Inspired by his mystical journeys, Jung resolved to change the way people looked at the human mind and spirituality. As Jung aged, he plunged deeper into the mystical side of his personality.

In January 1923, Jung experienced a "frightening dream" involving the German god Wotan. In his nightmare, Wotan ordered a gigantic wolfhound to carry away a human soul. The next morning, Jung learned his mother had died. Two months after dreaming that Wotan had claimed his mother's soul, Jung began building a stone tower near the sleepy Swiss village of Bollingen. After three decades, he had built a sprawling complex of buildings beside the shallow upper end of Lake Zürich. Jung claimed that the logical side of his personality had built the first tower as a maternal structure, a tribute to his mother and his wife, Emma. In 1931, Jung initiated the construction of a second tower, inspired by the mystical side of his personality. The second tower became Jung's "place of spiritual concentration." No one came in without his permission. Jung's spiritual retreat became known as "Bollingen Tower" or simply *Der Turm* (the Tower). The

Bollingen facility was so important to Jung that he dedicated a chapter in his autobiography to *Der Turm* (Jung, 1961/1973).

Jung's work is presented in the twenty-volume collection titled *The Collected Works of C. G. Jung* (Bollingen Series No. 20, Princeton University, 1953–1979). Many current journals such as the *Journal of Analytic Psychology* publish scholarly research, theoretical papers, and book reviews on Jung's psychology, and many appreciative and critical biographies of Jung exist (Elms, 2005). In addition, a number of professional organizations and institutes are dedicated to the advancement of Jungian thought (Samuels, 1994). The best-known institute is the C. G. Jung Institute located in Zürich. Helpful secondary sources on Jung include books by Hall and Nordby (1973), Humbert (1988), Mattoon (1981), and Bishop (1999). Jung's later years were particularly productive, even after a heart attack in 1944. He died on June 6, 1961.

Jung's Analytic Psychology

In terms of methodology and content, Jung's approach to science and psychology was broad. He called his system a science, but he knew that it did not fit general notions of scientific psychology (Jones, 2014). On the methodological side, he gained many insights from his patients, but also believed in the value of experimental work. He was also interested in cross-cultural comparisons of symbols and their meanings. Jung might best be characterized as a methodological pluralist because he found legitimacy and value in a variety of approaches to knowledge.

Jung was suspicious of ideologies and theories that may limit our field of vision. He acknowledged the heuristic value of theories so long as they are used in a proper way. His concern was that human beings can be *used* by theories; the proper approach was that theory should enhance vision, but we should be ready at any turn to discard a theory. Jung (1910/1954b) once said, "Theories in psychology are the very devil" (p. 7).

He was referring to situations where, in his words, "we have not even established the empirical extent of the psyche's phenomenology" (p. 7).

Jung's approach to content was as broad as his approach to methodology. His **analytic psychology** encompassed many things: the unconscious, an elaborate view of the structure of personality, psychotherapy, and even paranormal phenomena. Jung drew insights from diverse areas including Gnosticism, literature, Eastern religion, art, and pagan mythology. Ideas garnered from historical studies led Jung (1961/1973) to declare that "without history there can be no psychology, and certainly no psychology of the unconscious" (pp. 205–206).

During his exhaustive studies, Jung (1944/1953, 1967) discovered the ancient practice of **alchemy**. Although often stereotyped as pseudoscientists bent on changing base metals like lead into gold, alchemists pursued more important challenges. Jung discovered that the alchemists were dedicated to spiritual values and psychological transformation. Another goal involved finding a universal cure for disease, an *elixir of life* that could transform a person and even grant immortality.

At first, Jung regarded alchemy as nonsense. After immersing himself in alchemical lore, he found himself "condemned to study alchemy" as he tried to decipher its riddles and mysteries. In time, Jung (1961/1973) realized that the "experiences of the alchemists were, in a sense, my experiences, and their world was my world. This was, of course, a momentous discovery: I had stumbled upon the historical counterpart of my psychology of the unconscious" (p. 205). He studied secret doctrines as if he were "trying to solve the riddle of an unknown language" (1961/1973, p. 205). He discovered that alchemy "gave substance to my psychology," leading to a critical insight:

> Only after I had familiarized myself with alchemy did I realize that the unconscious is a *process*, and that the psyche is transformed or developed by the relationship of the ego to the contents of the unconscious . . . Through understanding of alchemical symbolism I arrived at the central concept of my psychology: *the process of individuation*.
>
> (Jung, 1961/1973, p. 209)

For Jung, **individuation** is the process of becoming a psychological individual, a self-realization that signals a coming to selfhood. He did not view his theory as finished but rather as a set of ideas to inspire others to additional inquiry (Hogenson, 2013), and Jung's alchemical ideas have remained fertile for psychologists (Mathers, 2014). Let's turn now to an overview of Jung's key concepts in psychology.

THE STRUCTURE OF PERSONALITY Jung used the term **psyche** to refer to the totality of human personality. Indeed, for Jung, *psyche* and *personality* are interchangeable terms referring to the compendium of what we are at both conscious and unconscious levels. Jung determined several interacting components in the psyche.

The Ego The ego, according to Jung, is the *I* or *me* of the personality and, as such, is the center of consciousness. As in Freud's system, the ego negotiates with the outer world and has the task of forming an accurate picture of the world.

Unconscious Processes Jung used the term **personal unconscious** to refer to the storehouse of repressed materials that are unavailable to consciousness as well as suppressed materials that can be called into consciousness. We might also find unimportant or irrelevant materials here. Like fingerprints, the personal unconscious is different for every person. Word-association methods can be used to document information in this realm of the unconscious. In contrast with the personal unconscious, Jung believed we all share in a **collective unconscious**, drawn from our common ancestors' biological past in the form of images and response predispositions. The collective unconscious ties us together with all other human beings.

The collective unconscious includes **archetypes**, a term similar to *pattern*, *model*, *copy*, and

410

prototype. Jung believed archetypes have their origin in the history of the experiences of humans and are present in each of us as potential modes or patterns of thought. For example, the species has had millions of years of experience with darkness, power, death, mothers, fathers, and so forth. It was inconceivable to Jung that collective experience is unrepresented in the life of the individual or in mythology. For example, when Jung visited the United States in 1912 (without Freud), he perceived universal archetypes in reported dreams of African-American men in residential treatment; he did not raise questions about lack of privilege or about cultural differences in the meanings of dreams (Brewster, 2013). It is important to point out that an archetype is not initially a so-called picture in the head; rather, it is a primordial image or a kind of universal pattern or form that sets us to think or act in characteristic ways. As we will see, the archetypes in Jung's theory play an important role in the overall structure of the personality.

The Shadow The **shadow** is an important component of the psyche that appears antagonistic to consciousness and to the goals of the ego. The shadow is not just the dark or evil side of the personality; it is the antagonist for whatever is publicly dominant in the personality. The shadow includes repressed materials from the personal unconscious and primitive materials from the collective unconscious that may provoke fear, awe, or anger. The shadow forces dialogue in consciousness by challenging conventional niceties and norms. Jung believed the shadow can be a doorway to reality and wholeness. It is not all evil because a negative quality in the shadow can be transposed into a positive quality in attitude and behavior. Thus, as noted by Mattoon (1981), "Anger can become assertiveness and . . . vulnerability can become sensitivity to the needs of others" (p. 27). Jung believed we can never achieve wholeness if we deny the positive lessons gained by confronting the dark and primal side of life. On the contrary, the failure to allow expression of darker images and motives may show up later in undesirable emotional explosions.

The Persona Literally, the term **persona** refers to the play-actor's mask, but psychologically, the term as used by Jung refers to the public image or the mask that we wear in front of others. Normally, the persona is the socially acceptable counterpart of the shadow. It is our public appearance, professional mannerisms, the roles we play, and our public profile. The persona is not just conditioned; indeed, it includes powerful unconscious components. The persona of an individual as a father is tied to the father archetype. The persona may become so dominant in personality that it attempts to murder the ego. In such cases, an individual can no longer discriminate social roles from other dimensions of his or her true self. When this happens, the persona appropriates and dominates everything and the individual is robbed of wholeness.

The Self Sharing affinities with Jamesian psychology, Jung believed the **self** is the great unifying principle in the psyche. He believed that *self-actualization* or self-realization is a major goal of life; those processes that direct us toward wholeness, integration, and assimilation are functions of the self. The self and the ego, in Jung's psychology, perform different functions but are interdependent. The ego is the *I* or *me*, the center of consciousness. Its immediate concerns are more pressing than the concerns of the self. The ego shows up early in personality development, but the self emerges later to integrate personality into the larger scheme of things. The claims of the ego may need to be subordinated to the claims of the self to achieve wholeness and unity. The self is symbolized by a **mandala**, "a magic circle" that represents a need to express selfhood such as in the Tibetan Wheel of Becoming.

The Anima and the Animus Jung could not accept that male and female sexuality are bipolar opposites. Though there is a male consciousness and a female consciousness, each is complemented by its counterpart. Both males and females come out of a long history marked by both masculine and feminine awareness, and Jung documented a feminine dimension in male consciousness and a male dimension in

411

feminine consciousness. The **anima** is a female archetype in men and the **animus** is a male archetype in women. In his concern for wholeness, Jung saw it as important that the anima find expression in men and that the animus find expression in women. Unfortunately, the persona and social conditioning may work against such awareness, locking the individual into a narrow consciousness with regard to sexuality. One may raise questions about the theoretical basis of the anima and animus as archetypes, but Jung was consistent with contemporary views when he challenged bipolar theories of sexuality. His work opens the door to further thoughtful and potentially productive questions about whether the subordination of women in many organizations and institutions interferes with the healthy development of the anima in males.

ATTITUDES AND FUNCTIONS Jung is perhaps best known for his concepts of extroversion and introversion, which he thought of as **attitudes**. Both extroversion and introversion refer to the direction of psychic energy in our lives. **Extroversion** is marked by a concentration of interest in the external world. The extrovert usually has an active, outgoing preference for social company and a strong presence around others. An extroverted person would "feel energized" in a large group of people but might experience diminished energy when spending time alone. By contrast, **introversion** is marked by inwardness, withdrawal, shyness, and a preference for quiet time alone or with select company. An introvert might experience energy while reading a book or playing a videogame at home but notice decreased energy when interacting with a group. Jung believed that both introverts and extroverts have latent unconscious wishes for the opposite orientation. Most of us display both attitudes, but one is usually dominant. These ideas from Jung, developed in correspondence with Hans Schmid-Guisan, continue to form the basis of widely used personality tests (Jung et al., 2013).

Jung believed in four basic psychological **functions**: thinking, feeling, sensation, and intuition.

All functions are prevalent in all people, but there are nevertheless strong preferences so that a given function may be clearly dominant in a given personality. A *thinking type* prefers rational discourse and problem solving whereas a *feeling type* tunes to the arousal of positive or negative emotions in every situation. Jung believed that the functions and the attitudes combine in various ways that give insight into the nature of an individual's conscious orientation. For example, an *introverted-thinking* type seeks seclusion and gets lost in a world of ideas that are enjoyed in their own right. By contrast, the sensation function combined with extroversion is illustrated in an individual who relishes company and the polite ceremony of a fine meal served in beautiful surroundings.

COMPLEXES Jung claimed that a **complex** involves conscious materials accompanied by emotional or perceptual distortions. For example, an inferiority complex is based on perceptual distortions regarding personal adequacy. Jung used the word-association test to identify complexes in his early work. When given stimulus terms such as *sex*, *God*, *father*, or *mother*, some subjects had difficulty finding an association. A complex, according to Jung, may result when the shadow fails to find expression in awareness. In his view, wisdom and dimensionality come with an awareness of the full spectrum of human nature, including both light and dark sides.

CAUSALITY Jung believed that teleology, or final causation, complements the roles played by material, efficient, and formal causation in human life. He stressed the importance of plans, expectations, and meaning orientation and argued that psychology is incomplete without these concepts. Jung stressed causality from several sources, including those from the personal and the collective unconscious, but also argued that there "exist psychic contents which are produced or caused by an antecedent act of the will, and which must therefore be regarded as products of some intentional, purposive and conscious activity" (Jung, 1926/1954a, p. 91). Jung recognized the difficulties attending the problem of free will as he referred to the "popular illusion concerning the 'arbitrariness of psychic processes'" (p. 91). He thus rejected hard-core determinism and popular notions of free will based on arbitrariness. He was open to a kind of free will born in wholeness and expanded consciousness.

In addition to his beliefs in causality and teleology, Jung embraced the controversial concept of **synchronicity**, in which simultaneous events appear related, even though their occurrence cannot be explained by the usual principles of causality (Cambray, 2009). Two events may not be linked in a causal way, but they're meaningful nonetheless. For example, you might pick up the phone to call a friend at the very moment she's calling you. Or a person might dream about someone dying before learning that the person had just passed away. We know synchronous events exist, but are they anything more than coincidence? Though Jung did not wish to apply the principle of synchronicity to paranormal phenomena such as clairvoyance or mental telepathy, he was also interested in these areas because they are a part of human experience. Although controversial, synchronicity is a part of Jung's theory that cannot be dismissed.

PSYCHOTHERAPY As in alchemy, Jung believed the goal of psychotherapy was transformation. His approach to psychotherapy is less structured and standardized than Freud's psychoanalysis. Jung relied on standard Freudian approaches, but also analyzed dreams, used the word-association test, asked the analysand to paint pictures of mandalas, or just engaged the person in dialogue. His approaches also reflected the times; for example, he considered people with schizophrenia to have a weakened ego rather than alterations in brain function or biochemistry (Abramovitch, 2014). Jung varied his approach as a function of the client's personality and problems. Because no one method fits all people in working toward wholeness, the analyst must be prepared to adjust to the needs

and abilities the analysand brings to therapy. An extroverted-feeling type of client may require a different form of therapy than an introverted-thinking type.

Evaluation

Jung's concepts of introversion and extroversion have long been a part of mainstream psychology. Jung's early work on the word-association test may also be counted as an important contribution with a continuing influence. Jung's approach to therapy also remains as a small but significant part of the work of mental health professionals. His great breadth with respect to content and methodology may also be viewed as a strength. Despite waves of continued scholarship, some argue that Jung has yet to receive the attention he deserves (Bishop, 2014). As already noted, however, there are any number of controversial concepts in Jung's psychology that have been the subject of severe criticism: the collective unconscious, archetypes, the principle of synchronicity, and the vagueness of many terms in his theory. Jung's broad approach to science and his interest in the occult have also been sources of concern. Perhaps the cardinal weakness of Jung's psychology has been its failure to generate meaningful experimental studies.

Karen Danielsen Horney

Like Adler and Jung, **Karen Danielsen Horney (1885–1952)** (*HORN eye*) initially found value in Freud's ideas but in time grew dissatisfied with the traditional assumptions of psychoanalysis. She challenged Freud's ideas about human sexuality, neurosis, and therapy. As a result, she incorporated a more sociocultural perspective into psychoanalytic thinking.

Karen Clementina Theodora Danielsen was born in Eilbek, Germany, on September 15, 1885. Although close to her mother, she felt alienated from her father, a steamship captain who was

413

often away at sea (Quinn, 1987). At an early age, she declared an interest in medicine. In 1901, she became one of the first girls to attend the Hamburg Realgymnasium (an accelerated high school), and later she became one of the first women in Germany to study medicine. She met Oskar Horney, a student of economics and political science, at the University of Freiburg. The young couple married in 1909 and moved to Berlin. She earned her medical degree in 1915 from the University of Berlin and delivered her first paper on psychoanalysis two years later. She underwent psychoanalysis with the renowned analyst Karl Abraham (1877–1925), who recognized her brilliance and wrote to Freud about her potential (Sayers, 1991). In time, she became the first female professor at the Berlin Psychoanalytic Institute, though her ideas were already at odds with traditional psychoanalysis.

In 1932, Horney emigrated to the United States, where she interacted with a diverse mix of scholars including Erich Fromm, Margaret Mead, Harry Stack Sullivan, and Max Wertheimer. In 1939, Karen and Oscar Horney were divorced after years of separation, and the ensuing period marked a time of great independence in her thinking. That same year, she published *New Ways in Psychoanalysis*. Her book took a critical stand against Freud, souring her relations with col-

leagues in the exclusive New York Psychoanalytic Society (Rubins, 1978). She resigned from the Society in 1941 and helped found the Association for the Advancement of Psychoanalysis (Sayers, 1991). She also served as a founder and Dean of the American Institute for Psychoanalysis and founder and editor of the *American Journal of Psychoanalysis* (Galdi, 2015). Karen Danielsen Horney died of cancer on December 4, 1952, in New York City.

Horney's System of Thought

Horney's powerful determination affected her approach to scholarship as well as her life (Eckardt, 2006). She was an innovative thinker and prolific critic of Freudian theory, as evidenced in her first book *The Neurotic Personality of Our Time* (1937). She revised and refined her personality theory in subsequent books including *Self-Analysis* (1942), *Our Inner Conflicts* (1945), and *Neurosis and Human Growth* (1950). Following emigration from Europe to the United States, Horney became attuned to sociocultural influences in the development of personality, especially in the shaping of neurosis. She believed that neurotic behavior did not develop from psychic tension between the ego and unconscious forces, but instead from conflict in interpersonal and social relationships. In her view, the *neurotic person of our times* was not the victim of sexual instincts, as suggested by traditional psychoanalysis, but rather a product of the sociocultural context of childhood.

BASIC ANXIETY AND NEUROSIS During the course of development, children naturally look to their caregivers for security and satisfaction. This process fosters the development of the **real self**, that "central inner force common to all humans and yet unique in each, which is a deep source of growth" (Horney, 1950, p. 17). Although children are born with a sense of real self, some parents may undermine a child's security through excessive isolation, rejection,

Karen Horney

414

indifference, hostility, or ridicule. As a result, the child may experience a sense of **basic anxiety**, a "terrible feeling of being isolated and helpless in a potentially hostile world" (Horney, 1945, p. 39). Such debilitating anxiety is counterproductive to growth because it stifles and distorts a person's view of the real self.

Horney believed that basic anxiety was a universal aspect of childhood that could manifest itself in adult neurosis. In time, a person may develop certain **neurotic trends** or irrational strategies of coping against basic anxiety. Horney (1942) believed that her study of neurotic trends set her apart from other scholars in the psychodynamic school:

> Freud believed that the [neurotic] disturbances generate from a conflict between environmental factors and repressed instinctual impulses. Adler, more rationalistic and superficial than Freud, believes that they are created by the ways and means that people use to assert their superiority over others. Jung, more mystical than Freud, believes in collective unconscious fantasies which, though replete with creative possibilities, may work havoc because the unconscious strivings fed by them are the exact opposite of those in the conscious mind. My own answer is that in the center of psychic disturbances are unconscious strivings developed in order to cope with life despite fears, helplessness, and isolation. I have called them "neurotic trends."
>
> (p. 40)

During the course of neurotic trends, individuals may develop an insatiable need for affection, approval, power, perfection, social recognition, or prestige. Likewise, they may feel a need to exploit others, to restrict their life and goals to narrow borders, or to seek a partner who will assume control of their life. Although all people possess such needs to some degree, neurotic people adopt these trends as absolute needs that dominate their lives and relationships.

In *Our Inner Conflicts* (1945), Horney elaborated on three unconscious *movements* that neurotic individuals rely on to deal with basic anxiety. A **compliant type** of individual is motivated to reduce the anxiety of helplessness by *moving toward* other people in a style of interaction characterized by dependence and unassertiveness. According to Horney (1945), "This type needs to be liked, wanted, desired, loved; to feel accepted, welcomed, approved of, appreciated; to be needed, to be of importance to others, especially to one particular person; to be helped, protected, taken care of, guided" (p. 51). The **hostile type** is likely to use a more aggressive coping style of *moving against* people through exploitation and dominance. For the hostile type, any "situation or relationship is looked at from the standpoint of 'What can I get out of it?'—whether it has to do with money, prestige, contacts, or ideas" (Horney, 1945, p. 65). Finally, the **detached type** employs an interpersonal coping strategy based on withdrawal and detachment from society by *moving away* from people. Horney (1945) believed that this social resignation arises from an "inner need to put emotional distance between themselves and others. More accurately, it is their conscious and unconscious determination not to get emotionally involved with others in any way, whether in love, fight, co-operation, or competition. They draw around themselves a kind of magic circle which no one may penetrate" (p. 75).

Unfortunately, such neurotic strategies further alienate the person from his or her real self and establish an **idealized self**, a fictitious view of neurotic selfhood that substitutes for the real self. Indeed, Horney noted that her patients often demonstrated a "neurotic search for glory," a powerful need to establish the idealized self even to the point of developing a "neurotic pride" about this false selfhood. To this end, a person struggling with neurosis may develop *blind spots* by denying any experiences that are inconsistent with the idealized self. Horney (1945) illustrated this "refusal to see" with a case study:

A patient, for example, who had all the characteristics of the compliant type and thought of himself as Christlike, told me quite casually that at staff meetings he would often shoot one colleague after another with a little flick of his thumb. True enough, the destructive craving that prompted these figurative killings was at that time unconscious; but the point here is that the shooting, which he dubbed "play," did not in the least disturb his Christlike image.

(p. 132)

Blind spots and neurotic pride, together with cynicism, rationalization, and other neurotic *solutions*, have potentially destructive effects for healthy personality growth. Horney used the term *self-hatred* to describe the neurotic tendency to despise one's real self. This self-contempt was sometimes mixed with a relentless drive for perfection governed by an unrealistic *tyranny of the should*. For example, a woman struggling with a neurosis may be driven by rigid and unrealistic expectations about how she *should* be a better student, *should* train more for her sports team, or *should* be more outgoing. Ultimately, such artificial harmony built around one's idealized self-image will foster neurotic pride and self-hatred but will also push the individual deeper into neurosis.

Horney provided a compelling alternative to psychoanalysis (Leslie, 1996). She believed the goal of psychotherapy should be oriented around helping people resolve their inner conflicts by reestablishing the real self over the idealized self. In *Self-Analysis* (1942), she maintained that such *self-realization* decreases conflict and anxiety and helps individuals strive for truth, productivity, and harmony with others and themselves. Near the end of her life, Horney became interested in Zen Buddhism and tried to incorporate it with her ideas about psychoanalysis (DeMartino, 1991).

FEMININE PSYCHOLOGY Between 1923 and 1936, Horney wrote a series of fourteen papers that constituted an aggressive counter

to Freud's theory of female sexual development; the posthumous collection of essays appeared in 1967 under the title *Feminine Psychology*. Freud publicly condemned Horney's sociocultural theory, but she was undeterred by his criticism (O'Connell, 1990), and she continued to promote her individualistic approach (Mitchell, 2014).

She took particular issue with Freud's belief that "anatomy is destiny." Horney concluded that culture, not anatomy, produces differences between women and men, and she found psychoanalysis to be excessively male-oriented and phallocentric in matters of gender development (Gilman, 2001). For example, psychoanalysts discuss *penis envy* but disregard the possibility of *womb envy* despite evidence from several cultures and mythologies that men envy women's ability to bear and nurse children (see Bayne, 2011). Indeed, Horney (1967) asserted that the professional accomplishments of men may serve as compensation for an inability to bear children (see Bayne, 2011). As her ideas about feminine psychology developed, she placed increasing emphasis on the cultural influences on female personality (Rubins, 1978).

For Horney, personality development and tensions between men and women were due to environmental, not biological, conditions. In particular, she believed that women's sense of inferiority is not constitutional but acquired from masculine society and psychology. Horney (1967) challenged society's "dread of women," which results in disparaging and hostile attitudes that define women as emotionally and intellectually inferior to men. To illustrate the prevalence of this patriarchal dread, she surveyed historical examples of female persecution ranging from biblical admonishments to the senseless slaughter of witches. She called for a new understanding of women but recognized the discouraging stereotypes of her day:

Woman's efforts to achieve independence and enlargement of her field of activities are continually met with a skepticism which insists that such efforts should be made only in the face of economic necessity, and that they run counter to her inherent character and natural tendencies. Accordingly, all efforts of this sort are said to be without any vital significance for women, whose every thought should center upon the male or motherhood.

(Horney, 1934, p. 605)

Taken as a whole, Horney's work represents an important step in advancing the psychological study of women, a field that gained momentum in the 1960s (Eckardt, 1991; Symonds, 1991). In addition, her ideas about psychotherapy and personality have influenced cognitive and rational-emotive therapy as well as the study of literature (O'Connell, 1990; Paris, 1991; Pelusi, 2016).

Unlike Adler and Jung, Horney did not replace psychoanalysis with a new theory of personality but rather challenged (Eckardt, 2005) and restructured the fundamental assumptions of the Freudian model to fit a different time and culture (Wallace, 1993). Her insightful work on cultural influences of personality and feminine psychology opened new frontiers and broadened the scope of psychoanalytic theory (Gilman, 2001; Ingram, 1985).

Other Developments

Fine (1990) observed that psychoanalysis has been beset with "innumerable inner conflicts, so similar in many ways to the inner conflicts that psychoanalysts find in their patients" (p. 3). Psychoanalysts are divided on a variety of issues including the autonomy of the ego, female sexuality, and the role of social and cultural influences in experience and behavior (Bergmann, 2004).

One of the most important developments in psychoanalytic theory has been the attempt to "mate a new ego and an old id" (Klein, 1983, p. 505). Though he had recognized ego instincts or drives, Freud emphasized the id as the primary source of motivation. A major movement within the

psychoanalytic tradition, known as ego psychology, has emphasized ego functions that are autonomous. This movement received its impetus from a seminal work by Heinz Hartmann (1894–1970) titled *Ego Psychology and the Problem of Adaptation* (1939). Since the publication of Hartmann's work, a great deal of work (see Holt, 1967) has examined the relation of the ego to Freud's classic drive theory. Such work has led to the claim that there is much more room in Freud's expanded theory for a model of human freedom and rationality (see Macklin, 1976). The ego psychologists remind classical theorists of Freud's statement in the final chapter of *The Future of an Illusion* that "the voice of the intellect is a soft one, but it does not rest till it has gained a hearing" (Freud, 1927/1961c, p. 53). The importance of a stronger ego with independent functions is supported by another post-Freudian development that emphasizes social and cultural factors in human experience.

In addition to the neglect of ego functions, there has also been widespread agreement that classical psychoanalytic theory neglected social and cultural influences on personality. Freud's focus was on individual psychological processes and, as noted by Munroe (1955), he "profoundly distrusted environmentalist theories that attempt to explain 'everything' by social and economic causes" (p. 117). He was critical of the Soviet communist system, arguing that "the psychological premises on which it is based are an untenable illusion" (see Freud, 1930/1961a, pp. 112–113). Freud's distrust of all-pervasive environmentalist viewpoints may have contributed to his neglect of more moderate approaches. Post-Freudians such as Erich Fromm (1941, 1947), Harry Stack Sullivan (1953), Erik H. Erikson (1963), and Joost A. M. Meerloo (1956) have added the necessary correctives for the neglect of social influences.

Freud's daughter Anna became a prominent figure in the psychoanalytic community in her own right (Young-Bruehl, 2008), and she gained recognition for her work on ego defenses (Meerloo, 1956) and sibling relationships (Pretorius, 2014). In 1941, she opened the Hampstead War

417

Nurseries for children orphaned by the war, and she then launched the Hampstead Child Therapy Course and Clinic in the late 1940s; this charitable institute was committed to the study and care of children (Pretorius, 2012). She pioneered analysis of children based on extensive clinical research (Midgley, 2012; Tischler, 2014), and she excelled as a teacher, trainer of analysts, and representative of psychoanalysis (Young-Bruehl, 2012).

As noted earlier in the chapter, Freud's views on female sexuality have also been subject to extensive criticism. He joined notable figures such as Friedrich Nietzsche and Charles Darwin, who, for all their important contributions, believed negative stereotypes in which women were regarded as inferior and subordinate to men.

Review Questions

1. The text outlined six general characteristics of Freud's thought. What kind of evidence might Freud have advanced for each characteristic?

2. Compare and contrast Freud and Jung with respect to their views on the structure of personality. Which view seems more adequate? Why?

3. Briefly review the posthypnotic phenomena that impressed Freud and that contributed to his view on the importance of unconscious processes.

4. Contrast Freud and Jung with respect to their positions on the unconscious.

5. Outline the four basic components of instincts according to Freud.

6. Distinguish between the three varieties of anxiety proposed by Freud.

7. Define *repression projection*, *reaction formation*, and *sublimation*. Why did Freud consider repression to be the most basic?

8. Critically evaluate Freud's stages of psychosexual development.

9. Distinguish between the manifest and latent content of dreams. Also briefly describe Freud's approach to psychotherapy, making sure you cover topics such as transference, free association, and countertransference.

10. Contrast Freud and Einstein with respect to their approaches to the causes of war.

11. Outline some of the new materials you encounter in the work of Freud that are not included in other systems of psychology.

12. Outline major criticisms of Freud's system of thought.

13. Contrast Jung and Freud with respect to their approaches to therapy.

14. What role did the ancient practice of alchemy play in shaping Jung's psychology?

15. Jung believed that the shadow can be a doorway to reality. What did he mean by this? He also believed that encounters with the materials in the shadow can lead to wisdom and wholeness. Do you agree with him? Why?

16. What did Jung mean by the term *archetype*? Give some examples. Briefly argue the pros and cons of the concept of archetypes.

17. Outline the four functions and two attitudes in Jung's psychology.

18. Discuss Jung's general approach to the problem of causality, including his position on teleology and a brief statement regarding his concept of synchronicity.

19. Outline some of the strengths and weaknesses encountered in Jung's system of thought.

20. Contrast Adler and Freud with respect to their approaches to motivation.

21. Contrast compensation and overcompensation in Adler's theory.

22. Briefly outline Adler's approach to the question of causation. Argue the pros and cons of Adler's teleological approach in contrast with an approach that places stronger emphasis on material and efficient causation.

23. Distinguish between the real self and the idealized self. What role does basic anxiety play in isolating the real self?

24. Briefly review Horney's ideas about the compliant, hostile, and detached neurotic types.

25. Compare and contrast Freud and Horney with respect to their position on feminine development.

Glossary

Adler, Alfred (1870–1937) Founder of a system of psychological thought known as individual psychology, Adler emphasized the importance of overcoming early feelings of inferiority. He focused on the purposive or goal-directed nature of behavior and on the capacity of the individual to identify with the goals of society at large.

alchemy The ancient practice of transformation. Jung found inspiration in alchemical practices, believing they gave substance to his psychology, spiritual values, and ideas about psychological transformation.

anal stage According to Freud, in the second and third years of life, the child develops a deep awareness of the pleasures associated with relief of bowel and bladder tension. The expression of this pleasure may be in conflict with societal norms and thus create special difficulties that must be negotiated with care if the child is to develop normally.

analytic psychology The name of the system of psychology advanced by Carl Gustav Jung.

anima In Jung's theory, the female archetype in men.

animus In Jung's theory, the male archetype in women.

archetype According to Jung, archetypes exist in the collective unconscious. They are patterns or forms that help mold thinking about experiences with topics such as power, death, darkness, mothers, fathers, and so on. Jung assumed that the vast experiences of the entire species with such topics do not go unrepresented in the psychological apparatus of each individual.

attitudes According to Jung, an attitude is a pervasive social orientation. Jung identified two attitudes: introversion and extroversion.

basic anxiety An overwhelming feeling of helplessness and isolation in a threatening and hostile world.

Breuer, Joseph (1842–1925) German physiologist and colleague of Sigmund Freud. Breuer's treatment of Bertha Pappenheim (*Anna O.*) played a central role in the early development of Freud's psychoanalysis.

Brücke, Ernst (1819–1892) Famous physiologist who had a powerful influence on Sigmund Freud. Brücke emphasized the importance of a thoroughgoing, physical–chemical approach to the study of psychological topics.

Charcot, Jean-Martin (1825–1893) French physician and neurologist who had a strong influence on the development of Freud's thought. Charcot emphasized the psychological basis of some physical symptoms.

collective unconscious A controversial concept advanced by Carl Jung. He believed that the human mind includes unconscious memories from the biological past of topics such as darkness, death, and power. Most of what is in the collective unconscious is associated with topics that strongly influence survival.

compensation In Adler's psychology, the normal attempts to overcome specific inferiorities by developing strengths in alternative areas (e.g., a person who is not athletic may excel in the classroom).

complex A term employed by Jung to refer to conscious materials that are strongly associated with emotional or perceptual distortions. For example, in Jung's view, an inferiority complex results partly from perceptual distortions regarding personal adequacy.

compliant type A neurotic attempt to reduce anxiety by *moving toward* people.

countertransference In Freud's psychology, the emotional attachment of a therapist to a patient.

detached type A neurotic attempt to reduce anxiety by *moving away from* people.

ego In Freud's system, the ego is the *I* or *me* of the personality—the center of organization and integration that must adapt to the demands

419

of reality. Jung uses the term to refer to a component of personality that is closely associated with conscious processes.

extroversion In Jung's psychology, a quality of personality marked by love of other people and social interaction.

fictional final goals According to Adler, fictions play major roles in the subjective world of the individual. Fictional final goals are those things that we wish to achieve. Such wishes are not necessarily grounded in realistic considerations.

fixation A strong attachment to a specific stimulus in Freud's theory of instinct. For example, a childhood trauma may result in an oral fixation that might manifest itself in adulthood as a habit of smoking cigars.

free association Therapeutic method developed by Sigmund Freud and marked by the uninhibited sharing of whatever happens to be in the center stage of consciousness at a given time.

Freud, Sigmund (1856–1939) Founder of psychoanalysis, which is both a major system of psychology and a therapeutic technique.

function According to Jung, a function is an expression of the psychic apparatus. He identified four functions: thinking, feeling, sensation, and intuition. He believed that, for many people, specific functions (e.g., thinking) are dominant features of the personality.

genital stage According to Freud, this stage is associated with the adolescent years and is marked by the development of emotional ties with members of the opposite sex.

Horney, Karen Danielsen (1885–1952) German American psychoanalyst who enlarged the domain of psychoanalysis with her study of sociocultural factors in neurosis and gender development.

hostile type A neurotic attempt to reduce anxiety by *moving against* people.

id In Freudian theory, the id is the most primitive component of the personality. It represents powerful biological needs and demands instant expression and immediate gratification.

idealized self A fictitious view of neurotic selfhood that replaces the real self.

identification In Freudian psychology, a defense mechanism of the ego marked by imitation of another person. The ego attempts to borrow from the success or adequacy of another individual.

individual psychology The name of the system of psychology founded by Alfred Adler.

individuation The name Carl Jung gave to describe the process of becoming a complete psychological individual, a self-realization that signals a coming to selfhood.

inferiority complex According to Adler, children are inadequate or inferior with respect to most functions. Overcoming inferiority is a task for all people. An inferiority complex is an intense or unusually strong manifestation of feelings that all people experience.

instinct This term is often used as the translation for Freud's term *Trieb*, which is close in meaning to the term *drive*. According to Freud, *Trieb* is an internal stimulus that persists until it finds satisfaction. It has a somatic source, a strength, an aim (its own satisfaction), and an object (that which will help it achieve its aim).

introversion According to Jung, an attitude marked by preference for inwardness and for minimal or highly selected social contact.

Jung, Carl Gustav (1875–1961) Founder of a system of psychology known as analytic psychology.

latency period According to Freud, the period between the phallic stage and the genital stage. In the latency period there is no obvious localization of erotic interest.

latent content of a dream According to Freud, the symbolic way a dream expresses an unconscious wish or drive.

mandala According to Jung, a "magic circle" or symbol that expresses selfhood.

manifest content of a dream According to Freud, the dream as described by the dreamer; the apparent content of a dream as censored by the ego.

420

moral anxiety According to Freud, anxiety associated with the threat that the irrational demands of the superego might overcome the ego.

neurotic anxiety According to Freud, this arises when the irrational demands of the id threaten to overwhelm the ego.

neurotic trends Neurotic needs that form strategies of protection designed to counter basic anxiety.

objective anxiety Objective threats from the world or from other people that threaten to overpower the ego.

Oedipus complex A young boy's desire for his mother along with feelings of competition with his father. The term is used more generally to refer to strong emotional attachment to the parent of the opposite sex and feelings of competition with the parent of the same sex.

oral stage In Freud's psychology, the first stage of psychosexual development. In this stage, the child's interactions with the world are primarily via the oral cavity and there is primitive learning about the responsiveness of the world to oral activities such as crying and sucking.

overcompensation According to Adler, overcompensation involves attempts to develop great strength in the very area that is most beset with difficulties (e.g., an individual with a physical disability who becomes a great athlete).

penis envy According to Freud, during the phallic period, the young girl is envious of the protruding sex organ of her father. Freud argued that the young girl holds her mother responsible for her own "castrated condition."

persona Literally, the play-actor's mask. In Jung's psychology, the persona is that part of the psychic structure that is most visible socially.

personal unconscious Jung's term for the storehouse of materials based on each individual's experiences that are not immediately available to consciousness.

phallic stage In Freud's psychology, that period from ages three to five when the child develops an interest in his or her sex organs and the sex organs of the parent. Freud believed that, at this time, the child begins to identify with the opposite-sexed parent.

pleasure principle Freud argued that the pleasure principle is the dominant feature of the human mental apparatus. The pleasure principle calls for immediate release of tension and acquisition of those goals that fulfill needs.

preconscious A feature of the mental apparatus, according to Freud, containing materials not now in consciousness but readily available to consciousness.

primary process Freud's term for images and memories of objects that serve to satisfy needs. A dream rich in imagery is an example of primary process material.

projection A defense mechanism of the ego manifested when personal faults or weaknesses are externalized or ascribed to objects, events, or other people. Thus, a married person tempted to be unfaithful may ascribe the wish to be unfaithful to the spouse.

psyche According to Jung, the totality of a human personality.

psychoanalysis The system of psychology and/or the treatment procedure set forth by Sigmund Freud. The term also has a broader meaning, referring sometimes to any group of psychologies that share some of the basic concepts associated with Freud's psychology.

rationalization Defense mechanism of the ego marked by the practice of employing false but logical or even plausible explanations designed to excuse weaknesses or errors.

reaction formation A defense in which the ego masks awareness of an anxiety-provoking motive by emphasizing its opposite. For example, a parent who harbors hostility toward a child, may become overly indulgent or overprotective.

reality principle Social and environmental demands, constraints, or pressures that place limitations on alternative modes of action.

real self In Horney's theory, the true source of healthy and positive growth in a human being.

regression Return or retreat to an earlier stage of development and reinstatement of attitudes or behaviors characteristic of an earlier stage.

repression An ego defense mechanism in which dangerous thoughts, memories, or perceptions are forced out of consciousness and into the unconscious realm.

resistance Failure to cooperate with the therapist presumably because of the trauma of dealing with unconscious materials that are about to be brought to the surface.

secondary process According to Freud, plans and strategies of the ego that provide compromised means for the expression of id impulses.

self According to Jung, the self is the unifying component of the psychic apparatus. The self is that which seeks optimal development, integration, and wholeness.

shadow According to Jung, the dark side of the personality that appears antagonistic to the social goals of the ego. Includes primitive materials from the collective unconscious; these materials may provoke negative emotions such as fear or anger.

social interest The term employed by Adler referring to the capacity of the individual to identify with the larger social good and the altruistic goals of society.

style of life Adler's term referring to unique personality qualities (including plans, strategies, and projects) designed to accomplish specific goals in life.

sublimation According to Freud, any of a variety of socially acceptable activities such as work, play, or philanthropic activities that represent a rechanneling of sexual energy into socially acceptable forms. In general, sublimation involves the substitution of a higher, more socially acceptable activity for a less socially acceptable one.

superego According to Freud, that part of the personality consisting of internalized social norms, values, and ideals. Like the id, the superego is not rational. It serves the goal of perfection and attempts to appropriate ego activities to serve its goal.

synchronicity A term employed by Jung that describes unlikely simultaneous occurrences or events not easily explained by the usual principles of causality.

transference According to Freud, this term refers to emotional attachments that patients may develop for their therapists.

16 Humanistic Psychologies

The darkness is habitable.

—Michael Novak (1970)

There is legitimate room to doubt whether any of the systems of psychology do justice to the richness, complexities, and mysteries of human experience. Psychologists affiliated with the humanistic school reject the narrow singularities and reductionism they encounter in many of the other systems of psychology. They have been particularly vocal in their criticisms of behaviorism and psychoanalysis (DeCarvalho, 1992). The basic concepts (conditioning and unconscious processes) associated with these two systems are important but, according to humanistic psychologists, these concepts are overextended. The criticism is that behaviorists and psychoanalysts have been so enamored with their core concepts of conditioning and unconscious processes that they have lost sight of the primary subject of interest—human beings.

The criticism of behaviorism does not deny that conditioning plays an important role in human life, but it is argued that humans have the capacity to operate at a meta-level of awareness that makes it possible to overcome or reverse the effects of conditioning. The defiant capacity, the ability to neutralize or even transcend conditioning, is, according to the humanistic psychologist, a unique feature of human nature.

A similar criticism is leveled at the classical psychoanalytic school. Unconscious forces may be at work, producing unexplained ideas or desires. Some individuals may act blindly on those ideas or desires, but most people are more conscious than unconscious. By overgeneralizing from a small sample of individuals with special kinds of illnesses, early psychoanalysts advanced a distorted view of human beings—a view that fails to differentiate between normal human beings and emotionally disturbed individuals who provided data for Freud's theories.

The humanistic viewpoint gained momentum in the 1960s when behaviorism and psychoanalysis were dominant forces. After rapid growth, the humanistic viewpoint was hailed as the "third force" in psychology because it stood in contrast with the two older schools (Gelso et al., 2014). Behaviorism and psychoanalysis were deterministic, whereas humanistic psychologists emphasized the capacity for free will (Barton, 1992). The claim is that behaviorism and psychoanalysis aped the methods of other sciences, whereas **third-force psychology** represented a broader epistemology adapted to the unique subject matter of interest. Thus, one might employ scientific, historical, philosophical, literary, or even artistic methods in studying human beings. Humanistic psychologists also argued for a broader concept of the subject matter of psychology. In addition to the traditional study of fear, aggression, learning, memory, and so on, it was argued that psychologists should study topics such as suffering, wisdom, growth, joy, meaning, authenticity, dignity, and peak experiences.

The humanistic psychologists asked nothing less of psychology than that it find ways to come to terms with human life, affectively, cognitively, and volitionally, and to recognize the variability and uniqueness of individual people (Ryback, 2012). The youthful discipline of psychology had been too narrow in terms of content, epistemology, and values; it had carved out too small a domain for itself. As a result, it lost contact with the fundamental issues of human nature and was in danger of becoming a sterile discipline.

Intellectual Traditions

The deep and rich intellectual background of humanistic psychology is encountered in the works of scholars who emphasized the importance of inner experience, the various meanings of freedom, and the experience of intentionality and activity of mental processes (Moss, 2015). In what follows, we review some of the dominant historical intellectual forces that influenced the development of third-force psychologies.

William James

The psychology and philosophy of **William James (1842–1910)** are important in the intellectual background of humanistic psychology for several reasons (Hoffman, 2010). First, the stream of experience played an important role in his philosophical vision (May, 1961/1969). According to James, an adequate psychology

cannot close the door on anything experienced. For all his background in physiology, medicine, and chemistry, James realized that experience deserves to be studied in its own right. Clearly, we can identify physiological and biochemical underpinnings and correlates of experience, but from a Jamesian viewpoint, experience, as it occurs, is a domain in itself with qualities that cannot be completely understood in terms of other underlying processes.

According to James, psychology ceases to be empirical when it strays too far from experience or attempts to explain away experience as completely reducible to, or nothing but the product of, a more fundamental process. From James's view, classical behaviorism could not qualify as an empirical psychology because it denies the role of experience altogether. The exclusion of experience as a proper subject matter is based on an intellectualist philosophy that tells us what to count and what not to count. James rejected simplistic attempts to reduce all things to one thing. Humanistic psychologists would agree.

James was a forerunner of humanistic psychology because he was a methodological pluralist. He was also open about what counts as the subject matter of psychology. He embraced robust notions of the self (1890/1981) and inspired his student, Mary Whiton Calkins (1916), to further develop self psychology. He hoped for psychology to make a practical difference in the world. He was interested in the application of psychology to daily life, the problems of education, the world of work, and the problems of people suffering emotional distress. His interest in questions of value and meaning ran deep (Rathunde, 2001) and is illustrated in his major works.

Existentialism

Humanistic psychology's ancestry is rooted in philosophers who devoted themselves to an understanding of the emotional, social, and intellectual issues of life. Such philosophers were concerned with the daily issues and concerns of human

424

beings as they live their lives. **Existentialism** is a philosophical orientation marked by such concerns. The focus is on the individual and on the capacity of the individual to exercise freedom to rise above environmental and social constraints. Let us examine some teachings of selected existential philosophers.

MIGUEL DE UNAMUNO   The Spanish philosopher and novelist **Miguel de Unamuno (1864–1936)** was born on September 29, 1864, in the Basque city of Bilbao. He had little interest in the abstract metaphysical problems of philosophy but great interest in what he called "the man of flesh and blood." Indeed, this expression is the title of the first chapter of Unamuno's classic book *The Tragic Sense of Life* (1913/1972). Sounding a theme consistent with the later humanistic psychologists, Unamuno lamented science and philosophy's failure to address the issues of human life. Science and philosophy fail, according to Unamuno, when specialization blocks the larger vision. In characteristic pejorative style, Unamuno reminded his reader that the specialist runs the danger of "murdering his humanity and burying it in the specialty" (Unamuno, 1913/1972, p. 36). Specialization breeds detachment, cold professionalism, and partial perspectives that do violence to human nature. The specialist can too easily treat another human being as an "it" rather than as a living "thou."

Science and philosophy also fail, according to Unamuno, when they place too great an emphasis on a purely cognitive intellectual analysis of human beings. He spoke with disdain for those who intellectualize; as he warned, "the people who think only with their brain turn into definition-mongers" (Unamuno, 1913/1972, p. 18). For Unamuno, cognition and thinking are not enough; we must also recognize the centrality of emotion in human life. A philosophy or psychology that neglects the affective dimension is too quick to dismiss or reduce important dimensions of existence. Unamuno pleaded for a perspective that recognizes the role of feeling in human life.

He wants scholars to think not just with their brains but "with their whole body and soul, with their blood, with the marrow of their bones, with their heart and lungs and viscera, with their whole life" (p. 18).

According to Koestenbaum (1967), Unamuno "extols the agony and the importance of the individual [and] the importance of personal integrity" (p. 183). Unamuno called for a new emphasis on emotional and intellectual honesty. Meaning orientation, truthfulness, practicality, and personhood are central themes in the works of Unamuno, just as they are in humanistic psychology.

SØREN AABYE KIERKEGAARD   **Søren Kierkegaard (1813–1855)** is sometimes called the "Danish Socrates" and is regarded as a founder of existentialism. Kierkegaard was born in Copenhagen on May 5, 1813. An orthodox Lutheran and successful businessman, Kierkegaard's father viewed it as an irony that he prospered despite an earlier period in his life when he cursed God. His tortured analysis was that God would punish him through his wealth. He was convinced he suffered the retributive anger of God through the misfortunes of several of his seven children. Two died in childhood, another died at age twenty-four, and two of his daughters died in early adulthood while giving birth. Young Kierkegaard labored under the stern tutelage of his domineering father who was bent on instilling a proper Christian perspective in the child. His mother, according to Lowrie (1970), "counted for little in the household. Whereas the father occupies so large a place in S. K.'s books and journals, not a single mention is made of his mother" (p. 24).

Though he struggled throughout his life with physical and potentially mental illnesses (Schioldann & Søgaard, 2013), Søren Kierkegaard showed early signs of brilliance. After attending a private school, he enrolled at the University of Copenhagen. He studied under Frederik Christian Sibbern, who, well before Wundt founded the laboratory in Leipzig, argued that a psychologist should also be a poet (Pind, 2016). Kierkegaard followed this recommendation as he studied theology, philosophy, history, and language but had difficulty focusing on any one topic. Indeed, he became something of a professional student and did not take his degree until 1840, two years after his father's death. He inherited a considerable sum of money from his father, making it possible to pursue the career of his choice—writing.

Kierkegaard typically wrote under a pseudonym and produced works that occupy a prominent place in existentialism. Among the many books were *Either/Or: A Fragment on Life* (1843/1987), *Fear and Trembling* (1843/1983), *Philosophical Fragments* (1844/1985), *Stages on Life's Way* (1845/1967), *Concluding Unscientific Postscript* (1846/1941), and *The Sickness Unto Death* (1849/1989).

In Kierkegaard's later years, he launched a bitter attack on the Danish Church, maintaining that church officials neglected the religion embraced by Jesus. Kierkegaard was more and more embittered and isolated by the counterattacks that followed. He died in 1855, leaving the simple but fitting epitaph, "That Individual." Kierkegaard was ignored or ridiculed in his own time, but his work continues to enjoy prominence in the twenty-first century. His philosophical views have had enormous influence in philosophy, religion, psychology, and literature. In a comment on Kierkegaard's influence, Taylor (1987) noted that "the insights of this lonely Dane pervade contemporary thought and shape the way many people now understand their lives" (p. 300).

Kierkegaard is understood partly in terms of his rejection of rationalism. Systematic conceptual schemes are inadequate because experience is not yet finished. Furthermore, truths that are simply grasped by the intellect have little to do with the real issues of life. If we focus exclusively on rational truths, we do not achieve real selfhood. Instead, we remain in the mode of the herd, marked by passive unexamined existence.

In his major works, Kierkegaard examined three modes of existence: the aesthetic, the ethical, and the religious. Each mode has a characteristic

dominant goal as well as an ironic element that exposes certain absurdities. The **aesthetic mode of existence** is marked either by sensual goals or by rational–intellectual goals. The sensualist may be in love with love, but incapable of real loving commitment to another person. Instead, other individuals are used as means for the sensualist's pleasures. Such an individual has no strong ties to the past or the future; it is only the temporary joy of the passing moment that counts.

In a similar manner, the rational–intellectualist is interested only in abstractions. Individuals become lost in the vague generalizations of the intellect. As noted by Schrag (1982), "Just as for the sensualist every girl is a woman in general, so for the intellectualist all reality is dissolved into general categories. Speculative thought sees only the general movement of history, explained through the mediation of logical categories, but forgets the individuals who [apprehend themselves] within their particular and concrete history" (p. 1296). Both the sensualist and the intellectualist can be insulated from the agonizing and vexing decisions in concrete real-life situations. Both can remain aloof because of all-encompassing definitions and clean logical categories that efficiently and coldly dictate a course of action with no regard for the host of particularities confronting each individual. According to Kierkegaard, the aesthetic mode of existence breeds indifference, which may collapse into boredom. Such boredom results in a quest for new diversions, but when the excitement of a new diversion has run its course, one is confronted with emptiness, melancholy, and despair.

The **ethical mode of existence**, according to Kierkegaard, is marked by a deep concern for justice, universal good, and genuine moral commitment. Unlike those in the aesthetic mode, those in the ethical mode are reflective and oriented toward a careful evaluation of the future consequences of their actions. The ethical stage is characterized by the growth of selfhood and a shouldering of responsibility. The ethicist recognizes the critical role of freedom in human life. Thus, the necessity and anxiety associated with choices have been confronted and accepted as one of the demands placed on a truly integrated self. Clearly, the ethicist is developmentally ahead of the aestheticist in the quest for selfhood.

Whereas aestheticism collapses into emptiness, melancholy, and despair, the ethical mode can lead to a profound sense of irony. The ethicist may become aware of moral complexities, of the difficulties of balancing conflicting claims, and of according proper weights to differing points of view. As a consequence, the ethicist may develop a deep sense of the many faces of irony in human life. Complete justice, balance, and equity—the primary goals of the ethical mode—are, in the end, impossible.

The **religious mode of existence**, according to Kierkegaard, is marked by sensitivity to one's contingency and complete dependence on God. In the religious mode, one is confronted with the crisis of the demands of faith versus human rational demands. Faith may require the impossible and the absurd, and one may collapse in terror at the prospect of faith flying in the face of reason. Authentic selfhood surfaces in the religious mode when one accepts responsibility for adjudicating between the claims of faith and those of reason.

Kierkegaard's modes are not necessarily stage-like or successive and rarely does one live exclusively in one mode. Rather, all of these modes operate in human life, and in the lives of most individuals one may see evidence of the operation of all three modes with one more dominant than another at a given time, but another more dominant later. Kierkegaard had a deep interest in the practical issues of life and in the ways human beings cope with their problems (Watkin, 1998), particularly the anxiety that appears fundamental for humans (Sharpless, 2012) and the ways in which people create meaning (Proulx, 2013). In these ways, he has shaped views of multiple generations of existentialists and existential therapists (de Feijoo & Protasio, 2015; Lippitt, 2016). His work contains a kind of psychological philosophy much different from earlier philosophical systems in which the focus

was on more rarefied problems such as the ultimate stuff of the universe, the existence of God, or the nature of truth.

MARTIN HEIDEGGER **Martin Heidegger (1889–1976)** was one of the most important and original existentialists of the twentieth century. Following the work of Unamuno and Kierkegaard, he focused on questions that influenced philosophy, psychology, sociology, religion, and literature.

Heidegger was born on September 26, 1889, in Messkirch, Germany. Reared in a Catholic family, he developed interests in history and theology. For a brief period, he was a novitiate in the Jesuit Order but he later pursued a Ph.D. in philosophy at Freiburg. He had had a long-standing interest in the experiential ideas of Franz Brentano (Gantt & Thayne, 2013). After completing his Ph.D. in 1915, he studied with Brentano's student, Edmund Husserl.

During the early 1930s, in the initial stages of his academic career, Heidegger's deep loyalty to Germany compelled him to favor National Socialism. For a time, he joined the Nazi party and even supported Hitler in speeches; these activities continue to raise questions about his ideas (Faye, 2009; O'Brien, 2010; Stolorow et al., 2010). Later, he changed his views, leading to tensions with the Nazi government and loss of his university position; he was forced into common labor. After the defeat of Hitler in World War II, Heidegger was restored to his professorial post at Freiburg, though his position was never secure because of his earlier affiliation with the Nazi movement. Heidegger's masterpiece is *Being and Time* (1927/1962), a classic book in existential metaphysics in twentieth-century philosophy. Heidegger died on May 26, 1976.

Heidegger's first concern was ontology or the nature of being. More specifically, he was concerned with the meaning of individual existence. He was also concerned with the practical questions of *how* we exist in this world. What is an authentic mode of being? How do we get trapped in unauthentic modes of being?

427

In his *Being and Time*, Heidegger employed the German term **Dasein**, which literally means "being there." We may find ourselves in a world not of our own choosing and we must navigate the norms and social realities of our culture (Koo, 2016). Three hallmarks of this condition include factuality, existentiality, and fallenness. *Factuality* refers to the bare fact of our being in the world. *Existentiality* surfaces in the broader framework of time. Not only are we in the world, but we are directional creatures, always going somewhere with real possibilities. *Fallenness* refers to breakdowns in existentiality. We simply drift, filling time with vacuous or meaningless activities. Outside forces propel us, leaving us with no real sense that we appropriate things for our own ends.

To lead an authentic existence, we must recognize and confront our existence and our existentiality. More than anything else, we must come to grips with our own finitude—the fact that we are going to die. This sobering fact leaves many with anxiety and dread. Unfortunately, such emotions work against our efforts to lead an authentic existence.

Heidegger believed the challenge for every human being is to exercise freedom and accept responsibility for the future. Taking such a stand, unfortunately, will produce anxiety, a fundamental experience for Heidegger (Elkholy, 2008). But if we fail to assume responsibility, we will be haunted by lingering guilt (because we know that we should be striving to accept responsibility). Anxiety and guilt are not attractive or admirable, but that they can inspire the courage to accept and use whatever freedom we possess is the mark of an authentic life.

Heidegger used the term *Dasein* to reflect his belief that the person and the world are inseparable. He analyzed the world in terms of regions that impose restrictions on our quest for authenticity. The **Umwelt** (the environment) refers to the surrounding world or the world of events and things. One person's world may be yielding or malleable, but for another it may be restrictive and uncompromising. Another region is the **Mitwelt** (the community) or our life with other people. The Mitwelt, like the Umwelt, may be yielding and responsive or rigid and constrictive. Dasein must be understood in the context of the Mitwelt and the Umwelt. Appropriation, movement, and authenticity must often be forged in difficult circumstances.

Heidegger recognized the powerful role of causal forces in human life. Circumstances in our life and environment may place restrictions on authenticity. He used the term **throwness** to refer to conditions, forces, or facts that do not easily yield to human effort. But according to Heidegger, the authentic individual who is aware of her or his own Dasein may produce real effects even when the Umwelt and Mitwelt seem almost overwhelming.

In addition to major impacts on existentialism, including the philosophy of Sartre and others (Mascolo, 2016), as well as philosophy in general (Emad, 2007), Heidegger's work has important implications for psychiatry (Bracken, 1999; Burston, 1998), especially his method of understanding being-in-the-world, known as *Daseinsanalysis*, which in turn inspired Ludwig Binswanger to develop an existential therapeutic perspective by that name (Holzhey-Kunz & Fazekas, 2012). Heidegger lamented that humans are so concerned with gadgets and technology that we fail to study the most important thing of all—our being-in-the-world.

FRANZ BRENTANO Franz Brentano (1838–1917) had a profound influence on Husserl and phenomenological psychology as well as others who shaped humanistic perspectives. In Chapter 11, we saw that Brentano embraced numerous variations on scientific procedure. He viewed voluntary and involuntary behaviors such as blushing as practical guides to inner processes. Brentano talked about the importance of genetic studies (e.g., studies of the actions of infants) and comparative studies that examine traditional as well as modern societies. He spoke about the importance of applied psychology and stressed the proactive, intentional,

428

or forward-looking aspects of human life. In addition to his experimental rigor and his applied focus, his primary contributions to humanistic psychology, both directly and through his many students, flow from his emphasis on experience. His emphasis on intentional, active experience and on the unity of consciousness provides a foundation for humanistic and existential perspectives in psychology.

Phenomenology

Scholars have used the term **phenomenology** in multiple ways (see Gavin, 1976; Schmitt, 1967), but as used here, it refers to a philosophical movement and to a way of studying or a method of approaching a subject. Literally, the term *phenomenon* means appearance, but it refers more specifically to that which is given in experience. The phenomenological method seeks to discover that which is given in experience as opposed to that which is dictated by the investigator's presuppositions, theories, or culture, and phenomenology has affected many areas of psychological science and practice (Ashworth & Chung, 2009; Westerlund, 2014). It may prove difficult to lay aside prejudices, theories, and assumptions that have guided past inquiries, but phenomenological investigations demand that the researcher make such an effort. Phenomenology also provided the foundation for later qualitative research (Wertz, 2014).

EDMUND HUSSERL The German philosopher **Edmund Husserl (1859–1938)** is commonly regarded as the founder of phenomenology (Staiti, 2014). He was born in Prossnitz, Moravia. Though trained in mathematics and science, Husserl shifted to philosophy after studying with Franz Brentano in Vienna. He taught at the University of Halle from 1887 to 1901, at Göttingen from 1901 to 1916, and at Freiburg from 1916 to 1929.

Like earlier philosophers such as Bacon and Descartes, Husserl was concerned about sources of error that interfere with knowledge. He argued

for a deep epistemic awareness marked by a persistent quest for clarity. Nothing was taken for granted or accepted as truth without painstaking scrutiny. Husserl was critical of experimental psychologists when they ignored consciousness (Giorgi, 2010a). He believed our knowledge of the world and our knowledge of ourselves begin with an experiential examination of human consciousness. Whatever is given, regardless of the nature of the inquiry, is given in consciousness. What is given in consciousness may be missed because of the narrowness of an investigation or the observer's prejudices. The phenomenological method calls for a different approach, one characterized as a kind of **disciplined naïveté** (see MacLeod, 1968b, p. 69). Husserl's ideal was to approach consciousness while suspending presuppositions so things can be captured in their givenness. In this way he moved to direct perception of his own inner states and away from Brentano's emphasis on observation of external responses to learn about internal states (Gantt & Thayne, 2013).

Husserl's phenomenology had numerous implications for psychology (Mays, 1998; Nissim-Sabat, 1999). First, it opposed any theory that restricts the range of human nature. Psychology from a phenomenological perspective should include the enormous varieties of consciousness and lived experience (Wertz, 2015). Another implication comes in the belief that the phenomena of consciousness cannot be compared with anything else. Computer or animal models, at best, only approximate human life. At worst, they dehumanize us. Phenomenological psychology also opposed reductionism (Giorgi, 2012). What is given in consciousness is a legitimate subject for investigation in its own right. Another implication for phenomenological psychology is methodological. Phenomenology calls for new kinds of *seeing*, a new way of exploring consciousness (see Natsoulas, 1990), and many methodological variations exist (Giorgi, 2010b). The method should not be confused with Titchener's introspection. MacLeod (1964) noted that, "there is no place in introspective analysis for meaning, except insofar as meanings can be reduced to elements and their attributes. For the phenomenologist, meaning is central and inescapable" (p. 54). The phenomenological method, unlike introspection, encourages the subject to report what is naturally there including the content, impressions, meanings, and associations.

In 1969, a journal titled *Journal of Phenomenological Psychology* was established to promote the discipline's appeal and research. In this journal one might encounter articles on methodological issues in the phenomenological framework or on topical areas such as "boredom" (Bargdill, 2000), "not belonging" (Clegg, 2006), or "the experience of spontaneous altruism" (Mastain, 2006). An examination of the journal reveals an emphasis on the daily world of lived experience. Though phenomenology does not represent a major school of psychology, it remains influential (Staiti, 2015; Salice & Schmid, 2016). In the words of Mruk (1989), phenomenology reminds "psychology that it is foremost a human science, and can no more afford the stifling presence of intellectual monopolies than can any other genuinely scientific endeavor" (p. 37).

The Formal Emergence of Humanistic Psychologies

Following World War II, many psychologists were unhappy with behaviorism's pessimistic view of human nature (DeCarvalho, 1990). A relatively small number of psychologists advocated a broader methodology and expansion of topics along with a focus on healthy human beings rather than animals or poorly adjusted human beings. Founded in 1961, the *Journal of Humanistic Psychology* provided a formal support structure for the new orientation, as did the American Association of Humanistic Psychology, later renamed the Association of Humanistic Psychology. The 1960s provided fertile soil for humanistic perspectives (Grogan, 2013). In the early 1970s, the American Psychological Association (APA) established Division 32, the

Division of Humanistic Psychology. DeCarvalho (1990) noted, "Within the space of a decade, humanistic psychology has earned a small but official place within mainstream psychology" (p. 31). In the 1970s and 1980s, there were educational programs that provided graduate courses and degrees with an emphasis on the humanistic orientation. We turn now to some of the founders of humanistic psychology.

Abraham Maslow

Abraham Maslow (1908–1970) was born on April 1, 1908. He became introverted and lonely during his time growing up in Brooklyn, New York. By his own account, his cold and domineering mother cast a shadow over his childhood. At times, Rose Maslow could be demeaning and even cruel. Maslow's father dreamed his son would become a lawyer, but Maslow was drawn to psychology. Around the same time, he married his cousin, Bertha Goodman. The shy young man attended the University of Wisconsin at Madison, where he became the first graduate student of Harry Harlow (1905–1981). Under Harlow's supervision, Maslow conducted research on primate dominance and sexuality. After earning his Ph.D. in 1934, he held positions at Columbia University, Brooklyn College, and Brandeis University. He had a remarkable education in psychology, working with notable figures such as Harlow, E. B. Titchener, Edward Thorndike, Erich Fromm, Karen Horney, and Max Wertheimer. In the summer of 1938, he worked with anthropologist Ruth Fulton Benedict (1887–1948) to study motivation in a tribe of Native Americans; this experience had only limited effects on his later psychology (Smith & Feigenbaum, 2013). Maslow served as APA president in 1968. Two years later, Maslow sustained a massive heart attack while jogging. He died on June 8, 1970.

Maslow's best-known books include *Motivation and Personality* (1954), *Toward a Psychology of Being* (1962), and *Religion, Values, and Peak Experiences* (1964). Throughout his major works, Maslow

Abraham Maslow

muscle twitch, or unconscious memory. Instead, the fundamental datum in psychology is something larger, a whole rather than a part. He insisted that he was not attacking science, but an attitude toward science. He believed science could be approached from a holistic-analytic standpoint rather than from a reductive-analytic perspective. In the holistic-analytic orientation, the scientist studies part of a whole rather than the isolated part itself.

MOTIVATION   Maslow's focus on the dynamic and purposive dimensions of human life emerged in his well-known hierarchical theory of motivation. His motivation theory found its way into mainstream psychology and remains his best-known contribution. Although he saw his theory as consistent with both experimental and clinical psychology, Maslow disagreed with monistic theories of motivation that emphasize single or exclusive determinants of behavior. Instead he emphasized a pluralistic hierarchical approach.

Biological Needs At the bottom of the hierarchy, we find basic *biological needs* such as hunger, thirst, and sleep that all creatures must meet to survive. Even at this level, needs are individually tailored by basic blood biochemistry (e.g., fat content, acid level, calcium content). Thus, appetite is based on a great many influences, most of which are unconscious.

Safety Needs The next step in Maslow's hierarchy is safety needs. Safety needs cannot be a dominant force in life until physiological needs are gratified. A hungry or thirsty animal may be forced to forgo safety to satisfy a physiological need. But once physiological needs are met, safety may become the dominant feature of life.

Psychological Needs Following the gratification of biological and safety needs, the individual seeks to fulfill *psychological needs* for love, affection, and belonging. The search for authentic emotional ties with others may now become the dominant force in life. Maslow (1954) contended that the person "may even forget that once, when he was hungry, he sneered at love as unreal or unnecessary or unimportant" (p. 89).

criticized the methodological and substantive narrowness of behaviorism and psychoanalysis. He set out to formulate a holistic system of psychology sensitive to the unique features of human experience. He designed a system of psychology that was *problem-centered* rather than *means-centered*. According to Maslow, a means-centered approach emphasizes methodology, techniques, apparatus, and orthodoxy, with an overemphasis on premature quantification, and a tendency to work on "safe problems" rather than significant ones. For Maslow, questions should be placed in higher priority than methods. He accepted the challenge of redrawing and expanding the discipline's boundaries into more humanistic territory without compromising scientific credibility (Nicholson, 2001).

As stated in his book *Motivation and Personality*, his goal was to create a perspective that was "holistic rather than atomistic, dynamic rather than static, dynamic rather than causal, purposive rather than simple-mechanical" (Maslow, 1954, p. 27). He disliked the idea that the fundamental unit in psychology is a reflex, simple sensation,

He believed that failure to gratify the needs for love and belonging is the most common force in human adjustment problems.

Esteem Needs The fourth set of needs in Maslow's hierarchy includes needs for esteem and recognition. Here we find a need for feelings of worth, competence, recognition for achievement, and adequacy. Maslow claimed Adler recognized such needs even as Freud neglected them. Maslow contended that failure to satisfy these needs diminishes personality, leading to a sense of weakness, inferiority, and helplessness.

Self-Actualization In the early development of his work, Maslow conceived **self-actualization** as the pinnacle of his need hierarchy. The Gestalt psychologist Kurt Goldstein had coined the term and, as mentioned in Chapter 15, it occupied a place in Jung's psychology. According to Maslow, self-actualization refers to self-fulfillment that comes from realizing or accomplishing our individual potential; similar ideas of personal fulfillment exist across many religions and cultures (D'Souza & Gurin, 2016). For one person, self-actualization may come from achievements in aesthetic activities (e.g., dancing, music, or art), whereas for another it may come about through achievements in cognitive activities (e.g., philosophy or science). Maslow suggested that self-actualization is delayed until other needs (i.e., physiological, safety, belonging, and self-esteem) have been satisfied.

As noted, in his early theory, Maslow placed self-actualization at the top of his need hierarchy. It has been argued, however (see Koltko-Rivera, 2006; Guest, 2014), that in his later work, Maslow intended that **self-transcendence** or intrinsic values might occupy a still higher place in human need structures. Self-transcendence points to the capacity of an individual to examine her or his worldview and its limitations in relation to more comprehensive multicultural perspectives and to seek values that transcend self-interest (Guest, 2014; Maslow, 1943). Self-transcendence allows for the development of a kind of epistemic humility and a deeper understanding of the complexity of things. Such transcendence can be a source of wisdom, "peak experiences," and an innovative

spirituality that rises above self-centered and culturally bound perspectives (Maslow, 1964).

Maslow's hierarchical theory of motivation represented a challenge to more monistic theories that emphasize the all-pervasive influence of one dominant motivational trend (e.g., sex, power, economic motivation). Not surprisingly, his hierarchical theory has drawn the attention of critics (see Winston, 2016). Shaw and Colimore (1988), for example, argued that the theory is contradictory in that it "contains both democratic and elitist worldviews" (p. 51). They used it as an illustration of how socioeconomic and political contexts can condition psychological theory. Such a criticism may be valid, but it also raises questions. Einstein's physics was, on more than one occasion, accused of being Jewish (see Gimbel, 2012). Cognitive work, even if conditioned by political or religious context, may nevertheless be applicable to a larger domain. If self-actualization is an innate need, as Maslow believed, then his theory could have considerable generality regardless of its origins.

A related criticism is that Maslow's theory is so individualistic that it leads to a kind of self-seeking and to a neglect of emphasis on the common good. In this context, Daniels (1988) claimed that "the central issue here is whether self-actualization is a goal to be sought directly or whether it emerges as a 'by-product' of living" (p. 21). The tensions between self-actualization and deep ecological and social awareness remain a central issue in motivation theory. Maslow found no necessary contradiction between being a self-actualized person and one with deep sensitivities to the larger good. Indeed, it is the person who is frustrated with respect to the gratification of lower-level needs who is a potential danger.

In his book *Toward a Psychology of Being*, Maslow (1962) contrasted the terms *being* and *deficiency* in relation to a variety of psychological functions such as love, motivation, and cognition. For example, *deficiency-love* and *being-love* (expressed by Maslow as D-love and B-love) are different. B-love is non-possessive, joyful, and less selfish and demanding. It takes pride in the being of another person and it shares in the achievements and accomplishments of the other person. D-love, by contrast, is more likely to be selfish, to use the other person for one's own need satisfaction. D-love is interested more in its own gratification than in the gratification of the needs of another person. It is more likely to include jealousy, possessiveness, and unrealistic expectations.

Maslow's application of the D and B concepts to motivation and cognition counters the idea that his theory is overly individualistic. For example, as one grows in B-cognition, one is more likely to be ecologically and socially aware and insightful. By contrast, D-cognition is marked by a more truncated and selective approach to information, such that one is informed by only a single issue or a single system of thought. Under such conditions, information is often used as a means of reducing anxiety rather than for achieving true growth.

THE SELF-ACTUALIZING PERSON During the 1930s, Maslow attended Max Wertheimer's lectures at the New School for Social Research and discovered a refreshing alternative to the mechanistic assumptions of behaviorism and psychoanalysis. Wertheimer promoted Maslow's interest in the role of values in human experience as well as the importance of studying healthy individuals. Around the same time, Maslow noticed that another prominent mentor, Ruth Fulton Benedict, with whom he worked extensively in 1938, shared remarkable characteristics with Wertheimer. Like Wertheimer, Benedict was a passionate champion of holism over reductionism. Both scholars offered a glimpse into a unique form of personality development. Secretly, Maslow examined Benedict and Wertheimer. He noted that these observations

> started out as the effort of a young intellectual to try to understand two of his teachers whom he loved, adored, and admired and who were very, very wonderful people. It was a kind of high-IQ devotion. I could not

be content simply to adore, but sought to understand why these two people were so different from the run-of-the-mill people in the world.

> (Maslow, 1971, pp. 41–42)

Maslow realized his training in psychology could not put proper perspective on the bold and unusual character of his mentors (Frick, 2000). Maslow hosted a party and was delighted when both Wertheimer and Benedict attended. Following this stimulating evening at his home, he tried to find a common theme in their personalities:

> When I tried to understand them, think about them, and write about them in my journal and my notes, I realized in one wonderful moment that their two patterns could be generalized. I was talking about a kind of person, not about two noncomparable individuals . . . I tried to see whether this pattern could be found elsewhere, and I did find it elsewhere, in one person after another.
>
> (Maslow, 1971, pp. 41–42)

Although crude and informal, Maslow's initial observations evolved into a disciplined undertaking that he recorded in a *GHB* (Good Human Being) notebook from 1945 through 1949 (Lowry, 1973). Maslow (1943) believed that his analysis of a life well lived was "in the functionalist tradition of James and Dewey, and is fused with the holism of Wertheimer, Goldstein, and Gestalt psychology, and with the dynamicism of Freud and Adler" (p. 371).

After rejecting terms such as *good human being*, *saintly person*, *self-fulfilling person*, or the unwieldy *almost ideally healthy human being*, Maslow seized on Kurt Goldstein's concept of *self-actualization* as a descriptor for his observations. Maslow read biographies and autobiographies of historically eminent women and men, searching for common characteristics of healthy-minded people. In developing his criteria of healthy people, Maslow (1954) was "fairly sure" he had discovered nine people who were self-actualizing individuals, and his list slowly expanded over time. Initially, it included luminaries such as Jane Addams, Albert Einstein, Aldous Huxley, William James, Eleanor Roosevelt, Albert Schweitzer, Benedict Spinoza, and Max Wertheimer. Finally, Maslow decided on thirty-seven potential cases of self-actualizing people. Although scholars question Maslow's exploratory biographical methods (Fuller, 2013), his criteria and his list of individuals continue to inspire discussion.

Maslow believed that fifteen positive or favorable characteristics could be identified in self-actualizing people, including a realistic and problem-centered perception of the world, a refreshing sense of spontaneity and simplicity, and a genuine acceptance of one's self as well as others. He observed that such *good specimens* have a mature, unhostile sense of humor together with a quality of detachment and a fierce need for privacy and autonomy resulting in deep interpersonal relations with only a few friends. Nonetheless, Maslow believed that self-actualizing persons have a great need to identify with all of humanity, roughly analogous to Alfred Adler's concept of social interest (McFarland et al., 2012). Additionally, they have a strong ethical sense and belief in democratic values that fosters resistance to the stifling effects of enculturation and obedience. In this context, the Asian schools of Taoism and Zen Buddhism influenced Maslow's investigations of transcendent states of consciousness (Cleary & Shapiro, 1996). For example, the self-actualizing person's need for creative expression and continued freshness of appreciation and wonder about the world may manifest itself in periodic mystical or *peak experiences* (Maslow, 1964). Maslow observed many of these traits in Wertheimer, for example, as he would play on the floor with his children or leap onto a desk for emphasis during a lecture (Hoffman, 1988).

Despite the admirable personality characteristics of self-actualizing people, Maslow cautioned against the belief that anyone ever achieves perfection. Indeed, there are traits in self-actualized people that may be perceived in a less than favorable way by others. For example, in their quest for truth, such individuals may exhibit periodic absentmindedness, unexpected ruthlessness, and *surgical coldness*. They are not free of conflict, occasional self-doubt, mistakes, regrets, and the like. In balance, however, their lives are guided by a realistic, coherent, productive, healthy, and forward-looking perspective.

OTHER CHARACTERISTICS OF MASLOW'S PSYCHOLOGY Maslow believed there is more to be gained by studying healthy self-actualizing people than by studying nonhuman models or people who are unwell. In his view, the study of healthy people will broaden the subject matter of psychology. New topical areas will, for example, include play, love, values, mystical experiences, humor, meanings of freedom, competence, and aesthetic needs. In other words, psychology should focus at least as much on the positive as on the negative dimensions of life. One of the most important topics in Maslow's vision of the discipline is to understand *meta-level awareness*. Such awareness refers to a capacity for meaningful self-appraisal that fosters growth in the direction of meaningful and realistic personal goals. Above all, Maslow advocated a positive psychology, which he called Eupsychia (the *well-being of the psyche*, as Coon, 2006, defines it), as an alternative to the negative emphasis in other systems. His positive emphasis may account for the theory's enormous popularity. As noted by Coon (2006), Maslow had a significant influence in the field of psychology, but his impact on the business community, particularly on the field of consulting (O'Roark, 2007), and in the emergence of management ideas (Cooke et al., 2005), in educational circles, the women's movement, and the broader American culture, was even greater. There has been a continuing belief that the motivation hierarchy has considerable theoretical and practical utility.

Gordon Allport

In the tradition of William James, **Gordon Allport (1897–1967)** emphasized individual experience. He advocated a psychology consistent with democracy and freedom and opposed any system that restrains us in methodological or substantive straitjackets. Although distinguished in several areas, the psychology of personality became the hallmark of Allport's career.

Allport was born in Montezuma, Indiana, on November 11, 1897. He and his older brother, Floyd H. Allport (1890–1978), were raised in a hardworking Midwestern home. While Gordon completed undergraduate studies at Harvard, Floyd earned his Ph.D. in 1919 under E. B. Holt and Hugo Münsterberg. Floyd suggested that Gordon consider devoting his dissertation to the study of personality, an unorthodox subject in American psychology at the time (Nicholson, 2000). After completing his doctoral degree at Harvard in 1922, Gordon traveled to Europe,

Gordon Allport

where he had positive encounters with Carl Stumpf, Max Wertheimer, and Wolfgang Köhler among others. (Allport had met Sigmund Freud years before but came away unimpressed with the man and his depth psychology.) He returned from Europe and accepted a position at Harvard, where he worked for most of the next four decades.

During the early 1920s, the Allport brothers worked together on the classification and measurement of personality traits, culminating in their 1928 Ascendance-Submission (A-S) Scale. By 1924, however, their collaboration soured over theoretical differences as Floyd embraced a more objective behavioral approach and Gordon rejected it (Nicholson, 2000). In time, Gordon became the principal architect of American personality theory (Barenbaum & Winter, 2013), and Floyd assumed a significant role in founding social psychology (he wrote an early book in the area and directed America's first doctoral program in social psychology at Syracuse University). Gordon Allport served as APA president in 1939 and received the Distinguished Scientific Contribution Award from that organization in 1964. He died at the age of seventy in 1967.

Allport's book *Personality: A Psychological Interpretation*, published in 1937, ranks as one of the important classics in the field (see Craik et al., 1993). His better-known works in personality include *Becoming: Basic Considerations for a Psychology of Personality* (1955) and *Pattern and Growth in Personality* (1961). His personality scholarship, particularly his emphasis on individuals as unique beings, contributed substantially to the emerging notions of self in the mid-twentieth century (Nicholson, 1998). He also published a work with P. E. Vernon and G. Lindzey titled *A Study of Values* (1951). Among his other works are the classics *The Nature of Prejudice* (1954) and *The Individual and His Religion* (1950).

In his book *Becoming*, Allport distinguished between the **Leibnizian tradition** and the **Lockean tradition** in psychology. The former emphasizes the proactive (purposive or goal-directed) nature of human life and the latter emphasizes the reactive (mechanistic) dimensions of life. Allport said that the Lockean tradition is evident in S–R behavioristic psychologies with their emphasis on animal models, machine theory, conditioning, and determinism. He preferred a Leibnizian tradition that argued for an active intellect, integrative self-actualizing capacities, and the important role of expectation or the forward-looking tendencies in human beings.

Allport also distinguished between **idiographic** and **nomothetic** orientations, a persistent divide in psychological science (Zachar, 2013). The former places emphasis on individual experience (such as case studies) and the latter concentrates on statistical abstractions such as group norms, means, standard deviations, and the like. Allport did not deny the importance of the nomothetic orientation but was concerned that in the rush to be scientific, psychology might neglect the most important reality—namely, individual experience in all of its uniqueness and complexity. His work in nomothetic traditions is reflected in his enduring work on prejudice (Allport, 1954; Dovidio et al., 2005), particularly in the 1950s, when prejudice formed integral parts of the legal, constitutional, economic, and educational landscapes in the United States (Loewen, 2005). Although scholars had examined these ideas before Allport, he developed attitude measures and brought these ideas into the psychological mainstream (Webster et al., 2010). He examined social factors that decrease prejudice, including the conditions under which intergroup contact reduced prejudice (Tropp, 2006), and he also emphasized idiographic factors in prejudice, including the first proposal attempting to identify the nature of a prejudiced personality (Roets & Van Hiel, 2011).

Allport was interested in the subject of motivation. He strongly rejected Freud's views (Anderson, in press), and he believed biological drives, learned motives, and concepts of homeostasis and maintenance cannot do justice to the dynamic qualities of human motivation. He coined the term **functional autonomy** to mean that an activity is independent of its original source and is now motivating in its own right.

He gave the example of a person who goes to sea to earn a living by fishing or transporting goods. In time, however, going to sea may be motivating in its own right so that the person enjoys being on the sea even after becoming financially independent. Allport believed that human motivation is not just a matter of maintaining equilibrium, nor just a matter of satisfying basic biological urges. On the contrary, it is often oriented toward growth, risk, novelty, and adventure.

Allport saw habit as an important early determiner of activity but believed that human beings make selections and live in terms of superordinate goals and motives. As we mature, we develop traits that provide stability to personality. In his book *Becoming* (1955) and in his classic, *The Individual and His Religion* (1950), Allport discussed the conditions that contribute to radical personality changes, and he examined other individual differences in religious beliefs and behaviors (Walborn, 2014). In *Becoming*, Allport (1955) wrote, "It sometimes happens that the very center of organization of personality shifts suddenly and apparently without warning. Some impetus coming perhaps from a bereavement, an illness, or a religious conversion, even from a teacher or a book, may lead to a reorientation" (p. 87). In *The Individual and His Religion*, Allport discussed the effects of battle experiences on such recentering. His perspectives on the study of religion shaped much of the social psychology of religion that followed (Nielsen et al., 2013; Titov, 2013). Allport proposed a broad system of psychology that challenged the behaviorist and psychoanalytic traditions. He was a prominent figure in the founding of third-force or humanistic psychology.

Carl R. Rogers

The founder of a new approach to therapy (first called *nondirective*, then *client-centered*, and finally *person-centered therapy*), **Carl R. Rogers (1902–1987)** was an innovative almost revolutionary figure in the third-force movement. He received world acclaim for a new approach to psychology that continues to influence psychotherapy, education, and personality theory (Rogers, 2013).

Rogers was born in Chicago on January 8, 1902 and completed his undergraduate degree at the University of Wisconsin. At age twenty, he became one of ten college students selected to represent the United States at the World Student Christian Federation Conference in Peking, China, and his six-month journey exposed him to experiences that were rare for undergraduates in his day (Cornelius-White, 2012). He continued his education at Union Theological Seminary and then at Columbia University, where he earned a Ph.D. in psychology in 1931. Rogers held positions at the Rochester Guidance Center, the Ohio State University, the University of Chicago, and the University of Wisconsin. From 1964 until his death in 1987, he worked in La Jolla, California, at the Center for the Study of the Person, an organization he helped found. In 1947, Rogers served as APA president. In 1956, he was among the first (alongside Wolfgang Köhler and Kenneth Spence) to receive the APA's Distinguished Scientific Contribution Award. Rogers's best-known books are *Client-Centered Therapy* (1951) and *On Becoming a Person* (1961). Rogers died on February 4, 1987.

Gendlin (1988) enumerated Rogers's contributions in terms of the ways he challenged

Carl Rogers

established psychology. The first amounted to an assault on the mystery and secrecy of psychotherapy. Rogers was the first to insist on a wedding of psychotherapy with the objective techniques of experimental psychology. He made the first recordings of psychotherapy sessions (with the client's permission) and assessed improvement by employing tests before and after therapy and by comparing his clients to control groups (Cain, 2010; Braakmann, 2014). In the words of Gendlin (1988), it was nothing less than "war against monolithic authority" (p. 127). In the end, however, Rogers's experimental approach prevailed and contributed to substantial changes in the discipline (O'Hara, 1995). Indeed, following Rogers's work, research on the effects of psychotherapy became commonplace. No longer was psychotherapy a mysterious secret reserved for an elite priesthood. Behavior therapists, though theoretically at odds with Rogers, were also major contributors to the new, more open approach to psychotherapy (see Suinn & Weigel, 1975).

Gendlin suggested that another challenge to the profession came in Rogers's stance on diagnosis in the treatment of emotional problems. In the medical model of Rogers's day, diagnosis of a patient's illness precedes treatment, but Rogers was concerned about the negative effects of labeling, and he viewed his therapeutic work as empowering clients instead of diagnosing patients (Zucconi, 2008). As a consequence, he skipped diagnosis and proceeded to the business of listening to his clients. His emphasis on listening is reflected in his development of nondirective interviewing as a therapeutic technique (Lee, 2011).

Rogers's psychology focused on the entire range of experiences that constitute a person's life, what he referred to as the **phenomenal field**. The phenomenal field consists of a differentiated and organized region called the *self*, which, according to Rogers, includes all the ways we evaluate ourselves, the ways we evaluate others, and the ways we relate to objects in the environment. He pointed to the possible tensions between the self as it is and the self as one would like it to be, or the **ideal self**. The greater the congruence between the two, for most people, the greater the health.

Rogers outlined the difference between **unconditional positive regard** and the conditional love to which many children are subjected, as well as the role of unconditional positive regard in therapy (Bozarth, 2007, 2013). Unconditional positive regard conveys a belief in the intrinsic worth of the child. It creates the feeling that the child is loved simply in his or her very existence. The individual does not have to earn such love; it is a gratuity. Conditional love, by contrast, carries the connotation of "I will love you if . . ." (if you are a better student, conform, dress properly, develop the correct interests, etc.). Rogers's central ideas, including person-centered therapy as well as the importance of empathy, unconditional positive regard, and genuineness, have become the "core conditions" of successful therapy (see, for example, Wampold, 2001; Elliott & Freire, 2010; Witty & Adomaitis, 2014) and continue to shape therapeutic practice in the United States (Kirschenbaum & Jourdan, 2005; Cain, 2014).

Rogers believed in a drive toward self-actualization and that we have the capacity to choose and to appropriate things that contribute to our growth. The task of the therapist is to provide an accepting atmosphere marked by unconditional positive regard. Rogers believed that if the proper relationship could be established between client and therapist, the client would gain insight and freedom, and these would produce growth and the ability to assume responsibility for effecting desirable personal changes.

Described as "A person of enormous energy and devotion to making a difference" (Barrett-Lennard, 2013, p. 42), Rogers has had a continuing influence on the discipline of psychology, manifested by an outpouring of scholarly articles and by an extension of his principles into other fields such as education and politics. In education, he advocated a student-centered rather than a teacher-centered pedagogy (Lemberger & Cornelius-White, 2016; Rogers et al., 2014).

He hoped to contribute to the humanization of political systems so often driven by rigid, uncompromising, self-serving ideologies as opposed to open and honest quests for truth in the service of the public good. A Rogerian approach to politics calls for leaders to listen and respond carefully to the voices and needs of the public. He opposed shams and appearances and valued personal qualities such as authenticity, honesty, and openness. He was especially critical of institutional structures that undermine individuality and block the potential for growth.

Viktor Frankl

The Viennese psychiatrist **Viktor E. Frankl (1905–1997)** developed **logotherapy**, a system of thought that embodies a clear expression of third-force psychology. Frankl was born in Vienna, Austria, on March 26, 1905. He had a unique experience as a teenager; he sent a paper he had written to a famous scholar whom he revered. Sigmund Freud not only responded to the young man, but he also submitted Frankl's paper to the *International Journal of Psychoanalysis*. They agreed to publish Frankl's work in 1924 (Frankl, 1997). He received an M.D. and a Ph.D. from the University of Vienna and served as professor of neurology and psychiatry at the University of Vienna Medical School. As a young neurologist, Frankl was not afraid of debating respected figures, including his greatest mentor, Alfred Adler (Frankl, 1997). Early in his career, Frankl broke with Adler and founded his own school based on logotherapy. Following the schools of Freud and Adler, Frankl's theory became known as the "Third Viennese School of Psychotherapy" (Barnes, 2000; Längle, 2012). He enjoyed a prosperous career as a psychiatrist in Vienna. As with other Jewish intellectuals at the time, the rise of Adolf Hitler threatened not only Frankl's career but also his life.

During the Holocaust, the Nazi regime imprisoned several members of Frankl's family who did not survive. His experiences in four different

Viktor Frankl

prison camps contributed to his perspectives on psychology. Frankl's best-known book, *Man's Search for Meaning* (1985), described his concentration-camp experiences and sketched his system of therapy. His book became an international bestseller. Following the war, Frankl held many positions, most notably as Professor of Logotherapy at the United States International University (San Diego). Frankl died in September 1997.

In the preface to *Man's Search for Meaning* (1985), Gordon Allport called attention to the fact that Frankl's "father, mother, brother, and his wife died in camps or were sent to the gas ovens" (p. 9). Allport asked how Frankl, in the face of such losses, in the expectation of his own death, and in the midst of barbarous indignities, could go on living. Allport offered the opinion that one who has survived such an ordeal is worthy of our attention. Although Frankl's ideas about meaning and life predated his Holocaust experience (Frankl, 1985; Pytell, 2007), his concentration-camp experiences solidified his ideas.

Frankl referred to several polls that ask people to list priorities in their lives. In each case, the leading answer involved living a purposeful or meaningful existence. The human need for meaningful existence is a core concept in Frankl's system. It is a need that is easily frustrated, sometimes by the very psychological and philosophical systems designed to alleviate human suffering. Frankl argued that people experience despair and meaninglessness if taught that they are products of conditioning or little more than a battleground of unconscious forces. He believed that behaviorism and classical psychoanalysis exercise a dehumanizing influence.

Frankl did not deny the role of conditioning in human life or that some human problems originate in the frustration of drives toward pleasure. He argued, however, that many human problems have their origin in the failure to find a meaning or purpose in life. In addition to psychogenic neuroses (those that result from the frustration of basic drives), Frankl describes **noogenic neuroses** (the Greek word *noos* means "mind"). He uses the term *noogenic* to refer to neuroses resulting from existential distress and the failure to find a sense of personal worth. These neuroses often include anxieties that are physical and also metaphysical and spiritual (Costello, 2011).

Frankl's logotherapy was a therapeutic intervention system for treating noogenic neurosis. The Greek term *logos* refers to a reason or a controlling principle. Logotherapy seeks to assist the individual in discovering the logos of existence. It assumes that human beings have a unique capacity to work at a kind of meta-level above the ongoing events of life. Unlike the Freudian emphasis on past experiences, logotherapy seeks a balanced solution to human concerns in the moment (Frankl, 1997). We may get caught up in the monotony of an everyday routine, but we can adopt a positive attitude about our day-to-day lives. Our perspective—be it healthy or unhealthy—can have a powerful effect on the meaning of our daily lives and work. We often have little choice about events in our daily lives, but we have the responsibility and freedom to choose how a situation will affect us (Gerwood, 1998). Frankl discovered that even in concentration camps, certain people could find meaning in their suffering. Indeed, those who found meaning were more likely to survive the unspeakable trauma. We may find ourselves, as did Frankl, in overpowering circumstances that we did not choose, for example, facing disease or life-changing injury. He argued, however, that there is an arena in which choice can be real. We can take a stance toward our suffering, we can see it in a larger context, or we can find some possible and meaningful goal that it may serve. As Leslie (1996) observed, Frankl was an unapologetic optimist "in spite of everything."

Frankl believed that humans have a capacity for what he called **paradoxical intention**. The expression refers to doing the very opposite of what we would like most to do. People who have an irrational fear may consciously engage in the very thing they fear. Through several repetitions, the fear may subside. Frankl believed that the capacity for the defiant or even heroic stance lies dormant in all people and counts as a unique feature of being human.

In logotherapy, Frankl worked on meaning orientation by helping his clients search for alternative perspectives. In one case, a client was unable to overcome the grief associated with his wife's death. Rejecting standard psychoanalytic interpretations, Frankl helped the elderly client find meaning in his loss. One day, Frankl asked the widower to discuss what might have happened had he died before his wife. The man announced that this was a horrible thought because his wife would have had to endure the suffering he now experienced. Suddenly, the client saw the whole matter in a different light. By outliving his wife, she had been spared the suffering he now endured. Frankl (1985) noted that "suffering ceases to be suffering at the moment it finds a meaning" (p. 135). Logotherapy is designed to help clients explore the range of possible meanings relevant to their situation. Given this perspective, researchers have found logotherapy to be effective in many contexts.

Frankl rejected the idea that one meaning orientation can be relevant to all people. Rather, all individuals must authentically explore the possible meanings in their particular situation. Imitation, secondhand interpretations, rationalizations, and so forth must be rejected in favor of a genuine quest. With his individual and experiential emphasis, Frankl's methods can provide foundations for *autoethnography*, a form of self-study that examines an individual's experiences (Esping, 2010). Later scholars extended Frankl's emphasis on meaning into experimental studies (Crumbaugh & Maholick, 1964; Steger, 2009; Batthyany & Russo-Netzer, 2014).

Frankl's system embodies many tenets of existential and third-force psychology. He opposed determinism, reductionism, and all forms of what he called "nothingbutness." He emphasized those things that are uniquely human, including the capacity to take a stance toward the daily events of our lives. Novak's quotation at the beginning of this chapter captures the defiant human spirit so central to Viktor Frankl's thinking. As one trained in neurology and pharmacology, Frankl did not underestimate neurochemical causes. At the same time, he declared that the error begins when we believe human beings are "nothing but" neurochemical mechanisms. He elevated the role of psychology, mental processes, and values in the overall scheme of things. Frankl's psychology is not pessimistic nor is it naïvely optimistic (Leslie, 1996); instead, it offers a middle road of hope that, both individually and collectively, people can discover meaningful beliefs with survival value. Contemporary scholarly work on his system is encountered in numerous journals and specifically in the *International Forum for Logotherapy*, a journal, as the name implies, that focuses on Frankl's continuing intellectual legacy.

Joseph F. Rychlak

As we will see, a major criticism of humanistic or third-force psychologies is that they lack the rigor associated with scientific studies. Some members of the third-force movement would not deny the legitimacy of the criticism. They might argue, however, that theories meeting the test of scientific rigor have dealt with trivial questions that bear little relation to our lives. Their preference is for a psychology with ecological validity that speaks to issues confronting us here and now. In this spirit, **Joseph F. Rychlak (1928–2013)**, described as "one of the last grand theorists" in psychology (Slife, 2013, p. 82), argued for a psychology both rigorous *and* humanistic.

Rychlak received his Ph.D. in clinical psychology from the Ohio State University in 1957. Much of his career was devoted to the quest for a rigorous and humanistic psychology. His position is set forth in many papers and in major works such as *The Psychology of Rigorous Humanism* (1988) and *Artificial Intelligence and Human Reason: A Teleological Critique* (1991). Those who knew him warmly remember that his humanistic perspectives also shaped his personal life and his interactions with his family, colleagues, and students (Slife & Stilson, 2013).

Rychlak believed that traditional psychologies, especially behaviorism, constructed a model of humans that is too narrow. The emphasis in such psychologies has always been on material and efficient causality (see Chapter 2). According to Rychlak, formal and final causes, as described by Aristotle, cannot be dismissed if we are to have an adequate understanding of events in our world. Even in physical systems, the central role of formal causes is critical. Rychlak accepted it as axiomatic that human beings live on the basis of their plans, anticipations, and expectations; in short, we are telic or purposive creatures. An adequate psychology, according to Rychlak, will embrace a broad concept of causality, emphasizing material, efficient, formal, and final causes. The neglect of any of these, in his view, will result in conceptual blind spots as well as strained and unnatural explanations. Recent scholarship on the "science of prospection" is consistent with Rychlak's position that our thoughts and behaviors are driven by future-oriented plans and not exclusively by the past (see Baumeister & Vohs, 2016).

Rychlak also emphasized the human capacity for oppositional thinking. In his view, like that of William James, relations are as fundamentally real as the things related. Events are not joined by mechanical association; instead, relations are often given in the flow and logic of experience itself. Indeed, some ideas simply come with their opposites (e.g., the concept *up* implies its opposite *down*). Human beings, in Rychlak's view, see alternatives and anticipate their consequences. We then act on the basis of anticipated consequences and are thus future-oriented creatures rather than machines (Rychlak, 2005, 2009).

Rychlak found no reason why these views must be antithetical to science or to scientific understanding, nor did he think psychologists need to alter their methods as they proceed with scientific work. What is needed, according to Rychlak, is a radically new orientation regarding the assumptions we make about human behavior in both science and psychotherapy (Rychlak, 2000). In his view, psychologists can recognize the capacity for oppositional thinking, teleology (or *telosponsivity* as he calls it), and even some degree of free will without sacrificing their scientific integrity. He argued that the so-called hard sciences, such as physics, no longer operate in terms of the Newtonian assumption that every connection in the universe is complete. Psychology, like physics, can proceed with its scientific work, even if there are uncertainties and arenas of random or chaotic events. According to Rychlak, human research data do not contradict the assumptions of a rigorous humanistic psychology. There is always variance for which the scientist cannot give an account.

Overview of Third-Force Psychologies: Major Positions and Criticisms

Third-force movements, methods, and topics of study occupy a small but significant niche in psychology (Serlin, 2011). There are journals, professional organizations, institutes, training programs, and a sizable literature, but, for reasons outlined in the criticisms that we will shortly review, the third-force movement remains on the periphery of mainstream psychology. Members of the third-force movement have profound disagreements with each other, but there are numerous points of agreement.

1. *Pluralistic methodology.* Third-force theorists believe that methods should be adapted to problems rather than vice versa. They might argue that science does not consist of a single well-defined method applicable in every situation. In the interest of understanding human beings, humanistic psychologists may also employ methods (e.g., literary or artistic methods) that are not in the scientific tradition. The persistence of humanistic psychologists has paid off. In the twenty-first century, the growth of qualitative research, phenomenological studies, and other experiential methods demonstrates the impact of humanistic perspectives on the larger field (Taylor & Martin, 2015).

2. *Opposition to reductionism.* Humanistic psychologists emphasize the uniqueness of human beings and argue against the adequacy of reductionism, models, and analogies (Silani et al., 2013). If we want to understand human nature, we should study humans.

3. *Emphasis on experience.* The primary subject matter for humanistic psychologists is not behavior, unconscious processes, a single dominant motive, learning, or the senses. Rather, the emphasis is on human experience in all its richness and variety. The humanistic psychologist does not leave out anything that is a demonstrable part of human experience (Hardy, 2016). A psychology that omits or reduces anything that is experienced is, to that extent, not an empirical psychology.

4. *Contextualism.* Humanistic psychologists advocate holistic studies that give due attention to natural context. They are concerned that artificial situations may produce effects that cannot be replicated in the everyday world. Though they admit that greater rigor is achieved in artificial situations, they emphasize testing findings in natural context.

5. *Free will.* Humanistic psychologists take the experience of free will at face value; however, they do not deny important and limiting biological and social constraints. Given such constraints, or what Heidegger called "throwness," they still argue for the human capacity to take a stance against opposition, misfortune, or constraint. Free will is tied to attitude or meaning orientation.

6. *Basic human nature.* Humanistic psychologists refuse the pessimistic assumption that human nature is nasty, brutish, and self-seeking. Instead, they believe people are growth-oriented and, in healthy circumstances, display goodness and altruism. Although the lack of discussion of evil by Maslow and Rogers was seen by existential psychologist Rollo May (1982) as a shortcoming that could support claims that humanistic psychology is simplistic (Bohart, 2013; Hoffman, 2009; Schmid, 2013), Rogers's view challenged both behaviorism and psychoanalysis.

7. *Emphasis on relevance.* Humanistic psychologists do not accept hard distinctions between basic and applied studies. They seek a problem-oriented discipline rooted in ecological validity. Their preference is for studies connected to real problems or at least having the promise of being connected to real problems. They do not promote abstract studies with little connection to daily life.

Despite such agreement, third-force psychology is not a coherent system. Many issues and points of disagreement emerge. For example, DeCarvalho (1990) outlined important distinctions between humanistic psychologists and dominant trends in European existentialism. The points outlined previously, however, summarize central themes in third-force psychology. We turn now to criticisms of humanistic psychology.

The third-force critique of behaviorism, psychoanalysis, and other psychologies did not go unanswered. Indeed, numerous counterarguments and criticisms surfaced in the literature (see Child, 1973; Wertheimer, 1978).

1. *What is humanistic psychology?* In a critique of humanistic psychology, Wertheimer (1978) called attention to contradictions and problems associated with the term *humanistic*. It is a term with multiple meanings from the time of the Renaissance. Further, there is the implication that behavioral or psychoanalytic traditions are not humane or humanistic. That problem was illustrated beautifully when the American Humanist Association named B. F. Skinner as their humanist of the year (see Skinner, 1972). Clearly, many psychologists and systems of psychology qualify as humanistic; humanistic psychologists perceive the diversity of practitioners and views to be a strength (Hoffman, 2016).

2. *Views of science.* From its inception, psychology cast its lot on the side of rigor and science. Other approaches (e.g., literary, artistic, philosophical) to the study of human beings have existed for centuries, but a truly rigorous scientific approach is novel and recent. Such an approach may not tell the whole story but deserves a chance, among other approaches, to see what it can accomplish. It is premature to denigrate experimental approaches.

3. *Attitude toward basic scientific studies.* The history of science provides ample evidence for the value of basic studies and the importance of pursuing knowledge for its own sake. The demand for relevance can have a narrowing effect on the intellectual process and thus interfere with the discovery mission of science. Many studies in the history of science would have failed the test of relevance, yet such studies provided the foundations for later breakthrough studies. The insistence on relevance is, at best, anti-intellectual; at worst, it interferes with discovery.

4. *Antireductionistic position.* Many scientists might agree that the study of part processes, or the use of analogies or models, can never do justice to any global phenomenon of interest. At the same time, they argue that science cannot neglect part processes. Indeed, it is the very nature of science to begin with simple elements. Any topic of interest, from a mechanical conveyance such as an automobile to a complex biological event such as a disease, must be approached with due emphasis on all the working parts. A scientific approach to human beings is no different. Wertheimer (1978) argued that the holistic approach of the humanistic psychologists is not consistent with the more informed and scientific holism of Gestalt psychology.

5. *Free will.* The celebration of free will may, in fact, impede progress by blinding psychologists to real but subtle causes. Many traditional psychologists may suspend judgment on whether there is or is not free will, but when they function as scientists, they look for causes. Humanistic belief in free will runs the risk of offering glib accounts of complex events and, thus, of interfering with scientific analysis.

Critics have voiced numerous additional concerns about third-force psychologies (Feltham, 2013). Wertheimer (1978) suggested that their therapeutic procedures are suspect in terms of effecting real change, and Child (1973) accused them of neglecting the hard work of systematic observation so essential in scientific work. In a friendly review of humanistic psychology, Smith (1990) commented on strands of this orientation that are affiliated with various countercultures and spiritual–mystical groups. Some might argue that such affiliations are natural consequences of the general philosophical orientation of this school of thought. In contrast, however, theorists such as Rychlak (1988, 1998) argue that the best of the humanistic tradition will surface in a fairly rigorous psychology that still does justice to the richness and complexity of human experience and behavior. Facets of humanistic psychology continue to shape many areas of practice and scholarship (Bargdill & Broomé, 2015).

Although humanistic psychology has remained on the margins of mainstream psychology, its influence is clearly evident in contemporary interest in positive psychology, as discussed in the next chapter.

Review Questions

1. Why was humanistic psychology referred to as a third force? What are some of the distinguishing features of third-force psychology?
2. Describe at least three features in the thought of William James that identify him as an intellectual forerunner of humanistic psychology.
3. What affinities can you find between third-force psychologies and the philosophy of Unamuno?
4. Identify Kierkegaard's three modes of existence and the specific ways that each one can collapse into an undesirable state.
5. Discuss the meaning of Heidegger's term *Dasein* and the significance of that term for psychology.
6. Define Heidegger's terms *throwness*, *Mitwelt*, and *Umwelt*.
7. Discuss the implications of Husserl's phenomenology for psychology.
8. Why is Franz Brentano included in the intellectual background of third-force psychologies?
9. Outline Maslow's hierarchical theory of motivation and discuss criticisms of the theory that you consider valid.
10. Discuss some of the defining characteristics of a self-actualizing person according to Maslow.
11. Define the concept of *functional autonomy* as employed by Allport. How might a behaviorist explain functional autonomy?
12. Some of Carl Rogers's major contributions to psychology were challenges to standard practices. Discuss two such contributions.
13. What did Rogers mean by *unconditional positive regard*?

14. Describe the major focus of Frankl's logotherapy and show how his concept of *paradoxical intention* might play a role in the treatment of a fear.
15. Advance arguments for or against Rychlak's contention that humanistic psychology can be rigorous.
16. Outline five major criticisms of humanistic psychologies.

Glossary

aesthetic mode of existence According to Kierkegaard, the emphasis on sensual or intellectual pleasure. This mode breeds indifference and boredom and the collapse into melancholy and despair.

Allport, Gordon (1897–1967) Well-known personality psychologist interested in the development of a psychology consistent with the principles of freedom and democracy. His individualistic psychology is consistent with many of the main themes of humanistic or third-force psychologies.

Brentano, Franz (1838–1917) Founder of act psychology (see Chapter 11), which emphasizes intentionality, the unity of consciousness, a broad methodology, and the application of psychology. Brentano's system shares numerous affinities with humanistic psychology.

Dasein Literally, the term refers to "being-in-the-world." The term was employed by Heidegger to refer to a kind of authentic self-awareness along with a deep awareness of the surrounding environment and one's role in that environment.

disciplined naïveté The attempt to approach the phenomena of consciousness while suspending presuppositions so that such phenomena may be captured in their givenness.

ethical mode of existence According to Kierkegaard, the ethical mode of existence is marked by deep concerns for justice, genuine and caring moral concerns, and a capacity to shoulder responsibility. In the face of moral complexities and absurdities, the ethical mode of existence may collapse into a profound sense of irony.

existentialism A philosophical orientation typically traced to the work of Kierkegaard and Unamuno, marked by an emphasis on the centrality of experience, the role of freedom in human life, the irreducible uniqueness of each person, rejection of reductionism, and the quest for authenticity in the face of all of the absurdities and forces that threaten human dignity.

Frankl, Viktor E. (1905–1997) Viennese psychiatrist and founder of a humanistic orientation known as logotherapy. Frankl emphasized the importance of the quest for meaning and the human capacity to construct alternative meaning orientations.

functional autonomy A concept employed by Gordon Allport referring to the possibility that an activity may become independent of its original motivational source and may now become reinforcing in its own right. An example is the person who originally goes to sea to make a living but soon enjoys going to sea in its own right.

Heidegger, Martin (1889–1976) German philosopher and one of the most important existentialists of the twentieth century. Heidegger's work focused on the theoretical meaning of existence and the practical questions of how we should exist individually and collectively in the world.

Husserl, Edmund (1859–1938) German philosopher and founder of phenomenology. He emphasized the uniqueness of consciousness, the dangers of reductionism, and an approach to the study of consciousness that attempts to describe what is naturally there in terms of content, impressions, and meanings.

ideal self According to Rogers, the self as one would like it to be.

idiographic According to Gordon Allport, an approach to the study of personality that emphasizes individual experience. This approach makes use of techniques such as case studies, verbal reports, and interviews.

James, William (1842–1910) American psychologist and philosopher (see Chapter 12) who emphasized the centrality of experience, individualism, a plurality of methods, and the dangers of reductionism. Some of the intellectual traditions in his work are reflected in the work of humanistic psychologists.

Kierkegaard, Søren (1813–1855) Danish philosopher commonly regarded as one of the founders of existentialism. Kierkegaard rejected the concern of rationalist philosophy with the abstractions of the intellect and instead called attention to the daily practical issues that individuals encounter and the problems of coping with those issues in an authentic way.

Leibnizian tradition According to Allport, a tradition that emphasizes the proactive (purposive or goal-directed) nature of human life.

Lockean tradition Allport's expression referring to deterministic and mechanistic approaches to psychology according to which human beings are regarded as primarily reactive or as mere products of social conditioning.

logotherapy Viktor Frankl's approach to psychotherapy emphasizing meaning orientation and the capacity of the individual to appropriate alternative meanings for the events of life.

Maslow, Abraham (1908–1970) One of the important founders and leaders of third-force psychology. Maslow is remembered, among other things, for his hierarchical theory of motivation, his studies on self-actualization, and his emphasis on studying healthy people as a means of building an appropriate database for an adequate psychology.

Mitwelt Heidegger's term for the community or our life with other people.

nomothetic Allport's term for a research orientation that emphasizes statistical abstractions (e.g., means, standard deviations).

noogenic neuroses Frankl's expression referring to the anxiety associated with loss of meaning or a feeling of worthlessness.

paradoxical intention Frankl's expression referring to the capacity to do the very opposite of what one would most like to do. Thus, one who is fearful of flying might prefer to stay home but instead chooses to fly.

phenomenal field An expression employed by Rogers to refer to the entire range of experiences that are part of a person's life.

phenomenology A philosophical orientation and a method for approaching a subject of interest. The method seeks to discover what is given directly in experience itself in contrast to intellectualized content.

religious mode of existence Kierkegaard's expression for an orientation to life marked by a deep sensitivity to one's contingency and dependence on God.

Rogers, Carl R. (1902–1987) One of the most innovative figures in the tradition of humanistic psychology, remembered for his revolutionary attempts to wed psychotherapy with more traditional experimental psychology. His radical emphasis on the person represented a unique war against the authorities of institutions and systems.

Rychlak, Joseph F. (1928–2013) A leader in the humanistic psychology tradition who argued for a rigorous humanistic psychology. He saw no necessary contradictions between humanistic psychology and rigorous scientific practices.

self-actualization A term employed by psychologists such as Kurt Goldstein, Carl Gustav Jung, and Abraham Maslow. The term generally refers to fulfillment of positive potentials.

self-transcendence The capacity of an individual to critically examine her or his worldview and its limitations in relation to more comprehensive and inclusive multicultural perspectives.

third-force psychology A term commonly employed to refer to humanistic psychology viewed as an alternative to behaviorism and psychoanalysis.

throwness Heidegger's term referring to those conditions, forces, or facts that do not easily yield to human effort.

Umwelt Literally, *the world around*. Refers to the physical world or the environment.

Unamuno, Miguel de (1864–1936) Spanish philosopher who was deeply concerned about the dangers of specialization and reductionism. Unamuno also stressed the importance of affect and warned against a purely cognitive or intellectual approach to the problems of psychology.

unconditional positive regard Rogers's term for a belief in the intrinsic worth of another individual. Unconditioned positive regard contrasts with the kind of acceptance or love that comes with conditions.

446

17 Beyond the Systems of Psychology

Psychology is now characterized by a pluralism of conceptual and methodic posit, and of research interest, so great as to suggest a new humility before the actual complexities of the psychological universe: problems are being addressed, rather than—as in the past—evaded or liquidated by premanufactured explanations.
—Sigmund Koch (1986)

The history of psychology from the formal founding in the late nineteenth century to the middle of the twentieth century was commonly understood in terms of dominant and competing systematic visions. We have covered the most influential systems in previous chapters but must now turn to a period of history that witnessed major transitions in the development and organization of the new discipline. The post-World War II era from about 1950 was an age of dynamic transformation in nearly every facet of Western civilization. Scientific, technological, economic, educational, aesthetic, political, and religious enterprises all exhibited accelerating changes. Even more than before, psychology developed at an extraordinary pace, but with few excep-

tions there was less emphasis on the grand old systems and a new emphasis on the development of expertise on more highly focused problems. It was an age of specialization; accelerating knowledge in every field (e.g., medicine, law, biology, physics, psychology) foreclosed on the possibility of grasping the whole of things. With the dawn of the space age and the information age, specialists were replacing generalists. A multitude of innovative instruments, techniques, and ideas came forward resulting in substantive advances in accelerating numbers of content areas of basic experimental psychology and in growing numbers of applications of psychology.

There is no easily accessible way, even for the most knowledgeable generalist, to capture or grasp the enormous details of the growing popularity, breadth, and reach of psychology in the latter half of the twentieth century. By the 1970s and 1980s psychology was often the most popular major on college and university campuses. Suddenly, almost overnight, it seemed psychology was everywhere. The unprecedented proliferation of new interest areas had forced psychology out of the cloistered world of academia and into the wider public domain. Psychology, writ large, has natural ties with all human activities and with a great range of classic academic subjects such as neurology, physiology, the social sciences, business, industry, engineering, architecture, philosophy, and other humanities. Powerful feminist and multicultural movements influenced all the subdisciplinary areas of psychology and fostered productive new ways to think about theory, research, and applications of knowledge. The same can be said for the effects of a growing emphasis on animal rights and for the emergence of ecology as an urgent multidisciplinary area of concern.

The latter half of the twentieth century also witnessed a rediscovery of consciousness, experience, and mind as legitimate topics for scientific and professional psychology. This rediscovery will be discussed shortly in a section on cognitive psychology. If psychology started as a basic science, its very nature proved highly relevant to almost everything associated with human and animal life. Little wonder then that the discipline, like medicine, would ultimately include a basic science component along with an enormous professional component.

The Systems of Psychology in Retrospect

In what follows, we discuss some of the specialties that were dominant in the latter half of the twentieth century. These include: clinical psychology and related fields, biopsychology, social psychology, and industrial–organizational psychology. Few psychologists identified with structuralist, functionalist, and Gestalt systems though there were significant numbers who continued to identify with psychoanalytic, humanistic, and neobehaviorist schools of thought. Even within these orientations, however, there were remarkable variations with respect to methodologies, assumptions, and the kinds of problems to be addressed. Before moving to a discussion of some of the dominant specialties, we briefly explore

the continuing influence of psychoanalytic, humanistic, and neobehaviorist orientations as well as the more pervasive influence of cognitive psychology.

Psychoanalysis

Throughout his life, Sigmund Freud encountered both rejection and acceptance of his work. The political climate in Germany during the 1930s was not conducive to the advancement of psychoanalysis. Jahoda (1969) pointed out, "In October 1933 psychoanalysis was banned from the Congress of Psychology in Leipzig as a 'Jewish science'; soon after that psychoanalytic literature was burned, and the community of practicing psychoanalysts dispersed rapidly to save their lives and livelihoods" (p. 420). This unfortunate trend escalated after Freud's death in 1939 (Gitre, 2011). Despite a troubled history, psychoanalysis achieved gains in Western psychology and remained a significant force in psychotherapy during the 1950s (Lazarus, 2000; Kuriloff, 2014).

A proliferation of journals attest to the endurance of psychoanalysis in the West following World War II. In 1909, Sigmund Freud and Eugen Bleuler (1857–1939) established the first psychoanalytic periodical, the *Jahrbuch für Psychoanalytische und Psychopathologische Forschungen*. Later, psychoanalytic journals such as *Imago* (1912) and the *Internationale Zeitschrift für Psychoanalyse* (1913) struggled during Freud's lifetime. However, since that time a large number of psychoanalytic publications have continued to flourish in the English-speaking world including the *Psychoanalytic Review* (1913), *American Imago* (1944), the *American Psychoanalytic Association Journal* (1952), the *Journal of Analytic Psychology* (1955), *Contemporary Psychoanalysis* (1964), and *Modern Psychoanalysis* (1976). Noteworthy for psychologists, the American Psychological Association launched the journal *Psychoanalytic Psychology* in 1984 to serve as the official publication of the Division of Psychoanalysis. Lewis

(1984) noted that the purpose of the journal was to integrate research and clinical work and to "pursue questions wherever they may lead." The *Encyclopedia of Associations* (see Burek et al., 1989) listed over forty national and international psychoanalytic societies. As noted in Chapter 16, psychoanalytic theory and practice evolved from the time of Freud and are now marked by increasingly pluralistic perspectives with some common ground (see Gabbard et al., 2012; Gideon, 2016; Katz, 2014; Newirth, 2015; Rudnytsky, 2011).

Nevertheless, some scholars are skeptical about the future of psychoanalysis. Eissler (1965) long ago warned that psychoanalysis was vulnerable to attacks from religion, government, biological and sociological perspectives, and especially medical orthodoxy. Recognizing the validity of such criticism, many psychoanalysts have worked to nullify such dangers (Kirsner, 2001). For example, the American Psychoanalytic Association established criteria during the 1930s that required psychoanalysts to attend medical school. However, in a landmark 1988 out-of-court decision against medical orthodoxy, psychoanalysts began recognizing the right of Ph.D.s to seek psychoanalytic training (Buie, 1988). This bold step broadened the base of psychoanalysis and helped ensure its future; questions of appropriate training continue to raise questions in psychoanalysis (Helmut, 2015).

The advancement of psychodynamic theory may depend upon its unique contributions to research (Weinberger et al., 2000). Gilgen (1982) claimed that psychoanalysis has made numerous contributions to the post-World War II study of developmental psychology, motivation, personality, and abnormal psychology. Silverman (1976) reported several psychoanalytic programs that have found scientific evidence for the relationship between psychopathology and unconscious wishes. Furthermore, Baars (1986) claimed that experimental psychologists have too often ignored psychodynamic theory, making it "the single greatest neglected topic in contemporary scientific psychology" (p. 412). Although the American fascination with psy-

choanalysis remains (Roth, 1998), its influence on psychotherapy has been diminished by the growth of humanistic psychology, expansion of behavior and cognitive therapies, and the growing intersection of psychiatry and neuroscience (Goldberg, 2015).

Humanistic Psychology

In an overview of the history of humanistic psychologies, DeCarvalho (1990) noted that "Some psychologists during the 'golden age' of behaviorism of post World War II, discontented with behaviorism's view of human nature and method, drew on a long tradition linking psychology with humanities and in a rebellious manner institutionally founded humanistic psychology" (pp. 22–23). This rebellious manner began with an informal 1954 mailing list distributed by Abraham Maslow to 125 psychologists who identified with the humanistic rejection of psychoanalysis and neobehaviorism.

As the list of followers grew, plans were made to establish an official humanistic psychology organization (DeCarvalho, 1992). The institutional support structure for the new orientation included the founding of the *Journal of Humanistic Psychology* in 1961 and the founding of the American Association of Humanistic Psychology (AAHP), later renamed the Association of Humanistic Psychology. James F. T. Bugental (1915–2008) was elected as the AAHP's first president. Over one hundred members attended the first national meeting, held in Philadelphia in 1963. In November 1964, the premier figures in humanistic psychology attended a conference held in Old Saybrook, Connecticut. Abraham Maslow, James Bugental, Carl Rogers, Gordon Allport, Jacques Barzun, Charlotte Bühler, George Kelly, Rollo May, Gardner Murphy, and Henry Murray were among the participants (DeCarvalho, 1990). In the early 1970s, a coalition of over three hundred psychologists established Division 32 of the American Psychological Association (APA), titled the Division of Humanistic Psychology.

Although institutionalized by U.S. psychologists, humanistic psychology has broad appeal in other countries. DeCarvalho (1991) claimed that "Outside of the United States, primarily in South America, humanistic psychology has been as popular as behaviorism has been inside the United States" (p. 151). Indeed, recent decades have witnessed ambitious efforts to promote humanistic psychology on an increasingly global level; for example, in September 1983, 150 North American psychologists visited the former Soviet Union as delegates for the Association of Humanistic Psychology (Hassard, 1990). In the following years, AHP and Soviet exchange conferences were held in Moscow, Leningrad, Tblisi, Vilnius, and Kiev. In 1986, Carl Rogers gave the keynote address to two thousand North American and Soviet psychologists and educators at the USSR Academy of Pedagogical Science. Such multicultural projects have shared insights into practice and theory, fostered collaboration on mutual problems, and produced international recognition for humanistic psychology.

In the 1970s and 1980s, an increasing number of educational programs provided graduate courses and degrees with a humanistic orientation. Additional social support structures have emerged, including institutes, correspondence courses, and seminars. With this growth and the prompting of Rychlak (1988) and others, humanistic psychologists have considered adopting more rigorous and scientific methods (Cain, 2002; Schneider et al., 2001; Sheldon & Kasser, 2001). In his presidential address to Division 32, M. Brewster Smith (1990) argued that the natural sciences play a complementary role in the development of humanistic psychology. At present, several humanistic centers, such as Saybrook University, have established programs that offer challenging new directions for humanistic psychology in the twenty-first century. Humanistic psychologists have also called for greater interactions with other fields, including neuroscience and anthropology (Houston, 2013), and integration of humanistic and positive psychology has been fruitful for both fields (Friedman, 2013).

Humanistic psychology and closely related fields such as existential psychology and phenomenological psychology remain somewhat on the periphery of the larger discipline, especially in the United States. Nevertheless, there are significant numbers of scholars and practitioners who remain dedicated to this orientation.

Neobehaviorism and the Psychology of Learning

Neobehaviorism prospered as the dominant orientation in American psychology in the latter part of the twentieth century (see Mackintosh, 1997). The neobehaviorism movement attained its apex of popularity under B. F. Skinner, possibly the most celebrated psychologist in the last half of the twentieth century. Gilgen (1982) reported that a random sampling of scholars in the history of psychology and members of the APA rated Skinner as both the most important person and the most important influence in U.S. psychology during the post-World War II period (see also "Visible Scientists," 1975). Rutherford (2009) shows how Skinner's laboratory work migrated to the public arena, especially from the 1950s to the 1970s. For some, the Skinnerian approach to psychology amounted to nothing less than a philosophical worldview. Skinner's experimental behavior analysis attracted countless researchers and practitioners (Staddon, 2014). Based on careful observation, perseverance, and serendipity, Skinner compiled a corpus of work that revolutionized the study of learning and contributed to applied and clinical psychology (Gitre, 2011).

Aside from Skinner's ascendancy, other neobehaviorists prioritized the psychology of learning but with radically different approaches. As noted in Chapter 13, there were varieties of theoretical orientations within the neobehaviorist movement. The psychologies of Clark Hull, Edward Tolman, and Edwin Guthrie focused on a considerable range of problems such as habit breaking, the role and nature of reinforcement, the minimal conditions required for learning, and the transfer effects from one problem to another.

Another important approach to learning was inspired by linguist Noam Chomsky (1959) and by Harvard professor Jerome Bruner who called attention to the role of language or verbal learning in human learning. Bruner (1964), in a lead article in the *American Psychologist*, celebrated the enormous flexibility in learning afforded by language, noting that "language provides a means, not only for representing experience, but also for transforming it . . . Not only, if you will, did the dog bite the man, but the man was bitten by the dog" (p. 4). Language provides the natural mediating basis for such a transformation as it affords easy leaps from one idea or behavior to another. A new emphasis on language, and what was sometimes referred to as transformation grammars, challenged the adequacy of the strict mechanistic explanations preferred by behavioristic psychologies. Other approaches to learning, somewhat tangential to neobehaviorism, surfaced in the late twentieth century. Examples are found in the work of Harry Harlow and Albert Bandura.

Harry Fredrick Harlow (1905–1981) was born in Fairfeld, Iowa, and received an English degree at Stanford University. He started his academic career in English, but later switched to psychology. He was awarded a Ph.D. in experimental psychology from Stanford University in 1930. Shortly after graduating, Harlow was hired as an assistant professor at the University of Wisconsin at Madison, where he founded the Primate Laboratory and directed it until 1974 (Blum, 2011). Harlow served as editor of the *Journal of Comparative and Physiological Psychology* from 1951 to 1963, and as president of the APA in 1958. He published numerous books and articles on topics such as learning, motivation, and social isolation.

Among other things, Harlow is remembered for the importance of his emphasis on learning to learn. A phrase such as "learning to learn" has intuitive appeal for those who were once poor learners, but who experienced a turnaround to suddenly become good learners. Harlow (1949) tested form discrimination in monkeys using an apparatus he invented known as the **Wisconsin General Test Apparatus**. Monkeys were confined in a cage while a variety of stimulus objects were presented on a horizontal tray inserted through a small opening in the cage. The stimulus objects were placed over small depressions that contained a desirable food reward. The monkey was trained to select a particular object; if the object sheltered a food reward, the animal could remove the object and eat the food reward. A screen could also be lowered to allow the experimenter to create a new pattern of objects and stimuli. Although the task proved difficult at first, the monkey eventually made fewer and fewer errors. According to Harlow, the primate had formed a **learning set**; the monkey's previous experience had facilitated the ability to discriminate among new stimuli. Harlow's research on learning sets, or learning to learn, was a promising method for the study of learning ability in primates and humans. The procedures he employed became part of a typical testing procedure in clinical neuropsychology (see Eling & Maes, 2008).

Another of Harlow's enduring contributions was the study of attachment in baby monkeys. Harlow's work demonstrated the learning of affectional ties based on the quality of tactile stimulation. His work suggested that we learn to love and we learn to bond based on the quality of our surroundings. In a famous study, Harlow (1958) employed "mother surrogates" constructed of either wire or terry cloth. From a psychological standpoint wire is much colder to the touch than cloth and much less desirable. Harlow demonstrated that the quality of tactile stimulation afforded by a cloth figure produced greater attachment and better adjustment for baby monkeys than the colder features of a wire figure (Vicedo, 2009). Harlow also documented the detrimental effects of isolation on social interaction in young rhesus monkeys, as well as the persistence of these effects into adulthood (Kobak, 2012; Vicedo, 2010, 2013).

There were additional new developments in the psychology of learning. For example,

Albert Bandura (b. 1925) was born in Canada to hard-working immigrant parents, whose values about work shaped his life and career (Ortiz, 2015). He advanced a social learning theory focused on observational learning and modeling. According to Bandura, learning is not based exclusively on simple mechanical S–R connections or reinforcement–response connections. Bandura showed that we learn through observation and imitation, and that reinforcement does not always have to be directly experienced. We can learn vicariously through observing effects on others. As with Skinner, Bandura's ideas have found successful application in clinical settings (see Follette & Callaghan, 2011; Schunk, 2012) and career counseling (Lent, 2016).

We turn next to a very broad movement inspired partly by the neobehaviorists, verbal learning theorists, and the work of people such as Harlow and Bandura. The movement, known as cognitive psychology, has touched virtually all the subdisciplinary areas of psychology.

Cognitive Psychology

According to the Oxford English Dictionary the term *cognitive* as an adjective refers in a wide sense to processes of knowing, and these processes presumably include sensing, perceiving, remembering, recognizing, apprehending, and thinking. The related adjective *cognizant* has often been used in a legal sense to include a wide conscious awareness of context as well as awareness of the causal forces active in a given situation. Cognitive psychology brings us back to the interior mental world of consciousness and experience. Recall that John B. Watson, who stood at the headwaters of American behaviorism, had argued that the mental world, including consciousness, is altogether unfit for scientific study. Another early behaviorist, Albert P. Weiss, saw psychology as a branch of physics. In both

cases, we basically study only the exterior world of structures and movements.

But in the 1960s and 1970s there was growing discontent among many psychologists with the narrowness of behavioristic psychologies. Explanations based purely on external forces seemed artificial, contrived, thin, and anemic. Something was clearly missing. Classically, the word *empirical* was basically a synonym for the word *experience*. Extreme mechanistic psychologies had departed from their original empirical roots. Wilhelm Wundt along with other early pioneers studied consciousness, and the study of experience was a central organizing feature of the psychology and philosophy of William James. Gestalt psychologist Wolfgang Köhler was especially vocal in his intense critical treatment of behavioristic psychologies.

The new emphasis on cognitive psychology was illustrated in the work of numerous scholars (e.g., Bermúdez, 2010; Brook, 2006; Gardner, 1985; Robins et al., 1999) who explored a great range of topics such as memory, pattern recognition, reasoning, child and adult development, and artificial intelligence (Gardner, 1985). According to Neisser (1967), "The term 'cognition' refers to all the processes by which the sensory input is transformed, reduced, elaborated, stored, recovered, and used" (p. 4). Lachman, Lachman, and Butterfield (1979) noted that the cognitive psychologist is "a scientist motivated to understand a natural system consisting of the human higher mental processes" (p. 6). In what follows, we will consider dominant themes, substantive areas, and critiques of cognitive psychology. But first we will consider some of the influences that led to the founding of this orientation.

Intellectual Traditions

The study of mental events dates from the time of the pre-Socratic philosophers, but the experimental approach to cognitive processes is a product of the nineteenth and twentieth centuries (Greenwood, 1999). As we have seen in previous chapters, the writings of pioneers such as Franz Brentano, William James, Wilhelm Wundt, John Dewey, and Sigmund Freud all exhibited keen interest in mental events as central to a science of human nature. We look now in a little more detail at the work of some of the precursors of cognitive psychology.

HERMANN EBBINGHAUS   Prior to the work of Hermann Ebbinghaus there had been suspicions that basic memorial processes could not be studied scientifically. But with the use of nonsense syllables, Ebbinghaus was able to neutralize the contaminating effects of previous associations on memory and to experimentally study such problems as number of repetitions required to memorize a list of materials as well as retention of learned materials as a function of time. Complex mental events were thus quantified, and experimental findings could be replicated. A classic behaviorist could argue that Ebbinghaus was studying nothing but behavior, but the cognitive psychologist could argue that Ebbinghaus had found a way to subject previously private mental events to scientific and public scrutiny.

FREDERICK C. BARTLETT   Another important pioneer in the study of cognitive psychology was Sir **Frederick Charles Bartlett (1886–1969)**, who strongly rejected the idea that thinking, memory, and other cognitive processes are based on the mechanical laws of association or simple stimulus–response connections. According to Bartlett, cognitive themes or *schemas* govern mental processes and these schemas exert a compelling influence on the way original information is processed and later retrieved. For example, tell a person a short story and then ask the person to remember the story. The initial processing of the story will not take place on a blank slate. The person will process the story in a complex schema consisting of predispositions, mental sets, a worldview, stereotypes, religious and political prejudices, and more. Now ask the person to remember the story at various later time intervals. Bartlett (1932) found that as greater

intervals of time passed, participants made more errors in retrieval and substitution. A short story with a political theme is likely to be processed, elaborated, and remembered differently by a conservative Republican than a liberal Democrat. Bartlett believed his results demonstrated thematic frameworks that modified and organized new information. Some scholars argue that Bartlett's investigations of illusions in memory mark the beginning of the study of false memories (Neuschatz et al., 2007).

Bartlett accepted the objective method of the behaviorists but was critical of behaviorism, which he likened to a dangerous religious movement (Bartlett, 1923). Although a prominent figure in early British psychology (Collins, 2006), Bartlett, because of his mentalistic orientation, was largely ignored during the neobehaviorist era of the 1940s and 1950s. However, cognitive researchers interested in schematic and reconstructive processes in memory have rediscovered his ideas (Brewer, 2000; Iran-Nejad & Winsler, 2000; Neisser, 1982).

JEAN PIAGET AND COGNITIVE DEVELOPMENT Born in Neuchâtel, Switzerland, **Jean Piaget (1896–1980)** was a devoted student of biology and zoology. Although he was trained in the biological sciences, Piaget's interest in developmental psychology was evident in his first psychology article titled "Relationship between Psychoanalysis and Child Psychology," published in 1920. Two decades later, he had published six major books on developmental topics such as language, intelligence, moral judgment, reasoning, causality, and the construction of reality in children as well as sociological perspectives on child development (Hsueh, 2004). Beginning with his early research on intelligence, Piaget conducted extensive interviews with children rather than administering tests in a standardized manner, and his clinical methods developed as he worked (Mayer, 2005; Hill & Millar, 2015). He also pursued cross-cultural studies (Oesterdiekhoff, 2013). According to Gruber and Vonèche (1977), this unorthodox study of cognition proved to be insightful: "What had been at the outset nothing but a boring and annoying test situation became a real dialogue with suggestions and counter suggestions, an argument developed, a deepening of the child's thought, a new method of interrogating children was born" (p. 53).

Such methods led Piaget to develop a general theory of genetic epistemology that stressed the activation of schemas within serially progressive structural stages (Ferrari et al., 2001). He insisted that cognition develops in a sequence from sensory-motor coordination to abstract reasoning. In 1940, as professor at the University of Geneva, he continued studying the genesis of human knowledge (Burman, 2012). His ideas continue to inspire thought and debate (Martí & Rodríguez, 2012).

Although regarded for his contributions, Piaget was not the first psychologist to advance a cognitive theory of development. As we have seen, Charles Darwin, G. Stanley Hall, Kurt Koffka, and James Mark Baldwin also offered insight into the intellectual development of children.

GESTALT PSYCHOLOGY AND EDWARD TOLMAN Like Bartlett, the Gestalt psychologists rejected the rigid associationism encountered in behaviorism. The influences and similarities between Gestalt theory and cognitive psychology have not gone unnoticed. Indeed, Neisser credited the Gestalt psychologists with providing the early impetus for the study of cognition (see Baars, 1986, p. 274). Several research areas exhibit a Gestalt orientation, including memory and cognition (German & Defeyter, 2000; Kelley & Nairne, 2001; Murray, 1995), human factors research (Foley & Moray, 1987), visual neuroscience (Wertheimer, 1999), evolutionary psychology (Murray & Farahmand, 1998), organizational theories of learning (Baddeley, 1990), artificial intelligence (Guberman & Wojtkowski, 2001), and perception (Chen, 2001; Kellman, 2000).

Edward Tolman, also influenced by the Gestalt tradition, was a key figure in the history of cognitive psychology. Tolman forged an uneasy alliance with neobehaviorism but did not acquiesce to popular explanations of psychology based on material and efficient causality. His concept of purpose presented a fresh theoretical alternative to neobehaviorism (Dewsbury, 2000; Fuller, 2013). Indeed, Tolman's penchant for cognition is evident in concepts such as cognitive maps, sign expectancies, and means–end hierarchies (Innis, 1999; Tolman, 1932). His legacy is evident in later research in computer science and cognitive neuroscience (Goldman, 1999).

Themes and Content Areas of Cognitive Psychology

Cognitive psychology can be distinguished by several dominant themes. The first involves the early influence of the **information-processing metaphor**, the idea that mental events operate in much the same way as a computer (Bower, 2000). More specifically, the organism is conceived as a sophisticated processor of information. For example, memory might entail the processing of information in successive stages or levels (such as sensory memory, working memory, and long-term memory) before the execution of a response. For this reason, cognitive psychology was sometimes referred to as *information-processing psychology*.

The information-processing approach enjoyed early support within the cognitive framework (Garnham, 2009). For example, cognitive psychologists depicted theoretical representations of cognition by using flowcharts, a method borrowed from computer science, which characterize the serial processing of information into various stages. The nomenclature of the cognitivists also exhibited a distinct computer flavor. The term *stimulus* was occasionally replaced with *cue* or *input*, and *response* was replaced with *output process*. The memory concepts of *encoding*, *storage*, and *retrieval* reflected the bond between cognitive psychology and computer science. According to Lachman and colleagues (1979), this new nomenclature was more than just substitution; the terms "are pointers to a conceptual infrastructure that defines an approach to a subject matter . . . It implies different beliefs about the behavior's origin, its history, and its explanation" (p. 99).

A second theme in cognitive psychology concerns the role of the participant in cognitive experimentation. Many neobehaviorists conceptualized the individual as a passive receiver of information in whom associative bonds guide the organization of material in a linear fashion. By contrast, the cognitive psychologists followed the Gestalt psychologists and Tolman by assigning a more dynamic role to the organism. The individual is viewed as an active organizer of information using hierarchical schemas or other processes.

Finally, it would be naïve to assume that cognitive psychology evolved without some residue of influence from verbal learning and neobehaviorism (Lachman et al., 1979). From these approaches, cognitive psychology inherited a robust empirical approach grounded in laboratory research, and it also inherited learning as a topic area but with renewed interest in cognitive phenomena and explanations (Gardner, 1985; Leahey, 2013). In general, cognitive psychology has further adopted from its predecessors a nomothetic or general explanation of cognitive phenomena rather than an idiographic perspective.

From its inception, cognitive psychology has been characterized as one of the most pluralistic and interdisciplinary movements in the history of psychology. Indeed, cognitive research has spilled over and intertwined with growing cognitive interest in other areas, so that on occasion the larger field has been called "cognitive science" to reflect its interdisciplinary orientation (Gardner, 1985). Cognitive science is an apt title because scholars in philosophy, anthropology, engineering, neuroscience, linguistics, artificial intelligence, and computer science have identified in one way or another with the study of cognitive processes (Gentner, 2010). Research on memory, attention, problem solving, judgment and decision making, concept formation, language, pattern recognition, artificial intelligence,

and human development have all emerged as mainstream fields of cognitive science. Advances in methodology and technology, including new brain-imaging techniques, allow greater interdisciplinary connections (Boden, 2006). Additionally, research in behavioral genetics and neuroscience holds great promise for the emerging field of cognitive neuroscience (Kolb, 1999). Likewise, information processing has become almost an addiction among some social psychologists who study social cognition (Schneider, 1991).

Critical Appraisal of Cognitive Psychology

Norman (1980) wrote a perceptive article that outlined twelve issues that have been neglected by cognitive scientists. He argued that the science of cognition has neglected but should not ignore belief systems, consciousness, development, emotion, interaction, language, learning, memory, perception, performance, skill, and thought. Norman called for both a reconsideration of some popular research areas (e.g., memory, language, and perception) and a further examination of skill and interaction. It should also be noted that one of the definitions of the term *cognition* in the Oxford English Dictionary emphasizes processes of knowing including sensation, perception, and conception as distinguished from emotion and motivation. In contrast with purely mechanical systems, we are creatures with empathic qualities; we feel and we strive toward ends with aesthetic qualities. Can cognitive science separate reason from emotion and continue to claim to study humans (Maiese, 2016)? These ideas are problematic for the computer and information processing metaphor so often invoked in the cognitive movement.

THE COMPUTER METAPHOR In the Victorian era, Cambridge mathematician Charles Babbage (1792–1871) devoted years toward the invention of calculating machines. In 1834, he

455

introduced his most ambitious invention, the Analytical Engine. Ada B. Lovelace (1815–1852), although born the daughter of Lord Byron, rejected poetry in favor of mathematics and science. In 1843, she wrote a paper about Babbage's Analytical Engine, which became the "first published example of what could be called a computer program—written over a century before the emergence of the technology needed to run it" (Woolley, 1999, pp. 1–2). As Green (2001a) observed, the work of Babbage and Lovelace also introduced the possibility of a nineteenth-century cognitive science.

During the mid-twentieth century, the computer metaphor of mind liberated cognitive psychology from neobehaviorism. In this context, a computational cognitive science provided a rigorous account of intentionality (Green, 2000) and addressed a growing frustration with the narrow disciplinary vision of neobehaviorism (Crowther-Heyck, 2000). One serious limitation of computer models of humans is that computers cannot (yet) readily model irrational behavior (Krueger, 2012). Among others, Roediger (1980) found value in the computer metaphor, but warned of other erratic trends in the history of psychology:

> The information processing approach has been an important source of models and ideas, but the fate of its predecessors should serve to keep us humble concerning its eventual success. In 30 years, the computer-based information processing approach that currently reigns may seem as invalid a metaphor to the human mind as the wax-tablet or telephone-switchboard models do today. Unless today's technology has somehow reached its ultimate development, and we can be certain it has not, then we have not reached the ultimate metaphor for the human mind, either.
> (p. 244)

MENTALISM Among a number of critics (Uttal, 2000), B. F. Skinner was a resolute antagonist of the mentalistic foundation of cognitive psychology. Skinner (1963) voiced early concern about cognitive psychology's dependence on a mental rather than behavioral orientation. Troubled by the terminology of cognitive psychologists, Skinner (1987c) argued against the faddish nature of mentalistic language: "A curve showing the appearance of the word *cognitive* in the psychological literature would be interesting. A first rise could probably be seen around 1960; the subsequent acceleration would be exponential. Is there any field of psychology today in which something does not seem to be gained by adding that charming adjective to the occasional noun?" (p. 783).

He further asserted that science should have a language, but one that is founded on objectively defined terminology. Skinner (1989) used etymological data to demonstrate that cognitive terms are not novel descriptors but merely reformulations of previous physical and behavioral nomenclature. Thus, words such as *mind*, *thinking*, *doing*, *waiting*, and *sensing* do not warrant inclusion in the psychologist's vocabulary.

Skinner (1977) believed that cognitive psychology was a threatening obstacle in the evolution of a scientific psychology. In his final publication, he found similarity in the tension between cognitive psychology and radical behaviorism and the older dissension between creationist explanations and evolutionary theory. Like Darwin, Skinner (1990) advanced a position that was plagued with opposition:

> After almost a century and a half, evolution is still not widely understood . . . A creation science has been proposed to be taught in its place. The role of variation and selection in the behavior of the individual suffers from the same opposition. Cognitive science is the creation science of psychology, as it struggles to maintain the position of mind.
> (p. 1209)

Meanwhile, Skinner (1987b) concluded, "Let us bring behaviorism back from the Devil's Island to which it was transported for a crime it never committed, and let psychology become once again a behavioral science" (p. 111).

ECOLOGICAL VALIDITY Although recognized as a founder of cognitive psychology, Ulric Neisser has voiced concern about the artificial nature of this orientation. After numerous discussions with J. J. Gibson (1904–1979), a leader in the field of perception, Neisser revised many early ideas in his landmark text on cognitive psychology. Borrowing from Gibson's approach, Neisser (1976) claimed that **ecological validity** is absent in cognitive psychology research. In other words, many cognitive experiments on mental events are artificial; they are hard to generalize to real-world experience. Neisser (1976) declared that "The study of information processing . . . has not yet committed itself to any conception of human nature that could apply beyond the confines of the laboratory" (p. 6).

Neisser (1982) edited *Memory Observed: Remembering in Natural Contexts*, a volume of ecologically valid research on topics such as flashbulb memories (vivid memories of salient events such as John Kennedy's assassination or the 2001 terrorist attack on the World Trade Center), mnemonics (memory aids that promote efficient retrieval), memorists (people with exceptional memory), and eyewitness testimony. Neisser's plea for ecological soundness provides an intriguing challenge for cognitive psychologists.

Finally, we may ask whether cognitive psychology signifies a paradigm shift. Despite cognitive psychology's relatively short existence, historical treatises on the so-called cognitive revolution have been written (Baars, 1986; Gardner, 1985); but the idea of a revolution has been challenged (e.g., Leahey, 1992). An accurate evaluation of cognitive psychology must wait until a later date to be based on an adequate perspective.

Clinical Psychology and Related Fields

At present, the largest divisions of the APA include: Division 12 (Society of Clinical Psychology), Division 42 (Division of Independent Practice), Division 40 (Clinical Neuropsychology), Division 29 (Psychotherapy), and Division 39 (Psychoanalysis). Clinical psychology and related areas such as counseling and school psychology play a critical and increasingly visible role in contemporary society. Interest in clinical problems and the challenges of adjustment has been a part of psychology from its earliest days. Prior to the formal founding of psychology there were varieties of practitioners providing counseling and assessment, including phrenologists and spiritualists among others (Cautin et al., 2013). Near the nineteenth century's end, abnormal psychology came of age during unprecedented reform in the United States (Reisman, 1991). In the 1890s William James was teaching a course at Harvard titled "Mental Pathology." Richardson (2006) notes that the course was "what would today be called abnormal psychology" (p. 334). Inspired by William James, the Boston School of "psychotherapeutics" included scholars such as Henry Bowditch (1808–1892), Richard Cabot (1868–1939), Morton Prince (1854–1929), James Jackson Putnam (1846–1918), and Boris Sidis (1867–1923). *Psychotherapeutics* reflected the optimism and social activism of the Progressive Era (King et al., 2013). As the center for psychotherapeutics, the Boston School became the foremost authority on scientific psychotherapy during the period (Taylor, 2000).

Developments in Europe, especially Sigmund Freud's founding of psychoanalysis, demonstrated a growing responsiveness to psychological problems of living. Despite Freud's medical training, he rejected the medical model he encountered in Meynert's clinic in Vienna. After the failure of his *Project for a Scientific Psychology*, Freud turned his attention to a more psychological approach to issues encountered in his clinic.

Although Wilhelm Wundt's research focused on the senses as windows to the mind, his larger vision may have influenced students and associates such as Emil Kraepelin and Lightner Witmer to study theoretical and practical problems of adjustment (Routh, 2011). As noted in Chapter 10, the lead article in Witmer's journal, *The Psychological Clinic*, called for a new discipline to be named "clinical psychology" (see McReynolds, 1987, p. 852). Witmer envisioned a discipline that would involve both testing and treatment. In its earliest incarnation, however, clinical psychology was identified far more with testing than therapy in the formal sense.

Critical Developments

Psychological testing existed prior to 1914, but the testing movement didn't gain momentum until World War I. During that period, psychologists demonstrated the value of their skills in vital areas such as assessment, selection, research, and leadership. Subsequently, the applied branches of the discipline enjoyed strong positions in academic training programs and in the industrial world. Several early scholars attempted to establish standards for training for clinical psychologists (Farreras, 2016), and in 1917, a handful of clinicians formed the American Association of Clinical Psychologists (AACP). The organization was short-lived, but the AACP stimulated professional changes, leading to the creation of the Clinical Section of the APA in 1919. Despite clinical psychology's modest inroads in personality and intelligence testing, psychiatry continued to dominate the more prestigious therapeutic side of the helping professions.

During World War II, however, clinical psychology discovered a new momentum (Routh, 2013). With an escalating number of Allied troops suffering from "shell-shock," an earlier term for what is now called *posttraumatic stress disorder* (Monson et al., 2007), psychiatrists were forced to relinquish their stranglehold on the mental health field. Consequently, more and more psychologists were pressed into service to evaluate *and* treat enlisted soldiers and veterans. In some cases, experimental psychologists with no clinical training contributed to the effort; many found the work so rewarding that it produced a "mass exodus" from the laboratory to the clinic (Hathaway, 1958).

In many respects, World War II provided a vital catalyst for the birth of clinical psychology in the modern sense (Street, 2006). As psychologists enjoyed greater responsibility as therapists, the area experienced a surge in interest. The Allied effort during the war enlisted the aid of around 1,500 psychologists, the majority coming from the academic or government sector. However, about three times as many psychologists worked in clinical settings in the postwar environment compared to the years leading up to the war (Andrews & Dreese, 1948). Clinical psychology was experiencing growing pains.

In response to rising interest, the APA established accreditation standards and evaluations for graduate training programs. American psychologist **David Shakow (1901–1980)** became the principal architect of clinical training after World War II (Barlow, 2011; Cautin, 2006). During a career that spanned six decades, Shakow developed methods for clinical research and contributed extensively to the literature on schizophrenia (Cautin, 2008). Additionally, Shakow (1942) envisioned a graduate curriculum in clinical psychology that included an internship in the third year. His wartime article also called for the establishment of a specialty board to certify clinical psychologists. (Following his lead, the APA later established the American Board of Examiners in Professional Psychology.) Impressed with his work, APA president Carl Rogers asked Shakow to chair a committee charged with defining educational and training standards for the emerging discipline of clinical psychology. Based on the committee's recommendations, the "Shakow Report" was presented at the 1947 APA convention and later adopted as APA policy.

Despite swelling interest in clinical psychology, many postwar Veterans Administration hospitals were understaffed and unprepared to meet the demand of treating veterans with psychiatric disorders (Farreras et al., 2016). Cautin (2006) observed that the "training of clinical psychologists thus became an immediate priority—and not just within the field of psychology. Governmental agencies such as the U.S. Public Health Service (USPHS) and the Veterans Administration also recognized this imperative; the former was primarily interested in developing a national mental health policy, and the latter in meeting the clinical needs of its clients" (p. 216).

The agencies took action, making a push to fund graduate programs in clinical psychology (Cautin & Baker, 2014). In 1949, David Shakow traveled to Colorado where he joined seventy colleagues for the two-week Boulder Conference on Graduate Education in Clinical Psychology (Petersen, 2007). Organized by the APA and subsidized by the USPHS, the conference goal was to determine training models and practices for clinical psychology. The "Shakow Report" set the agenda for the famous Boulder Conference (Baker & Benjamin, 2000). Hosted by University of Colorado psychologist Victor C. Raimy (1950), the conference addressed the pressing need to establish guidelines for clinical training in the postwar environment. In what became known as the **Boulder model**, it recommended that doctoral programs train clinical psychologists as research-practitioners (Petersen, 2007). The model's authors advised that students develop solid backgrounds in general and clinical psychology through classroom instruction, learn applied professional skills through extensive supervised experience, and acquire training in research. Within this view, clinical research and clinical practice are not separate fields but inform each other (Antony & Roemer, 2011).

In addition to solidifying clinical psychology's identity as separate from psychiatry, the Boulder model promoted professional clinicians who were solid researchers and could adapt their clinical work to emerging findings in a changing scientific field. In 1992, directors of an overwhelming majority of ninety doctoral programs in clinical psychology claimed to follow the Boulder model (O'Sullivan & Quevillon, 1992), and enthusiasm for the model persists into the twenty-first century (Norcross et al., 2005).

In the wake of the Boulder Conference, ethical guidelines were established to direct practicing therapists. In 1953, the APA adopted a Code of Ethical Standards of Psychologists and, since that time, Handelsman and colleagues (2005; Anderson & Handelsman, 2009; Knapp, Gottlieb, & Handelsman, 2015) and others have emphasized the importance of teaching ethics to clinicians and other psychologists. Around the same time, a proliferation of journals emerged with titles such as the *Journal of Clinical Psychology*, the *Journal of Counseling Psychology*, and many others.

Despite its popularity, numerous critics have attacked the Boulder model. A persistent objection came from students who wanted a graduate education grounded more in practical clinical experience than in clinical scholarship. Almost a quarter-century after the Boulder Conference, Colorado hosted another seminal conference when the National Conference on Levels and Patterns of Professional Training in Psychology was held in Vail in July 1973. Unlike the Boulder Conference, the Vail conferees were not composed of clinical psychology's "establishment." In fact, the majority of the one hundred attendees were students, women, and minority-group members and their dissatisfaction with the Boulder model was palpable (Stricker, 1975). Although they recommended that the classic scientist–practitioner model continue in Ph.D. programs, the Vail Conference endorsed a new professional degree known as the Doctor of Psychology (Psy.D.; see Strickler, 2016). Whereas the Boulder Conference emphasized science in graduate clinical training, the Vail Conference stressed practice. As noted by Bell and Hausman (2014), training models offer important advantages but may also separate graduate education programs into different identities based on their preferred models.

Another postwar development that influenced clinical psychology came in the establishment of norms for diagnostic psychiatric categories. In

1952, the American Psychiatric Association, formerly the Association of Medical Superintendents of American Institutions for the Insane (Silver, 2009), introduced the *Diagnostic and Statistical Manual of Mental Disorders* (*DSM*). The *DSM* was a categorical classification system designed to provide uniform assessment and diagnoses across the field of psychiatry, but it did not meet with universal favor (Berrios, 2006). Few psychologists contributed to the first two versions of the *DSM* (Gurley, 2009), and some critics charged that the first two versions of the *DSM* were vague (due in part to psychoanalytic concepts) and unreliable. Subsequent versions, the *DSM-III* in 1980 and *DSM-IV* in 1994, focused on symptoms rather than theory but faced ongoing criticisms about validity, reliability, and cultural bias. In 2000, the American Psychiatric Association published the fourth edition of the *DSM*, the *DSM-IV-TR*. When the fifth edition was introduced in May 2013, the American Psychiatric Association dropped Roman numerals from the designated acronym, making it the *DSM-5*. The format, development, and values of the *DSM* continue to inspire discussion and criticism (Demazeux & Singy, 2015; Greenberg, 2013; Scott, 2015).

JOSEPH WOLPE Numerous directions in psychotherapy emerged in the last half of the twentieth century. **Joseph Wolpe (1915–1997)**, inspired by Pavlov's work on experimental neurosis and the work of Mary Cover Jones on the experimental elimination of fear (see Chapter 13), was a pioneer in *behavior therapy*, a revolutionary approach to psychotherapy based on the principles of learning. Wolpe argued that if anxiety and other adjustment problems could be learned, they could also be unlearned. In 1958, Wolpe's landmark book *Psychotherapy by Reciprocal Inhibition* appeared in print, laying the groundwork for a behavioral therapy based on learning theory. Garfield and Bergin (1994) echoed the sentiment of many clinicians when they called his book the first to establish therapy in the formal sense.

Wolpe (1958) used the term *reciprocal inhibition* to describe the process of extinguishing learned neurotic reactions in anxiety-provoking situations. This work provided the genesis for his model of **systematic desensitization**. Let's say a client meets with a behavioral therapist to treat a phobia. After identifying the fear response, the therapist trains the client in relaxation methods as a coping strategy (in this case, the relaxed state becomes the dominant response that competes with and weakens the anxiety response). After learning progressive-relaxation training, the therapist helps the client construct an *anxiety hierarchy*, a graduated sequence of anxiety-provoking situations (ranging from 0 for "comfortable and relaxed" to 100 for "extremely tense and anxious"). For example, a person with arachnophobia might rate hearing the word "spider" as a 5 and seeing a picture of a spider in a magazine as a 15, moving all the way up to the thought of venomous spiders crawling over one's face at the hierarchy's apex. While relaxed, the client imagines a series of anxiety-provoking situations, beginning with the least disturbing situation. After gradual exposure, the person learns to reach the highest point on the hierarchy without anxiety. In later years, Wolpe drew on his groundbreaking work to develop assertiveness training programs.

AARON T. BECK Another approach to psychotherapy, known as cognitive therapy, was developed by Aaron T. Beck. Frustrated with his initial experiences with psychoanalytic therapy, Beck sought to employ more effective and experimentally grounded approaches (Rosner, 2012). A fundamental tenet of his cognitive therapy is that depression is the product of unrealistic negative views about our self, our world, and our future (Wills, 2009); these views have deep roots in many philosophical traditions, including Stoicism, Buddhism, and Taoism (Murguia & Díaz, 2015). Beck (1963) observed that his depressed patients were haunted by *automatic thoughts*, streams of spontaneous negative cognitions that fueled depression and other emotional difficulties. As he helped patients identify and correct cognitive distortions, they developed more realistic self-perceptions that inspired happiness and productivity.

Beck is viewed as the founder of cognitive therapy (Scott & Freeman, 2010). His method of psychotherapy has played a leading role in treating people with depression, anxiety disorders, personality disorders, and other conditions (Dobson, 2012). His *Beck Depression Inventory* (BDI) remains a popular self-report inventory designed to measure the severity of depression. First introduced in 1961, it has undergone a major revision, resulting in the BDI-II in 1996. Beck is the only psychiatrist to receive research awards from both the APA and the American Psychiatric Association. He has published over five hundred articles and authored or co-authored twenty-two books.

Although not as influential in academic clinical psychology as Beck, other theorists have contributed to a cognitive perspective that emphasizes the effects of cognition on behavior and emotional change (Keegan & Holas, 2010). Albert Ellis (1913–2007) developed **Rational Emotive Behavior Therapy (REBT)** as a comprehensive treatment that works to resolve irrational thoughts that lead to conflict and self-defeating thinking (Ellis, 2004). Scholars have found roots of REBT in Stoicism (Still & Dryden, 2012; Pelusi, 2016) and the ideas of Epicurus (Reiss, 2003).

MARSHA M. LINEHAN   Although not as closely tied to laboratory research as behavior and cognitive therapies, "mindfulness-based" treatments pioneered by **Marsha M. Linehan (b. 1943)** constituted another approach to psychotherapy (Linehan & Wilks, 2015). While treating clients with borderline personality disorder and suicidal tendencies, Linehan (1993) developed *Dialectical Behavior Therapy* (DBT), a blend of Eastern perspectives of healing and Western behavioral therapy (Neacsiu et al., 2012). Her treatment has its roots in contemporary behavioral science as well as the concept of *radical acceptance* (according to Linehan, 1993, p. 148, this is "acceptance from deep within"),

Marsha Linehan

inspired from Eastern meditative practices, Western contemplative spirituality, and the phenomenological and humanistic traditions in psychology (Felder et al., 2014). DBT draws on Zen practices to encourage people to foster compassion, wisdom, and **mindfulness**, the practice of observing thoughts without letting them entangle us (Linehan & Lungu, 2012). Essentially, mindfulness is a sense of being centered and conscious in the present moment when we see reality and ourselves without delusion or judgment. The practice of mindfulness and radical acceptance form the core of DBT. Linehan and her colleagues have applied DBT models to treat depression, anxiety, suicidal behaviors, drug abuse, and borderline personality disorder as well as impulsive behaviors involving eating disorders, substance abuse, compulsive gambling, and overspending.

Recently, Linehan revealed some of her motivation. She admitted her own youthful struggles and extensive inpatient treatment, and she connected her past with her burning drive to treat those who may be viewed as beyond help. As a teenager, while sitting in her solitary room in residential treatment, she made a promise that shaped the rest of her career: "When I get out, I'm going to come back and get others out of here" (Carey, 2011, ¶29). More than forty years later, her status as a survivor lends additional support to her empirically validated therapies.

In the tradition of the mindfulness practice movement, Segal et al. (2001) conducted seminal work on a mindfulness-based treatment of depression. DBT, along with Steven C. Hayes's related treatment known as *Acceptance and Commitment Therapy* (ACT), constitutes a third wave that has influenced psychotherapists perhaps more than academic clinical psychologists.

As with any intellectual enterprise, a number of debates have swirled around clinical psychology. In 1952, British psychologist Hans Jürgen Eysenck (1916–1997) published "The Effects of Psychotherapy: An Evaluation," an open challenge to the effectiveness of psychotherapy. Based on his controversial analysis of twenty-four studies, Eysenck determined that more than two-thirds of "severe neurotics" recovered through "spontaneous remission" without the aid of psychotherapy. His work sparked a firestorm of critical reaction and aggressive debate. These debates have extended through the present (Lambert, 2010; Routh, 2013), and the persistent gap between researchers and practitioners reflects these tensions (Cautin, 2011). The question of psychotherapy's efficacy underscores the need for clinicians to evaluate treatments with sound methodology. In his provocative book *The Great Psychotherapy Debate*, Wampold (2001) notes:

> There are over 250 distinct psychotherapeutic approaches, which are described, in one way or another, in over 10,000 books. Moreover, tens of thousands of books, book chapters, and journal articles have reported research conducted to understand psychotherapy and to test whether it works. It is no wonder that, faced with the literature on psychotherapy, confusion reigns, controversy flourishes, converging evidence is sparse, and recognition of psychotherapy as a science is tenuous. Any scientific endeavor will seem chaotic if the explanatory models are insufficient to explain the accumulation of facts. If one were to ask prominent researchers to list important psychotherapeutic principles that have been scientifically established and generally accepted by most psychotherapy researchers, the list would indeed be short.

On the other hand, an enumeration of the results of psychotherapy studies would be voluminous. How is it that so much research has yielded so little knowledge?

(p. 1)

Wampold insists that research findings are insightful if clinical psychologists work at the proper level of abstraction and skill to discover the scientific foundation of psychotherapy. He also argues that the common factors of treatment (such as empathy and warmth) are more important than the specific theoretically driven factors like systematic desensitization in behavior therapy or cognitive restructuring in cognitive therapy. Along these same lines, others (e.g., Magnavita & Anchin, 2014) are focusing on the possibilities of the unification of psychotherapy and of psychology in general (Henriques, 2008, 2013). We will turn to a consideration of the problems of unification and pluralism in the final chapter.

The continuing vibrancy of clinical and counseling psychology as a field is seen in the growing numbers of psychologists working in hospitals, schools, academic departments, and private practice. The need for clinicians has not diminished. Despite Patricia Churchland's (1989) radical claim that clinical psychology will become an applied branch of neuroscience, it continues to grow and to incorporate perspectives from other fields including social psychology, educational psychology, psychology and the law, and cultural psychology. Churchland's claim may, however, be applicable to the work of psychiatrists who increasingly focus exclusively on medication management for patients with emotional problems. A paradigm shift from psychiatrists as psychotherapists to psychiatrists as medication managers has been prompted in part by insurance companies who resist paying for long-term psychotherapy. As a consequence, psychologists increasingly engage patients in "talk therapies" and behavioral therapies, but again, because of insurance costs, such therapies are short-term.

Biopsychology

As the neurosciences came of age in the late eighteenth century, scholars became increasingly aware of the brain's role in diseases, cognition, emotion, and behavior (Whitaker et al., 2007). Biopsychology has emerged as a formal discipline in its own right, but also as a significant part of an unprecedented collection of academic disciplines that together comprise the brain sciences. University campuses now witness extensive collaborations of scholars from fields such as anatomy, physiology, genetics, pharmacology, biochemistry, computer science, engineering, psychology, and philosophy. Armed with a proliferation of new methods, accelerating numbers of researchers, and increased levels of funding, the brain sciences have risen to public prominence, manifested most noticeably in 2013 by the president's "Brain Initiative." The initiative prioritized the scientific and economic benefits of much deeper understandings of the role of the central nervous system in diseases such as Alzheimer's, epilepsy, schizophrenia, autism, and amyotrophic lateral sclerosis (ALS or Lou Gehrig's disease). Such diseases, along with brain and spinal injuries from accidents and contact sports, result in untold suffering and a significant drain on societal resources. Accordingly, the initiative called for massive public and private investments to explore the causes and potential cures of diseases and injuries with devastating individual, social, and economic consequences.

Psychology, from its inception and by its nature, has been a key player in attempts to understand the biological underpinnings of behavior. Earlier, we spoke of the growth of specialization and this is nowhere better illustrated than in the great range of topics explored by biopsychologists. In what follows we explore selected trends in biopsychology in the latter half of the twentieth century.

Biological perspectives in psychology are codified in the American Psychological Association under several divisions including: Division 6, Behavioral Neuroscience and Comparative Psychology (Dewsbury, 1996); Division 40, Society for Clinical Neuropsychology; and Division 55, American Society for the Advancement of Pharmacotherapy.

Though our focus here is on selected advances in biological psychology in the latter half of the twentieth century, it is important to remind ourselves of major early breakthroughs with the work of Camillo Golgi and Ramón y Cajal who shared the Nobel Prize in 1906 for their work on the microscopic structure of the nervous system (see Chapter 8). The latter half of the century witnessed a veritable explosion of advances that together have constituted a revolution in the ways we think about ourselves and others. In what follows we explore some of the most important breakthroughs in the brain sciences.

Enriched Environment Studies

A host of studies in the second half of the twentieth century explored the effects of simple vs. enriched environments on brain morphology and chemistry as well as behavior. Canadian neuroscientist **Donald Olding Hebb (1904–1985)** (1949) was among the first to demonstrate the detrimental effects of simple environments on the later abilities of rats. Following Hebb's work, other researchers (e.g., Bennett et al., 1964) compared the effects on the brains and behaviors of rats from enriched environments vs. impoverished environments. An enriched environment typically included the social stimulation of other rats, mazes, tunnels, and various toys. Litter-mates were reared alone without the benefit of environmental and social stimulation. The brains of the animals were compared following weeks of exposure in the different environmental circumstances. Animals from the enriched conditions had developed impressively larger brains than their litter-mates from the impoverished conditions. Growth of the brains resulted from many changes including increased dendritic branching and the proliferation of synapses and nutritive glial cells. Early research was conducted on young rats, but similar salutary benefits of enriched environments were found in later research projects on older rats and with other animals.

An optimistic fallout from enriched environment studies is illustrated in the subtitle of an article on "Environment and Brain Plasticity" (Sale et al., 2014). The subtitle of the article, "Towards an Endogenous Pharmacotherapy," suggests that by exercise, social contacts, and intellectual enrichment programs the brain can be enlarged and enhanced. The most obvious conclusion from enriched environment studies is that the brain is not a fixed or static entity but rather should be viewed as a work in progress. Enriched environment studies were presumed to have educational implications, and led to the introduction of the Head Start and Early Start Programs. There is still much to be learned concerning the transfer of findings from controlled animal studies to humans in their day-to-day environments, but enriched environment studies provide an optimistic outlook for understanding and productive control of the neural underpinnings of emotional, cognitive, and motivational activities.

Split-Brain Research

Roger W. Sperry (1913–1994) and colleagues performed numerous studies on animals with surgically separated brains (Sperry, 1961). Additionally, Sperry and others did extensive research with humans who had surgery to lesion the corpus callosum to ease epileptic symptoms not otherwise treatable in the 1960s. This work led to increased understanding of the common and separate functions of right and left hemispheres of the brain (see Springer & Deutsch, 1985). In 1981, Sperry was awarded the Nobel Prize in Medicine for his split-brain research. Under Sperry's guidance, Michael S. Gazzaniga (b. 1939) played a critical role in this research and later became a founding figure in the discipline of *cognitive neuroscience*. He has written for both the scientific community and general audiences, including neuroscientific consideration of the

issue of free will (Gazzaniga, 2011). This classical issue in psychology remains relevant in the twenty-first century.

Studies of Synaptic Transmission

Australian neurophysiologist and philosopher Sir **John C. Eccles (1903–1997)** won the Nobel Prize in 1963 for his detailed groundbreaking work on the synapse. Early in his career, he believed synaptic transmission to be of an electrical (mechanical) nature, but in time, his research demonstrated that transmission across the synapse is sometimes chemical. The distinction between electrical and chemical synapses was extremely important. The two types do very different things. Initially, it was believed there were far more electrical synapses, but later it was understood that chemical synapses far outnumber mechanical synapses. Electrical synapses are far faster and more precise and are more likely to be involved in autonomic activities and simple and defensive behaviors. Chemical synapses are slower, much more complex, and variable. They are based on neurotransmitters and are more likely to underpin higher cognitive functions. **Eric Kandel (b. 1929)**, winner of the 2000 Nobel Prize in Physiology or Medicine, demonstrated that memory functions are associated with changes in synaptic connections between neurons; that short-term and long-term memory formations are distinct processes; and that genetically modified animal models (e.g., mice) could better illustrate the roles of specific proteins and genes in the formation of memories.

Direct Electrical Stimulation of the Brain

Recall earlier discussions (Chapter 8) of the pioneering work of Gustav Theodor Fritsch and Julius Eduard Hitzig who helped establish the field of electrophysiology by applying small electrical currents to the brain of a dog. Fritsch and Hitzig were able to demonstrate regions of the cortex responsible for specific movements of the dog. Studies on electrical brain stimulation (EBS) were refined in the second half of the twentieth century, resulting in unprecedented advances. Neurosurgeon Wilder Penfield (1952) applied electrical stimulation to the cortex of patients who were awake and who were undergoing various neurosurgical procedures. Under the influence of such stimulations, patients experienced vivid earlier memories. If Penfield moved the electrical probe to a slightly different region, a different memory would be evoked. These findings raised questions about memory storage. Additionally, stimulation of the cortex did not typically evoke emotions, but deeper probes into the limbic system did evoke emotions. James Olds (1922–1976), for example, discovered areas in the limbic system that reliably produced profound pleasure. In the 1970s and 1980s there were a great many laboratories employing EBS techniques in animal studies and in medical settings. Such studies played important roles in mapping the brain and in exploring underlying structures associated with sensory, motor, emotional, and cognitive functions.

It should be noted that there is still much to learn about the long-standing issue concerning the localization of function vs. brain plasticity. Recall from Chapter 8 that discoveries such as the specialization of spinal nerves, the discovery of the speech areas of the brain, differences between left and right brain functions, and the localization of respiration functions suggested that many functions are highly localized in the nervous system. These assumptions supported Penfield's findings of localized memories. On the other hand, the early research of Pierre Flourens and the later work of Karl Lashley on the cortical basis of learning challenged the idea of "brain centers." Lashley's work suggested that a memory could be evoked in any of a number of locations. Perhaps, a memory is part of a complex circuit or a neural assembly. Further, it is known from work on brain injuries that one part of a brain can sometimes take over the work of another part

that was injured. At present it appears that both part processes and collective or holistic processes are at work in the brain.

Measuring Brain Activity

Donald B. Lindsley (1907–2003) was an early cognitive and behavioral neuroscientist and a pioneer in the study of the electrical activity of the brain (Eason, 2004). In the late 1930s, the electroencephalogram was just emerging in psychiatry and psychology as an important new research and clinical tool (see Kreezer, 1938). German psychiatrist Hans Berger (1873–1941) is credited with the invention of the electroencephalogram (EEG) and was the first to document different brain wave patterns (including the *alpha wave*, also known as *Berger's wave*). Lindsley (1936) published groundbreaking results in *Science* magazine of his examinations of EEG patterns in children and adults. He followed this work with many other applications of neurophysiological recording, including in utero fetal EEG recordings (Lindsley, 1942), now a common procedure. He is also remembered for his investigations of the role of the brain stem in sleep, attention, and arousal (Chalupa, 2005). Later advances involved the measurement of local brain electrical activity in response to specific events by recording event-related potentials (ERPs).

A proliferation of new ways to measure brain activity continues to drive progress in biological psychology. The advent of single-neuron recording and stimulation opened the door to many research topics including visual and auditory processing and long-term potentiation in memory. Although researchers such as Lashley and Hebb studied larger functions of the brain, many neuroscientists moved toward single-cell recording. The movement prompted Wolfgang Köhler (1967/1971) to lament that "The micro-electrode inserted in an individual cell seems to have abolished all interest in more molar functions of the nervous system" (p. 122). Single-cell research remains common, but despite these concerns, biological psychology has also moved forward with new methods that allow investigation into the brain as a whole.

With the advent of structural and functional imaging, no area of psychology has benefited more from advances in technology than neuroscience. Developed in the late 1970s, computed tomography (CT) scans allowed researchers, neurologists, and other physicians to view the brain and potential brain injuries in live participants (Roberts et al., 1978). Soon after, in the mid-1980s, magnetic resonance imaging (MRI) allowed observers to view the brain in higher levels of resolution than were possible with CT scans (DeWitt, 1985). By the end of the twentieth century, emerging functional imaging technology allowed neuroscientists to observe the brain in action in real time. For example, positron emission tomography (PET) scans permit the observation of blood flow during cognitive activities (Bunney et al., 1983); in 1991, functional magnetic resonance imaging (fMRI) techniques provided researchers with high-resolution images of brains in action in real time (Bandettini, 2007). PET scans and fMRIs help scholars identify areas of the brain that are relatively active or inactive during specific operations. These results aid in the assessment and treatment of brain injuries in addition to serving research functions. The use of PET scans and fMRIs to describe the localization of brain functions has led some contemporary critics to argue that these approaches comprise "modern phrenology" (Raichle, 1999, p. 107). Many dispute these allegations (Frith, 2006). These tools are continuously expanding into new areas, such as lie detection (Choi, 2015), bringing additional questions in their wake. The descriptive and predictive value of advanced imaging techniques is clear even if the ability to draw causal inferences remains in contention.

Psychopharmacology

The study of the effects of drugs on thought and behavior made significant advances based on research about how neurons communicate with one another. Between the twentieth century's world wars, many scholars investigated psychological drugs using methods from experimental psychology (Schmied et al., 2006). Since the discovery of the neurotransmitter acetylcholine, many scholars have investigated its properties (Sourkes, 2009), and the discovery of monoamines—neurotransmitters including dopamine, serotonin, and norepinephrine—soon followed. These discoveries have revolutionized our understanding of the brain and the rest of the nervous system as well as pharmacological treatments for people with mental illness.

By the late 1950s, despite some false starts related to the uses of hallucinogens as treatments for people with some psychological disorders, particularly schizophrenia (Mills, 2010), this basic research knowledge had been translated into practice in the form of psychopharmacological treatments for mental illness (Kline & Saunders, 1959; Kuhn, 1958). In the late 1970s and early 1980s, neurotransmitter research expanded to include investigation of neuropeptides, peptides that communicate information between neurons (see Krivoy et al., 1977).

Drawing on discoveries from neurotransmitter research, clinical psychology benefited from advances in psychopharmacology. The use of medications to treat people with psychological disorders began in 1949 when Australian psychiatrist John Cade (1912–1980) used lithium salts to treat individuals with bipolar disorder (Cole & Parker, 2012; Mitchell, 1999; Schioldann, 2009). Despite its success, lithium did not enjoy widespread acceptance in psychiatry, particularly in the United States, until two decades after Cade's treatment (Shorter, 2009). (Two decades before Cade, lithium was used as an original ingredient in a soft drink called "Bib-Label Lithiated Lemon-Lime Soda"; in time, the unwieldy name was shortened to "7Up Lithiated Lemon Soda" before evolving into the more familiar "7Up.")

Following Cade's work, the field gained momentum with the development of tricyclics (Kuhn, 1958) and monoamine oxidase inhibitors

(Kline & Saunders, 1959) to treat depression. Following a discovery by French physician Henri Laborit (1914–1995) that a specific group of antihistamine drugs calmed users, researchers developed a medication known as chlorpromazine. Marketed as Thorazine in the 1950s, it became the first antipsychotic drug, revolutionizing the prognosis and treatment of individuals with severe psychiatric disorders (López-Muñoz et al., 2005).

Since the 1980s, the field of psychopharmacology has exploded, and the range of available medications to treat people with mental disorders has rapidly expanded. With improved medications, many individuals with mental illnesses can function at higher levels and are more likely to adapt to life outside residential treatment. Increase in availability of psychopharmaceuticals influenced the general move away from institutionalization. This move brought success and independence to many people who formerly had debilitating mental illnesses. The unfortunate side of this trend, however, is that some patients did not adjust to life outside residential treatment; many became homeless or incarcerated (Gilligan, 2001). Important questions linger about medication, helping people continue their use of medication, and long-term responsibilities of caregivers, treatment centers, and government agencies. These issues continue to guide basic and applied biological research in psychology.

Behavioral Genetics

Still another breakthrough in biological psychology includes the study of the role of genes in cognition and behavior. It is clear that human social behaviors, like the behaviors of other animals, have genetic roots that are adaptive for survival. For example, there exist strong cross-cultural norms for reciprocity and altruism. Dawkins (2006) suggests that human willingness to give back to others and to help others results from evolutionary selection of genes for these social traits. The work of Dawkins, among others, led to the emergence of evolutionary psychology as a self-conscious discipline (Buss, 2005).

Behavioral genetics has deep roots in the history of psychology (Maxson, 2007) and has inspired controversy throughout its existence (Panofsky, 2014). In his controversial work *Hereditary Genius* (1869/2006), Francis Galton argued for the hereditary basis of intelligence. His perspective informed much of the early work in intelligence, and many early psychologists, including H. H. Goddard, Lewis Terman, Robert M. Yerkes, and Catherine Cox Miles, argued that intelligence was entirely hereditary (see Gould, 1981). The emphasis on genetics was powerful and carried significant consequences. Let's say intelligence is completely genetic. If some are more economically or socially successful than others, it follows that successful people owe their success to hereditary superiority. According to this thinking, people who are not successful are limited by their genetics and cannot be educated to succeed. Unfortunately, such perspectives helped justify and perpetuate the existing racism and segregation in American society (see Sussman, 2014; Winston, 2003).

Other early psychologists regarded the relative influence of nature and nurture as an open question, and this question persists today. For example, Barbara Stoddard Burks (1902–1943) evaluated the relative contributions of genetics and environment to an organism's traits through comparisons of the traits of children and the traits of their biological parents and foster parents (Burks, 1927, 1928; King et al., 1996). To address these questions, Thomas J. Bouchard Jr. (b. 1937) evaluated the relative similarity of monozygotic and dizygotic twins raised together and apart (Bouchard et al., 1984). As director of the Minnesota Center for Twin and Adoption Research, his work continues to inspire replication, support, and criticism.

In recent decades, increasing power and availability of genetic manipulation techniques have allowed researchers to pursue important psychological questions in nonhuman species. The use of animal models allows researchers to investigate questions with more experimental control and more invasive procedures. For example, researchers have investigated the role of genes in individual differences related to alcohol consumption (Rhodes et al., 2007), genetic influence on sex-specific courtship behaviors of fruit flies (Manoli et al., 2006), and genetic influences on the actions of psychotropic drugs (Duman et al., 2007). Behavioral genetics also addresses psychopathology, with research on people with disorders such as schizophrenia and antisocial behavior (Carey, 2003).

Psychoneuroimmunology

The study of the interactions between the brain, behavior, the immune system, and the social and physical environments emerged in the 1970s with the work of Robert Ader and colleagues. Ader and Cohen (1975) classically conditioned rat immune systems by pairing saccharine-flavored water with an immune system suppressant. They found that when the immune suppression agent was removed from the saccharine solution, rats still showed immune system suppression. Following this work, the field was formalized with the 1981 publication of *Psychoneuroimmunology*, now in its fourth edition (Ader, 2006; see also Kusnecov & Anisman, 2014).

The area has exploded with the recognition that social, behavioral, and neurological factors can influence the immune system and that the immune system communicates with neurons via cytokines and other chemicals. Additionally, stress, attitudes, and perceived control influence immune reactions, and immune responses affect and interact with much of human and animal behavior (Fleshner & Laudenslager, 2004). The discipline has offered insight into how organisms adapt to a variety of challenges, with critical implications for real-world applications such as the control and prevention of chronic pain (Watkins & Maier, 2005). The journal *Brain, Behavior, and Immunity* was founded in 1986 to provide synthesis across the fields of psychology, neuroscience, and immunology. Central features

include "the role of the brain and behavior in modulating immunity and the role of immune processes in the regulation of neural and endocrine functions and behavior" (Ader & Kelley, 2007, p. 20). Psychoneuroimmunology continues to grow, particularly as part of the interdisciplinary field of health psychology (Belar et al., 2013). Additionally, the field provides an example of the decreasing insularity in psychology; basic and applied psychologists are reaching into hospitals, recovery rooms, and long-term care facilities, among other places, where people seek healing.

The future is wide open for the fields of psychoneuroimmunology, behavioral and cognitive neuroscience, and behavioral genetics. Although some scholars (Churchland, 1989) claim that biological approaches will eventually eclipse psychology, leading it to become a branch of applied neuroscience, others expect both fields to grow in unison. Researchers continue to develop new methodologies that expand potential knowledge in the field, and the overlap between psychology and other disciplines such as biology, neurology, and ethology will continue to stimulate new paradigms and knowledge.

Social Psychology

In an address celebrating the twenty-fifth anniversary of the APA, John Dewey (1917) argued that the development of social psychology was important to general psychology and to a more complete understanding of human experience and behavior. Early classics by scholars such as Baldwin (1911), Dewey (1922), Bartlett (1923), Dunlap (1925), and McDougall (1926) set the stage for what would later become one of the dominant subdisciplinary areas of psychology.

Intellectual Traditions

Scholars have long attempted to investigate social phenomena empirically (Jahoda, 2007;

Kruglanski & Stroebe, 2012), and, as mentioned in Chapter 16, **Floyd H. Allport (1890–1971)** was a significant figure in the formal emergence of the discipline and is often regarded as the founder of experimental social psychology (Katz, 1979). At Harvard, Hugo Münsterberg had encouraged Allport to focus his doctoral research on the "behavior of individuals acting alone versus their action together in groups" (Allport, 1974, p. 3). Following Münsterberg's advice, Allport (1920) devoted his dissertation to the topic, establishing it as one of the first studies on conformity. In 1924, he published a landmark book on social psychology that was important because it provided "an objectively conceived and somewhat systematic presentation of the subject from the psychological rather than the sociological point of view; and second, it suggested at least by implication the possibility of a new experimental science of social psychology" (Allport, 1974, p. 9). In later years, he conducted research on social influence, cultural change, political structures, Nazi propaganda and persuasion, attitudes, and anti-Semitic prejudice. Despite his interest in the last area, he couldn't always liberate himself from the biases of his day. In his social psychology textbook, Allport (1924) wrote, "The intelligence of the white race is of a more versatile and complex order than that of the black race . . . [and] probably superior also to that of the red or yellow races" (p. 386). Such biases pervade much of the psychological study of groups and of individual differences from this time period (Guthrie, 2003; Winston, 2003).

Social psychology has centered on three primary topical areas: within- and between-group processes, attitudes and beliefs, and social- and self-perception (Ross et al., 2010). In what follows, we will examine several pivotal studies in social influence, a topic that has shaped the history of the field (Prislin & Crano, 2012). Social influence is but one area of social psychology, but it is an important part that reveals why social psychology occupies such a prominent place in contemporary psychology.

Muzafer Sherif and the Autokinetic Effect

Muzafer Sherif (1908–1988), one of the pioneers in the development of social psychology, was motivated by many life experiences, including the time he was held without charge in solitary confinement in a Turkish prison for his outspoken criticism of the Nazi movement (Harvey, 1989). Among other acts, he had supported a Jewish student and written a book advocating against racism. There is now a growing awareness of Sherif's role as an international political activist as well as a psychologist (Kayaoğlu et al., 2014). Research questions concerning prejudice, intergroup conflict, and destructive group influence fascinated Sherif.

Sherif earned B.A. and M.A. degrees in his native Turkey and an M.A. degree at Harvard followed by a Ph.D. at Columbia under the direction of Gardner Murphy. He also studied with Wolfgang Köhler in Berlin. (Gestalt psychology's influence is evident in his mature research and in his classroom teaching.) Sherif is remembered for his text *An Outline of Social Psychology*, originally published in 1948 and revised in 1956 and 1969 with the help of his wife Carolyn Wood Sherif (1922–1982), also a social psychologist. Sherif's famous boys' camp research in intergroup conflict and conflict reduction (Gaertner et al., 2000; Reicher & Haslam, 2014) was set forth in *Groups in Harmony and Tension*, which he also co-authored with Carolyn Sherif (see Sherif & Sherif, 1953) when he was at Yale University, and a follow-up book titled *Intergroup Conflict and Cooperation: The Robbers Cave Experiment* (see Sherif et al., 1961), which he published when he was at the University of Oklahoma. Sherif was also the recipient of many awards including the Distinguished Scientific Contribution Award in 1968 from the APA (see Harvey, 1989).

Following Allport's work on conformity, Sherif (1936) conducted early studies on a phenomenon known as the **autokinetic effect**, an illusion of apparent movement. Imagine you're in a darkened room, staring at a stationary pinpoint of light (Abrams & Levine, 2012). Though stationary, the light appears to move. Astronomers noted that if we focus on a star or a planet on a dark night while blocking other lights from the field of vision, the star in focus will move in irregular or erratic ways. Such apparent movement has been suggested as a possible explanation for flying saucer sightings.

Under the guise of a visual perception experiment, Sherif conducted systematic studies on the autokinetic effect in individual and group settings. Alone in a darkened room, participants estimated the movement of a motionless pinpoint of light. Later, they engaged in the same task while participating in three-person groups. They initially diverged in their estimates, but after working together over many trials, they established a group norm so that all reported about the same amount of movement. This classic study demonstrated that a simple perception in an unstructured or ambiguous situation is conditioned or shaped by group influence. If basic perceptions are shaped in social context, how much more may beliefs, attitudes, opinions, and the like be subject to social influences that might be below our threshold of awareness?

Solomon Asch and Conformity

Solomon Asch (1907–1996) was born in Warsaw, Poland. He emigrated with his family to the United States in 1920. Asch was an introverted child who mastered English after an intensive reading of Charles Dickens's novels. He flourished in his studies and earned his master's degree under Robert Sessions Woodworth at Columbia University. Asch received his Ph.D. from Columbia in 1932. He was captivated by the Gestalt orientation and became acquainted with Max Wertheimer shortly after his immigration to the United States. When Wertheimer died in 1943, Asch replaced him as chair of psychology at the New School for Social Research (McCauley & Rozin, 2003). Two years later, Asch joined Wolfgang Köhler and Clara Mayer (dean

Solomon Asch

at the New School) in editing the first edition of *Productive Thinking* (Wertheimer, 1945/1982). Asch stayed at the New School until moving to Swarthmore College in 1947, where he established a strong relationship with Köhler. In 1966, he headed the Institute for Cognitive Studies at Rutgers University, then moved to the University of Pennsylvania, where he retired in 1979. He died on February 20, 1996.

In a classic social influence study, Asch demonstrated group influences on individual behavior in a more structured situation than that employed in Sherif's autokinetic studies. In Asch's classic conformity studies, volunteer participants believed they were participating in an experiment on visual perception. The participant and several confederates inspected white cards displaying vertical lines. One card displayed a single vertical line (a standard) and the other displayed three lines of varying length to be compared with the standard. One of the comparison lines provided a clear "best fit" in terms of length with the standard line. In the typical experimental scenario, the volunteer sat in a small room with six confederates.

Though there were numerous variations in the experimental conditions, the central purpose of the study was to examine behaviors of the volunteer participant when the confederates, who had received prior instructions, made a wrong choice that flew in the face of direct visual evidence. What would the participant do when all the confederates, speaking one at a time, declared that the appropriate matching stimulus was a line that was longer or shorter than the standard? About three-quarters of Asch's participants conformed at least once; choosing the wrong line in the face of contradictory evidence caused less distress than publicly disagreeing with a group of strangers. Asch's findings have practical consequences in many areas such as marketing, crowd behavior, and jury decision making; people's willingness to conform to statements that are obviously false (as in Asch's line-length studies) justifies significant concerns about conformity in decisions involving more complex legal stimuli (Kruglanski & Stroebe, 2012).

Stanley Milgram and Destructive Obedience

Born to Jewish immigrants in the Bronx, New York, **Stanley Milgram (1933–1984)** attended James Monroe High School with a classmate who was also destined to become a social psychologist, Phillip G. Zimbardo (b. 1933). Milgram studied political science at Queens College but never took a psychology course as an undergraduate (Blass, 2004). Harvard University rejected Milgram as a graduate candidate due to his insufficient background in psychology. After taking six courses in the area, he was finally accepted, and he earned his Ph.D. from Harvard in 1960. Milgram spent an influential postdoctoral year studying with Solomon Asch (McCauley & Rozin, 2003). Gordon Allport also played a critical role in shaping Milgram's psychological perspective.

Milgram joined the faculty at Yale University in the fall of 1960 and received a two-year National Science Foundation grant for a study on obedience the next year (Blass, 2004). He completed data collection during the 1960–1961 academic year, drawing on a participant pool from the New Haven, Connecticut area. His research was inspired in part by the destructive actions of Adolf Eichmann, the Gestapo chief of Jewish Affairs, who was responsible for mass deportation of Jewish citizens to ghettos and extermination camps in Nazi-occupied Eastern Europe. Eichmann was apprehended in Argentina. When Eichmann was placed on trial in Jerusalem in 1961, he insisted, in his own defense, that he was only following orders during his time as a high-ranking Nazi official (Cesarani, 2007). Eichmann's words haunted the young Yale psychologist and, among other factors, inspired one of the most controversial experiments in the history of psychology (Blass, 2009).

The question Milgram raised was simple: How far would a person go to obey authority? The studies required extensive development and pretesting (Russell, 2011), and the answer was disturbing and complex. Acting as the "teacher," the participant worked with a forty-seven-year-old man with a heart condition who served as a "learner" (in reality, he was Milgram's accomplice). After the learner was strapped to a chair and rigged with electrodes, the teacher moved to an adjoining room to begin the experiment. Milgram (1963) promoted the study as an exploration of the role of punishment on forgetting, ordering the teacher to administer an electrical shock to the learner for every mistake he made on the test. Given the power of the situation, many teachers felt social pressure to obey authority. But how many people would actually administer the maximum 450 volts? Despite violent protests from the learner, 65 percent of Milgram's participants gave what they believed were harmful shocks. Outcomes from a more recent and more ethical replication were consistent with Milgram's findings (Burger, 2009, 2011), and, tragically, history provides too many examples of destructive obedience (Navarick, 2012).

The repercussions were as staggering as the study itself. Critics blasted the research, demanding greater ethical standards in psychology research (Baumrind, 1964, 2015). Blass (2004) noted that when Milgram tried to join the APA, his application was put on hold pending an investigation into the ethics of his research (satisfied, the APA later allowed him to join). Undeterred, Milgram conducted a series of variations on his obedience experiments that stimulated other researchers. Recent years have seen an explosion of historical scholarship on Milgram (Brannigan et al., 2015; Martin, 2016; Reicher et al., 2014) as well as a feature film (Singer et al., 2015).

In August 1971, Zimbardo created a "prison" in the basement of Stanford University's psychology building to study the psychology of authoritarian roles in prison life. Conceived as a two-week experiment, the Stanford Prison Experiment was cut short after only six days. During the simulation, participants who acted as "guards" became cruel and sadistic, while the "prisoners" grew demoralized and despondent. Like Milgram's research, Zimbardo's study produced devastating findings that mirror destructive social influence too often encountered in the real world (Haney & Zimbardo, 1998), including the tragic abuses of detainees in the Iraqi prison Abu Ghraib (Drury et al., 2012; Zimbardo, 2007). This study has also experienced a surge of interest and a feature film (Alvarez, 2015). The studies by Milgram and Zimbardo continue to play significant roles in shaping public perceptions of psychology (Bartels et al., 2016; De Vos, 2010).

Current Developments

Social psychology gained ground in basic research departments with the work of Sherif, Asch, Milgram, Zimbardo, and others, and the field expanded to include questions related to attributions, attitudes, and culture. Today, the field explores many broad research areas, including interpersonal attraction, social perception, prejudice, aggression, persuasion, and altruism, among others (Fiske et al., 2010).

Social psychology has also blended into other broad paradigms in psychology. For example,

rather than separating social psychology from cognitive psychology, some researchers investigate *social cognition*, the ways people think about themselves and others in social situations (Fiske & Taylor, 1991, 2008; North & Fiske, 2012; Haidt, 2012). Evolutionary psychologists generate hypotheses about adaptive human social interaction and then test these hypotheses with methods from social psychology (Buss, 2000). Although health psychology has its roots in psychodynamic and physiological approaches, some health psychologists today employ methods from social psychology to evaluate social and contextual effects on health behaviors (Belar et al., 2013). Additionally, some basic and applied fields of psychology emerged, in whole or in part, as subfields of social psychology. Parts of the broad fields of industrial-organizational psychology, with early roots in Münsterberg's *Psychology and Industrial Efficiency* (1913), apply social psychology to questions in the workplace. Environmental psychology, a field that formally emerged in the 1960s in response to increased concerns about questions of human population and degrading environmental health, uses some approaches from social psychology to evaluate the effects of built or natural environments on behavior and cognition (Richards, 2000). Some areas of psychology and the law, as discussed later, have roots in questions about the influence of eyewitnesses and other social factors.

At present, eight divisions of the APA are devoted in one way or another to the study of the effects of social influences on experience and behavior. Among the most prominent are the Society for Personality and Social Psychology (Division 8) and the Society for the Psychological Study of Social Issues (Division 9), whose social justice orientation reflects the moralistic roots that inspired much of early psychology (Morawski & Bayer, 2013). Other related divisions of the APA include: Population and Environmental Psychology (Division 34); Society for the Study of Peace, Conflict, and Violence: Peace Psychology Division (Division 48); and Family Psychology (Division 43). Early studies on topics such as the senses, reaction times, individual differences, and the physiological underpinnings of behavior were important, but there is increasing awareness that social context determines much of who we are and what we do. All APA-accredited Ph.D. programs in clinical and counseling psychology require that students receive training in the social forces that shape our lives. Moreover, social psychology is one of the more dominant areas for doctoral-level studies.

Social psychology continues to grow in basic fields as well as applied fields and in overlap between traditional social psychology and other areas of psychological science and practice.

Industrial-Organizational Psychology

Pioneers such as Sigmund Freud and Dorothea Lynde Dix agreed on the vital role that work plays in human adjustment. Dix (1845/1971) argued, "Of all the remedies for 'razing out the written troubles of the brain' none can compare with labor, wherein I include all useful employment" (p. 39). In her campaign to improve the therapeutic climate for people with mental illnesses, she repeatedly highlighted the therapeutic value of meaningful work. Freud (1930/1961a) noted that "No other technique for the conduct of life attaches the individual so firmly to reality as laying emphasis on work" (p. 27). He believed the capacities to love and work are two of the most important indicators of mental health. The field of industrial-organizational psychology is the study of behavior, cognition, and experience in work settings. As such, this field touches many topics that are central to human happiness and well-being.

Intellectual Traditions

In Chapter 12, we discussed Hugo Münsterberg's critical role in establishing industrial-organizational psychology. His classic book *Psychology and Industrial Efficiency* (1913) helped launch the discipline and covered areas still vital to the industrial-organizational field, although the field has grown more complex and specialized since his seminal work (Bryan & Vinchur, 2012, 2013). Around the same time, American social worker **Mary Parker Follett (1868–1933)** conducted early work on political psychology that addressed issues relating to the human side of government and democracy, drawing the admiration of Theodore Roosevelt and other politicians. She also explored crowd psychology during two decades of civic work in Boston's immigrant neighborhoods.

In the 1920s, Follett focused on corporate issues, particularly adult learning to improve individual and corporate outcomes (Wheelock & Callahan, 2006; Mott, 2015). She was recognized as a leading management consultant, and she offered America's first executive development seminars in New York City (Tonn, 2003). In her writings, lectures, and seminars, she popularized phrases such as "conflict resolution," "power sharing," and the "task of leadership." Her work strongly influenced James Webb, who led the National Aeronautics and Space Administration (NASA) in the 1960s (Davis, 2015), and her legacy remains evident in discussions concerning worker empowerment, collaborative leadership, conflict resolution, and corporate social responsibility (Stout & Love, 2015).

Walter Dill Scott (1869–1955) joined other students of Wilhelm Wundt, including Lightner Witmer and James McKeen Cattell, as pioneers in applied psychology (Landy, 1997). A pioneer in the world of business psychology (Vinchur & Koppes, 2007), Scott was critical in calling for managers to improve workers' attitudes and motivation in order to increase productivity.

After completing a doctorate with Wundt in 1900, Scott joined the faculty at Northwestern University, where he served as president from 1920 to 1939. He was founder and president of the Scott Company, the first personnel consulting firm, and served as APA president in 1919. Von Mayrhauser (1989) called attention to the similarities between

473

Binet's and Scott's approaches to intelligence testing and to Scott's crucial role in developing successful group tests.

Strong (1955) argued that Scott "may properly be called the father of applied psychology for no one else applied psychology to such a variety of business problems as he did and at so early a date" (p. 682). If Scott had a favorite topical area in academic psychology, it was undoubtedly motivation, but his interest in theoretical problems in motivation was complemented by an interest in practical motivational problems. Some of his earliest contributions in applied psychology were books and articles on advertising (Kuna, 1976). In an early popular article written for *Atlantic Monthly*, Scott (1904) reviewed the history and growth of advertising and argued that there was a significant role for psychologists in this field. He wrote about the roles of mental imagery, motivation, and suggestion in advertising and showed that psychologists, by virtue of their training, have relevant expertise for the field. Scott's other applied interests included the psychology of public speaking, the psychology of argument and persuasion, prediction of vocational interests and skills, methods of improving work efficiency, and management techniques.

Scott and Münsterberg were not alone in expressing enthusiasm for applied psychology. Despite occasional concerns about premature application, well-known scholars filled books and periodicals with suggestions on how psychology might be useful. For example, Royce (1898) pointed out that psychology might be useful to educators in finding ways to combat fatigue, boredom, and poor work habits. Seashore (1911), in a *Popular Science Monthly* article, offered the optimistic opinion that there was a need for consulting psychologists in a great range of human endeavors, including the arts, science, the professions, and industry. Others wrote on topics such as the value of humor (Kline, 1908), the importance of play and relaxation (Patrick, 1914), and the effects of strong emotions (Cannon, 1922). Psychology, almost from the beginning, had a

promising potential that captured the attention and imagination of the public.

Lillian Gilbreth (1878–1972) was born Lillian Evelyn Moller in Oakland, California. Undeterred by her family's bias against higher education for women, Gilbreth earned a master's degree in literature and was close to finishing a Ph.D. at the University of California at Berkeley. Following marriage to Frank Gilbreth in 1904, her graduate studies were delayed for the better part of a decade. After her husband's consulting firm relocated to Providence, Rhode Island, Gilbreth studied psychology at Brown University where she earned a Ph.D. in 1915.

Lillian and Frank Gilbreth were pioneers in the field of ergonomics, the study of how the workplace can be designed for maximum safety, productivity, and worker satisfaction. Their books on the topics of fatigue (Gilbreth & Gilbreth, 1916) and motion (Gilbreth & Gilbreth, 1917)

Lillian Gilbreth

474

addressed the problems of wasted time and effort in a variety of settings, and they were among the first to use film to study workers' motions (Hindmarsh, 2009). They sensitized the public and industrial leaders to the financial and psychological value of meta-level thinking about how work is and should be performed to maximize safety, productivity, and satisfaction. The results were salutary for both workers and employers and set the stage for the scientific and professional efforts of generations of industrial and organizational psychologists. The Gilbreths' work on fatigue represents their approach to other problems. They employed questionnaires and engaged in on-site inspections, examining effects of lighting, heating, ventilation, length of rest periods, arrangement of materials, seating arrangements, and type of clothing on worker fatigue. They argued that fatigue is a psychological and a physiological problem that accounts for enormous losses of time and money and a perennial waste of human energy.

In their book *Management in the Home*, Gilbreth, Thomas, and Clymer (1954/1962) provide fruitful discussions on topics such as how to eliminate unnecessary work, how to think about sequence of operations, how to simplify operations, and how to use tools with maximal efficiency. As mentioned, they were the first to use film to examine workers in motion in order to improve efficiency (Belliveau, 2012). Many of their ideas for energy-saving kitchens are still in effect. According to Koppes (2000), two of Gilbreth's "most notable inventions were the shelves inside refrigerator doors and the foot-pedal trash can" (p. 499).

Gilbreth and Gilbreth were also interested in structural and procedural suggestions for homemakers and workers with disabilities. The creation of helpful and efficient settings, tools, and procedures for veterans and others with disabilities were set forth in their book *Motion Study for the Handicapped* (Gilbreth & Gilbreth, 1920). In this context, they explored topics such as how an oral hygienist can work with one arm or with other movement limitations. Additional topics included studies of typing with one hand, jobs

that could be carried out effectively by people who are blind, and the need for reeducation programs for those who have acquired disabilities due to injuries or illness. After Frank Gilbreth died in 1924, Lillian Gilbreth continued these endeavors with characteristic vigor (see Yost & Gilbreth, 1944).

With the visibility of her work, Gilbreth gained recognition as an early figure to publicly embrace a successful career and a successful marriage (Vasquez, 2007). She held appointments at Rutgers, Purdue University, and the Massachusetts Institute of Technology, where she was appointed lecturer when she was eighty-six years old. She once noted that for Frank, "time was always an opportunity" (Gilbreth, 1928/1951, p. 16), but the same was true for her. Gilbreth's contributions extend beyond industrial-organizational psychology to include diverse arenas such as military psychology, educational psychology, management, sports medicine, and engineering psychology. Her breadth and larger philosophic perspective mark her as a premier example of a general psychologist (see Perloff & Naman, 1996). She received over a dozen honorary doctorates and, according to Koppes (2000), she served "on a number of committees appointed by Presidents Hoover, Roosevelt, Truman, Eisenhower, Kennedy, and Johnson" (p. 499). Books published by two of her twelve children, *Cheaper by the Dozen* (Gilbreth & Carey, 1948) and *Belles on Their Toes* (Gilbreth & Carey, 1950), celebrated life in the Gilbreth family. Their books inspired several successful Hollywood movies.

In early 1972, Lillian Moller Gilbreth died at the age of ninety-three. She was a unique and creative pioneer who extended the reach of psychology by exploring problems that gave the discipline a public face along with the promise of a productive dialogue with other disciplines such as mechanical engineering and business. Gilbreth is among the few psychologists who exemplify the empirical, pragmatic, and functionalist traditions set forth by William James, Hugo Münsterberg, John Dewey, and Walter Dill Scott.

Current Developments

As a subfield of psychology, industrial-organizational psychologists study topics such as fatigue, rest periods, leadership, motivation, performance appraisal, evaluation of job applicants, and all of the various dimensions of the workplace including lighting, motion studies, incentives, worker morale, job satisfaction, advertising, hiring, and compensation issues. Since the spread of graduate training following World War II (Lowman et al., 2007), there are now over sixty programs in the United States that offer doctorates in industrial-organizational psychology, far more programs offering master's level training in the area, and a national organization, Division 14 of the APA, Society for Industrial-Organizational Psychology (SIOP). Industrial-organizational psychologists are also some of the best-paid professionals in the United States, and they work in a great variety of settings including private consulting, universities, consulting firms, and large organizations that require assistance on topics such as employee training, selection, quality of work life, consumer issues, and efficiency issues associated with assembly lines and human–machine interactions. In an increasingly technological age, it is likely there will be increasing demand for workers who are skilled in this subdisciplinary area of psychology.

Review Questions

1. Outline some of the developments of psychoanalysis in the United States following World War II.
2. Identify major events in the institutionalization of humanistic psychology. What attempts have been made to increase the international and scientific appeal of humanistic psychology?
3. What were the main contributions of Harry Harlow's research? How is his work incongruent with the neobehaviorism of B. F. Skinner?
4. Describe specific developments that contributed to the advance of cognitive psychology.
5. Briefly discuss three major themes in cognitive psychology.
6. What are the main arguments for and against the computer metaphor?
7. In your opinion, does cognitive psychology represent a paradigm shift or revolution? What evidence would you employ in defending your position?
8. Why would you endorse a unified psychology? Why would you support a pluralistic one?
9. Describe criticisms of cognitive psychology. Are these criticisms valid?
10. What are the historical roots of clinical psychology? What historical thinkers considered clinical questions before the advent of psychology as a formal discipline?
11. What were critical events in the emergence of clinical psychology as a subfield of psychology and a formal profession?
12. Describe the components of the Boulder model. Why do you think these factors were chosen?
13. Name three cognitive or cognitive-behavioral therapists. How are their views similar? How are their perspectives different?
14. Name two reductionistic biological psychologists. Name two biological psychologists who emphasize systems or holistic approaches. What methodological and topical differences are there between these perspectives?
15. Describe three productive topics of study in biological psychology.
16. Is the use of fMRI and PET scan information to locate areas of the brain that correlate with specific cognitive functions the "new phrenology," or do these approaches provide valid methods to evaluate the relationship between cognition and neurology?
17. In what ways has biological psychology benefited from infusions of ideas and researchers from other disciplines?
18. What possible social and cultural problems can arise from the study of genes and behavior, specifically intelligence and genetics?

19. Describe similarities and differences in the methodologies and research topics of Muzafer Sherif, Solomon Asch, and Stanley Milgram.
20. Which early applied psychologist, in your opinion, provided the strongest foundation for early industrial and organizational psychology? How would you defend your choice?

Glossary

Allport, Floyd H. (1890–1971) A founder of experimental social psychology, Allport pioneered research in conformity, social influence, and prejudice.

Asch, Solomon (1907–1996) A social psychologist in the Gestalt tradition, Asch performed classic conformity studies in which participants often conformed to strangers' mistaken perceptions of the length of a clearly visible line.

autokinetic effect The tendency of a fixed point of light to appear to move. Muzafer Sherif examined the ways that social norms influenced the perceived degree of movement.

Bandura, Albert (b. 1925) Psychologist who studied vicarious or observational learning.

Bartlett, Frederick Charles (1886–1969) British psychologist who stressed the role of representations or schemas in memory and cognition.

Beck, Aaron T. (b. 1921) An early cognitive therapist who helped clients reduce negative thoughts and more accurately perceive themselves. He developed the Beck Depression Inventory.

behavioral genetics The study of the role of genes in cognition and behavior.

Boulder model The model for current clinical training that recommends doctoral programs train clinical psychologists as research-practitioners with solid backgrounds in general and clinical psychology, extensive supervised experience, and research experience.

cognitive psychology A broad interdisciplinary effort to study the processing of information in memory, problem solving, judgment, and other forms of cognition. Also known as cognitive science or information-processing psychology.

computer metaphor The use of computers to model and study cognitive functions of humans and animals.

Eccles, John C. (1903–1997) Received the 1963 Nobel Prize for his work on synaptic transmission.

ecological validity The view that psychologists should study real-world, everyday events about the human condition. Cognitive psychology has been criticized for its lack of ecological validity.

Follett, Mary Parker (1868–1933) An early industrial-organizational psychologist who applied her background in political psychology to corporate issues and seminal executive development seminars.

Gilbreth, Lillian (1878–1972) Called the "Mother of Industrial and Organizational Psychology," she and her husband Frank Gilbreth helped launch the field of ergonomics. She studied many diverse topics including worker efficiency and effective management.

Harlow, Harry Frederick (1905–1981) American psychologist noted for his creative contributions to learning theory and the formation of attachment.

Hebb, Donald Olding (1904–1985) A pioneer in the neurobiology of learning, he provided a testable explanation of associationist learning and evaluated the effects of the environment on rats' neurological development.

information-processing metaphor The view that cognition involves the processing of information in a sophisticated manner or sequence. Also known as the computer metaphor.

Kandel, Eric (b. 1929) A biological psychologist taking reductionistic approaches to the physiological aspects of memory in animal models.

learning set Harlow's finding that previous experience can facilitate a primate's ability to discriminate among stimuli. Harlow also referred to this process as *learning to learn*.

Lindsley, Donald B. (1907–2003) An early cognitive and behavioral neuroscientist, he helped launch the electrical study of the brain, particularly with his application of the EEG to psychological research.

Linehan, Marsha M. (b. 1943) Developer of DBT, a blend of Western scientific approaches to behavior and Eastern mindfulness practices.

mentalism The use of words such as *mind*, *intention*, and *cognition* in the study of science. This aspect of cognitive psychology was challenged by B. F. Skinner.

Milgram, Stanley (1933–1984) A social psychologist who examined participants' willingness to obey an authority's orders to injure or even apparently kill another human.

mindfulness The practice of observing thoughts without letting them entangle us; being centered and conscious in the present moment without delusion or judgment.

Piaget, Jean (1896–1980) Swiss epistemologist who advanced a popular developmental theory of serially progressive stages of human cognition.

psychoneuroimmunology The study of the interactions between the brain, behavior, the immune system, and the social and physical environments. The field was launched by Robert Ader and colleagues in the 1970s and 1980s.

psychopharmacology The use of pharmaceuticals to treat individuals with psychological disorders.

Rational Emotive Behavior Therapy (REBT) An early form of cognitive-behavioral therapy developed by Albert Ellis. Initially called Rational Therapy, this system gained its formal name in 2004.

Scott, Walter Dill (1869–1955) American psychologist and a critical early figure in the study of applied and industrial psychology as well as the psychology of advertising.

Shakow, David (1901–1980) A prominent clinical psychologist who developed training models for clinical psychologists that included internship and certification standards. His "Shakow Report" formed the core of the Boulder model of clinical education.

Sherif, Muzafer (1908–1988) An early social psychologist in the Gestalt tradition. He studied social norms with the autokinetic effect, and he organized the famous boys' camp studies of prejudice.

Sperry, Roger W. (1913–1994) Biological researcher who studied the effects of split-brain operations on animals and humans with epilepsy.

systematic desensitization Joseph Wolpe's popular behavior therapy based on Pavlovian conditioning. Originally called *reciprocal inhibition*, the methodology involves progressive-relaxation techniques paired with an anxiety hierarchy.

Wisconsin General Test Apparatus An apparatus designed by Harry Harlow to study form discrimination in primates.

Wolpe, Joseph (1915–1997) Psychiatrist and founding figure of behavior therapy. His work on systematic desensitization revolutionized therapy for anxiety disorders and placed him at the forefront of the "first wave" of psychotherapy.

18 Prospects for the Twenty-First Century

Thou shalt behold / The worlds beyond thy little world

—Lord Byron, 1821/1970

William James and Wilhelm Wundt, as well as many other founders, understood the potential breadth and reach of the new psychology, but the discipline has clearly exceeded their most optimistic expectations. Expansion has been driven by internal disciplinary developments and discoveries but also by the rapid unfolding of external events that could not have been easily foreseen or anticipated when the discipline was in its infancy. The space age called for psychologists to think about life in confined and esoteric environments; the demands of an increasingly crowded world along with climate change have fostered a need for the development of environmental or ecopsychology; changing age demographics and expanded life spans have forced attention to the psychological problems of aging; and once secure categories such as male and female have given way to entirely new ways to think about the multiple meanings of gender and personal identity. A host of additional external developments are shaping all academic disciplines in multiple directions.

Psychology, like all other disciplines, finds itself in a world that is both shrinking and expanding. Dizzying accelerations of speed in computation, transportation, and communication over the past century have shrunk the world and dramatically altered the meanings of space and time. Modern computer technology requires new time and distance measures such as the nanosecond (a billionth of a second). A nanosecond was difficult to imagine until computer scientist Grace Hopper (2012) provided a visual aid by pointing out that electricity travels just under twelve inches in a billionth of a second. Paradoxically, the speeds involved in micro technologies have contributed to a rapidly expanding world, with electronic libraries larger by orders of magnitude than the greatest libraries of the past. The difference is that electronic libraries reduce travel to and within the library and are readily available to anyone with access to the nearest computer, tablet, or smartphone. The epigraph that opens this chapter (Byron, 1821/1970, p. 529) has never been more applicable or relevant than it is in the opening years of the twenty-first century.

The previous chapter explored some of the most dominant topical areas and characteristics of psychology in the latter half of the twentieth century. In this final chapter, we explore trends that are surfacing in the early decades of the twenty-first century. Some of the trends touch on basic scientific and philosophical issues, but most focus on applications of psychology and real-world needs and problems. Topics such as globalization, health, disciplinary identity, legal issues, education, and faith enter the picture in this final chapter. We also address important recent events in psychology as characterized in the **Hoffman Report** (2015). We begin with the problem of disciplinary as well as personal identity in the context of increasing global perspectives and multiculturalism.

Globalization and Multiculturalism: Psychology in an Expanding World

Critical psychologists question traditional methods and assumptions in psychology and emphasize social justice and equality. In his discussion of **critical psychology**, Teo (2015) asks you to engage in the following thought experiment: "Assume you were born in the 5th century—would you think, feel, want, and do the same things you do now?" (p. 245). Consider also how you would have been shaped had you been born in a country and culture radically different from your current location. Consider different identities; would you want the same things if you identified with a different ethnicity, gender, or level of income? Such questions sharpen sensitivity to the effects of time and context on thought processes, along with awareness of our subjectivity, including our sense of who we are, what we believe, how we think, and what we desire. Such awareness inevitably has consequences for the ways we conduct our lives and the ways we think about others.

Teo notes that critical psychology is an international movement supported by scholarly journals (e.g., *Annual Review of Critical Psychology*), numerous books, a four-volume encyclopedia, and various conferences. The problem of subjectivity is one of the major concerns addressed by academicians and practitioners concerned with critical psychology. Advocates of critical psychology hope to promote a deeper and wider consciousness of the relations between our actions and the ways we perceive the world and ourselves. Habitual, local, time-bound, authority-based, "one-size-fits-all" solutions are called into question. The new emphasis is on awareness of the plurality of legitimate interests and the need for ameliorating actions that abound in a world marked, in the words of Teo, by "inequality, alienating institutions, and power struggles" (2015, p. 250).

Trends toward globalization and multiculturalism have implications for organizations as well as individuals. Psychology, as a formal discipline, was born in Europe and extended quickly to the United States. The temporal and spatial location of the discipline was highly relevant to methodologies, assumptions, and the nature of the topics to be investigated. There was, however, an early awareness that psychological thought exceeds the boundaries of time and place. Virginia Staudt Sexton and Henryk Misiak (1976), in their edited book *Psychology around the World*, reminded readers that psychology is international as they called attention to the development and status of psychology in forty countries. Gardner and Lois Murphy (1968), in their book *Asian Psychology*, explored psychological thought in India, China, and Japan. Numerous other writers published articles on the development of psychological thought in a variety of geographic locations (see Viney et al., 1979). A new and much stronger emphasis on globalization of psychology has been apparent in recent years.

There is a growing awareness that psychologists have largely studied people in societies that are **W.E.I.R.D.**: Western, Educated, Industrialized, Rich, and Democratic (Heinrich et al., 2010). Only about 12 percent of the earth's population lives in this context. Additionally, by studying predominantly university undergraduates, psychologists have further narrowed the base of their scholarship. How well do psychological findings represent the larger world population? In the early 1990s, scholars opened the door to these questions (Markus & Kitayama, 1991), which have continued to gain prominence and to generate extensive criticism in the process (Suedfeld, 2016).

Spatial boundaries and sensitivities have evolved throughout history as a result of changes in mobility and technology. We are now creatures who live locally, regionally, nationally, globally and cosmically. The reasons for transitions from one location to the next have always been of interest to historians. Each transition results in profound social, psychological, political, philosophical, and religious mutations (Mesoudi et al., 2016). Claire Colebrook (2002, p. 133), describing the philosophy of Gilles Deleuze, speaks of "transversal becomings" to describe the ongoing, abrupt, and unexpected changes in the ways we see the external world and the ways we see ourselves and others. Astronauts speak of near mystical experiences as they regard the earth from the vantage point of space. The transitions from one location to another always result in new perspectives, unexpected questions, novel ways to organize things, expanding understandings of who we are, and sometimes a rejection of modernity based on frightening dislocations and nostalgia for lost locations once regarded as secure.

On the other hand, globalized societies are inevitably enriched and challenged in their exposure to the perspectives, foods, practices, and ideas of other cultures. It is understandable that there are exclusionary and defensive reactions based on beliefs about preserving what has been enduring in a given culture. Clashes over topics such as dress modes, the display of symbols, appropriate interpersonal spaces, gender roles, legal issues, sacred spaces and practices, appropriate political structures, immigration, and tolerance for differences remain continuing challenges.

Greater difficulties surface in questions of personal identity. Who are we, and how do our local singularities and values fit in an expanding pluralistic world? How can psychology help with these difficult questions?

There is increasing awareness that an adequate modern psychology in a globalized world must be informed by robust multiple engagements. Accordingly, psychologists as scientists and as practitioners are increasingly bringing global perspectives to a great range of topical areas, including women's issues (Tan, 2016; Fulu & Miedema, 2016), television content (Chalaby, 2016), health equity (Schrecker, 2016), and income inequality (Sheng, 2015). The range of topics that are being explored covers much of what has been included in traditional psychological and sociological studies, but globalization expands horizons and challenges earlier philosophical and cultural singularities and certitudes. Philosopher A. C. Grayling (2015) argues that "Simplicity" is an idea that must die and that nature itself is probably not that interested in simplicity. Grayling's critique of simplicity is aimed largely at biological reductionism that sees "nothing in the pearl but the disease of the oyster," but critiques of simplicity are all the more applicable in the case of psychological, political, and social phenomena that have to date been regarded from largely local perspectives. Psychology in the opening decades of the twenty-first century is increasingly informed by an awareness of the limitations of purely local, regional, or even national perspectives.

Changing Perspectives on Gender

Throughout this book we have visited and revisited historical highlights of sex and gender issues. If anything, these questions will continue into the twenty-first century because of ignorance and deeply entrenched discriminatory patterns that prevail through much of the world. Through much of the history of psychology, scholars have confounded **sex** (which is biological) and

481

gender, "the attitudes, feelings, and behaviors that a culture associates with a person's biological sex" (American Psychological Association, 2011, p. 11). Psychologists have long assumed that people assigned male at birth based on visual inspection of genitalia would be men, that people assigned female at birth would be women, and that men and women must be essentially different (see Braaten & Viney, 2000). Despite the prevalence of these views, physicians have long known that these supposedly biological categories present problems; for example, after an extensive review of records, Blackless et al. (2000) concluded that up to 2 percent of live births involve a child who is intersex or who shows sexual variation of some kind. Beyond physical variations, it has long been recognized that people may not fit the biological category to which they were assigned at birth. Throughout history, people transitioned across genders, publicly or privately. For example, Horwitz (1998) describes a man who served in combat in the Civil War and then lived much of the rest of his life as a carpenter (a field largely closed to women at that time) despite being assigned female at birth. In 1952, Christine Jorgenson underwent the first sexual reassignment surgery, and she inspired questions as well as extensive backlash for her public transition (Jorgenson & Stryker, 1967/2000). We are now growing in our recognition that two categories of gender do not capture human experience, and perhaps more importantly, that two categories of gender have *never* been adequate (see Viney & Woody, 2017). Few cultural notions about personal identity have changed as quickly as our ideas about gender, inspiring intense cultural, religious, and legal debates about school and bathroom access as well as the consequences of discrimination (Rankin et al., 2010; Seelman, 2016). Psychologists have worked to enhance scientific, practical, and ethical approaches to people who identify outside of the gender binary (American Psychological Association, 2015; Singh & dickey, 2016). We expect debates to continue and practices to be challenged alongside the growing recognition of the extensive variation in human gender identity and expression.

Intersectionality in the Psychology of Prejudice and Privilege

The landscape of the psychology of prejudice and privilege has changed rapidly in recent years. There is a growing recognition that prejudice and privilege are inseparable. Rather than seeing only some people facing disadvantage, for example due to their ethnicity, we now recognize that relative disadvantage can only exist in the presence of relative advantage or **privilege** (Weekes, 2009). For example, if people with some identities are less likely to be hired, then people with privileged identities are more likely to be hired. Additionally, scholars are now recognizing the complexity of individual identities. The notion of **intersectionality** reflects the growing awareness that each of us carries multiple privileged and devalued identities and that the effects of these identities vary with context (Else-Quest & Hyde, 2016). For example, if I identify as a woman who is Asian, my gender may feel more salient and negative in my engineering classes than in my psychology classes (where a majority of students are women); my ethnicity may fit advantageous stereotypes about my math ability; and, as a traditional college student, my age may negatively shape the reactions of my neighbors when I move into my new apartment. How we experience the world rests on multiple facets of our identities and the context (Collins & Bilge, 2016). The scholarship continues to grow to capture more of human experience, particularly as we grow in our awareness of the complex interactions of environments and individual identities.

Health Psychology

The modern world, from about 1600, has witnessed seismic shifts in understanding of the causes, prevention, and cure of diseases. The ignorance and gloomy fatalism of earlier eras have been replaced by justifiable hope and optimism based on the clearly demonstrated powers of modern science to enhance the quality of life. Imagine going to a dentist in previous centuries prior to the development of local anesthetics and prior to interventions in the control of gum disease, and tooth decay. Think of the many ways we can now preserve or enhance eyesight and hearing. Joint replacements, organ transplants, life-saving surgical interventions, prosthetics, and antibiotics are among the interventions that create expectations for comforts and quality of life unavailable and unimaginable to previous generations.

The very success of the health care industry has created new moral sensitivities about equity of access to all those services that enhance the quality of life. The role of profit in the health care industry has been called into question in many countries where access to health maintenance is increasingly viewed as a basic human right comparable to police and fire protection. The trend has been toward an ideal of quality of life based on health care as an entry-level benefit bestowed by society on each child and as a continuing benefit through the life span of the individual. There is also growing sensitivity to the fact that health maintenance is not just medical; it is multidimensional with social, political, philosophical, and psychological components.

The psychology of health and health maintenance—**health psychology**—has been one of the fastest growing interest areas in the larger discipline. In the late 1970s the American Psychological Association established Division 38, Society for Health Psychology (Belar et al., 2003), to emphasize the study of psychological and behavioral aspects of health and health maintenance. Subsequently, the APA, in recognition of the need for further academic and professional support structures, established the journal *Health Psychology*, initially published on a quarterly basis. The rapid growth of scholarly and professional work in the area resulted in a transition to bimonthly publication, but continued growth

of interest has now resulted in monthly publication of this important journal. There are additional scholarly journals such as *The Journal of Health Psychology* and *The British Journal of Health Psychology*, as well as a growing number of programs offering degrees in health psychology.

Health psychologists move back and forth almost seamlessly between science and practice. Ecology has been viewed as a moral science and the same can be said for health science. Basic discoveries often have obvious and immediate implications for personal and social interventions. The "is" and the "ought" are not easily separated in this field.

Health psychologists explore an enormous range of issues and problems that relate to health and health maintenance. Studies on topics such as obesity and weight control, coping styles with cancer, smoking behavior, drug use, and the many problems of aging are common in the literature, but there are all kinds of creative studies pertinent to health that might not have been anticipated. For example, there is some evidence that generosity (prosocial spending or the tendency to give to others) may be associated with lower blood pressure (Whillans et al., 2016). Basic attitudes are also relevant to health. For example, there is often a major difference between "subjective age" (how old we feel) and chronological age. One study (Yannick et al., 2016) found that subjective age predicts hospitalization in the elderly. How old we feel ourselves to be may often have greater implications for basic health than chronological age.

As noted in Chapter 16, positive subjective orientations are critical to optimal human functioning. Subjective well-being, relations with others, meaningful work, economic stability, and environmental quality all relate to health (see Diener et al., 2015). The field of *positive psychology* (Seligman, 2004) is included as an important part of health psychology as well as other subdisciplines. Health and its maintenance has always been the major goal of the medical sciences and these sciences are now joined, supplemented, and enhanced by the behavioral and social sciences.

483

Positive Psychology

At the end of the twentieth century and into the new millennium, scholars have promoted **positive psychology**, the study of positive experience and the strengths of individuals and human communities (Seligman & Csikszentmihalyi, 2000). Although some historical psychologists, such as Jung, Frankl, and Maslow (McLafferty & Kirylo, 2001), emphasized optimal functioning in their work, Seligman and Csikszentmihalyi (*CHICK sent me high*) responded to criticisms that psychology has been excessively problem-focused. This rapidly growing movement has roots in traditional psychological research, such as studies of conditioning.

In the last three decades, several enterprising researchers have employed operant and Pavlovian conditioning principles to reveal intriguing new findings about learning. Martin E. P. Seligman (b. 1942) and his colleagues documented that laboratory animals may learn helplessness if the consequences of their behavior appear independent of that behavior. Seligman has applied his findings on learned helplessness to the study of depression (Seligman & Csikszentmihalyi, 2000). Similarly, the research of Robert A. Rescorla (b. 1940) on contingencies (learning relations among events) has expanded the fundamental principles of Pavlovian conditioning (Rescorla, 2002). Research with animals produced impressive advances in the understanding of learning and its neurophysiological underpinnings, but prohibitive costs, animal rights activism, and legitimate moral issues have increasingly challenged such research. Positive psychology includes studies of optimal experience or flow (Csikszentmihalyi, 1990) and has now expanded into health psychology and social psychological research as well as into existential psychology and ecopsychology (Passmore & Howell, 2014).

Ecopsychology

The origin of the prefix "eco" goes back to ancient times with words such as the Latin *oeco* and the Greek *oikos* meaning house, dwelling, household, or place of residence. The term ecology, in contemporary usage, refers not just to our local habitat, but to larger physical and biological environments. The term *ecology*, literally the science of living things in relation to each other and their environments, was coined in the 1860s by the German zoologist Ernst Haeckel. Studies in ecology accelerated rapidly in the second half of the twentieth century, but there were tensions over how to prioritize the great varieties of ecological studies. For example, plant ecology and animal ecology obviously overlap in many distinctive ways, but each is a highly specialized study requiring different kinds of skills, methodologies, and vocabularies. Within plant ecology, there is also forest ecology that sometimes stands in contrast with range or grassland ecology. Other specialty areas include ocean, atmospheric, agricultural, river, and architectural ecologies, among many others. In recent years there has been growing interest in a field known as **ecopsychology**. The term *ecopsychology* entered the English language in 1963 in an article by J. B. Calhoun on "population dynamics and social organization on the vertebrate level." Calhoun (1963) pointed to the necessity of a "coalescent discipline, ecopsychology." The reach of such a coalescent discipline was set forth by Theodore Roszak (1993) in his classic book titled *The Voice of the Earth: An Exploration of Ecopsychology*. Ecopsychology is a topical area that relates closely to our earlier discussions of globalization and health psychology, and this is an area that will, and must, grow significantly as we move further into the problems that will be encountered in the twenty-first century.

Ecopsychology is possibly the most complex of the various subdisciplines of ecology and therefore the most difficult to define. Human ecology includes physical, temporal, personal, social, economic, experiential, and cultural influences. Physical influences include geographic, technological, architectural, and meteorological variables that promote, constrain, or limit the course and possibilities for human life. On the temporal side, we are creatures who live in time. It takes little imagination to consider how different life might have been, say, five hundred years ago: no airplanes, automobiles, life-saving antibiotics, or all the daily conveniences resulting from the harnessing of electricity such as smartphones, refrigerators, computers, radio, and television. Contemporary technological advances go a long way toward defining life as we know it today, including the ways we think and feel, what we believe and value, and how we adjust. We are situated in time with emerging capacities to discern potential ecocidal as well as eco-friendly developments. In addition to physical and temporal influences, human ecology includes social and cultural variables such as family, friends, language, aesthetic expressions, religious institutions, political and economic structures, and philosophical or metaphysical systems.

The complexity of human ecology is illustrated by the fact that human beings can live in the most favorable physical circumstances but remain ecologically compromised and in poor health because of toxic economic, social, and cultural circumstances. The field of ecopsychology, sensitive to the multidimensional influences in human life, calls for a radical revisioning of psychology that includes and goes beyond many of the ideas we have encountered in some of the earlier systems of psychology. The reach of ecopsychology extends to architecture that includes building designs that are nature-oriented. As noted by Joye (2012), architectural structures can be a kind of second nature making use of light, openness, fresh air, and a sense of wholeness and well-being. The philosopher Charles Hartshorne (1991) valorized the role of aesthetics in philosophical visions, quoting with approval Beethoven's claim that tones made by musical instruments are "primordial feelings of nature" (p. 600).

There were numerous precursors of ecopsychology in the earlier systems of psychology, including the Gestalt school with its rejection of piecemeal, atomistic, and elementaristic approaches to the world. Humanistic, phenomenological, and existential psychologies with their emphasis on the primacy of human experience also play out in the background of ecopsychology (see May, 1953; Passmore & Howell, 2014). William James, with his emphasis on experience, diversity of relations, intimacy, and the conflation of self and world, also figures in the intellectual background of ecopsychology. There are extensive additional precursors encountered in earlier intellectual developments across multiple fields such as evolution, philosophy, political movements such as the counterculture of the 1960s, and science (see Buzzell & Chalquist, 2015; Kahn & Hasbach, 2012).

The radical new vision of ecopsychology demands deeper sensitivities to the width and depth of the complexities of our human household. The new vision is illustrated in the concept of **ecotherapy** (Buzzell & Chalquist, 2009; Tudor, 2014). The older notion of psychotherapy, with its emphasis on exploration of the inner world and salutary behavioral adjustments, is not rejected, but is complemented by holistic sensitivities to the relations of the inner world of experience and connections with nature and with the social and physical architectures of our surroundings. The inner world of experience cannot be separated from the multiple settings in which it is situated. Simple shifts in external structures often have salutary or toxic consequences. For example, a simple shift from one school to another or one teacher to another may have life-altering implications for the lives of students. In an article on ecotherapy, Hasbach (2012) emphasizes the salutary and healing effects of contacts with nature. In response to questions about what ecotherapists do, she notes that they listen and talk and recognize the many problems that arise from a great host of social or interpersonal pathologies. But nature itself is always a backdrop for the ecotherapist. Alienation or dissociation from nature, especially in our frenzied technological age, is an important source of problems.

Kahn (2013) calls attention to the "evolutionary architecture of our bodies, minds, and spirits and our deep-seated needs for multiple and sustained connections with our natural habitat" (p. 163). These needs have been severely compromised in our hurried technological world.

There are now major peer-reviewed academic journals and multiple reference sources for ecopsychology. The journal *Ecopsychology* was inaugurated in 2009 and publishes scholarly empirical research articles as well as theoretical, philosophical, and teaching articles (e.g., Mace et al., 2012). There is also a *European Journal of Ecopsychology*, and there are emerging possibilities for education and training in this important endeavor. Ecopsychology, if it is a system at all in the sense of our earlier definition of systems, could become the most pluralistic and comprehensive approach to the problems of living that we have encountered to date (Buzzell, 2014). It extends the meanings of context well beyond the meanings encountered in any of the systems of psychology. It can be characterized in terms of a practical pluralism from the standpoint of ontology, epistemology, and axiology. On the theoretical side, however, ecopsychology emphasizes a thorough-going, even radical, interrelatedness. In the words of William James, "There can *be* no difference anywhere that doesn't *make* a difference elsewhere" (James, 1907/1975b, p. 30).

Psychology and the Law

The intersection of psychological and legal themes played out long before the emergence of psychology as a formal discipline. For centuries, observers have speculated that human motives could contaminate legal outcomes. In the seventeenth century, Francis Bacon noted tensions between legal goals of justice and human drives for revenge. Hoping to separate vengeance from the legal system, he wrote that "Revenge is a kind of wild justice, which the more Man's nature runs to, the more ought the law to weed it out" (Bacon, 1625/1857, p. 46).

Intellectual Traditions

From the mid-1700s to modern times, legal systems in Western nations shifted from brutal to more lenient punishments with a greater role for extenuating factors such as the mental state of the defendant (Foucault, 1979). Early cases in English common law established distinct judgments for people with mental illnesses who may not recognize the difference between right and wrong (Brigham & Grisso, 2003). However, questions about mental illness and expert testimony came to the forefront of public perception in England with the trial of Daniel M'Naughton.

In 1843, M'Naughton tried to assassinate Sir Robert Peel, the prime minister of England, but due to an error, he shot and killed Edward Drummond, the prime minister's secretary (Rychlak & Rychlak, 1990a). To aid the jury in its decision regarding M'Naughton's behavior and psychological state, the court invited nine medical professionals to address the court. After considering the recommendations of the experts, the jury found M'Naughton not guilty by reason of insanity. M'Naughton spent the remainder of his life institutionalized, first at Bethlem Royal Hospital and then at Broadmoor. The landmark M'Naughton case established the role of expert psychological testimony in questions of mental illness.

Additional legal events shaped the relationship between psychology and law. Eight years before becoming a Supreme Court Justice, Louis D. Brandeis (1856–1941) brought social psychology into the legal system in a brief for a 1908 court case (Ogloff & Finkelman, 1999). In the early twentieth century, the state of Oregon, like much of the United States, regulated male and female labor differently. The state pressed criminal charges and convicted the owner of a laundry who mandated that his female workers had to spend more than ten hours a day on the job. The owner appealed to the U.S. Supreme Court, and Brandeis, an eminent attorney who would later serve on the Supreme Court, wrote a lengthy brief in support of the state's position.

The brief provided only a cursory review of legal arguments; a majority of Brandeis's materials presented data from social science to support the state's claims that long working hours were particularly detrimental to women. Brandeis based his arguments on claims of women's physical and psychological inferiority, and later scholars view the social science underlying Brandeis's work as rather poor (Monahan & Walker, 1994). Despite these limitations, the Supreme Court upheld the laundry owner's conviction and the laws supporting gender differences in working hours. This case affected the legal system in important ways. First, the phrase "Brandeis brief" continues to describe any collection of scientific or other non-legal materials submitted to support one side in a court case. Second, Brandeis paved the way for increasing contributions to legal decisions from social scientists.

The famous desegregation case, *Brown v. Board of Education* (1954), increased the prominence of psychology and motivated more interaction between psychologists and the legal system. In what Monahan and Walker (1994) referred to as "the best-known use of social science in any area of law" (p. 148), a group of thirty-five researchers in psychology, psychiatry, and other fields compiled and signed a Brandeis brief arguing that segregation causes consistent, significant, and preventable harm to children (Brigham & Grisso, 2003). Psychologists were not unified in their attack on segregation, however; Henry Garrett, chair of psychology at Columbia University and Mamie Clark's dissertation advisor, had testified in a previous case in support of continued racial segregation in education (Jackson, 2000; see Garrett, 1930). Given the impact of psychological testimony on the outcome of *Brown*, which ended "separate but equal" practices in the United States, psychologists guaranteed their continued involvement with the legal system.

In the late 1800s and early 1900s, psychologists initiated basic and applied research into legal issues, including well-known scholars such as Münsterberg, Jung, and Wertheimer as well as lesser-known scholars such as Arnold (1906; see

Bornstein & Penrod, 2008). Carl Jung and Max Wertheimer engaged in an extended dispute over who should receive credit for pioneering the use of free association techniques to detect lies; Jung's paper was published first, but Wertheimer had submitted his work first (see King & Wertheimer, 2005). In the same year as Brandeis's famous brief, Hugo Münsterberg (1908) opened the door to topics such as false confessions, including those that the false confessor believed to be true, and the role of hypnosis in memory and crime prevention (Kassin, 2016). Questions related to false or coerced confessions have exploded in recent years with documentaries, increased news coverage, and changing case law (Burns et al., 2013; Starr, 2015a, 2015b). Across psychology and law, one of Münsterberg's most enduring legacies came in his work on eyewitness testimony.

Hugo Münsterberg and Eyewitness Testimony

The accuracy of eyewitness testimony was an early interest for forensic investigators such as the German criminologist Franz von Liszt (1851–1919). As described by Münsterberg (1908), during class, von Liszt's students unexpectedly witnessed an intense argument culminating in an actual gunshot (the pistol had been loaded with a blank round). When von Liszt asked his students to describe the people and the events in question, students' reports varied and often proved inaccurate. Imagine being in the classroom for that demonstration! We can only wonder if the experience affected the students' hearing and emotional welfare along with their eyewitness memories.

In 1906, Münsterberg (1908) brought a similar demonstration to a scientific convention of "jurists, psychologists, and physicians, all, therefore, men well trained in careful observation" (p. 51). During Münsterberg's presentation, a commotion erupted as an individual in a brightly colored clown suit rushed into the meeting followed by a black man; there was a struggle and a gunshot before the confederates ran from the meeting. First, as Münsterberg stated, the attendees at the meeting were all men, and second, the black man was particularly distinctive because the audience, which included scholars who had attended universities that excluded applicants based on race, was composed entirely of white men. After this unusual interruption, Münsterberg asked the attendees to write descriptions of the event. In the reports, he found extensive disagreement, errors, and missing details. In fact, many eyewitnesses had added false information to their testimony. Münsterberg's pioneering studies raised important legal questions about eyewitnesses as well as scientific questions about memory (Memon et al., 2008).

Münsterberg's success as a teacher, researcher, and writer in psychology and law helped the area gain popularity and inspired greater student enrollment in many fields of basic and applied psychology (Sporer, 2006). He was also a pioneer in encouraging courts to consider psychological research (Bornstein & Meissner, 2008), and, as we discussed in Chapter 12, his student, William Moulton Marston, remained interested in lie detection and continued Münsterberg's popularization of psychology (Bunn, 1997). Unfortunately, the intrusion of cultural history lessened his impact on psychology, reducing scholarly interest in psychology and the law. Münsterberg had protested U.S. entry into World War I, he never became a U.S. citizen, and he consistently praised his native Germany, further straining his relations with some American citizens (Spillmann & Spillmann, 1993). Other influences also affected the viability of research in psychology and law; Münsterberg ended his career without graduate students, stifling subsequent research. At the same time, his critics gained favor in psychological and legal circles. The American jurist John Henry Wigmore (1863–1943) publicly assailed Münsterberg with a parody of his research. In his satire, Wigmore (1909) described a fictitious civil trial held on April Fool's Day. At this trial, Münsterberg and "Mr. X Perry Ment" were found liable for damaging the reputation of the legal profession and were assessed damages of $1 (see Sporer, 2006).

Elizabeth F. Loftus

Eyewitness testimony, along with other research topics in psychology and the law, faded to the background of psychology until **Elizabeth F. Loftus (b. 1944)** and other researchers led a "renaissance" in the 1970s (Sporer, 2006, p. i). Loftus's seminal work, *Eyewitness Testimony* (1979/1996), described the field at the time, provided testable hypotheses for future research, and, perhaps most importantly, inspired other researchers. Like Münsterberg, Loftus (1993, 2003) has faced cultural hostilities based on intense cultural and scholarly resistance to her work, especially her investigations into repressed

Elizabeth F. Loftus

488

memories, one of the most contentious psycho-logical issues of the 1990s and one that continues to generate controversy (Patihis et al., 2014). Since the 1970s, the field of eyewitness testimony has grown through the systematic efforts of psy-chologists who have generated a well-developed body of research on eyewitness testimony (Wells et al., 2006). Findings from this research have not remained insulated in psychology; psychologists who are experts in these areas formed an integral part of the working group that assisted the U.S. Department of Justice (1999) in writing guide-lines for collecting evidence from eyewitnesses.

Current Developments

As in the M'Naughton case of old, contemporary forensic psychologists inherited the role of expert witnesses in the American legal system (Brigham & Grisso, 2003). Typically trained as clinicians, forensic psychologists work in the legal system to answer questions about defendants and other individuals interacting with the law (Nicholson, 1999) and address applied issues in criminal and civil trials. In contrast with researchers such as Loftus who apply psychological methods to legal questions, the professional activities of forensic psychologists vary and may include determining whether an individual is mentally ill, assessing the psychological harm of a crime or an injury, assessing a defendant's competency to stand trial, or evaluating a juvenile to determine whether he or she should be transferred to the adult court system (Grisso & Brigham, 2013). The growing role of forensic psychologists in the law, partic-ularly since the 1970s (Packer & Borum, 2013), can be seen in the increasing number of active forensic psychologists and the growing number of training programs for forensic psychology, par-ticularly joint law-and-psychology programs with forensic emphases (Bersoff, 1999).

Social and cognitive psychologists continue to investigate questions of legal importance. Basic and applied researchers study a wide range of topics including but not limited to eyewitness testimony (Wells et al., 2006), interrogation and confession (Kassin & Gudjonsson, 2004; Kassin, 2016), pretrial publicity (Studebaker & Penrod, 1997), and civil and criminal jury decision making (Greene & Bornstein, 2003; Nietzel et al., 1999).

The field of psychology and the law, includ-ing its research and clinical areas, received a major boost in 1969 when Eric Dreikurs and Jay Ziskin gathered interested researchers, expert wit-nesses, and practitioners to form the American Psychology-Law Society (Pickren & Fowler, 2003). Since the late 1960s, psychology and the law has exploded into one of the fastest-growing and most diverse research and applied areas in psy-chology. The continued increase in the public and legal status of the field can be seen in the increas-ing number of psychological experts testifying in court, the growth of psychological consultants in the law, and the increasing citation of psycho-logical research to justify legal decisions (Ogloff & Finkelman, 1999).

Resurgence of Motivation

Most of the classic systems of psychology treated motivation as a central topical area along with sen-sation, perception, and learning. Motivation, for example, was a central organizing principle in the psychologies of Freud and Adler. Learning theo-rists in the behaviorist tradition spoke of drives, goals, anticipatory responses, and drive reduction. Humanistic psychologists such as Maslow, Allport, and Frankl were known primarily for their theoreti-cal treatments of motivation. In the mid-twentieth century, psychology curricula commonly included courses with titles such as Motivation and Emotion, Biogenic Motives, Sociogenic Motives, and Theories of Motivation. However, with the advent of the cognitive movement in psychology, the topic of motivation was deemphasized and courses in motivation were often dropped from curricula (Ferguson, 2000, p. xv).

The cognitive approach to psychology and espe-cially the ascendance of the computer metaphor contributed to the changing status of motivation.

Computers do many things including the basic functions of processing, storing, and retrieving information, but, with the exception of science fiction stories, it is difficult to think of computers as possessing motives or emotions. Motivation is perhaps irrelevant if living things function largely like computers. At the turn of the twenty-first century, however, there were growing suspicions, as noted by Higgins and Kruglanski (2000), that "the cognitive approach cannot explain the intricacies of human psychology" (p. 1). They note that the term motivation can be characterized partly by "the verb 'to want'" (p. 2). The term also refers to goal-directed behavior based on needs and wants. Courses in motivation and emotion include scientific approaches to the physiological, social, and cognitive basis of needs and wants.

Reduction of interest in motivation may also have had deeper philosophical roots. Classic sciences such as physics and chemistry are based exclusively on material, efficient, and formal causes. There is no room for teleological explanations in these sciences. Motivation, often defined as goal-directed behavior, is based on such concepts as anticipation, plans, and desires. Recall that teleology (Aristotle's final cause) focuses on purposes, intentions, and anticipated end states. It can be argued that motivational studies are inherently teleological and therefore incompatible with classic sciences. If psychology is to be a science, should it also avoid teleological concepts?

Recently, however, there has been a resurgence of interest in motivational concepts, marked by recognition that humans and other living creatures live not simply in the past or in the present. Rather we live with an eye to possible future scenarios that have causal consequences for present decisions and actions. Humans act for the sake of reaching a particular kind of future. Furthermore, life includes a deliberative dimension in which possible futures or outcomes are explored in terms of personal or social goals. Recently there has been a significant emphasis on a "science of prospection" (see Baumeister & Vohs, 2016). The language of this science is somewhat different from the language employed by earlier motivation theorists, but the focus is comparable. Concepts such as prospection and motivation are essential to understanding directional vectors in human behavior along with such topics as social judgments, risk taking, addictions, motivated reasoning, aggression, and analysis of attributions. The twenty-first century is likely to witness a return to studies on the interdependence of cognition and motivation.

Evolving Scientific Methodologies

Recall the declaration of Francis Bacon that "the art of discovery may advance as discoveries advance" (1620/1960, p. 120). By almost any measure the art of discovery accelerated in the twentieth century and the acceleration continues in the twenty-first century. As noted in Chapter 2, evolving scientific methodologies have led numerous scholars to declare that there is no longer such a thing as a single scientific method or procedure. Swan (2015) argues that "The scientific idea most ready for retirement is the scientific method itself. More precisely, it's the idea that there's only *one* scientific method" (p. 392). Scientific methodologies have indeed advanced beyond the imaginative capacities of Francis Bacon. From the time of the discovery of x-rays there has been a continuing proliferation of remarkable new instruments of observation. The term **phrontistery**, from the Greek *Phrontisterion*, meaning "thinking place," refers to the ever-growing list of technical tools and ways to observe and measure an enormous range of phenomena in the macro and micro worlds. There are well over four hundred entries in the phrontistery of instruments employed by scientists (Chrisomalis, 2014). These tools have greatly extended the reach and the methods of scientific observation. The scientific revolution has made it possible to literally see with new and fresh eyes things that were completely unknown to our remote and even our more recent ancestors.

The evolution of science is understood not simply by the development of new technical tools of observation, but by new quantitative methods to measure and organize vast data sets. Massive readily available cloud-based data sets are now broken down and unpacked in polyvariate multicolored displays that reveal previously unimagined ways of discerning patterns, relations, and interactions in the content areas of all the sciences, from economics to physics (Ahmadi et al., 2016). The dynamic nature of new scientific methodologies is commonly illustrated in multicolored weather maps based on complex interactions of temperatures, air pressures, humidity gradients, wind direction vectors, and terrain characteristics. Such methodologies make it possible to compute probabilities of the locations, characteristics, and directions of specific kinds of storms for specific geographic regions for specified temporal intervals. Such polyvariate technologies are now employed in all the sciences, including the history of psychology (Pettit, 2016). There is still use for well-controlled univariate or even multivariate studies that result in conclusions based on small carefully collected data sets. Such studies however, may themselves become part of meta-analytic work designed to enhance confidence levels of scientific conclusions. A poll of polls may be more accurate than any single poll.

In addition to large-scale quantitative methods, **qualitative research** methods have come into their own in recent decades. Although many early psychologists started their inquiries with rich and descriptive examinations of human experience, including Freud, Wundt (Brinkmann, 2015), and particularly William James, who used his own experiences as the starting point for many psychological questions (Leary, 2014; see also James, 1899/1983b), the study of human experience quickly lost ground in the early twentieth century (Wertz, 2014). Between the late 1960s and the 1990s, however, scholars across fields refined the tools for qualitative analysis, and

in the 1990s there occurred what Wertz (2014) called "a revolutionary institutionalization of qualitative methods" (p. 4), which gained further support and legitimacy. Leary (2014) argues that qualitative study remains essential for the future success of psychology and should guide scholarship across fields, including experimental fields in psychology and neuroscience.

It should also be noted that modern scientific methodologies have moved far beyond the mere description of natural processes. Description and control have always been central to scientific activities, but new and dramatic possibilities for control are increasingly manifested in fields such as synthetic biology, robotics, and genetic engineering. Early pioneers in the philosophy of science such as Bacon, Descartes, and Galileo would have difficulty grasping the surprising extensions of the epistemology they so highly prized. None of this is to imply, however, that there are not widely accepted beliefs about what counts as science. For example, procedures must be set forth with clarity and results must be replicable.

Science and Faith

The Pew Research Center has conducted demographic studies of religious affiliation in over 230 countries around the world. According to these studies, roughly 80 percent of the world's population identifies with one religion or another. Religion is a powerful force in the daily lives of masses of people and in its institutional and individual expressions it plays significant and sometimes decisive roles in almost every political and social dimension of life. A robust psychology can ill afford to ignore the influence of religion in the lives of individuals and society. Indeed it can be argued that psychology, as a human science, would be remiss and seriously incomplete if it ignored the multiple roles religion plays in human cognitive, emotional, and social functions. Early pioneers in psychology such as William James (1902/1985), Edwin D. Starbuck

491

(1899), and James Leuba (1896, 1912/1969, 1925) understood this simple fact and argued for empirical approaches to the study of religious beliefs and practices and their effects. Their work, in any treatment of the history of psychology, should not be ignored.

The psychology of religion has been a significant part of the history of psychology. This part of psychology must play a significant role in the twenty-first century. Beliefs have consequences both for the individual and for society. Consider the clinical or counseling psychologist working with clients whose adjustments to life cannot be separated from their religious beliefs and practices, or the social scientist who wishes to understand the role religion might play in acceptance of LGBT (lesbian, gay, bisexual, and transgender) communities or in the voice and roles of women within religious communities. Neither can we ignore the possible role of selected religious beliefs in violence and terrorism (see Kimball, 2002; Nelson-Pallmeyer, 2003). Polls continue to show that women generally are more religious than men, but in many traditions they have no access to top leadership roles within faith communities. The relation of religion to sex and gender issues is thus an important topic.

The role of religion in human life has been recognized by the American Psychological Association in the Association's support of Division 36, Society for the Psychology of Religion and Spirituality. There are also numerous journals, including *The Journal for the Scientific Study of Religion*, that support scholarly research on a great variety of religious issues and questions. Significant numbers of contemporary psychologists continue to study religion in the tradition established by the founders. Psychologists, as psychologists, must accept methodological naturalism and bracket any questions regarding non-natural approaches to causality. But there is still great value in empirical studies on topics such as the roles faith might play in topical areas such as: general happiness and a sense of well-being, ways of handling grief and loss, assimilation of new discoveries and beliefs, economic equalities and inequalities, access to health care, and also the roles religious beliefs might play in violence. Religion is not irrelevant and it cannot reasonably be ignored. Studies in the psychology of religion (Hood et al., 2009; Spilka & Ladd, 2013) and science and religion (e.g., Lindberg & Numbers, 1986; Kurtz, 2003; Viney & Woody, 2017) will inevitably enhance understandings of history and of life in the twenty-first century.

Recent Events: EITs and the Hoffman Report

As we near the conclusion of this history of psychology and look to the future, we must consider the immediate and long-term impacts of a recent series of important events. In the first decade of the new millennium, journalists began to report that psychologists were participating in **enhanced interrogation techniques** (EITs) at Guantanamo Bay and elsewhere (see Bloche, 2011; Risen, 2014, for reviews). EITs included stress positions, long-term exposure to cold, sleep deprivation, and waterboarding, among other tactics. Licensed psychologists worked with the Department of Defense (DoD) in the development, implementation, and assessment of the EITs. How could these activities be compatible with the ethics code of the American Psychological Association (2002)?

The APA actively denied any role in these events, but accusations persisted from journalists and others. Finally, to quell the rumors, the APA brought in external evaluators. After an extensive investigation, Hoffman et al. (2015) revealed that "key APA officials, primarily the APA Ethics Director . . . colluded with important DoD officials to have APA issue loose, high-level ethical guidelines that did not constrain DoD in any greater fashion than existing DoD interrogation guidelines" (p. 24). When Hoffman et al. examined motives, they concluded "that APA's principal motive in doing so was to align APA and curry favor with DoD . . . and to keep the growth of psychology unrestrained in this area" (p. 24).

Hoffman et al. concluded that there was "a pattern of secret collaboration with DoD officials" (p. 24) to ensure that the APA ethical guidelines did not preclude psychologists' participation in EITs.

This public relations nightmare exploded in the APA leadership hierarchy, with some APA leaders leaving the organization (Ackerman, 2015) and, finally, a strong statement that prevented participation in "Acts of Torture and Cruel, Inhuman, or Degrading Treatment or Punishment in All Settings" (APA, 2013, ¶1). The recovery of the reputation of the APA and of individual psychologists across the United States remains a long-term project.

Sadly, some psychologists have long feared these possibilities. In 1951, Joost A. M. Meerloo, a Dutch psychoanalyst who had survived torture by the Nazis during his escape from occupied Holland in World War II, warned us. He presciently cautioned that governments would ask psychologists to apply their knowledge of interrogation to what he called *menticide*, the psychological destruction of individuals for political purposes, which he noted would be "unworthy of a 'free democratic psychiatry'" (1951, p. 594). As the APA leadership stated at the release of the Hoffman Report, "What happened never should have" (McDaniel & Kaslow, 2015, ¶2). As we look to the future, we must remain vigilant about applications of our ethics, decisions of our leadership, and our own integrity. The echoes of this event will reverberate into the future of psychology.

Diversity and Pluralism in Modern Psychology

The expansion and reach of contemporary psychology can be characterized as a kind of *diaspora*, the Greek word for "scattering." As we have seen throughout this book, the diaspora is reflected in the pluralistic content of modern psychology, the variety of methodologies employed, and the diversity of professional and scientific organiza-

tions. As of 2016, the American Psychological Association listed fifty-six divisions that reflect an enormous range of activities, from basic research in classic content areas to ever-growing applications in every imaginable arena of life. It seems that psychology is everywhere. Because of its very expansive nature, it was never destined to be an insular and obscure science isolated in the laboratories and lecture halls of academia.

Applications of the discipline were surfacing from the outset of the formal founding in the 1870s (Camfield, 1973) and were particularly obvious in the work of psychologists in World War I and the expansion of clinical psychology in World War II (Gilgen, 1982). However, the rise of applied psychology resulted in tensions within the larger discipline, resulting in the formation of several scientific societies formed in protest against psychology's growing professionalism. A group of experimental psychologists founded the Psychonomic Society in the early 1960s, spawning several outstanding journals, including *Psychonomic Science* (founded in 1964 and changed to the *Bulletin of the Psychonomic Society* in 1973), *Perception and Psychophysics* (1967), *Behavior Research Methods, Instruments and Computers* (1969), and *Memory and Cognition* (1973). The American Psychological Society (APS) also emerged from the strain between professional and scientific psychology. Following a decade of unsuccessful campaigns to reorganize the APA, the Assembly for Scientific and Applied Psychology formally elected to establish the APS in 1988. This national organization, devoted explicitly to scientific psychology, held the first APS convention in 1989. *Psychological Science*, the first APS journal, began publication the following year.

Does the diversity of psychology damage or promote the health and reputation of the discipline and does diversity contribute to disunity? Some psychologists have expressed concerns about disunity in psychology (see Sternberg, 2005), including the claim that disunity undermines the status of the discipline (Staats, 1999, 2005). Such concern is understandable and has resulted in an outpouring of scholarly efforts to find ways to unify or integrate all the branches of the psychological sciences. There has been a stream of anthologies (Grinker, 1956; Royce, 1970; Sternberg, 2005) setting forth arguments pro and con unification. An entire issue of the *Review of General Psychology* was devoted to nineteen different approaches to unification (Candland, 2013). More recently Gaj (2016), in his book *Unity and Fragmentation in Psychology*, has explored varieties of unity along with various approaches to unification.

Concerns over disunity and fragmentation are fueled partly by claims that the more mature sciences are unified and coherent disciplines. For example, Staats (1989) has argued that "Each science undergoes a transition from early disunification to later unification" (p. 143). He noted that this transition has produced considerable consensus regarding theory, methodology, and philosophy in the natural sciences whereas the behavioral sciences are disunited and therefore "relatively backward" (p. 148).

There has, however, been intense disagreement in recent years over the unity or disunity of the sciences. There are thoughtful reminders of the extensive unities to be found in all the sciences from physics, to biology, to evolutionary psychology (Pombo et al., 2014). Others argue that unities between and within the sciences are overestimated (Dupré, 1993; Galison & Stump, 1996; Cartwright, 1999; Clarke, 1998; Kellert et al., 2006). There are vast differences in the content areas of the various sciences and major differences in methodologies. The observational methods of astronomers and field biologists are different from the hands-on experimental manipulations of chemists, and these methods are still different from the methods employed in historical sciences such as paleontology.

In terms of administrative and organizational structures, psychology is as unified as many of the sciences and more unified than some. Undergraduate programs in psychology are typically administered out of a single, usually large department. By contrast, it is now common to encounter twenty or more separate departments

in the various branches of the biological sciences, including botany, horticulture, range science, forestry, zoology, anatomy, animal science, microbiology, biophysics, and biochemistry. Perhaps psychologists overestimate the unity of other sciences; if so, such overestimation may result in an unfortunate devaluing of the scientific and professional status of psychology (see Viney, 1996a). Nevertheless, there is value in exploring various kinds of disciplinary unity (e.g., methodological unity, conceptual unity, unity of language, and unity of purpose). It remains problematic as to whether there is a grand unity that somehow brings together all the great problems of epistemology, axiology, and ontology. In the meantime, and in the spirit of William James, there may be value in celebrating the values that pluralism affords for psychology (Viney, 1989; Viney et al., 1992; Woody & Viney, 2009). If there is a unity to be found, perhaps it will surface from the bottom up rather than from the top down, or in the words of Green (2015b), from "a series of fragments, and then we will see what becomes of the larger psychology as a result" (p. 479).

It is important to think critically about pluralism and fragmentation, but it is equally important to think critically about monistic philosophies, singularities, and the effects of various religious, political, and scientific unification efforts encountered in history. With the rise of Hitler in Germany, Jewish scholars were released from universities and scientists were forced to conceive of science in terms of Aryan politics (see Gimbel, 2012). There was, of course, a mass exodus from Germany of scientists, with predictable consequences for the progress of science in a country that, prior to Hitler, was world-famous for its scientific accomplishments. In the former Soviet Union, there were attempts to force all academic disciplines into a Marxist radical environmentalist framework. The results were especially disastrous for Russian biology and agriculture. There have been attempts to unify the sciences (see Hafling, 1981; Rescher, 1985) and, as noted earlier, numerous proposals for the unification of psychology. To date there has been

494

no unification scheme with the reach or even the promise of a consolidation that satisfies all interest groups. In addition to the importance of exploring the advantages of unification, it may also be beneficial to explore the values of pluralism, especially in the light of the continuing changes that occur over time.

To date, diversity and pluralism form the bedrock for psychology's unfolding expansion. As we have seen, the discipline has undergone unprecedented growth in the decades following World War II. Innovative ways of thinking have emerged while older perspectives have undergone reinterpretation for a new age. Dramatic technologies have opened fresh vistas while revealing the architecture and action of the brain. By design, psychology plays a role in the exploration and understanding of problems and issues that challenge us individually and collectively. Time after time, the ambitions of experimental and applied psychology have transformed how we look at ourselves as well as the world around us. As psychologists, we face a formidable test, as William James (1900/2010) said, "to get human life in its wild intensity" (p. 168). At its best, psychology exposes the trials and rich possibilities of existence, from suffering and pain to joy and fulfillment. Traveling deeper into the century, we anticipate a continuing fascination with a discipline that speaks so directly to the problems confronting the complicated world of human experience and behavior.

Conclusion

It is altogether fitting that a lengthy overview of the history of a discipline should be followed by speculation about the future. But future developments of any discipline do not take place in a vacuum. Political and economic preferences, discoveries in other sciences, and the larger ecosphere will set the context for the future. There are also questions about human tolerance for change. Human beings like stability, but also value innovation; we are torn between conserva-

tive and progressive agendas. Which agenda will prevail? If it is progressive, will rate of change accelerate or will it decline?

In this chapter, we have identified a number of topical areas we see on the horizon. Of course, there are other worthy candidates. We are in a space age with lofty ambitions for exploration. Psychological factors will play highly significant roles in a human-based voyage to Mars or in the development and social structure of habitable space colonies. Climate change will result in large-scale physical and geological changes with inevitable requirements for social and psychological adjustments. It is very possible that the human population will double by 2030, as other life forms disappear or are depleted.

The largest questions we face are social and psychological. The early decades of the twenty-first century witness a host of exclusivist narrow-gauge political and religious systems of thought that often foster violence and terrorism. Fundamental questions now center on the human capacity to examine all belief structures in a deeply critical manner. The task is painful. Frederick Nietzsche (1887/1956) observed the irony that "We knowers are unknown to ourselves" (p. 149). Can we now learn to know ourselves and can we identify the conditions that promote survival, growth, and well-being? These questions underscore the relevance of the human sciences in the twenty-first century.

Review Questions

1. What questions do critical psychologists ask, and why do they raise these questions?
2. What are the consequences when psychologists study a narrow slice of humanity, particularly those who live in countries that are W.E.I.R.D.?
3. How have psychologists and others confounded sex and gender?
4. How do sex and gender differ?
5. How have our views of gender changed in recent history?

6. What are potential benefits of studying intersectionality?
7. How has health psychology expanded into traditional health fields?
8. Describe the roots of positive psychology.
9. What are the primary concerns and hopes of ecopsychologists?
10. What famous legal cases led to the direct involvement of psychologists in the legal system, and how did psychologists contribute to each case?
11. What are some critical social and contextual differences that affected the successes and failures of Hugo Münsterberg and Elizabeth Loftus?
12. What factors have led to a resurgence of motivation studies?
13. How did qualitative research methods emerge in psychology?
14. How do faith and religion affect the lives and experiences of believers and nonbelievers?
15. What are the most important consequences of the Hoffman Report?

Glossary

critical psychology An approach that challenges traditional methods and assumptions in psychology to promote social justice.

ecopsychology The study of the relationships between humans and the natural world, emphasizing principles of psychology and ecology.

ecotherapy A form of therapy that blends traditional therapy and ecopsychology with particular emphasis on human health in the natural world.

enhanced interrogation techniques A series of tactics employed by psychologists against prisoners at Guantanamo Bay and elsewhere, including stress positions, long-term exposure to cold, sleep deprivation, and waterboarding, among others.

gender The attitudes, feelings, and behaviors that a culture associates with a person's biological sex.

health psychology The study of psychological and behavioral aspects of health and health maintenance.

Hoffman Report The independent report that verified the APA's collusion with the Department of Defense to maintain an ethics code for psychologists that would not preclude psychologists' participation in enhanced interrogation techniques.

intersectionality The notion that each of us has multiple privileged and devalued identities and that these interact with our contexts to impact our experiences of advantage or disadvantage in the world.

Loftus, Elizabeth F. (b. 1944) She led the return to questions of eyewitness testimony that helped to revitalize the study of psychology and the law.

phrontistery A list of technical observation and measurement tools and techniques.

positive psychology The scientific study of positive human experience, positive human functioning, and fulfillment among individuals, families, and communities.

privilege The cultural advantages that come to some individuals based on their perceived identities, such as gender, ethnicity, and income.

qualitative research A collection of research methods that incorporate rich and deep examinations of human experience.

sex The biological category to which children are assigned at birth. Typically male, female, or intersex.

W.E.I.R.D. Western, Educated, Industrialized, Rich, and Democratic—almost all participants in psychological research live in nations that are W.E.I.R.D. This limits psychological scholarship to a small proportion of people in the world.

References

Aaen-Stockdale, C. (2008). Last but not least: Ibn Al-Haytham and psychophysics. *Perception, 37*, 636–638.

Abramovitch, Y. (2014). Jung's understanding of schizophrenia: Is it still relevant in the 'era of the brain'? *The Journal of Analytical Psychology, 59*, 229–244.

Abrams, D., & Levine, J. M. (2012). Norm formation: Revisiting Sherif's autokinetic illusion study. In J. R. Smith & S. A. Haslam (Eds.), *Social psychology: Revisiting the classic studies* (pp. 57–75). Thousand Oaks, CA: Sage Publications.

Academy of Sciences of the U.S.S.R. & Academy of Medical Sciences of the U.S.S.R. (1951). *Scientific session on the physiological teaching of academician I. P. Pavlov, June 28–July 4, 1950*. Moscow, U.S.S.R.: Foreign Languages Publishing House.

Ackerman, S. (2015, July 14). Three senior officials lose their jobs at APA after US torture scandal. *The Guardian*. Retrieved January 5, 2016 from www.theguardian.com/us-news/2015/jul/14/apa-senior-officials-torture-report-cia

Adams, N. (2012). Skinner's Walden Two: An anticipation of positive psychology? *Review of General Psychology, 16*, 1–9.

Ader, R. (Ed.). (2006). *Psychoneuroimmunology* (4th ed.). Burlington, MA: Academic Press.

Ader, R., & Cohen, N. (1975). Behaviorally conditioned immunosuppression. *Psychosomatic Medicine, 37*, 333–340.

Ader, R., & Kelley, K. W. (2007). A global view of twenty years of Brain, Behavior, and Immunity. *Brain, Behavior, and Immunity, 21*, 20–22.

Adler, A. (1929). *The science of living*. Garden City, NY: Garden City Publishing.

Adler, A. (1938). *Social interest: A challenge to mankind* (J. Linton & R. Vaughan, Trans.). London: Faber and Faber.

Adler, A. (1957). *Understanding human nature* (W. B. Wolfe, Trans.). New York: Premier Books, Fawcett World Library.

Adler, A. (1964a). The differences between individual psychology and psychoanalysis. In H. L. Ansbacher & R. R. Ansbacher (Eds.), *Alfred Adler: Superiority and social interest* (pp. 205–218). Evanston, IL: Northwestern University Press. (Original work published 1931)

Adler, A. (1964b). *The practice and theory of individual psychology* (P. Radin, Trans.). London: Routledge & Kegan Paul.

Adler, H. E. (1996). Gustav Theodor Fechner: A German Gelehrter. In G. A. Kimble, C. A. Boneau, & M. Wertheimer (Eds.), *Portraits of pioneers in psychology* (Vol. 2, pp. 1–13). Washington, DC: American Psychological Association.

Adler, H. E. (1998). Vicissitudes of Fechnerian psychophysics in America. In R. W. Rieber & K. Salzinger (Eds.), *Psychology: Theoretical-historical perspectives* (2nd ed., pp. 3–14). Washington, DC: American Psychological Association.

Afnan, S. M. (1958). *Avicenna, his life and works*. London: Allen.

Aggarwal, N. (2011). Melancholia in Chahâr Maqâle, a 12th-century Persian text. *The British Journal of Psychiatry, 198*, 378.

Ahmadi, M., Dileepan, P., & Wheatley, K. K. (2016). A SWOT analysis of big data. *Journal of Education for Business, 91*, 289–294.

Aiton, E. J. (1985). *Leibniz: A biography*. Boston: Adam Hilger.

Ajit, N. (2008). On the way to theory: A processual approach. *Organizational Studies, 29,* 173–190.

Alavi, H. R. (2007). Al-Ghazali on moral education. *Journal of Moral Education, 36,* 309–319.

Aleksandrova-Howell, M., Abramson, C. I., & Craig, D. (2012). Coverage of Russian psychological contributions in American psychology textbooks. *International Journal of Psychology, 47,* 76–87.

Alexander, F. G., & Selesnick, S. T. (1966). *The history of psychiatry.* New York: Harper & Row.

Al-Ghazali. (1963). *Al-Ghazali's Tahafut Al-Falasifah* [Incoherence of the philosophers] (Sabih Ahmad Kamali, Trans.). Lahore: Pakistan Philosophical Congress. (Original work published c. 1095)

Ali, S. H. (2012). Learning ecological ethics from Plato. *Science, 335,* 797–798.

Allen, G. (1878a). Hellas and civilization. *The Gentleman's Magazine, 245,* 156–170.

Allen, G. (1878b). Nation-making: A theory of national characters. *The Gentleman's Magazine, 245,* 580–591.

Allen, G. W. (1967). *William James: A biography.* New York: Viking.

Allett, J. (1996). Crowd psychology and the theory of democratic elitism: The contribution of William McDougall. *Political Psychology, 17,* 213–227.

Allik, J. (2007). History of experimental psychology from an Estonian perspective. *Psychological Research, 71,* 618–625.

Allport, F. H. (1920). The influence of the group upon association and thought. *Journal of Experimental Psychology, 3,* 159–182.

Allport, F. H. (1924). *Social psychology.* Boston: Houghton Mifflin.

Allport, F. H. (1974). Floyd H. Allport. In G. Lindzey (Ed.), *A history of psychology in autobiography* (Vol. 6, pp. 3–29). Englewood Cliffs, NJ: Prentice Hall.

Allport, G. W. (1937). *Personality: A psychological interpretation.* New York: Henry Holt.

Allport, G. W. (1943). The productive paradoxes of William James. *Psychological Review, 50,* 95–120.

Allport, G. W. (1950). *The individual and his religion.* New York: Macmillan.

Allport, G. W. (1954). *The nature of prejudice.* Cambridge, MA: Addison-Wesley.

Allport, G. W. (1955). *Becoming: Basic considerations for a psychology of personality.* New Haven, CT: Yale University Press.

Allport, G. W. (1961). *Pattern and growth in personality.* New York: Holt, Rinehart and Winston.

Allport, G. W. (1985). Preface. In V. E. Frankl (Author), *Man's search for meaning* (pp. 9–13). New York: Washington Square Press.

Allport, G. W., Vernon, P. E., & Lindzey, G. (1951). *A study of values* (Rev. ed.). Boston: Houghton Mifflin.

Almond, P. C. (2014). *The Devil: A new biography.* Ithaca, NY: Cornell University Press.

Altus, D. E., & Morris, E. K. (2009). B. F. Skinner's utopian vision: Behind and beyond Walden Two. *The Behavior Analyst, 32,* 319–335.

Alvarez, K. P. (Producer & Director). (2015). *The Stanford Prison Experiment.* IFC Films, USA.

American Psychiatric Association. (2013). *Diagnostic and statistical manual of mental disorders* (5th ed.). Arlington, VA: American Psychiatric Publishing.

American Psychological Association. (1958). American Psychological Association distinguished scientific contribution awards: 1957. *American Psychologist, 13,* 155–158.

American Psychological Association. (2002). Ethical principles of psychologists and code of conduct. *American Psychologist, 57,* 1060–1073.

American Psychological Association. (2011). Guidelines for psychological practice with lesbian, gay, and bisexual clients. *American Psychologist, 67,* 10–42.

American Psychological Association. (2015). Guidelines for psychological practice with transgender and gender nonconforming people. *American Psychologist, 70,* 832–864.

Anderson, F. H. (Ed.). (1960). *Francis Bacon: Baron of Verulam, Viscount St. Albans.* New York: Liberal Arts Press.

Anderson, J. W. (in press). An interview with Henry A. Murray on his meeting with Sigmund Freud. *Psychoanalytic Psychology.*

Anderson, S. K., & Handelsman, M. M. (2009). *Ethics for psychotherapists and counsellors: A proactive approach.* Malden, MA: Wiley.

Andresen, J. (1991). Skinner and Chomsky 30 years later: The return of the repressed. *Behavior Analyst, 14,* 49–60.

Andrews, T. G., & Dreese, M. (1948). Military utilization of psychologists during World War II. *American Psychologist, 3,* 533–538.

Angell, F. (1913). Gustav Theodor Fechner. *Popular Science Monthly, 83,* 40–49.

Angell, F. (1921). Wilhelm Wundt. *American Journal of Psychology, 32,* 161–178.

Angell, J. R. (1909). The influence of Darwin on psychology. *Psychological Review, 16,* 152–169.

Angell, J. R. (1961). James Rowland Angell. In Carl Murchison (Ed.), *A history of psychology in autobiography* (Vol. 3, pp. 1–38). New York: Russell and Russell. (Original work published 1930)

Angioli, A., & Kruger, P. (2015). A genealogy of ideas in Alfred Adler's psychology. *The Journal of Individual Psychology, 71,* 236–252.

Anonymous. (1916). Some suggestions relative to a study of the mental attitude of the Negro. *Pedagogical Seminary, 23,* 199–203.

Ansbacher, H. L. (1994). Was Adler a disciple of Freud? A reply. *Journal of Adlerian Theory, Research and Practice, 50,* 496–505.

Ansbacher, H. L., & Ansbacher, R. R. (Eds.). (1956). *The individual psychology of Alfred Adler.* New York: Basic Books.

Ansbacher, R. R. (1997). Alfred Adler, the man, seen by a student and friend. *Individual Psychology: Journal of Adlerian Theory, Research and Practice, 53,* 270–274.

Antony, M. M., & Roemer, L. (2011). History. In *Behavior therapy* (pp. 7–14). Washington, DC: American Psychological Association.

Araujo, S. d. F. (2012). Why did Wundt abandon his early theory of the unconscious? Towards a new interpretation of Wundt's psychological project. *History of Psychology, 15,* 33–49.

Araujo, S. d. F. (2014a). Bringing new archival sources to Wundt scholarship: The case of Wundt's assistantship with Helmholtz. *History of Psychology, 17,* 50–59.

Araujo, S. d. F. (2014b). The emergence and development of Bekhterev's psychoreflexology in relation to Wundt's experimental psychology. *Journal of the History of the Behavioral Sciences, 50,* 189–210.

Araujo, S. d. F. (2016). *Wundt and the philosophical foundations of psychology: A reappraisal.* Cham, Switzerland: Springer.

Aristotle. (1908). Nicomachean ethics. In W. D. Ross (Ed.), *The works of Aristotle* (Vol. 9). Oxford: Clarendon Press.

Aristotle. (1931a). De anima. In W. D. Ross (Ed.), *The works of Aristotle* (Vol. 3). Oxford: Clarendon Press.

Aristotle. (1931b). On dreams. In W. D. Ross (Ed.), *The works of Aristotle* (Vol. 3). Oxford: Clarendon Press.

Aristotle. (1931c). On memory and reminiscence. In W. D. Ross (Ed.), *The works of Aristotle* (Vol. 3). Oxford: Clarendon Press.

Aristotle. (1931d). On prophesying by dreams. In W. D. Ross (Ed.), *The works of Aristotle* (Vol. 3). Oxford: Clarendon Press.

Arnett, J. J. (2006). G. Stanley Hall's *Adolescence*: Brilliance and nonsense. *History of Psychology, 9,* 186–197.

Arnheim, R. (1943). Gestalt and art. *Journal of Aesthetics, 2,* 71–75.

Arnheim, R. (1962). *The genesis of a painting: Picasso's Guernica.* Berkeley & Los Angeles: University of California Press.

Arnheim, R. (1966). *Toward a psychology of art.* Berkeley & Los Angeles: University of California Press.

Arnheim, R. (1974). *Art and visual perception: A psychology of the creative eye.* Berkeley & Los Angeles: University of California Press.

Arnheim, R. (1986). *New essays on the psychology of art.* Berkeley & Los Angeles: University of California Press.

Arnold, G. F. (1906). *Psychology applied to legal evidence and other constructions of law.* Calcutta, India: Thacker, Spink & Co.

Asch, S. E. (1955). Opinions and social pressure. *Scientific American, 193,* 31–35.

Asch, S. E. (1968). Wolfgang Köhler: 1887–1967. *American Journal of Psychology, 81,* 110–119.

Ash, M. G. (1985). Gestalt psychology: Origins in Germany and reception in the United States. In C. E. Buxton (Ed.), *Points of view in the modern history of psychology* (pp. 295–344). New York: Academic Press.

Ash, M. G. (1995). *Gestalt psychology in German culture, 1890–1967: Holism and the quest for objectivity.* New York: Cambridge University Press.

Ash, M. G., & Woodward, W. R. (Eds.). (1987). *Psychology in twentieth-century thought and society.* New York: Cambridge University Press.

Ashworth, P., & Chung, M. C. (Eds.). (2009). *Phenomenology and psychological science: Historical and philosophical perspectives.* New York: Springer.

Asprem, E. (2010). A nice arrangement of heterodoxies: William McDougall and the professionalization of psychical research. *Journal of the History of the Behavioral Sciences, 46,* 123–143.

Asthana, H. S. (2015a). Founder of modern experimental psychology. *Psychological Studies, 60,* 108–113.

Asthana, H. S. (2015b). Wilhelm Wundt. *Psychological Studies, 60,* 244–248.

Augustine, A. (1955). *Augustine: Confessions and Enchiridion* (A. C. Outler, Ed. and Trans.). Philadelphia: Westminster Press.

Austin, C. R. (1989). *Human embryos: The debate on assisted reproduction.* New York: Oxford University Press.

Averill, L. A. (1990). Recollections of Clark's G. Stanley Hall. *Journal of the History of the Behavioral Sciences, 26,* 107–113.

Averroës. (2008). *Tahafut Al-Tahafut* [The Incoherence of the Incoherence] (S. Van Den Bergh, Trans.). Cambridge, UK: Cambridge University Press. (Original work published c. 1180)

Baars, B. J. (1986). *The cognitive revolution in psychology.* New York: Guilford.

Babkin, B. P. (1949). *Pavlov: A biography*. Chicago: University of Chicago Press.

Backe, A. (2001). John Dewey and early Chicago functionalism. *History of Psychology, 4*, 323–340.

Bacon, F. (1857). Essay IV: Of revenge. In R. Whately (Ed.), *Bacon's essays: With annotations*. London: John W. Parker and Son. (Original work published 1625)

Bacon, F. (1960). *The new organon*. New York: Liberal Arts Press. (Original work published 1620)

Baddeley, A. (1990). *Human memory: Theory and practice*. Boston: Allyn & Bacon.

Baer, J., Kaufman, J. C. Y., & Baumeister, R. F. (Eds.). (2008). *Are we free? Psychology and free will*. Oxford: Oxford University Press.

Bailey, R. E., & Gillaspy, J. A., Jr. (2005). Operant psychology goes to the fair: Marian and Keller Breland in the popular press, 1947–1966. *The Behavior Analyst, 28*, 143–159.

Bailly, J.-S., Franklin, B., De Bory, G., Lavoisier, A., Majault, M.-J., Sallin, M., D'Arcet, J., Guillotin, J.-I., & Le Roy, A. (2002). Secret report on mesmerism or animal magnetism. *International Journal of Clinical and Experimental Hypnosis, 50*, 364–368. (Original work published 1784)

Bakan, D. (1958). *Sigmund Freud and the Jewish mystical tradition*. Princeton, NJ: Van Nostrand.

Baker, D. B., & Benjamin, L. T., Jr. (2000). The affirmation of the scientist-practitioner: A look back at Boulder. *American Psychologist, 55*, 241–247.

Baker, S. C., & Serdikoff, S. L. (2013). Addressing the role of animal research in psychology. In D. S. Dunn, R. A. R. Gurung, K. Z. Naufel, & J. H. Wilson (Eds.), *Controversy in the psychology classroom: Using hot topics to foster critical thinking* (pp. 105–112). Washington, DC: American Psychological Association.

Bakewell, S. (2010). *How to live: Or a life of Montaigne in one question and twenty attempts at an answer*. London: Chatto & Windus.

Baldwin, J. M. (1894). The origin of right-handedness. *Popular Science Monthly, 44*, 606–615.

Baldwin, J. M. (1895). *Mental development in the child and the race*. New York: Macmillan.

Baldwin, J. M. (1911). *The individual and society: Or, psychology and sociology*. Boston: Badger.

Baldwin, J. M. (1913). *History of psychology: A sketch and an interpretation* (2 vols.). New York: G. P. Putnam.

Ball, L. C. (2012). Genius without the "Great Man": New possibilities for the historian of psychology. *History of Psychology, 15*, 72–83.

Ball, P. (2012). *Curiosity: How science became interested in everything*. Chicago: University of Chicago Press.

Bandettini, P. (2007). Functional MRI today. *International Journal of Psychophysiology, 63*, 138–145.

Barenbaum, N. B., & Winter, D. G. (2013). Personality. In D. K. Freedheim & I. B. Weiner (Eds.), *Handbook of psychology, Vol. 1: History of psychology* (2nd ed., pp. 198–223). Hoboken, NJ: John Wiley & Sons Inc.

Bargdill, L. (2000). The study of life boredom. *Journal of Phenomenological Psychology, 31*, 188–219.

Bargdill, R., & Broomé, R. (Eds.) (2015). *Humanistic contributions for psychology 101: Growth, choice, and responsibility*. Colorado Springs, CO: University Professors Press.

Barlow, D. H. (2011). A prolegomenon to clinical psychology: Two 40-year odysseys. In D. H. Barlow (Ed.), *The Oxford handbook of clinical psychology* (pp. 3–20). New York: Oxford University Press.

Barnes, J. (Ed.). (1984). *The complete works of Aristotle* (Vol. 1). Princeton, NJ: Princeton University Press.

Barnes, R. C. (2000). Viktor Frankl's logotherapy: Spirituality and meaning in the new millennium. *Texas Counseling Association, 28*, 24–31.

Baron-Cohen, S. (2015). Radical behaviorism. In J. Brockman (Ed.), *This idea must die: Scientific theories that are blocking progress* (pp. 204–207). New York: HarperCollins.

Barratt, B. B. (2013). *What is psychoanalysis? 100 years after Freud's "secret committee."* New York: Routledge.

Barrett-Lennard, G. T. (2013). Origins and evolution of the person-centred innovation in Carl Rogers' lifetime. In M. Cooper, M. O'Hara, P. F. Schmid, & A. C. Bohart (Eds.), *The handbook of person-centred psychotherapy and counselling* (2nd ed., pp. 32–45). New York: Palgrave Macmillan.

Bartels, J. M., Milovich, M. M., & Moussier, S. (2016). Coverage of the Stanford prison experiment in introductory psychology courses: A survey of introductory psychology instructors. *Teaching of Psychology, 43*, 136–141.

Bartholomew, D. J. (2012). Social statistics. In N. Balakrishnan (Ed.), *Methods and applications of statistics in the social and behavioral sciences* (pp. 329–334). Hoboken, NJ: John Wiley & Sons Inc.

Bartlett, F. C. (1923). *Psychology and primitive culture*. Cambridge, MA: Cambridge University Press.

Bartlett, F. C. (1932). *Remembering: A study in experimental and social psychology*. New York: Macmillan.

Bartol, C. R., & Bartol, A. M. (1999). History of forensic psychology. In A. K. Hess & I. B. Weiner (Eds.), *The handbook of forensic psychology* (pp. 3–23). New York: Wiley.

Barton, A. (1992). Humanistic contributions to the field of psychotherapy: Appreciating the human and liberating the therapist. *Humanistic Psychologist, 20,* 332–348.

Batthyany, A., & Russo-Netzer, P. (2014). Psychologies of meaning. In A. Batthyany & P. Russo-Netzer (Eds.), *Meaning in positive and existential psychology* (pp. 3–22). New York: Springer Science + Business Media.

Baumeister, R. F., & Vohs, K. D. (2016). Introduction to the special issue: The science of prospection. *Review of General Psychology, 20,* 1–2.

Baumrind, D. (1964). Some thoughts on ethics of research: After reading Milgram's "Behavioral Study of Obedience." *American Psychologist, 19,* 421–423.

Baumrind, D. (2015). When subjects become objects: The lies behind the Milgram legend. *Theory and Psychology, 25,* 690–696.

Bayne, E. (2011). Womb envy: The cause of misogyny and even male achievement? *Women's Studies International Forum, 34,* 151–160.

Bazan, A. (2016). The role of biology in the advent of psychology: Neuropsychoanalysis and the foundation of a mental level of causality. In J. De Vos & E. Plutyh (Eds.), *Neuroscience and critique: Exploring the limits of the neurological turn* (pp. 173–187). New York: Routledge.

Beach, F. A. (1955). The descent of instinct. *Psychological Review, 62,* 401–410.

Beatty, B. (1998). From laws of learning to a science of values: Efficiency and morality in Thorndike's educational psychology. *American Psychologist, 53,* 1145–1152.

Beatty, B. (2005). The rise of the American Nursery School: Laboratory for a science of child development. In D. V. Pillemer & S. H. White (Eds.), *Developmental psychology and social change: Research, history and policy* (pp. 264–287). New York: Cambridge University Press.

Beck, A. T. (1963). Thinking and depression: Idiosyncratic content and cognitive distortions. *Archives of General Psychiatry, 9,* 324–333.

Beck, H. P., Levinson, S., & Irons, G. (2009). Finding Little Albert: A journey to John B. Watson's infant laboratory. *American Psychologist, 64,* 605–614.

Beck, H. P., Levinson, S., & Irons, G. (2010). The evidence supports Douglas Merritte as Little Albert. *American Psychologist, 65,* 301–303.

Beck, J. (1968). Herman von Helmholtz. In D. L. Sills (Ed.), *International Encyclopedia of the Social Sciences* (Vol. 6, pp. 345–350). New York: Macmillan and Free Press.

Becker, K., Steinberg, H., & Kluge, M. (2016). Emil Kraepelin's concepts of the phenomenology and physiology of sleep: The first systematic description of chronotypes. *Sleep Medicine Reviews, 27,* 9–19.

Beenfelt, C. (2013). *The philosophical background and scientific legacy of E. B. Titchener's psychology: Understanding introspectionism.* New York: Springer Science + Business Media.

Begley, S. (2007, March 19). Beyond stones & bones. *Newsweek,* 52–58.

Behrens, R. R. (1998). On Max Wertheimer and Pablo Picasso: Gestalt theory, cubism and camouflage. *Gestalt Theory, 20,* 111–118.

Beins, B. C. (2010). Teaching measurement through historical sources. *History of Psychology, 13,* 89–94.

Beins, B. C. (2012). Jean Piaget: Theorists of the child's mind. In W. Pickren, D. A. Dewsbury, & M. Wertheimer (Eds.), *Portraits of pioneers in developmental psychology* (pp. 89–108). New York: Psychology Press.

Belar, C. D., McIntyre, T. M., & Matarazzo, J. D. (2013). Health psychology. In D. K. Freedheim & I. B. Weiner (Eds.), *Handbook of psychology: History of psychology* (Vol. 1, 2nd ed., pp. 488–506). Hoboken, NJ: Wiley.

Bell, D. J., & Hausman, E. M. (2014). Training models in professional psychology doctoral programs. In W. B. Johnson & N. J. Kaslow (Eds.), *The Oxford handbook of education and training in professional psychology* (pp. 33–51). New York: Oxford University Press.

Belliveau, A. R. (2012). Psychology's first forays into film. *Monitor on Psychology, 43*(5), 26–27.

Ben-Noun, L. (2004). Mental disorder that afflicted King David the Great. *History of Psychiatry, 15,* 467–476.

Benjamin, L. T., Jr. (1974). Prominent psychologists: A selected bibliography of biographical sources. *Journal Supplement Abstract Service. Catalog of Selected Documents in Psychology, 4,* 1 (Ms. No. 535).

Benjamin, L. T., Jr. (1975). The pioneering work of Leta Hollingworth in the psychology of women. *Nebraska History, 56,* 493–505.

Benjamin, L. T., Jr. (1997). *A history of psychology: Original sources and contemporary research.* New York: McGraw-Hill.

Benjamin, L. T., Jr. (2001). American psychology's struggles with its curriculum; Should a thousand flowers bloom? *American Psychologist, 56,* 735–742.

Benjamin, L. T., Jr. (2006). Hugo Münsterberg's attack on the application of scientific psychology. *Journal of Applied Psychology, 91,* 414–425.

Benjamin, L. T., Jr., & Baker, D. B. (2009). Recapturing a context for psychology: The role of history. *Perspectives on Psychological Science, 4,* 97–98.

Benjamin, L. T., Jr., & Heider, K. L. (1976). History of psychology in biography: A bibliography. *Journal*

Supplement Abstract Service. Catalog of Selected Documents in Psychology, 6, 61 (Ms. No. 1276).

Benjamin, L. T., Jr., & Nielsen-Gammon, E. (1999). B. F. Skinner and psychotechnology: The case of the heir conditioner. *Review of General Psychology, 3,* 155–167.

Benjamin, L. T., Jr., Pratt, R., Watlington, D., Aaron, L., Bonar, T., Fitzgerald, S., et al. (1989). *A history of American psychology in notes and news, 1883–1945: An index to journal sources.* Millwood, NY: Kraus International.

Benjamin, L. T., Jr., & VandenBos, G. R. (2006). The window on psychology's literature: A history of Psychological Abstracts. *American Psychologist, 61,* 941–954.

Benjamin, L. T., Jr., Whitaker, J. L., & Ramsey, R. M. (2007). John B. Watson's alleged sex research: An appraisal of the evidence. *American Psychologist, 62,* 131–139.

Benn, S. I. (1967). Punishment. In P. Edwards (Ed.), *The encyclopedia of philosophy* (Vol. 7, pp. 29–36). New York: Macmillan and Free Press.

Bennett, E. L., Diamond, M. C., Krech, D., & Rosenzweig, M. R. (1964). Chemical and anatomical plasticity of the brain. *Science, 146,* 610–619.

Benzaquén, A. (2015). Educational designs: The education and training of younger sons at the turn of the eighteenth century. *Journal of Family History, 40,* 462–484.

Berenda, C. W. (1965). *World visions and the image of man: Cosmologies as reflections of man.* New York: Vantage Press.

Bergmann, G. (1956). The contribution of John B. Watson. *Psychological Review, 63,* 265–276.

Bergmann, M. S. (Ed.). (2004). *Understanding dissidence and controversy in the history of psychoanalysis.* New York: Other Press.

Bergsma, A., Poot, G., & Liefbroer, A. C. (2008). Happiness in the garden of Epicurus. *Journal of Happiness Studies, 9,* 397–423.

Berkeley, G. (1935). *Three dialogues between Hylas and Philonous.* Chicago: Open Court. (Original work published 1713)

Berkeley, G. (1948). An essay towards a new theory of vision. In A. A. Luce (Ed.), *The works of George Berkeley, Bishop of Cloyne* (Vol. 1, pp. 141–240). London: Thomas Nelson & Sons. (Original work published 1709)

Berkeley, G. (1957). *Treatise concerning the principles of human knowledge.* Indianapolis, IN: Bobbs-Merrill. (Original work published 1710)

Berlucchi, G., & Buchtel, H. A. (2009). Neuronal plasticity: Historical roots and evolution of meaning. *Experimental Brain Research, 192,* 307–319.

Berman, K. M., & Schultz, R. A. (2013). Leta Stetter Hollingworth: As curricularist Mrs. Pilgrim in the classroom. In E. A. Romey (Ed.), *Finding John Galt: People, politics, and practice in gifted education* (pp. 3–24). Charlotte, NC: Information Age Publishing.

Bermúdez, J. L. (2010). The prehistory of cognitive science. In *Cognitive science: An introduction* (pp. 4–27). Cambridge, UK: Cambridge University Press.

Bernard, L. L. (1924). *Instinct: A study in social psychology.* New York: Henry Holt.

Bernard, W. (1972). Spinoza's influence on the rise of scientific psychology: A neglected chapter in the history of psychology. *Journal of the History of the Behavioral Sciences, 8,* 208–215.

Berrios, G. E. (2005). On the fantastic apparitions of vision by Johannes Müller [introduction]. *History of Psychiatry, 16,* 229–246.

Berrios, G. E. (2006). Classifying madness: A philosophical examination of the Diagnostic and Statistical Manual of Mental Disorders. *Social History of Medicine, 19,* 153–155.

Berrios, G. E. (2014). The historiography of lithium usage in psychiatry. *Annales Médico-Psychologiques, 172,* 164–169.

Berrios, G. E. (2015). Introduction to Classic Text No. 101: David Hartley's views on madness. *History of Psychiatry, 26,* 105–116.

Bersoff, D. N. (1999). Preparing for two cultures: Education and training in law and psychology. In R. Roesch, S. D. Hart, & J. R. P. Ogloff (Eds.), *Psychology and the law: The state of the discipline* (pp. 375–401). New York: Kluwer Academic/Plenum.

Bettmann, O. L. (1974). *The good old days—They were terrible!* New York: Random House.

Bickerton, D. (2014). *More than nature needs: Language, mind, and evolution.* Cambridge, MA: Harvard University Press.

Bickhard, M. H. (2001). The tragedy of operationalism. *Theory and Psychology, 11,* 35–44.

Biddle, W. (1995). *A field guide to germs.* New York: Henry Holt.

Billock, V. A., & Tsou, B. H. (2011). To honor Fechner and obey Stevens: Relationships between psychophysical and neural nonlinearities. *Psychological Bulletin, 137,* 1–18.

Binet, A., & Féré, C. (1891). *Animal magnetism* (3rd ed.). London: Kegan Paul, Trench, Trübner. (Original work published 1887)

Bireta, T. J., & Neath, I. (2008). Age-related differences in the von Restorff isolation effect. *The Quarterly Journal of Experimental Psychology, 61,* 345–352.

Bishop, P. (1999). *Jung in contexts: A reader*. Florence, KY: Taylor & Francis/Routledge.

Bishop, P. (2014). *Carl Jung*. London: Reaktion Books.

Bitterman, M. E. (2006). Classical conditioning since Pavlov. *Review of General Psychology, 10*, 365–376.

Bjork, D. W. (1993). *B. F. Skinner: A life*. New York: Basic Books.

Bjornsson, A. S. (2004). *The foundations of the scientific revolution in ancient times and the Middle Ages*. Reykjavik: University of Iceland Press.

Blackless, M., Charuvastra, A., Derryck, A., Fausto-Sterling, A., Lauzanne, K., & Lee, E. (2000). How sexually dimorphic are we? Review and synthesis. *American Journal of Human Biology, 12*, 151–166.

Blackmore, J. (2013). Social justice in education: A theoretical overview. In B. J. Irby, G. Brown, R. Lara-Alecio, & S. Jackson (Eds.), *The handbook of educational theories* (pp. 1001–1009). Charlotte, NC: Information Age Publishing.

Bland, E. D., & Strawn, B. D. (Eds.). (2014). *Christianity and psychoanalysis: A new conversation*. Downers Grove, IL: InterVarsity Press.

Blass, T. (2004). *The man who shocked the world: The life and legacy of Stanley Milgram*. New York: Basic Books.

Bloche, G. (2011). *The Hippocratic myth*. New York: Palgrave MacMillan.

Bloom, H. (Ed.). (1987). *Michel de Montaigne*. New York: Chelsea House.

Bloom, P. (2014). The war on reason. *Atlantic, 313*, 64–70.

Blum, D. (2011). *Love at Goon Park: Harry Harlow and the science of affection* (2nd ed.). New York: Perseus.

Blumenthal, A. L. (1975). A reappraisal of Wilhelm Wundt. *American Psychologist, 30*, 1081–1088.

Blumenthal, A. L. (1979). The founding father we never knew. *Contemporary Psychology, 24*, 547–550.

Blumenthal, A. L. (1998). Leipzig, Wilhelm Wundt, and psychology's gilded age. In G. A. Kimble & M. Wertheimer (Eds.), *Portraits of pioneers in psychology* (Vol. 3, pp. 31–48). Washington, DC: American Psychological Association.

Bochner, S. (1973). Mathematics in cultural history. In P. P. Wiener (Ed.), *Dictionary of the history of ideas* (Vol. 3, pp. 177–185). New York: Scribner.

Boden, M. (2006). *Mind as machine: A history of cognitive science* (Vols. 1 & 2). New York: Oxford University Press.

Bohan, J. S. (1992a). *Re-placing women in psychology: Readings toward a more inclusive history*. Dubuque, IA: Kendall/Hunt.

Bohan, J. S. (1992b). *Seldom seen, rarely heard: Women's place in psychology*. Boulder, CO: Westview Press.

Bohart, A. C. (2013). Darth Vader, Carl Rogers, and self-organizing wisdom. In A. C. Bohart, B. S. Held, E. Mendelowitz, & K. J. Schneider (Eds.), *Humanity's dark side: Evil, destructive experience, and psychotherapy* (pp. 57–76). Washington, DC: American Psychological Association.

Bonacchi, S. (2009). Editorial. *Gestalt Theory, 31*, 100.

Boring, E. G. (1927). Edward Bradford Titchener. *American Journal of Psychology, 38*, 489–506.

Boring, E. G. (1942). *Sensation and perception in the history of experimental psychology*. New York: Appleton-Century-Crofts.

Boring, E. G. (1950). *A history of experimental psychology* (2nd ed.). Englewood Cliffs, NJ: Prentice Hall.

Boring, E. G. (1953). John Dewey: 1859–1952. *American Journal of Psychology, 66*, 145–147.

Boring, E. G. (1961). *Psychologist at large*. New York: Basic Books.

Boring, E. G. (1963). *History, psychology, and science: Selected papers*. New York: Wiley.

Boring, E. G. (1966). Introduction. In G. T. Fechner (Author), *Elements of psychophysics* (Vol. 1, H. E. Adler, Trans., D. H. Howes & E. G. Boring, Eds., pp. ix–xvii). New York: Holt, Rinehart & Winston.

Bornstein, B. H., & Meissner, C. A. (2008). Introduction: Basic and applied issues in eyewitness research: A Münsterberg centennial retrospective. *Applied Cognitive Psychology, 22*, 733–736.

Bornstein, B. H., & Penrod, S. D. (2008). Hugo who? G. F. Arnold's alternative early approach to psychology and law. *Applied Cognitive Psychology, 22*, 759–768.

Botting, E. H. (2006). Mary Wollstonecraft's enlightened legacy: The "modern social imaginary" of the egalitarian family. *American Behavioral Scientist, 49*, 687–701.

Bouchard, T. J., Jr., Lykken, D. T., McGue, M., Segal, N. L., & Tellegen, A. (1990). Sources of human psychological differences: The Minnesota study of twins reared apart. *Science, 250*, 223–228.

Boudewijnse, G. A. (2005). Christian von Ehrenfels (1859–1932) and Edgar Rubin (1886–1951). *Gestalt Theory, 27*, 29–49.

Boudewijnse, G. A., Murray, D. J., & Bandomir, C. A. (1999). Herbart's mathematical psychology. *History of Psychology, 2*, 163–193.

Boudewijnse, G. A., Murray, D. J., & Bandomir, C. A. (2001). The fate of Herbart's mathematical psychology. *History of Psychology, 4*, 107–132.

Bovaira, F., & Augustin, A. (Producers), Amenabar, A. (Writer/Director), & Gil, M. (Writer). (2010). *Agora* [Motion Picture]. Santa Monica, CA: Lionsgate.

Bower, G. H. (1962). An association model for response

and training variables in paired-associate learning. *Psychological Review, 69,* 347–353.

Bower, G. H. (2000). A brief history of memory research. In E. Tulving & F. I. M. Craik (Eds.), *The Oxford handbook of memory* (pp. 3–32). New York: Oxford University Press.

Boyer, R. W. (2014). Unless we are robots, classical and quantum theories are inadequate. *NeuroQuantology, 12,* 102–105.

Bozarth, J. (2007). Unconditional positive regard. In M. Cooper, M. O'Hara, P. F. Schmid, & G. Wyatt (Eds.), *The handbook of person-centred psychotherapy and counseling* (pp. 182–193). New York: Palgrave Macmillan.

Bozarth, J. D. (2013). Unconditional positive regard. In M. Cooper, M. O'Hara, P. F. Schmid, & A. C. Bohart (Eds.), *The handbook of person-centred psychotherapy and counseling* (2nd ed., pp. 180–192). New York: Palgrave Macmillan.

Bozeman, T. W. (1977). *Protestants in an age of science: The Baconian ideal and ante-bellum American religious thought.* Chapel Hill: University of North Carolina Press.

Braakmann, D. (2014). Historical paths in psychotherapy research. In O. C. G. Gelo, A. Pritz, & B. Rieken (Eds.), *Psychotherapy research: Foundations, process, and outcome* (pp. 39–65). New York: Springer-Verlag.

Braaten, E. B., & Viney, W. (2000). Some late nineteenth-century perspectives on sex and emotional expression. *Psychological Reports, 86,* 575–585.

Bracken, P. J. (1999). The importance of Heidegger for psychiatry. *Philosophy, Psychiatry, & Psychology, 6,* 83–85.

Brackman, A. C. (1980). *A delicate arrangement: The strange case of Charles Darwin and Alfred Russel Wallace.* New York: Times Books.

Brailsford, H. N. (1963). Mary Wollstonecraft. In E. R. A. Seligman (Ed.), *Encyclopedia of the social sciences* (Vol. 15, pp. 436–437). New York: Macmillan.

Brannigan, A., Nicholson, I., & Cherry, F. (2015). Introduction to the special issue: Unplugging the Milgram machine. *Theory and Psychology, 25,* 551–563.

Breitenfeld, T., Jurasic, M. J., & Breitenfeld, D. (2014). Hippocrates: The forefather of neurology. *Neurological Sciences, 35,* 1349–1352.

Breland, K., & Breland, M. (1961). The misbehavior of organisms. *American Psychologist, 16,* 681–684.

Brennan, B. P. (1968). *William James.* New York: Twayne.

Brentano, F. (1973). *Psychology from an empirical standpoint.* (A. C. Rancurello, D. B. Terrell, & L. L. McAlister, Trans.). London: Routledge & Kegan Paul. (Original work published 1874)

Brett, G. S. (1965). *A history of psychology* (2nd rev. ed.) (Edited and abridged by R. S. Peters). Cambridge, MA: MIT Press. (Original work published 1912–1921)

Brewer, W. F. (2000). Bartlett, functionalism, and modern schema theories. *Journal of Mind and Behavior, 21,* 37–44.

Brewster, F. (2013). Wheel of fire: The African-American dreamer and cultural consciousness. *Jung Journal: Culture and Psyche, 7,* 70–87.

Brian, D. (1997). *Einstein: A life.* New York: Wiley.

Brickhouse, T. C., & Smith, N. D. (1990). What makes Socrates a good man? *Journal of the History of Philosophy, 28,* 169–179.

Bridges, J. H. (1976). *Life and work of Roger Bacon: An introduction to the Opus Majus.* Merrick, NY: Richwood.

Bridgman, P. W. (1927). *The logic of modern physics.* New York: Macmillan.

Bridgman, P. W. (1954). Remarks on the present state of operationism. *The Scientific Monthly, 79,* 224–226.

Bridgman, P. W. (1955). *Reflections of a physicist.* New York: Philosophical Library.

Brigham, J. C., & Grisso, J. T. (2003). Forensic psychology. In I. B. Weiner (Series Ed.) & D. K. Freedheim (Vol. Ed.), *Handbook of psychology, Vol. 1: The history of psychology* (pp. 391–411). New York: Wiley.

Bringmann, W. G., Bringmann, M. W., & Early, C. E. (1992). G. Stanley Hall and the history of psychology. *American Psychologist, 47,* 281–289.

Bringmann, W. G., Bringmann, N. J., & Balance, W. D. G. (1980). Wilhelm Maximilian Wundt 1832–1874: The formative years. In W. G. Bringmann & R. D. Tweney (Eds.), *Wundt studies: A centennial collection* (pp. 13–32). Toronto: C. J. Hogrefe.

Bringmann, W. G., Bringmann, N. J., & Ungerer, G. A. (1980). The establishment of Wundt's laboratory: An archival and documentary study. In W. G. Bringmann & R. D. Tweney (Eds.), *Wundt studies: A centennial collection* (pp. 123–157). Toronto: C. J. Hogrefe.

Brinkmann, S. (2013). *John Dewey: Science for a changing world. History and theory of psychology.* Piscataway, NJ: Transaction Publishers.

Brinkmann, S. (2015). Perils and potentials in qualitative psychology. *Integrative Psychological & Behavioral Science, 49,* 162–173

Bromberg, W. (1959). *The mind of man: A history of psychotherapy and psychoanalysis.* New York: Harper Torchbacks.

Brook, A. (Ed.). (2006). *The prehistory of cognitive science.* Basingstoke, UK: Palgrave Macmillan.

Brooke, J. H. (2013). "Ready to aid one another": Darwin

on nature, God, and cooperation. In M. A. Nowak & S. Coakley (Eds.), *Evolution, games, and God: The principle of cooperation* (pp. 37–59). Cambridge, MA: Harvard University Press.

Brooks-Gunn, J., & Johnson, A. D. (2006). G. Stanley Hall's contribution to science, practice and policy: The child study, parent education, and child welfare movements. *History of Psychology, 9,* 247–258.

Broome, M. R., Harland, R., Owen, G. S., & Stringaris, A. (2012). Franz Brentano (1838–1917): Editors' introduction. In M. R. Broome, R. Harland, G. S. Owen, & A. Stringaris (Eds.), *The Maudsley reader in phenomenological psychiatry* (pp. 3–5). New York: Cambridge University Press.

Brown, F. J., & Gillard, D. (2015). The 'strange death' of radical behaviourism. *The Psychologist, 28,* 24–27.

Brown, J. A. C. (1964). *Freud and the post-Freudians.* Baltimore: Penguin.

Brown, L. (1993). *The new shorter Oxford English Dictionary* (2 vols.). New York: Oxford University Press.

Brown-Sequard, C. E. (1890). Have we two brains or one? *Forum, 9,* 627–643.

Brown v. Board of Education, 347 U.S. 483 (1954).

Brožek, J. (1972). Russian contributions on brain and behavior. In J. Brozek & D. I. Slobin (Eds.), *Psychology in the USSR: An historical perspective.* White Plains, NY: International Arts and Sciences Press. Also published in (1966) *Science, 152,* 930–932.

Bruce, D. (1998). Lashley's rejection of connectionism. *History of Psychology, 1,* 160–164.

Bruner, J. S. (1964). The course of cognitive growth. *American Psychologist, 19,* 1–15.

Brush, S. G. (1974a). The prayer test. *American Scientist, 62,* 561–563.

Brush, S. G. (1974b). Should the history of science be rated X? *Science, 183,* 1164–1172.

Bryan, L. L. K., & Vinchur, A. J. (2012). A history of industrial and organizational psychology. In S. W. J. Kozlowski (Ed.), *The Oxford handbook of organizational psychology* (Vol. 1, pp. 22–75). New York: Oxford University Press.

Bryan, L. L. K., & Vinchur, A. J. (2013). Industrial-organizational psychology. In D. K. Freedheim & I. B. Weiner (Eds.), *Handbook of psychology, Vol. 1: History of psychology* (2nd ed., pp. 407–428). Hoboken, NJ: John Wiley & Sons.

Bryan, M. L. M., Bair, B., & DeAngury, M. (Eds.). (2003). *The selected papers of Jane Addams: Preparing to lead, 1860–81* (Vol. 1). Champaign: University of Illinois Press.

Buchanan, J. R. (1885). *Manual of psychometry: The dawn of a new civilization* (2nd ed). Boston: Dudley M. Holman.

Buckingham, H. W. (2006). The Marc Dax (1770–1837)/Paul Broca (1824–1880) controversy over priority in science: Left hemisphere specificity for seat of articulate language and for lesions that cause aphemia. *Clinical Linguistics & Phonetics, 20,* 613–619.

Buckingham, H. W., & Finger, S. (1997). David Hartley's psychobiological associationism and the legacy of Aristotle. *Journal of the History of the Neurosciences, 6,* 21–37.

Buckley, K. W. (1989). *Mechanical man: John Broadus Watson and the beginnings of behaviorism.* New York: Guilford.

Buckman, S. S. (1895). Babies and monkeys. *Popular Science Monthly, 46,* 371–388.

Buffon, C. de. (1977). *Selections from natural history general and particular* (Vol. 1). New York: Arno Press. (Original work published 1780–1785)

Buie, J. (1988, November). Psychoanalysis barriers tumble: Settlement opens doors to non-MDs. *American Psychological Association Monitor, 19*(11), 1, 15.

Bulkeley, K. (2008). *Dreaming in the world's religions: A comparative history.* New York: New York University Press.

Buncombe, M. (1995). *The substance of consciousness: An argument for interactionism.* Aldershot, UK: Avebury.

Bunn, G. C. (1997). The lie detector, *Wonder Woman,* and liberty: The life and work of William Moulton Marston. *History of the Human Sciences, 10,* 91–119.

Bunn, G. C. (2007). Spectacular science: The lie detector's ambivalent powers. *History of Psychology, 10,* 156–178.

Bunney, W. E., Garland, B., & Buchsbaum, M. S. (1983). Advances in the use of visual imaging: Techniques in mental illness. *Psychiatric Annals, 13,* 420–426.

Buranelli, V. (1975). *The wizard from Vienna: Franz Anton Mesmer.* New York: Coward, McCann & Geoghean.

Burek, D. M., Koek, K. E., & Novallo, A. (Eds.). (1989). *Encyclopedia of associations* (24th ed.). Detroit, MI: Gale Research.

Burger, J. M. (2009). Replicating Milgram: Would people still obey today? *American Psychologist, 64,* 1–11.

Burger, J. M. (2011). Alive and well after all these years. *The Psychologist, 24,* 654–657.

Burke, R. B. (Trans.). (1962). *The Opus Majus of Roger Bacon* (2 vols.). New York: Russell and Russell.

Burks, B. S. (1927). Foster parent-foster child comparisons as evidence upon the nature-nurture problem. *Proceedings of the National Academy of the Sciences of the United States of America, 13,* 846–848.

Burks, B. S. (1928). The relative influence of nature and nurture upon mental development: A comparative study of foster parent-foster child resemblance and true parent-true child resemblance. *27th Yearbook of the National Society for the Study of Education*, Part 1, 219–316.

Burman, J. T. (2012). Jean Piaget: Images of a life and his factory. *History of Psychology, 15,* 283–288.

Burman, J. T. (2015). Neglect of the foreign invisible: Historiography and the navigation of conflicting sensibilities. *History of Psychology, 18,* 146–169.

Burnes, B. (2007). Kurt Lewin and the Harwood studies: The foundations of OD. *Journal of Applied Behavioral Science, 43,* 213–231.

Burnes, B., & Cooke, B. (2013). Kurt Lewin's field theory: A review and re-evaluation. *International Journal of Management Reviews, 15,* 408–425.

Burnham, J. (Ed.). (2013). *After Freud left: A century of psychoanalysis in America*. Chicago: University of Chicago Press.

Burns, J. E. (2014). The nature of causal action: Qualities needed to enable a causal action, such as free will, that is initiated in a mental realm to produce a change in the physical world. *Journal of Consciousness Studies, 21,* 60–73.

Burns, K., McMahon, D., & Burns, S. (Directors) & McMahon, D., Burns, K., & Burns, S. (Producers). (2013). *The Central Park Five*. Public Broadcasting Service, USA.

Burns, W. E. (2003). *Witch hunts in Europe and America: An encyclopedia*. Westport, CT: Greenwood Press.

Burston, D. (1998). Laing and Heidegger on alienation. *Journal of Humanistic Psychology, 38,* 80–93.

Burton, J. H. (1967). *Life and correspondence of David Hume* (Vol. 2). New York: Burt Franklin. (Original work published 1846)

Buss, A. R. (1977). In defense of a critical-presentist historiography: The fact-theory relationship and Marx's epistemology. *Journal of the History of the Behavioral Sciences, 13,* 252–260.

Buss, D. M. (2000). *The dangerous passion: Why jealousy is as necessary as love and sex*. New York: Free Press.

Buss, D. M. (2002). Human mate guarding. *Neuroendocrinology Letters, 23,* 23–29.

Buss, D. M. (Ed.). (2005). *The handbook of evolutionary psychology*. Hoboken, NJ: Wiley.

Buss, D. M. (2013). Seven tools for teaching evolutionary psychology. In D. S. Dunn, R. A. R. Gurung, K. Z. Naufel, & J. H. Wilson (Eds.), *Controversy in the psychology classroom: Using hot topics to promote critical thinking*. Washington, DC: American Psychological Association.

Buss, D. M. (2016). *Evolutionary psychology: The new science of mind* (5th ed.). New York: Taylor & Francis.

Buss, D. M., & Duntley, J. D. (2006). The evolution of aggression. In M. Schaller, J. A. Simpson, & D. T. Kenrick (Eds.), *Evolution and social psychology: Frontiers of social psychology*. Madison, CT: Psychosocial Press.

Buss, D. M., & Shackelford, T. K. (1997). From vigilance to violence: Mate retention strategies in married couples. *Journal of Personality and Social Psychology, 72,* 346–361.

Busse, B., Hashem-Wangler, A., & Tholen, J. (2015). Two worlds of participation: Young people and politics in Germany. *The Sociological Review, 63,* 118–140.

Butera, G. (2010). Thomas Aquinas and cognitive therapy: An exploration of the promise of the Thomistic psychology. *Philosophy, Psychiatry, & Psychology, 17,* 347–366.

Buzzell, L. (2014). Ecopsychology as a big tent: Staying open to multiple modes of exploration. *Ecopsychology, 6,* 60–61.

Buzzell, L., & Chalquist, C. (2009). *Ecotherapy: Healing with nature in mind*. San Francisco, CA: Sierra Club Books.

Buzzell, L., & Chalquist, C. (2015). Ecopsychology and the long emergency: Fostering sanity as the world goes crazy. *Ecopsychology, 7,* 183–184.

Byron, Lord (1970). Cain: A mystery. In F. Page (Ed.), *Lord Byron Poetical Works* (pp. 520–545). New York: Oxford University Press. (Original work published 1821)

Cadwallader, T. C. (1987). Origins and accomplishments of Joseph Jastrow's 1888-founded Chair of Comparative Psychology at the University of Wisconsin. *Journal of Comparative Psychology, 101,* 231–236.

Cain, D. J. (Ed.). (2002). *Humanistic psychotherapies: Handbook of research and practice*. Washington, DC: American Psychological Association.

Cain, D. J. (2010). *Person-centered psychotherapies*. Washington, DC: American Psychological Association.

Cain, D. J. (2014). Person-centered therapy. In G. R. VandenBos, E. Meidenbauer, & J. Frank-McNeil (Eds.), *Psychotherapy theories and techniques: A reader* (pp. 251–259). Washington, DC: American Psychological Association.

Calder, R. (1970). *Leonardo and the age of the eye*. New York: Simon and Schuster.

Calhoun, J. B. (1963). Ecology and sociology of the Norway rat (Public Health Service Publication, No. 1008), 285/1.

Calkins, M. W. (1893). Statistics of dreams. *American Journal of Psychology, 5,* 311–343.

Calkins, M. W. (1906). A reconciliation between structural and functional psychology. *Psychological Review, 13,* 61–81.

Calkins, M. W. (1916). The self in recent psychology: A critical summary. *Psychological Bulletin, 13,* 20–27.

Cambray, J. (2009). *Synchronicity: Nature and psyche in an interconnected universe.* College Station, TX: Texas A & M University Press.

Camfield, T. M. (1973). The professionalization of American psychology, 1870–1917. *Journal of the History of the Behavioral Sciences, 9,* 67–68.

Campbell, K. (1967). Materialism. In P. Edwards (Ed.), *The encyclopedia of philosophy* (Vol. 5, pp. 179–188). New York: Macmillan and Free Press.

Candland, D. K. (2013). Introduction to the special issue. *Review of General Psychology, 17,* 123.

Cannon, W. B. (1922). What strong emotions do to us. *Harper's Magazine, 145,* 234–241.

Cantor, N. F. (2001). *In the wake of the plague: The Black Death and the world it made.* New York: Free Press.

Capehart, J., Viney, W., & Hulicka, I. M. (1958). The effect of effort upon extinction. *Journal of Comparative and Physiological Psychology, 53,* 79–82.

Capra, F. (1988). The role of physics in the current change of paradigms. In R. F. Kitchener (Ed.), *The world view of contemporary physics* (pp. 144–155). Albany: State University of New York Press.

Carey, B. (2011, June 23). Expert on mental illness reveals her own fight. *New York Times, 165.* Retrieved July 20, 2016 from www.nytimes.com/2011/06/23/health/23lives.html?pagewanted=all&_r=0

Carey, G. (2003). *Human genetics for the social sciences.* Thousand Oaks, CA: Sage.

Carlson, E. T. (1977). Benjamin Rush and mental health. *Annals of the New York Academy of Sciences, 291,* 95–103.

Carlson, E. T. (1981). The history of multiple personality in the United States: I. The beginnings. *American Journal of Psychiatry, 138,* 666–668.

Carlson, E. T., & Simpson, M. M. (1964). The definition of mental illness: Benjamin Rush (1745–1813). *American Journal of Psychiatry, 121,* 209–214.

Carlson, E. T., Wollock, J. L., & Noel, P. S. (Eds.). (1981). *Benjamin Rush's lectures on the mind.* Philadelphia: American Philosophical Society.

Carlson, J., & Maniacci, M. P. (Eds.). (2012). *Alfred Adler revisited.* New York: Routledge.

Carlson, J., Watts, R. E., & Maniacci, M. (2006). *Adlerian therapy: Theory and practice.* Washington, DC: American Psychological Association.

Carol, M., & Owens, S. (2007). Qualitative research in psychology: Could William James get a job? *History of Psychology, 10,* 301–324.

Carr, H. A. (1925). *Psychology: A study of mental activity.* New York: Longmans, Green and Co.

Carr, H. A. (1961). Harvey A. Carr. In C. Murchison (Ed.), *A history of psychology in autobiography* (Vol. 3, pp. 69–82). New York: Russell and Russell. (Original work published 1930)

Carroll, D. W. (2012). The regents versus the professors: Edward Tolman's role in the California loyalty oath controversy. *Journal of the History of the Behavioral Sciences, 48,* 218–235.

Carron, A. V., & Brawley, L. R. (2008). Group dynamics in sport and physical activity. In T. S. Horn (Ed.), *Advances in sport psychology* (3rd ed., pp. 213–237, 452–455). Champaign, IL: Human Kinetics.

Cartwright, N. (1999) *The dappled world: A study of the boundaries of science.* Cambridge, UK: Cambridge University Press.

Cary, P. (2007). A brief history of the concept of free will: Issues that are and are not germane to legal reasoning. *Behavioral Sciences and the Law, 25,* 165–181.

Cassedy, S. (2008). A history of the concept of the stimulus and the role it played in the neurosciences. *Journal of the History of the Neurosciences, 17,* 405–432.

Cassirer, E. (1981). *Kant's life and thought* (J. Haden, Trans.). New Haven, CT: Yale University Press.

Castiglioni, A. (1941). *A history of medicine* (E. B. Krumbhaar, Ed. and Trans.). New York: Knopf.

Caston, V. (2015). Perception in ancient Greek philosophy. In M. Matthen (Ed.), *The Oxford handbook of the philosophy of perception* (pp. 29–50). New York: Oxford University Press.

Catani, M., & Sandrone, S. (2015). *Brain Renaissance: From Vesalius to modern neuroscience.* New York: Oxford University Press.

Cattell, J. M. (1890). Mental tests and measurements. *Mind, 15,* 373–381.

Cattell, J. M. (1992). Retrospect: Psychology as a profession. *Journal of Consulting and Clinical Psychology, 60,* 7–8. (Original work published 1937)

Cautin, R. L. (2006). David Shakow. In D. A. Dewsbury, L. T. Benjamin, & M. Wertheimer (Eds.), *Portraits of pioneers in psychology* (Vol. 6, pp. 207–221). Washington, DC: American Psychological Association.

Cautin, R. L. (2008). David Shakow and schizophrenia research at Worcester State Hospital: The roots of the scientist-practitioner model. *Journal of the History of the Behavioral Sciences, 44,* 219–237.

Cautin, R. L. (2011). Invoking history to teach about

the scientist-practitioner gap. *History of Psychology, 14,* 197–203.

Cautin, R. L., & Baker, D. B. (2014). A history of education and training in professional psychology. In W. B. Johnson & N. J. Kaslow (Eds.), *The Oxford handbook of education and training in professional psychology* (pp. 17–32). New York: Oxford University Press.

Cautin, R. L., Freedheim, D. K., & DeLeon, P. H. (2013). Psychology as a profession. In D. K. Freedheim & I. B. Weiner (Eds.), *Handbook of psychology, Vol. 1: History of psychology* (2nd ed., pp. 32–54). Hoboken, NJ: John Wiley & Sons Inc.

Cavalli, T. F. (2016). The alchemical Osiris: From Ra to radium. *Psychological Perspectives, 59,* 46–70.

Celesia, G. G. (2012). Alcmaeon of Croton's observations on health, brain, mind, and soul. *Journal of the History of the Neurosciences, 21,* 409–426.

Cesarani, D. (2007). *Becoming Eichmann: Rethinking the life, crimes, and trial of a "desk murderer."* Cambridge, MA: Da Capo Press.

Cézilly, F. (2015). Preference, rationality and interindividual variation: The persisting debate about female choice. In T. Hoquet (Ed.), *Current perspectives on sexual selection: What's left after Darwin?* (pp. 191–209). Dordrecht, Netherlands: Springer Science + Business Media.

Chalaby, J. K. (2016). Television and globalization: The TV content global value chain. *Journal of Communication, 66,* 35–59.

Chalupa, L. M. (2005). Donald B. Lindsley. *American Psychologist, 60,* 193–194.

Chan, W. (1967). Confucius. In P. Edwards (Ed.), *Encyclopedia of philosophy* (Vol. 2, p. 189). New York: Macmillan and Free Press.

Chance, P. (1999). Thorndike's puzzle boxes and the origins of the experimental analysis of behavior. *Journal of the Experimental Analysis of Behavior, 72,* 433–440.

Chang, Z., & Ota Wang, V. (2014). Lamark was right: Nurturing nature and naturing nurture. In F. T. L. Leong, L. Comas-Diaz, G. C. Nagayama Hall, C. V. McLoyd, & J. E. Trimble (Eds.), *APA handbook of multicultural psychology* (Vol. 1, pp. 313–337). Washington, DC: American Psychological Association.

Charland, L. C. (2002). Tuke's healing discipline: Commentary on Erica Lilleleht's "Progress and power: Exploring the disciplinary connections between moral treatment and psychiatric rehabilitation." *Philosophy, Psychiatry, & Psychology, 9,* 183–186.

Charland, L. C. (2007). Benevolent theory: Moral treatment at the York Retreat. *History of Psychiatry, 18,* 61–80.

Charles, E. P. (2013). Special Issue: Unifying approaches to psychology. *Review of General Psychology, 17,* 123–242.

Chaturvedi, S. K. (2015). Religious, spiritual, and cultural aspects of psychiatric ethics in Hinduism. In J. Z. Sadler, W. C. W. van Staden, & K. W. M. Fulford (Eds.), *The Oxford handbook of psychiatric ethics* (Vol. 1, pp. 616–633). New York: Oxford University Press.

Chen, L. (2001). Perceptual organization: To reverse back the inverted (upside-down) question of feature binding. *Visual Cognition, 8,* 287–303.

Child, I. L. (1973). *Humanistic psychology and the research tradition: Their several virtues.* New York: Wiley.

Choi, O. (2015). Using fMRI for lie detection: Ready for court? In K. J. Weiss & C. Watson (Eds.), *Psychiatric expert testimony: Emerging applications* (pp. 84–101). New York: Oxford University Press.

Chomsky, N. (1959). A review of Skinner's Verbal Behavior. *Language, 35,* 26–58.

Chrisomalis, S. (2014). Scientific instruments. Retrieved July 20, 2016 from http://phrontistery.info/instrum.html.

Christen, D. (1984). *The genesis of misogynism and woman's subordination within the Christian church.* Unpublished senior honors thesis, Colorado State University Library.

Churchland, P. (2006). Do we have free will? *New Scientist, 192,* 42–45.

Churchland, P. S. (1989). *Neurophilosophy: Toward a unified science of mind-brain.* Cambridge, MA: MIT Press.

Ciabattari, J. (2014). Does Freud still matter? Retrieved July 12, 2016 from www.bbc.com/culture/story/20140421-does-freud-still-matter.

Cipriani, G., Dolciotti, C., Picchi, L., & Bonuccelli, U. (2011). Alzheimer and his disease: A brief history. *Neurological Sciences, 32,* 275–279.

Clanchy, M. T. (1997). *Abelard: A Medieval life.* Malden, MA: Blackwell.

Clark, D. O. (2005). From philosopher to psychologist: The early career of Edwin Ray Guthrie, Jr. *History of Psychology, 8,* 235–254.

Clark, E. (1972). Eduard Hitzig. In C. C. Gillispie (Ed.), *Dictionary of scientific biography* (Vol. 6, pp. 440–441). New York: Scribner.

Clark, R. W. (1971). *Einstein: The life and times.* New York: World.

Clarke, D. M. (1982). *Descartes' philosophy of science.* University Park: University of Pennsylvania Press.

Clarke, E., & O'Malley, C. D. (1968). *The human brain and spinal cord: A historical study illustrated by writings from antiquity to the twentieth century.* Berkeley & Los Angeles: University of California Press.

Clarke, S. (1998). *Metaphysics and the disunity of scientific knowledge*. Farnham, UK: Ashgate.

Clauser, B. E. (2007). The life and labors of Francis Galton: A review of four recent books about the father of behavioral statistics. *Journal of Educational and Behavioral Statistics, 32,* 440–444.

Cleary, T. S., & Shapiro, S. I. (1996). Abraham Maslow and Asian psychology. *Psychologia: An International Journal of Psychology in the Orient, 39,* 213–222.

Clegg, J. W. (2006). A phenomenological investigation of the experience of not belonging. *Journal of Phenomenological Psychology, 37,* 53–83.

Clements, R. D. (1967). Physiological-psychological thought in Juan Luis Vives. *Journal of the History of the Behavioral Sciences, 3,* 219–235.

Cleveland, G. (1905). Would woman suffrage be unwise? *The Ladies Home Journal, 22,* 7–8.

Clodd, E. (1972). *Pioneers of evolution from Thales to Huxley: With an intermediate chapter on the causes of the arrest of the movement*. New York: Books for Libraries Press. (Original work published 1897)

Cobb, M. (2006). *Generation: The seventeenth-century scientists who unraveled the secrets of sex, life, and growth*. New York: Bloomsbury.

Cochran, M. (Ed.). (2010). *The Cambridge companion to Dewey*. New York: Cambridge University Press.

Coe, G. A. (1900). *The spiritual life: Studies in the science of religion*. New York: Eaton & Mains.

Cohen, D. (2009). *The escape of Sigmund Freud*. New York: Overlook Press.

Cohen, D. (2012). *Freud on coke*. London: Cutting Edge Press.

Cole, C. W., Oetting, E. R., & Hinkle, J. E. (1967). Nonlinearity of self-concept discrepancy: The value dimension. *Psychological Reports, 21,* 58–60.

Cole, N., & Parker, G. (2012). Cade's identification of lithium for manic-depressive illness—The prospector who found a gold nugget. *Journal of Nervous and Mental Disease, 200,* 1101–1104.

Cole, T. R. (1993). The prophecy of "Senescence": G. Stanley Hall and the reconstruction of old age in twentieth-century America. In K. W. Schaie & W. A. Achenbaum (Eds.), *Societal impact on aging: Historical perspectives* (pp. 165–181). New York: Springer.

Colebrook, C. (2002). *Gilles Deleuze*. New York: Routledge.

Coleman, S. R. (1981). Historical context and systematic functions of the concept of the operant. *Behaviorism, 9,* 207–226.

Collins, A. (2006). The embodiment of reconciliation: Order and change in the work of Frederic Bartlett. *History of Psychology, 9,* 290–312.

Collins, A. F. (1999). The enduring appeal of physiognomy: Physical appearance as a sign of temperament, character, and intelligence. *History of Psychology, 2,* 251–276.

Collins, P. H., & Bilge, S. (2016). *Intersectionality*. Cambridge, UK: Polity Press.

Colp, R., Jr. (1986). Confessing a murder: Darwin's first revelations about transmutation. *Isis, 77,* 9–32.

Compton, W. C., & Hoffman, E. (2013). *Positive psychology*. Belmont, CA: Wadsworth.

Connors, C. (2000). Freud and the force of history: "The Project for a Scientific Psychology." In M. Rossington & A. Whitehead (Eds.), *Between the psyche and the polis: Refiguring history in literature and theory* (pp. 59–73). Aldershot, UK: Ashgate.

Constant, J. (2014). Jean Marc Gaspard Itard (1774–1838). *Neuropsychiatrie de l'Enfance et de l'Adolescence, 62,* 128–130.

Cooke, B., Mills, A. J., & Kelley, E. S. (2005). Situating Maslow in Cold War America: A recontextualization of management theory. *Group & Organization Management, 30,* 129–152.

Coon, D. J. (1992). Testing the limits of sense and science: American experimental psychologists combat spiritualism, 1880–1920. *American Psychologist, 47,* 143–151.

Coon, D. J. (1993). Standardizing the subject: Experimental psychologists, introspection, and the quest for a technoscientific ideal. *Technology and Culture, 34,* 757–783.

Coon, D. J. (1994). "Not a creature of reason": The alleged impact of Watsonian behaviorism on advertising in the 1920s. In J. T. Todd & E. K. Morris (Eds.), *Modern perspectives on John B. Watson and classical behaviorism* (pp. 37–63). Westport, CT: Greenwood Press.

Coon, D. J. (1996). "One moment in the world's salvation": Anarchism and the radicalization of William James. *The Journal of American History, 83,* 70–99.

Coon, D. J. (2006). Abraham H. Maslow: Reconnaissance for Eupsychia. In D. A. Dewsbury, L. T. Benjamin, & M. Wertheimer (Eds.), *Portraits of pioneers in psychology* (Vol. 6, pp. 255–271). Washington, DC: American Psychological Association.

Cooper, S. J. (2005). Donald O. Hebb's synapse and learning rule: A history and commentary. *Neuroscience and Biobehavioral Reviews, 28,* 851–874.

Copleston, F. (1962). *A history of philosophy: Vol. 2. Medieval philosophy, Part II*. New York: Image Books.

Coralli, A., & Perciaccante, A. (2016). Leonardo's recurrent stroke? *The Lancet Neurology, 7,* 667.

509

Coren, S. (2003). Sensation and perception. In I. B. Weiner (Series Ed.) & D. K. Freedheim (Vol. Ed.), *Handbook of psychology, Vol. 1: History of psychology* (pp. 85–108). New York: Wiley.

Cornel, T. (2014). Matters of sex and gender in F. J. Gall's organology: A primary approach. *Journal of the History of the Neurosciences, 23,* 377–394.

Cornelius-White, J. H. D. (2012). *Carl Rogers: The China diary.* Ross-on-Wye, UK: PCCS Books.

Costello, S. J. (2011). An existential analysis of anxiety: Frankl, Kierkegaard, Voegelin. *International Forum for Logotherapy, 34,* 65–71.

Cottingham, J. (1979). Varieties of retribution. *Philosophical Quarterly, 29,* 238–246.

Cottingham, J., Stoothoff, R., & Murdoch, D. (1984–1985). *The philosophical writings of Descartes* (2 vols.). Cambridge, UK: Cambridge University Press.

Craik, K. H., Hogan, R., & Wolfe, R. N. (Eds.). (1993). *Fifty years of personality psychology: Perspectives on individual differences.* New York: Plenum Press.

Cravens, H. (2006). The historical context of G. Stanley Hall's *Adolescence* (1904). *History of Psychology, 9,* 172–185.

Crawford, C., & Krebs, D. (Eds.). (2008). *Foundations of evolutionary psychology.* New York: Lawrence Erlbaum Associates.

Crews, F. (1996). The verdict on Freud. *Psychological Science, 7,* 63–68.

Crick, F. H. C. (1994). *The astonishing hypothesis: The scientific search for the soul.* New York: Scribner.

Crochetière, K., Vicker, N., Parker, J., King, D. B., & Wertheimer, M. (2001). Gestalt theory and psychopathology: Some early applications of Gestalt theory to clinical psychology and psychopathology. *Gestalt Theory, 23,* 144–154.

Crombie, A. C. (1961). *Augustine to Galileo* (2nd ed.). Cambridge, MA: Harvard University Press.

Crosby, D. A. (1996). Experience as reality: The ecological metaphysics of William James. In D. A. Crosby & C. D. Hardwick (Eds.), *Religious experience and ecological responsibility* (pp. 67–87). New York: Peter Lang.

Crosby, D. A., & Viney, W. (1990, August). *Toward a psychology that is radically empirical.* Paper presented at the annual meeting of the American Psychological Association, Boston.

Crossman, E. K. (1991). Schedules of reinforcement. In W. Ishaq (Ed.), *Human behavior in today's world* (pp. 133–138). New York: Praeger.

Croston, R., Branch, C. L., Kozlovsky, D. Y., Dukas, R. & Pravosudov, V. V. (2015). Heritability and the evolution of cognitive traits. *Behavioral Ecology, 26,* 1447–1459.

Crowther-Heyck, H. (2000). Mystery and meaning: A reply to Green (2000). *History of Psychology, 3,* 67–70.

Crumbaugh, J. C., & Maholick, L. T. (1964). An experimental study in existentialism: The psychometric approach to Frankl's concept of noogenic neurosis. *Journal of Clinical Psychology, 20,* 200–207.

Crutchfield, R. S. (1961). Edward Chace Tolman: 1886–1959. *American Journal of Psychology, 74,* 135–141.

Csikszentmihalyi, M. (1990). *Flow: The psychology of optimal experience.* New York: Harper & Row.

Cubelli, R., & De Bastiani, P. (2011). 150 years after Leborgne: Why is Paul Broca so important in the history of neuropsychology? *Cortex: A Journal Devoted to the Study of the Nervous System and Behavior, 47,* 146–147.

Cucina, J. M., Hayes, T. L., Walmsley, P. T., & Martin, N. R. (2014). It is time to get medieval on the overproduction of pseudotheory: How Bacon (1267) and Alhazen (1021) can save industrial–organizational psychology. *Industrial and Organizational Psychology: Perspectives on Science and Practice, 7,* 356–364.

Cunha, M. P., Clegg, S., & Rego, A. (2013). Lessons for leaders: Positive organization studies meets Niccolò Machiavelli. *Leadership, 9,* 450–465.

Curley, E. (Ed. & Trans.). (1985). *The collected works of Spinoza* (Vol. 1). Princeton, NJ: Princeton University Press.

Curry, O. (2006). Who's afraid of the naturalistic fallacy? *Evolutionary Psychology, 4,* 234–247.

Cusher, B. E. (2014). How does law rule? Plato on habit, political education, and legislation. *Journal of Politics, 76,* 1032–1044.

Dain, N. (1964). *Concepts of insanity in the United States, 1789–1865.* New Brunswick, NJ: Rutgers University Press.

Dally, A. (2004). Sargant, William Walters (1907–1988). In *Oxford dictionary of national biography.* Oxford: Oxford University Press. www.oxforddnb. com. source.unco.edu/view/article/40195

Dalton, J. H., Hill, J., Thomas, E., & Kloos, B. (2013). Community psychology. In D. K. Freedheim & I. B. Weiner (Eds.), *Handbook of psychology, Vol. 1: History of psychology* (2nd ed., pp. 468–487). Hoboken, NJ: John Wiley & Sons Inc.

Daly, M. (1968). *The church and the second sex.* New York: Harper & Row.

Damasio, A. (2003). *Looking for Spinoza: Joy, sorrow, and the feeling brain.* New York: Harcourt.

D'Amato, R. C., Zafiris, C., McConnell, E., & Dean, R. S. (2011). The history of school psychology: Understanding the past to not repeat it. In M. A. Bray & T. J. Kehle (Eds.), *The Oxford handbook of school psychology* (pp. 9–46). New York: Oxford University Press.

Damjanovic, A., Milovanovic, S. D., & Trajanovic, N. N. (2015). Descartes and his peculiar sleep patter. *Journal of the History of the Neurosciences, 24,* 396–407.

Daniels, M. (1988). The myth of self-actualization. *Journal of Humanistic Psychology, 28,* 7–38.

Danto, E. A. (in press). Trauma and the state with Sigmund Freud as witness. *International Journal of Law and Psychiatry.*

Danziger, K. (1979). The positivist repudiation of Wundt. *Journal of the History of the Behavioral Sciences, 15,* 205–230.

Danziger, K. (2001). Sealing off the discipline: Wilhelm Wundt and the psychology of memory. In C. D. Green & M. Shore (Eds.), *The transformation of psychology: Influences of 19th-century philosophy, technology, and natural science* (pp. 45–62). Washington, DC: American Psychological Association.

Darwin, C. (1877). A biographical sketch of an infant. *Mind, 2,* 285–294.

Darwin, C. (1897). *Journal of researches into the natural history and geology of the countries visited during the voyage of the H. M. S. Beagle round the world under the command of Capt. Fitz Roy, R.N.* New York: D. Appleton & Co.

Darwin, C. (1958). *The autobiography of Charles Darwin 1809–1882* (N. Barlow, Ed.). London: Collins.

Darwin, C. (1998). *The expression of emotions in man and animals.* New York: Oxford University Press. (Original work published 1872)

Das Neves, J. C., & Melé, D. (2013). Managing ethically cultural diversity: Learning from Thomas Aquinas. *Journal of Business Ethics, 116,* 769–780.

Davies, B. (2013). The Zombie Ward: The chilling story of how 'depressed' women were put to sleep for months in an NHS hospital room—leaving mental scars that remain 40 years on. Retrieved November 30, 2015 from www.dailymail.co.uk/femail/article-2386477/NHS-Zombie-Ward-How-depressed-women-sleep-months-Londons-Royal-Waterloo-Hospital.html

Davis, A. M. (2015). When Webb met Follett: Negotiation theory and the race to the moon. *Negotiation Journal, 31,* 267–283.

Dawkins, R. (2006). *The selfish gene* (30th anniversary ed.). New York: Oxford University Press.

Deason, G. B. (1986). Reformation theology and the mechanistic conception of nature. In D. C. Lindberg & R. L. Numbers (Eds.), *God and nature: Historical essays on the encounter between Christianity and science* (pp. 167–191). Berkeley: University of California Press.

deBeer, G. (1964). *Charles Darwin: Evolution by natural selection.* New York: Doubleday.

DeCarvalho, R. J. (1990). A history of the "third force" in psychology. *Journal of Humanistic Psychology, 30,* 22–44.

DeCarvalho, R. J. (1991). *The founders of humanistic psychology.* New York: Praeger.

DeCarvalho, R. J. (1992). The institutionalization of humanistic psychology. *Humanistic Psychologist, 20,* 124–135.

de Chardin, T. (1961). *The phenomenon of man* (B. Wall, Trans.). New York: Harper & Row.

de Feijoo, A. M. L. C., & Protasio, M. M. (2015). Kierkegaard's ideas on clinical psychology and psychotherapy. *Existential Analysis, 26,* 145–153.

Delahunty, R. J. (1985). *Spinoza.* Boston: Routledge & Kegan Paul.

Delaunay, P. (1958). Humanism and encyclopedism. In R. Taton (Ed.) & A. J. Pomerans (Trans.), *History of science: The beginnings of modern science.* New York: Basic Books.

Delheye, P. (2014). Statistics, gymnastics and the origins of sport science in Belgium (and Europe). *European Journal of Sport Science, 14,* 652–660.

DeMartino, R. J. (1991). Karen Horney, Daisetz T. Suzuki, and Zen Buddhism. *American Journal of Psychoanalysis, 51,* 267–283.

DeMause, L. (Ed.). (1974). *The history of childhood.* New York: Psychohistory Press.

Demazeux, S., & Singy, P. (Eds.). (2015). *The DSM-5 in perspective: Philosophical reflections on the psychiatric Babel.* New York: Springer Science + Business Media.

de Melo, C. M., de Castro, M S. L. B., & de Rose, J. C. (2015). Some relations between culture, ethics and technology in B. F. Skinner. *Behavior and Social Issues, 24,* 39–55.

Demeter, T. (2012). Liberty, necessity and the foundations of Hume's "science of man." *History of the Human Sciences, 25,* 15–31.

Dennett, D. C. (1991). *Consciousness explained.* Boston: Little, Brown.

Dennis, M. (1985). William Preyer (1841–1897) and his neuropsychology of language of acquisition. *Developmental Neuropsychology, 1,* 287–315.

Dennis, W. (Ed.). (1948). *Readings in the history of psychology.* New York: Appleton-Century-Crofts.

DeRosa, P. (1988). *Vicars of Christ: The dark side of the papacy.* New York: Crown.

Descartes, R. (1985a). Discourse and essays (J. Cottingham, R. Stoothoff, & D. Murdoch, Trans.). *The philosophical writings of Descartes* (Vol. 1, pp.

511

109–175). Cambridge, UK: Cambridge University Press. (Original work published 1637)

Descartes, R. (1985b). The passions of the soul (J. Cottingham, R. Stoothoff, & D. Murdoch, Trans.). *The philosophical writings of Descartes* (Vol. 1, pp. 324–404). Cambridge, UK: Cambridge University Press. (Original work published 1649)

Descartes, R. (1985c). Treatise on man (J. Cottingham, R. Stoothoff, & D. Murdoch, Trans.). *The philosophical writings of Descartes* (Vol. 1, pp. 99–108). Cambridge, UK: Cambridge University Press. (Original work published 1664)

Descartes, R. (2010). *Meditations on first philosophy* (7th ed.). J. Veitch (Ed. & Trans.). Seaside, OR: Watchmaker Publishing.

Deutsch, M., & Coleman, P. T. (2012). Psychological components of sustainable peace: An introduction. In P. T. Coleman & M. Deutsch (Eds.), *Psychological components of sustainable peace* (pp. 1–14). New York: Springer Science + Business Media.

Deutsch, M., & Collins, M. E. (1951). *Interracial housing: A psychological evaluation of a social experiment*. Minneapolis: University of Minnesota Press.

De Vos, J. (2010). From Milgram to Zimbardo: The double birth of postwar psychology/psychologization. *History of the Human Sciences, 23,* 156–175.

deVries, M. W., Müller, N., & Möller, H. (2008). Emil Kraepelin's legacy: Systematic clinical observation and the categorical classification of psychiatric diseases. *European Archives of Psychiatry and Clinical Neuroscience, 258,* 1–2.

Dewalque, A. (2013). Schema of the Brentano school intellectual progeny. *Phenomenology and the Cognitive Sciences, 12,* 445.

Dewey, J. (1896). The reflex arc concept in psychology. *Psychological Review, 3,* 357–370.

Dewey, J. (1917). The need for social psychology. *Psychological Review, 24,* 266–277.

Dewey, J. (1922). *Human nature and human conduct: An introduction to social psychology*. New York: Henry Holt.

DeWitt, L. D. (1985). MRI and the study of aphasia. *Neurology, 35,* 861–865.

Dewsbury, D. A. (Ed.). (1989). *Studying animal behavior: Autobiographies of the founders*. Chicago: University of Chicago Press.

Dewsbury, D. A. (1990). Whither the introductory course in the history of psychology? *Journal of the History of the Behavioral Sciences, 26,* 371–379.

Dewsbury, D. A. (1992). William James and instinct theory revisited. In M. E. Donnelly (Ed.), *Reinterpreting the legacy of William James* (pp. 263–291). Washington, DC: American Psychological Association.

Dewsbury, D. A. (1993). The boys of summer at the end of summer: The Watson-Lashley correspondence of the 1950s. *Psychological Reports, 72,* 263–269.

Dewsbury, D. A. (1996). A history of Division 6 (behavioral science and comparative psychology): Now you see it. Now you don't. Now you see it. In D. A. Dewsbury (Ed.), *Unification through division* (Vol. 1: Histories of the divisions of the American Psychological Association, pp. 41–65). Washington, DC: American Psychological Association.

Dewsbury, D. A. (1998). Celebrating E. L. Thorndike a century after "Animal Intelligence." *American Psychologist, 53,* 1121–1124.

Dewsbury, D. A. (2000). Comparative cognition in the 1930s. *Psychonomic Bulletin and Review, 7,* 267–283.

Dewsbury, D. A. (2003). James Rowland Angell: Born administrator. In G. A. Kimble & M. Wertheimer (Eds.), *Portraits of pioneers in psychology* (Vol. 5, pp. 55–71). Washington, DC: American Psychological Association.

Dewsbury, D. A. (2006). *Monkey farm: A history of the Yerkes Laboratories of Primate Biology, Orange Park, Florida, 1930–1965*. Cranbury, NJ: Bucknell University Press.

Dewsbury, D. A. (2013). John B. Watson's early work and comparative psychology. *Revista Mexicana de Análisis de la Conducta, 39,* 10–33.

Diamond, S. (1971). Gestation of the instinct concept. *Journal of the History of the Behavioral Sciences, 7,* 323–336.

Diamond, S. (1974a). Four hundred years of instinct controversy. *Behavior Genetics, 4,* 237–252.

Diamond, S. (Ed.). (1974b). *The roots of psychology: A source book in the history of ideas*. New York: Basic Books.

Diamond, S. (1977). Francis Galton and American psychology. *Annals of the New York Academy of Sciences, 291,* 47–55.

Diamond, S. (1980). Wundt before Leipzig. In R. W. Rieber (Ed.), *Wilhelm Wundt and the making of a scientific psychology* (pp. 3–70). New York: Plenum Press.

Diamond, S., Balvin, R. S., & Diamond, F. R. (1963). *Inhibition and choice*. New York: Harper & Row.

Diehl, L. A. (1986). The paradox of G. Stanley Hall: Foe of coeducation and educator of women. *American Psychologist, 41,* 868–878.

Diener, E., Oishi, S., & Lucas, R. E. (2015). National accounts of subjective well-being. *American Psychologist, 70,* 234–242.

Digby, A. (1983). Changes in the asylum: The case of York, 1777–1815. *The Economic History Review, 36,* 218–239.

Digdon, N., Powell, R. A., & Smithson, C. (2014). Watson's alleged Little Albert scandal: Historical breakthrough or new Watson myth? *Revista de Historia de la Psicología, 35,* 47–60.

Diriwächter, R. (2012). Völkerpsychologie. In J. Valsiner (Ed.), *The Oxford handbook of culture and psychology* (pp. 43–57). New York: Oxford University Press.

Diriwächter, R., & Valsiner, J. (Eds.). (2008). *Striving for the whole: Creating theoretical syntheses.* Piscataway, NJ: Transaction Publishers.

Dix, D. L. (1971). Memorial soliciting a state hospital for the insane submitted to the Legislature of New Jersey. In D. J. Rothman (Ed.), *Poverty U.S.A.: The historical record* (pp. 1–46). New York: Arno Press. (Original work published 1845)

Dixon, T. (2012). "Emotion": The history of a keyword in crisis. *Emotion Review, 4,* 338–344.

Dobson, K. S. (2012). History. In *Cognitive therapy* (pp. 7–10). Washington, DC: American Psychological Association.

Dols, M. W. (2006). Medical madness. *Journal of Muslim Mental Health, 1,* 77–95.

Domenjo, B. A. (2000). Thoughts on the influences of Brentano and Comte on Freud's work. *Psychoanalysis & History, 2,* 110–118.

Donahoe, J. W. (1999). Edward L. Thorndike: The selectionist connectionist. *Journal of the Experimental Analysis of Behavior, 72,* 451–454.

Donahoe, J. W., & Vegas, R. (2011). Respondent (Pavlovian) conditioning. In W. W. Fisher, C. C. Piazza, & H. S. Roane (Eds.), *Handbook of applied behavior analysis* (pp. 17–33). New York: Guilford Press.

Dovidio, J. F., Glick, P., & Rudman, L. A. (Eds.). (2005). *On the nature of prejudice: Fifty years after Allport.* Malden, MA: Blackwell.

Drury, S., Hutchens, S. A., Shuttlesworth, D. E., & White, C. L. (2012). Philip G. Zimbardo on his career and the Stanford Prison Experiment's 40th anniversary. *History of Psychology, 15,* 161–170.

D'Souza, J., & Gurin, M. (2016). The universal significance of Maslow's concept of self-actualization. *The Humanistic Psychologist, 44,* 210–214.

DuBois, P. H. (1970). *A history of psychological testing.* Boston: Allyn & Bacon.

Duman, C. H., Schlesinger, L., Kodama, M., Russell, D. S., & Duman, R. S. (2007). A role for MAP kinase signaling in behavioral models of depression and antidepressant treatment. *Biological Psychiatry, 61,* 661–670.

Duncan, C. P. (1980). A note on the 1929 International Congress of Psychology. *Journal of the History of the Behavioral Sciences, 16,* 1–5.

Duncker, K. (1945). On problem solving. *Psychological Monographs, 58,* 1–113.

Dunlap, K. (1925). *Social psychology.* Baltimore: William & Wilkins.

Dunn, D. S. (2011). Situations matter: Teaching the Lewinian link between social psychology and rehabilitation psychology. *History of Psychology, 14,* 405–411.

Dupouy, S. (2011). The naturalist and the nuances: Sentimentalism, moral values, and emotional expression in Darwin and the Anatomists. *Journal of the History of the Behavioral Sciences, 47,* 335–358.

Dupré, J. (1993). *The disorder of things: Metaphysical foundations of the disunity of science.* Cambridge, MA: Harvard University Press.

Duran, J. (2006). *Eight women philosophers: Theory, politics, and feminism.* Urbana, IL: University of Illinois Press.

Durant, W. (1950). *The story of civilization: Part IV, The age of faith.* New York: Simon and Schuster.

Durant, W. (1954). *The story of civilization: Part I, Our Oriental heritage.* New York: Simon and Schuster.

Durant, W., & Durant, A. (1961). *The story of civilization: Part VII, The age of reason begins.* New York: Simon and Schuster.

Durant, W., & Durant, A. (1967). *The story of civilization: Part X, Rousseau and revolution.* New York: Simon and Schuster.

Dvorsky, G. (2013). Why Freud still matters, when he was wrong about almost everything. Retrieved July 12, 2016 from 109.gizmodo.com/why-freud-still-matters-when-he-was-wrong-about-almost1055800815.

Eacker, J. N. (1972). On some elementary philosophical problems in psychology. *American Psychologist, 27,* 553–565.

Eacker, J. N. (1975). *Problems of philosophy and psychology.* Chicago: Nelson-Hall.

Eagleman, D. M. (2011). *Incognito: The secret lives of the brain.* New York: Vintage Books.

Earle, W. J. (1967). William James. In P. Edwards (Ed.), *The encyclopedia of philosophy* (Vol. 4, pp. 240–249). New York: Macmillan and Free Press.

Eason, R. G. (2004). Donald Benjamin Lindsley. *American Journal of Psychology, 117,* 611–619.

Ebbinghaus, H. (1913). *Memory: A contribution to experimental psychology.* (H. A. Ruger & C. E. Bussenius, Trans.). New York: Teachers College Press, Columbia University. (Original work published 1885)

Eckardt, M. H. (1991). Feminine psychology revisited: A historical perspective. *American Journal of Psychoanalysis, 51,* 235–243.

Eckardt, M. H. (2005). Karen Horney: A portrait: The

120th anniversary, Karen Horney, September 16, 1885. *American Journal of Psychoanalysis, 65,* 95–101.

Eckardt, M. H. (2006). Karen Horney: A portrait. *American Journal of Psychoanalysis, 66,* 105–108.

Edelman, G. (1992). *Bright air, brilliant fire: On the matter of the mind.* New York: Basic Books.

Edwards, D. C. (1999). *Motivation and emotion: Evolutionary, physiological, cognitive, and social influences.* Thousand Oaks, CA: Sage.

Ehrman, B. (2003). *Lost Christianities: The battles for scripture and the faiths we never knew.* New York: Oxford University Press.

Eig, J. (2014). *The birth of the pill: How four crusaders reinvented sex and launched a revolution.* New York: W. W. Norton & Co.

Einstein, A. (1964). Why war? In J. Strachey (Ed.), *The standard edition of the complete psychological works of Sigmund Freud* (Vol. 22, pp. 199–202). London: Hogarth Press. (Original work published 1932)

Einstein, G. O., McDaniel, M. A., & Scullin, M. K. (2012). Prospective memory and aging: Understanding the variability. In M. Naveh-Benjamin & N. Ohta (Eds.), *Memory and aging: Current issues and future directions* (pp. 153–179). New York: Psychology Press.

Eiseley, L. C. (1957). Charles Darwin. In D. Flanagan (Ed.), *Lives in science.* New York: Simon and Schuster.

Eisenberg, L. (2007). Furor therapeuticus: Benjamin Rush and the Philadelphia yellow fever epidemic of 1793. *American Journal of Psychiatry, 164,* 552–555.

Eissler, K. R. (1965). *Medical orthodoxy and the future of psychoanalysis.* New York: International Universities Press.

Ekstein, D., & Kaufman, J. A. (2012). The role of birth order in personality: An enduring intellectual legacy of Alfred Adler. *The Journal of Individual Psychology, 68,* 60–61.

Eling, P. (2012). Neurognostics answer. *Journal of the History of the Neurosciences, 21,* 119–125.

Eling, P. (2016a). Broca's faculté du langage articulé: Language or praxis? *Journal of the History of the Neurosciences, 25,* 169–187.

Eling, P. (2016b). Neuroanniversary 2016. *Journal of the History of the Neurosciences, 25,* 213–217.

Eling, P., Draaisma, D., & Conradi, M. (2011). Gall's visit to the Netherlands. *Journal of the History of the Neurosciences, 20,* 135–150.

Eling, P., & Finger, S. (2015). Franz Joseph Gall on greatness in the fine arts: A collaboration of multiple cortical faculties of mind. *Cortex: A Journal Devoted to the Study of the Nervous System and Behavior, 71,* 102–115.

Eling, P., & Maes, R. (2008). On the historical and conceptual background of the Wisconsin Card Sorting Test. *Brain and Cognition, 67,* 247–253.

Elkholy, S. N. (2008). *Heidegger and a metaphysics of feeling.* London: Continuum.

Elliott, R., & Freire, E. (2010). The effectiveness of person-centered and experiential therapies: A review of the meta-analyses. In M. Cooper, J. C. Watson, & D. Holldampf (Eds.), *Person-centered and experiential therapies work: A review of the research on counseling, psychotherapy, and related practices* (pp. 1–15). Ross-on-Wye, UK: PCCS Books.

Ellis, A. (2004). *The road to tolerance: The philosophy of rational emotive behavior therapy.* Amherst, NY: Prometheus Books.

Elmer-DeWitt, P. (1993, November 8). Cloning: Where do we draw the line? *Time,* pp. 64–70.

Elms, A. C. (2005). Jung's lives. *Journal of the History of the Behavioral Sciences, 41,* 331–346.

Else-Quest, N. M., & Hyde, J. S. (2016). Intersectionality in quantitative psychological research: I. Theoretical and epistemological issues. *Psychology of Women Quarterly, 40,* 155–170.

Emad, P. (2007). *On the way to Heidegger's contributions to philosophy.* Madison, WI: The University of Wisconsin Press.

Emerson, R. W. (1969). *Essays: Second series.* Columbus, OH: Merrill. (Original work published 1841)

Emerson, R. W. (1981). Self reliance. In D. McQuade (Ed.), *Selected writings of Emerson* (pp. 129–153). New York: Modern Library. (Original work published 1841)

English, A. R. (2013). *Discontinuity in learning: Dewey, Herbart, and education as transformation.* Cambridge, UK: Cambridge University Press.

Engstrom, E. J. (1991). Emil Kraepelin: Psychiatry and public affairs in Wilhelmine Germany. *History of Psychiatry, 2,* 111–132.

Engstrom, E. J., & Kendler, K. S. (2015). Emil Kraepelin: Icon and reality. *American Journal of Psychiatry, 172,* 1190–1196.

Erikson, E. H. (1963). *Childhood and society* (2nd ed.). New York: Norton.

Ernst, C., & Angst, J. (1983). *Birth order: Its influence on personality.* Berlin: Springer-Verlag.

Ervin, S. M. (2015). History of nursing education in the United States. In S. B. Keating (Ed.), *Curriculum development and evaluation in nursing* (3rd ed., pp. 5–32). New York: Springer Publishing Co.

Esper, E. A. (1964). *A history of psychology.* Philadelphia: W. B. Saunders.

Esper, E. A. (1966). Max Meyer: The making of a scientific isolate. *Journal of the History of the Behavioral Sciences, 2,* 341–356.

Esping, A. (2010). Autoethnography and existentialism: The conceptual contributions of Viktor Frankl. *Journal of Phenomenological Psychology, 41,* 201–215.

Esping, A., & Plucker, J. A. (2015). Alfred Binet and the children of Paris. In S. Goldstein, D. Princiotta, & J. A. Naglieri (Eds.), *Handbook of intelligence: Evolutionary theory, historical perspective, and current concepts* (pp. 153–161). New York: Springer Science + Business Media.

Estes, W. K. (1950). Toward a statistical theory of learning. *Psychological Review, 57,* 94–107.

Evans, R. B. (1972). E. B. Titchener and his lost system. *Journal of the History of the Behavioral Sciences, 8,* 168–180.

Evans, R. B. (1991). E. B. Titchener on scientific psychology and technology. In G. A. Kimble, M. Wertheimer, & C. L. White (Eds.), *Portraits of pioneers in psychology* (pp. 89–103). Washington, DC: American Psychological Association.

Evans, R. B. (2000). Psychological instruments at the turn of the century. *American Psychologist, 55,* 322–325.

Evans, R. I. (1968). *B. F. Skinner: The man and his ideas.* New York: Dutton.

Eysenck, H. J. (1952). The effects of psychotherapy: An evaluation. *Journal of Consulting Psychology, 16,* 319–324.

Eysenck, M. W. (1986). Ebbinghaus: An evaluation. In F. Klix & H. Hagendorf (Eds.), *Human memory and cognitive capacities: Mechanisms and performances.* Amsterdam: Elsevier Science.

Fagan, T. K. (1992). Compulsory schooling, child study, clinical psychology, and special education: Origins of school psychology. *American Psychologist, 47,* 236–243.

Fagan, T. K. (1996). Witmer's contributions to school psychological services. *American Psychologist, 51,* 241–243.

Fancher, R. E. (1977). Brentano's psychology from an empirical standpoint and Freud's early metapsychology. *Journal of the History of the Behavioral Sciences, 13,* 207–227.

Fancher, R. E. (1996). *Pioneers of psychology* (3rd ed.). New York: Norton.

Fancher, R. E. (2000). Snapshots of Freud in America, 1899–1999. *American Psychologist, 55,* 1025–1028.

Fancher, R. E. (2009). Scientific cousins: The relationship between Charles Darwin and Francis Galton. *American Psychologist, 64,* 84–92.

Fancher, R. E., & Schmidt, H. (2003). Gottfried Wilhelm Leibniz: Underappreciated pioneer of psychology. In G. A. Kimble & M. Wertheimer (Eds.), *Portraits of pioneers in psychology* (Vol. 5, pp. 1–17). Washington, DC: American Psychological Association.

Farr, R. (1983). Wilhelm Wundt (1832–1920) and the origins of psychology as an experimental social science. *British Journal of Social Psychology, 22,* 289–301.

Farreras, I. G. (2016). Early history of clinical psychology (1896–1949). In J. C. Norcross, G. R. Vandenbos, D. K. Freedheim, & M. M. Domenech Rodríguez (Eds.), *APA handbook of clinical psychology: Roots and branches* (Vol. 1, pp. 3–18). Washington, DC: American Psychological Association.

Farreras, I. G., Routh, D. K., & Cautin, R. L. (2016). History of clinical psychology following World War II. In J. C. Norcross, G. R. Vandenbos, D. K. Freedheim, & M. M. Domenech Rodríguez (Eds.), *APA handbook of clinical psychology: Roots and branches* (Vol. 1, pp. 19–40). Washington, DC: American Psychological Association.

Faye, E. (2009). *Heidegger: The introduction of Nazism into philosophy* (M. B. Smith, Trans.). New Haven, CT: Yale University Press.

Fearing, F. (1970). *Reflex action: A study in the history of physiological psychology.* Cambridge, MA: MIT Press.

Fechner, G. (1966). *Elements of psychophysics* (H. E. Adler, Trans., D. H. Howes & E. G. Boring, Eds.). New York: Holt, Rinehart and Winston. (Original work published 1860)

Felder, A. J., Aten, H. M., Neudeck, J. A., Shiomi-Chen, J., & Robbins, B. D. (2014). Mindfulness at the heart of existential-phenomenology and humanistic psychology: A century of contemplation and elaboration. *The Humanistic Psychologist, 42,* 6–23.

Fellows, O. E., & Milliken, S. F. (1972). *Buffon.* New York: Twayne.

Feltham, C. (2013). The past and future of humanistic psychology. In R. House, D. Kalisch, & J. Maidman (Eds.), *The future of humanistic psychology* (pp. 3–7). Ross-on-Wye, UK: PCCS Books.

Ferguson, E. D. (2000). *Motivation: A biosocial and cognitive integration of motivation and emotion.* New York: Oxford University Press.

Ferguson, E. D. (2010). Adler's innovative contributions regarding the need to belong. *The Journal of Individual Psychology, 66,* 1–7.

Fernberger, S. W. (1935). Fundamental categories as determiners of psychological systems: An excursion into ancient Chinese psychologies. *Psychological Review, 42,* 544–554.

Ferrari, M., & Pinard, A. (2006). Death and resurrection of a disciplined science of consciousness. *Journal of Consciousness Studies, 13,* 75–96.

Ferrari, M., Pinard, A., & Runions, K. (2001). Piaget's framework for a scientific study of consciousness. *Human Development, 44,* 195–213.

Ferster, C. S., & Skinner, B. F. (1957). *Schedules of reinforcement.* New York: Appleton-Century-Crofts.

Festinger, L. (1962). *A theory of cognitive dissonance.* Stanford, CA: Stanford University Press.

Feyerabend, P. K. (1975). *Against method.* London: NLB.

Feyerabend, P. K. (1988). *Farewell to reason.* London: Verso.

Fine, R. (1990). *The history of psychoanalysis.* New York: Continuum.

Finger, S., & Wade, N. J. (2002). The neuroscience of Helmholtz and the theories of Johannes Müller: Part 2: Sensation and perception. *Journal of the History of the Neurosciences, 11,* 234–254.

Fischer, G., Viney, W., Knight, J., & Johnson, N. (1968). Response decrement as a function of effort. *Quarterly Journal of Experimental Psychology, 20,* 301–304.

Fisher, H. A. L. (1936). *A history of Europe.* Toronto: Longmans, Green & Co.

Fiske, S. T., Gilbert, D. T., & Gindzey, G. (Eds.). (2010). *Handbook of social psychology.* Hoboken, NJ: John Wiley & Sons.

Fiske, S., & Taylor, S. (2008). *Social cognition: From brains to culture.* New York: McGraw-Hill.

Fiske, S. T., & Taylor, S. E. (1991). *Social cognition* (2nd ed.). New York: McGraw-Hill.

Fissette, D. (2009). Stumpf and Husserl on phenomenology and descriptive psychology. *Gestalt Theory, 31,* 175–190.

Fitzek, H. (2013). Artcoaching: Gestalt theory in arts and culture. *Gestalt Theory, 35,* 33–46.

Flescher, A. M., & Worthen, D. L. (2007). *The altruistic species: Scientific, philosophical, and religious perspectives of human benevolence.* Philadelphia, PA: Templeton Foundation Press.

Fleshner, M., & Laudenslager, M. L. (2004). Psychoneuroimmunology: Then and now. *Behavioral and Cognitive Neuroscience Reviews, 3,* 114–130.

Foley, P., & Moray, N. (1987). Sensation, perception, and systems design. In G. Salvendy (Ed.), *Handbook of human factors.* New York: Wiley.

Follette, W. C., & Callaghan, G. M. (2011). Behavior therapy: Functional-contextual approaches. In S. B. Messer & A. S. Gurman (Eds.), *Essential psychotherapies: Theory and practice* (3rd ed., pp. 1–37). New York: Guilford Press.

Ford, J. E. (1990). Systematic pluralism: Introduction to an issue. *The Monist, 73,* 335–349.

Forrest, D. W. (1974). *Francis Galton: The life and work of a Victorian genius.* New York: Taplinger.

Forrester, J., & Cameron, L. (1999). "A cure with a defect": A previously unpublished letter by Freud concerning "Anna O." *International Journal of Psycho-Analysis, 80,* 929–942.

Forsdyke, D. R. (2015). "A vehicle of symbols and nothing more". George Romanes, theory of mind, information, and Samuel Butler. *History of Psychiatry, 26,* 270–287.

Forsyth, D. R., & Diederich, L. T. (2014). Group dynamics and development. In J. L. DeLucia-Waack, C. R. Kalodner, & M. T. Riva (Eds.), *Handbook of group counseling and psychotherapy* (2nd ed., pp. 34–45). Thousand Oaks, CA: Sage Publications.

Foucault, M. (1979). *Discipline and punish: The birth of the prison.* London: Vintage Books.

Frame, D. M. (Trans.). (1960). *The complete essays of Montaigne* (2 vols.). Garden City, NY: Anchor Books, Doubleday.

Frank, R. H. (2011). The strategic role of the emotions. *Emotion Review, 3,* 252–254.

Frankl, V. E. (1985). *Man's search for meaning* (Rev. ed.). New York: Washington Square Press.

Frankl, V. E. (1997). *Viktor Frankl recollections: An autobiography.* New York: Insight/Plenum Press.

Fraser, A. C. (Ed.). (1959). *An essay concerning human understanding.* New York: Dover.

Freud, S. (1950). Project for a scientific psychology. In J. Strachey (Ed.), *The standard edition of the complete psychological works of Sigmund Freud* (Vol. 1, pp. 283–397). London: Hogarth Press. (Original work published 1895)

Freud, S. (1955). A difficulty in the path of psycho-analysis. In J. Strachey (Ed.), *The standard edition of the complete psychological works of Sigmund Freud* (Vol. 17, pp. 136–144). London: Hogarth Press. (Original work published 1917)

Freud, S. (1957a). Instincts and their vicissitudes. In J. Strachey (Ed.), *The standard edition of the complete psychological works of Sigmund Freud* (Vol. 14, pp. 111–140). London: Hogarth Press. (Original work published 1915)

Freud, S. (1957b). Leonardo da Vinci and a memory of his childhood. In J. Strachey (Ed.), *The standard edition of the complete psychological works of Sigmund Freud* (Vol. 11, pp. 57–137). London: Hogarth Press. (Original work published 1910)

Freud, S. (1957c). On the history of the psycho-analytic movement. In J. Strachey (Ed.), *The standard edition of the complete psychological works of Sigmund Freud* (Vol. 14, pp. 3–66). London: Hogarth Press. (Original work published 1914)

Freud, S. (1959a). An autobiographical study. In J. Strachey (Ed.), *The standard edition of the complete psychological works of Sigmund Freud* (Vol. 20, pp. 7–70). London: Hogarth Press. (Original work published 1924)

Freud, S. (1959b). Family romances. In J. Strachey (Ed.), *The standard edition of the complete psychological works of Sigmund Freud* (Vol. 9, pp. 235–241). London: Hogarth Press. (Original work published 1908)

Freud, S. (1961a). Civilization and its discontents. In J. Strachey (Ed.), *The standard edition of the complete psychological works of Sigmund Freud* (Vol. 21, pp. 55–145). London: Hogarth Press. (Original work published 1930)

Freud, S. (1961b). The ego and the id. In J. Strachey (Ed.), *The standard edition of the complete psychological works of Sigmund Freud* (Vol. 19, pp. 1–66). London: Hogarth Press. (Original work published 1923)

Freud, S. (1961c). The future of an illusion. In J. Strachey (Ed.), *The standard edition of the complete psychological works of Sigmund Freud* (Vol. 21, pp. 3–56). London: Hogarth Press. (Original work published 1927)

Freud, S. (1961d). A religious experience. In J. Strachey (Ed.), *The standard edition of the complete psychological works of Sigmund Freud* (Vol. 21, pp. 167–172). London: Hogarth Press. (Original work published 1927)

Freud, S. (1964a). New introductory lectures on psycho-analysis. In J. Strachey (Ed.), *The standard edition of the complete psychological works of Sigmund Freud* (Vol. 22, pp. 3–182). London: Hogarth Press. (Original work published 1932)

Freud, S. (1964b). An outline of psycho-analysis. In J. Strachey (Ed.), *The standard edition of the complete psychological works of Sigmund Freud* (Vol. 23, pp. 141–207). London: Hogarth Press. (Original work published 1938)

Frick, P. L. (1928). Behaviorism and its anti-religious implications. *Methodist Review, 111,* 509–521.

Frick, W. B. (2000). Remembering Maslow: Reflections on a 1968 interview. *Journal of Humanistic Psychology, 40,* 128–147.

Fridlund, A. J., Beck, H. P., Goldie, W. D., & Irons, G. (2012a). Little Albert: A neurologically impaired child. *History of Psychology, 15,* 302–327.

Fridlund, A. J., Beck, H. P., Goldie, W. D., & Irons, G. (2012b). Little Albert—Answering the criticism. *The Psychologist, 25,* 258.

Friedman, H. L. (2013). Reconciling humanistic and positive psychology: Bridging the cultural rift. In R. House, D. Kalisch, & J. Maidman (Eds.), *The future of humanistic psychology* (pp. 17–22). Ross-on-Wye, UK: PCCS Books.

Friedrich, O. (1982). *The end of the world: A history.* New York: Fromm International.

Frith, C., & Rees, G. (2007). A brief history of the scientific approach to the study of consciousness. In M. Velmans & S. Schneider (Eds.), *The Blackwell companion to consciousness* (pp. 9–22). Malden, MA: Blackwell Publishing.

Frith, C. D. (2006). The value of brain imaging in the study of development and its disorders. *Journal of Child Psychology and Psychiatry, 47,* 979–982.

Froese, T. (2009). Hume and the enactive approach to mind. *Phenomenology and the Cognitive Sciences, 8,* 95–133.

Frolov, Y. P. (1938). *Pavlov and his school.* London: Kegan Paul, Trench, Trubner.

Fromm, E. (1941). *Escape from freedom.* New York: Rinehart and Co.

Fromm, E. (1947). *Man for himself.* New York: Rinehart and Co.

Fry, H. (2009). *Freud's war.* Stroud, UK: The History Press.

Fuchs, A. H., & Viney, W. (2002). The course in the history of psychology: Present status and future concerns. *History of Psychology, 5,* 3–15.

Fuller, J. L., & Thompson, W. R. (1960). *Behavior genetics.* New York: John Wiley and Sons.

Fuller, S. (2013). History of the psychology of science. In G. J. Feist & M. E. Gorman (Eds.), *Handbook of the psychology of science* (pp. 21–45). New York: Springer.

Fulu, E., & Miedema, S. (2016). Globalization and changing family patterns: Family violence and women's resistance in Asian Muslim countries. *Sex Roles, 74,* 480–494.

Furumoto, L. (1979). Mary Whiton Calkins (1863–1930) fourteenth president of the American Psychological Association. *Journal of the History of the Behavioral Sciences, 15,* 346–356.

Furumoto, L., & Scarborough, E. (1986). Placing women in the history of psychology: The first American women psychologists. *American Psychologist, 41,* 35–42.

Fusa-Poli, P., Howes, O., & Borgwardt, S. (2009). Johann Cristian Reil on the 200th anniversary of the first description of the insula (1809). *Journal of Neurology, Neurosurgery & Psychiatry, 80,* 1409.

Gabbard, G. O., Litowitz, B. E., Bonnie, E., & Williams, P. (Eds.). (2012). *Textbook of psychoanalysis* (2nd ed.). Washington, DC: American Psychiatric Publishing.

Gaertner, S. L., Dovidio, J. F., Banker, B. S., Houlette, M., Johnson, K. M., & McGlynn, E. A. (2000). Reducing intergroup conflict: From superordinate goals to decategorization, recategorization, and mutual differentiation. *Group Dynamics: Theory, Research, and Practice, 4,* 98–114.

517

Gaj, N. (2016). *Unity and fragmentation in psychology: The philosophical and methodological roots of the discipline.* New York: Routledge.

Galdi, G. (2015). Celebrating the 75th anniversary of the American Journal of Psychoanalysis. *American Journal of Psychoanalysis, 75,* 1–2.

Gale, B. G. (2016). *Love in Vienna: The Sigmund Freud–Minna Bernays affair.* Santa Barbara, CA: Praeger/ABC-CLIO.

Gale, M. C., & Gale, H. (1902). Children's vocabularies. *Popular Science Monthly, 61,* 45–51.

Galef, B. G., Jr. (1998). Edward Thorndike: Revolutionary psychologist, ambiguous biologist. *American Psychologist, 53,* 1128–1134.

Galison, P., & Stump, D. J. (Eds.). (1996). *The disunity of science: Boundaries, context and power.* Stanford, CA: Stanford University Press.

Galton, F. (1872). Statistical inquiries into the efficacy of prayer. *Fortnightly Review, 12,* 125–135.

Galton, F. (1885, June 25). The measure of fidget. *Nature, 32,* 174–175.

Galton, F. (1907). *Inquiries into human faculty and its development.* New York: Dutton. (Original work published 1883)

Galton, F. (1909). Anthropometric laboratories. In *Memories of my life* (pp. 244–258). New York: E. P. Dutton and Co.

Galton, F. (2006). *Hereditary genius: An inquiry into its laws and consequences.* Amherst, NY: Prometheus Books. (Original work published 1869)

Gangestad, S. W. (2012). Evolutionary perspectives. In K. Deaux & M. Snyder (Eds.), *The Oxford handbook of personality and social psychology* (pp. 151–181). New York: Oxford University Press.

Gantt, E. E., & Thayne, J. L. (2013). A conceptual history of self-observation in the phenomenological tradition: Brentano, Husserl, and Heidegger. In J. W. Clegg (Ed.), *Self-observation in the social sciences. History and theory of psychology* (pp. 147–171). Piscataway, NJ: Transaction Publishers.

Gantt, W. H. (1928). Ivan P. Pavlov: A biographical sketch. In W. H. Gantt (Ed.), *Lectures on conditioned reflexes* (Vol. 1 by Ivan P. Pavlov). New York: International.

García-Penagos, A., & Malone, J. C. (2013). From Watson's 1913 manifesto to complex human behavior. *Revista Mexicana de Análisis de la Conducta, 39,* 135–154.

García-Valdecasas, M. (2005). Psychology and mind in Aquinas. *History of Psychiatry, 16,* 291–310.

Gardner, H. (1985). *The mind's new science: A history of the cognitive revolution.* New York: Basic Books.

Gardner, H. (2008). Obituary for Rudolf Arnheim (1904–2007). *Psychology of Aesthetics, Creativity, and the Arts, 2,* 61–62.

Gardner-Thorpe, C. (2006). Erasmus Darwin (1731–1802): Neurologist. *Neurology, 66,* 1913–1916.

Garfield, S. L. (1992). Comments on "Retrospect: Psychology as a profession" by J. McKeen Cattell. *Journal of Consulting and Clinical Psychology, 60,* 9–15.

Garfield, S. L., & Bergin, A. E. (1994). Introduction and historical overview. In A. E. Bergin & S. L. Garfield (Eds.), *Handbook of psychotherapy and behavior change* (pp. 3–18). New York: Wiley.

Garforth, F. W. (Ed.). (1964). *John Locke: Some thoughts concerning education.* New York: Baron's Educational Series.

Garnham, A. (2009). Cognitivism. In J. Symons & P. Calvo (Eds.), *The Routledge companion to philosophy of psychology* (pp. 99–110). New York: Routledge.

Garraty, J. A., & Carnes, M. C. (1999). *American national biography* (Vol. 19). New York: Oxford University Press.

Garrett, H. E. (1930). *Great experiments in psychology.* New York: The Century Company.

Gates, A. I. (1968). James McKeen Cattell. In D. L. Sills (Ed.), *International encyclopedia of the social sciences* (Vol. 2, pp. 344–347). New York: Macmillan and Free Press.

Gaukroger, S. (1997). *Descartes: An intellectual biography.* New York: Oxford University Press.

Gavin, E. A. (1976). What is phenomenological psychology? *Philosophical Psychologist, 10,* 1–4.

Gavin, E. A. (1987). Prominent women in psychology, determined by ratings of distinguished peers. *Psychotherapy in Private Practice, 5,* 53–68.

Gay, P. (1988). *Freud: A life for our time.* New York: Norton.

Gaynor, J. F. (1973). The "failure" of J. M. G. Itard. *Journal of Special Education, 7,* 439–445.

Gazzaniga, M. S. (2011). *Who's in charge? Free will and the science of the brain.* New York: Ecco.

Geary, D. C. (1998). *Male, female: The evolution of human sex differences.* Washington, DC: American Psychological Association.

Gelfand, T., & Kerr, J. (Eds.). (1992). *Freud and the history of psychoanalysis.* Hillsdale, NJ: Analytic Press.

Gelso, C. J., Nutt Williams, E., & Fretz, B. R. (2014). *Counseling psychology* (3rd ed.). Washington, DC: American Psychological Association.

Gendlin, E. T. (1988). Carl Rogers (1902–1987). *American Psychologist, 43,* 127–128.

Gendzel, G. (2011). What the progressives had in common. *The Journal of the Gilded Age and Progressive Era, 10,* 331–339.

518

Gengerelli, J. A. (1976). Graduate school reminiscences: Hull and Koffka. *American Psychologist, 31,* 685–688.

Gentner, D. (2010). Psychology in cognitive science: 1978–2038. *Topics in Cognitive Science, 2,* 328–344.

George, S. (Executive Producer), & Donner, C. (Director). (1988). *Stealing heaven* [Film]. Los Angeles: Virgin Vision.

Gerard, E. O. (1966). Medieval psychology: Dogmatic Aristotelianism or observational empiricism? *Journal of the History of the Behavioral Sciences, 2,* 315–329.

Gergen, K. J. (2008). On the very idea of social psychology. *Social Psychology Quarterly, 71,* 331–337.

German, T. P., & Defeyter, M. A. (2000). Immunity to functional fixedness in young children. *Psychonomic Bulletin & Review, 7,* 707–712.

Gerwood, J. B. (1998). The legacy of Viktor Frankl: An appreciation upon his death. *Psychological Reports, 82,* 673–674.

Gesundheit, B., Or, R., Gamliel, C., Rosner, F., & Steinberg, A. (2008). Treatment of depression by Maimonides (1138–1204): Rabbi, physician, and philosopher. *American Journal of Psychiatry, 165,* 425–428.

Geuter, U. (1992). *The professionalization of psychology in Nazi Germany* (R. J. Holmes, Trans.). New York: Cambridge University Press. (Original work published 1984)

Gezundhajt, H. (2007). An evolution of the historical origins of hypnotism prior to the twentieth century: Between spirituality and subconscious. *Contemporary Hypnosis, 24,* 178–194.

Gibbon, C. (1878). *The life of George Combe* (Vol. 1). London: Macmillan & Co.

Gibby, R. E., & Zickar, M. J. (2008). A history of the early days of personality testing in American industry: An obsession with adjustment. *History of Psychology, 11,* 164–184.

Gibson, E. J., & Walk, R. D. (1960). The "visual cliff." *Scientific American, 202,* 64–72.

Gideon, L. (2016). The question of aims: Psychoanalysis and the changing formulations of the life worth living. *Psychoanalytic Psychology, 33,* 312–333.

Gielen, U. P., & Raymond, J. (2015). The curious birth of psychological healing in the Western world (1775–1825). In G. J. Rich & U. P Gielen (Eds.), *Pathfinders in international psychology* (pp. 25–51). Charlotte, NC: Information Age Publishing.

Gilbert, A. R. (1968). Franz Brentano in the perspective of existential psychology. *Journal of the History of the Behavioral Sciences, 4,* 249–253.

Gilbert, F. (1967). Niccoló Machiavelli. In P. Edwards (Ed.), *The encyclopedia of philosophy* (Vol. 5, pp. 119–121). New York: Macmillan and Free Press.

Gilbreth, F. B., & Gilbreth, L. M. (1916). *Fatigue study: The elimination of humanity's greatest unnecessary waste.* New York: Sturgis & Walton.

Gilbreth, F. B., & Gilbreth, L. M. (1917). *Applied motion study: A collection of papers on the efficient method to industrial preparedness.* New York: Sturgis & Walton.

Gilbreth, F. B., & Gilbreth, L. M. (1920). *Motion study for the handicapped.* London: Routledge.

Gilbreth, F. B., Jr., & Carey, E. G. (1948). *Cheaper by the dozen.* New York: Grosset & Dunlap.

Gilbreth, F. B., Jr., & Carey, E. G. (1950). *Bells on their toes.* New York: Bantam.

Gilbreth, L. M. (1951). *Living with our children.* New York: Norton. (Original work published 1928)

Gilbreth, L. M., Thomas, O. M., & Clymer, E. (1962). *Management in the home.* Binghamton, NY: Dodd, Mead. (Original work published 1954)

Gilderhus, M. T. (1992). *History and historians: A historiographical introduction.* Englewood Cliffs, NJ: Prentice Hall.

Gilgen, A. R. (1982). *American psychology since World War II: A profile of the discipline.* Westport, CT: Greenwood Press.

Gilligan, J. (2001). The last mental hospital. *Psychiatric Quarterly, 72,* 45–61.

Gilman, S. L. (2001). Karen Horney, M.D., 1885–1952. *American Journal of Psychiatry, 158,* 1205.

Gimbel, S. (2012). *Einstein's Jewish science: Physics at the intersection of politics and religion.* Baltimore: Johns Hopkins University Press.

Ginn, S. R., & Lorusso, L. (2008). Brain, mind, and body: Interactions with art in Renaissance Italy. *Journal of the History of the Neurosciences, 17,* 295–313.

Giorgi, A. (2010a). Phenomenological psychology: A brief history and its challenges. *Journal of Phenomenological Psychology, 41,* 145–179.

Giorgi, A. (2010b). Phenomenology and the practice of science. *Existential Analysis, 21,* 3–22.

Giorgi, A. (2012). The descriptive phenomenological psychological method. *Journal of Phenomenological Psychology, 43,* 3–12.

Gitre, E. J. K. (2011). The great escape: World War II, Neo-Freudianism, and the origins of U.S. psychocultural analysis. *Journal of the History of the Behavioral Sciences, 47,* 18–43.

Gleick, J. (1987). *Chaos: Making a new science.* New York: Viking.

Gleitman, H. (1991). Edward Chace Tolman: A life of scientific and social purpose. In G. A. Kimble, M. Wertheimer, & C. White (Eds.), *Portraits of pioneers in psychology* (pp. 227–241). Washington, DC: American Psychological Association.

Gleitman, H., Rozin, P., & Sabini, J. (1997). Solomon E. Asch (1907–1996): Obituary. *American Psychologist, 52,* 984–985.

Goddard, M. J. (2012). On certain similarities between mainstream psychology and the writings of B. F. Skinner. *The Psychological Record, 62,* 563–576.

Goldberg, A. (2015). *The brain, the mind and the self: A psychoanalytic road map.* New York: Routledge.

Goldman, M. S. (1999). Expectancy operation: Cognitive-neural models and architectures. In I. Kirsch (Ed.), *How expectancies shape experience* (pp. 41–63). Washington, DC: American Psychological Association.

Goldstein, R. (2006). *Betraying Spinoza: The renegade Jew gave us modernity.* New York: Schocken Books.

Gollaher, D. (1995). *Voice for the mad: The life of Dorothea Dix.* New York: Free Press.

Gondermann, T. (2007). Progression and retrogression: Herbert Spencer's explanations of social inequality. *History of the Human Sciences, 20,* 21–40.

Gonin, M. (2015). Adam Smith's contribution to business ethics, then and now. *Journal of Business Ethics, 129,* 221–236.

Goodwin, C. G. (2005). Reorganizing the experimentalists: The origins of the Society of Experimental Psychologists. *History of Psychology, 8,* 347–361.

Goodwin, C. J. (1985). On the origins of Titchener's experimentalists. *Journal of the History of the Behavioral Sciences, 21,* 383–389.

Gordon, B. L. (1959). *Medieval and Renaissance medicine.* New York: Philosophical Library.

Gorfein, D., & Hoffman, R. R. (Eds.). (1987). *Learning and memory: The Ebbinghaus centennial conference.* Hillsdale, NJ: Erlbaum.

Goshen, C. E. (1967). *Documentary history of psychiatry.* New York: Philosophical Library.

Gotesky, R. (1967). Rudolf Hermann Lotze. In Paul Edwards (Ed.), *Encyclopedia of philosophy* (Vol. 5, pp. 87–89). New York: Macmillan and Free Press.

Goudge, T. A. (1973). Evolutionism. In P. P. Wiener (Ed.), *Dictionary of the history of ideas* (Vol. 2, pp. 174–189). New York: Scribner.

Gould, S. J. (1981). *The mismeasure of man.* New York: Norton.

Grace, R. C. (2001). On the failure of operationism. *Theory and Psychology, 11,* 5–33.

Gray, J. (1999). Ivan Petrovich Pavlov and the conditional reflex. *Brain Research Bulletin, 50,* 433.

Gray, P. H. (1967). The nature of man or man's place in nature? Bruno, Spinoza, and La Mettrie. *Journal of General Psychology, 76,* 183–192.

Grayling, A. C. (2005). *Descartes: The life and times of a genius.* New York: Walker.

Grayling, A. C. (2015). Simplicity. In J. Brockman (Ed.), *This idea must die* (pp. 9–10). New York: HarperCollins.

Green, C. D. (1998). The thoroughly modern Aristotle: Was he really a functionalist? *History of Psychology, 1,* 8–20.

Green, C. D. (2000). Dispelling the "mystery" of computational cognitive science. *History of Psychology, 3,* 62–66.

Green, C. D. (2001a). Charles Babbage, the analytical engine, and the possibility of a 19th-century cognitive science. In C. D. Green & M. Shore (Eds.), *The transformation of psychology: Influences of 19th-century philosophy, technology, and natural science* (pp. 133–152). Washington, DC: American Psychological Association.

Green, C. D. (2001b). Operationism again: What did Bridgman say? What did Bridgman need? *Theory and Psychology, 11,* 45–51.

Green, C. D. (2003). Where did the ventricular localization of mental faculties come from? *Journal of the History of the Behavioral Sciences, 29,* 131–142.

Green, C. D. (2009). Darwinian theory, functionalism, and the first American psychological revolution. *American Psychologist, 64,* 75–83.

Green, C. D. (2015a). Hall's developmental theory and Haeckel's recapitulationism. *European Journal of Developmental Psychology, 12,* 656–665.

Green, C. D. (2015b). Why psychology isn't unified and probably never will be. *Review of General Psychology, 19,* 207–214.

Green, C. D., & Feinerer, I. (2015). The evolution of the American Journal of Psychology 1, 1887–1903: A network investigation. *American Journal of Psychology, 128,* 387–401.

Green, C. D., & Groff, P. R. (2003). *Early psychological thought: Ancient accounts of the mind and soul.* Westport, CT: Praeger.

Green, M. (1985). *Descartes.* Minneapolis: University of Minnesota Press.

Greenberg, G. (2013). *The book of woe: The DSM and the unmaking of psychiatry.* New York: Blue Rider Press.

Greene, E., & Bornstein, B. (2003). *Determining damages: The psychology of jury awards.* Washington, DC: American Psychological Association.

Greenwood, J. D. (1999). Understanding the "cognitive revolution" in psychology. *Journal of the History of the Behavioral Sciences, 35,* 1–22.

Greenwood, J. D. (2016). All the way up or all the way down? Some historical reflections on theories of psychological continuity. *Journal of Comparative Psychology, 130,* 205–214.

Gregoriou, Z., & Papastephanou, M. (2013). The utopianism of John Locke's natural learning. *Ethics and Education, 8,* 18–30.

Gregory, R. L. (1974). Choosing a paradigm for perception. In E. C. Carterette & M. P. Friedman (Eds.), *Handbook of perception* (Vol. 1, pp. 255–283). New York: Academic Press.

Gregory, R. L. (2007). Editorial essay: Helmholtz's principle. *Perception, 36,* 795–796.

Grendler, P. F. (1988). Printing and censorship. In C. B. Schmitt (Ed.), *The Cambridge history of Renaissance philosophy* (pp. 25–53). New York: Cambridge University Press.

Grey, L. (1998). *Alfred Adler, the forgotten prophet: A vision for the 21st century.* Westport, CT: Praeger Greenwood.

Gribben, J. (2006). *History of western science 1543–2001.* London: Folio Society.

Griggs, R. A. (2015). Psychology's lost boy: Will the real Little Albert please stand up? *Teaching of Psychology, 42,* 14–18.

Grimsley, D. L., & Windholz, G. (2000). The neurophysiological aspects of Pavlov's theory of higher nervous activity: In honor of the 150th anniversary of Pavlov's birth. *Journal of the History of the Neurosciences, 9,* 152–163.

Grinker, R. R. (1956). *Toward a unified theory of human behavior.* New York: Basic Books.

Grisso, T., & Brigham, J. C. (2013). Forensic psychology. In D. K. Freedheim & I. B. Weiner (Eds.), *Handbook of psychology, Vol. 1: History of psychology* (2nd ed., pp. 429–447). Hoboken, NJ: John Wiley & Sons Inc.

Grmek, M. D. (1974). Francois Magendie. In C. C. Gillispi (Ed.), *Dictionary of scientific biography* (Vol. 9, pp. 7–11). New York: Scribner.

Groethuysen, B. (1963). Michel de Montaigne. In E. R. A. Seligman & A. Johnson (Eds.), *Encyclopedia of the social sciences* (Vol. 10, pp. 634–635). New York: Macmillan and Free Press.

Grogan, J. (2013). *Encountering America: Humanistic psychology, sixties culture and the shaping of the modern self.* New York: HarperPerennial.

Grose, A. (2014). The unconscious from Freud to Lacan. In A. Gessert (Ed.), *Introductory lectures on Lacan* (pp. 1–21). London: Karnac Books.

Gross, C. G. (2007). The discovery of motor cortex and its background. *Journal of the History of the Neurosciences, 16,* 320–331.

Gruber, H. E., & Vonèche, J. J. (1977). *The essential Piaget.* New York: Basic Books.

Gsueh, Y. & Guo, B. (2012). China. In D. B. Baker (Ed.), *The Oxford handbook of the history of psychology: Global perspectives* (pp. 81–124). New York: Oxford University Press.

Guberman, S., & Wojtkowski, W. (2001). Reflections on Max Wertheimer's "Productive Thinking": Lessons for AI. *Gestalt Theory, 23,* 132–143.

Guest, H. S. (2014). Maslow's hierarchy of needs—The sixth level. *The Psychologist, 27,* 982–983.

Gullan-Whur, M. (1998). *Within reason: A life of Spinoza.* New York: St. Martin's Press.

Gundlach, H. (2014). Max Wertheimer, *habilitation* candidate at the Frankfurt Psychological Institute. *History of Psychology, 17,* 134–148.

Gurley, J. R. (2009). A history of changes to the criminal personality in the DSM. *History of Psychology, 12,* 285–304.

Guski-Leinwand, S. (2009). Becoming a science: The loss of the scientific approach of Völkerpsychologie. *Zeitschrift für Psychologie/Journal of Psychology, 217,* 79–84.

Guthrie, E. R. (1935). *The psychology of learning.* New York: Harper & Brothers.

Guthrie, E. R. (1944). Personality in terms of associative learning. In J. M. Hunt (Ed.), *Personality and the behavioral disorders: A handbook based on experimental and clinical research* (Vol. 1, pp. 49–68). New York: Ronald Press.

Guthrie, R. V. (2003). *Even the rat was white: A historical view of psychology* (2nd ed.). Boston: Allyn & Bacon.

Guthrie, W. K. C. (1960). *The Greek philosophers from Thales to Aristotle.* New York: Harper & Row.

Gutmann, J. (Ed.). (1949). *Ethics; preceded by On the improvement of the understanding.* New York: Hafner.

Gutterman, S. S. (1970). *The Machiavellians.* Lincoln: University of Nebraska Press.

Haeckel, E. H. P. K. (1905). *The evolution of man* (5th ed., Vol. 1). (J. McCabe, Trans.). New York: G. P. Putnam.

Hafling, O. (1981). *Logical positivism.* New York: Columbia University Press.

Hagner, M. (2012). The electrical excitability of the brain: Toward the emergence of an experiment. *Journal of the History of the Neurosciences, 21,* 237–249.

Haidt, J. (2012). *The righteous mind: Why good people are divided by politics and religion.* New York: Pantheon.

Haight, A. L. (1978). *Banned books 387 B.C. to 1987 A.D.* (4th ed.). Updated and enlarged by C. B. Grannis. New York: Bowker.

Hall, C. S., & Nordby, V. J. (1973). *A primer of Jungian psychology.* New York: Taplinger.

Hall, G. S. (1890). Children's lies. *American Journal of Psychology, 3,* 59–70.

Hall, G. S. (1891). The contents of children's minds on entering school. *Pedagogical Seminary, 1,* 139–173.

Hall, G. S. (1904). *Adolescence*. New York: D. Appleton and Co.

Hall, G. S. (January 29, 1907; April 30, 1907). Josiah Morse: Student correspondence, B1-6-8. G. Stanley Hall Papers, Clark University Archives.

Hall, G. S. (1910). A children's institute. *Harper's Magazine, 120,* 620–624.

Hall, G. S. (January 14, 1921). Josiah Morse: Professional correspondence, B1-3-2. G. Stanley Hall Papers, Clark University Archives.

Hall, G. S. (1922). *Senescence: The last half of life.* New York: D. Appleton and Co.

Hall, G. S. (1923). *Life and confessions of a psychologist.* New York: D. Appleton and Co.

Hall, G. S., & Browne, C. E. (1903). Children's ideas of fire, heat, frost and cold. *Pedagogical Seminary, 10,* 27–85.

Hall, G. S., & Motora, Y. (1887). Dermal sensitiveness to gradual pressure changes. *American Journal of Psychology, 1,* 72–98.

Hall, G. S., & Smith, T. L. (1903). Showing off and bashfulness as phases of self-consciousness. *Pedagogical Seminary, 10,* 159–199.

Hall, G. S., & Wallin, J. E. W. (1902). How children and youth think and feel about clouds. *Pedagogical Seminary, 9,* 460–506.

Hall, J. R. (2009). *Apocalypse: From antiquity to the empire of modernity.* Malden, MA: Polity Press.

Hall, V., Jr. (1950). Life of Julius Caesar Scaliger. *Transactions of the American Philosophical Society, 4,* 85–170.

Hallie, P. P. (1967). Stoicism. In P. Edwards (Ed.), *The encyclopedia of philosophy* (Vol. 8, pp. 19–22). New York: Macmillan.

Hamilton, D. L., & Carlston, D. E. (2013). The emergence of social cognition. In D. E. Carlston (Ed.), *The Oxford handbook of social cognition* (pp. 16–32). New York: Oxford University Press.

Handelsman, M. M., Gottlieb, M. C., & Knapp, S. (2005). Training ethical psychologists: An acculturation model. *Professional Psychology: Research and Practice, 36,* 59–65.

Haney, C., & Zimbardo, P. G. (1998). The past and future of U.S. prison policy: Twenty-five years after the Stanford Prison Experiment. *American Psychologist, 53,* 709–727.

Hardcastle, J. (2009). Vygotsky's enlightenment precursors. *Educational Review, 61,* 181–195.

Hardy, A. (2016). The case for a humanistic psychology. *The Humanistic Psychologist, 44,* 242–255.

Harlow, H. F. (1949). The formation of learning sets. *Psychological Review, 56,* 51–65.

Harlow, H. F. (1958). The nature of love. *American Psychologist, 13,* 673–685.

Harman, O. (2014). A history of the altruism-morality debate in biology. In F. B. M. de Waal, P. Smith Churchland, T. Pievani, & S. Parmigiani (Eds.), *Evolved morality: The biology and philosophy of human conscience* (pp. 147–165). Leiden, Netherlands: E. J. Brill.

Harms, E. (1967). *Origin of modern psychiatry.* Springfield, IL: Charles C. Thomas.

Harris, A. L., & Vitzthum, V. J. (2013). Darwin's legacy: An evolutionary view of women's reproductive and sexual functioning. *Journal of Sex Research, 50,* 207–246.

Harris, B. (1979). Whatever happened to little Albert? *American Psychologist, 34,* 151–160.

Harris, B. (1999). John Broadus Watson. In *American National Biography* (pp. 795–797). New York: Oxford University Press.

Harris, B. (2011). Letting go of Little Albert: Disciplinary memory, history, and the uses of myth. *Journal of the History of the Behavioral Sciences, 47,* 1–17.

Harris, J. C. (2010). Galileo Galilei: Scientist and artist. *Archives of General Psychiatry, 67,* 770–771.

Harris, M. (1974). *Cows, pigs, wars, and witches: The riddles of culture.* New York: Random House.

Harris, S. (2012). *Free will.* New York: Free Press.

Harrison, L. E. (2006). *The central liberal truth: How politics can change a culture and save it from itself.* New York: Oxford University Press.

Harrison, P. (2001). Curiosity, forbidden knowledge, and the reformation of natural philosophy in early modern England. *Isis, 92,* 265–290.

Harrower, M. (1984). *Kurt Koffka: An unwitting self-portrait.* Gainesville, FL: University Press of Florida.

Hartley, D. (1966). *Observations on man, his frame, his duty and his expectations.* Demar, NY: Scholars' Facsimiles & Reprints. (Original work published 1749)

Hartmann, H. (1939). *Ego psychology and the problem of adaptation.* New York: International University Press.

Hartshorne, C. (1934). *The philosophy and psychology of sensation.* Port Washington, NY: Kennikat Press.

Hartshorne, C. (1991). A reply to my critics. In Lewis Edwin Hahn (Ed.), *The philosophy of Charles Hartshorne* (pp. 598–600). La Salle, IL: Open Court.

Harvey, O. J. (1989). Muzafer Sherif. *American Psychologist, 44,* 1325–1326.

Hasbach, P. H. (2012). Ecotherapy. In Peter H. Kahn Jr. and Patricia H. Hasbach (Eds.), *Ecopsychology: Science, totems, and the technological species* (pp. 115–140). Cambridge, MA: MIT Press.

Hassard, J. (1990). The AHP Soviet exchange project: 1983–1990 and beyond. *Journal of Humanistic Psychology, 30,* 6–51.

Hatami, H., Afjei, E., Hatami, M., & Hatami, N. (2014). Monotheistic and spiritual style literature in traditional medicine's resources. *Journal of Religion and Health, 53,* 438–448.

Hatami, H., Hatami, M., & Hatami, N. (2013a). The religious and social principles of patients' rights in holy books (*Avesta, Torah, Bible,* and *Quran*) and in traditional medicine. *Journal of Religion and Health, 52,* 223–234.

Hatami, H., Hatami, M., & Hatami, N. (2013b). The socio-political situation of Avicenna's time and his spiritual messages: On the occasion of 1031st birth anniversary of Avicenna (23 August 980). *Journal of Religion and Health, 52,* 589–596.

Hatfield, G. (2009). Rationalist roots of modern psychology. In J. Symons & P. Calvo (Eds.), *The Routledge companion to philosophy of psychology* (pp. 3–20). New York: Routledge.

Hathaway, S. R. (1958). A study of human behavior: The clinical psychologist. *American Psychologist, 13,* 257–265.

Haupt, E. J. (1998). Origins of American psychology in the work of G. E. Müller: Classical psychophysics and serial learning. In R. W. Rieber & K. Salzinger (Eds.), *Psychology: Theoretical-historical perspectives* (2nd ed., pp. 17–75). Washington, DC: American Psychological Association.

Haupt, E. J. (2001). Laboratories for experimental psychology: Göttingen's ascendancy over Leipzig in the 1890s. In R. W. Rieber & D. K. Robinson (Eds.), *Wilhelm Wundt in history: The making of a scientific psychology* (pp. 205–250). New York: Kluwer Academic/Plenum Publishers.

Hawkins, S. L. (2014). William James and the "theatre" of consciousness. In C. U. M. Smith & H. Whitaker (Eds.), *Brain, mind and consciousness in the history of neuroscience* (Vol. 6, pp. 185–206). New York: Springer Science + Business Media.

Hayman, R. (2001). *A life of Jung.* New York: Norton.

Häyry, M. (2005). The tension between self governance and absolute inner worth in Kant's moral philosophy. *Journal of Medical Ethics, 31,* 645–647.

Healy, D. (1993). One-hundred years of psychopharmacology. *Journal of Psychopharmacology, 7,* 207–214.

Healy, D., Harris, M., Farquhar, F., Tschinkel, S., & Le Noury, J. (2008). Historical overview: Kraepelin's impact on psychiatry. *European Archives of Psychiatry and Clinical Neuroscience, 258,* 18–24.

Hebb, D. O. (1949). *The organization of behavior: A neuropsychological theory.* New York: Wiley.

Hebb, D. O. (1959). A neuropsychological theory. In S. Koch (Ed.), *Psychology: A study of science* (Vol. 1, pp. 622–643). New York: McGraw-Hill.

Heft, H. (2001). *Ecological psychology in context: James Gibson, Roger Barker, and the legacy of William James's radical empiricism.* Mahwah, NJ: Erlbaum.

Heidbreder, E. (1933). *Seven psychologies.* New York: Appleton-Century-Crofts.

Heidegger, M. (1962). *Being and time* (J. Macquarrie & E. Robinson, Trans.). New York: Harper & Row. (Original work published 1927)

Heidigger, M., & Fink, E. (1979). Heraclitus seminar 1966/67. C. H. Seibert (Trans.). Tuscaloosa, AL: University of Alabama Press. (Original work published 1970)

Heinrich, J., Heine, S. J., & Norenzayan, A. (2010). Most people are not WEIRD. *Nature, 466,* 29.

Helmholtz, H. L. von. (1896). *Handbuch der physiologischen Optik* (2nd ed.). Hamburg and Leipzig: L. Voss.

Helmholtz, H. L. von. (1971). The origin and correct interpretation of our sense impressions. In R. Kahl (Ed.), *Selected writings of Hermann Ludwig von Helmholtz* (pp. 501–512). Middletown, CT: Wesleyan University Press. (Original work published 1894)

Helmut, T. (2015). Remarks on the first century of the International Psychoanalytic Association and a utopian vision of its future: Part 2. *International Forum of Psychoanalysis, 24,* 120–132.

Helson, H. (1972). What can we learn from the history of psychology? *Journal of the History of the Behavioral Sciences, 8,* 115–119.

Henderson, D. (2015). Freud and Jung: The creation of the psychoanalytic universe. *Psychodynamic Practice: Individuals, Groups and Organisations, 21,* 167–172.

Henle, M. (1976). Why study the history of psychology? *Annals of the New York Academy of Sciences, 270,* 14–20.

Henle, M. (1977). The influence of Gestalt psychology in America. *Annals of the New York Academy of Sciences, 291,* 3–12.

Henle, M. (1978a). Gestalt psychology and Gestalt therapy. *Journal of the History of the Behavioral Sciences, 14,* 23–32.

Henle, M. (1978b). One man against the Nazis—Wolfgang Köhler. *American Psychologist, 33,* 939–944.

Henle, M. (1984). Isomorphism: Setting the record straight. *Psychological Research, 46,* 317–327.

Henle, M. (1985). Rediscovering Gestalt psychology. In S. Koch & D. E. Leary (Eds.), *A century of psychology as science* (pp. 100–120). New York: McGraw-Hill.

Henle, M. (1986). The influence of Gestalt psychology in America. In M. Henle (Ed.), *1879 and all that: Essays in the theory and history of psychology* (pp. 118–137). New York: Columbia University Press. (Original work published 1977)

Henle, M. (1989). Two disciplines, one name? *Contemporary Psychology, 34,* 857–858.

Henle, M. (1993). Man's place in nature in the thinking of Wolfgang Köhler. *Journal of the History of the Behavioral Sciences, 29,* 3–7.

Henle, M., Jaynes, J., & Sullivan, J. J. (Eds.). (1973). *Historical conceptions of psychology.* New York: Springer.

Henley, T. B., & Thorne, B. M. (2005). The lost millennium: Psychology during the Middle Ages. *Psychological Record, 55,* 103–113.

Henriques, G. R. (2008). The problem of psychology and the integration of human knowledge: Contrasting Wilson's consilience with the tree of knowledge system. *Theory and Psychology, 18,* 731–755.

Henriques, G. R. (2013). Evolving from methodological to conceptual unification. *Review of General Psychology, 17,* 168–173.

Henshaw, J. M. (2006). *Does measurement measure up?* Baltimore: Johns Hopkins University Press.

Herbart, J. F. (1977). The science of education (H. M. Felkin & E. Felkin, Trans.). In D. N. Robinson (Ed.), *Significant contributions to the history of psychology 1750–1920: Series B, Psychometrics and Educational Psychology* (Vol. 1, pp. 57–268). Washington, DC: University Publications of America (from 1902 edition).

Herlihy, D. (1997). *The Black Death and the transformation of the West.* Cambridge, MA: Harvard University Press.

Herrmann, D. J., & Chaffin, R. (Eds.). (1988). *Memory in historical perspective: The literature before Ebbinghaus.* New York: Springer-Verlag.

Herrnstein, R. J., & Boring, E. G. (Eds.). (1966). *A sourcebook in the history of psychology.* Cambridge, MA: Harvard University Press.

Hertberg-Davis, H. (2014). Leta Stetter Hollingworth: A life in schools (1886–1939). In A. Robinson & J. L. Jolly (Eds.), *A century of contributions to gifted education: Illuminating lives* (pp. 79–100). New York: Routledge.

Hess, E. H. (1962). Ethology: An approach toward the complete analysis of behavior. In R. Brown, E. Galanter, E. H. Hess, & G. Mandler (Eds.), *New directions in psychology* (pp. 157–266). New York: Holt, Rinehart and Winston.

Hess, M. (1967). Action at a distance and field theory. In P. Edwards (Ed.), *The encyclopedia of philosophy* (Vol. 1, pp. 9–15). New York: Macmillan.

Hesse, M. (1967). Models and analogy in science. In P. Edwards (Ed.), *The encyclopedia of philosophy* (Vol. 5, pp. 354–359). New York: Macmillan.

Hewstone, M., Schut, H. A. W., De Wit, J. B. F., Van Den Bos, K., & Stroebe, M. S. (Eds.). (2007). *The scope of social psychology: Theory and applications.* New York: Psychology Press.

Higgins, E. T. & Kruglanski, A. W. (2000). *Motivational science: Social and personality perspectives.* Philadelphia, PA: Taylor and Francis.

Hildebrand, J. H. (1957). *Science in the making.* New York: Columbia University Press.

Hilgard, E. R. (1996). History of educational psychology. In D. C. Berliner & R. C. Calfee (Eds.), *Handbook of educational psychology* (pp. 990–1004). New York: Macmillan Library Reference.

Hilgard, E. R., & Bower, G. H. (1966). *Theories of learning* (3rd ed.). New York: Appleton-Century-Crofts.

Hill, S., & Millar, N. (2015). Case study research: The child in context. In O. N. Saracho (Ed.), *Handbook of research methods in early childhood education: Review of research methodologies* (Vol. 1, pp. 523–545). Charlotte, NC: Information Age Publishing.

Hillman, J., & Shamdasani, S. (2013). *Lament of the dead: Psychology after Jung's Red Book.* New York: W. W. Norton & Co.

Hindmarsh, J. (2009). Work and the moving image: Past, present and future. *Sociology, 43,* 990–996.

Hiroshi, I. (Ed.). (2002). *Origin and development of scientific psychology in different parts of the world: Retrospect and prospect at the turn of the century.* New York: Psychology Press.

Hobbes, T. (1962a). Human nature. In W. Molesworth (Ed.), *The English works of Thomas Hobbes* (Vol. 4, pp. 1–76). London: Scientia Aalen. (Original work published 1650)

Hobbes, T. (1962b). Leviathan. In W. Molesworth (Ed.), *The English works of Thomas Hobbes* (Vol. 3, pp. 1–714). London: Scientia Aalen. (Original work published 1651)

Hocutt, M. (2013). A behavioral analysis of morality and virtue. *The Behavior Analyst, 36,* 239–249.

Hodgson, B. (1988). Economic science and ethical neutrality II: The intransigence of evaluative concepts. *Journal of Business, 7,* 321–335.

Hoff, P. (1998). Emil Kraepelin and forensic psychiatry. *International Journal of Law and Psychiatry, 21,* 343–353.

Hoff, P. (2012). Eugen Bleuler's concept of schizophrenia and its relevance to present-day psychiatry. *Neuropsychobiology, 66,* 6–13.

Hoffeld, D. R. (1980). Mesmer's failure: Sex, politics, personality and the Zeitgeist. *Journal of the History of the Behavioral Sciences, 16,* 377–386.

Hoffman, D. H., Carter, D. J., Viglucci Lopez, C. R., Benzmiller, H. L., Guo, A. X., Latifi, S. Y., & Craig, D. C. (2015). Report to the Special Committee of the Board of Directors of the American Psychological Association: Independent review relating to APA ethical guidelines, national security interrogations, and torture. Retrieved January 5, 2016 from www.apa.org/independent-review/APA-FINAL-Report-7.2.15.pdf

Hoffman, E. (1988). *The right to be human: A biography of Abraham Maslow.* Los Angeles: Tarcher.

Hoffman, E. (2009). Rollo May on Maslow and Rogers: "No theory of evil." *Journal of Humanistic Psychology, 49,* 484–485.

Hoffman, E. (2010). Introduction to the William James memorial issue. *Journal of Humanistic Psychology, 50,* 407–409.

Hoffman, L. (2016). Multiculturalism and humanistic psychology: From neglect to epistemological and ontological diversity. *The Humanistic Psychologist, 44,* 56–71.

Hoffman, R. R., & Deffenbacher, K. A. (1992). A brief history of applied cognitive psychology. *Applied Cognitive Psychology, 6,* 1–48.

Hogan, J. D. (2003). G. Stanley Hall. In G. A. Kimble & M. Wertheimer (Eds.), *Portraits of pioneers in psychology* (Vol. 5, pp. 19–36). Washington, DC: American Psychological Association.

Hogenson, G. B. (2013). Philosophy, the thinking function, and the reading of Jung. In J. Kirsch & M. Stein (Eds.), *How and why we still read Jung: Personal and professional reflections* (pp. 161–177). New York: Routledge.

Hollingworth, L. S. (1914). *Functional periodicity: An experimental study of the mental and motor abilities of women during menstruation.* Contributions to Education (No. 69). New York: Teachers College Press, Columbia University.

Hollingworth, L. S. (1920). *The psychology of subnormal children.* New York: Macmillan.

Hollingworth, L. S. (1928). *The psychology of the adolescent.* New York: Appleton.

Hollingworth, L. S. (1942). *Children above 180 I.Q.* Yonkers, NY: World Book.

Hollon, S. D., & DiGiuseppe, R. (2011). Cognitive theories of psychotherapy. In J. C. Norcross, G. R. VandenBos, & D. K. Freedheim (Eds.), *History of psychotherapy: Continuity and change* (2nd ed., pp. 203–241). Washington, DC: American Psychological Association.

Holt, R. R. (1967). Ego autonomy re-evaluated. *International Journal of Psychiatry, 3,* 481–536.

Holzhey-Kunz, A., & Fazekas, T. (2012). Daseinsanalysis: A dialogue. In L. Barnett & G. Madison (Eds.), *Existential therapy: Legacy, vibrancy and dialogue* (pp. 35–51). New York: Routledge.

Honeycutt, H. (2011). The "enduring mission" of Zing-Yang Kuo to eliminate the nature-nurture dichotomy in psychology. *Developmental Psychobiology, 53,* 331–342.

Hood, R. W., Jr. (2013). Methodological diversity in the psychology of religion and spirituality. In K. I. Pargament, J. J. Exline, & J. W. Jones (Eds.), *APA handbook of psychology, religion, and spirituality, Vol. 1: Context, theory, and research* (pp. 79–102). Washington, DC: American Psychological Association.

Hood, R. W., Jr., Hill, P. C., & Spilka, B. (2009). *The psychology of religion* (4th ed.). New York: Guilford Press.

Hooley, J. M., Maher, W. B., & Maher, B. A. (2013). Abnormal psychology. In D. K. Freedheim & I. B. Weiner (Eds.), *Handbook of psychology, Vol. 1: History of psychology* (2nd ed., pp. 340–376). Hoboken, NJ: John Wiley & Sons.

Hopper, G. (2012). Grace Hopper – Nanoseconds. Retrieved July 1, 2016 from www.youtube.com/watch?V=JEpsKnWZr18.

Hoquet, T. (Ed.). (2015). *Current perspectives on sexual selection: What's left after Darwin?* Dordrecht, Netherlands: Spring Science + Business Media.

Hoquet, T., & Levandowsky, M. (2015). Utility v. beauty: Darwin, Wallace and the subsequent history of the debate on sexual selection. In T. Hoquet (Ed.), *Current perspectives on sexual selection: What's left after Darwin?* (pp. 19–44). Dordrecht, Netherlands: Spring Science + Business Media.

Horgan, J. (1996, December). Why Freud isn't dead. *Scientific American,* pp. 106–111.

Hornday, W. T. (1883). Mental capacity of the elephant. *Popular Science Monthly, 23,* 497–509.

Horney, K. (1934). The overvaluation of love: A study of a common present-day feminine type. *Psychoanalytic Quarterly, 3,* 605–638.

Horney, K. (1937). *The neurotic personality of our time.* New York: Norton.

Horney, K. (1939). *New ways in psychoanalysis.* New York: Norton.

Horney, K. (1942). *Self-analysis.* New York: Norton.

Horney, K. (1945). *Our inner conflicts.* New York: Norton.

Horney, K. (1950). *Neurosis and human growth.* New York: Norton.

Horney, K. (1967). *Feminine psychology.* New York: Norton.

Horton, J. O., & Horton, L. E. (2005). *Slavery and the making of America*. New York: Oxford University Press.

Horwitz, T. (1998). *Confederates in the attic: Dispatches from the unfinished Civil War*. New York: Vintage.

Hosseini, H. (2011). George Katona: A founding father of old behavioral economics. *The Journal of Socio-Economics, 40*, 977–984.

Hothersall, D. (1995). *History of psychology*. New York: McGraw-Hill.

Houston, G. (2013). The future of humanistic psychology. In R. House, D. Kalisch, & J. Maidman (Eds.), *The future of humanistic psychology* (pp. 131–135). Ross-on-Wye, UK: PCCS Books.

Hsueh, Y. (2004). "He sees the development of children's concepts upon a background of sociology": Jean Piaget's honorary degree at Harvard University in 1936. *History of Psychology, 7*, 20–44.

Hsueh, Y., & Guo, B. (2012). China. In D. B. Baker (Ed.), *The Oxford handbook of the history of psychology: Global perspectives* (pp. 81–124). New York: Oxford University Press.

Huarte, J. (1959). *The examination of men's wits* (M. Camillo & R. Carew, Trans.). Gainesville, FL: Scholars Facsimiles and Reprints. (Original work published 1594)

Huddleson, S., & Russell, G. A. (2015). Richard Dadd: The patient, the artist, and the "face of madness." *Journal of the History of the Neurosciences, 24*, 213–228.

Huemer, W., & Landerer, C. (2010). Mathematics, experience and laboratories: Herbart's and Brentano's role in the rise of scientific psychology. *History of the Human Sciences, 23*, 72–94.

Hui, A. (2013). *The psychophysical ear: Musical experiments, experimental sounds, 1840–1910*. (Transformations: Studies in the history of science and technology). Cambridge, MA: MIT Press.

Hull, C. L. (1943). *Principles of behavior*. New York: D. Appleton-Century.

Hull, C. L. (1952). Clark L. Hull. In E. G. Boring, H. Werner, R. M. Yerkes, & H. S. Langfeld (Eds.), *A history of psychology in autobiography* (Vol. 4, pp. 143–162). New York: Russell and Russell.

Humbert, E. G. (1988). *C. G. Jung: The fundamentals of theory and practice* (R. G. Jalbert, Trans.). Wilmette, IL: Chiron.

Hume, D. (1978). *A treatise of human nature*. Oxford: Clarendon Press. (Original work published 1739–1740)

Humphrey, T. (1983). *Immanuel Kant—Perpetual peace and other essays on politics, history, and morals*. Indianapolis, IN: Hackett.

Hunt, J. M. (1956). Walter Samuel Hunter. *Psychological Review, 63*, 213–217.

Hunter, W. S. (1928). *Human behavior*. Chicago: University of Chicago Press.

Hunter, W. S. (1952). Walter S. Hunter. In E. G. Boring, H. Werner, R. M. Yerkes, & H. S. Langfeld (Eds.), *A history of psychology in autobiography* (Vol. 4, pp. 163–187). New York: Russell and Russell.

Huxley, T. H. (1874). Are animals automatons? *Popular Science Monthly, 5*, 724–734.

Huxley, T. H. (1898). *Hume with helps to the study of Berkeley*. New York: D. Appleton and Co.

Hyam, J. A., Paterson, D. J., Azoz, T. Z., & Green, A. L. (2011). Depiction of the neuroscientific principles of human motion 2 millennia ago by Lucretius. *Neurology, 77*, 1000–1004.

Ingram, D. H. (1985). Karen Horney at 100: Beyond the frontier. *American Journal of Psychoanalysis, 45*, 305–309.

Innis, N. K. (1992). Tolman and Tryon: Early research on the inheritance of the ability to learn. *American Psychologist, 47*, 190–197.

Innis, N. K. (1999). Edward C. Tolman's purposive behaviorism. In W. O'Donohue & R. Kitchener (Eds.), *Handbook of behaviorism* (pp. 97–117). San Diego, CA: Academic Press.

Innis, N. K. (2003). William McDougall: "A major tragedy?" In G. A. Kimble & M. Wertheimer (Eds.), *Portraits of pioneers in psychology* (Vol. 5, pp. 91–108). Washington, DC: American Psychological Association.

Iran-Nejad, A., & Winsler, A. (2000). Bartlett's schema theory and modern accounts of learning and remembering. *Journal of Mind and Behavior, 21*, 5–35.

Irizar, L. B. (2014). The role of courage in intellectual work. *Psychology, 5*, 1019–1023.

Irwin, T. (2013). Mental health as moral virtue: Some ancient arguments. In K. W. M. Fulford, M. Davies, R. G. T. Gipps, G. Graham, J. Z. Sadler, G. Stanghellini, & T. Thornton (Eds.), *The Oxford handbook of philosophy and psychiatry: International perspectives in philosophy and psychiatry* (pp. 37–46). New York: Oxford University Press.

Jablensky, A., Hugler, H., von Cranach, M., & Kalinov, K. (1993). Kraepelin revisited: A reassessment and statistical analysis of dementia praecox and manic-depressive insanity in 1908. *Psychological Medicine, 23*, 843–858.

Jackson, J. P., Jr. (2000). The triumph of the segregationists? A historical inquiry into psychology and the *Brown* litigation. *History of Psychology, 3*, 239–261.

Jackson, J. P., Jr. (2006). Kenneth B. Clark: The complexities of activist psychology. In D. A. Dewsbury, L. T. Benjamin, Jr., & M. Wertheimer (Eds.), *Portraits of pioneers in psychology* (Vol. 6, pp. 273–286). Washington, DC: American Psychological Association.

Jackson, P. W. (1998). *John Dewey and the lessons of art.* New Haven, CT: Yale University Press.

Jackson, S. W. (1969). Galen—On mental disorders. *Journal of the History of the Behavioral Sciences, 5,* 365–384.

Jacobi, J. (1958). *Paracelsus: Selected writings.* New York: Pantheon Books.

Jacobs, D. (2001). *Her own woman: The life of Mary Wollstonecraft.* New York: Simon and Schuster.

Jacoby, S. (2016). *Strange gods: A secular history of conversion.* New York: Pantheon Books.

Jager, M., & VanHoorn, W. (1972). Aristotle's opinion on perception in general. *Journal of the History of the Behavioral Sciences, 8,* 321–327.

Jahoda, G. (1992). *Crossroads between culture and mind: Continuities and change in theories of human nature.* Cambridge, MA: Harvard University Press.

Jahoda, G. (2000). Piaget and Lévy-Bruhl. *History of Psychology, 3,* 218–238.

Jahoda, G. (2006). Johann Friedrich Herbart: Urvater of social psychology. *History of the Human Sciences, 19,* 19–38.

Jahoda, G. (2007). *A history of social psychology: From the eighteenth-century Enlightenment to the Second World War.* New York: Cambridge University Press.

Jahoda, G. (2009). The metaphysical mechanics of the mind. *The Psychologist, 22,* 558–559.

Jahoda, M. (1969). The migration of psychoanalysis. In D. Fleming & B. Bailyn (Eds.), *The intellectual migration: Europe and America, 1930–1960* (pp. 371–419). Cambridge, MA: Harvard University Press.

Jahoda, M. (1977). *Freud and the dilemmas of psychology.* New York: Basic Books.

James, W. (unsigned). (1875). Notice of Wilhelm Wundt's principles of physiological psychology. *North American Review, 121,* 195–201.

James, W. (unsigned). (1876a). Notice of F. von Holtzendorff's psychology of murder. *Nation, 22,* 16.

James, W. (1876b, September 21). The teaching of philosophy in our colleges. *The Nation,* pp. 178–179.

James, W. (1880). Great men, great thoughts and the environment. *Atlantic Monthly, 46,* 441–459.

James, W. (1884a). The dilemma of determinism. *Unitarian Review, 22,* 193–224.

James, W. (1884b). What is an emotion? *Mind, 9,* 188–205.

James, W. (1890). *The principles of psychology* (Vol. 1). New York: Henry Holt.

James, W. (1894). The physical basis of emotion. *Psychological Review, 1,* 516–529.

James, W. (1898). *Human immortality: Two supposed objections to the doctrine.* New York: Houghton, Mifflin and Company.

James, W. (1911). The college bred. In *Memories and studies* (pp. 312–313). New York: Longman's Green & Co.

James, W. (1920a). Invalidism in Cambridge. In H. James (Ed.), *The letters of William James* (Vol. 1, pp. 140–164). Boston: Atlantic Monthly Press.

James, W. (1920b). Letter to Mrs. Henry Whitman. In H. James (Ed.), *The Letters of William James* (Vol. 2, p. 90). Boston: Atlantic Monthly Press. (Original letter written 1899)

James, W. (1975a). *The meaning of truth.* Cambridge, MA: Harvard University Press. (Original work published 1909)

James, W. (1975b). *Pragmatism.* Cambridge, MA: Harvard University Press. (Original work published 1907)

James, W. (1976). *Essays in radical empiricism.* Cambridge, MA: Harvard University Press. (Original work published 1912)

James, W. (1977). *A pluralistic universe.* Cambridge, MA: Harvard University Press. (Original work published 1909)

James, W. (1978). Pluralistic mystic. *Essays in philosophy* (pp. 172–190). Cambridge, MA: Harvard University Press. (Original work published 1910)

James, W. (1979a). The dilemma of determinism. In F. H. Burkhardt (Ed.), *The will to believe* (pp. 114–140). Cambridge, MA: Harvard University Press. (Original work published 1884)

James, W. (1979b). *The will to believe.* Cambridge, MA: Harvard University Press. (Original work published 1897)

James, W. (1980). Letter to John Dewey. In E. Hardwick (Ed.), *The selected letters of William James* (pp. 203–204). Boston: David R. Godine. (Original letter sent 1903)

James, W. (1981). *Principles of psychology.* Cambridge, MA: Harvard University Press. (Original work published 1890)

James, W. (1983a). *The physical basis of emotion: Essays in psychology* (pp. 299–314). Cambridge, MA: Harvard University Press. (Original work published 1894)

James, W. (1983b). *Talks to teachers and to students on some of life's ideals.* Cambridge, MA: Harvard University Press. (original work published 1899)

James, W. (1985). *The varieties of religious experience.* Cambridge, MA: Harvard University Press. (Original work published 1902)

James, W. (1986a). Letter to Charles William Elliot. In F. J. D. Scott (Ed.), *William James: Selected unpublished correspondence 1885–1910* (pp. 151–153). Columbus: Ohio State University Press. (Original letter dated February 21, 1897)

James, W. (1986b). Letter to James McKeen Cattell. In F. J. D. Scott (Ed.), *William James: Selected unpublished correspondence 1885–1910* (pp. 312–313). Columbus: Ohio State University Press. (Original letter dated June 10, 1903)

James, W. (2010). What makes a life significant? In R. Richardson (Ed.), *The heart of William James* (pp. 164–182). Cambridge, MA: Harvard University Press. (Original work published 1900)

Jansz, J. (2004). Psychology and society: An overview. In J. Jansz & P. van Drunen (Eds.), *A social history of psychology* (pp. 12–44). Malden, MA: Blackwell.

Jarius, S., & Wildemann, B. (2016). And Pavlov still rings a bell: Summarising the evidence for the use of a bell in Pavlov's iconic experiments on classical conditioning. *Journal of Neurology, 262,* 2177–2178.

Jastrow, J. (1903). Helen Keller: A psychological autobiography. *Popular Science Monthly, 63,* 71–83.

Jaynes, J. (1973a). Introduction: The study of the history of psychology. In M. Henle, J. Jaynes, & J. J. Sullivan (Eds.), *Historical conceptions of psychology*. New York: Springer.

Jaynes, J. (1973b). The problem of animate motion in the seventeenth century. In M. Henle, J. Jaynes, & J. J. Sullivan (Eds.), *Historical conceptions of psychology* (pp. 166–179). New York: Springer.

Jeremias, J. (1975). *Jerusalem in the time of Jesus: An investigation into economic and social conditions during the New Testament period* (F. H. & C. H. Cave, Trans.). Philadelphia: Fortress Press.

Jesseph, D. M. (2004). Galileo, Hobbes, and the book of nature. *Perspectives on Science, 12,* 191–211.

Johannsen, D. E. (1971). Early history of perceptual illusions. *Journal of the History of the Behavioral Sciences, 7,* 127–140.

Johnson, D. F. (2000). Cultivating the field of psychology: Psychological journals at the turn of the century. *American Psychologist, 55,* 1144–1147.

Johnson, W. H. (1927). Does the behaviorist have a mind? *Princeton Theological Review, 25,* 40–58.

Joireman, J., & Van Lange, P. A. M. (2015). Launch a paradigm shift: Challenge existing assumptions and test competing theories. In J. Joireman & P. A. M. Van Lange (Eds.), *How to publish high quality research* (pp. 121–143). Washington, DC: American Psychological Association.

Jonçich, G. (1968). Edward L. Thorndike. In D. L. Sills (Ed.), *International encyclopedia of the social sciences* (Vol. 16, pp. 8–14). New York: Macmillan and Free Press.

Jonçich, G. (1988). *The sane positivist: A biography of Edward L. Thorndike*. Middletown, CT: Wesleyan University Press.

Jones, D. N. (2016) The nature of Machiavellianism: Distinct patterns of misbehavior. In V. Zeigler-Hill & D. K. Marcus (Eds.), *The dark side of personality: Science and practice in social, personality, and clinical psychology* (pp. 87–107). Washington, DC: American Psychological Association.

Jones, E. (1953). *The life and work of Sigmund Freud* (Vol. 1). New York: Basic Books.

Jones, E. (1955). *The life and work of Sigmund Freud* (Vol. 2). New York: Basic Books.

Jones, E. (1957). *The life and work of Sigmund Freud* (Vol. 3). New York: Basic Books.

Jones, M. C. (1924a). The elimination of children's fears. *Journal of Experimental Psychology, 7,* 383–390.

Jones, M. C. (1924b). A laboratory study of fear: The case of Peter. *Pedagogical Seminary, 31,* 308–315.

Jones, R. A. (Ed.). (2014). *Jung and the question of science*. New York: Routledge.

Jorgensen, C., & Stryker, S. (2000). *Christine Jorgensen: A personal autobiography*. San Francisco, CA: Cleis Press. (Original work published 1967)

Joye, Y. (2012). Can architecture become second nature? An emotion-based approach to nature-oriented architecture (pp. 195–218). In P. H. Kahn, Jr. & P. H. Hasbach (Eds.), *Ecopsychology: Science, totems, and the technological species*. Cambridge, MA: MIT Press.

Juhasz, J. B. (1971). Greek theories of imagination. *Journal of the History of the Behavioral Sciences, 7,* 39–58.

Jung, C. G. (1953). Psychology and alchemy. In R. F. C. Hull (Trans.), *The collected works of C. G. Jung* (Vol. 12). New York: Pantheon. (Original work published 1944)

Jung, C. G. (1954a). Analytic psychology and education. In H. Read, M. Fordham, & G. Adler (Eds.), *The collected works of C. G. Jung* (Vol. 17, pp. 63–132). New York: Pantheon Books. (Original work published 1926)

Jung, C. G. (1954b). Psychic conflicts in a child. In H. Read, M. Fordham, & G. Adler (Eds.), *The collected works of C. G. Jung* (Vol. 17, pp. 1–35). New York: Pantheon Books. (Original work published 1910)

Jung, C. G. (1967). *Alchemical studies*. In H. Read, M. Fordham, & G. Adler (Series Eds.), *The collected works of C. G. Jung* (Vol. 13). Princeton, NJ: Princeton University Press.

Jung, C. G. (1973). *Memories, dreams, and reflections* (A. Jaffé, Ed., R. Winston & C. Winston, Trans.). New York: Pantheon. (Original work published 1961)

Jung, C. G., Schmid-Guisan, H., Beebe, J. (Ed.), & Falzeder, E. (Ed.). (2013). *The question of psychological types: The correspondence of C. G. Jung and Hans Schmid-Guisan, 1915–1916.* Princeton, NJ: Princeton University Press.

Jung, J. (1968). *Verbal learning.* New York: Holt, Rinehart and Winston.

Junior, A. S., Araujo, S. d. F., & Moreira-Almeida, A. (2013). William James and psychical research: Towards a radical science of mind. *History of Psychiatry, 24,* 62–78.

Kahl, R. (1967). Hermann von Helmholtz. In P. Edwards (Ed.), *The encyclopedia of philosophy* (Vol. 3, pp. 469–471). New York: Macmillan and Free Press.

Kahl, R. (Ed.). (1971). *Selected writings of Hermann von Helmholtz.* Middletown, CT: Wesleyan University Press.

Kahn, P. H., Jr. (2013). The next phase of ecopsychology: Ideas and directions, *Ecopsychology, 5,* 163–166.

Kahn, P. H., Jr., & Hasbach P. H. (Eds.). (2012). *Ecopsychology: Science, totems, and the technological species.* Cambridge, MA: MIT Press.

Kandel, E. R. (2001). *Eric R. Kandel–Biographical.* Retrieved August 23, 2013 from www.nobelprize. org/ nobel_prizes/medicine/laureates/2000/kandel-bio. html

Kant, I. (1952). *The critique of judgment* (J. C. Meridith, Trans.). Oxford: Oxford University Press. (Original work published 1790)

Kant, I. (1956). *Critique of practical reason* (L. W. Beck, Trans.). Indianapolis, IN: Bobbs-Merrill. (Original work published 1788)

Kant, I. (1960). *Religion within the limits of reason alone* (T. M. Greene & H. H. Hudson, Trans.). New York: Harper. (Original work published 1793)

Kant, I. (1965). *Critique of pure reason* (N. K. Smith, Trans.). New York: St. Martin's Press. (Original work published 1781)

Kaplan, K. J., Flicker, L., Wallrabenstein, I., Dodge, N., Laird, P., Theil, K., et al. (2007). Why does Zeno the Stoic hold his breath? "Zenoism" as a new variable for studying suicide. *Omega, 56,* 369–400.

Kaplan, R. M. (2008). Being Bleuler: The second century of schizophrenia. *Australian Psychiatry, 16,* 305–311.

Kaplan, R. M. (2012). Johann Christian Reil and the naming of our specialty. *Australasian Psychiatry, 20,* 157–158.

Kashima, Y. (2000). Recovering Bartlett's social psychology of cultural dynamics. *European Journal of Social Psychology, 30,* 383–403.

Kassin, S. M. (2016). False confessions: From colonial Salem, through Central Park, and into the twenty-first century. In C. Willis-Esqueda & B. H. Bornstein (Eds.), *The witness stand and Lawrence S. Wrightsman, Jr.* (pp. 53–74). New York: Springer Science + Business Media.

Kassin, S. M., & Gudjonsson, G. H. (2004). The psychology of confessions: A review of the literature and issues. *Psychological Science in the Public Interest, 5,* 33–67.

Kastenbaum, R. (1995). "How far can an intellectual effort diminish pain?": William McDougall's journal as a model for facing death. *Omega: Journal of Death and Dying, 32,* 123–164.

Katona, G. (1940). *Organizing and memorizing: Studies in the psychology of learning and teaching.* New York: Columbia University Press.

Katona, G. (1959). The psychology of the recession. *American Psychologist, 14,* 135–143.

Katona, G. (1979). Toward a macropsychology. *American Psychologist, 34,* 118–126.

Katona, G. (2002). The evolution of the concept of psyche from Homer to Aristotle. *Journal of Theoretical and Philosophical Psychology, 22,* 29–44.

Katz, D. (1979). Floyd H. Allport (1890–1978). *American Psychologist, 34,* 351–353.

Katz, S. M. (Ed.) (2014). *Metaphor and fields: Common ground, common language, and the future of psychoanalysis.* New York: Routledge.

Kaukua, J. (2014). Avicenna on the soul's activity in perception. In J. F. Silva & M. Yrjönsuuri (Eds.), *Active perception in the history of philosophy: From Plato to modern philosophy* (pp. 99–116). Cham, Switzerland: Springer International Publishing.

Kayaoğlu, A., Batur, S., & Aslıtürk, E. (2014). The unknown Muzafer Sherif. *The Psychologist, 27,* 830–833.

Keegan, E., & Holas, P. (2010). Cognitive-behaviorial therapy: Theory and practice. In R. A. Carlstedt (Ed.), *Handbook of integrative clinical psychology, psychiatry, and behavioral medicine: Perspectives, practices, and research* (pp. 605–629). New York: Springer Publishing Co.

Keen, S. (1973). *Apology for wonder.* New York: Harper & Row.

Keller, F. S., & Sherman, J. G. (1974). *The Keller plan handbook: Essays on a personalized system of instruction.* Menlo Park, CA: Benjamin.

Keller, M. (1943). The first American medical work on the effects of alcohol: Benjamin Rush's "An inquiry into the effects of ardent spirits upon the human body and mind." *Quarterly Journal of Studies on Alcohol, 4,* 321–341.

Kellert, S. H., Longino, H. E., & Waters, C. K. (2006). *Scientific pluralism: Minnesota studies in the philosophy of science XIX*. Minneapolis: University of Minnesota Press.

Kelley, M. R., & Nairne, J. S. (2001). Von Restorff revisited: Isolation, generation, and memory for order. *Journal of Experimental Psychology: Learning, Memory, and Cognition, 27*, 54–66.

Kellman, P. J. (2000). An update on Gestalt psychology. In B. Landau & J. Sabini (Eds.), *Perception, cognition, and language: Essays in honor of Henry and Lila Gleitman* (pp. 157–190). Cambridge, MA: MIT Press.

Kelly, J. (2005). *The great mortality: An intimate history of the Black Death, the most devastating plague of all time*. New York: HarperCollins.

Kelly-Gadol, J. (1977). Did women have a Renaissance? In R. Bridenthal & C. Koontz (Eds.), *Becoming visible: Women in European history* (pp. 139–164). Boston: Houghton Mifflin.

Kemp, S. (1990). *Medieval psychology*. Westport, CT: Greenwood Press.

Kemp, S. (1996). *Cognitive psychology in the Middle Ages*. Westport, CT: Greenwood Press.

Kemp, S. (1998). Medieval theories of mental representation. *History of Psychology, 1*, 275–288.

Kendler, K. S. (2016). The transformation of American psychiatric nosology at the dawn of the twentieth century. *Molecular Psychiatry, 21*, 152–158.

Kenny, A. (Ed. & Trans.). (1970). *Descartes' philosophical letters*. Oxford: Clarendon Press.

Keshavan, M. S. (2015). The Asclepian rod and the return of psychiatry to its home in medicine and neuroscience. *Asian Journal of Psychiatry, 16*, 87–88.

Kesselring, J. (2013). Helmholtz and Goethe—Controversies at the birth of modern neuroscience. *European Neurology, 69*, 152–157.

Kett, J. F. (2015). Historical perspectives on self-regulation in adolescence. In G. Oettingen & P. M. Gollwitzer (Eds.), *Self-regulation in adolescence* (pp. 103–122). New York: Cambridge University Press.

Kieckhefer, R. (1976). *European witch trials*. Berkeley: University of California Press.

Kierkegaard, S. (1941). *Concluding unscientific postscript* (D. F. Swenson & W. Lowrie, Trans.). Princeton, NJ: Princeton University Press. (Original work published 1846)

Kierkegaard, S. (1967). *Stages on life's way* (W. Lowrie, Trans.). New York: Schocken Books. (Original work published 1845)

Kierkegaard, S. (1983). *Fear and trembling* (H. V. Hong & E. H. Hong, Eds. & Trans.). Princeton, NJ: Princeton University Press. (Original work published 1843)

Kierkegaard, S. (1985). *Philosophical fragments* (H. V. Hong & E. H. Hong, Eds. & Trans.). Princeton, NJ: Princeton University Press. (Original work published 1844)

Kierkegaard, S. (1987). *Either/or: A fragment on life* (H. V. Hong & E. H. Hong, Eds. & Trans.). Princeton, NJ: Princeton University Press. (Original work published 1843)

Kierkegaard, S. (1989). *The sickness unto death* (A. Hannay, Trans.). London: Penguin Books. (Original work published 1849)

Kihlstrom, J. F., & Cantor, N. (2011). Social intelligence. In R. J. Sternberg & S. B. Kaufman (Eds.), *The Cambridge handbook of intelligence* (pp. 564–581). New York: Cambridge University Press.

Kilmartin, C. T., & Dervin, D. (1997). Inaccurate representation of the Electra complex in psychology textbooks. *Teaching of Psychology, 24*, 269–270.

Kim, Y. (2014). "Boundaries" and "thresholds": Conceptual models of the musical mind in the history of music psychology. *Psychology of Music, 42*, 671–691.

Kimball, C. (2002). *When religion becomes evil*. San Francisco, CA: Harper.

Kimble, G. A. (1996). Ivan Mikhailovich Sechenov: Pioneer in Russian reflexology. In G. A. Kimble, C. A. Boneau, & M. Wertheimer (Eds.), *Portraits of pioneers in psychology* (Vol. 2, pp. 33–45). Washington, DC: American Psychological Association.

King, B. M. (2013). Freud's Empedocles: The future of a dualism. In V. Zajko & E. O'Groman (Eds.), *Classical myth and psychoanalysis: Ancient and modern stories of the self* (pp. 21–37). New York: Oxford University Press.

King, D. B. (1992). Evolution and revision of the principles of psychology. In M. E. Donnelly (Ed.), *Reinterpreting the legacy of William James* (pp. 67–75). Washington, DC: American Psychological Association.

King, D. B. (2000). George Croom Robertson and Mind: The story of psychology's first editor. In G. A. Kimble & M. Wertheimer (Eds.), *Portraits of pioneers in psychology* (Vol. 4, pp. 33–48). Washington, DC: American Psychological Association.

King, D. B., Cox, M., & Wertheimer, M. (1998). Karl Duncker: Productive problems with beautiful solutions. In G. A. Kimble & M. Wertheimer (Eds.), *Portraits of pioneers in psychology* (Vol. 3, pp. 163–178). Washington, DC: American Psychological Association.

King, D. B., Montañez-Ramirez, L. M., & Wertheimer, M. (1996). Barbara Stoddard Burks: Pioneer behavioral geneticist and humanitarian. In G. A. Kimble, C. A. Boneau, & M. Wertheimer (Eds.), *Portraits of pioneers in psychology* (Vol. 2, pp. 213–225). Washington, DC: American Psychological Association.

King, D. B., Niess, A. B., Maddi, A. E., & Perkins, L. S. (2013). The rise of abnormal psychology during the progressive era: Reflections from an American scientific periodical. In T. G. Plante (Ed.), *Abnormal psychology across the ages* (Vol. 1, pp. 73–86). Santa Barbara, CA: Praeger.

King, D. B., & Viney, W. (1992). Modern history of pragmatic and sentimental attitudes toward animals and the selling of comparative psychology. *Journal of Comparative Psychology, 106,* 190–195.

King, D. B., & Wertheimer, M. (2005). *Max Wertheimer and Gestalt theory*. New Brunswick, NJ: Transaction.

King, D. B., Wertheimer, M., Keller, H., & Crochetière, K. (1994). The legacy of Max Wertheimer and Gestalt psychology. *Social Research, 61,* 907–935.

Kintsch, W. (1985). Reflections on Ebbinghaus. *Journal of Experimental Psychology: Learning, Memory and Cognition, 11,* 461–463.

Kirk, G. S., & Raven, J. E. (1957). *The presocratic philosophers*. Cambridge, UK: Cambridge University Press.

Kirkbride, T. S. (1994). A sketch of the history, buildings, and organization of the Pennsylvania Hospital for the Insane, extracted principally from the reports of Thomas S. Kirkbride, M.D., physician to the institution. *American Journal of Psychiatry, 151,* 21–26.

Kirsch, I. (1978). Demonology and the rise of science: An example of the misperception of historical data. *Journal of the History of the Behavioral Sciences, 14,* 149–157.

Kirsch, T., & Hogenson, G. (Eds.). (2014). The Red Book: *Reflections on C. G. Jung's Liber Novus*. New York: Routledge.

Kirschenbaum, H., & Jourdan, A. (2005). The current status of Carl Rogers and the person-centered approach. *Psychotherapy: Theory, Research, Practice, Training, 42,* 37–51.

Kirsner, D. (2001). The future of psychoanalytic institutes. *Psychoanalytic Psychology, 18,* 195–212.

Kissinger, S. C. (2008). Christian von Ehrenfels. In R. Diriwächter & J. Valsiner (Eds.), *Striving for the whole: Creating theoretical syntheses* (pp. 13–20). Piscataway, NJ: Transaction Publishers.

Kitcher, P. (1982). *Abusing science*. Cambridge, MA: MIT Press.

Klautke, E. (2010). *The mind of the nation: Völkerpsychologie in Germany, 1851–1955*. New York: Berghahn Books.

Klein, A. G. (2000). Fitting the school to the child: The mission of Leta Stetter Hollingworth, founder of gifted education. *Roeper Review, 23,* 97–103.

Klein, M. I. (1983). Freud's drive theory and ego psychology: A critical evaluation of the Blancks. *Psychoanalytic Review, 70,* 505–517.

Klempe, S. H. (2011). The role of tone sensation and musical stimuli in early experimental psychology. *Journal of the History of the Behavioral Sciences, 47,* 187–199.

Kline, L. W. (1908). The nature, origin and function of humor. *Popular Science Monthly, 73,* 144–156.

Kline, N. S., & Saunders, J. C. (1959). Drugs for treatment of depression. *Neurology, 9,* 224–227.

Knapp, S. J., Gottleib, M. C., & Handelsman, M. M. (2015). *Ethical dilemmas in psychotherapy: Positive approaches to decision making*. Washington, DC: American Psychological Association.

Knapp, T. J. (1995). A natural history of the behavior of organisms. In J. T. Todd (Ed.), *Modern perspectives on B. F. Skinner and contemporary behaviorism* (pp. 7–23). Westport, CT: Greenwood Press.

Knowles, D. (1967). Anicius Manlius Severinus Boethius. In P. Edwards (Ed.), *The encyclopedia of philosophy* (Vol. 1, pp. 328–330). New York: Macmillan and Free Press.

Knowlton, S. (1867). The silence of women in the churches. *The Congregational Quarterly, 9,* 329–334.

Kobak, R. (2012). Attachment and early social deprivation: Revisiting Harlow's monkey studies. In A. M. Slater & P. C. Quinn (Eds.), *Developmental psychology: Revisiting the classic studies* (pp. 10–23). Thousand Oaks, CA: Sage Publications.

Koch, S. (1986). Afterword. In S. Koch & D. E. Leary (Eds.), *A century of psychology as science* (pp. 928–950). New York: McGraw-Hill.

Koestenbaum, P. (1967). Miguel de Unamuno y Jugo. In P. Edwards (Ed.), *Encyclopedia of philosophy* (Vol. 8, pp. 182–185). New York: Macmillan.

Koffka, K. (1922). Perception: An introduction to the Gestalt-Theorie. *Psychological Bulletin, 19,* 531–585.

Koffka, K. (1935). *Principles of Gestalt psychology*. New York: Harcourt.

Koffka, K. (1980). *Growth of the mind*. New Brunswick, NJ: Transaction Books. (Original work published 1924)

Köhler, W. (1938). Simple structural functions in the chimpanzee and in the chicken. In W. D. Ellis (Ed.), *A source book of Gestalt psychology* (pp. 217–227). London: Kegan Paul, Trench, Trubner & Company.

Köhler, W. (1940). *Dynamics in psychology*. New York: Liveright.

Köhler, W. (1947). *Gestalt psychology*. New York: Liveright. (Original work published 1929)

Köhler, W. (1966). *The place of value in a world of facts.* New York: Liveright. (Original work published 1938)

Köhler, W. (1969). *The task of Gestalt psychology.* Princeton, NJ: Princeton University Press.

Köhler, W. (1971). Gestalt psychology. In M. Henle (Ed.), *The selected papers of Wolfgang Köhler* (pp. 108–122). New York: Liveright. (Original work published 1967)

Köhler, W. (1976). *The mentality of apes.* New York: Liveright. (Original work published 1925)

Köhler, W., & Restorff, H. von. (1935). Analyse von Vorgangen in Spurenfeld. *Psychologische Forschung, 13,* 293–364.

Kohlman, M. J. (2012). Evangelizing eugenics: A brief historiography of popular and formal American eugenics. *Alberta Journal of Educational Research, 58,* 657–690.

Kohn, D. (Ed.). (1985). *The Darwinian heritage.* Princeton, NJ: Princeton University Press.

Kolb, B. (1999). The twentieth century belongs to neuropsychology. *Brain Research Bulletin, 50,* 409–410.

Koltko-Rivera, M. E. (2006). Rediscovering the later version of Maslow's hierarchy of needs: Self-transcendence and opportunities for theory, research, and unification. *Review of General Psychology, 10,* 302–317.

Kontantin, R. (1960). The problem of measurement in the psychology of the eighteenth century. *American Psychologist, 15,* 256–265.

Koo, J.-J. (2016). Early Heidegger on social reality. In A. Salice & H. B. Schmid (Eds.), *The phenomenological approach to social reality: History, concepts, problems. Studies in the philosophy of sociality* (Vol. 6, pp. 91–119). Cham, Switzerland: Springer International Publishing.

Koops, W. (2015). Haeckel and levels of development. *European Journal of Developmental Psychology, 12,* 640–655.

Koppes, L. L. (2000). Lillian Gilbreth. In Alan E. Kaszdan (Ed.), *Encyclopedia of psychology* (Vol. 3, pp. 498–500). Washington, DC: American Psychological Association.

Korteweg, S. F. S., Van de Graf, R. C., & Werker, P. M. N. (2010). Sir Charles Bell was not affected by facial paralysis himself! *Arquivos de Neuro-Psiquiatria, 68,* 321–322.

Kovel, J. (1990). Beyond the future of an illusion: Further reflections on Freud and religion. *Psychoanalytic Review, 77,* 69–87.

Kramer, H., & Sprenger, J. (1971). *The malleus maleficarum* (M. Summers, Trans.). New York: Dover. (Original work published 1486)

Kranz, D. L. (2005). Hull's *Principles of behavior* and psychology's unity. *PsycCRITIQUES, 50*(37).

Krasner, J. (2016). On the origins and persistence of the Jewish identity industry in Jewish education. *Journal of Jewish Education, 82,* 132–158.

Krech, D. (1968). Edward C. Tolman. In D. L. Sills (Ed.), *International encyclopedia of the social sciences* (Vol. 16, pp. 95–98). New York: Macmillan.

Kreezer, G. (1938). The electro-encephalogram and its use in psychology. *American Journal of Psychology, 51,* 737–759.

Kressley, R. A. (2006). Gestalt psychology: Its paradigm-shaping influence on animal psychology. *Gestalt Theory, 28,* 259–269.

Krivoy, W. A., Kroeger, D. C., & Zimmermann, E. (1977). Neuropeptides: Influence of acute and chronic effects of opiates. *Psychoneuroendocrinology, 2,* 43–51.

Krueger, J. I. (2012). The (ir)rationality project in social psychology: A review and assessment. In J. I. Krueger (Ed.), *Social judgment and decision making* (pp. 59–75). New York: Psychology Press.

Kruger, L., Otis, T. S., & Shtrahman, M. (2011). Golgi in retrospect: A historiographic examination of contextual influence in tracing the constructs of neuronal organization. *Brain Research Reviews, 66,* 68–74.

Kruglanski, A. W., & Stroebe, W. (Eds.). (2012). *Handbook of the history of social psychology.* New York: Psychology Press.

Kruta, V. (1976). Ernst Heinrich Weber. In C. C. Gillispie (Ed.), *Dictionary of scientific biography* (Vol. 14, pp. 199–202). New York: Scribner.

Kuhlmann, H. (2005). *Living Walden Two: B. F. Skinner's behaviorist utopia and experimental communities.* Champaign, IL: University of Illinois Press.

Kuhn, R. (1958). The treatment of depressive states with G-22355 (imipramine hydrochloride). *American Journal of Psychiatry, 115,* 459–464.

Kuhn, T. S. (1970). *The structure of scientific revolutions* (2nd ed.). Chicago: University of Chicago Press.

Kuhse, H., & Singer, P. (1993). Individuals, humans and persons: The issue of moral status. In P. Singer, H. Kuhse, S. Buckle, K. Dawson, & P. Kasimba (Eds.), *Embryo experimentation: Ethical, legal, and social issues* (pp. 65–75). Cambridge, UK: Cambridge University Press.

Külpe, O. (1973). *Outlines of psychology* (E. B. Titchener, Trans.). New York: Arno Press. (Original work published 1893)

Kumar, N. (2010). Karl Popper, psychology and philosophy. *Psychological Studies, 55,* 270–274.

Kuna, D. P. (1976). The concept of suggestion in the

early history of advertising psychology. *Journal of the History of the Behavioral Sciences, 12,* 347–353.

Kuo, Z. Y. (1921). Giving up instincts in psychology. *Journal of Philosophy, 18,* 645–666.

Kuo, Z. Y. (1924). A psychology without heredity. *Psychological Review, 31,* 427–448.

Kuriloff, E. A. (2014). *Contemporary psychoanalysis and the legacy of the Third Reich: History, memory, tradition.* New York: Routledge.

Kurtz, P. (Ed.). (2003). *Science and religion: Are they compatible?* Amherst, NY: Prometheus Books.

Kusnecov, A. W., & Anisman, H. (Eds.). (2014). *The Wiley-Blackwell handbook of psychoneuroimmunology.* Hoboken, NJ: Wiley-Blackwell.

Lachman, R., Lachman, J. L., & Butterfield, E. C. (1979). *Cognitive psychology and information processing: An introduction.* Hillsdale, NJ: Erlbaum.

Laertius, D. (1972). *Lives of eminent philosophers.* R. D. Hicks (Ed & Trans.). Cambridge, MA: Loeb Classical Library.

Laird, S. (2008). *Mary Wollstonecraft: Philosophical mother of co-education.* London: Bloomsbury Academic.

Lambert, M. J. (2010). *Prevention of treatment failure: The use of measuring, monitoring, and feedback in clinical practice.* Washington, DC: American Psychological Association.

Lamdan, E., & Yasnitsky, A. (2016). Did Uzbeks have illusions? The Luria-Koffka controversy of 1932. In A. Yasnitsky & R. van der Veer (Eds.), *Revisionist revolution in Vygotsky studies* (pp. 175–200). New York: Routledge.

La Mettrie, J. O. (1912). *Man a machine.* La Salle, IL: Open Court. (Original work published 1747)

Lamiell, J. T. (2013a). Translator's preface. *History of Psychology, 16,* 195–196.

Lamiell, J. T. (2013b). On psychology's struggle for existence: Some reflections on Wundt's 1913 essay a century on. *Journal of Theoretical and Philosophical Psychology, 33*(4), 205–215.

Landon, H. C. R. (1990). *The Mozart compendium: A guide to Mozart's life and music.* New York: Schirmer.

Landy, F. J. (1992). Hugo Münsterberg: Victim or visionary? *Journal of Applied Psychology, 77,* 787–802.

Landy, F. J. (1997). Early influences on the development of industrial and organizational psychology. *Journal of Applied Psychology, 82,* 467–477.

Lane, M. (2012). *Eco-Republic: What the ancients can teach us about ethics, virtue, and sustainable living.* Princeton, NJ: Princeton University Press.

Lange, C. G. (1922). *The emotions.* Baltimore: Williams & Wilkins. (Original work published 1885)

Langfeld, H. S. (1937). Carl Stumpf. *American Journal of Psychology, 49,* 316–320.

Langfeld, H. S. (1946). Edwin Bissell Holt: 1873–1946. *Psychological Review, 53,* 251–258.

Längle, A. (2012). The Viennese school of existential analysis: The search for meaning and affirmation of life. In L. Barnett & G. Madison (Eds.), *Existential therapy: Legacy, vibrancy and dialogue* (pp. 159–170). New York: Routledge.

Lanska, D. J. (2014). Vesalius on the anatomy and function of the recurrent laryngeal nerves: Medical illustration and reintroduction of a physiological demonstration from Galen. *Journal of the History of the Neurosciences, 23,* 211–232.

LaPointe, L. L. (2013). *Paul Broca and the origins of language in the brain.* San Diego, CA: Plural Publishing.

LaPointe, L. L. (2014). Paul Broca and French brains: Portraits from the life of an eminent neuroscientist. *Communication Disorders Quarterly, 36,* 29–34.

Larrimore, M. (2008). Antinomies of race: Diversity and destiny in Kant. *Patterns of Prejudice, 42,* 341–363.

Larson, C. A. (1979). Highlights of Dr. John B. Watson's career in advertising. *Journal of Industrial/Organizational Psychology, 16,* 3.

Lashley, K. (1942). An examination of the "continuity theory" as applied to discriminative learning. *Journal of General Psychology, 26,* 241–265.

Lashley, K. S. (1950). In search of the engram. *Symposia of the Society for Experimental Biology, 4,* 454–482.

Latham, R. E. (1959). Introduction. In R. E. Latham (Trans.), *Lucretius on the nature of the universe* (pp. ix–xxxii). Baltimore: Penguin.

Latham, R. E. (1967). Lucretius. In P. Edwards (Ed.), *The encyclopedia of philosophy* (Vol. 5, pp. 99–101). New York: Macmillan and Free Press.

Lattal, K. A. & Rutherford, A. (2013). John Watson's Behaviorist Manifesto at 100. *Revista Mexicana de Análisis de la Conducta, 39,* 1–9.

Laver, A. B. (1972). Precursors of psychology in ancient Egypt. *Journal of the History of the Behavioral Sciences, 8,* 181–195.

Lawrence, D. H., & Festinger, L. (1962). *Deterrents and reinforcement. The psychology of insufficient reward.* Stanford, CA: Stanford University Press.

Lawton, G., & Churchland, P. (2013). At peace with my brain. *New Scientist, 220,* 30–31.

Layton, D. (1998). *Seductive poison: A Jonestown survivor's story of life and death in the People's Temple.* New York: Anchor Books.

Lazarus, A. A. (2000). Will reason prevail? From classical psychoanalysis to New Age therapy. *American Journal of Psychotherapy, 54,* 152–155.

Lea, H. C. (Ed.). (1957). *Materials toward a history of witchcraft* (Vol. 3). New York: Thomas Yoseloff.

Leahey, T. H. (1981). The mistaken mirror: On Wundt's and Titchener's psychologies. *Journal of the History of the Behavioral Sciences, 17,* 273–282.

Leahey, T. H. (1992). The mythical revolutions of American psychology. *American Psychologist, 47,* 308–318.

Leahey, T. H. (2001). Back to Bridgman? *Theory and Psychology, 11,* 53–58.

Leahey, T. H. (2005). Mind as a scientific object: A historical philosophical exploration. In C. E. Erneling & D. M. Johnson (Eds.), *The mind as a scientific object: Between brain and culture.* New York: Oxford University Press.

Leahey, T. H. (2013). Cognition and learning. In D. K. Freedheim & I. B. Weiner (Eds.), *Handbook of psychology, Vol. 1: History of psychology* (2nd ed., pp. 129–154). Hoboken, NJ: John Wiley & Sons Inc.

Leary, D. E. (1980). The intentions and heritage of Descartes and Locke: Toward a recognition of the moral basis of modern psychology. *Journal of General Psychology, 102,* 283–310.

Leary, D. E. (2014). Overcoming blindness: Some historical reflections on qualitative psychology. *Qualitative Psychology, 1,* 17–33.

Lee, R. M. (2011). "The most important technique . . .": Carl Rogers, Hawthorne, and the rise and fall of nondirective interviewing in sociology. *Journal of the History of the Behavioral Sciences, 47,* 123–146.

Lehrer, K. (1989). *Thomas Reid.* New York: Routledge.

Leiber, J. (2011). Descartes: The smear and related misconstruals. *Journal for the Theory of Social Behaviour, 41,* 365–376.

Lemberger, M. E., & Cornelius-White, J. H. D. (2016). Introduction to the Special Issue on person-centered approaches in schools. *Person-Centered and Experiential Psychotherapies, 15,* 1–4.

Lent, R. W. (2016). Self-efficacy in a relational world: Social cognitive mechanisms of adaptation and development. *The Counseling Psychologist, 44,* 573–594.

Lepoutre, T., & Villa, F. (2015). Freud with Charcot: Freud's discovery and the question of diagnosis. *The International Journal of Psychoanalysis, 96,* 345–368.

Lequyer, J. (1998). The dialogue of the predestinate and the reprobate. In D. W. Viney (Ed. and Trans.), *Translation of works of Jules Lequyer* (pp. 51–156). Lewiston, NY: Edwin Mellen. (Original work published 1865)

Lerner, R. M. (2009). The scientific study of adolescent development: Historical and contemporary perspectives. In R. M. Lerner & L. Steinberg (Eds.), *Handbook of adolescent psychology, Vol. 1: Individual bases of adolescent development)* (3rd ed., pp. 3–14). Hoboken, NJ: John Wiley & Sons.

LeRoy, H. (2008). Harry Harlow: From the other side of the desk. *Integrative Psychological & Behavioral Science, 42,* 348–353.

LeRoy, H., & Kimble, G. A. (2003). Harry Frederick Harlow: And one thing led to another . . . In G. A. Kimble & M. Wertheimer (Eds.), *Portraits of pioneers in psychology* (Vol. 5, pp. 279–297). Washington, DC: American Psychological Association.

Leslie, J. C. (2006). Herbert Spencer's contributions to behavior analysis: A retrospective review of Principles of Psychology. *Journal of the Experimental Analysis of Behavior, 86,* 123–129.

Leslie, R. C. (1996). Karen Horney and Viktor Frankl: Optimists in spite of everything. *International Forum for Logotherapy, 19,* 23–28.

Leuba, J. H. (1896). A study in the psychology of religious phenomena. *American Journal of Psychology, 7,* 309–385.

Leuba, J. H. (1925). *The psychology of religious mysticism.* New York: Harcourt, Brace, & Company.

Leuba, J. H. (1928). Morality among the animals. *Harper's Magazine, 157,* 97–103.

Leuba, J. H. (1969). *A psychological study of religion: Its origin, function, and future.* New York: AMS Press. (Original work published 1912)

Levine, H. G. (1978). The discovery of addiction: Changing conceptions of habitual drunkenness in America. *Journal of Studies on Alcohol, 39,* 143–174.

Levine, M., & Wishner, J. (1977). The case records of the Psychological Clinic at the University of Pennsylvania (1896–1961). *Journal of the History of the Behavioral Sciences, 13,* 59–66.

Levy, E. (1986). A Gestalt theory of paranoia. *Gestalt Theory, 8,* 230–255.

Lewin, K. (1931). The conflict between Aristotelian and Galileian modes of thought in contemporary psychology. *Journal of Genetic Psychology, 5,* 141–177.

Lewin, K. (1935). *A dynamic theory of personality: Selected papers* (D. K. Adams & K. E. Zener, Trans.). New York: McGraw-Hill.

Lewin, K. (1937). Carl Stumpf. *Psychological Review, 44,* 189–194.

Lewin, R. (1984). *Hitler's mistakes.* New York: William Morrow.

Lewis, H. B. (1984). Psychoanalytic Psychology: Editorial. *Psychoanalytic Psychology, 1,* 1–5.

Lewis, P. (2012). In defense of Aristotle on character: Toward a synthesis of recent psychology, neuroscience and the thought of Michael Polanyi. *Journal of Moral Education, 41,* 155–170.

Libet, B. (1985). Unconscious cerebral initiative and the role of conscious will in voluntary action. *Behavioral and Brain Sciences, 8,* 529–566.

Liddell, A. F. (1933). Instructed ignorance: The philosophy of Nicholas of Cusa. *Psychological Bulletin, 30,* 606–607.

Lifton, R. J. (1968). *Revolutionary immortality. Mao TseTung and the Chinese cultural revolution.* New York: Random House.

Lilleleht, E. (2015). "Assuming the privilege" of bridging divides: Abigail Fowler-Chumos, practical phrenology, and America's Gilded Age. *History of Psychology, 18,* 414–432.

Lincoln, A. (1950). Letter to W. H. Herndon. In A. H. Shaw (Ed.), *The Lincoln encyclopedia* (p. 149). New York: Macmillan. (Original work published 1856)

Lincoln, M. R., & Ebers, G. C. (2012). Robert Whytt, Benjamin Franklin, and the first probable case of multiple sclerosis. *Annals of Neurology, 72,* 307–311.

Lindberg, D. C., & Numbers, R. L. (1986). *God and nature: Historical essays on the encounter between Christianity and science.* Berkeley: University of California Press.

Lindenfeld, D. (1978). Oswald Külpe and the Würzburg School. *Journal of the History of the Behavioral Sciences, 14,* 132–141.

Lindsley, D. B. (1936). Brain potentials in children and adults. *Science, 83,* 354.

Lindsley, D. B. (1942). Heart and brain potentials of human fetuses in utero. *American Journal of Psychology, 55,* 412–416.

Linehan, M. (1993). *Cognitive-behavioral treatment of borderline personality disorder.* New York: Guilford.

Linehan, M., & Wilks, C. R. (2015). The course and evolution of dialectical behavior therapy. *American Journal of Psychotherapy, 69,* 97–110.

Linehan, M. M., & Lungu, A. (2012). Compassion, wisdom, and suicidal clients. In C. K. Germer & R. D. Siegel (Eds.), *Wisdom and compassion in psychotherapy: Deepening mindfulness in clinical practice* (pp. 205–220). New York: Guilford Press.

Link, S. W. (1994). Rediscovering the past: Gustav Fechner and signal detection theory. *Psychological Science, 5,* 335–340.

Lippitt, J. (2016). What can therapists learn from Kierkegaard? In M. Bazzano & J. Webb (Eds.), *Therapy and the counter-tradition: The edge of philosophy* (pp. 23–33). New York: Routledge.

Lippman, T. W. (1995). *Understanding Islam: An introduction to the Muslim world.* New York: Meridian.

Lipsitt, D. R. (2016). Drugs, dreams, and psychosomatics. *Psychosomatics: Journal of Consultation and Liaison Psychiatry, 57,* 113–114.

Ljungqvist, F. C. (2012). Female shame, male honor: The chastity code in Juan Luis Vives' De institutione feminae Christianae. *Journal of Family History, 37,* 139–154.

Lloyd, P., & Fernyhough, C. (Eds.). (1999). *Lev Vygotsky: Critical assessments: Vygotsky's theory.* Florence, KY: Taylor & Francis/Routledge.

Locke, J. (1959). *An essay concerning human understanding* (A. C. Fraser, Ed.). New York: Dover. (Original work published 1690)

Locke, J. (1989). *Some thoughts concerning education* (J. W. Yolton & J. S. Yolton, Eds.). Oxford: Clarendon Press. (Original work published 1693)

Loehlin, J. C. (2009). History of behavior genetics. In Y.-K. Kim (Ed.), *Handbook of behavior genetics* (pp. 3–11). New York: Springer Science + Business Media.

Loewen, J. W. (2005). *Sundown towns: A hidden dimension of American racism.* New York: Touchstone.

Loewen, J. W. (2007). *Lies my teacher told me: Everything your American history textbook got wrong* (2nd ed.). New York: Simon & Schuster.

Loftus, E. (1993). The reality of repressed memories. *American Psychologist, 48,* 518–537.

Loftus, E. F. (1996). *Eyewitness testimony.* Cambridge, MA: Harvard University Press. (Original work published 1979)

Loftus, E. F. (2003). The dangers of memory. In R. J. Sternberg (Ed.), *Psychologists defying the crowd: Stories of those who battled the establishment and won* (pp. 104–117). Washington, DC: American Psychological Association.

Logan, F. A. (1968). Clark L. Hull. In D. L. Sills (Ed.), *International encyclopedia of the social sciences* (Vol. 6, pp. 535–539). New York: Macmillan.

Lombrozo, T. (2015). The mind is just the brain. In John Brockman (Ed.), *This idea must die* (pp. 271–273). New York: Harper.

Longo, M. R., & Haggard, P. (2011). Weber's illusion and body shape: Anisotropy of tactile size perception on the hand. *Journal of Experimental Psychology: Human Perception and Performance, 37,* 720–726.

López-Muñoz, F., Alamo, C., Cuenca, E., Shen, W. W., Clervoy, P., & Rubio, G. (2005). History of the discovery and clinical introduction of chlorpromazine. *Annals of Clinical Psychiatry, 17,* 113–135.

López-Muñoz, F., Boya, J., & Alamo, C. (2006). Neuron theory, the cornerstone of neuroscience, on the centenary of the Nobel Prize award to Santiago Ramón y Cajal. *Brain Research Bulletin, 70,* 391–405.

Lorch, M. (2011). Re-examining Paul Broca's initial presentation of M. Leborgne: Understanding the impetus for brain and language research. *Cortex: A Journal Devoted to the Study of the Nervous System and Behavior, 47*, 1228–1235.

Lorusso, L. (2008). Neurological caricatures since the 15th century. *Journal of the History of the Neurosciences, 17*, 314–334.

Lotze, H. (1973). *Outlines of psychology*. New York: Arno Press. (Original work published 1881)

Louckx, K., & Vanderstraeten, R. (2014). State-istics and statistics: Exclusion categories in the population census (Belgium, 1846–1930). *The Sociological Review, 62*, 530–546.

Lovejoy, A. D. (1922). Paradox of the thinking behaviorist. *Philosophical Review, 31*, 135–147.

Lowman, R. L., Kantor, J., & Perloff, R. (2007). A history of I-O psychology educational programs in the United States. In L. L. Koppes (Ed.), *Historical perspectives in industrial and organizational psychology* (pp. 111–137). Mahwah, NJ: Lawrence Erlbaum Associates.

Lowrie, W. (1970). *Kierkegaard* (Vol. 1). Gloucester, MA: Peter Smith.

Lowry, R. J. (1973). *A. H. Maslow: An intellectual portrait*. Monterey, CA: Brooks/Cole.

Luccio, R. (2010). Anent isomorphism and its ambiguities: From Wertheimer to Köhler and back to Spinoza. *Gestalt Theory, 32*, 219–262.

Luchins, A. S., & Luchins, E. H. (1982). An introduction to the origin of Wertheimer's Gestalt psychology. *Gestalt Theory, 4*, 145–171.

Luchins, A. S., & Luchins, E. H. (2015). Isomorphism in Gestalt theory: Comparison of Wertheimer's and Köhler's concepts. *Gestalt Theory, 37*, 69–99. (Original work published 1999)

Lucretius. (1959). *On the nature of the universe* (R. E. Latham, Trans.). Baltimore: Penguin.

Lurie, A. T. (1979). The weeping Heraclitus by Hendrick Terbrugghen in the Cleveland Museum of Art. *The Burlington Magazine, 121*, 279–287.

Luther, M. (1967). Table talk. In H. T. Lehmann (Ed.), *Luther's works* (Vol. 54, pp. 358–359). Philadelphia: Fortress Press.

MacCormac, E. R. (1990). Metaphor and pluralism. *The Monist, 73*, 411–420.

MacCorquodale, K. C. (1970). On Chomsky's review of Skinner's Verbal Behavior. *Journal of the Experimental Analysis of Behavior, 13*, 83–100.

MacCorquodale, K. C., & Meehl, P. E. (1954). Edward C. Tolman. In W. K. Estes, S. Koch, K. MacCorquodale, P. E. Meehl, C. G. Muller, Jr., & W. N. Schoenfeld et al. (Eds.), *Modern learning theory* (pp. 177–266). New York: Appleton-Century-Crofts.

MacDonald, P. (2007). Francis Bacon's behavioral psychology. *Journal of the History of the Behavioral Sciences, 43*, 285–303.

Mace, B. L., Woody, W. D., & Berg, L. (2012). Teaching environmental psychology by doing it: Explorations in the natural world. *Ecopsychology, 4*, 81–86.

Mach, E. (1959). *The analysis of sensations* (5th ed.). (C. M. Williams, Trans.). New York: Dover. (Original work published 1886; 5th ed. published 1905)

Machiavelli, N. (1977). *The prince* (R. M. Adams, Trans. & Ed.). New York: Norton. (Original work published 1532)

Machleidt, W., & Sieberer, M. (2013). From Kraepelin to a modern and integrative scientific discipline: The development of transcultural psychiatry in Germany. *Transcultural Psychiatry, 50*, 817–840

Mackintosh, N. J. (1997). Has the wheel turned full circle? Fifty years of learning theory, 1946–1996. *Quarterly Journal of Experimental Psychology, 50*, 879–898.

Mackler, B., & Hamilton, K. (1967). Benjamin Rush: A political and historical study of the "Father of American Psychiatry." *Psychological Reports, 20*, 1287–1306.

Macklin, R. (1976). A psychoanalytic model for human freedom and rationality. *Psychoanalytic Quarterly, 45*, 430–454.

MacLeod, R. B. (1964). Phenomenology: A challenge to experimental psychology. In T. W. Wann (Ed.), *Behaviorism and phenomenology: Contrasting bases for modern psychology* (pp. 47–73). Chicago: University of Chicago Press.

MacLeod, R. B. (1968a). Johannes Müller. In D. L. Sills (Ed.), *International encyclopedia of the social sciences* (Vol. 10, pp. 525–527). New York: Macmillan and Free Press.

MacLeod, R. B. (1968b). Phenomenology. In D. L. Sills (Ed.), *International encyclopedia of the social sciences* (Vol. 12, pp. 68–72). New York: Macmillan and Free Press.

MacLeod, R. B. (Ed.). (1969). *William James: Unfinished business*. Washington, DC: American Psychological Association.

MacLeod, R. B. (1975). *The persistent problems of psychology*. Pittsburgh, PA: Duquesne University Press.

MacMillan, M. (1991). *Freud evaluated: The completed arc*. Amsterdam: North-Holland.

Macnamara, J. (1993). Cognitive psychology and the rejection of Brentano. *Journal for the Theory of Social Behavior, 23*, 117–137.

Madden, G. J., Dube, W. V., Hackenberg, T. D., Hanley, G. P., & Lattal, K. A. (Eds.). (2012). *APA handbook of behavior analysis, Vol. 1: Methods and principles*. Washington, DC: American Psychological Association.

Madigan, S., & O'Hara, R. (1992). Short-term memory at the turn of the century: Mary Whiton Calkins's memory research. *American Psychologist, 47,* 170–174.

Magiorkinis, E., Sidiropoulou, K., & Diamantis, A. (2010). Hallmarks in the history of epilepsy: Epilepsy in antiquity. *Epilepsy & Behavior, 17,* 103–108.

Magnavita, J. J., & Anchin, J. C. (2014). *Unifying psychotherapy: Principles, methods, and evidence from clinical science*. New York: Springer.

Mahaffy, J. P. (1969). *Descartes*. Freeport, NY: Books for the Libraries Press. (Original work published 1902)

Maher, W. B., & Maher, B. A. (2003). Abnormal psychology. In I. B. Weiner (Series Ed.) & D. K. Friedheim (Vol. Ed.), *Handbook of psychology, Vol. 1: History of psychology* (pp. 303–336). New York: Wiley.

Mahoney, M. J. (1989). Scientific psychology and radical behaviorism: Important distinctions based in scientism and objectivism. *American Psychologist, 44,* 1372–1377.

Maiese, M. (2016). The reason/emotion divide in contemporary philosophy of psychology. In M. C. Amoretti & N. Vassallo (Eds.), *Meta-philosophical reflection on feminist philosophies of science* (pp. 113–132). Cham, Switzerland: Springer International Publishing.

Mak, G., & Waaldijk, B. (2009). Gender, history, and the politics of Florence Nightingale. In R. Buikema & I. van der Tuin (Eds.), *Doing gender in media, art and culture* (pp. 207–222). New York: Routledge.

Malone, J. C. (2014). Did John B. Watson really "found" behaviorism? *The Behavior Analyst, 37,* 1–12.

Manchester, W. (1992). *A world lit only by fire: The Medieval mind and the Renaissance: Portrait of an age*. Boston: Little, Brown.

Mandler, G. (2003). Emotion. In I. B. Weiner (Series Ed.) & D. K. Freedheim (Vol. Ed.), *Handbook of psychology, Vol. 1: History of psychology* (pp. 157–175). New York: Wiley.

Mandler, J. M., & Mandler, G. (1969). The diaspora of experimental psychology: The Gestaltists and others. In D. Fleming & B. Bailyn (Eds.), *The intellectual migration: Europe and America, 1930–1960* (pp. 371–419). Cambridge, MA: Harvard University Press.

Manning, L., & Thomas-Antérion, C. (2011). Marc Dax and the discovery of the lateralisation of language in the left cerebral hemisphere. *Revue Neurologique, 167,* 868–872.

Manoli, D. D., Meissner, G. W., & Baker, B. S. (2006). Blueprints for behavior: Genetic specification of neural circuitry for innate behaviors. *Trends in Neurosciences, 29,* 444–451.

Markel, H. (2011). *An anatomy of addiction: Sigmund Freud, William Halsted, and the miracle drug cocaine*. New York: Pantheon Books.

Markus, H. R., & Kitayama, S. (1991). Culture and the self: Implications for cognition, emotion, and motivation. *Psychological Review, 98,* 224–253.

Marneros, A. (2009). The history of bipolar disorders. In C. A. Zarate, Jr. & H. K. Manji (Eds.), *Bipolar depression: Molecular neurobiology, clinical diagnosis and pharmacotherapy* (pp. 3–16). Cambridge, MA: Birkhäuser.

Marrow, A. J. (1969). *The practical theorist: The life and work of Lewin*. New York: Basic Books.

Marsh, C. (2013). Social harmony paradigms and natural selection: Darwin, Kropotkin, and the metatheory of mutual aid. *Journal of Public Relations Research, 25,* 426–441.

Marshall, P. (2015). Why we are conscious of so little: A neo-Leibnizian approach. In E. F. Kelly, A. Crabtree, & Marshall, P. (Eds.), *Beyond physicalism: Toward reconciliation of science and spirituality* (pp. 387–422). Lanham, MD: Rowman & Littlefield.

Marston, W. M. (1917). Systolic blood pressure symptoms of deception. *Journal of Experimental Psychology, 2,* 117–163.

Martens, J. W., Koehler, P. J., & Vijselaar, J. (2013). Magnetic flimmers: "Light in the electromagnetic darkness." *Brain: A Journal of Neurology, 136,* 971–979.

Martí, E., & Rodríguez, C. (Eds.). (2012). *After Piaget: History and theory of psychology*. Piscataway, NJ: Transaction Publishers.

Marti, F. (1983, April 1). *The social and political question of demythologizing*. Talk delivered before the Southern Society for Philosophy and Psychology, Atlanta, GA.

Martin, J. (2016). Ernest Becker and Stanley Milgram: Twentieth-century students of evil. *History of Psychology, 19,* 3–21.

Martinez, J. L., Jr., & Mendoza, R. H. (1984). *Chicano psychology*. New York: Academic Press.

Martinich, A. P. (1999). *Hobbes: A biography*. Cambridge, UK: Cambridge University Press.

Mascolo, A. (2016). L'évasion de l'être. Jean-Paul Sartre and the phenomenology of temporality. In F. Santoianni (Ed.), *The concept of time in early twentieth-century philosophy: A philosophical thematic atlas. Studies in applied philosophy, epistemology and rational ethics* (Vol. 24, pp. 77–84). Cham, Switzerland: Springer International Publishing.

Maslow, A. H. (1943). A theory of human motivation. *Psychological Review, 50,* 370–396.

Maslow, A. H. (1954). *Motivation and personality.* New York: Harper and Brothers.

Maslow, A. H. (1962). *Toward a psychology of being.* Princeton, NJ: Van Nostrand.

Maslow, A. H. (1964). *Religion, values, and peak experiences.* New York: Viking.

Maslow, A. H. (1971). *The farther reaches of human nature.* New York: Viking.

Masrour, F. (2013). Phenomenal objectivity and phenomenal intentionality: In defense of a Kantian account. In U. Kriegel (Ed.), *Phenomenal intentionality* (pp. 116–136). New York: Oxford University Press.

Massey, D. S. (2015). Brave new world of biosocial science. *Criminology, 53,* 127–131.

Masson, J. M. (1991). *Final analysis: The making and unmaking of a psychoanalyst.* Reading, MA: Addison-Wesley.

Mastain, L. (2006). The lived experience of spontaneous altruism: A phenomenological study. *Journal of Phenomenological Psychology, 37,* 25–52.

Mathers, D. (Ed.). (2014). *Alchemy and psychotherapy: Post-Jungian perspectives.* New York: Routledge.

Mathews, N. (1996). *Francis Bacon: The history of a character assassination.* New Haven, CT: Yale University Press.

Matson, W. I. (1982). De corpore. In F. N. McGill (Ed.), *World philosophy* (Vol. 2, pp. 851–856). Engelwood Cliffs, NJ: Salem Press.

Mattern, S. (2011). Galen and his patients. *The Lancet, 378,* 478–479.

Mattoon, M. A. (1981). *Jungian psychology in perspective.* New York: Free Press.

May, E. T. (2010). *America and the pill: A history of promise, peril, and liberation.* New York: Basic Books.

May, R. (1953). *Man's search for himself.* New York: Norton.

May, R. (1969). The emergence of existential psychology. In R. May (Ed.), *Existential psychology* (2nd ed., pp. 1–48). New York: McGraw-Hill.

May, R. (1982). The problem of evil: An open letter to Carl Rogers, *Journal of Humanistic Psychology, 22,* 10–21.

Mayer, A. (2014). *Sites of the unconscious: Hypnosis and the emergence of the psychoanalytic setting* (C. Barber, Trans.). Chicago: University of Chicago Press.

Mayer, S. J. (2005). The early evolution of Jean Piaget's clinical method. *History of Psychology, 8,* 362–382.

Mayrhauser, R. T. von. (1989). Making intelligence functional: Walter Dill Scott and applied psychological testing in World War I. *Journal of the History of the Behavioral Sciences, 25,* 60–72.

Mays, W. (1998). Genetic explanation in Husserl and Piaget. *New Ideas in Psychology, 16,* 1–10.

McCarthy-Jones, S. (2011). Seeing the unseen, hearing the unsaid: Hallucinations, psychology, and St. Thomas Aquinas. *Mental Health, Religion & Culture, 14,* 353–369.

McCauley, C., & Rozin, P. (2003). Solomon Asch: Scientist and humanist. In G. A. Kimble & M. Wertheimer (Eds.), *Portraits of pioneers in psychology* (Vol. 5, pp. 249–261). Washington, DC: American Psychological Association.

McCool, G. A. (1990). Why St. Thomas stays alive. *International Philosophical Quarterly, 30,* 275–287.

McDaniel, S., & Kaslow, N. J. (2015, July 24). Letter to APA members from APA President-Elect Susan McDaniel, PhD, and APA Past President Nadine J. Kaslow, PhD, ABPP, members of the Special Committee for the Independent Review. Retrieved January 5, 2016 from www.apa.org/independent-review/letter-members-apology.pdf

McDermott, J. J. (Ed.). (1968). *The writings of William James.* New York: Modern Library.

McDougall, W. (1905). *Physiological psychology.* London: J. M. Dent.

McDougall, W. (1908). *An introduction to social psychology.* Mineola, NY: Dover.

McDougall, W. (1923). *Outline of psychology.* Boston: Scribner.

McDougall, W. (1926a). *An introduction to social psychology.* Boston: Luce.

McDougall, W. (1926b). Men or robots? *Pedagogical Seminary, 33,* 71–102.

McDougall, W. (1960). *An introduction to social psychology.* London: Methuen. (Original work published 1908).

McFarland, S., Webb, M., & Brown, D. (2012). All humanity is my ingroup: A measure and studies of identification with all humanity. *Journal of Personality and Social Psychology, 103,* 830–853.

McGaugh, J. L. (2000). Memory: A century of consolidation. *Science, 287,* 248–251.

McHenry, L. C. (1969). *Garrison's history of neurology.* Springfield, IL: Charles C. Thomas.

McInerny, R. (1990). *A first glance at St. Thomas Aquinas.* Notre Dame, IN: University of Notre Dame Press.

McKerchar, T. L., Morris, E. K., & Smith, N. G. (2011). A quantitative analysis and natural history of B. F. Skinner's coauthoring practices. *The Behavior Analyst, 34,* 75–91.

McLafferty, C. L., Jr., & Kirylo, J. D. (2001). Prior positive psychologists proposed personality and spiritual growth. *American Psychologist, 56,* 84–85.

McReynolds, P. (1987). Lightner Witmer: Little known founder of clinical psychology. *American Psychologist, 42,* 849–858.

McReynolds, P. (1996). Lightner Witmer: A centennial tribute. *American Psychologist, 51,* 237–240.

McReynolds, P. (1997). *Lightner Witmer: His life and times.* Washington, DC: American Psychological Association.

McWhirter, P. T., & McWhirter, J. J. (1997). Lightner Witmer: Father and grandfather? *American Psychologist, 52,* 275.

Meade, M. (1979). *Stealing heaven: The love story of Heloise and Abelard.* New York: Soho Press.

Medawar, P. B. (1984). *The limits of science.* New York: Harper & Row.

Meehan, W. (2009). Partem totius naturae esse: Spinoza's alternative to the mutual incomprehension of physicalism and mentalism in psychology. *Journal of Theoretical and Philosophical Psychology, 29,* 47–59.

Meerloo, J. A. M. (1951). The crime of menticide. *American Journal of Psychiatry, 107,* 594–598.

Meerloo, J. A. M. (1956). *Rape of the mind: The psychology of thought control, menticide, and brainwashing.* Cleveland, OH: World Publishing Company.

Meischner-Metge, A. (2010). Gustav Theodore Fechner: Life and work in the mirror of his diary. *History of Psychology, 13,* 411–423.

Meissner, W. W. (1984). *Psychoanalysis and religious experience.* New Haven, CT: Yale University Press.

Melville, H. (1976). *Moby-Dick, or the whale.* New York: Norton. (Original work published 1851)

Memon, A., Mastroberardino, S., & Fraser, J. (2008). Münsterberg's legacy: What does eyewitness research tell us about the reliability of eyewitness testimony? *Applied Cognitive Psychology, 22,* 841–851.

Mendelowitz, E. (2008). Meditations on dissociation: Kristina and the enigmatic self. In K. J. Schneider (Ed.), *Existential-integrative psychotherapy: Guideposts to the core of practice* (pp. 245–266). New York: Routledge.

Merchant, C. (1979). The vitalism of Anne Conway: Its impact on Leibniz's concept of the monad. *Journal of the History of Philosophy, 17,* 255–269.

Meredith, A. (1986). Later philosophy. In J. Boardman, J. Griffin, & O. Murray (Eds.), *The Oxford history of the classical world* (pp. 708–714). New York: Oxford University Press.

Merenda, P. F. (1987). Toward a four-factor theory of temperament and/or personality. *Journal of Personality Assessment, 51,* 367–374.

Merlan, P. (1967). Plotinus. In P. Edwards (Ed.), *The encyclopedia of philosophy* (Vol. 6, pp. 351–359). New York: Macmillan and Free Press.

Mesoudi, A., Magid, K., & Hussain, D. (2016). How do people become W.E.I.R.D.? Migration reveals the cultural transmission mechanisms underlying variation in psychological processes. *PLoS ONE, 11,* Article e0147162.

Messias, E. (2014). Standing on the shoulders of Pinel, Freud, and Kraepelin: A historiometric inquiry into the histories of psychiatry. *Journal of Nervous and Mental Disease, 202,* 788–792.

Meymandi, A. (2010). Baruch Spinoza: The philosopher's philosopher. *Psychiatry, 7,* 47–50.

Michell, J. (1999). *Measurement in psychology: A critical history of a methodological concept.* New York: Cambridge University Press.

Michelmore, P. (1962). *Einstein, profile of the man.* New York: Dodd, Mead.

Midgley, N. (2012). Peter Heller's A Child Analysis with Anna Freud: The significance of the case for the history of child psychoanalysis. *Journal of the American Psychoanalytic Association, 60,* 45–70.

Milar, K. S. (1999). "A coarse and clumsy tool": Helen Thompson Wooley and the Cincinnati Vocation Bureau. *History of Psychology, 2,* 219–235.

Miles, W. (1949). James Rowland Angell, 1869–1949, Psychologist-educator. *Science, 110,* 1–4.

Milgram, S. (1963). Behavioral study of obedience. *The Journal of Abnormal and Social Psychology, 67,* 371–378.

Mill, J. S. (1969). *Autobiography* (J. Stillinger, Ed.). Boston: Houghton Mifflin. (Original work published 1873)

Mill, J. S. (1974). A system of logic ratiocinative and inductive. In J. M. Robson (Ed.), *Collected works of John Stuart Mill* (Vol. 8). Toronto: Routledge & Kegan Paul. (Original work published 1843)

Mill, J. S. (1988). *The subjection of women.* Indianapolis, IN/Cambridge, MA: Hackett. (Original work published 1869)

Miller, J. (1981). Interpretations of Freud's Jewishness, 1924–1974. *Journal of the History of the Behavioral Sciences, 17,* 357–374.

Millon, T. (2012). On the history and future study of personality and its disorders. *Annual Review of Clinical Psychology, 8,* 1–19.

Mills, J. (2006). Reflections on the death drive. *Psychoanalytic Psychology, 23,* 373–382.

Mills, J. (2013). Freedom and determinism. *The Humanistic Psychologist, 41,* 101–118.

Mills, J. A. (1988). The genesis of Hull's Principles of Behavior. *Journal of the History of the Behavioral Sciences, 24,* 392–401.

Mills, J. A. (1998). *Control: A history of behavioral psychology.* New York: New York University Press.

Mills, J. A. (2010). Hallucinogens as hard science: The adrenochrome hypothesis for the biogenesis of schizophrenia. *History of Psychology, 13,* 178–195.

Mintz, S. I. (1962). *The hunting of Leviathan.* Cambridge, UK: Cambridge University Press.

Miranda, M., Slachevsky, A., & Garcia-Borreguero, D. (2010). Did Immanuel Kant have dementia with Lewy bodies and REM behavior disorder? *Sleep Medicine, 11,* 586–588.

Misiak, H. K., & Sexton, V. S. (1966). *History of psychology: An overview.* New York: Grune & Stratton.

Mitchell, J. (2014). *Individualism and moral character: Karen Horney's depth psychology.* New Brunswick, NJ: Transaction Publishers.

Mitchell, P. B. (1999). On the 50th anniversary of John Cade's discovery of the anti-manic effect of lithium. *Australian and New Zealand Journal of Psychiatry, 33,* 623–628.

Miyata, Y. (2009). Pavlov's Nobel Prize in physiology or medicine. *Japanese Journal of Physiological Psychology and Psychophysiology, 27,* 225–234.

Mohl, J. C. (2012). Seeing the future by looking at the past: Comment on Kirsch et al. *Contemporary Hypnosis & Integrative Therapy, 29,* 169–174.

Molnár, Z., & Brown, R. E. (2010). Insights into the life and work of Sir Charles Sherrington. *Nature Reviews Neuroscience, 11,* 429–436.

Monahan, J., & Walker, L. (1994). *Social science in law: Cases and materials* (3rd ed.). Westbury, NY: Foundation Press.

Monson, C. M., Friedman, M. J., & La Bash, H. A. (2007). A psychological history of PTSD. In M. J. Friedman, T. M. Keane, & P. A. Resick (Eds.), *Handbook of PTSD: Science and practice* (pp. 37–52). New York: Guilford Press.

Montaigne, M. (1960). Apology for Raimond Sebond. In D. M. Frame (Trans.), *The complete essays of Montaigne* (Vol. 2, pp. 112–308). Garden City, NY: Doubleday.

Moore, J. (2005). Some historical and conceptual background to the development of B. F. Skinner's "Radical Behaviorism"—Part I. *Mind and Behavior, 26,* 65–94.

Moore, J. (2011). Behaviorism. *The Psychological Record, 61,* 449–464.

Moore, J. (2013). Tutorial: Cognitive psychology as a radical behaviorist views it. *The Psychological Record, 63,* 667–679.

Moore, J. (2015). Methodological behaviorism from the standpoint of a radical behaviorist. *The Behavior Analyst, 36,* 197–208.

Moore, K. G. (1946). Theory of imagination in Plotinus. *Journal of Psychology, 22,* 41–51.

Mora, G. (2008). Mental disturbances, unusual mental states, and their interpretation during the Middle Ages. In E. R. Wallace, IV & J. Gach (Eds.), *History of psychiatry and medical psychology: With an epilogue on psychiatry and the mind-body relation* (pp. 199–226). New York: Springer Science + Business Media.

Morawski, J. G. (1983). Hugo Münsterberg on the possibilities for psychology and society. *American Psychologist, 38,* 1259–1260.

Morawski, J. G., & Bayer, B. M. (2013). Social psychology. In D. K. Freedheim & I. B. Weiner (Eds.), *Handbook of psychology, Vol. 1: History of psychology* (2nd ed., pp. 248–278). Hoboken, NJ: John Wiley & Sons Inc.

Moray, N. (2007). Attention: From history to application. In A. F. Kramer, D. A. Wiegmann, & A. Kirlik (Eds.), *Attention: From theory to practice* (pp. 3–15). New York: Oxford University Press.

Morens, D. M. (1999). Death of a president. *New England Journal of Medicine, 341,* 1845–1849.

Morgan, C. L. (1977). *Comparative psychology.* Washington, DC: University Publications of America. (Original work published in 1894)

Morgan, C. T. (1968). Karl S. Lashley. In D. L. Sills (Ed.), *International encyclopedia of the social sciences* (Vol. 9, pp. 27–30). New York: Macmillan.

Morris, D. (1967). *The naked ape.* New York: McGraw-Hill.

Morris, E. A., & Todd, J. T. (1999). Watsonian behaviorism. In W. O'Donohue & R. Kitchener (Eds.), *Handbook of behaviorism* (pp. 15–69). San Diego, CA: Academic Press.

Morris, E. K., Smith, N. G., & Altus, D. E. (2005). B. F. Skinner's contributions to applied behavior analysis. *The Behavior Analyst, 28,* 99–131.

Moses/Morse, J. (January 7, 1907; January 25, 1907). Josiah Morse: Student correspondence, B1-6-8. G. Stanley Hall Papers, Clark University Archives.

Moses/Morse, J. (September 6, 1920). Josiah Morse: Student correspondence, B1-6-8. G. Stanley Hall Papers, Clark University Archives.

Moskowitz, M. J. (1977). Hugo Münsterberg: A study in the history of applied psychology. *American Psychologist, 32,* 824–842.

Moss, D. (2015). The roots and genealogy of humanistic psychology. In K. J. Schneider, J. F. Pierson, & J. F. T. Bugental (Eds.), *The handbook of humanistic psychology:*

Theory, research, and practice (2nd ed., pp. 3–18). Thousand Oaks, CA: Sage Publications.

Mott, V. W. (2015). Mary Parker Follett: A paradox of adult learner and educator. In S. Imel & G. T. Bersch (Eds.), *No small lives: Handbook of North American early women adult educators, 1925–1950* (pp. 125–132). Charlotte, NC: Information Age Publishing.

Mozans (pseudonym for) Zahm, J. A. (1913). *Women in science*. New York: Appleton.

Mruk, C. J. (1989). Phenomenological psychology and the computer revolution: Friend, foe or opportunity? *Journal of Phenomenological Psychology, 20,* 20–39.

Muckle, J. T. (Trans.). (1992). *The story of Abelard's adversities*. Toronto: Pontifical Institute of Medieval Studies.

Müller, G. E., & Pilzecker, A. (1900). Experimental contributions to the theory of memory. In S. Diamond (Ed.), *The roots of psychology* (pp. 271–273). New York: Basic Books.

Müller, U., Fletcher, P. C., & Steinberg, H. (2006). The origin of pharmacopsychology: Emil Kraepelin's experiments in Leipzig, Dorpat and Heidelberg (1882–1892). *Psychopharmacology, 184,* 131–138.

Mumford, L. (1934). *Techniques and civilization*. New York: Harcourt Brace.

Munroe, R. L. (1955). *Schools of psychoanalytic thought*. New York: Holt, Rinehart and Winston.

Münsterberg, H. (1908). *On the witness stand: Essays on psychology and crime*. New York: Clark Boardman.

Münsterberg, H. (1909). *Psychotherapy*. New York: Moffat, Yard.

Münsterberg, H. (1913). *Psychology and industrial efficiency*. New York: Houghton Mifflin.

Münsterberg, H. (1916). *The photoplay: A psychological study*. New York: Appleton.

Murguia, E., & Díaz, K. (2015). The philosophical foundations of cognitive behavioral therapy: Stoicism, Buddhism, Taoism, and Existentialism. *Journal of Evidence-Based Psychotherapies, 15,* 37–50.

Murphy, C. (2012). *God's jury: The inquisition and the making of the modern world*. Boston: Houghton Mifflin Harcourt.

Murphy, G. (1963). Robert Sessions Woodworth, 1869–1962. *American Psychologist, 18,* 131–133.

Murphy, G., & Murphy, L. B. (Eds.). (1968). *Asian psychology*. New York: Basic Books.

Murray, D. J. (1993). A perspective for viewing the history of psychophysics. *Behavioral and Brain Sciences, 16,* 115–186.

Murray, D. J. (1995). *Gestalt psychology and the cognitive revolution*. New York: Harvester Wheatsheaf.

Murray, D. J., & Farahmand, B. (1998). Gestalt theory and evolutionary psychology. In R. W. Rieber & K. Salzinger (Eds.), *Psychology: Theoretical-historical perspectives* (2nd ed., pp. 255–287). Washington, DC: American Psychological Association.

Murray, D. J., & Ross, H. E. (1982). Vives (1538) on memory and recall. *Canadian Psychology, 23,* 22–31.

Musikantow, R. (2011). Thinking in circles: Power and responsibility in hypnosis. *American Journal of Clinical Hypnosis, 54,* 83–85.

Nadel, L. (2013). Cognitive maps. In D. Waller & L. Nadel (Eds.), *Handbook of spatial cognition* (pp. 155–171). Washington, DC: American Psychological Association.

National Science Teachers Association. (2013). NTSA position statement: The teaching of evolution. Retrieved June 1, 2016 from www.nsta.org/docs/PositionStatement_Evolution.pdf

Natsoulas, T. (1990). Reflective seeing: An exploration in the company of Edmund Husserl and James J. Gibson. *Journal of Phenomenological Psychology, 21,* 1–31.

Navarick, D. J. (2012). Historical psychology and the Milgrim paradigm: Test of an experimentally derived model of defiance using accounts of massacres by Nazi Reserve Police Battalion 101. *Psychological Record, 62,* 133–154.

Neacsiu, A. D., Ward-Ciesielski, E. F., & Linehan, M. M. (2012). Emerging approaches to counseling intervention: Dialectical behavior therapy. *The Counseling Psychologist, 40,* 1003–1032.

Neary, F. (2001). A question of "peculiar importance": George Croom Robertson, *Mind* and the changing relationship between British psychology and philosophy. In G. C. Bunn, A. D. Lovie, & G. D. Richards (Eds.), *Psychology in Britain: Historical essays and personal reflections* (pp. 54–71). Leicester, UK: The British Psychological Society.

Neider, C. (Ed.). (1959). *The autobiography of Mark Twain*. New York: Harper.

Neisser, U. (1967). *Cognitive psychology*. New York: Appleton-Century-Crofts.

Neisser, U. (1976). *Cognition and reality*. San Francisco: Freeman.

Neisser, U. (1982). *Memory observed: Remembering in natural contexts*. New York: Freeman.

Nelson-Pallmeyer, J. (2003). *Is religion killing us? Violence in the Bible and the Quran*. New York: Trinity Press International.

Neuschatz, J. S., Lampinen, J. M., Toglia, M. P., Payne, D. G., & Cisneros, E. P. (2007). False memory research: History, theory, and applied implications.

In M. P. Toglia, J. D. Read, D. F. Ross, & R. C. L. Lindsay (Eds.), *The handbook of eyewitness psychology, Vol. I: Memory for events* (pp. 239–260). Mahwah, NJ: Lawrence Erlbaum Associates.

Newbold, S. P., & Schortgen, A. C. (2011). Connecting the past with the present: Moses Maimonides' contribution to democratic theory, public administration, and civil society. *Administration & Society, 43,* 147–170.

Newell, A. (1985). Duncker on thinking: An inquiry into progress in cognition. In S. Koch & D. Leary (Eds.), *A century of psychology as science* (pp. 392–419). New York: McGraw-Hill.

Newirth, J. (2015). Psychoanalysis' past, present, and future: Sherlock Holmes, Sir Lancelot, and the Wizard of Oz. *Psychoanalytic Psychology, 32,* 307–320.

Newman, E. J., & Loftus, E. F. (2012). Updating Ebbinghaus on the science of memory. *Europe's Journal of Psychology, 8,* 209–216.

Newman, S. (2006). "Study of several involuntary functions of the apparatus of movement, gripping, and voice" by Jean-Marc Gaspard Itard (1825). *History of Psychiatry, 17,* 333–339.

Newman, S. (2010). J-M. G. Itard's 1825 study: Movement and the science of the human mind. *History of Psychiatry, 21,* 67–78.

Nicholson, I. A. M. (1998). Gordon Allport, character, and the "culture of personality," 1897–1937. *History of Psychology, 1,* 52–68.

Nicholson, I. A. M. (2000). "A coherent datum of perception": Gordon Allport, Floyd Allport, and the politics of "personality." *Journal of the History of the Behavioral Sciences, 36,* 463–470.

Nicholson, I. A. M. (2001). "Giving up maleness": Abraham Maslow, masculinity, and the boundaries of psychology. *History of Psychology, 4,* 79–91.

Nicholson, R. A. (1999). Forensic assessment. In R. Roesch, S. D. Hart, & J. R. P. Ogloff (Eds.), *Psychology and the law: The state of the discipline* (pp. 121–173). New York: Kluwer Academic/Plenum.

Nicholson, S. (1995). The expression of emotional distress in Old English prose and verse. *Culture, Medicine and Psychiatry, 19,* 327–338.

Nicolas, S., Andrieu, B., Sanitioso, R. B., Vincent, R., & Murray, D. J. (2015). Alfred Binet and Crépieux-Jamin: Can intelligence be measured scientifically by graphology? *L'Année Psychologique, 115,* 3–52.

Nicolas, S., Coubart, A., & Lubart, T. (2014). The program of individual psychology (1895–1896) by Alfred Binet and Victor Henri. *L'Année Psychologique, 114,* 5–60.

Nicolas, S., Gounden, Y., & Sanitioso, R. B. (2014). Alfred Binet, founder of the science of testimony and psycho-legal science. *L'Année Psychologique, 114,* 209–229.

Nicolas, S., & Sanitioso, R. B. (2012). Alfred Binet and experimental psychology at the Sorbonne laboratory. *History of Psychology, 15,* 328–363.

Nicolas, S., & Söderlund, H. (2005). The project of an international congress of psychology by J. Ochorowicz (1881). *International Journal of Psychology, 40,* 395–406.

Nielsen, M. E., Hatton, A. T., & Donahue, M. J. (2013). Religiousness, social psychology, and behavior. In R. F. Paloutzian & C. L. Park (Eds.), *Handbook of the psychology of religion and spirituality* (2nd ed., pp. 312–329). New York: Guilford Press.

Nietzel, M. T., McCarthy, D. M., & Kern, M. J. (1999). Juries: The current state of the empirical literature. In R. Roesch, S. D. Hart, & J. R. P. Ogloff (Eds.), *Psychology and law: The state of the discipline* (pp. 23–52). New York: Kluwer Academic/Plenum.

Nietzsche, F. (1956). *The birth of tragedy and the genealogy of morals.* New York: Anchor Books. (Original work published 1887)

Nightmare in Jonestown. (1978, December 4). *Time, 112*(23), 16–21.

Nikolaeva, V. V. (2011). B.W. Zeigarnik and pathopsychology. *Psychology in Russia: State of the Art, 4,* 176–192.

Nissim-Sabat, M. (1999). Phenomenology and mental disorders: Heidegger or Husserl? *Philosophy, Psychiatry, & Psychology, 6,* 100–104.

Noel, P. S., & Carlson, E. T. (1970). Origins of the word "phrenology." *American Journal of Psychiatry, 127,* 694–697.

Noel, P. S., & Carlson, E. T. (1973). The faculty psychology of Benjamin Rush. *Journal of the History of the Behavioral Sciences, 9,* 369–377.

Norcross, J. C., Karpiak, C. P., & Santoro, S. O. (2005). Clinical psychologists across the years: The division of clinical psychology from 1960 to 2003. *Journal of Clinical Psychology, 61,* 1467–1483.

Norena, C. G. (1970). *Juan Luis Vives.* The Hague: Nijhoff.

Norena, C. G. (1975). *Studies in Spanish Renaissance thought.* The Hague: Nijhoff.

Norman, D. A. (1980). Twelve issues for cognitive science. *Cognitive Science, 4,* 1–32.

North, M. S., & Fiske, S. T. (2012). A history of social cognition. In A. W. Kruglanski & W. Stroebe (Eds.), *Handbook of the history of social psychology* (pp. 81–99). New York: Psychology Press.

Northoff, G. (2012). Immanuel Kant's mind and the brain's resting state. *Trends in Cognitive Sciences, 16,* 356–359.

Novak, M. (1970). *The experience of nothingness.* New York: Harper & Row.

Nutton, V. (2006). The rise of medicine. In R. Porter (Ed.), *The Cambridge history of medicine* (pp. 46–70). New York: Cambridge University Press.

Obiols, J. E., & Barrios, G. E. (2009). The historical roots of Theory of Mind: The work of James Mark Baldwin. *History of Psychiatry, 20,* 377–392.

O'Brien, G. V. (2013). Margaret Sanger and the Nazis: How many degrees of separation? *Social Work, 58,* 285–287.

O'Brien, M. (2010). Re-assessing the 'affair': The Heidegger controversy revisited. *The Social Science Journal, 47,* 1–20.

O'Connell, A. N. (1990). Karen Horney (1885–1952). In A. N. O'Connell & N. F. Russo (Eds.), *Women in psychology: A bio-bibliographic sourcebook* (pp. 184–196). New York: Greenwood Press.

O'Connell, A. N., & Russo, N. F. (Eds.). (1983). *Models of achievement: Reflections of eminent women in psychology.* New York: Columbia University Press.

O'Connell, A. N., & Russo, N. F. (Eds.). (1988). *Models of achievement: Reflections of eminent women in psychology* (Vol. 2). Hillsdale, NJ: Erlbaum.

O'Connell, A. N., & Russo, N. F. (Eds.). (1990). *Women in psychology: A bio-bibliograhic sourcebook.* New York: Greenwood Press.

Oesterdiekhoff, G. W. (2013). Relevance of Piagetian cross-cultural psychology to the humanities and social sciences. *American Journal of Psychology, 126,* 477–492.

Ogden, R. M. (1951). Oswald Külpe and the Würzburg school. *American Journal of Psychology, 64,* 4–19.

Ogloff, J. P. R., & Finkelman, D. (1999). Psychology and the law: An overview. In R. Roesch, S. D. Hart, & J. R. P. Ogloff (Eds.), *Psychology and the law: The state of the discipline* (pp. 1–20). New York: Kluwer Academic/ Plenum.

O'Hara, M. (1995). Carl Rogers: Scientist and mystic. *Journal of Humanistic Psychology, 35,* 40–53.

Okin, S. S. (Ed.). (1988). *The subjection of women.* Indianapolis/Cambridge: Hackett. (Original work published 1869)

Olds, J. (1954). A neural model for sign-gestalt theory. *Psychological Review, 61,* 59–72.

Ollendick, T. H., & Muris, P. (2015). The scientific legacy of Little Hans and Little Albert: Future directions for research on specific phobias in youth. *Journal of Clinical Child and Adolescent Psychology, 44,* 689–706.

O'Neil, W. M. (1984). The Wundt's myths. *Australian Journal of Psychology, 36,* 285–289.

O'Neil, W. M. (1995). American behaviorism: A historical and critical analysis. *Theory and Psychology, 5,* 285–305.

Oon, Z. (2008). A critical presentation of the life and work of Franz Anton Mesmer MD and its influence on the development of hypnosis. *European Journal of Clinical Hypnosis, 8,* 32–40.

Ophuls, W. (2011). *Plato's revenge: Politics in the age of ecology.* Cambride, MA: MIT Press.

Orgel, S. (1990). The future of psychoanalysis. *Psychoanalytic Quarterly, 59,* 1–20.

O'Roark, A. M. (2007). The best of consulting psychology 1900–2000: Insider perspectives. *Consulting Psychology Journal: Practice and Research, 59,* 189–202.

Ortiz, K. (2015). Albert Bandura. In D. L. Dobbert & T. X. Mackey (Eds.), *Deviance: Theories on behaviors that defy social norms* (pp. 119–124). Santa Barbara, CA: Praeger/ABC-CLIO.

O'Shea, G., & Bashore, T. R., Jr. (2012). The vital role of the American Journal of Psychology in the early and continuing history of mental chronometry. *American Journal of Psychology, 125,* 435–448.

O'Sullivan, J. J., & Quevillon, R. P. (1992). 40 years later: Is the Boulder model still alive? *American Psychologist, 47,* 67–70.

Otte, M. (2009). The analytic/synthetic distinction in Kant and Bolzano. In B. Sriraman & S. Goodchild (Eds.), *Relatively and philosophically earnest: Festschrift in honor of Paul Ernest's 65th birthday* (pp. 39–55). Charlotte, NC: Information Age Publishing.

Overholser, J. C. (2010). Psychotherapy that strives to encourage social interest: A simulated interview with Alfred Adler. *Journal of Psychotherapy Integration, 20,* 347–363.

Oviedo, G. L. (2012). Colombian approaches to psychology in the 19th century. *History of Psychology, 15,* 291–301.

Pace, E. A. (1921). In memory of Wilhelm Wundt. *Psychological Review, 28,* 159–162.

Packer, I. K., & Borum, R. (2013). Forensic training and practice. In R. K. Otto & I. B. Weiner (Eds.), *Handbook of psychology, Vol. 11: Forensic psychology* (2nd ed., pp. 16–36). Hoboken, NJ: John Wiley & Sons.

Pagels, E. (2003). *Beyond belief: The secret gospel of Thomas.* New York: Random House.

Palha, A. P., & Esteves, M. F. (1997). The origin of dementia praecox. *Schizophrenia Research, 28,* 99–103.

Palma, J.-A., & Palma, F. (2012). Neurology and Don Quixote. *European Neurology, 68,* 247–257.

Palmer, D. C. (2006). On Chomsky's appraisal of

Skinner's Verbal Behavior: A half century of misunderstanding. *The Behavior Analyst, 29,* 253–267.

Palmieri, P. (2012). Signals, cochlear mechanics and pragmatism: A new vista on human hearing? *Journal of Experimental & Theoretical Artificial Intelligence, 24,* 527–545.

Panofsky, A. (2014). *Misbehaving science: Controversy and the development of behavior genetics.* Chicago: University of Chicago Press.

Panourias, I. G., Stranjalis, G., Stravrinou, L. C., & Sakas, D. E. (2011). The Hellenic and Hippocratic origins of the spinal terminology. *Journal of the History of the Neurosciences, 20,* 177–187.

Panteliadis, C., Panteliadis, P., & Vassilyadi, F. (2013). Hallmarks in the history of cerebral palsey: From antiquity to mid-20th century. *Brain and Development, 35,* 285–292.

Papanicolaou, A. C. (1989). *Emotion: A reconsideration of the somatic theory.* New York: Gordon and Breach.

Paris, B. J. (1991). A Horneyan approach to literature. *American Journal of Psychoanalysis, 51,* 319–337.

Pariser, D. A. (2008). Rudolf Julius Arnheim (1904–2007). *American Psychologist, 63,* 55.

Park, R. J. (2010). Prologue: Reaffirming Mary Wollstonecraft! Extending the dialogue on women, sport, and physical activities. *The International Journal of the History of Sport, 27,* 1105–1112.

Passmore, H., & Howell, A. (2014). Eco-existential positive psychology: Experiences in nature, existential anxieties, and well-being. *The Humanistic Psychologist, 42,* 370–388.

Pastore, N. (1965). Samuel Bailey's critique of Berkeley's theory of vision. *Journal of the History of the Behavioral Sciences, 1,* 321–337.

Patihis, L., Ho, L. Y., Tingen, I. W., Lilienfeld, S. O., & Loftus, E. F. (2014). Are the "memory wars" over? A scientist-practitioner gap in beliefs about repressed memory. *Psychological Science, 25,* 519–530.

Patrick, G. T. W. (1914). The psychology of relaxation. *Popular Science Monthly, 84,* 590–604.

Pauley, P. J. (1986). G. Stanley Hall and his successors: A history of the first half-century of psychology at Johns Hopkins. In S. H. Hulse & B. F. Green, Jr. (Eds.), *One hundred years of psychological research in America* (pp. 21–51). Baltimore: Johns Hopkins University Press.

Pavlov, I. P. (1928). *Lectures on conditioned reflexes* (Vol. 1) (W. H. Gantt, Trans. & Ed.). New York: International.

Pavlov, I. P. (1941). *Lectures on conditioned reflexes* (Vol. 2) (W. H. Gantt, Trans. & Ed.). New York: International.

Pavlov, I. P. (1955). *I. P. Pavlov: Selected works* (J. Gibbons, Ed., S. Belsky, Trans.). Moscow: Foreign Languages Publishing House.

Payne, C., & Sacks, O. (2009). *Asylum: Inside the closed world of mental hospitals.* Cambridge, MA: MIT Press.

Peach, B. (1982). Leviathan. In F. N. Magill (Ed.), *World philosophy* (Vol. 2, pp. 839–846). Englewood Cliffs, NJ: Salem Press.

Pearce, J. M. S. (2009a). Marie-Jean-Pierre Flourens (1794–1867) and cortical localization. *European Neurology, 61,* 311–314.

Pearce, J. M. S. (2009b). The ophthalmoscope: Helmholtz's augenspiegel. *European Neurology, 61,* 244–249.

Pearce, J. M. S. (2015). Early observations on facial palsy. *Journal of the History of the Neurosciences, 24,* 319–325.

Pearson, K. (1897). *The chances of death and other studies in evolution.* New York: Edward Arnold.

Pearson, K. (1914). *The life, letters, and labors of Francis Galton* (Vol. 1). London: Cambridge University Press.

Peck, C. (2013). Freedom through control: B. F. Skinner and classroom management theory. In B. J. Irby, G. Brown, R. Lara-Alecio, & S. Jackson (Eds.), *The handbook of educational theories* (pp. 691–698). Charlotte, NC: Information Age Publishing.

Pelusi, N. (2016). Rational emotive behavior therapy. In I. Marini & M. A. Stebnicki (Eds.), *The professional counselor's desk reference* (2nd ed., pp. 207–210). New York: Springer Publishing Co.

Penfield, W. (1952). Memory mechanisms. *Archives of Neurology and Psychiatry, 67,* 178–198.

Perloff, R., & Naman, J. L. (1996). Lillian Gilbreth: Tireless advocate for a general psychology. In G. A. Kimble, C. A. Boneau, & M. Wertheimer (Eds.), *Portraits of pioneers in psychology* (Vol. 2, pp. 107–116). Washington, DC: American Psychological Association.

Perper, T. (2010). Will she or won't she: The dynamics of flirtation in Western philosophy. *Sexuality & Culture, 14,* 33–43.

Perry, G. (2013). *Behind the shock machine: The untold story of the notorious Milgram psychology experiments.* New York: New Press.

Perry, R. B. (1954). *The thought and character of William James: Briefer version.* New York: George Braziller.

Peters, R. S. (Ed.). (1965). *Brett's history of psychology.* Cambridge, MA: MIT Press.

Petersen, C. A. (2007). A historical look at psychology and the scientist-practitioner model. *American Behavioral Scientist, 50,* 758–765.

Pettit, M. (2016). Historical time in the age of big data: Cultural psychology, historical change, and the

Google Books Ngram Viewer. *History of Psychology, 19,* 141–153.

Pettit, M., & Davidson, I. (2014). Can the history of psychology have an impact? *Theory and Psychology, 24,* 709–716.

Petzold, M. (1987). The social history of Chinese psychology. In M. G. Ash & W. R. Woodward (Eds.), *Psychology in twentieth-century thought and society* (pp. 213–231). Cambridge, UK: Cambridge University Press.

Phillips, A. (2014). *Becoming Freud: The making of a psychoanalyst.* New Haven, CT: Yale University Press.

Phillips, L. (2000). Recontextualizing Kenneth B. Clark: An Afrocentric perspective on the paradoxical legacy of a model psychologist-activist. *History of Psychology, 3,* 142–167.

Piaget, J. (1952). Jean Piaget. In E. G. Boring (Ed.), *A history of psychology in autobiography* (Vol. 4, pp. 237–256). New York: Russell and Russell.

Piaget, J., & Garcia, J. (1989). *Psychogenesis and the history of science* (H. Feider, Trans.). New York: Columbia University Press. (Original work published 1983)

Pickenhain, L. (1999). The importance of I. P. Pavlov for the development of neuroscience. *Integrative Physiological & Behavioral Science, 34,* 85–89.

Pickren, W. E. (2012). Internationalizing the history of psychology course in the USA. In F. T. L. Leong, W. E. Pickren, M. M. Leach, & A. J. Marsella (Eds.), *Internationalizing the psychology curriculum in the United States* (pp. 11–28). New York: Springer Science + Business Media.

Pickren, W. E., & Dewsbury, D. A. (2002). *Evolving perspectives on the history of psychology.* Washington, DC: American Psychological Association.

Pickren, W. E., & Fowler, R. D. (2003). Professional organizations. In I. B. Weiner (Series Ed.) & D. K. Freedheim (Vol. Ed.), *Handbook of psychology, Vol. 1: The history of psychology* (pp. 535–554). New York: Wiley.

Pilcher, L. D. (Executive Producer), & Garner, K. V. (Director). (2004). *Iron Jawed Angels* [Motion Picture]. New York: Home Box Office Inc.

Pind, J. L. (2013). *Edgar Rubin and psychology in Denmark: Figure and ground.* Cham, Switzerland: Springer.

Pind, J. L. (2016). The psychologist as a poet: Kierkegaard and psychology in 19th century Copenhagen. *History of Psychology, 19,* 352–370.

Pinel, P. (1977). A treatise on insanity (D. D. Davis, Trans.). In D. N. Robinson (Ed.), *Significant contributions to the history of psychology, 1750–1920:* Series C. (Vol. III). Washington, DC: University Publications of America. (Original work published 1806)

Pivnicki, D. (1969). The beginnings of psychotherapy. *Journal of the History of the Behavioral Sciences, 5,* 238–247.

Plato. (1961a). Apology (H. Tredennick, Trans.). In E. Hamilton & H. Cairns (Eds.), *The collected dialogues of Plato including the letters* (pp. 3–26). Princeton, NJ: Princeton University Press.

Plato. (1961b). The Phaedo (H. Tredennick, Trans.). In E. Hamilton & H. Cairns (Eds.), *Plato: The collected dialogues, including the letters* (pp. 40–98). Princeton, NJ: Princeton University Press.

Plekhanov, G. V. (1967). *Essays in the history of materialism.* New York: H. Fertig.

Plotinus. (1956). *The Enneads* (S. MacKenna, Trans.). London: Faber & Faber.

Plummer, B. L. (1970). Benjamin Rush and the Negro. *American Journal of Psychiatry, 127,* 793–798.

Poffenberger, A. T. (1962). Robert Sessions Woodworth: 1869–1962. *American Journal of Psychology, 75,* 677–689.

Pollard, J. H. (2012). Mathematical theory of population. In N. Balakrishnan (Ed.), *Methods and applications of statistics in the social and behavioral sciences* (pp. 242–248). Hoboken, NJ: John Wiley & Sons, Inc.

Poma, A. (2013). *The impossibility and necessity of theodicy: The "essais" of Leibniz.* Dordrecht: Springer.

Pombo, O., Torres, J. M., Symons, J., & Rahman, S. (Eds.). (2014). *Special sciences and the unity of science.* New York: Springer.

Pomerantz, J. R. (2006). Colour as a Gestalt: Pop out with basic features and with conjunctions. *Visual Cognition, 14,* 619–628.

Popkin, R. H. (1967). Michel Eyquem de Montainge. In P. Edwards (Ed.), *The encyclopedia of philosophy* (Vol. 5, pp. 366–368). New York: Macmillan.

Popkin, R. H. (1979). *The history of skepticism from Erasmus to Spinoza.* Berkeley: University of California Press.

Poppen, R. (1996). *Joseph Wolpe.* Thousand Oaks, CA: Sage.

Popper, K. R. (1959). *The logic of scientific discovery.* London: Hutchinson.

Popplestone, J. A. (1995). *Recent variations on a theme by Descartes.* Paper presented at the meeting of the American Psychological Association, New York.

Porfeli, E. J. (2009). Hugo Münsterberg and the origins of vocational guidance. *The Career Development Quarterly, 57,* 225–236.

Posner, M. I., Rueda, M. R., & Kanske, P. (2007). Probing the mechanisms of attention. In J. T. Cacioppo, L. G. Tassinary, & G. G. Berntson (Eds.), *Handbook of psychophysiology* (3rd ed., pp. 410–432). New York: Cambridge University Press.

Postman, L. (1973). Hermann Ebbinghaus. In M. Henle, J. Jaynes, & J. J. Sullivan (Eds.), *Historical conceptions of psychology* (pp. 220–229). New York: Springer. Also published in (1968) *American Psychologist, 23*, 149–157.

Powell, R. A. (2010). Little Albert still missing. *American Psychologist, 65*, 299–300.

Powell, R. A. (2011). Research notes: Little Albert, lost or found: Further difficulties with the Douglas Merritte hypothesis. *History of Psychology, 14*, 106–107.

Powell, R. A., Digdon, N., Harris, B., & Smithson, C. (2014). Correcting the record on Watson, Rayner and Little Albert: Albert Barger as "psychology's lost boy." *American Psychologist, 69*, 600–611.

Pratola, S. (1974). Up with our foremother. *American Psychologist, 29*, 780.

Pretorius, I.-M. (2012). From the Hampstead War Nurseries to the Anna Freud Centre. In N. T. Malberg & J. Rapael-Leff (Eds.), *The Anna Freud tradition: Lines of development—Evolution of theory and practice over the decades* (pp. 30–37). London: Karnac Books.

Pretorius, I.-M. (2014). "From egocentricity to companionship": Anna Freud's understanding of sibling relationships. In D. Hindle & S. Sherwin-White (Eds.), *Sibling matters: A psychoanalytic, developmental, and systemic approach* (pp. 49–65). London: Karnac Books.

Preyer, W. (1888). The imitative faculty of infants. *Popular Science Monthly, 33*, 249–255.

Price, E. H. (2012). Do brains think? Comparative anatomy and the end of the Great Chain of Being in 19th-century Britain. *History of the Human Sciences, 25*, 32–50.

Pridmore, S. (2014). Herodotus on conversion disorder. *Australian and New Zealand Journal of Psychiatry, 48*, 1170.

Prislin, R., & Crano, W. D. (2012). A history of social influence research. In A. W. Kruglanski & W. Stroebe (Eds.), *Handbook of the history of social psychology* (pp. 321–339). New York: Psychology Press.

Proctor, R. W., & Evans, R. (2014). E. B. Titchener, women psychologists, and the experimentalists. *American Journal of Psychology, 127*, 501–526.

Proulx, T. (2013). Beyond mortality and the self: Meaning makes a comeback. In K. D. Markman, T. Proulx, & M. J. Lindberg (Eds.), *The psychology of meaning* (pp. 71–87). Washington, DC: American Psychological Association.

Pubols, B. H., Jr. (1959). Jan Swammerdam and the history of reflex action. *American Journal of Psychology, 72*, 131–135.

Puglisi, M. (1924). Franz Brentano: A biographical sketch. *American Journal of Psychology, 35*, 414–419.

Pytell, T. (2006). Transcending the angel beast: Viktor Frankl and humanistic psychology. *Psychoanalytic Psychology, 23*, 490–503.

Pytell, T. (2007). Extreme experience, psychological insight, and Holocaust perception: Reflections on Bettelheim and Frankl. *Psychoanalytic Psychology, 24*, 641–657.

Quételet, J. A. (1968). *A treatise on man and the development of his faculties*. New York: B. Franklin. (Original work published 1842)

Quick, T. (2014). From phrenology to the laboratory: Physiological psychology and the institution of science in Britain (c.1830–80). *History of the Human Sciences, 27*, 54–73.

Quinn, S. (1987). *A mind of her own: The life of Karen Horney*. New York: Summit.

Quinn, S. O. (2012). Credibility, respectability, suggestibility, and spirit travel: Lurena Brackett and animal magnetism. *History of Psychology, 15*, 273–282.

Raad, R., & Makari, G. (2010). Samuel Tuke's description of the retreat. *American Journal of Psychiatry, 167*, 898.

Radice, B. (1974). *The letters of Abelard and Héloise*. London: Penguin.

Radler, J. (2015). Bringing the environment in: Early Central European contributions to an ecologically oriented psychology of perception. *History of Psychology, 18*, 401–413.

Raichle, M. E. (1999). Modern phrenology: Maps of human cortical function. In D. C. Grossman & H. Valtin (Eds.), *Great issues for medicine in the twenty-first century* (pp. 107–118). New York: New York Academy of Sciences.

Raimy, V. C. (Ed.). (1950). *Training in clinical psychology*. Englewood Cliffs, NJ: Prentice Hall.

Rakhshani, A., Nagarathna, R., Sharma, A., Singh, A., & Nagedra, H. R. (2015). A holistic antenatal model based on yoga, Ayurveda, and Vedic guidelines. *Health Care for Women International, 36*, 256–275.

Rakos, R. F. (2013). John B. Watson's 1913 "Behaviorist manifesto": Setting the stage for behaviorism's social action legacy. *Revista Mexicana de Análisis de la Conducta, 39*, 99–118.

Rambo, L. R. (1980). Ethics, evolution, and the psychology of William James. *Journal of the History of the Behavioral Sciences, 16*, 50–57.

Rancurello, A. C. (1968). *A study of Franz Brentano*. New York: Academic Press.

Rand, N. (2004). The hidden soul: The growth of the unconscious in philosophy, psychology, medicine, and literature, 1750–1900. *American Imago, 61,* 257–289.

Ranke-Heinemann, U. (1990). *Eunuchs for the kingdom of heaven* (P. Heinegg, Trans.). New York: Penguin.

Rankin, S., Weber, G., Blumenfeld, W., & Frazer, S. (2010). *2010 state of higher education for lesbian, gay, bisexual & transgender people.* Charlotte, NC: Campus Pride.

Rapport, R. (2005). *Nerve endings: The discovery of the synapse.* New York: Norton.

Rashotte, M. E., & Amsel, A. (1999). Clark L. Hull's behaviorism. In W. O'Donohue & R. Kitchener (Eds.), *Handbook of behaviorism* (pp. 119–158). San Diego, CA: Academic Press.

Rathunde, K. (2001). Toward a psychology of optimal human functioning: What positive psychology can learn from the "experimental turns" of James, Dewey, and Maslow. *Journal of Humanistic Psychology, 41,* 135–153.

Rauch, J. (1993). *Kindly inquisitors: The new attacks on free thought.* Chicago: University of Chicago Press.

Ray, W. J. (2013). *Evolutionary psychology: Neuroscience perspectives concerning human behavior and experience.* Thousand Oaks, CA: Sage.

Razran, G. (1968). Ivan M. Sechenov. In D. L. Sills (Ed.), *International encyclopedia of the social sciences* (Vol. 14, pp. 129–130). New York: Macmillan and Free Press.

Read, N. (2010). Visionary or disaster? A perspective on William Sargant. Retrieved November 30, 2015 from www.nickread.co.uk/articles/2010/03/visionary-or-disaster-a-perspective-on-william-sargant/

Reagan, L. S. (2012). Mimesis in Thomas Hobbes's *Leviathan* (1651). *History of the Human Sciences, 25,* 25–42.

Reck, A. J. (1990). An historical sketch of pluralism. *The Monist, 73,* 367–387.

Reed, D. D., & Luiselli, J. K. (2009). Antecedents to a paradigm: Ogden Lindsley and B. F. Skinner's founding of "Behavior therapy." *The Behavior Therapist, 32,* 82–85.

Reicher, S., & Haslam, S. A. (2014). Camps, conflict and collectivism. *The Psychologist, 27,* 826–828.

Reicher, S. D., Haslam, S. A., & Miller, A. G. (2014). What makes a person a perpetrator? The intellectual, moral, and methodological arguments for revisiting Milgram's research on the influence of authority. *Journal of Social Issues, 70,* 393–408.

Reid, T. (1786). *Essays on the intellectual powers of man.* Dublin: L. White.

Reid, T. (1790). *Essays on the active powers of man.* Dublin: P. Byrne and J. Milliken.

Reid, T. (1970). *An inquiry into the human mind* (T. Duggan, Ed.). Chicago: University of Chicago Press. (Original work published 1764)

Reik, M. M. (1977). *The golden lands of Thomas Hobbes.* Detroit, MI: Wayne State University Press.

Reisenzein, R., & Schonpflug, W. (1992). Stumpf's cognitive-evaluative theory of emotion. *American Psychologist, 47,* 34–45.

Reisman, J. M. (1991). *A history of clinical psychology* (2nd ed.). New York: Brunner-Routledge.

Reiss, S. (2003). Epicurus: The first rational-emotive therapist. *The Behavior Therapist, 26,* 405–406.

Reppen, J. (Ed.). (2006). Special issue: The relevance of Sigmund Freud for the 21st century. *Psychoanalytic Psychology, 23,* 415–451.

Rescher, N. (Ed.) (1985). *The heritage of logical positivism.* Lanham, MD: University Press of America.

Rescorla, R. A. (2001). Experimental extinction. In R. R. Mowrer & S. B. Klein (Eds.), *Handbook of contemporary learning theories* (pp. 119–154). Mahwah, NJ: Lawrence Erlbaum Associates.

Rescorla, R. A. (2002). Extinction. In L. Bäckman & C. von Hofsten (Eds.), *Psychology at the turn of the millennium, Vol. 1: Cognitive, biological, and health perspectives* (pp. 219–244). Hove, UK: Psychology Press.

Resende, L. A. L., & Weber, S. A. T. (2010). "Sir Charles Bell was not affected by facial paralysis himself!": The authors reply. *Arquivos de Neuro-Psiquiatria, 68,* 322.

Rhodes, J. S., Ford, M. M., Yu, C. H., Brown, L. L., Finn, D. A., Garland, T., Jr., et al. (2007). Mouse inbred strain differences in ethanol drinking to intoxication. *Genes, Brain, and Behavior, 6,* 1–18.

Riccio, M. (2012). From sensation to consciousness: Suggestions in modern philosophy. In F. Paglieri (Ed.), *Consciousness in interaction: The role of the natural and social context in shaping consciousness* (pp. 289–299). Amsterdam: John Benjamins Publishing Co.

Richards, G. (1987). Of what is history of psychology a history? *British Journal for the History of Science, 20,* 201–211.

Richards, J. M., Jr. (2000). A history of division 34 (population and environmental psychology). In D. A. Dewsbury (Ed.), *Unification through division: Histories of the divisions of the American Psychological Association* (Vol. 5, pp. 113–135). Washington, DC: American Psychological Association.

Richards, R. J. (1980). Wundt's early theories of unconscious inference and cognitive evolution in their relation to Darwinian biopsychology. In W. G. Bringmann & R. D.

Tweney (Eds.), *Wundt studies: A centennial collection* (pp. 42–70). Toronto: C. J. Hogrefe.

Richards, R. J. (1987). *Darwin and the emergence of evolutionary theories of mind and behavior*. Chicago: University of Chicago Press.

Richardson, H. S. (1990). Measurement, pleasure, and the practical science in Plato's Protagoras. *Journal of the History of Philosophy, 28,* 7–32.

Richardson, R. D. (2006). *William James: In the maelstrom of American modernism*. Boston: Houghton Mifflin.

Richeson, A. W. (1940). Hypatia of Alexandria. *National Mathematics Magazine, 15,* 73–82.

Richter, J. P. (Ed.). (1970). *The literary works of Leonardo da Vinci* (3rd ed., 2 vols.). London: Phaidon.

Rieber, R. W., & Robinson, D. K. (Eds.). (2003). *Wilhelm Wundt in history: The making of a scientific psychology*. New York: Kluwer Academic/Plenum.

Riese, W. (1951). Philippe Pinel (1745–1826): His views on human nature and disease. His medical thought. *Journal of Nervous and Mental Disease, 114,* 313–323.

Riese, W. (1959). *A history of neurology*. New York: MD Publications.

Rilling, M. (2000a). How the challenge of explaining learning influenced the origins and development of John B. Watson's behaviorism. *American Journal of Psychology, 113,* 275–301.

Ringer, F. K. (1969). *The decline of the German mandarins: The German academic community, 1890–1933*. Cambridge, MA: Harvard University Press.

Risen, J. (2014). *Pay any price: Greed, power, and endless war*. Boston, MA: Houghton Mifflin Harcourt.

Roback, A. A. (1937). *Behaviorism at twenty-five*. Cambridge, MA: Sci-Art Publishers.

Roback, A. A., & Kiernan, T. (1969). *Pictorial history of psychology and psychiatry*. New York: Philosophical Library.

Robert, J. (2015). Pa/enser bien le corps: Cognitive and curative language in Montaigne's *Essais. Journal of Medical Humanities, 36,* 241–250.

Roberts, M. A., McGeorge, A. P., & Caird, F. I. (1978). Electroencephalography and computerized tomography in vascular and non-vascular dementia in old age. *Journal of Neurology, Neurosurgery, and Psychiatry, 41,* 903–906.

Robins, R. W., Gosling, S. D., & Craik, K. H. (1999). An empirical analysis of trends in psychology. *American Psychologist, 54,* 117–128.

Robinson, D. K. (2010). Fechner's "inner psychophysics." *History of Psychology, 13,* 424–433.

Robinson, D. N. (1977). *Significant contributions to the history of psychology, 1750–1920: Series C* (Vol.

III). Washington, DC: University Publications of America.

Robinson, D. N. (1982). *Toward a science of human nature*. New York: Columbia University Press.

Robinson, D. N. (1989a). *Aristotle's psychology*. New York: Columbia University Press.

Robinson, D. N. (1989b). Thomas Reid and the Aberdeen years: Common sense at the Wise Club. *Journal of the History of the Behavioral Sciences, 29,* 154–162.

Robinson, D. N. (2013). Historiography in science: A note on ignorance. *Theory and Psychology, 23,* 819–828.

Robinson, D. N. (2014). Kant: Intuition and the synthetic a priori. In L. B. Osbeck & B. S. Held (Eds.), *Rational intuition: Philosophical roots, scientific investigations* (pp. 114–130). New York: Cambridge University Press.

Rocca, J. (2007). William Cullen (1710–1790) and Robert Whytt (1714–1766) on the nervous system. In H. Whitaker, C. U. M. Smith, & S. Finger (Eds.), *Brain, mind and medicine: Essays in eighteenth century neuroscience* (pp. 85–98). New York: Springer Science + Business Media.

Rock, I. (Ed.). (1990). *The legacy of Solomon Asch: Essays in cognition and social psychology*. Hillsdale, NJ: Erlbaum.

Rock, I., & Palmer, S. (1990). The legacy of Gestalt psychology. *Scientific American, 263,* 84–90.

Rodis-Lewis, G. (1999). *Descartes: His life and thought* (J. M. Todd, Trans.). Ithaca, NY: Cornell University Press.

Roediger, H. L. (1980). Memory metaphors in cognitive psychology. *Memory and Cognition, 8,* 231–246.

Roets, A., & Van Hiel, A. (2011). Allport's prejudiced personality today: Need for closure as the motivated cognitive basis of prejudice. *Current Directions in Psychological Science, 20,* 349–354.

Rogers, A. (2013). Absence and presence—Carl Rogers in 2013. In R. House, K. Kalisch, & J. Maidman (Eds.), *The future of humanistic psychology* (pp. 62–69). Ross-on-Wye, UK: PCCS Books.

Rogers, A. K. (1912). *A student's history of philosophy*. New York: Macmillan.

Rogers, C. (1959). Introduction. In *The examination of men's wits by Juan Huarte* (M. C. Camilli & R. Carew, Trans.). Gainesville, FL: Scholars Facsimiles and Reprints. (Original work published 1594)

Rogers, C. R. (1951). *Client-centered therapy*. Boston: Houghton Mifflin.

Rogers, C. R. (1961). *On being a person: A therapist's view of psychotherapy*. Boston: Houghton Mifflin.

Rogers, C. R., Lyon, H. C., Jr., & Tausch, R. (2014). *On

becoming an effective teacher: Person-centered teaching, psychology, philosophy, and dialogues with Carl R. Rogers and Harold Lyon. New York: Routledge.

Rogers, E. M. (1960). *Physics for the inquiring mind.* Princeton, NJ: Princeton University Press.

Rogers, T. B. (1989). Operationism in psychology: A discussion of contextual antecedents and an historical interpretation of its longevity. *Journal of the History of the Behavioral Sciences, 25,* 139–153.

Rogow, A. A. (1986). *Thomas Hobbes: Radical in the service of reaction.* New York: Norton.

Rohles, F. H. (1992). Orbital bar pressing: A historical note on Skinner and the chimpanzees in space. *American Psychologist, 47,* 1531–1533.

Roith, E. (1987). New library of psychoanalysis: 4. In David Tuckett (General Ed.), *The riddle of Freud: Jewish influences on his theory of female sexuality.* New York: Tavistock.

Romand, D. (2012). Fechner as a pioneering theorist of unconscious cognition. *Consciousness and Cognition, 21,* 562–572.

Romanes, G. J. (1881). Intelligence of ants. *Popular Science Monthly, 19,* 495–510, 816–829.

Romanes, G. J. (1883). *Mental evolution in animals.* London: Kegan Paul, Trench & Co.

Ronan, C. A. (1982). *Science: Its history and development among the world's cultures.* New York: Facts on File.

Root, M. J. (2008). The evolution of psychologists' recommended childrearing practices in the United States. In D. G. Wiseman (Ed.), *The American family: Understanding its changing dynamics and place in society* (pp. 97–111). Springfield, IL: Charles C. Thomas.

Rose, F. C. (2009). Cerebral localization in antiquity. *Journal of the History of the Neurosciences, 18,* 239–247.

Rosenfield, L. C. (1968). *From beast-machine to man-machine: Animal soul in French letters from Descartes to La Mettrie.* New York: Octagon Books.

Rosenzweig, S. (1987). The final tribute of E. G. Boring to G. T. Fechner: Concerning the date October 22, 1850. *American Psychologist, 42,* 787–790.

Rosner, R. I. (2012). Aaron T. Beck's drawings and the psychoanalytic origin story of cognitive therapy. *History of Psychology, 15,* 1–18.

Ross, D. (1972). *G. Stanley Hall: The psychologist as prophet.* Chicago: University of Chicago Press.

Ross, L., Lepper, M., & Ward, A. (2010). History of social psychology: Insights, challenges, and contributions to theory and application. In S. T. Fiske, D. T. Gilbert, & G. Lindzey (Eds.), *Handbook of social psychology* (Vol. 1, pp. 3–50). Hoboken, NJ: John Wiley & Sons.

Roszak, T. (1993). *The voice of the earth: An exploration of ecopsychology.* New York: Touchstone.

Rotenberg, M., & Diamond, B. L. (1971). The biblical conception of psychopathology: The law of the stubborn and rebellious son. *Journal of the History of the Behavioral Sciences, 7,* 29–38.

Roth, M. S. (1998). *Freud: Conflict and culture.* New York: Knopf.

Roth, P. A. (2004). Hearts of darkness: "Perpetrator history" and why there is no why. *History of the Human Sciences, 17,* 211–251.

Rotter, J. B. (1954). *Social learning and clinical psychology.* New York: Prentice Hall.

Routh, D. K. (2011). A history of clinical psychology. In D. H. Barlow (Ed.), *The Oxford handbook of clinical psychology* (pp. 23–33). New York: Oxford University Press.

Routh, D. K. (2013). Clinical psychology. In D. K. Freedheim & I. B. Weiner (Eds.), *Handbook of psychology, Vol. 1: History of psychology* (2nd ed., pp. 377–396). Hoboken, NJ: John Wiley & Sons Inc.

Royce, J. (1898). The new psychology and the consulting psychologist. *Forum, 26,* 80–96.

Royce, J. R. (Ed.). (1970). *The first Banff conference on theoretical psychology.* Toronto: University of Toronto Press.

Rozin, P. (2001). Social psychology and science: Some lessons from Solomon Asch. *Personality and Social Psychology Review, 5,* 2–14.

Rubenstein, J., & Slife, B. (1988). *Taking sides: Clashing views on controversial psychological issues* (5th ed.). Guilford, CT: Dushkin.

Rubenstein, R. E. (2003). *Aristotle's children: How Christians, Muslims, and Jews rediscovered ancient wisdom and illuminated the Dark Ages.* New York: Harcourt.

Rubins, J. L. (1978). *Karen Horney: Gentle rebel of psychoanalysis.* New York: Dial.

Rudnytsky, P. L. (2008). Inventing Freud. *American Journal of Psychoanalysis, 68,* 117–127.

Rudnytsky, P. L. (2011). *Rescuing psychoanalysis from Freud and other essays in revision; the history of psychoanalysis series.* London: Kamac Books.

Ruggiero, G. (2007). *Machiavelli in love: Sex, self, and society in the Italian Renaissance.* Baltimore, MD: Johns Hopkins University Press.

Rush, B. (1806). *Essays, literary, moral, and philosophical* (2nd ed.). Philadelphia: Thomas and William Bradford.

Rush, B. (1818). *Medical inquiries and observations upon the diseases of the mind* (2nd ed.). Philadelphia: John Richardson. (Original work published 1812)

Russell, B. (1959). *Wisdom of the west.* New York: Crescent Books.

Russell, J. B. (1980). *A history of witchcraft*. London: Thames and Hudson.

Russell, N. J. C. (2011). Milgram's obedience to authority experiments: Origins and early evolution. *British Journal of Social Psychology, 50,* 140–162.

Rutherford, A. (2000). Radical behaviorism and psychology's public: B. F. Skinner in the popular press, 1934–1990. *History of Psychology, 3,* 371–395.

Rutherford, A. (2003). B. F. Skinner's technology of behavior in American life: From consumer culture to counterculture. *Journal of the History of the Behavioral Sciences, 29,* 1–23.

Rutherford, A. (2006). Mother of behavior therapy and beyond: Mary Cover Jones and the study of the "whole child." In D. A. Dewsbury, L. T. Benjamin, & M. Wertheimer (Eds.), *Portraits of pioneers in psychology* (Vol. 6, pp. 189–204). Washington, DC: American Psychological Association.

Rutherford, A. (2009). *Beyond the box: B. F. Skinner's technology of behavior from laboratory to life, 1950s–1970s*. Toronto: University of Toronto Press.

Ryback, D. (2012). Humanism and behaviorism. In L. L'Abate (Ed.), *Paradigms in theory construction* (pp. 297–315). New York: Springer Science + Business Media.

Rychlak, J. F. (1988). *The psychology of rigorous humanism* (2nd ed.). New York: New York University Press.

Rychlak, J. F. (1991). *Artificial intelligence and human reason: A teleological critique*. New York: Columbia University Press.

Rychlak, J. F. (1994). *Logical learning theory: A human teleology and its empirical support*. Lincoln: University of Nebraska Press.

Rychlak, J. F. (1998). How Boulder biases have limited possible theoretical contributions to psychotherapy. *Clinical Psychology: Science and Practice, 5,* 233–241.

Rychlak, J. F. (2000). A psychotherapist's lessons from the philosophy of science. *American Psychologist, 55,* 1126–1132.

Rychlak, J. F. (2005). In search and proof of human beings, not machines. *Journal of Personality Assessment, 85,* 239–256.

Rychlak, J. F. (2009). In search and proof of human beings, not machines. In L. P. Mos (Ed.), *History of psychology in autobiography* (pp. 211–240). New York: Springer Science + Business Media.

Rychlak, J. F., & Rychlak, R. J. (1990a). The insanity defense and the question of human agency. *New Ideas in Psychology, 8,* 3–24.

Rychlak, J. F., & Rychlak, R. J. (1990b). Free will is a verifiable assumption: A reply to Garrett and Viney. *New Ideas in Psychology, 8,* 43–51.

Sahakian, W. S. (Ed.). (1968). *History of psychology: A sourcebook in systematic psychology*. Itasca, IL: F. E. Peacock.

Sahakian, W. S., & Sahakian, M. L. (1975). *John Locke*. Boston: Twayne.

Sajadi, M. M., Sajadi, M. M., & Tabatabaie, S. M. (2011). The history of facial palsy and spasm: Hippocrates to Razi. *Neurology, 77,* 174–178.

Sakuma, A. (1999). Gestalt psychology in Japan. *Japanese Psychological Review, 42,* 326–345.

Sale, A., Berardi, N., & Maffei, L. (2014). Environment and brain plasticity: Towards an endogenous pharmacotherapy. *Physiological Reviews, 94,* 189–234.

Salice, A., & Schmid, H. B. (Eds.). (2016). *The phenomenological approach to social reality: History, concepts, problems*. Cham, Switzerland: Springer International Publishing.

Salkovskis, P. (1998). Changing the face of psychotherapy and common sense: Joseph Wolpe, 20 April 1915–4 December 1997. *Behavioural and Cognitive Psychotherapy, 26,* 189–191.

Salzinger, K. (1994). On Watson. In J. T. Todd & E. K. Morris (Eds.), *Modern perspectives on John B. Watson and classical behaviorism* (pp. 151–158). Westport, CT: Greenwood Press.

Samelson, F. (1985). Organizing for the kingdom of behavior: Academic battles and organizational policies in the twenties. *Journal of the History of Behavioral Sciences, 21,* 33–47.

Samelson, F. (1994). John B. Watson in 1913: Rhetoric and practice. In J. T. Todd & E. K. Morris (Eds.), *Modern perspectives on John B. Watson and classical behaviorism* (pp. 3–18). Westport, CT: Greenwood Press.

Samoilov, V. O. (2007). Ivan Petrovich Pavlov (1849–1936) (V. Zayas, Trans.). *Journal of the History of the Neurosciences, 16,* 74–89.

Samuel, L. R. (2013). *Shrink: A cultural history of psychoanalysis in America*. Lincoln, NE: University of Nebraska Press.

Samuels, A. (1994). The professionalization of Carl G. Jung's analytical psychology clubs. *Journal of the History of the Behavioral Sciences, 30,* 138–147.

Sanati, A., & Abou-Saleh, M. T. (2012). Avicenna's no health without mental health. *Arab Journal of Psychiatry, 23,* 185–187.

Sargant, W. (1957). *Battle for the mind*. New York: Harper & Row.

Sartre, J. P. (1965). Reply to Albert Camus. In J. P. Sartre (Ed.) & B. Eisler (Trans.), *Situations* (pp. 69–106). New York: George Braziller.

Sato, T., Nakatsuma, T., & Matsubara, N. (2012).

Influence of G. Stanley Hall on Yuzero Motora, the first psychology professor in Japan: How the kymograph powered Motora's career in psychology. *American Journal of Psychology, 125*, 395–407.

Sawyer, T. F. (2000). Francis Cecil Sumner: His views and influence on African American higher education. *History of Psychology, 3*, 122–141.

Sayers, J. (1991). *Mothers of psychoanalysis*. New York: Norton.

Scarborough, E. (2000). Margaret Floy Washburn. In A. Kazdin (Ed.), *Encyclopedia of psychology* (Vol. 8, pp. 230–232). Washington, DC: American Psychological Association, and New York: Oxford University Press.

Scarborough, E., & Furumoto, L. (1987). *Untold lives: The first generation of American women psychologists*. New York: Columbia University Press.

Schabas, M. (2015). John Stuart Mill: Evolutionary economics and liberalism. *Journal of Bioeconomics, 17*, 97–111.

Scherer, L. B. (1975). *Slavery and the churches in early America: 1619–1819*. Grand Rapids, MI: Eerdmans.

Scherez, G. (1976). Niels Stensen also known as Nicolaus Steno. In C. Gillispie (Ed.), *Dictionary of scientific biography* (Vol. 13, pp. 30–35). New York: Scribner.

Schillace, B. (2014). Seeing is believing: New York Academy of Medicine's Vasalius 500th year celebrations. *Culture, Medicine, and Psychiatry, 38*, 712–715.

Schioldann, J. (2009). *History of the introduction of lithium into medicine and psychiatry: Birth of modern psycho-pharmacology 1949*. Adelaide: Adelaide Academic Press.

Schioldann, J., & Søgaard, I. (2013). Søren Kierkegaard (1813–55): a bicentennial pathographical review. *History of Psychiatry, 24*, 387–398.

Schliemann, H. (1968). *Troy and its remains*. New York: Benjamin Blom. (Original work published 1875)

Schlinger, H. D. (2008). The long good-bye: Why B. F. Skinner's *Verbal Behavior* is alive and well on the 50th anniversary of its publication. *The Psychological Record, 58*, 329–337.

Schlosberg, H. (1954). Walter S. Hunter: Pioneer objectivist in psychology. *Science, 120*, 441–442.

Schlosser, M. E. (2012). Causally efficacious intentions and the sense of agency: In defense of real mental causation. *Journal of Theoretical and Philosophical Psychology, 32*, 135–160.

Schmid, P. F. (2013). Whence the evil? A personalistic and dialogic perspective. In A. C. Bohard, B. S. Held, E. Mendelowitz, & K. J. Schneider (Eds.), *Humanity's dark side: Evil, destructive experience, and psychotherapy* (pp. 35–55). Washington, DC: American Psychological Association.

Schmied, L. A., Steinberg, H., & Sykes, E. A. B. (2006). Psychopharmacology's debt to experimental psychology. *History of Psychology, 9*, 144–157.

Schmitt, R. (1967). Phenomenology. In P. Edwards (Ed.), *The encyclopedia of philosophy* (Vol. 6, pp. 135–151). New York: Macmillan and Free Press.

Schneck, J. M. (1978). Benjamin Rush and animal magnetism, 1789 and 1812. *International Journal of Clinical and Experimental Hypnosis, 26*, 9–14.

Schneider, D. J. (1991). Social cognition. *Annual Review of Psychology, 42*, 527–561.

Schneider, K. J., Bugental, J. F. T., & Pierson, J. F. (Eds.). (2001). *The handbook of humanistic psychology: Leading edges in theory, research, and practice*. Thousand Oaks, CA: Sage.

Schneider, W. H. (1992). After Binet: French intelligence testing, 1900–1950. *Journal of the History of the Behavioral Sciences, 28*, 111–132.

Schochow, M., & Steger, F. (2014). Johann Christian Reil (1759–1813): Pioneer of psychiatry, city physician, and advocate of public medical care. *American Journal of Psychiatry, 171*, 403.

Schrag, C. O. (1982). Either/or. In F. N. Magill (Ed.), *World philosophy* (Vol. 3, pp. 1294–1306). Englewood Cliffs, NJ: Salem Press.

Schrecker, T. (2016). Globalization, austerity and health equity politics. Taming the inequality machine and why it matters. *Critical Public Health, 26*, 4–13.

Schuchhardt, K. (1971). *Schliemann's excavations: An archaeological and historical study* (E. Sellers, Trans.). New York: Benjamin Blom. (Original work published 1891)

Schulte, H. (1938). An approach to a Gestalt theory of paranoic phenomena. In W. D. Ellis (Ed.), *A source book of Gestalt psychology* (pp. 362–369). London: Kegan Paul, Trench, Trubner & Company.

Schunk, D. H. (2012). Social cognitive theory. In K. R. Harris, S. Graham, T. Urdan, C. B. McCormick, G. M. Sinatra, & J. Sweller (Eds.), *APA educational psychology handbook, Vol. 1: Theories, constructs, and critical issues* (pp. 101–123). Washington, DC: American Psychological Association.

Schwarz, K. A., & Pfister, R. (2016). Scientific psychology in the 18th century: A historical rediscovery. *Perspectives on Psychological Science, 11*, 399–407.

Scott, C. (Ed.). (2015). *DSM-5© and the law: Changes and challenges*. New York: Oxford University Press.

Scott, J., & Freeman, A. (2010). Beck's cognitive therapy. In N. Kazantzis, M. A. Reinecke, & A. Freeman (Eds.), *Cognitive and behavioral theories in clinical practice* (pp. 28–75). New York: Guilford Press.

Scott, W. D. (1904). The psychology of advertising. *Atlantic Monthly, 93,* 29–36.

Scott, W. D. (1921). In memory of Wilhelm Wundt. *Psychological Review, 28,* 183.

Searle, J. R. (1992). *The rediscovery of the mind.* Cambridge, MA: MIT Press.

Searle, J. R. (1995a, November 2). The mystery of consciousness. *New York Review,* pp. 60–66.

Searle, J. R. (1995b, November 16). The mystery of consciousness: Part II. *New York Review,* pp. 54–61.

Seashore, C. E. (1911). The consulting psychologist. *Popular Science Monthly, 78,* 283–290.

Seelman, K. L. (2016). Transgender adults' access to college bathrooms and housing and the relationship to suicidality. *Journal of Homosexuality, 61,* 1–22.

Seeskin, K. (2008). Plato and the origin of mental health. *International Journal of Psychiatry and Law, 31,* 487–494.

Segal, Z. V., Williams, J. M. G., & Teasdale, J. D. (2001). *Mindfulness-based cognitive therapy for depression: A new approach to preventing relapse.* New York: Guilford.

Seidel, G. E., Jr., & Elsden, R. P. (1989). *Embryo transfer in dairy cattle.* Milwaukee, WI: Hoard & Sons.

Seligman, M. (2004). The new era of positive psychology. Ted Talk. Posted February 2004. Retrieved July 2, 2016 from www.ted.com/talks/martin_seligman_on_the_state_of_psychology?language=en

Seligman, M. E. P., & Csikszentmihalyi, M. (2000). Positive psychology: An introduction. *American Psychologist, 55,* 5–14.

Serlin, I. (2011). The history and future of humanistic psychology. *Journal of Humanistic Psychology, 51,* 428–431.

Seward, G. H., & Seward, J. P. (1968). Robert S. Woodworth. In D. L. Sills (Ed.), *International encyclopedia of the social sciences* (Vol. 19, pp. 561–564). New York: Macmillan and Free Press.

Sexton, V. S., & Misiak, H. K. (Eds.). (1971). *Historical perspectives in psychology: Readings.* Monterey, CA: Brooks/Cole.

Sexton, V. S., & Misiak, H. K. (Eds.). (1976). *Psychology around the world.* Monterey, CA: Brooks/Cole.

Seymore, M. (2001). *Mary Shelley.* New York: Grove Press.

Shakespeare, W. (1964). *Measure for measure* (E. Leisi, Ed.). New York: Hafner. (Original work published 1604–1605)

Shakow, D. (1942). The training of the clinical psychologist. *Journal of Consulting Psychology, 6,* 277–288.

Shamdasani, S. (Ed.). (2009). *The red book: Liber novus.* New York: W. W. Norton.

Shamdasani, S. (2012). *C. G. Jung: A biography in books.* New York: W. W. Norton & Co.

Shamdasani, S. (2015a). 'S.W.' and C.G. Jung: Mediumship, psychiatry and serial exemplarity. *History of Psychiatry, 26,* 288–302.

Shamdasani, S. (2015b). Jung's practice of the image. *Journal of Sandplay Therapy, 24,* 7–22.

Shapira, M. (2013). *The war inside: Psychoanalysis, total war, and the making of the democratic self in postwar Britain.* Cambridge, UK: Cambridge University Press.

Sharpless, B. (2012). Kierkegaard's conception of psychology. *Journal of Theoretical and Philosophical Psychology, 33,* 90–106.

Shaw, R., & Colimore, K. (1988). Humanistic psychology as an ideology: An analysis of Maslow's contradictions. *Journal of Humanistic Psychology, 28,* 51–74.

Shea, W. R. (1986). Galileo and the church. In D. C. Lindberg & R. L. Numbers (Eds.), *God and nature: Historical essays on the encounter between Christianity and science* (pp. 114–135). Berkeley: University of California Press.

Sheldon, K. M., & Kasser, T. (2001). Goals, congruence, and positive well-being: New empirical support for humanistic theories. *Journal of Humanistic Psychology, 41,* 30–50.

Sheldon, K. M., & King, L. (2001). Why positive psychology is necessary. *American Psychologist, 56,* 216–217.

Sheng, L. (2015). Theorizing income inequality in the face of financial globalization. *The Social Science Journal, 52,* 415–424.

Shereshevskii, A. M. (1994). The mystery of the death of V. M. Bekhterev. *Journal of Russian and East European Psychiatry, 27,* 103–113.

Sherif, M. (1936). *The psychology of social norms.* New York: Harper.

Sherif, M., Harvey, O. J., White, B. J., Hood, W. R., & Sherif, C. W. (1961). *Intergroup conflict and cooperation: The Robbers Cave experiment* (2nd ed.). Norman, OK: University Book Exchange.

Sherif, M., & Sherif, C. W. (1953). *Groups in harmony and tension: An integration of studies of intergroup relations.* Oxford: Harper & Brothers.

Shermer, M. (2002). *Why people believe weird things: Pseudoscience, superstition, and other confusions of our time.* New York: Henry Holt.

Shields, S. A. (1975). Ms. Pilgrim's progress: The contributions of Leta Stetter Hollingworth to the psychology of women. *American Psychologist, 30,* 852–857.

Shields, S. A. (1991). Leta Stetter Hollingworth: "Literature of opinion" and the study of individual differences. In G. A. Kimble, M. Wertheimer, & C. White (Eds.), *Portraits of pioneers in psychology* (Vol. 1, pp. 243–255). Washington, DC: American Psychological Association.

Shields, S. A., & Bhatia, S. (2009). Darwin on race, gender, and culture. *American Psychologist, 64*, 111–119.

Shimamura, A. P. (2012). Toward a science of aesthetics: Issues and ideas. In A. P. Shimamura & S. E. Palmer (Eds.), *Aesthetic science: Connecting minds, brains, and experience* (pp. 3–30). New York: Oxford University Press.

Shoja, M. M., & Tubbs, R. S. (2007). The disorder of love in the canon of Avicenna (A.D. 980–1037). *American Journal of Psychiatry, 164*, 228–229.

Shon, P. C. H., & Barton-Bellesa, S. (2015). The assumption of rational choice theory in Alfred Adler's theory of crime: Unraveling and reconciling the contradiction in Adlerian theory through synthesis and critique. *Aggression and Violent Behavior, 25*, 95–103.

Shook, J. R. (1995). Wilhelm Wundt's contribution to John Dewey's functional psychology. *Journal of the History of the Behavioral Sciences, 31*, 347–369.

Shorter, E. (2009). The history of lithium therapy. *Bipolar Disorders, 11*, 4–9.

Shorter, E. (2013). The history of the DSM. In J. Paris & J. Phillips (Eds.), *Making the DSM-5: Concepts and controversies* (pp. 3–19). New York: Springer Science + Business Media.

Shorto, R. (2008). *Descartes' bones: A skeletal history of the conflict between faith and reason*. New York: Doubleday.

Siewert, C. (2015). Phenomenological approaches. In M. Matthen (Ed.), *The Oxford handbook of philosophy of perception* (pp. 136–150). New York: Oxford University Press.

Silani, G., Zucconi, A., & Lamm, C. (2013). Carl Rogers meets the neurosciences: Insights from social neuroscience for client-centered therapy. In J. H. D. Cornelius-White, R. Motschnig-Pitrik, & M. Lux (Eds.), *Interdisciplinary handbook of the person-centered approach: Research and theory* (pp. 63–78). New York: Springer Science + Business Media.

Silva, J. F. (2014). Augustine on active perception. In J. F. Silva & M. Yrjönsuuri (Eds.), *Active perception in the history of philosophy: From Plato to modern philosophy* (pp. 79–98). Cham, Switzerland: Springer International Publishing.

Silver, A-L. S. (2009). Pioneers of the psychoanalytically oriented treatment of psychosis in the USA. In Y. O. Alanen, M. González de Chávez, A-L. S. Silver, & B. Martindale (Eds.), *Psychotherapeutic approaches to schizophrenic psychoses: Past, present and future* (pp. 56–64). New York: Routledge.

Silverman, L. H. (1976). Psychoanalytic theory: "The reports of my death are greatly exaggerated." *American Psychologist, 31*, 621–637.

Silverman, S. (2010). The death of Socrates: A holistic reexamination. *Omega, 6*, 71–84.

Simanek, D. E. (2014). The dangers of analogies. Retrieved June 20, 2016 from www.lhup.edu/~dsimanek/scenario/analogy.htm

Simon, B. (1972). Models of mind and mental illness in ancient Greece: II. The Platonic model. Section 1. *Journal of the History of the Behavioral Sciences, 8*, 389–404.

Simon, D. A. (2013). Spaced and massed practice. In J. Hattie & E. M. Anderman (Eds.), *International guide to student achievement* (pp. 411–413). New York: Routledge.

Simon, L. (1998). *Genuine reality: A life of William James*. New York: Harcourt Brace.

Singer, U., Golombeck, F., Schoof, A., Robbins, I., Abeckaser, D. A., Melita, P., & White, J. (Producers), & Almereyda, M. (Director). (2015). *Experimenter: The Stanley Milgram story*. BB Film Productions, USA.

Singh, A. A., & dickey, l. m. (2016). Implementing the APA guidelines on psychological practice with transgender and gender nonconforming people: A call to action to the field of psychology. *Psychology of Sexual Orientation and Gender Diversity, 3*, 195–200.

Singleton, M. M. (2014). The "science" of eugenics: America's moral detour. *American Journal of Physicians and Surgeons, 19*, 122–125.

Sizer, N., & Drayton, H. S. (1892). *Heads and faces and how to study them*. New York: Fowler & Wells.

Skinner, B. F. (1938). *The behavior of organisms: An experimental analysis*. New York: Appleton-Century.

Skinner, B. F. (1948). *Walden two*. New York: Macmillan.

Skinner, B. F. (1953). *Science and human behavior*. New York: Macmillan.

Skinner, B. F. (1956). A case study in scientific method. *American Psychologist, 11*, 221–233.

Skinner, B. F. (1957). *Verbal behavior*. New York: Appleton-Century-Crofts.

Skinner, B. F. (1958). Teaching machines. *Science, 128*, 969–977.

Skinner, B. F. (1960). Pigeons in a pelican. *American Psychologist, 15*, 28–37.

Skinner, B. F. (1963). Behaviorism at fifty. *Science, 140*, 951–958.

Skinner, B. F. (1967). B. F. Skinner. In E. G. Boring & G. Lindzey (Eds.), *A history of psychology in autobiography*

(Vol. 5, pp. 387–413). New York: Appleton-Century-Crofts.

Skinner, B. F. (1968). *The technology of teaching*. Englewood Cliffs, NJ: Prentice Hall.

Skinner, B. F. (1971). *Beyond freedom and dignity*. New York: Knopf.

Skinner, B. F. (1972). Humanism and behaviorism. *The Humanist, 32*(4), 18–20.

Skinner, B. F. (1974). *About behaviorism*. New York: Knopf.

Skinner, B. F. (1976). *Particulars of my life*. New York: Knopf.

Skinner, B. F. (1977). Why I am not a cognitive psychologist. *Behaviorism, 5*, 1–10.

Skinner, B. F. (1979). *The shaping of a behaviorist*. New York: Knopf.

Skinner, B. F. (1983a). *A matter of consequences*. New York: Knopf.

Skinner, B. F. (1983b). Origins of a behaviorist. *Psychology Today, 17*, 22–23.

Skinner, B. F. (1984). The shame of American education. *American Psychologist, 39*, 947–954.

Skinner, B. F. (1987a). Controversy? In S. Modgil & C. Modgil (Eds.), *B. F. Skinner: Consensus and controversy* (pp. 15–18). New York: Falmer.

Skinner, B. F. (1987b). *Upon further reflection*. Englewood Cliffs, NJ: Prentice Hall.

Skinner, B. F. (1987c). Whatever happened to psychology as the science of behavior? *American Psychologist, 42*, 780–786.

Skinner, B. F. (1989). The origins of cognitive thought. *American Psychologist, 44*, 13–18.

Skinner, B. F. (1990). Can psychology be a science of mind? *American Psychologist, 45*, 1206–1210.

Skinner, B. F., & Vaughn, M. E. (1983). *Enjoy old age: Living fully in your later years*. New York: Warner.

Skolnick, M. (2008). On identity as multiple and basic assumption. In G. M. Saiger, S. Rubenfeld, & M. D. Dluhy (Eds.), *Windows into today's group therapy* (pp. 45–53). New York: Routledge.

Skues, R. (2012). Clark revisited: Reappraising Freud in America. In J. Burnham (Ed.), *After Freud left: A century of psychoanalysis in America* (pp. 49–84). Chicago: University of Chicago Press.

Slife, B. D. (2005). The Kant of psychology: Joseph Rychlak and the bridge to postmodern psychology. *Journal of Constructivist Psychology, 18*, 297–306.

Slife, B. D. (2013). Joseph F. Rychlak (1928–2013). *American Psychologist, 69*, 82.

Slife, B. D., & Stilson, S. R. (2013). The rigorous humanist: Joseph F. Rychlak: December 17, 1928 – April 16, 2013. *The Humanistic Psychologist, 41*, 400–404.

Smith, B. (2009). Toward a realistic science of environments. *Ecological Psychology, 21*, 121–130.

Smith, C. U. M. (1987). David Hartley's Newtonian neuropsychology. *Journal of the History of the Behavioral Sciences, 23*, 123–136.

Smith, C. U. M. (2010a). The triune brain in antiquity: Plato, Aristotle, Erasistratus. *Journal of the History of the Neurosciences, 19*, 1–14.

Smith, C. U. M. (2010b). Darwin's unsolved problem: The place of consciousness in an evolutionary world. *Journal of the History of the Neurosciences, 19*, 105–120.

Smith, C. U. M. (2014). Herbert Spencer: Brain, mind, and the hard problem. In C. U. M. Smith & H. Whitaker (Eds.), *Brain, mind and consciousness in the history of neuroscience* (pp. 125–145). New York: Springer Science + Business Media.

Smith, L. S. (2003). Freud and Adler on agency and determinism in shaping personality. *The Journal of Individual Psychology, 59*, 263–280.

Smith, M. B. (1990). Humanistic psychology. *Journal of Humanistic Psychology, 33*, 6–21.

Smith, N. W. (1971). Aristotle's dynamic approach to sensing and some current implications. *Journal of the History of the Behavioral Sciences, 7*, 375–377.

Smith, N. W. (1974). The ancient background to Greek psychology and some implications for today. *Psychological Record, 24*, 309–324.

Smith, R. A., & Feigenbaum, K. D. (2013). Maslow's intellectual betrayal of Ruth Benedict? *Journal of Humanistic Psychology, 53*, 307–321.

Soble, A. (2009). A history of erotic philosophy. *Journal of Sex Research, 46*, 104–120.

Sokal, M. M. (1980a). Graduate study with Wundt: Two eyewitness accounts. In W. G. Bringmann & R. D. Tweney (Eds.), *Wundt studies: A centennial collection* (pp. 210–225). Toronto: C. J. Hogrefe.

Sokal, M. M. (1980b). Science and James McKeen Cattell, 1894–1945. *Science, 209*, 43–52.

Sokal, M. M. (1984). The Gestalt psychologists in behaviorist America. *American Historical Review, 89*, 1240–1263.

Sokal, M. M. (Ed.). (1987). *Psychological testing and American society: 1890–1930*. New Brunswick, NJ: Rutgers University Press.

Sokal, M. M. (1990). G. Stanley Hall and the institutional character of psychology at Clark, 1889–1920. *Journal of the History of the Behavioral Sciences, 26*, 114–124.

Sokal, M. M. (1992). Origins and early years of the American Psychological Association. *American Psychologist, 47*, 111–121.

Sokal, M. M. (1995). Stargazing: James McKeen Cattell, "American Men of Science," and the reward structure of the American scientific community, 1906–1944. In F. Kessel (Ed.), *Psychology, science, and human affairs: Essays in honor of William Bevan* (pp. 64–86). Boulder, CO: Westview Press.

Sokal, M. M. (1997). Baldwin, Cattell and the Psychological Review: A collaboration and its discontents. *History of the Human Sciences, 10,* 57–89.

Sokal, M. M. (2001). Practical phrenology as psychological counseling in the 19th-century United States. In C. D. Green & M. Shore (Eds.), *The transformation of psychology: Influences of 19th-century philosophy, technology, and natural science* (pp. 21–44). Washington, DC: American Psychological Association.

Sokal, M. M. (2006). James McKeen Cattell: Achievement and alienation. In D. A. Dewsbury, L. T. Benjamin, & M. Wertheimer (Eds.), *Portraits of pioneers in psychology* (Vol. 6, pp. 19–35). Washington, DC: American Psychological Association.

Sokal, M. M. (2009). James McKeen Cattell, Nicholas Murray Butler, and academic freedom at Columbian University 1902–1923. *History of Psychology, 12,* 87–122.

Sokal, M. M. (2011). Cattell, Columbia, and academic freedom: Rarely used sources enrich analyses of this significant episode. *History of Psychology, 14,* 100–104.

Sokal, M. M. (2016). Launching a career in psychology with achievement and arrogance: James McKeen Cattell at the Johns Hopkins University, 1882–1883. *Journal of the History of the Behavioral Sciences, 52,* 5–19.

Sokal, M. M., & Rafail, P. A. (1982). *A guide to manuscript collections in the history of psychology and related areas.* Millwood, NY: Kraus International.

Soles, D. E. (1985). Locke's empiricism and the postulation of unobservables. *Journal of the History of Philosophy, 23,* 339–369.

Soltis, J. F. (1971). John Dewey. In L. C. Deighton (Ed.), *The encyclopedia of education* (Vol. 3, pp. 81–85). New York: Macmillan.

Sommer, A. (2012). Psychical research and the origins of American psychology: Hugo Münsterberg, William James and Eusapia Palladino. *History of the Human Sciences, 25,* 23–44.

Sourkes, T. L. (2009). Acetylcholine—from Vagusstoff to cerebral neurotransmitter. *Journal of the History of the Neurosciences, 18,* 47–58.

Southall, J. P. C. (Ed.). (1962). *Helmholtz's treatise on physiological optics.* New York: Dover.

Southard, M. M. (1927). *The attitude of Jesus toward women.* New York: George H. Doran.

Spalding, D. A. (1873, February). Instinct. With original observations on young animals. *Macmillan's Magazine, 27,* 282–293.

Spence, K. W. (1937). The differential response in animals to stimuli varying within a single dimension. *Psychological Review, 44,* 430–444.

Spence, K. W. (1952). Clark Leonard Hull: 1884–1952. *American Journal of Psychology, 65,* 639–646.

Spencer, H. (1873). *Study of sociology.* New York: D. Appleton & Co.

Sperry, R. W. (1961). Cerebral organization and behavior. *Science, 133,* 1749–1757.

Spilka, B., & Ladd, K. L. (2013). *The psychology of prayer: A scientific approach.* New York: Guilford.

Spillmann, J., & Spillmann, L. (1993). The rise and fall of Hugo Münsterberg. *Journal of the History of the Behavioral Sciences, 29,* 322–338.

Sporer, S. L. (2006). The science of eyewitness testimony has come of age. *Psychological Science in the Public Interest, 7,* i–ii.

Sprengnether, M. (1990). *The spectral mother: Freud, feminism, and psychoanalysis.* Ithaca, NY: Cornell University Press.

Springer, S. P., & Deutsch, G. (1985). *Left brain, right brain* (Rev. ed.). New York: Freeman.

Sprung, H., & Sprung, L. (1996). Carl Stumpf (1848–1936), a general psychologist and methodologist, and a case study of a cross-cultural scientific transition process. In W. Battmann & S. Dutke (Eds.), *Processes of the molar regulation of behavior* (pp. 327–342). Lengerich, Germany: Pabst Science Publishers.

Sprung, L., & Sprung, H. (2000). George Elias Müller and the beginnings of modern psychology. In G. A. Kimble & M. Wertheimer (Eds.), *Portraits of pioneers in psychology* (Vol. 4, pp. 71–91). Washington, DC: American Psychological Association.

Staats, A. W. (1989). Unificationism: Philosophy for the modern disunited science of psychology. *Philosophical Psychology, 2,* 143–164.

Staats, A. W. (1999). Unifying psychology requires new infrastructure, theory, method, and a research agenda. *Review of General Psychology, 3,* 3–13.

Staats, A. W. (2005). A road to and philosophy of unification. In R. J. Sternberg (Ed.), *Unity in psychology: Possibility or pipedream?* (pp. 159–178). Washington, DC: American Psychological Association.

Stace, W. T. (1962). *A critical history of Greek philosophy.* New York: St. Martin's Press.

Staddon, J. E. R. (2014). *The new behaviorism* (2nd ed.). London: Psychology Press.

Stahnisch, F. W. (2008). Instrument transfer as knowledge transfer in neurophysiology: François Magendie's

(1783–1855) early attempts to measure cerebrospinal fluid pressure. *Journal of the History of the Neurosciences, 17,* 72–99.

Staiti, A. (2014). Husserl's transcendental phenomenology: Nature, spirit, and life. Cambridge, UK: Cambridge University Press.

Staiti, A. (Ed.). (2015). *Commentary on Husserl's ideas I.* Berlin: De Gruyter.

Starbuck, E. D. (1899). *The psychology of religion: An empirical study of the growth of religious consciousness.* London: Walter Scott.

Starr, D. (2015a, March 5). Remembering a crime you didn't commit. *The New Yorker.* Retrieved April 30, 2016 from www.newyorker.com/tech/elements/false-memory-crime

Starr, D. (2015b, May 22). Juan Rivera and the dangers of coercive interrogation. *The New Yorker.* Retrieved April 30, 2016 from www.newyorker.com/news/news-desk/juan-rivera-and-the-dangers-of-coercive-interrogation

Starr, R. (2012). Should we be writing essays instead of articles? A psychotherapist's reflection on Montaigne's marvelous invention. *Humanistic Psychology, 52,* 423–450.

Steger, M. F. (2009). Meaning in life. In S. J. Lopez & C. R. Snyder (Eds.), *Oxford library of psychology. Oxford handbook of positive psychology* (2nd ed.) (pp. 679–687). New York: Oxford University Press.

Steinberg, H. (2015). Emil Kraepelin's ideas on transcultural psychiatry. *Australasian Psychiatry, 23,* 531–535.

Steinberg, H., & Himmerich, H. (2013). Emil Kraepelin's habilitation and his thesis: A pioneer work for modern systematic reviews, psychoimmunological research and categories of psychiatric diseases. *The World Journal of Biological Psychiatry, 14,* 248–257.

Steiner, G. (2006). Descartes, Christianity, and contemporary speciesism. In P. Waldau & K. Patton (Eds.), *A communion of subjects: Animals in religion, science, and ethics* (pp. 117–131). New York: Columbia University Press.

Steinert, T. (2014). Regaining complex perception: Gestalt thinking in 20th century architectural theory. *Gestalt Theory, 36,* 325–338.

Stephen, L. (1993). Mrs. Mary Wollstonecraft Godwin. In L. Stephen & S. Lee (Eds.), *The dictionary of national biography* (Vol. 8, pp. 60–62). New York: Oxford University Press.

Stephen, L., & Lee, S. (Eds.). (1960). *Dictionary of national biography* (Vol. 9). London: Oxford University Press.

Stephens, J. (1975). *Francis Bacon and the style of science.* Chicago: University of Chicago Press.

Stern, C. (1949). *Children discover arithmetic: An introduction to structural arithmetic.* New York: Harper.

Sternberg, R. J. (Ed.). (2005). *Unity in psychology: Possibility or pipedream?* Washington, DC: American Psychological Association.

Steudel, J. (1974). Johannes Peter Müller. In C. C. Gillispie (Ed.), *Dictionary of scientific biography* (Vol. 9, pp. 567–584). New York: Scribner.

Stevens, G., & Gardner, S. (Eds.). (1982). *The women of psychology: Pioneers and innovators.* Cambridge, MA: Schenkman.

Stevens, S. S. (1951). Mathematics, measurement, and psychophysics. In S. S. Stevens (Ed.), *Handbook of experimental psychology* (pp. 1–49). New York: Wiley.

Stevens, S. S. (1961). To honor Fechner and repeal his law. *Science, 133,* 80–86.

Stewart, D. (1802). *Elements of the philosophy of the human mind.* London: T. Cadell Jun. and W. Davies in the Strand, and W. Creech in Edinburgh. (Original work published 1792)

Stewart, M. (2006). *The courtier and the heretic: Leibniz, Spinoza, and the fate of God in the modern world.* New York: Norton.

Stewart, M. (2014). *Nature's God: The heretical origins of the American republic.* New York: Norton.

Still, A., & Dryden, W. (2012). *The historical and philosophical context of rational psychotherapy: The legacy of Epictetus.* London: Karnac Books.

Stocking, G. W. (1965). On the limits of "presentism" and "historicism" in the historiography of the behavioral sciences [editorial]. *Journal of the History of the Behavioral Sciences, 1,* 211–218.

Stolorow, R. D., Atwood, G. E., & Orange, D. M. (2010). Heidegger's Nazism and the hypostatization of being. *International Journal of Psychoanalytic Self Psychology, 5,* 429–450.

Stone, M. H. (2011). The meaning of life and Adler's use of fictions. *The Journal of Individual Psychology, 67,* 13–30.

Stout, M., & Love, J. M. (2015). *Integrative process: Follettian thinking from ontology to administration.* Anoka, MN: Process Century Press.

Strachey, J. (Ed.). (1953–1974). *The standard edition of the complete psychological works of Sigmund Freud.* London: Hogarth Press.

Strandh, S. (1979). *A history of the machine.* New York: A. W. Publishers.

Street, W. R. (2006). Foundations of national security psychology. In A. D. Mangelsdorff (Ed.), *Psychology in the service of national security* (pp. 29–40). Washington, DC: American Psychological Association.

Stricker, G. (1975). On professional schools and professional degrees. *American Psychologist, 30,* 1062–1066.

Strickler, G. (2016). PsyD training in clinical psychology. In J. C. Norcross, G. R. Vandenbos, D. K Freedheim, & M. M. Domenech Rodríguez (Eds.), *APA handbook of clinical psychology: Roots and branches* (Vol. 1, pp. 49–67). Washington, DC: American Psychological Association.

Stromberg, W. H. (1989). Helmholtz and Zoellner: Nineteenth century empiricism, spiritism, and the theory of space perception. *Journal of the History of the Behavioral Sciences, 25,* 371–383.

Strong, E. K. (1955). Walter Dill Scott: 1869–1955. *American Journal of Psychology, 68,* 682–683.

Strous, R. D., Opler, A. A., & Opler, L. A. (2016). Reflections on "Emil Kraepelin: Icon and reality." *American Journal of Psychiatry, 173,* 300–301.

Studebaker, C. A., & Penrod, S. D. (1997). Pretrial publicity: The media, the law, and common sense. *Psychology, Public Policy, and the Law, 2–3,* 428–460.

Stumpf, C. (1895). Herman von Helmholtz and the new psychology. *Psychological Review, 2,* 1–12.

Stumpf, C. (1930). Carl Stumpf. In C. Murchison (Ed.), *A history of psychology in autobiography* (Vol. 1, pp. 389–441). Worcester, MA: Clark University Press.

Stumpf, C. (2012). *The origins of music* (D. Trippett, Trans.). New York: Oxford University Press. (Original work published 1911)

Suedfeld, P. (2016). On the road from WEIRD to STEM, psychology hits a bump. *Canadian Psychology, 57,* 60–64.

Suibhne, S. M. (2009). "Wrestle to be the man philosophy wished to make you": Marcus Aurelius, reflective practitioner. *Reflective Practice, 10,* 429–436.

Suinn, R. M., & Weigel, R. G. (1975). *The innovative psychological therapies: Critical and creative contributions.* New York: Harper & Row.

Sukhodolsky, D. G., Tsytsarev, S. V., & Kassinove, H. (1995). Behavior therapy in Russia. *Journal of Behavior Therapy and Experimental Psychiatry, 26,* 83–91.

Sullivan, H. S. (1953). *The interpersonal theory of psychiatry.* New York: Norton.

Sulloway, F. J. (1979). *Freud, biologist of the mind: Beyond psychoanalytic legend.* New York: Basic Books.

Sully, J. (1886). Development of the moral faculty. *Popular Science Monthly, 29,* 23–33.

Sully, J. (1894, 1895, 1896). Studies of childhood. *Popular Science Monthly, 45,* 323–330, 577–588, 733–742; *46,* 186–197, 348–363, 433–446, 781–792; *47,* 1–11, 340–353, 648–664, 808–817; *48,* 105–113, 166–180, 381–395.

Summers, M. (1965). *The geography of witchcraft.* New York: University Books.

Summers, M. (Trans.). (1971). *The malleus maleficarum of Heinrich Kramer and Jacob Sprenger.* New York: Dover.

Sussman, E. J. (1962). Franz Brentano—Much alive, though dead. *American Psychologist, 17,* 504–506.

Sussman, R. W. (2014). *The myth of race: The troubling persistence of an unscientific idea.* Cambridge, MA: Harvard University Press.

Swammerdam, J. (1758). *The book of nature* (T. Flloyd, Trans.). London: C. G. Seyffert.

Swan, M. (2015). The scientific method. In John Brockman (Ed.), *This idea must die* (pp. 392–395). New York: Harper.

Swazey, J. P. (1975). Charles Scott Sherrington. In C. C. Gillispi (Ed.), *Dictionary of scientific biography* (Vol. 12, pp. 395–403). New York: Scribner.

Symonds, A. (1991). Gender issues and Horney theory. *American Journal of Psychoanalysis, 51,* 301–312.

Szasz, T. (1970). *The manufacture of madness: A comparative history of the Inquisition and the mental health movement.* New York: Harper & Row.

Taine, H. A. (1876). Lingual development in babyhood. *Popular Science Monthly, 9,* 129–137.

Tan, A. M. (2016). Review of gender oppression and globalization: Challenges for social work. *Social Work and Christianity, 42,* 497–498.

Tansaz, M., Memarzadehzavareh, H., Qaraaty, M., Eftekhar, T., Tabarrai, M., & Kamalinejad, M. (2016). Menorrhagia management in Iranian traditional medicine. *Journal of Evidence-Based Complementary & Alternative Medicine, 21,* 71–76.

Tateo, L. (2013). Generalization as creative and reflective act: Revisiting Lewin's conflict between Aristotelian and Galileian modes of thought in psychology. *Theory and Psychology, 23,* 518–536.

Tauber, A. I. (2009). Freud's dreams of reason: The Kantian structure of psychoanalysis. *History of the Human Sciences, 22,* 1–29.

Taylor, B. (2003). *Mary Wollstonecraft and the feminist imagination.* New York: Cambridge University Press.

Taylor, E. (2000). Psychotherapeutics and the problematic origins of clinical psychology in America. *American Psychologist, 55,* 1029–1033.

Taylor, E. (2010). William James on a phenomenological psychology of immediate experience: The true foundation for a science of consciousness? *History of the Human Sciences, 23,* 119–130.

Taylor, E. (2011). William James's radical empiricism: Did E. B. Holt get it right? In E. P. Charles (Ed.), *A new look at New Realism: The psychology and philosophy of*

E. B. Holt (pp. 105–126). Piscataway, NJ: Transaction Publishers.

Taylor, E. I., & Martin, F. (2015). Humanistic psychology at the crossroads. In K. J. Schneider, J. F. Pierson, & J. F. T. Bugental (Eds.), *The handbook of humanistic psychology: Theory, research, and practice* (2nd ed., pp. 19–25). Thousand Oaks, CA: Sage Publications.

Taylor, G. R. (1983). *The great evolution mystery*. New York: Harper & Row.

Taylor, M. C. (1987). Søren Kierkegaard. In M. Eliade (Ed.), *The encyclopedia of religion* (Vol. 8, pp. 298–301). New York: Macmillan.

Taylor, R. (1967a). Causation. In P. Edwards (Ed.), *The encyclopedia of philosophy* (pp. 56–66). New York: Macmillan.

Taylor, R. (1967b). Determinism. In P. Edwards (Ed.), *The encyclopedia of philosophy* (pp. 359–373). New York: Macmillan.

Teilhard de Chardin. (1961). *The phenomenon of man* (B. Wall, Trans.). New York: Harper & Row.

Telles-Correia, D., & Marques, J. G. (2015). Melancholia before the twentieth century: Fear and sorrow or partial insanity? *Frontiers in Psychology, 6,* article no. 81.

Teo, T. (2015). Critical psychology: A geography of intellectual engagement and resistance. *American Psychologist, 70,* 243–254.

Terman, L. M. (1917). The intelligence quotient of Francis Galton in childhood. *American Journal of Psychology, 28,* 209–215.

Thomas, R. K. (2001). *Lloyd Morgan's canon: A history of misinterpretation*. Retrieved March 24, 2007 from http://htpprints.yorku.ca/archive/00000017/00/MCWeb.htm

Thompson, D., Hogan, J. D., & Clark, P. M. (2012). *Developmental psychology in historical perspective*. Malden, MA: Wiley-Blackwell.

Thompson, J. C. (2010). Women in ancient Egypt. Retrieved March 5, 2016 from www.womenintheancientworld.com

Thompson, T. (2014). Autism and behavior analysis: History and current status. In F. K. McSweeney & E. S. Murphy (Eds.), *The Wiley-Blackwell handbook of operant and classical conditioning* (pp. 483–508). Malden, MA: Wiley-Blackwell.

Thorndike, E. L. (1905). Measurements of twins. *Archives of Philosophy, Psychology, and Scientific Method, 1,* 1–64.

Thorndike, E. L. (1920). The psychology of the half-educated man. *Harper's Magazine, 140,* 666–670.

Thorndike, E. L. (1922). The psychology of labor. *Harper's Magazine, 144,* 799–806.

Thorndike, E. L. (1924). Mental discipline in high schools. *Journal of Educational Psychology, 15,* 1–22, 83–98.

Thorndike, E. L. (1936). The psychology of the profit motive. *Harper's Magazine, 173,* 431–437.

Thorndike, E. L., & Woodworth, R. S. (1901). The influence of improvement in one mental function upon the efficiency of other functions. *Psychological Review, 8,* 247–261, 384–395, 553–564.

Thorne, J. O. (Ed.). (1969). *Chambers' biographical dictionary*. New York: St. Martin's Press.

Thornhill, R., & Adcock, J. (1983). *The evolution of insect mating systems*. Cambridge, MA: Harvard University Press.

Thorpy, M. (2015). Sleep in the seventeenth and eighteenth centuries. In S. Chokroverty & M. Billiard (Eds.), *Sleep medicine: A comprehensive guide to its development, clinical milestones, and advances in treatment* (pp. 69–72). New York: Springer Science + Business Media.

Thurston, H. (1994). *Early astronomy*. New York: Springer-Verlag.

Tigiripalli, K. K., & Kadarla, L. K. (2009). Religion and human rights: A historical and contemporary assessment. In A. Sharma (Ed.), *The world's religions after September 11, Vol. 2: Religion and human rights* (pp. 27–35). Westport, CT: Praeger Publishers.

Tilman, R., & Knapp, T. (1999). John Dewey's unknown critique of marginal utility doctrine: Instrumentalism, motivation, and values. *Journal of the History of the Behavioral Sciences, 35,* 391–408.

Tinker, M. A. (1980). Wundt's doctorate students and their theses, 1875–1920. In W. G. Bringmann & R. D. Tweney (Eds.), *Wundt studies. A centennial collection* (pp. 269–272). Toronto: C. J. Hogrefe.

Tischler, L. (2014). Anna Freud: A new look at development. *British Journal of Psychotherapy, 30,* 154–168.

Titchener, E. B. (1892). The Leipsig school of experimental psychology. *Mind, 1* (new series), 206–234.

Titchener, E. B. (1898). A psychology laboratory. *Mind, 7,* 311–331.

Titchener, E. B. (1910). *A textbook of psychology*. New York: Macmillan.

Titchener, E. B. (1921). Wilhelm Wundt. *American Journal of Psychology, 32,* 161–177.

Titov, R. S. (2013). Gordon Allport: The concept of personal religious orientations. *Cultural-Historical Psychology, 1,* 2–12.

Toates, F. (2009). *Burrhus F. Skinner: Shaper of behaviour*. London: Palgrave Macmillan.

Toccafondi, F. (2009). Stumpf and Gestalt psychology: Relations and differences. *Gestalt Theory, 31,* 191–211.

Todes, D. P. (2014). *Ivan Pavlov: A Russian Life in Science.* New York: Oxford University Press.

Todman, D. (2008). Epilepsy in the Graeco-Roman world: Hippocratic medicine and Asklepian Temple medicine compared. *Journal of the History of the Neurosciences, 17,* 435–441.

Tolman, E. C. (1922). A new formula for behaviorism. *Psychological Review, 22,* 44–53.

Tolman, E. C. (1932). *Purposive behavior in animals and men.* New York: Century.

Tolman, E. C., & Honzik, C. H. (1930). Introduction and removal of reward and maze performance in rats. *University of California Publications in Psychology, 4,* 257–273.

Tomlinson, S. (2005). *Head masters: Phrenology, secular education, and nineteenth-century social thought.* Tuscaloosa: University of Alabama Press.

Tong, B. R. (2003). Taoist mind–body resources for psychological health and healing. In S. G. Mijares (Ed.), *Modern psychology and ancient wisdom: Psychological healing practices from the world's religious traditions.* New York: Haworth Integrative Healing Press.

Tonn, J. C. (2003). *Mary P. Follett: Creating democracy, transforming management.* New Haven, CT: Yale University Press.

Torrey, C. W. (1867). Women's sphere in the church. *The Congregational Quarterly, 9,* 163–171.

Toth, K., & King, B. H. (2010). Intellectual disability (mental retardation). In M. K. Dulcan (Ed.), *Dulcan's textbook of child and adolescent psychiatry* (pp. 151–171). Arlington, VA: American Psychiatric Publishing.

Toulmin, S. (1972). *Human understanding* (Vol. 1). Princeton, NJ: Princeton University Press.

Triarhou, L. C., & del Cerro, M. (2012). Ramón y Cajal erroneously identified as Camillo Golgi on a souvenir postage stamp. *Journal of the History of the Neurosciences, 21,* 132–138.

Tropp, L. R. (2006). Stigma and intergroup contact among members of minority and majority status groups. In S. Levin & C. van Laar (Eds.), *Stigma and group inequality: Social psychological perspectives* (pp. 171–191). Mahwah, NJ: Lawrence Erlbaum Associates.

Trueman, C. N. (2015). Ancient Egyptian medicine. Retrieved July 2, 2016 from www.history learningsite.co.uk/a-history-of-medicine/ancient-egyptian-medicine/n

Tsagareli, M. B. (2012). Ivane Tarkhnishvili (Tarchanoff): A major Georgian figure from the Russian physiological school. *Journal of the History of the Neurosciences, 21,* 393–408.

Tsanoff, R. A. (1964). *The great philosophers* (2nd ed.). New York: Harper & Row.

Tudor, K. (2014). Person-centered psychology and therapy, ecopsychology and ecotherapy. *Person-Centered and Experiential Psychotherapies, 12,* 315–329.

Tuke, D. H. (1872). *Illustrations of the influence of the mind upon the body in health and disease.* Philadelphia: Lindsay and Blakiston.

Tuke, D. H. (1878). *Insanity in ancient and modern life, with chapters on its prevention.* London: Macmillan.

Tuke, D. H. (1892). *A dictionary of psychological medicine.* London: J. & A. Churchill.

Tuke, S. (1813). *Description of the Retreat: An institution near York for insane persons of the Society of Friends.* Philadelphia, PA: Isaac Peirce.

Tuominen, M. (2014). On activity and passivity in perception: Aristotle, Philoponus, and Pseudo-Simplicius. In J. F. Silva & M. Yrjönsuuri (Eds.), *Active perception in the history of philosophy: From Plato to modern philosophy* (pp. 55–78). Cham, Switzerland: Springer International Publishing.

Turner, R. S. (1972). Hermann von Helmholtz. In C. C. Gillispie (Ed.), *Dictionary of scientific biography* (Vol. 6, pp. 241–253). New York: Scribner.

Turner, R. S. (1977). Hermann von Helmholtz and the empiricist vision. *Journal of the History of the Behavioral Sciences, 13,* 48–58.

Turner, R. S. (1994). *In the eye's mind: Vision and the Helmholtz-Hering controversy.* Princeton, NJ: Princeton University Press.

Tye, M. (1995). *Ten problems of consciousness: A representational theory of the phenomenal mind.* Cambridge, MA: MIT Press.

Tylor, E. B. (1872). Quételet on the science of man. *Popular Science Monthly, 1,* 45–55.

Unamuno, M. (1972). *The tragic sense of life* (A. Kerrigan, Trans.). Princeton, NJ: Princeton University Press. (Original work published 1913)

U.S. Department of Justice. (1999). *Eyewitness evidence: A guide for law enforcement.* Washington, DC: Author.

Ussher, J., Pierce, L., & Pierce, M. (2003). *Annals of the world: James Ussher's classic survey of world history.* Green Forest, AR: Master Books. (Original work published 1650)

Uttal, W. R. (2000). *The war between mentalism and behaviorism: On the accessibility of mental processes.* Mahwah, NJ: Erlbaum.

Uttal, W. R. (2001). *The new phrenology: The limits of localizing cognitive processes in the brain.* Cambridge, MA: MIT Press.

Uttal, W. R. (2011). *Mind and brain: A critical appraisal of cognitive neuroscience.* Cambridge, MA: MIT Press.

Uttal, W. R. (2013). *Reliability in cognitive neuroscience: A meta-meta-analysis.* Cambridge, MA: MIT Press.

Uytman, J. D. (1967). William McDougall. In P. Edwards (Ed.), *The encyclopedia of philosophy* (Vol. 5, pp. 226–227). New York: Macmillan and Free Press.

Valenstein, E. S. (2005). *The war of the soups and the sparks: The discovery of neurotransmitters and the dispute over how nerves communicate.* New York: Columbia University Press.

Valsiner, J. (2007). Returning to the future of psychology: Cultural psychology and the study of mental self-regulatory processes. *Intellectica, 46–47,* 251–268.

Vande Kemp, H. (1992). G. Stanley Hall and the Clark School of Religious Psychology. *American Psychologist, 47,* 290–298.

van Drunen, P., & Jansz, J. (2004). Child-rearing and education. In J. Jansz & P. van Drunen (Eds.), *A social history of psychology* (pp. 45–92). Malden, MA: Blackwell.

van Leeuwen, C. (2007). Towards an interdisciplinary science of visual Gestalten. *Gestalt Theory, 29,* 213–222.

van Steenburgh, J. J., Fleck, J. I., Beeman, M., & Kounios, J. (2012). Insight. In K. J. Holyoak & R. G. Morrison (Eds.), *The Oxford handbook of thinking and reasoning* (pp. 475–491). New York: Oxford University Press.

VanTassel-Baska, J. (2013). Sir Francis Galton: The Victorian polymath (1822–1911). In A. Robinson & J. L. Jolly (Eds.), *A century of contributions to gifted education: Illuminating lives* (pp. 8–22). New York: Routledge.

Vartanian, A. (1967). Julien Offray de La Mettrie. In P. Edwards (Ed.), *The encyclopedia of philosophy* (Vol. 4, pp. 379–382). New York: Macmillan.

Vasquez, M. J. T. (2007). Lillian Evelyn Moller Gilbreth: The woman who "had it all." In E. A. Gavin, A. Clamar, & M. A. Siderits (Eds.), *Women of vision: Their psychology, circumstances, and success* (pp. 45–60). New York: Springer Publishing Co.

Vedral, V. (2006). Is the universe deterministic? *New Scientist, 192,* 52–55.

Veehoven, R. (2011). Can we get happier than we are? In I. Brdar (Ed.), *The human pursuit of well-being: A cultural approach* (pp. 3–14). New York: Springer Science + Business Media.

Ventegodt, S., & Merrick, J. (2013). Reflections from a study tour to Hippocrates' Asklepieion on the island of Kos. In J. Merrick (Ed.), *Alternative medicine research yearbook 2012. Health and human development* (pp. 251–254). Hauppauge, NY: Nova Biomedical Books.

Ventriglio, A., & Bhugra, D. (2015). Descartes' dogma and damage to Western psychiatry. *Epidemiology and Psychiatric Sciences, 25,* 368–370.

Verstegen, I. (2000). Gestalt psychology in Italy. *Journal of History of the Behavioral Sciences, 36,* 31–42.

Verstegen, I. (2005). *Arnheim, Gestalt and art: A psychological theory.* Vienna: Springer-Verlag.

Verstegen, I. (2007). Rudolf Arnheim's contribution to Gestalt psychology. *Psychology of Aesthetics, Creativity, and the Arts, 1,* 8–15.

Verstegen, I. (2015). Editorial. *Gestalt Theory, 37,* 213–215.

Vicedo, M. (2009). Mothers, machines, and morals: Harry Harlow's work on primate love from lab to legend. *Journal of the History of the Behavioral Sciences, 45,* 193–218.

Vicedo, M. (2010). The evolution of Harry Harlow: From the nature to the nurture of love. *History of Psychiatry, 21,* 190–205.

Vicedo, M. (2013). The *nature and nurture of love: From imprinting to attachment in Cold War America.* Chicago: University of Illinois Press.

Vidal, F. (1987). Jean Piaget and the liberal protestant tradition. In M. G. Ash & W. R. Woodward (Eds.), *Psychology in twentieth-century thought and society* (pp. 271–294). Cambridge, UK: Cambridge University Press.

Viljanen, V. (2014). Spinoza on activity in sense perception. In J. F. Silva & M. Yrjönsuuri (Eds.), *Active perception in the history of philosophy: From Plato to modern philosophy* (pp. 241–254). Cham, Switzerland: Springer International Publishing.

Vinchur, A. J., & Koppes, L. L. (2007). Early contributors to the science and practice of industrial psychology. In L. L. Koppes (Ed.), *Historical perspectives in industrial and organizational psychology* (pp. 37–58). Mahwah, NJ: Lawrence Erlbaum Associates.

Viney, D. W. (1984). William James on free will and determinism. *Journal of Mind and Behavior, 7,* 555–556.

Viney, D. W. (1997). William James on free will: The French connection. *History of Philosophy Quarterly, 14,* 29–52.

Viney, W. (1989). The cyclops and the twelve-eyed toad: William James and the unity–disunity problem in psychology. *American Psychologist, 44,* 1261–1265.

Viney, W. (1990). The tempering effect of determinism in the legal system: A response to Rychlak and Rychlak. *New Ideas in Psychology, 8,* 31–42.

Viney, W. (1991). Charles Hartshorne's philosophy and the psychology of sensation. In L. E. Hahn (Ed.), *The philosophy of Charles Hartshorne. The library of living philosophers* (Vol. 20, pp. 91–112). LaSalle, IL: Open Court.

Viney, W. (1992). A study of emotion in the context of radical empiricism. In M. E. Donnelly (Ed.),

Reinterpreting the legacy of William James (pp. 243–250). Washington, DC: American Psychological Association.

Viney, W. (1996a). Disunity in psychology and other sciences: The network or the block universe? *Journal of Mind and Behavior, 17,* 31–43.

Viney, W. (1996b). Dorothea Dix: An intellectual conscience for psychology. In G. A. Kimble, C. A. Boneau, & M. Wertheimer (Eds.), *Portraits of pioneers in psychology* (Vol. 2, pp. 15–31). Washington, DC: American Psychological Association.

Viney, W. (2001). The radical empiricism of William James and philosophy of history. *History of Psychology, 4,* 211–227.

Viney, W. (2010, April). *The adaptive features of historical consciousness.* Paper presented at the Rocky Mountain Psychological Association, Denver, CO.

Viney, W., & Bartsch, K. (1984). Dorothea Lynde Dix: Positive or negative influence on the development of treatment for the mentally ill. *The Social Science Journal, 21,* 71–82.

Viney, W., & Burlingame-Lee, L. (2003). Margaret Floy Washburn: A quest for the harmonies in the context of a rigorous scientific framework. In G. A. Kimble & M. Wertheimer (Eds.), *Portraits of pioneers in psychology* (Vol. 5, pp. 73–88). Washington, DC: American Psychological Association.

Viney, W., King, C. L., & King, D. B. (1992). William James on the advantages of a pluralistic psychology. In M. E. Donnelly (Ed.), *Reinterpreting the legacy of William James* (pp. 91–100). Washington, DC: American Psychological Association.

Viney, W., King, D. B., & Berndt, J. (1990). Animal research in psychology: Declining or thriving? *Journal of Comparative Psychology, 104,* 322–325.

Viney, W. & Mullen, M. (2017). Tempering the foolish faiths: William James and ecology. *Ecopsychology.*

Viney, W. & Parker, E. (2016). Necessity as a nightmare or as a pathway to freedom: Freud's dilemma, a human dilemma. *Psychoanalytic Psychology, 33,* 299–311.

Viney, W., Wertheimer, M., & Wertheimer, M. L. (1979). *History of psychology: A guide to information sources.* Detroit, MI: Gale Research.

Viney, W., & Woody, W. D. (1995). Psychogeny: A neglected dimension in teaching the mind–brain problem. *Teaching of Psychology, 22,* 173–177.

Viney, W., & Woody, W. D. (2017). *Science and religion: Neglected perspectives.* New York: Routledge.

Virués-Ortega, J., Buela-Casal, G., Carrasco-Lazareno, M. T., Rivero-Dávila, P. D., & Quevedo-Blasco, R. (2011). A systematic archival inquiry on Juan Huarte

de San Juan (1529–88). *History of the Human Sciences, 24,* 21–47.

Visible scientists. (1975, May). *Time, 105,* 44.

Vlastos, G. (1967). Zeno of Elea. In P. Edwards (Ed.), *Encyclopedia of philosophy* (Vol. 8, pp. 369–379). New York: Macmillan and Free Press.

Voeks, V. (1950). Formalization and clarification of a theory of learning. *Journal of Psychology, 30,* 341–362.

Voeks, V. (1968). Edwin R. Guthrie. In D. L. Sills (Ed.), *International encyclopedia of the social sciences* (Vol. 6, pp. 296–302). New York: Macmillan.

Voltaire. (1991). *Candide, or optimism* (2nd ed.). (R. M. Adams, Ed. & Trans.). New York: Norton. (Original work published 1759)

Voltaire, F. M. (1980). *Letters on England* (L. Tancock, Trans.). Harmondsworth, UK: Penguin. (Original work published 1733)

Vrooman, J. R. (1970). *René Descartes: A biography.* New York: G. P. Putnam.

Wade, N. (2014). *A troublesome inheritance: Genes, race, and human history.* New York: Penguin Books.

Wade, N. J. (1994). Hermann von Helmholtz (1821–1894). *Perception, 23,* 981–989.

Wade, N. J. (2005). *Perception and illusion: Historical perspectives.* New York: Springer.

Wade, N. J. (2008). Guest editorial essay: Natural historians. *Perception, 37,* 479–482.

Wade, N. J. (2009a). Galileo's vision. *Cortex, 45,* 793–794.

Wade, N. J. (2009b). Guest editorial essay: Berkeley's essay. *Perception, 38,* 317–320.

Wade, N. J. (2010a). The Darwins and Wells: From revolution to evolution. *Journal of the History of the Neurosciences, 19,* 85–104.

Wade, N. J. (2010b). Guest editorial essay: Reid on perception. *Perception, 39,* 443–446.

Wade, N. J. (2012a). Scotland. In D. B. Baker (Ed.), *The Oxford handbook of the history of psychology: Global perspectives* (pp. 462–495). New York: Oxford University Press.

Wade, N. J. (2012b). Artistic precursors of Gestalt principles. *Gestalt Theory, 34,* 329–348.

Wade, N. J. (2015). How were eye movements recorded before Yarbus? *Perception, 44,* 851–883.

Wade, N. J., & Finger, S. (2001). The eye as an optical instrument. From camera obscura to Helmholtz's perspective. *Perception, 30,* 1157–1177.

Wade, N. J., Ono, H., & Lillakas, L. (2001). Leonardo da Vinci's struggles with representations of reality. *Leonardo, 34,* 231–235.

Wade, N. J., Sakurai, K., & Kyoba, J. (2007). Guest editorial essay: Whither Wundt? *Perception, 36,* 163–166.

Wagemans, J., Elder, J. H., Kubovy, M., Palmer, S. E., Peterson, M. A., Singh, M., et al. (2012a). A century of Gestalt psychology in visual perception: I. Perceptual grouping and figure-ground organization. *Psychological Bulletin, 138,* 1172–1217.

Wagemans, J., Feldman, J., Gepshtein, S., Kimchi, R., Pomerantz, J. R., van der Helm, P. A., et al. (2012b). A century of Gestalt psychology in visual perception: II. Conceptual and theoretical foundations. *Psychological Bulletin, 138,* 1218–1252.

Wagner, E. J. (2006). *The science of Sherlock Holmes. From Baskerville Hall to the valley of fear, the real forensics behind the great detective's greatest cases*. Hoboken, NJ: John Wiley & Sons, Inc.

Waithe, M. E. (1987a). Arete, Asclepigenia, Axiothea, Cleobulina, Hipparchia, and Lasthenia. In M. E. Waithe (Ed.), *A history of women philosophers* (pp. 197–209). Boston: Martinus Nijhoff.

Waithe, M. E. (1987b). Early Pythagoreans: Themistoclea, Theana, Arignote, Myia, and Damo. In M. E. Waithe (Ed.), *A history of women philosophers* (pp. 11–18). Boston: Martinus Nijhoff.

Waithe, M. E. (1989). Heloise. In M. E. Waithe (Ed.), *A history of women philosophers, Vol. II: Medieval, Renaissance and Enlightenment women philosophers A.D. 500–1600* (pp. 67–83). Boston: Kluwer Academic.

Walborn, F. (2014). *Religion in personality theory*. San Diego, CA: Elsevier Academic Press.

Walker, P. N. (1973). *Punishment: An illustrated history*. New York: Arco.

Wallace, W. A. (1993). *Theories of personality*. Boston: Allyn & Bacon.

Wallerstein, R. S. (2006). One psychoanalysis or many? In A. M. Cooper (Ed.), *Contemporary psychoanalysis in America: Leading analysts present their work* (pp. 691–720). Arlington, VA: American Psychiatric Publishing, Inc. (Original work published 1988)

Walusinski, O. (2012). A case of Charcotian grande hystérie: Observation by Julien Offray de La Mettrie in 1738. *European Neurology, 67,* 98–106.

Wampold, B. E. (2001). *The great psychotherapy debate: Models, methods, and findings*. Mahwah, NJ: Erlbaum.

Wang, S., Lilienfeld, S. O., & Rochat, P. (2015). The uncanny valley: Existence and explanations. *Review of General Psychology, 19,* 393–407.

Wapner, S. (1990). Introduction [to a series of papers on psychology at Clark University]. *Journal of the History of the Behavioral Sciences, 26,* 107–109.

Warburton, N. (2011). *A little history of philosophy*. New Haven, CT: Yale University Press.

Ward, J. (1876). An attempt to interpret Fechner's law. *Mind,* old series *1,* 452–466.

Ward, L. (2010). *John Locke and modern life*. New York: Cambridge University Press.

Ware, M. E. (2006, November). *Oral presentation*. Joint Nebraska Psychological Society/Association for Psychological and Educational Research in Kansas Teaching Conference, Fort Hays, KS.

Warren, H. (1921). In memory of Wilhelm Wundt. *Psychological Review, 28,* 166–169.

Washburn, D. A. (1997). The MacKay–Skinner debate: A case for "nothing buttery." *Philosophical Psychology, 10,* 473–479.

Washburn, D. A. (2010). The animal mind at 100. *The Psychological Record, 60,* 369–376.

Washburn, M. F. (1908). *The animal mind: A textbook of comparative psychology*. New York: Macmillan.

Washburn, M. F. (1916). *Movement and mental imagery*. New York: Houghton Mifflin.

Wasserman, E. A. (2013). Comparative cognition. In R. J. Nelson, S. J. Y. Mizumori, & I. B. Weiner (Eds.), *Handbook of psychology, Vol. 3: Behavioral neuroscience* (2nd ed., pp. 480–508). New York: John Wiley & Sons.

Wassmann, C. (2014). "Picturesque incisiveness": Explaining the celebrity of James's theory of emotion. *Journal of the History of the Behavioral Sciences, 50,* 166–188.

Watkin, J. (1998). Søren Kierkegaard's psychology of the self. *Journal of Psychology and Christianity, 17,* 362–373.

Watkins, J. W. N. (1965). *Hobbes's system of ideas*. London: Hutchinson University Library.

Watkins, L. R., & Maier, S. F. (2005). Glia and pain: Past, present, and future. In H. Merskey, J. D. Loeser, & R. Dubner (Eds.), *The paths of pain 1975–2005* (pp. 165–177). Seattle, WA: International Association for the Study of Pain Press.

Watrin, J. P., & Darwich, R. (2012). On behaviorism in the cognitive revolution: Myth and reactions. *Review of General Psychology, 16,* 269–282.

Watson, C. A. (2004). The sartorial self: William James's philosophy of dress. *History of Psychology, 7,* 211–224.

Watson, F. (1915). The father of modern psychology. *Psychological Review, 22,* 333–353.

Watson, J. B. (1912, February). Instinctive activity in animals. *Harper's Magazine, 124,* 376–382.

Watson, J. B. (1913). Psychology as the behaviorist views it. *Psychological Review, 20,* 158–177.

Watson, J. B. (1919). *Psychology from the standpoint of a behaviorist*. Philadelphia: Lippincott.

562

Watson, J. B. (1924a). *Behaviorism*. New York: Norton.

Watson, J. B. (1924b). The place of kinesthetic, visceral and laryngeal organization in thinking. *Psychological Review, 31,* 339–347.

Watson, J. B. (1924c). The unverbalized in human behavior. *Psychological Review, 31,* 273–280.

Watson, J. B. (1926). What the nursery has to say about instincts. In C. Murchison (Ed.), *Psychologies of 1925* (pp. 1–34). Worcester, MA: Clark University Press.

Watson, J. B. (1928). *Psychological care of infant and child*. New York: Norton.

Watson, J. B. (1961). John Broadus Watson. In C. Murchison (Ed.), *A history of psychology in autobiography* (Vol. 3, pp. 271–281). New York: Russell and Russell.

Watson, J. B., & Rayner, R. (1920). Conditioned emotional reactions. *Journal of Experimental Psychology, 3,* 1–14.

Watson, J. B., & Rayner, R. (1928). *Psychological care of the infant and child*. New York: W. W. Norton & Co.

Watson, J. D. (1968). *The double helix*. New York: New American Library.

Watson, R. I., Sr. (1966). The role and use of history in the psychology curriculum. *Journal of the History of the Behavioral Sciences, 2,* 64–69.

Watson, R. I. (Ed.). (1974/1976). *Eminent contributors to psychology* (2 vols.). New York: Springer.

Watson, R. I. (1978). *The history of psychology and the behavioral sciences: A bibliographic guide*. New York: Springer.

Watson, R. I., & Evans, R. B. (1991). *The great psychologists: A history of psychological thought* (5th ed.). New York: HarperCollins.

Watt, W. M. (1965). Al-Ghazali. In B. Lewis, Ch. Pellat, & J. Schacht (Eds.), *Encyclopedia of Islam* (Vol. 2, pp. 1038–1041). London: Luzac.

Watts, R. E. (1998). The remarkable parallel between Rogers's core conditions and Adler's social interest. *The Journal of Individual Psychology, 54,* 4–9.

Weber, E. H. (1978). *The sense of touch* (H. E. Ross, Trans.). New York: Academic Press. (Original work published 1834)

Weber, M. M. (1997). Alois Alzheimer, a coworker of Emil Kraepelin. *Journal of Psychiatric Research, 31,* 635–643.

Webster, R. J., Saucier, D. A., & Harris, R. J. (2010). Before the measurement of prejudice: Early psychological and sociological papers on prejudice. *Journal of the History of the Behavioral Sciences, 46,* 300–313.

Webster, S., & Coleman, S. R. (1992). Hull and his critics: The reception of Clark L. Hull's behavior theory. *Psychological Reports, 70,* 1063–1071.

Weekes, K. (Ed.). (2009). *Prejudice and privilege: Twenty years with the invisible knapsack*. Newcastle upon Tyne, UK: Cambridge Scholars Society.

Wegner, D. M. (2002). *The illusion of conscious will*. Cambridge, MA: MIT Press.

Weik, E. (2010). Bourdieu and Leibniz: Mediated dualisms. *Sociological Review, 58,* 486–496.

Weinberger, J., Siegel, P., & Decamello, A. (2000). On integrating psychoanalysis and cognitive science. *Psychoanalysis & Contemporary Thought, 23,* 147–175.

Weiner, B. (2013). Little-known truths, quirky anecdotes, seething scandals, and even some sciences in the history of (primarily achievement) motivation. *Personality and Social Psychology Review, 17,* 293–304.

Weiner, D. B. (1992). Philippe Pinel's "memoir on madness" of December 11, 1794: A fundamental text of modern psychiatry. *American Journal of Psychiatry, 149,* 725–732.

Weinstein, C. E., & Way, P. J. (2003). Educational psychology. In I. B. Weiner (Series Ed.) & D. K. Freedheim (Vol. Ed.), *Handbook of psychology, Vol. 1: History of psychology* (pp. 269–277). New York: Wiley.

Weishaar, M. E. (1993). *Aaron T. Beck*. Thousand Oaks, CA: Sage.

Weiss, A. P. (1924). Behaviorism and behavior I. *Psychological Review, 31,* 32–50.

Weiss, A. P. (1928). Behaviorism and ethics. *Journal of Abnormal and Social Psychology, 22,* 388–397.

Weiss, K. J. (2012). Classics in psychiatry and the law: Francis Wharton on involuntary confessions. *Journal of the American Academy of Psychiatry and Law, 40,* 67–80.

Weiss, R. (1989). The hedonic calculus in the Protagoras and the Phaedo. *Journal of the History of Philosophy, 27,* 511–529.

Welles, S. (Ed.). (1957). *The world's great religions*. New York: Time.

Wells, G. L., Memon, A., & Penrod, S. D. (2006). Eyewitness evidence: Improving its probative value. *Psychological Science in the Public Interest, 7,* 45–75.

Wennberg, B.-A., & Hane, M. (2005). Kurt Lewin's heritage: A possible breakthrough? *Gestalt Review, 9,* 245–270.

Wentworth, P. A. (1999). The moral of her story: Exploring the philosophical and religious commitments in Mary Whiton Calkins' self-psychology. *History of Psychology, 2,* 119–131.

Wertheimer, M. (Max). (1912). Experimentelle studien über das Sehen von Bewegung. *Zeitschrift für Psychologie, 61,* 161–265.

Wertheimer, M. (1934). On truth. *Social Research, 1,* 135–146.

Wertheimer, M. (1935). Some problems in the theory of ethics. *Social Research, 2,* 353–367.

Wertheimer, M. (1937). On the concept of democracy. In M. Ascoli & F. Lehmann (Eds.), *Political and economic democracy* (pp. 271–283). New York: Norton.

Wertheimer, M. (1940). A story of three days. In R. N. Anshen (Ed.), *Freedom: Its meaning* (pp. 555–569). New York: Harcourt Brace.

Wertheimer, M. (1950). Numbers and numerical concepts in primitive peoples. In W. D. Ellis (Ed.), *A source book of Gestalt psychology* (pp. 265–273). New York: Humanities Press. (Original work published 1912)

Wertheimer, M. (1982). *Productive thinking* (M. Wertheimer, Ed.). Chicago: University of Chicago Press. (Original work published 1945)

Wertheimer, M. (Michael). (1961). Psychomotor coordination of auditory and visual space at birth. *Science, 134,* 1962.

Wertheimer, M. (1972). *Fundamental issues in psychology.* New York: Holt, Rinehart and Winston.

Wertheimer, M. (1978). Humanistic psychology and the humane but tough minded psychologist. *American Psychologist, 33,* 739–745.

Wertheimer, M. (1980a). Historical research—why? In J. Brozek & L. J. Pongratz (Eds.), *Historiography of modern psychology* (pp. 3–23). Toronto: C. J. Hogrefe.

Wertheimer, M. (1980b). Max Wertheimer, Gestalt prophet. *Gestalt Theory, 2,* 3–17.

Wertheimer, M. (1983). Gestalt theory, holistic psychologies and Max Wertheimer. *Personale Psychologie, 5,* 32–49.

Wertheimer, M. (1985). A Gestalt perspective on computer simulations of cognitive processes. *Computers in Human Behavior, 1,* 19–33.

Wertheimer, M. (1986). The annals of the house that Ebbinghaus built. In F. Klix & H. Hagendorf (Eds.), *Human memory and cognitive capacities: Mechanisms and performance.* Amsterdam: Elsevier Science.

Wertheimer, M. (1987). *A brief history of psychology* (3rd ed.). New York: Holt, Rinehart and Winston.

Wertheimer, M. (1991). Personal communication.

Wertheimer, M. (2014a). Music, thinking, and perceived motion: The emergence of Gestalt theory. *History of Psychology, 17,* 131–133.

Wertheimer, M. (2014b). Max Wertheimer centennial celebration in Germany. *History of Psychology, 17,* 129–130.

Wertheimer, M., King, D. B., Peckler, M. A., Raney, S., & Schaef, R. W. (1992). Carl Jung and Max Wertheimer on a priority issue. *Journal of the History of the Behavioral Sciences, 28,* 45–56.

Wertheimer, M., & Schulte, H. (Trans.). (1986). An attempt at a theory of the paranoid ideas of reference and delusion formation. *Gestalt Theory, 8,* 231–255. (Original work published 1924)

Wertsch, J. V. (1985). *Vygotsky and the social formation of mind.* Cambridge, MA: Harvard University Press.

Wertz, F. J. (2014). Qualitative inquiry in the history of psychology. *Qualitative Psychology, 1,* 4–16.

Wertz, F. J. (2015). Phenomenology: Methods, historical development, and applications in psychology. In J. Martin, J. Sugarman, & K. L. Slaney (Eds.), *The Wiley handbook of theoretical and philosophical psychology: Methods, approaches, and new directions for social sciences* (pp. 85–101). Hoboken, NJ: Wiley-Blackwell.

Westerlund, F. (2014). What is a transcendental description? In S. Heinämaa, M. Hartimo, & T. Miettinen (Eds.), *Phenomenology and the transcendental* (pp. 257–275). New York: Routledge.

Westheimer, G. (1999). Gestalt theory reconfigured: Max Wertheimer's anticipation of recent developments in visual neuroscience. *Perception, 28,* 5–15.

Westman, R. S. (1986). The Copernicans and the churches. In D. C. Lindberg & R. L. Numbers (Eds.), *God and nature: Historical essays on the encounter between Christianity and science* (pp. 76–113). Berkeley: University of California Press.

Weston, S. (2009). Positive-normative distinction in British history of economic thought. In J. Peil & I. van Staveren (Eds.), *Handbook of economics and ethics* (pp. 366–373). Northampton, MA: Edward Elgar Publishing.

Wheeler, W. M. (1906). The queen ant as a psychological study. *Popular Science Monthly, 68,* 291–299.

Wheelock, L. D., & Callahan, J. L. (2006). Mary Parker Follett: A rediscovered voice informing the field of human resource development. *Human Resource Development Review, 5,* 258–273.

Whillans, A. V., Dunn, E. W., Sandstrom, G. M., Dickerson, S. S., & Madden, K. M. (2016). Is spending money on others good for your heart? *Health Psychology, 35,* 574–583.

Whitaker, H., Smith, C. U. M., & Finger, S. (Eds.). (2007). *Brain, mind, and medicine.* New York: Springer.

White, A. D. (1910). *A history of the warfare of science with theology in Christendom* (2 vols.). New York: D. Appleton and Co. (Original work published 1896)

White, A. D. (1978). *A history of the warfare of science with theology in Christendom* (2 vols.). Gloucester, MA: Peter Smith. (Original work published 1896)

White, S. H. (1992). G. Stanley Hall: From philosophy to developmental psychology. *Developmental Psychology, 28,* 25–34.

Whitehead, A. N. (1968). *Modes of thought.* New York: Free Press. (Original work published 1938)

Whitehead, A. N. (1971). *The concept of nature*. New York: Cambridge University Press. (Original work published 1920)

Whitehead, A. N. (1979). *Process and reality*. New York: Free Press.

Wichler, G. (1961). *Charles Darwin, the founder of the theory of evolution and natural selection*. New York: Pergamon Press.

Wiggins, B. J. (2009). William James and methodological pluralism: Bridging the qualitative and quantitative divide. *Mind and Behavior, 30,* 165–184.

Wight, R. D. (1993). The Pavlov-Yerkes connection: What was its origin? *Psychological Record, 43,* 351–359.

Wigmore, J. H. (1909). Professor Münsterberg and the psychology of testimony. *Illinois Law Review, 3,* 399–445.

Wilkins, J., & Matson, J. L. (2009). History of treatment in children with developmental disabilities and psychopathology. In J. L. Matson, F. Andrasik, & M. L. Matson (Eds.), *Treating childhood psychopathology and developmental disabilities* (pp. 3–28). New York: Springer Science + Business Media.

Wills, F. (2009). *Beck's cognitive therapy: Distinctive features*. New York: Routledge.

Wilson, A. N. (1997). *Paul: The mind of the apostle*. New York: Norton.

Wilson, E. O. (2000). *Sociobiology: The new synthesis* (25th anniversary ed.). Cambridge, MA: Belknap Press. (Original work published 1975)

Windholz, G. (1984). Pavlov vs. Köhler: Pavlov's little known primate research. *Pavlovian Journal of Biological Science, 19,* 23–31.

Windholz, G. (1997). Ivan P. Pavlov: An overview of his life and psychological work. *American Psychologist, 52,* 941–946.

Winston, A. S. (1990). Robert Sessions Woodworth and the "Columbia Bible": How the psychological experiment was redefined. *American Journal of Psychology, 103,* 391–401.

Winston, A. S. (2003). *Defining difference: Race and racism in the history of psychology*. Washington, DC: American Psychological Association.

Winston, A. S. (2006). Robert S. Woodworth and the creation of an eclectic psychology. In D. A. Dewsbury, L. T. Benjamin, & M. Wertheimer (Eds.), *Portraits of pioneers in psychology* (Vol. 6, pp. 51–66). Washington, DC: American Psychological Association.

Winston, C. N. (2016). An existential-humanistic-positive theory of human motivation. *The Humanistic Psychologist, 44,* 142–163.

Winter, I. J. (1976). *Montaigne's self-portrait and its influence in France, 1580–1630*. Lexington, KY: French Forum.

Wisdom, J. O. (1943). Determinism and psychoanalysis. *International Journal of Psychoanalysis, 24,* 140–147.

Wither, J. K. (2010). Warfare, trends in. In G. Fink (Ed.), *Stress of war, conflict and disaster* (pp. 225–235). San Diego, CA: Elsevier.

Witt, J. K., South, S. C., & Sugovic, M. (2014). A perceiver's own abilities influence perception, even when observing others. *Psychonomic Bulletin & Review, 21,* 384–389.

Witt, J. K., & Sugovic, M. (2013). Catching ease influences perceived speed: Evidence for action-specific effects from action-based measures. *Psychonomic Bulletin & Review, 20,* 1364–1370.

Witty, M. C., & Adomaitis, R. (2014). Carl Rogers and client-centered counseling. In R. D. Parsons & N. Zhang (Eds.), *Counseling theory: Guiding reflective practice. Counseling and professional identity* (pp. 171–199). Thousand Oaks, CA: Sage Publications, Inc.

Wolberg, A. (1989). Pilgrim's process through the psychoanalytic maze. *Psychoanalysis and Psychotherapy, 7,* 18–26.

Wolf, T. H. (1973). *Alfred Binet*. Chicago: University of Chicago Press.

Wollstonecraft, M. (1929). *A vindication of the rights of woman*, published with John Stuart Mill, *The subjection of women*. New York: Dutton. (Original work published 1792)

Wolpe, J. (1958). *Psychotherapy by reciprocal inhibition*. Stanford, CA: Stanford University Press.

Wolpe, J., & Plaud, J. J. (1997). Pavlov's contributions to behavior therapy: The obvious and the not so obvious. *American Psychologist, 52,* 966–972.

Wong, W. (2010). Retracing the footsteps of Wilhelm Wundt: Explorations in the disciplinary frontiers of psychology and in Völkerpsychologie. *History of Psychology, 12,* 229–265.

Wood, D. (2010). Epicueanism and the poetics of consumption. *International Journal of Consumer Studies, 34,* 369–374.

Wood, N. (1968). Niccolò Machiavelli. In D. Sills (Ed.), *International encyclopedia of the social sciences* (Vol. 9, pp. 505–511). New York: Macmillan and Free Press.

Woodworth, R. S., & Schlosberg, H. (1954). *Experimental psychology* (Rev. ed.). New York: Henry Holt.

Woody, W. D. (2001). Gestalt psychology and William James. In F. Columbus (Ed.), *Advances in psychology research* (Vol. 4, pp. 33–48). Huntington, NY: Nova Science.

Woody, W. D. (2003). Varieties of religious conversion: William James in historical and contemporary contexts. *Streams of William James, 5,* 7–11.

Woody, W. D. (2009). The use of "cult" in the teaching of psychology. *Psychology of Spirituality and Religion, 1*, 218–232.

Woody, W. D., & Viney, W. (2009). A pluralistic universe: An overview and implications for psychology. *Mind and Behavior, 30*, 107–120.

Wooley, H. T., & Hart, H. (1921). Feeble-minded ex-school children; a study of children who have been students in Cincinnati Special Schools. *Studies from the Helen S. Trounstine Foundation, 1*, 237–264.

Woolley, B. (1999). *The bride of science: Romance, reason, and Byron's daughter*. New York: McGraw-Hill.

Worburton, N. (2011). *A little history of philosophy*. New Haven, CT: Yale University Press.

Workman, L., & Reader, W. (2008). *Evolutionary psychology: An introduction*. New York: Cambridge University Press.

Wright, P. (2005). George Combe—phrenologist, philosopher, psychologist (1788–1858). *Cortex: A Journal Devoted to the Study of the Nervous System and Behavior, 41*, 447–451.

Wundt, W. (1876). Central innervation of consciousness. *Mind*, old series *1*, 161–178.

Wundt, W. (1901). *Ethics* (E. B. Titchener, J. H. Guilliver, & M. F. Washburn, Trans.). New York: Macmillan. (Original work published 1892)

Wundt, W. (1907). *Lectures on human and animal psychology* (J. Creighton & E. B. Titchener, Trans.). New York: Macmillan. (Original work published 1863)

Wundt, W. (1916). *Elements of folk psychology* (E. L. Schaub, Trans.). New York: Macmillan.

Wundt, W. (1969a). *Outlines of psychology* (C. H. Judd, Trans.). St. Clair Shores, MI: Scholarly Press. (Original work published 1897)

Wundt, W. (1969b). *Principles of physiological psychology* (5th ed., Vol. 1). (E. B. Titchener, Trans.). New York: Kraus Reprint Co. (Original work published 1873; 5th ed. published 1910)

Wundt, W. (1973). *An introduction to psychology*. New York: Arno Press. (Original work published 1912)

Wundt, W. (1977). Lectures on human and animal psychology. In D. N. Robinson (Ed.), *Significant contributions to the history of psychology 1750–1920: Series D: Comparative psychology* (Vol. 1). Washington, DC: University Publications. (Original work published 1894)

Wundt, W. (2013). Psychology's struggle for existence: Second edition, 1913. (J. T. Lamiell, Trans.). *History of Psychology, 16*(3), 197–211. (Original work published 1913)

Wyatt, W. J. (2000). Behaviorial science in the cross-hairs: The FBI file on B. F. Skinner. *Behavioral and Social Issues, 10*, 101–109.

Yanjiao, L, Yuping, W., Fanq, W., Xue, Y., Yue, H., & Sasha, L. (2015). Sleep medicine in ancient and traditional China. In S. Chokroverty & M. Billiard (Eds.), *Sleep medicine: A comprehensive guide to its development, clinical milestones, and advances in treatment* (pp. 29–33). New York: Springer Science + Business Media.

Yannick, S., Sutin, A. R., & Terracciano, A. (2016). Feeling older and risk of hospitalization: Evidence from three longitudinal cohorts. *Health Psychology, 35*, 634–637.

Yasnitsky, A. (2016). A transnational history of "The beginning of a beautiful friendship": The birth of the cultural-historical Gestalt psychology of Alexander Luria, Kurt Lewin, Lev Vygotsky, and others. In A. Yasnitsky & R. van der Veer (Eds.), *Revisionist revolution in Vygotsky studies* (pp. 201–225). New York: Routledge.

Yerkes, R. M. (1900). The formation of habits in the turtle. *Popular Science Monthly, 58*, 519–525.

York, G. K., III. (2011). Comment: Lucretius the Epicurian neurologist. *Neurology, 77*(10), 1003.

Yost, E., & Gilbreth, L. M. (1944). *Normal lives for the disabled*. New York: Macmillan.

Young, J. L. (2013). A brief history of self-report in American psychology. In J. W. Clegg (Ed.), *Self-observation in the social sciences* (pp. 45–65). Piscataway, NJ: Transaction Publishers.

Young, J. L., & Green, C. D. (2013). An exploratory digital analysis of the early years of G. Stanley Hall's *American Journal of Psychology* and *Pedagogical Seminary*. *History of Psychology, 16*, 249–268.

Young, P. T. (1972). An eclectic in psychology. In T. S. Krawiec (Ed.), *The psychologists* (Vol. 1, pp. 325–355). New York: Oxford University Press.

Young, R. M. (1966). Scholarship and the history of the behavioral sciences. In A. C. Crombie & M. A. Hoskin (Eds.), *History of science* (Vol. 5). Cambridge: W. Heffner & Sons.

Young-Bruehl, E. (2008). *Anna Freud: A biography* (2nd ed.). New Haven, CT: Yale University Press.

Young-Bruehl, E. (2012). Anna Freud: The teacher, the clinician, the person. In N. T. Malberg & J. Rapael-Leff (Eds.), *The Anna Freud tradition: Lines of development— Evolution of theory and practice over the decades* (pp. 10–13). London: Karnac Books.

Youniss, J. (2006). G. Stanley Hall and his times: Too much so, yet not enough. *History of Psychology, 9*, 224–235.

Yun, S. H. (2012). An analysis of Confucianism's yin-yang harmony with nature and the traditional oppression of women: Implications for social work practice. *Journal of Social Work, 13,* 582–598.

Zachar, P. (2013). Why the one and the many will not go away. *Philosophy, Psychiatry, & Psychology, 20,* 131–136.

Zagorin, P. (1968). Thomas Hobbes. In D. L. Sills (Ed.), *International encyclopedia of the social sciences* (Vol. 6, pp. 481–487). New York: Macmillan.

Zargaran, A., Borhani-Haghighi, A., Faridi, P., Daneshamouz, S., & Mohagheghzadeh, A. (2016). A review on the management of migraine in the Avicenna's Canon of Medicine. *Neurological Sciences, 37,* 471–478.

Zargaran, A., Mehdizadeh, A., Yarmohammadi, H., & Mohagheghzadeh, A. (2012). Zoroastrian priests: Ancient Persian psychiatrists. *American Journal of Psychiatry, 169,* 255.

Zeigarnik, A. Z. (2007). Bluma Zeigarnik: A memoir. *Gestalt Theory, 29,* 256–268.

Zeigler-Hill, V. Welling, L. L. M., & Shackelford, T. K. (Eds.). (2015). *Evolutionary perspectives on social psychology.* Cham, Switzerland: Springer International.

Zeitler, W. (2013). *The glass armonica: The music and the madness.* San Bernardino, CA: Musica Arcana.

Zentall, T. R. (2011). Animal intelligence. In R. J. Sternberg & S. B. Kaufman (Eds.), *The Cambridge book of intelligence* (pp. 309–327). New York: Cambridge University Press.

Zhuravel, V. A. (1995). From the history of the Bekhterev Psychoneurological Institute. *Journal of Russian and East European Psychiatry, 27,* 115–129.

Ziegler, P. (1991). *The black death.* London: Bath Press. (Original work published 1969)

Zilbersheid, U. (2013). The historical character of human nature in Freud's theories. *American Journal of Psychoanalysis, 73,* 184–204.

Zilboorg, G. (1941). *A history of medical psychology.* New York: Norton.

Zilboorg, G. (1961). *Freud and religion.* Westminster, MD: Westminster Press.

Zilio, D. (2016). On the autonomy of psychology from neuroscience: A case study of Skinner's radical behaviorism and behavior analysis. *Review of General Psychology, 20,* 155–170.

Zimbardo, P. G. (2007). *The Lucifer effect: Understanding how good people turn evil.* New York: Random House.

Zitzlsperger, U. (2006). Women's identity and authoritarian force: Women pamphleteers of the German reformation. In H. Chambers (Ed.), *Violence, culture and identity: Essays on German and Austrian literature, politics and society* (Vol. 1, pp. 65–83). New York: Peter Lang Publishing.

Zohalinezhad, M. E., & Zarshenas, M. M. (2015). Rhazes and an early case with possible hypertensive or reversible encephalopathy. *Journal of the History of the Neurosciences, 24,* 408–410.

Zubov, V. P. (1968). *Leonardo da Vinci* (D. H. Kraus, Trans.). Cambridge, MA: Harvard University Press.

Zucconi, A. (2008). From illness to health, well-being and empowerment: The person-centered paradigm shift from patient to client. In B. E. Levitt (Ed.), *Reflections on human potential: Bridging the person-centered approach and positive psychology* (pp. 131–146). Ross-on-Wye, UK: PCCS Books.

Zudini, V. (2011). The Euclidean model of measurement in Fechner's psychophysics. *Journal of the History of the Behavioral Sciences, 47,* 70–87.

Zusne, L. (1975). *Names in the history of psychology: A biographical sourcebook.* New York: Wiley.

Zusne, L. (1984). *Biographical dictionary of psychology.* Westport, CT: Greenwood Press.

Illustration Credits

Line portraits are by Jonathan Williams, Oxford Designers & Illustrators.

Chapter 3: p. 48: Courtesy of the National Library of Medicine; p. 53: Courtesy of the National Library of Medicine; p. 55: Lyrl Ahern; p. 62: Lyrl Ahern

Chapter 4: p. 71: Courtesy of the National Library of Medicine; p. 77: Hypatia, Alfred Seifert, Wikimedia Commons; p. 82: Lyrl Ahern; p. 85: Courtesy of the National Library of Medicine

Chapter 5: p. 104: Courtesy of the National Library of Medicine; p. 107: Painting by Federico Faruffini, Library of Congress, Prints and Photographs Division, [LC-USZ62-100795]; p. 111: Courtesy of the National Library of Medicine; p. 114: Courtesy of the National Library of Medicine

Chapter 6: p. 126: Courtesy of the National Library of Medicine; p. 129: Courtesy of the National Library of Medicine; p.141: Worthington (artist) and S. Freeman (engraver), Courtesy of the National Library of Medicine; p. 143: John Opie (artist) and James Heath (engraver), Courtesy of the Library of Congress, Prints and Photographs Division, [LC-USZ62-64309]

Chapter 7: p. 153: Courtesy of the National Library of Medicine; p. 156: Courtesy of the National Library of Medicine; p. 162: Courtesy of the National Library of Medicine

Chapter 8: p. 173: Courtesy of the Library of Congress, Prints and Photographs Division, [LC-USZ62-41264]; p. 183: Courtesy of the National Library of Medicine; p. 183: Courtesy of the Library of Congress, Prints and Photographs Division, [LC-B2-5926-1]; p. 191: Courtesy National Library of Medicine

Chapter 9: p. 203: Courtesy National Library of Medicine; p. 211: Courtesy of the National Library of Medicine; p. 221: Robert-Fleury (artist), Courtesy of the National Library of Medicine; p. 222: Courtesy of the National Library of Medicine; p. 225: Courtesy of the National Library of Medicine; p. 228: Bill Woody

Chapter 10: p. 241: Courtesy of the National Library of Medicine; p. 246: Courtesy of the National Library of Medicine

Chapter 11: p. 264: Courtesy of the National Library of Medicine; p. 273: Courtesy of the National Library of Medicine; p. 282: Courtesy of the National Library of Medicine

Chapter 12: p. 289: Courtesy of the National Library of Medicine; p. 299: Courtesy of Wikimedia Commons; p. 317: Courtesy of the National Library of Medicine

Chapter 13: p. 324: Courtesy of the National Library of Medicine; p. 329: Courtesy of Wikimedia Commons

Chapter 14: p. 360: Courtesy of Michael Wertheimer

Chapter 15: p. 386: Courtesy of the Library of Congress, Prints and Photographs Division, [LC-USZ62-139124]; p. 388: Courtesy of Clark University Archives; p. 405: Lyrl Ahern; p. 414: Lyrl Ahern

Chapter 16: p. 437: Lyrl Ahern

Chapter 17: p. 461: Courtesy of Marsha M. Linehan

Chapter 18: p. 488: Courtesy of Elizabeth F. Loftus

Index

a posteriori knowledge 14–15, 16, 35
a priori knowledge 14–15, 16, 35, 83, 170; Kant 163–164; rationalism 151–152, 168
AACP *see* American Association of Clinical Psychologists
Abelard, Peter 89–91, 92, 96, 97
ablation 185, 194
abnormal psychology 307, 457
About Behaviorism (Skinner) 348
Abraham, Karl 414
absolutism 8, 133, 141, 318
the Academy 58, 61, 67
Acceptance and Commitment Therapy (ACT) 462
Ach, Kaspar 282
acoustics 248, 278, 279
ACT *see* Acceptance and Commitment Therapy
act psychology 274–275, 280, 286
action at a distance 325, 355
active imagination 408
active mind, theory of the 152, 159, 164, 169
adaptation 209–210, 211, 253–254, 273, 308–309
Addams, Jane 184, 434
Ader, Robert 468
Adler, Alfred 405–407, 408, 419, 420, 421, 422; Frankl and 438; Horney on 415; Maslow on 432, 433; motivation 489

Adler, H. E. 243
adolescence 304, 399–400, 420
Adolescence (Hall) 304
Adorno, Theodor 238
The Advancement of Learning (Bacon) 126
advertising 339–340, 354, 474
Aesara 49, 67
Aesculapius (Asclepius) 52, 67
aesthesiometer 240, 259
aesthetic mode of existence 426, 427, 444
aestheticism 17, 35
aesthetics: ecopsychology 485; Fechner 278; James 295; Külpe 281–282; Stumpf 279
affect 271, 272, 286, 375
affections 268, 272, 286, 334
afferent 179, 194
Afnan, S. M. 85, 86
African-Americans 5, 302–303, 317–318, 321, 411
afterlife 391
Against Method (Feyerabend) 22
Agassiz, Louis 290
age, subjective and chronological 483
aggression 397, 403, 490
aging 201, 305, 479
Agnew, Spiro 353
agnosia 381
aircrib 350–351
Aiton, E. J. 161

Al-Ghazali 40, 87, 96, 106
Al-Razi, Abu Bakr (Rhazes) 84–85
Albers, Josef 380
alchemy 410, 419
Alcmaeon 52, 67
alcohol 223, 258
Alcott, Louisa May 184
Alexander, F. G. 42, 43, 86, 159
Alhazen 40, 86–87, 96
Allen, Ethan 323
Allen, Grant 10
Allin, Arthur 308
Allport, Floyd H. 435, 469, 477
Allport, Gordon 312, 435–436, 444, 445, 449; on Frankl 439; free will 25; historical timeline 238; influence on Milgram 471; motivation 489; teleology 24
Alzheimer, Alois 258
Alzheimer's disease 34, 258, 463
American Association for the Advancement of Science 274
American Association of Clinical Psychologists (AACP) 458
American Association of Humanistic Psychology 430, 449
American Humanist Association 443
American Imago (journal) 448
American Journal of Psychoanalysis 414
American Journal of Psychology 12

The American Journal of Psychology 302, 310
American Medical Association 231
American Men and Women of Science (Cattell) 311
American Naturalist (journal) 310
American Psychiatric Association 52, 222, 228, 233, 238, 460, 461
American Psychoanalytic Association 449
American Psychoanalytic Association Journal 448
American Psychological Association (APA) 238, 308; African-Americans 303; Allport 435; Beck 461; biopsychology 463; Calkins 314; Cattell 311; clinical psychology 457, 458, 459; Code of Ethical Standards of Psychologists 459; diversity and pluralism 493; Division of Humanistic Psychology 430, 449; enhanced interrogation techniques 492–493; Guthrie 344; Hall 303; Harlow 451; health psychology 483; history of psychology 11–12; Hull 341; industrial-organizational psychology 476; Köhler 362; Milgram 472; *Psychological Review* 310; religion 492; Rogers 437; sex/gender distinction 481–482; Sherif 469; Skinner 348; social psychology 472–473; Thorndike 329; Titchener 265; Tolman 345; Washburn 274; Woodworth 313
American Psychological Society (APS) 238, 493
American Psychologist (journal) 12
American Psychology-Law Society 489
American Revolution 164
anal stage 398–399, 419
analogy 33, 267
The Analysis of Sensations (Mach) 364
Analysis of the Phenomena of the Human Mind (Mill) 145
analytic a priori knowledge 163, 169
analytic psychology 409–413, 419

Anaximander of Miletus 47, 53, 67, 77, 198
Anaximenes 47, 67
Angell, Frank 251, 253
Angell, James Rowland 207, 243, 306, 307–308, 319, 341
anger: Bacon 128; Brentano 276; destructiveness 402; James-Lange theory of emotion 271; Sabuco 118; shadow 411; Watson 337; Wundt 256
Angyal, Andras 378
anima 411–412, 419
Animal Behavior Enterprises (ABE) 352
Animal Intelligence (Romanes) 208
animal magnetism 217–219, 223, 243
The Animal Mind (Washburn) 273
animal spirits 72, 73, 96, 175–176, 177, 178
animals: behavioral genetics 467–468; comparative psychology 207–208; Descartes 176, 177; enriched environment studies 463–464; ethology 338; Hume 137–138; James 298; Köhler 370; La Mettrie 181; Magendie 182; Montaigne 115; operant conditioning 349, 350, 352–353; reflex actions 178, 180; research on 182, 324–328, 330, 350, 451, 463–464, 484; Spinoza 158; split-brain research 464; Thorndike 330; Titchener 267; Washburn 273; Watson 337; Wundt 254
animism 216
animus 411–412, 419
Anna O. case 387, 419
Ansbacher, H. L. 405
Ansbacher, R. R. 405
Anthony, Susan B. 184, 230
anthropomorphism 208
Antiphon 56
Antoinette, Marie 218
anxiety: anxiety hierarchy 460; Avicenna 86; basic 415, 419; cognitive therapy 461; death 83, 305; Dialectical Behavior Therapy 461; ethical mode of

existence 426–427; Freud 395–396, 397, 400, 421; Heidegger 428; Horney 414–415; James 290; Watson 337
APA *see* American Psychological Association
aphasia 186
Apology for Raimond Sebond (Montaigne) 40, 114–115, 119
apperception 161, 165, 169, 255–256, 260
apperceptive mass 165, 169
applied psychology 285, 314–318, 373; behaviorism 354–355, 450; Brentano 276, 428; Dewey 306–307; Ebbinghaus 283; Freud 390; Gestalt psychology 380–381; legal issues 489; Mill 147; Müller 280; Münsterberg 299, 300, 301; Scott 473, 474; Skinner 350–353; social psychology 472
approach-approach conflict 376, 382–383
approach-avoidance conflict 376, 383
APS *see* American Psychological Society
aptitude 106, 118, 276
Aptitude Testing (Hull) 354
Aquinas, Thomas 40, 79, 93–95, 96
Araujo, S. d. F. 257
archetypes 410–411, 412, 413, 419
Arete 57, 67
Aristarchus of Samos 104
Aristippus 57, 67
Aristotle 36, 53, 61–66, 67; association 111; Averroës on 87, 88; causality 23–24, 33, 138, 148, 441; Christian church's position on 93; color 247; functionalism 308; geocentric cosmology 103; Hall on 304; on Heraclitus 50; historical timeline 40; Hsün Tzu compared with 42; hylomorphism 63, 68; influence of Socrates 57; influence on Aquinas 93, 94; influence on Augustine 82; influence on Huarte 119;

psychology's debt to 269; reason 91; teleology 37; Tertullian's critique of 81; on Thales 47; Whitehead on 289
Army Alpha and Beta tests 238, 317
Arnett, J. J. 304
Arnheim, Rudolf 380
Arnold, G. F. 487
Arnold, Matthew 53
art 102, 112, 380, 382, 388, 391
Artificial Intelligence and Human Reason: A Teleological Critique (Rychlak) 441
Ascendance-Submission (A-S) Scale 435
Asch, Solomon 362, 378, 470–471, 477
Asclepiades 71, 96
Ash, M. G. 374
Asian Psychology (Murphy & Murphy) 480
association: empiricism 151, 152; Guthrie 344; Hume 138; James Mill 145; John Stuart Mill 146; Jung 408; Müller 280; Titchener 268, 269–270; Vives 111; Wundt 255–256, 260
Association for the Advancement of Psychoanalysis 414
Association of Humanistic Psychology 449
associationism 111, 323; behaviorism 454; Hartley 140–141, 145, 149; Titchener 270; Wertheimer's critique of 368; Wundt's critique of 256
astrology 71, 76, 80, 185
astronomy 77, 103, 104, 106, 120, 121, 198, 226
asylums 224
atomic theory 51, 67, 75, 84, 97, 323
attention 268, 269, 287, 455
attitudes 412, 419
attributes of elementary mental processes 268, 286
attributive pluralism 30, 35
Augustine, Aurelius 40, 79, 81–84, 96, 116
Aurelius, Marcus 74, 96

authenticity 428, 438, 445
The Authoritarian Personality (Adorno) 238
authority 16–17, 33, 35; diffusion of 101–102; emotions and 18–19; Hobbes 173; Montaigne 117; obedience to 471–472; Renaissance 98
autism 229, 463
autoethnography 440
autokinetic effect 469–470, 477, 478
automatic thoughts 460
autonomy: functional 312, 319, 436, 445; Kant 164, 169
average man 190
Averill, L. A. 301
Averroës 87–88, 96
Avesta 45–46, 67
Avicenna 40, 79, 85–86, 93, 96, 113
avoidance-avoidance conflict 376, 383

Baars, B. J. 449
Babbage, Charles 455–456
Babkin, Boris 324
Babylonia 42–43
Bacon, Francis 125–129, 149, 156, 173, 349, 429; acquisition of knowledge 151; art of discovery 490; curiosity 167–168; empiricism 17, 119, 145, 148; historical timeline 40, 124; influence of Montaigne 115, 116, 121; influence on Voltaire 138; law and revenge 486; Leonardo da Vinci compared with 113; philosophy of science 19, 491; pragmatism 17–18
Bacon, Roger 80, 87, 92–93, 96, 102
Baddeley, A. 378
Bailly, Jean-Sylvain 218
Bain, Alexander 147, 149, 269–270
Bakewell, S. 115, 117
Baldwin, James Mark 310, 454, 468
Ball, L. C. 11
Ball, P. 168
Bandura, Albert 452, 477
Barger, Albert 336
Baron-Cohen, S. 353

Barrett-Lennard, G. T. 438
Bartlett, Frederick Charles 453, 468, 477
Barton, Clara 184
Barzun, Jacques 449
basic anxiety 415, 419
Battle for the Mind (Sargant) 328
BDI *see Beck Depression Inventory*
Beagle voyage 203–204
Beck, Aaron T. 460–461, 477
Beck Depression Inventory (BDI) 461
Beck, H. P. 336
Beck, J. 248
Becoming: Basic Considerations for a Psychology of Personality (Allport) 435, 436
becoming, philosophy of 49, 50
Bedlam 224
Beecher, Henry Ward 184
behavior, measurement of 188–192
The Behavior of Organisms (Skinner) 238, 348, 349
Behavior Research and Therapy (journal) 354
A Behavior System (Hull) 342
behavior therapy 328, 336, 340, 352, 354, 437, 449, 460, 462, 478
Behavior Therapy (journal) 354
behavioral genetics 347, 455, 467–468, 477
behaviorism 9, 322–358; applied psychology 354–355; Bartlett's critique of 453; causation 24; definition of 355; functionalism 318; Gestalt psychology critique of 359, 362, 369, 370, 372, 454; Guthrie 344–345; Helvétius 139; Hobbes as forerunner to 174; Hull 341–344; humanistic critiques of 423, 430–431, 439, 442, 449; James' critique of 424; Köhler's critique of 452; La Mettrie 181; learning 15–16, 390, 489; neobehaviorism 340–354, 448, 449, 450–452, 453, 454, 455, 456; Pavlov 323–329; present facts 264; reflex actions 180; rise of 269; Skinner 347–354, 456–457; Thorndike 329–331; Tolman 345–347; Watson 332–340

Behaviorism (Watson) 334–335, 337, 348
Behaviorist Manifesto 333
"A Behaviorist's Utopia" (Watson) 351–352
Behrens, R. R. 380
being: being-in-the-world 427–428; Maslow 432–433; philosophy of 49, 68
Being and Time (Heidegger) 427–428
Bekhterev, Vladimir Mikhailovich 257, 323, 355
beliefs: Freud 393–394; Mill 145; Montaigne 115; religious 492
Bell, Alexander Graham 310
Bell, Charles 181–182, 194
Bell, D. J. 459
Bell-Magendie Law 181, 194
bell-shaped curve 189
Belles on their Toes (Gilbreth & Carey) 475
Ben-Noun, L. 45
Benedict, Ruth Fulton 430, 433
Benjamin, L. T., Jr. 11, 315
Bentham, Jeremy 57, 141–142, 145, 146, 148, 149, 150
Berger, Hans 465
Bergin, A. E. 460
Bergmann, M. S. 340
Berkeley, George 28, 124, 132–135, 136, 140, 148, 149, 166
Berlin Psychological Institute 361, 373, 374, 375
Bernard, L. L. 338
Bernays, Martha 386, 387, 388
Bernheim, Hippolyte 393
Bethlehem Hospital 224
Bettmann, O. L. 9
Beyond Freedom and Dignity (Skinner) 348, 353
Bible 101, 103, 106; *see also* Christianity; scripture
Binet, Alfred 218–219, 238, 305, 310, 316–317, 319, 473–474
Binswanger, Ludwig 428
biochemistry 34
biological needs 431
biopsychology 463–468
bipolar disorder 258, 466
birth control 231, 232, 234
birth order 406, 407

Bishop, P. 409
Bjornsson, A. S. 95
Black Death 98–100
Blackless, M. 482
Blass, T. 472
Bleuler, Eugen 258, 408, 448
blind spots 415–416
bloodletting 223
Bloom, H. 114
Blumenthal, A. L. 257, 258
Boas, Franz 302
Bochner, S. 102
body: Aquinas 93–94; Aristotle 62–63; Avicenna 86; Descartes 155, 158, 175–177; early Chinese psychology 42; Egyptians 43; Fechner 242; Freud 391; Galen 73; James 297; James-Lange theory of emotion 271; Leibniz 170; Leonardo da Vinci 113; Lucretius 74–75; Mill 147; Plotinus 76; specific energies of nerves 183; Spinoza 158, 170; Titchener 269; Vesalius 121; Vives 110; Weber's illusion 241; Wundt 252; *see also* mind-body problem
body language 406
Boerhaave, Hermann 180
Bonaparte, Napoleon 6
The Book of Nature (Swammerdam) 177
Book of Optics (Alhazen) 40, 86, 87, 96
Borgia, Cesare 107, 108, 112
Boring, E. G.: on Dewey 306; great-person theory 10; on Helmholtz 172; intelligence 192; on Leonardo da Vinci 112; on Müller 280; nerves 183, 248; on Reid 167; on Titchener 264, 265; on Whytt 179
Born, Max 364
Boston School 457
Botting, E. H. 143
Bouchard, Thomas J. Jr. 467
Boulder model 459, 477
Bowditch, Henry 457
Bower, G. H. 343, 347
Boyle, R. W. 131
Bozeman, T. W. 138
Braaten, E. B. 143

Braid, James 219
Brailsford, H. N. 144
brain 463–466; ablation 185, 194; Alcmaeon 52; Avicenna 86; Descartes 176, 177–178; Egyptians 43; electrical stimulation 186, 464–465; emergentism 29–30; enriched environment studies 463–464; Galen 72–73; Gall 167; Hartley 141; Hippocrates 54; Huarte 119; isomorphism 373; La Mettrie 180–181; lateralization of function 8–9; localization of function 181–186, 194, 465; measuring brain activity 465–466; pluralism 30; psychoneuroimmunology 468, 478; split-brain research 464, 478; synaptic transmission 464; Titchener 269; ultramaximal inhibition 327; Unzer 180; *see also* neuropsychology; neuroscience
Brain, Behavior and Immunity (journal) 468
Brandeis, Louis D. 486–487
Breland, Keller 352–353
Breland, Marian 351, 352–353
Brentano, Franz 262, 274–278, 280, 286, 287, 295, 427; applied psychology 285; Freud as student of 386; historical timeline 124; humanistic psychology 428–429, 444; influence of 360, 365; mental events 453
Brett, G. S. 110, 128
Breuer, Joseph 386–387, 419
Bridges, J. H. 92
Bridgman, Percy W. 21–22, 340, 355–356
Bringmann, W. G. 250, 251
British Journal of Health Psychology 483
Broca, Paul 185–186, 194
Bromberg, W. 214
Brown-Sequard, C. E. 9
Brown v. Board of Education (1954) 238, 303, 487
Browne, James C. 207
Brücke, Ernst 188, 245, 386, 419

Bruner, Jerome 451
Bruno, Giordano 16, 40
Brush, S. G. 22
Buddha 44
Buddhism 198, 416, 434, 460
Buffon, Comte de 198–199, 200–201, 232
Bugental, James F. T. 449
Bühler, Charlotte 449
Burks, Barbara Stoddard 467
Burton, R. 114
business psychology 434
Buss, A. R. 8
Buss, D. M. 207
Butler, Louisa 191
Butterfield, E. C. 452
Byron, George Gordon 114, 219, 456, 479

Cabot, Richard 457
Cade, John 466
Cajal, Ramón y 463
Calhoun, J. B. 484
Calkins, Mary Whiton 238, 274, 313–314, 319, 424
Calvin, John 101–102, 106
Camus, Albert 9
Candide (Voltaire) 161
Cannon, W. B. 311
Canon of Medicine (Avicenna) 85
capital punishment 179–180, 200
Capra, Fritjof 381–382
Carnap, Rudolf 341
Carr, Harvey A. 306, 308–309, 318, 319
Cartwright, N. 22
Cassirer, E. 163
Castiglioni, A. 42
castration 399
catastrophe theory 199, 232
categories of understanding 164, 169
Catherine of Aragon 110
Cattell, James McKeen 257, 309–311, 319, 388; applied psychology 473; historical timeline 238; influence of Darwin 210; intelligence testing 316, 317; National Academy of the Sciences 308; Thorndike and 329
Cattell, Josephine Owen 311

causality 23–24; Adler 406; Al-Ghazali 87; Aristotle 33, 36, 62; Copernican revolution 106; emergentism 29–30; epiphenomenalism 28; free will and determinism 25, 26; Freud 389, 400; historical 10–11; Hume 136–137, 138, 148, 149; James 292; Jung 412–413; Kant 163–164, 169, 363; Leibniz 160–161; Piaget 453; psychophysical parallelism 29; Reid 167; Rychlak 441; voluntaristic psychology 253
Cautin, R. L. 459
Cavendish, Henry 372
Cavendish, William 173
Center for Evolutionary Psychology (CEP) 207
Chamberlain, Houston Stewart 251
chance 188–189, 206
change 117, 161–162, 200, 235
Channing, William Ellery 226
chaos: chaos hypothesis 9–10, 13; repeated patterns in 382
character 145
Charcot, Jean-Martin 219, 387, 419
Charron, P. 154
Cheaper by the Dozen (Gilbreth & Carey) 475
Cheiron 12
Chiarugi, Vincenzo 225, 232
Child, I. L. 443
children: Anna Freud's work 417–418; Augustine 82–83; authority 19; birth order 407; developmental psychology 208–209; disabled 228–229; fear conditioning 335–336; Freud 403; Hall 304–305; Helmholtz 247; Huarte 118–119; ideational learning 371–372; imitation 371; intelligence testing 317; Jewish philosophy 45; Locke 129, 132; Montaigne 116; Oedipus conflict 394; perceptual abilities 15; Piaget 453–454; Plato 61; psychosexual development 398–399; speech 338–339; Stumpf 279; unconditional

positive regard 438; Witmer 259; Wollstonecraft 144
Chinese psychology 41–42
Chomsky, Noam 350, 353, 451
Christianity 40, 45; Abelard 91; Aquinas 94; Augustine 82, 83; Bacon 92, 93; baptism 256; Brentano 275; early 78–79; Galen's ideas 73; Galileo 105, 106; Huarte 119; Hypatia of Alexandria 77; influence of Greek philosophy on 93; Jung 408; Kierkegaard 426; Leibniz 159; medieval period 79, 80; Montaigne 114, 115; neo-Platonism 76; Petrarch 107; Plotinus 76; Reformation 101–102, 115, 120, 121; Renaissance 101; rise of 78; Rush 222; sacred theory of origins 200; stoicism compared with 74; Tertullian 81; Vives 109; see also Church
Christina, Queen of Sweden 154
Church 79, 93, 101, 105, 106, 120, 124
Churchland, Patricia 462
Cicero, Marcus Tullius 7
Civilization and Its Discontents (Freud) 390, 401
Clanchy, M. T. 91
Clark, E. 186–187
Clark, Kenneth B. 303
Clark, Mamie Phipps 303, 487
Clark University 302, 303, 387, 388
Clarke, D. M. 155–156
Clarke, E. 179
Clarke, Edward 131
Classics in the History of Psychology (website) 12
Claus, Carl 386
Clements, R. D. 110
Cleveland, Grover 230
client-centered therapy 436
Client-Centered Therapy (Rogers) 437
clinical psychology 457–462, 478; Bandura 452; behaviorism 450; Gestalt model 381; Maslow 431; Münsterberg 300; psychopharmacology 466;

religious beliefs 492; social psychology 473; Tolman 347; Witmer 259

Clodd, E. 199

closure 367–368, 383

Clymer, E. 475

cocaine 386, 391

Code of Ethical Standards of Psychologists (APA) 459

Code of Manu 44

Coe, G. A. 82

cognition 452, 454, 455; early Chinese psychology 42; Gestalt psychology 382, 454; Henle 4; James 295, 297; motivation and 490; Unamuno 425

cognitive development 14, 453–454, 478

cognitive disabilities 228–229, 259, 315

cognitive maps 346–347, 356, 454

cognitive neuroscience 464

cognitive psychology 452–457, 477; critical appraisal of 455–457; Gestalt psychology 374, 378; intellectual traditions of 452–454; legal issues 489; motivation 489–490; themes and content areas 454–455; Tolman 347, 358; Wundt 257

Cognitive Psychology (Neisser) 238

cognitive revolution 355, 457

cognitive therapy 417, 449, 460–461, 462

cognitivism 355

Cohen, N. 468

Colebrook, Claire 481

Colimore, K. 432

collective unconscious 410–411, 412, 413, 415, 419

Collins, M. E. 377

color 131, 183, 246, 247–248; isomorphism 373; Maxwell 260; Mill 146; Müller 280; Wundt 256; Young-Helmholtz trichromatic theory 248, 260, 261

"Columbia Bible" 312

Columbia University 309–313, 315, 318, 319, 329, 437

Columbus, Christopher 40, 92, 121

Combe, George 184

commonsense philosophy 29, 64, 166–167, 169, 294

community psychology 377

comparative psychology 207–208, 211, 265, 267, 273, 335

comparison, explanation by 33

compensation 407, 419

completion tests 283

complexes 412, 419; *see also* inferiority complex; Oedipus complex

compliant types 415, 416, 419

computed tomography (CT) 466

computer metaphor 454, 455–456, 477, 489–490

computer science 454, 455, 456

Comstock, Anthony 231

Conan Doyle, Arthur 184, 191

Concerning Matters of Heaven and the Hereafter (Fechner) 243

Condillac, Étienne Bonnot de 138, 139, 148, 149, 219, 323

conditioned inhibition 343

conditioned reflex (CR) 324, 325–326, 356

Conditioned Reflexes (Pavlov) 141, 348

conditioned stimulus (CS) 325–326, 336, 356

conditioning 325–326, 356, 484; empiricism 151; humanistic critiques of 423, 439; James 297; Mill 145; Pavlov 325, 357; Skinner 349–350, 351, 352, 354, 357; Watson 334, 335, 337

Confessions (Augustine) 81–82, 83

conflict 376, 382–383, 469

conformity 470–471

Confucius 41–42, 67, 198

connectionism 330, 356, 369

consciousness 9, 27; Brentano 277, 287, 429; Calkins 314; Freud 393, 400; Husserl 429; idealism 28; James 295; Jung 410; Külpe 282; Plato 59; psychogenic emergentism 32; psychogeny 31; Stumpf 278; Titchener 268, 269, 270; twentieth-century developments in psychology 448; Unzer 179; Washburn 272–274, 287; Wundt 255, 452

conservatism 264

Constantine 79

Contemporary Psychoanalysis (journal) 448

context theory of meaning 270, 286

contextualism 442

contiguity, law of 344

Contributions to a Theory of Sensory Perception (Wundt) 250

Conversations on Common Things (Dix) 226

Conway, Anne 160

Coon, D. J. 291, 434

Copernican revolution 104, 105–106, 126, 133

Copernicus, Nicolaus 40, 104, 105, 106, 120, 153, 394

Copleston, F. 94

correlation 24, 192, 194, 210

cosmogony 46, 198, 232

cosmology 46–51, 198; definition of 120; Lucretius 75; Renaissance 103–104

counseling 457; career 452; religious beliefs 492; social psychology 473; Witmer 259

Counseling and Psychotherapy (Rogers) 238

countertransference 401, 419

The Courtier and the Heretic (Stewart) 160

CR *see* conditioned reflex

craniometry 4, 185, 192

creative synthesis 256, 260

crime 141, 189, 258, 406

critical empiricism 341, 357

critical psychology 480, 496

critical realism 281

Critique of Judgement (Kant) 163

Critique of Practical Reason (Kant) 163

Critique of Pure Reason (Kant) 124, 126, 162, 163

Crombie, A. C. 86, 88

CS *see* conditioned stimulus

Csikszentmihalyi, M. 484

CT *see* computed tomography

cultural context 417

cumulative recorder 350

curiosity 18, 84, 91, 115, 167–168

Curiosity: How Science Became Interested in Everything (Ball) 168

Cuvier, Georges 199, 232
cyclical hypothesis 8–9, 13
Cyrenaics 57

Da Vinci, Leonardo 40, 102, 111–113, 120
D'Ailly, Pierre 92
Dain, N. 227
Dale, Henry Hallett 238
Damasio, A. 157
D'Amato, R. C. 259
Damjanovic, A. 153
Daniels, M. 432
Dante Alighieri 80, 103, 130
Darrow, Clarence 6
Darwin, Charles 53, 182, 201, 202–206, 232, 233, 394; child development 454; developmental psychology 209; functionalism 308; Galton and 191; historical timeline 124; individual differences 210; influence of Bacon 126; influence on American psychology 210; influence on Hull 341; influence on Pavlov 324; influence on Spencer 211; natural selection 234; uniformitarianism 199; on women 418; Wundt and 253–254
Darwin, Erasmus 201, 202, 233
Dasein 428, 444
Daseinanalysis 428
data collection 6, 128; see also methods
Dawkins, R. 467
day view 243
DBT see Dialectical Behavior Therapy
De Anima (Aristotle) 63, 64, 65
De Anima et Vita (On Soul and Life) (Vives) 110, 121
De l'espirit (On the Mind) (Helvétius) 140
De Rerum Natura (Lucretius) 74
De Witt, Jan 157
Deason, G. B. 106
death 180
death anxiety 83, 305
deBeer, G. 205
DeCarvalho, R. J. 430, 442, 449, 450

deception 109
deductive argument 151, 152, 156, 163, 169
defense mechanisms 391, 396–398, 403, 421, 422
deficiency 432–433
Delahunty, R. J. 158
Delaunay, P. 100
delayed conditioning 325–326
Delbrück, Max 360
Deleuze, Gilles 481
delirium 220
delusions 71, 220, 381
DeMause, L. 116
dementia 220, 258
democracy 307, 360, 435
Democritus 27, 51, 67, 75, 84, 97, 323
DeMoivre, Abraham 189
demonology 97, 113, 197–198, 212; Babylonia 42–43; definition of 233; Jewish philosophy 45; Spinoza 158, 168, 216; witchcraft 213, 215–216
depression: Avesta 46; Avicenna 86; cognitive therapy 461; Dialectical Behavior Therapy 461; Freud 400; Hall 303; James 290; Mill 146; Münsterberg 300; Pinel 220; psychopharmacology 466–467; Sabuco 118
Der Turm (Jung) 409
Descartes, René 130, 152–156, 163, 194, 429; analogy 33; animal-machine model 181; Berkeley's critique of 135; curiosity 168; demonology 216; dualism of body and soul 158; emotion 271; historical timeline 40, 124; influence of Bacon 126; influence of Montaigne 115, 116, 121; influence of Vives 110, 111; interactionism 29; Leonardo da Vinci compared with 113; moral basis for psychology 139; movement 175–177, 178; philosophy of science 19, 491; rate of nervous transmission 188; rationalism 17, 119, 168, 169, 233; reason 277; sensory

and motor nerves 177–178; solar system 198; Spinoza compared with 159; Stensen's critique of 195
The Descent of Man (Darwin) 206
desires 277, 286, 390
destructiveness 402, 403
detached types 415, 419
determinism 25–27, 35, 423; Carr 309, 318; Democritus 51; Freud 389, 400–401; James 291, 292; Jung 413; La Mettrie 181; Lucretius 75; Skinner 349; Spinoza 158; Watson 358
Deutsch, M. 377
developmental psychology 208–209, 211; Freud 390, 403; functionalism 308; Gestalt psychology 370–372; James 289; Stumpf 279
deviance 19
Dewey, John 306–307, 308, 309, 319, 475; historical timeline 238; influence of Darwin 210; Maslow on 433; mental events 453; social psychology 468
Dewsbury, D. A. 8, 297
diagnosis 437, 459–460
Diagnostic and Statistical Manual of Mental Disorders (DSM) 228, 238, 460
Dialectical Behavior Therapy (DBT) 461–462
Dialogue Concerning the Two Chief World Systems—Ptolemaic and Copernican (Galileo) 105, 124, 153
Diamond, B. L. 45
Diamond, S. 119, 192, 249, 250, 280
Dickens, Charles 219, 470
Diderot, Denis 198
Die Seele des Kindes (The Mind of the Child) (Preyer) 209, 234
difference threshold 240, 260
"The Differences between Individual Psychology and Psychoanalysis" (Adler) 406
Dirac, Paul 17
disabilities 228–229, 475
disciplined naïveté 429, 444

Discourse on Method (Descartes) 154, 155
The Discourses (Machiavelli) 108
discrimination 326–327, 356
Diseases of the Mind (Rush) 124
dissociation 51, 295
dissociative identity disorder 223
Divine Comedy (Dante) 80, 103
Division 26 (History of Psychology) 11–12
Dix, Dorothea Lynde 124, 193, 217, 220, 221, 225–228, 229, 233, 473
doctrine of formal discipline 331, 356
The Doctrine of Muscular Movement (Wundt) 250
Dollinger, Ignaz von 275
double-aspect monism 28, 35, 253, 269
The Double Helix (Watson) 17
Doubts Concerning Galen (Rhazes) 84
dreams: Adler 406; Aesculapius 52; Aristotle 65; Augustine 83; Bacon 128; Calkins 314; Freud 387, 400, 401, 420; Hippocrates 54; Judaism 88; Jung 409, 411, 413; Locke 130; Middle Ages 80; regression 397; Woodworth 312
Dreikurs, Eric 489
drive 342, 356
drives: Allport 436; behaviorism 489; Frankl 439; Freud 393, 395, 396, 397, 400, 403, 420
Drives Toward War (Tolman) 354
Drury, John 131
DSM *see Diagnostic and Statistical Manual of Mental Disorders*
dualism 27, 28–30, 31, 35; demonology 216; Descartes 158, 176; Persia 46; Watson 333; Wundt 252
DuBois-Reymond, Emil 183, 188, 245, 250, 290, 302
Duncker, Karl 361, 370, 378, 383
Dunlap, K. 468
Durant, A. 115
Durant, Will 41, 88, 90, 115
dynamic psychology 312
Dynamics in Psychology (Köhler) 362

Earle, W. J. 291
Ebbinghaus forgetting curve 284, 285, 286
Ebbinghaus, Hermann 238, 270, 279, 282–285, 286, 298, 381, 453
EBS *see* electrical brain stimulation
Eccles, John C. 464, 477
ecological validity 457, 477
ecology 298–299, 484–485
ecopsychology 289, 479, 484–486, 496
Ecopsychology (journal) 486
ecotherapy 485, 496
Edison, Thomas A. 184, 310
education: Dewey 307; Dix 226; empiricism 148; Gestalt psychology 380–381; Hall 305; Helvétius 140; Herbart 165, 168; history as contribution to liberal 4; Hollingworth 315–316; Huarte 118–119; James 294; Kant 164; Lewin 376; Locke 129, 131–132; Maslow 434; Mill 145; Montaigne 116; Plato 60; Rogers 438; Rush 222; Skinner 351; Thorndike 331; Vives 111; Wertheimer 360; Wollstonecraft 144
educational psychology: clinical psychology and 462; Huarte 118; James 289; Katona 381; Münsterberg 300; Thorndike 331; Wooley 316
Educational Psychology (Guthrie) 345, 354
EEG *see* electroencephalogram
effect, law of 330, 357
efferent 179, 180, 194
efficient cause 23, 36
ego 390, 394, 417; anxiety 395–396; defense mechanisms 396, 397, 398, 403, 421, 422; definition of 419–420; drives 395; goal of therapy 400, 401; James 296; Jung 410, 411; structure of personality 392–393
The Ego and the Id (Freud) 398
ego psychology 417
Ego Psychology and the Problem of Adaptation (Hartmann) 417

Egypt 43–44
Ehrenfels, Christian von 275, 360, 364–365, 384
Eichmann, Adolf 471
Einstein, Albert 368, 389, 432; determinism 26; emigration to the United States 360; influence of Spinoza 159; influence on Gestalt psychology 364; Maslow on 434; on war 401–402
Eiseley, L. C. 205
Eissler, K. R. 449
EITs *see* enhanced interrogation techniques
elderly people 305, 351
Eleatics 49
Electra complex 399
electrical brain stimulation (EBS) 186, 464–465
electroencephalogram (EEG) 465, 478
electrophysiology 186, 194, 195, 464–465
electrotherapy 387
elements 52–54, 67, 255, 260, 266, 268, 286
Elements of Psychophysics (Fechner) 124, 243, 260, 283
Elements of the Philosophy of the Human Mind (Stewart) 167
Ellis, Albert 74, 461, 478
embryo research 31
emergentism 29–30, 36; psychogenic 32, 37
Emerson, Ralph Waldo 10, 98, 114, 289
Émile (Rousseau) 182
emotional disorders: Münsterberg 300; naturalistic approaches 212, 217, 232; Persia 46; reform in the treatment of 217–224; Rogers 437; witchcraft 213; *see also* mental disorders
emotions: Aquinas 93, 94; Augustine 83; Avicenna 86; Bacon 128; Bell 181; early Chinese psychology 41; empiricism 148; facial expressions 207; Heraclitus 50; Hume 136, 137–138, 148; industrial-organizational psychology 474; James-Lange

theory of emotion 271, 286, 296–297, 299, 320; Jung 412; knowledge and 18–19; Montaigne 115, 116; Pythagoreans 48; Sabuco 118, 121; Spinoza 158–159; Stumpf 279; Titchener 268, 269, 270, 271–272, 286; tridimensional theory of feeling 256, 257, 261; Unamuno 425; Vives 110, 111; Watson 334, 337; Woodworth 313; Wundt 256

The Emotions and the Will (Bain) 147

empathy 8, 140–141, 165, 455

Empedocles 52–53, 54, 67, 84, 198

Empirical Psychology (Hickok) 17

Empirical Psychology (Wolff) 17, 162, 168, 171

empiricism 16, 17, 119, 125–140, 323; Aquinas 94; Aristotle 62; Bacon 125–129; Berkeley 132–135; birth of psychology 216; Brentano 274; continental 138–140; contributions of 148; curiosity 167; definition of 36, 149; Gestalt psychology 363; Gilbreth 475; Heraclitus 50; Hobbes 173, 174; Hume 135–138, 162; James 293, 298, 320, 365; Kant 165, 363; Koffka 371; Locke 129–132; Lucretius 75; Mill 147; nativism versus 15; rationalism compared with 151; Reid 166–167; Renaissance 102; Rhazes 84; senses 152; Washburn 272; Wollstonecraft 142–143; Wundt's critique of 256; *see also* experience

Empiricus, Sextus 77–78, 96

Encyclopedia of Associations (Burek et al.) 449

energy 246

enhanced interrogation techniques (EITs) 492–493, 496

Enjoy Old Age (Skinner and Vaughan) 351

Enneads (Plotinus) 76, 97

enriched environment studies 463–464

environmental influences: field theory 375; Helvétius 140;

Locke 131–132; Pinel 221; Watson 334

environmental psychology 472, 479

Epictetus 73–74, 96

Epicureanism 66, 73, 74–75, 96, 97

Epicurus of Samos 74, 96, 323

epilepsy 54, 75, 84, 217, 463, 464, 478

epiphenomenalism 28, 30, 36, 272

epistemology 14–23, 494; a priori and a posteriori knowledge 14–15; aestheticism 17; authority 16–17; Bacon 92–93; Brentano 276; definition of 36; ecopsychology 486; emotions 18–19; empiricism 17; experience 365; genetic 14, 36; Hobbes 174; instinct versus learning 15–16; Külpe 281; Locke 129; Middle Ages 80; Montaigne 115; nativism versus empiricism 15; Paracelsus 113; philosophy of science 491; pragmatism 17–18; rationalism 17; relativism 54–55; relevance to psychology 23; Renaissance 119; Sabuco 118; science and 19–22; skepticism 18; Spinoza 157; Xenophanes 49; *see also* knowledge

equity 483

equivalent phase 327, 356

Erasmus, Desiderius 110

ergonomics 474–475

Erikson, Erik H. 417

Eros 61, 402

ERPs *see* event-related potentials

Escher, M. C. 380

Esper, E. A. 323

An Essay Concerning Human Understanding (Locke) 124, 129, 130

An Essay on the Principle of Population (Malthus) 124, 205, 233

An Essay Towards a New Theory of Vision (Berkeley) 124, 135

Essays in Radical Empiricism (James) 290, 296

Essays on the Active Powers of Man (Reid) 166

Essays on the Intellectual Powers of Man (Reid) 166

Essays on the Mind (Helvétius) 124

essentialism 143, 149

Essentials of Behavior (Hull) 342

esteem needs 432

Estes, William K. 345, 351

ethical mode of existence 426–427, 444–445

ethics: APA Code of Ethical Standards 459; behaviorist 334; enhanced interrogation techniques 492–493; Milgram's experiment 471–472; self-actualization 434; Wertheimer 360; *see also* morality

Ethics (Spinoza) 157, 158

Ethics (Wundt) 253

ethology 147, 338

Euclid 71, 102

eugenics 210, 231, 258

Eupsychia 434

European Journal of Ecopsychology 486

Eustachio, Bartolommeo 102

Evans, R. B. 101–102, 179, 265, 268, 272

Even the Rat Was White (Guthrie) 317–318

event-related potentials (ERPs) 465

evil: Hartley 141; humanistic psychology 442; La Mettrie 181; neo-Platonism 76; theodicy 161; Zarathustra 46

The Evolution of Man (Haeckel) 209

evolutionary psychology 467, 472

Evolutionary Psychology (journal) 207

evolutionary theory 197, 198–211, 233; birth of psychology 216; Darwin 202–206; Empedocles 53; Freud 389; functionalism 308; geological evolution 198–199; Gestalt psychology 379–380, 454; Hall 301; intellectual discourse 199–200; organic evolution 200–202, 235; significance for psychology 207–211; solar system 198; Washburn 273

Examen de Ingenios para las Sciencias (The Examination of Men's Wits) (Huarte) 118
excitation 327, 328
exercise, law of 330
existence 130–131, 167
existentialism 424–429, 442, 445, 450, 484; Brentano 278; ecopsychology 485; Heraclitus 51; James 289
existentiality 428
expectancy 346
expectations 26–27
experience 14–15, 17, 125, 151, 452; Allport 436; Berkeley 134; Brentano 274, 276, 277, 429; Descartes 155, 156; Dewey 306; Gestalt psychology 365, 380; Hobbes 173; humanistic psychology 442; Hume 136; idealism 28; James 289, 292, 293, 424, 452; Kant 162, 163–164, 170, 363; Montaigne 115, 116–117; rationalism 168; Titchener 266, 269; twentieth-century developments in psychology 448; Wundt 252–253; *see also* empiricism
experimental extinction 343, 346
experimental neurosis 327
experimental psychology 165, 172; Fechner 242, 244, 245; Galton 192; Helmholtz 248; Hull 341–342; Külpe 280, 282; Maslow 431; Müller 279–280; Münsterberg 301; neobehaviorism 341; psychodynamic theory ignored by 449; qualitative research 491; Rogers 437; twentieth-century transformations 447; Washburn 272; Weber 241; Woodworth 312–313; Wundt 250, 254, 257
Experimental Psychology (Woodworth) 312–313, 321
expert testimony 300, 486, 489
explanation, problem of 32–35
The Expression of Emotions in Man and Animals (Darwin) 207

extinction 326, 340, 343, 344, 346, 356
extrinsic teleology 24, 36, 37
extroversion 412, 413, 419, 420
eye of the soul 59, 67
eyewitness testimony 487–489, 496
Eyewitness Testimony (Loftus) 238, 488
Eysenck, Hans Jürgen 462

The Fabric of the Human Body (Vesalius) 102
facial expressions 207
factuality 428
faculties 184
fallenness 428
Fallopio, Gabriello 102
false confessions 487
falsifiability 20
"Family Romances" (Freud) 401
family size 230–231
Fancher, R. E. 277
fatalism 10, 45, 291
fatigue 343, 356, 475, 476
fear: Bacon 128; conditioning 335–336, 356–357; Guthrie 344–345; Hobbes 174; Hume 138; James-Lange theory of emotion 271; Lucretius 75; paradoxical intention 440; Plato 60; Sabuco 118; Spinoza 158; Watson 335–336, 337; Wundt 256
Fearing, F. 179
Fechner, Gustav Theodor 165, 240, 242–245, 249, 260; aesthetics 278; historical timeline 124; idealism 28; influence on Ebbinghaus 283
Fechner's law 244, 260
Feigl, Herbert 341
Feminine Psychology (Freud) 416
femininity 42, 411–412
feminism 448; Mill 147, 150; Wollstonecraft 143, 144
Féré, C. 218–219
Ferster, Charles 350
Feyerabend, Paul K. 21–22, 23, 36
fictional final goals 406, 420
field forces 364
field theory 364, 375–376, 383

figure-ground 367, 383
final cause 24, 36
Fine, R. 417
Fisher, H. A. L. 9
fixation 395, 398, 420
Flourens, Peter Jean Marie 185, 186, 194, 465
flow 484
fMRI *see* functional magnetic resonance imaging
Follett, Mary Parker 473, 477
forensic psychology 301, 489
forgetting 284, 285, 286, 298
forgiveness 101
form qualities 364
formal cause 23, 36
forms, theory of 58, 68–69, 83
formulae 34, 165, 244, 342, 375; *see also* mathematics
fossils 200
four-factor personality theory 54
Fowler, Lorenzo and Orson 184–185
Frank, Philipp 341
Frankenstein (Shelley) 145, 201
Frankl, Victor E. 438–440, 445, 484, 489
Franklin, Benjamin 124, 218, 223
Frederick the Great 163, 180
free association 55, 401, 420, 487
free will 25–27, 33, 253; Carr 309, 318; definition of 36; Freud 400; humanistic psychology 423, 442, 443; James 292; Jung 413; Lucretius 75; Rychlak 441; Spinoza 158; Wundt 254; Zarathustra 46
freedom: Allport 435; Carr 309; existentialism 425, 445; Freud 389, 417; James 291, 292; Kant 164; Kierkegaard 426; Spinoza 158; Wertheimer 360; Wundt 253
French Revolution 164, 180, 218
Freud, Anna 389, 417–418
Freud, Sigmund 10, 166, 219, 333, 340, 385–405, 420, 421–422; Adler and 405, 406, 407; Allport and 435, 436; anxiety 395–396; appreciative overview 403; assumptions 263; biography 385–389;

childhood 305; consciousness 255; continuing influence of 448; critical overview 403–404; defense mechanisms 396–398; descriptive examinations 491; determinism 25; dreams 312, 314; emotional disorders 300; on Empedocles 52; esteem needs 432; female sexuality 399, 404, 418; freedom 158; future perspectives 404–405; general characteristics of thought 389–390; Hall and 303; historical timeline 124, 238; on history 3, 6; Horney on 415, 416; humanistic critiques of 423; influence of Brentano 275; influence on Hull 341; Jung and 407–408; on Leonardo da Vinci 112; Maslow on 433; mental events 453; Montaigne compared with 114; motivation 393–395, 417, 489; Plato and 61; pleasure and pain 116, 142; pleasure principle 390–392; psychoanalysis as therapeutic technique 400–401; psychosexual development 398–400; rejection of medical model by 457; social psychology 401–403; structure of personality 392–393; unconscious mind 263; Watson on 332; Wertheimer on 381; work 473

Fridlund, A. J. 336

Fritsch, Gustav Theodor 186, 194, 464–465

From Beast-Machine to Man-Machine (Rosenfield) 177

Fromm, Erich 16, 414, 417, 430

functional autonomy 312, 319, 436, 445

functional concepts 371

functional fixedness 378, 383

functional magnetic resonance imaging (fMRI) 466

functionalism 266, 278, 288–321, 448; Angell 307–308; Calkins 313–314; Carr 308–309; criticisms of 318; Darwin 254; definition of 319–320;

Dewey 306–307; Gilbreth 475; Hall 301–305; influence of 318; James 288–299; Maslow 433; Münsterberg 299–301; Spencer 211, 234; thinking 368; Thorndike 329; University of Chicago 305–309; Watson's critique of 334; Woodworth 311–313; Wooley 316

functions, psychological 412, 420

Furumoto, L. 314

The Future of an Illusion (Freud) 3, 391, 417

Gaj, N. 494

Galapagos Islands 204

Galen (Claudius Galenus) 71–72, 79, 84, 96, 97; historical timeline 40; influence on Avicenna 85, 86; influence on Huarte 119; temperament 271, 327

Galileo Galilei 104–106, 120, 126, 131; historical timeline 124; influence on Descartes 153; influence on Hobbes 173, 174; law of inertia 368; philosophy of science 491; primary and secondary qualities 131; probability theory 189; rationalism 17

Gall, Franz Joseph 162, 167, 184, 185, 194, 195

Galton, Francis 190–192, 194, 201, 317, 467; Cattell and 310; individual differences 210, 233, 316; quantification 34, 172; word-association tests 408

Ganzheit 225

Gardner, S. 227

Garfield, S. L. 460

Garforth, F. W. 131

Gauss, Carl Friedrich 189, 369

Gautama, Siddhartha 44

Gay, P. 387, 389, 397, 404, 405

Gazzaniga, Michael S. 464

Gelb, Adhémar 381

gender: anima and animus 411–412; Aquinas 93; changing perspectives on 479, 481–482; definition of 496; essentialism 143; Hall 302; Hollingworth

320; Horney 416–417; Huarte 119; intersectionality 482; Mill 147; phrenology 185; religious beliefs 492; stereotypes 229–230; variability hypothesis 315, 321; Wooley 316; working hours and the law 486–487; *see also* women

Gendlin, E. T. 437

Genesis 200

genetic epistemology 14, 36

genetics 192, 202, 329, 330; behavioral 347, 455, 467–468, 477

genital stage 399–400, 420

genius 140, 210

geocentric cosmology 103, 104–105, 120, 121

geological evolution 198–199

geometry 173–174

Gerard, E. O. 94, 95

Gestalt psychology 266, 275, 359–384, 448; applied psychology 380–381; Brentano 278; cognitive psychology and 454, 455; common misunderstandings 379–380; definition of Gestalt 359, 383; Ehrenfels 364–365; extension of Gestalt principles 378–379; fundamentals of 365–372; historical timeline 238; influence of 373–374; intellectual background of 363–365; isomorphism 373; Koffka 362–363; Köhler 360–362; levels of explanation 34; Lewin 374–377; Maslow 433; as precursor to ecopsychology 485; relevance of 381–382; scientific holism 443; scientific method 372–373; structuralism 279; Wertheimer 282, 359–360

Gestalt Psychology (Köhler) 362, 372

Gestalt therapy 379, 381, 383

Gibson, E. J. 15

Gibson, J. J. 457

gifted children 315–316

Gilbreth, Frank 474–475

Gilbreth, Lillian 474–475, 477

Gilderhus, M. T. 5

Gilgen, A. R. 449, 450

Gleitman, H. 347

globalization 480, 481

God: Abelard 90, 91; Al-Ghazali 87; Aquinas 94; Aristotle 24, 65; Augustine 82; Bacon 92; Berkeley 134; causal power 106; Descartes 176; Einstein 26; Freud 393–394; Hartley 141; Hebrew language 200; Héloise 92; Hobbes 174; Islam 84; Judaism 45; Leibniz 161, 170; Locke 130–131; Middle Ages 80; plague 99, 100; religious mode of existence 427; Spinoza 157, 158, 159, 170, 216; theodicy 30; two-domain theory 81; *see also* religion

Goddard, H. H. 192, 317, 467

gods 42, 49, 51, 56, 251

Godwin, William 144

Goethe, Wolfgang 6, 376, 380, 391

Goldstein, Kurt 378, 381, 432, 433, 446

Goldstein, R. 157

Golgi, Camillo 187, 194, 463

Gollaher, D. 226

good continuation 367, 368, 383

The Good Old Days—They Were Terrible (Bettmann) 9

goodness: Aristotle 65–66; Hartley 141; Spencer 211; Zarathustra 46

Gordon, B. L. 84, 85, 86–87

Goshen, C. E. 54

Goudge, T. A. 198, 199, 211

Gould, S. J. 190, 192, 318

gratification 391, 392

Grayling, A. C. 481

great-person theory 10, 13

The Great Psychotherapy Debate (Wampold) 462

Greece, ancient 40, 44, 46–66, 88; antecedents of behaviorism 323; cosmology 46–51; evolutionary theory 198; Golden Age of 55–66; historical consciousness 5; holistic perspectives 363; influence during the Renaissance 100; influence on Huarte 119;

medicine 51–54, 71; reason 91; relativism 54–55; Tertullian's critique of 81

Green, C. D. 456, 494

grief 83

Griggs, R. A. 336

Grmek, M. D. 182

Groethuysen, B. 114

Grosseteste, Robert 89

group dynamics 377, 383

Groups in Harmony and Tension (Sherif) 469

Growth of the Mind (Koffka) 362–363, 370–371

Gruber, H. E. 453–454

Guantanamo Bay 492, 496

Guide for the Perplexed (Maimonides) 89, 97

Guillotin, Joseph Ignace 180, 194, 218

Gullan-Whur, M. 157

Gundlach, H. 366

Gutenberg, Johannes 98, 101

Guthrie, Edwin Ray 344–345, 354, 356, 450

Guthrie, R. V. 302, 317–318

Guthrie, W. K. C. 56, 62, 66

Gutterman, S. S. 109

gyrator 223

Habilitation project (Wertheimer) 366

habit: Allport 436; Aristotle 66; Augustine 83; Bacon 93; habit strength 342, 356; Hume 138; James 294, 297; Watson 335; Whytt 179

Haeckel, Ernst Heinrich 209, 233, 484

hagiography 11

Hales, Stephen 178, 194

Hall, C. S. 409

Hall, Granville Stanley 301–305, 306, 318, 320; Cattell and 309; child development 209, 454; Freud and 387, 388; historical timeline 238; influence of Darwin 210; journals 310; National Academy of the Sciences 308

Hallie, P. P. 74

hallucinations 71, 93

Handbook of Physiological Optics (Helmholtz) 246

Handbuch der Physiologie des Menschen (Müller) 182–183

happiness: Adler 406; Aristotle 65, 66; Freud 391; Hartley 140; Kant 163; La Mettrie 181; Montaigne 116; Paracelsus 113; Plotinus 76; religion and 492; Sabuco 118; social psychology 142; stoicism 73

hardening 132, 149

Harlow, Harry Frederick 430, 451, 477, 478

harmony 160, 161, 162, 170

Harris, B. 335

Harris, M. 215–216

Harrison, P. 84, 167

Hartley, David 124, 140–141, 145, 146, 148, 149, 323

Hartmann, Heinz 417

Hartshorne, Charles 485

Harvard University 289, 290, 299, 301–302, 345, 348, 362, 435

Harvey, William 174

Hasbach, P. H. 485

Haupt, E. J. 280

Hausman, E. M. 459

Hawking, Stephen 407

Hawthorne, Nathaniel 184

Hayes, Steven C. 462

health psychology 181, 472, 482–483, 496

Health Psychology (journal) 483

hearing 248

Hebb, Donald Olding 463, 465, 477

Hebrews 44–45

hedonic calculus 142

hedonism 57, 140, 142, 150

Heidbreder, Edna 269, 305

Heidegger, Martin 427–428, 442, 445, 446

Heider, Fritz 378

heliocentric cosmology 104, 105, 106, 120, 394

Hell, Maximillian 217

Helmholtz, Herman L. F. von 194–195, 245–248, 249, 260; colors 183; Hall and 302; James and 290; law and order 239; materialism 27; speed of a nervous impulse 172, 188; Wundt and 250

Helmont, F. M. von 160

Héloise 90, 91–92, 97

Helson, H. 4

Helvétius, Claude-Adrien 124, 138, 139–140, 149, 323

Henle, Mary 3, 4–5, 361, 362, 374, 378, 382

Henri, V. 310

Henry, Edward 191

Henry VIII, King of England 110, 224

Heraclitus 50–51, 59, 67, 77, 295

Herbart, Johann Friedrich 165–166, 168, 169

Herbert of Cherbury 116

Herder, Johann Gottfried 163

Hereditary Genius (Galton) 210, 467

heredity 192, 202, 204, 210, 467

Herodotus 5, 13

Herrnstein, R. J. 179

Herschel, William 201

heterogony of ends 256, 260

heteronomy 164, 169–170

heterosexuality 399

heuristic theory 197–198, 233

heuristic value 34, 197–198, 409

Hickok, Laurens 17

hierarchy of needs 431–432

Higgins, E. T. 490

Hildebrand, J. H. 21, 22

Hilgard, E. R. 343, 347

Hippocrates 53–54, 67–68, 71, 79, 84, 119, 219, 223

Hispanics 5

Histoire Naturelle (Buffon) 198

Historia Calamitatum (Story of My Calamities) (Abelard) 89–90

historiography 5–11, 13

history 3–13; chaos hypothesis 9–10; cyclical hypothesis 8–9; definitions of 6–7, 13; Gestalt psychology 380; Hall 304; historical consciousness 5–6; Jung 410; linear-progressive hypothesis 9; objectivity of 7; of psychology 11–13; reasons for studying 3–5; tyranny of the present 8

History of India (Mill) 145

History of Life and Death (Bacon) 126

History of Psychology (journal) 12

History of the Human Sciences (journal) 12

History of the Peloponnesian War (Thucydides) 5

History of the Winds (Bacon) 126

Hitler, Adolf 238, 361, 374, 389, 427, 438, 494

Hitler's Mistakes (Lewin) 360

Hitzig, Julius Eduard 186–187, 194, 195, 464–465

Hobbes, Thomas 27, 40, 124, 172–175, 195, 269–270, 323

Hoffman, D. H. 492–493

Hoffman Report (2015) 238, 480, 492–493, 496

holistic perspectives 363, 443

Hollingworth, Leta Stetter 230, 314, 315–316, 320, 321

Holocaust 5, 9, 389, 438–439

Holt, Edwin Bissell 332, 435

Holtzendorff, Franz von 288

homeostasis 52

Homer 49, 52

homme moyen 190

homosexuality 397

Honzik, C. H. 346

Hooker, Joseph 205–206

Hopper, Grace 479

Hornbostel, Erich Moritz von 279, 360

Horney, Karen Danielsen 413–417, 420, 421, 430

Horwitz, T. 482

hospitals 221, 224, 225, 227, 228

hostile types 415, 420

Howe, Samuel Gridley 227

Hsün Tzu 42, 68

Huarte, Juan 118–119, 120

Hull, Clark 263, 341–344, 349, 356, 450; applied psychology 354; Koffka and 362; Köhler and 370; operant conditioning 350; opposition to teleology 24; Tolman's rejection of 345

human ecology 484–485

human nature: Avicenna 85; behaviorism 430; Freud 389, 403; Hobbes 174; Hsün Tzu 42; humanistic psychology 423, 442; Machiavelli 108–109; Mill 147; Petrarch 107; Renaissance psychology 106; Sabuco 118; Spinoza 156

Human Nature and the Social Order (Thorndike) 331

humanism, Renaissance 102, 106–107, 115–116, 121

humanistic psychology 4, 263, 353, 423–446, 448, 449–450; Allport 435–436; criticisms of 442–443; Dialectical Behavior Therapy 461; Frankl 438–440; future hopes 264; intellectual traditions of 424–430; Maslow 430–434; motivation 489; Pinel as forerunner to 221; as precursor to ecopsychology 485; Rogers 436–438; Rychlak 440–441

humanitarian reform movements 216–232

Humbert, E. G. 409

Hume, David 133, 135–138, 140, 148, 149; association 270; curiosity 168; historical timeline 124; Kant's rejection of 162; Protagorean relativism 55; Reid on 166–167; sensations 277

humors 44, 54, 71–72, 84, 86, 119

hunger drive 340

Hunter, Walter Samuel 273, 332

Husserl, Edmund 275, 279, 427, 429–430, 445

Huxley, Aldous 114, 434

Huxley, T. H. 136, 175, 182

hylomorphism 63, 68

hylozoism 252, 260

Hypatia of Alexandria 40, 76–77, 97

hypnosis 219, 234, 354; Bernheim 393; Freud 387, 400; Münsterberg 300

Hypnosis and Suggestibility (Hull) 354

hysteria 43, 217, 386–387

id 392–393, 396, 398, 400, 401, 417, 420

Idea of a New Anatomy of the Brain (Bell) 181

ideal self 437–438, 445

idealism 27–28, 31, 133–135; Aristotle 63; Calkins 314; definition of 36; James 293; Külpe 281

idealized self 415, 416, 420

ideas 130, 133, 134; Condillac 139; Hume 136, 137; Locke 141; Mill 146; Wundt 253, 255

ideational learning 371–372

identical elements transfer theory 331, 356

identification 398, 399, 403, 420

identity 19; Egyptians 43; Freud 402; Heraclitus 51; Hume 136–137; intersectionality 482, 496; Leibniz 162; psychogenic identity theory 31–32, 37; see also personal identity; self

idiographic orientation 436, 445

idiotisme 220

Idols 126–127, 149

ignorance 57, 60, 61; Abelard 91; Bacon 92–93; Wollstonecraft 144

illness 51–54, 67–68; see also medicine; mental illness

illusions 127, 391

imageless thought 281, 286

images 112, 268, 270, 272, 281

imagination: active 408; Aristotle 65; Bacon 128; Hartley 140; Hume 137; Locke 130; Quételet 190; Spinoza 158

Imago (journal) 448

imitation 371, 452

Imlay, Gilbert 144

immune system 468, 478

impetus 395

impressions 136, 137, 173, 247, 270, 330

incentive 342–343

incest 397

The Incoherence of the Incoherence (Averroës) 87–88

The Incoherence of the Philosophers (Al-Ghazali) 40, 87

inconsistency of human action 117

indeterminism 26, 36

Index of Forbidden Books 101, 108, 120, 136

Indian philosophy, ancient 44

The Individual and His Religion (Allport) 238, 435, 436

individual differences 106, 192, 210, 211; Galton 233, 316; Hollingworth 315; Huarte 118, 119; Locke 131

individual psychology 405, 419, 420

individualism 289, 291, 432, 433, 444, 445

individuation 410, 420

inductive argument 151, 152, 170

inductivism 128, 349

indulgences 101, 120

industrial-organizational psychology 259, 300, 472, 473–476, 477

industrial psychology 300, 301

inequality 142, 147, 480, 481, 492

infanticide 45, 78

inferiority complex 406–407, 419, 420

information processing 455, 456, 457; information-processing metaphor 454, 477; La Mettrie 181

inheritance of acquired characteristics 201–202, 233

inhibition: Hull 343, 356; Müller 280; Münsterberg 300; Pavlov 326, 327, 328, 358; reciprocal 460, 478; ultramaximal 327, 328; Weber 240–241; Wundt 254

inner perception 276

An Inquiry into the Human Mind (Reid) 166

Inquisition 105, 109, 117, 124, 153, 157, 198, 213

insight 343, 347, 370, 383

Instinct: A Study in Social Psychology (Bernard) 338

instincts 15–16, 36; Freud 395, 420; James 297; Watson 337–338

"Instincts and their Vicissitudes" (Freud) 395, 397

institutions 221, 225, 227, 228

The Integrative Action of the Nervous System (Sherrington) 187

intellectualists 426

intelligence: Aquinas 93; Galton 467; measurement of 192; memory 111; Piaget 453; racial bias 469; Renaissance psychology 106; Washburn 273

intelligence testing 316–318, 319, 351, 458; historical timeline 238; Hollingworth 315–316; Köhler 364; racism 192–193; Scott 473–474; see also mental tests

interactionism 29, 36, 160, 161, 269, 272, 333, 335

interdisciplinarity 403, 455

Intergroup Conflict and Cooperation: The Robbers Cave Experiment (Sherif) 469

intergroup contact 436

International Forum for Logotherapy (journal) 440

International Journal of Psychoanalysis 438

International Society for the History of Behavioral and Social Sciences (Cheiron) 12

Internationale Zeitschrift für Psychoanalyse (journal) 448

The Interpretation of Dreams (Freud) 238, 314, 387, 408

interrogation techniques 492–493, 496

intersectionality 482, 496

intervening variables 345–346, 356

intoxication 391

intrinsic teleology 24, 36, 37

Introduction to the Principles of Morals (Bentham) 142

introspection 55, 286, 355; Brentano 276; Carr 309; Montaigne 116; Sabuco 118; Stumpf 279; Titchener 267, 270, 333, 429; Washburn 272–273; Watson 333; Wundt 263

introversion 412, 413, 419, 420

intuition 412

invariant dynamics 379–380

inventive ideation 347

involuntary action 177, 179, 180, 276

IQ 192, 315, 317; see also intelligence

irony 427, 444–445

Islam 78, 79; Bacon 92; Middle Ages 80, 84–88; women's roles 230
isomorphism 373, 383
Israel 45
Italian city-states 108
Itard, Jean-Marc Gaspard 229, 233

Jackson, Andrew 184
Jackson, S. W. 72
Jacobs, D. 143, 144
Jager, M. 63, 64
Jahoda, M. 448
Jahrbuch für Psychoanalytische und Psychopathologische Forschungen (journal) 448
jails 226–227
James, Henry 289
James-Lange theory of emotion 271, 286, 296–297, 299, 320
James, William 288–299, 306, 320, 445, 475, 479; abnormal psychology 457; absolutism 8, 318; Angell on 307; biography 289–290; Brentano's affinity with 278; Calkins and 313–314; consciousness 255, 452; descriptive examinations 491; Ebbinghaus compared with 283; emotions 271, 286, 296–297; free will 25, 27; Freud on 387–388; general characteristics of thought 291–294; Gestalt psychology 365; habit 66, 294; Hall and 301–302, 304; historical causality 10–11; historical timeline 124, 238; on history 6; history of psychology 11; humanistic psychology 424; influence of Darwin 210; instincts 297; intensity of human life 495; interrelatedness 486; legacy of 298–299; levels of explanation 34; Maslow on 433, 434; memory 298; mental events 453; methodology 373; National Academy of the Sciences 308; pluralism 494; pragmatism 18, 37; as precursor to ecopsychology

485; ranking of psychologists 311; rationalism 168; relations 441; religion 491–492; the self 295–296, 321; stoicism 74; stream of thought 294–295, 321; strenuous life concept 407; Stumpf and 279; Thorndike and 329; Woodworth and 311
Janet, Pierre 408
Jastrow, Joseph 208
Jaynes, J. 4, 175–176
Jefferson, Thomas 323
Jenner, Edward 124
Jesus Christ 79
Jesus Christ, in the Light of Psychology (Hall) 305
Johnson, D. F. 310
Jonçich, G. 330
Jones, E. 385, 386, 389
Jones, James Earl 407
Jones, Mary Cover 336–337, 356–357, 460
Jorgenson, Christine 482
Journal for the Scientific Study of Religion 492
Journal of Analytic Psychology 409, 448
Journal of Applied Behavior Analysis 350, 354
Journal of Applied Psychology 303
Journal of Clinical Psychology 459
Journal of Comparative and Physiological Psychology 342, 451
Journal of Consulting Psychology 311
Journal of Counseling Psychology 459
Journal of Experimental Physiology 182
Journal of Experimental Psychology 342
Journal of Health Psychology 483
Journal of Humanistic Psychology 430, 449
Journal of Man 184
Journal of Phenomenological Psychology 430
Journal of Religious Psychology 303
Journal of the History of the Behavioral Sciences 11, 12
Journal of the History of the Neurosciences 12
Joye, Y. 485

Judaism 44–45, 76, 78, 79; Clark University 302; Freud 385; Jewish scholars 494; Lewin 375; Middle Ages 80, 88–89; scapegoating of Jews 99; Spinoza 156, 157; Vives 109; witch trials 213
judgment 277, 286
Juhasz, J. B. 52, 59, 60, 65
Jung, Carl G. 388, 407–413, 419, 420, 422; biography 408–409; Electra complex 399; free will 25; Hall and 303; on history 7; Horney on 415; legal issues 487; optimal functioning 484; self-actualization 432, 446
just noticeable difference (jnd) 241–242, 244, 260, 261

Kahl, R. 246
Kahn, P. H. 486
Kandel, Eric 464, 477
Kandinsky, Vassily 380
Kant, Immanuel 162–165, 169, 170, 242; Angell on 307; historical timeline 124; influence of Bacon 126; influence on Gestalt psychology 363; rationalism 17; solar system 198, 233
Kaslow, N. J. 493
Katona, George 381, 383
Keller, Fred S. 351
Keller, Helen 184
Kelley, K. W. 468
Kelly, George 449
Kelly, J. 99
Kelly-Gadol, J. 119
Kepler, Johannes 104, 120
Kieckhefer, R. 214
Kierkegaard, Søren Aabye 425–427, 444, 445, 446
Kiernan, T. 282–283
Kirkbride, Thomas S. 228, 233
Kirsch, I. 212
Kitcher, P. 20
Klee, Paul 380
Klein, M. I. 417
knowledge 14–15, 35; acquisition of 140, 151; Aquinas 94; Bacon 126, 127, 128; Condillac 139; Descartes 155; emotions

and 18–19; empiricism 17; Hobbes 173, 174; Kant 162, 163–164, 170; Locke 130, 131; Montaigne 114–115, 117; Plato 58; rationalism 151–152; Sabuco 118; shift in worldviews 381; skepticism 18; Socrates 57; Xenophanes 49; *see also* epistemology
Koch, Sigmund 447
Koestenbaum, P. 425
Koffka, Kurt 282, 359, 362–363, 374, 383; child development 454; developmental concepts 370–371; *Habilitation* project 366; perceptual organization 366–367; Stumpf and 279
Köhler, Wolfgang 359, 360–362, 374, 381, 383, 384; Allport and 435; analysis 379; Asch and 470; Berlin Psychological Institute 373; criticism of behaviorism 452; *Habilitation* project 366; historical timeline 238; invariant dynamics 379–380; isomorphism 373; learning 369, 370; Lewin and 375; nervous system 465; Pavlov and 328; science 363–364; scientific method 372; Sherif and 469; Stumpf and 279; von Restorff effect 378
Koppes, L. L. 475
Koran 167
Kraepelin, Emil 219, 258, 260, 458
Kramer, Heinrich 40, 212–213, 214–215, 233
Kries, Johannes von 362
Kruglanski, A. W. 490
Kruta, V. 240–241
Kuhn, Thomas S. 20–21, 23, 36, 340
Kuhse, H. 31
Külpe, Oswald 280–282, 286–287, 360, 362
Kuo, Zing-Yang 15, 338

La Mettrie, Julien Offray de 27, 180–181, 195, 323
labor 331, 473–477
labor movements 216–217

laboratory research 262, 263; Calkins 313; cognitive psychology 455; Müller 279–280; Titchener 268; Wundt 253, 254–255; *see also* experimental psychology
Laborit, Henri 467
Lachman, J. L. 452
Lachman, R. 452, 454–455
The Ladies Home Journal 230
Laertius, D. 73
Lafayette, Marquis de 218
Lamarck, Jean-Baptiste 202, 233
Lange, Carl 271, 286, 296, 320
Langfeld, H. S. 279
language: brain areas 186; Bruner 451; Chomsky 350; cognitive psychology 455; Condillac 139; double-aspect monism 28; Huarte 118–119; ideational learning 371–372; La Mettrie 181; Lucretius 75; origin of 199–200; Piaget 453; Spinoza 170; Wundt 251
L'Année Psychologique (journal) 316
Laplace, Pierre Simon de 189, 198, 233
Lashley, Karl 369, 465
latency period 399, 420
latent content of a dream 400, 420
latent learning 346, 357
Latham, R. E. 75
Lauenstein, Otto von 361
Lavoisier, Antoine-Laurent 218
law 472, 486–489; Bentham 142; Comstock Law 231; epistemology 16; medieval universities 89; Münsterberg 300; Wundt 251
law of effect 330, 357
law of exercise 330, 357
law of Prägnanz 368, 383
Lea, H. C. 216
leadership 377, 476
learning: Aristotle 66; behaviorism 335, 340, 390, 450–451, 489; definition of 36; Ebbinghaus 284; empiricism 148; Gestalt psychology 369–370, 371–372, 454; Guthrie 344–345; Hull 343; instinct versus 15–16; James 298; Katona 381; latent

346, 357; "learning to learn" 451, 477; Montaigne 116; Plato 60, 61; Renaissance psychology 106; social learning theory 452; Thorndike 330; Tolman 346, 347, 357; Vives 111; Woodworth 313
learning sets 451, 477
Leary, D. E. 491
Leclerc, George-Louis (Comte de Buffon) 198–199, 200–201, 232
Lectures on Conditioned Reflexes (Pavlov) 238, 357
Lectures on Human and Animal Psychology (Wundt) 250, 253
Lehrer, K. 167
Leibniz, Gottfried Wilhelm 159–162, 168, 170, 178, 289; differential calculus 50; psychophysical parallelism 29; rationalism 17; Spinoza and 157
Leibnizian tradition 435–436, 445
Leonardo da Vinci 40, 102, 111–113, 120
Leonardo da Vinci and a Memory of His Childhood (Freud) 112
Lequier, Jules 292
Leslie, R. C. 440
Letters Concerning the English Nation (Voltaire) 132
Leuba, James 44, 492
Leucippus 51, 67, 68, 75, 323
Leviathan (Hobbes) 124, 173, 174
Levy, E. 381
Lewin, Kurt 279, 361, 374–377, 380, 383
Lewin, R. 360
Lewis, H. B. 448–449
LGBT communities 492
liberalism 145, 264
libido 392
Life and Confessions of a Psychologist (Hall) 303
life space 375–376, 383
life-span development 304, 305
The Limits of Science (Medawar) 22
Lincoln, Abraham 6, 7, 124, 184
Lindenfeld, D. 281
Lindsley, Donald B. 465, 478
Lindsley, Ogden 352
Lindzey, G. 435

linear-progressive hypothesis 9, 13
Linehan, Marsha M. 461, 478
Linnean Society 206
Liszt, Franz von 487
lithium 466
Locke, John 129–132, 140, 145, 149–150, 207, 323; acquisition of knowledge 151; child development 208; curiosity 168; historical timeline 124; influence of Bacon 126; influence on Pinel 219; influence on Voltaire 138; innate ideas 141; Kant compared with 164; Leibniz compared with 161; material substance 134; moral basis for psychology 139; perception of temperature 276; qualities 131, 133; senses 17; white paper hypothesis 129–130, 143, 148
Lockean tradition 435–436, 445
Loeb, Jacques 24
Loeb, Morris 302
Loewi, Otto 238
Loftus, Elizabeth F. 488–489, 496
Logan, F. A. 341, 342
The Logic of Modern Physics (Bridgman) 340, 355–356
The Logic of Scientific Discovery (Popper) 19, 37
logical positivism 341, 357
logotherapy 438, 439, 440, 445
Longfellow, Henry Wadsworth 184
Lorenz, Konrad 16
Lotze, R. H. 271, 278
love: Avicenna 86; Bacon 128; Empedocles 52, 53, 67; Freud 391, 403, 473; Héloise 91–92; James-Lange theory of emotion 271; *Malleus Maleficarum* 213; Maslow 432–433; Plato 61; Sabuco 118; Spinoza 159; Watson 337; Wollstonecraft 144
Lovelace, Ada B. 219, 456
Lowrie, W. 425
Luccio, R. 373
Lucretius 74–75, 97, 323
Ludwig, Karl 188, 245, 302
Lunar Society 201
Luria, Alexander 362, 375
Lurie, A. T. 51

Luther, Martin 40, 101, 106, 120, 121
Lyceum 62, 68
Lyell, Charles 124, 161, 199, 205–206, 233

MacCormac, E. R. 30
MacCorquodale, Kenneth 350
Mach, Ernst 364, 384
Machiavelli, Niccolò 40, 107–108, 112, 120, 121
Machiavellianism 109, 121
MacKay, Donald 348
MacLeod, R. B. 46, 98, 102, 182, 290, 429–430
Magellan, Ferdinand 40, 100, 121, 194
Magendie, François 181, 182, 195
magnetic resonance imaging (MRI) 466
magnetism, animal 217–219, 223, 243
Mahaffy, J. P. 154–155
Mahoney, M. J. 353
Maimonides, Moses 79, 88–89, 93, 97, 102
Malebranche, Nicolas 271
Malleus Maleficarum (Kramer & Sprenger) 40, 212–215, 233
Malone, J. C. 332
Malthus, Thomas Robert 124, 205, 233
Man a Machine (La Mettrie) 180, 195, 323
Man and His Works (Thorndike) 331
Man for Himself (Fromm) 16
Management in the Home (Gilbreth) 475
mandalas 411, 413, 420
Mandler, G. 378
Mandler, J. M. 378
mania 54, 72, 220
manic-depressive psychosis 258
manifest content of a dream 400, 420
Mann, Horace 184, 227
Man's Search for Meaning (Frankl) 439
Mao Tse-tung 7
Marcus Aurelius 74, 96
Marrow, A. J. 375

Marston, William Moulton 301, 320, 488
Martel, Charles 40, 84
Marx, Karl 184
Marxism 202, 323, 329, 368, 494
masculinity 42, 411–412
Maslow, Abraham 49, 430–434, 442, 445, 446, 449, 484, 489
mate guarding 207
material cause 23, 36
material self 295, 320
materialism 27, 36, 133, 134, 323; Aristotle 63; Fechner 243; Helvétius 139–140; Hobbes 174; James 293; Lucretius 75; Rush 222; Watson 358
Mathematico-Deductive Theory of Rote Learning (Hull) 342
mathematics: Augustine 83; Bacon 92; Carr 309; Condillac 139; Descartes 154; Herbart 165; Hull 341; Leonardo da Vinci 113; Pythagoras 48; Renaissance 102; *see also* formulae
Mathews, N. 125
Matson, W. I. 173, 174
A Matter of Consequences (Skinner) 348
Mattoon, M. A. 409, 411
Maudsley, H. 271
Maxwell, James Clerk 248, 260
May, Rollo 442, 449
Mayer, Clara 470
Mayrhauser, R. T. von. 473–474
McDaniel, S. 493
McDougall, William 15, 24, 202, 332, 338, 468
McHenry, L. C. 178, 179
McInerny, R. 94
McReynolds, P. 259
Mead, Margaret 414
Meade, M. 90
meaning 429–430; Frankl 439, 440; Titchener 270–271, 286
The Meaning of Truth (James) 290
means-centered approach 431
measurement 172–196; applications of new techniques 192–193; of behavior 188–192; brain activity 465–466; Cattell 310; Descartes 175–177; Ebbinghaus 283; Fechner 244;

Galton 310; Hales 178; Hobbes 172–175; Köhler 372; nervous system and brain areas 181–186; observational techniques 186–188; Offray de la Mettrie 180–181; operationism 340–341; Planck 364; psychophysics 240; speed of a nervous impulse 188; Stensen 178; Swammerdam 177–178; Unzer 179–180; Whytt 178–179; *see also* quantification

Mechanical Man: John B. Watson and the Beginnings of Behaviorism (Buckley) 323

mechanistic philosophy 174, 180, 181, 452

Medawar, P. B. 22

median 192

Medical Inquiries and Observations upon Diseases of the Mind (Rush) 222, 234

medication 462, 466–467

medicine: ancient Greek 51–54, 71; Averroës 88, 96; Avicenna 86; La Mettrie 181; Magendie 182; Maimonides 88–89; Middle Ages 79–80, 89; Rhazes 84–85; Romans 71–73; Whytt 178–179; *see also* physiology

medieval period 79–95, 97; Augustine 81–84; geocentric cosmology 103; Islam 84–88; Judaism 88–89; rise of the European universities 89–95

Meditations on First Philosophy (Descartes) 154

Meerloo, Joost A. M. 417, 493

Meinong, Alexius 275

melancholia: Avicenna 86; Galen 72; Hippocrates 54; Pavlov 328; Pinel 220; Rhazes 84

Melville, Herman 10

memory: Adler 406; Aristotle 63–64; Augustine 83; authority 19; Bacon 128; cognitive psychology 452, 453, 454, 455, 457; Ebbinghaus 283–284, 453; Gestalt psychology 378, 454; Hartley 141; Heraclitus 50; history as 4; Huarte 119;

intelligence testing 317; James 298, 320; localization of functions in the brain 465; Mill 145; Müller 280; Plato 60; psyche 37; Quételet 190; repressed memories 488–489; synaptic transmission 464; Titchener 268; Vives 110–111; von Restorff effect 378, 384; Woodworth 313; Wundt 255, 257

Memory: A Contribution to Experimental Psychology (Ebbinghaus) 238, 283

Memory Observed: Remembering in Natural Contexts (Neisser) 457

menstruation 315

mental disorders: Dix 226–228; Galen 72; humanitarian reform 217; Hypatia of Alexandria 77; Kraepelin 258; Pinel 219–221; Plato 60–61; psychopharmacology 467; Reil 225; Roman period 71; Rush 222–224, 234; Spinoza 158; Tuke 224–225; Zeigarnik 377; *see also* emotional disorders; mental illness; psychiatry; psychopathology

Mental Evolution in Animals (Romanes) 208

Mental Evolution in Man (Romanes) 208

mental illness: Avicenna 86; Freud 391; Jewish philosophy 45; law 486, 489; measurement 193; Pinel 220–221; Watson 335; *see also* mental disorders; psychiatry; psychopathology

mental phenomena 275–276, 277, 278, 282, 283

mental processes: cognitive psychology 453; cognitive revolution 355; Frankl 440; Freud 393; James, William 294; Kant 363; Mill 145; Titchener 268–269, 286

mental sets 281, 287

mental tests 310, 316–318, 334; *see also* intelligence testing

Mental Tests and Measurements (Cattell) 238

mentalism 456, 478

The Mentality of Apes (Köhler) 238, 361, 370

menticide 493

Meredith, A. 73

Merlan, P. 76

Merritte, Douglas 336

Mesmer, Franz Anton 113, 217–219, 223, 234

mesmerism 4, 124, 185, 217–219, 234

meta-level awareness 434

method of average error 245, 260

method of constant stimuli 245, 260

method of limits 244–245, 260

methods: behaviorism 340; Brentano 276; Carr 309; cognitive psychology 455; diversity of 494; Ebbinghaus 283; evolving scientific methodologies 490–491; Feyerabend 22; Gestalt psychology 371, 372–373; humanistic psychology 442; James 292; Jung 409; Plato 58; systems 263; Titchener 266–267; Watson 334–335

Meyer, Max Frederick 332

Meynert, Theodore 386

Michaels, John 310

Michelson, Albert A. 302

Middle Ages 79–95, 97; Augustine 81–84; demonology 212; geocentric cosmology 103; Islam 84–88; Judaism 88–89; neo-Platonism 76; rise of the European universities 89–95

Milar, K. S. 316

Miles, Catherine Cox 467

Miles, W. 307, 308

Milgram, Stanley 471–472, 478

military projects 351

Mill, James 141, 145, 150

Mill, John Stuart 55, 141, 145–147, 148, 150, 229

Mills, Hannah 224

Milton, John 131

mind 27–28; active 152, 159, 164, 169; Aristotle 63; Descartes 155; early Chinese psychology 42; Fechner 242; Kant 164; Leibniz

161, 170; Lucretius 74–75; Mill 147; Plato 59; psychogeny 31; rationalism 151, 152; Reid 167; specific energies of nerves 183; Spinoza 158, 159, 170; Titchener 269; twentieth-century developments in psychology 448; Unzer 179; Wundt 252–253; *see also* brain

mind-body problem 27–32; Aristotle 63, 68; dualism 28–30; Gestalt psychology 373, 383; Leibniz 160, 161; Lucretius 74–75; monism 27–28; pluralism 30–31; psychogeny 31–32; Spinoza 158, 160

Mind (journal) 147, 209, 254, 262

The Mind of the Child (Preyer) 305

mindfulness 461–462, 478

Mintz, S. I. 174

Misiak, Henryk 480

The Mismeasure of Man (Gould) 192, 318

misogyny 81, 82

Mitwelt 428, 445

M'Naughton, Daniel 124, 486, 489

Moby-Dick (Melville) 10

models, as explanations 33–34

moderation 48–49, 52, 66, 96, 118, 121

Modern Psychoanalysis (journal) 448

Mohammed 40, 84

molar behavior 345, 357

monadology 160–161, 170

Monahan, J. 487

monism 27–28, 30, 289, 494; definition of 36; double-aspect 28, 35, 253, 269; James 292, 293, 298; Leibniz 160, 170

monkeys, experiments with 451

Montaigne, Michel de 40, 78, 113–117, 119, 121, 138, 154, 168

mood 224, 293

Moore, K. G. 76

Mora, Masahiro 322

moral anxiety 396, 421

moral therapy 221

morality: in animals 208; Darwin 211; determinism 26; free will 25–26; Herbart 165; James

292–293; Kant 164, 170; Machiavelli 109; Piaget 453; *see also* ethics

More, Thomas 110

Morgan, Conwy Lloyd 197, 208, 234

Morris, Desmond 16

Morse, Samuel F. B. 184

Moses, Samuel 302

motion 50, 69, 133, 173, 174; Descartes 175–177; Stensen's critique 178; Washburn 273–274; Whytt 179

Motion Study for the Handicapped (Gilbreth & Gilbreth) 475

motivation: Allport 436; Aristotle 65; empiricism 148; Freud 390, 393–395, 402, 403, 404, 417; functionalism 308–309; Gestalt psychology 374; Hull 341, 342; industrial-organizational psychology 476; Lewin 375; Maslow 431–433, 434; Plato 60; resurgence of 489–490; Scott 474; self-interest 195; Tolman 346, 347; Woodworth 312, 313; Wundt 256

Motivation and Personality (Maslow) 430, 431

motor theory of consciousness 273–274, 287

Movement and Mental Imagery (Washburn) 273

Mozans (J. A. Zahm) 55

Mozart, Wolfgang Amadeus 218

MRI *see* magnetic resonance imaging

Mruk, C. J. 430

Müller, Friedrich 250

Müller, Georg Elias 279–280, 281, 287, 360, 381

Müller, Johannes 182–183, 188, 195, 245, 248, 250

multiculturalism 480

multiple levels of analysis 291–292

multiple personality disorder 223

Munroe, R. L. 417

Münsterberg, Hugo 299–301, 313–314, 320, 435, 475; eyewitness testimony 487–488; historical timeline 238; industrial-organizational

psychology 472, 473; social psychology 469

Murphy, C. 214

Murphy, Gardner 312, 449, 469, 480

Murphy, Lois 480

Murray, Henry 449

music 278, 279

music therapy 77, 86, 97, 225

Myia 48–49, 68

myograph 188, 254

mysticism 408, 409

naïve realism 239, 240, 281

The Naked Ape (Morris) 16

names 43

narcissism 392, 394

narcosis therapy 328

National Academy of the Sciences 274, 308, 329

National Science Teachers Association 206–207

nativism 15, 16, 36, 371, 379–380

natural selection 53, 206, 234, 235

natural spirit 72, 96, 97

naturalism 197–198, 212; ancient Greeks 46, 51; birth of psychology 216; definition of 234; Dewey 306; disabilities 229; emotional disorders 217, 232; Freud 389; Gestalt psychology 372; Hippocrates 53, 54; origin of language 199–200; Spinoza 216; *see also* evolutionary theory

nature: Aristotle 65; ecotherapy 485; Empedocles 53; Leibniz 161; Lucretius 74; Paracelsus 113; Spinoza 158

nature-nurture distinction 15, 379

The Nature of Prejudice (Allport) 435

nature of the soul 59

Nazi Germany: Eichmann 471; Frankl 438–439; Freud 389; Gestalt psychology 360, 361, 363–364, 374, 375, 378, 380; Heidegger 427; Meerloo 493; Sherif 469

nebular hypothesis 198, 234

necessity 166, 167

needs, hierarchy of 431–432

Neisser, Ulrich 238, 452, 454, 457

neo-Platonism 61, 66, 73, 75–77, 82, 97
neobehaviorism 340–354, 448, 449, 450–452, 453, 454, 455, 456
nerves 175–176, 177–178, 179, 181, 195; specific energies of 182–184, 195, 248; speed of a nervous impulse 172, 188, 194–195, 260; Wundt 254
nervous system 181–186, 187–188, 195, 241, 267, 463, 465
Neumann, John von 360, 361
Neurath, Otto 341
neurochemistry 440
neurology 34, 54, 75, 177
neurophysiology 34, 182–183, 323
neuropsychology 118, 347, 451
neuroscience 34, 185, 463; brain hemispheres 8–9; cognitive 464; cognitive psychology and 455; free will and determinism 26, 27; Gestalt psychology 382, 454; humanistic psychology and 450; La Mettrie 181; language of 187; Pavlov 328; psychiatry and 449; qualitative research 491; technological developments 466; Vesalius 102; see also brain
neurosis: experimental 327; Eysenck 462; Horney 414, 415, 416; noogenic neuroses 439, 445
Neurosis and Human Growth (Horney) 414
neurotic anxiety 396, 421
The Neurotic Personality of Our Time (Horney) 414
neurotic trends 415, 421
neurotransmitters 466
New Philosophy on the Nature of Man (Sabuco) 40, 117–118
New Ways in Psychoanalysis (Horney) 414
Newton, Isaac 7, 165, 187, 206; "clockwork universe" concept 161; color 247; differential calculus 50, 159, 170; influence of Bacon 126; influence on Hartley 141; influence on Voltaire 138

Nicomachean Ethics (Aristotle) 66
Nietzsche, Friedrich 418, 495
night view 243
Nightingale, Florence 193
Ninety-Five Theses again Indulgences (Luther) 40
nominal fallacy 127
nominalism 174
nomothetic orientation 436, 445, 455
nondirective therapy 436
noogenic neuroses 439, 445
Nordby, V. J. 409
Norena, C. G. 110
normal science 21, 23, 36
Norman, D. A. 455
noumenal world 164, 170
Novak, Michael 423, 440
Novum Organum (Bacon) 124, 126, 148
numbers 48; see also mathematics
numerical explanations 34

obedience 471–472, 478
objective anxiety 395–396, 421
objectivity in history 7, 13
objects 395
observational techniques 186–188, 263; Carr 309; Gestalt psychology 372; Titchener 267; Watson 334–335; Wundt 253
Observations on Man, His Frame, His Duty and His Expectations (Hartley) 124, 140
obsession 86
occupational therapy 225
Ockham's Razor 95, 97
Oedipus complex 394, 399, 406, 421
Ogden, Robert Morris 281, 282
Okin, S. S. 147
Olds, James 465
O'Malley, C. D. 179
one-trial learning 344
On Becoming a Person (Rogers) 437
On Dreams (Aristotle) 65
On Magic (Weyer) 216
On Memory and Reminiscence (Aristotle) 63, 64
On the Diagnosis and Cure of the Soul's Passions (Galen) 40, 72

On the Nature of the Universe (Lucretius) 74–75
On the Origin of Species by Means of Natural Selection (Darwin) 124, 205, 206, 207, 208, 210, 211
On the Revolution of the Celestial Spheres (Copernicus) 40, 104, 105
On the Sensations of Tone (Helmholtz) 248
On the Structure of the Human Body (Vesalius) 40
On the Witness Stand (Münsterberg) 238, 300
ontogeny recapitulates phylogeny 209, 234, 304
ontology 27, 37, 494; ecopsychology 486; Heidegger 427; Hobbes 174; Külpe 281
operant conditioning 349–350, 351, 352, 354, 357, 484; see also conditioning
operationism 340–341, 357
ophthalmoscope 246–247, 260
oppositional thinking 441
Opus Majus (Bacon) 92
oral stage 398, 421
organic evolution 200–202, 235
Organizing and Memorizing (Katona) 381
Orgel, S. 393
Ortgeist 10, 13
Our Inner Conflicts (Horney) 414, 415
An Outline of Psycho-analysis (Freud) 400
An Outline of Social Psychology (Sherif) 469
overcompensation 407, 421

Pace, Edward A. 252
pain: Condillac 139; Epicureanism 74, 75, 96; hardening 132; Hartley 140–141; Helvétius 140; Hobbes 174; Hume 138; Montaigne 116; Plato 60; Unzer 180; utilitarianism 142; Witmer 259; Wolff 162; Wundt 256
paired associate method 314
Pakistan 44
Palmer, S. 379
Papanicolaou, A. C. 297

Pappenheim, Bertha 386–387, 419
Paracelsus 113, 121, 217
paradigms 21, 37
paradoxical intention 440, 445–446
paradoxical phase 328, 357
parallelism 29, 37, 160, 161, 269, 333
paranoia 54, 258, 381
parents: authority 16, 401; Horney 414–415; Oedipus complex 394, 399, 421
Parmenides 49–50, 52, 59, 68
part-whole problem 365, 366
Particulars of My Life (Skinner) 348
Pascal, Blaise 189
passions 72, 118, 136, 137–138
past-mindedness 8
patriarchy 416
Pattern and Growth in Personality (Allport) 435
Paul 74, 167
Paul, Alice 230
Pauley, P. J. 304
Pavlov, Ivan 323–329, 334, 336, 348, 357, 358; applied psychology 354; critique of Gestalt school 379; determinism 25; emotional disorders 300; Hartley compared with 141; historical timeline 238; influence on Hull 341; influence on Wolpe 460; materialism 27; reflexology 180, 257, 369
peak experiences 432, 434
Pearson, Karl 315
Pedagogical Seminary (journal) 302
Peirce, Charles Sanders 18, 37, 320
pendulum myograph 254
Penfield, Wilder 465
penis envy 399, 404, 416, 421
percentiles 192
perception: Alhazen 86–87; Aristotle 64–65; autokinetic effect 469–470; Berkeley 133–134, 135, 149; Brentano 276; cognition 455; figure-ground 383; Gestalt psychology 363, 366–368, 454; Helmholtz 246–247, 248; Leibniz 161; Leonardo da Vinci

112; Locke 131; nativism versus empiricism 15; neo-Platonism 76; Parmenides 49–50; *petites perceptions* 161, 170; Plato 60; Plotinus 76; psyche 37; psychophysics 239; social influence 470–471; Stumpf 279; Titchener 268; Watson 334; Wertheimer 383; Wundt 254, 255; *see also* sensation; senses
Perls, Fritz 379, 381, 383
Perry, R. B. 289
perseveration 280
Persia 45–46
person-centered therapy 436
persona 411, 412, 421
personal identity 19, 136–137, 296, 479, 482; *see also* identity
personal unconscious 410, 421
personalism 314
personality: Adler 406; Allport 435, 436; Aquinas 94; Babylonia 43; brain areas 184; four-factor theory 54; Freud 392–393; Galen 72; Gestalt psychology 374, 382; Guthrie 354; Horney 414, 417; Indian philosophy 44; Jung 410–412; psychogenic emergentism 32; testing 458; Watson 335
Personality: A Psychological Interpretation (Allport) 435
personality disorders 461
personality tests 313, 412
Personalized System of Instruction (PSI) 351
PET *see* positron emission tomography
petites perceptions 161, 170
Petrarch, Francesco 40, 106–107, 121
Petzold, M. 41
The Phaedo (Plato) 56
phallic stage 399, 421
phantasia 65
phenomena 294
phenomenal field 437–438, 446
phenomenal world 164, 170
phenomenological descriptions 55
phenomenological method 373, 429–430

phenomenology: Brentano 277–278; definition of 446; Dialectical Behavior Therapy 461; ecopsychology 485; humanistic psychology 429–430, 442, 445, 450; Jung 410; Stumpf 279
phi phenomenon 365–366, 384
Philebus (Plato) 60
Phillips, Wendell 6
Philosophical Essays Concerning Human Understanding (Hume) 136
Philosophical Studies (Wundt) 238, 251
philosophy: cognitive psychology and 455; definition of 47–48, 68; epistemology 14–23; existentialism 424–429; Gestalt psychology 363; Greek 46–51, 55–66; James 291; mind-body problem 27–32; Roman 73–78; Wertheimer 360; Wundt 255, 257; *see also* empiricism; epistemology; ontology; rationalism
Philosophy (Russell) 348
phobias 337
The Photoplay (Münsterberg) 299
phrenology 4, 184–185, 194, 195, 223–224, 457
phrontistery 490, 496
phylogeny 209, 234, 304
physics 344, 364, 441, 490; *see also* Newton
physiology: Brentano 274; Descartes 175–177; Freud 390; Hall 301–302; Helmholtz 246; humanitarian reform 216; Magendie 182; Thorndike 330; Titchener 272; Watson 334; *see also* biopsychology; brain; nervous system; neurophysiology; neuroscience
Piaget, Jean 14, 305, 453–454, 478
Picasso, Pablo 380
Pilzecker, Alfons 280
pineal gland 176, 177, 178, 195, 216
Pinel, Philippe 124, 219–221, 224, 227, 228, 229, 234
Pivnicki, D. 56

The Place of Value in a World of Facts (Köhler) 362
plague 98–100
Planck, Max 363–364
Plato 40, 58–61, 67, 68, 83; charioteer metaphor 392; classification schemes 277; on Heraclitus 50; idealism 28; influence of Parmenides 49; influence of Socrates 57; influence on Avicenna 86; influence on Stumpf 278; reason 91; Russell on 94; Tertullian's critique of 81; Whitehead on 289
Platonism 61
pleasure: Aristotle 65; Augustine 83; Condillac 139; Democritus 51; Epicureanism 74, 75, 96; Freud 390–392, 395, 398, 406; Hartley 140–141, 148; Helvétius 140; Herbart 165; Hobbes 174; Hume 138; Kant 163; Mill 146; Montaigne 116; Plato 60; Socrates 57; Spencer 211; utilitarianism 142; Wolff 162; Wundt 256
pleasure principle 142, 390–392, 398, 421
Plekhanov, G. V. 139–140
Plotinus 70, 76, 82, 97
pluralism 27, 30–31, 35; definition of 37, 320; Dewey 306; Gestalt psychology 365; humanistic psychology 442; James 289, 291, 292, 298, 320, 365; Maslow 431; in psychology 494, 495
A Pluralistic Universe (James) 290
pneuma 72, 73, 97, 175
Poe, Edgar Allan 184
Poffenberger, A. T. 311
politics 329, 438, 473
polygraph 301
polytheism 70
Poma, A. 161
Popkin, R. H. 115–116, 154
Popper, Karl Raimond 19–20, 21, 37, 281
Popular Science Monthly 310
positive psychology 434, 444, 450, 483, 484, 496

positivism 139, 278, 331, 341, 344, 357
positron emission tomography (PET) 466
Postman, L. 282, 283
posttraumatic stress disorder 458–459
poverty 231
Powers, Francis 345, 354
Poyen, Charles 219
The Practice and Theory of Individual Psychology (Adler) 405, 406
pragmatism 17–18, 117, 207; definition of 37, 320; Gilbreth 475; James 294, 298, 320
Pragmatism (James) 290
Prägnanz, law of 368, 383
Pratola, S. 314
precision orientation 208
preconscious 400, 421
preestablished harmony 160, 161, 162, 170
pregnancy 44
prejudice 407, 482; Allport 436, 469; Bacon's Idols of the Cave 127, 149
presentations 277, 287
presentism 8, 13
Pressey, Sidney L. 351
Preyer, William Thierry 209, 234, 305
Priestley, Joseph 201
primary attention 269, 287
primary memory 298, 320
primary processes 392, 421
primary qualities 131, 133, 134, 150
The Prince (Machiavelli) 40, 108
Prince, Morton 457
Principia (Newton) 187
Principles of Behavior (Hull) 342
Principles of Biology (Spencer) 211
Principles of Geology (Lyell) 161, 199, 233
Principles of Gestalt Psychology (Koffka) 363
Principles of Physiological Psychology (Wundt) 251, 252, 261, 288
Principles of Physiology (Unzer) 179
The Principles of Psychology (James) 238, 283, 290, 293, 307, 318, 320

Principles of Psychology (Spencer) 211
Principles of the Philosophy of René Descartes (Spinoza) 157
privilege 482, 496
probability theory 189
problem-centered approach 431, 434, 442
problem solving: cognitive psychology 455; Duncker 378; Gestalt psychology 382; intelligence testing 317; Köhler 370; Thorndike 331; Watson 339; Woodworth 313
productive thinking 368–369, 381, 384
Productive Thinking (Wertheimer) 238, 368, 381, 470
progressionism 202
Progressive Era 216
Project for a Scientific Psychology (Freud) 457
Project Pigeon 351
projection 397, 421
projective tests 55
proprioception 188
prospection 490
Protagoras 55, 57, 68
providential theories 9–10
"The Province of Functional Psychology" (Angell) 308, 319
proximity 367, 384
PSI *see* Personalized System of Instruction
psyche 31, 32; Aristotle 63; definition of 37, 68; Freud 396; Jung 410, 421; Plato 59, 61
psychiatry: Avesta 46; diagnostic categories 459–460; dominance of 458; first use of the term 225; Heidegger 428; Huarte 118; Kraepelin 258, 260; medical roots of 52; neuroscience and 449; roots in ancient Israel 45; Rush 224; *see also* mental disorders; mental illness
psychic compounds 255, 256
psychical reflex 325, 357
PsychINFO 11, 12, 238
psychoanalysis 10, 278, 333, 385–422; Adler 405–407; Angell 308; childhood trauma

263–264; continuing influence of 448–449; definition of 421; first use of the term 387; Hobbes as forerunner to 174; Horney 413–417; humanistic critiques of 423, 430–431, 439, 442, 449; Jung 407–413; Kraepelin's opposition to 258; Lewin 375; pluralism 404; *see also* Freud

Psychoanalytic Psychology (journal) 448

Psychoanalytic Review (journal) 448

psychodrama 225, 232

psychogenesis 282

psychogenic emergentism 32, 37

psychogeny 31–32, 37

Psychological Abstracts 11, 238

Psychological Care of Infant and Child (Watson) 337

The Psychological Clinic (journal) 259, 458

Psychological Corporation 311, 319

psychological hedonism 57, 142, 150

Psychological Index (journal) 310

Psychological Monographs (journal) 310

psychological needs 431–432

Psychological Review (journal) 310, 333

Psychological Science (journal) 493

Psychologische Forschung (journal) 373, 378

psychology: causality 24; definitions of 255, 263, 275, 294, 314, 334; diversity and pluralism in 493–495; first use of the term 162; future prospects 479–496; historical timelines 40, 124, 238; history of 11–13; influence of evolutionary theory 207–211; relevance of epistemology 23; twentieth-century transformations in 447–448; *see also* applied psychology; behaviorism; clinical psychology; cognitive psychology; developmental psychology; experimental

psychology; functionalism; Gestalt psychology; humanistic psychology; social psychology

Psychology and Industrial Efficiency (Münsterberg) 300, 472, 473

Psychology (Angell) 307, 319

Psychology around the World (Sexton & Misiak) 480

"Psychology as the Behaviorist Views It" (Watson) 238, 333, 354

Psychology from an Empirical Standpoint (Brentano) 124, 275, 277

Psychology from the Standpoint of a Behaviorist (Watson) 337

The Psychology of Human Conflict (Guthrie) 345

The Psychology of Rigorous Humanism (Rychlak) 441

The Psychology of the Adolescent (Hollingworth) 316

Psychology: The Study of Mental Activity (Carr) 309

Psychology (Woodworth) 312

psychoneuroimmunology 468, 478

Psychonomic Society 493

psychopathology: behavioral genetics 468; Freud 400; functionalism 308; Gestalt psychology 381; Hall 301–302; identification 398; James 289; naturalistic approaches 212; psychoanalysis 449; Reil 225; Rush 222; Wundt 257; *see also* mental disorders

psychopharmacology 258, 466–467, 478

psychophysical parallelism 29, 37, 160, 161, 269

psychophysics 239–248, 260, 261, 278; Köhler's critique of 372; Müller 280; Stumpf 279; Woodworth 313

psychosexual development 398–400, 421

psychosis 258, 396, 402

psychotherapeutics 457

psychotherapy: Boston School 457; debates on 462; experimental behavior analysis 352; Freud

403, 448; Galen 72; Gestalt psychology 381; Guthrie 354; Horney 417; Jung 410, 413; Münsterberg 300; Rogers 437; *see also* therapy

Psychotherapy by Reciprocal Inhibition (Wolpe) 238, 460

Psychotherapy (Münsterberg) 300

Ptolemy 103, 104, 121

Puglisi, M. 275

purposive behaviorism 345, 357

Putnam, James Jackson 457

Puységur, Marquis de 219

Pyrrho 77, 97

Pythagoras 47–49, 52, 68, 71, 102

Quakers 224

qualitative research 372, 442, 491, 496

qualities: Galen 71–72; primary and secondary 131, 133, 134, 150

quantification 34, 102, 172, 372, 491; Hobbes 174–175; Watson 334; Weber 242; *see also* measurement

Quételet, Jacques 189–190, 193, 195, 210

Rabelais, François 131

race: *Brown v. Board of Education* 487; craniometry 192; eugenics 210; intelligence 192–193, 469; intersectionality 482; phrenology 185; segregation 377, 467, 487; Spencer 211

racism 192–193, 210, 258, 302, 467, 469

radical acceptance 461

radical empiricism 293, 298, 320, 365

Rafail, P. A. 11

rage 337

Raimy, Victor C. 459

Rambo, L. R. 292

Ramón y Cajal, Santiago 187, 195

Rancurello, A. C. 275

Ranke-Heinemann, U. 228

Rational Emotive Behavior Therapy (REBT) 461, 478

rational emotive therapy 74, 417

Rational Psychology (Hickok) 17

Rational Psychology (Wolff) 17, 162, 168, 171
rationalism 17, 119, 125, 151–171; a priori knowledge 151–152; Aquinas 94; Avicenna 85; Bacon's critique of 128; birth of psychology 216; contributions of 168; curiosity 167–168; definition of 37, 170; Descartes 152–156; Gestalt psychology 363; Herbart 165–166; Hobbes 173, 174; Kant 162–165, 363; Kierkegaard's rejection of 426; Leibniz 159–162; Maimonides 89; Reid 166–167; Rhazes 84; Spinoza 156–159; Stensen 178; *see also* reason
rationalization 397–398, 421
Rauch, J. 18
Rayner, Rosalie 335, 339
reactance 83
reaction formation 117, 397, 421
reactive inhibition 343, 356
real self 414–415, 421
realism 94, 281
reality principle 392, 421
reason 17, 18; Abelard 90–91; Aquinas 93, 94–95; Aristotle 62, 63; Averroës 87–88; Avicenna 85–86; Bacon 93; cognitive psychology 455; Descartes 155, 277; Empedocles 52; faith versus 80–81, 90–91, 94, 153; Hobbes 174; Judaism 88; Kant 164, 165; Leibniz 159; Leonardo da Vinci 113; Locke 130–131; Lucretius 74; Maimonides 89; medieval universities 89; Montaigne 114–115; Parmenides 49, 50; Plato 60, 68–69; Quételet 190; skepticism 77; Socrates 57; Spinoza 159; Zeno of Elea 69; *see also* rationalism
reasoning 453, 454
REBT *see* Rational Emotive Behavior Therapy
reciprocal inhibition 460, 478
recollection 63–64, 111, 378, 384
The Red Book (Jung) 409
Reflections of a Physicist (Bridgman) 21–22

reflex actions 178, 179, 180, 187, 194, 195–196, 254
"The Reflex Arc Concept in Psychology" (Dewey) 306
Reflexes of the Brain (Sechenov) 323
reflexology 257, 323, 355, 357, 369
reform movements 216–232
Reformation 101–102, 115, 120, 121
regression 397, 422
Reid, Thomas 166–167, 169, 170
Reil, Johann Christian 225, 234
reinforcement 263, 356, 357; behaviorism 340; Guthrie 344; Hull 342–343; Skinner 349–350; Thorndike 330; Tolman 346
relations 441
relativism 54–55, 56, 68
relaxation methods 460
religion 491–492; Allport 436; Aquinas 93; Babylonia 42–43; Brentano 275; Democritus 51; Egyptians 43; epistemology 16; Freud 391, 393–394; Hall 305; Heraclitus 51; James 289, 291–292; Kant 163; Lucretius 75; Machiavelli 108; Middle Ages 80–81; Montaigne 115; motives 256; prayer experiments 192; providential theories 9–10; Pythagoreans 48; Stensen 178; Watson 335; women's roles 230; Xenophanes 49; *see also* Christianity; God; Islam; Judaism
Religion, Values and Peak Experiences (Maslow) 430
Religion Within the Limits of Reason Alone (Kant) 163
religious mode of existence 427, 446
Renaissance 98–121; Black Death 98–100; changing visions of the world 103–106; definition of 121; demonology 212; diffusion of authority during the 101–102; empirical studies 102; expansion of geographic knowledge 100; influence of the Greek classics 100; naturalism 197; psychological thought

106–119; quantification 102; skepticism 18; witch hunts 20
Renouvier, Charles 292
repressed memories 488–489
repression 393, 396–397, 399, 400, 402, 403, 422
reproductive thinking 368, 384
The Republic (Plato) 59–60, 61
Rescorla, Robert A. 484
resistance 401, 422
Resor, Stanley 339
respondent conditioning 349, 357
response compression 244, 261
Restorff, Hedwig von 361, 378, 384
retribution 142
revelation 80–81, 90–91, 94
Review of General Psychology (journal) 494
reward and punishment: Augustine 83; Bentham 141, 142, 148, 149; capital punishment 179–180, 200; Helvétius 140, 149; Judaism 45; Locke 131, 132; Montaigne 116; Rush 222; Skinner 349; Thorndike 330; Wundt 251
Reynolds, Mary 223
Rhazes 84–85, 97
Ribot, Théodule 298
Richardson, H. S. 57
Richardson, R. D. 289
richness orientation 208
rituals 19, 43
Roback, A. A. 282–283
Robertson, George Croom 147
Robinson, D. N. 64, 145, 146, 166, 167
robotics 322–323
Rock, I. 379
Roediger, H. L. 456
Rogers, A. K. 113
Rogers, Carl 353, 436–438, 445, 446, 449; clinical psychology 458; evil 442; free will 25; historical timeline 238; Soviet conferences 450
Rogers, Carmen 118
Rogers, E. M. 197
role models 398
Roman period 70–78; Christianity 79; fall of Rome 78; medicine 71–73; philosophy 73–78

Romanes, George John 208, 234
Ronan, C. A. 84, 85, 94, 102, 113
Röntgen, Wilhelm Conrad 21
Roosevelt, Eleanor 434
Roosevelt, Theodore 184, 407, 473
Rorschach inkblot test 10
Rosenfield, L. C. 177, 181
Ross, D. 301, 302, 303, 309
Roszak, Theodore 484
Rotenberg, M. 45
Rousseau, Jean-Jacques 182, 198, 208, 219
Royal Society 124
Royce, Josiah 307, 308, 314, 474
Rubenstein, R. E. 87
Rubin, Edgar 367
Rudnytsky, P. L. 404–405
Rush, Benjamin 124, 221–224, 234
Russell, Bertrand 94, 145, 348
Russell, J. B. 215, 216
Rutherford, A. 353, 450
Rychlak, Joseph F. 24, 440–441, 443, 446, 450
Rychlak, R. J. 24

S-O-R see stimulus-organism-response
S-R see stimulus-response
Sabuco, Miguel 117–118
Sabuco, Oliva 40, 117–118, 121
Sachs, Sadie 231
sacred theory of origins 200
safety needs 431
Sahakian, M. L. 131
Sahakian, W. S. 131
salivary activity 324–325, 328
Samelson, F. 335
Sanford, Edmund Clark 314
Sanger, Margaret 230–232, 234
Santayana, George 314
Sargant, W. 327, 328
Sartre, Jean-Paul 9, 428
Scarborough, E. 274
schemas 453, 454, 455
schizophrenia 258, 413, 458, 463, 466, 468
Schlick, Moritz 341
Schliemann, Heinrich 46
Schlosberg, H. 312
Schmid-Guisan, Hans 412
Schol, Franz 386
School and Society (journal) 310

school psychology 259
Schrag, C. O. 426
Schulte, Heinrich 381
Schumann, Friedrich 280, 360, 366
Schur, Max 389
Schweitzer, Albert 434
science: Aquinas 94, 95; Bacon 92, 125–126, 127–128; Brentano 276; Condillac 139; correlation 24; Descartes 154, 155, 156; determinism 26; epistemology 16, 19; evolution controversy 206–207; faith and 491–492; Feyerabend 21–22, 23, 36; Freud 400–401; Galileo 104–106; Gestalt psychology 363–364; Greek 46; Helmholtz 246; Hobbes 173–174; humanistic psychology 443; Hume 138; James 292; Kuhn 20–21, 36; Leibniz 159; Lewin 375; Maslow 431; Middle Ages 80; motivation 490; Pavlov 324; Popper 19–20, 37; Renaissance 102; Rhazes 97; Rychlak 441; shift in worldviews 381; simplicity 208; skepticism 18; Skinner 348–349; Stensen 178; Stumpf 278; Titchener 266–267, 268; twentieth-century developments in psychology 448; Unamuno 425; unity and diversity of the sciences 494; Wertheimer 360; see also biopsychology; medicine; neuroscience; physiology
Science and Human Behavior (Skinner) 348
Science (journal) 310, 311
The Science of Education (Herbart) 165, 168
The Science of Living (Adler) 406
Scientific American 124
scientific empiricism 341, 357
scientific method 372–373, 490–491
Scott, Walter Dill 252, 307, 473, 475, 478
scripture 80–81, 89, 90–91, 99, 103, 105, 167, 230; see also Bible

Seashore, C. E. 474
Sechenov, Ivan Mikhailovich 323, 327
secondary attention 269, 287
secondary memory 298, 320
secondary personal selves 295
secondary process 392, 422
secondary qualities 131, 133, 134, 150
The Secrets of Nature (Vanini) 153
Segal, Z. V. 461–462
segregation 377, 467, 487
Séguin, Édouard 229, 234
Selesnick, S. T. 42, 43, 86, 159
self: Brentano 277; Horney 414–415, 421; Hume 136–137, 138; ideal 437–438, 445; idealized 415, 416, 420; individuation 410; James 295–296, 321, 424; Jung 411, 422; real 414–415, 421; Rogers 437–438; see also identity
self-actualization 263, 402, 411, 432, 433–434, 436, 438, 446
Self-Analysis (Horney) 414, 416
self-esteem 296, 320
self-flagellation 99–100
self-hatred 416
self-interest 174, 195
self-knowledge 74, 76
self-preservation 109
self-psychology 314, 424
self-realization 416
Self-Reliance (Emerson) 10
self-transcendence 432, 446
Seligman, Martin E. P. 484
Semond, Raimond 114
Senescence (Hall) 303, 305
sensation: Aristotle 64; Berkeley 135; Brentano 277; cognition 455; Condillac 139, 149; definition of 261; Fechner 243–244; Hume 136; James 294–295; Jung 412; Locke 140; Lucretius 75; Mach 364; Müller 183; Plotinus 76; psyche 37; Reid 167; Spinoza 159; Stumpf 278; Titchener 268, 270, 271, 272; Watson 333, 334; Woodworth 313; Wundt 254, 255; see also perception
The Sense of Touch (Weber) 241, 261

senses: Aquinas 93, 94; Aristotle 63, 64, 65; Bacon 127, 128; Condillac 139; Descartes 155; empiricism 148, 152; Hartley 140, 141; Heraclitus 50; Hobbes 173, 174; Indian philosophy 44; Kant 163–164; Leibniz 161; Leonardo da Vinci 111, 112; Locke 17, 130, 131; Lucretius 74, 75; neurophysiology of the 182–183; Parmenides 49; Plato 58, 59, 60, 61, 68; Protagoras 55; skepticism 77; specific energies of nerves 183–184; structuralism 390; Titchener 268; Wolff 162; Wundt 458; Zeno of Elea 50, 69; *see also* perception

The Senses and the Intellect (Bain) 147

sensorimotor learning 371

sensualism 426

sentiments 271–272

Servetus, Michael 16, 101–102

Seward, G. H. 312

Seward, J. P. 312

sex: Augustine 83; definition of 496; sex/gender distinction 481–482

sexism 302

Sexton, Virginia Staudt 480

Sextus Empiricus 77–78, 96

sexual intimacy 407

sexual selection 207

sexuality 232, 417; Freud 398–400, 404, 418; Jung 412

Shackelford, T. K. 207

shadow 411, 422

Shakespeare, William 14, 16, 19, 114, 224

Shakow, David 458, 459, 478

The Shaping of a Behaviorist (Skinner) 348

Shaw, R. 432

Shelley, Mary 145, 201

Shelley, Percy Bysshe 145

Sherif, Caroline Wood 469

Sherif, Muzafer 378, 469–470, 477, 478

Sherrington, Charles 187–188, 195, 311

Shook, J. R. 306

Shorto, R. 153, 155

Sibbern, Frederik Christian 425–426

Sic et Non (Yes and No) (Abelard) 91, 96

Sidis, Boris 457

Silverman, L. H. 449

similarity 367, 384

Simon, B. 59, 60–61

Simon, Théodore 238, 316, 319

simplicity 208, 481

simultaneous conditioning 325–326

sin 84, 99, 100, 101, 181, 222

Singer, P. 31

Sizer, Nelson 184

skepticism 4, 18, 69, 77–78, 81, 133; Augustine 82; Bacon 126, 127; Berkeley 134; definition of 37, 97; Descartes 154; Montaigne 114–115, 117, 121, 138, 168; Renaissance 100, 119; Roman period 73; Xenophanes 49

Skinner, Burrhus Frederic 347–354, 357; American Humanist Association 443; applied psychology 350–353, 354; critique of cognitive psychology 456–457, 478; critique of Köhler 370; critiques of 353; determinism 25; historical timeline 238; influence of Bacon 128; Machiavelli as forerunner to 109; neobehaviorism 450; operant conditioning 349–350, 351, 352, 354; opposition to teleology 24; philosophy of behaviorism 348–349; reinforcement 263

sleep: Alcmaeon 52; Bacon 128; Kraepelin 258; Lucretius 75; narcosis therapy 328; Plato 59

Smith, Adam 166

Smith, C. U. M. 141

Smith, M. Brewster 443, 450

Smith, N. W. 57, 64

Smith, Theodate Louise 304–305

social cognition 378, 472

social influence 106, 108, 469–472

social interest 406, 407, 422, 434

Social Interest: A Challenge to Mankind (Adler) 405

social learning theory 452

social psychology 142, 462, 468–473; Allport (Floyd) 435, 469; Freud 401–403; Gestalt psychology 374, 382; Herbart 165; information processing 455; James 289; Kant 164–165; legal issues 489; Lewin 375; Titchener 285

social self 296, 321

socialization 109, 120, 400

Society for the History of Psychology 11–12

Society of Experimentalists 265–266

sociocultural psychology 251

Socrates 40, 55–57, 58, 60, 68; pleasure and pain 116; reason 91; Russell on 94; skepticism 77; Tertullian's critique of 81

Sokal, Michael M. 11, 12, 303, 304–305, 309–310, 374

solar system 198, 233

solipsism 135, 150, 239, 267

Soltis, J. F. 307

Some Thoughts Concerning Education (Locke) 129, 131

sophists 55, 56–57, 68

soul: Anaximenes 47; Aquinas 93–94; Aristotle 62–63; Augustine 83; Avicenna 86; Descartes 158, 176, 216; early Christianity 79; Empedocles 53; Fechner 242; Galen 73, 97; Hall 304; Heraclitus 50; Hippocrates 54; neo-Platonism 76; Plato 59, 60, 61, 67, 83; Plotinus 76; psychogeny 31; Pythagoreans 48; Thales 47; Wolff 162

Spalding, D. A. 297

spatial perception 112

specific energies of nerves 182–184, 195, 248

speech 186, 196, 338–339

Spence, Kenneth W. 342, 343–344, 370

Spencer, Herbert 10, 211, 234, 308

Sperry, Roger W. 464, 478

Spillmann, J. 300–301

Spillmann, L. 300–301

spinal column 179, 181, 182, 194, 195

Spinoza, Benedict (Baruch) 45, 151, 156–159, 168, 170, 178; curiosity 168; demonology 216; double-aspect monism 28, 253; emotion 271; experience and brain processes 373; holistic perspectives 363; Leibniz compared with 160; Maslow on 434

spirit 27–28, 31, 60, 113, 175

spiritual self 296, 321

split-brain research 464, 478

spontaneous recovery 326, 357

Sprenger, James 40, 212–213, 214–215, 233

Sprung, H. 280

Sprung, L. 280

Spurzheim, Johann Kaspar 184, 185, 195

St. Ambrose 99

St. Mary of Bethlehem Hospital 224

Staats, A. W. 494

Stace, W. T. 57, 61, 66

Stanford-Binet Intelligence Scale 317

Stanford Prison Experiment 472

Stanton, Elizabeth Cady 230

Starbuck, Edwin D. 491–492

statistics 188–189, 190, 194; birth of psychology 216; definition of 195; descriptive 193; Galton 210; social 193

Stealing Heaven (Meade) 90

Stensen, Niels (Steno) 178, 195

stereoscope 247, 261

stereotypes, gender 148, 229–230, 416, 418

Steudel, J. 182

Stevens, G. 227

Stewart, Dugald 167

Stewart, M. 160, 323

stimuli 179, 196; Fechner 243–244, 245; Freud 395; Helmholtz 247; just noticeable difference 241–242; method of average error 245, 260; method of constant stimuli 245, 260; method of limits 244–245, 260; Pavlov 325–326, 328;

psychophysics 239–240; Skinner 349; Titchener 269, 270, 286; Tolman 346; ultraparadoxical phase 358; Wundt 254

stimulus generalization 326, 357

stimulus intensity dynamism 342, 358

stimulus-organism-response (S-O-R) 312, 342, 345

stimulus-response (S-R): Calkins 314; Gestalt psychology 369, 370; Hull 342; Lockean tradition 436; Skinner 349; Tolman 346–347; Woodworth 312

Stocking, G. W. 8

stoicism 66, 73–74, 92, 96, 97, 460, 461

Stone, M. H. 406

Strandh, S. 175

stream of thought 294–295, 321

stress 327, 328

Strong, E. K. 474

structuralism 279, 288, 448; Calkins 313, 314, 319; definition of 287; Gestalt psychology critique of 372; senses 390; Titchener 266; Watson's critique of 334

The Structure of Scientific Revolutions (Kuhn) 20, 36

Studies in Hysteria (Breuer) 387

A Study of Values (Allport et al.) 435

Stumpf, Carl 278–279, 287, 360, 362, 365; Allport and 435; Berlin Psychological Institute 361; influence of Brentano 275; Lewin and 374

style of life 406, 422

The Subjection of Women (Mill) 147, 229

subjective well-being 483

subjectivity 480

sublimation 397, 422

suffering 391, 440

suicide 389, 402, 461

Sullivan, Harry Stack 414, 417

Sulloway, F. J. 389

Sully, James 209, 305

Summa Theologica (Aquinas) 93

Summers, M. 212, 214

Sumner, Charles 227

Sumner, Francis 302–303, 321

superego 392–393, 396, 398, 400, 401, 422

superstition: Babylonians 43; Bacon 127; Egyptians 43; Judaism 88; Lucretius 75; Middle Ages 79, 80, 95; Rhazes 84, 97; Roman period 70, 71; Spinoza 158; witchcraft 213

survival of the fittest 211

Sussman, E. J. 274

Swammerdam, Jan 177–178, 195

Swan, M. 22, 490

Swazey, J. P. 188

symbols 19, 43, 80

sympathy 140–141

synaptic transmission 464

synchronicity 413, 422

synthetic a priori knowledge 163, 170

systematic desensitization 460, 462, 478

systems 262–264, 287

Szasz, T. 216

Taine, Hippolyte Adolphe 305

Talks to Teachers (James) 290, 296, 320

Taoism 198, 460

tautology 163

Taylor, Franklin 351

Taylor, G. R. 202, 206

Taylor, Harriet 146, 147, 148, 150

Taylor, M. C. 426

Taylor, R. 26

technology 350, 479, 485, 495; neuroscience 466; new scientific methods 491; Titchener 268

The Technology of Teaching (Skinner) 348

teleology 24, 33, 36; Adler 406; definition of 37; Héloise 92; Jung 412; motivation 490; Rychlak 441

Teller, Edward 360

temperament: Galen 271, 327; Huarte 118, 119; Pavlov 327, 328; Renaissance psychology 106; Vives 110

tension systems 376–377

Teo, T. 480
Terman, Lewis 190, 192, 317, 467
Tertullian 81, 97
A Textbook of Psychology (Titchener) 268
Thales 46–47, 68
Thanatos 402
Theana 48, 68
theism 135, 174
theodicy 30, 161
Theologia Naturalis (*Natural Theology*) (Sebond) 114
Theophrastus 24
theory: Alhazen 86; Heraclitus 51; Jung 409–410; Popper 20
Theory and Psychology (journal) 12
theory of forms 58, 68–69, 83
therapy: ancient Greeks 52; Asclepiades 71; clinical psychology 458; cognitive therapy 417, 449, 460–461, 462; criticisms of psychoanalysis 404; ecotherapy 485, 496; Frankl 439, 440; Freud 400–401, 403; Gestalt 379, 381, 383; Hippocrates 54; moral therapy 221; Münsterberg 300; Reil 225; Rhazes 84; Rogers 436–437, 438; *see also* behavior therapy; psychotherapy
thinking: Bacon 128; Gestalt psychology 363, 368–369; Jung 412; Watson 338–339
third-force psychology 423–424, 436, 438, 440, 441–443, 446; *see also* humanistic psychology
This Week in the History of Psychology (podcasts) 12
Thomas, O. M. 475
Thomas, R. K. 208
Thomas, William I. 339
Thorndike, Edward Lee 329–331, 357, 358; connectionism 356, 369; influence on Hull 341; Maslow and 430; Skinner compared with 349; variability hypothesis 315; Woodworth and 311, 313
Thorne, J. O. 108
Three Dialogues between Hylas and Philonous (Berkeley) 133, 134

Three Essays, Moral and Political (Hume) 136
thresholds 161, 166, 168, 240, 241, 244, 245, 260, 261
throwness 428, 442, 446
Thucydides 5, 13
The Timaeus (Plato) 58, 60, 61
timelines of psychology 40, 124, 238
Tinbergen, Nikolaas 16
tip-of-the-tongue phenomena 298
Titchener, Edward Bradford 257, 264–272, 285, 286, 287, 388; consciousness 255; on Ebbinghaus 284; elementary sense qualities 183; Hall compared with 304; historical timeline 238; introspection 333, 429; Maslow and 430; on Wundt 252, 262
toilet training 398
Tolman, Edward Chace 345–347, 356, 357, 358, 450; applied psychology 354; cognitive psychology 455; Gestalt psychology 378, 454; teleology 24
Tonpsychologie (Stumpf) 278
Torquemada, Tomás de 109
Tourette Syndrome 229
Toward a Psychology of Being (Maslow) 430, 432
trace conditioning 326
The Tragic Sense of Life (Unamuno) 425
training 458, 459, 473, 476, 489
tranquilizing chair 223
transfer of learning 298, 313, 330–331, 356, 450–451
transference 401, 422
trauma 263–264
A Treatise of Human Nature (Hume) 124, 135–136, 137–138
A Treatise on Insanity (Pinel) 124, 220, 221
Treatise on Man (Descartes) 124, 175
Treatise on the Emendation of the Intellect (Spinoza) 157
trial by combat 80
tridimensional theory of feeling 256, 257, 261

Trieb 395, 420
truncated law of effect 330, 358
truth 7, 14–15, 16–18; Hobbes 174; Parmenides 49; relativism 54–55, 68; Spinoza 158; two-domain theory 81; Wertheimer 360
Tryon, Robert Choate 347
Tsanoff, R. A. 87, 137, 173
Tuke, Daniel Hack 224–225, 227, 234
Tuke, Samuel 224, 234–235
Tuke, William 224, 235
Turner, R. S. 246
Twain, Mark 185
twin studies 210, 329–330, 467
two-domain theory 81
Tylor, E. B. 189, 190
Tyndall, John 192
tyranny of the should 416

UCR *see* unconditioned reflex
UCS *see* unconditioned stimulus
Ueberwasser, Ferdinand 249
ultramaximal inhibition 327, 328, 358
ultraparadoxical phase 328, 358
Umwelt 428, 446
Unamuno, Miguel de 425, 445, 446
uncertainty 25, 26
unconditional positive regard 438, 446
unconditioned reflex (UCR) 325, 358
unconditioned stimulus (UCS) 325–326, 358
the unconscious: collective 410–411, 412, 413, 415, 419; Freud 263, 389–390, 393, 394, 400, 403; Herbart 166; Jung 409, 410, 412, 421; Woodworth 312
unconscious processes 168, 410, 423
Understanding Human Nature (Adler) 405
unification of psychology 494–495
uniformitarianism 161, 170, 199, 233, 235
unity 159, 160

Unity and Fragmentation in Psychology (Gaj) 494
universities 89–95
University of Chicago 305–309, 316, 318, 319, 332–333, 339, 437
University of Leipzig 40, 240–243, 249, 251, 254, 257, 258, 262, 264, 280–281, 309–310
Unzer, Johann August 179–180, 195–196
Upanishads 44, 69
U.S. Public Health Service (USPHS) 459
Ussher, James 199
utilitarianism 140, 142, 145, 146, 147, 149, 150

Vail Conference 459
valences 376, 384
validity 130, 457, 477
values: Bacon 92; Hume 138; James 295; Machiavelli 108; moral anxiety 396; self-actualization 434
VanHoorn, W. 63, 64
Vanini, Giulio Cesare 153
variability hypothesis 315, 321
The Varieties of Religious Experience (James) 290, 291, 294, 296, 297, 320
Vartanian, A. 180–181
Vaughan, Margaret 351
Vedas 44, 69
verbal behavior 350
Verbal Behavior (Skinner) 348, 350
Vernon, P. E. 435
Vesalius, Andreas 40, 73, 102, 121
Vienna Circle 341
A Vindication of the Rights of Woman (Wollstonecraft) 124, 143, 144, 229
Viney, W. 11, 143
virtue: Aristotle 65–66; La Mettrie 181; Montaigne 115; Plato 60; Socrates 57; stoicism 73
vision 111, 112, 135, 246–247
visual perception 86–87, 246–247, 248, 273
vital spirit 72, 97
vitalism 72, 183, 216
Vives, Juan Luis 109–111, 121, 131

Vlastos, G. 50
Voeks, V. 345
The Voice of the Earth: An Exploration of Ecopsychology (Roszak) 484
Völkerpsychologie 251
Voltaire, François-Marie Arouet de 132, 138, 150, 161, 198, 219
voluntarism 253, 257, 261
von Restorff effect 378, 384; *see also* Restorff, Hedwig von
Vonèche, J. J. 453–454
Vorschule der Aesthetic (Fechner) 243
Vrooman, J. R. 153
Vygotsky, Lev 375

Wade, N. J. 92, 363
Waithe, M. E. 48, 57, 92, 118
Walden Two (Skinner) 348, 352
Walk, R. D. 15
Walker, L. 487
Walker, P. N. 180
Wallach, Alfred Russel 202, 205–206, 233, 235
Wallach, Hans 378
Wampold, B. E. 462
Wang, S. 322
Wapner, S. 303
war 401–402
war veterans 458–459
Ward, L. 130
Warren, Howard 252
Washburn, David 273
Washburn, Margaret Floy 265, 266, 272–274, 287
Washington, Booker T. 184
Watson, F. 109
Watson, J. D. 17
Watson, John B. 266, 322, 332–340, 345, 348, 355, 358; "A Behaviorist's Utopia" 351–352; applied psychology 354; assumptions 263; biography of 323; denial of hereditary influences 140; determinism 25; functionalism 318; Gestalt psychology critique of 369; historical timeline 238; influence on Hull 341; Machiavelli as forerunner to 109; materialism 27; mental

world of consciousness 452; observable behavior 263; opposition to teleology 24
Watson, Robert I. 4, 11, 101–102, 179
Watt, Henry 282
Watt, James 201
Watt, W. M. 87
Webb, James 473
Weber, Ernst Heinrich 240–242, 243–244, 261, 278
Weber's illusion 241, 261
Weber's law 244, 261
Wechsler, David 192
Wedgwood, Emma 205
W.E.I.R.D. societies 480–481, 496
Weiss, Albert Paul 323, 332, 452
Weltanschaung 263
Wentworth, P. A. 314
Wernicke, Carl 186, 196
Wertheimer, M. L. 11
Wertheimer, Max 359–360, 362, 380, 384; Allport and 435; Asch and 470; Berlin Psychological Institute 361; criticism of humanistic psychology 443; education 381; Ehrenfels and 364–365; Einstein and 364; forensic work 408; on Freud 381; historical timeline 238; Horney and 414; law of Prägnanz 383; legal issues 487; Lewin and 375; Maslow and 430, 433; Maslow on 433, 434; Nazi Germany 374; phi phenomenon 365–366; productive thinking 368–369, 384; psychopathology 381; Spinoza and 157; as student of Külpe 282; Stumpf and 279
Wertheimer, Michael 359–360, 365, 372, 382; behaviorism 323; Gestalt therapy 379; on Helmholtz 246; history of psychology 11; holistic perspectives 363; perceptual abilities of infants 15; richness versus precision 208; thinking 368; on Wundt 257
Wertz, F. J. 491
Weyer, Johann 216
White, A. D. 79, 199–200

white paper hypothesis 129–130, 139, 143, 148
Whitehead, Alfred North 61, 208, 289
Whitman, Walt 184–185
Whytt, Robert 178–179, 196
Wichler, G. 202
Wigmore, John Henry 488
"wild boy of Aveyron" 229
will 24, 26, 106; *see also* free will
The Will to Believe (James) 290, 296
William of Champeaux 89
William of Ockham 95, 97
Wilson, Edward O. 16
Winston, A. S. 313
Wisconsin General Test Apparatus 451, 478
witch hunts 20, 26, 81, 213–216
witchcraft 212–216, 217
The Witches' Hammer (Kramer & Sprenger) 212–215
Witkin, Herman 378
Witmer, Lightner 258–259, 261, 458, 473
Wolf, T. H. 316, 317
Wolff, Christian von 17, 162, 168, 171
Wollstonecraft, Mary 124, 142–145, 148, 150, 229, 231
Wolpe, Joseph 238, 336, 460, 478
womb envy 416
women: anima 411–412; Augustine 82; Babylonia 43; Calkins 313; Egyptians 43–44; Freud 399, 404, 416, 418; global perspectives 481; historiography 5; Horney 416–417; Huarte 119; Indian philosophy 44; intellectual participation of 274; Jesus'

treatment of 79; Jewish philosophy 45; Maslow 434; mesmerism 219; Mill 145, 147, 148; Müller 280; phrenology 185; Pratola 314; Pythagoreans 48; reform movements 229–232; religious beliefs 492; Renaissance 119; Titchener's graduates 265, 266; variability hypothesis 315, 321; Vives 111; voting rights 238; witchcraft 213; Wollstonecraft 142–145, 150; working hours and the law 486–487; *see also* gender
Wood, N. 109
Woodworth, Robert Sessions 311–313, 321, 330–331, 470
Woody, W. D. 365
Wooley, Helen 316, 321
word-association tests 408, 410, 412, 413
The World (Descartes) 153
World War II 458, 493
worldviews 18, 100, 201, 263, 381–382
Wundt, Wilhelm 10, 165, 241, 245, 249–259, 261, 262, 479; biography 249–252; breadth of vision 253; consciousness 452; creative synthesis 256, 260; criticism of Romanes 208; Darwin and 253–254; descriptive examinations 491; Ebbinghaus compared with 282–283; on Fechner 243; Hall and 302; historical timeline 124, 238; history of psychology 11; influence on Dewey 306; influence on Titchener 264; James and 288, 290; key concepts 255–257;

Külpe and 280–281; laboratory research 253, 254–255; legacy of 256–259; mental events 453; mind and body 252–253; Müller compared with 280; Münsterberg on 299; rationalism 168; senses 458; students of 473; Stumpf on 279; systems 263; voluntarism 253
Würzberg School 281, 282

Xenophanes 49, 69, 77

Yerkes, Robert M. 192, 238, 317, 467
yin and yang 42, 69
yoga 44
York Retreat 224, 234, 235
Young-Helmholtz trichromatic theory 248, 260, 261
Young, P. T. 265
Young, Thomas 183, 247–248, 260, 261, 323
Your City (Thorndike) 331

Zagorin, P. 174
Zarathustra 45–46, 69
Zargaran, A. 46
Zeigarnik, Bluma 376–377
Zeigarnik effect 377, 384
Zeitgeist 10, 13, 130, 291
Zen Buddhism 416, 434, 461
Zend-Avesta (Fechner) 243
Zeno of Cyprus 73, 97
Zeno of Elea 50, 59, 69
Ziegler, P. 99
Zilboorg, G. 110
Zimbardo, Phillip G. 471, 472
Ziskin, Jay 489
Zoroastrianism 45–46, 69